CHICAGO SCHOOL

1920

PERSPECTIVE:
Social Structure and Disorganization

KEY THEORISTS:
Park, Burgess, Shaw, McKay

KEY THEORIES:
Ecological Impact Model, Social Disorganization

SOCIAL PROCESS

1940

PERSPECTIVE:
Social Process & Control Theories

KEY THEORISTS:
Sutherland, Glasser, Nye, Reckless, Matza, Hirschi

KEY THEORIES:
Differential Association, Control Theory, Techniques of Neutralization, Social Bonding

FEMINIST

1970

PERSPECTIVE:
Feminist Perspectives

KEY THEORISTS:
Adler, Simon, Chesney-Lind

KEY THEORIES:
Liberation Thesis, Power-Control Theory, Feminist criminology, Pathways

CLASSICAL

1975

PERSPECTIVE:
Resurgence of Classical School

KEY THEORISTS:
Becker, Gibbs

KEY THEORIES:
Deterrence

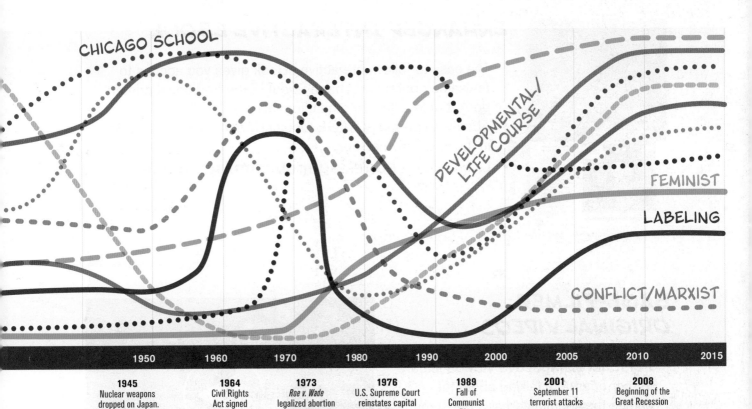

CHICAGO SCHOOL

DEVELOPMENTAL/ LIFE COURSE

FEMINIST

LABELING

CONFLICT/MARXIST

1950 | 1960 | 1970 | 1980 | 1990 | 2000 | 2005 | 2010 | 2015

1945
Nuclear weapons dropped on Japan. World War II ends. Cold War begins.

1964
Civil Rights Act signed

1973
Roe v. Wade legalized abortion nationally

1976
U.S. Supreme Court reinstates capital punishment

1989
Fall of Communist Bloc

2001
September 11 terrorist attacks

2008
Beginning of the Great Recession

1960

PERSPECTIVE:
Labeling Theory

KEY THEORISTS:
Lemert, Tannenbaum, Becker, Schur

KEY THEORIES:
Primary & Secondary Deviance, Dramatization of Evil

LABELING

1965

PERSPECTIVE:
Radical/Critical Criminology

KEY THEORISTS:
Quinney, Vold, Turk

KEY THEORIES:
Marxist Criminology, Group Conflict, Left Realism

CONFLICT/ MARXIST

1980

PERSPECTIVE:
Developmental-Life Course/ Biosocial Perspective

KEY THEORISTS:
Sampson, Laub, Thornberry, Moffitt

KEY THEORIES:
Transitions, Trajectories, Life-Course & Adolescence-Limited Offender, Biosocial Interaction Theory

DEVELOPMENTAL/ LIFE COURSE

The Tools You Need!

SAGE edge™

SHARPEN YOUR SKILLS WITH SAGE EDGE!

SAGE edge offers a robust online environment featuring an impressive array of tools and resources for review, study, and further exploration, keeping both instructors and students on the cutting edge of teaching and learning. SAGE edge content is open access and available on demand.

ENHANCED INTERACTIVE EBOOK

- The easy-to-follow interactive eBook gives you access to the same content and page layout of the traditional printed book, but in a flexible digital format.
- Access to premium SAGE Original Videos is only available in the interactive eBook.
- Learn more at **edge.sagepub.com/schram2e**

SAGE-FILMED ORIGINAL VIDEOS

- **Personal Perspective videos** feature former offenders talking about the crimes they committed and the steps they are taking to turn around their lives.

- **What Were They Thinking?! videos** profile unusual crimes that are related to chapter content.

- **Author videos** discuss concepts presented in each chapter to provide additional clarification and examples.

Lidia
Former Offender

A Fresh Approach to Criminology

WHY DO THEY DO IT?

OMAR MATEEN

Below is a modified CNN timeline of the Orlando, Florida nightclub shooting:

- Sunday (June 12, 2016), 2:02 a.m. ET: Shooting erupts at Pulse, a gay nightclub in Orlando, Florida. There are approximately 320 that evening enjoying the club's "Latin flavor" event. An officer working extra duty in full uniform at the club responds. He and two officers nearby open fire on the shooter, and a gun battle ensues. The shooter goes inside the club, where a hostage situation develops. Over 100 officers from Orange County Sheriff's Office and the Orlando Police Department respond to the scene.

- 2:09 a.m. ET: A standoff follows. Police say they had to wait three hours to access the situation, get armored vehicles on the scene, and ensure they had enough personnel.

- 2:22 a.m. ET: Shooter calls 911 to pledge allegiance to ISIS. He also mentions the Boston Marathon bombers.

- Approximately 5:00 a.m. ET: Heavily armed SWAT team members use an armored vehicle to smash down a door at the club, clearing the way for some 30 people inside to flee to safety. SWAT officers confront the suspect in the doorway, then shoot and kill him.[164]

At least 49 people were killed that evening, and over 50 individuals were injured. It was the worst mass shooting in U.S. history. As the news unfolded, many were asking what could motivate someone to engage in such a horrific crime.

People across the world, such as here in Seoul, South Korea, held vigils for the victims in the Orlando, Florida shooting.

Omar Mir Seddique Mateen was 29 years old. His parents are from Afghanistan; he was born in New York but lived in an apartment in Fort Pierce, Florida. Interviews with coworkers revealed that he was "scary." This was not just sometimes, but all the time. He had some anger management issues. Issues that would upset him revolved around women, race, or religion. In 2013, Mateen was interviewed two times by federal agents after co-workers reported he made "inflammatory" comments about radical Islamic propaganda. The next year, he raised concerns with the FBI because of his ties with an American who traveled to the Middle East to become a suicide bomber.

Sitora Yusufiy, Mateen's ex-wife, reported that he was a violent man and beat her. Not only did he physically abuse her, but he also isolated her from her family. They were married only a few months. They officially divorced in 2011. Mateen's father told reporters that Omar became enraged after a same-sex couple kissed in front of his family.[165]

THINK ABOUT IT:

1. Was this a terrorist act?

2. Was this a hate crime?

3. Frida Ghitis of CNN asked this very question: terrorism or homophobia? Her answer was "both."[166] Do you agree?

TOOLS DESIGNED FOR CLASSROOM ENGAGEMENT:

Applying Theory to Crime features help students integrate the concepts they learn with violent and property crimes and scenarios.

Why Do They Do It? cases give students an opportunity to critically analyze some of the most high profile cases they hear about in the news.

Chapter-Opening Case Studies present real-life examples that tie directly to the concepts learned in the chapter. These cases are revisited throughout the chapter as students learn additional theories and concepts.

Comparative Criminology boxes present transnational comparisons regarding crime rates and the systems other countries employ to deal with crime.

Helpful end-of-chapter pedagogical features include **theory comparisons**, **policy implications** and **critical thinking questions**.

A Fresh Approach to Criminology

introduction to criminology

SECOND EDITION

Los Angeles | London | New Delhi
Singapore | Washington DC | Melbourne

introduction to

SECOND EDITION

criminology

WHY DO THEY DO IT?

pamela j. schram
CALIFORNIA STATE UNIVERSITY, SAN BERNARDINO

stephen g. tibbetts
CALIFORNIA STATE UNIVERSITY, SAN BERNARDINO

Los Angeles | London | New Delhi
Singapore | Washington DC | Melbourne

FOR INFORMATION:

SAGE Publications, Inc.
2455 Teller Road
Thousand Oaks, California 91320
E-mail: order@sagepub.com

SAGE Publications Ltd.
1 Oliver's Yard
55 City Road
London EC1Y 1SP
United Kingdom

SAGE Publications India Pvt. Ltd.
B 1/I 1 Mohan Cooperative Industrial Area
Mathura Road, New Delhi 110 044
India

SAGE Publications Asia-Pacific Pte. Ltd.
3 Church Street
#10-04 Samsung Hub
Singapore 049483

Acquisitions Editor: Jessica Miller
eLearning Editor: Laura Kirkhuff
Editorial Assistant: Jennifer Rubio
Production Editor: Libby Larson
Copy Editor: Rachel Keith
Typesetter: C&M Digitals (P) Ltd.
Proofreader: Sally Jaskold
Indexer: Joan Shapiro
Cover Designer: Scott Van Atta
Marketing Manager: Amy Lammers

Printed in Scotland by Bell and Bain Ltd, Glasgow

Library of Congress Cataloging-in-Publication Data

Names: Schram, Pamela J., author. | Tibbetts, Stephen G., author.

Title: Introduction to criminology : why do they do it / Pamela J. Schram, California State University, San Bernardino, Stephen G. Tibbetts, California State University, San Bernardino.

Description: Second Edition. | Thousand Oaks : SAGE Publications, [2017] | Revised edition of the authors' Introduction to criminology, [2014] | Includes bibliographical references and index.

Identifiers: LCCN 2016040618 | ISBN 9781506347561 (pbk. : alk. paper)

Subjects: LCSH: Criminology.

Classification: LCC HV6025 .S38 2017 | DDC 364—dc23
LC record available at https://lccn.loc.gov/2016040618

This book is printed on acid-free paper.

MIX
Paper from responsible sources
FSC® C007785
www.fsc.org

18 19 20 21 10 9 8 7 6 5 4 3

BRIEF CONTENTS

DETAILED CONTENTS

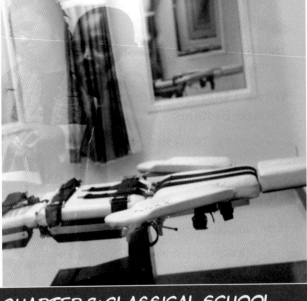

CHAPTER 2: MEASURING CRIME 28

CHAPTER 3: CLASSICAL SCHOOL OF CRIMINOLOGY THOUGHT 58

CHAPTER 5: EARLY POSITIVISM 110

CHAPTER 6: MODERN BIOSOCIAL PERSPECTIVES OF CRIMINAL BEHAVIOR 138

CHAPTER 7: PSYCHOLOGICAL/ TRAIT THEORIES OF CRIME 166

CHAPTER 11: LABELING THEORY AND CONFLICT/MARXIST/ RADICAL THEORIES OF CRIME 290

CHAPTER 12: FEMINIST THEORIES OF CRIME.................. 324

CHAPTER 15: HATE CRIMES, TERRORISM, AND HOMELAND SECURITY 422

CHAPTER 16: DRUGS AND CRIME 466

PREFACE

If you are considering a career in any aspect of criminal justice, and want to know more about the motivations and socio-psychological make-up of serious offenders, then this book is meant for you! *Introduction to Criminology: Why Do They Do It?* places a primary emphasis on applying the dominant theories in the existing criminological literature for why people commit crimes, and we also examine in detail many recent true (as well as many hypothetical) examples of serious crimes, and demonstrate theoretical applications for why they offended in those particular cases. While other textbooks do a decent job in discussing both the basic theories, as well as exploring the various types of crime, our book is distinctively unique in that it integrates various street crimes within each chapter, and applies theories that are appropriate in explaining such criminal activity. This is extremely important because most instructors never get to the latter typology chapters in a given semester or term. So our approach is to incorporate them into the theoretical chapters in which they apply directly to the theories that are being presented in the sections that they are most appropriate.

The emphasis on specific examples and true crime stories, such as notable serial killers and other recent crime stories, as well as utilizing established theoretical models to explain their offenses in each chapter, is another primary distinction of this book from that of most other criminology textbooks. Obviously, this book is meant to be used as a textbook in an introductory course in criminology, but due to the emphasis on applied theoretical explanations, this book is highly appropriate for higher-level undergraduate and graduate courses in criminological theory, as well as a reference for any person working in the field of criminal justice. This integration of true crimes (and some hypothetical examples) in this text occurs on both a general level, such as our Applying Crime to Theory section in each chapter, as well as more specific cases – the High Profile Crime sections—in each section, which often involve notable cases of serial killers, mass murderers, or other notorious example of offender/offending.

The subtitle of our book, "Why Do They Do It?" is the running theme in this book. Our goal in writing this book was to apply established theories of crime, which are often seen as abstract and hypothetical, to actual examples that have occurred, as well as to hypothetical examples that are quite likely to occur. To this end, we explore the various reasons of offending or the "why they do it" the subtitle for this book for various cases, from the first documented serial killers in the US—the Harpe Brothers in the late-1700s—to the most recent killers, such as California cop-killer/spree-killer Christopher Dorner in 2013 and Dylann Roof, a 21-year-old white male, entering the Emanuel African Methodist Episcopal Church in Charleston, South Carolina in 2015 and shooting numerous members. Importantly, theories will be applied throughout these discussions of the actual crimes. We shall see that some of the theories that applied to the earliest crimes also seem to apply to the most modern crimes as well.

Additionally, our textbook is unique from others because it does not include separate chapters on violent or property crimes, because we have worked those into each chapter, and applied them to the theories explored in those chapters. We strongly believe that by integrating discussions of such serious crimes—all of the FBI Index offenses of murder, rape, robbery, aggravated assault, burglary, motor vehicle theft, larceny, and arson, as well as other non-Index crimes such as simple assault and driving under the influence—into the theoretical chapters is the best approach toward explaining why individuals commit such offenses. And the flip side is good as well; by discussing the offenses with the theories, this also provides an example of how to apply theories toward explaining criminal behavior. Again, this goes back to our theme of "why do they do it?" Our integration of such specific offenses into the chapters that discuss relevant theories in explaining them is the best way to approach such material and demonstrates our goal: apply the appropriate theories for the specific crime.

Additionally, our book is distinguished from other textbooks in that we don't have an overwhelming amount of boxes and special sections that diverge from the text material. Rather, we narrowed down the special sections into three basic categories, largely based on the goal of this text, which are mostly dedicated to applying criminological theory to actual offenses, or true cases. We also added a special section in each chapter regarding international comparison of certain offenses (comparative criminology), with an emphasis on how various rates of such crimes differ across the world, especially as compared to the United States. The offenses we compare range widely, from homicide to human trafficking to the correlations of beer consumption and assaults (Ireland was a high outlier). We felt this was important for readers to see how the US compares to other nations in terms of various criminal offenses. So our goal is for readers to understand the ever-growing global nature of criminality, and where the United States is positioned regarding various rates and trends in illegal behavior.

This text is also unique from all of the others by providing a separate chapter on feminist criminology. Given that over half of our citizens are female, and there has been a recent increase in females committing certain crimes (e.g., simple assault), this is an important addition to the study of crime. Furthermore, while males are still universally responsible for the vast majority of violent acts—murder, robbery, aggravated assault—in all societies, if we can understand why females commit so much less violence, then maybe this will have significant implications for reducing male violence. So this separate chapter is vitally important for not only understanding female offenders, but also has implications for male criminals as well.

Another unique aspect of this book is that we devoted separate chapters on the developmental/life-course perspective, as well as modern biosocial approaches regarding propensities to commit crime. These two frameworks/perspectives have become some of the most accepted and valid frameworks on understanding why individuals engage in criminal behavior, but most other criminology textbooks do not examine these topics as closely as we do. A recent study that surveyed key criminologists in the field showed that the developmental/life-course perspective ranked as the second most accepted perspective in explaining chronic offending (and biosocial perspective ranked #6, out of 24+ theories), yet most other textbooks have only a small portion or shallow coverage of this perspective. This developmental/life-course perspective, as well as the biosocial perspective, currently is the "cutting edge" of the field right now, and our chapters on those frameworks highlights the importance of these theoretical models, as well as the recent empirical studies that have been done in those areas of study.

Our text does follow a somewhat traditional format in that it presents theories chronologically from the Classical School to the Positive School of Criminology, discussing all of the established theories in the areas of social structure, social process, and conflict theories as they became popular over time. However, we place much emphasis on examining why certain theories became popular at certain times, which is often due more to politics and societal trends than what empirical studies showed regarding the empirical validity of the given theory. These political and societal trends are vital in every aspect of our lives, and criminological theory is no different. So we tried to work that principle into the text throughout each chapter, showing how crime and theorizing about it is just one manifestation about society at that time period.

Finally, our special typology chapters, located in the last three chapters of the book, are dedicated to more contemporary topics, such as cybercrime, hate crimes, terrorism, white-collar/corporate crimes, drug-related offenses, as well as several others that do not fit into the FBI Index crimes. We have done our best to provide the most current research on these topics, and we hope that readers will gain far more insight on these topics. Furthermore, we believe that our coverage of these modern forms of offending are the most vital in understanding the current state of criminal offending occurring in our society.

Our book also provides an ancillary package with numerous resources to support instructors and students.

Digital Resources

SAGE edge offers a robust online environment featuring an impressive array of tools and resources for review, study, and further exploration, keeping both instructors and students on the cutting edge of teaching and learning. Learn more at **edge.sagepub.com/schram2e.**

Instructor Teaching Site

SAGE edge for Instructors supports your teaching by making it easy to integrate quality content and create a rich learning environment for students. A password-protected site, available at **edge.sagepub.com/schram2e,** features resources that have been designed to help instructors plan and teach their courses. These resources include an extensive test bank, chapter-specific PowerPoint presentations, lecture notes, sample syllabi for semester and quarter courses, class activities, web resources, and links to the video, audio, city and state rankings, author podcasts, and SAGE journal articles.

Student Study Site

SAGE edge for Students provides a personalized approach to help you accomplish your coursework goals in an easy-to-use learning environment. An open-access student study site is available at **edge.sagepub.com/schram2e.** This site provides access to the video, audio, city and state rankings, author podcasts, and SAGE journal articles as well as several study tools including eFlashcards, web quizzes, web resources and chapter outlines.

Available tools that can be found in the Interactive eBook:

 Videos: Links are provided to videos that correlate to the chapter content and increase student understanding.

 Premium videos: Available only in the Interactive eBook, original videos showcase author Stephen Tibbetts discussing real-world examples and strange crimes and a first-person view of the correctional system from former offenders.

 Journal articles: Articles from highly ranked SAGE journals such as *Crime and Delinquency, Theoretical Criminology, Criminal Justice Review,* and more can be accessed.

 Audio Links: Links are provided to audio clips that enhance student comprehension of chapter content.

 Web Links: Links are provided to relevant websites that further explore chapter-related topics.

Access SAGE premium video through the Interactive eBook!
Learn more at edge.sagepub.com/schram2e/access

Overall, we really hope you appreciate our unique approach to studying criminology, and hope you believe that after reading this book that you will have a better understanding of why offenders do what they do.

New to This Edition

As we mentioned previously, a constant theme of this book is "Why Do They Do It?" We explore different reasons of offending by presenting various cases, both hypothetical as well as actual cases, current as well as historical. For this edition, we have updated some of these materials, including more recent crime data as well as more current news stories. Other significant changes in this edition include the following:

- A more extensive discussion on victimization which focuses on victims of crime and presents key concepts in victimology.

- An entire chapter is dedicated to measuring crime (Chapter 2). This chapter provides students a strong, and essential, foundation to understanding and appreciating how crime data enhance our understanding of criminal activity.

- A new section on multicide examines the motivations behind mass murders, school shootings as well as issues of race and religious ideology linked to these types of crimes.

- Up-to-date coverage of contemporary issues such as gun control, mental health, disparity in the criminal justice system, cybercrime and internet fraud, hate crimes, and terrorism.

- Critical thinking questions have been included with other features of this text to help students understand the connection between the real-world examples and theory.

- The revised learning objectives follow Bloom's taxonomy and provide students with a clearer pedagogical framework.

Pamela J. Schram, PhD
Stephen G. Tibbetts, PhD
California State University, San Bernardino

ACKNOWLEDGMENTS

We would first like to thank Publisher Jerry Westby. It was Jerry's idea for us to write this book, and he has "gone to bat" for us numerous times regarding various unique things about this text, such as integrating the violent and property street crimes into the theoretical chapters, rather than just having separate chapters on these topics at the end of the book that instructors often don't get time to cover in a single term, as well as including separate chapters on feminist and developmental/life-course perspectives. This is a rather unorthodox approach, compared to other introduction to criminology textbooks, but Jerry was fully supportive, even at the outset. So we offer him the highest level of respect for his support in backing us on our rather deviant way of approaching this material.

We would also like to thank the staff at SAGE Publishing, for doing such a great job at putting the book together, which includes checking all of the mistakes we made in drafts of the chapters, as well as so many other things that go into producing this book. We specifically want to thank Associate Editor Theresa Accomazzo for all of her help in getting the drafts of the first edition in order to be sent to the copyeditor, and for giving advice on how to make the book far more polished than it was in its original draft. We also want to thank our copyeditor, <copyeditor>, who has gone to great lengths to make us sound much better than we are. She did a fantastic job, and it was a pleasure working with her. Also, we would like give a special thanks to Digital Content Editor Nicole Mangona and Laura Kirkhuff, who were invaluable in finding the various links to videos and other sources that were vital in the e-text version of the text and for pulling together the new original filming for the second edition. Overall, we give the greatest thanks to all of the SAGE staff that worked on this book!

Pamela Schram would like to acknowledge some very special people who had an influence on her life prior to her college years. First and foremost, she would like to thank her ninth grade English teacher, Mr. Joe Devlin. She remembers her first day of English class. Mr. Devlin said, "I can't learn you. First, that is poor English, and second, that is not how it works. I can teach you, but the learning part is on you." Obviously, this has "stuck" with her; it has been over 30 years and she still remembers his "opening" lecture. Later, he was Pam's Latin teacher; Pam continued to take Latin and she was the only student for Latin III. Mr. Devlin would stay after school to conduct this class. As you can imagine, this was not a popular after school activity. But, it taught Pam an important lesson as to how a truly dedicated teacher cares about his students.

Pam would also like to acknowledge Mrs. Frank. She was her second grade teacher. Mrs. Frank was one of those teachers who would incorporate learning with fun things, especially arts and crafts. Mrs. Frank encouraged Pam to write, especially short stories. These were the times when students learned cursive writing on paper with the various lines for lower and upper case. Pam still has some of those short stories written on the "special writing paper. " It brings back many fond memories as well as an appreciation for another special teacher who touched her life.

Pam would finally like to give a special thanks to her organ teacher, Mrs. Cessna. (As you can tell, Pam wasn't considered popular in school.) Mrs. Cessna was one of the most patient teachers Pam has ever had in terms of continuously giving her encouraging words. It may have also helped that Mrs. Cessna had some hearing difficulties. When most of her friends were taking piano, she decided to try organ lessons. She obviously endured some ridicule, especially from her brothers. Their words of encouragement were something like, "Well, with those lessons you can one day play at the Detroit Tiger stadium."

As Pam has gotten older, she has realized the numerous people that have touched her life in so many special ways. One of those special people is her co-author Steve Tibbetts. Steve is an extremely intelligent and well-respected criminologist in the field. He is also a wonderful friend with those important words of encouragement, usually with a sense of humor. He has been very patient and understanding with her not just when writing this book but during his years at CSUSB. Through his friendship, he has helped her to be a better person.

Stephen Tibbetts would like to thank some of the various individuals who helped him complete this book. First, he would like to thank some of the professors he had while earning his undergraduate degree in criminal justice at the University of Florida, who first exposed him to the study of crime and inspired him to become a criminologist. These professors include Ron Akers, Donna Bishop, and Lonn Lanza-Kaduce. He would also like to thank several professors who were key influences in his studies during his graduate studies at University of Maryland, such as Denise Gottfredson, Colin Loftin, David McDowell, Lawrence Sherman, and Charles Wellford. A special thanks goes to Raymond Paternoster, who was his mentor during his graduate studies at Maryland, and provided the best advice and support that any mentor could have given.

Tibbetts would also like to mention the support and influence that work with Alex Piquero, and his wife, Nicole Piquero, had on his career. He was lucky enough to share an office with Alex early on in graduate school, and the work that they did together early on in his career was key in inspiring him to do more work on biosocial and life-course criminology, which are both important portions of this book. Tibbetts' collaboration with Nicole Piquero on the issues of white-collar crime was also important, and has led to more recent studies in this often neglected topic of illegal behavior. He would also like to acknowledge several colleagues who have been important in his research in more recent years, such as John Paul Wright at University of Cincinnati, Nichole H. Rafter at Northeastern University, Chris L. Gibson at University of Florida, Kevin Beaver at Florida State University, and Cesar Rebellon at University of New Hampshire.

Tibbetts would also like to include a special acknowledgment to Jose Rivera, who has contributed much to this book in terms of both video and written sections. Jose has gone above-and-beyond in trying to contribute to the information provided in this book, given his experience as a former incarcerated inmate for over 9 years in various prisons in Southern California. He has shown that such inmates can excel after they have been incarcerated, not only by earning his Master's degree in Communication Studies, but by becoming a fantastic educator, which was proven when he was awarded the Graduate Teaching Assistant of the Year Award by his college at California State University, San Bernardino, in 2012. Jose also recently was a recipient of the President Obama's Presidential Volunteer Service Award in 2012 for his work in programs that promote educational opportunities for Latinos.

Finally, but most important, Tibbetts would especially like to thank his co-author on this book, Pamela Schram, for providing him with the inspiration, motivation, and collaboration for completing this project. Without Pam's constant support and advice, his work on this book could not have materialized. So he gives the highest acknowledgement to Pam; she will always be his most trusted *consigliere*.

Pam and Steve would like to thank the reviewers of the initial proposal for their advice and critiques. They would also like to express their sincere appreciation to their colleagues who reviewed the text and gave them invaluable feedback:

Reviewers of First Edition

Kevin Beaver, Florida State University—Tallahassee

Doris Chu, Arkansas State University—Jonesboro

Christopher Davis, Campbell University—Buies Creek

Melissa Deller, University of Wisconsin-Whitewater

Daniel Dexheimer, San Jose State University

Tina Freiburger, University of Wisconsin-Milwaukee

Chris L. Gibson, University of Florida

Jennifer Grimes, Indiana State University—Terre Haute

W. Bruce Johnson, Houston Community College/Northeast College

Michael A Long, Oklahoma State University

Scott Maggard, Old Dominion University—Norfolk

PJ McGann, University Of Michigan—Ann Arbor

Anna Netterville, University of Louisiana at Monroe

Angela Overton, Old Dominion University—Norfolk

Allison Payne, Villanova University—Villanova

Lacey Rohledef, University of Cincinnati

Anne Strouth, North Central State College—Mansfield

Patricia Warren, Florida State University—Tallahassee

Henriikka Weir, University Of Texas At Dallas—Richardson

Douglas Weiss, University of Maryland

Shonda Whetstone, Blinn College

Reviewers of Second Edition:

Marilyn S. Chamberlin, Western Carolina University

Dan Dexheimer, San Jose State University

Terri L. Earnest, University of Texas at San Antonio

Shanell Sanchez-Smith, Colorado Mesa University

Julie A. Siddique, University of North Texas at Dallas

Bradley Wright, University of Connecticut

Selena M. Respass, Miami Dade College

Charles Crawford, Western Michigan University

Tina L Freiburger, University of Wisconsin-Milwaukee

Frank P. Giarrizzi, Jr., Colorado Technical University

Lindsey Upton, Old Dominion University

Egbert Zavala, University of Texas at El Paso

Christopher Salvatore, PhD, Montclair State University

ABOUT THE AUTHORS

Pamela J. Schram has published articles on such topics as violent female offenders, female juvenile gang and non-gang members, as well as issues pertaining to women in prison, such as stereotypes about mothers in prison and vocational programming. She has co-authored three books on women in prison, theory and practice in feminist criminology, and a juvenile delinquency text. She is currently interested in issues pertaining to elderly prisoners. Dr. Schram has been involved in various research projects that have primarily focused on evaluating treatment effectiveness such as juvenile diversion options and programs for at-risk youths as well as programs for women in prison. Dr. Schram received her Ph.D. from Michigan State University. She is a professor in the Department of Criminal Justice. She is currently the Associate Dean of the College of Social and Behavior Sciences at California State University, San Bernardino.

Stephen G. Tibbetts is a professor in the Department of Criminal Justice at California State University, San Bernardino (CSUSB). He earned his undergraduate degree in criminology and law (with high honors) from the University of Florida, and his masters and doctorate degrees from the University of Maryland. For more than a decade, he worked as a sworn officer of the court (juvenile) in both Washington County, Tennessee, and San Bernardino County, California, providing recommendations for disposing numerous juvenile court cases. He has published more than 40 scholarly publications in scientific journals (including *Criminology, Justice Quarterly, Journal of Research in Crime and Delinquency, Journal of Criminal Justice,* and *Criminal Justice and Behavior*), as well as eight books, all examining various topics regarding criminal offending and policies to reduce such behavior. One of these books, *American Youth Gangs at the Millennium,* was given a Choice award by the American Library Association as an Outstanding Academic Title. Tibbetts received a Golden Apple award from the Mayor of San Bernardino for being chosen as the Outstanding Professor at the CSUSB campus in 2010. One of his recent books, *Criminals in the Making: Criminality Across the Life Course* (Sage, 2008), was recently lauded by *The Chronicle of Higher Education* as one of the key scholarly publications in advancing the study of biosocial criminology.

CHAPTER 1

Introduction to Criminology

Often, crimes such as the mass shooting in San Bernardino, California, lead people to ask, "Why do they do it?"

Francine Orr/Getty Images

INTRODUCTION

When introducing students to criminology, it is essential to stress how various concepts and principles of theoretical development are woven into our understanding of crime as well as policy. This chapter begins with a brief discussion of such concepts as *crime, criminal, deviant, criminology, criminal justice,* and *consensus and conflict perspectives of crime.* The following section presents a general summary of the different stages of the adult criminal justice system as well as the juvenile justice system. Next, this chapter illustrates how criminology informs policies and programs. Unfortunately, there are instances when policies lack evidence and are not founded on criminological theory and rigorous research but are more of a "knee-jerk" reaction. The concluding section provides students with an overview of victimology and various issues related to victims of crime.

KEY CONCEPTS IN UNDERSTANDING CRIMINOLOGY

What Is a Crime?

There are various definitions of crime. Many scholars have disagreed as to what should be considered a crime. For instance, if one takes a legalistic approach, then crime is that which violates the law. But should one consider whether certain actions cause serious harm? If governments violate the basic human rights of their citizens, are they engaging in criminal behavior?[4] As illustrated by these questions, the issue with defining crime from a legalistic approach is that one jurisdiction may designate an action as a crime while another does not recognize such an action as a crime. Some acts, such as murder, are against the law in most countries as well as in all jurisdictions of the United States. These are referred to as acts of *mala in se,* meaning the act is "inherently and essentially evil, that is immoral in its nature and injurious in its consequence, without any regard to the fact of its being noticed or punished by the law of the state."[5]

Other crimes are known as acts of *mala prohibita,* which means "a wrong prohibited; an act which is not inherently immoral, but becomes so because its commission is expressly forbidden by positive law."[6] For instance, prostitution is illegal in most jurisdictions in the United States. However, prostitution is legal, and licensed, in most counties of Nevada. The same can be said about gambling and drug possession or use.

This text focuses on both *mala in se* and *mala prohibita* offenses as well as other acts of deviance. Deviant acts are not necessarily against the law but are considered atypical and may be deemed immoral rather than illegal. For example, in Nevada in the 1990s, a young man watched his friend (who was later criminally prosecuted) kill a young girl in a casino bathroom. He never told anyone of the murder. While most people would consider this highly immoral, at that time, Nevada state laws did not require people who witnessed a killing to report it to authorities. This act was deviant, because most would consider it immoral; it was not criminal, because it was not against the laws of that jurisdiction. It is essential to note that as a result of this event, Nevada made withholding such information a criminal act.

BURKE AND HARE

During the 1820s, Edinburgh, Scotland, was a major center for those pursuing an education in medicine. Almost 60 years prior to Jack the Ripper, the first serial murderers, William Burke and William Hare, captured media attention. During a 12-month period, Burke and Hare killed 16 people in Edinburgh before being arrested in November 1828. What made these killings so sordid was that Burke and Hare committed them for the sole purpose of selling the cadavers to medical schools for dissection and medical research. They were assisted by Burke's companion, Helen M'Dougal, and Hare's wife, Margaret. Burke and Hare would lure their victims with alcohol. Then, they would suffocate their inebriated victims by lying on their chests and holding their mouths and nostrils closed. Subsequently, Burke and Hare would sell these cadavers, "no questions asked," to Dr. Robert Knox, a promising anatomist.

During the trial, Hare was granted immunity in return for testifying against Burke. Burke was found guilty and sentenced to death by hanging. He was hanged on January 28, 1829. Ironically, the next day, Burke's cadaver was donated to the University of Edinburgh, where Professor Alexander Monro conducted the dissection in the anatomical theater.[1] In fact, the University of Edinburgh Anatomical Museum has an exhibit of William Burke's skeletal remains. A description of the exhibit ends with a 19th-century children's rhyme:

Up the close and down the stair

In the house with Burke and Hare

Burke's the butcher

Hare's the thief

Knox the boy who buys the beef.[2]

In January 2016, Arthur and Elizabeth Rathburn from Grosse Point Park, Michigan (six miles outside Detroit), were indicted for running a black-market body part business. The Rathburns obtained most of the cadavers from two Chicago-area body donation labs. Many of the families who donated the bodies of their loved ones did so with the belief that they would go to science. A number of these cadavers were infected with HIV, hepatitis B, and other diseases. The Rathburns would use chainsaws, band saws, and reciprocating saws to butcher these cadavers for body parts. The Rathburns stored body parts from over 1,000 people inside a warehouse. Subsequently, they would sell these butchered body parts to medical and dental trainees. However, they sometimes did not disclose to their customers that these body parts were infected with disease.[3]

> WHAT MADE THESE KILLINGS SO SORDID WAS THAT BURKE AND HARE COMMITTED THEM FOR THE SOLE PURPOSE OF SELLING THE CADAVERS TO MEDICAL SCHOOLS FOR DISSECTION AND MEDICAL RESEARCH.

Over 180 years separate these two cases; the technological expertise needed to carry out these crimes significantly changed during this time. However, one consistent theme that links these two cases is motive—monetary gain. This is one of the most fascinating aspects to studying crime—although technology may have changed how crimes are committed (e.g., Internet fraud), have the explanations (i.e., "why they do it") changed?

Other acts of deviance are not necessarily seen as immoral but are considered strange and violate social norms, such as purposely belching at a formal dinner. These types of deviant acts are relevant even if not considered criminal under the legal definition, for individuals engaging in these types of activities reveal a disposition toward antisocial behavior often linked to criminal behavior. Further, some acts are moving from being deemed deviant to being declared illegal, such as using a cell phone while driving or smoking cigarettes in public. Many jurisdictions are moving to have these behaviors made illegal and have been quite successful, especially in New York and California.

While most *mala in se* activities are also considered highly deviant, this is not necessarily the case for *mala prohibita* acts. For instance, speeding on a highway (a *mala prohibita* act) is not deviant, because many people engage in this act. Thus, while this is illegal, it is not considered deviant. This book presents theories for all these types of activities, even those that do not violate the law.[7]

What Is Criminology and Criminal Justice?

The term *criminology* was first coined by the Italian law professor Raffaele Garofalo in 1885 (in Italian, *criminologia*). In 1887, French anthropologist Paul Topinard used it for the first time in French (*criminologie*).[8] In 1934, American criminologist Edwin Sutherland defined criminology as

> the body of knowledge regarding crime as a social phenomenon. It includes within its scope the process of making laws, of breaking laws, and of reacting toward the breaking of laws. . . . The objective of criminology is the development of a body of general and verified principles and of other types of knowledge regarding this process of law, crime, and treatment or prevention.[9]

Criminology is the scientific study of crime, especially why people engage in criminal behavior. While other textbooks may provide a more complex definition of crime, the word *scientific* distinguishes our definition from other perspectives and examinations of crime.[10] Philosophical and legal examinations of crime are based on logic and deductive reasoning—for example, by developing what makes logical sense. Journalists play a key role in examining crime by exploring what is happening in criminal justice and revealing injustices as well as new forms of crime. However, the philosophical, legal, and journalistic perspectives of crime are not scientific because they do not involve the use of the scientific method.

Criminal justice often refers to the various criminal justice agencies and institutions (e.g., police, courts, and corrections) that are interrelated and work together toward common goals. Interestingly, many scholars who referred to criminal justice as a system did so only as a way to collectively refer to those agencies and organizations rather than to imply that they were interrelated.[11] Some individuals argue that the term *criminal justice system* is an oxymoron. For instance, Joanne Belknap noted that she preferred to use the terms *crime processing*, *criminal processing*, and *criminal legal system*, given that "the processing of victims and offenders [is] anything but 'just.'"[12]

The Consensus and Conflict Perspectives of Crime

A consensus perspective of crime views the formal system of laws, as well as the enforcement of those laws, as incorporating societal norms for which there is a broad normative consensus.[13] The consensus perspective developed from the writings of late-19th- and early-20th-century sociologists such as Durkheim, Weber, Ross, and Sumner.[14] This perspective assumes that individuals, for the most part, agree on what is right and wrong as well as on how those norms have been implemented into laws and how those laws are

crime: there are various definitions of crime. From a legalistic approach, crime is that which violates the law.

mala in se: acts that are considered inherently evil.

mala prohibita: acts that are considered crimes primarily because they have been declared bad by the legal codes in that jurisdiction.

deviance: behaviors that are not normal; includes many illegal acts as well as activities that are not necessarily criminal but are unusual and often violate social norms.

criminology: the scientific study of crime and the reasons why people engage (or don't engage) in criminal behavior.

criminal justice: often refers to the various criminal justice agencies and institutions (e.g., police, courts, and corrections) that are interrelated.

consensus perspective: theories that assume that virtually everyone is in agreement on the laws and therefore assume no conflict in attitudes regarding the laws and rules of society.

Marsha Gay Reynolds, a JetBlue flight attendant, was accused of transporting $3 million worth of cocaine in her suitcase. What might have motivated such behavior?

conflict perspective: criminal behavior theories that assume most people disagree on what the law should be and that law is used as a tool by those in power to keep down other groups.

enforced. Thus, people obey laws not for fear of punishment but rather because they have internalized societal norms and values and perceive these laws as appropriate to observe rather than disobey.[15] The consensus perspective was more dominant during the early part of the 1900s. Since the 1950s, however, no major theorist has considered this to be the best perspective of law. Further, "to the extent that assumptions or hypotheses about consensus theory are still given credence in current theories of law, they are most apt to be found in 'mutualist' models."[16]

Around the 1950s, the conflict perspective was challenging the consensus approach.[17] The conflict perspective maintains that there is conflict between various societal groups with different interests. This conflict is often resolved when the group in power achieves control.

Several criminologists, such as Richard Quinney, William Chambliss, and Austin Turk, maintained that criminological theory has placed too much emphasis on explaining criminal behavior; rather, theory needs to shift its focus toward explaining criminal law. The emphasis should not be on understanding the causes of criminal behavior but on understanding the process by which certain behaviors and individuals are formally designated as criminal. From this perspective, one would ask different questions. For instance, instead of asking, "Why do some people commit crimes while others do not?" one would ask, "Why are some behaviors defined as criminal while others are not?" Asking these types of questions raises the issue of whether the formulation and enforcement of laws serve the interests of those in a more powerful position in society.[18]

THE CRIMINAL JUSTICE SYSTEM

According to the 1967 President's Commission on Law Enforcement and Administration of Justice,

> any criminal justice system is an apparatus society uses to enforce the standards of conduct necessary to protect individuals and the community. It operates by apprehending, prosecuting, convicting, and sentencing those members of the community who violate the basic rules of group existence.[19]

This general purpose of the criminal justice system can be further simplified into three goals: to control crime, to prevent crime, and to provide and maintain justice. The structure and organization of the criminal justice system has evolved in an effort to meet these goals. The structure and organization is often presented as three components: law enforcement, courts, and corrections.[20]

LEARNING CHECK 1.1

1. Crime that is evil in itself is referred to as _____.

2. Acts that are not necessarily against the law but are considered atypical and may be considered more immoral than illegal are _____ acts.

3. Criminology is distinguished from other perspectives of crime, such as journalistic, philosophical, or legal perspectives, because it involves the use of _____.

Answers located at www.edge.sagepub.com/schram2e

Law Enforcement

Law enforcement includes various organizational levels (i.e., federal, state, and local). One of the key features distinguishing federal law enforcement agencies from others is that they were often established to enforce specific statutes. Thus, their units are highly specialized and often associated with specialized training and resources.[21] Federal law enforcement agencies include the Federal Bureau of Investigation (FBI), the Drug Enforcement Administration (DEA), the U.S. Secret Service, the U.S. Marshals Service, and the Bureau of Alcohol, Tobacco, Firearms, and Explosives (ATF). Further, almost all federal agencies, including the Postal Service and the Forest Service, have some police power. In 2002, President George W. Bush restructured the federal agencies, resulting in the establishment of the Department of Homeland Security. This department was created in an effort to protect and defend the United States from terrorist threats.[22]

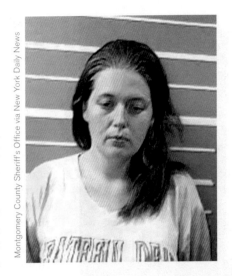 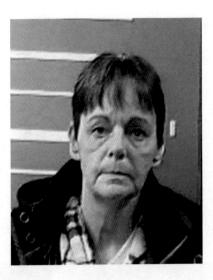

Montgomery County Sheriff's Office via New York Daily News

Law enforcement officials often find crime in unusual places. These two women were arrested after being accused of cooking meth inside a rural Illinois church.

The earliest form of state police agency to emerge in the United States was the Texas Rangers, founded by Stephen Austin in 1823 to protect settlers. By 1925, formal state police departments existed throughout most of the country. While some organizational variations exist among the different states, two models generally characterize the structure of these state police departments.

The first model can be designated as state police. States such as Michigan, New York, Pennsylvania, Delaware, Vermont, and Arkansas have a state police structure. These agencies have general police powers and enforce state laws as well as perform routine patrols and traffic regulation. Further, they have additional functions such as specialized units to investigate major crimes, intelligence units, drug trafficking units, juvenile units, and crime laboratories. The second model can be designated as highway patrol. States such as California, Ohio, Georgia, Florida, and the Carolinas have a highway patrol model. For these agencies, the primary focus is to enforce the laws that govern the operation of motor vehicles on public roads and highways. In some instances, this also includes not just enforcing traffic laws but investigating crimes that occur in specific locations or under certain circumstances, such as on state highways or state property.[23] Agencies on the local level are divided into counties and municipalities. The primary law enforcement office for most counties is that of county sheriff. In most instances, the sheriff is an elected position. The majority of local police officers are employed by municipalities. Most of these agencies comprise fewer than 10 officers. Local police agencies are responsible for the "nuts and bolts" of law enforcement responsibilities. For instance, they investigate most crimes and engage in crime prevention activities such as patrol duties. Further, these officers are often responsible for providing social services such as responding to incidents of domestic violence and child abuse.[24]

Courts

The United States does not have just one judicial system. Rather, the judicial system is quite complex. In fact, there are 52 different systems, one for each state, the District of Columbia, and the federal government. Given this complexity, however, one can

state police: agencies with general police powers to enforce state laws as well as to investigate major crimes; they may have intelligence units, drug trafficking units, juvenile units, and crime laboratories.

highway patrol: one type of model characterizing statewide police departments. The primary focus is to enforce the laws that govern the operation of motor vehicles on public roads and highways.

Andrew Harrer/Bloomberg via Getty Images

A black wool crepe is draped over Justice Antonin Scalia's bench chair in the Supreme Court courtroom. His death in 2016 left a vacancy on the Supreme Court bench.

characterize the United States as having a *dual court system*. This dual court system consists of separate yet interrelated systems: the federal courts and the state courts. While there are variations among the states in terms of judicial structure, usually a state court system consists of different levels or tiers, such as lower courts, trial courts, appellate courts, and the state's highest court. The federal court system is a three-tiered model: U.S. district courts (i.e., trial courts) and other specialized courts, U.S. courts of appeals, and the U.S. Supreme Court (see Figure 1.1).[25]

Before any case can be brought to a court, that court must have *jurisdiction* over those individuals involved in the case. Jurisdiction is the authority of a court to hear and decide cases within an area of the law (i.e., subject matter such as serious felonies, civil cases, or misdemeanors) or a geographic territory.[26] Essentially, jurisdiction is categorized as limited, general, or appellate:

Courts of limited jurisdiction. These are also designated as lower courts. They do not have power that extends to the overall administration of justice; thus, they do not try felony cases and do not have appellate authority.

Courts of general jurisdiction. These are also designated as major trial courts. They have the power and authority to try and decide any case, including appeals from a lower court.

Courts of appellate jurisdiction. These are also designated as appeals courts. They are limited in their jurisdiction decisions on matters of appeal from lower courts and trial courts.[27]

Every court, including the U.S. Supreme Court, is limited in terms of jurisdiction.

Corrections

limited jurisdiction: the authority of a court to hear and decide cases within an area of the law or a geographic territory.

probation: essentially an arrangement between the sentencing authorities and the offender requiring the offender to comply with certain terms for a specified amount of time.

jail: jails are often designated for individuals convicted of a minor crime and to house individuals awaiting trial.

After an offender is convicted and sentenced, he or she is processed in the corrections system. An offender can be placed on probation, incarcerated, or transferred to some type of community-based corrections facility. Probation is essentially an *arrangement* between the sentencing authorities and the offender. While under supervision, the offender must comply with certain terms for a specified amount of time to return to the community. These terms are often referred to as conditions of probation.[28] Examples of *general conditions* include the offenders regularly reporting to their supervising officer, obeying the laws, submitting to searches, and not being in possession of firearms or using drugs. *Specific conditions* can also be imposed, such as participating in methadone maintenance, urine testing, house arrest, vocational training, or psychological or psychiatric treatment.[29] There are also variations to probation. For instance, a judge can combine probation with incarceration, such as *shock incarceration*. This involves sentencing the offender to spend a certain amount of time each week, oftentimes over the weekend, in some type of institution like a jail; during the remaining time period, the offender is on probation.

Some offenders are required to serve their sentences in a corrections facility. One type of corrections facility is jail. Jails are often designated for individuals convicted of minor

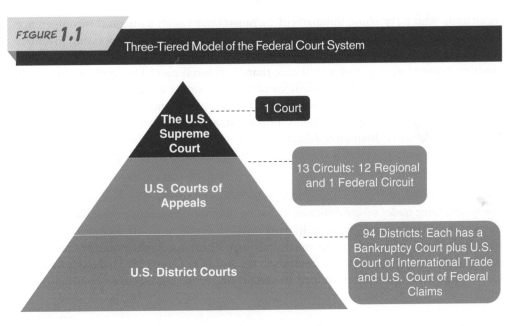

FIGURE **1.1**   Three-Tiered Model of the Federal Court System

The U.S. Supreme Court — 1 Court

U.S. Courts of Appeals — 13 Circuits: 12 Regional and 1 Federal Circuit

U.S. District Courts — 94 Districts: Each has a Bankruptcy Court plus U.S. Court of International Trade and U.S. Court of Federal Claims

Source: Adapted from http://judiciallearningcenter.org/our-programs/

crimes. Jails are also used to house individuals awaiting trial; these people have not been convicted but are incarcerated for various reasons, such as preventative detention. Another type of corrections facility is **prison**. Those sentenced to prison are often convicted of more serious crimes with longer sentences. There are different types of prisons based on security concerns, such as supermax, maximum, medium, and minimum security. Generally, counties and municipalities operate jails, while prisons are operated by federal and state governments.[30]

Given the rising jail and prison populations, there has been increased use of alternatives to traditional incarceration. For instance, examples of residential sanctions include halfway houses as well as work and study release. Examples of nonresidential sanctions include house arrest, electronic monitoring, and day reporting centers.[31]

The Juvenile Justice System

Prior to the establishment of the juvenile justice system, children were treated the same as adults in terms of criminal processing. Children were considered as "imperfect" adults or "adults in miniature." They were held to the same standards of behavior as adults. The American colonists brought with them the common law doctrine from England, which held that juveniles seven years or older could be treated the same as adult offenders. Thus, they were incarcerated with adults and could also receive similarly harsh punishments, including the death penalty. It should be noted, however, that youths rarely received such harsh and severe punishments.[32] Beginning in the early 1800s, many recognized the need for a separate system for juveniles.[33] For instance, Johann Heinrich Pestalozzi, a Swiss educator, maintained that children are distinct from adults, both physically and psychologically.

While there is some disagreement in accrediting the establishment of the first juvenile court, most acknowledge that the first comprehensive juvenile court system was initiated in 1899 in Cook County, Illinois. An essential component to understanding the juvenile justice system is the concept of **parens patriae**. This Latin term literally means "the parent of the country." This philosophical perspective recognizes that the state has both the right and the obligation to intervene on behalf of and to protect

prison: generally for those convicted of more serious crimes with longer sentences, who may be housed in a supermax-, maximum-, medium-, or minimum-security prison, based on security concerns.

parens patriae: a philosophical perspective that recognizes that the state has both the right and the obligation to intervene on behalf of its citizens in the case of some impairment or impediment such as mental incompetence or, in the case of juveniles, age and immaturity.

its citizens who have some impairment or impediment such as mental incompetence or, in the case of juveniles, immaturity. The primary objective of processing juveniles was to determine what was in the best interest of the child. This resulted in the proceedings resembling more of a civil case than a criminal case. The implication of this approach was that the juvenile's basic constitutional rights were not recognized; these rights included the right to the confrontation and cross-examination of the witnesses, the right to protection against self-incrimination, and compliance regarding the rules of evidence. Another distinctive feature separating the juvenile justice system and the adult criminal justice system is the use of different terms for similar procedures in each system (see Table 1.1).

During the 1960s, there was a dramatic increase in juvenile crime. The existing juvenile justice system came under severe criticism, including questions concerning the informal procedures of the juvenile courts. Eventually, numerous U.S. Supreme Court decisions challenged these procedures, and some maintained that these decisions would radically change the nature of processing juveniles. For instance, in the case *In re Gault* (1967), the U.S. Supreme Court ruled that a juvenile is entitled to certain due-process protections constitutionally

TABLE 1.1 Comparing Juvenile and Criminal Justice System Terms

JUVENILE JUSTICE SYSTEM TERM	CRIMINAL JUSTICE SYSTEM TERM
Adjudicated delinquent – Found to have engaged in delinquent conduct	**Conviction**
Adjudication hearing – A hearing to determine whether there is evidence beyond a reasonable doubt to support the allegations against the juvenile	**Trial**
Aftercare – Supervision of a juvenile after release from an institution	**Parole**
Commitment – Decision by a juvenile court judge to send the adjudicated juvenile to an institution	**Sentence to prison**
Delinquent act – A behavior committed by a juvenile that would have been a crime if committed by an adult	**Crime**
Delinquent – A juvenile who has been adjudicated of a delinquent act in juvenile court	**Criminal**
Detention – Short-term secure confinement of a juvenile for the protection of the juvenile or for the protection of society	**Confinement in jail**
Detention center – A facility designed for short-term secure confinement of a juvenile prior to court disposition or execution of a court order	**Jail**
Disposition – The sanction imposed on a juvenile who has been adjudicated in juvenile court	**Sentence**
Disposition hearing – A hearing held after a juvenile has been adjudicated	**Sentencing hearing**
Institution – A facility designed for long-term secure confinement of a juvenile after adjudication (also referred to as a training school)	**Prison**
Petition – A document that states the allegations against a juvenile and requests a juvenile court to adjudicate the juvenile	**Indictment**
Taken into custody – The action on the part of a police officer to obtain custody of a juvenile accused of committing a delinquent act	**Arrest**

Source: Taylor, R. W., & Fritsch, E. J. (2015). *Juvenile justice: Policies, programs, and practices* (4th ed.). New York, NY: McGraw-Hill Education, p. 9.

guaranteed to adults, such as a right to notice of the charges, right to counsel, right to confront and cross-examine witnesses, and right against self-incrimination. The case *In re Winship* (1970) decided that the standard of proof in juvenile delinquency proceedings is proof beyond a reasonable doubt. The first U.S. Supreme Court case to address juvenile court procedures was *Kent v. United States* (1966). The court ruled that juveniles who are facing a waiver to adult court are entitled to some essential due-process rights.

Although the major impetus for establishing the juvenile justice system was to emphasize rehabilitation, since the 1980s, there has been an emerging trend toward a more punitive approach to juveniles. This changing trend is due to various converging developments, such as broadening due-process protections of adults to include juveniles, the resurgence of retribution, and societal changes in perceptions about children's responsibility and accountability.[34] Another aspect to this more punitive trend is in reference to transfer provisions—waiving a juvenile offender from the juvenile justice system to the adult criminal justice system. The reasons for waivers have often been that the juvenile justice system cannot provide the needed treatment or protect the community from the offender. In reality, however, the reason for waivers is an immediate increase in the severity of response to the juvenile.[35]

Some states have had transfer provisions since the 1920s; other states have had such provisions since the 1940s.[36] Transfer provisions can be categorized into three types: judicial waiver, concurrent jurisdiction, and statutory exclusion.

> Judicial waiver: The juvenile court judge has the authority to waive juvenile court jurisdiction and transfer the case to criminal court. States may use terms other than *judicial waiver*. Some call the process *certification*, *remand*, or *bind over* for criminal prosecution. Others *transfer* or *decline* rather than waive jurisdiction.
>
> Concurrent jurisdiction: Original jurisdiction for certain cases is shared by both criminal and juvenile courts, and the prosecutor has discretion to file such cases in either court. Transfer under concurrent jurisdiction provisions is also known as *prosecutorial waiver*, *prosecutor discretion*, or *direct file*.
>
> Statutory exclusion: State statute excludes certain juvenile offenders from juvenile court jurisdiction. Under statutory exclusion provisions, cases originate in criminal rather than juvenile court. Statutory exclusion is also known as *legislative exclusion*.[37]

While all states have some type of provision that allows some juveniles to be tried in adult criminal court, 34 states have what is termed the "once an adult, always an adult" provision. Under this provision, juveniles who have been tried and convicted as adults *must* be prosecuted in criminal court for any subsequent offenses.

Introduction to Comparative Criminology

Another area of criminological research is the study of the nature and extent of crime and criminal justice systems across societies. This is an expanding area of research given

---

LEARNING CHECK 1.2

1. Law enforcement agencies on the state level that have general police powers as well as additional functions, such as investigating major crimes, are designated as the _____ model.

2. Law enforcement agencies on the state level whose primary focus is to enforce laws concerning public roads and highways are designated as the _____ model.

3. Every court, including the U.S. Supreme Court, is limited in terms of _____.

4. Recognizing that the state has both the right and an obligation to protect juveniles is referred to as _____.

Answers located at www.edge.sagepub.com/schram2e

---

judicial waiver: the authority to waive juvenile court jurisdiction and transfer the case to criminal court.

concurrent jurisdiction: original jurisdiction for certain cases is shared by both criminal and juvenile courts; the prosecutor has discretion to file such cases in either court.

statutory exclusion: excludes certain juvenile offenders from juvenile court jurisdiction; cases originate in criminal rather than juvenile court.

the complexities associated with crime, prevention, and detection in a high-tech, global environment.[38] There are various definitions for the term *comparative criminology*, some being more comprehensive in scope than others. Hardie-Bick, Sheptycki, and Wardak noted that comparative criminology should address questions such as the following:

- Why do some societies have lower crime rates?

- What are the differences and similarities in crime definition and control across social and cultural frontiers?

- How do theoretical models relating to crime translate across cultures?[39]

The comparative perspective is not a relatively new approach. In 1889, E. B. Taylor outlined the benefits of such an approach during his presentation to the Royal Anthropological Institute of Great Britain. But it was not until the mid-1950s that researchers outside anthropological studies, such as those in sociology, psychology, and political science, incorporated a more comparative approach in their research. Criminologists also began to incorporate this perspective in the late 1960s and early 1970s. While this approach has been relatively slow to gain prominence, a growing body of research incorporates this perspective.[40]

The study of comparative criminology is no longer considered an option but rather a necessity:[41]

> In our global village, crime problems are no longer a domestic concern. Many types of crime have international dimensions, and trends in crime and justice in different countries are increasingly interdependent. The international nature of markets for drugs, sexual services, and illicit firearms is generally recognized. Less well understood is the international nature of many other criminal markets such as that for stolen cars with an estimated half million stolen cars transported from developed to less developed countries annually. More and more criminal groups operate internationally through loose networks of partners in crime.[42]

As mentioned previously, although there is an increased appreciation for the study of comparative criminology, there are limitations regarding the availability of international statistics on crime and criminal justice. In recent years, there have been increasing efforts to enhance international statistics on global social issues such as diseases, infant mortality, and the consumption of illegal drugs. However, efforts to collect information on crime are limited. One explanation for the relative paucity of data on this global issue is that some governments do not want to be exposed to data that may reveal their countries in a negative light. Scholars are working to break this politically inspired *conspiracy of silence*.[43]

This text will include a series of boxes that compare the United States with foreign nations in terms of various aspects of criminology and criminal justice. Nearly every chapter in this textbook will include a Comparative Criminology box, and each will focus on a single type of serious crime; for example, the Comparative Criminology box in this chapter examines relative rates of motor vehicle theft. It is important to be aware of and understand where the United States stands in relative terms on crime rates, which enlightens us on how cultural and socioeconomic factors influence such rates. The same can be said of comparing various regions/states/cities across the United States, which some of the comparative boxes will also examine.

Most of the statistics in the various comparative criminology boxes of this book were obtained from *The World of Crime* by Jan Van Dijk, one of the best compilations of international crime statistics in that it synthesizes and reports on a variety of measures using both police reports and victimization surveys from a multitude of sources.

comparative criminology: the study of crime across various cultures to identify similarities and differences in crime patterns.

Applying Theory to Crime: *MOTOR VEHICLE THEFT*

A motor vehicle theft is defined as "the theft or attempted theft of a motor vehicle. . . . A motor vehicle is a self-propelled vehicle that runs on land surfaces and not on rails."[44] Examples of motor vehicles include sport utility vehicles, automobiles, trucks, buses, motorcycles, motor scooters, all-terrain vehicles, and snowmobiles. They do not, however, include farm equipment, bulldozers, airplanes, construction equipment, or watercraft. In 2014, about 689,527 motor vehicle thefts were reported in the United States. In that time, more than $4.5 billion was lost as a result of motor vehicle thefts; the average dollar loss per stolen vehicle was $6,537.

Slightly over 74% of all motor vehicle thefts were automobiles. According to the National Insurance Crime Bureau (NICB), the Honda Accord is stolen more often than any other car in the United States. This is followed by the Honda Civic, Ford pickup (full size), Chevrolet pickup (full size), Toyota Camry, Dodge Ram pickup (full size), Dodge Caravan, Nissan Altima, Acura Integra, and Nissan Maxima.[45] Further, the NICB noted that one should also consider vehicle theft fraud. In the past, vehicle thieves were focused on stealing cars and trucks the "old-fashioned way," such as by forced entry and circumventing ignitions. Today, there are new scams for stealing vehicles that involve fraud:

- Owner give-ups: The vehicle owner lies about the theft of the vehicle and then orchestrates its destruction to collect insurance money. He or she claims the vehicle was stolen, but then it is found burned or heavily damaged in a secluded area, submerged in a lake, or, in extreme cases, buried underground.

- Thirty-day specials: Owners whose vehicles need extensive repairs sometimes perpetrate the 30-day special scam. They will report the vehicle stolen and hide it for 30 days—just long enough for the insurance company to settle the claim. Once the claim is paid, the vehicle is often found abandoned.

- Export fraud: After securing a bank loan for a new vehicle, an owner obtains an insurance policy for it. The owner reports the vehicle stolen to a U.S. law enforcement agency but, in reality, has illegally shipped it overseas to be sold on the black market. The owner then collects on the insurance policy as well as any illegal profits earned through overseas conspirators who sell the vehicle.

- Phantom vehicles: An individual creates a phony title or registration to secure insurance on a nonexistent vehicle. The insured then reports the vehicle stolen before filing a fraudulent insurance claim. Often, antique or luxury vehicles are used in this scam, since these valuable vehicles produce larger insurance settlements.[46]

One interesting approach to addressing the problem of motor vehicle thefts, which has been popularized by the media, is the use of bait cars. The Los Angeles Police Department defines the use of a bait car as "an undercover operation where [they] bring in a plain motor vehicle and load it with desirable goods (iPod, GPS, cigarettes, etc.) and hope someone breaks into the car as [they] are watching."[47] On June 25, 2012, police in Albuquerque, New Mexico, were quite surprised when one of their bait cars was stolen by an 11-year-old boy. This boy wanted to take the car for a joy ride; on the way, he also decided to pick up two of his 10-year-old friends. A video camera had been placed in the bait car. In the video, the boy can be heard bragging to his friends about his driving skills. For instance, while turning up the radio to enjoy the music as he drives, the boy says, "I'm a good driver, huh?" During their joy ride, apparently one of the boys spotted a police officer; one of the boys said, "Quiet," while the other said, "Slow down."[48]

After reading about this youth, one might ask, "Why would he do that?" Some of you might consider that his 10-year-old peers somehow influenced his behavior, especially since it seems he wanted them to be a part of his criminal adventure. Others may argue that these boys lacked some form of adult supervision resulting from a dysfunctional family environment. Another possible explanation is that these boys lacked self-control, that they were thrill seekers who knew this was wrong, especially given their reaction when spotting the police. When we read about this type of behavior in a newspaper or hear about it on the news and ask, "Why would someone do that?" we are trying to find some kind of explanation. This is what theory attempts to do but in a more rigorous, scientific manner. Throughout this text, as we discuss various theories, we attempt to apply key points of those theories to either a real or hypothetical situation in boxes labeled "Applying Theories to Crime." For each of these special boxes, we begin with a brief discussion of a particular crime, such as motor vehicle theft, robbery, or murder. Subsequently, we apply the relevant theory or theories in that chapter to that particular crime. With this approach, you will obtain general information about particular offenses as well as apply key features of various theories to those crimes.

THINK ABOUT IT:

1. What kind of influence did peers have on this 11-year-old's behavior?

2. Do you think the lack of adult supervision could explain his behavior?

Comparative Criminology: *MOTOR VEHICLE THEFT*

Ranking Regions/Countries on Rates of Motor Vehicle Theft

The key measure of prevalence of motor vehicle theft in the world is the International Crime Victimization Survey (ICVS), which is a data bank that collects and standardizes police reports from more than 70 countries around the world. This measure has been conducted since 1987 and does have some weaknesses, but it is currently the best measure of most crimes in terms of cross-national comparisons.

The ICVS has collected many years' worth of data on motor vehicle theft. Van Dijk synthesized the data from ICVS regarding car theft from the years 1996 to 2005.[51] Some regions have very high numbers of stolen vehicles, but to make a fair

comparison across regions, rates of ownership should be accounted for. As seen in Figure 1.2, the countries with by far the highest percentages of car owners in urban areas who had been victimized by car theft were on the continent of Africa. A relatively distant second highest ranking area was countries in the region of Latin America/Caribbean.

To be more specific, we can examine the ranking of the countries in terms of their rates of vehicle theft. As can be seen in Figure 1.3, ICVS data show that Papua New Guinea had by far the highest rate (at 9.8% of car owners victimized each year), followed by Mozambique (7.5%) and then South Africa, Swaziland, and Brazil rounding out the top five. It is notable that the United States did not rank in the worst 15 countries for motor vehicle theft.

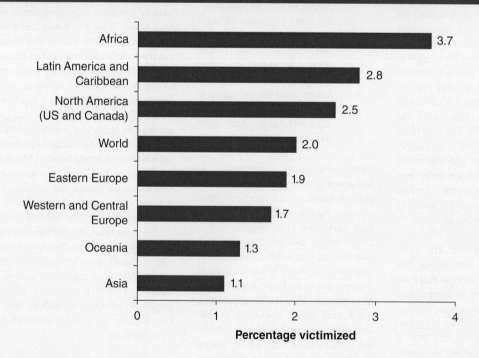

FIGURE 1.2

Percentages of Car Owners in Urban Areas Victimized by Car Theft or Joyriding During the Past 12 Months

Region	Percentage victimized
Africa	3.7
Latin America and Caribbean	2.8
North America (US and Canada)	2.5
World	2.0
Eastern Europe	1.9
Western and Central Europe	1.7
Oceania	1.3
Asia	1.1

Source: ICVS, 1996–2005, latest survey available.

FIGURE **1.3**

World Ranking of Countries According to Victimization of Car Owners in Urban Areas by Theft of a Car in the Course of One Year, Rank Number, and Percentage of Victims per Year

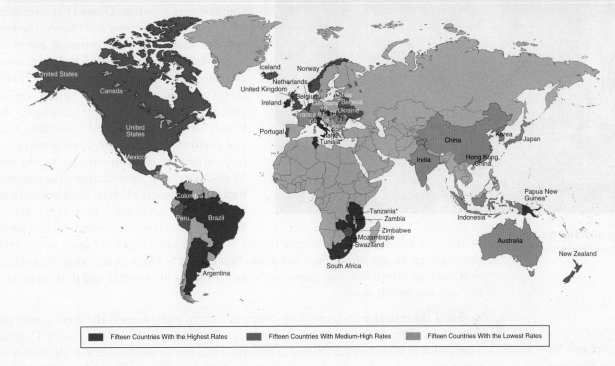

Fifteen Countries With the Highest Rates ■ Fifteen Countries With Medium-High Rates ■ Fifteen Countries With the Lowest Rates

Sources: ICVS, 1992, 1996–2005, latest survey available.

*Countries with data from ICVS, 1992.

It is not too surprising that motor vehicle theft tends to be higher (when accounting for rates of ownership) in some of the most deprived nations in the world, such as Africa and various Latin American/Caribbean countries. After all, in such extreme poverty, many individuals are driven to commit such crimes to survive. However, the results from the ICVS also reveal that vehicle theft actually happens quite a bit in many regions of the world (North America being ranked third), so motor vehicle theft is alive and well throughout virtually all societies.

THINK ABOUT IT:

1. According to the ICVS, what regions of the world had the highest rates of motor vehicle theft between 1996 and 2005?

2. Which regions had the lowest vehicle theft rates between 1996 and 2005?

3. Can you provide possible explanations for these differences across regions?

CRIMINOLOGICAL THEORY

Respected scientific theories in all fields of study, whether chemistry, physics, or criminology, tend to have the same characteristics. This is further illustrated by the scientific review process (i.e., blind peer review by experts) used in all fields to assess which studies and theoretical frameworks are of high quality. The criteria that characterize a good theory in chemistry are the same ones used to assess what makes a good criminological theory. These characteristics include parsimony, scope, logical consistency, testability, empirical validity, and policy implications.[49] Each of these characteristics is examined in the next section.[50]

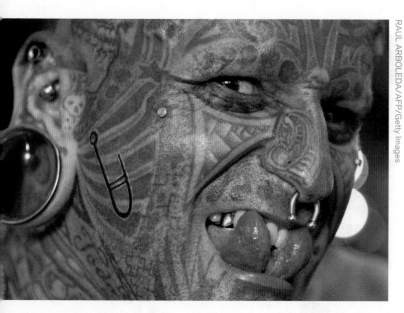

How would Lombroso classify this person?

RAUL ARBOLEDA/AFP/Getty Images

Characteristics of Good Theories

Parsimony is attained by explaining a phenomenon, such as criminal activity, in the simplest way possible. Other characteristics being equal, the simpler the theory, the better. The challenge with criminal behavior is that it is highly complex; however, some criminologists have attempted to explain this complex phenomenon using rather simplistic approaches. For instance, the theory of low self-control maintains that one personality factor—low self-control—is responsible for all criminal activity. As will be discussed in a later chapter, the originators of this theory, Michael Gottfredson and Travis Hirschi, contend that every act of crime and deviance is caused by this same factor: low self-control.[52] A simple theory is better than a more complex one. Given the complex nature of criminal behavior, however, it is likely that a simple explanation, such as identifying one factor to explain all types of criminal and deviant behavior, will not be adequate.

Scope is the trait that indicates how much of a given phenomenon the theory attempts to explain. Other traits being equal, the larger the scope, the better the theory. To some extent, this is related to parsimony in the sense that some theories, such as the theory of low self-control, seek to explain all crimes and all deviant acts. Thus, the theory of low self-control has a very wide scope. As we will discuss later, other theories of crime may attempt to explain only property crime, such as some versions of strain theory or drug use. However, the wider the scope of what a theory can explain, the better the theory.

Logical consistency is the extent to which a theory makes sense in terms of its concepts and propositions. Sometimes it is easier to illustrate this point with an example. Some theories do not make sense simply because of the face value of their propositions. For instance, Cesare Lombroso maintained that the most serious offenders are *born criminals*; they are biological throwbacks to an earlier stage of evolutionary development and can be identified by their physical features.[53] Lombroso, who is discussed later in this book, maintained that tattoos were one of the physical features that distinguished these born criminals. This does not make sense, or lacks logical consistency, because tattoos are not biological physical features (i.e., no baby has been born with a tattoo).

Testability is the extent to which a theory can be empirically and scientifically tested. Some theories simply cannot be tested. A good example of such a theory is Freud's theory of the psyche, discussed in more detail later in this book. Freud described three domains of the psyche—the conscious ego, the subconscious id, and the superego. None of these domains, however, can be observed or tested.[54] While some theories can be quite influential without being testable (e.g., Freud's theory), a theoretical model that is untestable and unobservable is at a considerable disadvantage. Fortunately, most established criminological theories can be examined through empirical testing.

Empirical validity is the extent to which a theoretical model is supported by scientific research. This is closely associated with the previous characteristic of testability. While almost all accepted modern criminological theories are testable, this does not mean they are equal in terms of empirical validity.

parsimony:
a characteristic of a good theory, meaning that it explains a certain phenomenon, such as criminal behavior, with the fewest possible propositions or concepts.

scope: refers to the range of criminal behavior that a theory attempts to explain.

logical consistency: the extent to which concepts and propositions of a theoretical model make sense in terms of face value and consistency with what is readily known about crime rates and trends.

testability: the extent to which a theoretical model can be empirically or scientifically tested through observation and empirical research.

For instance, deterrence theory proposed in part that offenders will not repeat their crimes if they have been caught and given severe legal punishment. If research finds that this is true for only a small minority of offenders or that punished offenders are only slightly less likely to repeat crimes than are unpunished offenders, then the theory has some, but not much, empirical validity.[55]

Thus, questions of empirical validity include these: "What degree of empirical support does the theory have?" "Do the findings of research provide weak or strong support?" "Does the preponderance of evidence support or undermine the theory?"[56]

Three Requirements for Determining Causality

Various criteria are involved in determining whether a certain variable causes another variable to change—in other words, causality. For this discussion, we will be referring to the commonly used scientific notation of a predictor variable—called X—as causing an explanatory variable—called Y. These variables are often referred to as an independent or predictor variable (X) and a dependent or explanatory variable (Y). These criteria are used for all scientific disciplines, whether chemistry, physics, biology, or criminology. The three criteria required to determine causality are temporal ordering, covariation or correlation, and accounting for spuriousness.

Temporal ordering requires that the predictor variable (X) precede the explanatory variable (Y) if one is attempting to determine that X causes Y. Although this issue of time order appears to be quite obvious, there are instances when this criterion is violated in criminological theories. For instance, a recent scientific debate has focused on whether delinquency is an outcome variable (Y) caused by associations with delinquent peers and associates (X) or whether delinquency (X) causes associations with delinquent peers and associates (Y), which then leads to more delinquent behavior. This is an example of temporal ordering, or "which came first, the chicken or the egg?" Research has revealed that both processes often occur, meaning that delinquency and associations with delinquent peers are likely to be both predictor and explanatory variables.

Correlation or covariation is the extent to which a change in the predictor (X) is associated with a change in the explanatory variable (Y). For instance, an increase in unemployment (X) is likely to lead to a rise in crime rates (Y). This would indicate a positive association, because both increased. Similarly, an increase in employment (X) is likely to lead to a decrease in crime rates (Y). This would be a negative, or inverse, association, because as one decreases, the other increases. The criterion of covariance is not met when a change in X does not produce any change in Y. Thus, if a significant change in X does not lead to a significant change in Y, this criterion is not met.

It is essential to stress, however, that correlation alone does not mean that X causes Y. For example, ice cream sales (X) tend to be highly associated with crime rates (Y). This does not mean that ice cream sales cause higher crime rates. Instead, other factors, such as warm weather, lead to an increase in both sales of ice cream and the number of people who are outdoors in public areas, which could lead to greater opportunities and tendencies to engage in criminal activity. This example leads to the final criterion for determining causality.

empirical validity: the extent to which a theoretical model is supported by scientific research.

temporal ordering: the criterion for determining causality; requires that the predictor variable (X) precede the explanatory variable (Y) in time.

correlation or covariation: a criterion of causality that requires a change in a predictor variable (X) to be consistently associated with some change in the explanatory variable (Y).

WHY DO THEY DO IT?

DIANE AND RACHEL STAUDTE

Greene County Sheriff's Office via AP

Diane and Rachel Staudte.

In an ABC *20/20* interview, Sarah Staudte stated that "she [her mother, Diane] had this journal that she wrote . . . her thoughts. She wrote the deaths of Shaun, my brother, and me. And that's what worried me . . . I was shocked." According to medical examiners, in April 2012, Mark Staudte, Sarah's father, died of "natural causes"; five months later, her brother's death was ruled as being due to "prior medical issues." Both bodies were cremated.[57] In June 2013, Sarah was taken to Cox South Hospital in Springfield, Missouri. While she exhibited flulike symptoms, the doctors discovered that her kidneys and brain were deteriorating. After running a number of tests, doctors still could not determine the cause of her kidney and brain failure. While she was hospitalized, Springfield police detective Neal McAmis received an anonymous tip. The caller stated that Diane could be responsible for Sarah's illness and might also have been involved in the deaths of Sarah's father and brother. Following this tip, Detective McAmis went to the hospital. One of the doctors stated that he was suspicious that this was a possible poisoning case. He further noted that Sarah was essentially given a "zero percent chance" of living; the question was not whether she was going to die, but when. The detective also talked to a nurse, who commented that Diane was acting strangely, given the severity of the situation. Diane was joking about Sarah's condition and was talking about her upcoming Florida vacation.[58]

Subsequently, Detective McAmis brought Diane Staudte in for questioning. During a four-hour interview, Diane admitted to fatally poisoning her husband and son as well as poisoning her daughter. She, along with her then 24-year-old daughter Rachel, had put antifreeze in Coca-Cola and Gatorade. During her taped interview, Diane made some startling comments in reference to why she had poisoned her family members. She stated that she "hated his [her husband's] guts." Below are portions of the interview between Detective McAmis and Diane regarding her son, Shaun:

"He was almost to the point of inappropriate at times," Diane Staudte said. "I mean he would walk into the bathroom if the door was shut. I mean just really bizarre stuff."

"He was such an interference and a bother that you just said you can't take it anymore?" McAmis prodded.

"He was more than a bother," Diane Staudte said.

"More than a bother, OK. Would a pest, would that be a good word for it?" McAmis asked.

"No, it was more than that," Diane Staudte said.[59]

Further into the interview, when asked about poisoning her daughter, Diane Staudte stated that Sarah was unemployed and therefore could not financially contribute to the household.

Detective McAmis then interviewed Diane's daughter, Rachel Staudte. Rachel stated that her mother initially brought up the idea, but soon after Rachel also became involved in the poisonings. When asked why she wanted to kill her father, Rachel stated, "[I]t was for a little peace." When asked about her brother, she said, "Shaun, because he was annoying." Finally, when asked about her sister, Sarah, Rachel stated "Sarah was just nosy. Very nosy." Rachel told the detective that they were planning to poison her then 12-year-old-sister.

Diane Staudte was sentenced to life in prison without the possibility of parole; Rachel, since she agreed to testify against her mother, was also sentenced to life, but she will be eligible for parole after serving over 42 years in prison.

Sarah Staudte did survive, but she suffered serious brain injury. She now has a guardian and lives in an assisted living facility.[60]

THINK ABOUT IT:

1. How does a mother involve her own daughter in the poisoning of family members?

2. If Diane and Rachel had not been caught, how many more individuals might have been poisoned?

In this text, we will be presenting what some may consider "high-profile" crimes. These are crimes that have received a great deal of media attention due to the individuals involved and/or the horrendous nature of the offense. In some instances, such as the Diane Staudte case, these types of crimes go beyond the question, "Why did she do it?"

Considering for **spuriousness** is a complicated way of saying, to determine that X causes Y, other factors (typically called Z factors) that could be causing the observed association must be accounted for before one can be sure that X is actually causing Y. In other words, these other Z factors may account for the observed association between X and Y. What often happens is that a third factor (Z) causes two events to occur together in time and place. Referring back to Lombroso, tattoos may have predicted criminality at the time he wrote. However, Lombroso did not account for an important Z factor—namely, associates or friends who also had tattoos. This Z factor caused the simultaneous occurrence of both other factors.

Charles Ommanney/Getty Images

Researchers in criminology are fairly good at determining the first two criteria of causality—temporal ordering and covariance or correlation. Most scientists can perform classical experiments that randomly assign participants either to receive or not to receive the experimental manipulation to examine the effect on outcomes. The problem for criminologists, however, is that the factors that appear to be important (according to police officers, parole agents, or corrections officers) are family variables, personality traits, employment variables, intelligence, and other similar characteristics that cannot be experimentally manipulated to control for possible Z factors. Thus, as criminologists, we may never be able to meet all the criteria for causality. Rather, we are often restricted to building a case for the factors we think are causing crime by amassing as much support as we can regarding temporal ordering and covariance or correlation, and perhaps accounting for other factors in advanced statistical models. Ultimately, social science, particularly criminology, is a difficult field in terms of establishing causality, and as we shall see, empirical validity of various criminological theories is hindered by such issues.

What aspects of this neighborhood would cause it to be classified as "disorganized"?

Theory Informs Policies and Programs

An essential aspect of a good theory is that it can help inform and guide policies that attempt to reduce crime. After all, a criminological theory is truly useful in the real world only if it helps reduce criminal offending. For instance, referring to the 11-year-old boy in Albuquerque who took the bait car for a joy ride, if one maintains that the reason he engaged in this criminal behavior was a lack of adult supervision, suggested policies and programs might be directed toward some type of after-school program. Many theories have been used as the basis of such changes in policy.

All major criminological theories have implications for, and have indeed been utilized in, criminal justice policy and practice. Every therapy method, treatment program, prison regimen, police policy, or criminal justice practice is based, either explicitly or implicitly, on some explanation of human nature in general or criminal behavior in particular.[61] In each chapter, we will present examples of how the theories of crime discussed have guided policy making.

One theoretical perspective we will be discussing is differential association. A central tenet of this theory is the influence of close peer groups or other role models. The major implication of this theory is to replace negative, antisocial role models with more positive, prosocial role models. The influence of this position is reflected in the

spuriousness: when other factors (often referred to as Z factors) are actually causing two variables (X and Y) to occur at the same time; it may appear as if X causes Y, when in fact they are both being caused by other Z factor(s).

conditions of probation or parole; offenders are required to stay away from convicted felons. Programs that bring juveniles together for positive purposes and positive interaction with others will face obstacles because "the lure of 'the streets' and of the friends they have grown up with remains a powerful countervailing force regarding rehabilitation."[62]

Another theory perspective we will be presenting focuses on social structure. If individuals live in an environment that is considered *disorganized*, such as one characterized by high unemployment and transiency, this could be deemed the *root cause* of crime. The challenge with implementing policies and programs with this perspective is that it does not necessarily focus on the individual but rather the community. Clifford Shaw argued that rather than treating individual offenders, one needs to focus on the community. Subsequently, he developed the Chicago Area Project. Shaw, along with his staff, organized various programs aimed at establishing or enhancing a sense of community with neighborhoods. He also obtained the assistance and cooperation of schools, churches, recreational clubs, trade unions, and businesses.[63]

VICTIMOLOGY

Victimology can be defined as the scientific study of victims.[64] Although this definition is quite simple, the range of specific topics and the depth to which they are examined can be complex. Specifically, the study of victims includes such widely varied topics as theoretical reasons that some individuals are more likely to be victimized, the legal rights of victims, and the incidence/spatial distribution of victimization in a given geographic area. These are just some of the many topics that fall under the general umbrella of victimology, and even these three topics can be broken into many categories of study. Before we discuss some of those areas, it is important to understand the evolution of the study of victims.

Victimology is a relatively new area of criminology, which is strange because there have been victims since the very beginning of human civilization. The earliest use of the term *victimology* is attributed to two scholars, Fredric Wertham in his book *The Show of Violence* (1949)[65] and Benjamin Mendelsohn, generally considered the Father of Victimology, in his 1956 article titled "Victimology" and published in a foreign journal.[66] This may not seem to many readers being that recent, but it is when you consider that most sciences, including criminology, had been studied for hundreds of years prior to the mid-20th century. Another indication that the science of victimology is very young is that the term *victimology* was not recognized as a correctly spelled word by spell checks in the most commonly used word-processing programs until the last few years.

However, the study of victims is a very insightful perspective for understanding crime. After all, for most crimes there is a victim, so to only try to understand the offender is to miss half the equation. As Wertham wrote:

> The murder victim is the forgotten man. With sensational discussions on the abnormal psychology of the murderer, we have failed to emphasize the unprotectedness of the victim and the complacency of the authorities. One cannot understand the psychology of the murderer if one does not understand the sociology of the victim. What we need is a science of victimology.[67]

It is also important to note that one of the most accurate measures of crime that exists is based on interviews with victims. Called the National Crime Victimization Survey (NCVS), it was begun in 1973 and is generally considered a more accurate estimate of crime in the United States than the Uniform Crime Reports collected by the police and FBI, especially for certain types of offenses, such as forcible rape and burglary. It is certainly the most important source for victimization data across the United States.

Victim Precipitation

One of the most basic underlying concepts of virtually all theoretical perspectives of victimology is that of victim precipitation.[68] Victim precipitation is when an individual does or doesn't do something that increases the risk that he or she will be victimized. For example, if someone does not lock their car and it gets stolen, this is known as *passive victim precipitation*, because it was something they did not or forgot to do. The other type, *active victim precipitation*, involves an individual actually doing something that increases their probability of being victimized. For example, if John yells a racial slur at Ron and then Ron attacks John, what Ron did is not justified, but John clearly increased his likelihood of being attacked, which is the reason why it is an active form of precipitation. The concept of victim precipitation is not about blame; rather, it is simply about raising the odds or risk of being victimized. To be clear, victims should not be blamed, but often what they did or didn't do made them more vulnerable to being targeted.

Marvin Wolfgang was a key researcher who conducted one of the first major studies of victim precipitation in the late 1940s and early 1950s, in which he found that a substantial percentage of homicides in Philadelphia involved situations in which the victim was the first to use force against the person(s) who killed them.[69] At the time, this was a key insight, because previously most researchers had assumed that most victims were completely innocent. Wolfgang's study showed that many of the victims of homicide were actually active precipitators of the crime. Many other theorists have expanded on this theory of victim precipitation, but none have really added to the original model and data provided by Wolfgang.

Incidence/Prevalence of Victimization

One of the most common misperceptions about rates of victimization involves the type of individual who is most likely to be victimized. Studies have shown that many people believe that the most likely individuals to be victims of violent crimes are elderly persons. Perhaps this is due to media coverage; when a grandmother gets raped or robbed, it makes the front page of every newspaper. In fact, however, older individuals are by far the least likely to be victimized by violence. The highest rates of violent victimization clearly occur among teenagers and young adults.[70] This is likely because young people are the ones who typically associate or "hang" with the most common offenders, namely young males.

The vast majority of victimization is intraracial, meaning that typically the offender is of the same race or ethnicity as the victim (see Figure 1.4). Research from the Department of Justice shows that this is true for homicide, for example. This makes sense because people of a given race or ethnicity tend to socialize with other people of the same race or ethnicity.[71]

The good news is that violent victimization has been falling drastically since the early 1990s. According to both the National Crime Victimization Survey and the Uniform Crime Reports (police reports summarized by the FBI), violent victimization has dropped by over 50% since 1993. The reasons for this huge decrease are still unknown, but both of these independent measures show it to be a fact. For example, New York City has seen a decrease from over 2,200 homicides per year in the early 1990s to fewer than 400 per

victim precipitation: the increased likelihood of an individual becoming a victim due to something they did (or did not do) that put them more at risk (e.g., not locking their car door).

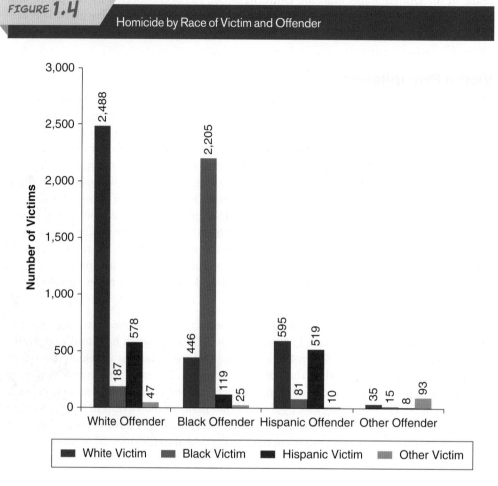

FIGURE **1.4**   Homicide by Race of Victim and Offender

Note: "Other" includes American Indian or Alaska Native, Asian, and Native Hawaiian or Other Pacific Islander.

Source: Crime in the U.S. 2014. FBI. Expanded Homicide Data Table 6.

year currently. Also, Los Angeles used to have well over 1,000 homicides per year in the early 1990s but is now averaging less than 500.

Child Abuse and Neglect

Rates of child abuse and neglect have decreased in the last few decades, probably due to more acknowledgment and awareness.[72] It is well known that in traditional times, police and other law enforcement felt that domestic issues should be best handled at the home. It should be noted that any citizen can make an anonymous claim about child abuse or neglect; to do so, they should call their local child protection agency. However, individuals working in a professional capacity must reveal their identity and agency if they report such accusations of abuse or neglect.

Several agencies have been created at the national level to measure rates of child abuse and to provide helpful services in such cases. One of the most prominent is the Attorney General's Defending Childhood Initiative, which is administered by the federal Office of Juvenile Justice and Delinquency Prevention (OJJDP), and its role is primarily to increase awareness about the long-term influence of children's exposure to violence and to seek solutions to address the problem. Additionally, the OJJDP's Internet Crimes Against Children (ICAC) task force program assists state and local enforcement in preventing and investigating technology-based sexual exploitation.[73] Also, the OJJDP works with the Office of Justice Programs to manage the AMBER Alert program, in which notices go out nationally to try to find abducted children; this program is credited with helping to rescue over 800 children.[74]

The Department of Justice has declared April to be National Child Abuse Prevention Month since 1983. Various agencies have been created to help children who are victims of crime and promote awareness of their rights and the services offered to them.

Compensation and Restitution

The main distinction between victim **compensation** and **restitution** is that the former is given by the state or government and the latter is given by the offender (typically as part of the sentence). New Zealand created the first victim compensation program in the world in 1963. California had the first state victim compensation program in the United States; it is still one of the largest and provides at least approximately $70,000 for victims of violent crime. Property crimes are not included because victims usually have some type of insurance for most of them; one big exception is drunk driving, which the organization MADD [Mothers Against Drunk Driving] lobbied hard for and got, so that is actually allowed in most compensation programs. Now all states have victim compensation programs and receive federal funding from legislated programs, most of them enacted in the 1980s.

Interestingly, the first historical record about victims goes back to the Code of Hammurabi in 1754 BC. This code had many laws, but the most relevant for this course is a portion that called for a restoration of equity between the offender and the victim as well as encouraged victims to forgive their offenders.[75]

Victim compensation programs are typically handled by the victims' services unit or department at local or county offices. Victims' services units are usually housed in the county district attorney's office, and they typically do a great job of helping victims, not just as first responders (where they counsel and give information about social services after a major crime) but also in helping victims fill out reports to apply for state compensation (for funeral services, medical expenses, etc.).

If an offender is required to pay *restitution* as part of his or her sentence, the victim will likely not fare well in actually receiving it. Most offenders are unemployed and/or moneyless and thus unable to pay their victims. There are cases in which victims do receive their court-mandated restitution (often because the offender is a juvenile and his or her parents pay the money), but these instances are the exception.

Roman Milert / Alamy Stock Phot

The Law Code of Hammurabi was inscribed on a seven-foot basalt stele. It is now on display in the Louvre Museum in Paris, France.

compensation: often paid to victims of violent acts; provided by crime that are provided by local, state, or federal governmental funds.

restitution: often ordered by the court to be paid to victims by the offender(s) as part of their sentence.

Here a woman is reading her victim impact statement during sentencing. Should the impact a crime has on a victim be given more consideration during a trial and sentencing?

Victim Impact Statements

Victim impact statements are reports of a victim (often a family member) to the court about how an offender affected their life. The first victim impact statement given in a court in the United States was reported in California in 1976. The admittance of victim impact statements to courts was challenged, and a number of cases made it to the U.S. Supreme Court, which wavered on the decision for many cases over the course of many years. However, the most definitive case is that of *Payne v. Tennessee* (1991), in which the highest court ruled that victim impact statements were relevant during the sentencing hearings. Nothing has really changed since that case; victim impact statements are still accepted under the law following a guilty verdict during the sentencing phase presented to judges or juries.[76]

It is important to note that victim impact statements can be given only during the sentencing phase of a trial, not when the jury is determining the verdict. Thus, in most trials only the judge actually hears and rules based on such victim impact statements, which is likely why most studies show that such impact statements do not have much impact on the sentencing outcome. The reason for this, according to the U.S. Supreme Court, is that it is believed that such victim impact statements would too strongly bias the jury at the verdict phase of the trial, preventing jurors from making an objective determination of guilt or innocence. However, the Court believes they are relevant at the sentencing phase of the trial, particularly in capital cases, that is, those in which the defendant is facing the death penalty.

Studies show that such victim impact statements have little effect despite the victims' families disclosing traumatic revelations of how the various crimes have affected their lives. Although some studies have found support for the influence of such victim impact statements on sentencing, most studies show no significant increase on the sentencing

victim impact statements: formal statements given by victims in court about the incident in which they were offended, often in person but also in other ways (e.g., a video or written statement read by the court reporter); these statements can be considered in determining the offender's sentence.

of the offender.[77] Still, such victim impact statements are largely deemed significant and important contributions to the judicial process, as the U.S. Supreme Court agrees, if only for providing a voice and some closure for victims and their families.

Victim Rights Awareness

April has been designated by the U.S. Department of Justice as National Crime Victims Awareness Month. Although different months bring awareness to specific offenses (such as September as Campus Safety Awareness Month, because that is the beginning of the academic year at many schools, or October as Domestic Violence Awareness Month), April is the most important month because it brings awareness to all victims of crime. Thus, you will likely see many candlelight vigils and parades during the month of April. It was first declared Crime Victims' Rights/Awareness Month in 1981 by President Ronald Reagan and was a good representation of the increase in attention to victims in the 1970s and 1980s.

Other examples of this increased attention to victims in the 1980s include the formation in 1983 of the Office of Victims of Crime (OVC), which was created by the U.S. Department of Justice to implement recommendations from the President's Task force on Victims of Crime initiated by President Reagan in 1982. Also, the Victims of Crime Act (VOCA) was passed in 1984, which established the Federal Crime Victims Fund to support state compensation funds and local victim service units and programs. The fund comprises various fines, penalties, forfeitures, and so forth collected by federal agencies.

Overall, far more attention has been given to victims of crime since the early 1970s. It is surprising that it took until the last five decades before victims were given such interest in terms of study and rights, especially when one considers that there have always been victims since the beginning of human civilization. In contrast, extensive scientific studies and theories of offenders have been conducted and promulgated for centuries. It has been beneficial to the field of criminology to add such study of victims, especially considering that they are nearly always half the equation when trying to determine why offenders attack.

LEARNING CHECK 1.4

1. Who is considered the Father of Victimology by most scholars?
   A. Lombroso
   B. Beccaria
   C. Sutherland
   D. Mendelsohn

2. When an individual does or does not do something that increases their risk of being victimized, this is referred to as victim
   A. anticipation.
   B. precipitation.
   C. expectation.
   D. consideration.

3. When an offender is ordered to pay money to the victim as part of sentencing, it is referred to as _____, whereas when the state or federal government provides funds to the victim for losses due to the crime, it is referred to as _____.
   A. compensation; restitution
   B. restitution; compensation

4. The U.S. Supreme Court has ruled that victim impact statements can be given during only what stage of a criminal trial?
   A. before the verdict but not after
   B. after the verdict and before the sentencing
   C. both before the verdict and before sentencing
   D. neither during the actual trial nor before sentencing; only after the sentence

Answers located at www.edge.sagepub.com/schram2e

CONCLUSION

The purpose of this chapter was twofold. First, we wanted to provide a general understanding of different aspects related to the field. We started with key concepts in understanding criminology, such as *crime*, *criminal*, *deviant*, and *victim*. We explored the difference between criminology and criminal justice as well as consensus and conflict perspectives of crime. Next, we provided a broad overview of the major components of the criminal justice system: law enforcement, courts, and corrections. When discussing the juvenile justice system, we reviewed fundamental differences between the adult criminal justice system and the juvenile justice system. Next, we introduced criminological theory by discussing what criteria are considered when assessing whether a theory is deemed good. We also briefly discussed the three requirements to show that a given factor causes changes in another factor. Next, we noted how theory should inform policies and programs. It is essential to stress that theory is not to be thought of as some abstract or out-of-touch scientific endeavor. Rather, theory has an important purpose in terms of developing policies and programs. As Ronald Akers noted:

> The question, then, is not whether policy can be or should be based on theory—it already is guided by theory—but rather, how well is policy guided by theory and how good is the theory on which the policy is predicated?[78]

While you are learning and critiquing the various theories presented in this text, it is essential to ask that question continually!

Finally, we presented an overview of victimology, or the study of victims. We briefly discussed such topics as victim precipitation, the incidence and prevalence of victimization, child abuse and neglect, and victim impact statements.

KEY TERMS

comparative criminology, 12

compensation, 23

concurrent jurisdiction, 11

conflict perspective, 6

consensus perspective, 5

correlation *or* covariation, 17

crime, 3

criminal justice, 5

criminology, 5

deviance, 3

empirical validity, 16

highway patrol, 7

jail, 8

judicial waiver, 11

limited jurisdiction, 8

logical consistency, 16

mala in se, 3

mala prohibita, 3

parens patriae, 9

parsimony, 16

prison, 9

probation, 8

restitution, 23

scope, 16

spuriousness, 19

state police, 7

statutory exclusion, 11

temporal ordering, 17

testability, 16

victim impact statements, 24

victim precipitation, 21

DISCUSSION QUESTIONS

1. How does criminology differ from other perspectives of crime?

2. Should criminologists emphasize only crimes made illegal by law, or should they also study acts that are deviant but not illegal? Explain why you feel this way.

3. Do you think the juvenile justice system procedures, as well as its philosophy, have changed since its inception in 1899? Why?

4. Would you consider the term *criminal justice system* an oxymoron? Explain your answer.

5. What characteristics of a good theory do you find most important? What are least important? Make sure to explain why you feel that way.

6. How much do you think an individual's behavior predicts their likelihood of being victimized? What types of circumstances do you think are most relevant?

7. If a member of your family was violently victimized, would you likely give a victim impact statement? Why or why not? Do you feel that such statements should be considered in the sentencing of offenders?

WEB RESOURCES

The Office for Victims of Crime website is the official website of the U.S. Department of Justice. The Office for Victims of Crime oversees programs that have been designed to benefit and assist crime victims (e.g., victims' rights, public awareness).

http://www.ovc.gov/

The Office for Victims of Crime fact sheet summarizes the amount of monies that are deposited into this fund from such sources as criminal fines, forfeited bail bonds, and penalty fees.

https://www.ncjrs.gov/ovc_archives/factsheets/cvfvca.htm

This website provides a general overview of the criminal justice system and a flowchart of events.

http://bjs.ojp.usdoj.gov/content/justsys.cfm/

STUDENT STUDY SITE

⑤SAGE edge™

WANT A BETTER GRADE ON YOUR NEXT TEST?

Get the tools you need to sharpen your study skills:

SAGE edge offers a robust online environment featuring an impressive array of tools and resources for review, study, and further exploration, keeping both instructors and students on the cutting edge of teaching and learning. Learn more at **edge.sagepub.com/schram2e**.

FOR FURTHER EXPLORATION AND APPLICATION, VISIT THE STUDENT STUDY SITE:

- Justice Department to Move Away from Using Private Prisons
- Proportion of Girls in Juvenile Justice System is Going Up, Studies Find
- Neighborhood variation in police stops and searches: A test of consensus and conflict perspectives
- Juvenile Justice: A system divided
- The comparative method in globalized criminology
- Why Study Criminology?
- Introduction to U.S. Court System
- They're not adults: NY seeks new approach to juvenile justice
- Through Our Eyes: Children, Violence, and Trauma
- Victimology and Motive: The Case of David Buller
- The Justice System
- Solitary Confinement
- Violence Against Women's Act Fact Sheet
- National Center for Victims of Crime

PREMIUM VIDEO:

Check out the Interactive eBook for premium videos, including videos from author Stephen Tibbetts, who discusses real-world examples and strange crimes; and videos from former offenders, who share their stories from a first-person view, and touch on key theories and concepts from the chapter.

CHAPTER 2

Measuring Crime

New York City memorializes the tenth anniversary of the September 11, 2001, terrorist attacks on September 11, 2011, at the World Trade Center site.

Andrew Burton/Getty Images

INTRODUCTION

One often hears on the news or reads in the newspaper about crime, such as that crime is increasing or decreasing in various communities, cities, or the country. Often, these reports are based on official crime statistics, or data on crime that has come to the attention of law enforcement. There are instances when crimes do not come to the attention of law enforcement or some other criminal justice agency. These undetected, or unreported, crimes are referred to as the *dark figure of crime* or, as illustrated in Figure 2.1, the *iceberg*. Later in this chapter, we will cover one approach to addressing these undetected or unreported crimes—surveying victims of crime.

When thinking further about this dark figure of crime, one may ask, "Do we truly want to know every crime that has been committed?" To do so may require "giving up" other aspects of our lives, such as privacy and freedom. Currently, there are millions of closed-circuit television (CCTV) cameras installed in streets and businesses worldwide. The major impetus of CCTVs is to reduce crime while increase public safety. However, some civil liberties groups have expressed concern (e.g., that they are susceptible to abuse).[4] There is a growing area of research focusing on the evaluation of CCTVs and reducing crime.[5] This illustrates the continuing growth of our technological abilities to *track*, *watch*, and *locate* different types of activity and behavior. Given these technological advances, do we also want to improve our ability to detect and count crime? By improving these abilities, would we be willing to "give up" our privacy?

Measuring crime is necessary for various reasons.[6] Some of these reasons include describing crime, explaining why crime occurs, and evaluating programs and policies. It is important to legislators, as well as concerned citizens, that crime statistics are available to describe, or gauge, criminal activity that can influence community well-being. Measuring crime is also needed for risk assessment of different social groups, including their potential for becoming offenders or victims. Another purpose of measuring crime is explanation. Identifying causes requires that differences in crime rates can be related to differences in people and their situations. Counting crime is also used to evaluate and justify programs and policies that try to address criminal activity (e.g., rehabilitation, incapacitation, deterrence).

This chapter examines various data collection methods used to enhance our understanding of criminal behaviors and patterns. The first portion describes various statistics collected by law enforcement agencies. The next portion provides an overview of the National Crime Victimization Survey. We then present a few examples of self-report surveys. The last portion summarizes additional approaches used to collect crime data, such as the National Youth Gang Survey and spatial analyses of crime.

CRIME DATA FROM LAW ENFORCEMENT AGENCIES

Law enforcement agencies throughout the United States gather a number of crime statistics. In this section, we look at five methods used to accomplish this.

SEPTEMBER 11, 2001, VICTIMS

On September 11, 2001, there were a total of 3,047 victims from the World Trade Center, the Pentagon, and Somerset County, Pennsylvania. In the 2001 report, *Crime in the United States*, it was decided that the victims of 9/11 would not be included in the general report as victims of murder. Rather, the Federal Bureau of Investigation provided a special report that focused on the terrorist attacks. This special report included summaries of the victims, including their race/ethnicity, sex, age, and location (i.e., the World Trade Center, the Pentagon, or Somerset County, Pennsylvania). Included with these victims were the 71 law enforcement officers killed in the line of duty:

- 37 officers with the Port Authority of New York and New Jersey Police Department
- 23 officers with the New York Police Department
- 5 officers with the New York Office of Tax Enforcement
- 3 officers with the State of New York Unified Court System
- 1 fire marshal with the New York City Fire Department
- 1 agent with the U.S. Secret Service
- 1 agent with the FBI[1]

According to the Federal Bureau of Investigation, the reason for not including these victims was, in part, as follows:

The statistics of September 11 are not a part of the traditional *Crime in the United States* publication because they are different from the day-to-day crimes committed in this country. Additionally, combining these statistics with our regular crime report would create many difficulties in defining and analyzing crime as we know it.[2]

Further, it was argued that the murder count was so large that if one were to combine this with what is considered *traditional crime statistics*, it would have what is called an outlier effect. An outlier is an extreme value that significantly differs from the rest of the distribution.

Some have argued that this was not an appropriate decision. In 2002, Dr. Paul Leighton, a professor of criminology, argued that "mass murder is still murder." He maintains that while it was reported that homicide increased just 3% from 2000 to 2001, it actually increased by 26%. Dr. Leighton contends that if the FBI had chosen to include the victims of 9/11, the various people who refer to the Uniform Crime Reports (e.g., bureaucrats, students, reporters) would have a visual reminder of the impact those terrorist attacks had on the country. Interestingly, the FBI had previously included the victims of other terrorist attacks (e.g., the first World Trade Center bombing and the bombing of Oklahoma City's Alfred P. Murrah Federal Building).[3]

THINK ABOUT IT:

Do you think that the victims of 9/11 should have been include in the *Crime in the United States* report?

> ON SEPTEMBER 11, 2001, THERE WERE A TOTAL OF 3,047 VICTIMS FROM THE WORLD TRADE CENTER, THE PENTAGON, AND SOMERSET COUNTY, PENNSYLVANIA.

FIGURE **2.1**

The Dark Figure of Crime

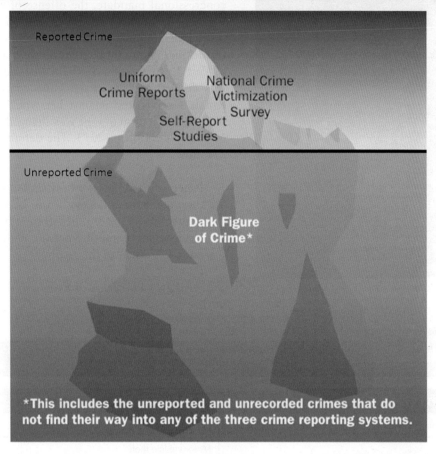

Source: https://mir-s3-cdn-cf.behance.net/project_modules/disp/9e0ca249724943.560866c4ba83e.jpg

They are the Uniform Crime Reports, the Supplementary Homicide Reports, the National Incident-Based Reporting System, Hate Crime Statistics, and the Law Enforcement Officers Killed and Assaulted Statistics.

Uniform Crime Reports (UCR)

HISTORICAL OVERVIEW. Between 1830 and 1930, the collection of crime statistics involved various agencies. Individual cities, regions, and states collected crime statistics for their respective regions in an effort to guide policy making. This resulted in the collection process being somewhat haphazard.[7] There was an interest in developing a crime reporting system among police chiefs. During the 1927 meeting of the International Association of Chiefs of Police (IACP), efforts were made to collect crime statistics in a consistent and uniform manner.[8] As a result, seven main classifications of crime were selected to assess fluctuations in crime rates. These classifications were later identified as Part I crimes. In 1930, only 400 agencies submitted their crimes reports; it was difficult during the beginning stages of the Uniform Crime Report (UCR) Program to assess the crime rate for the entire country. In 2014, the FBI reported that over 18,000 city, university, college, county, state, tribal, and federal law enforcement agencies voluntarily report data on those crimes brought to their attention.[9]

In 1960, these Part I crimes were termed the Crime Index. Part I crimes were those crimes most likely to be reported to the police, including murder, rape, robbery, aggravated assault, larceny, burglary, and motor vehicle theft. Information was collected on

Four members of the New York City Police Department's Honor Legion in the 1920s. How has police reporting of crime data changed since then?

additional categories of crimes, ranging from sex offenses to parking violations; these are designated as Part II crimes.[10] In 1979, by congressional mandate, the offense of arson was added as a Part I offense. In 2013, human trafficking/commercial sex acts and human trafficking/involuntary servitude were added as Part I offenses. Since 1929, *forcible rape* was defined as "the carnal knowledge of a female forcibly and against her will."[11] The modified definition of rape was changed prior to data collection in 2013. The definition is as follows:

> Penetration, no matter how slight, of the vagina or anus with any body part or object, or oral penetration by a sex organ of another person, without the consent of the victim.[12]

Table 2.1 provides a list of Part I and Part II offenses.

TABLE 2.1   Part I and Part II Offenses

PART I OFFENSES	
Criminal homicide	Larceny-theft (except motor vehicle theft)
Rape	Motor vehicle theft
Robbery	Arson
Aggravated assault	Human trafficking, commercial sex acts
Burglary	Human trafficking, Involuntary servitude
PART II OFFENSES	
Other assaults (simple)	Gambling
Forgery and counterfeiting	Offenses against the family and children
Fraud	Driving under the influence
Embezzlement	Liquor laws
Stolen property: buying, receiving, possessing	Drunkenness
Vandalism	Disorderly conduct
Weapons: carrying, possessing, etc.	Vagrancy
Prostitution and commercialized vice	All other offenses
Sex offenses (except rape and prostitution offenses)	Suspicion
Drug abuse violations	Curfew and loitering laws (persons under age 18)

Source: Federal Bureau of Investigation, Criminal Justice Information Services Division, Uniform Crime Reporting Program. (2013). *Summary Reporting System (SRS) user manual.* Washington, DC: U.S. Department of Justice, pp. 20–22.

FIGURE 2.2 Crime Clock

2014 CRIME CLOCK STATISTICS

A Violent Crime occurred every	26.3 seconds
One Murder every	36.9 minutes
One Rape every	4.5 minutes
One Robbery every	1.6 minutes
One Aggravated Assault every	42.5 seconds
A Property Crime occurred every	3.8 seconds
One Burglary every	18.2 seconds
One Larceny-Theft every	5.4 seconds
One Motor Vehicle Theft every	45.7 seconds

Source: Crime in the United States, 2015. FBI.

THE UCR PROGRAM. The primary objective of the Uniform Crime Reports (UCR) is to generate a consistent (or reliable) set of crime statistics that can be used in law enforcement administration, operation, and management. Over the years, however, the UCR has become one of the country's foremost indicators of crime. The UCR has provided information on fluctuations in the level of crime for criminologists, sociologists, legislators, municipal planners, and the media—information that has subsequently been used for both research and planning purposes (see Figure 2.2).[13]

The UCR has been used for a number of criminal justice studies, such as assessing the influence of gender equality on female homicide victimization;[14] evaluating the effect of home foreclosures on crime in Indianapolis, Indiana;[15] investigating the relationship between firearm ownership and violent crime;[16] comparing the influence of community policing in large and small law enforcement agencies on crime rates;[17] and assessing Weed and Seed Program effects on Part I offenses.[18]

In 2004, the FBI discontinued use of the Crime Index. The Crime Index had often been used to detect overall changes in crime across the country:

> The Crime Index and the Modified Crime Index were not true indicators of the degrees of criminality because they were always driven upward by the offense with the highest number, typically larceny-theft. The sheer volume of those offenses overshadowed more serious but less frequently committed offenses, creating a bias against a jurisdiction with a high number of larceny-thefts but a low number of other serious crimes such as murder and forcible rape.[19]

The FBI emphasizes that classifying and scoring crimes are the two most important functions of agencies participating in the Uniform Crime Reporting Program. Classifying is defined as determining the appropriate crime category in which to report an offense in the UCR. This is based on information resulting from an agency's investigation of the crime.[20] An important step in classification has been referred to as the hierarchy rule. Specifically, when more than one Part I offense is classified in a multiple-offense situation, the law enforcement agency must locate the offense that is highest on the hierarchy list and score that offense but not any of the other offenses.[21] There are some exceptions

Uniform Crime Reports: an annual report published by the Federal Bureau of Investigation in the U.S. Department of Justice. It is meant to estimate most of the major street crimes in the United States.

to this hierarchy rule. For example, the rule does not apply to arson, human trafficking/commercial sex acts, and human trafficking/involuntary servitude; these offenses are always reported, even in multiple-offense situations. See Table 2.2 for examples on how to classify multiple-offense situations.

Scoring is defined as counting the number of offenses after they have been classified. The two rules for scoring Part I crimes pertain to the two types of crimes involved (i.e., crimes against persons and crimes against property). For crimes against persons, one offense is scored for each victim. For crimes against property, one offense is scored for each distinct operation or attempt.[22]

TABLE **2.2** Examples of the Hierarchy Rule

The following scenarios illustrate the proper application of the hierarchy rule in reporting a multiple-offense incident.

SCENARIO	CRIMES COMMITTED	CRIME REPORTED
Two women broke into a new car dealership after closing hours. They took the cash from the dealership's office safe and two new automobiles from the garage.	1. A Burglary (Forcible Entry) 2. Motor Vehicle Theft	Following the hierarchy rule, only the Burglary (Forcible Entry), the highest of the offenses on the list of Part I offenses, must be scored.
A burglar broke into a home, stole several items, and placed them in a car belonging to the owner of the home. The homeowner returned and surprised the thief, who in turn knocked the owner unconscious by hitting him over the head with a chair. The burglar drove away in the homeowner's car.	1. A Burglary (Forcible Entry) 2. Robbery (Other Dangerous Weapon) 3. Aggravated Assault (Other Dangerous Weapon) 4. Motor Vehicle Theft (Auto)	After classifying the offenses, the reporting agency scores only one offense—Robbery (Other Dangerous Weapon)—the crime appearing first in the list of Part I offenses.
A white female, aged 23, was being arrested on charges of soliciting for prostitution. During the arrest, she pepper-sprayed the arresting officer's face. The officer's search incident to the arrest resulted in the recovery of a credit card belonging to an individual who had previously reported it stolen. There was no indication that the card had been used fraudulently.	1. Prostitution and Commercialized Vice 2. Stolen Property (Buying, Receiving, Possessing) 3. Aggravated Assault (Other Dangerous Weapon)	Following the hierarchy rule, only the Part I offense, Aggravated Assault (Other Dangerous Weapon), must be classified and scored. The Part II offenses are ignored in using the hierarchy rule.
EXCEPTIONS TO THE HIERARCHY RULE		
Someone stole a pickup truck that had a camper containing camping equipment attached to it. The police recovered the truck and camper but not the equipment.	1. Motor Vehicle Theft 2. Larceny-Theft	Motor Vehicle Theft is a special type of Larceny-Theft. It is a separate classification because of the volume of such thefts and the prevailing need of law enforcement for specific statistics on this offense. Therefore, when classifying, the reporting agency chooses between Larceny-Theft and Motor Vehicle Theft. In cases such as this, the agency classifies and scores the offense as Motor Vehicle Theft.
As a result of arson in an apartment building, six persons were found dead.	1. Murder 2. Arson	The Part I crimes of Murder and Arson are involved in this multiple-offense situation. The reporting agency counts six Criminal Homicide offenses (one for each victim) and Arson.

Source: Albert D. Biderman, A.D., & Reiss, A.J. (1967). On exploring the 'Dark Figure' of crime, *Annals*, pp. 1–15. Skogan, W.G. (1977). The 'Dark Figure' of unreported crime. *Crime and Delinquency, 23*, p. 41.

LIMITATIONS OF THE UCR. As early as 1931, there were criticisms concerning the UCR, and some of these still apply to the current UCR.[23] Even with these criticisms, the UCR continues to be a major source of information pertaining to crime in the United States.[24] Below is a brief overview of the criticisms and limitations concerning the UCR:

1. Some crimes do not come to the attention of those responsible for collecting this information. In reference to the UCR, this pertains to law enforcement agencies. As stated above, these *unknown* crimes constitute the dark figure of crime.[25] Potential problems with not counting these "unreported" crimes have been outlined by Wesley Skogan:

   • It restricts the deterrent capability of the criminal justice system by shielding offenders from police action.
   • It contributes to the misallocation of resources such as police manpower and equipment.
   • It can influence the police role when officers do not recognize certain types of criminal activity in their own environment. As a result, officers might overlook addressing these problems.
   • It can have a negative influence on victims of crimes who do not become "officially known" to the criminal justice system; for instance, these victims are ineligible for many supportive benefits from both public and private agencies.
   • It can influence the perceived "socialized" costs of crime; this misperception can influence private insurance premiums and the public cost of victim compensation programs.[26]

2. The UCR concentrates on conventional street crime (e.g., assaults, robbery) but does not adequately include other serious types of offenses such as corporate crime. This is illustrated by the priority given to the investigation and prosecution of such crimes within the federal government, including the collection of crime statistics.[27]

3. Crime statistics, such as the UCR, can be used for political purposes. Some argue that official crime statistics are a social construction.[28] In this vein, these statistics are perceived as an *objective reality* for program and policy purposes.[29] When these claims are stated and supported by powerful groups, this can influence public perceptions, which can then result in policy changes. One historical example are the efforts to warn individuals of marijuana use in the 1930s (see Photo 2.3).

4. Some law enforcement agencies may submit incomplete or delinquent reports. These incomplete or delinquent reports can be due to such reasons as: (a) an agency may have experienced a natural disaster that prevented the timely submission of the crime data; (b) due to budgetary restrictions, some police agencies may have had to limit some routine clerical activities, including the collection of crime statistics; and (c) changes in personnel experienced in preparing UCR data (as a result of, e.g., retirement, promotion) may result in problems with data reporting if the individual is replaced by someone who is not adequately trained and/or experienced with these activities.[30]

Underwood Archives/Getty Images

Efforts to warn people of the dangers of smoking marijuana in the 1930s included propaganda films such as *Reefer Madness*. How has the societal response to marijuana changed since then, and what impact has that had on its classification as a crime?

Comparative Criminology: *CHILD ABUSE*

Some Exploratory Studies on Child Abuse in Other Countries

Unfortunately, there is no systematic global data collection regarding child abuse; however, the World Health Organization (WHO, 2002) estimated that there were about 57,000 homicides of children under 15 in just the year 2000. This study also found that perpetrators of child abuse had witnessed violence against their mothers when they were young. This is consistent with studies that repeatedly find links between childhood exposure to domestic violence and violent offending at older ages (see discussion in Van Dijk, 2008, p. 88). This phenomenon is commonly referred to as the "cycle of violence."

Van Dijk (2008) points out that perhaps the most comprehensive studies of child abuse in modern times were done in Germany, surveying more than 11,000 teenagers about their experiences with domestic violence. One consistent finding was that children of immigrants reported significantly higher rates/percentages of violence against mothers, with extremely high rates among those from Turkey (32%), Yugoslavia (25%), and Russia (20%). Another interesting pattern was that the immigrant families that had resided in Germany for longer periods had higher rates of domestic violence, which Van Dijk claimed suggested "growing tensions between spouses after a longer exposure of

women to German norms and values concerning gender equality" (p. 88).

Also notable, WHO (2004) estimated that annual economic costs in the United States due to child abuse totaled about $94 billion. And although traditionally rare, there is a growing trend to punish much more severely parents and caretakers who abuse children, which also adds to the costs in terms of processing and incarcerating offenders. For example, in October 2012, a 23-year-old Texas woman was sentenced to 99 years in prison for such abuses as gluing her daughter's hands to the wall and beating her as punishment for potty-training setbacks. (Read more about this story here: http:// abcnews.go.com/US/texas-mom-glued-daughtershands- wall-99-years/story?id=17436643.)

THINK ABOUT IT:

1. In the 2008 German study of teenagers discussed in this section, what types of youths were consistently found to have higher rates of exposure to violence in the household?

2. What did this study show regarding living in Germany over time did to such rates, and what did the authors provide as an explanation for this trend?

Sources: Van Dijk, J. (2008). The world of crime. Thousand Oaks, CA: Sage; World Health Organization. (2002). World report on violence and health. Geneva: Author; World Health Organization. (2004). The economic dimensions of interpersonal violence. Geneva: Author.

5. Problems with the collection of UCR data can also occur because of clerical and data-processing errors. Based on his experience as a senior analyst in the New York Division of Criminal Justice Services, Henry Brownstein described how accuracy can be compromised due to clerical error.[31]

6. Changes in the legal code can influence subsequent crime reports and make later comparisons difficult. Thus, when a previously acceptable behavior is later criminalized or when a classification is altered (e.g., from misdemeanor to felony, or the reverse), this will likely result in a change in reported crimes.[32] For instance, some have argued that there are increasing efforts to *criminalize homelessness*. Some cities have implemented laws that make it illegal to sleep, eat, or sit in public spaces.[33]

It is essential to note that the UCR is a "summary-based system." These data are a summary, or total count, of crimes based on the reporting agencies. Thus, disaggregation of UCR data can occur only on the reporting agency level. The units of analysis are groups (i.e., reporting agencies). The UCR data are limited to the totals reported by each participating agency. The best-known summary UCR measures are numbers of Part I and

WHY DO THEY DO IT?

As mentioned in Chapter 1, throughout this text, we are presenting what some may consider "high-profile" crimes or crimes that have received a great deal of media attention, either due to the individuals involved or the outrageous nature of the offense. When reading or hearing about these crimes, many of us may ask ourselves, "Why do they do it?" For this particular chapter, however, we have decided to present what many may consider "odd" or "strange" types of offenses. While these crimes may not be as highly publicized as other offenses in later sections, they often evoke the same question, "Why do they do it?"

CONTAMINATED METH

The Granite Shoals (Texas) Police department posted the following to Facebook:

> Breaking News: Area Meth and Heroin Supply Possibly Contaminated With Ebola. Meth and Heroin recently brought in to Central Texas as well as the ingredients used to make it could be contaminated with the life threatening disease Ebola. If you have recently purchased meth or heroin in Central Texas, please take it to the local police or sheriff department so it can be screened with a special device. DO NOT use it until it has been properly checked for possible Ebola contamination! Contact any Granite Shoals PD officer for testing. Please share in hopes we get this information to anyone who has any contaminated meth or heroin that needs tested.

A few days later, Chastity Hopson brought her drugs to the Granite Shoals police station so it could be tested for Ebola. Subsequently, she was arrested and charged with possession of a controlled substance. The Facebook posting was a hoax.[36]

HOMEMADE LICENSE PLATE

Amanda Schweickert, of Buffalo, New York, was pulled over by Erie County Sheriff's officers. The officers noticed that there was something odd about her license plate. Upon further inspection, they noticed that she had painted a piece of cardboard in an attempt to make it look like a New York license plate. They also discovered that she was driving with a suspended license and no insurance. Ms. Schweickert was charged with possession of a forged instrument, driving with a suspended registration, and three traffic offenses.[37]

BEER-BATTERED FISH DEFENSE

John Przybyla, 75, was a serial drunk driver in Adams County, Wisconsin. He had nine previous charges of operating a vehicle while intoxicated. On October 12, 2015, he was pulled over for the 10th time. However, he explained to the officers that he had eaten some beer-battered fish and that that was the reason his blood alcohol level was above the legal limit.[38]

USHER STEALS OFFERINGS

Deputies from the Marion County Sheriff's Office (Florida) received a call from officials at the Blessed Trinity Catholic Church. The church officials had some suspicions that one of their ushers was stealing money. The deputies set up surveillance cameras in the church. The cameras caught Mario Condis, a 60-year-old church usher, stealing money from the church offering baskets while the congregation was in prayer. He would take the money from the baskets and place it in his pockets. Condis was arrested on one count of grand theft and three counts of petit theft.[39]

So, "why do they do it?" Do you think it may be due to mental illness? Alcohol abuse? Substance abuse? In the following chapters, we will present theories that try to understand and explain criminal behavior from various perspectives (e.g., sociological, psychological, biosocial). As you continue with the text, you will learn how criminologists throughout the centuries have attempted to understand and explain what is considered *criminal behavior*.

Answers located at www.edge.sagepub.com/schram2e

LEARNING CHECK 2.1

1. The UCR is based on offenses reported to _____.

2. *Unknown* crimes are referred to as _____.

3. When more than one Part I offense is classified, the law enforcement agency must locate the offense that is highest the list; this is referred to as the _____.

4. Exceptions to the hierarchy rule are _____.

Part II offenses. Additional summary data can include property recovered and weapons used in specific types of offenses as well as summary totals of arrests, classified by sex, race, and age grouping of offenders.[34]

Using UCR data, one can obtain total counts of crimes on a city or county level and move upward to a state or regional level. One cannot obtain information on individual crimes, offenders, or victims. The U.S. Department of Justice sponsors two types of crime measures that are based on incidents, rather than reporting agencies, as the units of analysis. The first crime measure is the Supplementary Homicide Reports; the second crime measure is the National Incident-Based Reporting System.[35]

Supplementary Homicide Reports

Homicides are less likely to be underreported compared to other crimes counted in the UCR. Homicides are also more likely to result in an arrest or to be cleared than other offenses. Finally, compared to other offenses such as forcible rape, robbery, and aggravated assault, homicide offense reports are more likely to have details about the incident, such as the victims and/or offenders.[40] Thus, in the 1960s, the FBI developed the Supplementary Homicide Reports (SHR). Since 1976, these data have been archived at the National Archive of Criminal Justice Data (NACJD), which is maintained by the University of Michigan's Inter-university Consortium for Political and Social Research (ICPSR).[41]

In the *Summary Reporting System (SRS) User Manual*, SHR collects additional information pertaining to the incident, including details of the murder victim and offender, their relationship to one another, the weapon used, and the circumstances in each criminal homicide.[42] For offenses of murder and nonnegligent manslaughter as well as manslaughter by negligence, reporting agencies include information such as the following: single or multiple victims; single, multiple, or unknown offenders; age, sex, race, and ethnicity of the victim and offender; description of the weapon and how it was used (e.g., if a bottle was used in the commission of a murder, the reporting agency must note whether the person was killed by beating, cutting, or stabbing); relationship of the victim to the offender (e.g., in a murder incident where a wife is killed by her husband, the relationship must be reported as "wife"); and circumstances (e.g., lover's quarrel, drunkenness, argument over money, revenge, narcotics, gangland killings).[43]

Modifications of the SHR have been put in place when unusual incidents reveal such a need. For instance, the underlying data structure of the SHR allows up to 11 victims and 11 offenders for each record. In those unusual incidents where a crime involves more than 11 homicides, the victim information is repeated over more than one record. If an individual does not have any knowledge of the specific incident, it may be difficult to determine the separate records involving the same incident:

Supplementary Homicide Reports: part of the UCR Program. These data provide more detailed information on the incident (e.g., the offender, the victim).

In April, 1995, an explosion at the Federal Building in Oklahoma City killed 168 individuals. At the time information was reported to the Supplementary Homicide Reporting Program, law enforcement believed three offenders were responsible for this act. Following reporting guidelines, the information on this incident in the FBI's 1995 SHR data file was spread over 16 records (15 containing 11 victims and the last containing 3 victims) with 3 offenders noted on each record.

Without extraordinary knowledge of this incident, an analysis of these records would yield 168 victims and 48 offenders. The data files underlying this analysis package have been adjusted to accurately reflect an incident with 168 victims and 3 offenders.[44]

In addition to the SHR, another national data collection system administered in the United States to collect detailed information on homicides is from the Centers for Disease Control and Prevention (CDC). They developed the National Vital Statistics System (NVSS). When comparing the SHR and the NVSS, there is substantial overlap in homicide reporting (see Table 2.3). Overall, the NVSS consistently demonstrates a higher number of homicides than the SHR. This is probably due to the variations in coverage and score as well as the voluntary versus mandatory reporting requirements.[45]

The SHR has been key in developing policy related to homicide, especially since these data include not only the number of homicides but also factors associated with these crimes (e.g., characteristics of the victims and offenders).[46] The SHR has also been used to enhance our understanding of patterns and trends pertaining to homicides, including the following: exploring sibling homicide, or siblicide;[47] examining choice of weapon in male sexual homicides;[48] comparing and understanding lethal violence in Finland and the United States;[49] and suggesting improvements of the SHR for collecting data on workplace homicides.[50] The SHR can also be considered the forerunner to the National Incident-Based Reporting System (NIBRS), since it provided additional information about incidents.[51]

Staff Sergeant Preston Chasteen, Department of Defense

The bombing of the Alfred P. Murrah Federal Building in Oklahoma City on April 10, 1995. What challenges do horrific incidents like this pose for the reporting of crime statistics?

TABLE 2.3 Comparing the NVSS Fatal Injury Reports and the UCR Supplementary Homicide Reports

	NVSS	SHR
Purpose	Track all deaths	Track crime statistics
Reporting source	State vital registrars	Law enforcement agencies
Initial report	Death certificate	Police report
Report responsibility	Medical examiners and coroners	Law enforcement officers
Homicide definition	Injuries inflicted by another person with intent to injure or kill by any means	Willful killing of one human being by another; includes murders and nonnegligent manslaughters
Reporting is:	Mandatory	Voluntary
Data collection methods	Manner/cause of death determined by medical examiners/coroners; demographic information is recorded by funeral directors on death certificates	In most states, reports from individual law enforcement agencies are compiled monthly by state-level agencies and then forwarded to the FBI

Source: Regoeczi, W., Banks, D., Planty, M., Langton, L., Annest, J. L., Warner, M., & Barnett-Ryan, C. (2014). *The nation's two measures of homicide.* Washington, D.C.: U.S. Department of Justice, p. 3.

The National Incident-Based Reporting System (NIBRS)

THE NIBRS PROGRAM.   Initially, the UCR was considered primarily a tool for law enforcement agencies. By the 1980s, it was evident that these data were being used by other entities involved with social planning and policy. Thus, there was a need to collect more detailed information on these data. The FBI, the Department of Justice Statistics (the agency responsible for funding criminal justice information projects), and other agencies and individuals from various disciplines were involved with setting in place the changes needed to update the program for collecting crime data.[52] After various stages of development and pilot programs, the FBI developed a draft of guidelines for this enhanced UCR Program, which is named the National Incident-Based Reporting System (NIBRS).

By the end of the 1980s, NIBRS was operational. By 2013, NIBRS was collecting data on each incident and arrest within 23 offense categories comprising 49 specific crimes (i.e., Group A). There are 10 Group B offenses for which only arrest data are collected (see Table 2.4). As of 2013, approximately 33% of law enforcement agencies reported data in the NIBRS format.[53]

There are two goals of the NIBRS data collection program: (1) to enhance the quantity, quality, and timeliness of crime statistical data collected by law enforcement entities; and (2) to improve the methodology used for compiling, analyzing, auditing, and publishing the collected crime data.[54] As a result of providing more "detailed, accurate, and meaningful data than those produced by the traditional UCR Program,"[55] NIBRS data have also been used to enhance criminological research. Examples of studies using NIBRS include the following: analyzing victims' injuries in robbery incidents;[56] examining elder abuse;[57] studying offender, victim, and incident characteristics of sibling sexual abuse;[58] comparing three hypotheses about intimate partner violence;[59] and examining sibling violence.[60]

Data Collection

To illustrate how NIBRS data are collected, this section includes some of the major differences between NIBRS and the UCR Program.[61]

- While the UCR Program collects counts on the number of criminal incidents involving eight offenses (i.e., Part I offenses), NIBRS expands the types of offenses reported (i.e., Group A and Group B).[62]

- Since NIBRS uses an incident-based reporting system, it includes a greater degree of detail in reporting (see Figure 2.3). The unit of analysis for the UCR is the reporting agency. For NIBRS data, however, there are six possible "units of analysis." Specifically, NIBRS data consist of six segments pertaining to the crime incident: administrative, offense, property, victim, offender, and arrestee. Within each segment, various information is collected on each incident. Examples of the various items collected for each segment include the following: *administrative*— incident number, incident date/hour; *offense*— attempted/completed, type of location, type of weapon or force involved; *property*—type of property loss, value of property; *victim*—type of injury, victim relationship to offender; *offender*—age, sex; *arrestee*—armed with weapon, resident status.[63]

- An incident can consist of multiple offenses. For NIBRS reporting procedures, the FBI defined an incident "as one or more offenses committed by the same offender, or group of offenders *acting in concert*, at the *same time and place*." *Acting in concert* was defined as follows: "[A]ll of the offenders to actually commit or assist in the commission of all of the crimes in an incident. The offenders must be aware of and consent to the commission of all of the offenses; or even

National Incident-Based Reporting System: an enhanced version of the UCR Program that collects more detailed information on incidents (e.g., the offenders, the victims).

TABLE **2.4**

NIBRS Offense Categories

GROUP A OFFENSES (REPORTED FOR ALL INCIDENTS)

1. Arson
2. Assault offenses
   - Aggravated assault
   - Simple assault
   - Intimidation
3. Bribery
4. Burglary/breaking and entering
5. Counterfeiting/forgery
6. Destruction/damage/vandalism of property
7. Drug/narcotic offenses
   - Drug/narcotic violations
   - Drug equipment violations
8. Embezzlement
9. Extortion/blackmail
10. Fraud offenses
    - False pretenses/swindle/confidence game
    - Credit card/automatic teller machine fraud
    - Impersonation
    - Welfare fraud
    - Wire fraud
11. Gambling offenses
    - Betting/wagering
    - Operating/promoting/assisting gambling
    - Gambling equipment violations
    - Sports tampering
12. Homicide offenses
    - Murder and nonnegligent manslaughter
    - Negligent manslaughter
    - Justifiable homicide
13. Human trafficking
    - Human trafficking, commercial sex acts
    - Human trafficking, involuntary servitude
14. Kidnapping/abduction
15. Larceny/theft offenses
    - Pocket-picking
    - Purse-snatching
    - Shoplifting
    - Theft from building
    - Theft from coin-operated machine or device
    - Theft from motor vehicle
    - Theft of motor vehicle parts or accessories
    - All other larceny
16. Motor vehicle theft
17. Pornography/obscene material
18. Prostitution offenses
    - Prostitution
    - Assisting or promoting
    - Purchasing prostitution
19. Robbery
20. Sex offenses
    - Rape
    - Sodomy
    - Sexual assault with an object
    - Fondling
21. Sex offenses, nonforcible
    - Incest
    - Statutory rape
22. Stolen property offenses
23. Weapon law violation

GROUP B OFFENSES (REPORTED FOR INCIDENTS PRODUCING ARRESTS)

1. Bad checks
2. Curfew/loitering/vagrancy violations
3. Disorderly conduct
4. Driving under the influence
5. Drunkenness
6. Family offenses, nonviolent
7. Liquor law violations
8. Peeping tom
9. Runaway*
10. Trespass of real property
11. All other offenses

*In January 2011, the FBI discontinued the collection of arrest data for runaways. Law enforcement agencies can continue to collect and report data on runaways, but the FBI will no longer use or publish the data.

Source: Federal Bureau of Investigation, Criminal Justice Information Services Division, Uniform Crime Reporting Program. (2013). *Summary Reporting System (SRS) user manual.* Washington, DC: U.S. Department of Justice, pp. 14–18.

if nonconsenting, their actions assist in the commission of all of the offenses."[64] Thus, all of the offenders in an incident are considered to have committed all the offenses that made up the incident. If one or more of the offenders, however, did not act in concert, then there is more than one incident.

- As mentioned in the previous section, the UCR Program uses the hierarchy rule with some exceptions. NIBRS does *not* use the hierarchy rule. Thus, if more than one crime was committed by the same person(s) and the time and space distinguishing these crimes were insignificant, *all* the crimes are reported within the same incident.

FIGURE **2.3**

The NIBRS Interactive Crime Map

Visit the NIBRS interactive map at: https://nibrs.fbi.gov/

Limitations of NIBRS

There are some limitations to NIBRS. Some of these limitations have slowed its widespread adoption.[65] A few of these limitations are listed below:

1. As with the UCR Program, NIBRS data include only crimes reported to law enforcement; unreported and unrecorded crimes are not included in NIBRS.

2. Since the NIBRS specifications were developed by a federal agency, participating local agencies may find it difficult to work with inflexible specifications and impose problems with reporting procedures.

3. Various organizations may have different goals and incentives. While the FBI and other national agencies are interested in a national monitoring system and national-level research applications, local and state agencies may have different organizational interests. For instance, local and state agencies may be more interested in local data collection requirements and analyses to support local operations, such as the deployment of law enforcement areas in certain problem areas.

4. While NIBRS data include more detailed information than the UCR Program, this is also a drawback. With this detailed information, the NIBRS record structure is more complex; researchers and analysts may find collecting this detailed information quite a challenge.

5. Currently, little is known about the extent of the errors made when collecting NIBRS data. While some errors can be addressed, other types of errors will be noted only after the NIBRS data collection program is adopted on a more widespread basis.

Hate Crime Data

On April 23, 1990, the president signed into law the "Hate Crime Statistics Act of 1990." This was due to increasing concern regarding these types of offenses. As part of the UCR

Program, the attorney general is required to develop guidelines and collect data about crimes that manifest evidence of prejudice based on race, religion, sexual orientation, or ethnicity. The UCR Program's first publication was titled *Hate Crime Statistics, 1990: A Resource Book.* This report was a collection of hate crime data from 11 states that compiled these data and volunteered to submit their data as a prototype. There have been significant changes to hate crime data collection since this time.

- The Violent Crime Control and Law Enforcement Act of 1994 amended the Hate Crime Statistics Act to include crimes committed against people with physical or mental disabilities that should also be viewed as hate crimes.

- The Church Arson Prevention Act was signed into law in 1996.

- The Matthew Shepard and James Byrd, Jr. Hate Crimes Prevention Act of 2009 was passed. This amendment included the collection of data for crimes motivated by any bias against gender or gender identity.

- In 2012, system modifications were implemented that allowed agencies to report up to four additional bias motivations per offense type.

- In 2013, bias types in the religion category were expanded to include all of those identified by the Pew Research Center and the U.S. Census Bureau. The program also started collecting data on anti-Arab bias.

- In 2015, law enforcement agencies were allowed to submit the following religious bias types: anti-Buddhist, anti-Eastern Orthodox (Greek, Russian, etc.), anti-Hindu, anti–Jehovah's Witness, anti-Mormon, anti–other Christian, and anti-Sikh. Also, the program started to collect data on race and ethnicity bias under the category of Race/Ethnicity/Ancestry.[66]

On June 17, 2015, Dylann Roof killed nine people while attending a prayer meeting at the Emanual African Methodist Episcopal Church in Charleston. What characterizes this as a hate crime?

Data Collection

To develop procedures for collecting national hate crime data, many emphasized avoiding any new data-reporting responsibilities on those law enforcement agencies participating in the UCR Program. Thus, the collection of hate crime data provides additional information on traditional UCR collection:

> Hate crimes are not separate, distinct crimes, but rather traditional offenses motivated by the offender's bias. For example, an offender may commit arson because of his/her racial bias. It is, therefore, unnecessary to create a whole new crime category. To the contrary, hate crime data can be collected by merely capturing additional information about offenses already being reported to UCR.[67]

Thus, if a traditional offense has been motivated by the offender's bias, the reporting agency is to complete the "Hate Crime Incident Report." Table 2.5 provides two examples of how hate crimes would be reported. Figure 2.4 provides a breakdown of hate crimes reported in 2014. When examining the bias for these single incidents, 47% are classified as racial bias.

hate crime data: the best-known hate crime data source is the Hate Crime Statistics, which collect information on traditional offenses, such as murder and vandalism, that have an additional factor of bias.

Joe Raedle/Getty Image

FIGURE 2.4

Bias Breakdown

Analysis of the 5,462 single-bias incidents reported by law enforcement during 2014 revealed the following biases:

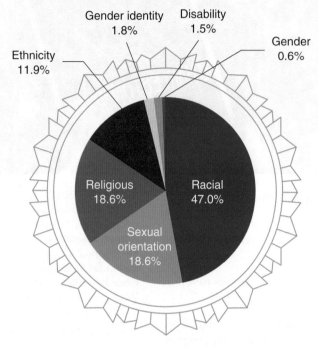

Gender identity
1.8%

Disability
1.5%

Gender
0.6%

Ethnicity
11.9%

Religious
18.6%

Racial
47.0%

Sexual
orientation
18.6%

Source: https://www.fbi.gov/news/stories/2015/november/latest-hate-crime-statistics-available/image/bias-breakdown-chart/@@images/a34d567e-641a-4f28-b390-436bf85c00de.jpeg

Law Enforcement Officers Killed and Assaulted Statistics

The FBI also collects data on the number of law enforcement officers killed and assaulted in the United States each year. This is important information that has been used for several reasons, including estimates of the risk involved in police work and analyses of what influences assaults against, and killings of, police officers. The UCR Program began gathering these data in 1972.[68]

Data Collection

Law Enforcement Officers Killed and Assaulted (LEOKA) is a supplementary data collection program of the UCR. LEOKA collects data from participating agencies on officer line-of-duty deaths and assaults. Information obtained from these data assist agencies in developing policies to enhance officer safety.

The UCR Program provided the following definitions to distinguish between *line-of-duty*, *felonious*, and *accidental* deaths:

> *Line-of-duty death*: This type of death occurs when the officer is on or off duty and acting in an official capacity while reacting to a situation that would ordinarily fall within the scope of his or her official duties as a law enforcement officer. Suicides and deaths caused by heart attacks or other natural causes as well as deaths occurring while the officer is acting in a military capacity are not included in this definition.

> *Felonious death*: This type of death occurs when an officer is killed because of or while performing his or her official duties and as a direct result of a criminal act by a subject.

> *Accidental death*: This type of death occurs when an officer dies as a result of an accident he or she is involved in while performing his or her duties (e.g., an officer is struck by a vehicle while directing traffic or drowns during a rescue attempt).[69]

Participating law enforcement agencies are required to report on officers who are killed or assaulted and meet the following criteria: (1) working in an official capacity, (2) having full arrest powers, (3) wearing a badge (ordinarily), (4) carrying a firearm (ordinarily), and (5) being paid from governmental funds allocated for payment of sworn law enforcement representatives. These officers are usually employed by local, county, state, tribal, or federal entities and working in occupations such as municipal or county police, constables, state police, highway patrol officers, sheriffs or deputies, marshals, or special agents. Officers usually not included are those involved with protective, prosecutorial, or confinement activities, such as federal judges, U.S. attorneys, probation officers, corrections officers, jailers, and prison officials.

The UCR Program includes a special form used to collect information on those incidents involving line-of-duty felonious or accidental killing of an officer or assault of an officer.

Law Enforcement Officers Killed and Assaulted: LEOKA is part of the UCR Program. LEOKA collects data on officer line-of-duty deaths and assaults.

TABLE 2.5   Example Scenarios of Hate Crimes

The following scenarios offer guidance on how to report hate crime. Based on the facts available, explanations after each scenario provide, as applicable, the known offense(s) and the bias type(s) that law enforcement would report. The number of victims has been added to some of the incidents for clarification.

SCENARIO	OFFENSES	REPORTING
An African-American man had just finished a midnight riverboat cruise with his fiancée and friends and was escorting his blind, male friend by the arm into a restroom while holding his girlfriend's purse. Inside the restroom, another man shouted anti-black and anti-gay insults at the men. The perpetrator followed them out of the restroom, continuing his verbal harassment. He then went to his car, retrieved a gun, returned to confront the men, and said, "Now what have you got to say?" The perpetrator fired the gun, killing one of the men.	• Murder (1 victim) • Aggravated Assault (1 victim)	This incident should be reported with an Anti-Black African-American Racial Bias and Anti-Gay (Male) Sexual Orientation Bias because the perpetrator used exclusively anti-black and anti-gay slurs and also acted out on his mistaken perception that the victim was gay.
An assailant ran by a Sikh pedestrian, shoved him to the ground, forcibly pulled his Dastaar (Sikh turban), and said, "Take that thing off your head— we don't want your kind in this neighborhood!" In the process of the attack, the victim suffered a concussion. When law enforcement responded to the scene, a witness to the attack recognized the offender as a clerk at a local convenience store near a predominantly Sikh community.	• Aggravated Assault	This incident should be reported with an Anti-Sikh Religious Bias because the evidence indicates that the victim was targeted due to his Dastaar and the assailant's ongoing dealings with the Sikh community.

Source: Federal Bureau of Investigation, Criminal Justice Information Services Division, Uniform Crime Reporting Program. (2015). *Hate crime data collection guidelines and training manual.* Washington, DC: U.S. Department of Justice, pp. 27 & 25.

In reference to officer assaults, the UCR emphasizes that reporting agencies must count all assaults. Even those incidents that involve more than verbal abuse or minor resistance to an arrest but do not result in the officer being injured need to be reported.[70]

CRIME DATA FROM VICTIMS OF CRIME: THE NATIONAL CRIME VICTIMIZATION SURVEY

While Canada and some European counties have surveyed individuals regarding their experiences of being victims of crimes, the United States has the longest and most extensive background with such surveys. Unofficial measures of crime, such as the National Crime Victimization Survey (NCVS), further broaden our understanding of crime with information from official measures of crime (e.g., Uniform Crime Reports).

The primary purpose of these data is to provide additional insight into what was referred to at the beginning of this chapter as the *dark figure* of crime (e.g., crimes unreported to law enforcement). Some of the reasons that victims failed to report these crimes to law enforcement include: (1) the victim believed nothing could be done about the incident; (2) the victim felt that the crime incident was not important enough to report to the police; (3) the victim perceived the incident was too private or personal; and (4) the victim thought that the police would not want to be inconvenienced with the crime incident.[71] The NCVS is also intended to (1) identify portions of the population at risk of victimization, (2) estimate multiple victimization rates, (3) provide data needed to evaluate

National Crime Victimization Survey: a primary measure of crime in the United States. It is collected by the Department of Justice and the Census Bureau and is based on interviews with victims of crime.

crime prevention programs, and (4) allow for comparisons of patterns, amounts, and locations of crime with the Uniform Crime Reports.[72]

The NCVS is used by various groups who are concerned about crime and crime prevention. Community groups and government agencies use these data to develop neighborhood watch programs as well as victim assistance and compensation programs. Law enforcement agencies use the NCVS for (1) enhancing citizen cooperation with officials in deterring and detecting crime, (2) establishing special police strike forces to combat those crimes that the NCVS reported as being most prevalent, and (3) developing street and park lighting programs in those areas with high reported crime rates. The print and broadcast media also use NCVS findings when reporting on various crime-related topics.[73]

Researchers also use the NCVS to prepare reports, to make policy recommendations, to provide testimony before Congress, and to present documentation in court.[74] The NCVS has also been used for various criminal justice research, such as examining the seasonal variation (i.e., the school calendar) in violent victimization;[75] exploring routine activity theory and lifestyle-exposure theory in terms of demographic characteristics and victimization risk;[76] investigating the epidemiology of self-defense gun use;[77] and studying the dynamics of elder victimization.[78]

From January 1971 to July 1972, the Census Bureau implemented the first nationwide victimization survey. The survey was included as a supplement to the existing Quarterly Household Survey (QHS). In July 1972, the National Crime Survey (NCS) evolved into a separate national sample survey. Due to a mandate, the Law Enforcement Assistance Administration (LEAA) was the first sponsor of the NCS. This mandate required that data be collected, evaluated, published, and disseminated regarding the progress of law enforcement in the United States.[79] In 1979, the NCS was moved to the Bureau of Justice Statistics (BJS) of the U.S. Department of Justice.

Various groups have had some serious reservations about collecting these data:

> Groups supportive of police-based crime statistics were already suspicious of this new data collection system. Academics began to raise questions about a multimillion-dollar data collection with few variables that could be used in testing theories of crime and that could not produce estimates for local jurisdictions. They also worried that this new data collection would take funds away from criminological research.[80]

To address these concerns, in the mid-1970s, the Law Enforcement Assistance Administration commissioned the Committee on Social Statistics of the National Academy of Sciences–National Research Council (NRC) to evaluate the victim surveys.[81] From 1979 to 1985, experts in criminology, survey design, and statistics conducted a detailed study of the NCS. Their findings recommended a redesign of the victim survey that would (1) increase the reporting of crime victimization and (2) include additional information on specific crime incidents. These recommendations were implemented in a two-stage process and were completed by July 1993. In addition to these changes, in 1991, BJS renamed the NCS the National Crime Victimization Survey (NCSV).

These major changes included the following:

1. The new questionnaire uses detailed cues to assist respondents in recalling and reporting incidents. These new questions and cues also encourage responses that include a broad continuum of incidents rather than just those involving weapons, severe violence, or strangers.

2. The NCVS includes multiple questions and cues on crimes committed by family members, intimates, and acquaintances.

3. Previously, only the categories of rape and attempted rape were measured in the survey. The NCVS broadened the scope of sexual incidents to include sexual assault (other than rape), verbal threats of rape or sexual assault, and unwanted sexual contact without force but involving threats or some type of harm to the victim.

Other changes have been made to the NCVS, including a series of hate crime questions as well as a series of identity theft questions. Also, in 2006, the NCVS converted to a computer-assisted personal interviewing (CAPI) environment.[82]

Any individual living in the United States and 12 years of age or older is eligible for participation in the NCVS. The households are selected by using scientific sampling methods. The NCVS collects data on individuals who have been the victims of crimes, whether or not these crimes were reported to law enforcement. The NCVS estimates the proportion of the various crime types reported to law enforcement; it also provides information as to why victims reported or did not report these crimes to law enforcement. The NCVS provides various information, including data about the victims (e.g., age, sex, race, ethnicity, marital status, income, and educational level), the offenders (e.g., sex, race, approximate age, and victim–offender relationship), and the crimes (e.g., time and place of occurrence, use of weapons, nature of the injury, and economic consequences). The victims are also asked about their experiences with the criminal justice system, if they used any self-protective measures, and possible substance abuse by offenders.[83]

Limitations of the NCVS

1. Crimes such as prostitution, drug dealing, and gambling are not often revealed in interviews for obvious reasons. Further, since murder victims cannot be interviewed, the most serious criminal offense is not included in the NCVS.[84] The NCVS also does not incorporate those situations when an individual is being victimized by drunkenness, disturbances of the peace, impaired driving, drug abuse, or sexual solicitation or procuring. The surveys cannot measure those situations where individuals are unaware they have been victimized, such as various types of fraud.[85]

2. Since the NCVS surveys only households, crimes committed against commercial businesses (e.g., stores) are not included. Thus, data on crimes such as burglaries, robberies, and vandalism are not collected.[86]

3. The validity of the NCVS is also an issue. Validity refers to whether an instrument is measuring what it intends to measure. The validity of the NCVS refers to whether is it measuring individuals who have been victims of crimes. Two different procedures have been used to test the validity of the participants' responses: forward record checks and reverse record checks. A forward record check begins with victims' reports, and these are subsequently checked against crimes known to police. A reverse record check starts with police records and then traces these back to victims to determine whether these crimes were reported to NCVS interviewers.[87]

Comparing the NCVS With the UCR

Since the NCVS was developed to complement the UCR, both data collection programs are similar in some respects. They both collect data on the same types of serious crimes; they collect information on rape, robbery, aggravated assault, burglary, theft, and motor vehicle theft. The definitions of rape, robbery, theft, and motor vehicle theft are practically the same for both programs. However, prior to 2013, the UCR measured rape as a crime against women *only*, while the NCVS measures rape as a crime against both sexes.

There are some meaningful differences between the UCR and the NCVS. First, each program was developed to serve different purposes. The UCR's primary purpose was to provide reliable criminal justice data for law enforcement administration, operation, and management. The purpose of the NCVS was to collect information that was previously unavailable on crime (e.g., crimes unreported to the police), victims, and offenders.

Second, while both programs collect information on overlapping types of crimes, these types of crimes are not necessarily identical. As mentioned previously, the NCVS collects data on crimes that were both reported and unreported to law enforcement. The UCR collects information on homicides, arson, commercial crimes, and crimes against children under the age of 12, whereas the NCVS does not collect these data.

Third, the UCR and the NCVS programs use different methods to collect crime data. Thus, for some crimes, they use different definitions. For instance, the UCR defines burglary as the unlawful entry or attempted entry of a structure to commit a felony or theft. Since the NCVS surveys individuals, it is difficult for the victims to ascertain offender motives; burglary is defined as the entry or attempted entry of a residence by a person who had no right to be in that residence.

Fourth, the two programs use different bases to calculate rates for certain crimes. For property crimes (e.g., burglary, theft, and motor vehicle theft), the UCR calculates rates using a per-capita rate based on 100,000 persons. The NCVS calculates rates for these crimes using a per-1,000-household rate. If the number of households does not grow at the same rate each year compared to the population, trend data for property crimes rates for these two programs may not be comparable.

Fifth, since the UCR and the NCVS implement different sampling procedures, there may be variations in estimates of crime. Estimates from the NCVS are obtained from interviews; thus, these data are susceptible to a margin of error. The NCVS uses rigorous statistical methods to calculate confidence intervals around all survey estimates. Trend data in the NCVS reports are listed as genuine only if there is at least a 90% certainty that the measured changes are not due to sampling variation. The UCR data are based on actual counts of those crimes reported by law enforcement agencies. There are instances when UCR data are estimated for nonparticipating jurisdictions or those jurisdictions reporting only partial data.

Thus, the UCR and the NCVS have unique strengths. One needs to realize the strengths and limitations of these programs to obtain a greater understanding of crime trends as well as the nature of crime in the United States.[88]

CRIME DATA FROM SELF-REPORT SURVEYS

Generally, surveys address four broad classes of questions: (1) the prevalence of attitudes, beliefs, and behaviors; (2) changes in these attitudes, beliefs, and behaviors over time; (3) differences between groups of people in their attitudes, beliefs, and behaviors; and (4) causal propositions about these attitudes, beliefs, and behaviors.[89] Self-report surveys collect data by asking respondents to provide information about themselves, usually as to whether they have engaged in certain forms of illegal behavior. Self-report information can be collected either through written questionnaires or through in-person interviews.

The earliest self-report studies were conducted in the 1940s. In 1946, a researcher wanted to compare male college students' involvement in illegal behavior with that of alleged juvenile delinquents. He compared the court records of these delinquents with the self-reported behavior of male college students enrolled at a southwestern university. The study revealed that all of the respondents in the college sample had been involved in at least one of the 55 offenses listed in the self-report questionnaire. He concluded that these college students had been involved in offenses that were as serious as those of these alleged delinquents, although these students may not have engaged in these behaviors as frequently as the juveniles.[90]

Research has continued to examine juveniles' involvement in delinquent behavior by using self-reporting procedures.[91] Self-report studies have also been administered to measure drug and alcohol use: for example, evaluating the Minnesota D.A.R.E. Plus Project;[92] examining drug use and violent offending;[93] and exploring the relationship between substance use and weapons aggression.[94] Research focusing on physical and sexual abuse has also used self-reporting procedures: examining the relation between dating violence and marijuana use;[95] investigating the correlation between abuse and other adverse childhood experiences among low-income women;[96] and exploring the prevalence of women's offending behavior and experiences with intimate partner violence.[97]

While there are no nationwide surveys implemented to collect self-report surveys of all types of crime, various types of self-report surveys have been implemented to collect data on specific types of behaviors. In addition to focusing on certain types of behavior, these surveys sometimes just focus on certain groups (e.g., juveniles). Three self-report surveys are discussed below: Monitoring the Future, the National Household Survey on Drug Abuse, and the National Youth Survey—Family Study.

Monitoring the Future

Substance abuse by adolescents continues to be an issue, not only because it is itself illegal and can pose a health risk, but also because it may be linked to other types of criminal activity. In 1975, the National Institute on Drug Abuse sponsored the annual self-report survey *Monitoring the Future: A Continuing Study of Lifestyles and Values of Youth*. It is sometimes referred to as Monitoring the Future (MTF). The MTF collects information to measure substance and alcohol use patterns among youths. While the survey initially sampled just 12th-grade students, in 1991, 8th- and 10th-grade students were also included in the annual survey.

Currently, the MTF survey of 12th-grade students contains about 1,400 variables. The survey measures use of drugs such as tobacco, alcohol, marijuana, hashish, LSD, hallucinogens, amphetamines, Ritalin, Quaaludes, barbiturates, cocaine, crack cocaine, GHB (gamma-hydroxybutyrate), and heroin.[98] The MTF also collects information on students' attitudes and beliefs about drugs, drug availability, and the social meanings of drug use. In addition to measuring issues of substance and alcohol use, the survey asks students about their attitudes on topics such as education, work and leisure, sex roles and family, population concerns (overpopulation and birth control), conservation, religion, politics, interpersonal relationships, race relations, and happiness.[99]

One limitation to the MTF research design is that it does not survey those youth who drop out of high school. This is a problem because certain behaviors, such as illegal drug use, occur at a higher-than-average rate in this group of individuals. However, it would be difficult to survey these individuals. Each spring, the data from students involve approximately 420 public and private high schools and middle schools. Within each school, up

Monitoring the Future: an annual self-report survey that collects information to measure substance and alcohol use patterns among youths.

There are often severe and tragic consequences associated with underage drinking and DUI-related automobile accidents.

to 350 students may be selected to participate in the survey. The surveys are administered by local Institute for Social Research representatives and their assistants. The questionnaires are group-administered in classrooms during a normal class period whenever possible.[100]

The National Survey on Drug Use and Health

Since 1971, the National Survey on Drug Use and Health (NSDUH; formerly, the National Household Survey on Drug Abuse) has been used to collect information annually on the use of illegal drugs by individuals in the United States. The NSDUH is currently sponsored by the Substance Abuse and Mental Health Services Administration of the Department of Health and Human Services; the data collection is conducted by RTI International (formerly the Research Triangle Institute).[101] The NSDUH is one of the largest surveys of drug use ever conducted in the United States.

The primary goal of NSDUH is to provide national as well as state-level estimates on the following:

- the level and patterns of alcohol, tobacco, and illegal substance use and abuse;
- trends in the use of alcohol, tobacco, and other types of drugs;
- the consequences of substance use and abuse; and
- groups at high risk for substance use and abuse.

These data are used by various government agencies, private organizations, and researchers as well as the public at large.[102] Numerous studies have used the NSDUH to examine issues pertaining to crime and criminal behavior: identifying the prevalence and correlates of group fighting among youths;[103] exploring the relationship between alcohol use and violence;[104] comparing the prevalence of externalizing behaviors (e.g., crime, violence, and drug use) and migration-related factors between immigrant and U.S.-born individuals;[105] and examining the extent of substance use, mental health issues, and criminal behavior among high school dropouts.[106]

National Youth Survey—Family Study

A major shortcoming of earlier juvenile delinquency research was that it concentrated on those youths who were already in the juvenile justice system. (This will be discussed in later chapters in reference to developing theories based on these data.) One reason that these data were used for such studies was that their records (e.g., police, juvenile hall) were easily accessible to researchers. The problem was that this research focused only on those juveniles who were formally processed in the system. Usually, these juveniles came from disadvantaged backgrounds and were more likely to come to the attention of the system, whereas juveniles from middle- or upper-class backgrounds were more likely to be diverted from the system.[107]

National Survey on Drug Use and Health: since 1971, the NSDUH been used to collect information annually on the use of illegal drugs by individuals in the United States.

Implementing self-report surveys is one approach to addressing problems associated with studying only those juveniles formally in the system. In 1977, researchers at the

University of Colorado implemented the National Youth Survey (NYS) with an initial sample of 1,725 male and female juveniles born between 1959 and 1965. Each respondent, along with his or her parents/legal guardians, was asked about various events and behaviors that had occurred the previous year. The study is ongoing. Thus, in 2011, the respondents were aged 46 to 55. In 1993, the partners and children of the original respondents were interviewed. As a result, in 2000, the name of the survey was changed to the National Youth Survey—Family Study.[108]

The NYS includes items that measure a respondent's involvement in criminal activity. It measures over 40 offenses that represent the full range of offenses reported in the UCR. The NYS also measures respondents' attitudes on issues such as level of community involvement, educational aspirations, employment skills, pregnancy, abortion, neighborhood problems, and the use of drugs and alcohol. The National Youth Survey—Family Study includes additional questions that cover the respondent's family, family relationships, educational attainment, and careers.

In regard to comparing data collected only on those youths who have come to the attention of the criminal justice system (i.e., official statistics) with self-report studies, researchers have cautioned that "to abandon either self-report or official statistics in favor of the other is 'rather shortsighted; to systematically ignore the findings of either is dangerous, particularly when the two measures provide apparently contradictory findings.'"[109] Thus, to obtain a full understanding of delinquent behavior, one should use both self-report surveys and official record research.

ADDITIONAL APPROACHES TO COLLECTING CRIME DATA

In this section, additional approaches to collecting crime data are briefly covered. It is important for those involved in the criminal justice field to realize that there are various types of data collection programs other than the UCR and NCVS. These additional data collection efforts are usually for a more specific purpose or target a more specific population. The National Youth Gang Survey and spatial analyses of crime are reviewed below.

The National Youth Gang Survey

In recent years, there has been an increase in the number of gangs and gang-related crime:

> Previous national surveys suggested growth in the number of cities, towns, and counties with gang problems, but there was no single source of uniform data that could be used to compare changes and trends over time.[110]

In response to this growing concern, the Office of Juvenile Justice and Delinquency Prevention and the Institute for Intergovernmental Research established the National Youth Gang Center (NYGC). One of NYGC's primary tasks was to implement periodic national surveys to collect data on problems associated with youth gangs. The first National Youth Gang Survey was conducted in 1995. For this initial survey, NYGC wanted to collect basic information concerning the gang problem in different jurisdictions. The survey was mailed to 4,120 police and sheriff's departments across the United States. Approximately 83% of the participating agencies responded to the survey.[111]

A key aspect to any research on gangs is how a "gang" is defined. The NYCG requires that participants report information for any "group of youths or young adults in your jurisdiction that you or other responsible persons in your agency or community are

National Youth Gang Survey: this survey collects basic information from law enforcement agencies concerning the gang problem in different jurisdictions.

Applying Theory to Crime: HATE CRIME

As noted previously, the UCR Program collects information on both single-bias and multiple-bias hate crimes. Law enforcement agencies are required to note at least one bias motivation. A single-bias incident is "an incident in which one or more offense types are motivated by the same bias." A multiple-bias incident is "an incident in which one or more offense types are motivated by two or more biases."[114]

In 2014, over 15,000 law enforcement agencies participated in the Hate Crime Statistics Program. Of these, 1,666 reported 5,479 hate crime incidents involving 6,418 offenses. Recall that hate crimes are not separate or distinct crimes; rather, they are traditional offenses but considered hate crimes when they are motivated by the offender's bias. Among the 6,418 hate crime offenses, 63.1% were crimes against persons and 36.1% were crimes against property. The remaining offenses were considered crimes against society (see Table 2.6).

As noted previously, in 2009, the Matthew Shepard and James Byrd Jr. Hate Crimes Prevention Act was passed. It was named after Matthew Shepard, a gay college student who was tortured and killed in 1998. His murder was motivated by the offenders' bias against gay men. James Byrd Jr., an African-American, was chained to a pickup truck and dragged to his death, also in 1998. His murder was motivated by the offenders' bias against African-Americans. The act expanded the definition of hate crimes to include violence based on gender, sexual orientation, gender identity, or disability.[115] In terms of sexual-orientation bias, law enforcement agencies reported 1,178 hate crime offenses based on sexual orientation bias in the *2014 Hate Crime Statistics*. Of these offenses:

- 58.0% were classified as anti-gay (male) bias.

Would you consider this hate speech?

- 23.6% were classified as anti-lesbian, -gay, -bisexual, or transgender (mixed-group) bias.

- 14.3% were classified as anti-lesbian bias.

- 2.6% were classified as anti-bisexual bias.

- 1.5% were classified as anti-heterosexual bias.[116]

One example of a violent offense that was subsequently considered a hate crime occurred in June 2015 in Sacramento, California. Timothy Brownell was accused of attacking three area musicians because they wore skinny jeans. Brownell allegedly yelled a homophobic slur at the musicians and subsequently assaulted them with a knife because of their skinny jeans. Later, he turned himself in at the county jail. Brownell's initial arrest was on suspicion of assault with a deadly weapon and possessing a firearm. However, the police later issued an arrest warrant when the attack was reclassified as a hate crime. One of the three victims, Alex Lyman, stated that Brownell approached

him without any provocation. Next, Brownell called him a homophobic slur and then began to stab him just because he was wearing skinny jeans.[117]

THINK ABOUT IT:

1. After examining the factors associated with this incident, such as "no provocation" and using a homophobic slur, what do you think would cause him to react in this manner?

2. What are some key factors that would indicate this offense should be classified as a "hate crime"?

As noted in the previous chapter, throughout this text we will attempt to apply key points of the theories to either real or hypothetical situations. For this particular example, it is essential to realize that while this offense was initially considered an assault, law enforcement later realized that motivation was a key aspect of this offense—Timothy Brownell had a bias toward what he *perceived* were gay men because they were wearing skinny jeans.

TABLE 2.6	Hate Crime Offenses by Persons, Property, or Society	
OFFENSE TYPE	**INCIDENTS**[A]	**VICTIMS**[B]
Total	**5,479**	**6,727**
Crimes against persons:	**3,303**	**4,048**
Murder and nonnegligent manslaughter	4	4
Rape (revised definition)[c]	9	9
Rape (legacy definition)[d]	0	0
Aggravated assault	599	770
Simple assault	1,307	1,514
Intimidation	1,378	1,745
Other[e]	6	6
Crimes against property:	**2,317**	**2,624**
Robbery	122	138
Burglary	162	208
Larceny-theft	239	256
Motor vehicle theft	22	22
Arson	26	39
Destruction/damage/vandalism	1,694	1,907
Other[e]	52	54
Crimes against society[e]	**53**	**55**

[a] The actual number of incidents is 5,479. However, the column figures will not add to the total because incidents may include more than one offense type, and these are counted in each appropriate offense category.

[b] The term *victim* may refer to a person, business, institution, or society as a whole.

[c] The figures shown in the rape (revised definition) row include only those reported by law enforcement agencies that used the revised Uniform Crime Reporting (UCR) definition of rape.

[d] The figures shown in the rape (legacy definition) row include only those reported by law enforcement agencies that used the legacy UCR definition or rape.

[e] Includes additional offenses collected in the National Incident-Based Reporting System.

Source: Federal Bureau of Investigation. (2015). *Uniform Crime Reports: 2014 hate crime statistics.* Washington, DC: U.S. Department of Justice.

willing to identify as a 'gang.'" Further, participating agencies are required to report such groups as motorcycle gangs, hate or ideology groups, prison gangs, and adult gangs.[112]

The 2012 NYGS consisted of two groups: (1) all police departments serving cities with a population of 50,000 or more and all suburban county police and sheriff's departments; and (2) a randomly selected sample of police departments serving cities with a population between 2,500 and 50,000 and a randomly selected sample of rural county police and sheriff's departments. Approximately 87% of the selected agencies responded to the survey. Key findings from this survey are as follows:

- Approximately 30% of all responding law enforcement agencies reported gang activity.

- Compared to 2011, slightly fewer jurisdictions had experienced gang activity (3,100 versus 3,300).

- Gang activity remained essentially concentrated in urban areas, with indications that it was occurring more than in previous years.

- Gang-related homicides had increased overall nationally, partly due to increased reporting by agencies.[113]

Spatial Analyses of Crime

Spatial analyses of crime focus on crime *places*. This interest in crime places "spans theory from the perspective of understanding the etiology of crime, and practice from the perspective of developing effective criminal justice interventions to reduce crime."[118] Thus, rather than attempting to understand crime from an individual perspective, spatial analysis also incorporates where and when crimes occur. This perspective can then assist in efforts to reduce future criminal activity.

Mapping crimes can provide such information as location, distance, direction, and pattern. Location is considered the most important piece of information. Understanding where crimes have occurred or what crimes may occur in the future is essential, especially when considering how to allocate police personnel and community resources. Distance is also a crucial element. For instance, distance can answer such questions as, "How far did the victim live from the place where she was attacked?" Direction is most helpful when considered along with distance. Usually, direction is referred to in a broader context, in statements such as, "Serial robberies are moving southeast" or "The east side is becoming a high-crime area." Finally, pattern is what crime analysts attempt to develop when using place-based crime data. Patterns are usually designated as random, uniform, clustered, or dispersed.[119]

Attempting to understand crime through location is not new. Law enforcement agencies have considered crime location to be an important component of crime control. In fact, the use of maps can be traced as far back as 1900 by the New York City Police Department.[120] Police departments would place pins on maps to represent crimes that occurred in various locations (see Photo 2.9). Thanks to technological advances, they now have more sophisticated and responsive ways to track this information (see Figure 2.5). Criminologists have also explored whether there is a relationship between criminal activity and location. These criminologists attempt to understand crime with what are called social ecological theories.[121] These criminologists examine how ecological conditions such as housing standards, poverty, and transient populations influence criminal activity.

Spatial analyses of crime: this type of analysis focuses on crime places. One major aspect is mapping crimes which provides information as location, distance, direction, and pattern.

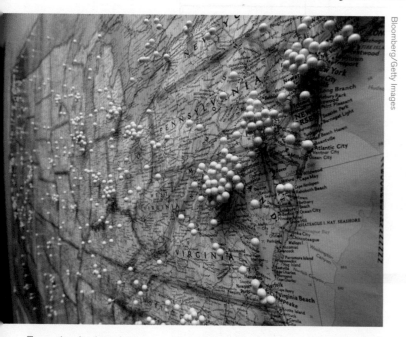

Bloomberg/Getty Images

Example of using pins on maps to represent crimes in a particular area. What are some advantages and some drawbacks of this method?

FIGURE **2.5**

FIGURE **2.5**   The San Jose Police Department Interactive Crime Map

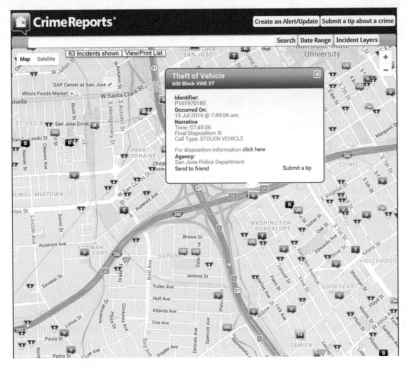

Visit the San Jose Police Department interactive crime map: http://www.sjpd.org/CrimeStats/CrimeReports.html

Since the 1990s, there have been major advances in the methods available for analyzing place-based crime data. These advances are primarily due to technological improvements, especially with computer capabilities. In addition to these computer capabilities, there have been major contributions from geographic information systems (GIS). GIS is a system made up of not only hardware but also incorporating computer software and data that are later used to analyze and describe information (e.g., crime). This information is then linked to spatial location. Further, law enforcement agencies continue to enhance the computerization of police records management systems as well as computer-aided dispatch systems (i.e., citizen calls to police).

Not only does spatial analyses of crime assist law enforcement, but researchers have also used these analyses to further our understanding of crime, such as by examining the relationship between school vicinity and criminal activity;[122] exploring community factors (e.g., poverty, ethnic diversity) and residents' perceptions of bias crime;[123] comparing the changes in the spatial patterns of automotive theft;[124] and examining the effects of population displacement after the demolition of an urban housing project.[125]

LEARNING CHECK 2.3

1. The _____ survey collects information on substance and alcohol use patterns among youths.

2. The _____ started with an initial sample of youths born between 1959 and 1965.

3. A key aspect of the National Youth Gang Survey is how the term _____ is defined.

4. _____ focuses on crime places.

Answers located at www.edge.sagepub.com/schram2e

CONCLUSION

This chapter began by reviewing various data collection procedures using law enforcement statistics. The Uniform Crime Reports Program is one of the best-known and most established data collection programs used to measure crime in the United States. The UCR Program also incorporates supplementary data procedures to collect information on homicides, hate crimes, and law enforcement officers who are killed and assaulted in the line of duty. To further enhance our understanding of crime in the United States, the National Incident-Based Reporting System was developed to provide additional information, especially pertaining to crime incidents and victims, that was not available with the UCR Program.

A major drawback to understanding crime using law enforcement statistics is that not all crimes come to the attention of police. In recognition of this "dark figure of crime," the National Crime Victimization Survey was developed in the 1970s.

The NCVS collects data from individuals who were victims of crime, regardless of whether or not they reported these crimes to law enforcement. The UCR and the NCVS are the two major data collection programs used to measure crime in the United States. While they have some similarities, there are also key differences. It is essential to stress that *both* data collection programs are necessary to understanding patterns and trends of criminal activity in the United States.

We also covered more specific data collection methods. These various methods are used primarily to collect data on certain issues related to criminal justice (e.g., Monitoring the Future and the National Survey on Drug Use and Health) or to collect data on certain populations (e.g., the National Youth Gang Survey). Finally, we briefly discussed a new technique, spatial analyses of crime, which is being explored not only for law enforcement purposes but for criminal justice research endeavors as well.

KEY TERMS

hate crime data, 43

Law Enforcement Officers Killed and Assaulted, 44

Monitoring the Future, 49

National Crime Victimization Survey, 45

National Incident-Based Reporting System, 40

National Survey on Drug Use and Health, 50

National Youth Gang Survey, 51

Spatial Analyses of Crime, 54

Supplementary Homicide Reports, 38

Uniform Crime Reports, 33

DISCUSSION QUESTIONS

1. How are the UCR collect data?

2. What are some key limitations to the UCR data, and how have these limitations been addressed?

3. How does the UCR collect information on homicides?

4. How does the UCR collect information on hate crimes?

5. How does the UCR collect information on law enforcement officers killed or assaulted in the line of duty?

6. What are some key differences between the UCR and NIBRS?

7. How does the NCVS attempt to measure the amount of crime that is not reported to law enforcement?

8. What are some similarities and differences between the UCR and the NCVS?

9. How do the various self-report surveys differ from the UCR and other types of law enforcement statistics?

10. What data collection program should be considered *the* source for understanding crime in the United States?

WEB RESOURCES

The FBI Uniform Crime Reporting website includes reports from various sources, such as the Uniform Crime Reports, Law Enforcement Officers Killed and Assaulted, and Hate Crime Data.

https://www.fbi.gov/stats-services/crimestats

The National Crime Victimization Survey can be located on the Bureau of Justice Statistics website, which provides information (such as methodology), questionnaires, and publications regarding this data source.

http://www.bjs.gov/index.cfm?ty=dcdetail&iid=245

The Monitoring the Future website provides information regarding their survey, such as press releases, publications, and tables and figures.

http://www.monitoringthefuture.org/

The National Gang Center website provides resources such as publications, training, as well as their newsletter.

https://www.nationalgangcenter.gov/survey-analysis

STUDENT STUDY SITE

WANT A BETTER GRADE ON YOUR NEXT TEST?

Get the tools you need to sharpen your study skills:

SAGE edge offers a robust online environment featuring an impressive array of tools and resources for review, study, and further exploration, keeping both instructors and students on the cutting edge of teaching and learning. Learn more at **edge.sagepub.com/schram2e**.

FOR FURTHER EXPLORATION AND APPLICATION, VISIT THE STUDENT STUDY SITE:

- FBI: Murders Up Nearly 11 Percent in 2015; Violent Crime Rose Slightly
- Historians Mine 400 Years of Crime Data at the Old Bailey
- Shooting for accuracy: Comparing data sources on mass murder.
- Missing data and imputation in the Uniform Crime Reports and the effects on National estimates
- Assessing the practice of hot spots policing: Surveying results from a national convenience sample of local police agencies
- Janet Lauritsen (1 of 3): What is the National Crime Victimization Survey
- What is a Hate Crime?
- Crime Statistics: The Dark Figure
- Study Highlights a New Epidemic of Drug Abuse that is a Growing Problem Among US Teens
- Not there for your children? Gangs will be
- Federal Bureau of Prisons - Inmate Statistics
- NIBRS
- Crime Mapping
- Prison Overcrowding
- Crime in the United States

PREMIUM VIDEO:

Check out the Interactive eBook for premium videos, including videos from author Stephen Tibbetts, who discusses real-world examples and strange crimes; and videos from former offenders, who share their stories from a first-person view, and touch on key theories and concepts from the chapter.

CHAPTER 3

The Classical School of Criminological Thought

INTRODUCTION

A 2009 report from the Death Penalty Information Center, citing a study based on FBI data and other national reports, showed that states with the death penalty have consistently higher murder rates than states without the death penalty.[4] The report highlighted the fact that if the death penalty were acting as a deterrent, the gap between these two groups of states would be expected to converge, or at least lessen over time. But that has not been the case. In fact, this disparity in murder rates has actually grown over the past two decades, with states allowing the death penalty having a 42% higher murder rate (as of 2007) compared with states that do not—up from only 4% in 1990.

Thus, it appears that in terms of deterrence theory, at least when it comes to the death penalty, such potential punishment is not an effective deterrent. This chapter deals with the various issues and factors that go into offenders' decision-making about committing crime. While many would likely anticipate that potential murderers in states with the death penalty would be deterred from committing such offenses, this is clearly not the case, given the findings of the study discussed above. This type of deterrence, or rather the lack thereof, regarding the death penalty and related issues makes up a key portion of this chapter.

This chapter examines explanations of criminal conduct that emphasize individuals' ability to make decisions based on the potential consequences of their behavior. The natural capability of human beings to make decisions based on expected costs and benefits was acknowledged during the Age of Enlightenment in the 17th and 18th centuries. This understanding of human capability led to what is considered the first rational theory of criminal activity—namely, deterrence theory. Of any other perspective to date, deterrence theory has had the most profound impact on justice systems in our nation. Furthermore, it is easy to see examples in contemporary life of offenders engaging in such rational decision-making, and a number of variations of this theoretical model have been developed that focus on the reasoning processes of people considering criminal acts.

Such theories of human rationality stand in stark contrast to the theories perpetuated for most of human civilization, up to the Age of Enlightenment—theories that focused on religious or supernatural causes of crime. Additionally, the Classical School theories of crime are distinguished from the other theories we examine in future chapters by their emphasis on free will and rational decision-making, which modern theories of crime tend to ignore. Specifically, the theoretical perspectives discussed in this chapter all focus on the human ability to choose one's own behavior and destiny, whereas paradigms popular before the Enlightenment and in contemporary times tend to emphasize the influence of external factors on individual choice. Therefore, the Classical School is perhaps the paradigm best suited for analysis of what types of calculations go on in someone's head before committing a crime.

As you read this chapter, consider the following topics:

- Identify the primitive types of "theories" explaining why individuals committed violent and other deviant acts for most of human civilization.

- Describe how the Age of Enlightenment drastically altered the theories for how and why individuals commit crimes as well as how it changed criminal justice policies.

- Explain how Cesare Beccaria's book in 1764 drastically influenced various criminal justice systems throughout the world, and be able to list the concepts and propositions recommended in his book.

- Summarize what Jeremy Bentham contributed to this movement toward the Classical School of criminological thought.

- Explain what the Neoclassical School of criminology contributed to the propositions of the Classical School that led most of the Western world (including the United States) to embrace this model as the major paradigm for the criminal justice system.

CASE STUDY

DEBORAH JEANE PALFREY

Deborah Jeane Palfrey, known as the "DC Madam," was brought up on charges of racketeering and money laundering related to running a prostitution ring in Washington, DC, and surrounding suburbs in Maryland and Virginia. The clientele of this prostitution ring included some notable politicians, such as state senators and other elected officials. Palfrey faced a maximum of 55 years in prison but likely would have received far less time had she not committed suicide before her sentencing. Her body was found in a storage facility at her mother's home in Tarpon Springs, Florida.

News reports revealed that she had served time before (for prostitution). Author Dan Moldea told *Time* magazine that she had contacted him for a book he was working on and told him "she had done time once before . . . and it damned near killed her. She said there was enormous stress—it made her sick, she couldn't take it, and she wasn't going to let that happen again."[1] The situation could have been worsened by the heightened media attention this case received; while most prostitution cases are handled by local or state courts, this one was handled by federal courts because it concerned Washington, DC.

It is quite likely that the impending maximum prison sentence led her to take her own life, given what she had said to Moldea. This shows the type of deterrent effect that jail or prison can have on an individual—in this case, possibly leading her to choose death over serving time. Ironically, Palfrey had commented to the press, after the suicide of a former employee in her prostitution network— Brandy Britton, who hanged herself before going to trial— "I guess I'm made of something that Brandy Britton wasn't made of."[2] It seems that Palfrey had the same concerns as Britton, and she ended up contradicting her bold statement when she ended her own life.

This case study provides an example of the profound effects legal sanctions can have on individuals. Legal sanctions are not meant to inspire offenders to end their lives, but this case does illustrate the potential deterrent effects of facing punishment from the legal system. We can see this on a smaller scale when a speeding driver's heart rate increases at the sight of a highway patrol or other police vehicle (which studies show happens to most drivers). Even though this offense would result in only a fine, it is a good example of deterrence in our everyday lives. We will revisit the Palfrey case at the conclusion of this chapter, after you have had a chance to review some of the theoretical propositions and concepts that make up deterrence theory.

Deborah Jeane Palfrey, known as the "D.C. Madam," committed suicide before being sentenced. Her case reveals the potentially powerful effects of formal sanctions on individuals' decision-making.

On a related note, a special report from the U.S. Department of Justice, Bureau of Justice Statistics, concludes that the suicide rate has been far higher among jail inmates than among prison inmates (see Figures 3.1 through 3.3).[3] Specifically, suicides in jails have tended over the past few decades to occur 300% (or three times) more often than among prison inmates.

A likely reason for this phenomenon is that many persons arrested and/or awaiting trial (which is generally the status of those in jail) have more to lose, such as in their relationships with family, friends, and employers, than do the typical chronic offenders that end up in prison. Specifically, many of the individuals picked up for prostitution and other relatively minor, albeit embarrassing, offenses are of the middle- and upper-class mentality and, thus, are ill-equipped to face the real-world consequences of their arrest. The good news is, this same Department of Justice report showed that suicides in both jails and prisons have decreased during the past few decades, likely due to better policies in correctional settings regarding persons considered at "high risk" for suicide.

> "SHE HAD DONE TIME ONCE BEFORE . . . AND IT DAMNED NEAR KILLED HER. SHE SAID THERE WAS ENORMOUS STRESS— IT MADE HER SICK, SHE COULDN'T TAKE IT, AND SHE WASN'T GOING TO LET THAT HAPPEN AGAIN."

THINK ABOUT IT:

1. Do you think that some of the clientele (e.g., notable politicians) should have also been charged for a criminal offense?

2. Do you think it made a difference that this case was handled by federal courts rather than local or state courts?

3. Do you think prostitution should be legal?

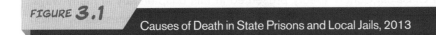

FIGURE 3.1

Causes of Death in State Prisons and Local Jails, 2013

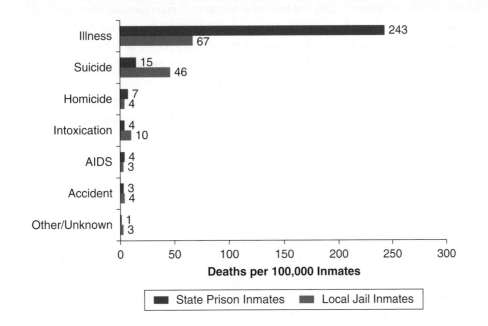

- Illness: 243 / 67
- Suicide: 15 / 46
- Homicide: 7 / 4
- Intoxication: 4 / 10
- AIDS: 4 / 3
- Accident: 3 / 4
- Other/Unknown: 1 / 3

Deaths per 100,000 Inmates

■ State Prison Inmates   ■ Local Jail Inmates

FIGURE 3.2

Suicide in State Prisons and Local Jails

Suicides per 100,000 inmates

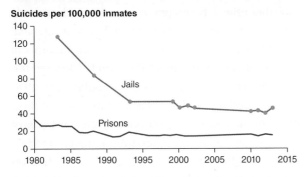

Suicide was the leading cause of death in local jails in 2013 (34% of all jail deaths) and has been the leading cause of death in local jails each year since 2000. The mortality rate for suicide among male jail inmates (43) was 1.5 times the rate for female inmates (28) from 2000 to 2013. Violent offenders in both local jails (92 per 100,000) and state prisons (19 per 100,000) had suicide rates more than twice as high as those of nonviolent offenders (31 and 9 per 100,000, respectively).

FIGURE 3.3

Homicide in State Prisons and Local Jails

Homicides per 100,000 inmates

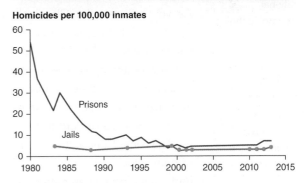

A third of homicides in state prisons in 2013 involved prisoners age 45 or older between 2001 and 2013. While 67% of homicide victims in state prisons had served at least two years, 37% had served at least five years.

Violent offenders were the victims of most state prison homicides (61%), and their jail homicide rate (5 per 100,000) was over twice that of nonviolent offenders (2 per 100,000).

Sources: Mumola, C. J. (2005, August). *Suicide and homicide in state prisons and local jails.* Washington, DC: U.S. Department of Justice, Office of Justice Programs; Noonan, M. (2015, August). *Mortality in local jails and state prisons, 2000–2013—Statistical tables.* Washington, DC: U.S. Department of Justice, Office of Justice Programs, Bureau of Justice Statistics.

The aspects of Classical School theory presented in this chapter vary in many ways, most notably in what they propose as the primary constructs and processes by which individuals determine whether or not to commit a crime. For example, some Classical School theories emphasize only the potential negative consequences of criminal actions, whereas others focus on the possible benefits. Still others concentrate on the opportunities and circumstances that predispose one to engage in criminal activity. Regardless of their differences, all the theories examined in this chapter emphasize a common theme: Individuals commit crimes because they identify certain situations and actions as beneficial due to a perceived lack of punishment and a perceived likelihood of profits, such as money or peer status. In other words, the potential offender weighs out the possible costs and pleasures of committing a given act and then behaves in a rational way based on the conclusions of that analysis.

The most important distinction of these Classical School theories, as opposed to those discussed in future chapters, is that they emphasize individual decision-making regardless of any extraneous influences on a person's free will, such as the economy or bonding with society. Although many outside factors may influence an individual's ability to rationally consider offending situations—and many of the theories in this chapter deal with such influences—primary responsibility rests on the individual to take all influences into account when deciding whether to engage in criminal behavior. Given this emphasis on individual responsibility, it is not surprising that Classical School theories are used as the basis for U.S. policies on punishment for criminal activity. After all, the Classical School theories are highly compatible and consistent with the conservative "get-tough" movement that has existed since the mid-1970s because they focus on individual responsibility. Thus, the Classical School still retains the highest influence in terms of policy and pragmatic punishment in the United States as well as throughout the Western world.

As you will see, the Classical School theoretical paradigm was presented as early as the mid-1700s, and it is still the dominant model of offending behavior in criminal justice systems. The Classical School paradigm remains the most popular theoretical framework among U.S. legislators and society and throughout the world. Although the Classical School theories have remained dominant in most Western societies, scientific and academic circles have somewhat dismissed many of the claims of this perspective. For reasons we explore in this chapter, the assumptions and primary propositions of the Classical School theories have been neglected by most recent theoretical models of criminology, which is likely premature given the impact this perspective has had on understanding human nature as well as its profound influence on most criminal justice systems, especially in the United States.

PRE-CLASSICAL PERSPECTIVES OF CRIME AND PUNISHMENT

For the vast majority of human civilization's history, people believed that criminal activity was caused by either supernatural or religious factors. Some primitive societies believed that crime increased during major thunderstorms or droughts. Most primitive cultures believed that when people engaged in behavior that violated the rules of the tribe or clan, the devil or evil spirits were making them do it.[5] For example, in many societies at that time, if a person had committed a criminal act, it was common to perform an exorcism

deterrence theory: theory of crime associated with the Classical School; proposes that individuals will make rational decisions regarding their behavior.

Age of Enlightenment: a period of the late 17th to 18th century in which philosophers and scholars began to emphasize the rights of individuals in society.

Classical School: a model of crime that assumes that crime occurs after a rational individual mentally weighs the potential good and bad consequences of crime and then makes a decision about whether to engage in a given behavior.

or primitive surgery, such as breaking open the offender's skull to release the demons thought to be lodged there. Of course, this almost always resulted in the death of the accused, but it was seen as a liberating experience for the defendant.

Exorcism was just one form of dealing with criminal behavior, but it epitomizes the nature of primitive cultures' understanding of what causes crime. However, as the movie *The Exorcist* showed, the Catholic Church, among other religious institutions, still uses exorcism in extreme cases. Exorcisms are performed in the 21st century by representatives of a number of religions, including Catholicism, "to get the devil out." For instance, in June 2005, a Romanian monk and four nuns acknowledged engaging in an exorcism that led to the death of a 23-year-old woman. During the procedure, the woman was chained to a cross, had a towel stuffed in her mouth, and was deprived of food for three days.[6] When the monk and nuns were asked to explain why they did this, they were defiant and said they were trying to take the devils out of the woman. Although they were prosecuted by Romanian authorities, many governments around the world still believe in and condone such practices and may not have prosecuted in this case.

One of the most common supernatural beliefs of primitive cultures was that the moon, in its fullest state, was a trigger for criminal activity. Then, as now, there was much truth to that theory. But in primitive times, this influence was believed to be caused by higher powers, such as the "destructive influence" of the moon itself. Modern studies have shown that this connection between the full moon and crime is primarily due to a Classical School theoretical model: There are simply more opportunities to commit crime when the moon is full. Specifically, there is more light during the full-moon phase, which means there are more people on the streets and more opportunities for crime. Also, nighttime is well established as a higher-risk period for adult crime, such as sexual assault.

Some of the primitive theories of crime had some validity in determining when crime was more likely to occur; however, virtually none of the primitive theories accurately predicted who would commit the offenses. During the Middle Ages and before, nearly all individuals were part of the lower classes, and only a subsection of that group engaged in offending against the normative society. So, for most of human civilization, there was close to no rational theoretical understanding for why certain individuals violated the laws of society.

Thus, for most of human civilization's history, people believed that crime was caused by supernatural or religious factors, leading to theories of crime such as "the devil made me do it." There were many variations on this perspective, such as crime caused by the full moon or excessive thunder. Due to the assumption that evil spirits were driving the motivations for criminal activity, punishments for criminal acts—especially for those deemed particularly offensive to the norms of a given society—were often quite inhumane by modern standards.

Punishments Under Pre-Classical Perspectives

For example, during the Middle Ages (Dark Ages), common punishments included beheading, torturing, burning alive at the stake, drowning, stoning (still used by many Islamic courts in portions of Africa and the Middle East), and quartering (in which the limbs of a convicted criminal are tied to four horses and then the horses are made to run in opposite directions, ripping limbs from the torso). These punishments seem harsh by contemporary standards, but given the context of the times, they were fairly standard and widely accepted.[7]

AP Photo

Medieval punishments were quite brutal, compared to how we execute offenders in current times. Most developed countries would never use such forms of execution today.

Although many would find primitive forms of punishment and execution quite barbaric, many societies still practice some of them. Recent examples can be seen among Islamic court systems (as well as in other religious/ethnic cultures), which are often allowed to carry out executions and other forms of corporal punishment. For instance, a number of offenders were flogged (i.e., whipped) for what is considered a relatively minor crime—or no crime at all—in most of the United States: gambling. Gambling was the most serious offense committed by the 15 individuals in Aceh, Indonesia (a highly conservative Muslim region of that country), who were publicly caned outside a mosque.[8]

It is interesting to note that a relatively recent Gallup Poll addressing the practice of caning (i.e., publicly whipping) convicted individuals revealed support for the practice from most of the American public. More extreme forms of corporal punishment, particularly the methods of public execution carried out by many religious courts and countries—such as stoning, in which persons are buried up to the waist and local citizens throw small stones (but not large stones, as those lead to death too quickly)—are drawn out and painful compared with modern forms of punishment in the United States. In most of the Western world, such brutal forms of punishment and execution were done away with in the 1700s due to the impact of the Age of Enlightenment.

THE AGE OF ENLIGHTENMENT

In the midst of the extremely draconian times of the mid-1600s, Thomas Hobbes, in his book *Leviathan* (1651), proposed a rational theory for why people are motivated to form democratic states of governance.[9] Hobbes proclaimed that people are rational, so they will logically organize a sound system of governance to create rules that will help alleviate the constant fear of offense by others. It is interesting that the very emotion (fear) that motivates individuals to cooperate in the formation of government is the same emotion that inspires these individuals to obey the laws of the government created—because they fear the punishment imposed for breaking the rules.

Hobbes clearly stated that until citizens in such societies received a certain degree of respect from their governing bodies, as well as from their justice systems, they would never fully buy in to the authority of government or the system of justice. Hobbes proposed a number of extraordinary ideas that came to define the Age of Enlightenment. He suggested a drastic paradigm shift with this new idea of social structure, which had extreme implications for justice systems throughout the world.

Specifically, Hobbes declared that human beings are rational beings who choose their destiny by creating a society. Hobbes further proposed that individuals in such societies democratically create rules of conduct that all members of society must follow. These rules that all citizens decide on become laws, and the result of not following these laws is a punishment determined by the democratically instituted government. It is clear from Hobbes's statements that the government, as instructed by the citizens, not only has the authority to punish individuals who violate the rules of the society but, more important, is bound by duty to punish such individuals. If such an authority fails to fulfill this duty, it can quickly result in a breakdown in the social order.

The arrangement of citizens agreeing to abide by the rules or laws set forth by a given society in return for protection is commonly referred to as the social contract. Hobbes introduced this idea, but it was emphasized by all the other Enlightenment theorists after him, such as Rousseau, Locke, Voltaire, and Montesquieu, and it embodies their underlying philosophies. Although all the Enlightenment philosophers had significant differences of belief, the one belief they had in common was that in the social contract. This idea that people invest in the laws of their society in exchange for the guarantee that they will be protected from others who violate those laws is universal across all the Enlightenment philosophers.

Another shared belief among Enlightenment philosophers was that each individual should have a say in the government, especially in the justice system. Virtually all the Enlightenment philosophers also emphasized fairness in determining who was guilty, as well as the appropriate punishments or sentences for misconduct. During the time in which they wrote, Enlightenment philosophers saw individuals who stole a loaf of bread to feed their families receive death sentences, while upper-class individuals who had stolen large sums of money or even committed murder were pardoned. This not only goes against common sense but also violates the social contract. After all, if citizens observe certain persons being excused from punishment for violation of the law, their belief in the social contract will break down. This same standard can be applied to modern times. For example, when Los Angeles police officers who were filmed beating a suspect were acquitted of criminal charges, a massive riot erupted among members of the community. This is a good example of the social contract breaking down, largely due to the realization that the government failed to punish members of the community (significantly, police officers) who had violated the rules.

Perhaps the most relevant concept the Enlightenment philosophers highlighted, as mentioned above, was the idea that human beings are rational and therefore have free will. The philosophers of this age focused on the ability of individuals to consider the consequences of their actions, and the philosophers assumed that people freely choose how to behave, especially in regard to criminal activity. We shall see that this was an extremely important part of Enlightenment philosophy, which the Father of Criminal Justice assumed in his formulation of what is considered to be the first bona fide theory for why people commit crime.

THE CLASSICAL SCHOOL OF CRIMINOLOGY

The foundation of the Classical School of criminological theorizing can be traced to the Enlightenment philosophers discussed above, but the more specific and well-known origin

social contract: an Enlightenment ideal or assumption that stipulates an unspecified arrangement among citizens in which they promise the state or government not to commit offenses against other citizens and in turn gain protection from being violated by other citizens.

LEARNING CHECK 3.1

1. According to the text, which type of theory was dominant throughout most of human civilization?
   a. Rational/deterrence
   b. Psychological/Freudian
   c. Supernatural/religious
   d. Positive/empirical

2. According to the text, what concept was NOT one of the key propositions of the Age of Enlightenment theorists?
   a. Democracy
   b. Social contract
   c. Determinism
   d. Free will
   e. Rationality

3. According to the text, which emotion did Hobbes claim was the motivation for groups of people both creating a state/government and enforcing its laws/rules?
   a. Shame
   b. Fear
   c. Guilt
   d. Empathy

Answers located at www.edge.sagepub.com/schram2e

http://commons.wikimedia.org/wiki/File:Cesare_Beccaria,_1738–1794.jpg

Cesare Beccaria (1738–1794), considered the Father of Criminal Justice, Father of Deterrence Theory, and Father of the Classical School of Criminology, due to the influence of his *On Crimes and Punishments* (1764).

of the Classical School is considered to be the 1764 publication of *On Crimes and Punishments* by Italian scholar Cesare Bonesana, Marchese di Beccaria (1738–1794), commonly known as Cesare Beccaria. He wrote this book at the age of 26 and published it anonymously, but after its almost instant popularity, he came forward as the author. Because of this significant work, most experts consider Beccaria not only the Father of Criminal Justice and the Father of the Classical School of Criminology but, perhaps most important, the Father of Deterrence Theory. All this will be explained in the following sections, in which we comprehensively survey the ideas and impact of Beccaria and the Classical School.

Influences on Beccaria and His Writings

As discussed previously in this chapter, the Enlightenment philosophers profoundly impacted the social and political climate of the late 1600s and 1700s. Growing up in this time, Beccaria was a child of the Enlightenment; as such, he was highly influenced by the concepts and propositions introduced by these great thinkers. The Enlightenment philosophy is readily evident in Beccaria's writing, and he incorporates many of these philosophers' assumptions into his work. As a student of law, Beccaria had a solid background for determining what was rational in legal policy as well as what was not. But his loyalty to the Enlightenment ideal is ever present throughout his work.

Specifically, Beccaria emphasized the social contract and incorporated the idea that citizens give up certain rights in exchange for protection from the state or government. He also claimed that actions or punishments carried out by the government that violate the overall sense of unity will not be accepted by the populace, largely due to the requirement that the social contract be a fair deal. Beccaria stated that laws are compacts of free individuals in a society. Additionally, he appealed to the ideal of the greatest happiness shared by the greatest number, otherwise known as utilitarianism. This, too, was a focus of the Enlightenment philosophers. Finally, the importance of free will and individual choice is key to his propositions and theorizing. Although these points are the main assumptions of his reforms and ideas on motives for committing crimes, taken directly from Enlightenment theorists, we shall see in the following sections that Enlightenment philosophy is present in virtually all his propositions, most clearly shown in his directly citing Hobbes, Montesquieu, and others in his work.[10]

Beccaria's Proposed Reforms and Ideas of Justice

Beccaria wrote at a time when authoritarian governments ruled the justice system, which was actually quite unjust. For example, back then, it was not uncommon for a person who stole food for his or her family to be imprisoned for life. A good example of this is the story of *Les Misérables*, in which the protagonist, Jean Valjean, receives a lengthy prison sentence after stealing a loaf of bread for his starving loved ones. On the other hand, a person at that time who had committed several murders could be excused by the judge if that person was from a prominent family.

As Beccaria claimed, "The true measure of crimes is namely the harm done to society"[11] (i.e., to the social contract). Thus, Beccaria was very clear that for a given act, a particular punishment should be administered as established by law, regardless of the contextual circumstances. (This point is the subject of much scrutiny later in this chapter.)

However, this principle did not take into account the offender's intent in committing the crime. In most modern justice systems, intent plays a key role in the charges and sentencing of defendants for many types of crimes. Most notably, the degrees of homicide

utilitarianism: a philosophical concept that relates to the idea of the greatest good for the greatest number.

in most jurisdictions of the United States include first-degree murder (which requires proof of planning or "malice aforethought"), second-degree murder (which typically involves no evidence of planning but, rather, is the spontaneous act of killing), and various degrees of manslaughter (which generally include some level of provocation on the part of the victim).

The degrees of homicide are just one example of the importance of intent—legally known as **mens rea** (literally, "guilty mind")—in most modern justice systems. Many types of offending are graded by degree of intent as opposed to the act itself—known legally as **actus reus** (literally, "guilty act"). Beccaria's propositions focus on only the actus reus, because he claimed that an act against society was harmful regardless of the intent, or mens rea. Despite his recommendation, most societies factor in the offender's intent in criminal activity. Still, this proposal that "a given act should be given equal punishment" certainly seemed to represent a significant improvement over the arbitrary punishments doled out by the regimes and justice systems of the 1700s.

Another sweeping reform Beccaria proposed was to do away with certain practices common in justice systems at the time. For example, he proposed that secret accusations not be allowed; rather, witnesses should be publicly confronted and cross-examined. Although some modern countries still accept and use secret accusations, as well as disallowing the cross-examination of so-called witnesses, Beccaria set the standard for most modern systems of justice in guaranteeing such rights to defendants in the United States and most other Western societies.

Additionally, Beccaria claimed that torture should not be used against defendants. Although some countries, such as Israel and Mexico, explicitly allow the use of torture for eliciting information and confessions, most countries now abstain from the practice. However, former U.S. Attorney General Alberto Gonzalez (the highest law enforcement rank in the country) wrote a memo stating that torture of terrorist suspects by the U.S. military is condoned. Despite this relatively recent change in U.S. philosophy regarding torture, the United States has traditionally agreed with Beccaria, who claimed that any information or oaths obtained under torture were relatively worthless. And our country apparently still agrees with Beccaria, at least in terms of domestic criminal defendants. Beccaria's belief in the worthlessness of torture is further expressed in this statement: "It is useless to reveal the author of a crime that lies deeply buried in darkness."[12]

Beccaria believed that this use of torture was one of the worst aspects of the criminal justice systems of his time and a manifestation of the truly barbaric acts common in feudal times in the Middle Ages (or "Dark Ages"). Beccaria expressed his doubt about the relevance of any information obtained via torture, a doubt best represented in this statement: "The impression of pain may become so great that, filling the entire sensory capacity of the tortured person, it leaves him free only to choose what for the moment is the shortest way of escape from pain."[13]

Beccaria addresses the possible policy implications of using torture in stating that, "of two men, equally innocent or equally guilty, the strong and courageous will be acquitted, the weak and timid condemned."[14]

Beccaria also asserted that defendants should be tried by fellow citizens or peers, not only by judges. He stated, "I consider an excellent law that which assigns popular jurors, taken by lot, to assist the chief judge . . . that each man ought to be judged by his peers."[15] Beccaria clearly felt that the responsibility for determining the facts of a case should be placed in the hands of more than one person (such as a judge). Related to prior discussions in this chapter, Beccaria's feelings on this subject were likely driven by his Enlightenment beliefs on democratic philosophy, in which citizens

mens rea: concept regarding whether offenders actually knew what they were doing and meant to do it.

actus reus: in legal terms, whether the offender actually engaged in a given criminal act.

Formal, public processing and trial of criminal defendants (rather than secret accusations and closed courtrooms) is a key part of Beccaria's proposed reforms of justice systems as well as of deterrence theory.

should have a voice and serve in judging the facts and in making ultimate justice decisions in criminal cases. This proposition is representative of Beccaria's overall philosophy toward fairness and democratic process, which all the Enlightenment philosophers shared.

Like other reforms discussed in this section, the right of all U.S. citizens to a trial by a jury of their peers is often taken for granted. It may surprise some readers to know that many modern developed countries have not provided this right. For example, Russia just recently held its first jury trials since Vladimir Lenin banished the practice 90 years ago. During Lenin's rule, the "bench-trials" of the old system produced almost a 100% conviction rate (99.6%, to be exact). This means that virtually every person convicted of a crime in Russia was found guilty, whether or not they were actually guilty. Given the relatively high percentage of persons found innocent of crimes (such as murder) in the United States—not to mention the numerous persons in our country recently released from death row after DNA analysis proved them not guilty—it is frightening to think of how many individuals were falsely convicted and unjustly sentenced in Russia over the past century.

Another important aspect of Beccaria's reforms involves his emphasis on making the justice system, particularly the laws and decisions made in processing, more public and understandable. After all, this fits the Enlightenment assumption that individuals are rational and that if individuals know the consequences of their actions, they will act accordingly. Specifically, Beccaria stated, "When the number of those who can understand the sacred code of laws and hold it in their hands increases, the frequency of crimes will be found to decrease."[16] In Beccaria's time, the laws were often unknown to the populace. This was somewhat due to widespread illiteracy but perhaps more due to current laws not being publicly declared. Even when laws were posted, they were often printed in languages (e.g., Latin) that the citizens did not read or speak. So Beccaria stressed the need for society to ensure that citizens were educated on current laws, explaining that this alone would lead to a significant decrease in law violations.

Furthermore, Beccaria believed that the important stages and decision-making processes of any justice system should be public knowledge rather than being held secretly or decided behind closed doors. As Beccaria stated, "Punishment . . . must be essentially public."[17] This statement has a highly democratic and Enlightenment feel to it, in the sense that citizens of a society have the right to know what vital judgments are being made. After all, in a democratic society, the citizens assign the government the profound responsibility of distributing punishment for crimes against the society. Citizens are entitled to know what decisions their government officials are making, particularly regarding justice. This provides not only knowledge and an understanding of what is going on but also a form of "checks and balances." Furthermore, the public nature of trials and punishments inherently produces a form of deterrence for those individuals who may be considering criminal activity, which is explored in the following sections of this chapter.

One of Beccaria's most profound and important proposed reforms is one of the least noted; in fact, it is largely ignored by every other review of his work. Specifically, Beccaria claimed to know the most certain way to reduce crime: "The surest but most difficult way to prevent crimes is by perfecting education."[18] Although he clearly expressed this as his primary recommendation for reducing crime, we know of no other review of his work that notes this hypothesis, which is amazing considering that most of the reviews are written for an educational audience. Furthermore, the importance placed on education makes sense given Beccaria's emphasis on knowledge of laws and consequences of criminal activity, as well as his focus on deterrence, which is explored in the following sections of this chapter.

©iStockphoto.com/stephen mulcahey

Beccaria's Ideas of the Death Penalty

Another primary area of Beccaria's suggested reforms dealt with the use—and, in his day, abuse—of the death penalty. First, let it be said that Beccaria was against the use of capital punishment. (Interestingly, he was not against corporal punishment, which he explicitly stated was appropriate for violent offenders.) Perhaps this was due to the times in which he wrote, when a large number of people were put to death, often by harsh methods. Still, Beccaria provided several rational reasons for why he felt the death penalty was not an efficient and effective punishment.

Although the United States typically uses torture methods only in times of war, such as in the recent war against terrorism, many countries still commonly use this practice against citizens accused of criminal activity.

First, Beccaria claimed that the use of capital punishment inherently violated the social contract:

> Is it conceivable that the least sacrifice of each person's liberty should include sacrifice of the greatest of all goods, life? . . . The punishment of death, therefore, is not a right, for I have demonstrated that it cannot be such.[19]

The second reason that Beccaria felt the death penalty was an inappropriate form of punishment was that the government's endorsing the death of a citizen would provide a negative example for the rest of society. Beccaria claimed, "The death penalty cannot be useful, because of the example of barbarity it gives men."[20] Although some studies show evidence that use of the death penalty in the United States deters crime,[21] most show no effect or even a positive correlation with homicide.[22] Researchers have called this increase of homicides after executions the brutalization effect, and a similar phenomenon can be seen at sporting events, such as boxing matches, hockey games, and soccer/football games, when violence breaks out among spectators. In recent years, there have even been notable incidents of fighting among spectators at youth sporting events.

To further complicate the possible contradictory effects of capital punishment, some analyses show that both deterrence and brutalization occur at the same time for different types of crime, depending on the level of planning or spontaneity of a given act. For example, one sophisticated analysis of homicide data from California examined the effects of a high-profile execution in 1992, largely because it was the first one in the state in 25 years.[23] As predicted, the authors of the study found that nonstranger felony-murders (which typically involve some planning) significantly decreased after the high-profile execution, whereas the level of argument-based stranger murders (typically more spontaneous) significantly increased during the same time period. Thus, the effects of both deterrence and brutalization were observed at the same time and in the same location following this execution.

brutalization effect: the predicted tendency of homicides to increase after an execution, particularly after high-profile executions.

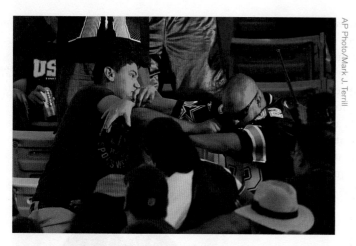

AP Photo/Mark J. Terrill

Fights among spectators at sporting events illustrate the type of "brutalization effect" Beccaria predicted in connection with the death penalty. Some individuals who see aggressive or violent acts are more likely to behave aggressively.

Another primary reason why Beccaria was against the use of capital punishment was that he believed it was an ineffective deterrent. Specifically, he thought that a quick punishment, such as the death penalty, could not be an effective deterrent compared with a more drawn-out penalty. As Beccaria stated, "It is not the intensity of punishment that has the greatest effect on the human spirit, but its duration."[24] Many readers can likely relate to this type of argument even if they do not necessarily agree with it; the idea of spending the rest of one's life in a cell is a scary one for most people. And for many, such a concept is more frightening than death, which supports Beccaria's idea that a more extended punishment may be a more effective deterrent than a short, albeit extremely severe, punishment such as execution.

This idea seems to be supported by the case study at the beginning of this chapter. As you will recall, Deborah Jeane Palfrey, known as the "D.C. Madam," committed suicide rather than go back to prison. So for many, prison is just as effective as a punishment as the death penalty; after all, Palfrey chose death over a lengthy prison sentence.

Beccaria's Concept of Deterrence and the Three Key Elements of Punishment

As noted previously in this chapter, Beccaria is widely considered the Father of Deterrence, and this is for good reason. After all, Beccaria was the first known scholar to write a work that summarized such extravagant ideas regarding the role of choice in human behavior as opposed to the influence of fate or destiny. Prior to his work, the common wisdom on the issue of human destiny in criminal behavior was that it was controlled by the gods or God. At that time, governments and society generally believed that certain persons were born either good or bad. Beccaria, as a child of the Enlightenment, defied this belief by proclaiming that persons freely choose their destinies and, thus, whether or not to engage in criminal behavior.

Specifically, Beccaria claimed that three characteristics of punishment make a significant difference in whether an individual will commit a criminal act—in other words, they deter crime. These vital deterrent characteristics of punishment include celerity (swiftness), certainty, and severity.

SWIFTNESS OF PUNISHMENT. The first of these characteristics is celerity, which we will refer to as swiftness of punishment. Beccaria claimed that swiftness of punishment was important for two reasons. The first dealt with Beccaria's claim, consistent with his reforms discussed previously in this chapter, that some defendants were spending many years awaiting trial. Often, this was a longer incarceration than their alleged offenses would have warranted, even if the maximum penalty were imposed. As Beccaria stated, "the more promptly and the more closely punishment follows upon the commission of a crime, the more just and useful will it be."[25] Thus, Beccaria's first reason for recommending swiftness of punishment was that reformation of punishment was severely lacking in the time when he wrote.

The second reason Beccaria emphasized swift sentencing was related to the deterrence aspect of punishment. At the time when Beccaria wrote, some accused individuals would spend years in detention awaiting trial. A swift trial and punishment were important because, as Beccaria stated, "privation of liberty, being itself a punishment, should not precede the sentence."[26] Not only was this unjust in the sense that some of these defendants would not have been incarcerated for as long even if they received the maximum sentence for the charges against them; it also was detrimental in terms of deterrence, because the individual did not link the sanction with the violation. Specifically, Beccaria believed that persons build an association between the pains of punishment and their criminal acts. As Beccaria stated,

> Promptness of punishments is more useful because when the length of time that passes between the punishment and the misdeed is less, so much the stronger and more lasting in the human mind is the association of these two ideas, crime and punishment . . . one as the cause, the other as the necessary inevitable effect.[27]

A parallel can be drawn with training animals or teaching children: You have to catch them in or soon after the act, or the punishment given does not matter because the offender does not know why he or she is being punished. Ultimately, Beccaria claimed that, for both reform and deterrent reasons, punishment should occur immediately after the act. Regarding the reform aspect, the defendant may spend a longer time in detention than the crime merits, and more important, the deterrent effect may be lost because the person will not relate the punishment with the negative act if punishment comes much later. Despite the commonsense aspects of swift punishment, this has not been examined by modern empirical research and is therefore the most neglected of the three elements of punishment Beccaria emphasized.

LEARNING CHECK 3.2

1. Beccaria's seminal work, published in 1764, regarding criminal justice reforms was titled (translated from Italian)

   a. *The Criminal Man.*

   b. *A General Theory of Crime.*

   c. *On Crimes and Punishments.*

   d. *Criminals in the Making.*

2. According to the text, Beccaria proposed the use of the following in his book to make the criminal justice system more effective.

   a. Jury trials

   b. Secret/anonymous accusations

   c. Public trials

   d. All of the above

3. According to the text, Beccaria believed that the death penalty/capital punishment could be used as an effective deterrent if done correctly. True or false?

4. According to the text, Beccaria claimed that punishments should be based on which of the following?

   a. Actus reus

   b. Mens rea

Answers located at www.edge.sagepub.com/schram2e

CERTAINTY OF PUNISHMENT. The second characteristic Beccaria felt was vital to the effectiveness of deterrence was certainty of punishment. Beccaria considered this the most important quality of punishment, which is evident in his statement, "Even the least of evils, when they are certain, always terrify men's minds."[28] It is obvious from this statement that Beccaria felt that certainty was the most important aspect of punishment—specifically, more important than severity and more important than swiftness/celerity by implication. He makes this clear when he says, "The certainty of punishment, even if it be moderate, will always make a stronger impression than the fear of another which is more terrible but combined with the hope of impunity."[29] As will be shown by scientific studies discussed later in this chapter, Beccaria was accurate in his assumption that perceived certainty or risk of punishment is the most important aspect of punishment.

It is interesting to note that the aspect of punishment Beccaria believed, and recent studies have shown (see below), to be most important in deterring crime—namely, certainty—is also the least likely to be enhanced in modern criminal justice policy. For example, over the past few decades, the rate of criminals being caught and/or arrested has not increased. Specifically, over the past few decades, law enforcement officials have been able to clear only about 21% of known felonies. Such clearance rates are based on the rate at which known suspects are apprehended for crimes reported to police. As shown in Figure 3.4, law enforcement officials are no better at solving serious crimes known to police than they were in past decades, despite increased knowledge and resources for solving such crimes.

swiftness of punishment: assumption that the faster punishment occurs after a crime is committed, the more an individual will be deterred in the future.

certainty of punishment: one of the key elements of deterrence; the assumption that when people commit a crime, they will perceive a high likelihood of being caught and punished.

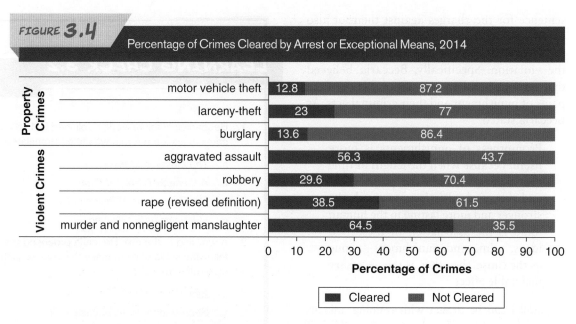

FIGURE 3.4

Percentage of Crimes Cleared by Arrest or Exceptional Means, 2014

Source: Federal Bureau of Investigation. (2015). *Crime in the United States 2014.* Washington, DC: Department of Justice.

SEVERITY OF PUNISHMENT. The third characteristic Beccaria emphasized was **severity of punishment.** Specifically, Beccaria claimed that in order for a punishment to be effective, the set penalty must outweigh the potential benefits (e.g., financial payoff) of the given crime. However, this came with a caveat: This aspect of punishment was perhaps the most complicated of the three, primarily because while the punishment must exceed any benefits expected from the crime, Beccaria thought too much severity would lead to more crime. Specifically, Beccaria stated,

> For a punishment to attain its end, the evil which it inflicts has only to exceed the advantage derivable from the crime; in this excess of evil one should include the . . . loss of the good which the crime might have produced. All beyond this is superfluous and for that reason tyrannical.[30]

Beccaria makes clear in this statement that punishments should equal or outweigh any benefits of a crime if they are to deter individuals from considering engaging in such acts; however, he also explicitly states that any punishments that exceed the reasonable punishment for a given crime not only are inhumane but also may lead to further criminality.

A modern example of how punishments can be taken to an extreme, thereby causing more crime rather than deterring it, is shown by current "three-strikes-you're-out" laws. Such laws have become common in many states, such as California. In such jurisdictions, individuals can be sentenced to life imprisonment for committing a crime, even a non-violent crime, that fits the state statutes' definition of a "serious felony" if it is their third offense. Such laws have been known to drive some relatively minor property offenders to wound or even kill people to avoid apprehension, knowing that they face life imprisonment if caught. The effectiveness of such "three-strikes" laws in reducing crime will be examined in a later chapter, but it is worthwhile to note here that a recent review of the impact of such laws across the nation shows them to be minimally effective; specifically, the authors analyzed the impact of three-strikes laws in virtually all large cities (188) in the 25 states with such laws and concluded that there was no significant reduction in crime rates due to the laws. Furthermore, the areas with three-strikes laws typically had higher homicide rates.[31]

severity of punishment: the assumption that a given punishment must be serious enough to outweigh any potential benefits gained from a crime.

Ultimately, Beccaria's philosophy on the three characteristics—swiftness, certainty, and severity—that make up a good punishment in terms of deterrence is still highly respected and adhered to in most Western criminal justice systems. Despite its contemporary flaws and caveats, perhaps no other traditional framework is followed as closely as Beccaria's— with only one exception, as we shall see in the coming sections.

Beccaria's Conceptualization of Specific and General Deterrence

Beyond the three characteristics of punishment Beccaria emphasized for improving the deterrent effect of punishment, he also developed the concepts of two identifiable forms of deterrence: specific deterrence and general deterrence. Although these two forms of deterrence tend to overlap in most sentences assigned by judges, they can be distinguished in terms of the intended target of the punishment. Sometimes the emphasis is clearly on one or the other, as Beccaria noted in his work.

Although Beccaria did not coin the terms *specific deterrence* and *general deterrence*, he makes the case that they are both important. Specifically, regarding punishment, Beccaria stated, "The purpose can only be to prevent the criminal from inflicting new injuries on its citizens and to deter others from similar acts."[32] The first portion of this statement, involving punishment preventing "the criminal" from reoffending, focuses on the defendant and only the defendant, regardless of any possible offending by others. Punishments that focus on the individual are considered *specific deterrence* (also referred to as special or individual deterrence). This concept is appropriately labeled because the emphasis is on the specific individual who offended. On the other hand, the latter portion of Beccaria's quote above emphasizes the deterrence of "others," regardless of whether the individual criminal is deterred. Punishments that focus primarily on potential criminals, and not on the criminal in the present case, are referred to as *general deterrence*.

Readers are probably wondering how a punishment would not be inherently both a specific and a general deterrent. After all, in today's society, virtually all criminal punishments for individuals (i.e., specific deterrence) are decided in court, a public venue; thus, other people are made somewhat aware of the sanctions (i.e., general deterrence). However, at the time in which Beccaria wrote in the 18th century, much if not most sentencing was done behind closed doors and was unknown to the public, thereby having no power to deter potential offenders. Therefore, Beccaria saw much utility in letting the public know what punishments were handed out for given crimes. This fulfilled not only the goal of general deterrence, which was essentially scaring others away from committing criminal acts, but also his previously discussed reforms of assuring the public that fair and balanced justice was being administered.

Despite the obvious overlap, there are some identifiable distinctions between specific and general deterrence in modern sentencing strategy. For example, some judges have chosen to hand down punishments that obligate defendants, as a condition of their probation/parole, to walk along the town's main streets wearing a sign that says something such as "Convicted Child Molester" or "Convicted Shoplifter." Other cities have implemented policies whereby pictures and identifying information of individuals arrested for prostitution or for soliciting prostitutes are printed in the paper or even displayed on billboards.

These punishment strategies are likely not much of a specific deterrent. After all, these individuals have now been labeled, so they may be psychologically encouraged to do what the public expects them to do (for more discussion and studies, see Chapter 11). So the specific deterrent effect may not be particularly strong in such cases. However, there is likely a strong general deterrent effect, which is what authorities are counting on in most of these cases. Specifically, they are expecting that many of the people who see these

specific deterrence: punishments given to an individual meant to prevent or deter that particular individual from committing crime in the future.

general deterrence: punishments given to an individual meant to prevent or deter other potential offenders from engaging in such criminal activity in the future.

Public arrest is a formal sanction due to the embarrassment and trauma of going through the booking process, even if charges are later dismissed. Arrest is a form of both specific deterrence and general deterrence.

REUTERS/Dominick Reuter

sign-laden individuals walking through the streets or publicly displayed in pictures are going to be frightened away from criminal activity.

On the other hand, numerous diversion programs, particularly for juvenile, first-time, and minor offenders, seek to punish offenders without engaging them in public hearings or trials. The goal of such programs is to hold the individuals accountable and have them fulfill certain obligations without dragging them through the often-public government system. The goal in such cases is specific deterrence, without using the person as a "poster child" for the public, which thus negates any possibility of general deterrence.

So while most judges likely invoke both specific *and* general deterrence in many of the criminal sentences they hand down, in notable cases either specific or general deterrence is emphasized, sometimes exclusively. Ultimately, Beccaria seemed to emphasize general deterrence and overall crime prevention, suggested by this statement: "It is better to prevent crimes than to punish them. This is the ultimate end of every good legislation."[33] In other words, he claimed that it is better to deter potential offenders before they offend rather than imposing sanctions after the fact. Beccaria's emphasis on prevention (rather than reaction) and general deterrence is also evident in his claim that education is likely the best way to reduce crime, as discussed previously in this chapter. After all, the more educated an individual is regarding the law and potential punishments as well as public cases in which offenders have been punished, the less likely he or she will be to engage in criminal activity. As mentioned previously, Beccaria did not coin the terms *specific deterrence* and *general deterrence*; however, his explicit identification of the differential emphases in terms of punishment was a key element in his work and is still considered important today.

Summary of Beccaria's Ideas and Influence on Policy

Ultimately, Beccaria summarized his ideas on reforms and deterrence with this statement:

> In order for punishment not to be, in every instance, an act of violence of one or of many against a private citizen, it must be essentially public, prompt, necessary, the least possible in the given circumstances, proportionate to the crimes, dictated by the laws.[34]

Beccaria is saying here that the processing and punishment administered by justice systems must be known to the public that delegates to the state the authority to make such decisions. Furthermore, he claims that the punishment must be appropriately swift, certain (i.e., necessary), and severe, in keeping with his concept of deterrence. Finally, he reiterates the need to standardize the punishments for given criminal acts as opposed to allowing arbitrary punishments imposed by a judge. These are just some of the many ideas Beccaria proposed, but he apparently saw them as being most important.

Although we, as U.S. citizens, take for granted the rights proposed by Beccaria and reviewed above, they were quite unique in the 18th century. In fact, the ideas Beccaria proposed were so revolutionary then that he published his book anonymously. He was worried that the church would accuse him of blasphemy and the government would persecute him for his views.

Regarding the first worry, Beccaria was right; the Roman Catholic Church excommunicated him when the book's authorship became known. In fact, his book remained on the list of condemned works until relatively recently (the 1960s). On the other hand, the government officials of the time embraced his work. Not only did the Italian government endorse Beccaria's book; most European and other world officials, particularly dictators, embraced it as well. Specifically, Beccaria was invited to visit many countries' capitals, even those of the most authoritarian states at that time, to help reform their criminal justice systems. For example, Beccaria was invited to meet with Catherine the Great, empress of Russia during the late 1700s, to help revise and improve that country's justice system. Most historical records suggest that Beccaria was not an ideal diplomat or representative of his ideas, largely because he was not physically or socially equipped for such endeavors. However, his ideas were strong and stood on their own merit.

It is likely that the reason dictators and authoritarian governments liked his reformatory framework so much was that it explicitly named treason as the most serious crime. Beccaria stated,

> The first class of crime, which are the gravest because most injurious, are those known as crimes of lese majeste [high treason]. . . . Every crime . . . injures society, but it is not every crime that aims at its immediate destruction.[35]

After all, treason was the criminal offense that most directly violated the government. To clarify, according to Enlightenment philosophy, not only are violations of law criminal acts against the direct victims, but such behaviors directly attack society as a whole by breaking the social contract. As Beccaria stated, the most heinous criminal acts are those that directly violate the social contract—treason and espionage. Therefore, it is not surprising that treason and similar offenses were considered the most serious crimes.

This is likely the reason why dictators of the time invited him to visit and presented him to the citizens as a "reformer" of their systems. These dictators likely saw a chance to pacify the revolutionary citizens, who the dictators could sense were about to overthrow their governments. In many of these cases, it was only a temporary solution. After all, the American Revolution occurred in the 1770s, the French Revolution in the 1780s, and other revolutions soon after this period.

We will see in later sections that governments that tried to apply Beccaria's ideas to the letter experienced problems, but most European (and American) societies that incorporated his ideas were more fair and democratic in their justice systems than those societies implementing any framework in existence prior to Beccaria. This is why he is, to this day, considered the Father of Criminal Justice.

LEARNING CHECK 3.3

1. According to the text, which element of deterrence did Beccaria believe was the most important in ensuring that individuals were deterred from committing crime?

    a. Swiftness of punishment

    b. Certainty of being caught

    c. Severity of punishment/sentences

    d. All were equally important

2. According to the text, Beccaria claimed which crime was the absolute worst offense?

    a. Murder

    b. Rape

    c. Robbery

    d. Treason

3. According to the text, Beccaria's book was well received by dictators around the world, even in those countries with more draconian criminal justice systems. True or false?

Answers located at www.edge.sagepub.com/schram2e

IMPACT OF BECCARIA'S WORK ON OTHER THEORISTS

As discussed above, Beccaria's work had an immediate impact on the political and philosophical state of affairs in the late 18th century. In addition to being invited to help reform other countries' justice systems, his propositions and theoretical model of deterrence were incorporated into many countries' newly formed constitutions, most written after major revolutions. The most notable of these was the U.S. Constitution and Bill of Rights.

It is apparent that the many documents constructed before and during the time of the American Revolution in the late 1700s were heavily influenced by Beccaria and other Enlightenment philosophers. Specifically, the concept that our government is "of the people, by the people, and for the people" makes it clear that the Enlightenment idea of democracy and having a voice in the government is of utmost importance in the United States. Another clear example is the emphasis on due process and individual rights in the U.S. Bill of Rights. Specifically, the important concepts of right to trial by jury, right to confront and cross-examine witnesses, right to a speedy trial, requirement that the public be informed of all decisions regarding their justice system (charges, pleas, trials, verdicts, sentences, etc.), and many other rights contained in our Constitution are all products of Beccaria's work.

Beyond the incredible influence the Enlightenment and Beccaria had on individual rights in the United States via the Constitution and Bill of Rights, the impact of Beccaria's propositions on the working ideology of our justice system cannot be overstated. Specifically, the public nature of our justice system comes from Beccaria, as does the emphasis on deterrence. After all, our criminal justice system (as well as those of virtually all Western countries) uses the method of increasing the certainty and severity of punishment to reduce crime. This system of deterrence remains the dominant model in criminal justice, in which the goal is to deter potential and previous offenders from committing crime by enforcing punishment that will make them reconsider the next time they think about engaging in such activity. This model assumes a rational thinking human being, as described by Enlightenment philosophy, who can learn from past experiences or from seeing others punished for offenses that he or she is rationally thinking about committing. Thus, Beccaria's work has had a profound impact on the philosophy and workings of the justice systems in most countries throughout the world.

Jeremy Bentham

Beyond his influence in the workings of justice systems, Beccaria also had a large impact on further theorizing about human decision-making related to criminal behavior. One of the more notable theorists inspired by Beccaria's ideas was Jeremy Bentham (1748–1832) of England, who has become a well-known Classical theorist in his own right, perhaps because he helped spread the Enlightenment/Beccarian philosophy to Britain. His influence in the development of Classical theorizing is debated, with a number of major texts not covering his writings at all.[36] Although he did not contribute a significant amount of theorizing beyond Beccaria's propositions regarding reform and deterrence, Bentham did further refine the ideas presented by previous theorists, and his legacy is well known.

One of Bentham's more important contributions was the concept of "hedonistic calculus," which was essentially the weighing of pleasure versus pain. This, of course, is strongly based on the Enlightenment/Beccarian concept of rational choice and utility. After all, if the expected pain outweighs the expected benefit of committing a given act, the rational individual is far less likely to do it. On the other hand, if the expected pleasure outweighs the expected pain, a rational person will likely engage in the act. Bentham listed a set of criteria that he thought would go into a rational individual's decision-making process. One analogy for this is a theoretical two-sided balance scale on which the pros and cons of crimes are weighed, with the individual then making a rational decision either to commit the crime or not.

Beyond the idea of hedonistic calculus, Bentham's contributions to the overall assumptions of Classical theorizing did not significantly revise the theoretical model. Perhaps the most important contribution he made to the Classical School was helping popularize the framework in Britain. Bentham became best known for his design of a prison structure, known as the "Panopticon," that was used in several countries, including the United States in early Pennsylvania penitentiaries. (This model used a type of wagon-wheel design, in which a post at the center allowed a 360-degree visual observation point for the various "spokes," or corridors, containing the inmate cells.) Thus, Beccaria remains the primary figure in the formation and articulation of the Classical School, and his conceptualization is the one that persisted for most of the late 18th and early 19th centuries.

THE NEOCLASSICAL SCHOOL OF CRIMINOLOGY

As discussed in prior sections, a number of governments, including the newly formed U.S. government, incorporated Beccaria's concepts and propositions in the development of their justice systems. However, the government that most strictly applied Beccaria's ideas—the French government after that country's revolution in the late 1780s—found that his concepts worked pretty well, with just one exception. Beccaria had claimed that every individual who committed a given act against the law should be punished in the same manner and to the same extent. Although equality in punishment sounds like a good philosophy, what the French quickly realized was that not everyone who commits a given act should be punished identically.

Specifically, the French system found that sentencing a first-time offender the same as a repeat offender did not make much sense, especially if the first-time offender was a juvenile. Furthermore, there were many cases in which malice did not appear to motivate the defendant's actions, such as when the defendant had limited mental capacity or committed a crime out of necessity. Perhaps most important, Beccaria's framework specifically dismisses the intent (i.e., mens rea) of criminal offenders and focuses only on the harm done to society by a given act (i.e., actus reus). French society—as well as most modern societies, including the United States—deviated from Beccaria's framework in considering the intent of offenders, often in a crucial way, such as in determining what types of charges should be filed against those accused of homicide (see the previous discussion on degrees of homicide in this chapter). Therefore, a new school of thought regarding the Classical/deterrence model developed, which became known as the Neoclassical School of criminology.

The only significant difference between the Neoclassical School and the Classical School is that the Neoclassical ("neo" means new) takes into account contextual circumstances of the individual or situation that allow for increases or decreases in the punishment. For example, would a society want to punish a 12-year-old, first-time shoplifter the same way as a 35-year-old, previous offender who shoplifted the same item? Additionally, does a society want to punish a mentally challenged, one-time car thief to the same extent as it would a normally functioning person who has been convicted of stealing more than a dozen cars? The answer to both is, probably not. At least that is what most modern criminal justice authorities, including those in the United States, have decided.

Public domain

Jeremy Bentham (1748–1832), one of the seminal theorists of the Classical and Neoclassical perspectives of criminology, insisted that his body be displayed at University College London. His preserved skeleton, with a wax head, sits there still.

Neoclassical School: assumes that aggravating and mitigating circumstances should be taken into account for purposes of sentencing and punishing an offender.

WHY DO THEY DO IT?

THE HARPE BROTHERS

The Harpe brothers, also known as the "Bloody Harpes," were likely the first notable serial killers in the United States and certainly the first sibling team of serial killers, if one marks our beginning as the colonial era. In the late 1700s, Micajah "Big" Harpe and Wiley "Little" Harpe were basically river pirates and highway robbers (in the traditional sense) who were active in various states in the Appalachian region of the southeastern United States, including Tennessee, Kentucky, North Carolina, Mississippi, and Illinois. Despite the financial gains from their various crimes, they seemed more motivated by the act of kidnapping, raping, and killing. They were known to butcher all their enemies and their enemies' families, including infants. In one notable incident, Micajah Harpe bashed his own daughter's head against a tree because of her constant crying. It is claimed that this was the only crime for which he actually showed remorse when he confessed.

The brothers also took part in the kidnap and rape of several teenage girls in North Carolina and pillaged (in every sense of the word) various farms. They later joined several different militias and Native American tribes, such as the renegade Creek and Chickamauga Cherokees (whom they had lived with at certain points), to attack frontier settlements and forts, such as Fort Nashborough (now Nashville, Tennessee). They were also known for kidnapping women and forcing them to become their wives. Given the time when they offended, little can be certain regarding the number of their victims or extent of their offenses, outside of the fact that historical records report they killed no fewer than 40 people and seemed to take great joy in doing so.

Regarding their demise, Micajah Harpe was killed by a revenge posse (after he killed a woman); he died after being shot and then attacked with a tomahawk. Legend has it that his head was hung on a pole at a crossroads known as Harpe's Head or Harpe's Head Road in Webster County, Kentucky. Wiley Harpe lived under an alias for a while to elude the local authorities but was captured, tried, and hanged in 1804.

So why did they do it? Aside from the psychological motivation to kidnap, rape, and kill so many people, the primary reason likely was because they could. This sounds crude and harsh, but there have always been evil people in the world. With no systematic formal justice system in the colonial period, especially in the frontier areas of Tennessee, Kentucky, and other pioneer regions in the 1700s, there was likely a sense of "do whatever you want." At that time, this was the Wild West of the colonies, and even if you violated local norms or rules, who was going to track you down and arrest you? After all, the first official law enforcement department did not form until the early 1800s in Texas (Texas Rangers, 1835), and the first municipal police force did not form until after that (Boston Police, 1838). Although some regions had a constable or similar officer who was supposed to enforce the rules or laws of that area, even such men were likely hesitant to go after two violent brothers who would likely attack anyone who came after them.

Without a certain formal policing authority, individuals can literally get away with murder. We have seen this happen in modern times when there is no stable law enforcement in place, such as in regions undergoing widespread chaos, whether it be Congo, Africa, or New Orleans, Louisiana, after Hurricane Katrina. The bottom line is that any time there is no formal, stable law enforcement authority in place, individuals can get away with any number of crimes without facing sanctions or accountability. This is perhaps why New Orleans recently ranked as the top city in the United States for violent crime; formal structures were thrown into complete chaos after the flooding and resulting disarray from Hurricane Katrina. So it is for this reason—the lack of any stable law enforcement or criminal justice system—that the Harpe brothers were able to get away with as much as they did, until they were finally apprehended by more informal authorities, such as the revenge posse made up of nonsworn individuals and local constables that had limited authority at that time. But by the time they were stopped, they had for years been brutalizing many victims without facing any accountability or formal sanctions for their crimes.

THINK ABOUT IT:

1. Can you think of a theory that would explain why the Harpe brothers committed their crimes?

2. Do you think if formal police authorities had been in that area at that time, the Harpe brothers would not have offended so much and for so long?

Sources: Musgrave, J. (1998, October 23). Frontier serial killers: The Harpes. American Weekend; Rothert, O. A. (1927). The Harpes, two outlaws in pioneer times. Filson Club Historical Quarterly, 1(4), 155–163.

Applying Theory to Crime: OTHER ASSAULTS (SIMPLE)

The FBI's Uniform Crime Report Program defines "other assaults," or "simple assaults," as "assaults and attempted assaults where no weapon was used or no serious or aggravated injury resulted to the victim. Stalking, intimidation, coercion, and hazing are included."[37] In 2014, there were a total of 1,093,258 simple assaults. From 2005 to 2014, the number of simple assaults by males decreased by 18.3%; for the same period, the number of simple assaults by females decreased by 3.7%.[38]

Based on 2014 National Crime Victimization Survey data, the Bureau of Justice Statistics reported that there were 3,318,923 victims of simple assault, which means 12.4 simple assaults per 1,000 persons age 12 or older. Comparing this rate with the rate of simple assaults for 2005 (i.e., 19.2) reveals a significant decrease (35.4%). Men and women reported similar rates of victimization (12.8 and 12.1, respectively); however, when examining the relationships between victims and offenders, some interesting differences appear.

For the male victims of simple assault, 39.2% were nonstranger, 52.2% were stranger, and the remaining were "relationship unknown." Within the 39.2% nonstranger simple assaults, 3.7% involved intimate partners (i.e., current or former spouses, boyfriends, or girlfriends), 8.6% involved another relative, and 26.9% were between friends or acquaintances. For the female victims of simple assault, 72.2% were nonstranger, 22.4% were stranger, and the remaining were "relationship unknown." Within the 72.2% nonstranger simple assaults, 18.5% involved intimate partners, 11.9% involved another relative, and 41.8% were between friends or acquaintances. When examining the rates of intimate

Police officers are a primary component of deterrence. Without the police, chaos might ensue, as seen during police strikes. However, studies show that concentrating officers in certain neighborhoods doesn't reduce crime in those areas.

partner violence by gender, 0.5 per 1,000 persons age 12 or older were male victims compared with 2.2 per 1,000 for female victims.[39]

It is essential to stress, however, that the scope and extent of domestic violence varies a great deal depending on the definition used to measure the incidence and prevalence of these assaults. Further, there is a general assumption that both official reports and self-reports understate the problem of domestic assault for a variety of reasons. For instance, a direct question pertaining to past victims or perpetrators of violence may not evoke a positive response. Some individuals may not remember or may not be willing to acknowledge or admit to illegal or inappropriate behavior.[40]

One area of study that has explored the application of deterrence theory is that of law enforcement responses to domestic violence. In the Minneapolis Domestic Violence Experiment, Sherman and Berk examined

the effects of police responses in deterring domestic assaults.[41] Officers were randomly assigned to respond in one of the following manners: (a) separate the parties and order one of them to leave, (b) inform the parties of various alternatives (e.g., mediating disputes), or (c) arrest the abuser. The results revealed that 10% of those arrested, 19% of those advised of alternatives, and 24% of those ordered to leave subsequently engaged in further violence. Thus, Sherman and Berk concluded that arresting perpetrators of domestic violence has the strongest deterrent effect. Some researchers, however, noted methodological shortcomings of the Minneapolis Domestic Violence Experiment. For instance, some officers involved in the experiment claimed to have prior knowledge of what type of action they were to take when responding to a domestic violence call. Thus, they would reclassify the offense in an effort to have it omitted from the study.[42]

(Continued)

(Continued)

The Minneapolis Domestic Violence Experiment had a tremendous policy impact:

> Within 1 year of the study's first publication, almost two thirds of major police departments had heard of the Minneapolis experiment, and three quarters of the departments correctly remembered its general conclusion that arrest was the preferable police response. Similarly, the number of police departments encouraging arrests for domestic violence tripled in 1 year from only 10% to 31%.[43]

It has also been suggested that the Minneapolis experiment was favorable among policy makers given the emerging support for deterrence theory. Due to the major policy impact of this experiment, the National Institute of Justice funded six experimental replications of the Minneapolis Domestic Violence Experiment; these have been collectively referred to as the "Replication Studies."[44] Essentially, these replications failed to confirm the earlier findings of the Minneapolis experiment. Buzawa and Buzawa contend that there may be a "middle ground." Specifically, deterrence may result for some offenders but not all offenders.[45]

To further highlight key aspects of deterrence theory, we apply this perspective to the crime of simple assault, specifically domestic violence. Doug and Emily have been living together for more than three years. They have a two-year-old son and are expecting their second child in a few months. Throughout their relationship, Doug has become increasingly violent toward Emily. At first, he would shout at and belittle her; soon after, he was pushing and shoving her. Now, Doug has started to hit, slap, and kick Emily. One evening, the violence became so overwhelming, Emily called the police. Following department policy, the officers arrested Doug for simple assault. Doug was convicted and sentenced to probation and mandatory counseling.

Doug's arrest incorporates the concepts associated with deterrence theory. For instance, the certainty of punishment is supported by the departmental policy to make an arrest in such instances of domestic violence. The concept of swiftness is also evident, with Doug being arrested soon after Emily called the police. One may ask, however, whether the punishment of probation and counseling was too severe or not severe enough. Also, one might consider whether such punishment will deter Doug from assaulting Emily again.

THINK ABOUT IT:

1. How do the rates of simple assault vary between males and females?

2. What did the Minneapolis Domestic Violence Experiment show regarding different ways to deal with cases of domestic violence?

3. What did the replication studies of domestic violence reveal about the original Minneapolis study on domestic violence?

This was also the conclusion of French society, and although French authorities for some time fully embraced the idea of equal punishment for a given act against society (i.e., equal harm done to society, as Beccaria advised), they quickly realized that the system was neither fair nor effective in terms of deterrence. So they came to acknowledge that circumstantial factors play an important part in how malicious or guilty a defendant is. A number of contextual factors either alleviate or increase the level of malicious intent involved in engaging in criminal activity.

Thus, the French revised their laws to take into account both mitigating and aggravating circumstances. This Neoclassical concept became the standard in all Western societies' justice systems. Fortunately, the United States also follows this model and considers such contextual factors in virtually all decision-making related to charges and sentences. For example, if a defendant is a juvenile, he or she is processed in a completely different system from the criminal court. Furthermore, first-time offenders are generally given the option of a diversion program or probation, as long as their offense is not serious.

The Neoclassical School is an important caveat to the previously important Classical School. Still, the Neoclassical School assumes virtually all the other concepts and propositions of the Classical School. For example, the Neoclassical School also endorses the idea of the social contract, due-process rights, and rational beings who are deterred by the certainty, swiftness, and severity of punishment. So, with the exception of aggravating and mitigating circumstances in sentencing and punishment, the Neoclassical School is identical to the Classical School. And this Neoclassical School is the model used by all Western societies in their justice systems. Thus, this framework had and continues to have an extremely important influence around the world.

LOSS OF DOMINANCE OF CLASSICAL/NEOCLASSICAL THEORY

For about 100 years after Beccaria wrote his book, the Classical/Neoclassical School was dominant in criminological theorizing. During this time, most governments, especially those in the Western world, shifted their justice frameworks toward the Neoclassical model. This has not changed, even in modern times. After all, virtually every society still uses the Neoclassical/Classical model as the framework for their systems of justice.

However, the Classical/Neoclassical framework lost dominance among academics and scientists in the 19th century, especially after Charles Darwin's publication of *The Origin of Species* in the 1860s, a book that introduced the concept of evolution and natural selection. This perspective shed new light on other influences of human behavior (e.g., genetics, psychological deficits) beyond that of free will and rational choice (covered in Chapters 5 and 6). Despite this shift in emphasis among academic and scientific circles, it remains true that the actual workings of the justice systems in most Western societies retained use of the Classical/Neoclassical model.

POLICY IMPLICATIONS

Even now, when authorities want to crack down on certain crimes such as drugs or gang activity, they focus on law enforcement and enhanced punishments to create more certainty and severity of being caught, respectively. So, although the Classical/Neoclassical perspective fell out of favor with researchers and academics over the past 150 years, it remains the primary model in terms of policy implications favored by most officials in the criminal justice system, legislators, and the general public. Many policies are based on deterrence theory: the premise that increasing punishment sanctions will deter crime. This is seen throughout the system of law enforcement, courts, and corrections.

This is interesting given the fact that Classical/deterrence theory has not been the dominant explanatory model among criminologists for decades. In fact, a recent poll of close to 400 criminologists in the nation ranked Classical theory as 22 out of 24 in terms of being the most valid explanation for serious and persistent offending.[47] Still, given the dominance of Classical/deterrence theory in most criminal justice policies, it is important to discuss the most common strategies.

For example, "three-strikes" laws have become prevalent in many states, as have police department gang units and injunctions (which condemn any observed loitering by or gathering of gang members in a specified region by listing members of established gangs). Furthermore, some states, such as California, have created gang enhancements in which juries decide whether the defendant is guilty of a given crime and also make a separate decision as to whether the person is a gang member. If a jury in California determines that the defendant is a gang member (usually with evidence provided by local police gang units), this automatically adds more time to any sentence assigned by the judge if the

Comparative Criminology: *HOMICIDE RATES*

Ranking Countries by Rate of Prison Population and Homicide Rates

This box continues the book's theme of comparing the United States with foreign nations in terms of various aspects of criminology and criminal justice (see Comparative Criminology 1.1 in Chapter 1, which provides an introduction to this feature). In this section, we will examine the findings and conclusions from the eighth United Nations Crime Survey,[46] specifically the portion dealing with rates of incarceration compared with rates of homicide in 89 countries. This comparison provides a recent analysis of the extent to which more severe sentences (as indicated by rate of incarceration) correlate with homicide rates in various countries. Readers should note that although most of the inmates in these countries were not convicted of

murder, it is assumed that the countries that incarcerate the most offenders are also the most likely to be punitive in terms of a serious offense such as murder—an assumption supported by empirical research.

According to the research findings from the eighth United Nations Crime Survey, the trend is that the higher the ranking of countries in terms of prison population, the higher the homicide rates (see Figure 3.5). As can be seen in the figure, a higher prison population in a given country is strongly and positively associated with the homicide rate in that country. The estimated correlation for this association was significant, and the estimated coefficient was strong to moderate ($r = 0.48$). To clarify, the rate of incarceration is positively correlated with the occurrence of murder in most of the reporting countries,

---

FIGURE 3.5

Ranking of Countries on Prison Population per 100,000 Population and on Homicide Rates per 100,000 Population

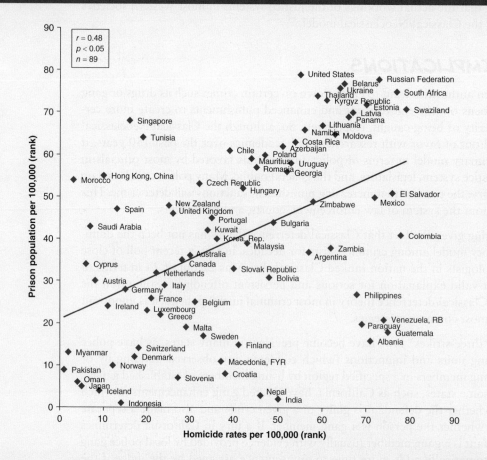

Sources: www.unodc.org; 8th UN Crime Survey; World Prison Population List (Seventh Edition), King's College, London, UK, 2007.

while the countries that reported the lowest incarceration rates are also the most likely to report the lowest murder rates. For example, the rate of incarceration is highest (of the 89 countries) in the United States, and the rate of homicide is also high. Regarding other countries, the Russian Federation, South Africa, Swaziland, Estonia, Latvia, Panama, Belarus, and Ukraine also have high rates of incarceration, as well as high rates of homicide (see Figure 3.5).

On the other hand, a number of countries have low rates of incarceration and low rates of murder. Such countries include Japan, Iceland, Indonesia, and Norway (see Figure 3.5). Again, countries that experience low levels of violence likely do not need to lock up such violent offenders; however, this analysis is done per capita, or by rate, so such comparisons are applicable. Of course, this observed association of countries that have the highest rates of murder tending to have the most punitive sanctions could be spurious, in the sense that sanctions in these countries are so punitive because they have higher rates

of violence. But the bottom line of this analysis is that despite more punitive sanctions in some countries (e.g., the United States, Russia), there appears to be no deterrent effect among individuals who commit murder. Perhaps this is due to the offenders not actually thinking about the sentences or penalties likely to result from the act of homicide, which will be explored more in the next section of this book.

THINK ABOUT IT:

1. When comparing various countries, how do incarceration rates correlate with homicide rates?

2. Which countries seem to incarcerate the most by rate? How do such nations tend to rank on homicide rates?

3. Which countries tend to have the lowest incarceration rates, and how do such countries rank on homicide rates?

Source: Van Dijk, J. (2008). *The world of crime*. Thousand Oaks, CA: SAGE.

individual is convicted of the crime. However, some states are starting to reconsider this hard-line approach to locking up offenders for life for nonviolent felonies, such as in the case of Shane Taylor in California, who was sentenced to life under the "three-strikes" law after being convicted of two burglaries (a property crime, according to the FBI definition) and then possession of 0.14 grams of methamphemine.[48]

Also, the still-common use of the death penalty and programs such as "scared straight" are based heavily on the deterrence framework of the Classical/Neoclassical perspective, despite much evidence showing that neither tends to be effective in deterring individuals from committing crimes and both may have even led to more recidivism by participants of such programs.[49] Furthermore, in terms of individuals' decision-making when it comes to crime, formal deterrence elements such as law enforcement or possible severe sanctions for a given act tend to have little impact. This is because such a model assumes people are rational and think carefully before engaging in criminal behavior, whereas most research findings suggest that people often engage in behaviors they know to be irrational or that offenders tend to engage in behaviors without rational decision-making, which criminologists often refer to as "bounded rationality." This means that individuals tend to be oblivious to many of the risks that may result from their behavior.[50] On the macro or group level, the same can be said for adding more officers to random street patrol in a given neighborhood or area, which shows negligible effects in crime reduction.[51] Rather, most deterrence effects and reductions of crime are more highly influenced by informal elements, such as families and communities having strong ties and "policing" their own neighborhoods, which we discuss in the next chapter.

These are just some examples of how the justice system in the United States, as well as most other Western systems, still relies primarily on deterrence of criminal activity through increased formal controls, such as law enforcement and enhanced sentencing, despite much evidence showing that these changes likely have little impact on individuals' decisions to engage in illegal behavior. The bottom line is that modern justice systems still base most of their ideology on the ability of individuals to be deterred by the certainty, severity, and swiftness of punishment—namely, the Classical/Neoclassical School of thought—despite the fact that this theoretical framework fell out of favor among scientists and philosophers in the mid- to late 1800s.

CONCLUSION

This chapter began with a discussion of the dominant perspectives throughout most of human civilization, which were supernatural- or religious-based theories. Once the Age of Enlightenment presented a more logical framework of individual decision-making and rationality in the 18th century, the Classical School of criminological thought became dominant, largely due to the propositions in Beccaria's *On Crimes and Punishments* (1764). Along with many proposed reforms, his perspective focused on the assumption that individuals have free will and make a rational choice to commit a given offense after first considering the risk of getting caught and punished, a proposition that established the deterrence theory of reducing offender behavior. Thus, the goal was to deter individuals from engaging in criminal activities by increasing their likelihood of being caught and/or punished via formal sanctions.

We also started this chapter with a case study of Deborah Jeane Palfrey, the "D.C. Madam," who committed suicide before she could be sentenced for her crimes. Although this is an extreme example, it shows the pressing influence of incarceration on the human psyche. Ms. Palfrey killed herself when facing a prison sentence, and given that she had been incarcerated before, this shows the negative effects of such a sentence. This is proof that there is a lot to be said for the deterrent effect of formal sanctions, which is the keystone of the Classical School. Thus, there is still a case to be made for the deterrent effects of formal sanctions, such as incarceration, among many potential offenders in our society.

The Classical School as originally proposed by Beccaria included some elements that virtually all countries had problems implementing, which led to the Neoclassical perspective that allowed for consideration of contextual aspects in sentencing decisions. This improved Neoclassical framework became the dominant model for close to a century, until the late 19th century, but is still commonly used as the basis for most criminal justice systems in the Western world, especially in the United States. We will see in the next chapter that the concepts and propositions of the Classical/Neoclassical framework were recently expanded to develop a more logically valid and empirically supported theory of offending behavior.

SUMMARY OF THEORIES IN CHAPTER 3

THEORY	CONCEPTS	PROPONENTS	KEY PROPOSITIONS
Supernatural/religious/ metaphysical theories	Full moon Lightning God/gods	Various pre-Classical groups Most common belief among societies prior to Enlightenment period	Belief that crime is caused by Satan (i.e., "the devil made them do it") or exceptional phenomena (e.g., full moon, thunderstorms)
Classical theory	Rationality Free will Social contract Deterrence theory Swiftness of punishment Certainty of punishment Severity of punishment	Cesare Beccaria Jeremy Bentham	Individuals have rational thought and decide to commit crime based on perceived risk of being caught/punished
Neoclassical perspective	Takes into account the contextual factors in a given crime in terms of punishment but assumes all other propositions of the Classical School (e.g., rationality, free will, deterrence)	No one key proponent, but this is the model all criminal justice systems in the Western world are based on (e.g., United States)	Same as Classical School but takes into account mitigating and aggravating factors when deciding the sentence for a given criminal activity

KEY TERMS

actus reus, 67

Age of Enlightenment, 59

brutalization effect, 69

certainty of punishment, 71

Classical School, 59

deterrence theory, 59

general deterrence, 73

mens rea, 67

Neoclassical School, 77

severity of punishment, 72

social contract, 65

specific deterrence, 73

swiftness of punishment, 70

utilitarianism, 66

DISCUSSION QUESTIONS

1. How do pre-Enlightenment perspectives of crime differ from those in the Age of Enlightenment?

2. What Enlightenment philosophy do you feel was most important for criminal policy?

3. Can you think of modern examples of violations of Enlightenment philosophy in criminal justice systems, or in society in general?

4. What concept/proposition of Beccaria's reforms do you find least practical? Most practical?

5. Which of the three elements of deterrence do you find to be most important? Least important?

6. Do you agree with Beccaria's assessment of the death penalty? What portions of his reasoning do you most agree or disagree with?

7. Can you define and explain the differences between general and specific deterrence? Give examples of each.

8. How did the Neoclassical school differ from the traditional Classical school? Do you believe it was an improvement? Why or why not?

9. What modern-day applications and policies do you think were inspired or influenced by Beccaria and Bentham?

WEB RESOURCES

For most of human civilization, theories of crime were based on supernatural or spiritual theories, such as "the devil made them do it."

http://www.salemweb.com/memorial/

The Age of Enlightenment established that individuals are rational and make decisions regarding their behavior, breaking from the belief that criminal behavior is caused by demons or other supernatural explanations.

http://history-world.org/age_of_enlightenment.htm

Hobbes was one of the first, and perhaps the most notable, Enlightenment theorists, in his focus on individuals being rational and having free will, thereby placing criminal behavior as a choice to be made and not up to fate.

http://www.philosophypages.com/hy/3x.htm

Beccaria was highly influenced by the Enlightenment and proposed the theory of deterrence and many reforms, which is why he is considered the Father of Deterrence as well as the Father of Criminal Justice and the Father of the Classical School of criminology.

http://www.constitution.org/cb/beccaria_bio.htm

Deterrence is one of the key propositions of the Classical School of criminology and assumes that individuals have free will and weigh out the benefits versus punishments of their behavior.

http://nij.gov/five-things/pages/deterrence.aspx

Bentham extended the ideas and concepts advanced by Beccaria and proposed a hedonistic calculus that further specified how individuals decide whether or not to commit crime based on a cost/benefit ratio.

http://www.utilitarianism.com/bentham.htm

http://www.ucl.ac.uk/Bentham-Project/who

The Neoclassical School of criminology added the consideration of aggravating and mitigating circumstances to sentencing of offenders, thus putting the context of the offense as a primary consideration, which the Classical School did not.

http://study.com/academy/lesson/neoclassical-criminology-school-theory.html

STUDENT STUDY SITE

$SAGE edge™

WANT A BETTER GRADE ON YOUR NEXT TEST?

Get the tools you need to sharpen your study skills:

SAGE edge offers a robust online environment featuring an impressive array of tools and resources for review, study, and further exploration, keeping both instructors and students on the cutting edge of teaching and learning. Learn more at **edge.sagepub.com/schram2e**.

FOR FURTHER EXPLORATION AND APPLICATION, VISIT THE STUDENT STUDY SITE:

- The `Shock of Confinement': The Grim Reality of Suicide in Jail

- Revisiting the Last Witch Trial

- Help Wanted: The Philippines Needs More Exorcists

- Deterrence or brutalization: What is the effect of executions?

- Boundary-crossing in perceptual deterrence: Investigating the linkages between sanction severity, sanction certainty, and offending

- Two hundred and fifty years since the publication of On Crimes and Punishments: The currency of Cesare Beccaria's thought

- Tracey Meares (1 of 6): Understanding Deterrence and Legitimacy in Law Enforcement

- Philosophy-Ethics: Utilitarianism, Part 1

- Crime and Punishment: Guilty as Charred Tony Robinson

- Death in Cell 49: How the Prison System Lost Track of Nelson Rodriguez

- Methods of Execution-Death Row: The Final 24 Hours

- Exorcism

- Stoning

- Torture

- Dismemberment

- Flagellation

PREMIUM VIDEO:

Check out the Interactive eBook for premium videos, including videos from author Stephen Tibbetts, who discusses real-world examples and strange crimes; and videos from former offenders, who share their stories from a first-person view, and touch on key theories and concepts from the chapter.

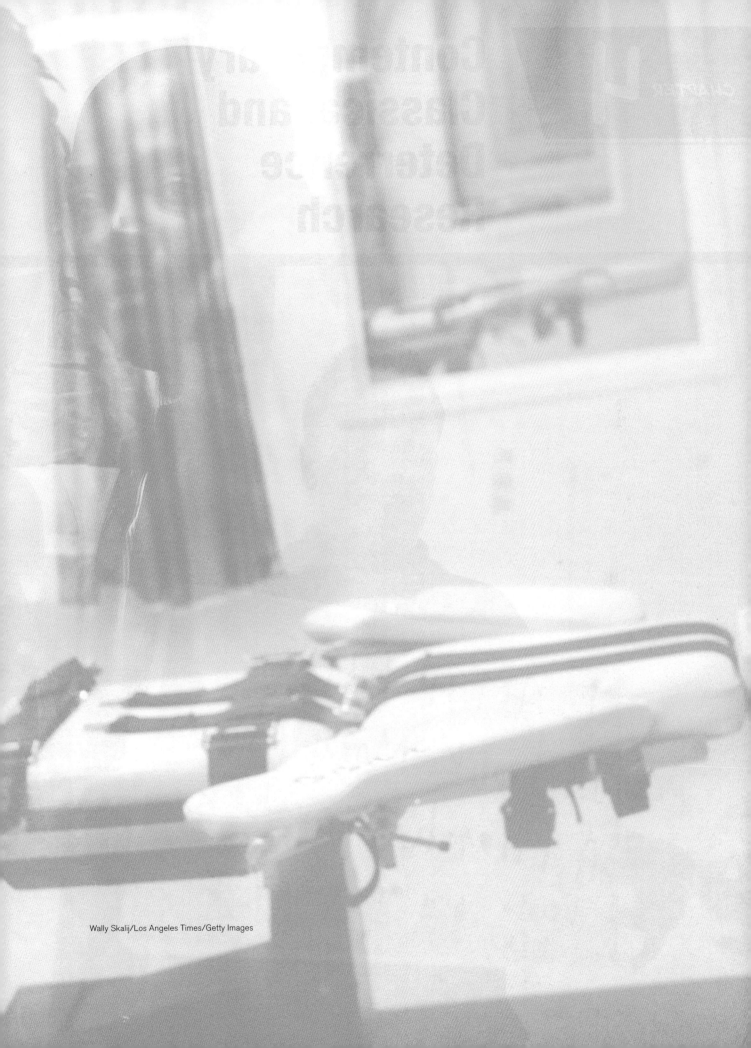

CHAPTER 4

Contemporary Classical and Deterrence Research

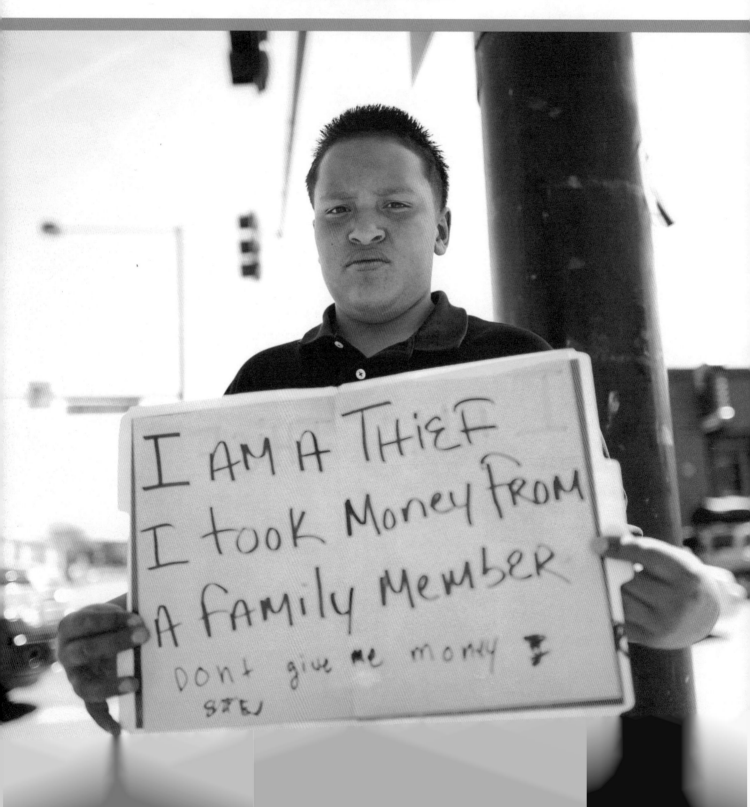

INTRODUCTION

On two separate days in August 2012, 13-year-old Brandon Mathison's mother forced him to wear a humiliating sign and walk along a busy intersection in Beaufort, South Carolina.[1] She made him do this because she had caught him smoking marijuana with his friends. The rather large placard he wore read, "Smoked pot, got caught! Don't I look cool? NOT!" on the front. On the back it read, "Learn from me, don't do drugs." This type of shaming strategy is an informal form of deterrence that stems from family, friends, and community as opposed to the formal sanctions of law enforcement, courts, and jail or prison. And for most individuals in society, the informal controls are what actually deter and reduce their likelihood of engaging in criminal activity, because they don't want to risk losing their friends and jobs and they care what their families and others think about them. The various theoretical models that emphasize such informal deterrent elements are examined in this chapter. But first, let's briefly review the previous chapter and see where we are headed in this one.

In the previous chapter, we examined the early history of theorizing about crime, which included pre–Classical School perspectives (e.g., religious, supernatural explanations) as well as early Classical School theorizing during and just after the Age of Enlightenment. Early theorizing by Cesare Beccaria and others during the late 18th century remained dominant in terms of academics and, more important, policy makers for close to 100 years. But the Classical framework as a model for understanding crime fell out of favor among academics and researchers in the late 19th century.

While the Classical model never stopped being the favorite of policy makers, virtually all dominant theories presented by scientists of the past century have been premised on assumptions and propositions that go against such Classical concepts as deterrence, free will/choice, and rational decision-making. However, Classical School concepts, assumptions, and propositions have experienced a "rebirth" in the past few decades. Furthermore, since the 1980s, several modern theoretical frameworks, such as rational choice, routine activities, and lifestyle perspectives, have given new life to the Classical perspective of criminological theorizing.

We will see that some of these more modern Classical School–based theories emphasize only the potential negative consequences of criminal actions, whereas other theories focus on the possible benefits. Still others concentrate on the opportunities and existing situations that predispose one to engage in criminal activity. Regardless of their differences, all the modern theoretical perspectives discussed in this chapter emphasize a common theme: Individuals commit crime because they identify certain situations and/or acts as beneficial due to the perceived low risk of punishment and perceived likelihood of profits, such as money or peer status. In other words, the potential offender weighs out the possible costs and pleasures of committing a given act and then behaves in a rational way based on this analysis of the situation.

© AP Photo/Joe Amon

LEARNING OBJECTIVES

As you read this chapter, consider the following topics:

- Explain the various types of research performed from the 1960s to the present to determine whether perceptions of sanctions had a significant impact on individual decisions to commit crimes.

- Name the components of rational choice theory that were not included or emphasized by traditional Classical/ deterrence theory in explaining criminal behavior.

- Compare and contrast formal and informal sanctions.

- List the three key elements of routine activities theory and be able to articulate which of the elements you think is most important.

- Describe which types of individuals are most likely to be deterred from committing most crimes, as well as which types of people are least likely to be deterred.

- Provide examples of modern-day applications and policies that most apply Beccaria's principles and the Classical school.

WAYNE

Wayne, raised in an upper-middle-class household in South Florida, was intelligent but also a risk taker, even at an early age. He was charismatic and made friends easily; even his teachers tended to like him, despite his sometimes deviant behavior. In high school, he engaged in many delinquent activities but nothing too serious. Although he had some encounters with police, it was usually for underage drinking or minor offenses, so he was never officially arrested. This is quite common, especially among teenage males.

This pattern took a more serious turn in college, when he was apprehended by police for a couple of incidents. However, these were also relatively minor, such as public intoxication, and even for these incidents, either charges were dismissed or he was never officially charged. But that is what it took to wake him up to the risks he was taking that could possibly jeopardize his future career. He wanted to be a lawyer, and he realized it would be difficult to get into law school, let alone be approved by the state bar association, if he had a criminal record. He was also potentially risking losing the respect of and strong bonds he had with family and friends.

So he realized around his junior year that he had to keep his nose clean and refocus his efforts on school, which he did. He eventually made the grades and test scores needed to gain entry into one of the top-tier law programs in the country, in Washington, DC—perhaps the best place to study law in our nation, given the opportunities and resources of that area. He did fantastically in law school and then moved back to Florida, where he became a respected and effective assistant district attorney. After a few years, he joined a private practice for a while, and within

about 10 years he started his own law firm, where he has continued to be successful.

We shall see in this chapter that most individuals in society grow out of teenage tendencies to engage in delinquent or criminal behavior, largely due not to the fear of going to jail but, rather, the fear of losing positive aspects of their lives that they have worked hard for, such as bonds with friends and family and, often most important, a great career.

We will follow up on Wayne at the conclusion of this chapter as a reminder to apply some of the theoretical models and concepts to explaining his change in behavior. These so-called informal elements of deterrence (e.g., family, friends, employers) are the ones that matter most for the vast majority of society—namely, the ones who have much to lose. And it is these types of considerations that the more traditional versions of Classical School/deterrence theory do not specify or take into account. Thus, the more modern versions of deterrence theory, such as rational choice theory, are far more robust and valid. But first, we will examine the rebirth of research in deterrence theory, which led to an evolution of theorizing and testing that resulted in the formation of these more fully specified explanations of criminal offending.

> THESE SO-CALLED INFORMAL ELEMENTS OF DETERRENCE (E.G., FAMILY, FRIENDS, EMPLOYERS) ARE THE ONES THAT MATTER MOST FOR THE VAST MAJORITY OF SOCIETY.

THINK ABOUT IT:

1. Why do you think Wayne did not have to serve a jail term and yet seemed to stop breaking the law?

2. Can you think of someone you know personally who committed minor delinquent/criminal acts when he or she was younger but eventually grew out of offending, as Wayne did?

The most important distinction of these Classical School theories, as opposed to those discussed in future chapters, is that they emphasize individual decision-making regardless of any extraneous influences on a person's free will, such as the economy or bonding with society. Although many outside factors may influence an individual's ability to rationally consider offending situations—and many of the theories in this chapter deal with such influences—the emphasis remains on the individual to consider all influences before making the decision to engage in or abstain from criminal behavior.

Given the focus on individual responsibility in modern times, it is not surprising that Classical School theories are still used as the basis for U.S. policies on punishment for criminal activity. Because they place responsibility on the individual, the modern Classical School theories discussed in this chapter are highly compatible and consistent with the conservative "get tough" movement that has existed since the mid-1970s. Thus, the Classical School still retains the highest influence in terms of policy and pragmatic punishment in the United States, as well as throughout all countries in the Western world. So the theories we examine in this chapter are the modern versions of the important assumptions, concepts, and propositions currently in use in virtually every system of justice in the Western world. Although most practitioners (even the judges who decide on sentences for a given illegal act) are likely not aware of these modern Classical theories of why individuals commit crimes (or do not), these modern perspectives represent the very types of concepts that all practitioners in our criminal justice system use to decide what is deserved or needed to reform an individual who has engaged in criminal activity.

REBIRTH OF DETERRENCE THEORY AND CONTEMPORARY RESEARCH

As discussed above, the Classical/Neoclassical framework fell out of favor among scientists and philosophers in the late 19th century, largely due to the introduction of Darwin's ideas on evolution and natural selection. However, virtually all Western criminal systems, particularly that of the United States, retained the Classical/Neoclassical framework for their models of justice. Despite the use of Beccaria's framework as the model for most justice systems, the ideology of his work was largely dismissed by academics and theorists after the presentation of Darwin's theory of evolution in the 1860s. Therefore, the Classical/Neoclassical model fell out of favor in terms of criminological theorizing for about 100 years. In the late 1960s and early 1970s, however, the Beccarian model of offending experienced a rebirth.

This rebirth was largely due to scientific reviews showing that the rehabilitation programs popular during the 1960s had virtually no impact in reducing recidivism among offenders, especially chronic offenders.[2] Specifically, Walter Bailey's review of 100 programs in the late 1960s revealed that very few showed beneficial outcomes in reducing offenders' recidivism. Even more attention was given to Robert Martinson's review of such rehabilitative programs, which concluded that "nothing works." Although this conclusion was a bit overstated, it was true that virtually none of the rehab programs significantly reduced offending among participants. Therefore, criminologists returned to their "roots" in focusing more on Classical/deterrence principles.

The Four Waves of Modern Deterrence Research

AGGREGATE STUDIES. In the late 1960s, several studies were published that used aggregate measures of crime and punishment and a deterrence model for explaining

A traditional electric chair. At one point in American history, electrocution was the primary method of execution, but it has since been largely replaced by lethal injection. Is the death penalty an effective deterrent?

aggregate studies: collections of studies, generally on a particular topic.

cross-sectional studies: a form of research design model in which a collection of data is taken at one point in time (often in survey format).

why individuals engage in criminal behavior.[3] These **aggregate studies** revealed a new interest in the deterrent aspects of criminal behavior and further supported the importance of certainty and severity of punishment in deterring individuals from committing crime, particularly homicide. Specifically, evidence showed that increased risk or certainty of punishment was associated with less crime for most serious offenses. Plus, most offenders who are arrested once never get arrested again, which lends some basic support for deterrence.

Many of these studies used statistical formulas to measure the degree of certainty and severity of punishment in given jurisdictions. Specifically, the measures of certainty of punishment often were determined by creating a ratio of the crimes reported to police compared with the number of arrests in a given jurisdiction. Another employed measure of certainty of punishment was the percentage of arrests that resulted in convictions, or findings of guilt, in criminal cases. Although other similar measures were employed, most of the studies showed the same result—namely, that an examination of both measures indicated that the higher the likelihood of arrest given reports of crime, or the higher the conviction rate after arrest, the lower the crime rate in a given jurisdiction. On the other hand, the scientific evidence regarding measures of severity, which such studies generally indicated by the length of the sentence for comparable crimes or a similar type of measure, did not show much impact on crime.

Additional aggregate studies examined the prevalence and influence of capital punishment and crime in given states.[4] The evidence largely showed that the states that had death penalty statutes also had higher murder rates than did non-death-penalty states. Furthermore, these studies showed that murderers in death penalty states who were not executed actually served less time than did murderers in non-death-penalty states. Thus, the evidence regarding increased sanctions, including capital punishment, was mixed. Still, a review by the National Academy of Sciences of the early deterrence studies concluded that there was more evidence for a deterrent effect than against it overall, although the Academy stated this in a tone that lacked confidence—perhaps cautious of what future studies would show.[5]

However, it was not long before critics noted that studies incorporating aggregate (i.e., macro-level) statistics are not adequate indicators or valid measures of the deterrence theory framework, largely because the model emphasizes the perceptions of individuals. After all, aggregate/group statistics are unreliable because different regions may have higher or lower crime rates than others, thereby creating bias in the level of ratios for certainty and/or severity of punishment. Further, the group measures produced by these studies provide virtually no information on the degree to which individuals in those regions perceive sanctions to be certain, severe, or swift. Therefore, the emphasis on the unit of analysis in deterrence research shifted from the aggregate level to a more individual level.

CROSS-SECTIONAL STUDIES. The following phase of deterrence research focused on individual perceptions of certainty and severity of sanctions, primarily drawn at one point in time—known as **cross-sectional studies**. A number of cross-sectional studies of individual perceptions of deterrence showed that perceptions of the risk or certainty of punishment were strongly associated with intentions to commit future crimes, but individual perceptions of severity of crimes were mixed. Furthermore, it was not clear whether perceptions were causing changes in behavior or whether behavior was causing changes in perception. This led to the next wave of research—longitudinal studies of individual perceptions and deterrence, which measured perceptions of risk and severity as well as behavior over time.[6]

LONGITUDINAL STUDIES. One of the primary concepts revealed by longitudinal research, which is studies that take certain measures over two or more time periods, was that behavior was influencing perceptions of the risk and severity of punishment more than perceptions were influencing behavior. This

Joe Raedle/Getty Images

Police conducting a field test with a suspected drunk driver. Driving under the influence is a popular topic in deterrence research because it tends to range across social status and racial/ethnic groups.

was referred to as the experiential effect, appropriately named because an individual's previous experience highly influences expectations regarding the chances of being caught and the resulting penalties. A common example is people who drive under the influence of alcohol (or other substances).

Studies show that when asked the chances of getting caught driving under the influence, most people who have never driven drunk predict an unrealistically high likelihood of arrest. However, if you ask persons who have been arrested for driving drunk—even those arrested several times for this offense—they typically predict that the chance of being caught is low. The reason for this is that chronic drunk drivers have typically been driving under the influence for many years, mostly without being caught. After all, it is estimated that drunk drivers traverse more than 1 million miles before one drunk driver is arrested.[7] If anything, this is likely a conservative estimate. Thus, people who drive drunk—some doing so every day—are not likely to be deterred even when arrested more than once, largely because they have been driving drunk for years by that time. In fact, H. L. Ross—perhaps the most notable expert on the deterrence of drunk drivers—and his colleagues concluded that drunk drivers who "perceive a severe punishment if caught, but a near-zero chance of being caught, are being rational in ignoring the threat."[8] Even the most respected scholars in this area admit that sanctions against drunk driving are nowhere certain enough, even if they are growing in severity.

A similar phenomenon is seen among white-collar criminals. Some researchers have used the measure of being caught by authorities for violating government rules—often enforced by the Securities and Exchange Commission (SEC)—as an indication that the organizations in violation will be less likely to commit future offenses.[9] However, organizations in violation of established practices that have been caught once by authorities have likely been committing these offenses for years, so they are more likely to continue doing so in the future than are organizations that have never violated the rules. Like the conclusion made regarding drunk driving, the certainty of punishment for white-collar violations is so low (and many would argue that the severity is also quite low) that it is rational for businesses and business professionals to take the risk.

It is interesting to note that of the many forms of criminal offending, white-collar crimes and drunk driving should be among the most likely to be deterred, due to their prevalence among citizens of the middle and upper socioeconomic classes. After all, if the extant research on deterrence has shown one thing, it is that individuals who have something

experiential effect: the extent to which previous experience affects individuals' perceptions of how severe criminal punishment will be when deciding whether or not to offend again.

to lose are the most likely to be deterred by sanctions. This makes sense because many unemployed, poor individuals will probably not be deterred by incarceration or other punishments, largely because they do not have much to lose. For some persons, particularly those of lower-class minority populations, incarceration does not present a significant departure from the deprived lives they already lead.

The fact that official sanctions are limited in deterring individuals—many of whom have a lot to lose—from drunk driving and white-collar crime is not a good indication of effectiveness for deterrence-based policies. This becomes even more questionable when other populations are considered, particularly the offenders in most predatory street crimes (e.g., robbery, burglary), who typically have nothing to lose because they come from poverty-stricken areas and are often unemployed. One recent study that examined the influence of sanctions showed that arrests had little effect on perceptions of certainty, whereas offending corresponded with decreases in such perceptions.[10]

Some individuals do not consider incarceration much of a step down in life, given the three meals a day, shelter, and relative stability entailed. This epitomizes one of the most notable paradoxes of the discipline: The individuals we most want to deter are the least likely to be deterred, primarily because they have nothing to fear. Even going back to early Enlightenment thought, Thomas Hobbes claimed that fear was the tool used to enforce the social contract; however, persons who don't fear punishment cannot be effectively deterred. Thus, it remains true that the individuals we most need to deter (chronic offenders) are the least likely to be deterred by the threatened punishments of our society, because they have so little to lose.

Along these same lines, studies have consistently shown that official deterrence is highly ineffective against criminal acts that involve immediate payoff, young male offenders, higher risk, low emotional/moral inhibitions, low self-control, and impulsivity.[11] Thus, many factors affect the extent to which official sanctions can deter crime. However, even among the most "deterrable" offenders, official sanctions exhibit failings, particularly when individuals in the highly deterrable categories have experience in the criminal behavior because they are rarely caught.

Identification and understanding of the experiential effect had a profound influence on evidence regarding the impact of deterrence. After all, any estimation of the influence of perceived certainty or severity of punishment must control for previous behaviors and experiences with such behavior to account for an experiential effect. Identification of the experiential effect was the primary contribution of the longitudinal studies of deterrence, but such studies faced even further criticism.

Longitudinal studies of deterrence provided a significant improvement over the preceding cross-sectional studies. However, such longitudinal studies typically involved designs in which measures of perception of certainty and severity of punishment were collected up to a year apart, including long stretches between the time of the criminal offense and when offenders were asked their perceptions of punishment. After all, psychological studies have clearly established that perceptions of the likelihood and severity of sanctions vary significantly from day to day, not to mention month to month and year to year.[12] Therefore, in the late 1980s and early 1990s, a new wave of deterrence research evolved that asked study participants to estimate their immediate intent to commit a criminal act in a given situation as well as requesting their immediate perceptions of certainty and severity of punishment in the same situation. This wave of research was known as scenario research, or vignettes.[13]

SCENARIO/VIGNETTE STUDIES. Scenario research was created to deal with the limitations of the previous methodological strategies for studying the effects of deterrence on criminal offending. Specifically, the critics of longitudinal research argued that

scenario research: studies that involve providing participants with specific hypothetical scenarios and then asking them what they would do in each situation.

vignettes: short, descriptive sketches.

individuals' perceptions of the certainty and severity of punishment changed drastically from one time to another, especially in different situations. The scenario method dealt with this criticism directly by providing a specific, realistic (albeit hypothetical) situation in which a person engages in a criminal act. The participant in the study was then asked to estimate the chances that he or she would engage in such an activity under the given circumstances as well as to respond to questions regarding his or her perceptions of the risk of getting caught (i.e., certainty of punishment) and the degree of severity of punishment expected.

© iStockphoto.com/enis izgi

Another important and valuable aspect of scenario research was that it promoted a contemporaneous (i.e., instantaneous) response regarding perceptions of the risk and severity of possible sanctions. In comparison, previous studies (e.g., aggregate, cross-sectional, longitudinal) had always relied on either group rates or individual measures of perception across long stretches of time. As discussed previously, individuals' perceptions regarding risk and/or severity of punishment vary significantly by time and situation, but the scenario method eliminates such criticisms. Some argue that the estimated likelihood of committing a crime given a hypothetical situation is not an accurate measure of what one would actually do. However, studies have shown an extremely high correlation between what one reports doing in a given scenario and what one would do in real life.[14] A recent review of criticisms of this method showed that one of the aspects where this research was lacking was in not allowing respondents to develop their own perceptions and costs associated with each offense.[15] Despite such criticisms, the scenario method appears to be the most accurate method we have to estimate the effects of individual perceptions on the likelihood of individuals engaging in a given criminal activity at a given time. This is something the previous waves of deterrence research—aggregate, cross-sectional, and longitudinal studies—could not estimate.

Formal and Informal Deterrence

Ultimately, the studies using the scenario method showed that participants were more affected by perceptions of certainty and less so—albeit sometimes significantly—by perceptions of severity. This finding supported previous methods of estimating the effects of formal/official deterrence (see Figure 4.1), meaning the deterrent effects of law enforcement, courts, and corrections (i.e., prisons and probation or parole). So the overall conclusion regarding the effects of official sanctions on individual decision-making remained unaltered. However, one of the more interesting aspects of scenario research is that it helped solidify the importance of extralegal variables in deterring criminal behavior, which had been neglected by previous methods.

These extralegal variables, called informal deterrence factors, include any factors beyond the formal sanctions of police, courts, and corrections—such as employment, family, friends, and community. These studies helped show that such informal sanctions are what provide most of the deterrent effect for individuals considering criminal acts. These findings coincided with the advent of a new model of deterrence, which became commonly known as rational choice theory.

The vast majority of findings on why people commit crimes are gained through self-report studies. Such studies explore factors (e.g., psychological, family life) that are not present in police reports or victimization studies.

formal/official deterrence: deterrent effects of law enforcement, courts, and corrections.

informal deterrence: factors like family, church, or friends that do not involve official aspects of criminal justice such as police, courts, and corrections (e.g., prisons).

rational choice theory: a modern, Classical School–based framework for explaining crime that includes the traditional formal deterrence aspects and other informal factors that studies show consistently and strongly influence behavior.

RATIONAL CHOICE THEORY

Rational choice theory is a perspective criminologists adapted from economists, who used it to explain a variety of individual decisions regarding different behaviors. This framework emphasizes all important factors that go into a person's decision to engage, or not engage, in a particular act. In terms of criminological research, the rational choice model emphasized official/formal forms of deterrence as well as the informal factors that influence individual decisions to engage in criminal behavior. This represented a profound advance in the understanding of human behavior. After all, as studies showed, most individuals are affected more by the influence of informal factors than by official/formal factors.

Although there were several previous attempts to apply the rational choice model to the understanding of criminal activity, the most significant work that brought rational choice theory into the mainstream of criminological research was Derek B. Cornish and Ronald V. Clarke's (1986) *The Reasoning Criminal: Rational Choice Perspectives on Offending*.[16] Furthermore, around the same time, Jack Katz (1988) published his work *Seductions of Crime*, which for the first time emphasized the benefits (mostly the inherent physiological pleasure) of committing crime.[17] Before Katz's publication, virtually no attention had been paid to the benefits of offending, let alone the "fun" people can have when engaging in criminal behavior. A recent study showed that the publication of Cornish and Clarke's book, as well as the timing of other publications such as Katz's, led to an influx of criminological studies based on the rational choice model in the late 1980s to mid-1990s.[18]

These studies on rational choice showed that while official/formal sanctions tend to have some effect on individuals' decisions to commit crime, they almost always are relatively unimportant compared with extra-legal/informal factors. Specifically, individual perceptions of how much shame or loss of self-esteem one would experience, even if no one else found out about the crime, was one of the most important variables in determining whether or not one would commit a crime.[19] Additional evidence indicated that females were more influenced by shame and moral beliefs when deciding to commit offenses than were males.[20] Recent studies have shown that levels of certain personality traits, especially low self-control and empathy, are likely the reason why males and females differ so much when it comes to engaging in criminal activity.[21] Finally, the influence of peers has a profound impact on individual perceptions of the pros and cons of offending—namely, by significantly decreasing the perceived risk of punishment when one sees friends getting away with crimes.[22]

LEARNING CHECK 4.1

1. According to the text, for which type of studies examining deterrence does the "experiential effect" pose the biggest threat of biased results?

   a. Longitudinal studies

   b. Aggregate studies

   c. Cross-sectional studies

2. According to the text, when looking at the results from the various waves of studies examining deterrence, which element of punishment has shown the most consistent deterrent effect?

   a. Perceived certainty of getting caught

   b. Perceived severity of the punishment/sentence

   c. Perceived swiftness of being punished

   d. They are all about equally important

3. According to the text, which type of studies by definition use data collected at one point in time?

   a. Longitudinal

   b. Aggregate

   c. Cross-sectional

Answers located at www.edge.sagepub.com/schram2e

FIGURE **4.1**

Formal Deterrence Versus Informal Deterrence

Formal Factors

Informal Factors

Law enforcement

Family and friends

Courts

Employment

Prisons and corrections

Community

Applying Theory to Crime: DRIVING UNDER THE INFLUENCE

The Uniform Crime Reporting (UCR) program separates criminal offenses into two categories: Part I and Part II crimes. Part I offenses include criminal homicide, forcible rape, robbery, aggravated assault, burglary, larceny-theft, motor vehicle theft, and arson. Part II offenses include fraud, vandalism, gambling, and driving under the influence (DUI). The UCR defines DUI as "driving or operating a motor vehicle or common carrier while mentally or physically impaired as the result of consuming an alcoholic beverage or using a drug or narcotic."[24] According to the Insurance Institute for Highway Safety, all 50 states and the District of Columbia have laws defining what constitutes "drunk driving." These laws designate a blood alcohol concentration (BAC) at or above a certain level; currently, this level is 0.08% (i.e., 0.08 grams of alcohol per 100 milliliters of blood).[25]

The FBI reported a total of 1,117,852 DUI arrests in the United States in 2014, with a national rate of 348.6 arrests per 100,000. When examining these rates by region, the West reported the highest rate (408.6), followed by the Midwest (373.3), the South (318.1), and the Northeast (285.4). Overall, there was a 21.8% decrease in DUI arrests from 2005 to 2014. Specifically, for those under 18 years of age, there was a 63.5% decrease; for those

18 years of age or older, there was a 26.4 decrease.[26]

The Centers for Disease Control and Prevention reported that every day, almost 28 people in the United States die due to motor vehicle accidents involving an alcohol-impaired driver. The annual cost of alcohol-related accidents totals more than $44 billion. At all BAC levels, young people are at a higher risk of being involved in an alcohol-related accident compared with older people. In 2014, three out of every 10 fatal crashes involved someone between 21 and 24 years of age (30%), followed by those between 25 and 34 (29%) and those between 35 and 44 (24%).[27]

One of the suggestions to prevent death and injury due to impaired driving is to reduce the legal BAC limit to 0.05%. "[The National Transportation Safety Board has] pushed for states to reduce the threshold for DWI/DUI to 0.05 BAC or lower because research clearly shows that most people are impaired by the time they reach 0.05."[28]

Another suggested prevention is to install ignition interlock devices in vehicles. This device is installed in the vehicle, usually in the glove compartment on the passenger's side. It is then wired to the engine's ignition system. In a vehicle with such a device installed, the driver has to blow about 1.5 liters of air into a

handheld alcohol sensor unit. If his or her BAC is over a preset limit, the car will not start. While these preset limits vary by state, they are usually between 0.02% and 0.04%.[29] All 50 states have some type of ignition interlock law. Twenty-three states have mandatory ignition interlock provisions for all offenses. California currently has a pilot program in four of its largest counties. While Colorado and Maine's laws are not mandatory for the first conviction, there are incentives to install the device on the first conviction.[30] For instance, in Florida, certain individuals convicted of DUI are required to install an ignition interlock device. The defendant has to contact specific vendors who install approved devices. If the court determines that the offender is unable to pay for the installation of the device, then a portion of the fine paid by the offender can be reallocated to the costs of the installation.[31]

THINK ABOUT IT:

1. Do you think these efforts, such as lowering the BAC or requiring offenders to install an ignition interlock program, deter individuals from driving while under the influence?

2. Do you think if these laws were removed "from the book," more people would drive while under the influence?

Another area of rational choice research dealt with the influence of an individual's behavior on other individuals. A recent review and test of perceived social disapproval showed that this was one of the most important variables in decisions to commit crime.[23] In addition to self-sanctions, such as feelings of shame and embarrassment, the perception of how loved ones and friends as well as employers would react is perhaps the most important factor in a person's decision to engage in criminal activity.

After all, these are the people we deal with every day, so it should not be too surprising that our perceptions of how they would react strongly affect how we choose to behave. And clearly this applies to the story at the very beginning of this chapter, namely, 13-year-old Brandon Mathison. His mother made him wear a humiliating sign and walk for two

Comparative Criminology: THREATS AND ASSAULTS

Ranking Countries by Rate of Beer Consumption and Rate of Threats/Assaults

In this section, we explore the association between rate of beer consumption and rate of violence—specifically, assaults and threats.

One of the modern versions of deterrence theory is rational choice theory. Rational choice theory assumes that individuals are rational and weigh the potential benefits against the potential costs of engaging in a criminal act. However, modern studies discussed in this chapter have shown that individuals often engage in activities, both legal and illegal, that are not rational. Many of these acts that appear quite irrational are committed by individuals who have been drinking alcohol. This

fits a concept known in the field as "bounded rationality," in the sense that individuals are sometimes not thinking clearly or at the level of the average person—a situation to which alcohol often contributes.

THINK ABOUT IT:

1. What is meant by "bounded rationality," and can you think of additional factors (other than alcohol) that may cause this?

2. Can you think of a true example of someone you know who appeared to have "bounded rationality" when he or she committed a delinquent/criminal act?

FIGURE **4.2**

Rates of Victimization by Threats/Assaults in 1996-2005 and Beer Consumption (Liters per Head) in Developed Countries (2004)

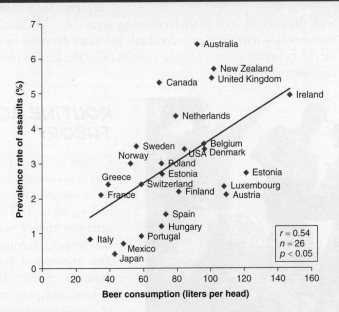

Sources: Van Dijk, J., van Kesteren, J., & Smit, P. (2007). *Criminal victimisation in international perspective: Key findings from the 2004–2005 ICVS and EU ICS*. Meppel, Netherlands: Boom Legal Publishers; The Hague, Netherlands: Ministry of Justice, Research and Documentation Center. World Advertising Research Center. (2004). *World drink trends*. Published in association with Commissie Gedistilleerd (Commission for Distilled Spirits). Henley-on-Thames, UK.

days along a busy intersection in his hometown because he smoked marijuana. This is also applicable to the case study we discussed earlier in the chapter, in which Wayne stopped offending due to informal considerations, such as jeopardizing his employment

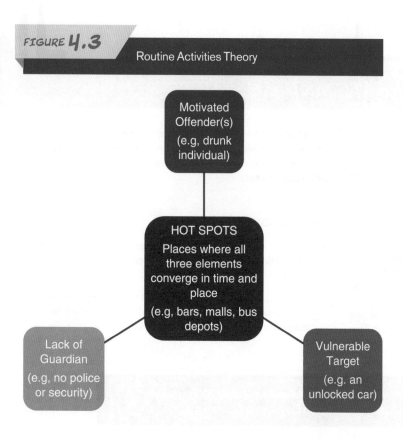

FIGURE **4.3**   Routine Activities Theory

Motivated Offender(s)
(e.g, drunk individual)

HOT SPOTS
Places where all three elements converge in time and place
(e.g, bars, malls, bus depots)

Lack of Guardian
(e.g, no police or security)

Vulnerable Target
(e.g. an unlocked car)

and the disapproval of family and friends if he continued offending.

Perhaps the most important finding of rational choice research was that the expected benefits, particularly the pleasure gained from offending, were one of the most significant influences in decisions to offend. Many other conclusions have been reached regarding the effect of extralegal/informal factors on criminal offending, but the ultimate conclusion is that these informal deterrent variables typically hold more influence in individual decision-making regarding deviant activity than do the official/formal deterrent factors emphasized by traditional Classical School models of behavior.

The rational choice model of criminal offending became the modern framework of deterrence. Even official authorities acknowledged the influence of extralegal/ informal factors, which is seen in modern efforts to incorporate the family, employment, and community in rehabilitation efforts. Such efforts are highly consistent with the current state of understanding regarding the Classical School/rational choice framework—namely, that individuals are more deterred by the impact of their actions on the informal aspects of their lives than by the formal punishments they may face in committing illegal acts.

Excessive alcohol consumption has been strongly linked to criminal offending, especially violent crimes.

©iStockphoto.com/Lifesizelmages

ROUTINE ACTIVITIES THEORY

Routine activities theory is another contemporary form of the Classical School framework in the sense that it assumes a rational, decision-making offender. The general model of routine activities theory was originally presented by Lawrence Cohen and Marcus Felson in 1979.[32] This theoretical framework emphasized the presence of three factors that come together in time and place to create a high likelihood of crime/victimization. These three factors are (1) motivated offender(s), (2) a suitable target, and (3) lack of guardianship (see Figure 4.3). Overall, the theory is appropriately named in the sense that it assumes that most crime occurs in the daily "routine" of people who happen to see tempting opportunities to commit crime and seize them. Studies tend to support this idea, as opposed to the idea that most offenders leave their homes knowing they are going to commit a crime; such offenders are called "hydraulic" and are relatively rare compared with the opportunistic type.

As seen in Figure 4.2, there is a strong correlation ($r = 0.54$) between beer consumption in a given country and the corresponding rates of threats and assaults. For example, New Zealand, the United Kingdom, and Ireland have relatively high rates of beer consumption and threats and assaults. On the other hand, Italy, Japan, France, and Portugal tend to have relatively low levels of both beer consumption and threats and assaults. Therefore, it is clear that certain countries display far more beer consumption than do other countries and that this likely contributes to higher rates of violence in those countries. So the bottom line of this analysis is that most of the countries that exhibit high levels of beer consumption, which is very likely to "bound" individuals' rational thinking before committing illegal acts, tend to show far higher rates of violence as measured by threat and assault rates. This adds to the empirical evidence supporting the limitations of rational choice/deterrence theory in the sense that individuals are not always rational, especially when they have consumed a good amount of beer.

The Three Elements of Routine Activities Theory

MOTIVATED OFFENDER(S). Regarding the first factor thought to increase the likelihood of criminal activity—a motivated offender—the theory of routine activities does not provide much insight. The model assumes that there are certain individuals who tend to be motivated and leaves it at that. Fortunately, we have many other theories, as discussed previously in this chapter and in the remainder of the book, that can fill this notable absence. The strength of routine activities theory is in its elaboration on the other two characteristics of a crime-prone environment: suitable targets and lack of guardianship.

SUITABLE TARGETS. Suitable targets can include a variety of situations—for example, a house in the suburbs left vacant over summer vacation. After all, data clearly show that burglaries more than double in the summer, when most families are on vacation (see Figure 4.4). Other suitable targets include anything from an unlocked car to a lone female carrying a lot of cash or credit cards and/or having purchased goods at a shopping mall, which is a common setting for victimization. Another likely location to be victimized is a bar or other place that serves alcohol, which has much to do with the fact that offenders have traditionally targeted drunk persons because they are less likely to be able to defend themselves—going back to rolling drunks for their wallets in the early part of the 20th century. This is only a short list of the many types of suitable targets available to motivated offenders in everyday life.

LACK OF GUARDIANSHIP. The third and final aspect of the routine activities model for increased likelihood of criminal activity is the lack of guardianship. Guardianship is often thought of as an on-duty police officer or security guard, which often is the case. However, there are many other forms of guardianship, such as a household dog, which studies demonstrate can be quite effective in home protection. Even a car or house alarm constitutes a form of guardianship. Furthermore, the presence of an adult, neighbor, or teacher can be quite effective in guarding an area against crime. Recent studies show that just increasing the lighting in an area can help prevent crime, with one study showing a 20% reduction in overall crime in areas randomly chosen to receive improved lighting compared with control areas that did not.[33] Regardless of the type of guardianship, the absence of adequate guardianship sets the stage for crime; on the other hand, each step taken toward protecting a place or person is likely to deter offenders from choosing that target over others. Locations that have a high convergence of motivated offenders, suitable targets, and lack of guardianship are typically referred to as "hot spots."

routine activities theory: explanation of crime that assumes crime and victimization are highest in places where three factors come together in time and place: motivated offenders, suitable or attractive targets, and absence of a guardian.

Applications of Routine Activities Theory

THE MINNEAPOLIS HOT SPOTS STUDY. Perhaps the most supportive study of routine activities theory and "hot spots" was that analyzing 911 calls for service in Minneapolis, Minnesota.[34] This study examined all serious calls (as well as total calls) to police in a one-year period. Of the top 10 locations police were called to, half were bars or other places where alcohol was served (see Table 4.1). As mentioned above, establishments that serve alcohol are often targeted by motivated offenders because of a high proportion of suitable targets. Furthermore, many bars have low levels of guardianship in relation to the number of people served. Many readers of this book can likely relate to this situation. After all, most college towns and cities have certain drinking establishments known for being "hot spots" for crime.

Still, the Minneapolis study showed that a lot of other types of establishments made the top 10 or ranked high on the list. These included bus depots, convenience stores, rundown motels and hotels, downtown malls and strip malls, fast-food restaurants, and towing companies. The common theme across these locations and the bars was the convergence of the three aspects described by routine activities theory as being predictive of criminal activity. Specifically, these are places that attract motivated offenders, largely because they feature a lot of vulnerable targets or lack sufficient levels of security or guardianship. The routine activities framework has been applied in many contexts and places, many of them international.[35]

CRIME MAPPING AND GEOGRAPHIC PROFILING. One of the many applications of routine activities theory is geographic profiling, which uses satellite positioning systems and is perhaps the most attractive and marketable aspect of criminological research in contemporary times. Essentially, such research applies global positioning systems (GPS) software to identify and plot the exact location of every crime in a given jurisdiction. Such information has been used to solve and/or predict various crimes; serial killers have been caught because victim locations were triangulated to reveal the most likely residence of the killer. Furthermore, such GPS software has also been used to predict where certain chronic offenders or crews/gangs will strike next. In police departments that use geographical mapping software to show where crimes take place or 911 calls for service originate (i.e., "hot spots"), this technology helps policing authorities determine where they should concentrate their efforts, such as where to assign more officers.

THE LIFESTYLES PERSPECTIVE. Another theory strongly related to routine activities theory is that of the lifestyles perspective. The lifestyles theory claims that individuals increase their probability of becoming victims (as well as offenders) according to the type of lifestyle they choose. However, some recent reviews of the literature have noted the strong, perhaps even redundant, relationship between lifestyles theory and the more established routine activities theory.[36] To clarify, such reviews have noted that "deviant lifestyles bear more risk of victimization than do conforming ones."[37] For example, elderly persons are far less likely to be victimized because they tend to stay indoors, especially at night. On the other hand, younger individuals (especially those in their teenage years and early 20s) are far more likely to be victimized, probably because they tend to go out late at night or hang out with other young persons, which significantly increases their probability of being victimized, since this is the age-group most likely to offend. Still, the bottom line in terms

© iStockphoto.com/Darren Mower

Routine activities theory focuses on the presence of suitable or vulnerable targets, such as a female walking alone in a secluded location.

FIGURE **4.4**

Violent Crime and Temperature

Violent crime in Columbus increases as the high temperature rises.

Average number of violent crimes in Columbus by a day's highest temperature:

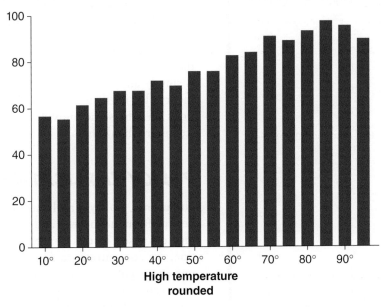

Source: Fox, J. A. (2010, July 6). Heat wave has a chilling effect on violent crime. *Boston.com*.

TABLE **4.1**

Top 10 Hot Spots in Minneapolis With 10 or More Predatory Crimes

RANK	DESCRIPTION	ROBBERIES, RAPES, AUTO THEFTS	ALL TYPES
1.	Intersection: bars, liquor, store, park	33	461
2.	Bus depot	28	343
3.	Intersection: homeless shelters, bars	27	549
4.	Downtown mall	27	445
5.	Intersection: adult bookstore, bars	27	431
6.	Bars	25	510
7.	Intersection: theater, mall, record store	25	458
8.	Hotel	23	240
9.	Convenience store	22	607
10.	Bar	21	219

Source: Sherman, L., Gartin, P., & Buerger, M. (1989). Hot spots of predatory crime: Routine activities and the criminology of place. *Criminology, 27,* 27–56.

of theorizing about lifestyles is that certain individuals tend to increase the likelihood of their own victimization by associating with the very individuals most likely to commit offenses (e.g., young males), hanging out in locales that tend to serve alcohol, or not taking adequate measures to protect themselves from being victimized. This is a perfect scenario for raising the risk of victimization according to routine activities theory, which shows how lifestyles theory is simply an extension of routine activities theory; by itself, it offers no new revelations for why some individuals are victimized more than others.[38]

LEARNING CHECK 4.2

1. According to the text, which theorists first proposed the rational choice theory of criminal behavior?

   a. Clarke and Cornish

   b. Gottfredson and Hirschi

   c. Sampson and Laub

   d. Cohen and Felson

   e. Sykes and Matza

2. According to the text, which theorists first proposed the routine activities theory of crime?

   a. Clarke and Cornish

   b. Gottfredson and Hirschi

   c. Sampson and Laub

   d. Cohen and Felson

   e. Sykes and Matza

3. According to the text, what is NOT one of the elements of routine activities theory that create a likely crime opportunity when they converge in time and place?

   a. Motivated offender

   b. Suitable/attractive target

   c. Time of day/night

   d. Absence of guardianship

Answers located at www.edge.sagepub.com/schram2e

POLICY IMPLICATIONS

Numerous policy implications can be derived from the theories and scientific findings discussed in this chapter. In this section, we concentrate on some of the most important policies. The "broken windows" perspective—which shares many assumptions with routine activities and rational choice theories—emphasizes the need for police to crack down on minor offenses to reduce major crimes.[39] Although many cities (such as New York and Los Angeles) have claimed reductions in serious crime after applying this theory, crime was reduced by the same amount across most cities during the same time period (from the late 1990s to the mid-2000s).

Other policies that can be derived from theories in this section include the "three-strikes-you're-out" policy, which assumes that offenders will make a rational choice not to commit future offenses if they could go to prison for life after committing three; in such a case, the negatives would certainly outweigh any expected benefits of the third crime. For deterrence to be most effective, punishment must be swift, certain, and severe. Where does the three-strikes policy fit into this equation? The bottom line is that it is much more severe than it is swift or certain. Given Beccaria's theory and philosophy (see Chapter 3), this policy will probably not work because it is not certain or swift; however, it is severe, in the sense that a person can be sentenced to life for committing three felony offenses over time.

A controversial three-strikes law was passed by voter initiative in California, and other states have adopted similar laws. This law sends third-time felons to prison for the rest of their lives regardless of the nature of that third felony. California first requires convictions for two "strikable" felonies—crimes such as murder, rape, aggravated assault, burglary, drug offenses, and so on. Then any third felony can trigger the life sentence. The cases of nonviolent offenders going to prison for life after stealing a piece of pizza or shoplifting DVDs, while rare, do occur.

The question we are concerned with here is, does the three-strikes policy work? As a specific deterrent, the answer is clearly yes; offenders who are imprisoned for life cannot commit more crimes on the street. In that regard, three strikes works well. Some people feel, however, that laws such as three strikes need to include a general deterrent effect to be considered successful, meaning that this law should deter everyone from engaging in multiple crimes. So is three strikes a general deterrent? Unfortunately, there are no easy answers to this question, because laws vary from state to state, the laws are used at different rates across counties in a given state, and so forth. There is at least some consensus in the literature, however.

©iStockphoto.com/sturti

Teens can increase the likelihood of being victimized by staying out late at night, hanging with the wrong crowd, or taking part in drinking or risky behavior.

One study from California suggests that three strikes reduced crime,[40] but the remaining studies show that three strikes either has no effect on crime or actually *increases* crime.[41] How could three strikes increase crime? The authors of those studies attributed an increase in homicide, following three strikes, to the possibility that third-strikers have more incentive to kill victims and any witnesses to avoid apprehension. Although this argument is tentative, it may be true.[42] This is just one of the many policy implications that can be derived from this section. We expect that readers of this book will come up with many more, but it is vital that they examine the empirical literature in determining policies' usefulness in reducing criminal activity. Other policy implications regarding the theories and findings discussed in this chapter are discussed in the final section of this book.

In another strategy strongly based on the rational choice model, a number of judges have started using shaming penalties to deter offenders from recidivating. They have ordered everything from posting pictures of men arrested for soliciting prostitutes to forcing offenders to walk down their towns' main streets wearing signs that announce their crimes. These are just two examples of an increasing trend that emphasizes the informal or community factors required to deter crime effectively. Unfortunately, to date there have been virtually no empirical evaluations of the effectiveness of such shaming penalties, although studies of expected shame for committing an act consistently show a deterrent effect.[43]

AP Photo/Damian Dovarganes

During a protest against California's "three strikes" law, Sequoia, Floyd, and Deonta Earl hold photos of their father, Floyd Earl, who is in jail for a term of 25 years to life. California voters and lawmakers approved the three-strikes law amid public furor over the 1993 kidnap and murder of 12-year-old Polly Klaas by Richard Allen Davis, a repeat offender on parole at the time of the kidnapping.

WHY DO THEY DO IT?

THE GREEN RIVER KILLER

Ridgway was caught after DNA from crime scenes was matched to a saliva test he had taken years before, when authorities had suspected him but didn't have enough evidence to make an arrest. So he continued his killing spree for many years, until they finally obtained further evidence linking him to some of the murders. Ridgway is now serving 480 years in prison for 48 life sentences, due to a bargain that got him out of the death penalty.

But why did he do it? Obviously, he has some psychological issues. But he passed the psychological test to determine readiness to stand trial, so he was not ruled legally insane. Virtually all his victims easily fit within his lifestyle, as he traveled around in his truck and picked up women in essentially the same area where he worked and lived. He never went far out of his way. In fact, none of his victims seemed to come from outside the Seattle area. And he would almost always dump or bury the bodies within a relatively limited radius in that region—hence his label, "the Green River Killer."

In one notable instance, he claimed that his son was with him in the truck when he picked up a woman. He had his son stay in the truck while he took the woman a distance away and killed her. But we know that he tended to pick up and kill these women as part of his daily routine, which included working at a truck-painting factory. Thus, this case applies to the routine activities theory and lifestyles perspective covered in this chapter. Also keep in mind that even at the time when he was apprehended for these murders, he had a relatively stable marriage, which is not atypical for serial killers. They often lead separate lives, and both lives can seem fairly routine despite extreme contradictions.

Gary Leon Ridgway was convicted and sentenced in 2003 after many decades of acting as the Green River Killer; he had stabbed his first victim at age 16, in 1965. He confessed to killing 71 victims (although he was convicted of only 48), virtually all of them women. He appeared to live separate lives. In one aspect of his life in the Seattle area, he was the father of a son and husband to his third wife. The other side involved picking up women, mostly prostitutes and strippers, who were willing to engage in sexual activity with him in remote locations.

He claimed that he would hide or bury the bodies of the victims he really "liked" because he knew he would want to go back and have sex with them later, which he did on occasion. He would also place various objects, such as a fish, bottle, or sausage, at the crime scene to throw off authorities, because these objects didn't match the modus operandi they were expecting to help link the crimes together. So he did appear to plan his crimes, at least in terms of manipulating the crime scenes (whether the primary scene, where the killing took place, or the secondary scene, where the body was dumped).

He also notably said, "I would choke them . . . and I was really good at it." But when asked by an investigator in an official interview where he ranked on a scale of evil from 1 to 5, he said he was a 3. So there appears to be a disconnect between the way he thinks and the way society at large thinks.

THINK ABOUT IT:

1. What was the Green River Killer's typical method of operation (MO), or how he carried out most of his killings?

2. How is the Green River Killer's case a good example of routine activities theory?

Sources: Jensen, J., & Case, J. (2011). *Green River Killer: A true detective story.* Milwaukie, OR: Dark Horse Books.

CONCLUSION

This chapter reviewed the rebirth of deterrence studies in criminological literature. This reemphasis on deterrence was largely a response to the failure of most rehabilitation programs to lower recidivism in criminals. Specifically, the empirical evidence from studies in the late 1960s and early 1970s regarding various rehabilitation programs showed that they were not effective in reducing recidivism, especially in chronic offenders. The first wave of research in this new focus on deterrence emphasized comparisons of jurisdictions (often various states in the United States) that tend to use more severe punishments than other jurisdictions. The subsequent waves of the rebirth of deterrence focused on longitudinal or panel studies that estimated how perceptions affect behavior, but this was quickly criticized by researchers who noted that the reverse is more likely: Behavior affects perceptions of being caught or punished. This led to the scenario methodology, in which individuals are asked their perceived likelihood of engaging in a specific situation at a given time, which is essentially where the current research on Classical/deterrence models remains.

We also examined more recent forms of Classical/deterrence theory, such as rational choice theory, which emphasizes the effects of informal sanctions (e.g., family, friends, employment) and the benefits of offending (e.g., the "fun" of offending). We also discussed routine activities theory, which explains why victimization tends to occur far more often in certain locations (i.e., "hot spots") due to the convergence of three key elements in time and place—motivated offender(s), vulnerable target(s), and lack of guardianship—which create an attractive opportunity for crime as individuals go about their everyday activities. Another theory closely related to routine activities theory is the lifestyles perspective. The common element across all these perspectives is the underlying assumption that individuals are rational beings who have free will and thus choose their behavior based on assessments of a given situation, such as the possible risks versus the potential payoff. The bottom line of these various modern theories is that the perceptions and decisions made by individuals often put them

at a much higher risk of engaging in criminal acts as well as becoming victims of such crimes.

To follow up on the case study of Wayne at the beginning of this chapter, you should be able to see how his story relates well to some of the theories and concepts presented in this chapter—most notably, rational choice theory. Just to remind you, Wayne had engaged in some delinquent/criminal acts in high school and college; it was nothing violent, but he had come close to being arrested in high school and was apprehended and held by police for a couple of incidents in college (all charges were dropped or dismissed). But he realized that he had a lot to lose, such as all the work he had put toward getting good grades and completing the pre-law curriculum. Furthermore, he realized that he wanted to maintain strong bonds with his family and friends, not to mention relationships with future employers, and they would likely lose some level of respect for him if he continued to be caught for various offenses. So he completely changed his life trajectory by focusing on his studies, career, and family life.

This is a hypothetical (and some may say prototypical) scenario of what the more modern versions of deterrence, such as rational choice theory, offer in terms of explanations for individuals' decision-making. But it is based on an actual case, according to the history of a good friend of one of the authors of this text. The point of this example is that each individual has the rationality and free will to examine the potential costs and benefits of his or her behavior and make decisions based on consideration of all major risks—both formal and informal sanctions—as well as perceived benefits. This goes well beyond the traditional Classical version of deterrence, which focused only on formal sanctions, and provides a far more robust and valid model for explaining criminal behavior—or in Wayne's case, the decision not to engage in such behavior. The assumptions of this type of theorizing will be contradicted in the following chapters, which discuss theories that assume there is virtually no rationality or free will, let alone calculated decision-making, involved in committing a crime.

SUMMARY OF THEORIES IN CHAPTER 4

THEORY	CONCEPTS	PROPONENTS	KEY PROPOSITIONS
Rational choice theory	Includes all traditional deterrence factors but adds • informal factors (e.g., family, friends, employers) • benefits of the crime (e.g., payoff and pleasure/thrill of offending)	Ronald V. Clarke and Derek B. Cornish	Assumes virtually all aspects of the traditional deterrence model but adds concepts that go into individuals' decisions to engage in criminal activity: The more a person believes his or her family, friends, and so forth will look down on the behavior, the more likely it is that he or she will be deterred. The more the expected pleasure or payoff of the crime, the less likely it is that a person will be deterred.

(Continued)

(Continued)

THEORY	CONCEPTS	PROPONENTS	KEY PROPOSITIONS
Routine activities theory	Likely opportunity for victimization, given three concepts: • Motivated offender • Attractive/suitable target • Absence of guardianship	Lawrence Cohen and Marcus Felson	Victimization/crime is much more likely to occur when three elements converge in time and place (see "Concepts"), typically as an individual is going about his or her daily activities, such as going to school or work or hanging out.
Lifestyles perspective	Risky lifestyles of offenders/victims	Various	Very similar propositions as routine activities theory but emphasizes the risky behavior (such as hanging out at seedy bars) of offenders as opposed to victims.

KEY TERMS

aggregate studies, 92

cross-sectional studies, 92

experiential effect, 93

formal/official deterrence, 95

informal deterrence, 95

rational choice theory, 95

routine activities theory, 100

scenario research, 94

vignettes, 94

DISCUSSION QUESTIONS

1. Do you think the deterrence model should have been rebirthed or left for dead? Explain why you feel this way.

2. Regarding the aggregate level of research in deterrence studies, do you find such studies valid? Explain why or why not.

3. In comparing longitudinal studies with vignette/scenario studies, which do you think offers the most valid method for examining individual perceptions regarding the costs and benefits of offending situations? Explain why you feel this way.

4. Can you relate to the experiential effect? If you can't, do you know someone who seems to engage in the behavior that results from this phenomenon? Make sure to articulate what the experiential effect is.

5. Regarding rational choice theory, would you rather be subject to formal sanctions if none of your family, friends, or employers found out that you engaged in shoplifting, or would you rather face the informal sanctions with no formal punishment (other than being arrested)? Explain your decision.

6. As a teenager, did you or family or friends get a "rush" out of doing things that were deviant or wrong? If so, did that feeling seem to outweigh any potential legal or informal consequences?

7. Regarding routine activities theory, which places, residences, or areas of your hometown do you feel fit this idea that certain places attract more crime than others (i.e., "hot spots")? Explain how you, friends, or others (including police) in your community deal with such areas. Does it work?

8. Regarding routine activities theory, which of the three elements of the theory do you feel is the most important to address in efforts to reduce crime in "hot spots"?

9. What types of lifestyle characteristics lead to the highest criminal/victimization rates? List at least five factors that lead to such propensities.

10. Find at least one study that uses mapping/geographical (GPS) data and report the conclusions of that study. Do the findings and conclusions fit the routine activities theoretical framework? Why or why not?

11. What types of policy strategies derived from rational choice and routine activities theories do you think would be most effective? Least effective?

WEB RESOURCES

The journal article at this site provides a good explanation of the key issues involved in modern longitudinal studies of deterrence, which were discussed in this chapter.

http://scholarlycommons.law.northwestern.edu/cgi/viewcontent.cgi?article=6586&context=jclc

This site is for the Death Penalty Information Center, which is one of the very best sources of facts and reports on the use and cost of capital punishment, as well as its limited effectiveness as a deterrent.

http://www.deathpenaltyinfo.org/reports

This site is a very thorough discussion by Robert Keel at the University of Missouri about the concepts and propositions that rational choice theory added to the traditional deterrence model.

http://www.umsl.edu/~keelr/200/ratchoc.html

The Center for Problem-Oriented Policing site has an excellent summary of routine activities theory and discusses its application to their approaches to policing and making high crime places safer.

http://www.popcenter.org/learning/pam/help/theory.cfm

This PowerPoint slideshow reviews routine activities theory and also discusses how some scholars have claimed that victims often raise the likelihood of their victimization because of their risky lifestyles.

http://www.slideshare.net/khadijahtgo/routine-activities-theory

STUDENT STUDY SITE

⑤SAGE edge™

WANT A BETTER GRADE ON YOUR NEXT TEST?

Get the tools you need to sharpen your study skills:

SAGE edge offers a robust online environment featuring an impressive array of tools and resources for review, study, and further exploration, keeping both instructors and students on the cutting edge of teaching and learning. Learn more at **edge.sagepub.com/schram2e**.

FOR FURTHER EXPLORATION AND APPLICATION, VISIT THE STUDENT STUDY SITE:

- Study Sheds Light on Criminal Activity During Time Change
- Training Helps Inmates Build a Bridge to Life Outside Prison Walls
- A reconceptualization of general and specific deterrence
- Decision making in the crime commission process: Comparing rapists, child molesters, and victim-cross-over sex offenders
- Lifestyle-routine activities and crime events
- Prison Rehabilitation
- Teen Who Stole Endures Public Punishment
- Jail Keeper Says California Three-Strikes Law Fails to Reduce Crime
- Dan Ariely: Crime and Irrationality
- Shaming
- The CDC on Drunk Driving
- Prison Sentencing
- Community Action
- Crime Mapping
- People V Brock Turner

PREMIUM VIDEO:

Check out the Interactive eBook for premium videos, including videos from author Stephen Tibbetts, who discusses real-world examples and strange crimes; and videos from former offenders, who share their stories from a first-person view, and touch on key theories and concepts from the chapter.

CHAPTER 5

Early Positivism

Biological Theories of Crime

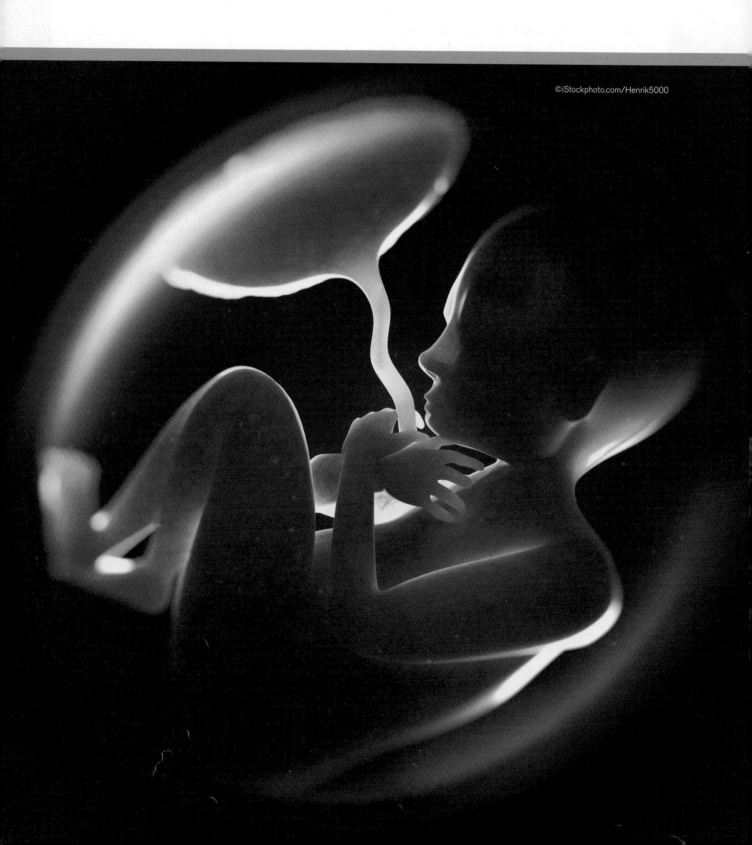

©iStockphoto.com/Henrik5000

INTRODUCTION

In the early 1940s, Charlie Follett was a teenage resident in California's Sonoma State Home, a placement facility for individuals deemed by the courts and other authorities to be undesirable, with the common "medical" terms being *feeble-minded* or *moron*.[1] This meant he scored relatively low on an IQ test. One day, facility workers told him to lie down on an operating table, and without telling him what was about to happen, they began his vasectomy. He was one of more than 20,000 Californians—most of them female—to be forcibly sterilized by the state from the early 1900s to 1963. Sometimes they never learned of the procedure, and sometimes they were lied to (for example, told that they had an appendectomy or some other medical procedure). This procedure was performed throughout the nation (Virginia had the second highest number of such sterilizations, at about 8,300), with the support of the U.S. Supreme Court via the 1927 decision in *Buck v. Bell*. Although California governor Gray Davis apologized much later, in 2003, no financial reparations had ever been offered to the victims of this misguided policy. This is one of the ways early theories of criminality were abused in terms of policy, but we discuss many others in this chapter.

This chapter examines the early formulations of scientific criminological testing and theorizing, referred to as the Positive School of criminology. The emphasis on science in criminology started in the mid-1800s and provided a basis for what continues today. First, we examine why criminological theories became the topic of scientists at that time, and then we examine the early explanations of criminal behavior as well as the many criticisms of such models, how such theories were tested, and especially the policy implications. We then discuss how Darwin's work inspired a giant change in how both academics and society viewed criminals.

We examine how the Father of Criminology developed his theory as well as how IQ testing impacted the field and policies, as noted in the story above. We will also explore how these two models merged to form body type theory. Then we will discuss how such theories inspired future models of criminality, with an emphasis on how such traditional frameworks have contributed to modern-day applications and explanatory frameworks.

EARLY BIOLOGICAL THEORIES OF BEHAVIOR

After many decades of dominance by the Classical School (see Chapter 3), academics and scientists were becoming aware that the deterrence framework was not explaining the distribution of crime. This restlessness led to new explanatory models of crime and behavior. Most of these perspectives focused on the fact that certain individuals or groups tend to offend more than others and that such "inferior" individuals should be controlled or even eliminated. This ideological framework fit a more general stance toward eugenics, which is the study of and policies related to improvement of the human race via control over selective reproduction (policies that were

LEARNING OBJECTIVES

As you read this chapter, consider the following topics:

- **Describe what distinguishes positivistic perspectives from the Classical/rational choice perspectives in terms of assumptions, concepts, and propositions.**

- **Explain how the early, pre-Darwinian theories, such as craniometry and phrenology, are different from (and similar to) later post-Darwinian theories, such as Lombroso's theory of offending.**

- **Identify the key assumptions, propositions, and weaknesses of Lombroso's theory of atavism and the born criminal.**

- **Explain the shift to more psychological areas, namely IQ testing, and how it affected the field in terms of policy and thinking about individuals' risk for criminality.**

- **Evaluate the key propositions, concepts, and weaknesses of Sheldon's body type theory, and how he measured the various body types of this perspective.**

CASE STUDY

JAVIER

Javier was born in an inner-city area in El Paso, Texas. Due to the lack of affordable prenatal and postnatal health care, his mother was largely on her own in taking steps to prevent developmental complications. She neglected to take any prenatal vitamins, and she did not have regular medical checkups to monitor the pregnancy. She gave birth prematurely, in the 34th week (the normal length of gestation is about 40 weeks). Everything seemed to go fine in the delivery, but as Javier grew he displayed many unusual physical features, including small, low-seated ears; a relatively large third toe and webbing between all his toes; a curved "pinky" finger; a cleft lip; and close-set eyes.

He had a relatively good home environment and a healthy diet, and he received constant attention and support from his mother and father. As he grew, he developed an athletic, muscular build. Even early on, his father noticed how athletic Javier was and signed him up for many local and school sports activities (e.g., soccer, football), where he excelled. However, his academic performance was problematic. In elementary and middle school, he performed better than average in math, but his verbal scores were low. Javier did well enough to advance to high school, where he became an outstanding linebacker on the school's football team.

Still, his verbal scores and grades were very low, and he became frustrated when writing papers and taking higher-level essay exams in high school, which greatly reduced his grade point average. Javier realized that his chances for getting a college scholarship were low, and he began to hang out more with his best friends, also standouts on the team, who had said they could make some money burglarizing homes they knew were unoccupied. He participated in more than a dozen of these crimes before he was caught and arrested, which further harmed his chances of getting a college scholarship, especially since he was kicked off the football team.

> JAVIER REALIZED THAT HIS CHANCES FOR GETTING A COLLEGE SCHOLARSHIP WERE LOW, AND HE BEGAN TO HANG OUT MORE WITH HIS BEST FRIENDS, ALSO STANDOUTS ON THE TEAM, WHO HAD SAID THEY COULD MAKE SOME MONEY BURGLARIZING HOMES THEY KNEW WERE UNOCCUPIED.

However, because Javier got caught only once, he was placed on probation and successfully completed it. He realized he should not commit such crimes in the future and cleaned up his act. While he never received any scholarships, upon graduation from high school, he got a job offer from his father's friend to work at a local automotive factory, which paid double the hourly minimum wage. So he took the job, and after a few years his good performance earned him a promotion. Ultimately, Javier outgrew his offending behavior streak, got married, and had two children, and he is now living happily with his family in a modest but nice house that he owns.

We discuss Javier again at the end of this chapter, where we apply some of the key theoretical concepts and propositions that specifically pertain to his experience. We also discuss some of the criticisms of these theories that do not seem to fit Javier's situation.

THINK ABOUT IT:

1. Do you think Javier's body type played a part in whom he hung out with?

2. How effective do you think probation and other diversion programs are for dealing with cases such as Javier?

explicitly mandated for certain groups, as we will see). Thus, the conclusion was that there must be notable variations across individuals (and groups) that can help determine those most at risk of offending.

So in the early to mid-1800s, several perspectives were offered regarding how to determine which individuals or groups are most likely to commit crime. Many of these theoretical frameworks were based on establishing a method for distinguishing the superior individuals and groups from the inferior individuals and groups. Such intentions were likely related to the increased use of slavery in the world during the 1800s as well as imperialism's fight to suppress rebellions. For example, slavery was at its peak in the United States during this period, and many European countries had taken over colonies that they were trying to control for profit and domain.

Craniometry

Perhaps the first example of this theory was represented by craniometry. **Craniometry** is the belief that the size of the brain or skull represents the superiority or inferiority of certain individuals or ethnic/racial groups.[2] The reason the size of both the brain and the skull were considered is that a person's skull was believed to perfectly conform to the brain structure; thus, the size of the skull was thought to match the size of the brain. Although modern science has somewhat dismissed this assumption, there is a significant correlation between the size of the skull and the size of the brain. Still, even according to the assumptions of the craniometrists, it is unlikely that much can be gathered from measuring the overall mass of the brain, and certainly not the size of the skull.

The scientists who studied this model would measure the various sizes, or circumferences, of the skull if they were dealing with living subjects. If they were dealing with recently dead subjects, they would measure the weight or volume of the brain itself. When dealing with subjects who had died long before, the craniometrists would pour seeds into the skull and then measure the volume by pouring the seeds into a graduated cylinder. Later, when these scientists realized that seeds were not a valid measure of volume, they moved toward using buckshot or ball bearings.

Most studies by craniometrists showed that subjects of white, Western European descent tended to be far superior to other ethnic groups in terms of larger skull circumference or brain size. Furthermore, the front portion of the brain (i.e., genu) was thought to be larger in the superior individuals and groups, and the hind portion of the brain/skull (i.e., splenium) was predicted to be larger in the lesser individuals and groups. Notably, these researchers typically knew to which ethnic/racial group the skulls/brains belonged before measuring them, making for an unethical and improper methodology of craniometry. Such biased measurements of brains and skulls continued throughout the 19th century and into the early 1900s.[3] These examinations were largely done with the intention of furthering the assumptions of eugenics, which aimed to prove under the banner of "science" that certain individuals and ethnic/racial groups were inferior to others.

This intent of noted craniometrists is supported by subsequent tests of some of these studies, conducted with the researchers not knowing which skulls/brains were from which ethnic/racial groups. These new studies showed only a small correlation between size of the skull/brain and certain behaviors or personality traits.[4] Furthermore, once some of the early "forefathers" of craniometry died, their brains showed average or below-average volume. The existing craniometrists then switched their postulates such that it was the more convoluted or complex structure of brains (those with more fissures and gyri

Craniometrists measured the size of brains and skulls and attempted to show that the larger the mass of the brain, the more superior the person or race.

Source: Cicely D. Fawcett and Alice Lee, "A Second Study of the Variation and Correlation of the Human Skull, With Special Reference to the Naqada Crania," *Biometrika*, Vol. 1, No. 4. (Aug., 1902).

Positive School: a perspective that assumes individuals have no free will to control their behavior.

eugenics: the study of and policies related to the improvement of the human race via discriminatory control over reproduction.

craniometry: field of study that emphasized the belief that the size of the brain or skull reflected superiority or inferiority, with larger brains and skulls being considered superior.

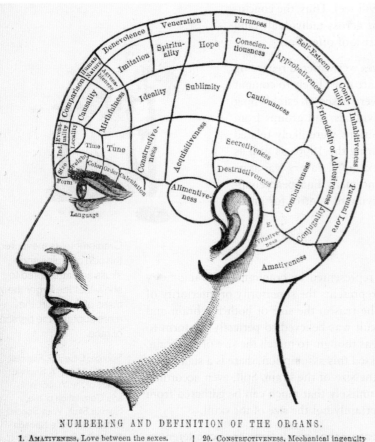

NUMBERING AND DEFINITION OF THE ORGANS.

1. AMATIVENESS, Love between the sexes.
A. CONJUGALITY, Matrimony—love of one. [etc.
2. PARENTAL LOVE, Regard for offspring, pets,
3. FRIENDSHIP, Adhesiveness—sociability.
4. INHABITIVENESS, Love of home.
5. CONTINUITY, One thing at a time.
E. VITATIVENESS, Love of life.
6. COMBATIVENESS, Resistance—defense.
7. DESTRUCTIVENESS, Executiveness—force.
8. ALIMENTIVENESS, Appetite—hunger.
9. ACQUISITIVENESS, Accumulation.
10. SECRETIVENESS, Policy—management.
11. CAUTIOUSNESS, Prudence—provision.
12. APPROBATIVENESS, Ambition—display.
13. SELF-ESTEEM, Self-respect—dignity.
14. FIRMNESS, Decision—perseverance.
15. CONSCIENTIOUSNESS, Justice, equity.
16. HOPE, Expectation—enterprise.
17. SPIRITUALITY, Intuition—faith—credulity.
18. VENERATION, Devotion—respect.
19. BENEVOLENCE, Kindness—goodness.

20. CONSTRUCTIVENESS, Mechanical ingenuity
21. IDEALITY, Refinement—taste—purity.
B. SUBLIMITY, Love of grandeur—infinitude.
22. IMITATION, Copying—patterning.
23. MIRTHFULNESS, Jocoseness—wit—fun.
24. INDIVIDUALITY, Observation.
25. FORM, Recollection of shape.
26. SIZE, Measuring by the eye.
27. WEIGHT, Balancing—climbing.
28. COLOR, Judgment of colors.
29. ORDER, Method—system—arrangement
30. CALCULATION, Mental arithmetic.
31. LOCALITY, Recollection of places.
32. EVENTUALITY, Memory of facts.
33. TIME, Cognizance of duration.
34. TUNE, Sense of harmony and melody.
35. LANGUAGE, Expression of ideas.
36. CAUSALITY, Applying causes to effect. [tion.
37. COMPARISON, Inductive reasoning—illustra-
C. HUMAN NATURE, Perception of motives.
D. AGREEABLENESS, Pleasantness—suavity.

A prototypical mapping of the skull by phrenologists. This shows the various characteristics believed to be influenced by abnormalities in certain parts of the brain.

phrenology: the science of determining human dispositions based on distinctions (e.g., bumps) in the skull, which is believed to conform to the shape of the brain.

than others) that distinguished superior brains from inferior ones.[5] However, this argument was even more tentative and vague than the former hypotheses of craniometrists and thus did not last long.

So craniometry itself did not last long, likely due to its noticeable lack of validity and the fact that Darwinian theory (not presented until the late 1800s) had not been presented or accepted at that time, so the model lacked a popular framework for basis. However, it is important to note that modern studies show that persons who have significantly larger brains do tend to score higher on intelligence tests.[6]

Phrenology

Despite the failure of craniometry to explain the difference between criminals and noncriminals, scientists were not ready to give up the assumption that this phenomenon could be explained by visual differences in the skull (or brain)—and they certainly weren't ready to give up the assumption that certain ethnic or racial groups were superior or inferior to others. Therefore, the experts of the time developed the perspective of phrenology. Phrenology is the science of determining human dispositions based on distinctions (e.g., bumps) in the skull, which are believed to conform to the shape of the brain (see photo on this page).[7] Readers should keep in mind that much of the theorizing of phrenologists was still targeted toward supporting the assumptions of eugenics and showing that certain individuals and groups were inferior or superior to others.

It is important to keep in mind that, like the craniometrists, phrenologists assumed that the shape of the skull conformed to the shape of the brain. Thus, a bump or other abnormality on the skull directly related to an abnormality in the brain. This assumption has been entirely refuted by modern scientific evidence, so it is not surprising that phrenology quickly fell out of favor in criminological thought. However, like its predecessor, phrenology did get some things right. Certain parts of the brain are indeed responsible for specific tasks.

For example, in the original phrenological map (see photo above), "destructiveness" was determined by the presence of abnormalities above the left ear. Modern scientific studies show that perhaps the most vital part of the brain in terms of criminality regarding trauma is that of the left temporal lobe, or the area above the left ear.[8] There are other indications that the phrenologists were right. After all, most readers are well aware of

FIGURE *5.1*

FIGURE *5.1*

Physiognomists attempted to show that criminals' facial profiles resembled those of animals, such as monkeys, apes, birds, and lions, implying they were a genetic "throwback" to an earlier, inferior stage of evolution.

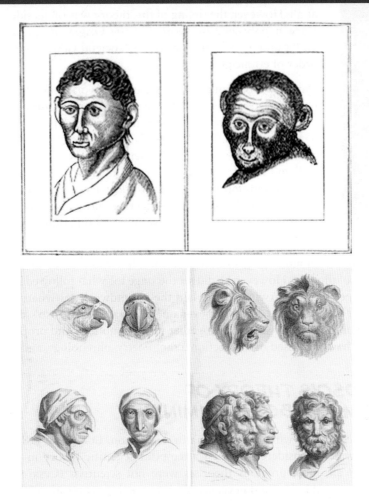

Illustration (anonym): *The Physiognomist's Own Book: an introduction to physiognomy drawn from the writings of Lavater,* Philadelphia; Pittsburg 1841.

© Charles Le Brun (heads).

the fact that specific portions of the brain govern the operation of individualized activities in our bodies. For example, a particular portion of the brain governs the action of our hands, whereas other areas govern our arms, legs, and so forth. So the phrenologists weren't completely wrong, but the extent to which they relied on bumps on the skull to indicate who would be most disposed to criminal behavior was inaccurate.

PHYSIOGNOMY

After phrenology fell out of favor among scientists, researchers and society still did not want to depart from the assumption that certain individuals or ethnic groups were inferior to others. Therefore, another discipline, known as physiognomy, became popular in the mid-1800s. **Physiognomy** is the study of facial and other bodily aspects to indicate developmental problems, such as criminality. Not surprisingly, early physiognomy studies focused on contrasting various racial/ethnic groups to prove that certain groups or individuals were superior or inferior, as illustrated in Figure 5.1.[9]

physiognomy: the study of facial and other bodily aspects to identify developmental problems, such as criminality.

© Cesar Lombroso

Cesare Lombroso (1836–1909) is considered the Father of Criminology and the Father of the Positive School for his contributions to the field in the late 19th century.

Using modern understandings of science, it should be obvious from the illustrations in Figure 5.1 that physiognomy did not last long as a respected scientific perspective of criminality. At any time other than the late 1800s, the importance of observed facial and bodily features in determining criminality would not be highly accepted for long, if at all. However, the timing of this theory was on its side. Specifically, Darwin published his work *On the Origin of Species* in the late 1800s and made a huge impact on societal views regarding the rank order of ethnic groups.

Darwin's model outlined a vague framework that proposed humans had evolved from more primitive beings, and that the human species (as all others) developed with a number of adaptations preferred by natural selection. In other words, some species are selected by their ability to adapt to the environment, whereas others do not adapt so well and die off, or at least become inferior in terms of dominance. This assumption of Darwin's work, which was suddenly accepted widely by both society and scientists throughout the world, falsely led to an inclination to believe that certain ethnic/racial groups are inferior or superior.

Darwin was not a criminologist, so he is not considered the father or theorist of any major schools of thought. However, he did set the stage for what followed in criminological thought. Specifically, Darwin's theory laid the groundwork for what would become the first major scientific theory of crime—namely, Cesare Lombroso's theory of born criminals. Lombroso's theory also tied together the assumptions and propositions of the disciplines we have discussed in this section: craniometry, phrenology, and physiognomy.

LOMBROSO'S THEORY OF ATAVISM AND BORN CRIMINALS

Informed largely by Darwin's theory of natural selection, Lombroso (1835–1909) created what is widely considered the first attempt at scientific theory in criminological thought. After all, most previous theorists were not scientists (Cesare Beccaria, for example, was trained in law and never went out to test his propositions) or did not specifically concentrate on explaining levels of criminality (such as the craniometrists and phrenologists). However, Lombroso was trained in medical science and oriented toward documenting his observations and scientific methodology. Furthermore, timing was on his side in the sense that Darwin's theory was published 15 years prior to the publication of Lombroso's major work and had time to become immensely popular with both scientists and the public.

Lombroso's Theory of Crime

The first edition of Lombroso's *The Criminal Man* was published in 1876 and triggered an immediate response from most Western societies in terms of both their ideas and policies related to crime and justice.[10] In this work, Lombroso outlined a theory of crime that brought together the pre-Darwinian theories of craniometry, phrenology, and physiognomy, discussed previously. Furthermore, Lombroso's theory was largely based on certain groups (and individuals) being "atavistic" and likely born to commit crime. Atavism means that a person or particular feature of an individual is a throwback to an earlier stage of evolutionary development. In other words, people who are serious criminals are manifestations of lower forms of humanity in terms of evolutionary progression. For example, Lombroso would likely suggest that chronic offenders are more

atavism: belief that certain characteristics or behaviors of a person are throwbacks to an earlier stage of evolutionary development.

similar to the earlier stages of humankind, such as the "missing link," than they are to modern humans.

Although Lombroso noted that there were other types of offenders, such as the mentally ill and "criminaloids," who committed minor offenses due to external or environmental circumstances, he specifically claimed that the "born criminals" were the ones who should be singled out in addressing crime. Specifically, Lombroso claimed that born criminals were the most serious and violent criminals in any society—those whom most criminologists now refer to as chronic offenders. Furthermore, Lombroso claimed that born criminals cannot deviate from their natural tendencies to be antisocial.

On the other hand, Lombroso claimed that despite the born criminal's inevitable tendency to commit crime, there was a way for societies to prevent or reduce these crimes—by identifying born criminals. According to Lombroso, the way for societies to identify born criminals, even early in life, is through stigmata. Stigmata are physical manifestations of the atavism of an individual, with such physical features indicating the prior evolutionary stages of development.

Lombroso's List of Stigmata

According to Lombroso, the manifestation of more than five stigmata indicates that an individual is atavistic and thus a born criminal. Readers may be wondering what these stigmata are, given the importance of these criteria. This is a great question, the answer to which was constantly changing according to Lombroso's list of what constitutes stigmata. In the beginning, this list was largely based on Lombroso's work as a physician and included such things as large eyes and large ears. It is hard to specify what exact criteria were listed as stigmata because Lombroso changed this list as he went along (which can be argued is very poor science), even up until the last edition of his book well into the 1900s.

For the most part, stigmata consisted of facial and bodily features that deviated from the norm—in other words, abnormally small or large noses, abnormally small or large ears, abnormally small or large eyes, abnormally small or large jaws, or almost anything that went outside the "bell curve" of normal physical development in human beings. Beyond deviant physical features, Lombroso also threw in some extraphysiological features, such as tattoos and a history of epilepsy (or other disorders) in the family.

Lombroso's documentation of some of the tattoos he saw on known criminal offenders included many tattoos that featured female names or some motto such as "born under an unlucky star" or "man of misfortune." Others were more intriguing, such as a tattoo on the penis of one offender that read "Entra Tutto," which means "it all goes in" or "it enters all."[11] Either translation is rather amusing. Although it is likely that these latter features are somewhat correlated to crime and delinquency, is it likely that they caused such antisocial behavior? Given Lombroso's model that persons are born criminal, it is quite unlikely that these factors are causally linked to criminality. After all, how many babies are born with tattoos? Regardless of the illogical nature of many of the stigmata, Lombroso professed that if a person had more than five of the physical features on his list, that person was indeed a born criminal and should be prevented from offending.

As a physician working for the Italian army, Lombroso examined the bodies of captured war criminals. According to Lombroso, he first realized the nature of the criminal when a particular war criminal was brought in for examination:

> This was not merely an idea, but a flash of inspiration. At the sight of that skull, I seemed to see all of a sudden, lighted up as a vast plain under a flaming sky, the problem of the nature of the criminal—an atavistic being who reproduces

stigmata: the physical manifestations of atavism (biological inferiority), according to Lombroso.

C. LOMBROSO — *L'homme criminel.*　PL. XLIX

RÉVOLUTIONNAIRES ET CRIMINELS POLITIQUES. — MATTOÏDES ET FOUS MORAUX.

Lombroso provided numerous profile images of criminals and claimed that his list of stigmata could identify a born criminal by facial features.

in his person the ferocious instincts of primitive humanity and the inferior animals. Thus were explained anatomically the enormous jaws, high cheek bones . . . solitary lines in the palms, extreme size of the orbits, handle-shaped ears found in criminals, savages and apes, insensibility to pain, extremely acute sight, tattooing, excessive idleness, love of orgies, and the irresponsible craving of evil for its own sake, the desire not only to extinguish life in the victim, but to mutilate the corpse, tear its flesh and drink its blood.[12]

While most laugh at his words now, at the time when he wrote this description it likely rang true to most readers, which is perhaps why his book was the dominant text in the criminological field for many decades. In the description above, Lombroso incorporates many of the core principles of his theory—namely, the idea of criminals being atavistic, or biological evolutionary throwbacks, and the stigmata that became so important in his theoretical model. Furthermore, Lombroso's theory synthesized the themes of craniometry, phrenology, and physiognomy. This theory came just a decade after Darwin, when society was ready to accept such a perspective, which was not too far removed from the dominant perspective of the slavery period in this country. Perhaps this is why his theoretical framework became so popular.

A good example of the popular acceptance of Lombroso's "scientific" stigmata appears in Bram Stoker's *Dracula*, in which the physical appearance of the Count (Dracula) is based on "Lombrosian" traits, such as the high bridge of the thin nose, arched nostrils, massive eyebrows, and pointed ears. This reference makes sense given the time when the novel was published (the late 1800s), when Lombroso's theory was highly dominant in society and science. This is just one indication of this theory's importance among academics, scientists, philosophers, fiction writers, and criminal justice policy during that period. The theory became popular for other reasons as well.

Not only did Lombroso claim that he could identify born criminals by their stigmata; he also claimed that he could identify certain types of criminals. For example, he claimed that certain stigmata could be identified among groups of anarchists, burglars, murderers, shoplifters, and so forth. Of course, if most readers are confused by their failure to distinguish one kind of offender from another, that is fine; virtually no one can. Lombroso's stigmata as a way to distinguish certain individuals as born criminals, let alone to identify certain forms of criminals, are quite invalid by modern research standards. However, as mentioned above, Lombroso's theory became extremely popular throughout the developed Western world, and much of this popularity was due to good timing.

Lombroso as the Father of Criminology and the Father of the Positive School

Lombroso's theory came a decade and a half after Darwin's work was published, so Darwin's views had already spread throughout the Western world. As mentioned previously, Lombroso's model coincided with much of the Western world's views on slavery and deportation at that time. Because of this good timing and because he became known as the first individual to test his hypotheses through observation, Lombroso is widely considered the Father of Criminology. This title is not assigned out of respect for his theory (which has been largely rejected) or his methods (which are considered highly invalid by modern standards) but is deserved because he was the first person to gain recognition in testing his theoretical propositions. Furthermore, his theory coincided with political movements popular at that time—the Fascist and Nazi movements of the early 1900s.

Lombroso is also considered the Father of the Positive School of criminology because he was the first to gain prominence in identifying factors beyond free will or free choice (i.e., the Classical School) that were predicted to cause crime. Although previous theorists had presented perspectives that went beyond free will, such as craniometry and phrenology, Lombroso was the first to gain widespread attention due to the popularity of Darwin's perspective at that time. The pre-Darwinian frameworks had not gained much attention due to the lack of a theoretical perspective conducive to these models. Lombroso's perspective was timed well (just after Darwin's), and it gained almost immediate support in all developed countries at that time, which is the most likely reason for why Lombroso is considered the Father of the Positive School of criminology.

It is important to understand the assumptions of positivism, which most experts consider somewhat synonymous with the term *determinism*. Determinism is the idea that most human behavior is determined by factors beyond free will and free choice (i.e., the Classical School). In other words, determinism (i.e., the Positive School) assumes that human beings do not decide how they will act by rationally thinking through the costs and benefits of a given situation. Rather, the Positive School is based on the fundamental belief that factors outside free will and choice—such as biological, psychological, and sociological variables—determine the choices we make regarding all types of behavior, especially decisions of whether or not to engage in criminal activity.

The majority of readers probably believe they have chosen their career paths as well as most other aspects of their lives. However, scientific evidence shows otherwise. For example, although most people consider religion one of the most important aspects of their lives, studies show that far more than 90% of the world's population have chosen their religious affiliation (e.g., Baptist, Buddhist, Catholic, Judaism) based on the religious affiliation of their parents or caretakers. Therefore, it is clear that what most people consider an extremely important decision—namely, what to believe regarding a higher being or force—is almost completely determined by their environment. To clarify, almost no one sits down and goes through a list of descriptions of various religions to decide which fits best. Rather, in almost all cases, religious affiliation is determined by culture, which dismisses the factor of free will/free choice assumed by the Classical School. The same type of argument can be made regarding the clothes we wear, the food we prefer, and the activities we enjoy.

determinism: the assumption that human behavior is caused by factors outside free will and rational decision-making.

LEARNING CHECK 5.1

1. What term means the study of and policies related to the improvement of the human race via control of selective reproduction?

    a. Cytogenetics

    b. Ethnographics

    c. Racionology

    d. Eugenics

    e. Fascionics

2. What is the 19th-century study of the size of the brain/skull that posited that the bigger the brain, the more superior the person or race?

    a. Phrenology

    b. Physiognomy

    c. Craniometry

    d. Skullography

    e. Cerebrotology

3. What is the 19th-century study of various bumps on portions of the skull believed to reveal weaknesses in terms of certain cognitive or personality traits?

    a. Phrenology

    b. Physiognomy

    c. Craniometry

    d. Skullography

    e. Cerebrotology

Answers located at www.edge.sagepub.com/schram2e

Another way to distinguish positivism and determinism is in the way scientists view human behavior, which can be understood using a chemistry analogy. Specifically, a chemist assumes that if a given element is subjected to certain temperatures, pressures, or mixtures with other elements, it will react in a predictable way. In a highly comparable way, a positivist assumes that when human beings are subjected to poverty, delinquent peers, low intelligence, or other factors, they will react in a predictable way. Therefore, there is virtually no difference between how a chemist feels about the behavior of particles and elements and how a positivistic scientist feels about human behavior.

In Lombroso's case, the deterministic factor was the biological makeup of individuals. However, we shall see in the next several chapters that positivistic theories focus on a wide range of variables, from biology to psychology to social aspects. For example, many readers likely believe that bad parenting, poverty, and associating with delinquent peers are some of the most important factors in predicting criminality. If you believe that such variables significantly influence decisions to commit crime, then you are likely a positive theorist; you believe that crime is caused by factors above and beyond free choice or free will.

Lombroso's Policy Implications

Beyond the theoretical aspects of Lombroso's theory of criminality, it is important to realize that his perspective had profound consequences for policy as well. For example, Lombroso was called in to testify in numerous criminal processes and trials to determine the guilt or innocence of suspects. Under the banner of science (in much the same way we view DNA or fingerprint analysis now), Lombroso was called in to determine the guilt of certain persons in key criminal testimony, often during trial.[13] Lombroso even wrote about many of the trials and official identifications he made as an "expert" witness, which often included identifying which suspect (often out of many) had committed a crime. Lombroso based such judgments solely on the visual stigmata evident in the line of suspects.[14] In one such account of Lombroso's experiences as an expert witness, he noted:

> [One suspect] was, in fact, the most perfect type of the born criminal: enormous jaws, frontal sinuses, and zygomata, thin upper lip, huge incisors, unusually large head, tactile obtuseness with sensorial manicinism. . . . He was convicted.[15]

WHY DO THEY DO IT?

DR. HAROLD SHIPMAN

been killing his patients for years without any apparent monetary incentive.

Despite his consistent denials of guilt, in 2000 he was convicted and sentenced to 15 consecutive life sentences with recommendation of no release. Notably, he was the only doctor in British legal history to be found guilty of killing his patients. Dr. Shipman hanged himself in his cell at Wakefield Prison in West Yorkshire, England, on January 13, 2004.

Dr. Harold Shipman is one of the top three most prolific serial killers on official record in the Western world. He is known to have killed more than 250 of his patients. The only serial killers on record that exceed him are both from Colombia: Pedro Lopez, the "Monster of the Andes," believed to have killed 300 people, and Luis Garavito, "Le Bestia" or the beast, believed to have killed more than 400 people, including more than 100 children. However, Shipman could rank number one if you break the list into categories of serial killers. After all, the others were predatory, hedonistic serial killers, but Dr. Shipman was an "Angel of Death." He was supposed to be helping his patients (indeed, he was paid to do so), but instead he killed them.

Shipman would typically inject his victims, almost always women, with lethal doses of diamorphine (i.e., heroin). It is believed he began killing patients in the late 1970s or early 1980s and continued until he was caught in the late 1990s. Investigators became suspicious when he was named in one of his victim's wills, which left him about 380,000 pounds. When it was discovered that he had forged this will, it triggered a much larger investigation. However, the desire for money is not believed to be his main motive, because an investigation of the records revealed that this forged will was an isolated case; he had

So why did he do it? BBC News recently released a report examining why he may have done it but essentially gave up trying to understand his motive.

> He has never revealed anything about the extent of his murderous career, and probably never will. . . . The experience of killing was personal and private to him, and he is never going to give that up. . . . We are never going to know the truth.

The best guess is from some of those present when he was tried in Preston Crown Court. They claimed that he likely "enjoyed exercising the power over life and death."

This explanation probably doesn't seem satisfactory to most readers, but the truth is that many serial killers kill simply because they enjoy it. A large part of that enjoyment is the power–control factor they hold over their victims. Fortunately, there are not many doctors who feel this way. But doctors are people, too. And where you have people, you will have killers.

Although this high-profile case is not specifically linked to any theories described in this chapter, it is presented here because the Father of Criminology, Lombroso, was also a medical doctor. In fact, it was during one of his criminal autopsies that he formulated his theoretical model.

THINK ABOUT IT:

1. What was the basic method of operation for Harold Shipman in how he killed his victims? This would make him what type or category of serial killer?

2. What is the best guess for why he committed his many killings?

Sources: The secret world of Harold Shipman. (2001, January 5). *BBC News.* Retrieved from http://news.bbc.co.uk/2/hi/uk_news/1102270.stm; Smith, J. D. (2004). *100 most infamous criminals.* New York, NY: MetroBooks.

When Lombroso was not available for such "scientific" determinations of guilty persons, his colleagues or students (often referred to as "lieutenants") were often sent. Some of these students, such as Enrico Ferri and Raphael Garrofalo, became quite active in the Fascist regime of Italy in the early 1900s. This model of government, like the Nazi party in Germany, sought to remove the "inferior" groups from society. Thus, Lombroso's theory was timed well in terms of both societal and governmental ideologies. This was another reason why Lombroso gained such prominence throughout the Western world throughout the late 1800s and early 1900s.

Another policy implication that was implemented in some parts of the world was identifying young children on the basis of observed stigmata, which tend to manifest in the first 5 to 10 years of life. This led to tracking or isolating certain children based on such criteria, largely physiological features. Although many readers may consider such policies ridiculous, modern medicine has supported the identification, documentation, and importance of certain physical features as indications of high risk for developmental problems.

For example, modern medicine identifies a number of what are termed **minor physical anomalies** (MPAs) that indicate developmental problems. These MPAs include

- head circumference out of the normal range,
- malformed ears,
- low-set ears,
- excessively large gap between the first and second toes,
- webbing between toes or fingers,
- no earlobes,
- curved fifth finger,
- asymmetrical ears,
- furrowed tongue, and
- simian crease (see Figure 5.2).[16]

Given the practice of correlating such visible physical aspects with developmental problems, including criminality, it is obvious that Lombroso's model of stigmata as predictors of antisocial problems has implications to the present day. Perhaps surprisingly, such implications are more accepted by modern medical science than they are in the criminological literature. For example, such minor physical anomalies (MPAs) are still used to diagnose and predict future development of young children. Such MPAs relate to the case study of Javier presented at the beginning of this chapter. Furthermore, some modern scientific studies have shown that being unattractive predicts criminal offending, which somewhat supports Lombroso's theory of crime.[17]

LEARNING CHECK 5.2

1. Who is considered the Father of Criminology, as well as the Father of the Positive School of criminological thought?
   a. Beccaria
   b. Binet
   c. Lombroso
   d. Sheldon
   e. Hirschi

2. What did the Father of Criminology say was a way to identify the most dangerous, chronic criminals?
   a. Those with bad parents
   b. Those who were poor
   c. Those who had delinquent peers
   d. Those who had stigmata
   e. Those who had weak ties to conventional society

3. What does the Positive School of criminology assume that clearly distinguishes it from the Classical School of criminology?
   a. Free will/free choice
   b. Rational decision-making in choosing behavior
   c. Determinism
   d. Hedonism
   e. Utilitarianism

Answers located at www.edge.sagepub.com/schram2e

minor physical anomalies: physical features, such as asymmetrical or low-seated ears, that are believed to indicate developmental problems.

About three decades after Lombroso's original work was published, and after a long period of dominance during that time, criminologists began to question his theory of atavism and stigmata. Furthermore, it became clear that there was more involved in criminality than just the way people looked, such as psychological aspects of individuals. However, scientists and societies were not ready to depart from theories, such as Lombroso's, that assumed that certain people or groups of people were inferior to others, so they simply chose another factor to emphasize—intelligence, or IQ.

AFTER LOMBROSO: THE IQ-TESTING ERA

Despite the evidence presented against Lombroso, his theorizing remained dominant until the early 1900s, when criminologists realized that stigmata and the idea of a "born" criminal were not valid. However, even at that time, theorists and researchers were not ready to give up the assumption that certain ethnic or racial groups were superior or inferior to others. Thus, a new theory emerged based on a more quantified measure originated by Alfred Binet in France. This new measure was IQ, which represents an individual's intelligence quotient. At that time, IQ was calculated as chronological age divided by mental age, which was then multiplied by 100—the average score being 100. This scale has changed enormously over time, but the bottom line is determining whether someone is above or below the base score of average (100).

Binet had good intentions in creating the concept of IQ scores in France, which he formulated to identify youth who were not performing up to par in educational skills. Binet was explicit in stating that IQ could be changed, which is why he proposed a score to identify slow learners so that they could be trained to raise their IQs.[18] However, when Binet's work on developing the idea and methods of scoring IQs was brought to the United States, his basic assumptions and propositions were twisted. One of the most prominent individuals who utilized Binet's IQ test in the United States for purposes of deporting, incapacitating, sterilizing, and otherwise ridding society of low-IQ individuals was H. H. Goddard.

Goddard's IQ Test

Goddard is generally considered the leading authority on the use and interpretation of IQ testing in the United States.[19] Goddard used the IQ test he adopted from Binet's model to examine immigrants coming into the United States. It is important to note that Goddard proposed quite different assumptions regarding intelligence or IQ than did Binet. To clarify, Goddard believed and claimed that IQ was static or innate, meaning that such levels could not be changed, even with training. The assumption of Goddard's perspective of intelligence was that it was passed from generation to generation, from parents to offspring.

Goddard is known for labeling this low IQ **feeble-mindedness**, which actually became a technical, scientific term in the early 1900s referring to those who had significantly below-average levels of intelligence. Of course, being a scientist, Goddard specified certain levels of feeble-mindedness, which were ranked based on the degree to which the

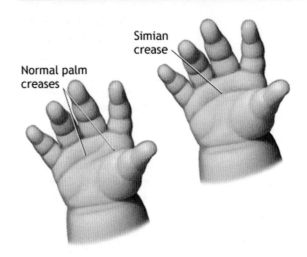

Simian crease

Normal palm creases

National Park Service Digital Image Archives

feeble-mindedness: technical, scientific term in the early 1900s meaning those who had significantly below-average levels of intelligence.

score was below average. In order from highest to lowest intelligence, the first group were the "morons," the second group were the "imbeciles," and the lowest group were the "idiots."

According to Goddard, from a eugenics point of view, the biggest threat to the progress of humanity was not the idiots. Rather, he believed the morons were the biggest threat to the genetic pool. In Goddard's words,

> The idiot is not our greatest problem. He is indeed loathsome. . . . Nevertheless, he lives his life and is done. He does not continue the race with a line of children like himself. . . . It is the moron type that makes for us our great problem.[20]

According to Goddard, of the three categories of feeble-mindedness, the morons are the group smart enough to slip through the cracks and reproduce, thus posing the biggest threat to humanity.

Goddard received many grants to fund his research, and he took his research team to Ellis Island in the early 1900s to identify the feeble-minded as they attempted to enter the United States. Much of his team was made up of women, who he believed were better at distinguishing the feeble-minded by sight:

> After a person has had considerable experience in this work, he almost gets a sense of what a feeble-minded person is so that he can tell one afar off. The people who are best at this work, and who I believe should do this work, are women. Women seem to have closer observation than men. It was quite impossible for others to see how . . . women could pick out the feeble-minded without the aid of the Binet test at all.[21]

Library of Congress

New York, Ellis Island. reg. No. 3163 E

Immigrants walk across pier from bridge on Ellis Island, where a large portion of immigrants were processed into the United States. Many of these immigrants were tested by Goddard and his research team for potentially being "feeble-minded."

Although Goddard never provided a good reason why, he insisted that women could pick out the feeble-minded better than men could, so he included them on his team of scientists stationed on Ellis Island.

Policy Implications

Regarding policy implications of his work, Goddard was proud of the increase in the deportations of potential immigrants to the United States. For example, Goddard enthusiastically reported that deportations for the reason of mental deficiency increased by 350% in 1913 and 570% in 1914 from the average of the preceding five years.[22] However, over time Goddard realized that his policy recommendations of deportation, incarceration, and sterilization were not based on accurate science.

Specifically, after consistently validating his IQ test on immigrants and mental patients, Goddard finally tested his intelligence scale on a relatively representative cross-section of American citizens—namely, draftees for military service during World War I. The results showed that many of these recruits scored as feeble-minded (i.e., lower than a mental age of 12) on the given IQ test. Therefore, Goddard changed (lowered) the criteria of what determined a person's feeble-mindedness; specifically, the criteria changed from a mental age of 12 to a mental age of 8. Although this appears to be a clear admission that his scientific method was inaccurate, Goddard continued to profess his model of the feeble-minded for many years, and societies utilized his ideas.

Toward the end of his career, Goddard did admit that intelligence could be improved, despite his earlier assumptions that it was innate and static.[23] In fact, Goddard actually claimed that he had "gone over to the enemy."[24] However, despite Goddard's admission that his assumptions and testing were not determinant of individuals' intelligence, the snowball had been rolling for too long and had gathered too much strength to fight even the most notable theorist's admonishment concerning the perspective.

STERILIZATION. Specifically, the sterilization of individuals, mostly females, based on scores from intelligence tests continued in the United States. Often, the justification was based not on the intelligence scores of the person being sterilized but on the scores of that person's mother or father. After all, as Goddard had proclaimed, the "germ-plasm" that determined feeble-mindedness was passed on from one generation to the next, so it inevitably resulted in feeble-minded offspring as well. Thus, the U.S. government typically sterilized individuals—again, mostly women—based on their parents' IQ scores.

This issue came to the highest court in the 1920s. The case of *Buck v. Bell* made its way to the U.S. Supreme Court in 1927, and the court discussed the issue of sterilizing individuals who had scored, or whose parents had scored, as mentally deficient on intelligence scales. The majority opinion, written by one of the court's most respected jurists, Oliver Wendell Holmes, Jr., stated,

> We have seen more than once that the public welfare may call upon the best citizens for their lives. It would be strange if it could not call upon those who already sap the strength of the state for these lesser sacrifices. . . . Three generations of imbeciles are enough.[25]

Thus, the highest court in the United States upheld the use of sterilization for the purposes of limiting reproduction among individuals deemed feeble-minded by a test score that even the creator and administrator of the test admitted was not valid or accurate.

Due to this approval from the court, such sterilizations continued for many years, up to the 1970s. Governors of many states, such as North Carolina, Virginia, and California, have since delivered public apologies for these policy practices. For example, in 2003 the governor of California, Gray Davis, apologized for the state law passed almost a century before that resulted in the sterilization of about 19,000 women in California.

Although this aspect of U.S. history is often hidden from the public, it did occur and it is important to acknowledge this blot on our nation's history, especially since it occurred at a time when we were supposed to be fighting the Nazis' and other regimes' abuses of civil rights.

Reexamining Intelligence

Ultimately, the sterilizations, deportations, and incarcerations based on IQ testing contributed to an embarrassing period in U.S. history. So for many decades, criminological researchers realized the atrocities that had been committed in the name of this theory, as well as the "Nazi" mentality of its assumptions, and IQ was not researched or discussed much in the literature. However, in the 1970s, an important study was published in which Travis Hirschi and Michael Hindelang examined the effect of intelligence on youths.[26] Hirschi and Hindelang found that even among youths in the same race and social class, intelligence has a significant effect on delinquency and criminality. This study, as well as others, showed that the IQs of delinquents or criminals are about 10 points lower than those of noncriminals.[27]

© Creatas/Thinkstock

Modern studies have shown a strong tie between low IQ, particularly verbal intelligence, and delinquency and criminality.

This study led to a rebirth in research regarding intelligence testing in criminological research. A number of recent studies have shown that certain types of intelligence are more important than others. Specifically, several studies have shown that low verbal intelligence has the most significant impact in predicting delinquent and criminal behavior.[28]

This tendency makes sense because verbal skills are important in virtually all aspects of life, from everyday interactions with significant others to filling out forms at work to dealing with people in the workplace and so on. In contrast, most people do not have to display advanced math or quantitative skills in their jobs or in day-to-day interactions, let alone spatial and other forms of intelligence that are more abstract. Thus, low verbal IQ is the type of intelligence that represents the most direct prediction of criminality, most likely due to the general need for such skills in routine daily activities. After all, persons who lack communication skills will likely find it hard to obtain or retain employment or to deal with family and social problems.

This rebirth in studies of the link between intelligence and criminality seemed to reach a peak with the publication of Richard Herrnstein and Charles Murray's *The Bell Curve* in 1994.[29] Although this publication eschewed the terminology of *moron*, *imbecile*, and *idiot* in favor of relatively benign terms (e.g., *cognitively disadvantaged*), their argument was consistent with that of the feeble-mindedness researchers of the early 20th century. Specifically, Herrnstein and Murray argued that persons with low IQ scores are somewhat destined to be unsuccessful in school, become unemployed, produce illegitimate children, and commit crime. They also suggested that IQ or intelligence is primarily innate, or genetically determined, with little chance of improvement. These authors also noted that African-Americans tend to score the lowest, whereas Asians and Jewish persons tend to score the highest. They provided results from social indicators that support their argument that these intelligence levels result in relative success in life in terms of group-level statistics.

Their book inspired a public outcry, resulting in symposiums at major universities and other venues during which the authors' postulates were largely condemned. As noted by other reviews of the impact of this work, some professors at public institutions were actually sued in court over their use of this book in their classes.[30] The book also received blistering reviews from other scientists.[31] However, none of these scientific critics have fully addressed the undisputed fact that African-Americans consistently score low on intelligence tests and that Asians and Jewish people score high. Furthermore, none have adequately addressed the issue that even within these populations, low IQ scores (especially on verbal tests) predict criminality. For example, in samples of only African-Americans, the group that scored lowest on verbal intelligence consistently committed more crime, and even among this population, the persons who scored low on IQ (especially the verbal portions) were more likely to become delinquent or criminal. So despite the harsh criticism of *The Bell Curve*, it is apparent that the authors' arguments carry some validity.

Applying Theory to Crime: BURGLARY

At the beginning of this chapter, we presented the case study of Javier. We will not repeat his history here, but as his major crime was burglary, we will discuss some facts about burglary.

The FBI (or Uniform Crime Reports) defines burglary as "the unlawful entry of a structure to commit a felony or theft" and classifies it as a serious Index Crime. Although burglaries are nonviolent by definition, they certainly pose much risk for becoming violent—for example, if the residents return while the burglary is taking place. Although some people may believe that burglary occurs only during the night, most police departments and certainly the FBI have moved beyond that common-law definition of this crime.

Burglary rates have decreased over the past decade, but this crime is still occurring millions of times each year.

Despite a steady decrease in burglaries over the past decade, the FBI recorded over 1.7 million burglaries in 2014. The vast majority of these burglaries involved some form of forced entry, and most were of home residences. Most burglaries occur during the hours of 6 a.m. and 6 p.m., when residents are most likely to be out. Still, even when victims do not encounter the burglar, the experience can be traumatic, given that victims know an offender has intruded into their home, often considered a place of refuge and security. In 2014, the average monetary/property loss of burglary per incident for a residence was $2,229; the average monetary/property loss of burglary per incident for a nonresidence was $2,312.

According to arrest reports, the vast majority (more than 80%) of burglary offenders are male, and a notable number (although not the majority) are under 18. Notably, the likelihood of an offender being caught for burglary is extremely low, perhaps because of the categorization of burglary as a property crime as well as the fact that there are no witnesses

(unlike most violent crimes). This is reflected in the low national clearance rate/arrest rate for burglary, which was less than 14% in 2014.

In an example of burglary's low priority with police, the San Diego Police Department wrote a press release in 1998 informing citizens that police would no longer investigate home burglaries. The department claimed that the low likelihood of catching anyone (i.e., the low clearance rate), as well as burglary's status as a nonviolent property crime, led them to decide they would rather spend their resources on more serious cases or those they had a greater chance of solving. In 2013, the Chicago Police Department officially stated that they would not actively investigate motor vehicle thefts home burglaries, and several other crimes in their jurisdiction due to their low priority compared to more violent offenses.[32] Although alarming, this reflects the opinion of many other police and sheriff departments throughout the country regarding incidents of burglary; specifically, most law enforcement officers find burglaries incredibly hard to solve,

even when reported, because they typically involve no witnesses or hard evidence.

In the case study at the beginning of this chapter, Javier realized he did not have much going for him in terms of education, so he decided to follow his friends in committing a number of burglaries. Javier was not a violent person, so he engaged in a property offense that he hoped would not result in violence. However, had he known the high potential for violence in a burglary—if, for instance, someone were sleeping in the back of the house or a homeowner returned unexpectedly—he may have thought twice.

THINK ABOUT IT:

1. What theoretical perspective discussed in this chapter best explains Javier's criminal behavior?

2. What aspects of this theoretical perspective in the previous question do not adequately apply to Javier's criminal behavior?

Sources: Associated Press. (1999, July 28). San Diego police may stop routine home burglary investigations. *Lodi News-Sentinel*, p. 8; Federal Bureau of Investigation. (2015). *Crime in the United States, 2014*. Washington, DC: U.S. Department of Justice; Walsh, A., & Ellis, L. (2007). *Criminology*. Thousand Oaks, CA: SAGE.

Comparative Criminology: *BURGLARY*

Ranking Regions/Countries as Most Likely for Burglary

In this section, we examine the findings and conclusions of various studies of burglary, which involves attempted or actual breaking and entering for the purpose of stealing goods, money, and so forth. What distinguishes burglary from larceny is that burglary, by definition, involves trespassing on property where the offender has no permission to enter, whereas larceny does not include trespassing (e.g., shoplifting). Furthermore, burglary can be distinguished from robbery, which by definition involves a threat of or actual violence in taking someone's possessions, whereas burglary does not involve violence, according to FBI and most other definitions.[33] The findings of recent studies regarding the prevalence of burglary across various regions and countries are enlightening in several ways.

The key measure of the prevalence of burglary in the world is the International Crime Victimization Survey (ICVS), a databank that collects and standardizes police reports from more than 70 countries around the world. This measure has been conducted since 1987. It does have some weaknesses, but it is currently the best international measure of crime for such cross-national comparisons.

The ICVS has collected many years' worth of data on burglary. Van Dijk synthesized the ICVS data on burglary for the years 1996 to 2005.[34] As seen in Figure 5.3, the countries with by far the highest percentages of households victimized by burglary in urban areas were countries in Africa. Distant second and third highest ranking were, respectively, countries in the region of Latin America/the Caribbean and Oceania (the islands near Southeast Asia and Australia).

It is not too surprising that burglary tends to be more common in some of the most deprived areas of the world, such as Africa and various Latin American/Caribbean countries. After all, in extreme poverty, many individuals are driven to commit such crimes to survive. However, the results from the ICVS reveal that burglary happens quite a bit in all regions of the world, so burglary is alive and well throughout virtually all societies, such as the United States (see Figure 5.4).

FIGURE 5.3

Percentages of the Public in Urban Areas Victimized by Household Burglary During the Past 12 Months, by World Region

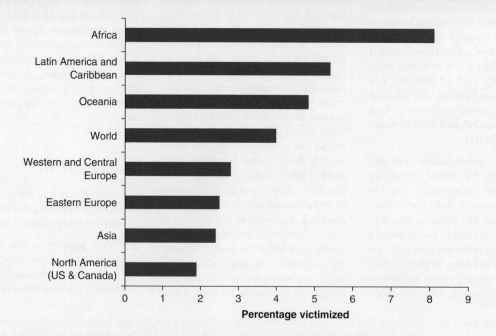

Source: International Crime Victimization Surveys (ICVS) 1996–2005.

FIGURE 5.4

Burglary Rate in 2014—U.S. Cities

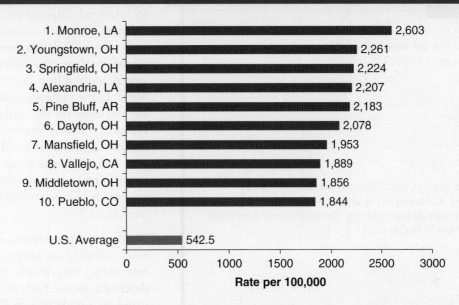

Source: Federal Bureau of Investigation. (2015). *Crime in the United States, 2014.* Washington, DC: U.S. Department of Justice

Note: Rate out of 100,000 population for cities with populations of 40,000 and higher

THINK ABOUT IT:

1. Would you have identified Monroe, Louisiana, as having the highest rate per 100,000 of burglaries in the United States?

2. How does this rate differ from the actual number of burglaries in the United States?

BODY TYPE THEORY: SHELDON'S MODEL OF SOMATOTYPING

Although numerous theories in the late 1800s and early 1900s were based on body types, such as Lombroso's theory and those of other criminal anthropologists, none of these perspectives had a more enduring impact than that of William Sheldon. In the mid-1940s, this new theoretical perspective merged the concepts of biology and psychology. Sheldon claimed that in the embryonic and fetal stages of development, there is an emphasis on the development of certain tissue layers.[35] According to Sheldon, these varying degrees of emphasis are largely due to heredity, which leads to the development of certain body types and temperaments or personalities. This theory, also known as somatotyping, became the best-known body type theory, for reasons we will discuss below.

According to Sheldon, all embryos must develop three distinct tissue layers, which are still acknowledged by perinatal medical researchers. The first layer of tissue is the endoderm, which is the inner layer of tissues and includes the internal organs, such as the stomach, large intestine, and small intestine. The middle layer of tissue, called the mesoderm, includes the muscles, bones, ligaments, and tendons. The ectoderm is the outer layer of tissue and includes the skin, capillaries, and much of the nervous system sensors.

somatotyping: the area of study, primarily linked to William Sheldon, that links body type to risk for delinquent and criminal behavior. Also, as a methodology, it is a way of ranking body types based on three categories: endomorphy, mesomorphy, and ectomorphy.

endoderm: medical term for the inner layer of tissue in our bodies.

LEARNING CHECK 5.3

1. According to the text, which theorist invented IQ testing in France in the early 1900s?

   a. Lombroso

   b. Binet

   c. Goddard

   d. Sheldon

   e. Hirschi

2. According to the text, which theorist was one of the key proponents of IQ testing in the United States in the early 1900s and had his research team identify "feeble-minded" persons at Ellis Island, New York City?

   a. Lombroso

   b. Binet

   c. Goddard

   d. Sheldon

   e. Hirschi

3. According to the text, which level of "feeble-mindedness" was considered the highest level of the feeble-minded and the biggest threat to society?

   a. Moron

   b. Idiot

   c. Imbecile

   d. Stupid

   e. Retarded

4. According to the text, what U.S. Supreme Court case (decided in 1927) ruled it constitutional for individuals to be sterilized based on IQ scores?

   a. *Miranda v. Arizona*

   b. *Buck v. Bell*

   c. *Mapp v. Ohio*

   d. *McKeiver v. Pennsylvania*

   e. *Breed v. Jones*

Answers located at www.edge.sagepub.com/schram2e

Sheldon used these medical facts regarding the three tissue layers to propose that some individuals tend to emphasize certain tissue layers relative to others, typically due to inherited dispositions. In turn, Sheldon believed that such emphases led to certain body types, such that persons who had a focus on their endoderm in development would inevitably become endomorphic, or obese. In the same way, individuals who had an emphasis on the middle layer of tissue typically became mesomorphic, or of an athletic or muscular build. Finally, someone who had an emphasis on the third layer of tissue in embryonic development would end up having an ectomorphic, or thin, build (see Figure 5.5).

Sheldon and his research team would grade each subject on three dimensions, corresponding respectively to the body types described above. Each body type was measured on a scale of 1 to 7, with 7 being the highest. Obviously, no one could score a 0 for any body type, because we all need our internal organs, bone/muscular structure, and outer systems (e.g., skin, capillaries). As stated above, each somatotype always had the following order: endomorphy, mesomorphy, ectomorphy.

So the scores on a typical somatotype might be 3-6-2 (a similar example is seen in Figure 5.5), which would indicate that this person scored a 3 (a little below average) on endomorphy, a 6 (high) on mesomorphy, and a 2 (relatively low) on ectomorphy. According to Sheldon's theory, this hypothetical subject would be a likely candidate for criminality, because he or she scored relatively high on the mesomorphy scale. In fact, the results from his data—as well as those from all studies that have examined the association of body types and delinquency and criminality—would support this prediction.

Perhaps most important, Sheldon proposed that these body types matched particular personality traits or temperaments. Specifically, Sheldon claimed that individuals who were endomorphic (obese) tended to be more jolly or lazy. The technical term for this temperament is viscerotonic. In contrast, persons who were mesomorphic (muscular) typically had a risk-taking and aggressive temperament, called somatotonic. Last, individuals who were ectomorphic (thin) tended to be introverted and shy, a personality type referred to as cerebrotonic. Obviously, it was the middle group, the mesomorphs, who had the greatest propensity for criminality, due to their risk-taking and aggressive dispositions.

FIGURE **5.5**

These three body types have been shown to have an influence on both temperament or personality and risk for criminality, with the mesomorph being at highest risk for delinquency or crime.

Somatotypes

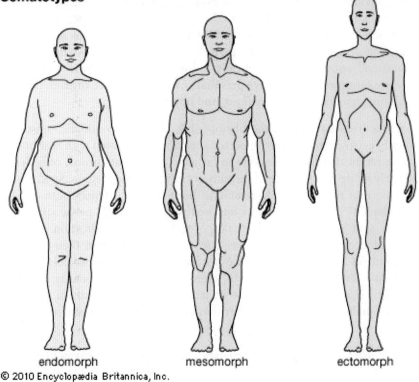

endomorph   mesomorph   ectomorph

© 2010 Encyclopædia Britannica, Inc.

Interestingly, many current and recent politicians were subjects in Sheldon's research. Specifically, most entering freshmen in Ivy League schools, especially Harvard, were asked to pose in the three positions for photos in Sheldon's studies. Many politicians who have been in the news in the past few years were participants in his studies. According to most sources, these subjects were told that posing naked in this way was for their own good (i.e., to check for medical conditions, such as scoliosis), when it was actually for Sheldon and his colleagues' research.[36]

Sheldon tested his theory using poor methodology. Specifically, he based his measures of individuals' body types on what he subjectively observed from three perspectives of each subject. He also had his trained staff view many of the photos and score these individuals in each body type category. Reliability among these scores was weak, meaning that the trained staff did not tend to agree with Sheldon or among themselves on the somatotype of each participant.

This is not surprising given the high level of variation in body types and the fact that Sheldon and his colleagues did not employ the technology used today, such as caliper tests and submersion in water tanks, that provides virtually all the information needed. After all, many readers have probably radically altered their weight and have gone from an ectomorphic or mesomorphic build to a more endomorphic form, or vice versa. Presented with the argument that individuals often alter their body types via diet and exercise, Sheldon's position was that he could tell what the "natural" body type

mesoderm: medical term for the middle layer of tissue in our bodies.

ectoderm: medical term for the outer layer of tissue in our bodies.

endomorphic: type of body shape associated with an emphasis on the inner layer of tissue (endoderm) during development.

mesomorphic: type of body shape associated with an emphasis on the middle layer of tissue (mesoderm) during development.

ectomorphic: type of body shape associated with an emphasis on the outer layer of tissue (ectoderm) during development.

of each individual was from the three pictures taken. This position is not a strong one, further confirmed by the poor interrater reliability shown among his staff. Therefore, Sheldon's methodology is questionable and raises concerns regarding the entire theoretical framework.

Despite the problematic issues of his methodology, Sheldon clearly showed that mesomorphs, or individuals who have muscular builds and tend to take risks, are more delinquent and criminal than are individuals of other body types/temperaments.[37] Furthermore, other researchers, even those who despised Sheldon's theory, found the same associations between mesomorphy and criminality as well as between related temperaments (i.e., somatotonia) and criminality.[38] Specifically, subsequent studies showed that mesomorphic boys were far more likely to have personality traits predictive of criminality, such as aggression, short temper, self-centeredness, and impulsivity.

Even recent theorists have noted the obvious link between an athletic, muscular build and the highly extroverted, aggressive personality often associated with that body type.[39] In fact, some recent theorists have gone so far as to claim that chronic offenders can be identified early in life by the shape of the muscles in their pelvic region. Specifically, these theorists claim that the most likely criminals (both male and female) can be identified by their "v-shaped" pelvic structure as opposed to a "u-shaped" pelvic structure.[40] The v-shaped pelvis, in both males and females, is seen to be an indication of a relatively high level of androgens (male hormones, such as testosterone) in their system, which predisposes individuals to crime. On the other hand, a more u-shaped pelvis is indicative of relatively low levels of androgens and, therefore, a lower propensity for aggression and criminality. Using this logic, it may be true that the more hair on an individual's arms (whether male or female), the higher that person's likelihood of committing crime. However, no research exists to address this particular factor.

Regarding the use of body types/characteristics to explain crime, many of the hard-line sociologists who have attempted to examine or replicate Sheldon's results have not been able to refute the association between mesomorphs and delinquency and criminality or the association between mesomorphy and somatotonic temperament toward risk-taking or aggression.[41] Thus, the association between being muscular or athletically built and engaging in criminal activities is undisputed and assumed to be true. Still, sociologists have taken issue with determinations of what causes this association.

Whereas Sheldon claimed this association was due to inherited traits for a certain body type, sociologists claimed it was due to societal expectations for muscular male youth to engage in risk-taking and aggressive behavior. For example, if a young male has an athletic build, he will be expected to be aggressive and will be encouraged to join sports teams and engage in high-risk behavior. After all, who would be most desirable to gangs? More muscular, athletic individuals are assumed to be better at fighting and other acts that require a certain degree of physical strength and stamina.

Ultimately, it is now established that mesomorphs are more likely to commit crime.[42] Furthermore, the personality traits linked to having an athletic or muscular build are dispositions toward risk-taking and aggressiveness, and few scientists dispute this correlation. No matter which theoretical model is adopted—whether it be that of the biopsychologists or the sociologists—the fact of the matter is that mesomorphs are indeed more likely to be risk-taking and aggressive and, thus, more likely to commit crime than individuals of other body types.

However, whether the explanation is biological or sociological is a question that shows the importance of theory in criminological research. After all, the link between mesomorphy and criminality is undisputed, but the explanation for why this link exists is still up for debate. Is it the biological influence or the sociological influence? The answer is

viscerotonic: the type of temperament or personality associated with an endomorphic (obese) body type; these people tend to be jolly, lazy, and happy-go-lucky.

somatotonic: the type of temperament or personality associated with a mesomorphic (muscular) body type; these people tend to be risk-taking and aggressive.

cerebrotonic: the type of temperament or personality associated with an ectomorphic (thin) body type; these people tend to be introverted and shy.

up to readers, and we hope they will be able to make their own determination—if not now, then later, after we have discussed other theories of crime.

Our position is that the answer is likely both biology *and* social environment, which interact with each other. Thus, it is most likely that both "nature and nurture" are at play in this association between mesomorphy and crime. This would mean both Sheldon and some of his critics were correct. There is often a middle ground to be found in theorizing on criminality, but people don't often see theory as such. It is important to keep in mind that theories in criminology, as a science, are always subject to falsification and criticism and can always be improved. Therefore, our stance on the validity and influence of this theory, as well as others, should not be surprising.

POLICY IMPLICATIONS

A variety of policy implications can be derived from the theories presented in this chapter. First, one could propose more thorough medical screening at birth and in early childhood, especially regarding MPAs such as Javier's in our hypothetical case study. The studies reviewed in this chapter implicate numerous MPAs in developmental problems (mostly originating in the womb). These MPAs are red flags signaling problems, especially in cognitive ability, which are likely to significantly impact criminal behavior.[44]

> ### LEARNING CHECK 5.4
>
> 1. According to the text, which theorist developed the most prominent theory on body types, known as somatotyping?
>   a. Lombroso
>   b. Binet
>   c. Goddard
>   d. Sheldon
>   e. Hirschi
> 2. According to the text, which body type is a muscular/athletic build and the most likely among individuals who tend to be delinquent or criminal?
>   a. Ectomorphic
>   b. Endomorphic
>   c. Mesomorphic
>   d. Klectomorphic
>   e. Candomorphic
> 3. According to the text, which type of personality is correlated with an ectomorphic body type?
>   a. Jolly/happy-go-lucky
>   b. Aggressive/extroverted
>   c. Shy/introverted
>   d. None of the above
>
> Answers located at www.edge.sagepub.com/schram2e

Other policy implications derived from the theories and findings of this chapter involve implementation of same-sex classes to allow for more focus on deficiencies shown to be specific to young boys or girls. For example, numerous school districts now have policies that prescribe same-sex math courses for female students. This same strategy might be considered for male students in English or literature courses, because males are biologically predisposed to have a lower aptitude in this area of study. Furthermore, far more screenings should be done regarding the IQ and aptitude levels of young children to identify which children require extra attention, because studies show that early intervention can make a big difference in improving IQ/aptitude.

A recent summary of the extant literature addressing what types of programs work best for reducing the long-term impact of early physiological risk factors for criminality noted the importance of diagnosing early head trauma and further concluded that the most consistently supported programs for at-risk children are those that involve weekly infant home visitations.[45] Another obvious policy implication derived from biosocial theory is mandatory health insurance for pregnant mothers and children, which is likely the most efficient way to reduce crime in the long term. Finally, all youth should be screened for abnormal levels of hormones, neurotransmitters, and toxins (especially lead).[46] These and other policy strategies are discussed in the last section of the book.

CASE STUDY REVISITED: JAVIER

At the beginning of this chapter, we discussed the case of Javier, who had engaged in more than a dozen burglaries when he was in high school. As you may recall, Javier had numerous MPAs (minor physical anomalies) that became evident as he grew up, such as small, low-seated ears; a relatively large third toe and webbing between all his toes; a curved "pinky" finger; a cleft lip; and narrow-set eyes. All these characteristics are currently used by medical doctors and researchers as "red flags" or predictors of developmental problems that begin in the womb or during delivery. They are also key indicators or predictors of future criminality, especially when more than five are present in one individual.[43] These MPAs, as well as Javier's history of offending, to some extent support the propositions of early positivistic theorists, such as physiognomists and, later, Lombroso, who claimed that physical features predict criminality.

In addition, Javier's low verbal aptitude supports the early "feeble-mindedness" theory researchers, such as Goddard, and even more modern research that implicates verbal/reading comprehension in predicting illegal behavior. In fact, modern studies show that verbal IQ scores have the greatest influence on criminality, which makes sense because we tend to use verbal and communication skills continuously, as opposed to mathematical skills, which are used more sporadically (and which Javier scored high in).

Finally, Javier developed an athletic, muscular physique. According to Sheldon, individuals (especially males) who are more muscular tend to be more likely to engage in criminal behavior. Whether it is due to an inherent aggressive or risk-taking temperament (as Sheldon claimed) or to being associated with or recruited by peers to engage in criminal activity (as more sociologically oriented theorists have claimed), Javier seemed to have both an aggressive personality (as an outstanding linebacker) and deviant peers (from his football team). Thus, Javier's experience seems to fit well with the body type perspective claiming that more muscular/athletic individuals will be more criminal on average.

However, you will also recall that Javier stopped his offending by the time he graduated high school. This defies virtually all the assumptions and propositions of the theories presented in this chapter. Specifically, all the theories assume that whether it be physical traits, IQ aptitude, or body type, individuals cannot change or reform from what they are destined to be. Javier's case study shows that, like many offenders, he actually did change the trajectory of his life and no longer offends. This happens more often than not and is perhaps the most important criticism of these theoretical perspectives. These early theories of the Positive School did not allow much room for the possibility of reform, because if a person has such physical anomalies, low IQ, or a certain body type, he or she is not likely to change much over time. Thus, these early theories do not hold much weight, in the sense that a vast majority of people who offend in their teenage or young adult years actually mature and stop committing crimes.

What are some policy implications that could help reduce the predictive effects of minor physical anomalies (MPAs)?

Why does Javier's growing out of offending pose a very important criticism or limitation of the theories presented in this chapter (e.g., low IQ, body types)?

CONCLUSION

This chapter discussed the early formation of the Positive School of criminology, which was a giant departure from the Classical School paradigm. The Classical School assumes free will/choice in criminal behavior, whereas the Positive School assumes that free will is not involved at all. Rather, according to the Positive School, our behavior is determined by factors other than free will/choice, such as bad parenting, poverty, and low intelligence. We started this chapter by discussing the earliest positive perspectives, which included craniometry, phrenology, and physiognomy. Thus, the early formation of criminology was largely based on examinations of the skull and brain (e.g., craniometry) in the early 1800s. But these disciplines did not become popular then, because Darwin had not yet presented his theory of evolution. The post-Darwinian explanations of the late 19th century, on the other hand, became very popular, largely because society was ready to accept them.

Once Darwin's theory spread worldwide, the ground was more fertile for a theory of crime that claimed that certain individuals (or groups) were more likely to become criminals, which led to a eugenics movement among both scientists and society as a whole. By far the most notable of these theories are Lombroso's (the Father of Criminology) and Goddard's theory of feeble-mindedness and IQ testing. Early policy implications of these perspectives were also examined. These studies ultimately inspired far more focus on the influence of inheritance and genetics in predisposing certain individuals

to criminal activity (which we also cover in the next chapter). This was supported by more recent studies on IQ testing and minor physical anomalies (MPAs) that show that individuals with low IQ scores and numerous MPAs do indeed engage in more criminal behavior than do their counterparts without MPAs.

Also, this chapter examined the connections between various body types, temperaments, and criminality, with recent research supporting a link between certain body types and criminal behavior. To some extent, these body type theories provide a bridge between the early emphasis on physical features (e.g., skull, stigmata, etc.) and the focus on psychological factors (e.g., temperament, personality). Thus, the body type theories appeared to advance the knowledge in criminological literature by emphasizing more than one dimension. Furthermore, most studies have supported the claim that body type actually does predict criminality, as well as the corresponding temperament or personality associated with certain body types most likely found among delinquents and criminals.

However, there are many criticisms of such early Positive School perspectives of crime. The next chapter sheds much more light on how valid these perspectives are, especially in terms of the empirical validity of the idea that biological or physiological factors influence criminality. Readers will likely be surprised by the results of these modern studies.

SUMMARY OF THEORIES IN CHAPTER 5

THEORIES	KEY PROPONENTS	FACTORS/CONCEPTS	KEY PROPOSITIONS
Craniometry	Various	Brain/skull size	Larger skull/brain superior
Phrenology	Various	Bumps on skull	Abnormalities on skull reveal deficiencies
Physiognomy	Various	Facial/bodily attributes	Certain facial or body features reveal inferiority
Atavism/ born criminal	Cesare Lombroso, Father of Criminology	Variety of stigmata identify "born criminals"	Stigmata reveal individuals likely to be born criminals
IQ testing/ feeble-mindedness	Alfred Binet, invented IQ; H. H. Goddard, used in United States	IQ identifies who is superior/ inferior	Low-IQ persons are likely criminals
Body type theories (we focused on the best known)	William Sheldon	Tissue-layer growth in embryonic stage leads to body type	Body type determines personality and behavior

KEY TERMS

atavism, 116

cerebrotonic, 130

craniometry, 113

determinism, 119

ectoderm, 129

ectomorphic, 130

endoderm, 129

endomorphic, 130

eugenics, 111

feeble-mindedness, 123

mesoderm, 129

mesomorphic, 130

minor physical
    anomalies, 122

phrenology, 114

physiognomy, 115

Positive School, 111

somatotonic, 130

somatotyping, 129

stigmata, 117

viscerotonic, 130

DISCUSSION QUESTIONS

1. What characteristics distinguish the Positive School from the Classical School regarding criminal thought? Which of these schools do you lean toward in your own perspective of crime, and why?

2. Name and describe the various positivistic theories that existed in the early to mid-1800s (pre-Darwin), as well as the influence they had on later schools of thought regarding criminality. Do you see any validity in these approaches (because modern medical science does)? Why or why not?

3. What was the significant reason(s) these early positivistic theories did not gain much momentum in societal popularity? Does this lack of popularity relate to the neglect of biological perspectives of crime in modern times?

4. What portion of Lombroso's theory of criminality do you find least valid? Which do you find most valid?

5. Most readers have taken the equivalent of an IQ test (e.g., SAT or ACT). Do you believe that this score is a fair representation of your knowledge as compared with others? Why or why not? Do your feelings reflect the criticisms of experts regarding the use of IQ in identifying potential offenders, such as in the feeble-mindedness theory?

6. In light of the scientific findings that show verbal IQ to be a consistent predictor of criminality among virtually all populations or samples, can you provide evidence from your personal experience for why this occurs?

7. Regarding Sheldon's body type theory, what portion of this theory do you find most valid? What do you find least valid?

8. If you had to give yourself a somatotype (e.g., 3-6-2), what would it be? Explain your choice, and note whether this score would make you a likely criminal in Sheldon's model.

9. Provide a somatotype for five of your family members or best friends. Does each somatotype have any correlation with criminality according to Sheldon's predictions? Describe your findings.

10. Ultimately, do you believe some of the positive theoretical perspectives presented in this section are valid, or do you think they should be entirely dismissed in terms of understanding or predicting crime? State your case.

11. What types of policies would you implement, if you were in charge, given the theories and findings in this chapter?

WEB RESOURCES

Phrenology/Craniometry

This site is an amazing and thorough review of phrenology, from its history to current usage to practical examples (Julius Cesar, Rasputin, etc.):

http://www.phrenology.org/index.html

A brief review of craniometry is presented, with some images:

http://skepdic.com/cranial.html

Cesare Lombroso

A concise, albeit detailed, biography of Lombroso:

http://www.cerebromente.org.br/n01/frenolog/lombroso
.htm

IQ Testing/Feeble-Mindedness

This site provides a review of eugenics and gives details of the use of IQ testing and "feeble-mindedness" in that context:

http://www.eugenicsarchive.org/html/eugenics/static/
themes/9.html

Body Type Theories/Somatotyping

A review providing more details and insight into the methodology of Sheldon's research on body types:

http://www.innerexplorations.com/psytext/shel.htm

A more current, applied approach to viewing different body types in everyday life:

http://www.uh.edu/fitness/comm_educators/3_
somatotypesNEW.htm

STUDENT STUDY SITE

WANT A BETTER GRADE ON YOUR NEXT TEST?

Get the tools you need to sharpen your study skills:

SAGE edge offers a robust online environment featuring an impressive array of tools and resources for review, study, and further exploration, keeping both instructors and students on the cutting edge of teaching and learning. Learn more at **edge.sagepub.com/schram2e**.

FOR FURTHER EXPLORATION AND APPLICATION, VISIT THE STUDENT STUDY SITE:

- Can Software That Predicts Crime Pass Constitutional Muster?
- IQ Isn't Set in Stone, Suggests Study That Finds Big Jumps, Dips in Teens
- Neurobiological determinism: Human freedom of choice and criminal responsibility
- IQ, handedness, and pedophilia in adult male patients stratified by referral source
- Crime and Violence: The Biological Behind Murder
- Cesare Lombroso, Left Handedness, and the Criminal Mind
- Phrenology- Studying the Shape of the Head
- Social Darwinism
- Eugenics
- Sterilization
- Phrenology
- Scientific Racism

PREMIUM VIDEO:

Check out the Interactive eBook for premium videos, including videos from author Stephen Tibbetts, who discusses real-world examples and strange crimes; and videos from former offenders, who share their stories from a first-person view, and touch on key theories and concepts from the chapter.

CHAPTER **6**

Modern Biosocial Perspectives of Criminal Behavior

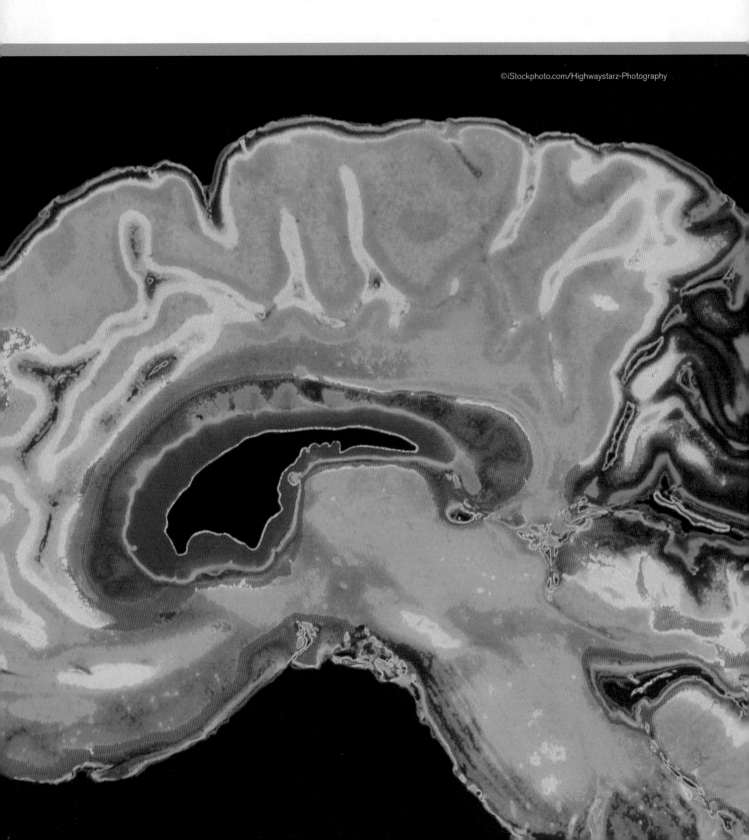

INTRODUCTION

In 1996, a pair of identical twin sisters in Orange County, California, made headlines because, despite their remarkable similarities—both were co-valedictorians of their high school, and both had criminal records for stealing from family and friends—one of the pair conspired to kill the other when they were 22 years old.[1] Sunny and Gina Han, both originally from South Korea, were virtually identical in terms of looks, personality, and criminality. But at a certain point, one wanted the other dead. Gina hatched a plot with two teenage boys to kill her sister. Sunny was tied up, forced to sit in a bathtub, and threatened for a while. Sunny survived, and Gina was later convicted and sentenced to 26 years to life in prison; after that, an appellate court upheld her sentence. During her sentencing hearing, she infamously said through tears, "Sunny is my flesh and blood."[2]

This chapter examines the modern perspectives on the biological aspect of criminality by exploring modern factors and theories of biosocial positivism in the current criminological literature. First, we will go back in time and explore some of the early waves of studies that specifically examined the influence of biology versus environment (i.e., nature vs. nurture), which include studies of identical twins such as the pair in the story above as well as family and adoption studies. We shall see that virtually all these studies support a more integrative approach of genetics/physiology via environment (i.e., nature via nurture). Then we will examine randomly occurring chromosomal mutations as well as discussing which mutations seem most likely to predict criminality among individuals.

Next, we will discuss the influence of various hormones, such as testosterone, and the level and activity of neurotransmitters (e.g., dopamine, serotonin) in how we behave in terms of criminality. Then we will discuss various parts of the brain that are most likely to show a high correlation to criminality when traumatized or otherwise hindered in performance. In relation to brain trauma, we will then explore the extreme importance of the functioning of the central nervous system, in which the brain plays a vital part. We will also review the findings from various studies regarding the autonomic nervous system, which is vital in many aspects of our everyday lives—especially in making decisions related to illegal behavior.

Finally, we will discuss in this chapter the integration of both physiology and environment in what are called interaction effects, which modern studies show have the greatest impact on our behavior, whether in illegal activities or more conventional activities. But before we dive into the actual theories, let's discuss a case study that applies some of the theoretical concepts, propositions, and criticisms presented in this chapter.

NATURE VERSUS NURTURE: STUDIES EXAMINING THE INFLUENCE OF GENETICS AND ENVIRONMENT

In the early 1900s, researchers became highly interested in testing the influence of heredity versus environment to see which of these two components

CASE STUDY

FAITH AND HOPE

Two identical twin girls, Faith and Hope, were born to a poor, teenage, single mother from Chicago's South Side. Their mother smoked and drank heavily throughout the pregnancy—somewhat due to stress and frustration at the father of the babies, who was completely absent (both physically and financially), and also ignorance regarding the damage she was doing to the babies. When the twins were born, they both had relatively low diagnostic scores on breathing, responsiveness, color, and so forth (i.e., Apgar scores). Still, their mother wanted to do her best to raise the twins.

After only a month, their mother realized she could not handle the burden of two babies, so she gave Hope up for adoption. This realization came after she accidently dropped Faith on her head while changing the girls' diapers on a bathroom counter. Hope was adopted relatively quickly by an upper-middle-class family living in the affluent northwest side of Chicago. Their mother readily signed off on this adoption, because she knew Hope was going to a good environment. Faith stayed with her mother and grew up without knowing she had an identical twin.

Faith showed many problems in early development, with low scores and grades in virtually all topics in school. School-mandated medical checkups found that she had a significantly lower heartbeat than most children her age. Furthermore, in middle school—with her mother working two full-time, minimum-wage jobs to support them—Faith ate an unhealthy diet of fast food and gained far more weight than normal for her age. This led to her becoming obese by age 11, at which time she also entered puberty, largely due to high levels of fats and proteins in her system. Faith developed breasts and quickly caught the attention of teenage boys at school. Following her mother's guidance, she avoided these boys' advances until she was in high school. When she was a freshman, a junior asked her to the junior prom, and she was so flattered and infatuated that she had sex with him in his car after the event.

Faith made him wear a condom, but as their relationship continued, she grew less cautious. She was pregnant by the end of her sophomore year. Once he found out, the father of the baby broke off all contact with Faith, so she explored other options to finance the cost of keeping the baby. She realized she would likely have to quit school and find a job because her mother's two minimum-wage jobs were not bringing in enough. Faith began stealing small items from local department stores and selling them online or to people she met. Not only did this not raise enough money, but she was caught by local police and arrested. The charges were dismissed because this was her first offense.

One of Faith's friends told her that she could make more money in one day distributing drugs than in an entire week at a minimum-wage job, so she met with a local gangster and he put her to work. She quickly began making some money, but she also ended up taking some of the methamphetamine they were selling so she could stay awake for the calls from her "boss" and "customers" who came at all times of the night. At one point, she got into an altercation with a customer who tried to take the drugs without paying. Because Faith knew she would have to pay her boss if she didn't get the money for the meth, she hit the customer in the head with a tree branch. The customer then called the police. Faith was arrested and charged with aggravated assault. Once the police interviewed the customer, she dropped the charges because she realized she had much to lose in the eyes of the court. Still, being charged with aggravated assault weighed heavily on Faith, because she never saw herself as a violent person.

> SHE QUICKLY BEGAN MAKING SOME MONEY, BUT SHE ALSO ENDED UP TAKING SOME OF THE METHAMPHETAMINE THEY WERE SELLING SO SHE COULD STAY AWAKE FOR THE CALLS FROM HER "BOSS" AND "CUSTOMERS" THAT CAME AT ALL TIMES OF THE NIGHT.

After a couple of months, Faith realized that her baby was in jeopardy and that she had become addicted to methamphetamine. She aborted the child and then tried to go back to high school through a continuation program. She graduated and is currently living with a relatively steady boyfriend and one child in an apartment in Chicago. We will revisit Faith at the end of this chapter as well as apply various theoretical concepts and propositions to her situation. We will also hear what happened to Hope, her twin sister.

THINK ABOUT IT:

1. How did very early physiological experiences lead to different developmental paths between the two sisters?

2. How did the social environment further compound the effects of such physiological differences between Faith and Hope?

Chapter 6: Modern Biosocial Perspectives of Criminal Behavior **141**

had the strongest effect on predicting criminality in people. This type of testing produced four waves of research: family studies, twin studies, adoption studies, and in recent years, studies of identical twins separated at birth. Each of these waves of research, some more than others, contributed knowledge to our understanding of how much criminality is inherited from our parents (or other ancestors) versus how much is due to cultural norms, such as family, community, and so forth. Ultimately, all have shown that the interaction between these two aspects—genetics and environment—is what causes crime among individuals and groups in society.

Family Studies

The most notable family studies were done in the early 1900s by Richard L. Dugdale, in his work with the Jukes family, and by the previously discussed researcher H. H. Goddard, who studied the Kallikak

The Hatfield clan poses in April 1897 at a logging camp in southern West Virginia. This family clan is part of the most infamous feud in American folklore, the long-running battle between the Hatfields and McCoys. Criminality tends to cluster in certain families, as the first wave of nature-versus nurture-studies showed.

family.[3] These studies were intended to test the proposition that criminality is more likely to be found in certain families, which would indicate that crime is inherited. Due to the similarity of the results from the two studies, we will focus here on Goddard's work with the Kallikak family.

Goddard's study of the Kallikak family showed that a high proportion of children from that family became criminals. Furthermore, Goddard claimed that many of the individuals (often children) from the Kallikak family actually looked like criminals, which fit Cesare Lombroso's theory of stigmata. In fact, Goddard had many members of this family photographed to back up these claims. However, follow-up investigations of Goddard's "research" show that many of these photographs were altered to make the subjects appear more sinister or evil—specifically by altering their facial features, most notably their eyes, to fit Lombroso's stigmata.[4]

Despite the despicable methodological problems with Goddard's data and subsequent conclusions, two important conclusions can be made from the family studies done in the early 1900s. The first is that criminality is indeed more common in some families; in fact, no study has ever shown otherwise. However, this tendency cannot be shown to be a product of heredity or genetics. After all, individuals from the same family are also products of a similar environment (often a bad one), so this conclusion of the family studies does little to advance knowledge regarding the relative influence of nature versus nurture in predicting criminality.

The second conclusion of family studies was more insightful and interesting. Specifically, the family studies showed that criminality in the mother (or head female caretaker) had a much stronger influence on future criminality of the children than did the father's criminality. This is likely due to two factors. The first is that the father is often absent while the children are being raised. But perhaps more important, it takes much more for a woman to transgress social norms and become a convicted offender, which indicates that the mother is highly antisocial and gives some (albeit limited) credence to the argument that criminality is inherited. Despite this conclusion, it should be apparent from the weaknesses in the methodology used in family studies that this finding did not hold much weight in the nature-versus-nurture debate. Thus, a new wave of research soon emerged that did a better job of measuring the influence of genetics versus environment—twin studies.

family studies:
studies that examine the clustering of criminality in a given family.

Members of the extended Kallikak family. Family studies such as Goddard's research on the Kallikak family were among the first attempts to examine the influence of genetics on deviant behavior.

Source: Henry H. Goddard's The Kallikak Family, 1912.

....

twin studies: studies that examine the relative concordance rates for monozygotic versus dizygotic twins.

monozygotic twins: twin pairs that come from a single egg (zygote) and thus share 100% of their genetic makeup.

dizygotic twins: twin pairs that come from two separate eggs (zygotes) and thus share only 50% of the genetic makeup that can vary.

concordance rates: rates at which twin pairs share either a trait (e.g., criminality) or lack of the trait.

Twin Studies

After family studies, the next wave of tests was called twin studies. These studies were specifically meant to determine, through examination of identical twin pairs versus fraternal twin pairs, the relative influence of nature and nurture on criminality. Identical twins are also known as monozygotic twins because they come from a single (hence "mono") egg (or zygote); they are typically referred to in the scientific literature as MZ (monozygotic) twins. Such twins share 100% of their genotype, meaning they are identical in terms of genetic makeup. On the other hand, fraternal twins are typically referred to as dizygotic twins because they come from two (hence "di") separate eggs (or zygotes); they are known in the scientific literature as DZ (dizygotic) twins. DZ twins share 50% of the genes that can vary, which is the same amount that any siblings from the same two parents share. DZ twins can be of different genders and may look and behave quite differently, as many readers have probably observed.

It follows that the goal of the twin studies was to examine concordance rates of delinquency for MZ twin pairs versus DZ twin pairs. Concordance is a count based on whether two people (or a twin pair) share a certain trait (or lack of a certain trait); for our purposes, the trait is criminal offending. Regarding a count of concordance, if one twin is an offender, then we look to see if the other is also an offender. If he or she is, then there is concordance given that the first twin is also a criminal offender. If neither of the twins is an offender, that also is concordant because they both lack the trait. However, if one twin is a criminal offender and the other is not, this is discordant because one has a trait that the other lacks.

Thus, the twin studies focused on comparing the concordance rates of MZ twin pairs with those of DZ twin pairs, with the assumption that any significant difference in concordance could be attributed to the similarity of the genetic makeup of the MZ twins (100%) to that of the DZ twins (50% [of what can vary in humans]). In other words, if genetics play a major role in determining the criminality of individuals, then MZ twins will be expected to have a significantly higher concordance rate for criminal offending than will DZ twins. After all, it is assumed that both the MZ twin pairs and DZ twin pairs compared in these studies were raised in the same relative environments, since they were raised in the same families at the same time.

The studies that have compared the concordance rates of MZ twins versus DZ twins clearly showed that MZ twins were far more similar in the trait of criminality than were DZ twins. Specifically, a number of studies were performed in the early and mid-1900s that examined the concordance rates between MZ and DZ twin pairs. These studies clearly showed that identical twins had far higher concordance rates than did fraternal (DZ) twins, with most studies showing twice as much or more concordance for MZ twins, even for serious criminality.[5]

However, these studies regarding comparisons between the twins were strongly criticized for reasons most readers see on an everyday basis. Specifically, identical twins, who look almost exactly alike, are typically dressed the same by their parents as well as treated the same by the public. In other words, they are not only treated the same by society but are generally expected to behave the same. This can be observed in any large public space, such as the local shopping mall or a theme park. When you see identical twins, they are often dressed the same, treated the same, and expected to act the same. However, this is not true for fraternal twins, who often look very different and quite often are of different genders.

This produced the foundation for criticisms of the twin studies, mainly that the higher rate of concordance among MZ twins could have been due to the extremely similar way they were treated, or were expected to behave, by society. Another criticism of the early twin studies pertained to identification of twins as fraternal or identical, which was often determined by sight in the early tests.[6] Although these criticisms were seemingly valid, the most recent meta-analysis, which examined virtually all the twin studies conducted up to the 1990s, concluded that the twin studies showed evidence of a significant hereditary basis for criminality.[7] Still, the criticisms of such studies were valid, so researchers in the early to mid-1900s involved in the nature-versus-nurture debate attempted to address these criticisms by moving on to another methodological approach for examining this debate—adoption studies.

Twin studies are vital in building an understanding of the influence of genetics on criminal behavior.

Adoption Studies

Due to the valid criticisms leveled at twin studies in determining the relative influence of nature (biology) versus nurture (environment), researchers in this area moved on to adoption studies that examined the predictive influence of the biological parents of adopted children versus that of the adoptive parents who raised the children from infancy to adulthood. It is important to realize that in such studies, the adoptees were typically given up for adoption prior to six months of age, meaning that these children had relatively no interaction with their natural parents; rather, they were raised almost completely from infancy by the adoptive parents.

Although there have been many adoption studies, perhaps the most notable was done by Sarnoff Mednick and his colleagues, who examined male children born in Copenhagen between 1927 and 1941 and adopted early in life.[8] In this study, as well as in other similar analyses, the findings can be considered as a 2-by-2 matrix, containing four cells that represent adoptees in various circumstances in terms of the criminality of their biological and/or adoptive parents (see Table 6.1).

As can be seen from Table 6.1, the primary questions posed in such studies regarding each adoptee are whether the biological parents are criminal (yes or no) and whether the adoptive

LEARNING CHECK 6.1

1. According to the text, family studies showed that the past criminality of which family member was the best predictor of whether or not others in the family would become criminals?

   a. Male siblings

   b. Grandfather

   c. Mother

   d. Father

   e. All of the above

2. According to the text, which type of twins share 50% of their genotype?

   a. MZ twins

   b. DZ twins

   c. XZ twins

   d. ZZ twins

3. According to the text, studies have consistently shown that which type of twins have the highest concordance rates in terms of criminality (as well as virtually all other behaviors and traits)?

   a. MZ twins

   b. DZ twins

   c. XZ twins

   d. ZZ twins

Answers located at www.edge.sagepub.com/schram2e

TABLE **6.1**

"Cross-Fostering" Analysis: Percentage of Adoptive Sons Who Have Been Convicted of Criminal Law Offenses

ARE BIOLOGICAL PARENTS CRIMINAL?	ARE ADOPTIVE PARENTS CRIMINAL?	
	NO	YES
No	13.5% (of 2,492)*	14.7% (of 204)
Yes	20.0% (of 1,226)	24.5% (of 143)

*Note: The numbers in parentheses are the numbers of cases in each cell, for a total sample of 4,065 adopted males.

Sources: Adapted from Mednick, S. A., Gabrielli, W. F., & Hutchings, B. (1984). Genetic influences in criminal convictions: Evidence from an adoption cohort. *Science, 224,* 891–894. Also reported in Wilson, J. Q., & Herrnstein, R. J. (1985). *Crime and human nature.* New York, NY: Simon & Schuster, p. 96.

parents are criminal (yes or no). The final question is what percentage of youths in each of these four cells end up becoming criminal.

This study, as well as virtually all others that have examined adoptees in this light, found that the highest predictability for future criminality by far was for adopted youths whose biological parents and adoptive parents were *both* convicted criminals. On the other hand, the adopted children for whom *neither* set of parents was criminal were the least likely to become criminal. Although these results should be the highlight for the studies, the researchers did not portray the results in these terms. Readers should realize that these findings support the major contentions of the authors of this textbook, because they fully back up the "nature-via-nurture" argument as opposed to the "nature-versus-nurture" argument; they support the idea that both biological *and* environmental factors contribute to the future criminality of youth.

adoption studies:
studies that examine the criminality of adoptees as compared with the criminality of their biological and adoptive parents.

selective placement:
the argument that adoptees tend to be placed in households that resemble those of their biological parents; for example, adoptees from rich biological parents are placed in rich adoptive households.

Unfortunately, the researchers who performed these studies focused on the other two groups (or cells) of youth—namely, only those who had either criminal biological parents or criminal adoptive parents. As can be seen in Table 6.1, the adoption studies found that the adoptees who had only criminal biological parents had a much higher likelihood of becoming criminal compared with the youths who had only criminal adoptive parents. In other words, when the influence of biological versus adoptive parents was compared, the biological parents had far more influence on the youth's future criminality. This was used to support the genetic influence in predisposing one toward criminality; however, this methodology was subject to criticism.

Perhaps the most notable criticism of adoption studies was that adoption agencies typically incorporated a policy of selective placement. Selective placement is when adoptees are placed with adoptive families similar to their biological parents in terms of demographics and background. Such selective placement of adoptees could bias the results of the adoption studies. However, recent analyses that have examined the impact of such bias have concluded that even when accounting for the influence of selective placement, the ultimate findings of the adoption studies are still somewhat valid.[9] Specifically, the biological parents of adopted children likely have more influence on the children than do the adoptive parents who raise the child from infancy to adulthood. Still, the criticism of selective placement was strong enough to encourage a fourth wave of research in the nature-versus-nurture debate—studies on identical twins separated at birth.

Twins Separated at Birth

The fourth, and final, wave of research that examined the relative influence of biological and environmental influences on individuals' criminality was twins separated at birth studies. Until recently, studies of identical twins separated at birth were virtually impossible because it was so difficult to find enough identical twins separated early in life. But since the early 1990s, such examinations have been possible. Readers should keep in mind that for many of the identical twin pairs studied in these investigations, the individuals did not know they had a twin. Furthermore, the environments in which they were raised were often extremely different, such as one twin being raised by a poor family in an urban environment while the other twin was raised by a middle- to upper-class family in a rural environment.

Some of the most advanced twin studies examine identical twins who were separated as infants, grew up in different environments, and yet often ended up sharing many personality traits and behavior patterns.

The studies on identical twins separated at birth—the most notable of these conducted at the University of Minnesota—found that the twin pairs often showed extremely similar tendencies for criminality, sometimes more than those seen in concordance rates for identical twins raised together.[10] This finding supported the profound influence of genetics and heredity, which is not surprising to most well-read scientists who now acknowledge the extreme importance of the inheritance of physiological and psychological aspects of human behavior. Perhaps more surprising was why separated identical twins who never knew they had a twin, and who were often raised in extremely different circumstances, had just as similar or even more similar concordance rates than did identical twins raised together.

The leading theory for this phenomenon is that identical twins who are raised together go out of their way to deviate from their natural tendencies in an effort to form their own identity separate from that of their identical twin, with whom they have spent their entire life. No significant criticism of this methodology has been presented. Thus, at this point, it is somewhat undisputed in the scientific literature that the studies of identical twins separated at birth have shown that genetics has a significant impact on human behavior, especially regarding criminal activity.

Ultimately, taking all the nature-versus-nurture methodological approaches and subsequent findings together, the best conclusion that can be made is that genetics and heredity both have a significant impact on criminality. After all, environment simply cannot account for all the consistent results from comparisons of identical twins and fraternal twins, nor for those of identical twins separated at birth, nor for those of adoptees with criminal biological parents versus those with noncriminal biological parents. Despite the taboo nature of and controversial response to the findings of such studies, it is quite clear that when nature and nurture are compared, biological factors, rather than environmental factors, tend to have the most influence on the criminality of individuals. Still, the authors of this book hope that readers will emphasize the importance of the interaction between nature and nurture (better stated as nature *via* nurture). After all, we hope that

twins separated at birth studies: studies that examine the similarities between identical twins who were separated in infancy.

LEARNING CHECK 6.2

1. According to the text, numerous adoption studies have shown which category of adoptees to have the highest likelihood of becoming criminals, based on the criminality of their biological and adoptive parents?

   a. Biological parents criminal/adoptive parents criminal

   b. Biological parents NOT criminal/adoptive parents criminal

   c. Biological parents criminal/adoptive parents NOT criminal

   d. NEITHER biological nor adoptive parents criminal

2. According to the text, numerous adoption studies have shown which of the following two categories of adoptees to have the highest likelihood of becoming criminals?

   a. Biological parents NOT criminal/adoptive parents criminal

   b. Biological parents criminal/adoptive parents NOT criminal

   c. Both categories have about the same rates of adoptees becoming criminals

3. According to the text, many studies have shown that identical twins separated at birth have far lower concordance rates in terms of criminality than do identical twins raised together. True or false?

Answers located at www.edge.sagepub.com/schram2e

we have shown quite convincingly through scientific study that the interplay between biology and the environment is what is most important in determining human behavior.

Perhaps in response to this nature-versus-nurture debate, a variety of new theoretical perspectives were offered in the mid- to late 1900s that merged biological and psychological factors in explaining criminality. Although leaning more toward the "nature" side of the debate, critics would use this same perspective to promote the "nurture" side; thus, this framework was useful in promoting the interaction between biological and sociological factors. One of the first of the various biosocial factors that will be examined is mutations of chromosomes (called cytogenetic abnormalities), which interact with environmental factors to increase the likelihood of criminality.

CYTOGENETIC STUDIES: THE XYY FACTOR

Beyond the body type theories, in the early 1900s another theory was proposed regarding biological conditions that predispose individuals toward crime: cytogenetic studies. Cytogenetic studies of crime focus on the genetic makeup of individuals, with a specific focus on abnormalities in their chromosomal makeup. Specifically, chromosomal abnormalities that occur randomly in the population are the primary focus of these types of studies. Many of the chromosomal mutations that have been studied (such as XYY) are typically not hereditary but rather largely due to random mutations in chromosomal formation.

First, we should begin with the basics of chromosomal makeup, which is probably a review for most readers but may be necessary for some. The normal chromosomal makeup for women is XX, which represents an X from the mother and an X from the father. The normal chromosomal makeup for men is XY, which represents an X from the mother and a Y from the father. However, as in many species of animals, genetic mutations often occur in human beings. Consistent with evolutionary theory, virtually all possible variations of chromosomes have been found in the human population, such as XXY, XYY, and many others. We will focus our discussion on the chromosomal mutations that have been most strongly linked to criminality.

One of the first chromosomal mutations recognized as a predictor of criminal activity was that of XYY. In 1965, Patricia A. Jacobs and her colleagues presented the first major study showing that this mutation was far more common in a Scottish male population of mental patients than in the general population.[11] Specifically, in the general population, XYY occurs in about 1 of every 1,000 males.

The first major study that examined the influence of XYY sampled about 200 men in the mental hospital, which would have predicted (assuming general population occurrences)

cytogenetic studies: studies of crime that focus on the genetic makeups of individuals, with a specific focus on abnormalities in chromosomal makeups.

about 1 occurrence. However, the study found 13 individuals who were XYY, which suggested that individuals who have mental disorders are more likely to have XYY chromosomes than those who do not have mental disorders. In other words, males who have XYY are at least 13 times (or 1,300%) as likely to have behavioral disorders as are those without this chromosomal abnormality. Subsequent studies examining this association have not been able to dismiss the effect of XYY on criminality but have concluded that this mutation is more linked with property crime than with violent crime.[12]

However, even knowing this relationship, can this help in policies regarding crime? Probably not, considering that 90% of the male mental patients in the study discussed above were not XYY. Still, this study showed the importance of looking at chromosomal mutations as a predictor of criminal behavior.

Such mutations include numerous chromosomal abnormalities, such as the following:

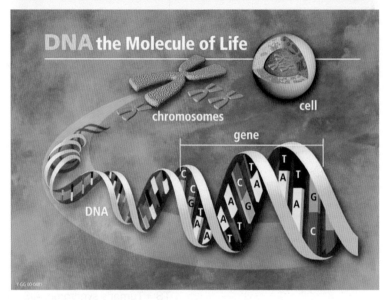

FIGURE 6.1

The Structure of DNA

Studies consistently show that our genetics play an important role in how we think and behave.

Source: U.S. Department of Energy, Office of Science. (2016). *Biological and Environmental Research (BER)*. Retrieved from science.energy.gov/ber/

- XYY—A male is given an extra Y chromosome, which makes him more "male-like." These individuals are often very tall but slow in terms of social and intelligence skills.

- XXY—Otherwise known as Klinefelter's syndrome, this mutation results in a higher likelihood for homosexuality and other behaviors but is not typically linked to criminality.

- XXX—Otherwise known as triple X syndrome, this mutation is a form of chromosomal variation characterized by the presence of an extra X chromosome. The condition occurs only in females. Females with triple X syndrome have three X chromosomes instead of two, and this occurs about once in every 1,000 female births. Unlike most other chromosomal mutation conditions, there is typically no distinguishable difference between women with triple X syndrome and the rest of the female population. This mutation has not been consistently linked with criminality.

- XO—Commonly referred to as Turner's syndrome, this is a mutation in which females are missing an entire sex chromosome. This is typically accompanied by physical mutations (such as a webbed neck) but has not been consistently linked with criminal behavior.

One study examined the relative criminality and deviance of a group of individuals in each of these groups of chromosomal mutations (see Figure 6.2).[13] This study found that the more the chromosomal mutation produced male hormones (androgens), the more likely the individuals were to commit crimes and deviant acts. On the other hand, the more the chromosomal mutation produced feminine hormones, the less likely the individuals were to commit criminal acts. Ultimately, all these variations in chromosomes

FIGURE **6.2**

Hypothetical Scattergram Relating Masculinity/Androgen Level (Designated by Karyotype) to Deviance

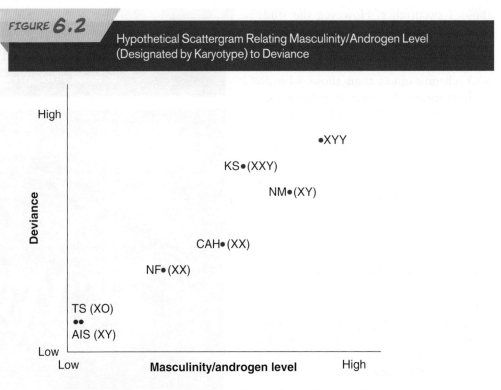

TS = Turner's syndrome. AIS = Androgen insensitivity syndrome.
NF = Normal female. KS = Klinefelter's syndrome. CAH = Congenital
adrenal hyperplasia. NM = Normal male. XYY = Jacob's (supermale) syndrome.

Source: Tibbetts, S., & Hemmens, C. (2010). *Criminological theory: text/reader.* Thousand Oaks, CA: SAGE, p. 254.

show that there is a continuum of degrees of "femaleness" and "maleness" and that the more male-like the individual is in terms of chromosomes, the more likely he or she will be to engage in criminal behavior.

Ultimately, the cytogenetic studies showed that somewhat random abnormalities in an individual's genetic makeup can profoundly influence that person's level of criminality. Whether or not this can or should be used in policy related to crime is another matter, but the point is that genetics do indeed contribute to dispositions toward criminality. Furthermore, most of the associations seen in these chromosomal mutations directly address the influence of increased male hormones or androgens, which predict a high level of criminal traits. This leads to the next section, which discusses the effects of hormones on behavior.

HORMONES AND NEUROTRANSMITTERS: CHEMICALS THAT DETERMINE CRIMINAL BEHAVIOR

Various chemicals in the brain and the body determine how we think, perceive, and react to a range of stimuli. Hormones, such as testosterone and estrogen, carry chemical signals to the body as they are released from certain glands and structures. Some studies have shown that a relative excess of testosterone in the body is consistently linked to criminal

Applying Theory to Crime: AGGRAVATED ASSAULT

Assault, especially aggravated assault, is a serious crime in terms of FBI/Uniform Crime Reports (UCR) standards and is categorized as an Index crime. After all, an aggravated assault is typically considered an unsuccessful murder, in the sense that it usually involves an inherent intent to do serious harm, such as use of a weapon or infliction of major bodily injury. This leads us to the FBI/UCR definition of aggravated assault as being "the unlawful attack by one person upon another for the purpose of inflicting severe or aggravated bodily injury on another."

According to recent reports by the FBI, aggravated assaults range from approximately 725,000 to 760,000 each year. The National Crime Victimization Survey reported between 850,000 and over 1,000,000 in recent years, but that is consistent with differences in methodology and accounts for the "dark figure of crime," as discussed in previous chapters. Reports of such assaults were highest in urban areas, which is not surprising since that is where homicide rates are highest. Some reviews have noted that aggravated assault occurs most often during the summer months, when people (including offenders) are more likely to be out and about.

One significant difference between most aggravated assaults and homicides is that the largest proportion of the former includes blunt objects, such as baseball bats, sticks, and so forth, as opposed to firearms, which is probably why the victims of aggravated assault do not die in the attack. Like most other Index crimes, assault rates have dramatically decreased over the past two decades. Although most of the time there is a living victim, the clearance rate of aggravated assault is close to or less than 50% for most years. This is likely due to victims not wanting to contribute to the investigation, because usually their attacker is a family member, good friend, or other associate. Also, the attacker may be a gang member or person in the community from whom the victim fears retaliation. Regardless of the reasons, aggravated assault is not typically reported when it happens, and even when it is, the offender is typically not formally prosecuted.

Relating back to our case study at the beginning of this chapter, Faith was charged with aggravated assault because she used a weapon—a tree branch she picked up off the street—to hit a drug "customer." Although it wasn't premeditated, the use of this weapon seemed to exhibit an intent to inflict bodily harm, so it does fit the definition of aggravated assault. That is why Faith was charged with this crime. Still, intent is subjective, so if this case went to trial—which it did not—a jury would have to decide if such severe bodily harm was intended, if Faith was simply trying to retrieve her money or drugs, or if she was acting in self-defense.

THINK ABOUT IT:

1. Do the recent national data indicate that aggravated assaults have increased or decreased over the past 20 years?

2. Given the FBI definition of aggravated assaults, do you think a jury would have found Faith guilty of this crime?

Source: FBI. (2015). *Crime in the United States, 2014.* Washington, DC: U.S. Department of Justice.

---

or aggressive behavior, with most studies showing a moderate relationship.[14] This relationship is seen even in the early years of life.[15] On the other side of the coin, studies have also shown that hormonal changes in females can cause criminal behavior. Specifically, studies have shown that a high proportion of the women in prison for violent crimes committed those crimes during their premenstrual cycle, at which time women experience a high level of hormones that make them more "male-like" due to relatively low levels of estrogen compared with progesterone.[16]

If anyone doubts the impact of hormones on behavior, they should examine the scientific literature regarding performance on intelligence tests taken at different times of day. Virtually all individuals perform better on spatial and mathematical tests early in the day, when they have relatively high levels of testosterone and other male hormones in their bodies. On the other hand, virtually all individuals perform better on verbal tasks in the afternoon or evening, when they have relatively high levels of estrogen or other female hormones in their systems.[17] Furthermore, studies have shown that individuals given shots of androgens (male hormones) before math tests tend to do significantly

Comparative Criminology: ASSAULT

Ranking Regions/Countries in Terms of Prevalence of Assault

In this section, we will examine the findings and conclusions of various studies regarding assault, which is defined by the International Crime Victimization Survey (ICVS) as personal attacks or serious threats without the purpose of stealing (Van Dijk, 2008, p. 78). The findings of recent studies regarding the prevalence of assault across various regions and countries of the world are enlightening in several ways.

The key measure of prevalence of assault in the world is the ICVS, a data bank that collects and standardizes police reports from more than 70 countries around the world. This measure has been conducted since 1987. It does have some weaknesses, but it is currently the best international measure of crime for such cross-national comparisons.

The ICVS has collected many years' worth of data on assault. Van Dijk (2008) synthesized the data from the ICVS regarding assault from the years 1996 to 2005. As seen in Figure 6.3, the countries with by far the highest percentages of persons victimized by assaults were those in Africa. Tied in

a distant second and third were, respectively, countries in North America and Oceania (the islands near Southeast Asia and Australia).

It is not too surprising that assault tends to be more common in some of the most deprived nations in the world, such as Africa, given the studies that have linked poverty to violence. In such extreme poverty, many individuals appear to be frustrated and take out their stress on others. After all, similar results are seen for homicide rates across countries, with Southern Africa having by far the highest rates (see Chapter 9). However, the results from the ICVS reveal that assault happens frequently in all portions of the world, so assault is somewhat prevalent in virtually all societies, especially in inner-city, poor areas.

THINK ABOUT IT:

1. Why do you think African nations have the highest rates of assault compared to other regions of the world?

2. What types of policies do you think could be used to reduce high rates of assault in countries that have such a significant problem with this type of offense?

Source: Van Dijk, J. (2008). The world of crime. Thousand Oaks, CA: Sage.

FIGURE 6.3   Percentages of the Public Victimized by Assaults in Urban Areas, by World Region

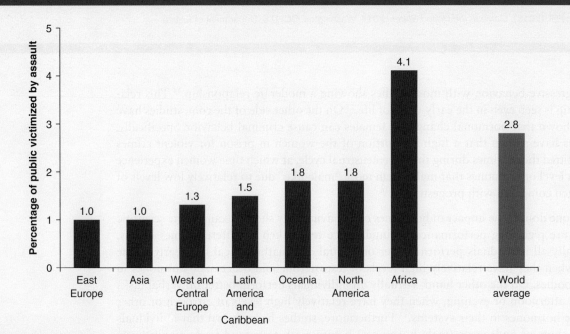

Source: International Crime Victimization Survey (ICVS), 1996–2005.

better on spatial and mathematics tests than they would otherwise. Studies show the same is true for persons given shots of female hormones prior to verbal/reading tests.

It is important to realize that this process of differential levels of hormones begins very early in life, specifically in about the fifth week after conception. It is at that time that the Y chromosome of the male tells the developing fetus that it is a male and to stimulate production of higher levels of testosterone. So even during the first few months of gestation, the genes on the Y chromosome significantly alter the course of genital, and thus hormonal, development.[18]

Not only does this level of testosterone alter the genitals of the fetus/embryo through gestation, but the changes in the genital area later produce profound increases in testosterone in the teenage and early adult years. This produces not only physical differences but also huge personality and behavioral alterations.[19] High levels of testosterone and other androgens tend to "masculinize" the brain toward risk-taking behavior, while lower levels typically found in females tend to result in the default feminine model.[20] These high levels of testosterone result in numerous consequences, such as lowered sensitivity to pain, enhanced seeking of sensory stimulation, and a right-hemisphere shift of dominance in the brain, which has been linked to higher levels of spatial aptitude but lower levels of verbal reasoning and empathy. This has profound implications for criminal activity and has been found to be more likely in males than females.[21]

FIGURE 6.4

The Role of Neurons

Neurons are the basic cell in the functioning of our nervous system, and studies have shown that levels of neurotransmitters (the chemicals that transfer the electric message across neural paths) are consistently linked to criminal behavior.

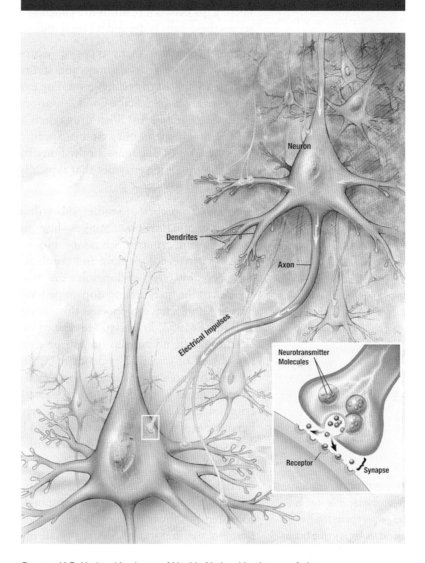

Source: U.S. National Institutes of Health, National Institute on Aging.

Ultimately, hormones have a profound effect on how individuals think and perceive their environment. It should be apparent that all criminal behavior, whether it is something we do or don't do, comes down to cognitive decisions in our 3-pound brain. So it should not be surprising that hormones play a highly active role in this decision-making process. Although hormones are a key part of the criminal process, they probably are secondary in terms of levels of neurotransmitters, which we will now discuss.

Neurotransmitters are chemicals in the brain and body that help transmit electric signals from one neuron to another. They can be distinguished from hormones in the sense that

neurotransmitters: nervous system chemicals in the brain and body that help transmit electric signals from one neuron to another.

hormones carry a signal that is not electric, whereas the signals neurotransmitters carry are indeed electric. Specifically, neurotransmitters are chemicals released when a neuron, which is the basic unit of our nervous system, wants to send an electric message to a neighboring neuron(s) (see Figure 6.4). When a message is sent from somewhere in the brain or body, it requires that the neural pathways be told of this message, which inherently necessitates that neurotransmitters be activated in processing the signal. Specifically, in immediate time, this requires that healthy levels of various neurotransmitters be allowed to pass messages from one neuron to the next across gaps between neurons. These gaps between neurons are called synapses, and the passing of the electric message across these gaps is dependent on a multitude of neurotransmitters.

Although there are many types of neurotransmitters, the most studied in relation to criminal activity are dopamine and serotonin. Dopamine is the neurotransmitter most commonly linked to feeling good. For example, dopamine is the chemical that tells us when we are experiencing good sensations, such as delicious food, sex, and other pleasurable activities. Most illicit drugs elicit a pleasurable sensation through enhancing the level of dopamine in our systems. Specifically, cocaine and methamphetamine work to raise the level of dopamine in the body by telling the body to produce more dopamine or by inhibiting the enzymes that typically "mop up" the dopamine in our system after it is used.

Although a number of studies show that low levels of dopamine are linked to high rates of criminality, other studies show no association or even a positive link between dopamine and criminal behavior.[22] However, it is likely that there is a curvilinear relationship between dopamine and criminal behavior, such that both extremely high and extremely low levels of dopamine are associated with deviance. Two of the most recent reviews of the literature on dopamine levels, by Wright, Tibbetts, and Daigle (2008) and Beaver (2008), have supported this curvilinear effect, as well as previous reviews such as Raine's (1993) archetypal review of the biological research up to the early 1990s.[23] Unfortunately, no conclusion can be drawn at this point about dopamine levels due to the lack of scientific evidence regarding this chemical. However, there have been a number of more recent studies by Kevin Beaver and his colleagues regarding various receptor genes of the dopaminergic system that have been shown to be associated with criminological behaviors, especially given certain alleles on an individual's genotype.[24] Furthermore, such studies by Beaver and his colleagues have shown how receptor genes of the dopaminergic system interact with environmental factors, thus creating a biosocial effect.[25]

On the other hand, a clear conclusion can be reached about the other major neurotransmitter that has been implicated in criminal offending: serotonin. Specifically, studies have consistently shown that low levels of serotonin are linked with criminal offending.[26] Serotonin is important in virtually all information processing, whether it be learning, emotional processing, and the like; thus, it is vital in most aspects of interactions with the environment. Those who have low levels of serotonin are likely to have problems in everyday communication and life in general. Therefore, it is not surprising that low levels of serotonin are strongly linked to criminal activity.

BRAIN INJURIES

Another area of physiological problems associated with criminal activity is that of trauma to the brain. As mentioned before, the brain is responsible for virtually every criminal act an individual commits, so any problems related to this structure have profound implications regarding behavior, especially deviance and criminal activity.

dopamine: a neurotransmitter that is largely responsible for good feelings in the brain; it is increased by many illicit drugs (e.g., cocaine).

serotonin: a neurotransmitter that is key in information processing and most consistently linked to criminal behavior in its deficiency; low levels are linked to depression and other mental illnesses.

Studies have consistently shown that damage to any part of the brain increases the risk of crime in the future. However, trauma to certain portions of the brain tends to have more serious consequences than trauma to other portions. Specifically, damage to the frontal lobe or temporal lobe (particularly on the left side) appears to have the most consistent associations with criminal offending.[27] These findings make sense, primarily because the frontal lobe (which includes the prefrontal cortex) is the area of the brain largely responsible for higher-level problem-solving and "executive" functioning.[28] Thus, the frontal lobe, and especially the left side of the frontal lobe, is the area that processes what we are thinking and is in charge of inhibiting us from doing what we are emotionally charged to do. After all, most of us have desires and emotional responses, but our (pre)frontal lobe, located just behind the forehead, inhibits us from acting on many of our natural instincts. Thus, any moral reasoning is reliant on this executive area of the brain because it is the region that considers long-term consequences of behavior.[29] Therefore, if there is damage to the frontal lobe, we will be far more inclined to act on our emotional urges without any logical inhibitions.

In a similar vein, the temporal lobe regions are highly related to the memory and emotional structures of the brain. To clarify, the temporal lobe covers and communicates almost directly with certain structures of the brain's limbic system. Certain limbic structures largely govern our memories (hippocampus) and emotions (amygdala). Any damage to the temporal lobe, which is generally located above the ear, is likely to damage these structures or the effective communication of these structures with other portions of the brain. Therefore, it is understandable why trauma to the temporal region of the brain is linked to future criminality.

Recent studies of brain structure and activity—using the latest, most sophisticated brain-scanning techniques (the most current form of functional MRI)—have investigated the brain as it makes moral choices.[30] These studies have shown that certain regions of the brain tend to be more active in making moral decisions (e.g., the medial frontal gyrus, an area related to the emotional portion/system of the brain) versus more rational, calculated decisions (e.g., the prefrontal cortex, the decision-making portion of the brain). Of course, it depends on the situation, but when it comes to crime, it is likely that both portions of the brain play a part. The criminal acts an individual finds morally offensive will likely be governed by the emotional centers of the brain, such as the medial frontal gyrus, whereas the crimes he or she finds less morally offensive will be governed by the higher-level, rational parts of the brain, such as the prefrontal cortex. It is likely that the latter instance is more about whether the individual can get

LEARNING CHECK 6.3

1. According to the text, which type of cytogenetic mutation has been most linked to criminality?

   a. XXY

   b. XXX

   c. XYY

   d. XX

2. According to the text, which type of neurotransmitter, when at low levels, has been consistently linked by virtually all studies to criminality?

   a. Norepinephrine

   b. GABA

   c. Serotonin

   d. Dopamine

   e. None of the above

3. According to the text, which type of neurotransmitter is likely to have a curvilinear effect on criminality, meaning that both very high and very low levels have been linked to deviant, antisocial behavior?

   a. Norepinephrine

   b. GABA

   c. Serotonin

   d. Dopamine

Answers located at www.edge.sagepub.com/schram2e

frontal lobe: the frontal region of the brain; most of the executive functions of the brain, such as problem solving, take place here.

temporal lobe: a region of the brain (on either side of the head) responsible for a variety of functions and located right above many primary limbic structures that govern our emotional and memory functions.

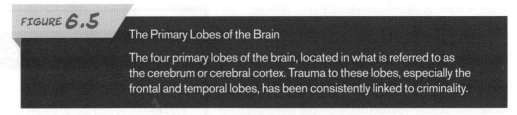

FIGURE **6.5**

The Primary Lobes of the Brain

The four primary lobes of the brain, located in what is referred to as the cerebrum or cerebral cortex. Trauma to these lobes, especially the frontal and temporal lobes, has been consistently linked to criminality.

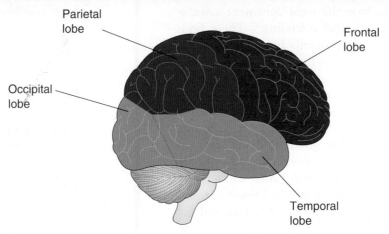

Parietal lobe

Frontal lobe

Occipital lobe

Temporal lobe

Source: U.S. National Library of Medicine, National Institutes of Health.

© AP Photo/M. SPENCER GREEN

Slices of brain from the autopsy of John Wayne Gacy, a serial killer who murdered at least 33 teenage boys and young men.

away with the act, whereas the former is so deeply based in a personal moral code that the person likely wouldn't commit the act even if he or she knew there was no chance of getting caught.[31] This is highly consistent with studies showing that moral beliefs typically trump any perceptions of getting caught for a given crime, no matter what the benefits or payout.[32] These types of brain activities, or lack thereof, are key in the next section we will discuss.

CENTRAL AND AUTONOMIC NERVOUS SYSTEM ACTIVITY

As has been mentioned in this chapter, the 3-pound mass that makes up our brain largely governs our decisions regarding whether to engage in criminal behavior. The brain is a key player in two different types of neurological systems that have been linked to criminal activity. The first we will discuss is the central nervous system, which encompasses our brain and spinal column and governs our voluntary motor activities.

The **central nervous system** (CNS) consists mostly of the brain and spinal column, which are largely responsible for what we as individuals choose to do, meaning our voluntary activities (see Figure 6.6). For example, that you are actually reading this sentence means you are in control of this brain-processing activity. Empirical studies of the influence of CNS functioning on criminality have traditionally focused on brain wave patterns, with most using electroencephalograms (EEGs). Although EEGs do not do a good job of describing which areas of the brain are active or inactive, they do reveal how much the brain as an entire organ is performing at certain times.

WHY DO THEY DO IT?

CHARLES WHITMAN

©iStockphoto.com/Gregg Mack

Charles Whitman's shooting spree is legendary and notorious for many reasons. He killed 15 people and injured 28 others from a landmark university tower at the University of Texas–Austin (the UT flagship campus). But what is almost more fascinating is his life story up until that fateful day.

Whitman was, by most accounts, a great person and a good soldier. He was one of the youngest Eagle Scouts ever to earn the honor. He graduated near the top of his class in high school and then went on to become a stellar member of the U.S. Marine Corps, earning the rating of sharpshooter. He used this skill when he went on his shooting rampage on August 1, 1966. It should be noted that the day before, he killed his wife and mother and left some letters (which will come up later). Then he planned out his attack on the university for the following day.

The day after Whitman killed his wife and mother, he proceeded to the main tower at UT–Austin, killed the receptionist, ascended the tower, and waited for classes to break; he then opened fire on the crowd of students. It is notable that he had taken with him a variety of materials that imply he was in it for the long haul. These items included toilet paper, spray deodorant, water canteens, gasoline, rope, and binoculars as well as a variety of weapons, such as a machete, a hatchet, a .357 Magnum revolver, a 12-gauge sawed-off shotgun, two rifles (one with a telescopic sight), 700 rounds of ammunition, and other weapons.

Whitman was shooting people on the run and in places only a trained sharpshooter could hit. He shot a pregnant woman, who later gave birth to a stillborn baby. He also shot a person crossing a street 500 yards away. This is the type of shot glorified in *Full Metal Jacket*, a Stanley Kubrick film that examined the Marine boot camps of the late 1960s. There is no doubt that Whitman was an expert sharpshooter and that the Marine Corps trained him well. Unfortunately, in this case his training was used against innocent targets. Whitman continued his mass killing for a couple of hours until several police officers were able to find a way through ground tunnels and then up to the top of the tower, where they shot and killed Whitman.

But why did he do it? The best guess we have, which directly relates to this chapter, began with one of his last letters. He wrote, "After my death, I wish an autopsy on me to be performed to see if there is any mental disorder." An autopsy was performed, and as Whitman sort of predicted, he did not simply have a mental disorder but a large brain tumor (about the size of a golf ball). As we examine how vulnerable our brain functioning can be to trauma, imagine the likely effects of a large tumor on thinking and processing skills.

THINK ABOUT IT:

1. Do you believe Whitman was insane? Give your reasons why you believe so or not.

2. Given how much planning went into his attack, how much of an effect do you believe his tumor had on him at the time of the attack?

Sources: Holmes, R. M., & Holmes, S. T. (2000). *Mass murders in the United States.* Upper Saddle River, NJ: Prentice Hall; Smith, J. D. (2003). *100 most infamous criminals.* New York, NY: MetroBooks.

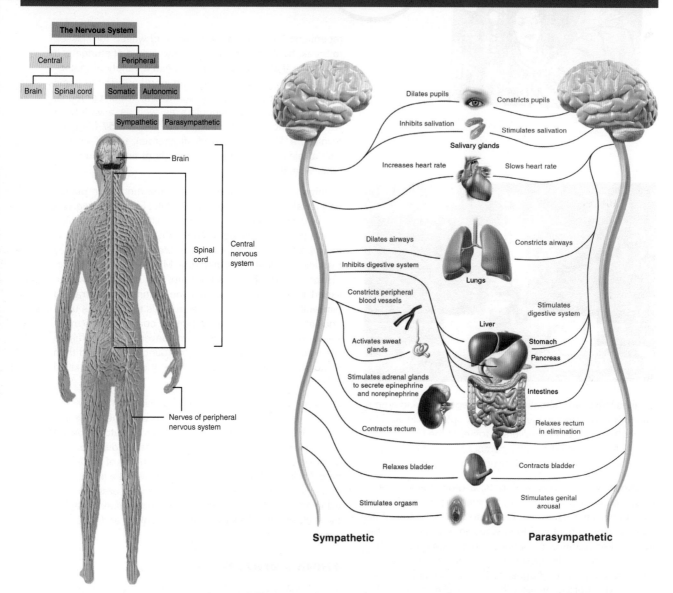

FIGURE **6.6**

Contrast Between the Central Nervous System (Primarily Brain and Spinal Cord, Voluntary Motor Activities) and the Autonomic Nervous System (Fight-or-Flight Responses, Involuntary Motor Activities)

central nervous system: the portion of the nervous system that largely consists of the brain and spinal column and is responsible for our voluntary motor activities.

Specifically, studies have emphasized comparing brain wave patterns of known chronic offenders (i.e., psychopaths, repeat violent offenders) with those of "normal" persons (i.e., those who have never been charged with a crime).[33] These studies consistently show that the brain wave patterns of chronic offenders are abnormal compared with the normal population, with most studies showing slower brain wave patterns in psychopaths compared with normals.[34] Specifically, there are four types of brain wave patterns found in individuals. From slowest to fastest, they are delta, theta, alpha, and beta.[35] Delta waves are often seen when people sleep, whereas theta waves are typically observed in times of lower levels of wakefulness, such as drowsiness. Relatively, alpha waves (which tend to be divided into "slow alpha" and "fast alpha" wave patterns, as are beta waves) tend to be related to more relaxed wakefulness, and beta waves are observed with high levels of wakefulness, such as in times of extreme alertness and particularly in times of excited activity.

The studies that have compared brain wave patterns among chronic offenders and "normals" have shown significant differences. Psychopaths tend to have more activity in the theta (or sometimes "slow alpha") patterns, whereas normals tend to show more activity in the "fast alpha" or beta types of waves. These consistent findings reveal that the cortical arousal of chronic offenders tends to be significantly slower than that of persons who do not typically commit crimes. Thus, it is likely that chronic offenders generally do not have the mental functioning that would dispose them toward making accurate assessments about the consequences of criminal behavior. For a recent review of various forms of brain trauma, as well as the effects of such trauma on the functioning of the CNS, see Boots,[36] who concluded that regarding traumatic brain injury (TBI), "there is compelling evidence of a connection between TBI, antisocial behaviors, and mental health disorders that has been produced over the past two decades."[37] Consistent with these relatively low levels of cortical activity in the CNS are the findings of studies examining the autonomic nervous system.

The second area of the nervous system that involves the brain and has been most linked to criminal behavior is the autonomic nervous system (ANS), which is primarily responsible for involuntary motor activities, such as heart rate, dilation of pupils, electric conductivity in the skin, and so forth (see Figure 6.6). This is the type of physiological activity that can be measured by a polygraph machine, or lie detector test. Polygraph measures capitalize on the inability of individuals to control these physiological responses to anxiety, which occur in most normal persons when they lie, especially regarding illegal behavior. However, such measures are not infallible, because the individuals who are most at risk of being serious, violent offenders are also the most likely to pass such tests even when they are lying (this will be further discussed below).

Consistent with the findings regarding CNS arousal levels, studies have consistently shown that individuals who have a significantly low level of ANS functioning are far more likely to commit criminal acts.[38] For example, studies consistently show that chronic violent offenders tend to have much slower resting heartbeats than do normal persons, with a number of studies estimating this difference at 10 heartbeats per minute slower for offenders.[39] This is a highly significant gap that cannot be explained away by alternative theories, such as that offenders are less excited in laboratory tests. However, one recent review by Armstrong argued that the lower heart rate among serious violent criminals may not be causal but, rather, a spurious effect from a more limited ability to regulate emotions via brain functioning.[40] But even if this position is true, Armstrong admits that criminality still likely relates back to brain functioning, which is perhaps the most important component in ANS theory.

Furthermore, persons who have such low levels of ANS arousal tend to experience what is known in the psychological literature as "stimulus hunger." Stimulus hunger is a phenomenon in which individuals who have a low level of ANS arousal constantly seek out experiences and stimuli that are risky and often illegal. Most readers have probably known children who could never seem to get enough attention, with some even seeming to enjoy being spanked or receiving other forms of harsh punishment. In other words, individuals who have a low level of ANS arousal constantly seek out stimuli, to the point that they feel no anxiety from punishment (even corporal punishment) and thus do not adequately learn right from wrong through normal forms of discipline. This is perhaps one of the reasons why children who are diagnosed with attention-deficit/hyperactivity disorder (ADHD) have a higher likelihood of becoming criminal than do their peers.

©iStockphoto.com/Lokibaho

A child experiencing a temper tantrum, which can often happen among children who have a low-functioning autonomic nervous system.

autonomic nervous system: the portion of the nervous system that consists of our anxiety levels, such as the fight-or-flight response, as well as our involuntary motor activities (e.g., heart rate).

After all, persons who are accurately diagnosed with ADHD have a neurological abnormality; specifically, they have a significantly low level of ANS arousal. This is why doctors prescribe stimulants (e.g., Ritalin) for such youths. Although it may seem counterintuitive to prescribe a "hyperactive" person a stimulant, what the medication does is boost the individual's ANS functioning to a normal level of arousal. This enables such individuals to experience a healthy level of anxiety related to wrongdoing. Assuming that the medication is properly prescribed and at the correct dosage, such persons tend to become more attuned to the discipline they face if they violate the rules.

All readers of this book have likely encountered children who do not seem to fear punishment at all. In fact, some of them do not feel anxiety even when being physically punished (e.g., spanked). Such children are likely to have lower-than-average levels of ANS functioning and are also likely to become chronic offenders if this disorder is not addressed. This is largely due to their lack of response to discipline and inability to consider long-term consequences of risky behavior. After all, if human beings do not fear punishment or negative consequences, what will stop them from engaging in selfish, greedy behavior? So it is important to address this issue when it becomes evident that children and teenagers do not seem to be deterred by traditional forms of punishment. On the other hand, children will be children, and ADHD and other disorders have been overdiagnosed in recent years. So it is up to a well-trained physician to determine whether an individual has such a low level of ANS functioning that medication and/or therapy is required to curb deviant behavior.

Individuals with significantly low levels of ANS arousal are likely to pass lie detector tests because they feel virtually no anxiety when they lie, so it is no surprise that many of these persons lie constantly. Thus, the very people that lie-detecting measures are meant to capture are the most likely to pass such tests, which is probably why these tests are typically not admissible in court. Only through medication and/or cognitive behavioral therapy can such individuals develop the ability to consider the long-term consequences of their decisions.

It is notable that individuals with low levels of ANS functioning are not always destined to become chronic offenders. In fact, some evidence has shown that persons with low levels of ANS arousal often become successful corporate executives, decorated military soldiers, world-champion athletes, and high-level politicians. After all, most of these occupations require persons who seek out exciting, risky behavior, and others require the ability to lie constantly and convincingly. So there are many legal and productive outlets for the natural tendencies of individuals with low levels of ANS functioning. These individuals could perhaps be steered toward such occupations and opportunities when they present themselves. It is clearly a better option than committing antisocial acts.

LEARNING CHECK 6.4

1. According to the text, which area of the brain seems most important in terms of trauma when considering the likelihood of criminality?

   a. Occipital lobe

   b. Parietal lobe

   c. Frontal lobe

   d. Cerebellum

2. According to the text, which type of nervous system deals with the involuntary motor skills and is key in the "fight-or-flight" responses we have when in danger?

   a. Central nervous system

   b. Gastronomic nervous system

   c. Autonomic nervous system

   d. Cerebral nervous system

3. According to the text, many studies have consistently shown that individuals who have a _____ heart rate and brain waves are more likely to be criminals.

   a. slower

   b. faster

Answers located at www.edge.sagepub.com/schram2e

Ultimately, abnormalities in the CNS and ANS systems are physiological aspects that contribute greatly to individuals' decisions regarding criminal activity, the general conclusion being that low levels of cortical arousal—in terms of both voluntary (CNS) and involuntary (ANS) activities—are clearly linked to a predisposition toward criminal activity. However, modern medical research and societal opportunities exist to help such individuals divert their tendencies toward more prosocial uses, often giving them an advantage in our competitive society.

BIOSOCIAL APPROACHES TO EXPLAINING CRIMINAL BEHAVIOR

Perhaps the most important, and most recent, perspective on how criminality is formed is that of biosocial approaches to explaining crime. Specifically, if any conclusion can be made regarding the previous theories and research in this chapter, it is that both genetics *and* environment influence behavior, particularly the interaction between the two. After all, even the most fundamental aspects of life can be explained by these two groups of factors.[41]

For example, we can predict with a great amount of accuracy how tall a person will be by looking at the individual's parents and other ancestors, because much of height is determined by a person's genotype. However, even for something as physiological as height, the environment plays a large role. As many readers will observe, individuals who are raised in poor, underdeveloped areas (e.g., Mexico, Asia) are shorter than U.S. citizens. However, individuals who descend from parents and relatives in these underdeveloped areas but are raised in the United States tend to be just as tall as (if not taller than) U.S. citizens. This is largely due to diet, which is an environmental factor.

In other words, genotype provides a certain range or "window" that determines the height of an individual, which is based on ancestral factors. But the extent to which an individual grows toward the maximum or minimum of that range is largely dependent on what occurs in the environment as he or she develops. This is why biologists make a distinction between genotype, which is directly due to genetics, and **phenotype**, which addresses the factors that are a manifestation of genetics interacting with the environment. Thus, diet influences height, as well as behavior, in human beings. The same type of biosocial effect is seen in connection with criminal behavior.

Over the past decade, a number of empirical investigations have examined the extent to which physiological variables interact with environmental variables, and the findings of these studies have shown consistent effects regarding criminality. Such studies have been more accurate than those that rely separately on either physiological/genetic variables or environmental factors. For example, findings from a cohort study in Philadelphia showed that individuals with a low birth weight were more likely to commit crime, primarily if they were raised in a lower-income family or a family with a weak social structure.[42] To clarify, if a person had a low birth weight but was raised in a relatively high-income household or a strong family structure, then the person was not likely to become criminal. Rather, it was the coupling of both a physiological deficiency (i.e., low birth weight) and an environmental deficit (i.e., weak family structure or low income) that had a profound effect on criminal behavior.

Consistent with these findings, other studies have shown that pre- and perinatal problems alone do not predict violence accurately. However, when perinatal problems were considered along with environmental deficits, such as weak family structure, this biosocial relationship predicted violent, but not property, crime.[43] Other studies have shown the effects on criminality of a biosocial interaction between the impact of physiological factors within the first minute of life, called Apgar scores, and environmental factors, such as exposure to cigarette smoke.[44] Additional studies have found that the interaction of

phenotype: an observed manifestation of the interaction of genotypical traits with the environment, such as height.

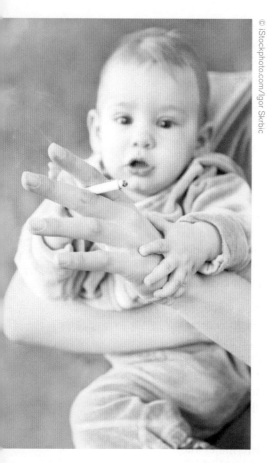

iStockphoto.com/Igor Skrbic

maternal cigarette smoking and father's absence in the household, especially early in life, is associated with criminal behavior, which is one of the biggest predictors of chronic offending in the future.[45] One of the most revealing studies showed that although only 4% of a sample of 4,269 individuals had both birth complications and maternal rejection, this relatively small group of persons accounted for more than 18% of the total violent crimes committed by the whole sample.[46] So studies have clearly shown that the interaction of biological factors and environmental deficiencies is the most consistent predictor of criminality.

Behavioral Genetics Studies

Another more modern approach to using identical twins to examine the influence of genetics and physiology on crime is the behavioral genetics approach, which estimates both the environmental and genetic influences on a given phenotype, such as criminal behavior.[47] These studies estimate heritability based on percentages derived from the variance of scores among identical versus fraternal twin pairs on a variety of characteristics and behaviors. This provides an approximate percentage of the influence in a given phenotype accounted for by genetic factors, shared environmental factors (i.e., the same across both twins in the pair, such as growing up in the same family), and nonshared environmental factors (i.e., accounting for different peer groups, significant events [e.g., employment, college education, arrests, etc.], and other nonshared environmental factors).[48]

Exposure to secondhand smoke during infancy has been consistently linked to future criminal behavior.

The meta-analyses (a methodological tool used to summarize all the studies on a particular topic) of the 80-plus studies of behavioral genetics regarding criminality or antisocial behaviors consistently show that heritability/genetic factors explain about 50% of the variance in antisocial behavior.[49] It is notable that this conclusion is based on several meta-analyses, which examined studies that included thousands of twin pairs. One further insightful conclusion from these studies is that heritability estimates appear to fluctuate over the life course, with such estimates being very high during early childhood, relatively low during adolescence (during which time peer and environmental influences, and sometimes parents, are likely to have their greatest influence), and much stronger again in adulthood.[50] It should also be noted that while the heritability estimates show about half of the variation in antisocial behavior and criminality, environmental factors—such as peer, familial, and community influence—also explained about half of such variation across these many studies. This finding goes a long way toward supporting a nature-via-nurture perspective as opposed to a nature-versus-nurture model—the latter of which was the dominant model for most of the history of criminological theorizing. As a recent summary in 2011 stated, the former perspective of biosocial interactions between physiology/genetics and environmental factors is the most accurate and current theoretical framework we have and can help us develop more fully specified models of criminality.[51]

Diet/Nutrition

In addition, studies have shown that when incarcerated juveniles were assigned to diets with limited levels of simple carbohydrates (e.g., sugars), their reported violations during incarceration declined by almost half (45%).[52] Such recent reviews of the existing studies on nutrition and criminal offending concluded that dietary deficiencies in iron, zinc, protein, riboflavin, and omega-3 are significantly related to criminality. Furthermore, other studies have reported that various food additives and dyes, such as those commonly found in processed foods, can also have a significant effect on criminal behavior. Thus, the old saying "You are what you eat" appears to have some scientific weight behind it, at least regarding criminal behavior.

Toxins

Additional studies have found that high levels of certain toxins, particularly lead, cadmium, and manganese, can have a profound effect on behavior, including criminality. Recent studies have found a consistent, strong connection between criminal behavior and exposure to high levels of lead. Unfortunately, medical studies have also found many everyday objects that contain lead, such as the play jewelry many children wear. Also unfortunate is that children, as with virtually every toxin, are the most vulnerable to lead poisoning and the most likely to be exposed to it. Even more unfortunate is that the populations (e.g., poor, urban, etc.) most susceptible to biosocial interactions are also the most likely to be exposed to high levels of lead, largely due to old paint in their homes and other household products that contain dangerous toxins.[53] Exposure to toxins and nutritional problems are some of the best examples of the biosocial nature of criminality; specifically, the way our environments impact our physiology has the greatest impact on how we will behave, including our decisions regarding criminal behavior.

CASE STUDY REVISITED: FAITH (AND HOPE)

At the beginning of this chapter, we discussed the case of Faith and how she had engaged in a number of larcenies after she dropped out of high school, later participating in the distribution of methamphetamine and eventually becoming addicted to it. As you may recall, she started life in deprived circumstances, as a twin born to a poor, inner-city mother in Chicago. And after their mother dropped Faith on her head while changing their diapers, she gave up Faith's identical twin sister, Hope, for adoption.

That Faith suffered an early head trauma may have had a significant impact on her subsequent behavior. Studies reviewed in this chapter show that the brain, at only 3 pounds, is even smaller and more vulnerable in early life, especially in the first few months of infancy. It is likely that Faith's early head injury affected her grades in school, which as you may recall were poor from even the earliest years of schooling. Such brain trauma, especially at an early age, is likely to impact the functioning of the CNS (central nervous system), which is key in governing one's voluntary motor skills.

During her elementary and middle school years, Faith was also found to have a very low heart rate, which is a key indicator of a low-functioning ANS (autonomic nervous system). Deficiencies in this ANS functioning are likely to have a vital impact on the discipline and development of individuals, because persons with low ANS functioning are far less likely to feel anxiety regarding punishment as well as more likely to engage in risk-taking behavior, such as illegal acts. Faith exhibited this type of behavior in suddenly quitting high school, committing acts of theft, and engaging in selling methamphetamine—not to mention using this drug. All these behaviors were acted out without any consideration for future consequences or long-term plans, which is often the case in individuals who have a lower-functioning ANS, as Faith appeared to have.

Cheap play jewelry has often been found to contain lead, a toxin that has been linked to criminality.

Faith was also raised by a single mother, who was largely absent because she had to work two jobs to make up for the father being physically and financially absent. This creates the prototypical interaction effect, whereby nurturing (or the environment) is weak and the nature (or physiological) portion is also weak. When an individual has weak support

Many household paints contain lead, a toxin that has been linked to criminal behavior. Such tainted paint is more commonly found in older homes, especially inner-city, urban homes.

in terms of both nature and nurture, it creates a "perfect storm" of factors that increase that person's likelihood of becoming a criminal.

Another example of this nature-via-nurture effect was seen in Faith becoming obese, largely from her fast-food diet. This obesity led to the early onset of puberty at age 11, which is a physiological factor. But this in turn led to the sociological factor of teenage males starting to seek her company, which increased the likelihood that she would engage in illegal behaviors (because teenage males have the highest rates of criminal offending in all societies). Thus, Faith's early menstruation (physiology) contributed to more attention from males (environment), which greatly increased her risk of criminality—thereby exemplifying the nature-via-nurture interaction.

Faith's identical twin sister, Hope, grew up fine in her upper-middle-class adoptive family. Although she, too, showed a relatively low heart rate in her medical checks and, like Faith, had problems with her grades early in school, she seemed to have a much easier time through high school and graduated on time. Hope did experiment with some drugs and alcohol, and she did find herself in one physical altercation with a classmate in her sophomore year (for which she was suspended from school for two days), but overall she did well in her teenage years and never earned a formal criminal record. She did not go to college but secured a job with the Chicago city government and is currently living in a small row house with a man and their child together. So Hope turned out to be in a similar situation as her identical twin sister, which supports the studies on identical twins reared apart. After all, both ended up taking drugs, engaging in violence, and so forth, but the social context for each was different. Ultimately, nature or biological factors tend to have an impact on behavior, often far more than the nurturing or environmental factors. All studies have been consistent in showing that. But the social environment always makes a large difference, especially in the way the same types of behaviors are handled (which will be discussed further in a later chapter).

POLICY IMPLICATIONS

Various policy implications have been introduced throughout this chapter, appropriate to the various biological or biosocial factors presented in each section. However, we feel that it is appropriate to emphasize one policy implication in particular—maternal/infant health care at all stages, including prenatal, postnatal, and in the first years of life. After reviewing all the extant research as well as other experts' reviews of this literature, there is no doubt that providing adequate health care for expecting mothers, as well as extended care for infants in their first years of life, is the most cost-effective way for any society to reduce future criminality. If such maternal health care during pregnancy is not available, the risk of a multitude of birth and delivery complications rises.[54]

In fact, we know of very few respected researchers in medicine, psychology, or any other field who do not believe that this policy recommendation should be followed. For every dollar spent on such maternal/infant health care, studies show that not only will many dollars in criminal justice processing and prison time be saved but many lives will be as well, due to the reduction in violence. There are many other policy implications, some discussed in this chapter, but we stand by maternal/infant health care in the perinatal stage as being the number-one priority for any society in preventing biological or biosocial factors that influence future criminality.

CONCLUSION

This chapter has examined a large range of explanations for criminal behavior that place most of the blame on biological and/or psychological factors, which are typically intertwined. These types of explanations were primarily popular in the early years of the development of criminology as a science but have also been shown in recent years to be quite valid as significant factors in individual decisions to commit crime. Specifically, this chapter discussed the early studies that explored the relative influence of nature versus nurture, such as the early family studies as well as the more robust subsequent wave of twin studies, adoption studies, and studies of identical twins raised apart. These studies revealed not only an answer to the nature-versus-nurture argument but also that "nature via nurture" should be emphasized when it comes to predicting criminality.

This chapter then examined the influence of hormones (e.g., testosterone) on human behavior, as well as the effect of variations in chromosomal mutations (e.g., XYY). Recent research has supported both of these theories in showing that persons with high levels of male androgens are far more likely to commit crime than are those who do not have high levels of these hormones. The link between brain trauma and criminality was also discussed, with an emphasis on the consistent association with damage to the left and/or frontal parts of the brain as well as trauma to special limbic structures involved in emotions and memory.

This chapter also examined theories regarding variations in levels of functioning of the CNS and the ANS, and all empirical studies have shown that low levels of functioning in these systems have links to criminality. Next, we explored the extent to which the interaction between physiological factors and environmental variables contributes to the most consistent prediction of criminal offending (hence, the importance of nature via nurture). Finally, we discussed how diet and nutrition as well as exposure to dangerous toxins have furthered our understanding of how the environment interacts with physiology to predict future criminality. Ultimately, it is interesting that the very theories that were key in the early years of criminology as a science, such as brain structure/functioning and other early diagnostics from the first year(s) of life (e.g., Apgar scores), are now showing strong evidence of being a primary influence on criminal behavior.

SUMMARY OF THEORIES IN CHAPTER 6

THEORIES	KEY PROPONENTS	CONCEPTS/FACTORS	KEY PROPOSITIONS
Family studies	Richard L. Dugdale, H. H. Goddard	Criminality	Criminality runs in families
Twin studies	Various	Concordance for criminality	MZ twins have higher concordance than DZ twins
Adoption studies	Sarnoff Mednick and colleagues	Criminality among various adoptees	Adoptees with criminal biological parents compared with criminal adoptive parents
MZ twins separated at birth	Various	Concordance rates of MZ twins raised apart	Criminality among MZ twins reared apart are similar
Cytogenetic studies	Patricia A. Jacobs	Chromosomal mutations	XYY individuals have more criminality
Hormonal theory	Various	Testosterone, estrogen levels	Higher levels of testosterone and lower levels of estrogen predict criminality
Neurotransmitters	Various	Dopamine, serotonin	Low levels of serotonin predict more criminality, whereas findings for other neurotransmitters are mixed
Brain injury	Various	Various lobes and brain structures	Trauma to certain portions of the brain (e.g., frontal lobe) and structures (e.g., limbic structures) predict criminality
Central nervous system functioning	Various	Brain wave patterns	Slower brain wave patterns predict criminality
Autonomic nervous system functioning	Various	Heart rate, sweating, and other indicators	Lower functioning predicts criminality
Biosocial interaction theory	Various	A variety of both physiological and developmental factors	Weak physiological factors interact with weak social and environmental factors to predict criminality

KEY TERMS

adoption studies, 143

autonomic nervous
   system, 157

central nervous system, 154

concordance rates, 142

cytogenetic studies, 146

dizygotic twins, 142

dopamine, 152

family studies, 141

frontal lobe, 153

monozygotic twins, 142

neurotransmitters, 151

phenotype, 159

selective placement, 144

serotonin, 152

temporal lobe, 153

twins separated at birth
   studies, 145

twin studies, 142

DISCUSSION QUESTIONS

1. Is there any validity to family studies in determining the role of genetics in criminal behavior? Why or why not?

2. Explain the rationale of studies that compare the concordance rates of identical twins and fraternal twins who are raised together. What do most of these studies show regarding the influence of genetics on criminal behavior? What are the criticisms of these studies?

3. Explain the rationale of studies that examine the biological and adoptive parents of adopted children. What do most of these studies show regarding the influence of genetics on criminal behavior? What are the criticisms of these studies?

4. What are the general findings in studies of identical twins separated at birth? What implications do these findings have for the importance of genetics or heritability regarding criminal behavior? Can you think of a criticism for such findings?

5. Explain what cytogenetic disorders are, and describe the related disorder that is most linked to criminal behavior. What characteristics of this type of disorder seem to be driving the higher propensity toward crime?

6. What types of hormones have been shown by scientific studies to be linked to criminal activity? Give specific examples that show this link to be true.

7. Explain what neurotransmitters are, and describe which neurotransmitters are key in predicting criminal offending. Provide support from previous scientific studies.

8. Which areas of the brain have shown the greatest vulnerability to trauma in terms of criminal offending? Does the lack of healthy functioning in these areas/lobes make sense? Why?

9. How do brain wave patterns differ between chronic, violent criminals and normal people? Does this make sense in biosocial models of criminality?

10. How does the autonomic nervous system differ between chronic, violent criminals and normal people? Does this make sense in biosocial models of criminality?

11. What types of policy implications would you support based on the information provided by empirical studies reviewed in this chapter?

WEB RESOURCES

Family/Twin/Adoption Studies

This site provides a concise historical review of twin studies, including some of the earliest in the late 19th century:

http://www.bookrags.com/research/twin-studies-wog/

This site provides an excellent review of adoption, family, and twin studies:

http://www.personalityresearch.org/papers/haimowitz.html

Cytogenetics

This site presents a study and findings regarding Klinefelter's syndrome, and more importantly XYY chromosomal mutation:

http://bmjopen.bmj.com/content/2/1/e000650.full

A good review of both past and modern cytogenetic studies and conclusions:

https://en.wikipedia.org/wiki/Cytogenetics

Hormones and Neurotransmitters

This site provides a discussion of the link between testosterone and aggression:

http://www.gender.org.uk/about/06encrn/63faggrs.htm

This site examines the disadvantages and advantages to using chemicals to castrate pedophiles:

http://serendip.brynmawr.edu/biology/b103/f02/web1/kamlin.html

In-depth review of how low levels of serotonin predict criminality:

http://law.jrank.org/pages/791/Crime-Causation-Biological-Theories-Serotonin.htmlAutonomic/central nervous systems

This site reviews several competing approaches to explaining the causes of criminality, particularly the interactions among different factors:

http://human-nature.com/nibbs/05/awalsh.html

This search provides a list of some of the best sources of reviews of the link between low central nervous system functioning and criminality:

https://www.google.com/#q=cns+criminality

Brain Trauma and Crime

This site reviews recent research that further supports a link between brain injury and criminality in young individuals:

http://www.medicalnewstoday.com/articles/251798.php

This site reviews research in which it was found that 60% of sampled prisoners had had traumatic brain injuries in their past:

http://www.traumaticbraininjury.net/does-brain-injury-contribute-to-criminal-behavior/

STUDENT STUDY SITE

$SAGE edge™

WANT A BETTER GRADE ON YOUR NEXT TEST?

Get the tools you need to sharpen your study skills:

SAGE edge offers a robust online environment featuring an impressive array of tools and resources for review, study, and further exploration, keeping both instructors and students on the cutting edge of teaching and learning. Learn more at **edge.sagepub.com/schram2e**.

FOR FURTHER EXPLORATION AND APPLICATION, VISIT THE STUDENT STUDY SITE:

- Great Pause' Among Prosecutors as DNA Proves Fallible
- Wild Chimps, Stick Dolls: What's at Play Here?
- The familial concentration and transmission of crime
- Adolescence: Does good nutrition = good behavior?
- UNM Study Probes Criminal Pattern
- Nature or Nurture? Twin Studies Provide Answers
- The Flight-or-Fight Response
- Jim Fallon: Exploring the Mind of a Killer
- Texas University Clock Tower Sniper 1966
- The Brain and Personality
- The Link Between the Brain and Morality
- Phineas Gage
- Modern-Day Lessons from Phineas Gage
- Brain Scans and Criminal Activity

PREMIUM VIDEO:

Check out the Interactive eBook for premium videos, including videos from author Stephen Tibbetts, who discusses real-world examples and strange crimes; and videos from former offenders, who share their stories from a first-person view, and touch on key theories and concepts from the chapter.

Psychological/Trait Theories of Crime

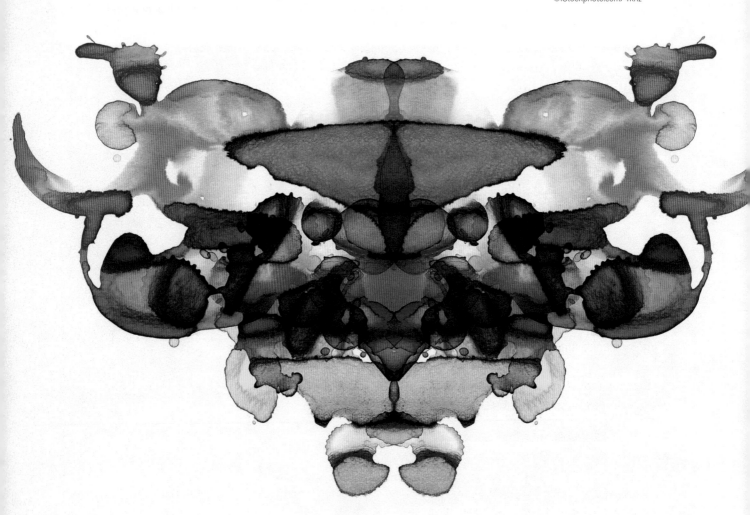

INTRODUCTION

Most sociological theories of crime focus on shared factors that influence offenders rather than factors that are unique to individuals:

> Individual difference variables are relegated to a minor, if not trivial, status in favor of influences that are thought to homogenize a collection of individuals into a population that is at risk for crime. At-risk populations are produced when social-cultural conditions combine to lower some groups' endorsement of legal norms and prohibitions.[5]

In contrast to sociological theories, psychological theories of crime focus on the influence of individuals' experiences or their emotional adjustment as well as on their personality traits and types.[6]

This chapter highlights various psychological theories, beginning with early psychological perspectives such as the theories developed by Sigmund Freud, Hans Eysenck, Lawrence Kohlberg, and John Bowlby. The next portion of this chapter reviews what are considered more contemporary psychological theories of criminal behavior. This section begins with a brief discussion on the controversial perspective concerning intelligence (e.g., IQ) and criminality. This section also discusses the theoretical perspective developed by James Q. Wilson and Richard J. Herrnstein. While these scholars never formally labeled their theory, one researcher suggested the name *operant-utilitarian theory of criminality*. Although Wilson and Herrnstein suggested that various factors influence criminal behavior, the most controversial aspect of their perspective was the biological factors, which include gender, low intelligence, impulsiveness, and body type. The following section explores research that has linked psychopathy with criminality. The last section in this chapter examines issues pertaining to mental illness and the criminal justice system. Specifically, we briefly discuss treatment, mental health courts, and the insanity defense.

EARLY PSYCHOLOGICAL THEORIZING REGARDING CRIMINAL BEHAVIOR

Freud's Model of the Psyche and Implications for Criminal Behavior

Sigmund Freud (1856–1939) originated psychoanalysis, which is founded on the perception of resistance used by individuals when therapists attempt to make them conscious of their unconscious.[7] The psychoanalytic perspective is both complex and extremely systematized. This discussion provides an overview of the general principles of psychoanalysis.

First, an individual's behavior is presumed to be due to the three aspects of his or her personality: the id, ego, and superego. The id is the source of instinctual drives; it contains everything that is present at birth.[8] Essentially, there are two types of instinctual drives: constructive and destructive. Constructive drives are usually sexual in nature. These drives make up the

LEARNING OBJECTIVES

As you read this chapter, consider the following topics:

- Identify the general principles of psychoanalysis and how psychoanalysis applies to criminal behavior.

- Describe the three dimensions associated with Hans Eysenck's theory of crime and personality.

- Identify some of the key distinctions of the various stages of moral development.

- Describe some of the essential features of attachment theory.

- Referring to James Q. Wilson and Richard J. Herrnstein, describe the three factors associated with street crime and human nature.

- List and describe the key features that distinguish a psychopath from other criminal offenders.

- Distinguish the M'Naghten rule, irresistible impulse test, Durham test, and American Law Institute's Model Penal Code.

CASE STUDY

ALBERT FISH

Albert Fish has been dubbed "America's boogeyman." From his physical appearance, many considered him a gentle, kind old man. Soon, it was revealed that this man was a serial killer, committing numerous depraved and unspeakable acts against children. Fish was brought to the attention of law enforcement after the 1928 kidnapping of a 12-year-old girl named Grace Budd. After befriending her parents, Fish told them that his niece was having a birthday party and asked if Grace would like to attend. Not suspicious of Fish's intentions, Mr. and Mrs. Budd gave their permission. Fish then escorted Grace to an isolated house in a northern suburb of New York City. He proceeded to strangle her and later mutilated her body and engaged in cannibalism.

The crime remained unsolved for six years. A New York City detective, William King, did not let up on the hunt for Grace's killer. He continued to question Fish during this time. Some contend that Fish would have gotten away with Grace's murder but was caught due to his arrogant and brazen behavior. In 1934, Fish sent a letter to Mrs. Budd, Grace's mother. The letter described, in gruesome detail, what he had done to Grace. Subsequently, King was able to link the letter to Fish.

While Fish was in custody, it soon became apparent that he was "a killer of unimaginable depravity, one who had spent his whole lifetime inflicting pain—on himself as well as others."[1] He considered the children he mutilated and murdered to be sacrificial offerings to the Lord. During his confession, Fish stated that he wanted to kill Edward Budd, but when he saw Edward's sister, Grace, he decided he wanted to kill her instead.[2] He later confessed to killing many children and molesting hundreds. Dr. Fredric Wertham, a New York City psychologist assigned to examine Fish, noted that he had engaged in "every sexual perversion known" as well as a few others that no one had heard of before that time.[3]

While the jurors at his trial acknowledged that Fish was insane, they maintained that he should be executed. Fish was executed in January 1936 in

Albert Fish, nicknamed "America's boogeyman," was a notorious serial killer in the 1930s.

> IT SOON BECAME APPARENT THAT HE WAS "A KILLER OF UNIMAGINABLE DEPRAVITY, ONE WHO HAD SPENT HIS WHOLE LIFETIME INFLICTING PAIN—ON HIMSELF AS WELL AS OTHERS."

Sing Sing Prison. He was 65 years old. It was reported that prior to his electrocution, Fish stated, "What a thrill it will be to die in the electric chair! It will be the supreme thrill—the only one I haven't tried."[4]

THINK ABOUT IT:

1. How would you explain Fish's criminal behavior? Some would maintain that his behavior exceeds other types of murder because of the brutal, perverse nature of his crimes as well as the fact that he preyed on children.

2. Why do you think Fish enjoyed inflicting pain?

3. How should the criminal justice system handle offenders like Fish (e.g., punishment, treatment)?

libido. Freud used the term *sex* in a broader context; thus, *sex* included those things, such as painting, that give people pleasure. The other type of instinctual drive is destructive. Destructive drives refer to such things as aggression, destruction, and death.[9]

The ego is the moderator between the demands of an instinct (i.e., the id), the superego, and reality. When discussing the relationship between the id and the ego, Freud noted that the ego characterizes what is referred to as reason and sanity, while the id refers to passions. Further, there are no conflicts in the id, whereas in the ego, conflicts between impulses need to be resolved.[10] The superego is also designated as a conscience. This evolves during the course of an individual's development, during which he or she learns the restrictions, mores, and values of society.

Second, *anxiety*, *defense mechanisms*, and the *unconscious* are also key principles of the psychoanalytical perspective. In terms of *anxiety*, this is considered a warning of looming danger or a painful experience. This results in the individual attempting to correct the situation. In most instances, the ego can cope with this anxiety through rational measures. When this does not work, however, the ego uses irrational measures, such as rationalization. These are referred to as *ego-defense mechanisms*:[11] (e.g., a woman harassed by her boss at work initiates an argument with her husband)[11] Discharging pent-up feelings, often of hostility, on objects less dangerous than those arousing the feelings, is an example of a *defense mechanism*.[12]

Freud maintained that large portions of the ego and superego can remain unconscious (see Figure 7.1). Further, it takes a great deal of effort for individuals to recognize their unconscious.[13] The unconscious can include disturbing memories, forbidden urges, and other experiences that have been repressed or pushed out of the conscious. While individuals may be unaware of their unconscious experiences, they continue to seek some form of expression, such as in fantasies and dreams. Until these unconscious experiences are brought to awareness, the individual could engage in irrational and destructive behavior.[14]

In reference to criminal behavior, Freud stated the following:

> I must work out an analogy between the criminal and the hysteric. In both we are concerned with a secret, with something hidden. . . . In the case of the criminal, it is a secret which he knows and hides from you, but in the case of the hysteric it is a secret hidden from him, a secret he himself does not know.[15]

One of the most well-known psychoanalysts to apply psychoanalysis to criminal behavior was August Aichhorn.[16] While most applications of psychoanalysis treated nervous disorders, he attempted to apply this method to uncover the unconscious motives of juveniles engaging in delinquent behavior. Aichhorn distinguished between *manifest* and *latent* delinquency. Delinquency is considered manifest when it results in antisocial behavior; latent delinquency is when the same state of mind exists but has not yet expressed itself through such behavior.[17]

Since Aichhorn, there have been various adaptations of Freudian theory to understanding delinquency; some of these adaptations differ a great deal from the work of Freud and Aichhorn. For instance, Erik Erikson examined adolescents struggling to discover their own ego identity while negotiating, learning, and understanding social interactions as well as developing a sense of morality and right and wrong.[18] David Abrahamsen maintained that criminal behavior is a symptom of more complex personality distortions; there is a conflict between the ego and superego as well as the inability to control impulsive and pleasure-seeking drives, because these influences are rooted in early childhood and later reinforced through reactions to familial and social stresses.[19] Like these theories,

psychoanalytic perspective: an individual's behavior is presumed to be due to the three aspects of his or her personality: the id, ego, and superego; anxiety, defense mechanisms, and the unconscious are also key principles of the psychoanalytical perspective.

id: a subconscious domain of the psyche, according to Freud, with which we are all born; it is responsible for our innate desires and drives (such as libido [sex drive]) and it battles the moral conscience of the superego.

ego: the only conscious domain of the psyche, according to Freud, it functions to mediate the battle between the id and superego.

superego: a subconscious domain of the psyche, according to Freud; it is not part of our nature but must be developed through early social attachments.

FIGURE **7.1**

Freud's Conception of the Human Psyche (The Iceberg Metaphor)

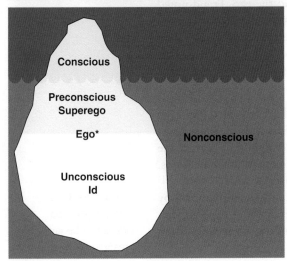

Conscious

Preconscious
Superego

Ego*

Nonconscious

Unconscious
Id

*Note: Ego is free-floating in all three levels

PEN model: discussions of this theory emphasize that human personality can be viewed in three dimensions: psychoticism, extroversion, and neuroticism.

psychoticism: individuals considered to have high psychoticism are associated with being aggressive, cold, egocentric, impersonal, impulsive, antisocial, unempathic, creative, and tough-minded; individuals with low psychoticism are characterized as being empathic, unselfish, altruistic, warm, peaceful, and generally more pleasant.

extroversion: in reference to the PEN model, traits associated with extroversion include being sociable, lively, active, assertive, sensation-seeking, carefree, dominant, surgent, and venturesome.

other psychoanalytic perspectives focused on family experiences that resulted in unconscious, internal conflicts during early childhood. These conflicts can explain why one engages in delinquent behavior.[20]

Hans Eysenck: Theory of Crime and Personality

For more than 20 years, Hans J. Eysenck developed a theory that linked personality to criminality.[21] Often, discussions of this theory emphasize that human personality can be viewed in three dimensions (i.e., the **PEN model**). He developed the Eysenck Personality Questionnaire to measure individuals on these three dimensions (see Table 7.1). The first dimension is **psychoticism**. Individuals considered to have high psychoticism are associated with being aggressive, cold, egocentric, impersonal, impulsive, antisocial, unempathic, creative, and tough-minded; individuals with low psychoticism are characterized as being empathic, unselfish, altruistic, warm, peaceful, and generally more pleasant.[22]

The second dimension is **extroversion**, with the associated traits of being sociable, lively, active, assertive, sensation-seeking, carefree, dominant, surgent, and venturesome. Introverts are usually characterized with the opposite type of traits (e.g., passive, cautious). Most individuals, however, are not exclusively extroverted or introverted; rather, these personality dimensions and associated traits are more on a continuum, with a majority of individuals being in the middle and not at the extremes. The last dimension is **neuroticism**, or instability, which is linked with such traits as anxiety, depression, guilty feelings, low self-esteem, tension, irrationality, shyness, moodiness, and emotionality.[23]

Nicole Hahn Rafter provided an insightful description of Eysenck's evolving development of linking criminality and personality.[24] Initially, Eysenck focused on two personality dimensions: neuroticism and extroversion. During this stage of theoretical development, he emphasized the extroversion dimension. Subsequently, he incorporated the psychoticism dimension. Thus, he moved "from his original concept of criminals as extroverts to identifying them with arch-villainous psychopaths."[25] In an effort to explain individual differences in criminality, Eysenck maintained that these can be understood in terms of biology. He offered three arguments: (1) genetics, (2) Pavlovian conditioning, and (3) neurophysiology.

In terms of genetics, or heredity, Eysenck drew on data collected from twins. He stated that "these data . . . demonstrate, beyond any question, that heredity plays an important, and possibly a vital part, in predisposing a given individual to crime."[26] This type of assertion, however, is what made many critics *distrustful* of Eysenck's conclusions.[27] The second argument, Pavlovian conditioning, is an essential part of his biological explanation, which is that

socialized and altruistic behavior had to be learned and that this learning was mediated by means of Pavlovian conditioning. The newborn and the young child have no social conscience and behave in a purely egocentric manner. They have to acquire a "conscience" through a process of conditioning.[28]

The argument was that it is more difficult to condition extroverts than introverts. Further, he maintained that classical conditioning is associated with moral behavior. Referring to

TABLE **7.1**	Example Questionnaire Items From the Eysenck Personality Questionnaire–Revised

EXTROVERSION

Do you like telling jokes and funny stories to your friends?

Do you prefer reading to meeting people?

Do you spontaneously introduce yourself to strangers at social gatherings?

NEUROTICISM

Are you a worrier?

Are you inclined to tremble and perspire when faced with a difficult task ahead?

Do you sometimes withhold your opinions for fear that people will laugh and criticize you?

PSYCHOTICISM

Do you enjoy hurting people you love?

Would it upset you a lot to see a child or an animal suffer?

Do people who drive carefully annoy you?

Do you get so excited and involved with new ideas that you never think of possible snags?

Source: Miles, J., & Hempell, S. (2004). The Eysenck personality scales: The Eysenck Personality Questionnaire–Revised (EPQ-R) and the Eysenck Personality Profiler (EPP). In M. J. Hilsenroth, D. L. Segal, & M. Hersen (Eds.), *Comprehensive handbook of psychological assessment: Personality assessment* (Vol. 2, pp. 99–100). Hoboken, NJ: Wiley.

These two examples illustrate how an extrovert and an introvert would react to staying home.

neuroticism: in reference to the PEN model, neuroticism is often linked with such traits as being anxious, depressed, tense, irrational, shy, moody, and emotional and having guilty feelings and low self-esteem.

various studies, Eysenck argued that "conscience is . . . a conditioned reflex."[29] The last type of argument was initially based on brain physiology. When he raised this argument, it was relatively undeveloped. Later, he noted that the differences between extroverted and introverted behavior were due to cortical arousal. Eysenck maintained that cortical arousal differs among individuals "with respect to the ease or difficulty with which their level of arousal can be increased (arousability), their usual level of arousal, and the ease with which this arousal level can be maintained."[30]

According to Eysenck, extroverts are characterized by a low level of cortical arousal. To achieve an ideal level of arousal, extroverts need more excitement and stimuli in their environment. Further, they are less susceptible to pain and punishment and experience less fear and anxiety. For neurotics, the biological link is in the sympathetic part of the autonomic nervous system, which involves the fight and flight reactions. Finally, the cortical arousal level is also associated with psychoticism. Like those scoring high on extroversion, those scoring high on psychoticism have low levels of cortical arousal and are more difficult to condition as well as more prone to developing antisocial behavior.[31]

Eysenck's model of personality and criminality has received mixed support.[32] For instance, individuals scoring high on psychoticism are often linked to criminal behavior regardless of the methodology (e.g., self-report among the general population or offender samples). Compared with the general population, neuroticism is higher among criminal offender samples. When employing self-report methods, extroversion is usually higher among the general population but not among criminal offender samples.[33]

Lawrence Kohlberg: Moral Development

A central feature of Lawrence Kohlberg's theory is that moral development occurs in stages.[34] According to Kohlberg, moral judgment evolves in children in a three-level progression, each level consisting of two stages (see Table 7.2). The preconventional level of morality is characteristic of designating what is considered "right" and "wrong"—for instance, "telling on your brother is wrong because it is 'tattling,' breaking into the druggist's store is wrong because 'you're not supposed to steal.'"[35] What is deemed "right" and "wrong" is defined by those in authority. Within this level, Stage 1 is characterized as a "punishment and obedience orientation"; rewards and punishments are key components of this stage. An individual follows the rules for his or her benefit as well as to avoid punishment.[36] Stage 2 is when one develops moral relativity. A person recognizes that different people have varying, yet just as valid, justifications for their claims of justice.[37] Thus, an individual views justice as an equal exchange of favors, such as "you scratch my back, I'll scratch yours." Or one may view justice as a "settling of scores," such as "an eye for an eye, a tooth for a tooth."[38]

preconventional level of morality: level of morality characteristic of designating what is considered "right" and "wrong."

conventional level of morality: level of morality considered the normal adult approach used to maintain the family and social order, such as the principle of the golden rule and appreciating social order.

postconventional level of morality: when a person attempts to establish a balance between individual rights and societal rules.

Stages 3 and 4 on the conventional level of morality are what Kohlberg considered the normal adult approaches used to maintain the family and social order. At Stage 3, individuals begin to understand and live by the principle of the golden rule; they appreciate such acts as generosity for those in need and forgiving those who do wrong. At Stage 4, these values of justice are expanded to the social order, such as establishing good citizenship, instilling a strong work ethic, and following the laws of society.[39] Kohlberg identified various types of justice as corrective justice (i.e., impartiality in the application of the law and the offender paying his or her debt to society) and commutative justice (i.e., the importance of contractual agreements for maintaining social order). Below is an example of commutative justice:

> Question—Is it important to keep a promise to someone you don't know well?

> Answer—Yes. Perhaps even more so than keeping a promise to someone you know well. A man is often judged by his actions in such situations, and to be described as being a "man of honour," or a "man of integrity" is very fulfilling indeed.[40]

On the postconventional level of morality, at Stage 5 an individual considers such "meta-ethical" issues as "why one should be moral." There is an attempt to establish a balance between an individual's rights and societal rules; this is considered a "social contract" perspective of morality.[41] Kohlberg designated Stage 6 "the moral point of view." A key aspect to this stage is that a person takes equal consideration of each individual's point of view in terms of the moral decision to be made. Various principles are characterized by

Stage 6, such as the principle of the maximum quality of life for each, equity or fairness in the distribution of goods and respect, and the principle of utility or benevolence.[42] Below is an example of Kohlberg's theory of moral development.

HEINZ'S DILEMMA. Heinz's wife was dying from cancer. Doctors said a new drug might save her. This drug had been discovered by a local chemist. Heinz desperately attempted to buy the drug, but the chemist was charging 10 times the money it cost to make the drug, and this was much more than Heinz could afford.

Even after family and friends tried to help Heinz, he could only raise half the money. He explained to the chemist that his wife was dying and asked if he could have the drug cheaper or pay the rest of the money later.

The chemist refused, saying that he had discovered the drug and was going to make money from it. The husband was desperate to save his wife, so later that night he broke into the chemist's and stole the drug.

TABLE 7.2   Heinz's Dilemma by Kohlberg's Stages of Morality

Below are typical answers to the Heinz's dilemma to illustrate the different stages of moral development:

STAGE	PRO	CON
PRECONVENTIONAL LEVEL OF MORALITY		
Stage 1	He should steal the drug. It isn't really bad to take it. It isn't as if he hadn't asked to pay for it first.	He shouldn't steal the drug. It's a big crime. He didn't get permission; he used force and broke and entered. He did a lot of damage, stealing a very expensive drug and breaking up the store, too.
Stage 2	It's all right to steal the drug, because his wife needs it and he wants her to live. It isn't that he wants to steal, but that's what he has to do to get the drug to save her.	He shouldn't steal it. The druggist isn't wrong or bad; he just wants to make a profit. That's what you're in business for—to make money.
CONVENTIONAL LEVEL OF MORALITY		
Stage 3	He should steal the drug. He is only doing something that is natural for a good husband to do. You can't blame him for doing something out of love for his wife. You'd blame him if he didn't love his wife enough to save her.	He shouldn't steal. If his wife dies, he can't be blamed. It isn't because he's heartless or that he doesn't love her enough to do everything that he legally can. The druggist is the selfish or heartless one.
Stage 4	You should steal it. If you did nothing, you'd be letting your wife die. It's your responsibility if she dies. You have to take it with the idea of paying the druggist.	It is a natural thing for Heinz to want to save his wife, but it's still always wrong to steal. He still knows that he's stealing and taking a valuable drug from the man who made it.
POSTCONVENTIONAL LEVEL OF MORALITY		
Stage 5	The law wasn't set up for these circumstances. Taking the drug in this situation isn't really right, but it's justified.	You can't completely blame someone for stealing, but extreme circumstances don't really justify taking the law into your own hands. You can't have people stealing whenever they are desperate. The end may be good, but the ends don't justify the means.
Stage 6	This is a situation that forces him to choose between stealing and letting his wife die. In a situation where the choice must be made, it is morally right to steal. He has to act in terms of the principle of preserving and respecting life.	Heinz is faced with the decision of whether to consider the other people who need the drug just as badly as his wife. Heinz ought to act not according to his particular feelings toward his wife, but considering the value of all the lives involved.

Source: Adapted from Kohlberg, L. (1969). Stage and sequence: The cognitive-developmental approach to socialization. In D. A. Goslin (Ed.), *Handbook of socialization theory and research*. Chicago, IL: Rand McNally; as cited in Lickona, T. (Ed.). (1976). *Moral development and behavior*. New York, NY: Holt.

An interesting facet to understanding moral development was Carol Gilligan's work, which explored gender differences in terms of moral orientations.[43] Gilligan distinguished between the moral orientations toward "care" and those toward "justice":

> In early childhood, girls often gravitate towards the morality of care, whereas boys often gravitate towards the morality of justice. . . . Males and females alike can develop an awareness of both care and justice; but because of widespread patterns of early experience, girls often orient more towards the former and boys towards the latter.[44]

Gilligan notes that women may construct a problem differently than do men. Thus, women may fail to develop within the constraints of Kohlberg's system of moral development.[45] She noted that Kohlberg's six stages of moral development were based on a study of 84 boys whose development Kohlberg followed for more than 20 years.[46]

John Bowlby: Attachment Theory

Development of attachment theory is the combined work of John Bowlby and Mary Ainsworth. Bowlby formulated the basic propositions of the theory; the roots of Bowlby's interest in studying separation are in his own early childhood and in his clinical experiences while training as a psychoanalyst prior to World War II.[47] Ainsworth implemented innovative methodology to test some of Bowlby's concepts as well as to further refine the perspective. While these scholars initially worked independently of each other, both were influenced by the work of Freud and other psychoanalytic theorists.[48] In discussing attachment theory, reference is often made to research examining the effects of separation on mother and infant monkeys. Bowlby cited this research and noted that these types of studies "show plainly not only that the attachment behaviour of young non-human primates is very similar to the attachment behaviour of young children but that their responses to separation are very similar also."[49]

attachment theory: there are seven essential features of this theoretical perspective focusing on attachment: specificity, duration, engagement of emotion, course of development, learning, organization, and biological function.

TABLE 7.3 Levels of Moral Development

LEVEL OF MORAL DEVELOPMENT	STAGE OF REASONING
Preconventional	Stage 1: Right is obedience to power and avoidance of punishment.
	Stage 2: Right is taking responsibility and leaving others to be responsible for themselves.
Conventional	Stage 3: Right is being considerate: "Uphold the values of other adolescents and adults' rules of society at large."
	Stage 4: Right is being good as defined by the values and norms of family and society at large.
Postconventional	Stage 5: Right is finding an inner "universal rights" balance between self-rights and societal rules—a social contract.
	Stage 6: Right is based on a higher order of applying principles to all humankind; being nonjudgmental and respecting all human life.

Source: Adapted from Kohlberg, L. (1986). The just community approach to corrections. *Journal of Correctional Education, 37,* 57–58.

Bowlby maintained that this theoretical perspective has seven essential features:

Specificity—Attachments are selective or "choosy"; these attachments are often focused on one or more individuals, usually with some order of preference.

Duration—Attachments are enduring and persistent; these attachments can sometimes last throughout a person's life.

Engagement of emotion—Some of the most intense and passionate emotions are associated with attachment relationships.

Course of development—In the first nine months of an infant's life, he or she develops an attachment to a primary figure. This primary figure is the person who provides the most fulfilling and pleasing social interaction.

Learning—While learning does have some influence on a person's attachments, the key component is social interaction.

Organization—Attachment behavior follows cognitive development as well as interpersonal maturation from birth.

Biological function—Attachment behavior has a biological function in terms of survival, which is supported by research on various species.[50]

For example, in terms of *engagement of emotion*, Bowlby discussed the emotion of fear:

In the presence of a trusted companion, fear of situations of every kind diminishes; when, by contrast, one is alone, fear of situations of every kind is magnified. Since in the lives of all of us our most trusted companions are our attachment figures, it follows that the degree to which each of us is susceptible to fear turns in great part on whether our attachment figures are present or absent.[51]

Bowlby's interest in early parent–infant interactions evolved from his clinical work with young offenders; his theoretical framework evolved from this work.[52] From 1936 to 1939, Bowlby assessed and treated 88 children between the ages of 5 and 16 at the London Child Guidance Clinic. In his study, "Forty-Four Juvenile Thieves," he stressed the importance of studying the mother–child relationship. As Bowlby noted, inquiries were made into not only the mother's conscious attitude but also her unconscious attitude. He developed a classification procedure to distinguish the various character types. Of the 44 juveniles in his study, 14 were classified as affectionless, followed by 13 classified as hyperthymic (i.e., children who tend toward constant overactivity) and 9 designated as depressed.[53] Below is a case history of one of the youths designated as *affectionless*.

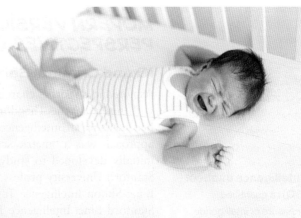

EXAMPLE CASE HISTORY: DEREK B.

History. He was the second of two boys, the elder being a cheerful, normal lad who had never got into trouble. He lived with his mother and father, whose marriage was happy and who appeared to treat the children sensibly and kindly and without discriminating between them. On enquiry into his early history it was found that he was a wanted child and had been breast-fed for three months, after which he throve on the bottle. Indeed he was said to be a happy normal child until the age of 18 months, when he got diphtheria. Because of this he was away in [the] hospital for nine months, during the whole of which he remained unvisited by his parents. In [the] hospital he was said to have been adored by everyone, but when he returned home he was a "little stranger." He refused all food and finally was left to starve for a while. His mother described how "it seemed like looking after someone else's baby. He did not know us, he called me 'nurse' and seemed to have no affection for us at all." She said it was fully 18 months before he settled down, although to an external eye it appeared that in fact he had never done so yet.

Personality. He seemed not to care for anyone except possibly his elder brother, but even with him there were spells of unreasonable temper. Usually he was happiest when playing alone. He was markedly undemonstrative and his schoolteacher commented that emotionally he was "very controlled for a young boy." The mother also remarked on this, saying that he was quite unmoved by either affection or punishment, and she had come to regard him as hard-boiled. On the other hand he was always fighting and was at times destructive of both his own and his brother's toys. The teacher complained particularly of his untruthfulness, "wanton destructiveness" and habits of annoying other children.

Stealing and Truanting. He began school at 4 1/2 and liked it at first. But later he disliked the teacher and wanted his brother's teacher. This led to truanting on and off for about a month. The pilfering was noticed soon after his beginning school. It seems to have been quite undiscriminating, for he was said to pilfer from children's pockets, the teacher's desk, from shops and from his mother. Any money he obtained he spent on sweets which he would share with his brother and other children, but not with his parents. He had been repeatedly beaten both by school authorities and at home for stealing, but the beating had no effect on him beyond making him cry for a few moments.

Examination. On tests he was found to have an [IQ] of 125 and to be slow, careful and deliberate in his work. To the psychiatrist he gave the impression of being an engaging, sociable kid. But in his play there was much violent destructiveness. On many occasions he pilfered toys from the Clinic.

Diagnosis. His superficial geniality was misleading at first. As time went on it was clear that his mother's and school-teacher's accounts of his detachment represented the truth. In view of this, his destructiveness, his hard-boiledness, and his unresponsiveness, he seemed to be a typical case of Affectionless Character. This was clearly related to his prolonged hospitalization.[54]

THINK ABOUT IT:

1. Applying Bowlby's attachment theory, what are some essential features that resulted in Derek being "affectionless"?

2. What are some possible treatments that could help Derek?

Source: Bowlby, J. (1944). Forty-four juvenile thieves: Their character and home-life. *International Journal of Psychoanalysis, 25,* 40–41.

MODERN VERSIONS OF PSYCHOLOGICAL PERSPECTIVES OF CRIMINALITY

IQ and Criminal Behavior

As noted in an earlier chapter, in the early 1900s, French psychologist Alfred Binet, along with his colleague Theodore Simon, developed what was considered a more quantified measure of intelligence—the intelligence quotient (IQ). Binet noted that this new approach was a "metric scale of intelligence." The Binet-Simon Intelligence Test was initially developed to study intellectual disabilities among French schoolchildren.[55] A Stanford University professor of educational psychology, Lewis M. Terman, revised the Binet-Simon Intelligence Test. Since its publication in 1916, it has been known as the Stanford-Binet Intelligence Test. Two American psychologists often considered Terman's

intelligence quotient (IQ): a quantified measure of intelligence.

rivals in the area of developing a scaled mental test were Henry H. Goddard and Robert Yerkes.[56]

Goddard is credited with bringing intelligence testing to the United States.[57] He translated and adapted Binet's model to study immigrants who were coming into the United States. An interesting difference between Goddard's and Binet's assumptions about intelligence or IQ was that Goddard maintained that intelligence or IQ was static or innate; thus, an individual's IQ could not change. He argued that intelligence was passed from generation to generation; intelligence was inherited from parents. As noted earlier in this book, Goddard labeled low IQ as "feeble-mindedness." There were specified levels of feeble-mindedness, such as *moron*, *imbecile*, and *idiot*.[58] Goddard's *The Kallikak Family: A Study in Hereditary Feeble-Mindedness* has been considered one of the major contributions to the menace, or threat, myth considered to be linked to feeble-mindedness, as well as to the eugenic prescriptions suggested to address such problems of poverty and crime.

Between 1888 and 1915, various researchers administered intelligence tests to prisoners and boys in reform schools. For instance, in the early 1900s, the Ohio Board of Administration was convinced that more than 40% of the juveniles incarcerated in the state reformatories were "definitely feeble-minded." Further, the board maintained that it was "folly" to try to reform these juveniles because they were not immoral; rather, they were unmoral.[59] There were critics, however, of such research and the subsequent findings. Edwin Sutherland maintained that the intelligence tests administered were inadequate and that there were too many variations of such tests. He also maintained that delinquency is associated more with social and environmental influences than with IQ or intelligence.[60]

James Q. Wilson and Richard J. Herrnstein: Crime and Human Nature

In their book *Crime and Human Nature*, Wilson and Herrnstein reviewed a considerable number of criminological studies that examined the influence of genetic and familial factors on criminal behavior.[80] Lawrence Wrightsman noted that such a shift in focus may be due to the changing political climate. During the 1960s, the dominant liberal political climate was one of optimism; there was a perception that any social problem could be solved. Environmental or sociological explanations of crime were more "palatable," while biological explanations "lost favor" among many social scientists. In the 1980s, however, there was a political shift to a more conservative perspective. Wrightsman maintained that this pendulum shift was more tolerant of hereditary factors being considered to explain criminal behavior.[81] In this vein, conservatives are more likely to consider causes

---

LEARNING CHECK 7.1

1. According to Freud, which of the following is also designated as a conscience?

   a. Ego

   b. Superego

   c. Libido

   d. Id

2. According to Kohlberg, which level of morality is characteristic of designating what is considered "right" and "wrong"?

   a. Preconventional

   b. Conventional

   c. Postconventional

   d. Nonconventional

3. According to Eysenck, which of the following is not associated with one of the three dimensions linked to criminality?

   a. Psychoticism

   b. Extroversion

   c. Anxiety

   d. Neuroticism

Answers located at www.edge.sagepub.com/schram2e

Applying Theory to Crime: RAPE

Many feminists maintain that when placing rape in a historical context, one needs to realize that women have historically been considered the property of either their fathers or their husbands and thereby denied equal status within patriarchal societies. Thus, rape has been considered only within the realm of the male's perspective (i.e., a violation of his property) rather than within the realm of a female's perspective (i.e., a violation of her body).[61] In ancient history, according to lex talionis—or the "an-eye-for-an-eye" philosophy when dealing with offenders—the father of a raped daughter was allowed to rape the rapist's wife. "Bride capture" involved a man raping a woman to establish a permanent relationship with her.[62]

Some feminists argue that the 19th-century approaches to protecting women (e.g., chivalry) were actually efforts among the middle class to control the activities of women working in the public sphere as opposed to the private sphere (i.e., the home). Anne Clark maintains that such efforts perpetuated the myth that as long as "proper" women remained in the home rather than "roaming the streets," they would not be vulnerable to rape.[63] During this time, it was even more difficult if women attempted to involve the court system to seek justice for the crime of rape.

Some have maintained "that the victim of a sexual assault is actually assaulted twice—once by the offender and once by the criminal justice system."[64] Since the increasing public awareness of rape in the 1970s, various legislative reforms have been enacted in an effort to modify rape statutes. Changes in the legal definitions of rape reflect society's changing attitudes regarding this crime. These changes have been especially influenced by the feminist movement. In 1975, the state of Michigan led the country in reforming rape laws. First, it replaced the term *rape* with *criminal sexual conduct*. Second, it identified four degrees of criminal sexual conduct, which were differentiated by the amount of force used, resulting injury, and the age as well as mental state of the victim. This change emphasized the force or coercion used by the perpetrator rather than focusing on the resistance (or lack thereof) of the victim. This shift in perspective incorporated rape with other violent offenses. For instance, a prosecutor does not have to prove beyond a reasonable doubt that a robbery victim did not consent to the offense; thus, why should the prosecutor have to prove beyond a reasonable doubt that a rape victim did not consent to the offense?[65]

A key issue in the definition of rape is whether to include the term *sexual*. One perspective maintains that it is essential to take the "sex out of" rape; rather, rape should be viewed as a crime of violence. Rape is no different than other crimes of violence such as murder and robbery. Another perspective argues that rape is essentially sexual in nature but also violent (i.e., sexual violence). Thus, "to take the sex out of rape is to make it something it is not."[66]

These variations have two important implications regarding measuring rape in the United States. First, because of these differing definitions and procedures, state comparisons are difficult. Second, while some states may have similar legal definitions, the enforcement, prosecution, and conviction procedures may emphasize different legal and possibly extralegal factors.[67]

In reference to the definition issues pertaining to rape, as noted in Chapter 2, the Uniform Crime Reports (UCR) changed the definition of rape starting in 2013. Previously the definition was for *forcible* rape: "the carnal knowledge of a female forcibly and against her will. Attempts or assaults to commit rape by force or threat of force are also included." Since 2013, the definition has been "penetration, no matter how slight, of the vagina or anus with any body part or object, or oral penetration by a sex organ of another person, without the consent of the victim." Attempts or assaults to commit rape are included, but statutory rape and incest are excluded.[68] In 2014, 84,041 rapes (legacy definition) were reported to law enforcement agencies. This was approximately 2.4% higher than in 2013.

The Behavioral Science Unit of the FBI has attempted to provide a classification of rapists. Researchers have also attempted to categorize various types of rapists.[69] One such typology was developed by Raymond Knight and Robert Prentky.[70] They classified rapists into four categories: compensatory, displaced-anger, exploitive, and sadistic rapists (see Table 7.4 for a more detailed description of each type).

Ian could be characterized as an exploitive rapist (see Table 7.4). As with many of these types of rapists, Ian was raised in various foster homes from the age of two. During this time, he was physically abused and neglected. In his adult years, Ian had difficulty establishing and maintaining relationships, especially with women. He had two failed marriages; he had three children by these two women but was not actively involved in their lives. He had a tendency to meet women in situations that did not involve a great deal of emotional intimacy, such as in clubs or casual dating online websites.

After his first failed marriage, Ian committed his first rape. He met the woman, Darlene, in a club. They were talking in the club and drinking quite heavily. Once the club closed, he suggested that Darlene meet him at his house. She agreed. Soon after they arrived at his house, Ian attacked Darlene. Ian later acknowledged that he

TABLE 7.4 Four Categories of Rapists

CATEGORY	DESCRIPTION	CHARACTERISTICS
Compensatory rapists	Compensatory rapists, also referred to as power-reassurance rapists, reveal the least amount of sexual and general aggression when compared with the other typologies. These individuals also demonstrate little evidence of childhood and adolescent impulsivity, such as running away, involvement in the juvenile justice system, or problems in grammar school. Compared with the other typologies, these offenders most often come from stable families with intact parental marriages; fewer of these individuals experienced neglect and physical abuse.	In reference to adult social characteristics, compensatory rapists average a 10th-grade education level. They often are single and live with either one or both parents; this type of rapist is most likely to be dominated by an aggressive and sometimes seductive mother. They are most likely employed in menial occupations and considered steady and reliable employees. In reference to sexual deviance, the compensatory rapist may be involved in transvestism or such behavior as voyeurism, fetishism, or excessive masturbation.[71]
Displaced-anger rapists	The displaced-anger, or anger-retaliation, rapists had the most chaotic and unstable childhoods. Compared with the other typologies, more of these rapists were either adopted or placed in foster homes. They often come from single-parent homes; as with the exploitive and sadistic groups, a number of these individuals were neglected and abused.[72] In reference to adult social characteristics, the displaced-anger group's primary reason to rape is to hurt their victim. Rapes by such individuals are characterized by: (1) the presence of a high degree of nonsexualized aggression or rage, expressed through verbal and physical assaults that clearly exceed what is necessary to force the compliance of the victim; (2) clear evidence, in verbalizations or behavior, of the intent to demean, degrade, or humiliate the victim; (3) no evidence that aggression is eroticized or that sexual pleasure is derived from injurious acts; (4) injurious acts are not focused on parts of the body that have sexual significance.[73]	This group averages a 9th-grade education. This type of offender perceives himself as athletic and masculine. Thus, he may engage in sports and work in an action-oriented occupation as well as engage in extramarital affairs. While this offender is often married, he is not violent toward his partner.
Exploitive rapists	Exploitive, or power-assertive, rapists are twice as likely to have some contact with youth services compared with the other groups. Many of these offenders were raised in single-parent families; almost one third lived in foster homes. As with the displaced-anger rapists, a large number of these offenders were physically abused.	In reference to adult characteristics, these rapists have many domestic issues; they also may have experienced a number of unhappy marriages. They are typically well dressed and may frequent clubs to pick up women. This type of offender may be employed in a traditionally male occupation, such as construction. He attempts to exude an image of masculinity in his physical appearance and demeanor.[74] For this offender, the "sexual behavior is hypothesized to be an impulsive, predatory act. . . . The victim seems to have little or no psychological meaning to the offender, and represents, hypothetically, a masturbatory object."[75]
Sadistic rapists	Of the various typologies, the sadistic rapist is the most dangerous. With this type of offender, as sexual arousal increases, the aggressive nature of the offense emerges; this usually results in the most bizarre and intense forms of sexually aggressive violence.[76] More than half of those designated as sadistic rapists were raised in single-parent homes. Many of these offenders were physically abused; a number of them also experienced some type of sexual deviance during childhood.	In reference to adult characteristics, the sadistic rapist is usually married, and some consider him to be a "good family man." He often lives in a middle-class residential area with low criminal activity; he typically has a better-than-average education and is employed in a white-collar occupation.

(Continued)

(Continued)

never "planned" on raping Darlene. Rather, he stated that it was more of an impulsive act—in the "spur of the moment." He had no ill feelings toward Darlene; in fact, Ian stated that "he had no feelings toward her whatsoever."

One theoretical perspective that could possibly be applied to this offense is Bowlby's attachment theory. Due to Ian's unstable childhood, he was unable to form healthy attachments, especially with his mother. Further, these attachments lacked specificity given the various foster homes he was placed in throughout childhood. Related to this, the attachments lacked duration; they were short-lived and sporadic, at best. The problems associated with Ian establishing healthy attachments in childhood were reflected during his adulthood. He had difficulty developing strong relationships, especially with women. This may also have contributed to his ability to rape by perceiving the victim as having "little or no psychological meaning."

THINK ABOUT IT:

1. Are there any other essential features of Bowlby's theory that could apply to Ian's behavior?

2. What approaches could be implemented to enhance Ian's relationships, especially with women?

of crime within the individual as well as to blame the behavior on the criminal's lack of moral sense; liberals are more likely to consider the causes of crime in society, such as unequal distribution of wealth. Thus, "conservatives are much more likely to see criminals as different from normal citizens, while liberals are more likely to see them as people who have simply reacted differently to different situations they find themselves in."[82]

Wilson (at the time, a Harvard University political scientist) and Herrnstein (a Harvard University psychologist) never explicitly "named" their theory,[83] but Jack Gibbs has suggested that they use the label *operant-utilitarian theory of criminality*, since they often use concepts associated with operant psychology.[84] They maintained that there had been an overemphasis on sociological explanations for criminal behavior:

> The existence of biological predispositions means that circumstances that activate criminal behavior in one person will not do so in another, that social forces cannot deter criminal behavior in 100 percent of a population, and that the distributions of crime within and across societies may, to some extent, reflect underlying distributions of constitutional factors. *Perhaps the simplest thing to say at this point is that crime cannot be understood without taking into account individual predispositions and their biological roots* [italics added].[85]

Wilson and Herrnstein attempted to explain street crime by demonstrating how human nature develops and evolves from the interaction of three factors:

1. *Social environment.* While broad societal values have often been neglected as explanations, they maintained that the shift in American culture from valuing restraint and discipline to the recent narcissistic "me-first" orientation has a strong influence on the individual level and has contributed to the increasing crime rate during the previous two decades.

2. *Family relationships.* Parents who are uncaring, inconsistent in the treatment of their children, or unskilled in dispensing rewards and punishments contribute to their children's criminal behavior. Further, being from a broken home or a single-parent household is not necessarily an influential factor; rather, it is the parent's failure to teach the child the consequences of his or her actions.

3. *Biological makeup.* Qualities considered influential include gender, low intelligence, impulsiveness, and body type. These are at least partly hereditary.[86]

Comparative Criminology: SEXUAL OFFENSES

Ranking of Countries According to Sexual Offenses or Incidents Against Women

Sexual assault/rape offenses are some of the most difficult crimes for which to obtain accurate numbers. This is especially problematic when comparing such offenses across various countries. Specifically, "perceptions as to what is unacceptable sexual behavior may differ significantly across countries, even in the current era of increasingly globalized norms and values."[77] One question on the International Crime Victimization Survey asked the following:

> People sometimes grab, touch, or assault others for sexual reasons in a really offensive way. This can happen either at home or elsewhere, for instance, in a pub, the street, at school, on public transport, in cinemas, on the beach, or at one's workplace. Over the past five years has anyone done this to you?[78]

In terms of victimization, only those incidents that occurred in the previous year were included. It is essential to stress that this item covers a broad range of behaviors; these range from rape and attempted rape to less serious offenses. Table 7.5 summarizes the rates of sexual offenses or incidents against women among the various countries.

Van Dijk (2008) highlighted a few key findings from these analyses. In the group with the highest rates, the first 10 countries are considered to be "low gender equality." Low gender equality is when the social position of women is rather weak; women are often considered inferior in various social contexts, such as the family and the workplace. When looking at countries such as Finland, Denmark, the United States, the Netherlands, Canada, Switzerland, the United Kingdom, Germany, and New Zealand, their rates are relatively high considering that these countries are deemed to have higher gender equality. Citing Kangaspunta's work,[79] Van Dijk states that this may be because individuals living in countries with a more liberal view of women are more likely to report such sexual incidents or crimes.

THINK ABOUT IT:

1. What are some of the reasons that sexual assault/rape offenses are so difficult to measure and compare across countries/cultures?

2. How do varying levels of gender equality play a role in rates of sexual assault?

3. Did any of the countries in the rankings surprise you by how high (or low) their rates of sexual assault were compared to those of other countries?

TABLE 7.5 Ranking of Countries According to Sexual Offenses or Incidents Against Women

FIFTEEN COUNTRIES WITH THE HIGHEST RATES					
1 Papua, New Guinea	11.8	6 Swaziland	6.2	11 Namibia	4.8
2 Colombia	10.2	7 Lesotho	5.7	12 Peru	4.7
3 Nigeria	8.8	8 Costa Rica	5.5	13 Serbia and Montenegro	4.6
4 India	7.0	9 Zambia	5.4	14 Finland	4.3
5 Albania	6.7	10 Botswana	5.0	15 Denmark	3.8
FIFTEEN COUNTRIES WITH MEDIUM-HIGH RATES					
16 United States	3.5	28 Germany	2.5	45 Austria	1.3
20 Netherlands	3.2	29 New Zealand	2.4	46 Brazil	1.3
21 Canada	3.1	36 Bolivia	1.8	49 Hong Kong, China	1.2
22 Switzerland	3.1	39 Mexico	1.7	51 Greece	1.1
25 United Kingdom	3.0	40 Japan	1.7	52 Italy	0.9

Sources: Van Dijk, J. (2008). *The world of crime: Breaking the silence on problems of security, justice, and development across the world.* Thousand Oaks, CA: SAGE, p. 85; ICVS, 1996–2005.

The third factor, *biological makeup*, is considered the most controversial aspect of Wilson and Herrnstein's theoretical perspective. They stressed that this theory was not one of predestination. Rather, they argued that the question of whether criminals are "born or made" is poorly phrased. The word *born* implies that some part of criminality may be due, categorically and permanently, to assigned constitutional factors (e.g., genetics); the word *made* implies that some aspect of criminality may be due, categorically and permanently, to social factors. They maintained that such a viewpoint "neglects, obviously, the complex interactions that exist between those causes."[87]

Wilson and Herrnstein contend that at any time, a person can choose between committing a crime and not committing a crime. The consequences of committing a crime consist of rewards and punishments. The greater the ratio of net rewards of crime to net rewards of noncrime, the greater the tendency to commit the crime.[88] Further, constitutional factors, such as intelligence and impulsivity, can influence an individual's ability to judge future and immediate rewards and punishments. Thus, "aggressive and impulsive males with low intelligence are at a greater risk for committing crimes than are young males who have developed 'the bite of conscience,' which reflects higher cognitive and intellectual development."[89] In reference to intelligence, Wilson and Herrnstein argued that social scientists have maintained that individuals identified as offenders have an average IQ of 92, which is about 8 points below the population average. Further, they contend that a low IQ may result in offenders' inability to think past "short-term" situations or difficulty understanding society's rules and the consequences of their actions.[90]

There have been various criticisms of Wilson and Herrnstein's theoretical perspective.[91] One is that they failed to empirically test their terms, such as *ratio of rewards*. Specifically, they did not adequately operationalize these terms; this makes it difficult for researchers to test their theory. Another concern was the focus on street and predatory crimes, such as murder, robbery, and burglary. They did not include other offenses such as white-collar crimes. As Gibbs asked, "Are some white-collar crimes predatory?"[92] Some argued that while Wilson and Herrnstein objectively selected and presented relevant literature, they may have actually selectively reviewed literature that supported their theory. Thus, "although readers were given the impression that the authors' arguments were based on solid *science* and, therefore, should be *believed*, critics asserted that, in more than one instance, these arguments were based on shaky evidence."[93]

Psychopathy and Crime

David Lykken distinguished between the terms *sociopath* and *psychopath*. Sociopath refers specifically to antisocial personalities attributed to social or familial dysfunction. Psychopath refers to individuals whose antisocial behavior may be a result of a defect or abnormality within themselves, rather than in their rearing or socialization. In his classic book *Mask of Sanity*, Hervey Cleckley maintained that psychopaths are intelligent, self-centered, glib, superficially charming, verbally shallow, and manipulative. In terms of emotions, these individuals lack essential human characteristics such as empathy and remorse. Behaviorally, psychopaths engage in irresponsible behavior, are prone to seek novelty and excitation, and often engage in moral transgressions or antisocial acts.[94]

While there were various attempts to develop an assessment tool measuring psychopathy, it was not until the mid-1980s that major advances were made. Robert Hare developed the Psychopathy Checklist–Revised (PCL-R) to examine psychopathy in adult samples. His scale adapted some of Cleckley's concepts of psychopathic individuals as well as including such factors as impulsivity and criminological components (e.g., criminal versatility).[95] The Hare PCL-R includes scales measuring two factors: (1) the callous, selfish, remorseless use of others, and (2) a chronically unstable and antisocial lifestyle.[96]

sociopath: refers specifically to antisocial personalities that are due to social or familial dysfunction.

psychopath: refers to individuals whose antisocial behavior may result from a defect or abnormality within themselves rather than in their rearing or socialization.

While a majority of the research on psychopathy has considered it as one construct, other studies in the adult literature have focused on possible subtypes or subgroups of psychopathy.[97] One subgroup is consistent with Cleckley's original concept of the *primary* psychopath:

> [An individual] who displays certain characteristics that are maladaptive and pathological (e.g., lack of conscience, irresponsibility, failure to learn from experience)—as well as key traits that appear ostensibly adaptive, or at least nonpathological (e.g., low anxiety, interpersonal charm, absence of irrational thinking).[98]

Another subgroup also has many of the same *maladaptive* traits as the primary psychopath. However, this subtype, or *secondary* psychopath, seems to be more prone to exhibit extensive symptoms of psychological turmoil and emotional reactivity. Also, these individuals tend to be more reactive, antagonistic, and impulsive; they are also more at risk for engaging in self- and other-destructive behavior such as drug use/abuse, suicidal ideation/gestures, and interpersonal aggression.[99]

Various theories have attempted to explain psychopathy. Lykken suggested the *low fear-quotient theory*. He maintained that all individuals have an innate propensity to fear certain stimuli, such as loss of support, snakes, or strangers. Individuals subsequently associate, or condition, fear of stimuli and situations that they have previously experienced with pain or punishment. This is referred to as an innate *fear quotient*; this fear quotient varies from person to person. Primary psychopaths are at the low end of this fear-quotient continuum. Further, most of the normal socialization process relies on punishing antisocial behavior. However, "someone who is relatively fearless will be relatively harder to socialize in this way"[100] (see Box 7.1).

BOX 7.1

Lykken provided the following example of a child who demonstrated fearlessness. The letter was written by the mother of a teenage daughter in response to an article Lykken wrote for a popular magazine:

> Your article on fearlessness was very informative. I was able to identify with many of the traits. However, being thirty-six and a single parent of three children, I have managed to backpack on the "edge" without breaking my neck. I have a 14-year-old daughter who seems to be almost fearless to anything in her environment. She jumps out second-story windows. When she was in first grade, I came home from work one afternoon and found her hanging by her fingers from our upstairs

window. I "calmly" asked her what she was doing. She replied that she was "getting refreshed." Later, she stated that she did things like that when she needed a lift—that she was bored and it made her feel better. Nancy is bright, witty, attractive, charismatic, and meets people easily. She tends to choose friends who are offbeat, antisocial, and into dope, alcohol, etc. During her month's visit here with me, she stole money from my purse, my bank card, etc., etc.[101]

THINK ABOUT IT:

How would you explain the link between this girl's "fearlessness" and her criminal behavior?

©iStockphoto.com/aluxum

Another explanation of psychopathy is *inhibitory defect* or *underendowment*. Some psychopathic individuals seem to act impulsively without assessing the situation, appreciating the dangers, or considering the consequences. This perspective maintains that lesions in certain areas of the brain can cause a decrease in inhibitory control in animals as well as humans. This view does not argue that *all* psychopaths have lesions or qualitative defects in their frontal cortex areas; rather, frontal lesions can produce a syndrome similar to psychopathy.[102]

The interpersonal and affective factors associated with psychopathy often are related to a socially deviant lifestyle, including irresponsible and impulsive behavior; these behaviors tend to ignore or violate social rules and mores. While not all psychopaths have any type of formal contact with the criminal justice system, the interpersonal, affective, and behavioral features of psychopathy place them at a high risk for aggression and violence.[103] With the widespread adoption of the PCL-R to assess psychopathy, there is empirical evidence on the association between psychopathy and criminal behavior.[104] Research has revealed that while psychopathy occurs in about 1% of the general population, these individuals make up a significant proportion of the prison population.[105]

Hare stressed that while psychopathy is closely associated with antisocial and criminal behavior, it should not be confused with criminality in general.[106] He noted that psychopaths are *qualitatively* different from other individuals involved in criminal behav-

Referring to Lykken's *low fear-quotient theory*, do you think this woman is more at the low- or high-end of the fear-quotient continuum?

ior. Specifically, he noted that psychopaths have a distinct criminal career in terms of the number and type of antisocial behaviors as well as the ages when they engage in these behaviors. Also, the motivation to engage in these antisocial behaviors differs between psychopaths and nonpsychopaths.

In terms of treatment of psychopaths, most clinicians and researchers are less than optimistic about successful outcomes. A major reason is that unlike most other types of offenders, psychopaths do not experience personal distress and do not appreciate the problems associated with their attitudes and behavior. Further, when they do seek treatment, it is usually in an effort to benefit their situation, such as seeking probation and parole, rather than to improve themselves. Thus, "it is not surprising that they derive little benefit from traditional treatment programs, particularly those aimed at the development of empathy, conscience, and interpersonal skills."[107]

MENTAL HEALTH AND THE CRIMINAL JUSTICE SYSTEM

The proportion of male and female jail detainees with a mental health disorder is significantly higher than the proportion of people with a mental health disorder in the general population.[108] Some have referred to the "in and out" of prison and/or jail among offenders with mental health disorders as "the revolving door."[109] According to the Treatment Advocacy Center:

Prisons and jails have become America's "new asylums": The number of individuals with serious mental illness in prisons and jails now exceeds the number in state psychiatric hospitals tenfold. Most of the mentally ill individuals in prisons and jails would have been treated in the state psychiatric hospitals in the years before the deinstitutionalization movement led to the closing of the hospitals, a trend that continues even today. The treatment of mentally ill individuals in prisons and jails is critical, especially since such individuals are vulnerable and often abused while incarcerated. Untreated, their psychiatric illness often gets worse, and they leave prison or jail sicker than when they entered.[110]

Various issues are associated with mental health and the criminal justice system. In this section, we briefly present some of these issues, beginning with treatment approaches.

Treatment

Different types of treatment methods have been implemented to address problems linked to criminality, including coping and problem-solving skills, conflict resolution, empathy, and relationships with peers, parents, and other adults.

For instance, in 1997 the Thinking for a Change program was developed by Bush, Glick, and Taymans in cooperation with the National Institute of Corrections. Thinking for a Change is an integrated cognitive behavioral change program that includes cognitive restructuring, social skill development, and development of problem-solving skills. The program was designed to be used with offender populations in prisons, jails, community corrections, and probation and parole settings.[111] Generally, cognitive intervention is

an approach that focuses on the ways that offenders think. Thinking includes a wide array of skills and processes, such as problem-solving skills, the ability to empathize with others and victims, the ability to formulate and then achieve plans for the future, and the ability to foresee the consequences of one's own behavior.[112]

A major impetus to developing this program was based on the experience that criminal behavior was more vulnerable to positive social change when offenders were able to apply, and incorporate, both cognitive restructuring and cognitive skills programs.[113]

In reference to studies evaluating the Thinking for a Change program, Golden, Gatchel, and Cahill's study revealed some "mixed" results concerning recidivism.[114] They concluded that the program does improve problem-solving skills among those who have completed the program. These skills may subsequently deter them from engaging in future criminal activity. The researchers also noted that future research might consider exploring whether "booster sessions," such as an aftercare group or relapse prevention measures, could further deter future criminal behavior. While cognitive behavioral

---

LEARNING CHECK 7.2

1. Goddard maintained that intelligence or IQ:

   a. was influenced by one's environment.

   b. was influenced by one's socialization.

   c. was static or innate.

   d. did not influence criminality.

2. Wilson and Herrnstein argued that street crime is associated with human nature and maintained that human nature develops and evolves from the interaction of three factors. Which of the following is **NOT** one of those three factors?

   a. Social environment

   b. Peer relationships

   c. Family relationships

   d. Biological makeup

3. According to Cleckley, which of the following is an individual who displays certain characteristics that are maladaptive and pathological, as well as key traits that appear ostensibly adaptive or at least nonpathological?

   a. Primary

   b. Secondary

   c. Sociopath

   d. Nonpsychopath

Answers located at www.edge.sagepub.com/schram2e

Thinking for a Change: an integrated cognitive behavioral change program that includes cognitive restructuring, social skill development, and the development of problem-solving skills.

WHY DO THEY DO IT?

ARIEL CASTRO

On May 6, 2013, the world learned of the horrific ordeal three young women endured at the house of Ariel Castro on Seymour Avenue in Cleveland, Ohio. The first woman, Michelle Knight, was abducted on August 23, 2002. She was 21 years old at the time. The second young woman, Amanda Berry, disappeared on April 21, 2003; she was almost 17 years of age at the time. The third adolescent, Georgina "Gina" DeJesus, went missing on April 2, 2004. She was 14 years old.[116] All three women suffered unimaginable sexual, physical, and emotional abuse for years. Amanda Berry described the conditions of her imprisonment. She was forced to sleep on a filthy mattress and had only a bucket for using the bathroom, resulting in a despicable odor. Castro would give her a bag of chips or crackers or some other food. However, this, along with other essentials such as a shower, was given at a price. Berry also mentioned that one of the cruelest deeds was when Castro would play "mind games." DeJesus stated that Castro made her play "Russian roulette."

On Christmas Day, 2006, Amanda Berry gave birth to a little girl, Jocelyn. As she grew older, Castro allowed Jocelyn certain freedoms that were not given to Knight, Berry, or DeJesus. While Jocelyn was often locked in with the three women, on occasion, Castro would allow her to go outside to play in the backyard or the park or attend Sunday services. Berry stated that "she loved him and he loved her." However, she was nervous because she was never sure if he would sexually abuse Jocelyn.

After 10 years, the women finally escaped. One day, Berry realized that the bedroom door was unlocked and Castro was not in the home. A neighbor, Charles Ramsey, helped Berry free herself from the padlocked storm door. Subsequently, Berry called 911. On August 1, 2013, Ariel Castro was sentenced to life plus 1,000 years. He pled guilty to 937 counts of kidnapping and rape. On September 3, 2013, he committed suicide by hanging himself in his prison cell.[117]

Findings from a report by a prison mental health clinician prior to Castro's suicide revealed that he believed that his victims were equally to blame for his crimes. He stated that his behavior was due to his addiction to pornography. The report noted that Castro was a deeply troubled man who was simultaneously pompous, demanding, happy, paranoid, and frustrated. While in prison, he was warned on numerous occasions to wear clothes in his cell when female corrections officers were present. He would ask for clean underwear and bedding while claiming, "Still nothing gets done. I don't know if I can take this neglect anymore, and the way I'm being treated. . . . I feel as though I'm being pushed over the edge, one day at a time." Castro was diagnosed with narcissistic personality disorder with antisocial features. However, he was not considered a high suicide risk.[118]

THINK ABOUT IT:

1. What should the criminal justice system do for offenders such as Castro?

2. Do you think there is a strong link between individuals with mental health issues and criminal behavior?

3. Should there be more coordination and collaboration between the criminal justice and mental health systems?

approaches have been applied to various types of programs such as case management, psychologically oriented treatments, and psychoeducational programs, such applications have, according to Wilson, resulted in there being no differences between offenders who participate in a problem-solving skills development program and those who do not.[115]

Six areas of treatment that have demonstrated some evidence of effectiveness for treatment offenders with mental illness include the following:

- Collaborative psychopharmacology—symptoms of mental illness improve when clients are included in the medical decision-making process.

- Assertive community treatment—providing services to clients in their community as opposed to a clinical setting such as an outpatient clinic or psychiatric hospital.

- Family psychoeducation—educating family members about mental illness as well as the effects of mental illness, enhancing interpersonal relations, and encouraging a supportive support system.

- Supported employment—assisting clients to obtain competitive employment and provide assistance when needed (e.g., skill development).

- Illness management and recovery—supporting clients to take responsibility for their recovery in an effort to manage their illness.

- Integrated dual disorders treatment—focusing on issues of mental illness and substance abuse simultaneously in an integrated approach.[119]

Bill Pugliano/Getty Images

The home of Ariel Castro.

Mental Health Courts

The concept of mental health courts developed from the drug court model in the late 1980s. The first mental health court was created in 1997 in Broward County, Florida. In 2000, President Clinton signed the America's Law Enforcement and Mental Health Project bill. This bill authorized the establishment of up to 100 mental health courts and allocated $10 million a year, for up to four years, to maintain these courts.[120] As with drug courts, a major reason for establishing mental health courts was to address the large proportion of individuals with mental illnesses involved in the criminal justice system. Thus, "like drug courts and other 'problem-solving courts,' . . . mental health courts move beyond the criminal court's traditional focus on case processing to address the root causes of behaviors that bring people before the court."[121] The goals of mental health courts include increasing public safety for communities, increasing treatment participation and quality of life for offenders, and enhancing the use of resources in various communities.[122]

Based on a "working definition," mental health courts share some common features. First, this is a specialized court for offenders with mental health illnesses. Second, as noted above, this court focuses more on problem-solving approaches. Third, participants in this court are identified through a series of mental health screenings and assessments. Fourth, these offenders voluntarily participate in a judicially supervised treatment plan. Finally, there are incentives for adherence to the treatment as well as sanctions for nonadherence.[123] There are, however, variations among the different mental health courts, such as target population, charge accepted (i.e., misdemeanor or felony), plea arrangement, intensity of supervision, program duration, and type of treatment available.

Most of the mental health court participants suffer from serious mental illnesses. The term *mental illness* covers a broad range of psychological disorders. Within the group of disorders considered serious are those illnesses that are severe and persistent, such as schizophrenia, schizoaffective disorder, bipolar disorder, severe depression, and anxiety

mental health courts: courts established to address the large proportion of individuals involved in the criminal justice system who have mental illnesses.

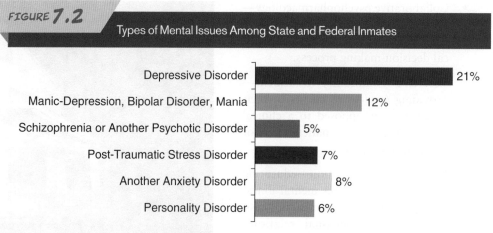

FIGURE 7.2

Types of Mental Issues Among State and Federal Inmates

Depressive Disorder	21%
Manic-Depression, Bipolar Disorder, Mania	12%
Schizophrenia or Another Psychotic Disorder	5%
Post-Traumatic Stress Disorder	7%
Another Anxiety Disorder	8%
Personality Disorder	6%

U.S. Department of Justice, Bureau of Justice Statistics 2007/Urban Institute

Source: http://www.theatlantic.com/health/archive/2015/04/more-than-half-of-prisoners-are-mentally-ill/389682/ but data from http://www.bjs.gov/content/pub/pdf/mhppji.pdf

disorders (see Figure 7.2). Most states, when determining the criteria for participating in mental health courts, consider offenders' level of functioning as well as "severe and persistent" disorders to prioritize their access to mental health services. Some mental health courts accept individuals with a broad range of mental conditions.

Insanity Defense

Society has often been challenged with the idea that a mentally ill person should not be held criminally responsible for his or her actions.[124] The idea of excusing offenders for their criminal actions due to a mental disease has been in existence for centuries.[125] Insanity is not a medical term; rather, it is a legal term. In this context, questions such as the following are raised:

insanity: the idea—which has been in existence for centuries—of excusing offenders for their criminal actions due to a mental disease; the term is not a medical term but rather a legal term.

- Is the person so insane that he or she cannot make a valid will?

- Is the person so insane that he or she should be civilly committed?

- Is the person so insane that he or she cannot be tried for his or her alleged crime?[126]

The general rationale for an insanity defense is that a person should not be punished for engaging in a criminal act if he or she could not refrain from committing the act. The law is established to punish those individuals who make the wrong choices; thus, those people who do not have free choice, due to a mental illness, should not be punished for such acts.[127]

Mental health courts, modeled after drug courts, attempt to address the issues that bring a person to court.

Craig F. Walker/The Denver Post/Getty Images

The standards for establishing an insanity defense vary extensively among the different states. Four states—Kansas, Montana, Idaho, and Utah—do not allow for an insanity defense. However, Montana, Idaho, and Utah do have a provision under which an offender can receive a guilty but insane, or mentally ill, verdict.[128] Among the states that do allow an insanity defense, there are essentially four types of tests—again, with modified versions as well. These include the M'Naghten rule, irresistible impulse test, Durham

TABLE 7.6 Various Insanity Defense Standards

TEST	LEGAL STANDARD BECAUSE OF MENTAL ILLNESS	FINAL BURDEN OF PROOF	WHO BEARS THE BURDEN OF PROOF
M'Naghten	"Didn't know what he was doing or didn't know it was wrong"	Varies between proof by a balance of probabilities on the part of the defense to proof beyond a reasonable doubt on the part of the prosecutor	
Irresistible impulse	"Could not control his conduct"		
Durham	"The criminal act was caused by his mental illness"	Beyond reasonable doubt	Prosecutor
Brawner–ALI	"Lacks substantial capacity to appreciate the wrongfulness of his conduct or to control it"	Beyond reasonable doubt	Prosecutor
Present federal law	"Lacks capacity to appreciate the wrongfulness of his conduct"	Clear and convincing evidence	Defense

Source: Morris, N. (n.d.). Crime file: Insanity defense. Washington, DC: U.S. Department of Justice, National Institute of Justice, p. 3. Retrieved from https://www.ncjrs.gov/pdffiles1/Digitization/100742NCJRS.pdf.

test, and American Law Institute's Model Penal Code (see Table 7.6). Table 7.7 is a brief summary of defenses related to mental health that have been attempted by defense attorneys.

THE M'NAGHTEN RULE. This is the oldest rule for determining insanity.[129] The M'Naghten case introduced the modern concept of insanity into English Common Law, which later influenced law in the United States. In 1843, Daniel M'Naghten shot Edward Drummond, who was the secretary to the British prime minister, Sir Robert Peel. M'Naghten thought that Peel, along with the "Tories," was involved in a conspiracy against him. He believed that the only feasible way to resolve this issue was to kill Peel. Unfortunately, M'Naghten mistook Drummond for Peel. The issue of insanity was formally introduced in M'Naghten's trial. He was subsequently acquitted by a jury on the grounds of insanity.[130] As noted in Table 7.6, the legal standard is that "he didn't know what he was doing or didn't know it was wrong." Specifically, the M'Naghten rule is as follows:

1. Every person is presumed sane unless the contrary can be proven.

2. A person suffering a "partial" delusion should be dealt with as if the circumstance of the delusion was real.

3. To establish a defence on the grounds of insanity, it must be clearly proved that
   - at the *time of committing the act,*
   - the accused was laboring under such a *defect of reason,*
   - from a *disease of the mind,*
   - as *not to know the nature and quality of the act he was doing*
   - and if he did know it (the nature and quality of the act he was doing), that *he did not know what he was doing was wrong.*[131]

THE IRRESISTIBLE IMPULSE TEST. In 1897, the federal courts, and subsequently many state courts, included the irresistible impulse test with the M'Naghten "right–wrong" test. With this test, offenders can claim that, due to a mental disease, they were unable to control their behavior.[132] The standard for this test is that the individual could not control

M'Naghten rule: the legal standard that "he didn't know what he was doing or didn't know it was wrong" resulting from the M'Naghten case, which introduced the modern concept of insanity into English Common Law.

irresistible impulse: one standard for the insanity defense; offenders can claim that, due to a mental disease, they were unable to control their behavior.

his or her conduct. One well-known case that used this defense was that of Lorena Bobbitt. In 1993, Lorena Bobbitt severed her husband's penis with a kitchen knife.

During the testimony, Mrs. Bobbitt stated that minutes after her drunken husband raped her, she was drinking a glass of water in the kitchen. It was at this time that she noticed a 12-inch knife. She picked up the knife and cut off her husband's penis while he was sleeping. She further testified that she had not realized what she had done until later. She noticed the knife in one hand and her husband's penis in the other. The defense argued that, given the abuse from her husband and also her various mental illnesses, after her husband raped her, Mrs. Bobbitt experienced an "irresistible impulse" to retaliate against him.[133]

THE DURHAM RULE. In the 1954 case *Durham v. United States*, the court included a volitional or free-choice component to the insanity defense. Thus, according to the Durham rule, offenders are not criminally responsible, even if they are aware of their conduct, if this behavior was the "product of mental disease or defect."[134] Judge David Bazelon noted that the M'Naghten rule was too narrow. The court argued that the test should incorporate the situation in which psychopathic disorders are qualifying conditions.[135]

AMERICAN LAW INSTITUTE'S MODEL PENAL CODE. About one year after the Durham decision, the American Law Institute's Model Penal Code (ALI/MPC) developed the substantial capacity test. Due to vague and contradictory rules about insanity, a number of states adopted the ALI test. The test includes the following, in Section 4.01 of the Model Penal Code:

> A person is not responsible for criminal conduct if at the time of such conduct as a result of mental disease or defect he lacks substantial capacity either to appreciate the criminality (wrongfulness) or his conduct or to conform his conduct to the requirements of the law.[136]

A key difference between the M'Naghten and ALI/MPC tests is that the M'Naghten test stipulates that the offender must demonstrate *total* mental impairment; the ALI/MPC test stipulates that the offender must demonstrate a lack of *substantial capacity*.

Durham rule: offenders are not criminally responsible, even if they are aware of their conduct, if this behavior was the "product of mental disease or defect."

American Law Institute's Model Penal Code (ALI/MPC): one standard for the insanity defense; the ALI/MPC test stipulates that the offender demonstrate a lack of substantial capacity.

TABLE **7.7**

DEFENSE	DESCRIPTION
Affluenza	In June 2013, then 16-year-old Ethan Couch was driving while under the influence. His car struck a stalled vehicle, killing four individuals. A psychologist, hired by the defense, testified that Couch was a product of "affluenza"—his privilege and upbringing did not provide him the ability to connect his actions with consequences.
Sleepwalking	In 1997, Scott Falater stabbed his wife 44 times and subsequently drowned her in their swimming pool. His defense was that he did not remember killing his wife because he was sleepwalking. Falater was convicted of first-degree murder and was sentenced to life in prison.
Television intoxication	In 1977, Ronny Zamora shot and killed his elderly neighbor because she caught him burglarizing her home. Zamora's attorney raised the television intoxication defense—his client could not distinguish between reality and fantasy due to his obsession with violent television shows, such as *Kojak*.
Twinkie	In 1978, after Dan White lost his job as a San Francisco supervisor, he consumed large amounts of junk food (e.g., candy and Coca-Cola). Because he was depressed, as supported by his large consumption of junk food, Dan White brought a gun into city hall. He killed Mayor Moscone and Supervisor Milk.
Premenstrual syndrome (PMS)	In 1984, Margaret Mileau was charged with aggravated assault and reckless driving in Florida. She claimed that premenstrual syndrome was the reason she went into a rage and rammed her car into the rear as well as the passenger's and driver's doors of a car in which her boyfriend was a passenger.

Mental Health Defenses Attempted by Defense Attorneys

POLICY IMPLICATIONS OF PSYCHOLOGICAL/TRAIT THEORIES

Although precise estimates on the number of offenders with mental disorders vary, the number of these individuals is quite high and has been increasing in recent years.[137] As noted earlier, some have referred to the "in and out" of prison and/or jail among offenders with mental health disorders as "the revolving door." Thus, a major policy implication would be to address this "revolving door." One suggested approach would be to implement primary, secondary, and tertiary prevention programs. Generally, primarily prevention focuses on eliminating influences that could potentially result in someone engaging in criminal activity.[138] For instance, teachers, employers, and family may make referrals to family therapy organizations, substance abuse clinics, and mental health associations.[139] Secondary prevention focuses on intervening for individuals who demonstrate a tendency toward criminal behavior.[140] In reference to mental health, these types of prevention programs can provide treatment such as psychological counseling to at-risk individuals.[141] Tertiary prevention deals with eliminating recidivistic behavior of offenders.[142] For offenders with mental health problems, tertiary prevention programs may involve requirement of a probation order or diversionary sentence as well as an aftercare program at the end of a prison sentence.[143]

Morgan and his colleagues examined various studies that focused on the treatment effects of service providers to offenders with mental illness. The results revealed that interventions with these types of offenders lessened symptoms of distress as well as improved offenders' ability to cope with their problems. These effects resulted in offenders demonstrating improved institutional adjustment and behavioral functioning. Further, these interventions revealed significant reductions in psychiatric and criminal recidivism. Morgan et al. noted that these results should be of great interest to policy and decision makers: "[T]he results of this review suggest that improvements in the *co-occurring dimensions of mental illness and criminalness are possible* [italics added]."[144]

U.S. Marshals Service

Justice. Integrity. Service.   U.S. Department of Justice

For Immediate Release
December 18, 2015

Contact:
Northern District of Texas (214) 767-0836;
USMS Office of Public Affairs (202) 307-9065

'Affluenza' Teen Wanted by U.S. Marshals

UPDATE: Ethan Couch was Apprehended in Mexico on December 29, 2015

Washington - The U.S. Marshals North Texas Fugitive Task Force is currently searching for fugitive Ethan Couch, 18, wanted for probation violation out of Tarrant County. Couch's case made national news in 2013 when he was sentenced to 10 years probation for the vehicular manslaughter of four people. On December 11th, a warrant was issued for Couch's arrest.

U.S. Marshals are working in conjunction with state, local, and federal agencies in the apprehension of Couch. A reward of up to five thousand dollars is being offered for information that leads to the arrest of Couch.

U.S. Marshals task forces combine the efforts of federal, state, and local law enforcement agencies to locate and arrest the most dangerous fugitives. In 2014, U.S. Marshals arrested more than 104,000 fugitives.

Additional information about the U.S. Marshals Service can be found at http://www.usmarshals.gov.

####

America's Oldest Federal Law Enforcement Agency

The "Wanted" poster for Ethan Couch. Couch's attorney argued that he was suffering from "affluenza" and should not be held accountable for his actions. Should this be a viable defense?

LEARNING CHECK 7.3

1. Some have referred to the "in and out" of prison and/or jail among offenders with mental health disorders as:

   a. the downward spiral

   b. the revolving door

   c. the elevator system of justice

   d. the inverted sieve

2. Mental health courts were modeled after:

   a. the American Psychological Association's Model Health Court

   b. civil court procedures

   c. drug courts

   d. family courts

3. For this standard, the court included a volitional or free-choice component to the insanity defense:

   a. M'Naghten rule

   b. Irresistible impulse

   c. Durham

   d. ALI/MPC

Answers located at www.edge.sagepub.com/schram2e

CONCLUSION

This chapter summarized theories that focus on psychological aspects of criminality rather than sociological aspects. According to Mischel, there are various fundamental assumptions of psychological theories of criminality.[145] Some of these assumptions include the following:

1. Personality is the major motivational element within individuals because it is the seat of drives and the source of motives.

2. Crimes result from abnormal, dysfunctional, or inappropriate mental processes within the personality.

3. Criminal behavior, although condemned by the social group, may be purposeful for the individual insofar as it addresses certain felt needs.

4. Normality is generally defined by social consensus.

5. Defective, or abnormal, mental processes may have a variety of causes, including a diseased mind, inappropriate learning or improper conditioning, the copying of inappropriate role models, and adjustment to inner conflicts.[146]

This chapter started with early psychological perspectives such as psychoanalysis, dimensions of an individual's personality (e.g., psychoticism, extroversion, and neuroticism) and criminal behavior, moral development, and attachment to significant others. The following section presented more current psychological perspectives, beginning with the controversial discussion concerning intelligence and criminality. Next, we reviewed the theoretical perspective some have named operant-utilitarian theory of criminality, which maintains that various factors influence criminal behavior, including biological factors such as gender, low intelligence, impulsiveness, and body type. We concluded this section with various issues pertaining to mental health in the criminal justice system.

At the beginning of this chapter, we presented the case of Albert Fish. It is interesting to note that while the jurors acknowledged that Fish was insane, they still argued he should be executed. This raises some interesting questions in terms of mental health and the criminal justice system. While this case was heard more than 70 years ago, these issues are central to many horrific crimes we read about in the newspaper or see on the news today. Can a person be insane but still guilty of committing a crime?

SUMMARY OF THEORIES IN CHAPTER 7

THEORY	CONCEPTS	PROPONENTS	KEY PROPOSITIONS
Psychoanalytic perspective	The id, ego, and superego; anxiety, defense mechanisms, and the unconscious	Sigmund Freud, August Aichhorn	Individuals may be unaware of their unconscious experiences; they seek some form of expression until these experiences are brought to their awareness. Attempt to uncover unconscious motives of individuals engaging in criminal behavior.
Theory of crime and personality	Personality can be viewed in three dimensions: psychoticism, extroversion, and neuroticism (the PEN model)	Hans Eysenck	Initially, Eysenck focused on two personality dimensions (neuroticism and extroversion) in terms of how they are linked to criminality; later, he incorporated the psychoticism dimension.
Moral development	Three levels of morality: preconventional, conventional, and postconventional. Within each level are two stages.	Lawrence Kohlberg	Depending on an individual's level of moral development, he or she will perceive issues such as right and wrong, avoiding punishment, responsibility, societal rules, and respecting human life in a different form of reasoning.
Attachment theory	Seven essential features: specificity, duration, engagement of emotion, course of development, learning, organization, and biological function.	John Bowlby, Mary Ainsworth	Individuals may react in certain ways if they experienced some type of separation or if they have weak attachments to significant others.
Operant-utilitarian theory of criminality	Overemphasis on sociological explanations; human nature develops and evolves from the interaction of three factors: social environment, family relationships, and biological makeup.	James Q. Wilson, Richard J. Herrnstein	Crime cannot be understood without considering the individual's predisposition and biological makeup. Constitutional factors, such as intelligence and impulsivity, can influence an individual's ability to judge future and immediate rewards and punishments.
Low fear-quotient theory	Fear quotient; fear-quotient continuum; normal socialization process; psychopathy	David Lykken	Individuals have an innate propensity to fear certain stimuli, or an innate fear quotient. Psychopaths are at the low end of this fear-quotient continuum.

KEY TERMS

American Law Institute's
    Model Penal Code (ALI/
    MPC), 190

attachment theory, 174

conventional level of
    morality, 172

Durham rule, 190

ego, 167

extroversion, 170

id, 167

insanity, 188

intelligence
    quotient (IQ), 176

irresistible impulse, 189

mental health courts, 187

M'Naghten rule, 189

neuroticism, 170

PEN model, 170

postconventional level of
    morality, 172

preconventional level of
    morality, 172

psychoanalytic
    perspective, 167

psychopath, 182

psychoticism, 170

sociopath, 182

superego, 167

Thinking for a Change, 185

DISCUSSION QUESTIONS

1. What are some of the key principles of Freud's psychoanalytic perspective?

2. How did Aichhorn apply some of these principles to juvenile offenders?

3. What is the PEN model?

4. How would you distinguish the various levels of moral development?

5. What are the key features of attachment theory?

6. What are some of the main issues regarding the link between intelligence and criminality?

7. According to Wilson and Herrnstein, what are the three factors associated with street crime and human nature?

8. How would you distinguish between a psychopath and other criminal offenders?

9. What are the key differences between the M'Naghten, irresistible impulse, Durham, and ALI/MPC tests?

WEB RESOURCES

The American Bar Association provides various resources on this website, such as publications including periodicals and the *ABA Journal*:

http://www.americanbar.org/aba.html

This website provides information on mental health courts for over 30 states:

www.ncsc.org/Topics/Alternative-Dockets/Problem-Solving-Courts/Mental-Health-Courts/State-Links.aspx

$SAGE edge™

WANT A BETTER GRADE ON YOUR NEXT TEST?

Get the tools you need to sharpen your study skills:

SAGE edge offers a robust online environment featuring an impressive array of tools and resources for review, study, and further exploration, keeping both instructors and students on the cutting edge of teaching and learning. Learn more at **edge.sagepub.com/schram2e**.

FOR FURTHER EXPLORATION AND APPLICATION, VISIT THE STUDENT STUDY SITE:

- Along With Assault and Arson, FBI Starts to Track Animal Abuse
- Gun Violence and Mental Health Laws, 50 Years After Texas Tower Sniper
- Reliability of scores from the Eysenck Personality Questionnaire: A reliability generalization study
- Adolescent parricide and psychopathy
- People with serious mental illness in the criminal justice system: Causes, consequences, and correctives
- Cannibal `Albert Fish' Documentary
- Science Bulletins: Attachment Theory-Understanding the Essential Bond
- Treatment or Lockup: Criminal Justice System Grapples with Mentally Ill
- Violent Minds: Standing at the Crossroads of Mental Health, Public Safety
- Exclusive: Rape in America: Justice Denied
- Albert Fish
- Dr. Petiot
- Weird Crimes at Walmart
- Attachment Theory
- Criminal Insanity

PREMIUM VIDEO:

Check out the Interactive eBook for premium videos, including videos from author Stephen Tibbetts, who discusses real-world examples and strange crimes; and videos from former offenders, who share their stories from a first-person view, and touch on key theories and concepts from the chapter.

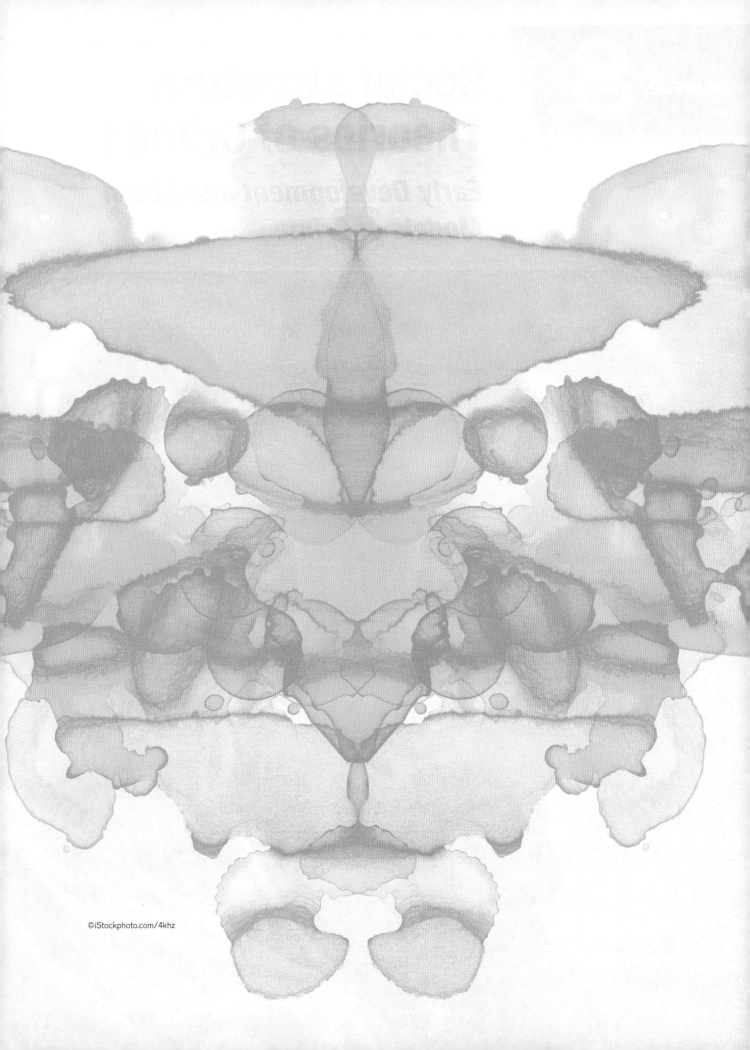

CHAPTER 8

Social Structure Theories of Crime I

Early Development and Strain Models of Crime

Reuters

INTRODUCTION

This chapter will examine explanations of criminal conduct that emphasize the differences among varying groups in societies, particularly in the United States. Such differences among groups are easy to see in everyday life, and many theoretical models have been developed that place the blame for crime on observed inequalities and/or cultural differences among groups. In contrast to the theories presented in previous chapters, social structure theories disregard any biological or psychological variations across individuals. Rather than emphasizing physiological factors, social structure theories assume that crime is caused by the way societies are structurally organized.

These social structure theories vary in many ways, most notably in what they propose as the primary constructs and processes causing criminal activity. For example, some structural models place an emphasis on variations in economic or academic success, whereas others focus on differences in cultural norms and values. Still others concentrate on the actual breakdown of the social structure in certain neighborhoods and the resulting social disorganization that occurs from this process (which we will examine in the next chapter). Regardless of their differences, all the theories examined in this chapter emphasize a common theme: Certain groups of individuals are more likely to break the law due to disadvantages or cultural differences resulting from the way society is structured.

The most important distinction of these social structure theories, as opposed to those discussed in previous chapters, is that they emphasize group differences instead of individual differences. In other words, structural models tend to focus on the macro level of analysis as opposed to the micro level (note: these units of analysis were discussed in the first chapters of this text). Therefore, it is not surprising that social structure theories are commonly used to explain the propensity of certain racial/ethnic groups to commit crime as well as the overrepresentation of the lower class in criminal activity.

As you will see, these theoretical frameworks were presented as early as the 1800s and reached their prominence in the early to mid-1900s, when the political, cultural, and economic climate of society was most conducive to such explanations. Although social structural models of crime have diminished in popularity in recent decades,[1] there is much validity to propositions in the theories discussed in this chapter, and there are numerous applications for social structure theories in contemporary society.

EARLY THEORIES OF SOCIAL STRUCTURE: EARLY TO LATE 1800S

Early European Theorists: Comte, Guerry, and Quetelet

Most criminological and sociological historians trace the origin of social structure theories to the research done in the early to mid-1800s by a number of European researchers, the most important including Auguste Comte,

CASE STUDY

THE BLACK BINDER BANDIT

A recent news story reported on a jobless man who was arrested for committing a dozen bank robberies across the Phoenix valley. The man, Cristian Alfredo Urquijo, 39, told authorities that he did it to survive and that "desperation was a great motivator." He was accused of robbing at least a dozen banks between 2010 and 2011. The criminal complaint noted that he had been laid off from work, was unable to find employment, and robbed the Phoenix-area banks to survive. He went on to say, "It's pretty simple. It's black and white. I don't have a job, I had to work, and I rob to survive." During his crime spree, authorities called him "The Black Binder Bandit" because he typically hid a revolver in a black binder and also would usually place the stolen money in this binder.

Urquijo pleaded guilty to nine counts of bank robbery, three counts of armed bank robbery, and one count of use of a firearm in a crime of violence, which carries an enhanced sentence. He had originally been charged with 16 counts of bank robbery, but as often happens in plea negotiations, the counts were reduced. He did admit that he had robbed at least 12 banks and also that he had obtained more than $49,000 from these bank robberies.

It is obvious that this man committed these crimes because he wanted to provide for himself in an economic recession. This is just one of many examples of individuals who are strongly motivated to commit crimes—even the major federal crime of bank robbery—to deal with the economic strain or frustration of not being able to "get ahead" or achieve the American Dream of success. This chapter discusses the evolution of theories that address this concept of trying to provide for oneself or succeed while dealing with societal and economic dynamics in American society. Specifically, this chapter reviews the development of anomie/ strain theory, starting with its origins among early social structure theorists, such as Durkheim, and moving to its further development by Merton. The chapter also examines the development of various strain models of offending as well as the most modern versions of strain theory (e.g., general strain theory). We will also examine the empirical research findings on this perspective, which reveal that this framework remains one of the dominant theoretical explanations of criminal behavior in modern times. We will finish this chapter by examining the policy implications suggested by this perspective for explaining criminal behavior, and we will further

discuss the case of "The Black Binder Bandit" toward the end of this chapter.

It should be noted that the Federal Bureau of Investigation (FBI) typically assigns nicknames (such as "The Black Binder Bandit") to serial bank robbers. The FBI does so for a very important reason: The public is more likely to take note of serial bank robbers when there is a catchy moniker or nick-

As surveillance photos show, Urquijo typically carried into the bank a black binder, in which he hid a revolver and the money he acquired from the bank robbery.

name attached to them. Apparently, this strategy is useful, because bank robbery actually has a much higher clearance rate than other types of robbery. Other notable nicknames of serial bank robbers in the past few years are the "Mesh-Mask Bandit" (still at large in Texas; wears a mesh mask), the "Geezer Bandit" (still at large in Southern California; authorities believe that the offender may be a young person disguising himself as an elderly person), and the "Michael Jackson Bandit" (still at large in Southern California; wears one glove during robberies). Although all these bank robbery suspects are still "at large," many others have been caught as a result of making their nicknames notable to the public.

> "IT'S PRETTY SIMPLE. IT'S BLACK AND WHITE. I DON'T HAVE A JOB, I HAD TO WORK, AND I ROB TO SURVIVE."

THINK ABOUT IT:

1. Can you articulate why the "Black Binder Bandit" seems to be a good example of Merton's strain theory?

2. Based on what he said to the police and his behavior, what adaptation of strain would you say best fits him?

3. Outside the nicknames already listed in this discussion, do you know of any other robbers the authorities have nicknamed and the reason(s) the robbers were given that moniker?

Public domain

Andre-Michel Guerry, and Adolphe Quetelet.[2] Although we will not discuss the various concepts, propositions, and research findings from their work, it is important to note that all their work was largely inspired by the social dynamics that resulted from the Industrial Revolution (defined by most historians as beginning in the mid-1700s and ending in the mid-1800s), which was in full swing at the turn of the 18th century and continued throughout most of the 1800s. Societies were quickly transitioning from primarily agriculture-based economies to more industrial-based economies, and this transition inevitably led to populations moving from primarily rural farmland to dense urban cities, which seemed to cause an enormous increase in social problems. These social problems ranged from failure to properly dispose of waste and garbage, to constantly losing children and not being able to find them, to much higher rates of crime (which continue to grow in urban areas compared with suburban and rural areas).

The problems associated with such fast urbanization, as well as the shift in economics, led to a drastic change in basic social structures in Europe as well as the United States. In addition to the extraordinary implications of the Industrial Revolution on the Western world, other types of revolutions were also affecting social structure. One of the first important theorists in the area of social structure theory was Auguste Comte (1798–1857); in fact, Comte is widely credited with coining the term *sociology*, because he was the first to be recognized for emphasizing and researching concepts based on more macro-level factors, such as social institutions (e.g., economic factors).[3] Although such conceptualization is elementary by today's standards, it had a significant influence on the sociological thinking that followed.

Soon after, the first modern national crime statistics were published in France in the early 1800s, and a French lawyer named André-Michel Guerry (1802–1866) published a report that examined these statistics and concluded that property crimes were higher in wealthy areas but violent crime was much higher in poor areas.[4] Some experts have claimed that this report likely represents the first study of scientific criminology,[5] and this was later expanded and published as a book. Ultimately, Guerry concluded that opportunity, in the sense that the wealthy had more to steal, was the primary cause of property crime. Interestingly, this conclusion is supported by recent U.S. Department of Justice statistics that show that property crime is just as common, if not more so, in middle- to upper-class households but that violent crime is not.[6] It is clear, as Guerry stated centuries ago, that there is more to steal in the wealthier areas and that poor individuals will use opportunities to steal goods and currency from wealthy households or establishments.

Adolphe Quetelet (1796–1874) was a Belgian researcher who, like Guerry, examined French statistics in the mid-1800s. Besides showing relative stability in the trends of crime rates in France, such as in age distribution and female-to-male ratios of offending, Quetelet also showed that certain types of individuals were more likely to commit crime.[7] Specifically, Quetelet showed that young, male, poor, uneducated, and unemployed individuals were more likely to commit crime than were their counterparts,[8] which has also been supported by modern research. Similar to Guerry, Quetelet concluded that opportunities, in addition to the demographic characteristics, had a lot to do with where crime tended to be concentrated.

However, Quetelet added a special component by identifying that greater inequality or gaps between wealth and poverty in the same place tend to excite temptations and passions. In other words, areas that exhibited large differences in wealth, with many poor and many wealthy in close proximity, had the biggest problems. This is a concept referred to as relative deprivation and is a quite distinctive condition from that of just a state of poverty.

For example, a number of deprived areas in the United States do not have high rates of crime, likely because virtually everyone is poor, so people are generally content with

relative deprivation: the perception that results when relatively poor people live in close proximity to relatively wealthy people.

their lives relative to their neighbors. However, in areas of the country where there are very poor people living in close proximity to very wealthy people, this causes animosity and feelings of deprivation compared with others in the area. Studies have supported this hypothesis,[9] and this is one of the likely explanations for why Washington, DC, which is perhaps the most powerful city in the world but also has a large portion of severely rundown and poor areas, has such a high crime rate compared with any other jurisdiction in the country.[10] Modern studies have also supported this hypothesis in showing a clear linear association between higher crime rates and localities with more relative deprivation. For example, in more modern times, David Sang-Yoon Lee found that crime rates were far higher in cities that had wider gaps in income; specifically, the larger the gap between the 10th and 90th percentiles, the greater the crime levels.[11]

People window-shopping and passing by a woman begging for money.

In addition to the concept of relative deprivation, Quetelet showed that areas with the most rapidly changing economic conditions also showed high crime rates (this will be discussed later in the chapter when we review Durkheim). Quetelet is perhaps best known for this comment: "The crimes . . . committed seem to be a necessary result of our social organization. . . . Society prepares the crime, and the guilty are only the instruments by which it is executed."[12] This statement makes it clear that crime is a result of societal structure and not of individual propensities or personal decision-making. Thus, it is not surprising that Quetelet's position was controversial at the time when he wrote (when most theorists were focusing on free will and deterrence) and that he was rigorously attacked by critics for removing all decision-making capabilities from his model of behavior. In response, Quetelet argued that his model could help lower crime rates by leading to social reforms that address the inequalities of the social structure (such as those between the wealthy and the poor).[13]

One of the essential points of Guerry's and Quetelet's work is the positivistic nature of their conclusions. Specifically, they both concluded that the distribution of crime is not random; rather, it is the result of certain types of persons committing certain types of crime in particular places, largely due to the way society is structured and distributes resources. This perspective of criminality strongly supports the tendency of crime to be clustered in certain places as well as among certain persons in these places. Such findings support a structural, positivistic perspective of criminality through which criminality is seen as being deterministic and, thus, caused by factors outside an individual's control. So in some ways, the early development of structural theories was in response to the failure of the Classical approach to crime control. We will see that as the 19th century drew to a close, Classical and deterrence-based perspectives of crime fell out of favor, while social structure theories and other positivistic theories of crime, such as the structural models developed by Guerry and Quetelet, attracted far more attention.

DURKHEIM AND THE CONCEPT OF ANOMIE

collective conscience: according to Durkheim, the extent to which people in a society share similarities or likeness; the stronger the collective conscience, the less crime in that community.

Although influenced by earlier theorists (e.g., Comte, Guerry, and Quetelet), Émile Durkheim (1858–1916) was perhaps the most influential theorist in modern structural perspectives on criminality.[14] As discussed above, like most other social theorists of the 19th century, he was strongly affected by the political (e.g., American and French) revolutions and the Industrial Revolution. In his doctoral dissertation (1893) at the University of Paris—the first sociological dissertation at that institution—Durkheim developed a general model of societal development largely based on the economic/labor distribution, in which societies are seen as evolving from a simplistic mechanical society toward a multilayered organic society (see Figure 8.1).

As outlined in Durkheim's dissertation, titled *The Division of Labor in Society*, primitive mechanical societies exist as those in which all members essentially perform the same functions, such as hunting (typically males) and gathering (typically females). Although there are a few anomalies (e.g., medicine men), virtually everyone experiences essentially the same daily routine. Such similarities in daily routine and constant interaction with like members of the society lead to a strong uniformity in values, which Durkheim called the **collective conscience**. The collective conscience is the degree to which individuals of a society think alike, or as Durkheim put it, the totality of social likenesses.

Due to very little variation in the distribution of labor in these primitive **mechanical societies**, or those with "mechanical solidarity," the individuals in such societies tend to share similar norms and values, which creates a simple-layered social structure with a strong collective conscience. Because people have more or less the same jobs and mostly interact with similar

---

LEARNING CHECK 8.1

1. Which early social structure theorist emphasized the concept of "relative deprivation"?

   a. Merton

   b. Guerry

   c. Durkheim

   d. Comte

   e. Quetelet

2. Which early social structure theorist is credited with coming up with the term *sociology*?

   a. Merton

   b. Guerry

   c. Durkheim

   d. Comte

   e. Quetelet

3. Early studies by social structure theorists/researchers found that there were higher rates of property crime in _____ neighborhoods but higher rates of violent crime in _____ neighborhoods (which still holds true in modern times).

   a. poor/wealthy

   b. wealthy/poor

Answers located at www.edge.sagepub.com/schram2e

---

individuals, they tend to think and act alike, which creates a strong solidarity among members. In mechanical societies, law functions to enforce the conformity of the group. However, as societies progress toward more modern, **organic societies** in the Industrial Age (most historians mark the Industrial Revolution as beginning in the 1750s and ending in the 1860s), the distribution of labor becomes more highly specified. There is still a form of solidarity in organic societies, called "organic solidarity," because people tend to depend on other groups in the society through the highly specified division of labor, and law's primary function is to regulate interactions and maintain solidarity among the groups.

For example, modern researchers at universities in the United States tend to be trained in extremely narrow topics, some as specific as the antennae of certain species of ants. On the other hand, some individuals are gathering trash from cans on the same streets every single day. The antennae experts probably have little interaction with or in common with the garbage collectors. According to Durkheim, moving from such universally shared roles in mechanical societies to such extremely specific roles in organic societies results in huge cultural differences, which leads to giant contrasts in normative values and attitudes across such groups. Thus, the collective conscience in such societies is weak, largely because there is little agreement on moral beliefs or opinions. Therefore, the preexisting solidarity among the members breaks down and the bonds are weakened, which creates a climate for antisocial behavior.

mechanical societies: in Durkheim's theory, these societies were rather primitive, with a simple distribution of labor (e.g., hunters and gatherers) and thus a high level of agreement regarding social norms and rules because nearly everyone was engaged in the same roles.

organic societies: in the Durkheimian model, those societies that have a high division of labor and thus a low level of agreement about societal norms, largely because everyone has such different roles in society.

Durkheim was clear in stating that crime is not only normal but necessary in all societies. Because Durkheim saw even crime as needed in society, his theory is often considered a good representation of functionalism, which assumes that virtually all types of behaviors or groups (such as crime and criminals) serve some important role in a given community. Specifically, he claimed that all social behaviors, especially crime, provide essential functions in a society. To clarify, Durkheim claimed that crime was needed for several reasons. First, crime is important because it defines the moral boundaries of societies. Few people know or realize what is against the societal laws until they see someone punished for a violation. This reinforces their understanding of both what the rules are and what it means to break the rules. Furthermore, the identification of rule breakers creates a bond among the other members of the society, perhaps through a common sense of self-righteousness or superiority.

This type of urban decay and deterioration is key in theories that emphasize neighborhood environment and how it contributes to high crime rates in certain city areas.

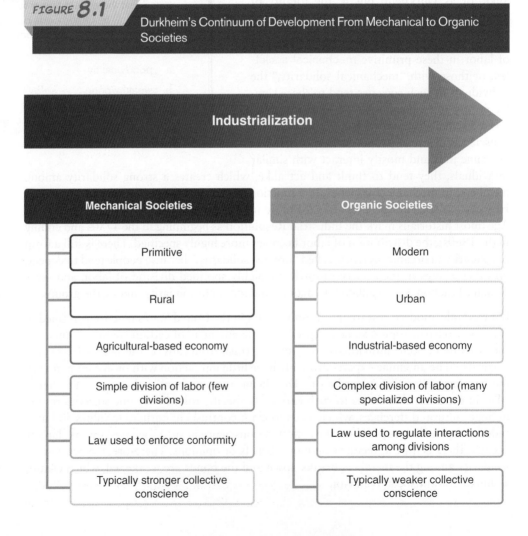

FIGURE **8.1**

Durkheim's Continuum of Development From Mechanical to Organic Societies

Industrialization

Mechanical Societies	Organic Societies
Primitive	Modern
Rural	Urban
Agricultural-based economy	Industrial-based economy
Simple division of labor (few divisions)	Complex division of labor (many specialized divisions)
Law used to enforce conformity	Law used to regulate interactions among divisions
Typically stronger collective conscience	Typically weaker collective conscience

In later works, Durkheim explained that this need for bonding is what makes crime so necessary in a society. Given the possibility that a community does not have any law violators, the society will change the legal definitions of what constitutes a crime to define some of its members as criminals. Examples of this are prevalent, but perhaps the most convincing is that of the Salem witch trials, in which hundreds of individuals were accused and tried for an almost laughable offense and more than a dozen were executed. Although this case is hard to relate to, Durkheim would say it was inevitable because crime was so low in the Massachusetts Bay Colony (historical records confirm this) that the society had to come up with a fabricated criterion for defining certain members of the population as offenders.

Other examples are common in everyday life, but the most readily apparent are those in which a group of people are thrown together. The fastest way for such a group to bond is to unite over a common enemy, which often means forming into cliques and ganging up on others in the group. As college students can usually relate to, in a group of three or more roommates, two or more of the individuals will quickly join together and complain about the others in the housing unit. This is an inevitable phenomenon of human interaction and group dynamics that has always existed throughout the world across time and place. As Durkheim said, even in

> a society of saints . . . crimes . . . will there be unknown; but faults which appear venial to the layman will create there the same scandal that the ordinary offense does in ordinary consciousnesses. . . . This society . . . will define these acts as criminal and will treat them as such.[15]

Public domain

Émile Durkheim's (1858–1916) theories on the progression of societies from mechanical to organic, as well as the "collective conscience" and "anomie," have heavily influenced many modern theories of crime.

This is why law enforcement should always be cautious in "cracking down" on gangs, especially during relatively inactive periods, because crackdowns will likely make the gangs stronger by giving members a common enemy. Like all societal groups, when a common enemy rears its head, the persons in the group (even those who do not typically get along) will come together and "circle the wagons" to protect themselves via strength in numbers. This usually produces a powerful bonding effect, and one that many sociologists and especially gang researchers have consistently observed.[16]

While traditional (mostly mechanical) societies could count on relative consensus in regard to moral values and norms, this sometimes led to too much control and stagnation of creative thought. However, Durkheim claimed that progress typically depends on deviating from established moral boundaries in a society, especially one in the more mechanical stage. There are many examples of this, including virtually all religious icons. For example, Jesus, Buddha, and Mohammed were all criminally persecuted for deviating from societal norms in the times when they preached. Political heroes have also been prosecuted and incarcerated as criminals, such as Mahatma Gandhi in India, Nelson Mandela in South Africa, and Dr. Martin Luther King Jr. in the United States. Perhaps one of the most compelling cases is that of scientist and astronomer Galileo, who proposed a theory that Earth was not the center of the universe. Even though he was right, he was persecuted for this theory because of the demand for strict adherence to the beliefs of his society. It is obvious that Durkheim was accurate in saying that the normative structure in some societies is so strong that it hinders progress and that crime is the price societies pay for progress.

In contrast to the problems of more primitive mechanical societies, modern societies do not have such extreme restraint against deviations from the established norms. Rather, almost the opposite is true; there are too many differences across groups because the division of labor is highly specialized. Thus, the varying roles in society, such as farmers versus scientific researchers, have become quite different due to the natural transition from primitive societies to more modern, specialized groups found in our contemporary societies. This leads to extreme differences in the cultural values and norms of the various groups. In other words, there is a breakdown in the collective conscience because there is really no longer a "collective" nature in society. Therefore, law no longer is primarily interested in defining the norms of society but rather is focused on governing the interactions that take place among the different classes. According to Durkheim, law provides a service in regulating such interactions as societies progress toward more organic (more industrial) forms.

Importantly, Durkheim emphasized that human beings, unlike other animal species that live according to their spontaneous needs, have no internal mechanism to signal when their needs and desires are satiated. Therefore, the selfish desires of humankind are limitless, and the more an individual has, the more he or she wants. In other words, people are greedy by nature, and without something to tell them what they need and deserve, they will never feel content.[17] According to Durkheim, it is society that provides the mechanism for limiting human individuals' insatiable appetite for more and more. Specifically, he claimed that only society has the power necessary to create laws that tell citizens where the limits are drawn on their selfishness and passions.

Durkheim also noted that in times of rapid change, society fails in this role of regulating desires and expectations. This rapid change can be due to numerous factors, such as war or social movements (such as the changes seen in the United States in the 1960s). For Durkheim, the transitions he likely had in mind were those that affected the time in which he wrote—namely, just after the American and French Revolutions, and also immediately following the Industrial Revolution. Durkheim claimed that with rapid change, the ability of society to serve as a regulatory mechanism breaks down and the selfish, greedy tendencies of individuals are uncontrolled, causing a state Durkheim called **anomie**, or "normlessness." Societies in such anomic states would experience increases in many social problems, particularly criminal activity.

Durkheim was clear that it really did not matter whether the rapid change was for good or bad; either way, it would have negative effects on society. For example, whether the U.S. economy was improving (such as in the late 1960s) or quickly tanking (such as in the 1930s, during the Great Depression), according to Durkheim both of these would produce more criminal activity due to the lack of stability in regulating human expectations and desires. Interestingly, both of these periods (the late 1960s and 1930s) showed the greatest crime waves of the 20th century, particularly for murder.[18] Another fact that supports Durkheim's predictions is that middle- and upper-class individuals have higher suicide rates than those from lower classes. This is consistent with the idea that it is better to have stability, even if it means always being poor, than it is to have instability at higher levels of income.

In his most widely known work, *Suicide*, Durkheim applied his theoretical model to an act that was (and often still is) considered an individual decision—namely, the taking of one's own life. This was a major step for several reasons. First, Durkheim took an act—suicide—that would seem to be the ultimate form of free choice or free will, and he showed that this decision to take one's own life is largely determined by external, social factors. To clarify, Durkheim claimed that suicide was a "social fact," meaning that it was a product of meanings and structural aspects that result from interactions among persons.

Specifically, Durkheim showed that the rate of suicide was significantly lower among individuals who were married, young, and adherents of religions that were more interactive and communal (e.g., Judaism). All these characteristics boil down to one aspect:

anomie: a concept originally proposed by Durkheim, which meant normlessness or the chaos that takes place when a society (e.g., economic structure) changes very rapidly.

The more social interaction and bonding with the community, the less suicide. So Durkheim concluded that variations in suicide rates are due to differences in social solidarity or bonding to society. Examples of this are still seen today, as in the recent reports of high rates of suicide among persons who live in extremely rural areas, such as Alaska (which has the highest rate of juvenile suicide), northern portions of Nevada, and Wyoming and Montana. Another way of looking at the implications of Durkheim's conclusions is that social relationships are what make people feel happy and fulfilled. If we are isolated or have weak bonds with society, we will likely be depressed and discontent with our lives.

The second reason Durkheim's examination of suicide was important was that he showed that in times of both rapid economic growth and rapid decline, suicide rates increased. Although researchers later argued that crime rates did not always follow this pattern,[19] he used quantified measures to test his propositions as the positivistic approach recommended. In the least, Durkheim created a prototype of how theory and empirical research could be combined in testing differences across social groups. This theoretical framework would be drawn on heavily for one of the most influential and accepted criminological theories of the 20th century—strain theory.

LEARNING CHECK 8.2

1. Durkheim's model emphasized the evolution of more primitive _____ types of societies to more advanced _____ types of societies.
   a. mechanical/organic
   b. organic/mechanical

2. Durkheim's proposed theory included the concept of "anomie," which can best be defined as:
   a. stability.
   b. normlessness.
   c. status quo.
   d. deprived.
   e. ritualistic.

3. Durkheim wrote an entire book on what type of behavior?
   a. Murder
   b. Robbery
   c. Rape
   d. Burglary
   e. Suicide

Answers located at www.edge.sagepub.com/schram2e

MERTON'S STRAIN THEORY

The one thing that all forms of strain theory have in common is their emphasis on a sense of frustration in crime causation, hence the name "strain" theory. Although the theories differ regarding what exactly is causing the frustration as well as in the way individuals cope (or don't) with such stress and anger, they all identify the strain placed on individuals as the primary causal factor in the development of criminality. Another common feature of strain theories is that they all trace their origin to the seminal theory of Durkheim as well as to Robert K. Merton's theoretical framework.

When formulating his theory of structural strain in the 1930s, Merton drew heavily on Durkheim's idea of anomie.[20] As we shall see in this chapter, although Merton altered the way anomie was defined, it is apparent that Durkheim's theoretical framework was a vital influence in the evolution of strain theory. By combining Durkheimian concepts and propositions with an emphasis on American culture, Merton's structural model became one of the most popular perspectives in criminological thought in the early 1900s and remains one of the most cited theories in the criminological literature.

Cultural Context and Assumptions of Strain Theory

Some have claimed that Merton's seminal piece in 1938 was perhaps the most influential theoretical formulation in the criminological literature and one of the most frequently

©iStockphoto.com/Craig McCausland

Virtually all Americans are raised to believe in the American Dream, in which we are led to believe that if we just work very hard we will gain financial success. However, this is certainly not the case, especially for those who are not given the educational and occupational opportunities that others are given, typically via heredity.

cited papers in sociology.[21] Although partially due to its strong foundation in previous structural theories, the popularity of Merton's strain theory is likely more related to the timing of its publication. As we have discussed previously, virtually every theory addressed in this book became popular when it did because the political and social climate at the time desired that type of theory for its fit with the current perspective on how the world works. Perhaps no theory better represents this phenomenon than strain theory.

Virtually all historians would agree that the most significant social issue in the 1930s was the economy. The Great Depression, largely a result of the stock market crash in 1929, affected virtually every aspect of life in the United States. Not only did unemployment and extreme poverty soar, but suicide rates rose and crime rates skyrocketed, particularly murder rates.[22] So it is not surprising that there was fertile ground in American society for a theory of crime that placed virtually all the blame on the economic structure in the United States.

Not only was society ready for a perspective such as strain theory, but on the other side of the coin, Merton was highly influenced by what he saw happening to the country during the Great Depression. Specifically, he observed how much the economic institution impacted almost all other social factors, particularly crime. He watched how the breakdown of the economic structure drove people to kill themselves or others, not to mention the rise in property crimes, such as theft. After all, many individuals who had once been successful were now poor, and some felt driven to crime for survival. Notably, Durkheim's hypotheses regarding crime and suicide were supported during this time of rapid change, and Merton apparently realized that the framework simply had to be updated and supplemented.

One of the key assumptions distinguishing strain theory from Durkheim's perspective is that Merton altered his version of what "anomie" means, a definition we will explore below. Specifically, Merton discussed the nearly universal socialization of the American Dream in U.S. society. To clarify, this is the idea that as long as someone works hard and pays his or her dues, that person will achieve every goal in the end. According to Merton, the socialized image of the goal is material wealth, whereas the socialized concept of the means of achieving the goal is hard work (e.g., education, labor). So the conventional model of the American Dream was consistent with the Protestant work ethic of working hard for a long time and knowing you will be repaid in the distant future.

Furthermore, Merton claimed that nearly everyone is socialized to believe in the American Dream, no matter what economic class they are raised in. There is some empirical support for this belief, which makes sense because virtually all parents, even if they are poor, want to instill in their children a hope for the future, particularly if one is willing to work hard in school and/or at a job. In fact, parents and society usually use celebrities as examples of this process—namely, those individuals who started off poor and rose to wealth. Modern examples include former secretary of state Colin Powell, Dallas Mavericks owner Mark Cuban, Oscar winner Hilary Swank, and Hollywood director/screenwriter Quentin Tarantino, not to mention Arnold Schwarzenegger, who went from teenage immigrant to Mr. Olympia and governor of California.

These stories epitomize the American Dream, but parents and society do not always teach the reality of the situation. As Merton points out, while a small percentage of persons can rise from the lower class to become materially successful, the vast majority of poor children really don't have much chance of ever obtaining such wealth. So it is this near-universal socialization of the American Dream, without it being obtainable in most cases, that causes most of the strain and frustration in American society. Furthermore, Merton claims that most of the strain and frustration is due not necessarily to the failure to achieve conventional goals (i.e., wealth) but rather to the differential emphasis placed on the material goals and the deemphasis of the importance of the conventional means.

MERTON'S CONCEPT OF ANOMIE AND STRAIN. Merton claimed that an ideal society would feature an equal emphasis on the conventional goals and means in society. However, in many societies, one of these aspects would be emphasized more than the other. Merton claimed that the United States epitomized the type of society that emphasizes goals far above means. This disequilibrium in emphasis between the goals and means of societies is what Merton called anomie. So, like Durkheim's, Merton's anomie was a negative state for society; however, the two men had different explanations for how this state of society came about. While Durkheim believed that anomie was primarily caused by a society transitioning too fast to maintain its regulatory control over members, for Merton, anomie represented too much focus on the goals of wealth in the United States at the expense of the conventional means.

There are numerous examples of how the goals are emphasized more than the means in our society, but perhaps the best way to illustrate this is through hypothetical situations. Which of the following two men would be more respected by youth (or even adults) in our society: (1) John, who has his PhD in physics but lives in a one-bedroom apartment because he can find only a job as a postdoctoral student for a stipend of $25,000 a year, or (2) Joe, who is a relatively successful drug dealer who owns a four-bedroom home, drives a Hummer, dropped out of school in the 10th grade, and makes about $90,000 a year? In years of asking this question in our classes, the answer, with few exceptions, is usually Joe, the drug dealer. After all, he appears to have obtained the American Dream.

Still another way of supporting Merton's idea that America is too focused on the goal of material success is to ask you, the reader, to think about why you are taking the time to read this chapter and/or to attend college. Specifically, the question is this: If you knew for a fact that you would not get a better employment position by studying this book or, furthermore, by earning a college degree, would you be learning this material just for your own edification? In more than a decade of posing this question to about 10,000 students in university courses, one of the authors of this book found that only about 5% (usually less) of respondents said yes. Interestingly, when asked the reason they would put all this work into attending classes, many of them said they would do it for the partying or social life. Ultimately, it appears that most college students would not be engaging in the hard work it takes to educate themselves if it weren't for some payoff at the end of the task. In some ways, this supports Merton's claim that the emphasis is on the goals, with little or no intrinsic value placed on the work itself (i.e., the means). This phenomenon is not meant to be disheartening or a negative statement; after all, it is only meant to exhibit the reality of American culture and to show that it is quite common in our society to place an emphasis on the goal of financial success as opposed to hard work for hard work's sake.

Merton went on to say that individuals, particularly those in the lower class, eventually realize that the ideal of the American Dream is a lie, or at least a false illusion for the vast majority of people. For example, people can work very hard in school and then get stuck in jobs that will never produce the type of material success promised them via the dream they were socialized to believe in. This revelation of the truth will likely take place when people are in their late teens to mid-20s, the time when crime tends to peak.

adaptations to strain: as proposed by Merton, the five ways that individuals deal with feelings of strain; see *conformity, innovation, rebellion, retreatism,* and *ritualism.*

conformity: in strain theory, an adaptation to strain in which an individual buys into the conventional means of success and also buys into conventional goals.

ritualism: in strain theory, an adaptation to strain in which an individual buys into the conventional means of success (e.g., work, school, etc.) but does not buy into the conventional goals.

innovation: in strain theory, an adaptation to strain in which an individual buys into the conventional goals of success but does not buy into the conventional means for getting to the goals.

retreatism: in strain theory, an adaptation to strain in which an individual does not buy into the conventional goals of success and also does not buy into the conventional means.

rebellion: in strain theory, an adaptation to strain in which an individual buys into the idea of conventional means and goals of success but does not buy into the current conventional means or goals.

According to Merton, this is when the frustration or strain is evident, which is consistent with the peak of offending at the approximate age of 17. Therefore, some individuals begin to innovate ways that they can achieve the goals of society (i.e., material success) without having to use the conventional means of attaining them. Obviously, this is often through criminal activity. However, not all individuals deal with strain in this way; after all, most people who are poor do not resort to crime. To Merton's credit, one of the good things about his theory is that he explained that individuals deal in different ways with the limited economic structure of society. Merton referred to these variations in dealing with the revelation of the economic structure as adaptations to strain.

ADAPTATIONS TO STRAIN. There are five adaptations to strain, according to Merton. The first of these is conformity, in which persons buy into the conventional goals of society but also buy into the conventional means of working hard in school or labor.[23] This would include the vast majority of the readers of this book, in the sense that, like most of you, conformists want to achieve material success and are willing to do so by conventional means such as educational effort and diligent work. As the label suggests, these individuals are conforming to the goals and means that society suggests. Another adaptation to strain is ritualism. Ritualists do not seek to achieve the goals of material success, probably because they know they don't have a realistic chance of obtaining such success. However, they do buy into the conventional means in the sense that they like to do their jobs or are happy just making ends meet. For example, studies have shown that some of the most content and happy people in society are those that don't seek to become rich; rather, they are quite content with their blue-collar jobs and often have a strong sense of pride in the work they do, even if it is sometimes menial. To clarify, such a person considers his or her work a type of ritual and performs it without a goal in mind; rather, the work itself is a form of intrinsic goal. Ultimately, conformists and ritualists tend to be at low risk for offending, in contrast to those who adopt other adaptations to strain.

The other three adaptations to strain are far more likely to lead to criminal offending: innovation, retreatism, and rebellion. Perhaps most likely to become predatory street criminals are the innovators, who Merton claimed greatly desire the conventional goals of material success but are not willing to engage in conventional means of obtaining those goals. Obviously, drug dealers and professional auto thieves, as well as many other variations of chronic property criminals (e.g., bank robbers), fit this adaptation. To clarify, as their name suggests, they are innovating ways to achieve material goals without doing the hard work usually needed to succeed. However, innovators are not always criminals. In fact, many of them are the most respected individuals in our society. For example, some entrepreneurs have used the capitalistic system of our society to produce useful products and services (e.g., the men who designed Google for the Internet) and have made a fortune at young ages without advanced college educations or years of work at a company. Another example is successful athletes who sign multimillion-dollar contracts at age 18. So it should be clear that not all innovators are criminals.

The fourth adaptation to strain is retreatism, in which individuals do not seek to achieve the goals of society or buy into the idea of conventional hard work. There are many varieties of this adaptation, such as persons who become homeless by choice or persons who isolate themselves in desolate places without human contact. A good example of a retreatist is Ted Kaczynski, the Unabomber, who left a good position as a professor at the University of California, Berkeley, to live in an isolated Montana cabin, which had no running water or electricity, and did not interact with humans for many months at a time. Other types of retreatists, perhaps the most likely to be criminal, are those who actively disengage from social life and try to escape via psychologically altering drugs. All these forms of retreatists seek to drop out of society altogether, thus refusing to buy into the means or goals of society.

The last adaptation to strain, according to Merton, is rebellion—the most complex of the five adaptations. Interestingly, rebels buy into the idea of societal goals and means, but they do not buy into the conventional goals and means currently in place. Most true rebels are criminals by definition, largely because they are trying to overthrow the established societal structure. For example, the founders of the United States were all rebels because they actively fought the governing state (English rule) and clearly committed treason in the process. Had they lost or been captured during the American Revolution, they would have been executed as the criminals they were by law. However, because they won the war, they became heroes and presidents. Another example is Karl Marx, who will be discussed later in this text. He bought into the goals and means of society, just not those of the current American culture. Rather, he proposed socialism/communism as a means to the goal of utopia. So there are many contexts in which a rebel can become a criminal, but sometimes rebels end up becoming heroes.

Merton also noted that one individual can represent more than one adaptation to strain. Perhaps the best example is the Unabomber, who started out as a conformist in that he was a respected professor at University of California, Berkeley, well on his way to tenure and promotion. He then seemed to shift to a retreatist state, isolating himself from society (as mentioned above). Later, he became a rebel who bombed innocent people in his quest to implement his own goals and means—as described in his manifesto, which he coerced several national newspapers to publish (and which subsequently resulted in his apprehension, because his brother read it and informed authorities that he thought his brother had written it!).

LEARNING CHECK 8.3

1. According to Merton's theory, which type of individual deals with strain by emphasizing the conventional goals of success without any consideration for the conventional means of gaining such success?

   a. Ritualists
   b. Conformists
   c. Retreatists
   d. Rebels
   e. Innovators

2. According to Merton's theory, which type of individual deals with strain by emphasizing the conventional means of gaining success without any consideration for the conventional goals of such success?

   a. Ritualists
   b. Conformists
   c. Retreatists
   d. Rebels
   e. Innovators

3. According to Merton's theory, which type of individual deals with strain by emphasizing the conventional goals of success as well as strongly considering the conventional means for gaining such success?

   a. Ritualists
   b. Conformists
   c. Retreatists
   d. Rebels
   e. Innovators

Answers located at www.edge.sagepub.com/schram2e

Finally, some have applied an athletic analogy to these adaptations, which often helps in translating them to actual, everyday behavior.[24] In a basketball game, conformists will play to win, but they will always play by the rules and won't cheat to win. Ritualists will play the game just because they like to play, and they don't care about winning. Innovators will play to win, and they will break any rules they can to triumph in the game. Retreatists don't like to play and obviously don't care about winning. Finally, rebels will not like the rules on the official court, so they will try to steal the ball and play by their own rules on another court. Although this is a somewhat simplistic analogy, it is likely to help readers remember the adaptations and perhaps enable them to apply these ways of dealing with strain to everyday situations, such as resorting to criminal activity.

Evidence and Criticisms of Merton's Strain Theory

Although Merton's framework, which emphasized the importance of the economic structure, appeared to have a high degree of face validity during the Great Depression, many scientific studies showed mixed support for strain theory. While research that examined the effects of poverty on violence and official rates of various crimes has found relatively consistent support (albeit weaker effects than strain theory implies), a series of studies of self-reported delinquent behavior found little or no relationship between social class and criminality.[25] Furthermore, the idea that unemployment drives people to commit crime has received little support.[26]

On the other hand, some experts have argued that Merton's strain theory is primarily a structural model of crime that is more a theory of societal groups than of individual motivations.[27] Therefore, some modern studies have used aggregated group rates (i.e., macro-level measures) to test the effects of deprivation as opposed to using individual (micro-level) rates of inequality and crime. Most of these studies provide some support for the hypothesis that social groups and regions with higher rates of deprivation and inequality have higher rates of criminal activity.[28] Furthermore, the case study provided at the beginning of this chapter, that of Cristian Alfredo Urquijo or the "Black Binder Bandit," clearly shows that in some cases economic desperation is a primary motivation in committing robberies for financial survival. In sum, there appears to be some support for Merton's strain theory when the level of analysis is the macro level and official measures are being used to indicate criminality.

However, many critics have claimed that these studies do not directly measure perceptions or feelings of strain, so they are only indirect examinations of Merton's theory. In light of these criticisms, some researchers have focused on the disparity in what individuals aspire to in various aspects of life (e.g., school, occupation, social life) versus what they realistically expect to achieve.[29] The rationale of these studies is that if an individual has high aspirations (i.e., goals) but also has low expectations of actually achieving the goals due to structural barriers, then that individual is more likely to experience feelings of frustration and strain. Furthermore, it was predicted that the larger the gap between aspirations and expectations, the stronger the sense of strain. Of the studies that examined discrepancies between aspirations and expectations, most did not find evidence linking a large gap between these two levels with criminal activity. In fact, several studies found that for most antisocial respondents, there was virtually no gap between aspirations and expectations. Rather, most of the subjects (typically young males) who reported the highest levels of criminal activity tended to report low levels of both aspirations and expectations.

Surprisingly, when aspirations were high, it seemed to inhibit offending, even when expectations to achieve those goals were unlikely. One interpretation of these findings is that individuals who have high goals will not jeopardize their chances for obtaining such aspirations, even when they realize their chances are slim. On the other hand, individuals who don't have high goals are likely to be indifferent to their future and, in a sense, have nothing to lose. So without a stake in conventional society, this predisposes them to crime. While this conclusion supports social control theories (discussed in the following chapters), it does not provide support for strain theory.

Some critics have argued that most studies on the discrepancies between aspirations and expectations have not been done correctly. For example, Farnworth and Leiber claimed that it was a mistake to examine the differences between educational goals and expectations, or differences between occupational goals and expectations, which is what most of these studies did.[30] Rather, they proposed testing the gap between economic aspirations (i.e., goals) and educational expectations (i.e., means of achieving these goals). Not only does this make sense, but Farnworth and Leiber found support for a gap between these two factors being predictive of criminality. However, they also report that persons who reported having low economic aspirations were more likely to be delinquent, which supports the previous studies they criticized. Another criticism of this type of strain theory study is that it is possible that simply reporting a gap between expectations and aspirations does not necessarily mean that the individuals actually feel strained; rather, researchers have simply, and perhaps wrongfully, assumed that a gap between the two measures indicates feelings of frustration.[31]

Other criticisms of Merton's strain theory include some historical evidence and its failure to explain the age–crime curve. Regarding the historical evidence, it is hard to understand why some of the largest increases in crime took place during a period of relative economic prosperity—namely, the late 1960s. Crime increased more than ever before (that we have measures for) between 1965 and 1973, which were generally good economic years in the United States. Therefore, if strain theory is presented as the primary explanation for criminal activity, it would probably have a hard time explaining this historical era. On the other hand, it can be argued that the growth in the economy in the 1960s and early 1970s may have caused even more disparity between rich and poor, thereby producing more relative deprivation.

The other major criticism of strain theory is that it does not explain one of the most established facts in the field: the age–crime curve. Specifically, in virtually every society in the world, across time and place, predatory street crimes (e.g., robbery, rape, murder, burglary, larceny, etc.) tend to peak sharply in the teenage years to early 20s and then drop off quickly, certainly before age 30. However, most studies show that feelings of stress and frustration tend to continue rising after age 30 and do not diminish significantly. For example, suicide rates tend to be just as high or higher as one ages, with persons over 55 showing the highest rates of suicide.

On the other hand, it can be argued that the reason why strain continues or even increases as one ages but the rates of crime go down is that individuals develop coping mechanisms for dealing with their frustrations. This idea seems to make sense, and while Merton never discussed (outside the adaptations) actual methods of coping with strain, a variation of Merton's theory—general strain theory—did emphasize this concept. Before we cover general strain theory, we will discuss two other variations of Merton's theory that were developed within a five-year period (1955–1960) to explain gang formation and behavior using a structural strain framework.

VARIATIONS OF MERTON'S STRAIN THEORY

Cohen's Theory of Lower-Class Status Frustration and Gang Formation

In 1955, Albert Cohen presented a theory of gang formation that used Merton's strain theory as a basis for why individuals resort to such group behavior.[32] In Cohen's model, young males from lower classes are at a disadvantage in school because they lack the normal interaction, socialization, and discipline instituted by educated parents of the middle class, which is in line with Merton's original framework of a predisposed disadvantage among underclass youth. According to Cohen, such youths are likely to experience failure in school due to this lack of preparation in conforming with middle-class values, so they fail to live up to what is considered the "middle-class measuring rod," which emphasizes factors such as motivation, accountability, responsibility, deferred gratification, long-term planning, respect for authority and property, and controlling emotions.

Like Merton, Cohen emphasized the youths' internalization of the American Dream and fair chances for success, leading to frustration when they fail to be successful according to this middle-class standard. This strain that they feel due to failure in school performance and respect among their peers, often referred to as "status frustration," leads them to develop a system of values that is contrary to middle-class standards and values. Some have claimed that this represents a Freudian defense mechanism known as **reaction formation**, which involves adopting attitudes or committing behaviors that are the opposite of what is expected—a form of defiance and avoidance of guilt for not living up to the assumed standards. According to Cohen, these lower-class male youths will adopt a normative value system that defies the very values they are expected to live up to. Specifically, instead of abiding by middle-class norms of obedience to authority, school achievement, and respect for authority, these youths change their normative beliefs to value the opposite characteristics: Namely, they value malicious, negativistic, and non-utilitarian delinquent activity.

For example, these youths will begin to value destruction of property and skipping school, not because these behaviors lead to a payoff or success in the conventional world but simply because they defy the conventional order. In other words, they turn the middle-class values upside down and consider activity that violates the conventional norms and laws, thereby psychologically and physically rejecting the cultural system placed on them without benefit of equal preparation and fair distribution of resources. Furthermore, Cohen claimed that while these behaviors do not appear to have much utility or value, they are quite valuable and important from the perspective of the strained youth. Specifically, they do these acts to gain respect from their peers (those who have gone through the same straining experiences and reactionary formation), which they could not gain through school performance and adherence to middle-class normative culture.

Cohen stated that he believed this tendency to reject middle-class values is the primary cause of gangs, because a number of these lower-class individuals who have experienced the same strains (i.e., status frustration) and experiences form a group—a classic example of "birds of a feather flock together." Cohen claimed that not all lower-class males resort to crime and join a gang in response to this structural disadvantage. Other variations, beyond that of the **delinquent boy**, are the **college boy** and the **corner boy**. The "college boy" responds to his disadvantaged situation by dedicating himself to overcoming the odds and competing in the middle-class schools despite his unlikely chances for success. On the other hand, the "corner boy" responds to the situation by accepting his place in society as a lower-class individual who will somewhat passively make the best of life at the bottom of the social order.

As compared with Merton's original adaptations, Cohen's delinquent boy is probably most similar to rebellion, because the delinquent boy rejects the means and goals (middle-class values and success in school) of conventional society and replaces them with new means and goals (negativistic behaviors and peer respect in a gang). Some would argue that delinquent boys should be seen as innovators, because their goal is ultimately the same: peer respect. But the peers involved completely change, so we argue that through the reaction formation process, the delinquent boy actually creates his own goals and means that go against the conventional, middle-class goals and means. Regarding the college boy, the adaptation that seems to fit best is conformity, because the college boy continues to believe in the conventional goals (i.e., financial success/achievement) and means (i.e., hard work via education/labor) of middle-class society. Finally, the corner boy probably best fits the adaptation of ritualism, because he knows that he likely will never achieve the goals of society, so he essentially resigns himself to not obtaining financial success. At the same time, he does not resort to predatory street crime but, rather, holds a stable blue-collar job or makes ends meet in other typically legal ways. Some corner boys who end up simply collecting welfare and giving up on work altogether may actually become more like the adaptation of retreatism, because they have virtually given up on the conventional means (hard work) of society as well as the goals.

reaction formation: a Freudian defense mechanism applied to Cohen's theory of youth offending, which involves adopting attitudes or committing behaviors that are opposite of what is expected.

delinquent boy: a type of lower-class male youth, identified by Cohen, who responds to strains and status frustration by joining with similar others in a group to commit crime.

college boy: a type of lower-class male youth who has experienced the same strains and status frustration as his peers but responds to his disadvantaged situation by dedicating himself to overcoming the odds and competing in the middle-class schools despite his unlikely chances for success.

corner boy: a type of lower-class male youth who has experienced the same strains and status frustration as others but responds to his disadvantaged situation by accepting his place in society as someone who will somewhat passively make the best of life at the bottom of the social order. As the label describes, such youth often hang out on corners.

At the time when Cohen developed his theory, official statistics showed that virtually all gang violence—and most violence, for that matter—was concentrated among lower-class male youths. However, with the development of self-report studies in the 1960s, his theory was shown to be somewhat overstated in the sense that middle-class youths were well represented in committing delinquent acts.[33] Other studies have also been critical of Cohen's theory, particularly the portions that deal with his proposition that crime rates will increase after youths drop out of school and join a gang. Although the findings are mixed, many studies have found that delinquency is often higher before the youths drop out of school and may actually decline once they drop out and become employed.[34] Some critics have pointed out that such findings discredit Cohen's

theory, but this is not necessarily true. After all, delinquency may be peaking right before the youths drop out because that is the time when they feel most frustrated and strained, whereas delinquency may be decreasing after they drop out because some of the youths are raising their self-esteem by earning a wage and taking pride in holding a job.

Still, studies have clearly shown that lower-class youths are far more likely to have problems in school and that school achievement is consistently linked with criminality.[35] Furthermore, there is little dispute that much of delinquency represents malicious, negativistic, and nonutilitarian activity. For example, what do individuals have to gain from destroying mailboxes or tagging walls? This is an act that will never gain much in the lines of money or any other form of payoff aside from peer respect. So, ultimately, it appears that there is some face validity to what Cohen proposed, in the sense that some youths engage in behavior that has no other value than earning peer respect, even though that behavior is negativistic and nonutilitarian according to the values of conventional society. Regardless of some criticisms of Cohen's model, he provided an important structural strain theory of the development of gangs and lower-class delinquency.

Cloward and Ohlin's Theory of Differential Opportunity

Five years after Cohen published his theory, Richard A. Cloward and Lloyd E. Ohlin presented yet another structural strain theory of gang formation and behavior.[36] Similar to Merton and Cohen, Cloward and Ohlin assumed that all youths, including those in the lower class, are socialized to believe in the American Dream and that when they realize they are blocked from conventional opportunities, they become frustrated and strained. What distinguishes Cloward and Ohlin's theory from the previous strain theories is that they emphasized three different types of gangs that form based on the characteristics of the social structure in the neighborhood. To clarify, the nature of gangs varies according to the availability of illegal opportunities in the social structure. So whereas previous strain theories focused only on lack of legal opportunities, Cloward and Ohlin's model emphasized *both legal and illegal* opportunities, and the availability (or lack) of these opportunities largely determined what type of gang would form in that neighborhood—hence the name *differential opportunity theory*. Furthermore, the authors acknowledged Edwin Sutherland's (see Chapter 10) influence on their theory, and this influence is evident in their focus on the neighborhood associations that largely determine what type of gang will form. According to differential opportunity theory, the three types of gangs are criminal gangs, conflict gangs, and retreatist gangs.

Organized crime syndicates are typically found in neighborhoods with more structured criminal organizations, which mentor youth in these neighborhoods and result in a prevalence of criminal gangs.

© iStockphoto.com/PointImage

Criminal gangs are those that form in lower-class neighborhoods that have an organized structure of adult criminal behavior. Such neighborhoods are so organized and stable that the criminal networks are often known and accepted by the conventional portion of individuals in the area. The adult gangsters in these neighborhoods mentor the youth and take them under their wing. This can pay off for the adult criminals, too, because youth can often be used to do the "dirty work" for the criminal enterprises in the neighborhood without risk of serious punishment if caught. The successful adult offenders supply the youth with the motives and techniques for committing crime. So while members of criminal gangs are blocked from legal opportunities, they are offered ample opportunities in the illegal realm.

Due to the strong organization and stability of such neighborhoods, criminal gangs tend to reflect this high degree of organization and stability. Therefore, criminal gangs primarily commit property or economic crimes, with the goal of making a profit through illegal behavior. These crimes can range from "running numbers" as local bookies to "fencing" stolen goods to running businesses that are a front for vice crimes (e.g., prostitution, drug trading). Regardless of the type, they all involve making a profit illegally, and there is often a system or structure in which the criminal activity takes place. Furthermore, these criminal gangs are most like the Merton adaptation of innovation (discussed previously in this chapter) because the members still want to achieve the goals of conventional society (financial success). Because of the strong organizational structure of these gangs, they are not as conductive to individuals who are highly impulsive or uncontrolled as they are to those who have self-control and are good at planning for the future.

Examples of criminal gangs are seen in movies depicting highly organized neighborhoods (often consisting of primarily one ethnicity)—movies such as *The Godfather*, *A Bronx Tale*, *State of Grace*, *Sleepers*, *New Jack City*, *Clockers*, *Goodfellas*, *Better Luck Tomorrow*, and many others that were partially based on real events. All these depictions involve a highly structured hierarchy in a criminal enterprise, which is largely a manifestation of the organization of the neighborhood. The Hollywood motion pictures also involve stories about the older criminals in the neighborhood taking younger males from the neighborhood under their wing and training them in the ways of the criminal network. Furthermore, virtually all ethnic groups have examples of this type of gang/neighborhood; for example, in looking at the list of movies above, there are Italian-American, Irish-American, African-American, and Asian-American representations. Thus, criminal gangs can be found across the racial and ethnic spectrum, largely because all groups have certain neighborhoods that exhibit strong organization and stability.

Conflict gangs are another type of gang that Cloward and Ohlin identified. Conflict gangs tend to develop in neighborhoods that have weak stability and little or no organization. In fact, the neighborhood often seems to be in a state of flux because people are constantly moving in and out of the area. Because the youth in the neighborhood do not have a solid crime network or adult criminal mentors, they tend to form together as a relatively disorganized gang. Due to this disorganization, they typically lack the skills and knowledge to make a profit through criminal activity. Therefore, the primary illegal activity of conflict gangs is violence. This violence is used to gain prominence and respect among themselves and the neighborhood, but due to the disorganized nature of the neighborhood as well as the gang itself, conflict gangs never quite achieve the respect and stability of criminal gangs. The members of conflict gangs tend to be more impulsive and lack self-control compared with members of criminal gangs, largely because there are no adult criminal mentors to control them.

According to Cloward and Ohlin, conflict gangs are blocked not only from legitimate opportunities but also from illegitimate opportunities. If applying Merton's adaptations, conflict gangs would probably fit the category of rebellion best, largely because none

criminal gangs: a type of gang identified by Cloward and Ohlin that forms in lower-class neighborhoods with an organized structure of adult criminal behavior. Such gangs tend to be highly organized and stable.

conflict gangs: a type of gang identified by Cloward and Ohlin that tends to develop in neighborhoods with weak stability and little or no organization; gangs are typically relatively disorganized and lack the skills and knowledge to make a profit through criminal activity.

of the other categories fits well. But it can be argued that conflict gangs have rejected the goals and means of conventional society and implemented their own values, which emphasize violence. Examples of motion pictures that depict this type of breakdown in community structure and result in a mostly violent gang culture include *Menace to Society*, *Boyz n the Hood*, *A Clockwork Orange*, *Colors*, *The Outsiders*, and others that emphasize the chaos and violence that results when neighborhood and family organization is weak.

Finally, if an individual is a "double failure" in both the legitimate and illegitimate worlds, meaning he or she can't achieve success in school or status in a local gang, that person may join other such people to form a retreatist gang. **Retreatist gangs** are made up of those individuals who have failed to succeed in the conventional world and also could not achieve status in the criminal or conflict gangs of their neighborhoods. Because members of retreatist gangs are no good at making a profit from crime (like criminal gang members) or at using violence to achieve status (like conflict gang members), their primary form of offending is usually drug usage. Like Merton's retreatist adaptation to strain, members of retreatist gangs often simply want to escape from reality. Therefore, the primary activity of the gang is usually getting high, which is well represented in such movies as *Trainspotting*, *Drugstore Cowboy*, and *Panic in Needle Park*. In all these movies, the only true goal of the gangs is to get stoned and escape from the world in which they have failed.

There were a number of empirical studies and critiques of Cloward and Ohlin's theory, with much of the criticism being similar to that of Merton's strain theory—specifically, that there is little evidence that gaps between what lower-class youth aspire to and expect to achieve are predictive of feelings of frustration and strain, or that such gaps are predictive of gang membership or criminality.[37] Another criticism of Cloward and Ohlin's theory is the inability to find empirical evidence that supports their model of the formation of three types of gangs and their specialization in offending. While some research supports the existence of gangs that appear to specialize in certain forms of offending, many studies find that the observed specialization of gangs is not exactly the way Cloward and Ohlin proposed.[38] Additional studies have shown that many gangs tend not to specialize but, rather, engage in a wider variety of offending behaviors.

Despite the criticisms of Cloward and Ohlin's model of gang formation, their theoretical framework inspired policy, largely due to the influence of their work for Attorney General Robert Kennedy. In fact, Kennedy asked Ohlin to assist in developing federal policies regarding delinquency, which resulted in the Juvenile Delinquency Prevention and Control Act of 1961. Cloward and Ohlin's theory was a major influence on the Mobilization for Youth project in New York City, which along with the federal legislation stressed creating education and work opportunities for youth. Although evaluations of this program showed little effect in reducing delinquency,[39] it was impressive that such theorizing about lower-class male youths could have such a large impact on policy interventions.

Ultimately, the variations of strain theory presented by Cohen and Cloward and Ohlin provided additional revisions that seemed at the time to advance the validity of strain theory. However, as discussed above, most of these revisions were based on official statistics that showed lower-class male youths as committing the most crime, which were

Many gangs thrive more on violence than on profit-making activities. Such gangs, called conflict gangs, tend to be more territorial and are often found in neighborhoods lacking the structure provided by established crime syndicates.

retreatist gangs: a type of gang identified by Cloward and Ohlin that tends to attract individuals who have failed to succeed in both the conventional world and the criminal or conflict gangs of their neighborhoods.

later shown by self-reports to be exaggerated.[40] Due to the realization that most of the earlier models of strain were not empirically valid for most criminal activity, strain theory became unpopular for several decades. But during the 1980s, another version of strain was devised by Robert Agnew, who rejuvenated the interest in strain theory by devising a theory that made the theory more general and applicable to a larger variety of crimes and forms of deviance.

GENERAL STRAIN THEORY

In the 1980s, Robert Agnew proposed general strain theory, which includes a much larger range of behavior due to not concentrating on simply the lower class and provides a more applicable model for the frustrations that all individuals feel in everyday life.[41] Unlike other strain theories, which all assumed the internalization of the American Dream and the resulting frustration when it was revealed as a false promise to those of the lower classes, general strain theory does not necessarily rely on this assumption. Rather, this theoretical framework assumes that people of all social classes and economic positions deal with frustrations in routine daily life, which virtually everyone can relate to.

Specifically, previous strain theories, such as the models proposed by Merton, Cohen, and Cloward and Ohlin, focused on individuals' *failure to achieve positively valued goals* that they had been socialized to work toward. Like these previous models, general strain theory also focuses on this source of strain; however, general strain theory emphasizes two additional categories of strain: *presentation of noxious stimuli* and *removal of positively valued stimuli* (see Figure 8.2). In addition to the failure to achieve one's goals, Agnew claimed that the presentation of noxious stimuli (i.e., bad things) in one's life could cause major stress and frustration. Examples of noxious stimuli would include an

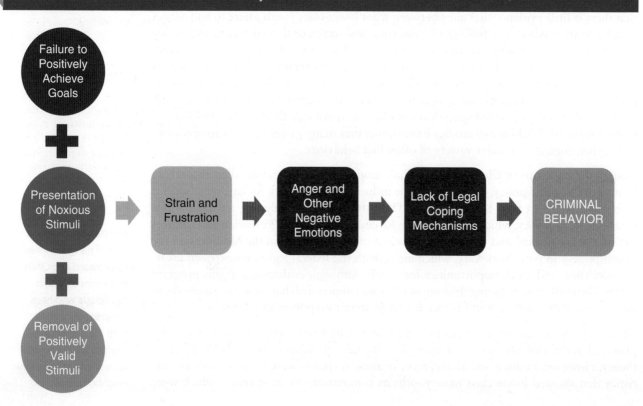

FIGURE **8.2** Model of General Strain Theory

U.S. Marshals Service photo

Christopher Dorner went on a shooting spree, killing police officers and innocent victims in retaliation for his termination from the LAPD.

In early February 2013, Christopher Dorner went on a killing spree in Southern California that resulted in four people dead, including two police officers, and three officers wounded. His intent was to murder as many law enforcement officers as possible, especially those whom he blamed for losing his job with the Los Angeles Police Department (LAPD), where he had served as an officer from 2005 to 2008. One of the initial victims of his killing spree included the daughter (and her fiancé) of the LAPD captain who unsuccessfully represented him in his appeal of charges of misconduct while on patrol.

Dorner made his intentions quite clear in a "manifesto" he wrote and posted on his Facebook page just before he began his killing spree. In this manifesto, he listed many individuals he planned to stalk and kill, as well as celebrities and others whom he claimed to admire, such as the actor Charlie Sheen. He also made very clear in the manifesto that his goal was to get the LAPD to admit that his termination was in retaliation for reporting excessive force by a fellow officer. After his initial killings, he fled to Big Bear, California, in San Bernardino County, where he burned his truck and holed up in a vacant residence.

Dorner's rampage led to one of the largest manhunts in LAPD history, involving many other agencies in the search. These agencies included the San Bernardino County Sheriff's Office and several federal agencies, such as the U.S. Fish & Wildlife agency, whose agent finally spotted Dorner and exchanged gunfire with him just before the siege that took place at the cabin near the small town of Angelus Oaks, California, in the San Bernardino National Forest.

Despite Dorner's killing of innocent victims, many people came out to support him for taking a stand against the LAPD. Although the authors of this book find it hard to believe, he did gain much support in stalking and killing police officers and their family members. Perhaps Dorner gained this support by articulating his reasons, albeit sometimes delusionally (e.g., praising drug-addicted, sex-crazed celebrities), in his manifesto.

Dorner shot himself in the head during the mountain siege, after an intense gun battle that killed two more officers. (It is notable that one of the coauthors of this book [Tibbetts] lives in Angelus Oaks. The official population, according to the 2010 Census, is 535.) Law enforcement authorities used incendiary devices to force Dorner out of the cottage, which elicited an outcry from some of Dorner's supporters, who saw this as an attempt to kill the suspect by whatever means available. Regardless of the motives of law enforcement officers, Dorner was neutralized.

So why did Dorner do it? Given the reasons laid out in his manifesto, he likely was feeling frustrated or strained after being fired from the LAPD as well as being relieved from his service in a U.S. Naval Reserve unit on February 1, 2013. So in addition to an unstable psychological state (which his manifesto reveals, along with documented past domestic issues with several of his former romantic partners), he was likely acting out a deep-seated anger that stemmed from his being fired by the LAPD. Thus, general strain theory, which places a focus on anger, as well as lack of more conventional coping mechanisms is likely the best theory for explaining why Dorner took out his frustrations by killing both law enforcement officers and innocent family members of persons against whom he wanted to exact revenge.

THINK ABOUT IT:

1. Can you articulate reasons why Dorner's case is a good example of strain/general strain theory?

2. Do you see any justification to Dorner's actions, based on the issues in his past and his frustrations?

Sources: Cart, J., & Stevens, M. (2013, February 12). Dorner manhunt: Fish and Wildlife officers make the big break. *Los Angeles Times.* Lloyd, J., Ebright, O., Pamer. M., & Tata, S. (2013, February 28). Charred human remains found in rubble of Big Bear–area cabin. *NBC News.*

abusive parent, a teacher who always picks on one student, or a boss who puts undue strain on one employee. These are just some of the many negative factors that can exist in one's life, and the examples of this category of strain are endless.

The other strain category Agnew identified was the removal of positive stimuli (i.e., good things), which is likely the largest cause of frustration. Examples of removal of positively valued stimuli include the loss of a good job, loss of the use of a car for a period of time, or loss of a loved one. Like the other two sources of strain, examples of removal of positive aspects are infinite, and these may have varying degrees of influence depending on the individual. To clarify, one person may not feel much frustration from losing a job or divorcing his or her spouse, whereas another person may experience severe anxiety or depression from such events.

Ultimately, general strain theory proposes that these three categories of strain (failure to achieve goals, noxious stimuli, and removal of positive stimuli) will lead to stress and a propensity to feel *anger.* Anger can be seen as a primary mediating factor in the causal model of the gender strain framework. In other words, it is predicted that to the extent that the three sources of strain cause feelings of anger in an individual, that individual will be predisposed to commit crime and deviance. However, Agnew was clear in stating that if an individual can somehow cope with this anger in a positive way, then such feelings do not necessarily have to result in criminal activity. These coping mechanisms vary widely across individuals, with certain strategies working better for some people than for others. For example, some people destress by working out or running, whereas others do so by watching television or a movie. One type of activity that has shown relatively consistent success in relieving stress is laughter, which psychologists are now prescribing as a release of stress. Another is yoga, which largely includes simple breathing techniques such as taking several deep breaths, which is physiologically shown to enhance release of stress (see any studies on stress reduction done in the past few decades).

Individuals experience stressors every day, and general strain theory emphasizes the importance of stress and anger in increasing the likelihood of engaging in criminal behavior, especially when individuals have not developed healthy coping mechanisms.

Although he did not originally provide details on how coping mechanisms work or explore the extant psychological research on these strategies, Agnew specifically pointed to such mechanisms in dealing with anger in prosocial ways. The primary prediction regarding coping mechanisms is that individuals who find ways to deal with their stress and anger in a positive way will no longer be predisposed to commit crime, whereas individuals who do not find a healthy, positive outlet for their anger and frustrations will be far more likely to commit crime. Obviously, the goal is to reduce the use of antisocial and negative coping with strain, such as drug usage, aggression, and so forth, which are either criminal in themselves or increase the likelihood of offending.

Evidence and Criticisms of General Strain Theory

Fortunately, recent research and theoretical development have more fully examined various coping mechanisms and their effectiveness in reducing anger and, thus, preventing criminal activity. Obviously, in focusing on individuals' perceptions of stress and anger as well as their personal abilities to cope with such feelings, general strain theory places more emphasis on the micro level of analysis. Still, due to its origins in structural strain theory,

©iStockphoto.com/Juanmonino

it is included in this chapter and is typically classified as belonging to the category of strain theories that includes the earlier, more macro-level-oriented theories. Additionally, recent studies and revisions of the theory have attempted to examine the validity of general strain theory propositions at the macro, structural level.[42]

Since general strain theory was first proposed in the mid-1980s, there has been a vast amount of research examining various aspects of the theory.[43] For the most part, studies have generally supported the model. Specifically, most studies find a link between the three categories of strain and higher rates of criminality as well as a link between the sources of strain and feelings of anger or other negative emotions (e.g., anxiety, depression).[44] However, there have been criticisms of the theory, and especially of the way the theory has been tested.

For example, similar to the problems with using objective indicators to measure perceptions of deterrence (as discussed in previous chapters), it is important for strain research to measure subjects' perceptions and feelings of frustration, not simply the occurrence of certain events themselves. Unfortunately, some studies have looked only at the latter, and the validity of such findings is questionable.[45] Fortunately, a number of other studies have directly measured subjective perceptions of frustration as well as personal feelings of anger.[46]

LEARNING CHECK 8.4

1. According to Agnew, which of the following is NOT one of the key reasons why individuals become strained or frustrated?

   a. Failure to acquire goals/expectations

   b. Dealing with negative stimuli

   c. Loss of positive stimuli

   d. Low self-control

2. Which type of adaptation to strain did Cohen NOT label/identify in his theory?

   a. Corner boy

   b. Drug boy

   c. College boy

   d. Delinquent boy

3. Which of the following types of gangs did Cloward and Ohlin NOT label/identify in their theory of gangs?

   a. Ritualistic gangs

   b. Conflict gangs

   c. Criminal gangs

   d. Retreatist gangs

Answers located at www.edge.sagepub.com/schram2e

Such studies have found mixed support for the hypothesis that certain events lead to anger[47] but less support for the prediction that anger leads to criminality, and this link is particularly weak for nonviolent offending.[48] On the other hand, the most recent studies have found support for the links between strain and anger as well as between anger and criminal behavior, particularly when coping variables are considered.[49] Still, many of the studies that do examine the effects of anger incorporate indicators of anger using time-stable "trait" measures, as opposed to incident-specific "state" measures that would be more consistent with the situation-specific emphasis of general strain theory.[50] This is similar to the methodological criticism, discussed in other chapters in this text, that has been leveled against studies of self-conscious emotions, particularly shame and guilt; namely, when it comes to measuring emotions such as anger and shame, criminologists should choose their measures carefully and make sure the instruments are consistent with the theory they are testing. Thus, future research on general strain theory should employ more effective, subjective measures of straining events and situational states of anger.

Regardless of the criticisms of general strain theory, it is hard to deny its face validity. After all, virtually everyone can relate to the tendency to react differently to similar situations based on what type of day they are having. For example, we all have days when everything seems to be going great—it is Friday, you receive accolades at work, and you are looking forward to a nice weekend with your friends or family. If someone says something derogatory to you or cuts you off in traffic on such a day, you will probably

WHY DO THEY DO IT?

GANG LU

Gang Lu was a PhD graduate at the University of Iowa in 1991 when he entered a meeting of his former academic department and shot and killed several faculty members (including the chair of his PhD dissertation committee and two other committee members). He also shot and killed a student, his former roommate and winner of the elite Spriestersbach Dissertation Prize—awarded to an outstanding PhD candidate for exemplary research in the field of physics, including a $2,500 reward and nomination as a candidate for a prize on the national level. After Lu shot these people, he proceeded to another building, where he shot and killed the associate vice president for academic affairs and the campus grievance officer, to whom Lu had made numerous complaints about not being nominated/chosen as a candidate for the Spriestersbach prize. In addition to the prize money, Lu believed that winning this award would have helped him get hired as a tenure-track professor.

He also shot a temporary student employee in the grievance office; she was paralyzed but survived the attack. Apparently, the president of the university was also on Lu's "hit list," but he happened to be out of town the day of the shootings. Lu was later found dead in a campus room, where he had shot himself in the head. Lu used a .38-caliber revolver in the attack.

So why did Lu perform this massacre? It is likely that one of the primary reasons can be explained by both traditional and general strain theories examined in this chapter. Specifically, he failed to obtain positively valued goals (the dissertation award) despite high expectations, which is consistent with the original version of strain theory proposed by Merton. However, anger over not winning the award and his complaints going unaddressed was clearly a key factor in his actions, and this anger is best explained by Agnew's general strain theory, which was also discussed in this chapter as a more recent and robust framework regarding how strain and frustration can increase propensities to commit crimes. Lu obviously did not deal or cope with this frustration and anger in a healthy way, which is also key in general strain theory; those with healthy coping mechanisms to strain and stress are typically fine, but those who can't deal with it in a positive way are likely to be predisposed to violence or other illegal activity.

A movie—titled *Dark Matter*—starring Meryl Streep and Aiden Quinn and largely based on this event was released in 2007 and won the Sloan Prize at the Sundance Film Festival that year. It is not a factual depiction of what occurred in this case, but it hits close to the mark in portraying why Lu might have committed this act.

THINK ABOUT IT:

1. Can you articulate why Gang Lu's case appears to be a good example of general strain theory?

2. Do you see a way that there could have been some early predictors or interventions that could have prevented Gang Lu's actions?

Sources: Beard, J. A. (1997, June 24). The fourth state of matter. *New Yorker.* Eckhardt, M. L. (2001, November 1). 10 years later: U. Iowa remembers fatal day. *Daily Iowan*; Marriott, M. (1991, November 3). Gunman in Iowa wrote of plans in five letters. *New York Times.*

be inclined to let it go. On the other hand, we also all have days when everything seems to be going horribly wrong—it is Monday, you get blamed for mishaps at work, and you have a fight with your spouse or significant other. On a day such as this, if someone yells at you or cuts you off in traffic, you may be more inclined to respond aggressively. Or perhaps more commonly, you will overreact and snap at a loved one or friend when he or she didn't do much to deserve it; this is a form of displacement in which a cumulative buildup of stressors causes us to lash out. In many ways, this supports general strain theory and its prevalence in everyday life.

Applying Theory to Crime: BANK ROBBERY

Bank robbery is a special type of robbery that, unlike the everyday "street" robberies we discussed in a previous chapter, is within the jurisdiction of the FBI as opposed to local police authorities. Robbery is defined by the FBI in its Uniform Crime Reports (UCR) as "the taking or attempting to take anything of value from the care, custody, or control of a person or persons by force or threat of force or violence and/or putting the victim in fear." Thus, bank robbery is a special form of robbery but robbery nonetheless. A working definition of bank robbery is the act of entering a bank when it is open (or when some person is on the premises) to take money or other goods, and then taking them by force or threat of force. It should be noted that if a break-in occurs at a bank and no one is there, it is typically defined as a burglary (see Chapter 5).

Each year, the FBI puts together a comprehensive review of the many thousands of bank robberies in the United States, which we will review below. But first, it is important to mention that there is no established, systematically collected database of bank robberies for other countries throughout the world. In fact, virtually all other countries simply include bank robberies with other types of robbery that occur in a given year. That said, the United States likely is well represented in the world in terms of bank robbery. We say that with confidence given the data from the FBI.

In 2015, the FBI reported that at least 4,030 bank robberies were committed in the United States. Notably, this did not include more than 50 bank burglaries (those occurring when the bank was closed); as you may recall from a previous chapter, robberies are inherently violent, so someone must be present for a robbery to occur.

Some interesting statistics about these bank robberies in 2015 (largely because such distributions do not tend to differ much from year to year) include gender and race of the offender, day of the week, time of day, type of bank, areas of the bank involved, and modus operandi. Regarding gender, the vast majority of bank robbers were male (4,388; note: this number exceeds the number of incidents because sometimes there are multiple offenders in these bank robberies) versus female (359). This statistic backs up data previously reviewed in the text showing that males commit the overwhelming majority of violent crimes; in this case, females made up less than 8% of all bank robbers. In terms of race, black robbers (2,121) outnumbered white offenders (1,919), despite making up only about 13.3% of the general population. This is likely due to their high rates of poverty in our nation, which makes sense especially in terms of the theories reviewed in this chapter.

Another notable factor in the etiology of bank robbery in the United States is that of day of the week as well as time of day. The modal category for day is Friday (789), which makes sense because offenders may be thinking about getting money for weekend activities. Friday is followed by Tuesday (710) followed by Monday (672) and Wednesday (672), perhaps because offenders didn't have the foresight to anticipate the weekend but feel that they need to make up for what they spent on the weekend (just an educated guess), or perhaps they believe the banks have the most money on hand those days. Consistent with this theory, Saturday is the least likely day for bank robberies.

One of the more consistent predictors of bank robbery is the time of

day when most robbers hit banks. In the report, as well as for the past few decades, bank robbers were most likely to offend between 9 a.m. and 1 p.m., with the highest peak coming in the hour between 10 a.m. and 11 a.m. A theory for why offenders seem to choose this time most often is that they want some of the money that flows in during the first hour (with most banks opening at 9 a.m.) but want to avoid the "lunch-hour" banking rush, when there are many witnesses.

Another factor highlighted by the FBI's 2015 report is that of the type of bank location robbed. In 2015, the main office was rarely robbed, whereas the primary robberies were among branch offices (3,926 robberies), with other locations such as in-store branches and other remote facilities being robbed infrequently. Also, in 2015, metropolitan banks were robbed far more often (1,940 robberies) than were banks in suburbs, small cities, or rural locations. Additionally, in 2015, nearly all the bank robberies were carried out at the bank counter (3,920 robberies) as opposed to the vault/safe, safe deposit boxes, office area, drive-in/walk-up, armored vehicles, or other areas.

Finally—and this may come as a surprise, given the current Hollywood depictions of "takeover robberies," such as in the movies *Heat* and *The Town*—the vast majority of bank robberies in 2015 (as well as for every year in the past few decades) were committed by a demand note (2,416) followed by an oral demand (2,146), usually presented to the teller at the counter.

It is likely that bank robbery is largely driven by unemployment and/or poverty, especially during hard economic times. In one notable recent incident, a jobless man was arrested for committing a dozen bank robberies across the

(Continued)

(Continued)

Phoenix valley. The man, Cristian Alfredo Urquijo, discussed in the case study at the beginning of this chapter, told authorities that he did it to survive and that "desperation was a great motivator."

Urquijo's case is reflective of some of the various theories discussed in this chapter, especially those regarding strain theory. After all, we are talking about a man who, up to that time, appeared to have a clean record. However, when he was suddenly unemployed, he innovated a new way to obtain the money he needed to survive. In addition, according to general strain theory, when positive stimuli are removed (such as a stable job), individuals are more likely to engage in criminal offending, especially when such illegal acts are attempts to replace the lost positive stimuli (in this case, income from work).

THINK ABOUT IT:

1. How do peak times of bank robberies differ from that of other robberies? Can you provide a reason or reasons for this?

2. Why do you think "takeover" bank robberies are far rarer than "oral command" or "passing note to the teller" bank robberies?

Sources: Federal Bureau of Investigation. (2016). *Bank crime statistics 2015: Federally insured financial institutions, January 1, 2015 – December 31, 2015*. Washington, DC: Author; Jobless Arizona bank robber says he "stole to survive." (2011, August 23). *Reuters*.

SUMMARY OF STRAIN THEORIES

The common assumption found across all variations of strain theory is that crime is far more common among individuals who are under a great degree of stress and frustration, especially those who can't cope with or handle such stress in a positive way. The origin of most variations of strain theory can be traced to Durkheim's and Merton's concepts of anomie, which essentially means a state of chaos or normlessness in society due to a breakdown in the ability of societal institutions to regulate human desires, thereby resulting in feelings of strain.

Although different types of strain theories were proposed and gained popularity at various points throughout the 20th century, they all became accepted during eras that were politically and culturally conducive to such perspectives, especially regarding the differences across the strain models. For example, Merton's formulation of strain, which emphasized the importance of the economic institution, was developed and became popular during the Great Depression. Then, in the late 1950s, two strain theories that focused on gang formation were developed by Cohen and by Cloward and Ohlin; they became popular among politicians and society due to the focus on official statistics suggesting that most crime at that time was being committed by lower-class, inner-city male youths, many of whom were gang members. Finally, Agnew developed his general strain model in the mid- to late 1980s, during a period when a number of general theories of crime were being developed (e.g., Gottfredson and Hirschi's low self-control theory and Sampson and Laub's developmental theory); thus, such models were popular at that time, particularly those that emphasized personality traits (such as anger) and experiences of individuals. So all the variations of strain, like all the theories discussed in this book, were manifestations of the periods in which they were developed and became widely accepted by academics, politicians, and society.

POLICY IMPLICATIONS OF STRAIN THEORY

Although this chapter deals with a wide range of theories regarding social structure, the most applicable policy implications are those suggested by the most recent theoretical models of this genre. Thus, we will focus on policies that are most relevant in contemporary times and are key factors in the most modern versions of this perspective.

Comparative Criminology: BANK ROBBERY

Ranking U.S. States on Bank Robbery and Notable Findings From Other Nations

There is no systematic database for occurrences of bank robbery across various nations. Thus, we are largely going to compare various states and regions of the United States and then discuss some findings from other foreign nations.

First, it must be said that bank robbery in the United States has declined significantly over the past two decades, which is consistent with other violent crimes (e.g., homicide) during this most recent time period. For the most recent year for which preliminary data are available (2010), bank robberies once again declined. In 2010, there were just over 5,600 bank robberies (a significant decrease [by about 400] from 2009), in which the offenders got away with about $42 million (of that, authorities recovered about $8 million). As in previous years, the vast majority of these offenses were committed at the bank counter via a demand note. Of course, there are many other types of bank robberies, such as "takeover" robberies (which usually include more than one armed offender forcing everyone in the bank to "get down"). But regardless of type or modus operandi of the robberies, they are all counted the same in most FBI data because they are all attempted or true bank robberies.

In 2010, California, as usual, recorded by far the most bank robberies, at 805 for the year; Texas was a distant second at 464. It should be said that California does have more people than any other state, but even when accounting for the population, California remains overrepresented in bank robberies compared with virtually all states. The other primary states that had high bank robbery numbers were Ohio (263) and Florida (243). Just for comparison among U.S. states, it is notable that North Dakota had only two bank robberies in 2010. Once again, it is important to note that North Dakota has a far lower population than the other states discussed above, but even when standardizing the rates per capita, North Dakota is far lower in bank robberies than those other jurisdictions.

Virtually no foreign nations keep, or at least release publicly, records on bank robbery (at least on the government level) as the FBI does in the United States. Rather, most countries tend to lump incidents of bank robbery in with other types of robbery. Therefore, in this comparative section, we will simply examine some of the statistics and findings that have been provided regarding bank robberies in various countries.

As in the United States, bank robberies in Canada in recent years took place in more urban areas. In fact, banks in only seven cities in Canada were responsible for about 66% of all bank robberies despite having only about 30% of bank branches. The same can be said for the United Kingdom; London has only about 10% of bank branches but reported about 39% of the bank robberies in the whole United Kingdom. The concentration of bank robberies in urban areas is largely attributed to their location, especially in terms of the nearby highways or freeways that allow for more opportunity to escape via fast-moving traffic. Furthermore, a recent study showed that one third of the banks robbed in the United Kingdom were robbed again soon after, specifically in the following three months. However, the same can be said for banks in the United States; if a particular bank is robbed, it greatly increases its chances of being robbed again, especially if the first robbery was successful (i.e., the offenders were not caught).

A study by the Australian Institute of Criminology examined more than 800 bank robberies that occurred in Australia between 1998 and 2002. It was found that the majority (55%) of the incidents were committed by a lone offender, similar to incidents in the United States. This study also found that pairs or multiple offenders inflicted the most injuries on victims at the scene and used disguises most often.

Overall, the trends regarding bank robberies in other similar, industrialized countries seem highly consistent with the trends in the United States. It is important to note that recent developments in crime prevention (e.g., bulletproof teller windows) and biometric technology (e.g., video, fingerprint scanners) make it much harder to access the vaults of various banks in the countries we have discussed. Perhaps this is why bank robberies have fallen dramatically in most of these countries, especially in the United States—even in Southern California, where bank robberies occur less than half as often as they did two decades ago.

Ultimately, although the rates of bank robberies vary across nations, many of the countries that are most like the United States (e.g., Canada, the United Kingdom, Australia) appear to have the same trends in the way bank robberies are committed. So perhaps the most intriguing conclusion is that offenders tend to think the same way across various countries. Still, given that most of the countries in the world do not report specific data on bank robberies, we are going only on what official data have been reported by the countries discussed above. Hopefully, in the future, there will be more readiness among nations to report rates and characteristics of bank robbery.

THINK ABOUT IT:

1. Are there more similarities or differences between other countries and the United States in terms of various issues regarding bank robberies? What specific factors are you examining to make your conclusion?

2. Do you think it is important to have a more systematic collection of data regarding bank robberies in countries around the world, or do you think the cultural differences are too different to compare them?

Sources: Australian Institute of Criminology. (2003, July). *Bank robbery in Australia.* Canberra, Australia: Author. Federal Bureau of Investigation. (2010). *Bank crime statistics 2009: Federal insured financial institutions, January 1, 2009–December 31, 2009.* Washington, DC: Author; Home Office. (n.d.). *Policy: Reducing and preventing crime.* Richey, W. (2011, April 5). Which state has the most bank robberies? FBI releases its annual report. *Christian Science Monitor.*

Specifically, the factors that are most vital for policy regarding social structure are those involving educational and vocational opportunities and programs that develop healthy coping mechanisms to deal with stress.

Empirical studies have shown that intervention programs that focus on educational and/ or vocational training and opportunities are needed for high-risk youths, because those that do not have much motivation for such endeavors can have a significant impact on reducing their offending rates.[51] Specifically, providing an individual with a job, or the preparation for such, is key to building a more stable life, even if the position is not a high-paying job. Thus, the individual is less likely to feel stressed or "strained." In modern times, people are lucky to have a stable job, and this must be communicated to our youth. And ideally they will find some intrinsic value in the work they perform.

Another key area of recommendations from this perspective involves developing healthy coping mechanisms to strain. After all, every individual deals with stress virtually every day. The key is not to avoid stress or strain, because that is impossible. Rather, the key is to develop healthy, legal ways to cope with such strain. Many programs have been created to train individuals on how to develop coping mechanisms for handling such stress without resorting to antisocial behavior. There has been some success in such "anger-management" programs, particularly the ones that take a cognitive-behavioral approach, which teaches individuals to think before they act and often involves role playing.[52]

CONCLUSION

This chapter examined the theories that emphasize inequitable social structure as the primary cause of crime. We examined early perspectives that established that societies vary in the extent to which they are stratified, as well as the consequences that result from inequalities and complexities of such structures. Early European researchers showed that certain types of crimes were clustered in different areas based on their socioeconomic levels. These early models set the stage for later theoretical development in social structure models of crime, especially strain theories.

Our examination of strain theories explored theoretical models stating that individuals and groups who are not offered equal opportunities for achieving success can experience feelings of stress and frustration and, in turn, develop dispositions toward committing crime. There have been many versions of strain theories proposed by scholars over the past century, with some focusing on economics and others emphasizing school performance, neighborhood dynamics, or many other factors beyond economic ones that can also produce frustration among individuals.

We also examined the policy recommendations suggested by the various strain theoretical models, which included the need to help provide individuals with educational and job opportunities as well as helping them to develop healthy coping mechanisms to deal with the daily stressors we all face. Some of these programs have shown success in reducing the level of criminality from stress and frustrations, especially recent programs that have helped high-risk individuals develop better coping mechanisms to deal with their stressors. These programs hold much promise for future interventions.

Finally, we followed up on our initial case study of a jobless man—Cristian Alfredo Urquijo, or the "Black Binder Bandit"—arrested for committing a dozen bank robberies across the Phoenix valley. He confessed to authorities that he engaged in these bank robberies to survive and that "desperation was a great motivator," as he had been laid off and could not find a stable job. This "Black Binder Bandit," so nicknamed because he often hid a revolver in a black binder, is a good representation of some of the theories discussed in this chapter, especially those regarding strain theory.

SUMMARY OF THEORIES IN CHAPTER 8

THEORY	CONCEPTS	PROPONENTS	KEY PROPOSITIONS
Early European social structure theories	Relative deprivation	Adolphe Quetelet	Areas that have the greatest differences in wealth in close proximity (i.e., very poor living near very rich) tend to have the highest crime rates.
Early European social structure theories		André-Michel Guerry	Violent crime rates tend to be highest in poor areas, whereas property crimes tend to cluster in wealthier areas.
Early strain theory	Mechanical vs. organic societies Anomie Collective conscience	Émile Durkheim	Societies evolve from mechanical to organic, with the former having a limited division of labor/roles, which strengthens the "collective conscience" of members. As the division of labor increases in the move to a more organic society, the collective conscience breaks down and results in "normlessness" or anomie.
Merton's strain theory	Anomie (different meaning from Durkheim's) Adaptations to strain	Robert K. Merton	U.S. economic structure causes a differential emphasis on the goals ("wealth") compared with the conventional means of obtaining the goals, which results in anomie. Individuals with limited access to success and wealth adapt to such strain in different ways, with many innovating ways to achieve the goals via illegal methods instead of through legitimate means.
Lower-class frustration theory	Reaction formation Corner boy College boy Delinquent boy	Albert Cohen	Lower-class youth are not prepared for school and are at a disadvantage because schools are based on middle-class norms. Due to failure at school, they socialize with other failures and defy the middle-class norms/rules ("reaction formation"), which leads to gang formation. Different adaptations to this frustration exist, with delinquent boys being the most likely to commit crimes.
Differential opportunities theory	Criminal gangs Conflict gangs Retreatist gangs	Richard A. Cloward and Lloyd E. Ohlin	Gangs in lower-class city areas are a manifestation of the type of neighborhood structure that exists there as well as the ability of youths to be accepted by adult criminal enterprises. Some youths are given opportunities to engage in illegal structures (e.g., the mafia), and others are blocked from these illegitimate opportunities as well as legitimate ones.

(Continued)

(Continued)

THEORY	CONCEPTS	PROPONENTS	KEY PROPOSITIONS
General strain theory	Failure to obtain goals Loss of positive stimuli Presentation of noxious stimuli Coping mechanisms (or lack thereof)	Robert Agnew	This greatly expanded the sources of strain to include everything that had been presented by previous models (economics, school frustration, etc.) and also added much more in the sense of having constant stressors (noxious stimuli) and the loss of positive aspects in one's life. It also added the component of coping mechanisms and individuals' ability to deal with stress in a healthy way.

KEY TERMS

adaptations to strain, 208

anomie, 204

collective conscience, 201

college boy, 212

conflict gangs, 214

conformity, 208

corner boy, 212

criminal gangs, 214

delinquent boy, 212

innovation, 208

mechanical societies, 201

organic societies, 201

reaction formation, 212

rebellion, 208

relative deprivation, 199

retreatism, 208

retreatist gangs, 215

ritualism, 208

DISCUSSION QUESTIONS

1. How does sociological positivism differ from biological or psychological positivism?

2. Which of the early sociological positivism theorists do you think contributed the most to the evolution of social structure theories of crime? Why? Do you think their ideas still hold up today?

3. Can you think of modern examples of Durkheim's image of mechanical societies? Do you think such societies have more or less crime than modern organic societies?

4. What type of adaptation to strain do you think fits you most? Least? What adaptation do you think best fits your professor? Your postal delivery worker? Your garbage collector?

5. Do you know people you went to school with who fit Cohen's model of status frustration? What did they do in response to the feelings of strain?

6. How would you describe the neighborhood where you or others you know grew up in terms of Cloward and Ohlin's model of organization/disorganization? Can you relate to the types of gangs they discussed?

7. If you were the attorney general of the United States, what types of policy recommendations would you give to help alleviate some of the financial (or other types of) strain on individuals or disadvantaged groups?

WEB RESOURCES

Émile Durkheim

A brief, but very insightful, review of Durkheim's personal and professional life:

http://durkheim.uchicago.edu/Biography.html

Strain Theory

This site provides a concise synopsis of key factors in Merton's strain theory:

https://www.boundless.com/sociology/textbooks/boundless-sociology-textbook/deviance-social-control-and-crime-7/the-functionalist-perspective-on-deviance-62/strain-theory-how-social-values-produce-deviance-375-6183/

This bibliographical site provides a basic introduction as well as a list of the key publications for classic strain theory and general strain theory:

http://www.oxfordbibliographies.com/view/document/obo-9780195396607/obo-9780195396607-0005.xml

WANT A BETTER GRADE ON YOUR NEXT TEST?

Get the tools you need to sharpen your study skills:

SAGE edge offers a robust online environment featuring an impressive array of tools and resources for review, study, and further exploration, keeping both instructors and students on the cutting edge of teaching and learning. Learn more at **edge.sagepub.com/schram2e**.

FOR FURTHER EXPLORATION AND APPLICATION, VISIT THE STUDENT STUDY SITE:

Ban the Box Laws,' Do They Help Job Applicants With Criminal Histories?

In Panama, Restoring Streets and Reforming Gangs at the Same Time

The maximizer: Clarifying Merton's theories of anomie and strain

An intersectional analysis of differential opportunity structure for community-based anticrime efforts

Toward an understanding of the emotional and behavioral reactions to stalking: A partial test of general strain theory

SOCIOLOGY - Émile Durkheim

Robert Agnew on Strain Theory and the American Society for Criminology

Christopher Dorner Manhunt: Search for Ex-LAPD Cop Goes On Amid California Snowstorms

A Community Safety Net to Prevent Rampage Shootings: Bernice Pescosolido at TEDxBloomington

Law Enforcement Tries to Curb Increasing Gang Violence in La, OC Counties

The Great Moldovan bank robbery

Strain theory

Extreme Body Modification

Robbery

PREMIUM VIDEO:

Check out the Interactive eBook for premium videos, including videos from author Stephen Tibbetts, who discusses real-world examples and strange crimes; and videos from former offenders, who share their stories from a first-person view, and touch on key theories and concepts from the chapter.

CHAPTER 9

Social Structure Theories of Crime II

Social Disorganization and Subcultures

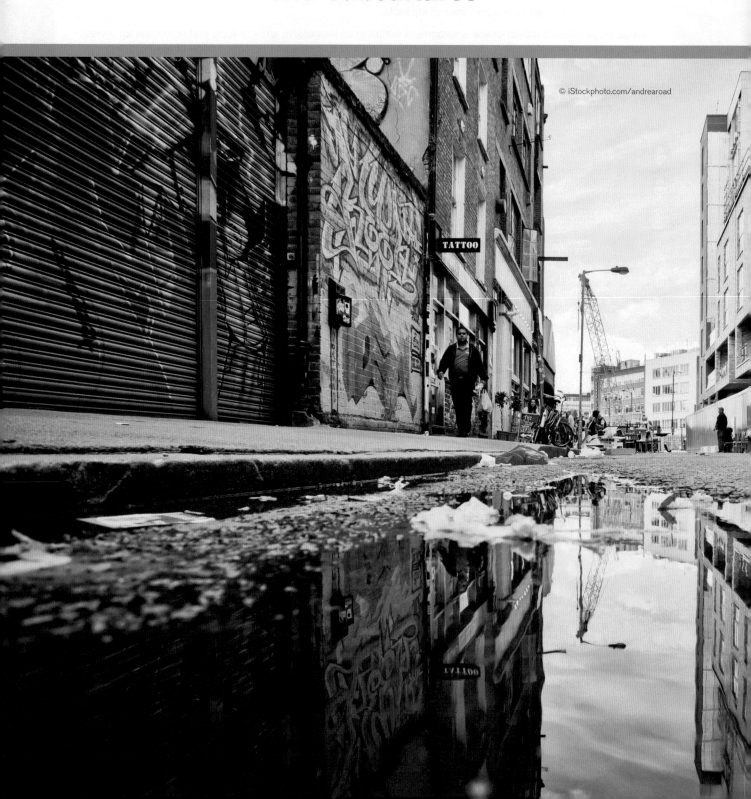

© iStockphoto.com/andrearoad

INTRODUCTION

This chapter will continue our survey of key social structure theories that have been proposed by criminologists to explain criminal behavior. The previous chapter discussed early social structure theories that evolved in Europe in the 19th century as well as more modern versions of strain theory. In this chapter, we will focus on a different type of social structure framework that emphasizes the risk factors and social dynamics in certain neighborhoods. Specifically, we will examine the Chicago School of criminology, which is otherwise known as the Ecological School or theory of social disorganization, for reasons that will become clear by the end of this chapter. The Chicago School perspective places a high emphasis on the impact of the neighborhood where a youth lives in determining his or her criminal behavior.

The Chicago School evolved in that location because the city at that time (late 19th century to early 20th century) desperately needed answers to dealing with its exponentially growing problem of delinquency and crime. Thus, this became a primary focus in the city. A significant portion of the Chicago perspective involved the transmission of cultural values to other peers and even intergenerational transmission, as the older youths relayed their antisocial values and techniques to the younger children. Thus, the cultural/subcultural perspective is also a key area of this theoretical model. This cultural aspect of the Chicago model will also be examined in this chapter, as will other subculture frameworks of offending behaviors.

THE ECOLOGICAL SCHOOL AND THE CHICAGO SCHOOL OF CRIMINOLOGY

Despite its name specifying one city, the Chicago School of criminology represents one of the most valid and generalizable theories we will discuss in this book in the sense that many of its propositions can be readily applied to the growth and evolution of virtually all cities around the world. The Chicago School, which is often referred to as the Ecological School or the theory of social disorganization, also represents one of the earliest examples of balancing theorizing with scientific analysis, along with guiding important programs and policy implementations that still exist and thrive in contemporary times. Perhaps most important, the development of the Chicago School of criminology was the epitome of using theoretical development and scientific testing to help improve conditions in society when it was most needed, which can be appreciated only by understanding the degree of chaos and crime that existed in Chicago in the late 1800s and early 1900s.

Cultural Context: Chicago in the 1800s and Early 1900s

Experts have identified 19th-century Chicago as the fastest-growing city in the history of the United States.[2] Census data show the town growing from about 5,000 people in the early 1800s to more than 2 million people by 1900; put another way, the population more than doubled every decade during the 19th century.[3] This massive rate of growth, which was much

CASE STUDY

LOS ANGELES GANGS

Although most case studies we review in this book are about individuals, in this case we concentrate on groups, which is fitting for this chapter because virtually all the theories we will cover in this section are macro- or group-level theories. A recent scientific study by researchers at the University of California, Los Angeles, showed that when Los Angeles gangs and incidents of gang activities are mapped, the places with the highest frequency of violence are on the borders between two or more rival gangs.[1]

This 2012 report showed that, contrary to popular belief, the most dangerous places to be in Los Angeles are not the regions deeply within the territory of a dominant gang but rather on the

WHEN LOS ANGELES GANGS AND INCIDENTS OF GANG ACTIVITIES ARE MAPPED, THE PLACES WITH THE HIGHEST FREQUENCY OF VIOLENCE ARE ON THE BORDERS BETWEEN TWO OR MORE RIVAL GANGS.

boundaries of gang territories, perhaps due to turf disputes or the increased likelihood of encountering rival factions. We shall see that this recently observed phenomenon among established gang territories was to some extent predicted and explained by Chicago School theories of crime and city growth proposed more than half a century ago. We will follow up on this case study toward the end of this chapter.

THINK ABOUT IT:

Why do you think the most violent areas of Los Angeles are those on the borders of rivaling gangs as opposed to regions that are strongly dominated by a single gang?

faster than that seen in other large U.S. cities such as Boston, Baltimore, New York, Philadelphia, and San Francisco, was due to Chicago's centrally located geographic position; in other words, it was in many ways "landlocked," because although it sits on Lake Michigan, there was no water route to the city from the Atlantic Ocean until the Erie Canal opened in 1825, which opened the Great Lakes region to shipping (including migration of people). Three years later, the Baltimore and Ohio Railroad—the first U.S. passenger train with a route from a mid-Atlantic city to central areas—started operating. These two transportation advancements created a continuous stream of (im)migration to the Chicago area, which only increased with the completion of the transcontinental railroad in 1869, linking both coasts with the midwestern portions of the country.[4]

National Archives and Records Administration (Chicago 1930s)

This type of run-down residential area was key in early theories of crime, such as the Chicago School of criminology, also known as the theory of social disorganization or Ecological School.

It is important to keep in mind that in the early to mid-1800s, many large U.S. cities had virtually no formal social agencies such as we have today to handle problems of urbanization. For example, there were no social workers, building inspectors, garbage collectors, or even police officers. Once police agencies did start in some of these cities, their duties often included tasks we associate with other agencies, such as finding lost children and collecting garbage, primarily because there weren't other agencies to perform these tasks. Therefore, communities were largely responsible for solving their own problems, including crime and delinquency. However, by the late 1800s, Chicago was largely made up of citizens who did not speak a common language and did not share one another's cultural values. This phenomenon is consistent with Census Bureau data from that era that show 70% of Chicago residents were foreign-born and another 20% were first-generation American. Thus, it was almost impossible for these citizens to organize themselves to solve community problems, because in most cases they could not even understand one another. This resulted in the type of chaos and normlessness that Durkheim predicted would occur when urbanization and industrialization occurred too rapidly (see previous chapter); in fact, Chicago represented the archetypal example of a society in an anomic state, with almost a complete breakdown in control. There were many manifestations of this breakdown in social control, but one of the most notable was that children were running wild on the streets in gangs, with little intervention from the adults in the neighborhoods. So delinquency was soaring, and it appeared that the gangs were controlling the streets as much as any other group.

So the leaders and people of Chicago needed theoretical guidance to develop solutions to their problems, particularly regarding the high rates of delinquency. This was a key factor in why the Department of Sociology at the University of Chicago became so important and dominant in the early 1900s. Essentially, modern sociology developed in Chicago because the city needed it to solve its social problems. Thus, Chicago became a type of laboratory for the sociological researchers, and they developed a number of theoretical models of crime and other social ills that are still empirically valid today.

Chicago School of criminology: theoretical framework of criminal behavior that emphasizes the environmental impact of living in a high-crime neighborhood, applies ecological principles to explain how cities grow, and highlights levels of neighborhood organization to explain crime rates.

Ecological Principles in City Growth and Concentric Circles

In the 1920s and 1930s, several new perspectives of human behavior and city growth were offered by sociologists at the University of Chicago. The first relevant model was proposed by Robert E. Park, who claimed that much of human behavior, especially the way cities grow, follows the basic principles of ecology that had been documented and applied to wildlife for many years at that point.[5] Ecology is essentially the study of the dynamics and processes through which plants and animals interact with the environment. In an application of Darwinian theory, Park proposed that the growth of cities follows a natural pattern and evolution.

Specifically, Park claimed that cities represent a type of complex organism that has a sense of unity formed from the interrelations among citizens and groups in the city. Park applied the ecological principle of symbiosis to explain the dependency of the various citizens and units on one another: Everyone is better off working together as a whole. Furthermore, Park claimed that all cities contain identifiable clusters, which he called natural areas, where the group has taken on a life or organic unity by itself. To clarify, many cities have neighborhoods that are primarily made up of one ethnic group or are distinguished by certain features. For example, Hell's Kitchen, Times Square, and Harlem represent areas of New York City that have each taken on a unique identity; however, each of them contributes to the whole—namely, the makeup and identity of the city. The same can be seen in other cities, such as Baltimore, which in a 2-mile area has the Inner Harbor, Little Italy, and Fells Point, with each area complementing the others. From Miami to San Francisco to New Orleans, all cities across America—and throughout the world, for that matter—contain these identifiable natural areas.

Kudzu covers other plants and hogs their sunlight. The Ecological/ Chicago School of criminology applied this type of natural process to show how a criminal element invades and comes to dominate certain areas.

Applying several other ecological principles, Park also noted that some areas (or species) may invade and dominate adjacent areas (species), causing the recession of previously dominant areas (species). The dominated area or species can either recede and migrate to another location or die off. In wildlife, this can be seen in the incredible proliferation of a weed called kudzu. Kudzu grows at an amazing pace and has large leaves. It grows on top of other plants, trees, fields, and even houses, covering everything in its path and stealing all the sunlight. Introduced in the 1800s at a world exposition, this weed was originally used to stop erosion but got out of control, especially in the southeastern region of the United States. Now this weed costs the government more than $350 million each year in destruction of crops and other fauna. This is a good example of a species that invades, dominates, and causes the recession of other species in the area. As is often the case, kudzu was not a completely natural phenomenon; it was synthetically introduced to this country at a world expo.

A similar example is the introduction of buffalo on Santa Catalina Island, off the coast of Southern California, in the 1930s. About three dozen buffalo were originally imported to the island for a movie shoot and the producers decided not to spend the money to remove them afterward, so they have remained and multiplied. Had this occurred in many other parts of the United States, it would not have caused a problem; however, the largest mammal native to the island before the buffalo "invaded" was a 4-pound fox. So the massive buffalo, which have multiplied into the many hundreds (to the point where officials recently deported several hundred to their native Western habitat), have destroyed much of the environment, driving to extinction some plants and animals unique to Catalina Island. Similar to the invasion of kudzu, the buffalo came to dominate the environment, and other species died off.

natural areas: the Chicago School's idea that all cities contain identifiable clusters, such as a Chinatown or Little Italy, and neighborhoods that have low or high crime rates.

Park claimed that a similar process occurs in cities, where some areas invade other zones or areas and the previously dominant area must succeed or die off. This is easy to see in modern times with what is known as *urban sprawl*. Geographers and urban planners have long acknowledged the detriment caused to traditionally stable residential areas when businesses move in. Some of the most recent examples involve the battles of longtime homeowners against the introduction of malls, businesses, and other industrial centers in a previously zoned residential district. The media have documented such fights, especially with the proliferation of such establishments as Walmart and Super Kmarts in areas where residents perceive (and perhaps rightfully so) their presence as an invasion. Such an invasion can create chaos in a previously stable residential community due to increased traffic, a transient population, and, perhaps most important, crime. Furthermore, some cities are granting power to such development through eminent domain, in which the local government can take land from the homeowners to rezone and import businesses.

© Stefan Didam (bison)

The American buffalo was introduced to Catalina Island for a movie shoot in the 1930s and destroyed much of the native plant life. This is an example of a foreign element creating chaos and destruction, as crime does in residential areas when they are invaded by industries or other factors.

At the time when Park developed his theory of ecology, he observed the trend of businesses and factories invading the traditionally residential areas of Chicago, which caused chaos and breakdown in stability in those areas. Readers, especially those who were raised in suburban or rural areas, can likely relate to this, in that when they go back to where they grew up or even currently live, they can often see fast growth. Such development can devastate the informal controls (i.e., neighborhood networks, family ties, etc.) in these areas due to the "invasion" of a highly transient group of consumers and residents who do not have strong ties to the area.

This leads to a psychological indifference toward the neighborhood, in which no one cares about protecting the community any longer. Those who can afford to leave the area do, and those who can't afford to leave will simply remain until they can save enough money to move. After all, especially in the time when Park presented his theory of ecology in the 1920s, when factories moved into the area, it often meant a lot of smoke billowing out of chimneys. No one wanted to live in such a state, particularly at a time when there was no real understanding of pollution and virtually no filters on such smokestacks. In fact, certain parts of Chicago, as well as all other cities in America, were perpetually covered by smog from these factories. In highly industrial areas, it appeared to be always snowing or overcast due to the constant and vast coverage of smoke and pollutants across the sky. So it is easy to see how such "invasions" by factories and businesses can completely disrupt the previously dominant and stable residential areas of a community.

Park's ideas became even more valid and influential with the complementary perspective offered by Ernest W. Burgess.[6] Burgess proposed a theory of city growth in which cities were seen as growing not simply on the edges but from the inside outward. To clarify, while it is easy to see cities growing on the edges, as in the example of urban sprawl described above, Burgess claimed that the source of the growth is in the center of the city. Specifically, the growth of the inner city puts pressure on the adjacent zones of the city, which in turn begin to grow into the next adjacent zones (following the ecological principle of "succession" identified by Park). This type of development is referred to as "radial growth," meaning it begins on the inside and ripples outward.[7]

© Stefan Didam (bison)

An example of radial growth can be seen by watching a drop of water fall into the center of a bucket filled with water. The waves from the impact will form circles that ripple outward. This is exactly how Burgess claimed that cities grow. Although the growth of cities is most visible on the edges, largely due to development of businesses and homes where only trees or barren land existed before, the growth on the edges originates from pressure forming in the very heart of the inner-city area. Another good analogy is the "domino effect," because pressure from the center leads to pressure to grow in the next zone, which leads to growth in the adjacent zones, and so forth.

The Chicago/Ecological model proposed that as factories invaded and dominated residential areas, the residents who could afford to leave did and those left were the poor and deprived, which increased the risk of crime.

To his credit, Burgess also specified the primary zones all cities appear to have, which include five pseudo-distinctive natural areas (in a constant state of flux due to growth). Burgess exhibited these zones as a set of concentric circles (see Figure 9.1). The first, center circle was called Zone I, the central business district (on the chart, it is labeled "The Loop" because that is what downtown Chicago is called, even today). This area of a city contains the large business buildings (modern skyscrapers), which include banking establishments, chambers of commerce, the courthouse, and other essential business and political centers such as police headquarters and the post office. The adjacent area, just outside the business district, is the "factory zone" (unnumbered), which is perhaps the most significant in terms of causing crime, because it invaded the previously stable residential zones in Zone II—identified as the transition zone or **zone in transition**. Zone II is appropriately named, because it was truly in a state of transition from residential to industrial, primarily because this was the area of the city where businesses and factories were invading residential areas. Zone II was the area most significantly subjected to the ecological principles suggested by Park—namely, invasion, domination, recession, and succession. This is the zone subsequent theorists focused on in criminological theorizing, and it is based on the encroachment of factories and/or businesses in areas that were previously stable residential communities.

zone in transition: in the Chicago School, this zone (Zone II) was once residential but is becoming more industrial because of invading factories; it tends to have the highest crime rates.

concentric circles: model proposed by Chicago School theorists that assumes that all cities grow in a natural way with the same five zones.

According to Burgess's theory of concentric circles, Zone III was the "workingmen's homes," largely made up of relatively modest homes and apartments; Zone IV consisted of higher-priced family dwellings and more expensive apartments; and Zone V was considered the suburban or commuter zone. These outer three zones identified by Burgess were of less importance in terms of distinction, primarily because as a general rule, the farther a family could move out of the city, the better in terms of social organization and the lower the rate of social ills (e.g., poverty, delinquency). The important point of this theory of concentric circles is that the growth of each inner zone puts pressure on the next zone to grow and push on the next zone.

It is easy for readers to see examples of this model of **concentric circles**. Whether you live on the East Coast, the West Coast, or in the middle regions of the United States, all you have to do is drive on a highway that enters a major city to see real-life evidence of the validity of this perspective. For example, whether you drive on

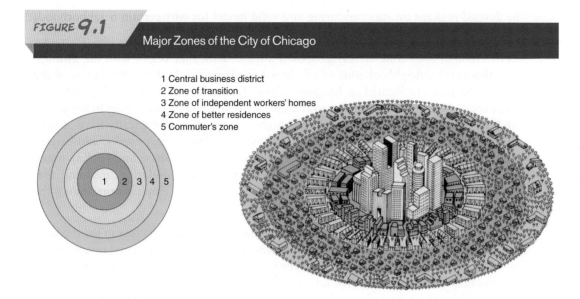

FIGURE 9.1   Major Zones of the City of Chicago

1 Central business district
2 Zone of transition
3 Zone of independent workers' homes
4 Zone of better residences
5 Commuter's zone

Interstate 95 through Baltimore or Interstate 10 through Los Angeles, you will see the same pattern of structures as you travel through the city. As you approach each of the cities, if you look closely you will see suburban wealth in the homes and buildings (often hidden by trees off the highway). As you get closer to the cities, you will see the homes and buildings deteriorate in terms of value. From the raised highway system near Baltimore and Los Angeles, it is readily apparent when you enter Zone II, due to the prevalence of factories and the highly deteriorated nature of these areas. Many of the factories developed through the 20th century have been abandoned or are limited in use, so many of these factory zones feature rusted-out or demolished buildings. This is also often the location of subsidized or public housing. In other words, this is where the people who can't afford to live anywhere else live. Finally, as you enter the inner-city area of skyscrapers, the conditions improve drastically, because this is where the major businesses have invested their money; it appears to be a relative utopia compared with Zone II.

This theory does not apply just to U.S. cities, and we challenge readers to find any major city throughout the world that did not develop this way. In modern times, some communities have tried to plan their development, and other communities have experienced the convergence of several patterns of concentric circles due to central business districts (i.e., Zone I) starting in what were previously suburban areas (i.e., Zone V). However, for the most part, the theoretical framework of concentric circles still has a great deal of support. In fact, even cities found in Eastern cultures have evolved this way. Therefore, Park's application appears to be correct: Cities grow in a natural way across time and place and abide by the natural principles of ecology.

SHAW AND MCKAY'S THEORY OF SOCIAL DISORGANIZATION

Clifford Shaw and Henry McKay drew heavily on their colleagues at the University of Chicago in devising their theory of social disorganization, which became known as the Chicago School theory of criminology.[8] Shaw had been producing excellent case studies on the individual (i.e., micro) level for years before he took on theorizing on the macro (i.e., structural) level of crime rates.[9] However, once he began working with McKay, he devised perhaps the most enduring and valid model for why certain neighborhoods have more social problems, such as delinquency, than others.

In this model, Shaw and McKay proposed a framework that began with the assumption that certain neighborhoods in all cities have more crime than other parts of the city—most of them located in Burgess's Zone II, which is the zone in the transition from residential to industrial, due to the invasion of factories. According to Shaw and McKay, the neighborhoods that have the highest rates of crime typically have at least three common problems (see Figure 9.2): physical dilapidation, poverty, and heterogeneity (which is a fancy way of saying a high cultural mix). Shaw and McKay noted other common characteristics, such as a highly transient population, meaning that people constantly move in and out of the area, as well as unemployment among the residents of the neighborhood.

As noted in Figure 9.2, other social ills are included as antecedent factors in the theoretical model. The antecedent social ills tend to lead to a breakdown in social organization, which is why this model is referred to as the theory of social disorganization. Specifically, it is predicted that the antecedent factors of poverty, heterogeneity, and physical dilapidation will lead to a state of social disorganization, which in turn will lead to crime and delinquency. This means that the residents of a neighborhood that fits the profile of having a high rate of poor, culturally mixed residents in a dilapidated area cannot come together to solve problems, such as delinquency among the neighborhood's youth.

One of the most significant contributions of Shaw and McKay's model was that they demonstrated that the prevalence and frequency of various social ills—be they poverty, disease, low birth weight, or other problems—tend to overlap with higher delinquency rates.

FIGURE 9.2 Model of Shaw and McKay's Theory of Social Disorganization

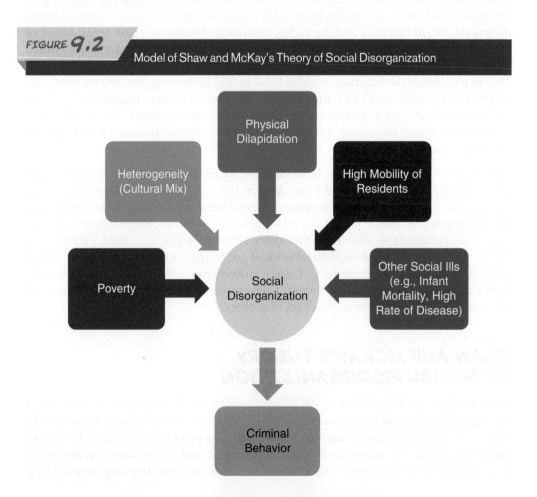

Regardless of what social problem is measured, higher rates of social problems are almost always clustered in the zone in transition. It was in this area that Shaw and McKay believed there was a breakdown in informal social controls and that children began to learn offending norms from their interactions with peers on the street through what they called "play activities."[10] Thus, the breakdown in the conditions of the neighborhood leads to social disorganization, which in turn leads to delinquents learning criminal activities from older youth in the neighborhood. Ultimately, the failure of the neighborhood residents to organize themselves allows the older youth to govern the behavior of the younger children. Basically, the older youth in the area provide a system of organization where the neighborhood cannot, so younger children follow them instead.

Shaw and McKay supplied data to support these theoretical propositions. Specifically, they demonstrated through data from the U.S. Census and city records that neighborhoods with high rates of poverty, physical dilapidation, and a high cultural mix also had the highest rates of delinquency and crime. Furthermore, the high rates of delinquency and other social problems were consistent with Burgess's framework of concentric circles, in that the highest rates were observed for the areas in Zone II, the zone in transition. However, there was an exception to the model; the Gold Coast area along the northern coast of Lake Michigan was notably absent from the high rates of social problems, particularly delinquency, that existed throughout the otherwise consistent model of concentric circles and neighborhood zones.

So Shaw and McKay's findings were as predicted, in the sense that high delinquency rates were apparent in the area of the city where factories were invading the residential district. Furthermore, Shaw and McKay's longitudinal data showed that it did not matter which ethnic groups lived in Zone II (zone in transition), because all groups (with the exception of Asians) who lived in that zone had high delinquency rates while they lived there. On the other hand, once most of each ethnic group moved out of Zone II, their delinquency rates decreased significantly.

This finding rejects the notion of social Darwinism, because it is obvious that the culture is not what influences crime and delinquency but, rather, the criminogenic nature of the environment. After all, if ethnicity or race made a difference, the delinquency rates in Zone II would fluctuate based on who lived in that area, but these rates did not differ. Rather, the zone determined the rates of delinquency regardless of what ethnic or racial groups were living there at the time.

Reaction and Research for Social Disorganization Theory

Over the past few decades, the Chicago School theoretical framework has experienced an enormous amount of attention from researchers.[11] Virtually all the research has supported Shaw and McKay's version of social disorganization and the resulting high crime rates in neighborhoods that exhibit such deprived conditions. Modern research has

---

LEARNING CHECK 9.1

1. In Shaw and McKay's theoretical model, which zone was predicted to be the highest in crime and delinquency rates, largely due to other social problems there?

   a. Central business district

   b. Zone in transition

   c. Zone VI

   d. Zone V

2. Which unit of analysis does Shaw and McKay's theory focus on?

   a. Macro level

   b. Micro level

   c. Situational level

Answers located at www.edge.sagepub.com/schram2e

supported the theoretical model proposed by Shaw and McKay, specifically in terms of the high crime rates in disorganized neighborhoods. Also, it is quite true that virtually every city that one can drive through on an elevated highway (e.g., Richmond, Virginia; Baltimore, Maryland; Los Angeles, California) supports Shaw and McKay's model of crime in concentric circles. Specifically, one can see while driving into almost all cities that the pattern of dilapidated structures surrounds the inner-city area, which is the zone of transition. Preceding (and following) this layer of dilapidated structures, one encounters a layer of houses and residential areas that seem to increase in quality as the driver gets closer to (or farther away from) the inner-city area.

However, critics have raised some valid concerns regarding the original model. Specifically, it has been argued that Shaw and McKay's original research did not actually measure their primary construct: social disorganization. Although this criticism was accurate in calling out Shaw and McKay on not measuring their primary intervening variable, recent research has shown that the model is valid even when measures of social disorganization are included in the model.[12] Such measures of social disorganization include simply asking members of the neighborhood how many neighbors they know by name or how often they observe unsupervised peer groups in the area.

Additional criticisms of Shaw and McKay's formulation of social disorganization also focus on the emphasis the theory places on the macro, or aggregate, level of analysis. After all, while their theory does a good job predicting which neighborhoods will have higher crime rates than others, the model does not even attempt to explain why most youths in the worst areas do not become offenders. Furthermore, their model does not attempt to explain why some, albeit a very small amount of, youths in the best neighborhoods (in Zone V) choose to commit crime. However, the previous case studies completed and published by Clifford Shaw attempted to address the individual (micro) level of offending.

Also, there was one notable exception to Shaw and McKay's proposition that all ethnic/racial groups would have high rates of delinquency and crime while they lived in Zone II. Evidence showed that when Japanese residents made up a large portion of residents in this zone in transition, they had very low rates of delinquency. Thus, as in most theoretical models in social science, there was an exception to the rule.

Perhaps the biggest criticism of Shaw and McKay's theory, which has yet to be adequately addressed, deals with their blatant neglect in targeting the most problematic source of criminality in the Zone II—transitional zone—neighborhoods. Their findings seem to point undoubtedly to the invasion of factories and businesses into residential areas as a problem, yet the researchers did not focus on slowing such invasions as a recommendation. This is likely due to political and financial concerns, being that the owners of the factories and businesses were financing their research and later funded their primary policy implementation. Furthermore, this neglect is represented in their failure to explain the exception of the Gold Coast in their results and conclusions.

Despite the criticisms and weaknesses of the Chicago School perspective on criminology, this theory resulted in one of the largest programs to date attempting to reduce delinquency rates. Clifford Shaw was put in charge of establishing the Chicago Area Project, which established centers in the most crime-ridden neighborhoods of Chicago. These neighborhood centers sought to create activities for youth as well as to establish ties between parents and officials in the neighborhood. Although this program was never scientifically evaluated, it still exists, and many cities have implemented programs based on this model. For example, Boston implemented a similar program that was evaluated by Walter Miller.[13] This evaluation showed that while this project was effective in establishing relationships and interactions between local gangs and community groups as well as providing more educational and vocational opportunities, the program appeared to

Applying Theory to Crime: STALKING

January is National Stalking Awareness Month, as designated by the U.S. Department of Justice. Although this suggests an unprecedented interest in stalking—including the first-ever national survey sponsored by the National Institute of Justice, a branch of the U.S. Department of Justice (Tjaden & Thoennes, 1998)—the number of studies on stalking is still limited. Despite a recent surge in laws to combat stalking passed in virtually every state and the District of Columbia, very little is known about the most common stalkers, how much stalking occurs, and so forth.

To define it, stalking generally refers to threatening or harassing behavior an individual repeatedly engages in (e.g., making harassing phone calls, following a person, leaving numerous messages, continuously appearing at a person's home or place of work). Unfortunately, legal definitions vary from state to state. However, regardless of the definition, there is a strong link between stalking and other forms of violence in intimate relationships (Tjaden & Thoennes, 1998), with 81% of women who were stalked by a current or former partner also having been physically abused by that person.

Women are significantly more likely to be stalked, with recent estimates showing that females are twice as likely as males to be victimized in this way (Tjaden & Thoennes, 1998). A recent study by the Bureau of Justice Statistics (Baum, Catalano, & Rand, 2009)

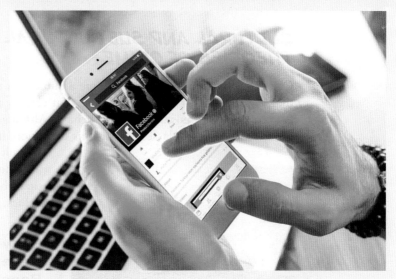
©iStockphoto.com/bombuscreative

concluded that a pattern of decreasing risk for such stalking victimization is evident for persons in higher-income households. This study also showed that a large portion of stalking victims experienced some form of cyberstalking, such as e-mail or text messages, and almost half (46%) of all victims felt fear of not knowing what would happen next. Importantly, more than half of stalking victims lost more than a week of work due to this victimization.

These findings relate to the theories covered in this chapter in the sense that with the advancement of technology and media, there seems to be a certain cultural element that encourages stalking. After all, Twitter, Facebook, and other social networking sites enable the "following" of individuals, and some individuals, given their unstable state,

tend to have problems drawing appropriate lines regarding intrusion into others' lives. Much more study must be done to determine how to discourage and decrease the recent surge in stalking, because the current increase in such cyber-related networking will likely only increase stalking in the near future. For example, a story from 2009 showed how a Bronx man was sentenced to 40 years in prison for international stalking, harassment, and so forth (see the FBI report for this case here: http://www.fbi.gov/newyork/press-releases/2009/nyfo091609.htm).

THINK ABOUT IT:

To what extent do you think social media and other modern technologies are increasing the risk for stalking? Do you know people who were stalked this way?

Sources: Baum, K., Catalano, S., & Rand, M. (2009). *Stalking victimization in the United States.* Washington, DC: Bureau of Justice Statistics; Tjaden, P., & Thoennes, N. (1998). *Stalking in America: Findings from the National Violence Against Women Survey.* Washington, DC: U.S. Department of Justice, National Institute of Justice.

fail in reducing delinquent or criminal behavior. Thus, the overall conclusion reached by experts was that the Boston project and other similar programs, such as the Chicago Area Project, typically fail to prevent criminal behavior.[14]

CULTURAL AND SUBCULTURAL THEORIES OF CRIME

Cultural/subcultural theories of crime assume that there are unique groups in society that socialize their children to believe that certain activities that violate conventional law are good and positive ways to behave. Although it is rather difficult to find large groups of people or classes that fit this definition, it is somewhat likely that there are subcultures or isolated groups of individuals who buy in to a different set of norms than the conventional, middle-class set of values.

Aaron Huey/National Geographic/Getty Images

Cultural/subcultural theorists claim that residents in such environments have a different normative code or moral values than do those in mainstream society, which often are counter to the law and conventional culture.

cultural/subcultural theory: a perspective on criminal offending that assumes that many offenders believe in a normative system distinctly different from and often at odds with the norms accepted by conventional society.

Early Theoretical Developments and Research in Cultural/ Subcultural Theory

One of the key developments of cultural theory has been largely attributed to the 1967 work of Franco Ferracuti and Marvin E. Wolfgang, who examined the violent themes of a group of inner-city youths from Philadelphia.[15] Ferracuti and Wolfgang's primary conclusion was that violence is a culturally learned adaptation to deal with negative life circumstances and that learning such norms occurs in an environment that emphasizes violence over other options.[16] These researchers based their conclusion on an analysis of data that showed great differences in rates of homicide across racial groups. However, Ferracuti and Wolfgang were clear that their theory was based on subcultural norms. Specifically, they proposed that no subculture can be totally different from or totally in conflict with the society of which it is a part.[17] This cultural/subcultural theory brings the distinction of culture and subculture to the forefront.

The distinction between a culture and a subculture is that a culture represents a distinct, separate set of norms and values among an identifiable group of people that are summarily different from those of the dominant culture. For example, communism is distinctly different from capitalism because it emphasizes equality over competition, and it values utopia (i.e., everyone gets to share all profits) over the idea that the best performer gets the most reward. So it can be said that communists have a different culture than capitalists. However, there is a substantial difference between a culture and a subculture, which is typically only a pocket of individuals who may have a set of norms that deviate from conventional values. Therefore, what Ferracuti and Wolfgang concluded is not so much a cultural theory as a subcultural theory.

This is also seen in the most prominent (sub)culture theory, which was presented by Walter Miller.[18] Miller presented a theoretical model that proposed that the entire lower class had its own cultural value system. In this model, virtually everyone in the lower class believed in and socialized the values of six focal concerns: fate, autonomy, trouble, toughness, excitement, and smartness. Fate was the concern of luck, or whatever life dealt you; it disregarded responsibility and accountability for one's actions. Autonomy was the value of independence from authority. Trouble was the concern of staying out of legal problems, as well as getting into and out of personal difficulties (e.g., pregnancy). Toughness was maintaining your reputation on the street in many ways. Excitement was the engagement in activities (some illegal) that helped liven up an otherwise mundane existence of being lower class. Smartness was an emphasis on "street smarts" or the ability to con others. Miller claimed that these six focal concerns were emphasized and taught by members of the lower class as a culture or environment (or "milieu," as stated in the title of his work).

A more recent subculture model proposed by Elijah Anderson has received a lot of attention in the past few years.[19] This theory focuses on African-Americans and claims that due to deprived conditions in the inner cities, black Americans feel a sense of hopelessness, isolation, and despair. Anderson clearly notes that while many African-Americans believe in middle-class values, these values have no value on the street, particularly among young males. According to Anderson, "the code of the streets"—also the title of his book—is to maintain one's reputation and demand respect. For example, to be disrespected ("dissed") is considered grounds for a physical attack. Masculinity and control of one's immediate environment are treasured characteristics; this is perceived as the only thing these young men can control, given the harsh conditions they live in (e.g., unemployment, poverty, etc.).

DISPARITIES OF RACE IN REGARD TO SUBCULTURAL THEORIES OF CRIME. Recent reviews of race and crime rates have shown that the most consistent predictor of crime rates in a given area is the percentage of blacks who live in the area, regardless of whether measured by comparison across neighborhoods, counties, states, or industrialized nations.[20] The race and crime relationship has been consistent over time, with virtually all studies finding that blacks have the highest crime rates (especially for violent crimes, such as homicide), followed by whites, and then Asians. As Wright has noted, "the undeniable fact is that blacks commit more crime than any other group; and they commit more violent crime than any other group . . . [T]he data on this fact could not be any clearer."[21]

For example, according to data from the Federal Bureau of Investigation, blacks commit 85% of all interracial crimes, and although 45% of violent crimes involve blacks offending whites, only 3% involve whites offending blacks. Furthermore, black youths account for 45% of all juvenile detention cases despite accounting for only approximately 15% of the juvenile population.[22] This supports the existence of a strong subculture of black youths in the United States, which supports Anderson's concept of subcultures that lead to a higher propensity for committing crime and being incarcerated.

LEARNING CHECK 9.2

1. Which theorist proposed the theory of lower-class focal concerns?
   a. Burgess
   b. Shaw
   c. Anderson
   d. Miller

2. Which theorist wrote a significant book on inner-city, African-American subculture titled *The Code of the Streets*?
   a. Burgess
   b. Park
   c. Anderson
   d. Miller

Answers located at www.edge.sagepub.com/schram2e

---

focal concerns: primary concept of Miller's theory, which asserts that all members of the lower class focus on concepts they deem important: fate, autonomy, trouble, toughness, excitement, and smartness.

Comparative Criminology: VIOLENCE AGAINST FEMALES

Cross-Regional Rates of Intimate Violence Committed Against Females

In this section, we compare various regions based on their rates of intimate violence against females. This box is relevant to the chapter because countries with higher rates of violence against females tend to have cultural norms that are more permissive of such violence within families.

As shown in Figure 9.3, the region of the world with by far the highest annual percentage of females 15 and over being victimized by violence from intimate partners was the Middle East. The second highest region was Africa, but it was a distant second. The leading theory for why these two regions, and especially the Middle East, are so high is the

extreme patriarchy—or dominance of males—prominent in most countries in those regions.

Consistent with this conclusion, Van Dijk (2008) points out that perhaps the most comprehensive studies of domestic abuse in modern times were done in Germany and surveyed more than 11,000 teenagers about their experiences with domestic violence in their homes. One consistent finding was that rates or percentages of violence against mothers reported by children of immigrants were significantly higher, with extremely high rates reported among those from Turkey (32%), Yugoslavia (25%), and Russia (20%). Another interesting pattern was that the immigrant families who had resided in Germany for longer periods had higher rates of violence, which Van Dijk claimed suggested "growing tensions between

FIGURE 9.3

Percentages of Women, 15 Years and Older, Victimized by Violence From Intimate Partners Over the Past 12 Months

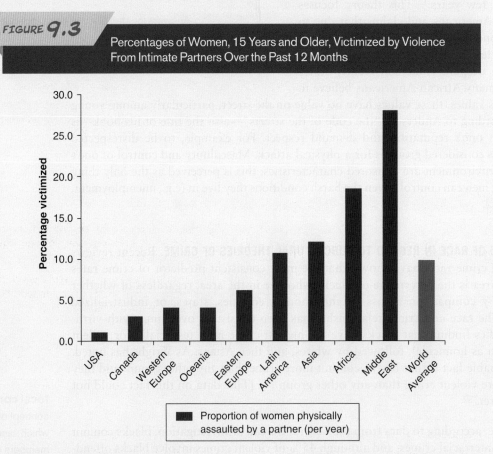

Sources: Independently run, dedicated surveys of violence against women in 72 countries; United Nations. (2006). *In-depth study on all forms of violence against women*. Report to the Secretary-General, New York, United Nations. (A/61/122/Add.1.)

FIGURE 9.4

Total Violent Crime and Intimate Partner Violence, 1993–2011
(Rate per 1,000 Persons Age 12 or Older)

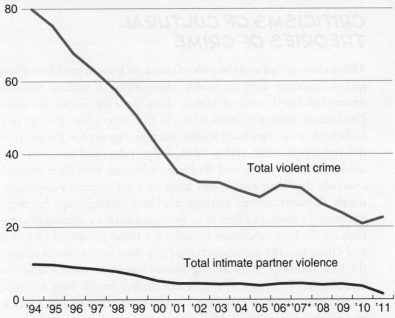

Note: Estimates based on two-year rolling averages beginning in 1993. Includes rape or sexual assault, robbery, aggravated assault, and simple assault committed by current or former spouses, boyfriends, or girlfriends.

* Due to methodological changes, use caution when comparing 2006 NCVS criminal victimization estimates to other years. See Criminal Victimization, 2007, NCJ 224390, BJS website, December 2008, for more information. Source: Bureau of Justice Statistics, National Crime Victimization Survey, 1993–2010.

spouses after a longer exposure of women to German norms and values concerning gender equality" (p. 88).

It is also notable that the World Health Organization (2004) estimated annual economic costs in the United States due to intimate partner violence at about $13 billion. One bit of good news is that intimate partner violence has dropped significantly in the United States in recent years (see Figure 9.4), showing a 72% drop between 1994 and 2011.

THINK ABOUT IT:

1. Why do you think that regions of the world with more permissive attitudes regarding females have higher rates of intimate violence toward them?

2. How do you think such societies with more liberating policies toward women could reduce the increase in their rates of domestic victimization?

Sources: Bureau of Justice Statistics. (2013). *Intimate partner violence, 1993–2011*. Washington, DC: U.S. Department of Justice; Van Dijk, J. (2008). *The world of crime*. Thousand Oaks, CA: SAGE; World Health Organization. (2004). *The economic dimensions of interpersonal violence*. Geneva, Switzerland: Author.

Consistent with previous research, a recent study conducted in the United Kingdom found that extreme disadvantage had more of a predictive effect of crime rates for black communities, but not for white or South Asian communities/boroughs. This supports the idea of subcultural influence, even among similarly deprived groups.[23] This is also seen on the other side of the fence regarding victims of crime, in which there is a consistently seen greater prevalence of intraracial crime (e.g., blacks violating blacks) compared to interracial crime (e.g., white violating blacks). Specifically, a recent study using the National Incident-Based Reporting System (NIBRS) for 2009 and 2010 for aggravated assault rates found that as racial residential segregation increased, the relative frequency of black intraracial assault to black interracial assault increased. On the other hand, there was no effect on the ratio of white intra- versus interracial assault.[24] This also supports a subcultural perspective, given that certain racial groups seem to respond differently to similar living conditions.

CRITICISMS OF CULTURAL THEORIES OF CRIME

The studies on cultural theories of crime, at least in the United States, show that no large groups blatantly deny the middle-class norms of society. Specifically, Miller's model of lower-class focal concerns simply does not exist across the entire lower class. Studies consistently show that most adults in the lower class attempt to socialize their children to believe in conventional values, such as respect for authority, hard work as positive, delayed gratification, and so forth, and not the focal concerns that Miller specified in his model. Even Ferracuti and Wolfgang admitted that their research findings led them to conclude that their model was more of a subcultural perspective and not one of a distinctly different culture. So there are likely small groups or gangs that have subcultural normative values, but that does not constitute a completely separate culture in society. Perhaps the best subculture theories are those presented by Cohen, as well as Cloward and Ohlin (see the previous chapter), in their variations of strain theory that emphasize the formations of gangs among lower-class male youths, which we discussed earlier in this chapter. Therefore, it can be concluded that if there are subcultural groups in our society, they seem to make up a small percentage of the population, which somewhat negates the cultural/subcultural perspective of criminality.

POLICY IMPLICATIONS

Many of the policy implications suggested by the theoretical models proposed in this chapter are rather ironic. Regarding social disorganization, a paradox exists in the sense that the very neighborhoods most desperately in need of becoming organized to fight crime are the same inner-city poor areas that are, by far, the most difficult places to cultivate such organization (e.g., neighborhood watch or "Block Watch" groups). Rather, the neighborhoods that do have high levels of organization tend to be those that already have low levels of crime, because the residents naturally "police" their neighbors' well-being and property since they have a stake in keeping the area crime free. Although there are some anecdotal examples of success in neighborhood watch programs, the majority of the empirical evidence is "almost uniformly unsupportive" of this approach's ability to reduce crime in such neighborhoods. Furthermore, many studies of these neighborhood watch programs find that in a notable number of communities, these groups actually increase the fear of crime, perhaps due to the heightened awareness of crime issues in such areas.

Also, as explained above, perhaps the most prominent program that resulted from the Chicago School/social disorganization model—the Chicago Area Project—and similar programs have been deemed failures in reducing crime rates among the participants. Still, there have been some advances in trying to get residents of high-crime areas organized to fight crime. To clarify, the more specific the goals of neighborhoods regarding crime reduction, such as more careful monitoring of high-level offenders (e.g., more intensive supervised probation) and better lighting in dark places, the more effective the implementation will be.

Regarding cultural/subcultural programs, some promising intervention and outreach programs have been suggested by such models of offending. There are now many programs that attempt to build prosocial attitudes (along with other health and opportunity aspects) among high-risk youth, often young children. For example, a recent program called Peace Builders, which focuses on children in early grades, was shown by a recent

WHY DO THEY DO IT?

WHITEY BULGER

Whitey Bulger (James Joseph "Whitey" Bulger Jr.) is perhaps the most notorious gangster from the South Boston area, which is saying a lot given the history and tradition of organized crime in "Southie," as they call it. Bulger was a key figure of a criminal organization from the early 1970s to the mid-1990s and head of this organization for much of that time. Under heat from authorities, he fled in 1994, and for 12 years he was on the FBI's "Ten Most Wanted" list. Bulger was apprehended with his long-term girlfriend, Catherine Greig, in Santa Monica, California, in 2011. He was sentenced on November 14, 2013 to two terms of life imprisonment, plus five years.

Bulger is believed to have been largely in charge of narcotics distribution and extortion rackets in the Southie area during most of the 1980s and early 1990s, along with the violence inherent to such a position. Interestingly, most sources show that he was also an FBI informant during much of this time period, which allowed him to essentially "get away with murder" and his other illegal activities.

Perhaps most related to this chapter, Bulger was seen locally as a type of Robin Hood figure, considered by most people on the streets as a sort of guardian protecting the interests of the neighborhood or local area. After all, Bulger had been a key element of organized crime in that area for many years, and this led to a subcultural/cultural climate placing him as an authority for all that happened in that locale. Furthermore, much of his business dealt with narcotics distribution and extortion, so his motives fit the other theories in this chapter of being largely based on finding criminal opportunities despite the relatively poor and deprived conditions of the South Boston region.

So why did he do it? As alluded to before, Bulger likely saw the draw of organized crime as being his only way to achieve the higher financial and/or social status that could be obtained in the South Boston area. After all, there were not many legitimate opportunities open to him given his early criminal record, not to mention the deprivation and lack of stable employment in that region. Furthermore, he probably also desired to become an important figure in the subculture/culture of that area, and the only likely way to do that was to become a prominent figure in the organized crime syndicates.

Whitey Bulger (1929–) was the head of one of the most notorious organized crime syndicates in Boston until he was apprehended in Southern California in 2011.

U.S. Marshals Service photo

THINK ABOUT IT:

1. Can you relate to Bulger's local community's attitude toward him as a type of hero?

2. How do you think such a subculture develops in local communities for such prominent gangsters?

Sources: MacKenzie, E., & Karas, P. (2004). *Street soldier: My life as an enforcer for "Whitey" Bulger and the Boston Irish Mob.* Hanover, NH: Steerforth; Weeks, K., & Karas, P. (2009). *Brutal: My life inside Whitey Bulger's Irish Mob.* New York, NY: HarperCollins.

evaluation to be effective in producing gains in conflict resolution, development of prosocial values, and reductions in aggression, and a follow-up showed that these attributes were maintained for a long period of time. Another recent anti-aggression training program for foster-home boys showed much success in increasing levels of empathy, self-efficacy, and attribution style among boys who had exhibited early-onset aggression. Ultimately, there are effective programs out there that promote prosocial norms and culture. More efforts should be devoted to promoting such programs that will help negate the antisocial cultural norms of individuals, especially among high-risk youths.

CONCLUSION

In this chapter, we examined theoretical perspectives proposing that the social organizations in neighborhoods that are broken down and dilapidated are unable to control delinquency and crime in those areas. Furthermore, we discussed how this model of crime was linked to processes derived from ecological principles. This type of approach has been tested numerous times, and virtually all studies show that the distribution of delinquents and crime activity is consistent with this model.

We then discussed the ability of cultural and subcultural theories to explain criminal activity. Empirical evidence shows that cultural values do make a contribution to criminal behavior but that the existence of an actual alternative culture in our society has not been found. However, some pockets of certain subcultures, particularly regarding inner-city youth gangs, certainly exist and provide some validity for the subculture perspective of crime. Furthermore, the Chicago perspective plays a role because it is typically in the inner-city areas (i.e., zones of transition) where these subcultural groups form.

We also examined some policy implications suggested by these theoretical models. Regarding social disorganization, we noted the paradox that exists: The very neighborhoods most desperately in need of becoming organized to fight crime are the same inner-city ghetto areas that are, by far, the most difficult places to cultivate such organization (e.g., neighborhood watch groups). On the other hand, the neighborhoods that do have high levels of organization tend to be those that already have low levels of crime, because the residents naturally "police" their neighbors' well-being and property since they have a stake in keeping the area crime free. Still, there have been some advances in organizing residents of high-crime areas to fight crime. Regarding the cultural and subcultural perspectives, we examined some of the intervention and outreach programs suggested by such models of offending.

Finally, it is important to follow up on the case study we discussed at the beginning of this chapter, which involved a 2012 UCLA-led study finding that the most dangerous areas of Los Angeles were not deep within established gang territories but rather near the boundaries or border areas among rival gangs. This makes sense and can be explained by several of the frameworks presented in this chapter. Specifically, the natural areas discussed by Park and the zones identified by Shaw and McKay seem to be relatively safe and sound when there is some stability; it is when they are disrupted—such as in the zone in transition, where residential areas are being invaded by factories or big-box stores—that chaos tends to ensue. It appears that this is exactly the same case in terms of gangs and gang territories. So although much of the Ecological/Chicago School framework was proposed more than 50 years ago, it can still be applied to contemporary city dynamics and crime rates in metro areas worldwide.

SUMMARY OF THEORIES IN CHAPTER 9

THEORY	CONCEPTS	PROPONENTS	KEY PROPOSITIONS
Ecological/Chicago School perspectives on city growth	Natural areas Concentric circles	Robert E. Park and Ernest W. Burgess	Virtually all cities grow in a natural way, whereby they form distinct areas that tend to grow in a radial fashion from the center outward, forming rings of concentric circles.
Social disorganization theory	Various zones in the city Zone in transition Factory zone	Clifford Shaw and Henry McKay	Nearly all cities experience large growth of factories around the city center, which invades residential areas and essentially creates a state of transition and instability, which leads to chaos and higher crime and delinquency rates.
Subcultural theories		Marvin E. Wolfgang and Franco Ferracuti; Elijah Anderson	Some groups of people have normative structures that deviate significantly from the mainstream culture, which inevitably leads to illegal behavior.
Lower-class focal concerns	Six focal concerns (that go against middle-class norms)	Walter Miller	The lower class has an entirely separate culture and normative value system (i.e., focal concerns), which in many ways values the opposite of many middle-class standards.

KEY TERMS

Chicago School of
   criminology, 229

concentric circles, 234

cultural/subcultural
   theory, 240

focal concerns, 240

natural areas, 232

zone in transition, 234

DISCUSSION QUESTIONS

1. Can you identify and discuss another example of the ecological principles of invasion, domination, and succession among animals or plants that was not discussed in this chapter?

2. Can you see examples of the various zones that Shaw and McKay described in the town or city where you live (or nearest you)? Try obtaining a map or sketching a plot of the town or city closest to your home and then draw the various concentric circles where you think the zones are located.

3. What forms of organization and disorganization have you observed in your own neighborhood? Try to supply examples of both if possible.

4. Can you provide modern-day examples of different cultures and subcultures in the United States? What regions, or parts of the country, would you say have cultures that are more conducive to crime?

5. Do you know people who believe most or all of Miller's focal concerns? What social class do they belong to? What are their other demographic features (age, gender, urban/rural, etc.)?

6. Do you know individuals who seem to fit either Ferracuti and Wolfgang's cultural theory or Anderson's model of inner-city youth street code? Why do you believe they fit such a model?

WEB RESOURCES

Chicago School of Criminology

This site provides a brief but well-applied video example of the theory of social disorganization/Chicago school perspective.

   http://study.com/academy/lesson/the-chicago-schools-
      social-disorganization-theory.html

This site provides a brief summary of the Chicago School of criminology and offers an extensive bibliographical list of key studies that have examined this perspective:

   http://www.oxfordbibliographies.com/view/document/obo-
      9780195396607/obo-9780195396607-0077.xml

Subcultural Theories

This site provides an excellent video that gives all the key concepts and propositions of subcultural theory in criminology:

   https://www.youtube.com/watch?v=P2Gn4ibhRLM

This site provides a good, published book review of Anderson's *Code of the Streets.*

   https://www.westga.edu/assetsCOSS/coss/Book_review-
      Code_of_the_Streets-Heather_Kelley.pdf

$SAGE edge™

WANT A BETTER GRADE ON YOUR NEXT TEST?

Get the tools you need to sharpen your study skills:

SAGE edge offers a robust online environment featuring an impressive array of tools and resources for review, study, and further exploration, keeping both instructors and students on the cutting edge of teaching and learning. Learn more at **edge.sagepub.com/schram2e**.

FOR FURTHER EXPLORATION AND APPLICATION, VISIT THE STUDENT STUDY SITE:

- Chicago Residents Fight Crime One Vacant Lot at a Time
- Does Crime Drop When Immigrants Move In?
- The sense of belonging in new urban zones of transition
- The effects of neighborhood context on youth violence and delinquency: Does gender matter?
- City of Imagination: Kowloon Walled City 20 Years Later
- A Community Safety Net to Prevent Rampage Shootings: Bernice Pescosolido at TEDxBloomington
- The safest cities in America
- President Obama declares January National Stalking Awareness Month
- Ending Violence Against Women and Girls: If Not You, Who?
- Subculture
- Social Disorganization
- Additional Subcultures

PREMIUM VIDEO:

Check out the Interactive eBook for premium videos, including videos from author Stephen Tibbetts, who discusses real-world examples and strange crimes; and videos from former offenders, who share their stories from a first-person view, and touch on key theories and concepts from the chapter.

CHAPTER 10

Social Process and Control Theories of Crime

INTRODUCTION

People learn rules, morals, and values through a process of socialization. Early socialization usually occurs with the family. During this stage, children start learning how to behave. Ideally, they learn what behavior is appropriate when at home and in public. Socialization also takes place later in life and outside the family context. As individuals grow older, other influential agents of socialization become school and peers. The workplace, community and religious organizations, and countless other entities also contribute to the socialization process.

Most people who have no understanding of criminological theory understand that socialization is important and, possibly, connected to how one behaves later in life. It is well-known, for instance, that broken homes,[1] poor parental control,[2] and child abuse and neglect[3] often lead to certain problems. For example, a child who suffers repeated abuse may be inclined to abuse his or her children in adulthood. Even if one is fortunate enough to grow up in a fully functional family, other outside factors—such as being bullied in school or ridiculed in the workplace—can contribute to inappropriate behavior.[4]

In short, people are influenced by numerous sources, which is why it is useful to examine the role of socialization in criminal behavior. Theories that claim socialization is linked to criminal activity are known as social process theories. Social process theories examine how individuals interact with other individuals and groups. These theories focus carefully on how behavior is learned, internalized, and transmitted between individuals.

This chapter begins with social process theories known as learning theories. Learning theories attempt to explain how and why individuals learn criminal, rather than conforming, behavior. Learning theorists believe that individuals are "socialized" in criminal behavior. For example, learning theorists argue that delinquent peers may contribute to a person's decision to violate the law. Next, we discuss control theories. Control theories focus on social or personal factors that prevent individuals from engaging in selfish, antisocial behaviors.

A useful way to distinguish between learning and control theories is as follows: Learning theories are concerned with why individuals are socialized into criminal activity (e.g., by witnessing domestic violence over a period of years and then acting abusively in adulthood). By contrast, control theories are concerned with why individuals are not socialized into conforming behavior. That is, what is it about one's surroundings and upbringing that leads one to follow the rules of society despite a natural disposition to offend?

LEARNING THEORIES

In this section, we review theories that explain the social processes of *how* and *why* people engage in criminal behavior through learning. Unlike other theories that assume we are born with offending tendencies (e.g., control theories), virtually all learning theories assume that our attitudes and behavioral decisions are acquired via communication after we are born; thus, individuals enter the world with a blank slate (often referred to as the tabula rasa). Thus, learning theories seek to explain how criminal and noncriminal

LEARNING OBJECTIVES

As you read this chapter, consider the following topics:

- Articulate what distinguishes learning theories of crime from other perspectives.

- Distinguish differential association theory from differential reinforcement theory.

- Evaluate the strengths and weaknesses of differential association and differential reinforcement theory.

- Define the five original techniques of neutralization and explain them.

- Discuss early forms of social control theory, such as those of Hobbes and Freud.

- Explain Reckless's containment theory.

- Explain Hirschi's social bonding theory, particularly the four elements of the bond.

- Describe the key tenets of integrated social control theories.

- Discuss low self-control theory, such as what personality traits are involved.

CASE STUDY

THE WEAVERS

Ward "Pete" Weaver Jr. was a long-haul truck driver, so he was away from home for lengthy periods of time. In 1978, Pete Weaver was sentenced to prison for a rape conviction. Later, in 1981, Pete Weaver was sentenced to 42 years in prison. He had picked up two runaways; he arranged for a friend to shoot the 18-year-old man and himself repeatedly raped the 15-year-old girl. Weaver Jr.'s truck routes corresponded to 26 unsolved hitchhiker homicides, but he was never charged with those cases. While Weaver Jr. was in prison, he confided to a cellmate that he had murdered another couple. He had beaten 18-year-old Robert Radford to death with a pipe and then kidnapped, raped, and strangled Radford's 23-year-old fiancée, Barbara Levoy. After killing Levoy, Weaver Jr. buried her behind his rented house in Oroville, California, where he later covered the grave with concrete and built a deck.[5] Weaver Jr. came from a family of extensive violence. He was known to be cruel to his siblings as well as animals.[6]

Ward Francis Weaver III, known as "Little Pete," is the son of Ward Weaver Jr. Like his father, he is a violent man. He was sentenced to three years in prison for assaulting his pregnant wife. After his release, Ward Weaver continued to be involved in volatile relationships. In 2001, he, along with his girlfriend, moved to Oregon City. One of his daughters befriended classmates at a middle school. These friends would regularly sleep over at the Weaver household. In August 2001, Weaver was accused of attempting to rape one of these girls, Ashley Pond. The claim was not immediately investigated by police. On January 9, 2002, Ashley disappeared. Two months later, another classmate, Miranda Gaddis, disappeared. Their whereabouts were unknown until Ward Weaver's son Francis dialed 911 because his father had raped his (Francis's) girlfriend. In that 911 call, Francis stated that his father

Flowers and letters placed at a fence bordering the crime scene that became a community memorial for the two slain Oregon City girls. Ward Weaver's house is seen in the background.

> WEAVER, JR., CAME FROM A FAMILY OF EXTENSIVE VIOLENCE. HE WAS KNOWN TO BE CRUEL TO HIS SIBLINGS AS WELL AS ANIMALS.

claimed to have raped and killed the two girls and buried them under a concrete patio. Subsequently, Miranda Gaddis's body was found in a shed in the backyard; Ashley Pond's body was buried under the concrete.

Francis Paul Weaver was the stepson of Ward Francis Weaver III. He was the person who turned his stepfather in during the 911 call. In March 2016, Francis Paul Weaver was convicted of the death of Edward Spangler. He, along with two others, had killed Spangler as a result of a drug deal that went bad. While not the actual shooter, Weaver was convicted and sentenced to life for his involvement.[7]

This case study brings up numerous questions, particularly those that focus on how someone's family can influence his or her behavior. Were these men "born" violent, or was violence something they learned firsthand?

THINK ABOUT IT:

1. Do you think that these men learned these violent tendencies from others in their family?

2. What other factors may have influenced these men (e.g., peers)?

behavior is learned through cultural values people internalize and acquaintances they make. A key feature of learning theories is recognizing the influence of peers and significant others on an individual's behavior. Three learning theories are discussed in this section, starting with differential association theory.

Differential Association Theory

Edwin H. Sutherland is considered one of the most influential criminologists of the 20th century. In the third edition of *Principles of Criminology*, Sutherland fully introduced his differential association theory.[8] He was especially interested in explaining how criminal values and attitudes could be culturally transmitted from one generation to the next. Sutherland was greatly influenced by Shaw and McKay's concept of social disorganization[9] (see previous chapter). He was also influenced by Gabriel Tarde's imitation theory,[10] which, as its name suggests, claims that people imitate one another. Tarde formulated three laws of imitation: (1) People imitate one another in proportion as they are in close contact, (2) often the superior is imitated by the inferior, and (3) when two mutually exclusive methods or approaches come together, one method can be substituted for another.[11]

ELEMENTS OF DIFFERENTIAL ASSOCIATION THEORY. Sutherland presented his theory of differential association with nine specific statements.[12] The statements are listed below in italics, and each statement is followed by a brief interpretation and clarification.

1. *Criminal behavior is learned.* Criminal behavior is not inherited; rather, a person needs to be trained, or educated, in crime.

2. *Criminal behavior is learned in interaction with other persons in a process of communication.* In most instances, this communication is verbal. However, communication can also be nonverbal in nature.

3. *The principal part of the learning of criminal behavior occurs within intimate personal groups.* Sutherland distinguished personal and impersonal groups. Personal communications between family and friends, he theorized, will have more of an influence than impersonal communications, such as those occurring with simple acquaintances as well as through the movies and other entertainment media.

4. *When criminal behavior is learned, the learning includes (a) techniques of committing the crime, which are sometimes very complicated, sometimes very simple; and (b) the specific direction of motives, drives, rationalizations, and attitudes.* Criminals learn from others the techniques, methods, and motives necessary to sustain their behavior.

5. *The specific direction of motives and drives is learned from definitions of the legal codes as favorable or unfavorable.* Individuals may associate with others who define the legal codes as rules that should be observed; these individuals, however, may also associate with others whose definitions favor violating these legal codes.

6. *A person becomes delinquent because of an excess of definitions favorable to violation of law over definitions unfavorable to violation of law.* Sutherland noted that this is the essence of differential association. Individuals can have associations that favor both criminal and noncriminal behavior patterns. A person will engage in criminal behavior when there is an *excess* of definitions that favor violating the law.

7. *Differential associations may vary in frequency, duration, priority, and intensity.* Frequency and duration refer to how often and how long associations occur. Priority refers to whether an individual has developed a strong sense of lawful behavior during early childhood. Intensity is not precisely defined.

learning theories: theoretical models that assume that criminal behavior of individuals is due to a process of learning from others the motivations and techniques for engaging in such behavior.

control theories: theories of criminal behavior that emphasize the assumption that humans are born selfish and that their tendencies toward aggression and offending must be controlled.

differential association theory: a theory of criminal behavior that emphasizes association with significant others (peers, parents, etc.) in learning criminal behavior.

8. *The process of learning criminal behavior by association with criminal and anti-criminal patterns involves all of the mechanisms that are involved in any other learning.* This statement asserts that the process of learning criminal behavior is similar to the process of learning other types of behavior.

9. *While criminal behavior is an expression of general needs and values, it is not explained by those general needs and values, since noncriminal behavior is an expression of the same needs and values.* Sutherland argued that motives, needs, and values as explanations for criminal behavior are inadequate because they are also explanations for noncriminal behavior. For instance, needing money is a motivation for a thief to steal as well as for a student to get a part-time job. This final proposition was largely an argument against the other dominant social theories of crime at the time when Sutherland wrote—namely, strain theory, which emphasized economic goals and means in predicting criminal activity.[13]

To further elaborate on these principles, it is important to understand the cultural context when Sutherland developed his theory in the early to mid-20th century. At that time, most academics, and society for that matter, believed that there was something abnormal or different about criminals. For example, Sheldon's body type theory was popular in the same time period, as was the use of IQ (intelligence quotient) to pick out persons who were of lower intelligence and predisposed to crime (both of these theories are covered in Chapter 5). Thus, the common assumption at the time when Sutherland created the principles of differential association theory was that there was something essentially wrong with individuals who committed crime.

In light of this common assumption, it was extremely profound for Sutherland to propose that criminality is learned just as any conventional activity is learned. He asserted that any normal individual, when exposed to definitions and attitudes favorable toward crime, will learn both the motivations and techniques for engaging in illegal behaviors. Furthermore, he proposed the idea that the various learning mechanisms and processes—namely, social interaction—involved in developing criminality are identical to the learning processes of virtually all conventional activities, such as reading, playing football, or riding a bike.

Almost everyone learns to swim or ride a bike from friends, parents, or teachers. In contrast, almost no one learns how to do these activities from reading a book. Instead, we typically learn the techniques (e.g., how to float in a pool or balance and turn on a bike) as well as motivations (e.g., it is pleasurable and fun to do with friends) for engaging in such activities from our significant others. According to Sutherland, crime is learned the same way—through interactions with individuals with whom we are close—and from them we learn both the techniques (e.g., how to hot-wire a car) and the motivations (e.g., taking a "joyride" in a stolen car can be a thrill). Although in modern times most people and researchers take it for granted that criminal behavior is learned, the idea was quite radical when Sutherland presented his theory of differential association.

Still, differential association theory is just as deterministic as were the earlier theories that emphasized biological factors (e.g., stigmata, body types) or psychological factors (e.g., low IQ). In other words, Sutherland strongly felt that if a person was receiving from significant others and internalizing a higher ratio of definitions that breaking the law is beneficial, then that person certainly would engage in illegal behavior (see principle 6 above). So there is virtually no room for any free choice or decision-making in this model of criminal activity. In contrast, individuals' propensities to commit crimes are determined through social interactions with significant others. Thus, individuals do not actually make decisions to commit (or not commit) criminal acts; rather, we are predetermined to do so, which makes differential association theory as highly positivistic (i.e., deterministic) as any of the preexisting positivistic theories we reviewed in Chapter 5 (e.g., Lombroso's theory of born criminals).

However, the primary distinction of differential association theory from the earlier positivistic theories is that instead of biological or psychological traits being emphasized as primary factors in causing criminality, it is social interaction and learning. In fact, Sutherland was quite clear in asserting that individual differences in terms of physiological functioning have nothing to do with the development of criminality. It should be noted at this point that this hard stance against biological and psychological factors being relevant as risk factors in criminal activity has been negated by the extant empirical research, which clearly shows that such variations in physiological functioning do in fact significantly influence criminal behavior. In defense of Sutherland, this body of research does suggest that such physiological factors may affect individuals' criminality largely due to the effects of such detriments on the learning processes of people in everyday life.

CLASSICAL CONDITIONING. At the time when he developed his theory of differential association, Sutherland used the dominant psychological theory of learning of the early 20th century. This learning model was called classical conditioning and was primarily developed by Pavlov.[14] Classical conditioning assumes that animals, as well as people, learn through associations between stimuli and responses. The organism, animal, or person is a somewhat passive actor in this process, meaning that the individual simply receives various forms of stimuli and responds in natural ways. Furthermore, the organism (or individual) will learn to associate certain stimuli with certain responses over time.

In developing the theory, Pavlov performed seminal research that showed that dogs, which are naturally afraid of loud noises, could be quickly conditioned not only to be less afraid of loud bells but actually to desire and salivate at their ringing. A dog naturally salivates when presented with meat, so when this unconditioned stimulus (meat) is presented, a dog will always salivate (unconditioned response) in anticipation of eating the meat. Pavlov demonstrated through a series of experiments that if a bell (conditioned stimulus) is always rung at the same time as the dog is presented with meat, then the dog will learn to associate what was previously a negative stimulus (loud bell) with a positive stimulus (food). Thus, the dog will quickly begin salivating at the ringing of a bell, even when meat is not presented. When this occurs, it is called an unconditioned response, because it is not natural; however, it is a powerful and effective means of learning, and it can sometimes take only a few occurrences of coupling the ringing bell with meat before the unconditioned response takes place.

A common, real-life example that virtually everyone can relate to is associations related to songs or smells. Specifically, probably every reader has heard a song on the radio that reminded her or him of a good (or bad) event that occurred years before while that same song was playing. It can seem as though we are reexperiencing that event in our minds when we hear the song. Similarly, people diagnosed with posttraumatic stress disorder can reexperience traumatic events from exposure to certain stimuli. For example, the sound of a car backfiring can remind a war veteran of being under fire in combat. A similar phenomenon occurs with odors, in the sense that a certain scent, such as a particular perfume or cologne, can remind us of someone we once dated. Another version of this experience is when a spouse has to leave for a long time and the pillow retains

©iStockphoto.com/Wavetop

How could you explain this dog salivating in terms of classical conditioning?

classical conditioning: a learning model that assumes that animals, as well as people, learn through associations between stimuli and responses.

his or her natural scent; this can hold a powerful association with memories and often elicits strong emotions (responses) in the partner or spouse left behind. On a simpler level, the smell of a turkey cooking in the oven may automatically remind us of Thanksgiving (or other holidays).

These are just a couple of the many types of associations typically experienced by people in everyday life, and there are many other forms of this type of learning that virtually all persons experience but may not realize they are experiencing. Still, all involve the primary components of classical conditioning in that they all include a stimulus (e.g., a song), an association with the stimulus, and the resulting response (e.g., good/bad feelings). This is still a highly supported learning model.

Another modern use of this learning model in humans is the prescribed administration of drugs that make people ill when they drink alcohol.[15] Alcoholics are often prescribed drugs that will make them feel sick, often to the point of throwing up, if they ingest any alcohol. The idea behind these drugs is primarily that users will learn to associate feelings of sickness with drinking and that this will thus curb the desire to consume alcohol. One important barrier to this strategy is that many alcoholics do not consistently take the drugs, so they often slip back into addiction. However, in defense of this strategy, if alcoholics were to maintain their prescribed drug regimen, it would likely work, because people do tend to learn effectively through association, which in this case is feelings of nausea (the response) associated with ingesting alcohol (the stimulus).

A similar form of the classical conditioning learning model was prominently used in the critically acclaimed 1964 novel (and subsequent motion picture) *A Clockwork Orange*. In this novel, the author, Anthony Burgess, tells the story of a juvenile murderer who is "rehabilitated" by doctors who force him to watch hour after hour of violent images while simultaneously giving him drugs that make him sick. In the novel, the protagonist is "cured" after only two weeks of this treatment, having learned to consistently associate violence with sickness. However, once he is released he lacks the ability to choose violence and other antisocial behavior, which is seen as losing his humanity. Therefore, the ethicists order a reversal treatment and make him back into his former self, a violent predator. Although a fictional piece, *A Clockwork Orange* is probably one of the best illustrations of the use of classical conditioning in relation to criminal offending and rehabilitation.

REACTION TO DIFFERENTIAL ASSOCIATION THEORY. Since Sutherland's nine statements were published, they have been subjected to significant scrutiny and interpretation. Researchers have been critical of his statements and have also pointed to several "misinterpretations" of his work.[16] For example, some people assume that Sutherland's theory is concerned only with associations between criminals. If this were the only relevant type of association, then the theory would be invalid, because some people have an association with criminals but are not considered criminals themselves. These people include police officers, corrections officers, and judges.

As indicated, Sutherland theorized that crime occurs when associations favorable to violation of the law "outweigh" associations favorable to conforming to the law. But measuring this ratio and understanding when the balance tips in favor of a criminal lifestyle is all but impossible.[17] Still, some empirical studies have found support for differential association variables, particularly in the area of white-collar crime. For example, one recent study involving a sample of 133 graduate business students found that participants would go against their friends' and professors' opinions and commit corporate crime if they felt that their coworkers and superiors at work agreed with the illegal behavior.[18] This study found that the influence of associating with people who have a different set of values—in this case, strong corporate attitudes—on a daily basis can have a powerful effect on criminal decision-making, even to the point where individuals will do things they know their family and friends feel are immoral. The context of this and other corporate crime studies is interesting because Sutherland actually coined the term *white-collar crime* and did much of the seminal work on that topic (for more discussion, see Chapter 14). So perhaps it is not so surprising that much of the support for differential association theory is found in the context of corporate crime.

On a related note, Sutherland theorized that criminal associations lead to crime but that the reverse is plausible. That is, one may commit crime and then seek out individuals with attitudes similar to one's own.[19] This is similar to the "Which came first, the chicken or the egg?" debate. Do youths learn to commit crime once they start hanging out with delinquent peers, or do the youths that commit crime start hanging out with similar people (i.e., "Birds of a feather flock together")? After a rather lengthy literary debate, most recent research points to the occurrence of both causal processes: Criminal associations cause more crime *and* committing crime causes more criminal associations.[20] Another interesting criticism that has been leveled at differential association theory is the argument that if criminal behavior is learned and people are born with a blank slate (i.e., tabula rasa), then who first committed crime if no one taught that person the techniques and motives for it? After all, if someone was the first to do it, then who could expose that person to the definitions favorable to violation of law? Furthermore, what factor(s) caused that individual to do it first if it was not learned? If the answers to these questions involve any factor(s) other than learning—which they must, because the theory's assumption is that there was no one to teach this behavior—then the action cannot be explained by learning theories. This is a criticism that cannot be addressed, so it is somewhat ignored in the scientific literature.

At the same time, however, some research is supportive of Sutherland's theory. For example, researchers have found that young criminals are "tutored" by older ones,[21] that criminals sometimes maintain associations with other criminals prior to their delinquent acts,[22] and that the deviant attitudes, friends, and acts are closely connected.[23] Unfortunately, many of Sutherland's principles are somewhat vague and cryptic, which does not lend the theory to easy testing.[24] Related to this issue, perhaps one of the biggest problems with Sutherland's formulation of differential association is that he used primarily one type of learning model—classical conditioning—to formulate most of his principles, which neglects the other important ways we learn attitudes and behavior from significant others. This may be an important reason why his principles are so hard to test, especially in light of more current models of his framework that have incorporated other learning models that are easier to test and provide more empirical validity.

©iStockphoto.com/mike mols

Finally, Sutherland was adamant that such learning about how and why to commit crime occurred *only* through social interaction with significant others and *not* via any media role models, such as those in movies or on the radio. Although not surprising in our modern times, it was not long before another theorist, Daniel Glaser, proposed an alternate theory that included the important influence that such media can play in behavior. We will now review Glaser's theory.

Do you think children are influenced by video games, movies, and other forms of media?

GLASER'S CONCEPT OF DIFFERENTIAL IDENTIFICATION. As stated above, Sutherland claimed that learning of criminal definitions could take place only through social interactions with significant others as opposed to reading a book or watching movies. However, in 1956, Daniel Glaser proposed the idea of differential identification, which allows for learning to take place not only through people close to us but also through other reference groups, even distant ones such as sports heroes or movie stars whom the individual has never actually met or corresponded with.[25] Glaser claimed that it did not matter much whether the individual had a personal relationship with the reference group(s); in fact, he claimed that they could even be imaginary, such as fictitious characters in a movie or book. Thus, "a person pursues criminal behavior to the extent that he identifies himself with real or imaginary persons from whose perspective his criminal behavior seems acceptable."[26] The important thing, according to Glaser, was that the individual identify with the person or character and thus behave in ways that fit the norm set of this reference group or person.

Glaser's proposition has been virtually ignored by subsequent criminological research, with the exception of Dawes's 1973 study of delinquency, which found that identification with persons other than parents was strong when youths reported a high level of rejection from their parents.[27] Given the profound influence of video games, movies, music, and television on today's youth culture, it is obvious that differential identification was an important addition to Sutherland's framework. Thus, far more research should examine the validity of Glaser's theory in contemporary society. Although Glaser and others modified differential association, the most notable, respected, and empirically valid variation of Sutherland's model is differential reinforcement theory.

Differential Reinforcement Theory

In the 1960s, a notable study reevaluated Sutherland's differential association theory and made some pointed criticisms. One of the primary criticisms was that the theory was incomplete without some attention to the more modern psychological models of learning.[28] That is, C. R. Jeffery called out the failure of Sutherland's model to include the concept that people can be conditioned, via rewards or punishments, into behaving in certain ways. Soon after this critical review, Robert Burgess and Ronald Akers criticized and refined Sutherland's work in 1966.[29] The product of this follow-up was what is now known as differential reinforcement theory. Burgess and Akers argued that by integrating Sutherland's work with contributions from the field of social psychology—namely, the learning models of operant conditioning and modeling/imitation—decisions to commit criminal behavior could be more clearly understood.

ELEMENTS OF DIFFERENTIAL REINFORCEMENT THEORY. In their 1966 article, Burgess and Akers presented seven propositions to summarize differential reinforcement theory (see Table 10.1)—often referred to as social learning theory in the criminological literature—which largely represent efficient modifications of Sutherland's original nine principles of differential association. The influence of the relatively new (in 1966) learning models proposed by social psychologists is illustrated in their first statement as well as throughout

differential identification: a theory of criminal behavior similar to differential association theory, the major difference being that this theory takes into account associations with persons and images presented in the media.

TABLE 10.1

Differential Reinforcement Theory Propositions

1. Criminal behavior is learned according to the principles of operant conditioning.
2. Criminal behavior is learned both in nonsocial situations that are reinforcing or discriminative and through that social interaction in which the behavior of other persons is reinforcing or discriminative for criminal behavior.
3. The principal part of the learning of criminal behavior occurs in those groups which comprise the individual's major source of reinforcements.
4. The learning of criminal behavior, including specific techniques, attitudes, and avoidance procedures, is a function of the effective and available reinforcers, and the existing reinforcement contingencies.
5. The specific class of behaviors which are learned and their frequency of occurrence are a function of the reinforcers which are effective and available, and the rules or norms by which these reinforcers are applied.
6. Criminal behavior is a function of norms which are discriminative for criminal behavior, the learning of which takes place when such behavior is more highly reinforced than noncriminal behavior.
7. The strength of criminal behavior is a direct function of the amount, frequency, and probability of its reinforcement.

Source: Burgess, R., & Akers, R. (1966). A differential association-reinforcement theory of criminal behavior. *Social Problems, 14,* 146.

the seven principles. Although differential reinforcement incorporates the elements of classical conditioning learning models in its framework, the first proposition clearly states that the essential learning mechanism in social behavior is operant conditioning; thus, it is vital to understand what operant conditioning is and how it is valid at all times in an individual's life. The inclusion of both modern models of learning (e.g., operant conditioning and modeling) and classic models of learning (e.g., classical conditioning) explains why differential reinforcement theory is also commonly referred to as the social learning theory of crime.

DIFFERENTIAL REINFORCEMENT THEORY PROPOSITIONS. Differential reinforcement theory may appear, in many ways, to be no different than rational choice theory (see Chapter 4). This is true to some extent, because both models focus on punishments and reinforcements that occur after an individual offends. Differential reinforcement theory, however, can be distinguished from the rational choice perspective in that it assumes humans are born with an innate capacity for rational decision-making, whereas the differential reinforcement perspective assumes individuals are born with a blank slate (i.e., tabula rasa) and thus must be socialized and taught how to behave through various forms of conditioning (e.g., classical and operant conditioning) and modeling. Also, differential reinforcement theory is far more deterministic than rational choice theory in the sense that the former assumes that individuals have virtually no free will or free choice (behavior is based on the definitions, beliefs, rewards, punishments, etc., that individuals are subject to after their previous behaviors), whereas the latter is based almost entirely on the assumption that individuals do indeed have the ability to make their own choices and tend to make calculated decisions based on the contextual circumstances of a given situation. Thus, it is clear that differential reinforcement theory has different assumptions, as well as distinctive concepts, that clearly distinguish it from rational choice models of behavior. We will now review some of the key concepts that differential reinforcement theory proposed that were important additions to the differential association model and that made it a far more robust and valid theory for explaining criminal behavior.

differential reinforcement theory: a theory of criminal behavior that emphasizes various types of social learning, specifically classical conditioning, operant conditioning, and imitation or modeling.

operant conditioning: a learning model based on the association between an action and feedback following the action.

modeling/imitation: a major factor in differential reinforcement theory that proposes that much social learning takes place via imitation or modeling of behavior.

Applying Theory to Crime: MURDER

In this section, we provide an example of a person (named Trent) who committed murder, largely due to influences from social interactions with his peers, who were fellow gang members. This illustrates an example of Sutherland's differential association theory, which will be discussed further below. But before we get to the actual example, it is important to understand murder or criminal homicide as well as some current statistics on this criminal act.

According to common law, as well as traditionally in the United States, the crime of murder is defined as the "unlawful killing of a human being by another human being with malice aforethought."[30] However,

proving malice aforethought is sometimes difficult, because, under the modern interpretation, it is not necessary to prove either malice as it is commonly defined, nor forethought. Therefore, it is preferable not to rely upon this misleading expression for an understanding of murder.[31]

According to the Federal Bureau of Investigation (FBI) Uniform Crime Reports (UCR), murder and nonnegligent manslaughter are defined as the "willful (nonnegligent) killing of one human being by another."[32] The UCR Program does not include such incidents as deaths caused by negligence, suicide, or accident; justifiable homicides; or attempts to murder or assaults to murder, which are counted as aggravated assaults.[33] Based on the 2014 report, the FBI summarized the following key findings concerning murder:

FIGURE 10.1

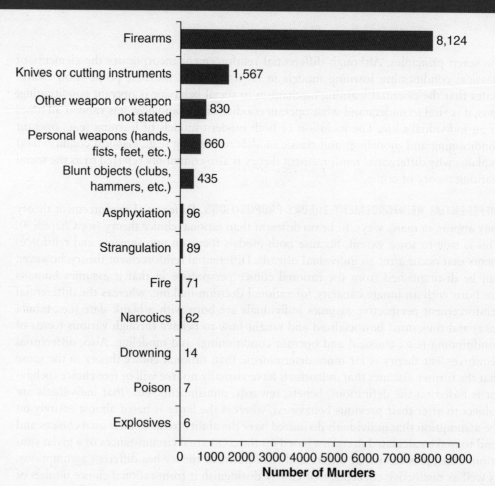

Murder by Weapon in 2014

Weapon	Number of Murders
Firearms	8,124
Knives or cutting instruments	1,567
Other weapon or weapon not stated	830
Personal weapons (hands, fists, feet, etc.)	660
Blunt objects (clubs, hammers, etc.)	435
Asphyxiation	96
Strangulation	89
Fire	71
Narcotics	62
Drowning	14
Poison	7
Explosives	6

Number of Murders

Source: Federal Bureau of Investigation. (2015). *Crime in the United States, 2014.* Washington, DC: U.S. Department of Justice, n.p.

- About 14,249 people were murdered nationwide in 2014. This is a 0.5% decrease from 2013 and a 3.2% decrease from 2010.

- Of the number of murders nationwide, 46.0% were in the South, 20.5% were in the Midwest, 20.5% were reported in the West, and 13.1% were reported in the Northeast.

Figure 10.1 provides a summary of the types of weapons used in these murders. Note that more than two thirds of the murders involved a firearm (67.9%), followed by knives or cutting instruments (13.1%).

There are instances when individuals, accused of murder, provide some type of defense to justify their criminal actions. For instance, self-defense is most often used as a defense in homicide cases. The defendant must show some evidence of the following to make such a claim:

- Unlawful force was threatened against him or her.

- Danger of harm was imminent.

- He or she was not the aggressor.

- He or she fully believed that danger existed.

- Force was necessary to avert the danger.

- The type and amount of force used was necessary.

The jury is then required to determine whether the defendant's perception

of the need of self-defense, or the degree of force used, was reasonable.[34] Another defense is the insanity defense. Throughout American history, the insanity defense has varied. We discuss this in more detail in Chapter 7. A well-known case using a diminished-capacity defense occurred in 1978, when Dan White shot and killed San Francisco mayor George Moscone and San Francisco supervisor Harvey Milk. His diminished-capacity defense was termed the "Twinkie Defense" by the media. It was based on psychological testimony revealing that Dan White's junk-food diet exacerbated a chemical imbalance in his brain. Thus, he was not deemed legally responsible for these deaths.[35]

To clarify key aspects of differential association, we apply this perspective to the crime of murder. Trent had a troubled family life and difficulties in school. He did not easily establish and maintain close relationships with his family or friends. When Trent was 12 years old, he was befriended by a couple of boys in his neighborhood. He would spend a great deal of time with these boys, and these boys were part of a local gang. In this gang, Trent learned how to shoplift, burglarize homes and businesses, and sell drugs. He also learned how to use a gun. Soon he began to incorporate beliefs such as, one has to "take what one wants" rather than "work hard and wait for the rewards." This attitude illustrates an excess of definitions favorable to violating the law over definitions unfavorable to violating the law.

When Trent was 16 years old, he and some of his fellow gang members spotted a man driving a very

expensive car. They decided to carjack the automobile at any cost. They waited until the man was at a red light and pulled their car alongside his. Given his previous internalization of the techniques and motivations provided by fellow gang members as well as their encouragement just prior to the incident, Trent got out through the passenger-side door and told the man to get out of his car. The man refused, so Trent shot him once in the head. Trent then dragged the man out of the car and slid into the driver's seat and drove away. A number of eyewitnesses immediately called 911. Two days later, Trent was arrested and charged with murder.

Incorporating Sutherland's differential association, we can argue that Trent learned to engage in criminal activity through his friends. This learning process also involved Trent being exposed to definitions and attitudes favorable toward crime, which ultimately resulted in Trent committing murder because he wanted an automobile "at any cost."

THINK ABOUT IT

By incorporating Sutherland's differential association, consider the following:

1. What influenced Trent to engage in criminal activity?

2. Was he more likely to be exposed to definitions favorable, or unfavorable, to crime?

3. What could have deterred Trent to engage in criminal activity?

PSYCHOLOGICAL LEARNING MODELS

Operant Conditioning

Operant conditioning was primarily developed by B. F. Skinner,[39] who coincidentally was just across campus from Edwin Sutherland when he was developing differential association theory at Indiana University; just as it is now, academia tended to be too intradisciplinary and intradepartmental. If Sutherland had been aware of Skinner's studies and theoretical development, he likely would have included it in his original framework of differential

Comparative Criminology: *HOMICIDE*

Homicide Rates per World Subregion

In this section, we examine findings from data provided by the sixth through eighth United Nations Crime Surveys and data from the World Health Organization[36] regarding homicide rates in various world subregions.[37]

The data in Figure 10.2 reveal that of the world subregions included in this study, Southern Africa has, by far, the highest rate of homicide at 31 (per 100,000/year). The second-highest region—Central America—is a not-so-distant second at 26.5, and the third-ranking subregion—South America—is close to the second at 23.5. It is also notable that the world average is 6.2, which would likely be significantly lower if there wasn't such a high outlier at the top (Southern Africa). In fact, if we removed the world ranking from this report, and chose to use the median (instead of the mean or average) as our measure of central tendency of the 16 subregions presented in the report, then the world average would be about 5.8 (per 100,000/year).

Also notable is North America (which of course includes the United States) at a rate of 6.8, which is below the world average (8.2). Perhaps most interesting is the rate reported for North Africa (0.8), which is the lowest reported, despite being on the same continent as the highest recorded rate (Southern Africa). This just goes to show how certain locations, often in close proximity, can be entirely different in terms of crime. This can also be seen on a more local level, such as in cities in Southern California (e.g., Mission Viejo, Thousand Oaks) that are some of the safest communities in the United States virtually every year, while some close cities in that region (e.g., Compton, San Bernardino) typically have some of the highest rates of crime. It is quite amazing that some of the cities in our nation or regions in the world can have such drastic differences regarding crime rates. This just goes to show how variant places can be, even if they are relatively close in proximity or in the same geographic area.[38]

FIGURE 10.2

Homicides per 100,000 Population per World Subregion

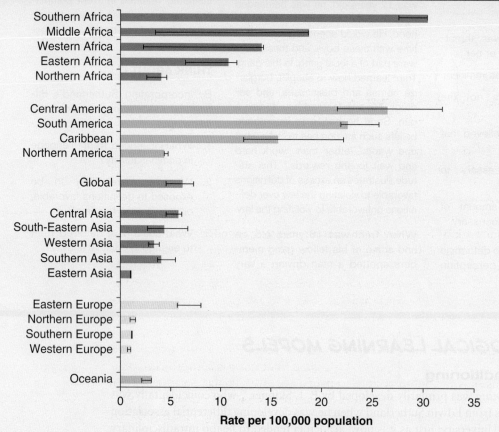

Source: 2013 Global Study on Homicide. United Nations Office on Drugs and Crime.

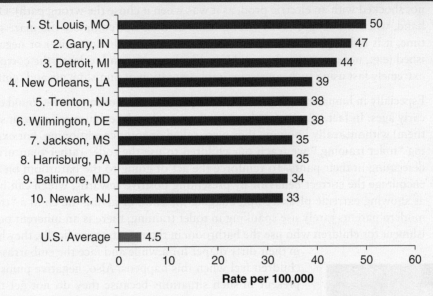

FIGURE 10.3 Top 10 U.S. Cities With the Highest Murder Rates in 2014*

City	Rate per 100,000
1. St. Louis, MO	50
2. Gary, IN	47
3. Detroit, MI	44
4. New Orleans, LA	39
5. Trenton, NJ	38
6. Wilmington, DE	38
7. Jackson, MS	35
8. Harrisburg, PA	35
9. Baltimore, MD	34
10. Newark, NJ	33
U.S. Average	4.5

Source: FBI. Crime in the US, 2014. Table 8.

*Only includes cities with populations over 40,000

association theory. However, operant conditioning was not well-known or researched at the time Sutherland developed his theory of differential association; rather, he simply incorporated the dominant learning model of his time—classical conditioning. So it was up to others, such as Burgess and Akers, to later incorporate operant conditioning (as well as Bandura's social learning principles, discussed below) into Sutherland's theoretical model.

To explain it simply, operant conditioning is concerned with how behavior is influenced by reinforcements and punishments. Operant conditioning assumes that the animal or human is a proactive player in seeking out rewards, not just a passive entity that simply receives stimuli, which is what classical conditioning assumes. Specifically, certain behaviors are encouraged through reward (**positive reinforcement**) or through avoidance of punishment (**negative reinforcement**). For example, if a child is given a toy or video game for doing well on his or her report card, that is a positive reinforcement. On the other hand, if a child who has been confined to his or her room after school for a week for not doing homework is then allowed to start playing with friends again after school because she or he did a good job on homework the following week, this is a negative reinforcement because the child is now being rewarded via the avoidance of something negative. Like different types of reinforcement, punishment also comes in two forms. Thus, behavior is discouraged, or weakened, via adverse stimuli (positive punishment) or lack of reward (negative punishment). A good example of positive punishment would be putting a child in a "time-out," where he or she is forced to sit alone for many minutes—a punishment that tends to be quite effective with young children. Another form of positive punishment—perhaps the best example—is "spanking," but this has been frowned on in recent times because it is certainly a positive form of a negative stimulus. So anything that directly presents negative sensations or feelings is a positive punishment. On the other hand, if parents take away their child's opportunity to go on an outing with friends (say to a movie or theme park) because he or she skipped school, this is an example of negative punishment because the parents are removing a positive aspect or reward.

positive reinforcement: a concept in social learning in which people are rewarded by receiving something they want.

negative reinforcement: a concept in social learning in which people are rewarded through removal of something they dislike.

One notable example of operant conditioning is teaching a mouse to successfully run a maze. When the mouse takes the right paths and finishes the maze quickly, it is either positively reinforced (e.g., rewarded with a piece of cheese) or negatively reinforced (e.g., not shocked with an electric prod, as it was when it chose the wrong path). On the other hand, when the mouse takes wrong turns or does not complete the maze in adequate time, it is either positively punished (e.g., shocked with electricity) or negatively punished (e.g., not given the cheese). Mice, like humans, tend to learn the correct behavior extremely fast using such consistent implementation of punishments and reinforcements.

Especially in humans, such principles of operant conditioning can be found even at very early ages. In fact, many of us have implemented such techniques (or been subjected to them) without really knowing they were called operant conditioning. For example, during "toilet training," we teach our children to use the toilet rather than urinating and defecating in their pants. To reinforce the act of going to the bathroom on a toilet, we encourage the correct behavior by presenting positive rewards, which can be as simple as showing extreme pleasure and hugging the child or giving the child a "treat." While modern parents rarely use spanking in toilet training, there is an inherent positive punishment for children who use the bathroom in their pants; specifically, they have to stay in their dirty diaper for a while and face the embarrassment most children feel when this happens. Also, negative punishments are present in such situations because they do not get the positive recognition or treats, so the rewards are absent as well.

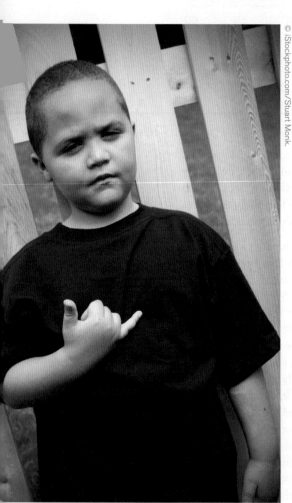

© iStockphoto.com/Stuart Monk.

A large amount of research has shown that humans learn attitudes and behavior best through a mix of punishments and reinforcements throughout life. For example, studies have clearly shown that rehabilitative programs that appear to work most effectively in reducing recidivism in offenders are those that have many opportunities for rewards as well as threats for punishments. To clarify, empirical research that has combined the findings from hundreds of studies of rehabilitation programs has demonstrated that the programs that are most successful in changing the attitudes and behavior of previous offenders are those that offer at least four reward opportunities for every one punishment aspect of the program.[40] So whether it is training children to use the toilet or altering criminals' thinking and behavior, operant conditioning is a well-established form of learning that makes differential reinforcement theory a more valid and specified model of offending than differential association.

Thus, whether deviant or conforming behavior occurs and continues "depends on the past and present rewards or punishment for the behavior, and the rewards and punishment attached to alternative behavior."[41] This is in stark contrast to Sutherland's differential association model, which looked only at what happens before an act (i.e., classical conditioning), not what happens after (i.e., operant conditioning). Burgess and Akers's model looks at both what occurs before the act and what occurs afterward. Thus, illegal behavior is likely to occur, as Burgess and Akers theorized, when its perceived rewards outweigh the potential punishments for committing such acts.

Referring to Bandura's theory of imitation/ modeling, do you think the boy pictured learned this hand sign by observing others?

BANDURA'S THEORY OF IMITATION/MODELING. Burgess and Akers emphasized another learning model in their formulation of differential reinforcement theory, which was *imitation and modeling*. Given that Sutherland's original formulation of differential association theory was somewhat inspired by Tarde's concept of imitation,[42] it is surprising that his nine principles did not adequately emphasize the importance of modeling in the process of learning behavior. Similar to the neglect of acknowledging Skinnerian models of operant conditioning, Sutherland's failure to focus on imitation and modeling was likely due to the fact that the primary work by Albert Bandura in this area had not become well-known at the time when differential association theory was being formulated.[43]

Bandura demonstrated, through a series of theoretical and experimental studies, that a significant amount of learning takes place absent virtually any form of conditioning or responses to a given behavior. To clarify, he claimed that individuals can learn even if they are not punished or rewarded for a given behavior (i.e., operant conditioning) or exposed to associations between stimuli and responses (i.e., classical conditioning). Instead, Bandura proposed that people learn much of their attitudes and behavior from simply observing the behavior of others—namely, through mimicking others. This type of phenomenon is often referred to as "monkey see, monkey do"—but not just monkeys do this. Social psychological research has clearly established that humans, as well as most animal species, are physiologically "hardwired" (meaning it is instinctive) to observe and learn the behavior of others, especially those older in years, to see what behavior is essential for success and survival.

The most important finding of Bandura's experiments was that simply observing the behavior of others, especially adults, can have profound learning effects on the behavior of children. To clarify, in Bandura's experiments, a randomized experimental group of children watched a video of adults acting aggressively toward a Bo-Bo doll (a blow-up plastic doll), and a control group of children did not watch such illustrations of adults beating up the dolls. These different groups of children were then sent into a room containing Bo-Bo dolls. The experimental group who had seen the adult behavior mimicked this behavior by acting far more aggressively toward the dolls than did the children in the control group, who had not seen the adults beating up the dolls. So although the experimental group was not provided with previous associations or rewards for being more aggressive toward the dolls, the children who had seen adults act more aggressively became far more aggressive themselves (compared with the control group) simply because they were imitating or modeling what they had seen the older people do.

In light of these findings, Bandura's theory of modeling and imitation has implications not only for the criminal behavior of individuals but also for the influence of television, movies, video games, and so on. The influences demonstrated by Bandura simply supported a phenomenon we can see in everyday life—namely, the source of fashion trends, such as wearing low-slung pants or baseball hats a certain way. These types of styles tend to ebb and flow based on respected persons (often celebrities) wearing clothing a certain way, which leads to many people, typically youth, mimicking that behavior. This can be seen very early in life, with parents having to be careful what they say and do because their children, as young as two years old, will imitate them. For example, this is why parents often must change their language when in the presence of toddlers. This continues throughout life, especially in teenage years, as young people imitate the "cool" trends and styles as well as behavior. Of course, sometimes this behavior is illegal, but individuals are often simply mimicking the way their friends or others are behaving, with little regard for potential rewards or punishments. Thus, Bandura's theory of modeling and imitation adds a great deal of explanation to a model of learning, and differential reinforcement theory included such influences; Sutherland's model of differential association did not, largely because the psychological perspective had not yet been developed.

REACTION TO DIFFERENTIAL REINFORCEMENT THEORY. Just as Sutherland's work has been interpreted and criticized, so too has that of Burgess and Akers. For instance, Reed Adams criticized the theory for incorrectly and incompletely applying the principles of operant conditioning. Further, Adams noted that the theory does not adequately address the importance of "nonsocial reinforcement."[44] Nonsocial reinforcement can be considered self-reinforcement. For example, if someone gets enjoyment out of abusing others, then the person can be considered "reinforced" through nonsocial means.

Perhaps the most important criticism of differential reinforcement theory is that it appears tautological, which means that the variables and measures used to test its validity are true by definition. To clarify, studies testing this theory have been divided into four groups of variables or factors: associations, reinforcements, definitions, and modeling. Some critics have noted that if individuals who report that they associate with those who offend are rewarded for offending, believe offending is good, and have seen many of their significant others offend, they will be more likely to offend. In other words, if your friends and/or family are doing it, there is little doubt that you will also do it.[45] For example, critics would argue that a person who primarily hangs out with car thieves, knows he will be rewarded for stealing cars, believes stealing cars is good and not immoral, and has observed many respected others stealing cars will inevitably commit auto theft himself. However, it has been well argued that such criticisms of tautology are not valid because none of these factors necessarily make offending by the respondent true by definition.[46]

Differential reinforcement theory has been criticized in the same way as Sutherland's theory has, in the sense that delinquent associations may take place after criminal activity rather than before. However, Burgess and Akers's model clearly addresses this area of criticism, because differential reinforcement covers what comes after the activity. Specifically, it addresses the rewards or punishments that follow criminal activity, whether those rewards come from friends, parents, or other members or institutions of society.

It is arguable that differential reinforcement theory may have the most empirical validity of any contemporary (nonintegrated) model of criminal offending, especially considering that studies have examined a variety of behaviors, ranging from drug use to property crimes to violence. The theoretical model has also been tested in samples across the United States, as well as in other cultures such as South Korea, with the evidence being quite supportive of the framework. Furthermore, a variety of age groups have been examined, ranging from teenagers to middle-aged adults to the elderly, with all studies providing support for the model.[47] Specifically, researchers have empirically tested differential association–reinforcement theory and found that the major variables of the theory have a significant effect in explaining marijuana and alcohol use among adolescents.[48] The researchers concluded that the "study demonstrates that central learning concepts are amenable to meaningful questionnaire measurement and that social learning theory can be adequately tested with survey data."[49] Other studies have also supported the theory when attempting to understand delinquency, cigarette smoking, and drug use.[50] One recent empirical study—a meta-analysis of virtually all the scientific studies that have tested differential reinforcement/social learning theory—concluded that there was considerable variation in the magnitude and stability of key variables in the theory.[51] Specifically, in this comprehensive study, the effects of all variables—differential association, definitions, modeling/imitation, and differential reinforcement—were typically significant predictors. However, the study showed that although the former two concepts (differential association and definitions) showed stronger magnitude in terms of explaining criminal behavior, the latter two (differential reinforcement and modeling/imitation) had only modest effects on such behavior. Overall, the model appeared to be relatively supported by the extant empirical evidence. Therefore, the inclusion of three psychological learning models—namely, classical conditioning, operant conditioning, and modeling/imitation—appears to have made differential reinforcement one of the most valid theories of human behavior, especially in regard to criminal behavior. Thus, it appears that differential reinforcement/social learning theory is one of the more valid theories in terms of explaining criminal behavior, perhaps due to the theory's incorporation of so many distinct concepts and learning theories in its primary assumptions and propositions.

NEUTRALIZATION THEORY

Neutralization theory is associated with Gresham Sykes and David Matza's *Techniques of Neutralization*[52] and Matza's *Drift Theory*.[53] Like Sutherland, both Sykes and Matza claimed that social learning influences delinquent behavior, but they also claimed that most criminals hold conventional beliefs and values. More specifically, Sykes and Matza argued that most criminals are still partially committed to the dominant social order. According to Sykes and Matza, youths are not immersed in a subculture committed to extremes of either complete conformity or complete nonconformity. Rather, these individuals vacillate, or *drift*, between these two extremes:

> The delinquent *transiently* exists in a limbo between convention and crime, responding in turn to the demands of each, flirting now with one, now the other, but postponing commitment, evading decision. Thus, he [or she] drifts between criminal and conventional action.[54]

While still partially committed to conventional social order, youths can *drift* into criminal activity and avoid feelings of guilt for these actions by justifying or rationalizing their behavior. Why is it called neutralization theory? People justify and rationalize behavior through "neutralizing" it, or making it seem less serious. In other words, individuals make up situational excuses for behavior they know is wrong, and they do this to alleviate the guilt they feel for committing such immoral acts. In many ways, this technique for alleviating guilt resembles Freud's defense mechanisms (see Chapter 6), which allow our mind to forgive ourselves for the bad things we do even though we know they are wrong. So the specific techniques of neutralization outlined by Sykes and Matza in 1957, which we consider next, are much like excuses for inappropriate behavior.

Techniques of Neutralization

Sykes and Matza developed methods, or techniques of neutralization,[55] that people use to justify their criminal behavior. These techniques allow people to neutralize their criminal and delinquent acts by making them look as though they are conforming to the rules of society. Individuals are then freed to engage in criminal activities without serious damage to their self-image. These five techniques of neutralization include the following:

1. *Denial of responsibility.* Denial of responsibility is more than just claiming that deviant acts are an accident. Rather, individuals may claim that due to outside forces (e.g., uncaring parents, bad friends, poverty), they are not responsible or accountable for their behavior. Statements such as "It wasn't my fault" are extremely common among both youth and adult offenders.

2. *Denial of injury.* Criminals may evaluate their wrongful behavior in terms of whether anyone was hurt by it. For instance, vandalism may be considered "mischief"; stealing a car may be viewed as "borrowing." Sometimes society agrees with people who evaluate their wrongfulness in this manner, designating these activities as "pranks."

3. *Denial of the victim.* While criminals may accept responsibility for their actions and admit these actions caused an injury, they neutralize them as being a rightful retaliation or punishment. Criminals may perceive themselves as avengers and the victim as the wrongdoer. For instance, vandalism is revenge on an unfair teacher, and shoplifting is retaliation against a "crooked" store owner. Another variation is when shoplifters claim that no one is getting hurt because the stores have theft insurance, failing to acknowledge that stores raise their prices to counteract such losses and higher insurance premiums.

techniques of neutralization: a theory that suggests that individuals, especially in their teenage years and early adulthood, make excuses to alleviate guilt related to committing certain criminal acts.

4. *Condemnation of the condemners.* Criminals may also shift the focus of attention from their deviant acts to the motives and behavior of those who disapprove of these actions. They may claim the condemners are hypocrites, deviants in disguise, or compelled by personal spite. For instance, one may claim that police are corrupt, teachers show favoritism, or parents "take it out" on their children. Thus, criminals neutralize their behavior through "a rejection of the rejectors."[56]

5. *Appeal to higher loyalties.* Criminals may sacrifice the rules of the larger society for the rules of the smaller social groups to which they belong, such as a gang or peer group. They do not necessarily deviate, because they reject the norms of the larger society. Rather, their higher loyalty is with these smaller groups; thus, they subscribe to the norms of these groups over general social norms. They may claim that one must "always help a buddy" or "never squeal on a friend." Another example of this neutralization technique is antiabortion radicals who shoot doctors who perform abortions; they claim they are appealing to a higher loyalty (a supreme being), which relieves them from responsibility and guilt.

Sykes and Matza emphasized that the techniques of neutralization may not be strong enough to protect individuals from their own internalized values and the reactions of conforming others. Instead, neutralization techniques lessen "the effectiveness of social controls" and "lie behind a large share of delinquent behavior."[57]

One area where techniques of neutralization have been applied is white-collar crime. Several studies have examined the tendency to use such excuses to alleviate guilt for engaging in behavior that professionals know is wrong. For example, a recent study that examined the decision-making of 133 students in a graduate business program found that not only did neutralizing attitudes have significant effects on the respondents' decisions to commit corporate crime (involving distributing a dangerous drug), but the older students—namely, those with more seniority and experience in the business world—were more likely to employ techniques of neutralization.[58]

©iStockphoto.com/Yuri_Arcurs

How would you would explain sending/reading personal texts while at work in terms of the various techniques of neutralization?

Furthermore, studies of corporate crime have identified two more common types of excuses that white-collar criminals use in their illegal activities.[59] Specifically, the two techniques of neutralization that experts have observed primarily among corporate criminals are "defense of necessity" and "metaphor of the ledger." *Defense of necessity* implies that an individual should not feel shame or guilt about doing something immoral as long as the behavior is perceived as necessary. Often in the corporate world, the climate puts pressure on the bottom line, and all that matters is making a larger profit, no matter what behavior is used; in other words, criminal activity is often seen as a necessity.

The other neutralizing technique found primarily in corporate settings is *metaphor of the ledger*, which essentially is the belief that an individual or group has done so much good (e.g., provided a useful product or service for public consumption) that he or she is entitled to mess up by doing something illegal (e.g., "cooking the books" or knowingly distributing a faulty, dangerous product). Many of us likely use this latter technique often, especially when it comes to studying or writing a paper right before the test or deadline. At times when we know we should be working, we may often say something along the lines of, "I worked hard yesterday, so even though I am not close to being finished, I deserve to go out with my friends to the beach today." This is a good example of using the fact that you did a good thing to justify doing something you know you probably shouldn't if you want to do well on the test or paper. So it is not just in corporate climates that these neutralizing techniques—seven altogether—are used to alleviate guilt. Regular people, especially college students and professors, use them all the time.

Reaction to Neutralization Theory

Studies that have attempted to empirically test neutralization theory are, at best, inconclusive. Robert Agnew argued that there are essentially two general criticisms of studies that support neutralization theory.[60] The first challenge is that several researchers have improperly measured the acceptance of neutralization techniques. Based on his research on neutralization among incarcerated adults, one researcher noted that

> the relationships between vocabularies of motive and criminal behavior are more subtle, complex, and situation-specific than previously recognized. The major tasks for subsequent neutralization research are to empirically distinguish between neutralization and unconventional commitment.[61]

Second, researchers have expressed concern that criminals may use techniques of neutralization *prior* to committing a criminal offense. This ordering, they claim, is just as plausible as when neutralization *follows* a criminal act.[62] This uncertain time-order problem is due to research conducted at a single point in time. Additional research conducted over time could prove supportive of neutralization theory. However, some would argue that the temporal ordering problem is not a major criticism of the theory, because some individuals may be predisposed to make up such rationalizations for their behavior regardless of whether they do it before or after the offending act. Such a propensity may be related to low self-control theory, which we examine later in this chapter.

CONTROL THEORIES

The learning theories discussed in the previous section assume that individuals are born with a conforming disposition, or at least a blank slate (i.e., tabula rasa). By contrast, control theories assume that all people would naturally commit crimes if not for restraints on the selfish tendencies that exist in every individual. Social control perspectives of criminal behavior thus assume that there is some type of basic human nature and that all human beings exhibit antisocial tendencies toward being violently aggressive and taking from others what they want. Therefore, such control theories are more concerned with

---

LEARNING CHECK 10.2

1. Burgess and Akers, in their differential reinforcement theory, integrated Sutherland's work with the learning models of _____ conditioning and modeling/imitation.

2. The differential reinforcement perspective assumes that individuals are born with a _____ _____.

3. According to Sykes and Matza, youths engaging in criminal behavior are still partially committed to the dominant _____ _____.

4. People use certain methods, or _____ _____, to justify their criminal behavior.

Answers located at www.edge.sagepub.com/schram2e

FIGURE **10.4**

Frequencies of Hitting, Biting, and Kicking at Ages 2 to 12 Years

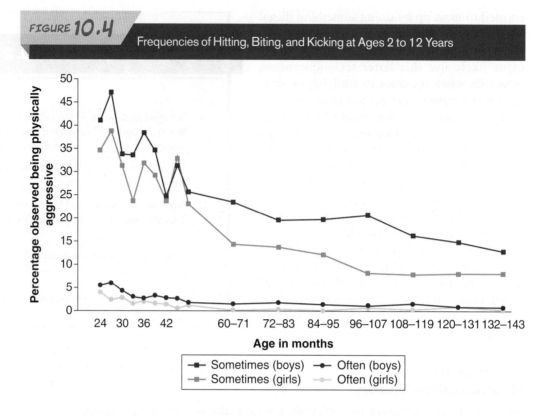

explaining why individuals *don't* commit crime or deviant behaviors. Specifically, control theorists rhetorically ask, "What is it about society, human interaction, and other factors that causes people *not* to act on their natural impulses?"

The assumption that people have innate antisocial tendencies is a controversial one because it is nearly impossible to test. Nevertheless, some recent evidence supports the idea that human beings are inherently selfish and antisocial by nature. Specifically, researchers have found that most individuals are oriented toward selfish and aggressive behaviors at a very early age, with such behaviors peaking at the end of the second year (see Figure 10.4).[63] Such studies are observational and examine children interacting with their peers. But it is clear from such studies that young individuals are predisposed toward selfish, physically aggressive behavior.

An example of antisocial dispositions appearing early in life was reported by Tremblay and LeMarquand, who found that for most young children (particularly boys), aggressive behaviors peaked at 27 months. These behaviors included hitting, biting, and kicking.[64] Their research is not isolated; virtually all developmental experts acknowledge that toddlers exhibit a tendency to show aggressive behaviors toward others. We are sure virtually all readers can relate to this, even if they don't have children of their own. All one needs to do is observe a typical preschool playground, and one will see numerous "felonies" occur in a short period of time. The bottom line is that the "terrible twos" is a true phenomenon; most individuals exhibit a high tendency toward violence, as well as stealing from others, at this time in life. This line of research would seem to support the notion that people are predisposed toward antisocial, even criminal, behavior.

Control theorists do not necessarily assume that people are predisposed toward crime in a way that remains constant throughout life. On the contrary, research shows that most individuals begin to desist from such behaviors after age two. This trend continues until about age five, with only the most aggressive individuals (i.e., chronic offenders) continuing into higher ages. Furthermore, this extreme desistance from engaging in such antisocial behavior supports the control perspective in explaining criminal behavior, especially in the long term, because it is clear from these scientific studies that something must be controlling virtually all individuals (who previously showed tendencies toward aggressive, antisocial behavior) to inhibit themselves from carrying out their natural propensities to fight and take at will.

When considering potential factors that inhibit individuals from following their instincts, it is important to note that at the same time selfish and aggressive behaviors decline, self-consciousness is formed. Specifically, it is around age two when individuals begin to see themselves as entities or beings; prior to age two, children have no understanding that they are people. Subsequently, during this second year, various social emotions—such as shame, guilt, empathy, and pride—begin to appear, largely because they become possible in children's knowing that they are part of a society.[65] This observation is critical because it is what separates control theories from the classical school of criminology and the predispositional theories that we already discussed. According to control theories, without appropriate socialization or personal inhibitions, people will act on their "pre-programmed" tendency toward crime and deviance.

In short, control theories claim that all individuals have natural tendencies to commit selfish, antisocial, and even criminal behavior. So what curbs this natural propensity? Many experts believe the best explanation is that individuals are socialized and controlled by social attachments and investments in conventional society. Others claim that there are internal mechanisms (such as self-control or self-conscious emotions, such as shame, guilt, etc.), but even those are likely a product of the type of environment in which one is raised. This assumption regarding the vital importance of early socialization is probably the primary reason why control theories are currently among the most popular and accepted theories for criminologists.[66] We will now discuss several early examples of these control theories.

Early Control Theories of Human Behavior

THOMAS HOBBES'S SOCIAL CONTRACT. Although control theories are found in a variety of disciplines, perhaps the earliest notable form of social control in explaining deviant behavior is found in a perspective offered by the 17th-century Enlightenment philosopher Thomas Hobbes (see Chapter 3). Hobbes claimed that the natural state of humanity was one of greediness and self-centeredness, which led to a chaotic state of constant warfare among individuals. In this state, Hobbes claimed that individuals were essentially looking out for their own well-being, and without any law or order there was no way to protect themselves.[67] But Hobbes also theorized that this constant state of chaos created such fear among many individuals that it resulted in them coming together to rationally develop a pact that would prevent such chaos. This became the concept of a society. Hobbes claimed that by creating a society and forming binding contracts (or laws), this would alleviate the chaos by deterring individuals from violating others' rights. However, despite such laws, Hobbes doubted that the innately greedy nature of humans would be completely eliminated. Rather, the existence of such innate selfishness and aggressiveness was exactly why the use of punishments was necessary, their purpose being to induce fear in the societal members who choose to violate the societal law. In a way, Hobbes was perhaps the first deterrence theorist in the sense that he was the first notable theorist to emphasize the use of punishment to deter individuals from violating the rights of others.

Most experts agree that toddlers, particularly boys, exhibit a tendency toward aggression.

ÉMILE DURKHEIM'S IDEA OF COLLECTIVE CONSCIENCE. Consistent with Hobbes's view of individuals being naturally selfish, Émile Durkheim proposed a theory of social control in the late 1800s that suggested humans have no internal mechanism to let them know when they are fulfilled.[68] To this end, Durkheim coined the terms *automatic spontaneity* and *awakened reflection*. Automatic spontaneity can be understood in reference to animals' eating habits. Specifically, animals stop eating when they are full and are content until they are hungry again; they don't start hunting again right after they have filled their stomachs. In contrast, awakened reflection concerns the fact that humans do not have such an internal regulatory mechanism. People often acquire resources beyond what is immediately required. Durkheim went so far as to say that "our capacity for feeling is in itself an insatiable and bottomless abyss."[69] This is one of the reasons Durkheim believed crime and deviance are quite normal, even essential, in any society.

Durkheim's "awakened reflection" has become commonly known as greed. People tend to favor better conditions and additional fulfillment because we apparently have no biological or psychological mechanism to limit such tendencies. As Durkheim noted, the selfish desires of mankind "are unlimited so far as they depend on the individual alone. . . . The more one has, the more one wants."[70] Thus, society must step in and provide the "regulative force" that keeps humans from acting too selfishly.

One of the primary elements of this regulative force is the collective conscience, which is the extent of similarities or likenesses that people share. For example, almost everyone can agree that homicide is a serious and harmful act that should be avoided in any civilized society. The notion of collective conscience can be seen as an early form of the idea of social bonding, which has become one of the dominant theories in criminology, discussed later in this chapter.[71] According to Durkheim, the collective conscience serves many functions in society. One such function is the ability to establish rules that inhibit individuals from following their natural tendencies toward selfish behavior. Durkheim also believed that crime allows people to unite together in opposition against deviants. In other words, crime and deviance allow conforming individuals to be "bonded" together in opposition against a common enemy, as can be seen in everyday life. This enemy consists of the deviants who have not internalized the code of the collective conscience.

Many of Durkheim's ideas hold true today. Just recall a traumatic incident you may have experienced with other strangers (e.g., being stuck in an elevator during a power outage, weathering a serious storm, being involved in a traffic accident). Incidents such as this bring people together and permit a degree of bonding that would not take place in everyday life. Crime, Durkheim argued, serves a similar function.

How is all this relevant today? Most control theorists claim that individuals commit crime and deviant acts not because they are lacking in any way but because certain controls have been weakened in their development. This assumption is consistent not only with Durkheim's theory but with a Freudian model of human behavior we discussed in Chapter 7.

FREUD'S CONCEPT OF THE ID AND SUPEREGO. Although psychoanalytic theory would seem to have few similarities with a sociological positivistic theory, in this case it is extremely complementary. One of Freud's most essential propositions is that all individuals are born with a tendency toward inherent drives and selfishness due to the id domain of the psyche.[72] According to Freud, not only are all people born with id drives; they all have an equal amount of such motivations toward selfishness. Another one of Freud's assumptions is that this inherent, selfish tendency must be countered by controls produced from the development of the superego. According to Freud, the superego, which is the domain of the psyche that contains our conscience (see Figure 10.5), is formed through the interactions that occur between a young infant/child and significant others. As you can see, the control perspective has a long history that can be found in many philosophical and scientific disciplines.

Early Control Theories of Crime

Throughout the 1950s and 1960s, criminologists borrowed and built on some of the ideas just discussed. Until that time, most research in the criminological literature was dominated by the learning theories discussed earlier in this chapter or by social structure theories, such as Merton's strain theory or the Chicago School perspective (see Chapters 8 and 9, respectively). While early control theories may not be particularly popular in this day and age, they were vitally important because they laid the groundwork for future theoretical development.

REISS'S CONTROL THEORY. One of the first control theories of crime was proposed by Albert Reiss in 1951. Reiss claimed that delinquency was a consequence of weak controls that resulted in weak ego or superego controls among juvenile probationers.[73] Reiss assumed that there was no explicit motivation for delinquent activity; rather, he claimed that it would occur in the absence of controls or restraints against such behavior.

Like Freud, Reiss believed that the family was the primary entity through which deviant predispositions were discouraged. Furthermore, Reiss claimed that a sound family environment would provide for an individual's needs and the essential emotional bonds that are so important in socializing individuals. Another important factor in Reiss's model was close supervision, not only by the family but also by the community. He claimed that individuals must be closely monitored for delinquent behavior and adequately disciplined when they break the rules.

Personal factors, such as the ability to restrain one's impulses and delay gratification, were also important in Reiss's framework. These concepts are similar to later, more modern concepts of control theory that have been consistently supported by empirical research.[74] For this reason, Reiss was ahead of his time when he first proposed his control theory. Although the direct tests of Reiss's theory have provided only partial support for it, Reiss's influence is apparent in many contemporary criminological theories.[75]

FIGURE **10.5**
Freud's Model of the Three Domains of the Psyche

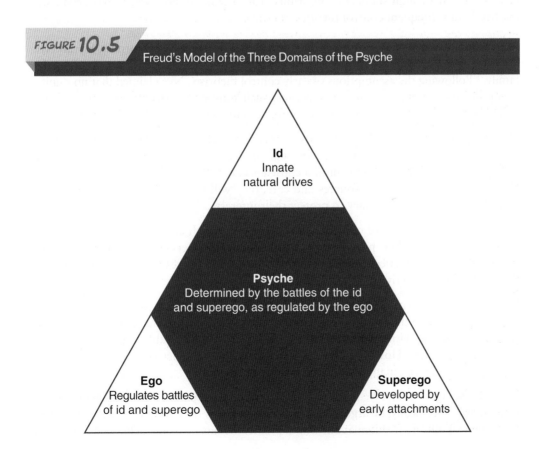

Id
Innate
natural drives

Psyche
Determined by the battles of the id
and superego, as regulated by the ego

Ego
Regulates battles
of id and superego

Superego
Developed by
early attachments

According to Reiss's model, close supervision by the family discourages deviant predispositions.

TOBY'S CONCEPT OF STAKE IN CONFORMITY. Soon after Reiss's theory was presented, a similar theory was developed. In 1957, Jackson Toby proposed a theory of delinquency and gangs.[76] He claimed that individuals were more inclined to act on their natural tendencies when the controls on them were weak. Like most other control theorists, Toby claimed that such inclinations toward deviance were distributed equally across all individuals. Further, he emphasized the concept of a *stake in conformity* that supposedly prevents most people from committing crime. The stake in conformity Toby was referring to is the extent to which individuals are *invested* in conventional society. In other words, how much is a person willing to risk by violating the law?

Studies have shown that stake in conformity is one of the most influential factors in individuals' decisions to offend. For example, individuals who have nothing to lose are much more likely to take risks and violate others' rights than are those who have relatively more invested in social institutions.[77]

One distinguishing feature of Toby's theory is his emphasis on peer influences in terms of both motivating and inhibiting antisocial behavior, depending on whether most of one's peers have low or high stakes in conformity. Toby's stake in conformity has been used effectively in subsequent control theories of crime.

NYE'S CONTROL THEORY. A year after Toby introduced the stake in conformity, F. Ivan Nye (1958) proposed a relatively comprehensive control theory that placed a strong focus on the family.[78] Following the assumptions of early control theorists, Nye claimed that no significant positive force causes delinquency, because such antisocial tendencies are universal and would be found in virtually everyone if not for certain controls usually found in the home.

Nye's theory consists of three primary components of control. The first component is *internal control*, which is formed through social interaction. This socialization, he claimed, assists in the development of a conscience. Nye further claimed that if individuals are not given adequate resources and care, they will follow their natural tendencies toward doing what is necessary to protect their interests.

Nye's second component of control is *direct control*, which consists of a wide range of constraints on individual propensities to commit deviant acts. Direct control includes numerous types of sanctions, such as jail and ridicule, and the restriction of one's chances to commit criminal activity.

Nye's third component of control is *indirect control*, which occurs when individuals are strongly attached to their early caregivers. For most children, it is through an intense and strong relationship with their parents or guardians that they establish an attachment to conventional society. However, Nye suggested that when the needs of an individual are not met by caregivers, inappropriate behavior can result.

As shown in Figure 10.6, Nye predicted a U-shaped curve of parental controls in predicting delinquency. Specifically, he argued that either no controls (i.e., complete freedom) or too much control (i.e., no freedom at all) would predict the most chronic delinquency. Instead, he believed that a healthy balance of freedom and parental control was the best strategy for inhibiting criminal activity. Some recent research supports Nye's prediction.[79] We will see later in this chapter that contemporary control theories, such as Tittle's control-balance theory, draw heavily on Nye's idea of having a healthy balance of controls and freedom.[80]

RECKLESS'S CONTAINMENT THEORY. Another control theory, known as containment theory, has been proposed by Walter Reckless.[81] This theory emphasizes both *inner containment* and *outer containment*, which can be viewed as internal and external controls. Reckless broke from traditional assumptions of social control theories by identifying predictive factors that *push* and/or *pull* individuals toward antisocial behavior. However, the focus of his theory remained on the controlling elements, which can be seen in the emphasis placed on "containment" in the theory's name.

Reckless claimed that individuals can be *pushed* into delinquency by their social environment, such as by a lack of opportunities for education or employment. Furthermore, he pointed out that some individual factors, such as brain disorders or risk-taking personalities, could push some people to commit criminal behavior. Reckless also noted that some individuals could be *pulled* into criminal activity by hanging out with delinquent peers, watching too much violence on television, and so on. All told, Reckless went beyond the typical control theory assumption of inborn tendencies. In addition to these natural dispositions toward deviant behavior, containment theory proposes that extra pushes and pulls can motivate people to commit crime.

Reckless further claimed that the pushes and pulls toward criminal behavior could be enough to force individuals into criminal activity unless they are sufficiently *contained* or controlled. Reckless claimed that such containment should be both internal and external. By *inner containment*, he meant building a person's sense of self. This would help the person resist the temptations of criminal activity. According to Reckless, other forms of inner containment include the ability of individuals to internalize societal norms. With respect to *outer containment*, Reckless claimed that social organizations, such as school, church, and other institutions, are essential in building bonds that inhibit individuals from being pushed or pulled into criminal activity.

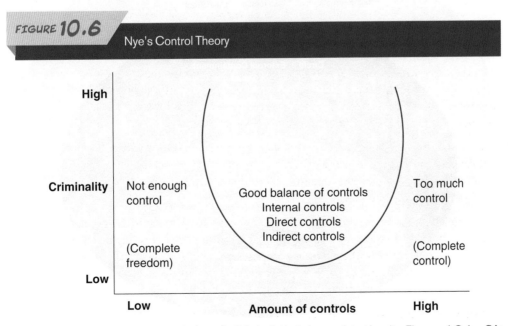

FIGURE 10.6   Nye's Control Theory

Source: Tibbetts, S., & Hemmens, C. (2010). *Criminological theory: A text/reader.* Thousand Oaks, CA: SAGE, p. 456.

Reckless described a visual image of containment theory, which we present in Figure 10.7. The outer circle (Circle 1) in the figure represents the social realm of pressures and pulls, whereas the innermost circle (Circle 4) symbolizes a person's individual-level pushes to commit crime. In between these two circles are the two layers of controls—namely, external containment (Circle 2) and internal containment (Circle 3). The structure of Figure 10.7 and the examples included in each circle are those specifically noted by Reckless.[82]

While some studies have shown more general support for containment theory, other studies have shown that some of the components of the theory, such as internalization of rules, seem to have much more support in accounting for variation in delinquency than do other factors, such as self-perception.[83] In other words, external factors may be more important than internal ones. Furthermore, some studies have noted weaker support for Reckless's theory among minorities and females. Thus, the model appears to be most valid for white males.[84]

One of the problems with containment theory is that it does not go far enough toward specifying the factors that are important in predicting criminality. For example, an infinite number of concepts exist that could potentially be categorized as either a "push" or "pull" toward criminality, or as an "inner" or "outer" containment of criminality. Thus, the theory could be considered too broad and not specific enough to be of practical value. To Reckless's credit, though, containment theory has increased the exposure of control theories of criminal behavior. And although support for containment theory has been mixed, there is no doubt that it has influenced other, more recent control theories.[85]

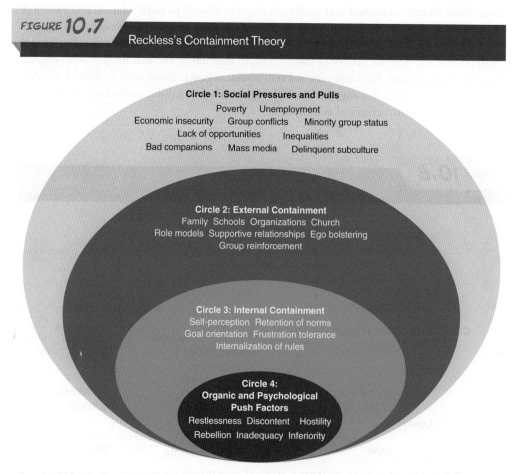

FIGURE **10.7** Reckless's Containment Theory

Source: Tibbetts, S., & Hemmens, C. (2010). *Criminological theory: A text/reader.* Thousand Oaks, CA: SAGE, p. 458.

Modern Social Control Theories

As the previous sections attest, control theory has been around, in various forms, for some time. Modern social control theories, to which we now turn our attention, build on these earlier versions of social control but also add a level of depth and sophistication. Two modern social control theories that we consider here are Matza's drift theory and Hirschi's social bonding theory.

MATZA'S DRIFT THEORY. The theory of *drift*, presented by David Matza in 1964, claims that individuals offend at certain times in their lives when social controls, such as parental supervision, employment, and family ties, are weakened.[86] In developing his theory, Matza criticized earlier theories and their tendency to predict too much crime. For example, theories such as those of the Chicago School would wrongfully predict that all individuals in bad neighborhoods will commit crime. Likewise, strain theory predicts that all poor individuals will commit crime. Obviously, this is not true. Thus, Matza claimed that there is a degree of determinism (i.e., Positive School) in human behavior but also a significant amount of free will (i.e., Classical School). He called this perspective soft determinism, which is the gray area between free will and determinism. This is illustrated in Table 10.2.

Returning to the basics of Matza's theory, he claimed that individuals offend at times in life when social controls are weakened. As is well-known, the time when social controls are most weakened for the majority of individuals is during their teenage years. It is at this time that parents and other caretakers stop having a constant supervisory role. At the same time, teenagers generally do not have too many responsibilities—such as careers or children—that would inhibit them from experimenting with deviance. This is consistent with the well-known age–crime relationship; most individuals arrested are in their teenage years (see Figure 10.8).[87] Once sufficient ties are developed, people tend to mature out of criminal lifestyles.

Matza further claimed that when supervision is absent and ties are minimal, the majority of individuals are the most "free" to do what they want. Where, then, does the term *drift* come from? As shown in Figure 10.8, it is during the times when people have few ties and obligations that they will "drift" in and out of delinquency. Matza pointed out that previous theories are unsuccessful in explaining this age–crime relationship. For example, he claimed that "most theories of delinquency take no account of maturational reform; those that do often do so at the expense of violating their own assumptions regarding the constrained delinquent."[88]

Matza insisted that "drifting" is not the same as a commitment to a life of crime. Instead, it is "experimenting" with questionable behavior and then rationalizing it. The way youth rationalize behavior that they know to be wrong is through the learning of techniques of neutralization, discussed earlier in this chapter.

TABLE **10.2**   Matza's Concept of Soft Determinism as the Middle-Ground Stance Between Two Extreme Assumptions of Criminal Behavior

ASSUMPTION OF COMPLETE FREE WILL	SOFT DETERMINISM	ASSUMPTION OF TOTAL ("HARD") DETERMINISM
Belief held by classical theorists	A sort of middle-ground position	Belief held by positive theorists
Assumes all behavior is the result of decisions freely chosen by a person		Assumes all behavior is the result of factors (e.g., economy, upbringing, peers) determining behavior

soft determinism: the assumption that both determinism and free will play a role in offenders' decisions to engage in criminal behavior.

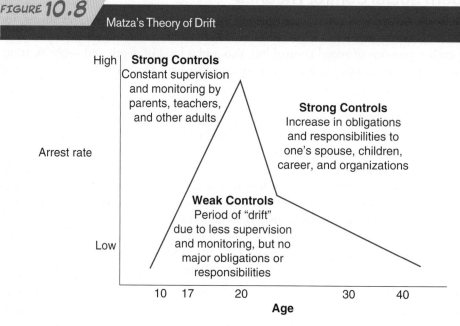

FIGURE 10.8 Matza's Theory of Drift

Strong Controls
Constant supervision and monitoring by parents, teachers, and other adults

Strong Controls
Increase in obligations and responsibilities to one's spouse, children, career, and organizations

Weak Controls
Period of "drift" due to less supervision and monitoring, but no major obligations or responsibilities

High

Arrest rate

Low

Age
10 17   20   30   40

Source: Tibbetts, S., & Hemmens, C. (2010). Criminological Theory: Text/Reader. Thousand Oaks, CA: SAGE Publications., p. 460.

Drift theory goes on to say that individuals do not reject the conventional normative structure. On the contrary, much offending is based on neutralizing or adhering to *subterranean values* that they have been socialized to use as a means of circumventing conventional values. This is basically the same as asserting one's independence, which tends to occur with a vengeance during the teenage years.

As discussed in Chapter 8, subterranean values are quite prevalent and underlie many aspects of our culture. For example, while it is conventional to believe that violence is wrong, boxing and other injury-prone sports are some of the most popular spectator activities. Such phenomena create an atmosphere that readily allows neutralization or rationalization of criminal activity.

We will see other forms of subterranean values when we discuss risk-taking and low self-control later in this chapter. In many contexts (such as business), risk-taking and aggressiveness are seen as desirable characteristics; so many individuals are influenced by such subterranean values. This, according to Matza, adds to individuals' likelihood of "drifting" into crime and delinquency.

Matza's theory of drift seems sensible on its face, but empirical research examining the theory has been mixed.[89] One of the primary criticisms of Matza's theory, which even he acknowledged, is that it does not explain the most chronic offenders, the people responsible for the vast majority of serious, violent crimes. Chronic offenders often

Is boxing a socially acceptable form of violence?

Daniel Shirey/Zuffa LLC/Getty Images

offend long before and well past their teenage years, which clearly limits the predictive value of Matza's theory.

Despite its shortcomings, Matza's drift theory does appear to explain why many people offend exclusively during their teenage and young adult years but then grow out of it. Also, the theory is highly consistent with several of the ideas presented by control theorists, including the assumption that (1) selfish tendencies are universal, (2) these tendencies are inhibited by socialization and social controls, and (3) the selfish tendencies appear at times when controls are weakest. The theory goes beyond the previous control theories by adding the concepts of soft determinism, neutralization, and subterranean values, as well as the idea that in many contexts selfish and aggressive behaviors are not wrong but are actually desirable behaviors.

HIRSCHI'S SOCIAL BONDING THEORY. Perhaps the most influential social control theory was presented by Travis Hirschi in 1969.[90] Hirschi's theory of social bonding takes an assumption from Durkheim that "we are all animals, and thus naturally capable of committing criminal acts."[91] However, as Hirschi acknowledged, most humans can be adequately socialized to become tightly bonded to conventional entities, such as families, schools, communities, and the like. Hirschi claimed also that the stronger a person is bonded to conventional society, the less prone to engaging in crime he or she will be. More specifically, the stronger the social bond, the less likely that an individual will commit criminal offenses.

As shown in Figure 10.9, Hirschi's social bond is made up of four elements: (1) attachment, (2) commitment, (3) involvement, and (4) beliefs. The "stronger" or more developed a person is in each of the four elements, the less likely he or she will be to commit crime. Let us now consider each element in detail.

The most important factor in the social bond is *attachment,* which consists of affectionate bonds between an individual and his or her significant others. Attachment is

social bonding: a control theory that assumes that individuals are predisposed to commit crime and that conventional bonds prevent or reduce offending. This bond is made up of four constructs: attachments, commitment, involvement, and moral beliefs regarding committing crime.

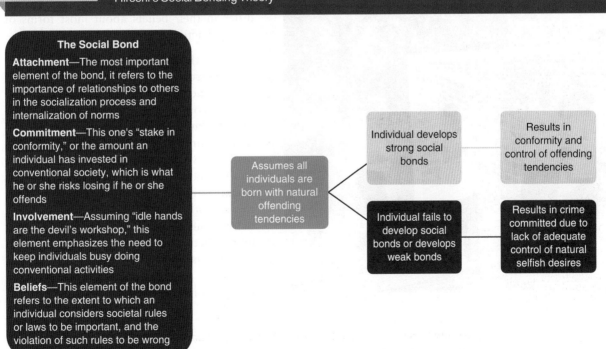

FIGURE 10.9 Hirschi's Social Bonding Theory

The Social Bond

Attachment—The most important element of the bond, it refers to the importance of relationships to others in the socialization process and internalization of norms

Commitment—This one's "stake in conformity," or the amount an individual has invested in conventional society, which is what he or she risks losing if he or she offends

Involvement—Assuming "idle hands are the devil's workshop," this element emphasizes the need to keep individuals busy doing conventional activities

Beliefs—This element of the bond refers to the extent to which an individual considers societal rules or laws to be important, and the violation of such rules to be wrong

Assumes all individuals are born with natural offending tendencies

Individual develops strong social bonds → Results in conformity and control of offending tendencies

Individual fails to develop social bonds or develops weak bonds → Results in crime committed due to lack of adequate control of natural selfish desires

Source: Tibbetts, S., & Hemmens, C. (2010). *Criminological theory: A text/reader.* Thousand Oaks, CA: SAGE, p. 462.

vitally important for the internalization of conventional values. Hirschi claimed that "the essence of internalization of norms, conscience, or superego thus lies in the attachment of the individual to others."[92] Hirschi made it clear, as did Freud, that strong early attachments are the most important factor in developing a social bond. Commitment, involvement, and belief, he argued, are contingent on adequate attachment to others. That is, without healthy attachments, especially early in life, the probability of acting inappropriately increases.

Commitment, the second element of Hirschi's social bond, is the investment a person has in conventional society. This has been explained as one's "stake in conformity," or what is at risk of being lost if one gets caught committing crime. If a person feels that much will be lost by committing crime, then he or she will probably not do so. In contrast, if someone has nothing to lose, what is to prevent that person from doing something he or she may be punished for? The answer is, of course, not much. And this, some theorists claim, is why it is difficult to control so-called "chronic offenders" who have nothing to lose. Trying to instill a "commitment" to conventional society in such individuals is extremely difficult.

Another element of the social bond is *involvement*, which is the time spent in conventional activities. The assumption is that time spent in constructive activities will reduce time devoted to illegal behaviors. This element of the bond goes back to the old adage that "idle hands are the devil's workshop."[93] Hirschi claimed that taking an active role in all forms of conventional activities can inhibit delinquent and criminal activity.

The last element of the social bond is *beliefs*, which have generally been interpreted as moral beliefs concerning the laws and rules of society. This is one of the most examined, and consistently supported, aspects of the social bond. Basically, individuals who feel that a course of action is against their moral beliefs are much less likely to pursue it than are individuals who don't see a breach of morality in such behavior. For example, we all probably know some people who see drunk driving as a serious offense because of the injury and death it can cause. However, we also probably know individuals who don't see a problem with such behavior. The same can be said about speeding in a car, shoplifting from a store, or using marijuana; people differ in their beliefs about most forms of criminal activity.

Hirschi's theory has been tested by numerous researchers and has, for the most part, been supported.[94] However, one criticism is that the components of the social bond may predict criminality only if they are defined in a certain way. For example, with respect to the "involvement" element of the bond, studies have shown that not all conventional activities are equal when it comes to preventing delinquency. Only academic or religious activities seem to have consistent effects on inhibiting delinquency. In contrast, many studies show that teenagers who date or play sports actually have an increased risk of committing crime.[95]

According to Hirschi, participating in conventional activities can inhibit delinquent and criminal activity.

©iStockphoto.com/monkeybusinessimages

Another major criticism of Hirschi's theory is that the effects of "attachments" on crime depend on whom one is attached to. As explained earlier in this chapter, studies have clearly and consistently shown that attachment to delinquent peers is a strong predictor of criminal activity.

Finally, some evidence indicates that social bonding theory may better explain reasons why individuals start offending but not reasons why people continue or escalate in their offending. One reason for this is that Hirschi's theory does not elaborate on what occurs after an individual commits criminal activity. This is likely the primary reason why some of the more complex integrated theories of crime (some of which are discussed below) often attribute the initiation of delinquency to a breakdown in the social bond. However, they typically see other theories (such as differential reinforcement) as better predictors of what happens after the initial stages of the criminal career.[96]

Despite the criticism it has received, Hirschi's social bonding theory is still one of the most accepted theories of criminal behavior.[97] It is a relatively convincing explanation for criminality because of the consistent support it has found among samples of people taken from all over the world.[98]

Integrated Social Control Theories

It is worthwhile to briefly discuss the two integrated models that most incorporate the control perspective into their frameworks. These two integrated models are control-balance theory and power-control theory. Both have received considerable attention in the criminological literature.

TITTLE'S CONTROL-BALANCE THEORY. Presented by Charles Tittle in 1995, control-balance theory proposes that (1) the amount of control to which one is *subjected* and (2) the amount of control one can *exercise* determine the probability of deviance occurring. The "balance" between these two types of control, he argued, can even predict the *type* of behavior likely to be committed.[99]

Tittle argued that a person is least likely to offend when he or she has a balance of controlling and being controlled. Further, the likelihood of offending will increase when these factors become imbalanced. If individuals are more controlled (Tittle calls this control deficit), then the theory predicts that they will commit predatory or defiant acts. In contrast, if an individual possesses an excessive level of control (Tittle calls this control surplus), then he or she will be more likely to commit acts of exploitation or decadence. Note that excessive control is not the same as excessive self-control. Tittle argues that people who are controlling—that is, who have excessive control over others—will be predisposed toward inappropriate activities.

Initial empirical tests of control-balance theory have reported mixed results, with both surpluses and deficits predicting the same types of deviance.[100] Additionally, researchers have uncovered differing effects of the control-balance ratio on two types of deviance that are contingent on gender. This finding is consistent with the gender-specific support found for Reckless's containment theory, described earlier in this chapter.[101]

HAGAN'S POWER-CONTROL THEORY. Power-control theory is another integrated theory, proposed by John Hagan and his colleagues.[102] The primary focus of this theory is on the level of patriarchal attitudes and structure in the household, which are influenced by parental positions in the workforce. Power-control theory assumes that in households where the mother and father have relatively similar levels of power at work (i.e., balanced households), mothers will be less likely to exert control over their daughters. These balanced households will be less likely to experience gender differences in the criminal offending of the children. However, households in which mothers and fathers have dissimilar levels of power in the workplace (i.e., unbalanced households) are more likely to suppress criminal activity in daughters. Additionally, assertiveness and risky activity among the males in the house will be encouraged. This assertiveness and risky activity may be a precursor to crime.

Power-control theory focuses on the patriarchal attitudes and structure in the household.

Most empirical tests of power-control have provided moderate support for the theory, while more recent studies have further specified the validity of the theory in different contexts.[103] For example, one recent study reported that the influence of mothers, not fathers, on sons had the greatest impact on reducing the delinquency of young males.[104] Another researcher has found that differences in perceived threats of embarrassment and formal sanctions varied between more patriarchal and less patriarchal households.[105] Finally, studies have also started measuring the effect of patriarchal attitudes on crime and delinquency.[106] Power-control theory is a good example of a social control theory in that it is consistent with the idea that individuals must be socialized and that the gender differences in such socialization affect how people will act throughout life.

We will revisit this theory again in Chapter 12.

A GENERAL THEORY OF CRIME: LOW SELF-CONTROL

In 1990, Hirschi, along with his colleague Michael Gottfredson, proposed a general theory of low self-control, which is often referred to as the general theory of crime.[107] This theory has led to a significant amount of debate and research in the field since its appearance, more so than any other contemporary theory of crime. Like the previous control theories of crime, this theory assumes that individuals are born predisposed toward selfish, self-centered activities and that only effective child rearing and socialization can create self-control among persons. As shown in Figure 10.10, without such adequate socialization (i.e., social controls) and reduction of criminal opportunities, individuals will follow their natural tendencies to become selfish predators. Furthermore, the general theory of crime assumes that self-control must be established by age 10. If it has not formed by that time, according to the theory, individuals will forever exhibit low self-control.

Although Gottfredson and Hirschi still attribute the formation of controls to the socialization process, the distinguishing characteristic of this theory is its emphasis on the individual's ability to control himself or herself. That is, the general theory of crime assumes that people can take a degree of control over their own decisions and, within certain limitations, "control" themselves.

The general theory of crime is accepted as one of the most valid theories of crime.[108] This is probably because it identifies only one primary factor that causes criminality—low self-control. But low self-control may actually consist of a series of personality traits, including risk taking, impulsiveness, self-centeredness, short-term orientation, and quick temper. For example, recent research has supported the idea that inadequate child-rearing practices tend to result in lower levels of self-control among children and that these low levels produce various risky behaviors, including criminal activity.[109]

Psychological Aspects of Low Self-Control

Criminologists have recently claimed that low self-control may be due to the emotional disposition of individuals. For example, one study showed that the effects of

low self-control:
a theory that proposes that individuals either develop self-control by age 10 or do not. Those who do not will manifest criminal or deviant behaviors throughout life.

low self-control on intentions to commit drunk driving and shoplifting were tied to individuals' perceptions of pleasure and shame. More specifically, the findings of this study showed that individuals who had low self-control had significantly lower levels of anticipated shame but significantly higher levels of perceived pleasure in committing both drunk driving and shoplifting.[110] These results suggest that individuals who lack self-control will be oriented toward gaining pleasure and taking advantage of resources but also toward avoiding negative emotional feelings (e.g., shame) that are primarily induced through socialization.

Physiological Aspects of Low Self-Control

Low self-control can also be tied to physiological factors. Interestingly, research has shown that chronic offenders show greater arousal toward danger and risk taking than toward the possibility of punishment.[111] This arousal has been measured by monitoring brain activity in response to certain stimuli. The research suggests that individuals are *encouraged* to commit risky behavior due to physiological mechanisms that reward their risk-taking activities by releasing "pleasure" chemicals in the brain.[112]

In a similar vein, recent studies show that chronic gamblers tend to get a physiological "high" (a sudden, intense release of brain chemicals similar to that following a small dose of cocaine) from the activity of betting, particularly when they are gambling with their own money and risking a personal loss.[113] Undoubtedly, there exists a minority

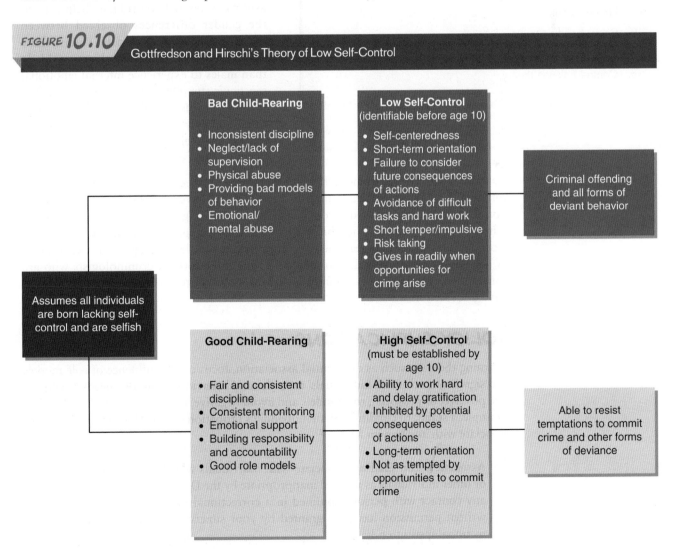

FIGURE **10.10** Gottfredson and Hirschi's Theory of Low Self-Control

group of individuals who thrive off of risk-taking behaviors significantly more than others do. This suggests that there are not just psychological differences among people but also physiological differences that may explain why certain individuals favor risky behaviors.

Researchers have also found that criminal offenders generally perceive a significantly lower level of internal sanctions (e.g., shame, guilt, embarrassment) than do nonoffenders.[114] So, in summary, a select group of individuals appear to derive physiological and psychological pleasure from engaging in risky behaviors while simultaneously being less likely to be inhibited by internal emotional sanctions. Such a combination, Gottfredson and Hirschi claimed, is dangerous and helps explain why some impulsive individuals often end up in prison.

Finally, the psychological and physiological aspects of low self-control may help explain the gender differences observed between males and females. Specifically, studies show that females are significantly more likely than males to experience internal emotional sanctioning for offenses they have committed.[115] In other words, there appears to be something innately different about males and females that helps explain the differing levels of self-control each possesses.

Control perspectives are among the oldest and most respected explanations of criminal activity. The fundamental assumption that humans have an inborn, selfish disposition that must be controlled through socialization distinguishes control theories from other theories of crime. The ability of the control perspective to remain among the most popular criminological theories demonstrates its legitimacy as an explanation of behavior. This is likely due to the dedication and efforts of criminologists who are constantly developing new and improved versions of control theory, many of which we have discussed here.

POLICY IMPLICATIONS

Learning theories, such as differential association, focus on the influence of role models and significant others on individuals' attitudes and behaviors. Thus, one needs to emphasize positive, or prosocial, role models and avoid negative, or antisocial, role models. For example, a standard condition of an individual's probation or parole is that he or she not associate with any known felons:[121]

> Associates: You shall not associate with individuals who have criminal records or other individuals as deemed inappropriate by the Division. You shall not have any contact with persons confined in a correctional institution unless specific written permission has been granted by your supervising officer and the correctional institution.[122]

WHY DO THEY DO IT?

JESSE POMEROY

AP Photo

Jesse Pomeroy was born on November 29, 1859, in Charlestown, Massachusetts. His father, Thomas, was a violent alcoholic. He would often go on drinking binges and then proceed to beat his two sons, Charles and Jesse. Jesse's mother, Ruth Ann, eventually divorced Thomas in the 1870s; divorce was extremely uncommon during this time. In fact, Ruth Ann revealed that she divorced her husband after one of these brutal beatings:

Jesse later admitted to his doctors that his father had made him go to his room and strip totally naked, whereupon Thomas had proceeded to lash out with a leather belt . . . [Jesse] realized the beatings . . . were not that bad, not nearly as horrific as the relentless pummeling he had received almost four years earlier, when his father had taken Jesse, just eight years old, to an abandoned shed in the woods. There Thomas had become so enraged that the blows from a horse-whip had nearly killed his son.[116]

Ruth Ann realized that Jesse was a strong-willed boy. Jesse was often made fun of at school, primarily because of a deformity in his right eye. Jesse's teacher complained of his problem behavior at school. The teacher noted that he was a loner; he preferred to read cheap "dime novels." During this time, these novels were full of violence, sex, battles, and mayhem. Eventually, Ruth Ann was asked to remove her son from school.

Jesse's problems were not restricted to just school. His mother brought home two yellow canaries; she would come home looking forward to their chirping in the wooden cage. One afternoon, she came home to find the two canaries dead—their necks were twisted off their bodies. Prior to this, a neighbor had told Ruth Ann that

her little kitten had gone missing. A few days later, Ruth Ann watched Jesse walking down a nearby street with the dead kitten in one hand and a kitchen knife in the other. In 1871, there were reports that children in the next city over, Chelsea, were being beaten by an older boy. Some of these children were sexually assaulted. The victims reported that this boy would offer them money and treats; then he would suggest they go to a remote locate. There he would abuse the children.[117] The newspapers referred to him as "The Boy Torturer" and "The Red Devil." After reading a description of this boy in the *Boston Globe*, Ruth Ann recognized this was her son; she moved her family to South Boston. In August of 1872, a young boy was found tortured in South Boston; a month later, a child was found beaten, assaulted, and tied up to a telephone pole. This victim, however, was able to give a very detailed description. This resulted in Jesse Pomeroy being arrested and sentenced to the State Reform School at Westborough for the remainder of his minor-status years (e.g., six years). Ruth Ann, however, diligently worked to have her son released earlier; Jesse was released months after.[118]

In March 1874, nine-year-old Katie Curran disappeared. During the investigation, it was revealed that the last place she had been seen was at the Pomeroys' shop; Jesse was interrogated, but there was no arrest at that time. In April, the body of four-year-old Horace Millen was found on the beach of Dorchester Bay. His throat had been cut and he had been stabbed 15 times; also, one of his eyes had been torn out. The police recalled the beatings of the other children two years earlier and arrested Jesse Pomeroy; he was 14 years old at the time. In July 1874, Jesse confessed to Horace Millen's murder. Jesse Pomeroy also confessed to the murder of Katie Curran. He had lured her into the basement of his mother's dress shop. He had then cut her throat and buried her body under an ash heap. When he was asked why he committed the murders, he stated, "I couldn't help it."[119] On September 7, 1876, Jesse Pomeroy was sentenced to death. Subsequently, his sentence was commuted to life in prison—solitary confinement. In 1916, he was released from solitary confinement and was allowed to mix with other prisoners at the Charlestown Prison. On September 29, 1932, he died at the age of 73 years.[120]

THINK ABOUT IT:

So why did he do it? As described by the theories presented in this chapter, specifically various social control

(Continued)

(Continued)

theories (such as Hirschi's theory of social bonding) and socialization theories (e.g., differential association theory, differential reinforcement theory), it appears that Jesse Pomeroy never had much of a chance to form strong social bonds with conventional society, nor was he adequately socialized. To clarify, his father was abusive. He was considered a loner at school. He began early in life to demonstrate cruel behavior to animals. Thus, do you think Jesse Pomeroy engaged in such behaviors out of selfishness and personal satisfaction, and without any empathy for his victims, because that was what his experience in the world taught him to do?

If you maintain that Jesse had low self-control so he engaged in these behaviors, then why did he have such low self-control?

What types of things could have been done to improve Jesse's low self-control?

Programs such as Head Start attempt to provide youths with more positive or favorable definitions of conventional behavior. Various school districts are incorporating conflict resolution programs into their curricula.[123] Tremblay and Craig maintained that the developmental prevention approach is primarily founded on the premise that criminal activity is influenced by behavioral and attitudinal patterns that are learned during an individual's development. In their review of various preventive interventions, however, they stated,

> It does appear that money invested in early (e.g., preschool) prevention efforts with at-risk families will give greater pay-offs than money invested in later (e.g., adolescence) prevention efforts with the same at-risk families. This general rule is not easy to apply, because juvenile delinquents attract much more public attention than high risk infants or toddlers.[124]

In reference to social control theories, policies focus on enhancing more crime and delinquency control measures. These types of efforts are often popular from the public perspective. In a similar vein, programs have been developed that attempt to engage youths in more conventional-type activities. Thus, programs such as Boy Scouts, Girl Scouts, 4-H clubs, and Little League baseball are examples of such programming.[125]

CONCLUSION

In the first section, we discussed learning theories. These theories focus on the process of how and why individuals learn criminal behavior, including the techniques, justifications, and underlying values. These theories also give substantial attention to significant people involved in the socialization process—specifically, family, friends, and important others. Learning theories continue to be helpful in our understanding of criminal behavior, as shown by virtually all empirical studies that have evaluated the validity of these theoretical models. If we theorize that individuals learn various techniques, justifications, and values that influence their potential to engage in criminal activity, then these individuals can also learn how to engage in law-abiding behavior.

In the latter half of this chapter, we examined a large number of control theories, which assume that individuals are essentially born naturally greedy and selfish and that we have to be controlled to resist acting on these inherent drives. Although the many different control theories have some unique distinctions, they all share one key underlying assumption: They all assume that people must be socialized in such a way that their learning of right and wrong will control the antisocial tendencies they are born with.

In this chapter, we discussed a wide range of theories that may appear to be quite different. However, it is important to remember that all the criminological theories covered in this chapter share an emphasis on social processes as the primary reason why individuals commit crime. This is true for the learning theories, which propose that people are taught to commit crime, as well as for the control theories, which claim that people offend naturally and must be taught not to commit crime. Despite their seemingly opposite assumptions of human behavior, the fact is that learning and control theories both identify socialization, or the lack thereof, as the key cause of criminal behavior.

SUMMARY OF THEORIES IN CHAPTER 10

THEORY	CONCEPTS	PROPONENTS	KEY PROPOSITIONS
Differential association	Criminal behavior is learned in interaction with other persons; learning occurs within intimate personal groups; learned definitions are favorable or unfavorable to the legal code; associations vary in frequency, duration, priority, and intensity.	Edwin Sutherland	Criminality is learned just like any conventional activity; any normal individual, when exposed to definitions and attitudes favorable toward crime, will learn both the motivations and techniques for engaging in illegal behaviors.
Differential reinforcement theory	Criminal behavior is learned according to the principles of operant conditioning and modeling/imitation; criminal behavior is learned in both nonsocial and social interactions; learning occurs in groups that make up the individual's major source of reinforcements.	Robert Burgess and Ronald Akers	Assumes individuals are born with a blank slate and socialized and taught how to behave through classical and operant conditioning as well as modeling; behavior occurs and continues depending on past and present rewards and punishments.
Techniques of neutralization	Criminals are still partially committed to the dominant social order; there are five techniques of neutralization to justify criminal behavior.	Gresham Sykes and David Matza	Individuals can engage in criminal behavior and avoid feelings of guilt for these actions by justifying or rationalizing their behavior; since they are partially committed to the social order, such justifications help them engage in criminal behavior without serious damage to their self-image.
Early control theories	Individuals are naturally born selfish and greedy, and they must be socialized by others to control their inherent desires and drives.	Sigmund Freud, Jackson Toby, Albert Reiss, F. Ivan Nye, Walter Reckless, and others	Most of the early theorists emphasized the need for external societal controls to counter people's inner drives; Reckless called such a process "containment," in the sense that if such drives are not contained, there is little to stop a person from doing what is natural, which is to offend.
Theory of drift	Soft determinism, meaning that offending behavior is the result of both free will/decision-making and deterministic factors outside our control.	David Matza	Offending typically peaks in the teenage years because that is the time when social controls are weakest; that is, we are no longer being monitored constantly by caretakers, and the adulthood control factors of marriage, employment, etc., have not yet kicked in.
Social bonding theory	The social bond is made up of four elements: attachments, commitment, involvement, and moral beliefs.	Travis Hirschi	A simple theory in the sense that as each of the four elements of the social bond grows stronger, the likelihood of offending lessens due to the individual's being more bonded to conventional society.
Control-balance theory	Control deficit and control surplus	Charles Tittle	Individuals who either are too controlled by others or have too much control over others are more likely to commit crimes, compared with people who have a healthy balance between the two.
Power-control theory	Balanced and unbalanced households	John Hagan	Households in which the parents have similar types of jobs are more balanced and tend to control their sons and daughters more equally than in unbalanced households, where the parents have different jobs, which leads to more controls placed on daughters than on sons.
Low self-control theory	Bad child rearing	Michael Gottfredson and Travis Hirschi	Bad parenting (abusive, inconsistent, lack of monitoring, neglectful) results in lack of development of self-control, which then leads to criminality and risky behaviors.

KEY TERMS

DISCUSSION QUESTIONS

1. What distinguishes learning theories from other criminological theories?

2. What distinguishes differential association from differential reinforcement theory?

3. What did differential identification add to learning theories?

4. Which technique of neutralization do you use/relate to the most? Why?

5. Which technique of neutralization do you find least valid? Why?

6. Which element of Hirschi's social bond do you find you have the highest levels of?

7. Which element of Hirschi's social bond do you find you have the lowest levels of?

8. Can you identify someone you know who fits the profile of a person with low self-control?

9. Which aspects of the low self-control personality do you think you fit?

10. Regarding Matza's theory of drift, do you think this relates to when you or your friends have committed crimes in your lives? Why or why not?

WEB RESOURCES

Social Learning Theories

http://sociology.about.com/od/Sociological-Theory/a/Social-Learning-Theory.htm

http://psychology.about.com/od/developmentalpsychology/a/sociallearning.htm

Control Theories

http://www.oxfordbibliographies.com/view/document/obo-9780195396607/obo-9780195396607-0091.xml

http://www.youtube.com/watch?v=pvwd8R5_OGs

http://www.everydaysociologyblog.com/2008/11/gottfredson-and.html

STUDENT STUDY SITE

WANT A BETTER GRADE ON YOUR NEXT TEST?

Get the tools you need to sharpen your study skills:

SAGE edge offers a robust online environment featuring an impressive array of tools and resources for review, study, and further exploration, keeping both instructors and students on the cutting edge of teaching and learning. Learn more at **edge.sagepub.com/schram2e**.

FOR FURTHER EXPLORATION AND APPLICATION, VISIT THE STUDENT STUDY SITE:

- Selling Kids on Veggies when Rules Like `Clean Your Plate' Fail
- To End the Cycle of Crime, Italian Judge Breaks Up Big-Time Mafia Families
- Preventing Juvenile Detention With a Blank Canvas and a Can of Spray Paint
- An examination of differential association and social control theory: Family systems and delinquency
- Techniques of neutralization and persistent sexual abuse by clergy: A content analysis of priest personnel files from the Archdiocese of Milwaukee
- A partial test of Agnew's general theory of crime and delinquency.
- Francis Weaver, Son Of Notorious Child Killer Ward Weaver III, Charged In Homicide
- Children, Violence, and Trauma—A Call to Action
- One of the Most Dangerous Schools in America-ABC World News Tonight-ABC News
- Hidden Camera Experiment: Young Kids Drawn to Guns-ABC World News- ABC News
- The Difference Between Classical and Operant Conditioning- Peggy Andover
- Bandura's Bobo Doll Experiment
- Aileen Wuornos
- Parents Take Guns to Schools
- Victim Fights Back
- Predictive Policing

PREMIUM VIDEO:

Check out the Interactive eBook for premium videos, including videos from author Stephen Tibbetts, who discusses real-world examples and strange crimes; and videos from former offenders, who share their stories from a first-person view, and touch on key theories and concepts from the chapter.

CHAPTER 11

Labeling Theory and Conflict/ Marxist/Radical Theories of Crime

INTRODUCTION

During the 1960s and 1970s, one of the most prominent paradigms to rival traditional theoretical explanations of crime was radical and/or critical criminology.[4] Traditional criminology theories (e.g., classical and positive) were considered a part of mainstream criminology; they had a tendency to support the status quo and the dominant ideologies of that time. Critical criminology, however, was initially based on a critique of both the state and the political economy of crime and crime control.[5] While this earlier radical criminological perspective continued for a relatively brief time, this framework is typically used as a gauge for assessing whether theories in the 1980s and 1990s were evolving or devolving.[6]

By the late 1980s and early 1990s, this radical perspective was transforming. First, the paradigm was designated as critical rather than radical. Second, while the earlier radical paradigm primarily focused on Marxist and neo-Marxist frameworks of class, state, and social control, the critical paradigm began to broaden its focus and diversify. A common feature of the earlier radical and subsequent critical perspectives, however, is their "anti-establishment stances or criticisms, their pursuits of transformation of one kind or another, and their relative appreciations for the political economy of crime and crime control."[7]

This chapter presents several critical criminology theories. We start with a discussion on labeling theory. Next, we focus on selected contributions to the conflict perspective, including the conservative (pluralist) and the Marxist/radical. Additional critical perspectives are reviewed, including peacemaking criminology, restorative justice, and left realism. This chapter concludes by presenting examples of policies and programs related to the labeling and conflict theories of crime.

LABELING THEORY

As with fashions, ideas can be influenced by changing fads, even ideas that attempt to explain crime.[8] Labeling theory came to the forefront during a time when various assumptions concerning societal authority were being questioned and reexamined. Near the end of the 1950s, the unfair and inequitable treatment of underprivileged individuals in society was becoming a widespread concern for many Americans. As a result, protests and demonstrations were held to fight for civil rights and women's rights. Others were also questioning the legitimacy of political authority regarding U.S. foreign policy in Vietnam. Thus, many protested the United States' involvement in the Vietnam War; a number of these protests were held on college campuses.

Within this broader societal context, scholars were also beginning to question existing explanations of crime. These scholars maintained that too much emphasis was placed on explaining individual characteristics contributing to criminal behavior. These scholars were concerned with the structure of social class and power; thus, the labeling perspective is not overly concerned with questions of why an individual engages in deviant

LEARNING OBJECTIVES

As you read this chapter, consider the following topics:

- Summarize the foundational ideas of labeling theory.

- Describe the basic assumptions of labeling theory.

- Evaluate the research and criticisms of labeling theory.

- Explain the key features of the consensus view of the law.

- State the distinguishing features of conservative (pluralist) and critical-radical perspectives.

- List the key features of Marxist theory as they relate to criminological theories.

- Evaluate the research and criticisms of labeling theory.

- Describe the key contributors of alternative perspectives such as peacemaking criminology, the restorative justice perspective, and left realism.

- Discuss the policy implications of labeling and conflict theories of crime.

CASE STUDY

THE FLINT, MICHIGAN, WATER CRISIS

To save money, in April 2014, the state of Michigan decided to switch Flint's water supply from the treated Detroit Water and Sewerage Department water to the Flint River. The Detroit water supply was essentially from Lake Huron and the Detroit River. However, the problem with the switch to water from the Flint River was that officials had failed to employ corrosion inhibitors. The switch was implemented during a time when the city of Flint was in a state of emergency. It was intended to be temporary; a new state-run supply line to Lake Huron was to be connected in approximately two years.

Soon, the residents of Flint began to notice that the water started to look, smell, and taste funny. Some thought it was sewage, but it was actually iron. What made things worse was that residents did not realize that a large number of water lines to their homes were made of lead. Since the water was not property treated, lead started to leach into the water supply. This continued for almost two years. Dr. Mona Hanna-Attisha, a pediatrician in Flint's Hurley Medical Center, was noticing more and more frantic parents concerned over their children's rashes and hair loss. By comparing blood lead levels in toddlers, Dr. Hanna-Attisha found that these levels had doubled, in some instances tripled, after switching the water supply to the Flint River. When she released her findings, initially officials denounced her work, accusing her of causing hysteria. A week later, they admitted her findings were correct.

In October 2015, the city switched back to using Detroit water, but this did not address the damage that was done to the lead pipes. The state then responded by distributing filters and bottled water. However, there are potential long-term health consequences. Dr. Hanna-Attisha stated that lead is "a well-known, potent neurotoxin. There's tons of evidence on what lead does to a child, and it is one of the most damning things that

you can do to a population. It drops your IQ, it affects your behaviour, it's been linked to criminality, it has multigenerational impacts. There is no safe level of lead in a child."[1]

In April 2016, criminal charges were filed against three officials:

- Mike Glasgow, Flint's Laboratory and Water Quality Supervisor
- Mike Prysby, a Michigan Department of Environmental Quality (DEQ) official
- Stephen Busch, Lansing district coordinator for the DEQ's Office of Drinking Water and Municipal Assistance

The various charges against these officials include misconduct in office; conspiracy—tampering with evidence; treatment violation—Michigan Safe Drinking Water Act; and willful neglect of duty.[2]

For over 30 years, Flint has been steadily declining given that the automotive industry was the foundation of that city. As a result, it has declined in population and employment while experiencing increases in poverty and violent crime.[3] Do you think this could have happened in a more affluent area? As one resident stated, "you can't treat cities the way you treat some corporation that you might just sort of sell off."

THINK ABOUT IT:

1. Do you think social class could explain how this situation was handled?

2. Do you think this could have happened in a more affluent area?

3. What would be some suggested policies/programs that could be developed that would prevent this from happening again in Flint or any other city?

> THERE'S TONS OF EVIDENCE ON WHAT LEAD DOES TO A CHILD, AND IT IS ONE OF THE MOST DAMNING THINGS THAT YOU CAN DO TO A POPULATION. IT DROPS YOUR IQ, IT AFFECTS YOUR BEHAVIOUR, IT'S BEEN LINKED TO CRIMINALITY, IT HAS MULTIGENERATIONAL IMPACTS. THERE IS NO SAFE LEVEL OF LEAD IN A CHILD.

behavior. Rather, this perspective focuses on such questions as, Who applies the deviant label to whom? Who establishes and enforces the rules?[9] Specifically, these scholars argued that it is important to understand how criminal, or deviant, behavior is defined or labeled. Furthermore, these scholars were interested in how society reacts to this labeled behavior.

Comparing water from the Flint River and the Detroit River. Which would you rather drink?

FOUNDATION OF LABELING THEORY

Labeling theory was influenced by symbolic interactionism, especially from the works of Charles Horton Cooley, William I. Thomas, George Herbert Mead, and Erving Goffman. Symbolic interactionism focuses on how an individual's personality and thought processes evolve through social interactions such as symbolic language and gestures. Cooley argued that an individual gains a sense of his or her social self through primary groups or significant others.[10] Thus, if a child learns how to spell a word correctly and a teacher tells her that she did an excellent job, that child will feel a sense of pride and pleasure. If, however, the child misbehaves in the classroom and the teacher reprimands her, she may feel a sense of shame and embarrassment. Cooley identified this process of obtaining one's self-image through the "eyes of others" as the *looking-glass self*. This also illustrates the influence of *primary groups*. Cooley noted that primary groups are those characterized by intimate and personal interactions.[11] Some of the most important primary groups are the neighborhood and play groups, and especially the family.[12]

While Cooley essentially focused on the process of self-formation during childhood, Thomas was concerned with the later years, specifically when the adult self is redefined.[13] Further, Thomas maintained that to understand human behavior, one needs to understand the "total situation," which consists of objective factors as well as an individual's subjective definitions of those factors.[14] One needs to understand the "definition of the situation."[15]

Mead identified two types of social interaction—nonsymbolic interaction and symbolic interaction. Nonsymbolic interaction occurs when individuals respond to gestures or actions. For instance, two dogs may go through a series of gestures (e.g., snarling, growling, baring teeth). The dogs are responding to each other's gestures. These responses are dictated by preexisting tendencies to respond in certain ways. These dogs are *not* responding to the intention of the gestures; therefore, these animal interactions are devoid of any conscious or deliberate meaning.[16] Symbolic interaction occurs when individuals interpret each other's gestures and act based on the meaning of those gestures. Mead was primarily interested in symbolic interaction. Specifically, Mead was concerned with the "*interpretation,* or ascertaining the meaning of the actions or remarks of the other person, and *definition,* or conveying indications to another person as to how he is to act [italics in original]."[17] Symbolic interactionism emphasizes how human behavior and social relationships are developed through social interactions. This perspective focuses on how an individual's behavior is intertwined with another's.

labeling theory:
theoretical perspective that assumes that criminal behavior increases because certain individuals are caught and labeled as offenders; their offending increases because they have been stigmatized.

symbolic interactionism:
proposes that many social interactions involve symbolism, which occurs when individuals interpret each other's words or gestures and act based on the meaning of those gestures.

An essential component of symbolic interactionism is that individuals who are stigmatized as being deviant are predisposed to take on a deviant self-identity.[18] Goffman defined stigma as an "attribute that is deeply discrediting" and that diminishes the individual "from a whole and usual person to a tainted, discounted one."[19] He maintained that stigmatized individuals differ from "normals" in terms of how society reacts to them. Subsequently, society attributes a wide range of deficiencies based on the original perceived flaw. In the next section, we further explore how symbolic interactionism influenced labeling theory.

Do you think some people would "label" this individual? What types of "labels" would some people apply to this individual?

Frank Tannenbaum: The Dramatization of Evil

Many scholars identify the origins of the labeling perspective in Frank Tannenbaum's 1938 publication, *Crime and the Community*. Drawing on the school of symbolic interactionism, Tannenbaum focused on the process that occurs after an individual has been caught and designated as violating the law. He maintained that there is a gradual shift from the definition of the specific act as evil to the definition of the individual as evil.[20]

The "community's point of view," or the social reaction to illegal behavior, is designated the **dramatization of evil**. According to Tannenbaum, the process of making the criminal involves tagging, defining, and identifying the individual as such, resulting with that person becoming the very thing he or she is described as being.[21] Tannenbaum contends that the first dramatization of evil has a greater influence on "making the criminal" than any other experience.

Along with the dramatization of evil, Tannenbaum argued that acts are not inherently good or bad; rather, there are differing degrees of good and bad. The social reactions also influence how those behaviors will be labeled. Furthermore, these behaviors are placed within a context that includes such factors as a person's social status and the social setting. For instance, society might react differently to an attorney drinking a glass of wine at dinner than to a homeless person drinking a bottle of wine on a street corner.

Edwin M. Lemert: Primary and Secondary Deviance

In his 1951 book, *Social Pathology*, Edwin Lemert made a significant contribution to the labeling perspective by distinguishing between primary deviance and secondary deviance. **Primary deviance** is behavior that is situational or occasional. A person uses excuses or rationalizations to justify his or her deviant behavior. These behaviors continue to be considered "primary deviations or symptomatic and situational as long as they are rationalized or otherwise dealt with as functions of a socially acceptable role."[22] Lemert argued that this process occurs either through *normalization* (i.e., a problem of everyday life) or through minimal controls that do not seriously hinder individuals' getting along with each other.[23] Thus, a person engaging in primary deviant behavior perceives the behavior as bad; this individual, however, does not perceive himself or herself as a bad person.

Secondary deviance is deviant behavior, or social roles based upon it, which becomes a means of defense, attack, or adaptation to the overt and covert

dramatization of evil: a concept proposed by Tannenbaum in relation to labeling theory; states that when relatively minor laws are broken, the community tends to dramatize it.

primary deviance: in labeling theory, the type of minor, infrequent offending people commit before they are caught and labeled as offenders.

problems created by the societal reaction to primary deviation. In effect, the original "causes" of the deviation recede and give way to the central importance of the disapproving, degradational, and isolating reactions of society.[24]

A person engaging in secondary deviant behavior uses this behavior as a way to defend against, or adjust to, the various problems related to the social reactions to his or her primary deviance.

The sequence of interaction that results in secondary deviation essentially consists of the following: (1) primary deviation; (2) social penalties; (3) further primary deviation; (4) stronger penalties and rejections; (5) further deviation, possibly with hostilities and resentment toward those imposing the penalties; (6) crisis reaching the tolerance quotient, expressed in formal action by the community stigmatizing the deviant; (7) strengthening of the deviant conduct as a reaction to the stigmatizing and penalties; and (8) ultimate acceptance of the deviant social status and efforts at adjusting to the associated role.[25] (See Figure 11.1 for an example of the process of secondary deviation.) A key aspect of secondary deviance is not only society's reaction to the individual's behavior but also the individual's response to that reaction. According to this perspective, when the societal reaction and label are integrated into an individual's self-image, they will likely lead to the amplification of deviance.

Howard S. Becker: The Dimensions of Deviance

In 1963, another major contribution to the labeling perspective was Howard S. Becker's *Outsiders: Studies in the Sociology of Deviance*. Becker argued that the term *outsiders* refers to those individuals considered by others to be deviant; these labeled individuals are deemed to be "outside" the circle of the "normal" members of the group.[26] Furthermore, deviance is created by society. Social groups create deviance by making the rules, whose infraction is considered deviance, and by applying those rules to particular people and labeling them as outsiders.[27] A key aspect to labeling deviance is realizing that certain groups have the power to impose rules, and subsequently labels, on other groups. This power differential results in groups with this "authority" to designate other individuals as deviants and outsiders.

Becker argued that deviance has two dimensions. One dimension is that only those behaviors considered deviant by others are truly deviant. The second dimension is whether a behavior or an act conforms to a certain rule. With this conceptual framework, Becker developed a typology of deviant behavior (see Table 11.1). Two of the four types of behavior are both correctly perceived by society. A person engaging in conforming behavior obeys the rules, and society perceives that person as obeying the rules. At the other extreme, the **pure deviant** is an individual who disobeys the rules and is perceived by society as doing so.

secondary deviance: in labeling theory, the more serious, frequent offending people commit after they have been caught and labeled as offenders.

pure deviant: based on Becker's typology, an individual who disobeys the rules and is perceived as doing so.

falsely accused: based on Becker's typology, when an individual has been identified as disobeying the rules but did not violate the rules.

secret deviant: based on Becker's typology, an individual who violates the rules of society but elicits no reaction from society.

TABLE 11.1 Typology of Deviant Behavior

	OBEDIENT BEHAVIOR	RULE-BREAKING BEHAVIOR
Perceived as deviant	Falsely accused	Pure deviant
Not perceived as deviant	Conforming	Secret deviant

Source: Becker, H. S. (1963). *Outsiders: Studies in the sociology of deviance.* New York: Free Press, p. 20.

FIGURE **11.1**

An Example of the Process of Secondary Deviation

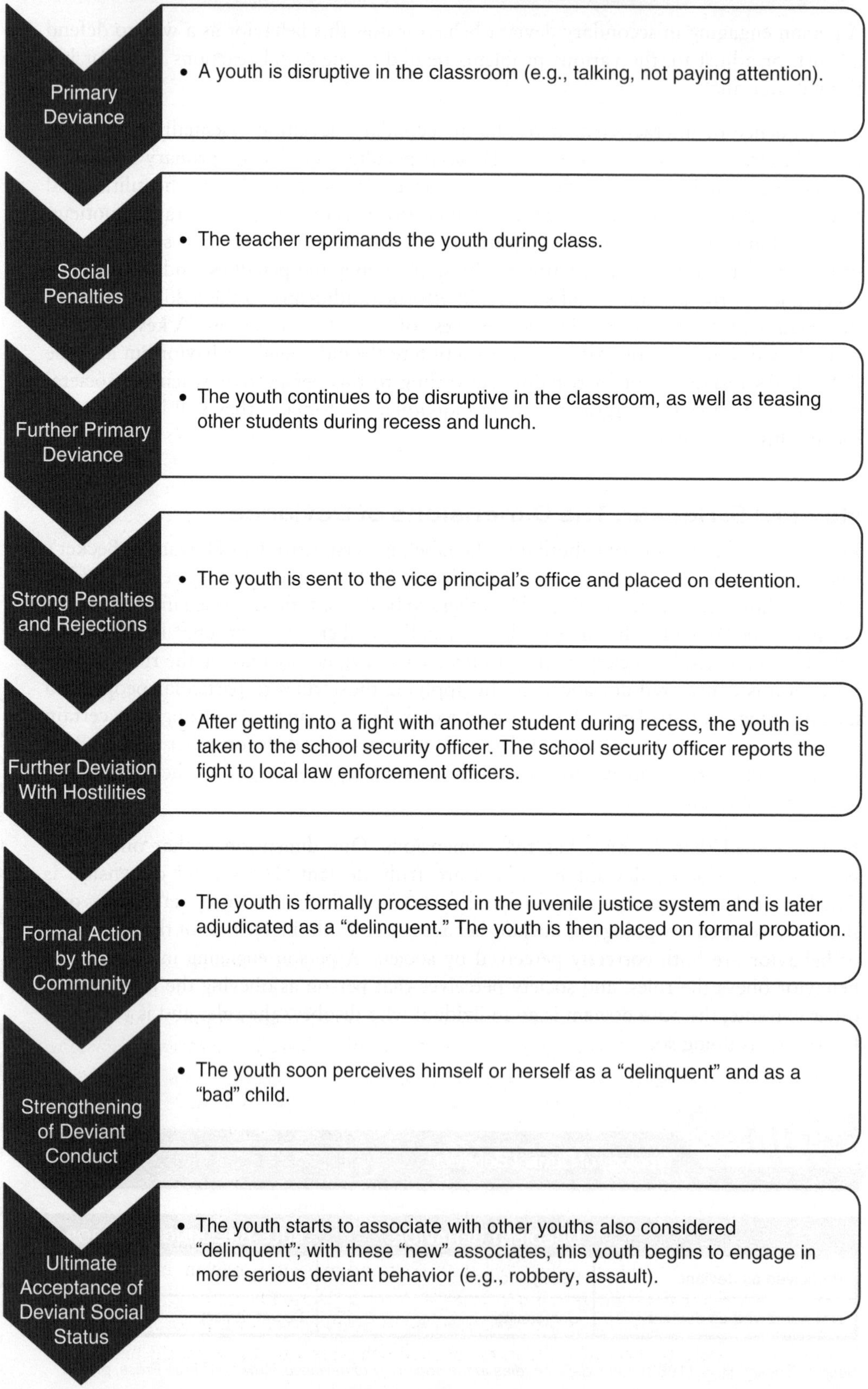

| Primary Deviance | • A youth is disruptive in the classroom (e.g., talking, not paying attention). |

| Social Penalties | • The teacher reprimands the youth during class. |

| Further Primary Deviance | • The youth continues to be disruptive in the classroom, as well as teasing other students during recess and lunch. |

| Strong Penalties and Rejections | • The youth is sent to the vice principal's office and placed on detention. |

| Further Deviation With Hostilities | • After getting into a fight with another student during recess, the youth is taken to the school security officer. The school security officer reports the fight to local law enforcement officers. |

| Formal Action by the Community | • The youth is formally processed in the juvenile justice system and is later adjudicated as a "delinquent." The youth is then placed on formal probation. |

| Strengthening of Deviant Conduct | • The youth soon perceives himself or herself as a "delinquent" and as a "bad" child. |

| Ultimate Acceptance of Deviant Social Status | • The youth starts to associate with other youths also considered "delinquent"; with these "new" associates, this youth begins to engage in more serious deviant behavior (e.g., robbery, assault). |

Source: Adapted from Lemert, E. M. (1951). *Social pathology: A systematic approach to the theory of sociopathic behavior.* New York, NY: McGraw-Hill, p. 77.

The remaining two types of behavior are more problematic. First, the falsely accused is an individual who has been identified as disobeying the rules when he or she did not violate the rules. For instance, a juvenile occasionally associates with a group of delinquents and is arrested with these youths one night on suspicion of burglary. This juvenile will show up in the official statistics as a delinquent, along with other juveniles who actually engaged in delinquent behavior. Researchers, using official data, will attempt to develop an understanding of delinquency, including this youth who was falsely accused. Second, the secret deviant is an individual who violates the rules of society, without society reacting to this behavior. These individuals are able to avoid detection; thus, they are not labeled as deviant. Self-report studies reveal that a large number of individuals fall into this group.[28]

Edwin M. Schur: Defining Deviance

In the late 1960s, Edwin M. Schur's work also made a significant contribution to the labeling perspective.[29] He addressed some of the criticisms and misunderstandings of the labeling perspective. First, he noted that some scholars maintained that this perspective failed to distinguish adequately between deviance and nondeviance. The labeling perspective, however, attempts to explain the *varieties of the deviant experience* rather than just the "mere counting and classifying of deviating acts and individuals."[30] Second, Schur mentioned that various criticisms argued that the labeling perspective was too narrow—for instance, that the focus was on the ascribed aspects of the deviant status rather than on the deviant motivation. Third, Schur cited critics who maintained that this perspective failed to explain some forms of deviance.

One reason for this confusion and controversy was the failure of labeling theorists to provide a concise definition of deviance that can be used when conducting research. He provided the following working definition:

> Human behavior is deviant *to the extent that* it comes to be viewed as involving a *personally discreditable* departure from a group's normative expectations, *and it elicits* interpersonal or collective reactions that serve to "isolate," "treat," "correct," or "punish" *individuals* engaged in such behavior [italics in original].[31]

Schur argued that the terms *deviant* and *delinquent* are what sociologists designate as an ascribed status and not an achieved status. Specifically, an ascribed status is a social position an individual occupies not only due to the consequence of that individual's actions but also as a result of the actions of others.[32]

Schur identified key factors in the labeling process, including stereotyping, retrospective interpretation, and negotiation. Stereotyping is usually associated with racial prejudice and discrimination. Citing the work of Piliavin and Briar,[33] Schur argued that stereotyping can also occur in police encounters with juveniles. During the various decision-making stages of these encounters (e.g., bringing the juvenile into the station, type of disposition to invoke), police react to various cues from the juvenile. These cues include the youth's group affiliations, age, race, grooming, dress, and demeanor.[34] The second key factor, retrospective interpretation, was defined as the process by which an individual is identified as a deviant and thereafter viewed in a "new light."[35] Through this process, an individual is given a new personal identity. The most dramatic way of initiating this process is through a public status-degradation ceremony, such as a criminal trial.[36] Schur contended that the individual's character, both past and present, is reexamined. In terms of youths adjudicated as delinquent, retrospective interpretation is applied through such terms as *delinquency proneness* and *predelinquent*. Studies focus on these adjudicated delinquents to identify certain "indicators" of such behavior after these youths have been labeled delinquent.

stereotyping: in labeling theory, usually associated with racial prejudice and discrimination.

retrospective interpretation: in labeling theory, the process by which an individual is identified as a deviant and thereafter viewed in a "new light."

status-degradation ceremony: the most dramatic way to initiate the process of giving an individual a new identity, such as a criminal trial.

The last key factor, **negotiation**, is more noticeable in cases involving adults rather than juveniles, usually in instances that use plea bargaining in criminal trials. This negotiation process, however, is still present when working with juveniles. For instance, alleged delinquents may try to influence their disposition by exploiting the relationship between the image they present and the probable outcome of their case. Citing Aaron Cicourel's work on juveniles,[37] Schur noted that a juvenile who is "appealing and attractive," wants to be liked, and relates in a friendly manner to those around him or her is a prime candidate for clinical interpretations rather than criminal imputations.[38]

Basic Assumptions of Labeling Theory

Referring to works such as those by Tannenbaum, Lemert, and Becker, Clarence Schrag identified the following basic assumptions of labeling theory:

1. *No act is intrinsically criminal.* The law designates an act as a crime; thus, crimes are defined by politically influential and organized groups.

2. *Criminal definitions are enforced in the interest of the powerful.* While the law incorporates detailed guidelines, as well as definitions and procedures, the implementation of the law can vary by decisions of local officials and other social leaders.

3. *A person does not become a criminal by violating the law.* Rather, a person becomes a criminal by authorities designating him or her as such.

4. *The practice of dichotomizing individuals into criminal and noncriminal groups is contrary to common sense and research.* Self-report and other unofficial sources reveal that most acts committed by criminals conform with the law, while some actions of "conformists" violate the law. Thus, the criminal label designates an individual's legal status and not his or her behavior.

5. *Only a few persons are caught in violating the law even though many individuals may be equally guilty.* The act of "getting caught" begins the labeling process. When an individual is labeled as a criminal, he or she may become one of a few that many can blame for the ills of society (i.e., a scapegoat).

6. *While the sanctions used in law enforcement are directed against the individual and not just the criminal act, the penalties for such an act vary according to the characteristics of the offender.* Therefore, the decisions of many authorities appear to reflect the perspective, "Once a criminal, always a criminal, but some are more criminal than others."

7. *Criminal sanctions also vary according to other characteristics of the offender.* Further, these sanctions tend to be more severe among males, the young, the unemployed or underemployed, the poorly educated, members of the lower classes, members of minority groups, transients, and residents of deteriorated urban areas.

8. *Criminal justice is founded on a stereotyped conception of the criminal as a pariah—a willful wrongdoer who is morally bad and deserving of the community's condemnation.* The criminal justice system is based on a free-will perspective that allows for the condemnation and rejection of the identified offender.

9. *Confronted by public condemnation and the label of an evil man, it may be difficult for an offender to maintain a favorable image of himself.* Thus, labeling is a process that produces, eventually, identification with a deviant image and subculture and, subsequently, the "rejection of the rejectors."[39]

negotiation: one of the key factors identified by Schur (i.e., labeling process); more noticeable in cases involving adults rather than juveniles (e.g., plea bargaining).

Although some might add to, or modify, these assumptions, the above represent a comprehensive analysis of labeling theory as it is generally discussed and used in criminological theory, research, and policy.[40]

EVALUATING LABELING THEORY

Research on Labeling Theory

Researchers from various disciplines have conducted empirical studies of labeling theory using different types of research methods. In the field of criminal justice, a central focus of research for a number of studies was the process of deviance amplification due to labeling an individual as a criminal or a delinquent. Examples of this line of research include examining the relationship between the severity of a juvenile court disposition and future offending,[41] parental labeling and delinquency,[42] perceived teacher disapproval and subsequent delinquency,[43] racial differences between negative labeling and criminal behavior,[44] labeling youth as delinquent or mentally ill based on their dress or taste in music (e.g., punk, heavy metal) and future criminal behavior,[45] the effects of processing status offenders and subsequent delinquent behavior,[46] and the influence of formal police intervention and increase in criminal involvement.[47]

As mentioned previously, research from various disciplines has used labeling theory to study different types of phenomena. Using a field experimental method, Richard Schwartz and Jerome Skolnick examined the effect of an employee's criminal court record on the reactions of potential employers.[49] The researchers constructed four employment folders that differed only with respect to the applicant's reported record of criminal court involvement. The results revealed that only one employer demonstrated an interest in the convicted folder, three in the tried-but-acquitted folder, six in the tried-but-acquitted folder (including a letter from the judge), and nine in the no-criminal-record folder. The researchers concluded that "the individual accused but acquitted has almost as much trouble finding even an unskilled job as the one who was not only accused of the same offense, but also convicted."[50]

Rosenhan examined how the label of "insanity" can influence the behavior and perceptions of hospital staff.[51] Eight individuals from various backgrounds, but deemed "sane," applied for admission to different mental hospitals. Upon their arrival at the hospitals, each individual pretended to hear voices, a symptom of schizophrenia. When questioned about their backgrounds and significant life events, they all gave truthful and accurate responses. All but one individual was labeled schizophrenic. After their admission, these individuals were responsible for demonstrating their sanity. The various hospital staff treated them as schizophrenic patients. Subsequently, these individuals were discharged from the hospital, with a diagnosis of schizophrenia "in remission."

Critiques of Labeling Theory

There have been various critiques of labeling theory, including the following:

1. The various propositions to be tested are not adequately specified. This lack of specificity does not allow researchers to empirically examine the relationship

---

LEARNING CHECK 11.1

1. According to Tannenbaum, the social reaction to illegal behavior is designated as the _____.

2. A person engaging in _____ behavior perceives the behavior as bad; this individual, however, does not perceive himself or herself as a bad person.

3. Becker maintained that the _____ is when an individual has been identified as disobeying the rules but did not violate the rules.

4. When an individual is given a new personal identity, the most dramatic way of initiating this process is through a public _____, such as a criminal trial.

Answers located at www.edge.sagepub.com/schram2e

WHY DO THEY DO IT?

BRIAN BANKS AND WANETTA GIBSON

An emotional Brian Banks upon hearing that his conviction was dismissed.

In the summer of 2002, Brian Banks was a senior at Long Beach Poly High; Wanetta Gibson was a sophomore. Brian Banks, a top college football prospect, was being heavily recruited by the University of South Carolina, University of California, Los Angeles, and other high-profile college football programs. While attending summer school, Banks left his classroom to make a phone call. He ran into Gibson. Banks stated that "they fooled around," but it was consensual. Subsequently, Gibson charged that Banks sexually assaulted her.

Rather than facing the possibility of a 41-years-to-life prison sentence, Banks pled no contest to one count of forcible rape. He spent five years in prison. Upon his release, he was required to register as a sex offender and wear an electronic monitoring bracelet. During this time, Gibson and her family sued the Long Beach schools. They settled the case for $1.5 million.

Around 2011, Gibson reached out to Banks on Facebook. Banks responded by asking if Gibson would meet with him and a private investigator. She agreed to the meeting. During the meeting, Gibson was secretly recorded, stating that she had lied and she was not raped. This triggered a

series of events. In May 2012, Brian Banks's conviction was dismissed.[48] Wanetta Gibson has been ordered to pay the $1.5 million plus an additional $1.1 million in fees. In January 2015, Brian Banks was working for the National Football League in New York City.

THINK ABOUT IT

In this example, the question "Why do they do it?" refers to those people who may have initially labeled Brian Banks.

1. What did Brian Banks experience being labeled a convicted sex offender? Subsequently, what may some now label Wanetta Gibson?

2. Did age, gender, and race play a part in establishing patterns of differential criminal justice decision-making?

between significant variables. Charles Tittle notes that advocates of labeling theory argue "that the particular strength of labeling theory lies in its resistance to formalization and in its vagueness and ambiguity, since such features alert us to important aspects of social life which are themselves relativistic and elusive."[52]

2. Due to the lack of satisfactory data and empirical research, evaluating the adequacy of labeling theory has been difficult. Furthermore, since the theory is vague with respect to its propositions, it is difficult to obtain additional information from research conducted for other purposes.[53] Additional refinement is needed, especially with respect to deviance amplification.[54]

3. Labeling theory focuses on the *reaction* to criminal and/or deviant behavior. It avoids the question of causation; specifically, why do some individuals commit a certain act while others do not?[55]

4. Labeling theory focuses on the "reactors" rather than the "actors." Thus, it views the "actor" or "labellee" as overly passive.[56] John Hagan emphasized that

labeling theory would likely benefit empirically from the recognition of a *reciprocal* relationship in terms of the actor and reactor, stimulus and response, and preexisting differences and "reaction effects."[57]

5. Labeling should be viewed as a perspective rather than a theory. Specifically, it is neither a theory in the strictest sense nor does it focus exclusively on the act of the labeling itself. Rather, it is one approach to studying a general area of human activity.[58] Erich Goode argues that labeling theory is not a theory; in fact, he also maintains that it may not even be a perspective. Instead of examining deviance in general, the theory examines specific features of deviance.[59]

If you saw this woman walking in a store, would you perceive her as a potential shoplifter? Why or why not?

In 1975, Charles Wellford argued that labeling theory had weaknesses as an explanatory model of criminal behavior.[60] Eighteen years later, along with his former student Ruth Triplett, Wellford commented on the future of labeling theory in understanding deviant and criminal behavior. They maintained that the future of labeling theory could be promising, especially in terms of social thought or symbolic interactionism.[61]

Some scholars have been examining more complex versions of labeling theory.[62] For instance, some are interested in *shaming*.[63] David R. Karp maintains that the previous terms associated with labeling theory (e.g., *primary* and *secondary deviance*) have been replaced with other terms, such as *shame*.[64] Specifically, the central issue now is the potential of shaming as a tool of formal social control. Shaming involves self-labeling or self-stigmatizing. The concept of shaming is not new, especially when we look at how society has dealt with individuals considered to be deviant and/or criminal (e.g., the stocks, the "scarlet letter").[65]

CONFLICT PERSPECTIVES

Most of the theories presented in the previous chapters are based on what are generally referred to as the consensus perspective of law. In the 18th and 19th centuries, consensus perspectives of law were identified as "social contract theories." These theories stressed that law serves a necessary social function (i.e., functionalism). A major proponent of this perspective, Thomas Hobbes, argued that without either law or the state, individuals would pursue their self-interests without considering how these pursuits could affect others. To avoid such a lawless condition, individuals enter into an agreement, or consensus, to sacrifice their self-interests in an effort to form a society for the common good of all people.[70] Criminologists from this consensus perspective maintain that (1) law reflects the need for social order, (2) law is a product of value consensus, (3) law is an impartial system that protects public rather than private interests, and (4) where differences between groups exist, law is the neutral mechanism that helps individuals resolve their conflicts.[71]

Around the 1950s, conflict theory began to challenge the assumptions associated with the consensus and functional models of criminology.[72] There are various conflict theoretical perspectives. They all share a critical position concerning the existing social order; they differ, however, as to their conceptualization of the nature of social order.[73] Generally, there are two forms of conflict theory: conservative (pluralist) and critical-radical. The primary focus of conservative (pluralist) conflict theories is power and the use of that power; this theoretical framework views society as consisting of diverse interest groups competing for power.[74] George Vold, Austin Turk, and Richard Quinney have made major contributions to the conservative (pluralist) conflict theoretical perspective. The other form of conflict theory, critical-radical, can be traced back to the writings of Karl Marx; this theoretical framework views contemporary society as being dominated by a unified,

Applying Theory to Crime: LARCENY-THEFT

Hammurabi, the King of Babylon in 1780 B.C., was the earliest known ruler to publicly provide the people with a body of laws. His "Code of Laws" includes various references to the crime of theft:

- If anyone steals the property of a temple or of the court, he shall be put to death, and also the one who receives the stolen thing from him shall be put to death.

- If anyone steals cattle or sheep, or an ass, or a pig or a goat, if it belonged to a god or to the court, the thief shall pay thirtyfold therefor; if they belonged to a freed man of the king he shall pay tenfold; if the thief has nothing with which to pay he shall be put to death.

- If anyone takes a male or female slave of the court, or a male or female slave of a freed man, outside the city gates, he shall be put to death.[66]

According to the Federal Bureau of Investigation (FBI) Uniform Crime Reports (UCR), larceny-theft is the "unlawful taking, carrying, leading, or riding away of property from the possession or constructive posses-sion of another." Examples of larceny-theft include "bicycles, motor vehicle parts and accessories, shoplifting, pocket-picking, or the stealing of any property or article that is not taken by force and violence or by fraud." Thus, such crimes as embezzlement, con-fidence games, forgery, and check fraud are not counted as theft.[67] Based on the 2014 report, the FBI summarized the following key find-ings concerning larceny-theft:

- There were an estimated 5,858,496 larceny-thefts nationwide.

- When comparing the 2013 and 2014 larceny-theft

rates, there was a drop of 2.7%.

- Larceny-thefts accounted for an estimated 70.8% of property crimes.

- The average value of prop-erty taken during larceny-thefts was $941 per offense. When the average value was applied to the esti-mated number of larceny-thefts, the loss to victims was an estimated $5.5 bil-lion. The largest portion of reported larcenies (22.9%) was thefts from motor vehi-cles (except accessories).[68]

Table 11.2 provides a summary of larceny-theft by type from the FBI's *Crime in the United States, 2014*.

The National Crime Victimization Survey (NCVS) collects data to provide additional insight into what is referred to as the dark figure of crime (e.g., crimes unreported to law enforcement). In reference to prop-erty crimes, such as larceny-theft, the NCVS does not include those affecting businesses or other com-mercial establishments; rather, the NCVS collects data on households. Some key summary findings, based on 2014 data, include the following:

- In 2014, 10.4 million house-holds experienced at least one or more property vic-timizations (this includes lar-ceny-theft as well as other types of property crimes).

- In 2014, 46.0% of prop-erty crimes were reported to police.

- About 118.1 per 1,000 households experienced property thefts in 2014.[69]

In an effort to further illustrate key aspects of labeling theory, we apply this perspective to the crime of larceny-theft. Jeff was a 15-year-old boy who was getting into some

"minor" trouble at home (e.g., not cleaning his room, talking back to his mother). At one point, Jeff's mother decided to punish him by taking away his allowance. Jeff was quite upset about this, because he was planning to buy an iPhone with his allowance. He decided to get this iPhone by shoplifting from a nearby discount store; however, Jeff got caught stealing. The police were called, and Jeff was formally processed in the juvenile justice system and adjudicated as a delin-quent. Afterward, many of Jeff's teachers, other kids at school, and neighbors knew he was caught stealing and processed through the juvenile justice system.

Initially, Jeff thought that he had made a "stupid" decision to steal the iPhone. He never considered himself a thief; he stole the iPhone in large part because he was angry that his mother took his allowance. However, after Jeff realized that many people around him, such as teachers, schoolmates, and neighbors, considered him a thief, he started to identify himself as a thief as well. So Jeff decided that if people were going to consider him a thief, he might as well start steal-ing more property. One evening, a neighbor left her garage door open. Jeff snuck in the garage and stole a bicycle. Identify some key fea-tures of labeling theory (e.g., self-fulfilling prophecy, secondary deviance, offense escalation) in this scenario.

THINK ABOUT IT:

1. What was the pivotal point when Jeff decided to engage in more criminal behavior?

2. How does labeling theory des-ignate this "pivotal point?"

3. What policies/programs should be implemented to address criminal/delinquent behavior that results from being labeled?

TABLE 11.2	Larceny-Theft by Type in 2014		
TYPE	NUMBER OF OFFENSES	PERCENTAGE DISTRIBUTION	AVERAGE VALUE
Pocket-picking	27,465	0.5%	$548
Purse-snatching	20,660	0.4%	$508
Shoplifting	1,097,444	21.5%	$204
From motor vehicles (except accessories)	1,172,876	22.9%	$835
Motor vehicle accessories	359,490	7.0%	$553
Bicycles	184,575	3.6%	$418
From buildings	626,572	12.3%	$1,333
From coin-operated machines	11,728	0.2%	$480
All others	1,610,734	31.5%	$1,530

Source: Federal Bureau of Investigation. (2015). *Crime in the United States, 2014.* Washington, D.C: U.S. Department of Justice.

capitalist ruling class.[75] William Chambliss and Robert Seidman, as well as Mark Colvin and John Pauly, have incorporated Marxist themes to understand crime and criminals.

THE CONSERVATIVE (PLURALIST) CONFLICT PERSPECTIVES

George Vold: Group Conflict Theory

In his 1958 book *Theoretical Criminology*,[76] George Vold introduced group conflict theory. Prior to introducing this theory, Vold provided an interesting evaluation of various theoretical perspectives.[77] He noted that, historically, there have been two basic types of criminological theories: *spiritualism* and *naturalism*. *Spiritual* explanations are influenced by "otherworld" powers. However, these explanations "cannot be considered scientific, even if some thoughtful and intelligent people believe that they represent the best explanation of crime." *Natural* explanations are more systematic and scientific. Vold identified three types of naturalistic theories: (1) those that focus on the individual, (2) those that emphasize group and intergroup relations, and (3) those that are "eclectical," including various factors that might explain criminal behavior.[78] In the preface of his book, Vold stated,

> No special plea is made for any particular theoretical position examined, though it should be clear that there is some preference for approaches that recognize and make more explicit the concept of crime as a by-product of the struggle for power in the group structure of society.[79]

group conflict theory: Vold argued that part of human nature is that people's lives are a part, and a product, of their group associations; groups come into conflict with one another due to conflicting and competitive interests.

Comparative Criminology: *LARCENY-THEFT*

Ranking Countries by Rate of Larceny-Theft

The FBI considers larceny a major Index crime in the United States. However, according to Van Dijk,[81] there is likely no suitable, or comparable, equivalent to larceny in the various world statistics. The closest equivalent presented is for pickpocketing, which is somewhat similar in that there is no threat of violence, which would then make the crime robbery.

The best and most recent data are drawn from the International Crime Survey (years 1996–2005), which is basically broken into different continental regions. As Figure 11.2 shows, Africa leads the world in pickpocketing rates, with Asia and Latin America and the Caribbean tying for a close second. Eastern Europe had the fourth highest rate. All these regions were shown to be quite high in terms of pickpocketing. This should not come as much of a surprise, given that these same regions (or countries within these regions) tend to have the highest scores regarding robbery and/or burglary.

It makes sense that countries or regions that have high rates on one type of property crime (such as burglary) will also have high rates for other forms of property crime, such as pickpocketing and larceny.

CRITICAL THINKING QUESTIONS:

1. Why do you think that countries or regions that have high rates of one type of property crime would also have high rates for other types of property crimes?

2. What other types of information would you like to consider crimes, or include, in understanding the link between countries or regions that have high rates of one type of property crime would also have high rates for other types of property (e.g., medium income, unemployment)?

Sign warning tourists of pickpockets

© iStockphoto.com/Antonio Ribeiro.

FIGURE **11.2**

Percentages of the Public in Urban Areas Victimized by Pickpocketing During the Past 12 Months, by World Region

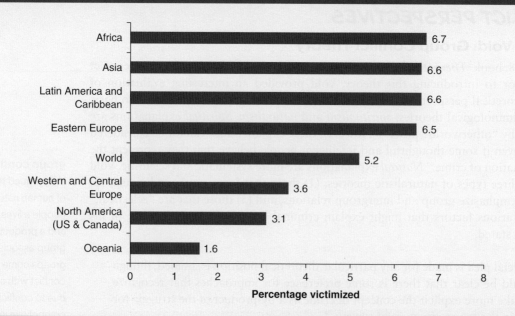

Region	Percentage victimized
Africa	6.7
Asia	6.6
Latin America and Caribbean	6.6
Eastern Europe	6.5
World	5.2
Western and Central Europe	3.6
North America (US & Canada)	3.1
Oceania	1.6

Percentage victimized

Thus, he focused on the issue of conflicting group interests. Vold argued that part of human nature is that people's lives are a part of, and a product of, their group associations. Individuals are fundamentally group-involved beings. These groups usually evolve out of situations in which individuals have common interests and common needs that can be further promoted through some type of collective action. Subsequently, "groups come into conflict with one another as the interests and purposes they serve tend to overlap, encroach on one another, and become competitive."[80]

A key aspect to group conflict theory is recognizing the *social process* view of society as a collection of various groups that are held together in a dynamic equilibrium of opposing group interests and efforts. This social process involves a continuous struggle to maintain, or enhance, the position of one's own group within the context of these other competing groups. Conflict is an essential component to this social process. Thus, "these social interaction processes grind their way through varying kinds of uneasy adjustment to a more or less stable equilibrium of balanced forces, called social order or social organization."[82] Vold stressed that the conflict between these groups to maintain, or enhance, their own interests is especially apparent through the legislative political process.

In reference to crime, Vold maintained that the process of lawmaking, lawbreaking, and law enforcement reflects essential and fundamental conflicts between group interests, as well as the struggles among groups for control of state police power. Subsequently, criminal behavior is the course taken by less powerful groups who could not promote and defend their interests and purposes in the legislative process.[83]

Group conflict theory focuses only on those situations in which criminal behavior is a result of conflicting group interests. Generally, these types of crimes include (1) crimes arising from political protest, (2) crimes resulting from labor disputes, (3) crimes arising from disputes between and within competing unions, and (4) crimes arising from racial and ethnic clashes.[84] Group conflict theory, however, does not explain more individual types of behavior such as rape and robbery.

The importance of Vold's contribution is that it offered another explanation of understanding crime—*critical criminology*. Like many new approaches to explaining crime, Vold's is not as well defined or soundly based as those that followed.[85] These are discussed below.

Austin Turk: The Power to Define Criminal Behavior

In his 1969 book, *Criminality and Legal Order*, Austin Turk stated that "nothing and no one is intrinsically criminal; criminality is a definition applied by individuals with the power to do so, according to illegal and extra-legal, as well as legal criteria."[86] While this appears to reflect the assumptions of labeling theory, Turk argued that one also needs to recognize the milieu that establishes the social categories.[87]

According to Turk, society is characterized by conflict arising among various groups seeking to establish or maintain control over one another. Thus, criminology should focus on differences between the status and role of legal *authorities* and *subjects*.[88] Individuals in society become accustomed to living with the social roles of authorities and subjects in such a manner that these roles are not questioned. While consensus theorists would contend that social order occurs through the internalization of the norms reflected in the law, Turk maintained that social order is based in a consensus–coercion balance preserved by the authorities.

Turk's "theory of criminalization" (i.e., the process of being labeled a criminal) occurs through the interaction between those who enforce the law and those who violate the law. This interaction is influenced by various social factors. One such social factor is the congruence of cultural and social norms.[89] Cultural norms are associated with verbal

Occupy Wall Street protesters on the steps of Federal Hall, across the street from the New York Stock Exchange.

formulations of values (e.g., the law as written); social norms are associated with actual behavior patterns (e.g., the law as enforced). Conflict will occur between authorities and subjects regarding the congruence of the cultural and social norms.

Two additional social factors are the level of organization and the level of sophistication of both the authorities and the subjects. It is assumed that authorities are organized, since organization is essential for establishing and maintaining power. Conflict is more likely when subjects are also organized. Turk defined sophistication as the understanding of patterns in the behavior of others, which is then used in an effort to manipulate them. When either the subjects or authorities are less sophisticated, conflict is more likely to occur. For instance, when authorities are less sophisticated, they may have to use more overt forms of coercion to achieve their goals, as opposed to more subtle approaches.[90]

Another social factor is the power differential between enforcers and violators. Criminalization will most likely occur when the enforcers (e.g., the police, prosecutors, and judges) have a great deal of power compared with the resisters. Finally, realism of moves is another essential social factor. Conflict will most likely occur when either the enforcers or resisters engage in inappropriate or unsuitable behavior. For instance, an unrealistic move would be a motorist, while driving her car alongside a highway patrol officer, lighting up a marijuana cigarette. A realistic move would be when she smokes a marijuana cigarette in the privacy of her home.

In a subsequent article, Turk attempted to develop a model of social deviance and proposed various "working premises."[91] Turk also stressed that his proposed **nonpartisan conflict perspective** differs from a **partisan conflict perspective**. For instance, Richard Quinney (discussed below) argued for the partisan conflict perspective:

> In understanding criminal justice—its theory and practice under capitalism—we provide a theory and a practice that has as its objective changing the world. The importance of criminal justice is that it moves us dialectically to reject the capitalist order and to struggle for a new society. We are engaged in socialist revolution.[92]

Turk stressed the importance of nonpartisan conflict theory. Specifically, he maintained that the ideological position or the political utilities of theories are irrelevant when assessing the validity of knowledge claims.[93] Thus, *truth* should be independent of an individual's political ideology or personal values.

nonpartisan conflict perspective: according to Turk, the ideological position or political utilities of theories are irrelevant when assessing the validity of knowledge claims; truth should be independent of political ideology or personal values.

partisan conflict perspective: according to Quinney, provides a theory and practice with the purpose of changing the world; associated political objective.

Richard Quinney: The Social Reality of Crime

Drawing from Vold's comments as well as from social interaction and labeling theory, Quinney provided a different explanation of criminal behavior. He set forth six propositions that described his social reality of crime. These propositions are as follows:

Proposition 1 (definition of crime): Crime is a definition of human conduct that is created by authorized agents in a politically organized society.

This proposition reflects assumptions of labeling theory. Quinney maintained that crime is created. Further, he argued that this proposition avoids the more commonly used "clinical perspective," which focuses on the quality of the act and assumes some type of individual pathology. Crime is considered a process that culminates in defining persons and behaviors as criminal.[94]

Proposition 2 (formulation of criminal definitions): Criminal definitions describe behaviors that conflict with the interests of the segments of society that have the power to shape political policy.

Quinney stressed that those groups who have the power to represent their interests in public policy are able to regulate the formulation of these criminal definitions. These interests are essentially based on desires, values, and norms. The formulation of criminal definitions is one of the most obvious indications of conflict in society. Specifically, formulating criminal law, such as legislative statutes, administrative rulings, and judicial decisions, allows these powerful segments of society to protect and perpetuate their own interests.[95]

Proposition 3 (application of criminal definitions): Criminal definitions are applied by the segments of society that have the power to shape the enforcement and administration of criminal law.

These interests of the powerful groups cannot be effectively protected by just formulating criminal law; rather, it is also essential that these groups protect their interests by *applying* these criminal definitions. Furthermore, the likelihood that criminal definitions will be applied differs according to the extent to which the behaviors of the powerless groups conflict with the interests of powerful groups. These powerful groups usually do not directly apply the criminal law. Instead, they delegate the enforcement and administration of law to authorized legal agents.[96]

Proposition 4 (development of behavior patterns in relation to criminal definitions): Behavior patterns are structured in segmentally organized society in relation to criminal definitions, and within this context persons engage in actions that have relative probabilities of being defined as criminal.

Individuals in segments of society that are not represented in formulating and applying the criminal definitions are more likely to act in a manner that will be defined as criminal. Individuals in segments of society that are represented in formulating and applying the criminal definitions are less likely to act in a manner that will be defined as criminal. As this process of formulating and applying criminal definitions continues, those individuals identified as criminal begin to perceive themselves as criminal and subsequently learn to play the role. This process results in these individuals engaging in behavior that increases their chances of being defined as criminal.[97]

Proposition 5 (construction of criminal conceptions): Conceptions of crime are constructed and diffused in the segments of society by various means of communication.

Quinney noted that the "real world" is a social construction. Social reality is constructed through various processes that include the type of "knowledge" they develop, the ideas they are exposed to, the manner in which they select information that fits the "world" they are developing, and how they interpret these conceptions. As a result, individuals behave in reference to the social meanings they attach to their experiences. Within this broader context of constructing social reality, the concept of crime is also constructed. These conceptions are constructed by communication. Furthermore, the most fundamental conceptions are those of the powerful segments of society; these conceptions are usually incorporated into the social reality of crime.[98]

Proposition 6 (the social reality of crime): The social reality of crime is constructed by the formulation and application of criminal definitions, the development of behavior patterns related to criminal definitions, and the construction of criminal conceptions.

FIGURE **11.3**   Model of the Social Reality of Crime

Formulation of criminal definitions

Application of criminal definitions

THE SOCIAL REALITY OF CRIME

Development of behavior patterns in relation to criminal definitions

Construction of criminal conceptions

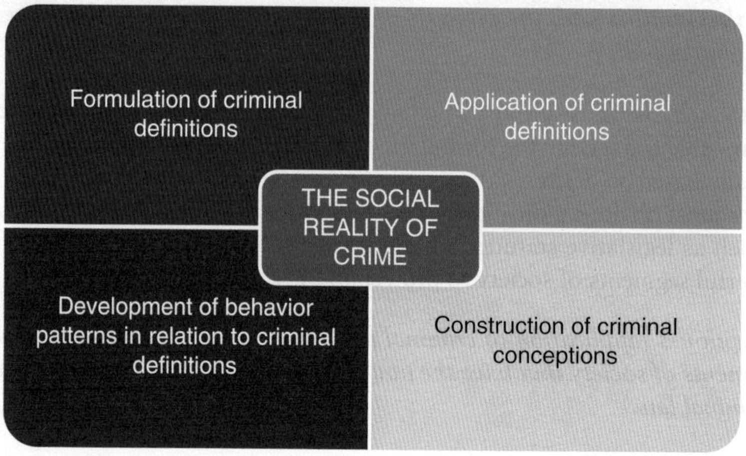

Source: Adapted from Quinney, R. (1970). *The social reality of crime*. Boston: Little, Brown, p. 24.

LEARNING CHECK 11.2

1. Group conflict theory does not explain more individual types of behavior such as _____.

2. According to Turk, social order is not maintained through consensus but, rather, a _____–_____ balance.

3. Unlike Quinney, Turk argued that the political use of a theory is irrelevant when assessing the validity of that theory; this has been designated as the _____ conflict perspective.

Answers located at www.edge.sagepub.com/schram2e

Quinney maintained that the previous five propositions can be accumulated into a composite. The theoretical framework for the social reality of crime describes, as well as explains, factors that increase the probability of crime in society, which subsequently results in the social reality of crime (see Figure 11.3).[99]

THE RADICAL CONFLICT PERSPECTIVES

While it is difficult to summarize the various conservative (pluralist) conflict perspectives, this is even more challenging with the radical conflict perspectives. Criminologists within this perspective have covered a broad range of interests, including Marxism (discussed below) and left realism (discussed at the end of this chapter). Regardless of these various positions, the recent radical conflict perspectives can be traced to the writings of Karl Marx.[100]

Marxist Criminology

Marx wrote very little about crime and criminal behavior. Radical criminologists, however, applied his ideas concerning social class to understanding crime. His philosophy was greatly influenced by the poor economic conditions following the Industrial Revolution. He argued that societies are characterized by class struggles. These class struggles are essentially based on the economic organization of a society.[101]

Marx focused on the means of production. Society is divided into two classes based on the means of production. The superordinate class, or **bourgeoisie**, owns the means of production (e.g., factories); the subordinate class, or **proletariat**, works for those who

bourgeoisie: a class or status Marx assigned to the dominant, oppressing owners of the means of production; believed to create and implement laws that helped retain their dominance over the working class

own the means of production. This division of labor results in class struggles:

> The division of labor offers us the first example . . . that . . . as long as a cleavage exists between the particular and the common interests, . . . man's own deed becomes an alien power opposed to him, which enslaves him instead of being controlled by him. For as soon as labor is distributed, each man has a particular, exclusive sphere of activity, which is forced upon him and from which he cannot escape.[102]

Awareness of common interests among members in a class was designated as *class consciousness*. Alternatively, not being aware of these common interests was identified as *false consciousness*. This false consciousness causes the proletariat to believe that maintaining the capitalist system is in their best interest, rather than in the interest of the bourgeoisie.

Generally, criminologists have incorporated Marxist ideology in three ways. First, they have maintained that the law is a tool of the ruling class. The law represents the interests of the ruling class, essentially perpetuating concepts of capitalism. Second, they argue that all crime, in capitalist countries, is a product of a class struggle. When the accumulation of wealth and property is emphasized, this produces individualism and competition, which can result in conflict between, as well as within, classes. Third, scholars need to address the relationships between the mode of production and understanding crime.[103]

This poster illustrates the social stratification by social class and economic inequality.

William Chambliss and Robert Seidman and the U.S. Criminal Justice System

In their book *Law, Order, and Power,* William Chambliss and Robert Seidman used a Marxist perspective to provide a critical understanding of the American justice system. Compared with the consensus perspective, the conflict perspective provides a very different framework when attempting to explain the criminal justice system. They argued that the myth (i.e., consensus perspective) regarding the operation of the law includes such concepts as, that it represents the values of society as a majority, it operates through a value-neutral government controlled by the people, and it serves the best interests of society.[104]

From a conflict perspective, Chambliss and Seidman stressed that society is made up of various groups that are in conflict. The law is a tool for those in power (i.e., the ruling class), functioning to provide coercive power in conflict.[105] They maintained that the myth of the operation of the law is revealed daily:

> We all know today that blacks and the poor are not treated fairly or equitably by the police. We know that judges have discretion and in fact make policy (as the Supreme Court did in the school desegregation cases). We know that electoral laws have been loaded in the past in favor of the rich, and the average presidential candidate is not a poor man, that one-fifth of the senators of the United States are millionaires.
>
> It is our contention that, far from being primarily a value-neutral framework within which conflict can be peacefully resolved, the power of the state is itself the principal prize in the perpetual conflict that is society.[106]

proletariat: in Marx's conflict theory, the oppressed group of workers exploited by the bourgeoisie; they never profit from their own efforts because the upper class owns and controls the means of production

TABLE 11.3 Functioning of Law Enforcement Agencies

1. The agencies of law enforcement are bureaucratic organizations.
2. An organization and its members tend to substitute for the official goals and norms of the organization's ongoing policies and activities, which will maximize rewards and minimize the strains on the organization.

3. This goal-substitution is made possible by:
  a. the absence of motivation on the part of the role-occupants to resist pressures toward goal-substitution.
  b. the pervasiveness of discretionary choice permitted by the substantive criminal law, and the norms defining the roles of the members of the enforcement agencies.
  c. the absence of effective sanctions for the norms defining the roles in those agencies.

4. Law enforcement agencies depend for resource allocation on political organizations.
5. It will maximize rewards and minimize strains for the organization to process those who are politically weak and powerless and to refrain from processing those who are politically powerful.
6. Therefore it may be expected that law-enforcement agencies will process a disproportionately high number of the politically weak and powerless, while ignoring the violations of those with power.

Source: Chambliss, W., & Seidman, R. (1971). *Law, order, and power.* Reading, MA: Addison-Wesley, p. 269.

They maintained that the relationship between power and the use of the law extends to various institutions such as the legislatures, law enforcement, and especially the appellate courts.

In reference to the appellate courts, judges make rulings that have a lasting effect on future cases. Through their socialization process and privileged social position, these judges "are necessarily biased in favor of ensuring that courts are more available to the wealthy than to the poor, and tend to produce solutions in the interests of the wealthy."[107] Chambliss and Seidman also examined how law enforcement agencies are connected to the powerful and wealthy political structure. The specific points of this assertion are listed in Table 11.3.

ADDITIONAL EXPLANATIONS OF CRIME USING A MARXIST FRAMEWORK

Colvin and Pauly's Integrated Structural-Marxist Theory

In their integrated structural-Marxist theory of delinquency, Mark Colvin and John Pauly maintain that structures of control have various "patterns associated with work, families, school, and peer groups and that those patterns form the mechanisms for the reproduction of the class structure."[108] Parents' socialization and discipline practices with their children are influenced by their workplace experiences. Working-class parents in an unstable workplace setting experience more coercive controls. As a result, these parents tend to enforce an uneven and erratic family control structure that fluctuates between being lax and highly punitive. Working-class parents with steadier, long-term employment tend to enforce a more utilitarian compliance structure in the family. Their children can usually expect predictable consequences for their behavior. Parents who are characterized as "white-collar workers" tend to enforce a more normative family compliance structure, which results in more positive bonds with their children. Such socialization and discipline practices influence delinquent behavior; specifically, there are significant positive associations between more physical and punitive parental discipline practices and delinquent behavior.[109]

Another essential aspect of the reproduction of labor and capitalist production relations is the school experience. Colvin and Pauly contend that

> parents' bonds engendered by workplace control structures are reproduced in the child through family controls; the child's initial ideological orientation toward authority is most likely to be reinforced in school control structures by mechanisms which render the child suitable for eventual placement in a workplace control structure similar to that of the parent. Thus, inequality and the class structure are subtly reproduced.[110]

Some studies have maintained that school control structures correlate with delinquent behavior. For instance, positive bonds with school have been associated with lower levels of delinquency.

In reference to peer associations, Colvin and Pauly suggest that such associations act as a mediator between delinquent behavior and the other control structures of family and school. Youths with similar bonds to family and school will be drawn to one another and subsequently share comparable values and experiences. For instance, juveniles in advanced educational tracks, which reinforce positive bonds, form peer associations that consist of more normative and compliant structures that discourage delinquent behavior. Alternatively, youths in lower educational tracks, characterized by more alienated bonds with family and school, form peer associations that reinforce more negative, delinquent behavior.[111]

The integrated structural-Marxist theory reveals how various theoretical perspectives have been incorporated in an attempt to provide a more comprehensive understanding of criminal behavior. This perspective begins with a "structural-Marxist" perspective, which opens with the premise that social relations are grounded in the process of capitalist material production. This perspective also incorporates aspects of learning theory, strain theory, control theories, and labeling theory.

Herman and Julia Siegel Schwendinger and Adolescent Subcultures

In their book *Adolescent Subcultures and Delinquency*, Herman Schwendinger and Julia Siegel Schwendinger incorporated a Marxist framework to explain adolescent subcultures and delinquency.[112] They based this theoretical explanation on extensive observations and interviews conducted from the 1950s through the 1980s. They argued that previous theoretical explanations of delinquency are inadequate and maintained that it is essential to incorporate structural conditions, especially economic conditions, under which certain peer groups develop and that promote delinquent behavior.

A capitalistic economic system is conducive to developing and maintaining various social class relationships that are primarily reproduced in individuals' places in the labor force. The Schwendingers contend that certain *stratified networks* of adolescent groups negotiate those relationships between the broader social context (e.g., socioeconomic conditions) and patterns of delinquent behavior among peer groups. These adolescent groups may be designated by such labels as "rich kids" and "poor kids." These groups may violate the law more often than other youths; however, both groups represent subcultures that have historically evolved with the rise of capitalism. Their lifestyles may reveal conspicuous consumption or other status accompaniments.[113]

For instance, these *stratified networks* can be enhanced in the public school system. Most adolescents in the United States attend public schools that help youths develop the skills needed to eventually participate in the labor force. Resources, however, are not equally distributed among youths. Some adolescents benefit more than others due to economic and cultural privileges awarded to certain ethnic, racial, or occupational groups.

Steven Spitzer and Problem Populations

Steven Spitzer applied a Marxian perspective to understanding deviance. He argued that one of the most essential functions of the superstructure in capitalist societies is the regulation and management of problem populations. These groups are problems when they question or disturb the following:

1. Capitalist modes of appropriating the product of human labor (e.g., when the poor "steal" from the rich)

2. The social conditions under which capitalist production takes place (e.g., those who refuse or are unable to perform wage labor)

3. Patterns of distribution and consumption in capitalist society (e.g., those who use drugs for escape and transcendence rather than sociability and adjustment)

4. The process of socialization for productive and non-productive roles (e.g., youth who refuse to be schooled or those who deny the validity of "family life")

5. The ideology that supports the functioning of capitalist society (e.g., proponents of alternative forms of social organization)[114]

Problem populations have similar characteristics, but a key factor is that their behavior, personal qualities, and/or position threatens the social relations of production.

Official control of these individuals is determined by how much of a problem they pose for the continuation of a capitalist society. Those individuals who are passive and do not attempt to disrupt society are viewed by the dominant class as *social junk*. Social junk rarely comes to the attention of officials except when attempts are made to regulate or contain these individuals. Examples of what Spitzer called social junk are the aged, handicapped, and mentally ill. Those individuals who question established relationships, especially relations to production and domination, are designated as *social dynamite*. Officials usually deal with social dynamite through the legal system. Examples of individuals considered to be social dynamite are political activists and criminals.[115]

LEARNING CHECK 11.3

1. According to Marx, the _____ owned the means of production; the _____ worked for those who owned the means of production.

2. _____ and _____ maintained that law enforcement agencies are connected to the powerful and wealthy political structure.

3. Colvin and Pauly contend that working-class parents in an unstable workplace environment experience more _____ controls.

Answers located at www.edge.sagepub.com/schram2e

EVALUATING CONFLICT THEORIES

Research on Conflict Theories

Research using a conflict perspective can be categorized into one of two broad approaches: (1) studies examining laws that are formulated in the interests of those in power and (2) studies examining the differential processing of certain individuals in the criminal justice system.[116] Research from the first approach includes examining vagrancy laws[117] and the Marihuana Tax Act.[118] One example of a more current study using the first approach is Amanda Robinson's research on public reaction to a domestic violence pro-arrest policy.[119]

Robinson hypothesized that there would be differences in support for the criminalization of domestic violence between powerful groups (i.e., middle- and upper-class white men) and less powerful groups (i.e., women, minorities, and the economically and educationally disadvantaged). The analyses revealed that there were differences by age, education, income, and gender; these differences supported the conflict perspective.

Various studies have used the second approach to examine differential processing of individuals in the criminal justice system. A number of studies have explored whether race and ethnicity are significant factors during various stages of criminal justice processing: intake diversion,[120] arrests,[121] juvenile justice dispositions,[122] and felony dispositions.[123]

Other aspects of the criminal justice system were examined using this approach. Malcolm Holmes hypothesized that the number of threatening acts and people was directly related to the number of police brutality civil rights criminal complaints filed with the U.S. Department of Justice.[124] The results revealed that the presence of threatening people (percentage black, percentage Hispanic, and majority/minority income inequality) was positively related to the mean number of civil rights criminal complaints. Mitchell Chamlin tested two hypotheses: (1) Increases in the size of threatening groups (e.g., blacks, Hispanics, and the poor) will increase the level of hostility between crime control agents (e.g., law enforcement officers) and civilians, and (2) these increased levels of hostility will enhance the volatility of police–citizen encounters, resulting in increased rates of police killings.[125] The results revealed that economic inequality did not have an effect on police killings. Support for the increase in population size of racial minorities, however, was related to "mutually suspicious interactions between civilians and police."

Critiques of Conflict Perspectives

George Vold and his colleagues presented some of the limitations associated with the conflict perspective.[126] First, while there have been advancements in research methodologies, especially with the use of more sophisticated techniques using multivariate analyses, there is still a fundamental problem when testing conflict theory; specifically, a similar finding may be interpreted in more than one way:

> If a direct effect of race on the decision to arrest or the length of a sentence is found, controlling for hosts of other factors, what does this mean? It could be evidence of widespread racial prejudice in society, manifested in unequal treatment of minorities by criminal justice system actors. On the other hand, it could represent systematic and institutionalized protection of those in power (whites) from the threatening group (blacks).[127]

Thus, some studies that reveal unequal treatment of individuals of different races haphazardly and erroneously assume support for conflict theory.

Second, some research studies testing conflict theory are unable to distinguish between alternative explanations. For instance, some studies (such as those discussed in the previous section) attempt to reveal that in areas where threatening groups (e.g., minorities and the poor) pose an increasing threat to those in power, there is an increase in law enforcement activity. These researchers, when finding such a positive relationship, argue that this supports conflict theory. There may, however, be alternative explanations. For example, nonwhites may *want* or *need* more law enforcement protection than do whites. Or nonwhites may encounter different types of social problems that require more social services.

Finally, few attempts have been made to develop and test well-constructed conflict theories. As demonstrated in the previous section, there are variations of the conflict perspective. As a result, many empirical studies do not adequately specify which conflict

WHY DO THEY DO IT?

TED KACZYNSKI

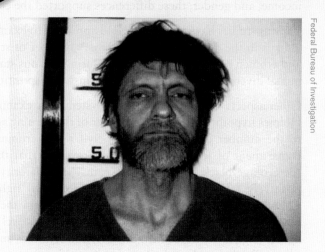

Mug shot of Theodore "Ted" Kaczynski.

Federal Bureau of Investigation

In 1978, the explosion of what was considered a primitive homemade bomb sent to a Chicago university started Theodore Kaczynski's "reign of terror." Over the next 17 years, these bombs were either hand-delivered or mailed, resulting in three deaths and 24 injuries. In 1979, an FBI task force, including the Bureau of Alcohol, Tobacco, Firearms, and Explosives and the U.S. Postal Inspection Service, was formed to investigate what was designated as the UNABOM (university and airline bombing targets) case. This task force, which grew to more than 150 full-time investigators, analysts, and others, attempted to recover bomb components and examined the lives of the victims in an effort to identify the bomber.[130]

In 1995, the unidentified "Unabomber" sent the FBI a 35,000-word essay that explained, from his perspective, the reasons for these bombs, as well as his views on the ills of modern society. The following is just one item among the 232 listed in the manifesto:

> 4. We therefore advocate a revolution against the industrial system. This revolution may or may not make use of violence; it may be sudden or it may be a relatively gradual process spanning a few decades. We can't predict any of that. But we do outline in a very general way the measures that those who hate the industrial system should take in order to prepare the way for a revolution against that form of society. This is not to be a POLITICAL revolution. Its object will be to overthrow not governments but the economic and technological basis of the present society.[131]

FBI director Louis Freeh and Attorney General Janet Reno agreed with the task force's recommendation to publish the essay, with the hope that a reader could identify the author. This manifesto was printed in the *Washington Post* and the *New York Times*.

While thousands of people offered various suspects, one stood out. In January 1996, in his family home in Illinois, David Kaczynski found papers, written by his brother Theodore (Ted), that contained Unabomer-like rhetoric. David Kaczynski notified the FBI. Linguistic analysis revealed that the author of these documents was most likely the author of the manifesto as well. On April 3, 1996, Ted Kaczynski was arrested in his remote mountain cabin in Stemple Pass, Montana. During the search of his cabin, investigators found a large number of bomb components, 40,000 handwritten journal pages, descriptions of Unabomer crimes, and one live bomb ready for mailing. Following his guilty plea in January of 1998, Ted Kaczynski was incarcerated in an isolated cell in a Colorado supermax prison.[132]

THINK ABOUT IT:

1. Are any features of this type of offense reflected in the various theories that have been discussed?

2. In reference to Steven Spitzer's work, would Ted Kaczynski be considered social dynamite? Why or why not?

propositions on conflict theory are being tested. Vold and his colleagues cited a study conducted by Lanza-Kaduce and Greenleaf, however, that addresses this problem by specifically identifying how Turk's theory of norm resistance can be operationalized and tested when examining encounters between police and citizens.[128] "Their effort is encouraging, in that it shows that a particular conflict theory can be tested empirically, if the researcher is careful to be true to the original theory."[129]

ADDITIONAL CRITICAL THEORIES

We finish up the chapter with a brief discussion of three other critical criminological theories: (1) peacemaking criminology, (2) the restorative justice perspective, and (3) left realism.

Peacemaking Criminology

Peacemaking criminology has incorporated three intellectual traditions: religious, feminist, and critical.[133] Generally, peacemaking criminology contends that rather than using punishment and retribution as a means of social control, society should attempt reconciliation through mediation and dispute settlement.[134] Individually and collaboratively, Harold Pepinsky and Richard Quinney have been involved in developing peacemaking criminology.[135] Figure 11.4 is a theoretical model of peacemaking criminology. This model consists of five basic elements—social structure, crimes, social harms, the criminal justice system, and peacemaking alternatives:

> Peacemaking criminology research, in its strictest sense, will opt to examine how people in our present times become affected by and, in turn, affect these five basic elements within the peacemaking criminology theoretical model. Leaving out an element would lead, in a peacemaking criminology view, to an incomplete understanding of crime and how to address crime in a humane way.[136]

peacemaking criminology: incorporates three intellectual traditions: religious, feminist, and critical; contends that society should attempt reconciliation through mediation and dispute settlement.

FIGURE 11.4

Theoretical Model of Peacemaking Criminology

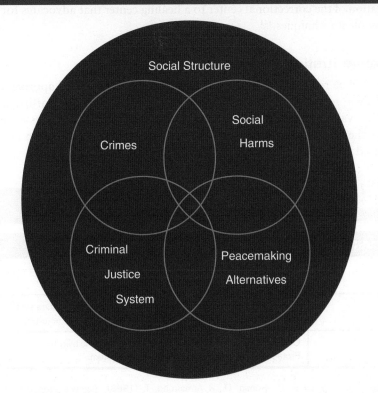

Source: Wozniak, J. F. (2001). Toward a theoretical model of peacemaking criminology: An essay in honor of Richard Quinney. *Crime and Delinquency, 48,* 221.

A key aspect to this model is recognizing that the world needs to be understood in terms of its interconnections rather than focusing on individual elements.

John Wozniak identified three predominate themes of peacemaking criminology. The first theme is types of crime and social harms. A common approach among peacemaking criminologists is to focus on different crimes (i.e., violation of a law) in the same context as other social harms (i.e., physical, mental, or social damages or injuries that are not violations of law in the strictest sense).[137] A key tenet of peacemaking criminology is to realize how different types of crime are inextricably related to different types of social harm.

The second theme is the types of peacemaking frameworks or perspectives. A general review of the literature reveals that many peacemaking criminology scholars tend to deviate from mainstream criminology theories in their research. Rather, they tend to focus on the type of theories that begin with questioning existing political, economic, and underlying ideologies of the status quo. They also maintain that answers to violence and social harm, as well as the injustices associated with such harm, are essentially outside the criminal justice system.[138] Not only is peacemaking criminology diverse; it is also optimistic. For instance, this approach encourages individuals working in the field of criminal justice to believe that society could be reorganized in a way that would result in human reactions conducted in a more humane manner.

The third theme is the types of peacemaking alternatives.[139] Peacemaking alternatives are quite diverse with respect to confronting crimes and social harms. Wozniak selected various examples to illustrate this point. Within the feminist tradition of peacemaking, he cited how researchers examining sexual assault led to the promise of community "Take Back the Night" marches, sexual assault centers, rape crisis programs, Men and Women Committed to Stopping Violence Against Women, and watchdog programs committed to monitoring the treatment of victims.[140] Another scholar's research endeavors directed attention toward the Alternatives to Violence Project for prisons, as well as transformation of the correctional center to a healing center that advocates for the teaching of nonviolent techniques.[141]

Restorative Justice Perspective

Retributive justice refers to the repair of justice through a one-sided approach of imposing punishment; restorative justice refers to the repair of justice by reaffirming a shared consensus of values, involving a joint or multisided approach.[142] Restorative justice emphasizes the victim, the community, and the offender. The restorative justice framework is based on the balanced approach (see Figure 11.5).

retributive justice: refers to the repair of justice through a one-sided approach of imposing punishment.

restorative justice: refers to the repair of justice by reaffirming a shared consensus of values involving a joint or multisided approach; emphasizes victim, community, and offender.

TABLE **11.4** Model of Restorative Justice

CLIENT/CUSTOMERS	GOALS	VALUES
Victims	Accountability	When an offense occurs, an obligation to victims and community incurs.
Youth	Competency Development	Offenders who enter the juvenile justice system should exit more capable than when they entered.
Community	Community Protection	Juvenile justice has a responsibility to protect the public from juveniles in the system.

Source: Adapted from Maloney, D., Romig, D., & Armstrong, T. (1988). *Juvenile probation: The balanced approach.* Reno, NV: National Council of Juvenile and Family Court Judges.

FIGURE **11.5**

FIGURE **11.5**   The Balanced Approach

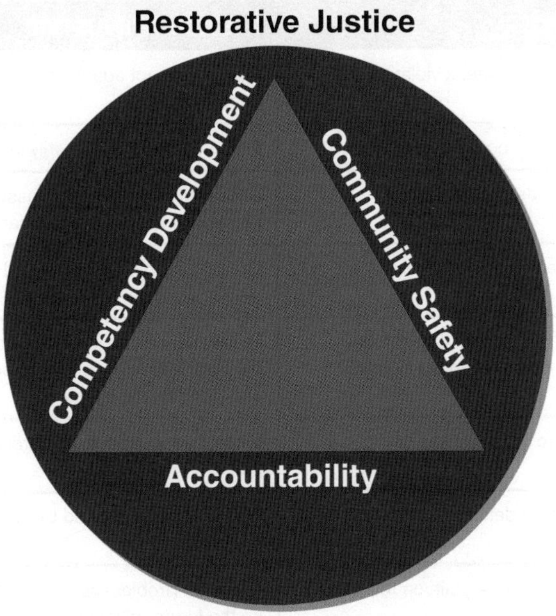

Restorative Justice

Competency Development

Community Safety

Accountability

Source: Bazemore, G., & Umbreit, M. (1997). *Balanced and restorative justice for juveniles: Framework for juvenile justice in the 21st century.* Washington, DC: Office of Juvenile Justice and Delinquency Prevention, p. 14.

The Balanced Approach mission addresses the public need for 1) sanctioning based on accountability measures which attempt to restore victims and clearly denounce and provide meaningful consequences for offensive behavior; 2) offender rehabilitation and reintegration; and 3) enhanced community safety and security. It does this by articulating three system goals directed toward the three primarily "client/customers" of the system—the victim, the offender, and the community. These system goals, which also govern the response to each offense, are: accountability; competency development; community protection.[143]

To further illustrate how the restorative justice perspective differs from a more traditional and retributive perspective, Gordon Bazemore and Mark Umbreit compared these two perspectives (see Table 11.5) and found key differences. For instance, retributive justice focuses on public vengeance as well as punishment exacted through an adversarial process. Restorative justice is more inclusive in that it considers not only the offender but the victim and the community.

Wheeldon argued that although there have been definitional challenges, existing restorative justice programs share key principles. The first is focusing on harms. Such harms include those suffered by communities. The second is to root procedures in the communities where such harms occurred. Such procedures or processes include understanding the community's part in crime commission as well as prevention. When the community is involved in this process, there is an acceptance that even those individuals not personally harmed by a specific crime continue to have an interest in the resolution of this offense. The third is the moral potential for restorative justice. This is related to the spiritual or religious traditions as well as a sense of humanism.[144]

TABLE *11.5*	Retributive and Restorative Justice Assumptions

RETRIBUTIVE JUSTICE	RESTORATIVE JUSTICE
Crime is an act against the state, a violation of a law, an abstract idea	Crime is an act against another person or the community
The criminal justice system controls crime	Crime control lies primarily in the community
Offender accountability defined as taking punishment	Accountability defined as assuming responsibility and taking action to repair harm
Crime is an individual act with individual responsibility	Crime has both individual and social dimensions of responsibility
Punishment is effect: (a) Threat of punishment deters crime; (b) punishment changes behavior	Punishment alone is not effective in changing behavior and is disruptive to community harmony and good relationships
Victims are peripheral to the process	Victims are central to the process of resolving a crime
The offender is defined by deficits	The offender is defined by capacity to make reparation
Focus on establishing blame or guilt, on the past (did he/she do it?)	Focus on problem solving, on liabilities/obligations, on the future (what should be done?)
Emphasis on adversarial relationship	Emphasis on dialogue and negotiation
Imposition of pain to punish and deter/prevent	Restitution as a means of restoring both parties; goal of reconciliation/restoration
Community on sideline, represented abstractly by state	Community as facilitator in restorative process
Response focused on offender's past behavior	Response focused on harmful consequences of offender's behavior; emphasis on the future
Dependence upon proxy professionals	Direct involvement by participants

Source: Bazemore, G., & Umbreit, M. (1997). *Balanced and restorative justice for juveniles: Framework for juvenile justice in the 21st century.* Washington, DC: Office of Juvenile Justice and Delinquency Prevention, p. 15.

Left Realism

Jock Young identified four major processes that have transformed criminological thinking: (1) the etiological crisis due to rising crime rates; (2) the crisis in penalty in terms of the failure of prisoners, as well as a reappraisal of the role of police; (3) the increased awareness of victimization and of crimes that had previously gone "unnoticed"; and (4) a growing public demand and criticism of public service efficiency and accountability.[145] In the 1980s, some theorists were questioning the narrow focus of Marxism and other radical theories.[146]

The major criticism was that these theoretical perspectives placed too much emphasis on the notion that crime is a result of the capitalist system and the abuses of those in the "elite" class. As a result, this focus fails to recognize that crime also exists in socialist countries; it ignores how crime challenges those in the lower classes who are often victims of violence; and this narrow emphasis results in weak crime-control approaches that do not adequately address the problem of crime. This critical perspective was identified as left realism. Realism contends that previous criminological theories are incomplete in that they emphasize only one part of the square of crime: the state (as in labeling theory, neoclassicism), the public (as in control theory), the offender (as in positivism), or the

left realism:

contends that previous criminological theories have been incomplete in that they emphasize only one part of the square of crime; attempts to provide an analysis of crime on all levels and develop a range of policy recommendations.

victim (as in victimology). One of the major goals of left realism is to provide an analysis of crime on all levels, as well as to develop a range of policy recommendations.[147]

Criminological realism refers to the notion of the *square of crime*. This term is "short-hand" and serves as a reminder that crime occurs at the intersection of a number of lines of force. One should not view crime solely in terms of victims and offenders without also including the role of the state and public opinion.[148] This square of crime is illustrated in Figure 11.6.

Left realists stress the necessity of a crime-control strategy in a capitalist society. It is essential that this crime-control strategy protect those individuals from the lower and working classes who are more vulnerable to becoming victims of crime and also experience a more intense fear of crime. In fact, this increased fear of crime has provided for the right wing to adhere to a "law-and-order" campaign that is repressive to many of these individuals.[149]

POLICIES RELATED TO LABELING AND CONFLICT THEORIES OF CRIME

A major policy implication of labeling research is that if deviance amplification occurs, the criminal justice agency, especially the juvenile justice system, should strive to divert certain individuals from formal processing to avoid the negative effects of such labeling.[150] In reference to policies related to the labeling perspective, a general approach

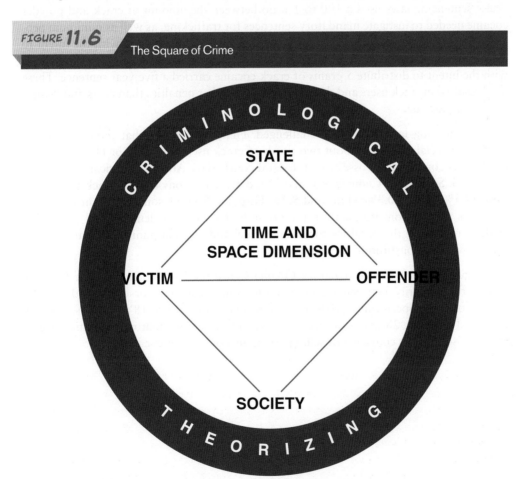

FIGURE 11.6   The Square of Crime

Source: Matthews, R., & Young, J. (1992). Reflections on realism. In J. Young & R. Matthews (Eds.), *Rethinking criminology: The realist debate* (pp. 1–23). London: SAGE, p. 20.

has been to incorporate diversion programs, particularly for juveniles. Diversion occurs when a juvenile is not formally processed in the juvenile justice system (e.g., adjudication or incarceration); rather, these youths may be referred to some type of program such as treatment or work. Some would maintain that when a youth is diverted out of the juvenile justice system, he or she avoids the *label* of "juvenile delinquent." Thus, "by keeping juveniles out of the system, the labeling impact of courts and judges will be reduced. Juveniles will also develop less of the secondary deviance patterns that result from being labeled by the system as 'delinquent.'"[151]

One example of a diversion program is youth courts (also known as peer courts or teen courts). Youth courts are typically for juveniles between the ages of 10 and 15 years old who have no prior arrests and are charged with less serious law violations (e.g., shoplifting, vandalism). In most cases, these youths are provided with an option to participate in this program rather than continue through the formal juvenile justice system. These courts differ from other programs in that the juveniles determine the disposition; however, adults do oversee the program.[152]

An example of policies that reflect the conflict theoretical perspective relates to crack and cocaine legislation.[153] In the mid-1980s, crack cocaine was becoming more prevalent and receiving a great deal of media attention. Crack was characterized as inducing violence, highly addictive, and a major problem in urban areas. This public perception led to the quick passage of two federal sentencing laws: the Anti–Drug Abuse Act of 1986 and the Omnibus Anti–Drug Abuse Act of 1988.

These sentencing laws used a 100-to-1 ratio between the amount of crack and powder cocaine needed to instigate mandatory sentences for trafficking, as well as minimum penalties for simple possession of crack cocaine. For instance, possession with the intent to distribute 500 grams or more of powder cocaine carried a five-year sentence; possession with the intent to distribute 5 grams of crack cocaine carried a five-year sentence. These laws resulted in crack users and dealers receiving harsher penalties than users and dealers of powder cocaine.

These sentencing laws have been challenged. First, some argue that these differences resulted in racial disparity. About two thirds of crack users are white or Hispanic; most individuals convicted of possession in federal courts were African-American. According to the U.S. Sentencing Commission, in 1994, defendants convicted of crack possession were 84.5% black, 10.3% white, and 5.2% Hispanic. Second, some maintained that the sentences were unconstitutional on the grounds that (1) they denied equal protection or due process, (2) the penalties constituted cruel and unusual punishment, and (3) the statutes were unconstitutionally vague.

On August 3, 2010, President Barack Obama signed the Fair Sentencing Act. This law lessens the disparity between mandatory minimum sentences for crack and powder cocaine offenses. Specifically, it reduces the sentencing disparity to 18 to 1. Thus, a person convicted of selling 28 grams of crack will face a five-year mandatory minimum, just as will a person who is convicted of selling 500 grams of powder cocaine.

CONCLUSION

An overriding theme of this chapter was to illustrate various theoretical perspectives that challenge the traditional criminological theories and dominant ideologies. These critical perspectives question various assumptions that were considered as "given" in the traditional perspectives. We started this chapter with labeling theory. A major aspect of the labeling perspective is critically examining how deviant behavior is defined and who has the power to define this behavior as such.

The next section presented various conflict perspectives. These different perspectives, however, share a common assumption—conflict is natural to society. While it is difficult to generally categorize these conflict perspectives, we grouped them in two categories. The first was conservative (pluralist) theories. Conservative (pluralist) conflict theories emphasize power and the use of power. The second was critical-radical theories. These perspectives have incorporated Marxist themes to understand crime and criminals. We concluded this chapter by presenting three additional critical perspectives—peacemaking criminology, the restorative justice perspective, and left realism.

It is essential that readers appreciate how these diverse criminological theories have evolved. A major contribution of these critical theoretical perspectives is that they provide an additional lens not previously considered in traditional, mainstream criminological theories. These critical perspectives also emphasize that attempts to understand individual criminal behavior need to incorporate the broader societal context.

After studying these theoretical perspectives, students should reconsider the case study on the Flint Water Crisis at the beginning of this chapter. Think about issues such as whether poverty is a key factor in how this crisis was ignored for quite some time and the lasting effects on the residents of Flint.

SUMMARY OF THEORIES IN CHAPTER 11

THEORY	CONCEPTS	PROPONENTS	KEY PROPOSITIONS
Labeling theory	Not overly concerned with questions of why an individual engages in deviant behavior; rather, it is important to understand how criminal, or deviant, behavior is defined or labeled, as well as how society reacts to this behavior.	Frank Tannenbaum, Edwin Lemert, Howard Becker, Edwin Schur	No act is intrinsically criminal; criminal definitions are enforced in the interest of the powerful; an individual does not become a criminal by violating the law; penalties for a criminal act vary according to the characteristics of the offender; criminal justice is based on a stereotyped conception of the criminal; public condemnation may make it difficult for an offender to sustain a positive self-image.
Conservative (pluralist) conflict perspectives	Conflict is an essential component; groups have competing interests; society is made up of groups with different levels of power; group interests are reflected in various aspects of society, especially in the legislative political process.	George Vold, Austin Turk, Richard Quinney	Conflict arises between various groups seeking to establish or maintain control over one another; the law is an essential tool used to reflect the interests of those powerful groups; differences in power are reflected in who defines behavior as criminal.
Radical conflict perspectives	Modes of production influence various aspects of the social structure, including the criminal justice system, family, and school.	Various	Similar propositions to those of conservative (pluralist) conflict perspectives, with an emphasis on wealth and social class.

KEY TERMS

bourgeoisie, 308

consensus perspective, 301

dramatization of evil, 294

falsely accused, 297

group conflict theory, 303

labeling theory, 291

left realism, 318

negotiation, 298

nonpartisan conflict perspective, 306

partisan conflict perspective, 306

peacemaking criminology, 315

primary deviance, 294

proletariat, 309

pure deviant, 295

restorative justice, 316

retributive justice, 316

retrospective interpretation, 297

secondary deviance, 294

secret deviant, 297

status-degradation ceremony, 297

stereotyping, 297

symbolic interactionism, 293

DISCUSSION QUESTIONS

1. What are the major assumptions of labeling theory?

2. According to Lemert, how does an individual get labeled as a "deviant"?

3. According to Becker, what two behaviors are incorrectly perceived by society?

4. Is labeling a theory, a perspective, or neither?

5. What key features distinguish the consensus model of law from the conflict model of law?

6. How has Marxist theory been incorporated to explain crime?

7. What are some of the limitations of conflict theories?

8. What are the key features of peacemaking criminology?

9. How has the restorative justice perspective incorporated the offender, victim, and community?

10. What are some examples of policies that reflect the labeling and conflict perspectives?

WEB RESOURCES

Critical criminology

This web resource provides additional information regarding critical criminology including the origins, principal and emerging strings, and well as the key concerns of critical criminology.

http://criminal-justice.iresearchnet.com/criminology/critical-criminology

Restorative Justice Online

This web resource provides a more comprehensive understanding of the mission, vision, and values associated with restorative justice in practice.

http://www.restorativejustice.org/

STUDENT STUDY SITE

$SAGE edge™

WANT A BETTER GRADE ON YOUR NEXT TEST?

Get the tools you need to sharpen your study skills:

SAGE edge offers a robust online environment featuring an impressive array of tools and resources for review, study, and further exploration, keeping both instructors and students on the cutting edge of teaching and learning. Learn more at **edge.sagepub.com/schram2e**.

FOR FURTHER EXPLORATION AND APPLICATION, VISIT THE STUDENT STUDY SITE:

- Tide Starts to Turn Against the `Crime' of Being Homeless
- Why the Public Perception of Crime Exceeds the Reality
- Outnumbering Boomers, Millennials Look for Economic Opportunity
- Interactionist labeling: Formal and informal labeling's effects on juvenile delinquency
- Crime, punishment, and the American dream: Toward a Marxist integration
- Justice league? Depictions of justice in children's superhero cartoons
- Drinking Water Crisis in Flint, Michigan, Prompts Federal Investigation
- Perspectives on Deviance: Differential Association, Labeling Theory, and Strain Theory
- Labeling Theory
- Long Beach School District Sues Banks Accuser
- "Why Marxism?" An Interview with C. Bradley Thompson
- Daniel Reisel: The Neuroscience of Restorative Justice
- Columbine
- Manifestos from Killers
- Black Lives Matter

PREMIUM VIDEO:

Check out the Interactive eBook for premium videos, including videos from author Stephen Tibbetts, who discusses real-world examples and strange crimes; and videos from former offenders, who share their stories from a first-person view, and touch on key theories and concepts from the chapter.

CHAPTER 12

Feminist Theories of Crime

public domain

INTRODUCTION

Feminist criminology evolved when various assumptions and stereotypes about women in criminal justice were being questioned. Such questions included women as professionals as well as women as offenders and victims. This chapter begins with a brief history of feminism in the United States. To provide a better understanding of feminist theories of crime, it is essential to stress that there is no one feminist perspective. Rather, there are various feminist perspectives. Some of these feminist perspectives are discussed in the subsequent section. Next, this chapter discusses traditional theories of female crime, followed by feminist critiques of previous research focusing on women. We then present issues pertaining to understanding crime and criminal behavior that have been raised in feminist research. Finally, we discuss various policy and program recommendations based on theories and research grounded in a feminist perspective.

A BRIEF HISTORY OF FEMINISM IN THE UNITED STATES

Feminism is a belief that women and men are inherently of equal worth. Because most societies privilege men as a group, social movements are necessary to achieve equality between women and men, with the understanding that gender always intersects with other social hierarchies.[3]

Most scholars contend that feminism has evolved in three major waves. The first wave of feminism started in the mid-1800s when women demanded the right to vote.[4] A major event associated with this first wave occurred in 1848. About 300 women and men met in Seneca Falls, New York. At the Seneca Falls Convention, these participants established a "Declaration of Sentiments" as well as 12 resolutions. This declaration was modeled after the Declaration of Independence. The Declaration of Sentiments stressed the need for reforms in marriage, divorce, property, and child custody laws. A major criticism of this convention was that the focus was primarily on white, upper-class women. Thus, working-class and black women were essentially invisible.

These "invisible" women, however, did contribute to the 19th century women's rights movement. For instance, Sojourner Truth delivered her well-known speech at an 1851 women's rights convention in Akron, Ohio.[5] She delivered an impromptu speech that included her well-known question, "Ain't I a woman?" In this speech, she attempted to persuade the audience to support women's rights. The feminist views were "taking a beating all evening." Eventually, a man claimed that women needed to be protected with chivalrous acts. It was at this time that Sojourner Truth rose and replied with her speech.[6]

The peak of the first wave was between 1870 and 1928. This time period is characterized by intense activity toward winning women the right to vote as well as achieving educational and social reforms. While many women from various backgrounds were involved in these reforms, those women who were particularly involved in the antislavery and temperance movements worked together to secure women the right to vote.[7] In 1920, the Nineteenth Amendment to the Constitution was passed, giving the vote to women. With the passage of the Nineteenth Amendment, many of the suffragists believed that women had indeed become men's equals.[8]

LEARNING OBJECTIVES

As you read this chapter, should consider the following topics:

- Compare and contrast the first, second, and third waves of feminism.

- Identify the key features of the various feminist perspectives.

- Describe how traditional theories of crime perceived female offenders.

- Identify some of the problems associated with traditional research methods.

- Identify the main tenets of the liberation thesis.

- Discuss how power-control theory attempts to explain gender differences in delinquency rates.

- Describe feminist pathways research.

- Evaluate the key critiques of feminist theories.

- Describe some of the key policies based on feminist theories of crime.

CASE STUDY

GERTRUDE BANISZEWSKI

When the police arrived at the home of Gertrude Baniszewski in October 1965, they found the lifeless body of 16-year-old Sylvia Likens. Sylvia's parents had found employment as carnival workers. This required them to move around, so Gertrude Baniszewski agreed to board Sylvia and her sister Jenny for $20 a week. When one of the checks arrived late, Baniszewski lashed out at the two girls. This was followed by three weeks of violent and sadistic attacks, especially on Sylvia. A number of Baniszewski's seven children, along with some neighborhood children, watched or actually joined in the torture. This was all done under the supervision of Baniszewski. No one reported the abuse.[1]

Sylvia's emaciated corpse was covered with over 150 wounds ranging from burns to cuts. Sylvia was burned with cigarettes numerous times; she was forced to dance naked in front of the other children; she took baths in scalding water; and she was constantly beaten and starved. On one horrible night, Baniszewski took a sewing needle and carved an "I" in Sylvia's abdomen. She then gave the needle to a neighbor boy and instructed him to spell the word "prostitute."

After this incident, Sylvia was dead and Baniszewski was arrested along with eight youthful offenders ranging in age from 11 to 17 years. The children stated that they participated in the torture of Sylvia because "Gertie" told them to. In 1966, Gertrude Baniszewski was convicted of first-degree murder; her daughter, Paula, was convicted of second-degree murder; and, the remaining offenders were found guilty of lesser homicide charges.[2]

public domain

A 1965 photograph of Sylvia Likens.

DO WE AS A SOCIETY PERCEIVE SUCH OFFENSES COMMITTED BY A MOTHER DIFFERENTLY THAN SIMILAR OFFENSES COMMITTED BY A FATHER?

THINK ABOUT IT:

1. Do we as a society perceive such offenses committed by a mother differently than similar offenses committed by a father?

2. Do we initially ask, "How could a mother do that to another child?"

The **second wave of feminism** developed in the 1960s when other marginalized groups were also challenging the status quo (e.g., civil rights movement, prisoners' rights movement).[9] Feminists of this wave argued that to be fully liberated, women needed to have equal access to economic opportunities and sexual freedoms as well as civil liberties. Some women advocated a reformist, liberal agenda, whereas others pushed for a more revolutionary, radical program of change and action.[10] The liberal political perspective was influenced by the Civil Rights Act of 1964, which banned racial discrimination as well as sex discrimination. The radical political perspective was influenced by both the civil rights and student movements of the 1960s.[11]

Many liberal feminists were joining emerging women's *rights* groups such as the National Organization for Women (NOW), the National Women's Political Caucus, and the Women's Equity Action League. Most radical feminists were involved with women's *liberation* groups, which were much smaller and more personally focused. Among these groups were the Women's International Terrorist Conspiracy from Hell (WITCH), the Redstockings, the Feminists, and the New York Radical Feminists.[12] It was in this social context, within these emerging political perspectives, that feminist criminology began to question assumptions and stereotypes concerning women in criminal justice. This included women as professionals as well as women as offenders and victims.

The **third wave of feminism** evolved around the late 1980s into the 1990s. This wave of feminism is an extension as well as a response to the shortcomings of the second wave.[13] Some have maintained that this third wave coincides with the birth of Generation X; in fact, the literature associated with the third wave often describes younger women's experiences of frustration with the second wave of feminism.[14] The one major theme of third wave feminism is willingness to accommodate difference, diversity, and change:

> They seem to be feminist sponges, willing and able to absorb some aspects of all the modes of feminist thought that preceded the third wave's emergence on the scene. Third-wave feminists are particularly eager to understand how gender oppression and other kinds of human oppression co-create and co-maintain each other . . . [D]ifference is the way things are. Moreover, contradiction, including self-contradiction, is expected and even willingly welcomed.[15]

More than any other group of feminists, the third-wave feminist perspective has provided a voice for many women who otherwise did not identify with previous feminist perspectives, especially women of color.

Key Terms of Feminist Perspectives

Before discussing the various feminist perspectives, it is essential for readers to appreciate key terms associated with these perspectives. A few of these key terms are *sex*, *gender*, *chivalry*, *paternalism*, and *patriarchy*.

Differences between women and men have usually been identified as either sex or gender differences. **Sex** differences typically refer to biological characteristics, such as reproductive organs and hormones. **Gender** differences usually refer to social definitions of what it

Everett Collection Inc/Alamy Stock Photo

Suffrage supporters demonstrating in Chicago on October 20, 1916.

first wave of feminism: started in the mid-1800s when women demanded the right to vote.

second wave of feminism: developed in the 1960s when other marginalized groups were also challenging the status quo (e.g., civil rights movement, prisoners' rights movement). Feminists of this wave argued that to be fully liberated, women needed to have equal access to economic opportunities and sexual freedoms as well as civil liberties.

third wave of feminism: evolved around the late 1980s and into the 1990s; an extension of as well as a response to the shortcomings of the second wave.

sex: sex differences typically refer to biological variations such as reproductive organs and hormones.

gender: gender usually refers to social definitions of what it means to be a woman or a man.

chivalry: pertains to behaviors and attitudes toward certain individuals that treat them as though they are on a pedestal.

paternalism: denotes that women need to be protected for their own good. In a broader social context, paternalism implies independence for men and dependence for women.

patriarchy: a social, legal, and political climate based on male dominance and hierarchy. A key aspect to this ideology is that women's nature is biologically, not culturally, determined.

means to be a "woman" or a "man." These social definitions may include characteristics such as appearance and occupation. It is confusing when the terms *sex* and *gender* are used interchangeably; sometimes individuals will use these terms imprecisely and assume that everyone understands the difference between sex and gender.[16]

West and Zimmerman illustrate the complexity of the concepts of sex and gender by distinguishing between *sex, sex category,* and *gender.*[17] As mentioned above, *sex* is determined through the use of socially agreed on biological criteria. An individual is located in a *sex category* by applying socially determined criteria of sex. By applying these criteria, society has defined sex as a binary category through sex categorization. *Gender* is not a set of characteristics or a variable or a role. Rather, gender is a product of social "doings." *Gender* is activity considered appropriate for a person's sex category. These activities are determined through social constructions of sex and sex category. "Doing gender" is a continuous activity embedded in everyday interactions. By understanding the independence of these constructs, people can question whether differences between women and men are due to sex or to social constructions of gender.

Chivalry pertains to behaviors and attitudes toward certain individuals that treat them as though they are on a pedestal.[18] Chivalrous behavior is more complex than just preferential treatment. Engaging in a chivalrous relationship usually entails a bartering system in which men hold a more powerful status than do women. Social class and race/ethnicity are also intertwined with such treatment. Women of certain social classes and racial/ethnic backgrounds are considered more worthy of chivalrous treatment than other women. This is best illustrated by Sojourner Truth's speech "Ain't I a Woman?" The idea of paternalism denotes that women need to be protected for their own good. In a broader social context, paternalism implies independence for men and dependence for women. Both chivalry and paternalism suggest that certain individuals or groups need protection because they are weak and helpless. This protection can also lead to various types of control.

The Latin word *pater* refers to the social role of a father as opposed to the biological role of a father. Patriarchal societies exclude women from the exercise of political responsibilities; patriarchy refers to the subordinate role of women and male dominance.[19] Thus, patriarchy is a social, legal, and political climate based on male dominance and hierarchy. A key aspect to this ideology is that women's nature is biologically, not culturally, determined.[20]

LEARNING CHECK 12.1

1. _____ is determined through the use of socially agreed on biological criteria.

2. _____ is a product of social "doings."

3. Engaging in a _____ relationship usually involves a bartering system in which men hold a more powerful status than do women.

4. The idea of _____ denotes that women need to be protected for their own good. _____ is a social, legal, and political climate founded on male dominance and hierarchy.

Answers located at www.edge.sagepub.com/schram2e

FEMINIST PERSPECTIVES ON GENDER

As noted previously, it is essential to provide readers with a general understanding that there is no *one* feminist perspective. Rather, there are various feminist perspectives. This section gives readers a summary of these different perspectives of gender. These summaries "are crude and oversimplified, but they offer a starting point for different ways of conceptualizing gender in social and political theory."[21]

Traditional or Conservative Perspective

Kathleen Daly and Meda Chesney-Lind highlighted key features of the traditional or conservative perspective. First, they maintained that from this perspective, the causes of gender inequality are due to biological sex differences, including hormonal differences (e.g., greater testosterone production in males) or reproductive capacities (e.g., female child bearing and lactation). Second, they identified the process of how gender is formed. The conservative perspective stresses that social behavior is based on these biological sex differences. These biological sex differences can be amplified to explain social behavior, such as greater strength and innate aggression among males as well as innate nurturing and caregiving among females. Unlike the other feminist perspectives, the conservative perspective does not offer any strategies for social change, since men's and women's behaviors reflect evolutionary adaptations of sex differences.[22]

Liberal Feminism

Liberal feminism, also termed *mainstream feminism*, is founded on political liberalism, which holds a positive view of human nature as well as the ideals of liberty, equality, justice, dignity, and individual rights. A major feature of liberal feminism is that women should receive the same rights and treatment as men.[23] This perspective purports that gender inequality is due to women's blocked opportunities to participate in various aspects of the public sphere, such as education, employment, and political activity.[24] (See Table 12.1 for an example of a liberal feminist agenda.) Strategies for social change are devised to

TABLE 12.1

NOW's 1967 Bill of Rights for Women

BILL OF RIGHTS FOR WOMEN
I. That the U.S. Congress immediately pass the Equal Rights Amendment to the Constitution to provide that "Equality of rights under the law shall not be denied or abridged by the United States or by any State on account of sex," and that such then be immediately ratified by the several States.
II. That equal employment opportunity be guaranteed to all women, as well as men, by insisting that the Equal Employment Opportunity Commission enforces the prohibitions against racial discrimination.
III. That women be protected by law to ensure their rights to return to their jobs within a reasonable time after childbirth without the loss of seniority or other accrued benefits, and be paid maternity leave as a form of social security and/or employee benefit.
IV. Immediate revision of tax laws to permit the deduction of home and child-care expenses for working parents.
V. That child-care facilities be established by law on the same basis as parks, libraries, and public schools, adequate to the needs of children from the pre-school years through adolescence, as a community resource to be used by all citizens from all income levels.
VI. That the right of women to be educated to their full potential equally with men be secured by Federal and State legislation, eliminating all discrimination and segregation by sex, written and unwritten, at all levels of education, including colleges, graduate and professional schools, loans and fellowships, and Federal and State training programs such as the Job Corps.
VII. The right of women in poverty to secure job training, housing, and family allowances on equal terms with men, but without prejudice to a parent's right to remain at home to care for his or her children; revision of welfare legislation and poverty programs which deny women dignity, privacy, and self-respect.
VIII. The right of women to control their own reproductive lives by removing from the penal code laws limiting access to contraceptive information and devices, and by repealing penal laws governing abortion.

Source: NOW Bill of Rights (adopted at NOW's first national conference, Washington, D.C., 1967). In R. Morgan (Ed.), *Sisterhood is powerful*. New York, NY: Random House, pp. 513–514. Reprinted with permission of the National Organization for Women.

traditional or conservative perspective: causes of gender inequality are due to biological sex differences, and social behavior is based on the biological sex differences; does not offer any strategies for social change since men's and women's behaviors reflect evolutionary adaptations of sex differences.

liberal feminism: one of the areas of feminist theories of crime that emphasize the assumption that differences between males and females in offending are due to the lack of female opportunities in education, employment, etc., compared with males.

free women from oppressive gender roles—for instance, performing only those jobs associated with the traditional feminine personality (e.g., nursing, teaching, and child care).[25]

There are generally two types of liberal feminists: classical and welfare. Both approaches rely a great deal on legal remedies to address gender inequality. Classical liberal feminists support limited government and a free market as well as political and legal rights. Central facets of this approach are freedom of expression, religion, and conscience. Welfare liberal feminists favor government involvement in providing citizens, particularly underprivileged individuals, with housing, education, health care, and social security. They also maintain that the market should be limited through significant taxes and restricting profits.[26]

A major criticism of the liberal feminist perspective is that it primarily focuses "on the interests of white, middle-class, heterosexual women."[27] Specifically, within the area of feminist criminology, some argue that the liberal perspective poses "men as the criminal yardstick." This results in equating justice with equality and not considering other influential standpoints such as race/ethnicity and social class.[28] Joanne Belknap maintains that

> prison reform for women would not be nearly as effective in achieving equality with men's prisons if the only goal was to allow the same access to health care, vocational, educational, legal, and treatment programs. While these would be significant advances, it is also necessary to request reforms that address women prisoners' experiences, needs, and histories that differ from male prisoners.[29]

Another area where the "equal treatment" doctrine is problematic is in sentencing. Specifically, sentencing reforms aimed at reducing race- and class-based disparities in sentencing for male offenders "may yield equality with a vengeance" for female offenders.[30] Thus, "equality defined as equal treatment of men and women . . . forestalls more fundamental change and in some instances may worsen women's circumstances."[31]

Radical Feminism

Radical feminism evolved from the women's liberation movement of the 1960s. This perspective emphasizes the importance of personal feelings, experiences, and relationships. Gender is a system of male dominance, and women's biology is the main cause of patriarchy.[32]

The cause of gender inequality, according to this perspective, is based on men's need or desire to control women's sexuality and reproductive potential. Further, the process of gender formation is founded on the power relations between men and women, in which boys and men view themselves as superior to and having a right to control girls and women. These relations are further intensified through heterosexual sexuality, as defined by men. [33]

Radical feminists maintain, in principle, that sexism is the first, most widespread form of human oppression. They do not, however, agree on the nature or function of this sexism or on what strategies are needed for social change. Rosemarie Tong identified two types of radical feminism: libertarian and cultural.[34] Radical-libertarian feminists assert that an exclusively feminine gender identity will most often limit a woman's development as a full human person. They encourage women to become androgynous individuals who embody both (good) masculine and (good) feminine characteristics. Radical-cultural feminists argue that women should be strictly female/feminine. They should not try to be like men. Women should emphasize such values and virtues as interdependence, community, connection, sharing, emotion, body, trust, absence of hierarchy, nature, immanence, process, joy, peace, and life. Alternatively, women should not emphasize such values as independence, autonomy, intellect, will, wariness, hierarchy, domination, culture, transcendence, product, asceticism, war, and death.

radical feminism: emphasizes the importance of personal feelings, experiences, and relationships; gender is a system of male dominance, and women's biology is the main cause of patriarchy.

Tong noted that this distinction, while not perfect,

> helps explain not only why some radical feminists embrace the concept of androgyny and others eschew it, but also why some radical feminists view both sex and reproduction as oppressive, even dangerous for women and why others view these aspects as liberating, even empowering for women. . . . *[R]adical feminists are not afraid to take exception to each other's views* [italics added].[35]

Suggested strategies for social change among some radical feminists include overthrowing patriarchal relations, developing methods of biological reproduction to permit women's sexual autonomy, and establishing women-centered social institutions and women-only organizations. Other radical feminists celebrate gender differences, particularly women's special capacities or talents; however, these feminists do not pose gender differences in the framework of power relations.[36]

One of the criticisms of radical-libertarian and radical-cultural feminism is that they need to reconcile the split between themselves in an effort to avoid polarization, particularly in the area of sexuality. Even though radical-libertarian feminists are hesitant about consensual heterosexuality, they maintain that these relationships can be pleasurable for women. Radical-cultural feminists warn against the dangers of heterosexuality and have implied that there is no such thing as consensual heterosexuality. Thus, according to this view, "only lesbians are capable of consensual sex in a patriarchal society."[37] Citing Ann Ferguson, a socialist feminist, Tong notes that there is no one universal "function" for human sexuality.[38]

Marxist and Socialist Feminism

Some scholars maintain that while it is possible to distinguish between Marxist feminism and socialist feminism, it is difficult, particularly because these two perspectives' differences are more an issue of emphasis than of substance.[39] Marxist feminism places gender in the context of production methods. The burdens of physical and social reproduction in the home are operated and reinforced in a male-dominated economic and political order.[40] The causes of gender inequality are due to hierarchical relations of control with the increase of private property and ownership among men. Class relations are primary, and gender relations are secondary.[41] An insightful example of such gender and class relations is housework. Traditionally, housework has been delegated to women; however, housework does not produce surplus value or profit. Thus, some do not consider this labor. van Hooff conducted semi-structured interviews to examine dual-career heterosexual couples' explanations and justifications for the division of housework that followed more traditional gender roles. Table 12.2 provides some examples of these explanations and justifications for both the men and women. Marxist feminism focuses essentially on work-related inequalities, as well as enhancing our understanding of the trivialization of women's work in the home (e.g., raising children, doing housework) and the tedious, poorly paid jobs predominately occupied by women.[42] The General Social Survey reveals that when asking males and females regarding their

Marxist feminism: a perspective of crime that emphasizes men's ownership and control of the means of economic production; similar to critical or radical feminism but distinguished by its reliance on the concept of economic structure.

socialist feminism: feminist theories that moved away from economic structure (e.g., Marxism) and placed a focus on control of reproductive systems; believes that women should take control of their own bodies and reproductive functions via contraceptives.

Photos 12 / Alamy Stock Photo

Women's Liberation Movement protesters marching down 5th Avenue in New York in 1970.

TABLE 12.2	Heterosexual Couples' Explanations and Justifications for the Division of Household Tasks

FEMALES	MALES
It's kind of ended up that I do the cleaning and shit, and I don't know how it happened, but it's like two years later I'm a 1950s housewife or something.	Ali would do most of it. We argue about it quite a lot. It's not fair, really, I should do more.
I don't think it was really a decision, but I am the cleaner in the relationship, just because I'm better at it.	Well, I would clean, but by the time I get there Chloe's already done it.
I do it. It's not something that we've ever discussed, I just sort of have done it, and neither of us is sort of bold enough to bring it up now, so instead I just do it.	Sara does do most of it, I've got to admit, but it's not because I think she should do it because she's a woman, it's just because she's got higher standards of cleanliness than me (laughs).

Source: van Hooff, J. H. (2011). Rationalising inequality: Heterosexual couples' explanations and justifications for the division of housework along traditionally gendered lines. *Journal of Gender Studies, 20,* pp. 21–22.

FIGURE 12.1	Who Does Household Cleaning Among Married Persons 18–65?

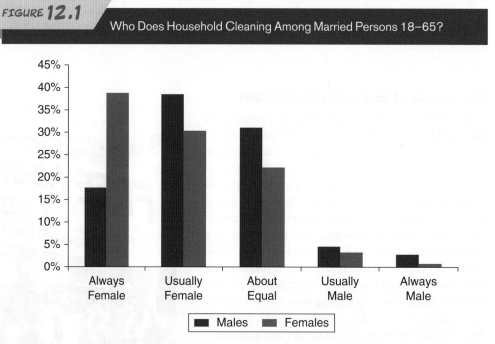

Source: "Modern Family: Division of Labor, Perception, and Reality, Austin Institute, December 17, 2014. http://www.austin-institute.org/research/modern-family-division-of-labor-perception-and-reality/

perceptions as to who does most of the cleaning in the household, there is an overwhelming response of either "always female" or "usually female" (see Figure 12.1).

Socialist feminism attempts to synthesize radical and Marxist feminism. This perspective attempts to integrate concepts such as male domination and political–economic relations. Social feminists focus on gender, class, and racial relations of domination. They differ from Marxist feminists in that both class and gender relations are deemed primary.[43] Within the socialist feminism perspective, there are two general themes: (1) two-system explanations of women's oppression and (2) interactive-system explanations of women's oppression. Under the two-system explanations, these emphases are less committed to the Marxist-founded framework. Rather, they maintain that patriarchy, not capitalism, may be women's ultimate worst enemy.[44] The interactive-system explanations attempt to illustrate that both capitalism and patriarchy are equal contributors to women's oppression; they are interdependent. These feminists use terms such as *capitalist patriarchy* or *patriarchal capitalism*.[45]

Postmodern Feminism

Postmodern feminism is a more contemporary intellectual movement that has been modified and adapted by feminist theory. This perspective rejects the traditional assumptions about truth and reality; the emphasis is more on the plurality, diversity, and multiplicity of women as distinct from men.[46] Tong argues that the relationship between postmodernists and feminists is "uneasy."[47] For instance, similar to all postmodernists, postmodern feminists reject ideas centered on an absolute world that is "male" in style (e.g., phallogocentric). They also reject any attempts to provide a single explanation or steps women must take to achieve liberation (i.e., a feminist "to-do list"). Those who identify themselves as postmodern feminists "invite each woman who reflects on their writings to become the kind of feminist she wants to be. There is, in their estimation, no single formula for being a 'good feminist.'"[48]

However, this emphasis on diversity, and "no single formula for being a 'good feminist,'" poses dilemmas for feminists:

> The emphasis on diversity in postmodernism, however, ignores the need for political entities . . . that can pursue collective political action on women's issues. If one calls for unity among women, one assumes that women are an entity that has "essentially" the same interests. . . . Thus, the marriage between postmodernism and feminism poses a threat to the political agenda of feminists.[49]

One suggested approach to addressing this dilemma is to adopt a stance of "positionality" or "both/and." An individual does not need to choose between the postmodern focus on multiplicity and feminist politics. Rather, when a person is engaged in politics, he or she can act as though women (or African-Americans or poor people) are a group united around a similar cause or purpose. In other situations, however, that person realizes and appreciates women's (or other groups') diversity.[50]

postmodern feminism: a perspective that says women as a group cannot be understood, even by other women, because every person's experience is unique; therefore, there is no need to measure or research such experiences.

Additional Feminist Perspectives

Additional feminist perspectives include ecofeminism as well as global and postcolonial feminism. Ecofeminism was developed around the 1980s to examine relations between environmental issues and women's issues. It sprang from the growing global environmental crisis. Ecofeminists perceive domination—of women, minority groups, animals, and the Earth—as the essential problem rather than patriarchy.[51] This perspective, however, contains many varieties, such as nature ecofeminism, radical-cultural ecofeminism, and spiritual ecofeminism.[52]

Global and postcolonial feminism emerged in the mid-1970s. This is an international women's movement founded in the commonalities

LEARNING CHECK 12.2

1. _____ feminism has also been termed mainstream feminism.

2. According to the _____ feminist perspective, gender is a system of male dominance, and women's biology is the main cause of patriarchy.

3. Some have maintained that there are two types of radical feminism: _____ and _____.

4. The _____ feminist perspective views class relations as primary and gender relations as secondary.

5. The _____ feminist perspective rejects the traditional assumptions about truth and reality and emphasizes the plurality, diversity, and multiplicity of women as distinct from men.

Answers located at www.edge.sagepub.com/schram2e

of women's lives, such as low economic status. This perspective critically explores the impact of development, patriarchal religions, international trafficking in women, and the Westernization of the Third World.[53] While feminists from First World nations (i.e., those nations that are heavily industrialized, located primarily in the Northern Hemisphere) are essentially interested in issues revolving around sexuality and reproduction, a number of Third World feminists (i.e., those in economically developing nations, located primarily in the Southern Hemisphere) are concerned not only with gender issues but with political and economic issues as well.[54]

In the next section, we provide a brief overview of the traditional theories of female criminality. This context will provide readers with a better understanding of the development of feminist criminology.

TRADITIONAL THEORIES OF FEMALE CRIME

From antiquity to the present, cultures have categorized women into "either/or" roles.[55] One such pervasive conceptualization is the Madonna/whore duality. This cultural ideology has been reflected and perpetuated by the criminal justice system. It is grounded in two contrasting perceptions of the female "nature" or sexuality. The Madonna image personifies women as faithful and submissive wives, as well as nurturing mothers. The whore image portrays women as temptresses who prey on a man's sexuality and self-control. Inherent in this dichotomization are class and racial/ethnic assumptions. The Madonna image was primarily restricted to women from white, middle- to upper-class backgrounds.[56]

Archive Image / Alamy Stock Photo

This photo of a Victorian woman illustrates what is referred to as the cult of true womanhood.

Young further argued that black women have not experienced this "good/bad" dichotomy.[60] Rather, stereotypes of black women have essentially been "bad." Young attempted to identify the gender role characterizations that have been attributed to black females. For instance, the characterization of the black female as a matriarch has revealed two negative images—the *Amazon* (domineering, strong, assertive, independent, and masculine) and the *sinister Sapphire* (dangerous, castrating, and treacherous toward black men). Another instance of contradictory images is founded on myths concerning a black woman's sexuality—*mammy* (long-suffering, patient, nurturing, and asexual) and *seductress* (loose, immoral, and sexually depraved).[61] Young argues that black women in American society have been victimized by their double status as blacks and as women. Specifically, discussions of blacks have focused on the black man and discussions of females have focused on the white woman. Rather than being considered as a primary focus, black women have been on the periphery of understanding in terms of their position relative either to black males or to white females. Thus, "these images have influenced the way in which black female victims and offenders have been treated by the criminal justice system."[62]

Another pervasive cultural perception is "femininity." The concept of femininity is made up of various traits such as gentleness, sensitivity, nurturance, and passivity. Comparatively, traits associated with masculinity include intelligence, aggressiveness, independence, and competitiveness.[63] These conceptualizations become problematic when such traits are assumed to be inherent to an individual's sex or are considered as "biological fact."[64] Gender roles guided by concepts of femininity and masculinity are considered to be sex-linked behaviors as well as traits.[65] Related to the conceptualization of femininity was the cult of true womanhood. The attributes of true womanhood comprised four virtues: piety, purity, submissiveness, and domesticity.[66]

Comparative Criminology: *TRAFFICKING IN PERSONS*

Ranking Regions/Countries as Most Likely for Trafficking in Persons

In this section, we examine the findings and conclusions of studies regarding trafficking in persons, largely collected by the U.N. Office on Drugs and Crime (UNODC). The findings of these recent studies regarding the prevalence of trafficking in persons in certain countries, including the main origin countries as well as the main transit and main destination countries, are enlightening in several ways. The majority of trafficking in persons cases are for the purpose of sexual exploitation (77%), followed by those for the purpose of labor exploitation (23%). More than 60% of the victims are female, and more than 30% are minors (mostly girls), as shown in Figure 12.2.

Van Dijk synthesized some of the data from the UNODC published in 2006,[57] as well as a study by Kriistina Kangaspunta regarding the prevalence of trafficking in persons in the year 2002.[58] As shown in Table 12.3, the top five countries with the highest frequencies of trafficking in persons for country of origin (starting with the highest) were Russia, Ukraine, Thailand, Nigeria, and the Republic of Moldova (notably, the United States did not make the top 10 countries of origin). The top five main transit countries (those through which trafficked persons were sent) were (starting with the highest) Albania, Bulgaria, Hungary, Poland, and Italy. Finally, the top five destination countries were (starting with the highest) Belgium, Germany, Greece, Italy, and the Netherlands. Notably, the United States ranked 10th in destination countries.

As with data collected through official sources, this information may be more a reflection of the investigative activities of the police, or lack thereof, than of the extent of such crimes. This may be due to various reasons. First, not all countries are committed, or able, to conduct investigations or prosecutions of such cases. Second, trafficking in persons is not criminalized in some countries, so prosecutions of these crimes may be designated as something other than trafficking. Van Dijk maintains that if governments are not forthcoming about such crimes, the international media can be a helpful resource. Further, since trafficking in persons is a transnational crime, "reports on cases of human trafficking coming from destination countries often provide information about where the victims were recruited and through which countries they were transported."[59] Thus, while some countries, such as countries of origin or transit, may not acknowledge such criminal activities, information obtained from destination countries can be useful.

THINK ABOUT IT

1. What are some of the problems associated with collecting accurate data on trafficking persons?

2. What are the ramifications of not having accurate data on trafficking persons?

TABLE 12.3 Most Frequently Cited Countries of Origin, Transit, and Destination of Trafficking in Persons (2002)

	MAIN COUNTRIES OF ORIGIN	MAIN TRANSIT COUNTRIES	MAIN DESTINATION COUNTRIES
1	Russian Federation	Albania	Belgium
2	Ukraine	Bulgaria	Germany
3	Thailand	Hungary	Greece
4	Nigeria	Poland	Italy
5	Republic of Moldova	Italy	The Netherlands
6	Romania	Thailand	Israel
7	Albania	–	Turkey
8	China	–	Japan
9	Belarus	–	Thailand
10	Bulgaria	–	United States
11	Lithuania	–	–

Sources: Kangaspunta, K. (2003). Mapping the inhuman trade: Preliminary findings of the database on trafficking in human beings. *Forum on Crime and Society, 3,* 81–105; United Nations Office on Drugs and Crime. (2006). *Trafficking in persons: Global patterns.* Vienna, Austria: Author.

FIGURE 12.2 Victims of Trafficking in Persons, by Age and Gender, 2011

WOMEN 49%

MEN 18%   BOYS 12%   GIRLS 21%

Source: United Nations Office on Drugs and Crime. (2014). *Global report on trafficking in persons, 2014.*

Theories of female criminality emerged within this cultural context and the prevailing assumptions regarding women (e.g., the Madonna/whore duality, femininity, and the cult of true womanhood). When contextualized, the development of such theoretical constructs illustrates that "those women who do commit offenses are judged to be either criminal by nature or pathological because they deviate from the 'true' biologically determined nature of women which is to be law abiding."[67] Nicole Rafter Hahn argued that a woman was usually deemed "bad" if she had one of the following characteristics: (1) She was indecisive and lacked "moral fortitude," (2) she was promiscuous, or (3) she was irresponsible, because she was loosening not only her morals and values but also those of her mate and descendants.[68]

The following sections briefly review some of the early theories of female crime that reflect and incorporate these negative perceptions. Specifically, we will discuss such theorists as Cesare Lombroso, W. I. Thomas, Sigmund Freud, and Otto Pollak.

Cesare Lombroso: Physical Attributes of Female Offenders

One of the earliest theorists focusing on the female offender was Cesare Lombroso.[69] In his book *The Female Offender*, Lombroso emphasized the physiological and psychological determinants of female criminality rather than socializing factors or social–structural constraints.[70] For instance, Lombroso summarized some of the anomalies associated with prostitutes and other female offenders. He noted that prostitutes essentially do not have any wrinkles but are more likely to have moles, hairiness, large jaws and cheekbones, and anomalous teeth (see Table 12.4). According to Lombroso, women who committed homicides often had cranial depressions as well as prominent cheekbones.

TABLE 12.4

An Example of Lombroso's Summary Data Collected on Female Offenders—Wrinkles

	14 TO 24 YEARS		25 TO 49 YEARS		50 YEARS AND OVER	
	NORMAL	CRIMINAL	NORMAL	CRIMINAL	NORMAL	CRIMINAL
	54. PERCENT	20. PERCENT	72. PERCENT	41. PERCENT	32. PERCENT	9. PERCENT
Deep frontal, horizontal wrinkles	9.2	25	41.7	53.6	90.6	88.8
Deep frontovertical wrinkles	1.8	–	6.9	7.3	40.6	71
Crow's-feet	5	12.5	20	33	78	88.8
Wrinkles under the eyelids	1.8	–	15	14.6	46.6	44.4
Nasolabial wrinkles	25.9	25	69.5	63.3	96.7	100
Zygomatic wrinkles	–	–	5.5	12.2	28.1	22.2
Goniomental wrinkles	–	25	36.1	31.7	53.1	44
Labial wrinkles	–	–	6.9	12.2	28.1	44

Source: Lombroso, C. (1898). *The female offender.* New York, NY: Appleton, p. 72.

Lombroso implemented a typology for female offenders similar to the one he did for male offenders. He begins the chapter "The Born Criminal" by citing sexist comments such as the following Italian proverb: "Rarely is a woman wicked, but when she is she surpasses the man."[71] Other traits of this born criminal include a lack of the maternal instinct (which was regarded as a biological trait) as well as an excessive desire for revenge, cruelty, greed and avarice, love of dress and ornaments, a lack of religious feeling, and untruthfulness. When summarizing traits of the occasional criminal, Lombroso notes that occasional offenders can be divided into two classes—one that includes the milder types of born criminals and another that differs only slightly from the normal, or "consisting of normal women in whom circumstances have developed the fund of immorality which is latent in every female."[72] Although this theory has been refuted, this "biological determinism" perspective is entrenched in some theories of female criminality. For instance, while more sophisticated and technical, this biological determinism is evident in premenstrual syndrome explanations of female crime.[73]

W. I. Thomas: The Biology of Female Offending

W. I. Thomas argued that there are basic biological differences between males and females. For instance, maleness is "katabolic," which denotes the animal force that uses the destructive release of energy, resulting in the potential for creative work. Femaleness is "anabolic," which denotes motionless, lethargic, and conservative energy.[74] Thus, females were seen as passive and motionless, while males were seen as active and dynamic.[75] In his subsequent work, Thomas focused on female delinquency. This work was noted for a transition from physiological explanations to more sophisticated theoretical explanations that incorporate physiological as well as psychological and social-structural explanations.[76]

Thomas maintained that humans essentially have four desires: (1) the desire for new experience, (2) the desire for security, (3) the desire for response, and (4) the desire for recognition.[77] The desire for new experience and the desire for response were the two wishes that influenced criminal behavior. Therefore, Thomas argued that a woman who went into prostitution did so to satisfy a desire for excitement and response; for a woman, prostitution was the most likely option to satisfy those needs.[78] Environmental factors were also incorporated in Thomas's work. For instance, he maintained that "when crime and prostitution appear as professions they are the last and most radical expressions of loss of family and community organization."[79]

Sigmund Freud: Female Inferiority

Many early theories of female deviance embraced the psychoanalytic writings of Sigmund Freud. Many of these theories evolved from two key concepts: (1) the structure of the personality and (2) the psychosexual stages of development of the child.[80] Freud perceived women as anatomically inferior—biologically destined to be wives and mothers. The basis for this inferiority is that women's sex organs are inferior to men's sex organs. This is further argued by noting that the girl assumes that she has lost her penis as a punishment; as a result of this assumption, she is traumatized and matures with a sense of envy and vengeance. The boy also realizes that the girl has lost her penis; he fears a similar punishment and is wary of the girl's envy and vengeance. Thus, "women are exhibitionistic, narcissistic, and attempt to compensate for their lack of a penis by being well dressed and physically beautiful."[81] The Freudian orientation is not just restricted to this form of penis envy for understanding female deviant behavior. Freud also maintained that women are inferior because they are more concerned with personal matters and have very little interest in social issues.[82]

Within this perspective, a deviant woman attempts to be a man. Such a woman is forcefully rebellious. This drive to accomplishment is due to her longing for a penis. Since this drive will never be fulfilled, the result is that the woman will become "neurotic."

According to the Freudian orientation, the best way to treat such a woman is to help her adjust to her sex role. Thus, this reflects "the notion of individual accommodation that repudiates the possibility of social change."[83]

Otto Pollak: Hidden Female Criminality

In his 1950 book *The Criminality of Women*, Otto Pollak's concluding statement was that "the criminality of women reflects their biological nature in a given cultural setting."[84] Pollak argued that women are more criminal in nature than many have generally perceived. He suggested that criminologists should address the following three questions: (1) Are those crimes in which women seem to participate exclusively, or to a considerable extent, offenses that are known to be greatly underreported? (2) Are women offenders generally less often detected than are men offenders? (3) Do women, if apprehended, meet with more leniency than do men?[85] This unknown criminality is essentially due to women's deceitful nature and the "masked" quality of female criminality. He maintained that "the criminality of women is largely masked criminality."[86]

Pollak supported his theory of "hidden" criminality by noting such factors as the relative weakness of a woman, which make deceit necessary as a defense; that all oppressed classes use subversion as a common tactic; that a woman's socialization teaches her to conceal many things, such as menstruation, aggression, and marital frustration; and that the biology of the female enables her to deceive (i.e., she can fake an orgasm, while a man cannot).[87]

> Man must achieve an erection in order to perform the sex act and will not be able to hide his failure. His lack of positive emotion in the sexual sphere must become overt to the partner, and pretense of sexual response is impossible for him, if it is lacking. Woman's body, however, permits such pretense to a certain degree and lack of orgasm does not prevent her ability to participate in the sex act.[88]

It is interesting to stress that while Pollak did consider biological factors, he incorporated sociological factors as well. Like the other theorists we have discussed above, these sociological factors were based on assumptions and prejudices.[89]

In her classic essay on female crime, Dorie Klein revealed that theorists such as Lombroso, Thomas, Freud, and Pollak focused primarily on women's biology (i.e., their sexuality) or some type of psychological problem. Klein argued that these theorists focused on women's sexuality or other stereotypical traits, such as women being manipulative, to explain criminal behavior. They did not, however, examine economic, political, or social factors that provide a more comprehensive understanding of female criminality.[90]

FEMINIST CRITIQUES OF PREVIOUS RESEARCH STUDYING WOMEN AND CRIME

Feminist scholars have argued that science reflects the social values and concerns of dominant societal groups.[91] Subsequently, research in the social sciences has often ignored women and issues of concern to women, or has created differences between

---

LEARNING CHECK 12.3

1. According to _____, the criminality of women is primarily due to their ability to mask or hide their criminal behavior.

2. _____ maintained that women are inferior to men; this is primarily due to women's sex organs being inferior to men's sex organs.

3. Lombroso's theory has been designated as _____ determinism.

4. According to Thomas, maleness is "katabolic" and femaleness is _____.

Answers located at www.edge.sagepub.com/schram2e

women and men, girls and boys that are not "natural, essential, or biological."[92] Studies of women and crime have also been either marginalized or "invisible."[93] In 1977, Carole Smart noted that women have not been *entirely* ignored in the study of crime and deviance. The quality of work, however, is questionable at best. She stressed the importance of contextualizing female criminality within a broader framework: moral, political, economic, and sexual spheres.[94]

From a critical, feminist perspective, Ngaire Naffine conducted an extensive review of the literature pertaining to female criminality. Her review examined such theoretical perspectives as strain theory, differential association, masculinity theory, the Control School, labeling theory,

REUTERS/Robert Galbraith

Does society view female offenders differently than male offenders?

and the women's liberation thesis (discussed below).[95] With the exception of the women's liberation thesis, female criminality was rarely a major focus of these various theoretical perspectives. In fact, these theories were primarily based on adult and juvenile male offenders. If female criminality was mentioned, in most instances these explanations were founded on sexist assumptions and biases.

It is essential to understand that the inclusion of women does not necessarily imply that the study is using a feminist framework. To illustrate this point, feminists note that research using either an "add-and-stir" approach or a sex roles approach do not incorporate key feminist concepts:

1. **Add women and stir.** One approach to eliminating the "male centeredness" (i.e., androcentrism) of traditional analyses is the "add-and-stir" approach. That is, one uses an existing theoretical perspective based on males and "adds" women. Feminists argue, however, that if one merely "adds women and stirs" in a perspective or schema established by an androcentric analysis, the experiences of women will be marginalized or ignored. Women's experiences would then be located "as compared to men's" perspective. Many scholars contend that a great deal of criminological research incorporates this approach. Thus, although women are not necessarily invisible, their experiences and representation are infrequent and distorted.[96]

2. **Sex roles.** Another approach to conducting research on women has been to focus on the social construction of *sex roles*, currently referred to as *gender roles*.[97] Research using this approach has been criticized primarily because there is a tendency to perceive these roles as being almost sex linked, without incorporating a larger context as to how these roles have been defined or "determined." This approach can lead to a form of biological determinism due to the limited explanation or theoretical understanding of the conceptualization of roles.[98] (The "Why Do They Do It?" case on page 300 further illustrates this idea of "the conceptualization of roles" as related to a sex offender.) Candace West and Don Zimmerman proposed that it is essential to move beyond this approach of sex role, or gender role, studies. Instead, the focus of research should be "what is involved in doing gender as an ongoing activity embedded in everyday interaction."[99]

add women and stir: when one uses an existing theoretical perspective based on males and "adds" women.

sex roles: research using the sex role approach has been criticized primarily because of the tendency to perceive these roles as being almost sex-linked, without incorporating a larger context for how these roles have been defined, leading to a form of biological determinism.

The first of the modern gender-based perspectives on crime tried to understand female criminality rather than provide a more gender-sensitive approach to criminal behavior. The liberation thesis is one example of such a theoretical perspective. Another example of a gender-based perspective is John Hagan's power–control theory. While this is not a feminist theory, it is an integrated theory informed by feminism.[100]

LIBERATION THESIS

The liberation thesis, also referred to as the emancipation hypothesis, attempts to link the women's liberation movement with female crime rates. While there were various explanations for the changing female crime rates, two predominant explanations were (1) the increased opportunities for women to participate in the labor force and, thus, increased opportunities to commit certain types of crime, and (2) the changing self-concept and identity of women and girls due to the consciousness-raising aspects of the movement.[101] Two often-cited scholars of this perspective are Freda Adler and Rita Simon. It is essential to stress that these perspectives were offered during the second wave of feminism. Thus, they were influenced by what was occurring in the broader social context of that time.

Applying Theory to Crime: FEMALE SEX OFFENDERS

According to the UCR, a total of 2,290 females were arrested for sex offenses in 2014 (excluding rape and prostitution).[102] Sex offenses were defined as "[o]ffenses against chastity, common decency, morals, and the like. Incest, indecent exposure, and statutory rape are included. Attempts are included." Below are a few reports of female teachers who were arrested for sexually abusing their students:

- Joy Morsi, a 40-year-old Queens, New York, gym teacher was charged with having sex with two underage students. She pled guilty to one count each of rape and criminal sexual act charges. She was ordered to attend an outpatient program for a diagnosed depressive disorder followed by 10 years of probation.[103]

- In Texas, a middle school English teacher was accused of sexually abusing a 13-year-old boy; she later turned herself in to authorities. The 24-year-old teacher, Alexandria Vera, was charged with the continuous sexual abuse of a child. Vera claims that she and the 13-year-old are in love.[104]

- Brianna Altice, a 35-year-old English high school teacher in Utah was accused of having sexual relationships with three of her students; one boy was 16 years old and the other two boys were 17 years old. She pled guilty to three counts of forcible sexual abuse in exchange for prosecutors dropping an additional eleven counts, some including first-degree felonies.[105]

Robert Tanner from the *Associated Press* wrote the following:

A 17-year-old girl in upstate New York is forced into sex by a male teacher. Instead of sympathy, the student gets harassed for causing trouble for a popular teacher, threatened and pushed around by other girls. Just six weeks before graduation, she quits school.

A 17-year-old boy in Colorado is seduced by his attractive female teacher. A neighbor tells the teen's mom it was a sexual conquest like "climbing Mt. Everest." He has to hide from the crush of media attention.

They are crimes and abuses, but often they're treated as entertainment. Girls are pressed into the role of seducer or naive victim. Boys are seen as studs. Sexual misconduct by teachers is remarkably common in American schools, an Associated Press investigation found. But how Americans react to it is deeply split depending on the victim's gender.[106]

THINK ABOUT IT

1. Some would argue that these women do not fit the stereotype of a sex offender. Do you think they are sex offenders?

2. Do some people view male sex offenders differently than they view female sex offenders?

In her 1975 book *Sisters in Crime*, Adler argued that as women continue to strive for equality with men, they will also have more opportunities to commit crimes that were previously unavailable to them due to occupational discrimination:

> Women are closing many of the gaps, social and criminal, that have separated them from men. The closer they get, the more alike they look and act. . . . The simplest and most accurate way to grasp the essence of women's changing patterns is to discard dated notions of femininity. That is a role that fewer and fewer women are willing to play. In the final analysis, women criminals are human beings who have basic needs and abilities and opportunities. Over the years these needs have not changed, nor will they. But women's abilities and opportunities have multiplied, resulting in a kaleidoscope of changing patterns whose final configuration will be fateful for all of us.[107]

As the position of women becomes similar to that of men, this will result in women obtaining not only legitimate opportunities in the labor force but illegitimate opportunities as well.[108]

In her 1975 book *Women and Crime*, Simon proposed a similar argument.[109] She did differ from Adler, however, with respect to the types of crime that would be influenced by the women's movement. Adler maintained that due to women's liberation, the violent crime rate among women would increase. Simon suggested that only the property crime rates among women would increase and that the violent crime rates among women would, in fact, decrease because women's frustrations would lessen as they were provided more opportunities in employment and education.[110]

Naffine outlined the assumptions of the women's liberation theory: (1) The liberation movement can be linked to an increase in female crime, (2) the increase in female crime is a function of women becoming more masculine, and (3) these increases in female crime are due to women becoming actively competitive with men.[111] There are various problems with these assumptions, including the assumption about the relation between enhanced structural opportunities and the increase in women's offending rates. Statistics have revealed that women have not achieved equality in those high-paying and managerial professions.[112] There have been additional criticisms of the liberation thesis, including the manipulation of statistics and attempts to support the assumption that gender equality "produces" increases in crime rates among women.[113]

POWER-CONTROL THEORY

John Hagan and his colleagues developed the **power-control theory**, incorporating a conflict-oriented theory with social control theory.[114] The power–control theory attempted to explain gender differences in delinquency rates by including family dynamics. Specifically, Hagan argued that youths from families characterized as patriarchal (i.e., mother has lower status than father) revealed greater gender differences in delinquency rates compared with youths from more egalitarian homes (i.e., parents have same status or mother is the only parent in the home).

The argument was that female youths from more egalitarian families were encouraged to engage in risk-taking behaviors—just as their brothers were. Risk-taking behavior is considered to be related to delinquent behavior. Alternatively, female youths from patriarchal families were encouraged to avoid risk-taking behavior—unlike their brothers. Thus, these female youths were less likely to engage in delinquent behavior.

An integral aspect to the relationship between family dynamics, gender, and delinquency rates was social class. Hagan and his colleagues stressed the importance of class structure

liberation thesis: also referred to as the emancipation hypothesis; attempts to link the women's liberation movement with female crime rates.

power-control theory: integrated theory of crime that assumes that, in households where the mother and father have relatively similar levels of power at work, mothers will be less likely to exert control over daughters, and in households where mothers and fathers have dissimilar levels of power in the workplace, mothers will be more likely to suppress criminal activity in daughters but not in sons.

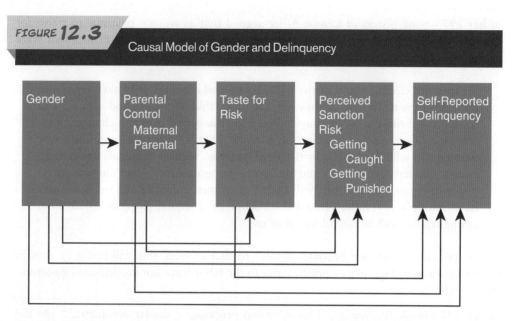

FIGURE **12.3**

Causal Model of Gender and Delinquency

Source: Hagan, J., Gillis, A. R., & Simpson, J. (1985). The class structure of gender and delinquency: Toward a power-control theory of common delinquent behavior. *American Journal of Sociology, 90,* 1157.

in the gender–delinquency relationship. While in all classes males are freer to engage in delinquent behavior than females, males in more powerful classes are the freest to engage in such behavior compared with males in less powerful classes.[115] As a result, individuals—especially those from various social classes—experience power relationships in the larger society differently. Specifically, the social reproduction of gender relations refers to those activities, institutions, and relationships that are involved in maintaining and reinforcing gender roles. These activities include those individuals responsible for caring for, protecting, and socializing children for their adult roles. According to this theoretical perspective, family class structure shapes the social reproduction of gender relations, which then influences rates of delinquency.[116] These power relationships in the larger society are reflected in the family relationships. Evaluations of the power-control theory reveal inconsistent findings;[117] others have maintained that the power-control theory is just a variation of the liberation thesis (i.e., the mother's liberation causes the daughter's criminal behavior).[118]

FEMINIST PERSPECTIVES ON UNDERSTANDING CRIME AND CRIMINAL BEHAVIOR

In 1987, Sandra Harding asked the question, "What's new in feminist analyses?" She provided three characteristics or features that distinguish feminist research.[119] The first feature is that the empirical and theoretical bases emanate from women's experiences. These bases, or resources, question as well as challenge traditional understandings of what has been considered human activity, as defined by white, European, middle-class men. By examining *women's experiences*, various issues are raised that contradict traditional research. The second feature of feminist analyses was the new purpose *for* women, whereas traditional analyses have primarily been for men. Research questions and answers are not "to pacify, control, exploit, or manipulate women." Furthermore, this research is implemented to meet the needs of women and to understand as well as

LAVINIA FISHER

Public domain

Built in 1802, the Old City Jail in Charleston, South Carolina, housed Lavinia Fisher and her husband, John.

On February 18, 1820, Lavinia Fisher and her husband, John Fisher, were hanged on the gallows in Charleston, South Carolina, for multiple robberies and murders. During the early 1800s, the Fishers operated a hotel called the Six Mile Wayfarer House, which was located 6 miles from Charleston, South Carolina. Men visiting Charleston started going missing—all after staying at the Six Mile Wayfarer House. After numerous reports of these missing men, authorities initiated an investigation. But given the couple's popularity and the lack of evidence, the authorities halted the investigation.

The local townspeople, however, were not satisfied and assembled a group of vigilantes, who attempted to stop the activities occurring at the hotel. Apparently, they were satisfied with their endeavors and returned to Charleston. At around the same time, John Peeples was traveling from Georgia to Charleston. He stopped at the Six Mile Wayfarer House to see if they had an available room. Lavinia greeted Mr. Peeples and informed him they did not have a room but invited him to tea and dinner. Mr. Peeples was attracted to Lavinia's beauty and charm. She asked him numerous questions. After some time, she informed Mr. Peeples that a room was available. During this time, Lavinia kept pouring tea for him; he did not like tea, but rather than appearing rude by refusing the tea, he poured it out when she was not looking.

Soon, Mr. Peeples grew uncomfortable. He noticed that Lavinia's husband, John, was shooting him odd glances while he talked to Lavinia; also, Mr. Peeples was worried that he had provided Lavinia with too much information and thought he might be a target for robbery. So he decided to rest in the chair by the door rather than in the bed. Later in the evening, he was awakened by a loud noise. He realized that the bed he should have been sleeping in had disappeared into a deep hole in the floor. Mr. Peeples jumped out the window and quickly informed the authorities. The police arrested John and Lavinia Fisher along with two men working with them. The police thoroughly searched the Six Mile Wayfarer House, uncovering hidden passages throughout the hotel, items that could be linked to various travelers who had been reported missing, tea laced with an herb that puts a person to sleep, a mechanism that opened the floorboards underneath the bed, and almost 100 sets of human remains in the basement.

THINK ABOUT IT

Some have considered Lavinia Fisher to be the first known female serial killer in the United States.

1. Why do you think Lavinia Fisher was involved with robbing and murdering numerous men visiting the Six Mile Wayfarer House?

2. Do you think there is a biological explanation? Do you think there may be a psychological explanation? Or do you think there are other factors that one should consider in explaining her criminal activity?

Source: South Carolina legends: Lavinia Fisher—First female American serial killer. See also Orr, B. (2010). *Six miles to Charleston: The true story of John and Lavinia Fisher*. Charleston, SC: History Press.

voice their experiences. The final characteristic of feminist research was locating the researcher in the same critical plane as the subject matter. Harding initiated this discussion by stressing that the sources of social power need to be examined. Specifically, she provided an example of how numerous studies have focused on the "peculiar mental and behavior characteristics" of women. Only recently, however, have there been studies on the "bizarre mental and behavioral characteristics of psychiatrists."[120]

Feminist scholars have raised various concerns with traditional research methods. Below, we briefly discuss two of these issues: (1) objectivity and subjectivity, and (2) qualitative "versus" quantitative analyses.

Objectivity and Subjectivity

Objectivity refers to being "neutral," "value free," or "unbiased." Feminist scholars challenge research claims of objectivity. In fact, they maintain that such claims are tautological; "value-free" (i.e., objective) research is a value. Furthermore, feminist scholars argue that the standards to assess objectivity are founded on biases established by, and for, individuals of privilege. Science and its practice are influenced by the values and experiences of its practitioners.[121] These practitioners are primarily from privileged backgrounds (i.e., white, middle-class males);[122] thus, androcentric and sexist biases are implicit in the standards implemented for conducting scientific research.[123] In the context of feminist jurisprudence, Catharine MacKinnon noted that "objectivity—the nonsituated, universal standpoint, whether claimed or aspired to—is a denial of the existence or potency of sex inequality that tacitly participates in constructing reality from the dominant point of view."[124]

Carolyn Wood Sherif provided additional challenges concerning "objective" research.[125] Her criticisms were primarily directed toward psychological research, but the issues that she raised can be directed to various types of social science research. She maintained that biases can occur at different points in the research process, including what to study, how to study the participants, and which behaviors or attitudes of the participants will be observed or ignored:

> The opportunity starts when a researcher decides what to study and it continues to widen during decisions about how to study the subject. . . . The researcher decides, of course, often in highly arbitrary ways dictated by custom in previous research, not by what the person does or is doing in daily life. . . . The researcher makes all of these decisions, often forgetting at times that he or she is a human being who is part of the research situation too.[126]

Feminist researchers acknowledge their biases and argue that other researchers need to do so as well. "In doing so, the false idealization of objectivity and the criticisms of subjectivity become meaningless and irrelevant."[127]

Qualitative "Versus" Quantitative Analyses

On the surface, the major distinction between these two types of analyses appears to be how the data are represented: qualitative is nonnumerical, and quantitative is numerical. But feminist researchers have raised questions regarding qualitative and quantitative methods. Toby Epstein Jayaratne and Abigail J. Stewart noted that quantitative methods translate individuals' experiences into predefined categories designated by the researchers. This method distorts women's experiences and results in "silencing women's own voices."[128] Those scholars advocating qualitative methods maintain that women's understandings, emotions, and actions must be explored in those women's own terms.

Researchers advocating quantitative methods maintain that although these methods can be, and have been, used to distort women's experiences, they need not be. As this

objectivity: refers to being "neutral," "value free," or "unbiased." Feminist scholars challenge research claims of objectivity.

qualitative: nonnumerical research methods; often compared with quantitative research methods.

quantitative: numerical research methods; often compared with qualitative research methods.

discourse continues, emphasizing *only* qualitative methods for feminist research has also been critiqued. For instance, Jacquelyn White and Richard Farmer conducted a study on sexual violence and implemented a multiple-strategic approach. They argued that it is essential to recognize that *both* the qualitative and quantitative methods have strengths and weaknesses:

> Empirical analytic methods cannot help us know the phenomenological experiences of a beautiful sunset, nor can we know the phenomenological experience of a rape survivor using traditional research paradigms. Conversely, subjective reports shed little light on the incidence and prevalence of sexual assault. There is, however, much that can be learned from both subjective methods and traditional scientific approaches when applied to the study of sexual aggression and victimization.[129]

It is essential to note that issues relevant to these types of research methods have been "politicized"—specifically, one method (i.e., quantitative) being deemed more "scientific" than the other (i.e., qualitative). However, one method is not "inherently" superior to the other; rather, these methods are only different approaches to understanding reality.

Feminist Criminology

Feminist criminology evolved, primarily from liberal feminists, with the realization and objection that gender was essentially ignored and excluded from criminological theory.[130] This exclusion was difficult to understand given that gender was such a strong predictor of criminal behavior.[131] Further, feminists recognized the limitations of critical and radical criminological perspectives given the primary focus on economic disparities without examining the issues of race and gender. Thus, "early feminist criminologists demanded that analyses of crime include consideration of gender in ways that had not occurred before."[132] Twenty years after her essay on female crime, Dorie Klein included an afterword; she maintained that feminist criminologists need to address three major challenges: (1) continue to search for the scientific basis of theories of men's and women's criminal behavior, (2) reexamine gender and racial/ethnic biases in the social sciences, and (3) develop a new definition of crime.[133] Joanne Belknap gave an overview of the potential of various traditional criminological theories to provide insight in examining gender differences and similarities in understanding criminal behavior. Some of the traditional criminological theories that do have some promise in this area of understanding include differential association theory and strain and general strain theory.[134]

Kathleen Daly and Meda Chesney-Lind identified the following five elements that distinguish feminist thought from other forms of social and political thought:

1. Gender is not a natural fact but a complex social, historical, and cultural product; it is related to, but not simply derived from, biological sex differences and reproductive capacities.

2. Gender and gender relations order social life and social institutions in fundamental ways.

3. Gender relations are constructs of masculinity and femininity and are not symmetrical but are based on an organizing principle of men's superiority and social and political–economic dominance over women.

4. Systems of knowledge reflect men's views of the natural and social world; the production of knowledge is gendered.

5. Women should be at the center of intellectual inquiry, not peripheral, invisible, or appendages to men.[135]

When addressing whether there can be a feminist criminology, Daly and Chesney-Lind maintained that feminist theories and research should be incorporated in any criminologist's study of crime. Incorporating such perspectives entails more than just a focus on women or sexism. Rather, these approaches provide an opportunity to study unexplored aspects of men's crime and forms of justice, as well as forms of theory construction and verification. Thus, they argued that the promise of feminist thought has barely been realized.[136]

Almost 20 years after Daly and Chesney-Lind's article on feminist criminology, Amanda Burgess-Proctor argued that for contemporary third-wave feminist criminologists, it is essential to build on the foundation laid by previous feminist criminologists.[137] Specifically, she maintained that feminist criminology needs to embrace all sources of oppression without prioritizing gender. Thus, feminist criminology should incorporate an intersectional framework, informed by multiracial feminism, which includes such defining social characteristics as race, class, gender, sexuality, nationality, and age.[138]

multiracial feminism: an intersectional framework that includes such defining social characteristics as race, class, gender, sexuality, nationality, and age.

pathways research: typically collects data, usually through interviews, at one point in time that provide retrospective inquiry as to an individual's life and life experiences.

One feminist framework that has been used to explore the experiences of women in the criminal justice system is pathways research:

> A feminist approach to understanding the etiology of females' (and sometimes males') offending is termed by some as "pathways to crime." . . . [T]his approach attempts to determine life experiences, particularly childhood ones, that place one at risk of offending. The pathways research indicates that traumas such as physical and sexual abuse and child neglect are not only defining features in the lives of many female offenders, but also these traumas are often related to one's likelihood of committing crimes.[139]

Whereas life course research collects longitudinal data over the course of an individual's life, pathways research typically collects data, usually through interviews, at one point in time that provides retrospective inquiry as to an individual's life and his or her life experiences.[140] Some feminists have argued that the pathways perspective has provided

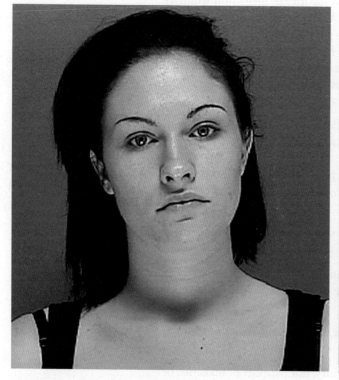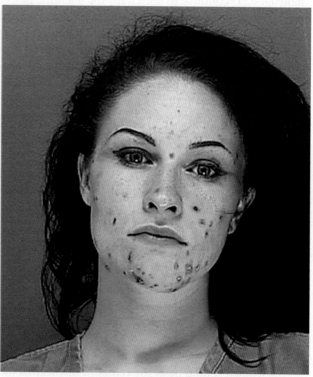

Before and after pictures of a woman who uses methamphetamine. One may question how this woman got to this point in her life—in other words, her pathway.

researchers with a greater understanding of how a woman's offending is influenced by the social conditions of her life as well as by her being a woman in a patriarchal society.[141]

Recently, a growing area of research has been using the pathways framework. Barbara Owen conducted what she termed a "quasi-ethnography" of women incarcerated in the Central California Women's Facility.[142] This methodology included in-depth interviews with these women as well as detailed observations of everyday life. When inquiring about these women's lives prior to prison, Owen identified three key issues that were central pathways to their incarceration—multiplicity of abuse in their pre-prison lives; family and personal relationships, especially those involving male partners and children; and their spiraling marginality and subsequent criminality.[143] A majority of these incarcerated women experienced various forms of physical, sexual, and emotional abuse in their lives. In addition, the abuse of drugs and alcohol was a key factor for many of these women prior to their incarceration. Many also experienced poverty as well as early parenthood. The spiraling marginality shared by many of these women included limited educational and vocational preparation, which resulted in a lack of employment opportunities. Owen concluded her book by noting that "this description of the lives of women in prison then is offered as a starting point for constructive dialogue and public policy concerning the lives and experiences of women on their own terms."[144]

Other examples of research focuses incorporating a pathways perspective include women incarcerated in an Iranian prison;[145] transferring female juveniles to adult court;[146] drug abuse among women;[147] sexual assault victimization and suicidal behavior;[148] the development of antisocial behavior;[149] the impact of serious mental illness and trauma in women's pathways to jail;[150] and risk factors among Arab female youths in Israel.[151]

CRITIQUES OF FEMINIST THEORIES

A number of criticisms concerning feminist theories have been raised by feminist scholars. In the 1960s, women of color challenged feminism by arguing that these perspectives essentially focused on the experiences of white middle-class women.[152] After reviewing feminist theory in sociology, Janet Saltzman Chafetz argued that the current topic among feminist scholars is the intersection of race, class, and gender.[153] A number of feminist scholars maintain that examining difference, rather than equality, is a major emphasis of current feminist studies.

While some feminist scholars maintain that this shift in focus has revitalized feminist theory,[154] others assert that it has introduced new conflicts in feminist studies.[155] Maxine Baca Zinn and Bonnie Thornton Dill stress, however, that while there may be problems when focusing on difference,

> our perspectives take their bearings from social relations. Race and class difference are crucial, we argue, not as individual characteristics . . . but insofar as they are primary organizing principles of a society which locates and positions groups within that society's opportunity structures.[156]

LEARNING CHECK 12.4

1. When one uses an existing theoretical perspective based on males and adds women, this is referred to as "_____."

2. The _____ is also referred to as the emancipation hypothesis.

3. The _____-_____ theory attempts to explain gender differences in delinquency rates by including family dynamics.

4. Some scholars maintain that approaches to assess _____ are based on biases established by, and for, individuals of privilege.

5. The _____ research approach attempts to determine life experiences, particularly childhood ones, that place one at risk of offending.

Answers located at www.edge.sagepub.com/schram2e

Some feminist scholars emphasize the importance of examining the interlocking, or intersection, of race, class, and gender.[157] The development of an intersectional perspective on gender and race is rooted in the work of scholars focusing on women of color.[158]

Amanda Burgess-Proctor identified key conceptual factors that distinguish multiracial feminism from other feminist perspectives.[159] First, multiracial feminism claims that gender relations do not exist in a vacuum; rather, men and women are also characterized by their race, class, sexuality, age, physical ability, and other social locations of inequality. Second, multiracial feminism stresses the importance of recognizing the ways intersecting systems of power and privilege interact on all social-structural levels. Third, multiracial feminism is founded on the concept of *relationality*; this "assumes that groups of people are socially situated in relation to other groups of people based on their differences."[160] Other key conceptual facets to multiracial feminism include appreciating the interaction of social structure and women's agency, implementing various methodological approaches, and an emphasis on understandings founded on the lived experiences of women. This evolving perspective uses various terms such as *multiracial feminism, multicultural feminism,* and *U.S. Third World feminism*.[161] Another issue that has been raised by feminist scholars is that, when conducting research on women, it is essential that one avoid placing these women as *either* offenders *or* victims. This has been referred to as the "blurred boundaries" theory of victimization and criminalization. As Mary Gilfus notes, "criminalization is connected to women's subordinate position in society where victimization by violence coupled with economic marginality related to race, class, and gender all too often blur the boundaries between victims and offenders."[162] This false categorization of women as *either* offenders *or* victims does not provide an enhanced understanding about women who commit crime.

Lisa Maher critiqued both traditional and feminist research with respect to the importance of not overemphasizing or ignoring women's agency.[167] The more traditional approach often overlooks the social locations of women's marginalization and places too much emphasis on female offenders as "active subjects" who pursue criminal opportunities. This places women with "overendowed" agency. On the other end of the spectrum, more associated with some feminist research, women are denied agency. Thus, "women are portrayed

women's agency: the more traditional approach overlooks social locations of women's marginalization and places too much emphasis on female offenders as "active subjects" who pursue criminal opportunities. On the other end, women are denied agency and situated as mere instruments for the reproduction of determining social structures.

Applying Theory to Crime: ROBBERY

Again, referring to the King of Babylon, Hammurabi, and the "Code of Laws," there are a few references to the crime of robbery:

- If a man has committed highway robbery and has been caught, that man shall be put to death.

- If the highwayman has not been caught, the man that has been robbed shall state on oath what he has lost and the city or district governor in whose territory or district the robbery took place shall restore to him what he lost.[163]

According to the FBI's Uniform Crime Reports, robbery is defined as "the taking or attempting to take anything of value from the care, custody, or control of a person or persons by force or threat of force or violence and/or by putting the victim in fear."[164] Below are some key findings on robbery; these are based on the FBI's report *Crime in the United States, 2014*:

- An estimated 325,802 robberies occurred nationwide in 2014.

- When comparing the 2013 and 2014 robbery rates, the rate decreased by 5.6%.

- An estimated $400 million in losses were attributed to robberies in 2014.

- The average dollar value amount of property stolen per reported robbery was $1,227. Banks were listed as the highest average dollar loss at $3,816 per offense.

- Strong-arm tactics were used in 43.0% of the robberies, firearms were used in 40.3%, knives and cutting instruments were used in 7.9%, and other dangerous weapons were used in 8.8% of robberies in 2014.

Table 12.5 is a summary of robbery by type from the FBI's *Crime in the United States, 2014.*

As noted previously, the National Crime Victimization Survey collects data to provide additional information concerning crime and victims in the United States. In reference to robberies, some key findings, based on 2014 data, are listed below:

- The number of robbery victims increased by less than 3% from 2013 (645,645) to 2014 (664,211).

- Among male robbery victims, 54% of offenders were strangers and 40% nonstrangers; among female robbery victims, 38% of offenders were strangers and 57% nonstrangers.

- In 2014, 48% reported there was no weapon involved in the robbery, compared with 45% who reported there was a weapon; less than 8% did not know.[165]

To illustrate key aspects of feminist pathways, we apply this perspective to the crime of robbery-theft. Emily was a 24-year-old woman incarcerated in a midwestern correctional facility for women. She was sentenced to 15 years for armed robbery. One may ask how Emily got to this point in her life. What pathways did she take during her life that resulted in her incarceration? To answer these questions, one could conduct an in-person interview with Emily and attempt to gain a more in-depth understanding of her life prior to being incarcerated.

After listening to Emily's past experiences, one obtains a greater understanding of how key aspects of her life led her down the pathway to incarceration. Emily was one of four children. Her father left her mother when she was two years old. She had a very unstable family life. When Emily was five years old, her mother married a man named John. Both her mother and John abused drugs and alcohol. John was physically abusive to Emily, her siblings, and her mother. John started sexually abusing Emily when she was 12 years old. During this time, Emily had a difficult time in school, both academically and socially.

At 15 years of age, Emily ran away. She was living on the streets and started abusing drugs, especially crack cocaine. When she was 17 years old, Emily met Matt, a 25-year-old involved in various criminal activities, including theft and drug sales. Although the relationship was quite tumultuous, Emily and Matt had a child. Eventually, Matt left Emily and the child. A year later, Emily lost custody of her child due to abuse and neglect. Emily continued to abuse drugs. To support her drug habit, Emily engaged in various criminal activities, including prostitution, shoplifting, burglary, and robbery.

THINK ABOUT IT

Critical thinking questions:

1. How does knowing Emily's "pathways" help us understand why she engages in criminal behavior?

2. What policies/programs could have been implemented to change Emily's "pathway" to incarceration? https://www.unodc.org/documents/data-and-analysis/glotip/GLOTIP_2014_full_report.pdf

TABLE **12.5**	Robbery by Location in the U.S. in 2014		
LOCATION	NUMBER OF OFFENSES (2014)	PERCENT DISTRIBUTION	AVERAGE VALUE
Street/highway	116,259	41.0%	$871
Commercial house	39,793	14.0%	$1,872
Gas or service station	7,095	2.5%	$1,026
Convenience store	15,276	5.4%	$699
Residence	47,569	16.8%	$1,466
Bank	5,220	1.8%	$3,816
Miscellaneous	52,608	18.5%	$1,235

Source: Federal Bureau of Investigation. (2015). *Crime in the United States, 2014.* Washington, DC: U.S. Department of Justice.

Comparative Criminology: *ROBBERY*

Rates of Robbery Across Different Continents and Regions of the World

Continuing with our comparisons between the United States and foreign nations in terms of various aspects in criminology and criminal justice, in this section, we examine findings from relatively recent data provided from the International Crime Victimization Survey.

As shown in Figure 12.4, Latin America and the Caribbean was the world region that reported the highest percentage of citizens who had been victims of robbery, which was three times higher than the global average. The second-highest was Africa, but this percentage was significantly lower than that of the leading region. Van Dijk noted that a high number of robberies in Latin America were committed with a firearm.

Furthermore, he pointed out Brazil, Mexico, and Argentina as having high rates of armed robberies. He also noted the most common form of robbery in modern times in these Latin American countries, which involves "express robberies," named after American Express credit cards. These robberies involve a victim being held at gunpoint or knifepoint until he or she withdraws money from the bank, typically from an automatic teller machine (ATM). Such chronic forms of these various types of robbery are likely the reason why Latin America and the Caribbean lead the world in terms of robbery.[166]

THINK ABOUT IT:

1. What policies/programs would you implement to deter these types of robberies (e.g., "express robberies")?

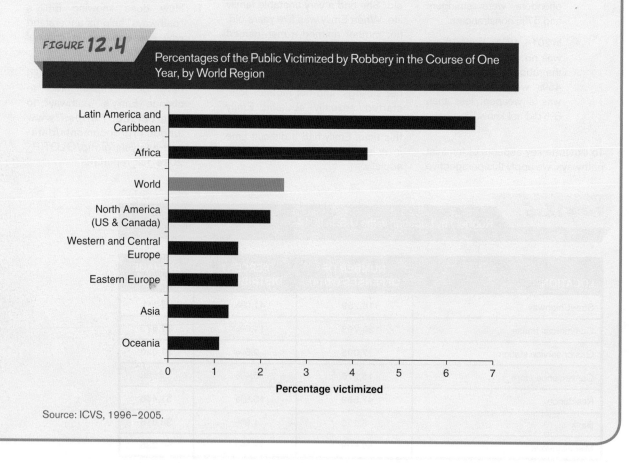

FIGURE 12.4 Percentages of the Public Victimized by Robbery in the Course of One Year, by World Region

Source: ICVS, 1996–2005.

as the passive victims of oppressive social structures, relations, and substances, or some combination thereof."[168] These women are then situated as submissive objects that are mere instruments for the reproduction of determining social structures.

POLICIES BASED ON FEMINIST THEORIES OF CRIME

A key aspect to understanding policies based on feminist theories of crime is that some policies are not always directly related to crime. Rather, feminist perspectives also incorporate broader social issues that are connected to criminal behavior.[169] Thus, aspects of policies related to feminist theories of crime are reflected in broader concepts of feminism. For instance, feminist researchers emphasize the importance of *reflexivity*.[170] This is when research empowers women; this form of research takes women's experiences seriously and centers on the idea that "the personal is the political":

> Feminist work has demonstrated that even the most apparently private interactions have political consequences and motivations. The inextricable connections between the personal and the political means that what happens to "the individual" is not merely the result of individual processes. As a consequence, it is unsatisfactory to treat individuals as if they were isolated from society—at the very least because this cannot give an accurate picture of people and their lives.[171]

This phrase "The personal is the political" refers to the notion that the "private sphere" (e.g., sexuality and domestic life) is as structured by power relations involving gender, sexuality, race, class, and age as the "public sphere" (e.g., waged work outside the home, party politics, and state institutions).[172]

Another aspect related to feminism is **praxis**. According to Donovan, praxis does not refer just to consciousness raising. Rather, praxis also refers to "the development of alternative arrangements that will themselves provide models for change and will in the process change consciousness.[173] Praxis also implies building alternative institutions, such as the establishment of rape crisis centers and shelters, as well as changes in personal relationships. Generally, praxis is when theory translates into action. One of the most essential opportunities for praxis centers on the pursuit of social justice.[174]

Influenced by the women's movement (i.e., the second wave of feminism), our understanding and the legal response to rape have undergone substantial changes.[175] For instance, the Schwendingers theorized how rape myths have pervaded the legal sphere of society, as exemplified by the belief that if a rape victim did not "fight back" or resist, as well as demonstrate physical evidence of such a confrontation, then she must have initially given her consent and afterward "changed her mind."[176] In the past, this myth has been significant in laws that required a demonstration of resistance. However, the Schwendingers provided the following analogy to elucidate the misconceptions associated with this myth:

> Businessmen may forcibly resist theft of their property. But no law *demands* this kind of personal resistance as a condition for the lawful protection of his property rights. Women's rights, on the other hand, seem to be another matter [italics in original].[177]

"The personal is the political": refers to the notion that the "private sphere" is as structured by power relations involving gender, sexuality, race, class, and age as the "public sphere."

praxis: refers not just to consciousness raising but also to the establishment of alternative arrangements that will provide models for change, which then change consciousness.

AP Photo/Detroit News, John T. Greilick

"SlutWalk Detroit" demonstrators protest against blaming and shaming victims of sexual violence.

Legislative reforms were enacted in an effort to modify state rape statutes. Searles and Berger asserted that the major goals of the legislative reforms included (1) increasing the reporting of rape and enhancing the prosecution and conviction in rape cases, (2) improving the treatment of rape victims involved in the criminal justice process, (3) achieving comparability between the legal treatment of rape and other violent offenses, (4) prohibiting a broader range of coercive sexual conduct, and (5) expanding the range of persons protected by the law.[178] Four major types of legislative reforms were identified: (1) redefinition of the offense, (2) evidentiary reforms, (3) statutory offenses, and (4) penal structure.[179]

Another example of how feminist criminologists have informed policies is in the area of **gender-specific programming**. The Office of Juvenile Justice and Delinquency Prevention established a funding opportunity to enhance programs specifically targeted to juvenile girls.[180] Such programming gives females an increased sense of community. This sense of community has been associated with juveniles developing and integrating a healthy identity.[181] Table 12.7 outlines factors associated with gender-specific programs for girls.

There have been efforts to incorporate these key factors of gender-specific services for female juvenile offenders. For instance, Bond-Maupin and her colleagues argued that intake officials recognized an appreciation of how gender, class, and race influence the lives of female juveniles.[182] Other studies have also recommended that agencies providing services to female juveniles incorporate gender-specific or gender-responsive programs.[183] Such programming has also been recommended for adult female offenders with substance abuse problems,[184] as well as for adult female prisoners.[185]

TABLE 12.7	Factors Associated With Gender-Specific Programs for Girls

THE VALENTINE FOUNDATION OUTLINED 14 FACTORS THAT SHOULD BE INCORPORATED IN A GENDER-SPECIFIC PROGRAM FOR GIRLS:
1. Ask girls who they are, what their lives are like, and what they need.
2. Allow girls to speak up and actively participate in the services they receive.
3. Assist girls with their family relationships and help them deal with family issues.
4. Assist girls in becoming grounded in some form of spirituality.
5. Allow staff more time and opportunity for building trusting relationships with girls.
6. Allow girls the safety and comfort of same-gender environments.
7. Provide girls with mentors who reflect girls' lives and who model survival, growth, and change.
8. Assist girls with child care, transportation, and safe housing issues.
9. Maintain a diverse staff who reflect the girls served.
10. Weave a multicultural perspective through programming.
11. Teach girls strategies to overcome domestic violence, physical and sexual abuse, and substance abuse.
12. Understand that relationships are central to girls' lives; help girls maintain important connections without sacrificing themselves to their relationships.
13. Connect girls with at least one capable and nonexploitive adult for an ongoing supportive relationship.
14. Promote academic achievement and economic self-sufficiency for girls.

Source: Valentine Foundation and Women's Way. (1990). *A conversation about girls.* Bryn Mawr, PA: Valentine Foundation.

gender-specific programming:

programs targeted to juvenile girls; gives females an increased sense of community that has been associated with developing and integrating a health identity.

CONCLUSION

In an effort to provide a context for feminist theories of crime, this chapter started with a brief history of feminism in the United States. Many describe this history in terms of waves (i.e., first, second, and third waves). As noted at the beginning of this chapter, it is essential for readers to understand that there is no one feminist perspective. Thus, this section presented various feminist perspectives, such as liberal feminism, radical feminism, Marxist and socialist feminism, and postmodern feminism.

The next portion of this chapter presented traditional theories of female crime. This brief overview gave readers an enhanced appreciation of the development of feminist criminology. These traditional theories were developed by such scholars as Cesare Lombroso, W. I. Thomas, Sigmund Freud, and Otto Pollak. The next section provided feminist critiques of previous research that focused on women and crime. Such critiques include using an "add-women-and-stir" approach and implementing a sex roles perspective.

Subsequently, we discussed various aspects pertaining to feminist perspectives on understanding crime and criminal behavior. This discussion included problems feminist scholars have raised pertaining to traditional research methods such as objectivity and subjectivity, as well as qualitative "versus" quantitative analyses. This section also presents a brief overview of multiracial feminism and how it differs from previous feminist perspectives. We also illustrate one example of research within a feminist perspective—feminist pathways. Key critiques of feminist theories were also raised in this section. These criticisms include earlier feminist theories focusing on the experiences of white, middle-class women; placing women as either offenders or victims; and ignoring women's agency.

We concluded this chapter with a discussion of policies based on feminist theories of crime. Two related concepts pertaining to any feminist research presented in this section were "the personal is the political" and praxis. We reviewed such policies as early rape reform efforts, as well as the current trend of providing gender-specific programs for female offenders.

At the beginning of this chapter, we presented the case study of Elizabeth Escalona, who pled guilty to injury to a child. We asked if some individuals would perceive such offenses committed by a mother differently than they would similar offenses committed by a father. Some may answer "yes" to this question; others may contend that this is due to stereotypes such as the perception that women have a biologically determined sense of maternal and nurturing capabilities. Also note that the case study discussion included references to Escalona's prior life experiences leading up to her abusing her daughter—in other words, pathways to crime.

SUMMARY OF THEORIES IN CHAPTER 12

THEORY	CONCEPTS	PROPONENTS	KEY PROPOSITIONS
Traditional theories of female crime	Dichotomize women into "either/or" roles in terms of sexuality; femininity; the cult of true womanhood; emphasize biological and psychological factors	Various (e.g., Cesare Lombroso, W. I. Thomas, Sigmund Freud, Otto Pollak)	Emphasized physiological and psychological explanations to understand female criminality, rather than social factors; particular emphasis on stereotypical assumptions of women and sexuality.
Liberation thesis	Increased opportunities for women to participate in the labor force; changing self-concept and identity of women; liberation movement	Freda Adler Rita Simon	As opportunities for women in the legal sphere are enhanced, so are opportunities for women in the illegal sphere; increases in female crime are due to women becoming actively competitive with men.
Power-control theory	Family dynamics; patriarchal families; egalitarian families; social class	John Hagan et al.	Youths from patriarchal families have greater gender differences in delinquency rates compared with youths from egalitarian families; individuals experience power relationships in the broader social context, especially those from different social classes.
Feminist criminology	Gender is not a natural fact but a complex social, historical, and cultural product; gender relations order social life; gender relations are constructs of masculinity and femininity based on organizing principle of men's superiority; systems of knowledge reflect men's view of the natural and social world; women should be at the center of intellectual inquiry	Various	Continue to search for the scientific basis of theories of men's and women's criminal behavior; reexamine gender and racial/ethnic biases in the social sciences; develop a new definition of crime; recognize the ways interesting systems of power and privilege interact on all social–structural levels.

KEY TERMS

add women and
   stir, 339

chivalry, 328

first wave of feminism, 354

gender, 327

gender-specific
   programming,
   352

liberal feminism, 329

liberation thesis, 340

Marxist feminism, 331

multiracial feminism, 346

objectivity, 344

paternalism, 328

pathways
   research, 346

patriarchy, 328

postmodern feminism, 333

power-control
   theory, 341

praxis, 351

qualitative, 344

quantitative, 344

radical feminism, 330

second wave of
   feminism, 327

sex, 327

sex roles, 339

socialist feminism, 331

"The personal is the
   political", 351

third wave of feminism, 327

traditional or conservative
   perspective, 329

women's
   agency, 348

DISCUSSION QUESTIONS

1. How would you distinguish the first, second, and third waves of feminism?

2. What are the key features of the various feminist perspectives?

3. How did traditional theories of crime perceive female offenders?

4. What are some of the problems associated with traditional research methods when studying gender?

5. What are some of the key concepts associated with feminist thought?

6. What is feminist pathways research?

8. What are some critiques of feminist criminological theories?

9. What is meant by "the personal is the political"?

10. What is praxis?

11. What are some of the major rape reforms?

12. What are the key factors of gender-specific programming?

WEB RESOURCES

National Organization for Women (NOW)

This web resource is the site for the National Organization for Women (NOW). NOW is dedicated to identifying the various issues, and implementing strategies, to women's rights.

http://now.org/

American Society of Criminology Division on Women and Crime

This web resource focuses on the increasing interest in the study of gender in terms of offenders, victims, and professional employees of the criminal justice systems.

http://ascdwc.com/

STUDENT STUDY SITE

WANT A BETTER GRADE ON YOUR NEXT TEST?

Get the tools you need to sharpen your study skills:

SAGE edge offers a robust online environment featuring an impressive array of tools and resources for review, study, and further exploration, keeping both instructors and students on the cutting edge of teaching and learning. Learn more at **edge.sagepub.com/schram2e**.

FOR FURTHER EXPLORATION AND APPLICATION, VISIT THE STUDENT STUDY SITE:

- Violent Crimes Prompt Soul-Searching in Korea About Treatment of Women

- At 75, Wonder Woman Lassos in a New Generation With An Ageless Fight

- Inner-city youth development organizations: Strengthening programs for adolescent girls

- Applicability of general power-control theory to prosocial and antisocial risk-taking behaviors among women in South Korea

- Feminist theory | Society and Culture | MCAT | Khan Academy

- Hard-hitting Interviews with Female Ex-offenders

- Five Arrested in Human Trafficking Ring Across Central, Southern California

- Philadelphia Mom Admitted Suffocating Her 2 Children in Florida, Police Say

- Girls Not Brides

- Child Abuse

- The Unslut Project

PREMIUM VIDEO:

Check out the Interactive eBook for premium videos, including videos from author Stephen Tibbetts, who discusses real-world examples and strange crimes; and videos from former offenders, who share their stories from a first-person view, and touch on key theories and concepts from the chapter.

CHAPTER 13

Developmental/Life-Course Perspectives of Criminality

INTRODUCTION

This chapter discusses the development of the life-course perspective in the late 1970s and its influence on modern research on criminal trajectories. During this period, criminological theorists and researchers began to realize that tracking the offending patterns of certain individuals over their lifetimes would add much to the understanding of why such individuals commit more offenses at certain points in their lives. The same type of examination also shows why individuals reduce, or even stop, offending after certain significant life events (e.g., getting a good job, getting married, having children).

Thus, this chapter focuses on explaining the various concepts in the life-course perspective, such as early onset, desistance, frequency of offending, and factors involved in criminal careers. Perhaps the best indicator for predicting future chronic, habitual offenders is when they were first arrested, labeled "early onset." To clarify, when an individual is arrested prior to age 14, this is likely the best indicator that the person is at high risk of becoming a habitual offender. Another important factor is when the person committed his or her most serious offenses. The other aspects of developmental theory are also insightful in our understanding of why individuals commit crime, especially in terms of when they commit most of their offenses (i.e., frequency), and perhaps more so regarding why they desist or stop offending. We will also discuss the criticisms and arguments against this developmental/life-course perspective. Finally, we will review the current state of research regarding the perspective of life-course or developmental theory.

To clarify, this chapter presents one of the most current and progressive approaches toward explaining why individuals engage in criminal activity—namely, developmental theories of criminal behavior. Developmental theories are explanatory models of criminal behavior that follow individuals throughout their life course of offending, thus explaining the development of offending over time. Such developmental theories represent a break with past traditions of theoretical frameworks, which typically focused on the contemporaneous effects of constructs and variables on behavior at a given point in time. Prior to the 1970s, virtually no traditional theories attempted to explain the various stages (e.g., onset, desistance) of individuals' criminal careers, and certainly no models differentiated the varying factors that are important at each stage. Developmental theories have been prominent in modern times, and we believe that readers will agree that developmental theories, also known as the life-course perspective, have added a great deal to our understanding and thinking about why people engage in criminal behavior.

BASIC CONCEPTS AND EARLY DEVELOPMENTAL THEORY

Developmental theories are distinguished by their emphasis on the evolution of individuals' criminality over time. Developmental theories tend to look at the individual as the unit of analysis, and such models focus on the various aspects of the onset, frequency, intensity, persistence/duration, desistance, and other aspects of the individual's criminal career. The onset of offending is

THE TEEN BURGLAR

A news story from the spring of 2012 reported that a 14-year-old boy had been arrested in Tennessee in connection with nearly 100 burglaries in the north Nashville area of Tennessee.[1] Officers said the teen was linked to these burglaries over the previous two years (making him 12 when he started offending). According to police, he had a specific and consistent modus operandi, or method of operation. Specifically, he would kick in back doors, enter, and steal whatever he could grab quickly, such as flat-screen TVs or video games. Officers noted his creativity and innovation, which included using a go-kart as his getaway vehicle, driving from house to house through back alleys. The police also mentioned that he had lost both parents and likely didn't have much guidance or anyone looking out for him. They had evidence tying him to the burglaries, such as fingerprints and items found inside his home, which likely is the reason he admitted to many of the break-ins. It is unfortunate that this boy had such a poor family life and so little parental supervision, but one must wonder what inspired him to commit more than 100 residential burglaries, starting when he was 12 years old! We will revisit this case in our conclusion, with additional insight into why he may have committed these crimes.

> ONE MUST WONDER WHAT INSPIRED HIM TO COMMIT MORE THAN 100 RESIDENTIAL BURGLARIES, STARTING WHEN HE WAS 12 YEARS OLD!

THINK ABOUT IT

1. Have you ever met or known about a child this young in your neighborhood doing so many crimes before the age of 10? If so, what do you think was the cause(s)?

2. How much do you think having poor parental supervision contributed to his crimes? Do you think he would have been prevented, or do you think he was driven to commit these crimes regardless of family supervision?

3. What do you think of his method of operation (i.e., modus operandi) in how he committed his burglaries? Do you see some intellectual skill in how he did it, given that he wasn't caught for 2 years?

when the offender first begins offending, and desistance is when an individual stops committing crime. Frequency refers to how often the individual offends at certain times, whereas intensity is the degree of seriousness of the offenses he or she commits at certain times in the offending career. Persistence or duration involves the length of an individual's criminal career in terms of time from onset to final offense. Finally, desistance refers to when the criminal career of an individual ends and he or she opts out of offending (or at least doesn't get caught again).

Experts have long debated and examined these various aspects of the development of criminal behavior. Perhaps the earliest notable focus on such development was presented in 1950 and after by Sheldon and Eleanor Glueck of Harvard University, who for more than 40 years performed research that examined the development of criminal careers among 1,000 boys (500 were persistent delinquents and 500 were not).[2] The Gluecks examined a plethora of variables, ranging from their subjects' IQ scores to their body types to their personalities, as well as multiple sociological factors. The data from this research have been utilized by researchers in modern times, primarily Robert Sampson, John Laub, and their colleagues, in exploring the various reasons why individuals offend early in life, as well as why some desist and others continue to offend, sometimes throughout their lives.[3] Many other studies have followed this model of examining a multitude of factors that may influence the development of individuals, especially in terms of criminality.

Virtually all studies on the life-course/developmental perspective show that most individuals who get arrested are never arrested again.[4] However, for those who offend many times, a certain pattern emerges. This pattern involves an escalation from minor-status offending (e.g., truancy, underage drinking, smoking tobacco), usually committed early in their preteen or early teenage years. This then leads to some higher level petty crimes (e.g., shoplifting, smoking marijuana) and then to far more serious criminal activity, such as robbery and aggravated assault, and eventually murder and rape. This development of criminality is shown across every study that has ever been performed and demonstrates that, with very few exceptions, people begin with relatively minor offending and progress toward more serious, violent offenses.[5]

Although this trend is undisputed, other issues remain unresolved. For example, studies have not yet determined when police contact or an arrest becomes *early onset*. Most empirical studies draw the line at age 14, so any arrest or contact prior to this time is considered early onset.[6] However, other experts disagree and say this line should be drawn earlier (say at 12 years old) or even later (such as at 16 years old). Still, however it is defined, early onset is one of the most important predictors of any of the measures we have for determining who is most at risk for developing serious, violent offending behavior. Given extensive research, the current "cut-off" age is still considered age 13.[7]

Another key area is persistence or duration of offending. This has become one of the most researched components of the developmental perspective.[8] A great example of persistence in offending is represented by the story of a 41-year-old man named Kevin Holder in Lincoln, Nebraska, who has been arrested 226 times.[9] Some may instantly think that Mr. Holder has just committed simple misdemeanors, but that is not the case. Rather, his

© iStockphoto.com/PIKSEL

Chronic offending often starts with minor offenses, such as truancy, smoking, and underage drinking, but then escalates to more serious offenses, such as burglary, robbery, and assault.

developmental theories: perspectives of criminal behavior that emphasize the evolution of individuals' criminality over time, with the individual as the unit of analysis.

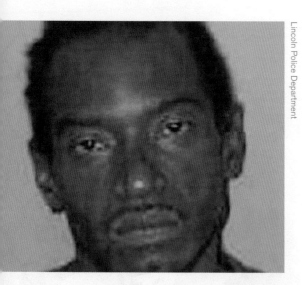

Lincoln Police Department

Kevin Holder has been arrested at least 226 times for a variety of offenses.

past offenses include assault, resisting arrest, assault on a police officer, and violation of a restraining order. What is even more shocking is that he was nowhere near the top rank in terms of number of arrests in that one county in Lincoln, Nebraska; he ranked number 40! Thus, there were 39 offenders in that county who had been arrested more frequently. In fact, the authorities there reported that a few had more than 500 arrests. This is an example, albeit extreme, of what is meant by persistence or duration of a criminal career.

Perhaps the most discussed and researched aspect of developmental theory is *offender frequency*, referred to as *lambda*. Estimates of lambda, or average frequency of offending by criminals over a year period, vary greatly.[10] Some estimates of lambda are in the high single digits, and some are in the triple digits. Given this large range, it does not do much good in estimating the frequency of most offenders. Rather, the frequency depends on many, many variables, such as what types of offenses the individual commits. Perhaps if we were studying only drug users or rapists, it would make sense to determine lambda, but given the general nature of most examinations of crime, such estimates are not typically useful. Thus, the frequency of offending, even within crime type, varies so widely across individuals that we question its use in understanding criminal careers.[11] Still, it can sometimes be useful to have an estimate of lambda or frequency, such as if a researcher is investigating a specific type of offense or particular group of offenders.

It is notable that the developmental/life-course perspective has recently become one of the most dominant theories in explaining criminality. A study conducted in 2008 surveyed 387 criminologists to discover which theories each of them considered the most viable explanations for serious/persistent criminal behavior.[12] This study found that life-course/developmental theory was ranked number 2 for most accepted theoretical explanation of serious crime (after social learning theory, which was ranked number 1). This perspective made a giant leap in ranking from similar surveys done in past years.[13]

Before we discuss the dominant models of developmental theory, it is important to discuss the opposing viewpoint, which is that of complete stability in offending. Such counterpoint views assume that the developmental approach is a waste of time because the same individuals who show antisocial behavior at early ages (before age 10) are those who will exhibit the most criminality in their teenage years, 20s, 30s, 40s, and so on. This framework is most notably represented by the theoretical perspective proposed by Gottfredson and Hirschi in their model of low self-control.

ANTIDEVELOPMENTAL THEORY: LOW SELF-CONTROL THEORY

In 1990, Travis Hirschi, along with his colleague Michael Gottfredson, proposed a general theory of low self-control as the primary cause of all crime and deviance (see prior discussion in Chapter 10); this is often referred to as the *general theory of crime*.[14] This theory has led to a significant amount of debate and research in the field since its appearance, more than any other contemporary theory of crime. Like other control theories of crime that we previously discussed (see Chapter 10), this theory assumes that individuals are born predisposed toward selfish, self-centered activities and that only effective child rearing and socialization can create self-control. Without such adequate socialization (i.e., social controls) and reduction of criminal opportunities, individuals will follow their natural tendencies to become selfish predators.

The general theory of crime assumes that self-control must be established by age 10. If it has not formed by that time, according to the theory, individuals will forever exhibit low self-control. This assumption of the formation of low self-control by age 10 is the oppositional feature of this theory compared with the developmental perspective. Once low self-control is set at age 10, there is no way to develop it afterward, the authors assert. In contrast, developmental theory assumes that people can, indeed, change over time.

Like others, Gottfredson and Hirschi attribute the formation of controls to socialization processes in the first years of life; the distinguishing characteristic of this theory is its emphasis on the individual's ability to control him- or herself. That is, the general theory of crime assumes that people can exercise a degree of control over their own decisions and, within certain limitations, control themselves. The general theory of crime is accepted as one of the most valid theories of crime.[15] This is probably due to the parsimony, or simplicity, of the theory, because it identifies only one primary factor that causes criminality—low self-control.

But low self-control may actually consist of a series of personality traits, including risk taking, impulsiveness, self-centeredness, short-term orientation, and quick temper. Recent research has supported the idea that inadequate child-rearing practices tend to result in lower levels of self-control among children and that these low levels of self-control produce various risky behaviors, including criminal activity.[16] It is important to note that even this theory has a developmental component in the sense that it proposes that self-control develops from parenting practices during the early years; thus, even this most notable antidevelopment theory actually includes a strong developmental aspect (see Figure 13.1).

In contrast to Gottfredson and Hirschi's model, one of the most dominant and researched frameworks of the past 20 years, another sound theoretical model shows that individuals can change their life trajectories in terms of crime. Research shows that certain events or realizations can lead people to alter their frequency or incidence of offending, sometimes to zero. To account for such extreme transitions, we must turn to the dominant life-course model of offending, which is Sampson and Laub's developmental model of offending.

LEARNING CHECK 13.1

1. According to the text, how do developmental/life-course theories of crime differ from traditional explanatory models?

   a. Developmental models focus more on group rates of crime.

   b. Developmental theories tend to put more emphasis on the state of the economy.

   c. Developmental models emphasize following individuals through various stages in their lives.

   d. Developmental theories focus more on the political changes that occur.

2. According to the text, which of the many concepts/factors in developmental theory seems to offer the best chance for predicting future criminality?

   a. Desistance

   b. Early onset

   c. Duration

   d. Frequency (lambda)

3. According to a study discussed in the text, a recent survey of 387 criminologists found that they ranked developmental/life-course theory where among all existing theoretical perspectives in ability to explain serious criminal behavior?

   a. No. 1

   b. No. 2

   c. No. 4

   d. No. 7

Answers located at www.edge.sagepub.com/schram2e

Comparative Criminology: *CHILD ABUSE*

Some Exploratory Studies on Child Abuse in Other Countries

Unfortunately, there is no systematic global data collection regarding child abuse; however, the World Health Organization (WHO, 2006) estimated that there were about 31,000 homicides globally of children under 15 in just the year 2002. This study also found that perpetrators of child abuse had witnessed violence against their mothers when they were young. This is consistent with studies that repeatedly find links between childhood exposure to domestic violence and violent offending at older ages (see discussion in Van Dijk, 2008, p. 88). This phenomenon is commonly referred to as the "cycle of violence." In terms of prevalence, a 2014 WHO report found that Estimates of child maltreatment indicate that nearly a quarter of adults (22.6%) worldwide suffered physical abuse as a child, 36.3% experienced emotional abuse and 16.3% experienced physical neglect (WHO, 2014).

Van Dijk (2008) points out that perhaps the most comprehensive studies of child abuse in modern times were done in Germany, surveying more than 11,000 teenagers about their experiences with domestic violence. One consistent finding was that children of immigrants reported significantly higher rates/percentages of violence against mothers, with extremely high rates among those from Turkey (32%), Yugoslavia (25%), and Russia (20%). Another interesting pattern was that the immigrant families that

had resided in Germany for longer periods had higher rates of domestic violence, which Van Dijk claimed suggested "growing tensions between spouses after a longer exposure of women to German norms and values concerning gender equality" (p. 88).

Also notable, WHO (2006) estimated that annual economic costs in the United States due to child abuse totaled about $94 billion. And although traditionally rare, there is a growing trend to punish much more severely parents and caretakers who abuse children, which also adds to the costs in terms of processing and incarcerating offenders. For example, in October 2012, a 23-year-old Texas woman was sentenced to 99 years in prison for such abuses as gluing her daughter's hands to the wall and beating her as punishment for potty-training setbacks. (Read more about this story here: http://abcnews.go.com/US/texas-mom-glued-daughters-hands-wall-99-years/story?id=17436643.)

THINK ABOUT IT

1. To what extent do you think that extreme child abuse leads to future criminality by the victims of such acts?

2. What type of parenting style is likely to be done by the child victims of such abuse when they become parents? Are they likely to continue the parenting style that they experienced?

Sources: Van Dijk, J. (2008). The world of crime. Thousand Oaks, CA: Sage; World Health Organization. (2006).

Preventing Child Maltreatment: a guide to taking action and generating evidence. Geneva: Author;. World Health Organization. (2014). GLOBAL STATUS REPORT ON VIOLENCE PREVENTION 2014.

MODERN DEVELOPMENTAL/ LIFE-COURSE PERSPECTIVES

Sampson and Laub's Developmental Model

One of the best-known and best-researched developmental theoretical models to date is that of Robert Sampson and John Laub.[17] Sampson and Laub have proposed a developmental framework largely based on a reanalysis of original data collected by Sheldon and Eleanor Glueck in the 1940s. As a prototype developmental model, individual stability and change are the primary foci of their theoretical perspective.

Most significantly, Sampson and Laub emphasized the importance of certain events and life changes that can alter an individual's decisions to commit (or not commit) criminal actions. Although based on a social control framework, this model contains elements of other theoretical perspectives. First, Sampson and Laub's model assumes, like other developmental perspectives, that early antisocial tendencies among individuals, regardless of social variables, are often linked to later adult criminal offending. Furthermore, some social-structure factors (e.g., family structure, poverty, etc.) also tend to lead to problems in social and educational development, which then lead to crime. Another key factor in

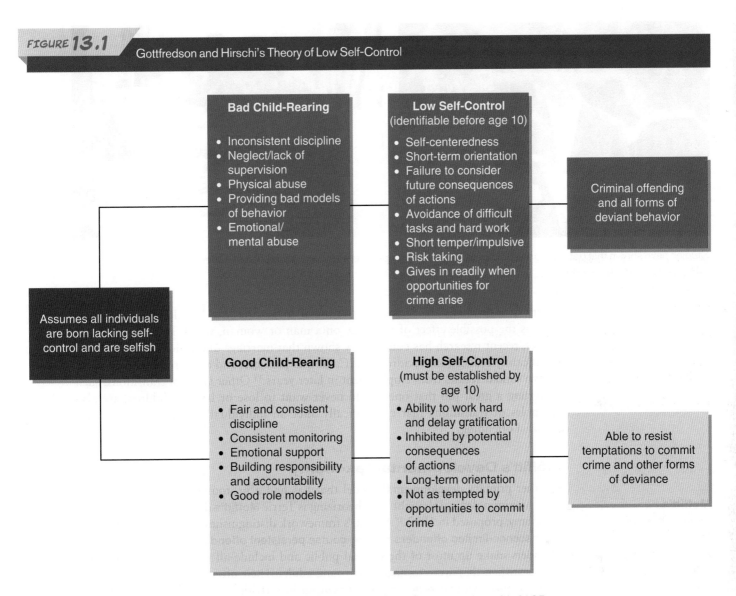

FIGURE **13.1**   Gottfredson and Hirschi's Theory of Low Self-Control

Source: Tibbetts, S. G. (2012). *Criminological theory: The essentials* (p. 602). Thousand Oaks, CA: SAGE.

this development of criminality is the influence of delinquent peers or siblings, which further increases an individual's likelihood for delinquency.

However, Sampson and Laub also strongly emphasize the importance of transitions, or specific events (e.g., marriage, stable employment) that are important in altering long-term trends in behavior, which are referred to as trajectories. Trajectories are more non-specific, longitudinal patterns of behavior either toward or away from committing crime and are typically the cumulative result of certain or many specific transitions, such as marriage, employment, having children, or enlisting in military service, which drastically change a person's criminal career. Sampson and Laub show sound evidence that many individuals who were once on a path toward a consistent form of behavior—in this case, serious, violent crime—suddenly (or gradually) halted due to such a transition or series of transitions. In some ways, this model is a more specified form of David Matza's theory of drift, which we discussed in Chapter 10, in which individuals tend to grow out of crime and deviance due to the social controls imposed by marriage, employment, and so on.

Still, Sampson and Laub's framework contributed much to the knowledge of criminal offending by providing a more specified and grounded framework that identified the

transitions: events important in altering trajectories toward or away from crime, such as marriage or employment.

trajectories: paths people take in life, often due to life transitions.

Studies have shown that getting married and obtaining steady employment significantly reduce the offending rates of even chronic offenders.

ability of individuals to change their criminal trajectories via life-altering transitions, such as the possible effect of marriage on a man or woman, which is quite profound. In fact, recent research has consistently shown that marriage and full-time employment significantly reduced the recidivism of California parolees, and other recent studies have shown similar results from employment in later years.[18] Other types of transitions, such as getting a great job that one would never want to lose or having children, are also examples of transitions that can radically alter an individual's trajectory away from criminal offending.

Moffitt's Developmental Taxonomy

Another primary developmental model that has had a profound effect on the current state of criminological thought and theorizing is Terrie Moffitt's developmental theory or taxonomy, proposed in 1993.[19] Moffitt's framework distinguishes two types of offenders: adolescence-limited offenders and life-course persistent offenders. Adolescence-limited offenders make up most of the general public and include all persons who committed offenses when they were teenagers or young adults. Their offending was largely caused by association with peers and a desire to engage in activities exhibited by the adults they were trying to emulate. Such activities are a type of rite of passage and quite normal among all people who have normal social interactions with their peers in teenage or young adult years. It should be noted that a small percentage (about 1% to 3%) of the population are nonoffenders who, quite frankly, do not have normal relations with their peers and therefore do not offend at all, even in adolescence.

On the other hand, there exists another, smaller group of offenders, referred to in this model as *life-course persistent offenders*. This small group, estimated to account for 4% to 8% of all offenders—albeit the most violent and chronic—commit the vast majority of the serious, violent offenses in any society, such as murder, rape, and armed robbery. In contrast to the adolescence-limited offenders, the disposition of life-course persistent offenders toward offending is caused by an entirely different model: an interaction between neurological problems and the disadvantaged or criminological environments in which they were raised.

For example, if an individual has only neurological problems or only came from a poor, disadvantaged environment, then that individual will be unlikely to develop a life-course persistent trajectory toward crime. However, if a person has both neurological problems and came from a disadvantaged environment, then that individual will have a very high

Moffitt's developmental theory or taxonomy: a theoretical perspective proposing that criminal acts are committed by (1) adolescence-limited offenders or (2) life-course persistent offenders.

adolescence-limited offenders: a type of offender who commits crimes only during adolescence and desists in his or her 20s or adulthood.

life-course persistent offenders: a type of offender who starts offending early and persists through adulthood.

WHY DO THEY DO IT?

HENRY EARL

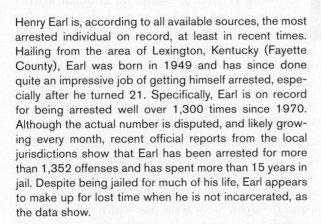

Henry Earl, arrested more than 1,300 times, is widely considered the most arrested individual in U.S. history.

Henry Earl is, according to all available sources, the most arrested individual on record, at least in recent times. Hailing from the area of Lexington, Kentucky (Fayette County), Earl was born in 1949 and has since done quite an impressive job of getting himself arrested, especially after he turned 21. Specifically, Earl is on record for being arrested well over 1,300 times since 1970. Although the actual number is disputed, and likely growing every month, recent official reports from the local jurisdictions show that Earl has been arrested for more than 1,352 offenses and has spent more than 15 years in jail. Despite being jailed for much of his life, Earl appears to make up for lost time when he is not incarcerated, as the data show.

Although many of his arrests were for public intoxication, he also had a number of more serious charges, including third-degree trespassing, and various charges of disorderly conduct. Readers are probably wondering how this man could still be on the streets, but the most likely explanation is that virtually all his arrests were for nonviolent, nontheft, and nondrug (except alcohol) violations, which tend not to get much jail time. However, one would think that after the first hundred arrests, not to mention the first thousand, the judges would try to put this public nuisance away for a long time. Apparently, that is not the case. Earl's last reported arrest was in November 2013, so he is seemingly still active and perhaps trying to achieve a record of arrests that may be hard for anyone to beat.

This goes to show a couple of things that relate to this chapter. First, if someone is highly motivated to commit crime, he or she can easily find ways to do so. After all, anyone can simply leave the house and commit numerous felonies against neighbors, people driving by on the street, and so forth—not to mention what that person is capable of outside of his or her neighborhood. Second, there is virtually no way to deter or stop a person from committing

a crime he or she is highly motivated to commit, especially if that person has nothing to lose. Obviously, Earl has nothing at stake in terms of conventional society.

This case is notable in the context of developmental/life-course criminology. Although a highly extreme case study, it reveals that normal development, such as key transitions in life, as noted by Sampson and Laub's theory, clearly don't apply in this case. Some individuals have an extremely high predisposition to offend, an even higher disposition than Gottfredson and Hirschi's theory of low self-control may have imagined possible. Regardless, this amazingly strong disposition toward such antisocial behavior is likely due to major failures in all areas of development throughout Earl's life course, beginning with his genetics, early development, and adolescence.

THINK ABOUT IT

1. Can you apply the life-course persistent label from Moffitt's theory to Henry Earl?

2. Can you think of any intervention or policy that would help Mr. Earl reduce his consistent arrests

Sources: Henry Earl: Setting the record straight. (2008, September 25). *Smoking Gun.* Lexington-Fayette Urban County Government, Division of Community Corrections. (n.d.). *JailWebsite.com.*

United States Department of Justice.

©iStockphoto.com/Vincent Shane Hansen

Terrie Moffitt developed the most renowned and studied developmental framework, which not only identified different types of offenders but also provided a causal etiology for why chronic, persistent offenders differ from relatively normal individuals who commit crime only during their adolescent years.

likelihood of becoming a chronic, serious, violent offender. This proposition, which has been supported by empirical studies,[20] suggests that it is important to pay attention to what happens early in life.

Because illegal behaviors are normal among teenagers or young adults, more insight can be gained by looking at the years prior to age 12 to determine who is most likely to become a chronic, violent offender. Life-course persistent offenders begin offending very early in life and continue to commit crime far into adulthood, even middle age, whereas adolescence-limited offenders tend to engage in criminal activity only during their teenage and young-adult years. Moffitt's model suggests that more than one type of development explains criminality. Furthermore, this framework shows that certain types of offenders commit crime due to entirely different causes and factors.

Thornberry's Interactional Model of Offending

A final major developmental theory was presented by Terrence Thornberry in 1987.[21] This model incorporated empirical evidence that addressed an extremely important aspect never before addressed in criminological theory. Specifically, Thornberry's interactional theory was the first to emphasize reciprocal, or feedback, effects in the causal modeling of the theoretical framework. To clarify, this was the first widely acknowledged model that presented certain factors, such as peer associations, both as a predictor variable and as a factor that is subsequently influenced by other factors that follow it temporally, such as offending. In other words, negative peer influences predict future offending, but such offending can then cause even more negative peer influence, thus leading to even more criminality.

As a basis for his model, Thornberry combined social control and social learning models. According to Thornberry, both of these theories try to explain criminality in a straightforward, causal process and are largely targeted toward a certain age population.[22] Thornberry uniquely claims that the processes of both social control and social learning theory affect each other in a type of feedback process.

Thornberry's interactional model incorporates five primary theoretical constructs, which are synthesized in a comprehensive framework to explain criminal behavior. These five concepts are commitment to school, attachment to parents, belief in conventional values (these first three are taken from social control and bonding theory), adoption of delinquent values, and association with delinquent peers (these last two are drawn from social learning and differential association–reinforcement theory). These five constructs, which most criminologists would agree are important in the development of criminality, are obviously important in a rational model of crime; so at first, it does not appear that Thornberry has added much to the understanding of criminal behavior. Furthermore, Thornberry's model clearly points out that different variables will have greater effects at certain times; for example, he claims that association with delinquent peers will have more effect in the mid-teenage years than at other ages.

What Thornberry adds beyond other theories is the idea of reciprocity or feedback loops, which no previous theory had mentioned, much less emphasized. In fact, much of the previous criminological literature spent much time debating whether individuals

Applying Theory to Crime: ARSON

Arson is a serious crime in terms of Federal Bureau of Investigation (FBI)/Uniform Crime Reports (UCR) standards; it is categorized as a Part I/Index crime. According to Winslow and Zhang, the FBI did not seriously consider arson an Index crime until around 1978, when it was realized that incidents of arson had increased more than 3,100% between the years 1951 and 1977. Thus, the authorities at the U.S. Department of Justice in charge of the FBI and UCR decided that arson should be added to the other seven Index crimes. The FBI definition of arson is "any willful or malicious burning or attempting to burn, with or without intent to defraud, a dwelling house, public building, motor vehicle, or aircraft, personal property of another, etc." As you can see, this is a wide definition, which is why there are so many different types of arson. After all, some youths start fires for excitement, some business owners start fires to cash in on insurance claims, and pyromaniacs light fires to fulfill a psychological compulsion to burn things, whereas others burn crime scenes to destroy evidence or to get revenge on others. There are even more reasons to start illegal fires, but they all fall under this category of arson.

The reason why we are discussing arson in this chapter is because it is the only Part I/Index offense primarily committed by young people (under 14). The vast majority of arsonists are male. Furthermore, early onset of offending (a key factor of the developmental perspective) is often seen in an act of arson—"boys playing with fire." And although such youths often do not realize the implications of their actions, it still often causes much property damage and sometimes costs lives. Given the prevalence and clustering of arson in young ages, we are discussing it in this chapter; however, the act of arson spans a variety of ages and motives.

According to recent reports by the FBI, there were about 42,934 official reports/incidents of arson in the United States in 2014. The average damage/loss due to arson in that year was $16,055. Arsons involving structures (e.g., residential, public, storage) accounted for about 45% of the total, whereas mobile property (e.g., vehicles) and other types of property (e.g., crops, fences) accounted for about 23% and 31%, respectively. This shows the need for further prevention of this Index offense and reveals why it is a top priority for the FBI and other agencies in the federal government.

Perhaps this is why many programs have been formed to prevent arson, especially among youths. Various types of intervention programs have been started to try to curb high-risk "fire-setters." And, as mentioned before, this is one of the early predictors or "red flags" that developmental/life-course researchers examine in determining the likelihood someone will become a chronic offender. As many readers have likely heard, serial killers often have a history of cruelty toward domesticated animals (such as dogs and cats), or a history of bed-wetting. Early engagement in arson is another of these early key predictors of a chronic criminal career, such as in the case of David "Son of Sam" Berkowitz, who killed at least six victims and wounded seven others with a .44 caliber handgun over the course of about a year (1976–1977) in New York City. Berkowitz had a long record of committing arsons earlier in his life.

On the other hand, some youths simply are bored or are being experimental and don't ever intend harm to anyone or anything. However, early incidents of arson are certainly a "red flag" in developmental theory and should be taken seriously.

THINK ABOUT IT

1. How do you see arson as a "red flag" for predicting habitual offending in the future?

2. Do you think arson should be considered one of the key Index/Part I offenses by the FBI in their annual national index of offending? Why or why not?

Sources: U.S. Department of Justice. (2015). *Uniform crime report, 2014.* Washington, DC: Author; Winslow, R., & Zhang, S. (2008). *Criminology: A global perspective.* Upper Saddle River, NJ: Pearson, p. 42.

become delinquent and then start hanging out with similar peers or whether individuals start hanging out with delinquent peers and then begin engaging in criminal activity. This has been the traditional "chicken-or-egg" question in criminology for most of the 20th century—namely, "Which came first, delinquency or bad friends?" It has often been referred to as the *self-selection* versus *social learning* debate; in other words, do certain individuals decide to hang out with delinquents based on their previous behavior, or do they learn criminality from delinquents with whom they associate? One of the major contributions of Thornberry's interactional model is that he directly answered this question.

Thornberry's interactional model: the first major perspective to emphasize reciprocal, or feedback, effects in the causal modeling of the theoretical framework

Specifically, Thornberry noted that most, if not all, contributors to delinquency (and criminal behavior itself) are related reciprocally. Thus, Thornberry postulated that engaging in crime leads to hanging out with other delinquents and that hanging out with delinquents leads to committing crimes. It is quite common for individuals to commit crime and then start hanging out with peers who are doing the same, and it is also quite common for people to start hanging out with delinquent peers and then start committing crimes. Furthermore, it is perhaps the most likely scenario for a person to be offending and also dealing with both the influences of past experiences and peer effects (see Figure 13.2).

As mentioned previously, Thornberry considers the social control and bonding constructs, such as attachments to parents and commitment to school, which are some of the most essential predictors of delinquency. Like other theoretical models of social bonding and control, Thornberry's model puts the level of attachment and commitment to conventional society ahead of the degree of moral beliefs that individuals hold regarding criminal offending. However, lack of such moral beliefs leads to delinquent behavior, which in turn negatively affects the level of commitment or attachment an individual may have built in his or her development. As Thornberry claimed,

> While the weakening of the bond to conventional society may be an initial cause of delinquency, delinquency eventually becomes its own indirect cause precisely because of its ability to weaken further the person's bonds to family, school, and conventional beliefs.[23]

©iStockphoto.com/rez-art

Terrence Thornberry proposed one of the most complex, albeit accurate, models for how various factors interact with one another in the development of individuals in terms of predicting delinquency and criminality.

Thus, the implications of this model are that variables relating to social control or bonding and other sources cause delinquency, which then becomes, in itself, a predictor and cause for the breakdown of other important causes of delinquency and crime.

A CASE STUDY AND EMPIRICAL EVIDENCE FOR THORNBERRY'S INTERACTIONAL MODEL. As an example case study, consider a person we shall call Johnny, who has an absent father and a mother who uses inconsistent discipline and sometimes inflicts harsh physical abuse on her son. He sees his mother's state of constant neglect and abuse as proof that belief in conventional values is wrong, and he becomes indifferent toward governmental laws; his main goal is to survive and be successful. Because of his mother's psychological and physical neglect, Johnny pays no attention to school and turns to his older peers for guidance and support. These peers guide him toward behavior that gives him both financial rewards (by selling what they steal) and status in their group (respect for performing well in illegal acts). At some point, Johnny gets caught, and this makes the peers who taught him how to engage in crime proud while also alienating him from the previous bonds he had with his school, where he may be suspended or expelled, and with his mother, who further distances herself from him. This creates a reciprocal effect, or feedback loop, to the previous factors—lack of attachment to his mother and lack of commitment to school. The lowered level of social bonding and control of conventional institutions and factors (mother, school) and increased influence of delinquent peers then leads Johnny to commit more frequent and more serious crimes.

Thornberry's theoretical model is based on reciprocal effects, meaning that what is an outcome variable (e.g., association with delinquent peers) also becomes a predictive variable, in that it influences previous variables (e.g., commitment to school). This figure shows how such relationships function, with negative signs (–) meaning that there is an inverse relationship between the two variables (e.g., the more association with delinquent peers is associated with less commitment to school), or positive (+) signs meaning that there is a direct positive association between two variables (e.g., belief in conventional values is associated with commitment to school). These variables tend to have a feedback loop, as represented in the figure.

Such a model, although complex and hard to measure, is logically consistent, and the postulates are sound. However, the value of any theory has to be determined by the empirical evidence supporting its validity. Much of the scientific evidence regarding Thornberry's empirical model has been contributed by Thornberry and his colleagues.

Although the full model has yet to be tested, the researchers "have found general support for the reciprocal relationships between both control concepts and learning concepts with delinquent behavior."[24] One test of Thornberry's model used the longitudinal Rochester Youth Development Study to test its postulates.[25] This study found that the estimates of previous unidirectional models (nonreciprocal models) did not adequately explain the variation in the data. Rather, the results supported the interactional model, with delinquent associations leading to increases in delinquency, delinquency leading to reinforcing peer networks, and both directional processes working through the social environment. In fact, this longitudinal study demonstrated that, once the participants had acquired delinquent beliefs from their peers, the effects of these beliefs had further effects on their future behavior and associations, which is exactly what Thornberry's theory predicts.[26]

Another empirical test of Thornberry's interactional model examined the age-varying effects of the theory.[27] This study incorporated hierarchical linear modeling in investigating a sample of the National Youth Survey. The results showed that, while the effects of delinquent peers were relatively close to predictions, peaking in the mid-teenage

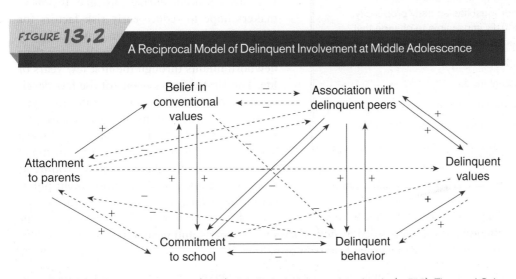

FIGURE 13.2   A Reciprocal Model of Delinquent Involvement at Middle Adolescence

Source: Tibbetts, S. G., & Hemmens, C. (2010). *Criminological theory: A text/reader* (p. 718). Thousand Oaks, CA: SAGE.

LEARNING CHECK 13.2

1. According to the text, which developmental theory focuses on transitions and trajectories in our life course as reasons for causing individuals to reduce their criminal offending—transitions such as getting married or obtaining a job one doesn't want to lose?

   a. Moffitt's developmental taxonomy

   b. Thornberry's interactional model

   c. Sampson and Laub's developmental theory

   d. Gottfredson and Hirschi's theory of low self-control

2. According to the text, which developmental theory focuses on two different types of offenders—namely, life-course persistent offenders and adolescence-limited offenders?

   a. Moffitt's developmental taxonomy

   b. Thornberry's interactional model

   c. Sampson and Laub's developmental theory

   d. Gottfredson and Hirschi's theory of low self-control

3. According to the text, which developmental theory focuses on certain factors having different influences at certain times in a person's life, as well as the reciprocal or feedback effects of subsequent variables or behaviors on the earlier antecedent factors, creating a feedback loop?

   a. Moffitt's developmental taxonomy

   b. Thornberry's interactional model

   c. Sampson and Laub's developmental theory

   d. Gottfredson and Hirschi's theory of low self-control

4. According to the text, which theoretical model is considered "antidevelopmental" in the sense that it proposes that once an individual has an early propensity toward criminality, it is virtually impossible to change that propensity and such a person will likely continue offending?

   a. Moffitt's developmental taxonomy

   b. Thornberry's interactional model

   c. Sampson and Laub's developmental theory

   d. Gottfredson and Hirschi's theory of low self-control

Answers located at www.sagepub.com/schram2e

years, the predictions regarding the effects of family on delinquency were not found to be significant in the periods expected, although family was important during adolescence.

Finally, it should be said that in many ways Thornberry's interactional model is far more developmental than others discussed here because it gives equal weight to the traditionally separate theoretical frameworks combined into his model, in the sense that both are considered antecedent and reciprocal in their effects on criminal behavior. Thornberry's model is likely the most convoluted framework we examine in this book, but it also sheds much light on what is happening in real life among individuals. After all, not only do certain factors, such as family influences, play a part in our peer influences, but peer influences come back and influence familial factors. So although readers may find such a model highly complicated, that is how human behavior works. We live in and experience a complicated world, with numerous interactions among a plethora of constantly occurring factors.

POLICY IMPLICATIONS

Many—perhaps an infinite number of—policy implications can be derived from developmental theories of criminality. Thus, we will focus on the most important, which are those policies emphasizing the prenatal and perinatal stages of life; the most significant and effective interventions can occur during this time. If policymakers hope to reduce early risk factors for criminality, they must insist on universal health care for pregnant women, as well as for their newborn infants through the first few years of life. The United States is one of the few developed nations that does not guarantee this type of maternal and infant medical care and supervision. Doing so would go a long way toward avoiding the costly damages (costly in many ways) of criminal behavior among youths at risk.[28] In fact, in one of the most recent publications regarding this issue, J. C. Barnes stated that "hundreds of studies have shown support for the notion that life-course-persistent offending is often preceded by deficiencies in pre-, peri-, and postnatal care that result in structural and/or functional brain abnormalities."[29]

Furthermore, there should be legally mandated interventions for pregnant women who are addicted to drugs or alcohol. Although this is a highly controversial topic, it appears

Comparative Criminology: *CRIME RATES*

Comparing Crime Rates of U.S. Cities

Given that this is the developmental theory chapter and we have explored all the major Part I or Index crimes in the UCR, as well as examining international comparisons for each of them, we thought it would be beneficial to concentrate on comparing various cities in the United States. So in this unique Comparative Criminology box, we are going to compare the crime rates of cities in the United States based on their total score on the UCR Crime Index for the year 2014. This measure includes rates for seven of the Index crimes for each city; these

seven are murder, forcible rape, aggravated assault, robbery, burglary, motor vehicle theft, and larceny-theft. Remember, these are comparisons based on rates per capita (not numbers), so they are somewhat fair comparisons regardless of the number of citizens in a given city. Notably, this study and ranking include only cities with populations of 75,000 or more.

Figure 13.3 shows cities with the top and bottom ten rankings on the total crime Index score for 2014. The "worst," or highest, ranking on this score was Miami Beach, Florida, followed by Salt Lake City, Utah; Spokane, Washington;

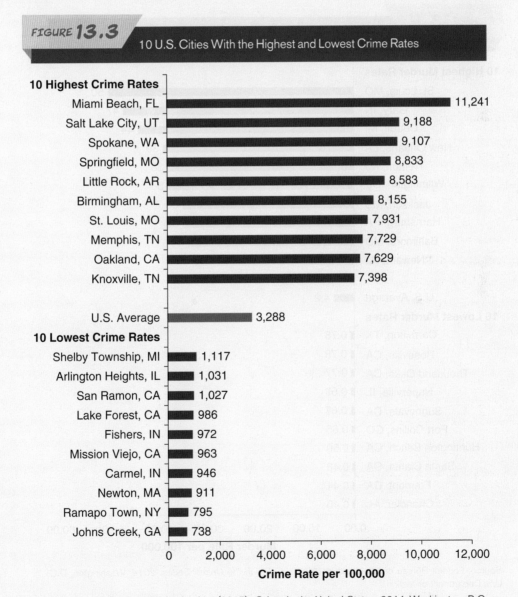

FIGURE 13.3 10 U.S. Cities With the Highest and Lowest Crime Rates

10 Highest Crime Rates

City	Crime Rate
Miami Beach, FL	11,241
Salt Lake City, UT	9,188
Spokane, WA	9,107
Springfield, MO	8,833
Little Rock, AR	8,583
Birmingham, AL	8,155
St. Louis, MO	7,931
Memphis, TN	7,729
Oakland, CA	7,629
Knoxville, TN	7,398
U.S. Average	3,288

10 Lowest Crime Rates

City	Crime Rate
Shelby Township, MI	1,117
Arlington Heights, IL	1,031
San Ramon, CA	1,027
Lake Forest, CA	986
Fishers, IN	972
Mission Viejo, CA	963
Carmel, IN	946
Newton, MA	911
Ramapo Town, NY	795
Johns Creek, GA	738

Crime Rate per 100,000

Source: Federal Bureau of Investigation. (2015). *Crime in the United States, 2014.* Washington, D.C: U.S. Department of Justice.

(Continued)

(Continued)

Springfield, Missouri; and Little Rock, Arkansas. It is notable that Missouri had two cities in the top ten on this ranking—perhaps a result of Missouri being "Ground Zero" for methamphetamine production in recent years.

On the other end of the list, the safest cities in the United States, according to this score, are Johns Creek, Georgia; Ramapo, New York; Newton, Massachusetts; Carmel, Indiana; and Mission Viejo, California. It is notable that California had three cities in the top ten "safest cities" (See Figure 13.3).

Breaking down the study to focus on only the most serious offense—murder—the rankings change quite a bit (see Figure 13.4). Specifically, in terms of murder rates in 2014, the city with the highest rank is St. Louis, Missouri, followed by Gary,

Indiana; Detroit, Michigan; New Orleans, Louisiana; Trenton, New Jersey; and Wilmington, Delaware. Notably, New Jersey had two cities in the top ten.

It is likely that the gross deprivation and poverty in virtually all these cities are key in their high murder rates. Many of these same cities seem to have been in the top 10 for murder over the past decade or so.

THINK ABOUT IT

1. What factors do you think factor most into why certain cities have such high rate of murder?

2. What factors do you think factor most into why certain cities have such low rates of murder/violent crimes?

FIGURE **13.4**

10 U.S. Cities With the Highest and Lowest Murder Rates*

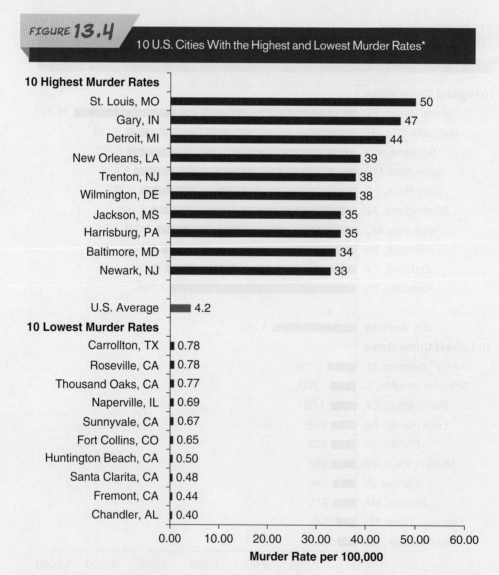

10 Highest Murder Rates

City	Murder Rate per 100,000
St. Louis, MO	50
Gary, IN	47
Detroit, MI	44
New Orleans, LA	39
Trenton, NJ	38
Wilmington, DE	38
Jackson, MS	35
Harrisburg, PA	35
Baltimore, MD	34
Newark, NJ	33
U.S. Average	4.2

10 Lowest Murder Rates

City	Murder Rate per 100,000
Carrollton, TX	0.78
Roseville, CA	0.78
Thousand Oaks, CA	0.77
Naperville, IL	0.69
Sunnyvale, CA	0.67
Fort Collins, CO	0.65
Huntington Beach, CA	0.50
Santa Clarita, CA	0.48
Fremont, CA	0.44
Chandler, AL	0.40

Source: Federal Bureau of Investigation. (2015). *Crime in the United States, 2014.* Washington, D.C: U.S. Department of Justice.

*Excludes cities that did not report any murders.

to be a no-brainer that women who suffer from such addictions may become highly toxic to the child they carry and should receive closer supervision and more health care. Perhaps no other policy implementation would have as much influence in reducing future criminality in children as making sure their mothers do not take toxic substances while pregnant.[30]

An additional concern is inadvertent exposure to toxins, such as lead, which has shown an alarming causal connection to persistent criminality. In a very recent review of the evidence regarding such toxins, particularly lead, John Wright stated that "a series of studies shows a consistent link between pre- and postnatal lead ingestion and delinquency in adolescence and criminal behavior in adulthood."[31] Although lead is just one of the many toxins likely to affect the development of an individual's brain, it is currently the most prominent of the various toxins that can predispose a young person toward criminality. Thus, the exposure to lead or any other toxins should be monitored, especially in certain areas where such toxins are known to exist.

Other policy implications include assigning special caseworkers for high-risk pregnancies, such as those involving low birth weight or low Apgar scores. Another advised intervention would be to organize a centralized medical system that provides a flag for high-risk infants who have numerous birth or delivery complications so that the doctors seeing them for the first time are aware of their vulnerabilities.[32] Finally, universal preschool should be funded and provided for all young children; studies have shown that this leads to better performance, both academically and socially, once they enter school.[33]

Ultimately, as the many developmental theories have shown, many concepts and stages of life can have a profound effect on the criminological trajectories lives can take. However, virtually all these models propose that the earlier stages of life are likely the most important in determining whether an individual will engage or not engage in criminal activity throughout life. Therefore, policymakers should focus their efforts on providing care and interventions within this time period.

CONCLUSION

This chapter presented a discussion of the importance of developmental or life-course theories of criminal behavior. This perspective is relatively new compared with other traditional theories explored in this text—becoming popular in the late 1970s—but did not become a mainstream or popular perspective until the 1990s to now. Ultimately, this is one of the most cutting-edge areas of theoretical development, and life-course theories are likely to be the most important frameworks in the future of the field of criminological theory.

- Developmental or life-course theory focuses on the individual and following such individuals throughout life to examine their offending careers. This perspective puts a lot of emphasis on life events, often referred to as transitions (such as getting married or becoming employed in a stable job), which significantly affect an individual's trajectory in criminal behavior. In-depth consideration of changes during the life course are of highest concern, especially regarding general conclusions that can be made about the factors that tend to increase or decrease someone's likelihood to continue offending.

- Life-course perspectives emphasize such concepts as onset, frequency of offending, duration of offending, seriousness of offending, desistance of offending, and other factors that play key roles in when individuals offend and why they do so—or don't do so—at certain times in their lives. There are many critics of the developmental or life-course perspective, particularly those who buy into the low self-control model. This model is antidevelopmental in the sense that it assumes that propensities for crime do not change over time but, rather, remain unchanged throughout life.

- One of the developmental models that has received the most attention is that of Sampson and Laub, which emphasizes transitions in life (e.g., marriage, military service, employment, etc.) that alter trajectories either toward or away from crime. Moffitt's developmental theory of chronic offenders (whom she labeled life-course persistent offenders) versus more normal offenders (whom she labeled adolescence-limited offenders) is the developmental model that has received the most attention over the past decade, and much of this research is supportive of the interactive effects of biology and environment combining to create chronic,

habitual offenders. Another key developmental theory is Thornberry's interactional model, which emphasizes different types of influences of certain factors at different times in our development, as well as the reciprocal or "feedback" effects of certain outcome variables on previous antecedent factors. This type of "feedback loop" can often result in a person becoming caught in a vicious cycle of criminality, which can become hard to escape.

- To follow up on the case study we discussed at the opening of this chapter, the Thornberry model is likely the best explanation for the case of the 14-year-old Tennessee boy arrested in connection with nearly 100 burglaries in the north Nashville area. Given that his parents had been absent for quite some time, as well as the rewards (or property) he was obtaining in stealing from these homes, the youth experienced success and then kept repeating the same illegal acts that allowed him to survive and be successful. There fore, this created a cycle in which he lacked support from society, which forced him to do what it took to stay alive. When this paid off the first time, he naturally kept doing the same thing, time after time. Although this example may seem rather extreme, it is likely that many more individuals also face extremely deprived conditions that essentially force them to engage in high levels of criminal activity.

- In this chapter, we also examined the policy implications of this developmental approach, which emphasize the need to provide universal care for pregnant mothers as well as their newborn infants. Other policy implications include legally mandated interventions for mothers who are addicted to toxic substances (e.g., alcohol, drugs) and assignment of caseworkers for high-risk infants and children, such as those with birth or delivery complications. Such interventions would go a long way toward sparing society from the many problems (e.g., financial, victimization, etc.) that will persist without such interventions. Ultimately, a focus on the earliest stages of intervention will provide the "biggest bang for our buck."

- Ultimately, the chapter discussed life-course/developmental theory as one of the most important perspectives in criminology today, in terms of empirical validity of the theoretical framework and the growing attention being given to the model in the research and discussion in criminological literature.

SUMMARY OF THEORIES IN CHAPTER 13

THEORY	CONCEPTS	PROPONENTS	KEY PROPOSITIONS
Developmental/ life-course theory	Early onset, duration, persistence, frequency, desistance from crime	Various	Focus is on following individuals through life.
Developmental/ life-course theory	Transitions and trajectories	Sampson and Laub	Individuals can change and stop offending despite early propensities, especially when positive transitions occur (e.g., marriage, employment).

(Continued)

(Continued)

THEORY	CONCEPTS	PROPONENTS	KEY PROPOSITIONS
Developmental/ life-course theory	Life-course persistent offenders and adolescence-limited offenders	Moffitt	There are two primary types of offenders. The life-course type are more chronic offenders who start early and continue throughout life; the adolescence-limited type offend only during teenage years to early 20s and then grow out of it.
Developmental/ life-course theory	Interactions among predictive factors and reciprocal effects	Thornberry	Key predictive factors have differential effects at certain times in life. These variables tend to influence or interact with each other and cause "feedback loops," or reciprocal effects, in which an outcome variable influences a prior antecedent variable, such as when being caught offending causes further tension in parental relationships.
Antidevelopmental theory	Low self-control	Hirschi and Gottfredson	Assumption that once low self-control disposition is formed by age 10, there is no way to change or develop away from criminality.

KEY TERMS

DISCUSSION QUESTIONS

1. What characteristic distinguishes developmental theories from traditional theoretical frameworks?

2. What aspects of a criminal career do experts consider important in such a model? Describe all the aspects they look at in a person's criminal career.

3. Discuss the primary criticisms regarding the developmental perspective, particularly that presented by Gottfredson and Hirschi. Which theoretical paradigm do you consider the most valid? Why?

4. What transitions or trajectories have you seen in your life or your friends' lives that support Sampson and Laub's developmental model? What events encouraged offending or inhibited it?

5. Given Moffitt's dichotomy of life-course persistent and adolescence-limited offenders, which of these should be given more attention in research? Why do you feel this way?

WEB RESOURCES

Overview of developmental theories of crime; discusses all the primary developmental theories:

http://www.sagepub.com/sites/default/files/upm-binaries/5182_Delisi_I_Proof_Chapter_3.pdf

Terrie Moffitt's theory

www.wpic.pitt.edu/research/famhist/PDF_Articles/APA/BF16.pdf

Sampson and Laub's model

http://harvardmagazine.com/2004/03/twigs-bent-trees-go-stra.html

Thornberry's interactional model

http://forensicpsychology.umwblogs.org/organized-crime/interactional-theory/http://www.jstor.org/stable/1143788?seq=12

STUDENT STUDY SITE

$SAGE edge™

WANT A BETTER GRADE ON YOUR NEXT TEST?

Get the tools you need to sharpen your study skills:

SAGE edge offers a robust online environment featuring an impressive array of tools and resources for review, study, and further exploration, keeping both instructors and students on the cutting edge of teaching and learning. Learn more at **edge.sagepub.com/schram2e**.

FOR FURTHER EXPLORATION AND APPLICATION, VISIT THE STUDENT STUDY SITE:

- In Tennessee, Giving Birth to a Drug-Dependent Baby Can Be a Crime

- Preschool Suspensions Really Happen and That's Not OK with Connecticut

- Opportunities, rational choice, and self-control: On the interaction of person and situation in a general theory of crime

- Young people's relations to crime: Pathways across ecologies

- Assessing long-term outcomes of an intervention designed for pregnant incarcerated women

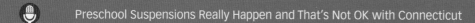

- Police Battling Career Criminals

- Child Abuse in the US: Cycle of violence

- String of Arsons in Lakeview Might Have Been Set by Children

- Jon Venables' Lawyer Recalls Representing the 8-year-old Killer

- Poverty

- Family Life and Delinquency of Crime

- Fatherless Families

- Jackson Katz

PREMIUM VIDEO:

Check out the Interactive eBook for premium videos, including videos from author Stephen Tibbetts, who discusses real-world examples and strange crimes; and videos from former offenders, who share their stories from a first-person view, and touch on key theories and concepts from the chapter.

CHAPTER 14

White-Collar Crime, Organized Crime, and Cybercrime

INTRODUCTION

This chapter examines a large group of offenses that do not generally fit in the traditional concept of predatory street crimes, such as murder, rape, assault, burglary, and motor vehicle theft. Rather, the types of offending examined in this chapter include various types of white-collar, organized, and computer (or cyber) crimes. Although these crimes do not receive nearly the amount of attention that traditional street crimes (e.g., murder) get on the evening news or in newspapers, readers may be surprised to learn that these forms of offending cause far more damage to society, in terms of both property/financial losses and violence, than do all the street crimes combined. The first section covers those crimes generally referred to as white-collar, corporate, or occupational. This section provides students with a general overview of such topics as defining, measuring, and curbing white-collar crime and discusses different types of crimes.

The next section presents various issues pertaining to organized crime, including types of organized crime groups and different criminal justice responses to these types of offenses. While in years past, clear distinctions were made between organized and white-collar crime, recently some researchers have maintained that these two types of offenses may be similar rather than fundamentally distinct.[6] The last portion of this chapter illustrates how difficult it is for the criminal justice system to "keep up" with technological advances, specifically in the area of cybercrime (also referred to as hi-tech crime, computer crime, e-crime, or electronic crime).

WHAT IS WHITE-COLLAR CRIME?

Despite years of being relatively ignored by researchers, white-collar crime is currently receiving much attention, probably due to high-profile chief executive officers (CEOs) and celebrities, such as Martha Stewart, being convicted of illegal business practices. Such types of corruption have existed since the earliest businesses formed many centuries ago, with historical records showing a high prevalence of unethical practices by businesses and governments throughout human civilization. However, white-collar crime is perhaps more emphasized today due to the global, multibillion-dollar nature of corporations in the modern world. Despite its presence throughout history, it is amazing that white-collar crime did not gain much attention from criminological researchers until the 1940s and remained a relatively low priority until the past few decades. This section examines the way the concept is defined and how it has evolved to the present day, with particular emphasis on its huge impact on modern societies, especially in the United States.

Definitions and History of White-Collar Crime

Experts in the area of white-collar crime consider it one of the most difficult concepts to define, with there being little consistency from researcher to researcher.[7] The first prominent acknowledgment of "white-collar crime" as an important concept for criminologists to study was presented at an American Sociological Society (later renamed the American Sociological Association, or ASA) conference in 1939 by Edwin Sutherland,[8] who coined the term *white-collar crime* and is generally considered the most prominent

CASE STUDY

WILLIAM T. WALTERS

Phil Mickelson is a professional golfer; he has won five major golf championships as well as garnered numerous endorsement agreements. Thomas Davis is a former investment banker; he has a Harvard education and lives a "country club lifestyle." Both men had something in common— they owed money to William Walters. William Walters was often considered the most successful sports gambler in the country. After an extensive investigation, the debts of Phil Mickelson and Thomas Davis have become the center of an insider trading scheme.[1]

WHAT'S CLEAR, ACCORDING TO DOZENS OF INTERVIEWS AND THOUSANDS OF PAGES OF LEGAL DOCUMENTS, IS THAT WALTERS BEATS THE ODDS EVERYWHERE—IN THE STOCK MARKET, REAL ESTATE, CRIMINAL PROCEEDINGS AND HIS TRUE WHEELHOUSE, SPORTS GAMBLING.[2]

Dean Foods, returned the favor by providing Walters "boardroom secrets." In an effort to conceal their scheme, Walters and Davis used disposable cellphones and developed a "secret code" when discussing Dean Foods. For instance, Dean Foods is a Dallas company. Thus, the two men referred to the company as "the Dallas Cowboys." Andrew Ceresney, director of the SEC's enforcement division, stated, "Davis breached his duty and broke the law as the result of being in dire financial straits. . . . Mr. Walters . . . was 'gambling on a sure thing.'"[5]

According to Mike Fish in a 2015 *ESPN* article, William Walters

. . . is thought to have bet more money more successfully than anyone in history, earning hundreds of millions of dollars. Federal and state investigators sniff around his operation regularly. Scores of bettors and bookies have tried to crack his methods so they can emulate him. . . . Walters has outrun them all.

In May 2016, federal prosecutors brought criminal charges against Walters, alleging that he used illegal stock tips from Thomas Davis to accumulate approximately $40 million in profits. Currently, Davis has pled guilty and is cooperating with prosecutors. Phil Mickelson has not been criminally accused of any wrongdoing. However, the Securities and Exchange Commission (SEC) has listed him in a civil complaint.[3] The SEC maintains that Mickelson earned almost $1 million from illegal stock tips. In a separate statement, Mickelson entered into an agreement with the SEC to repay those monies.[4] Thomas Davis, however, had debts that far exceeded Mickelson's. Walters lent Davis money. In return, Davis, who was chairman of

William T. Walters was considered the most successful sports gambler in the country.

THINK ABOUT IT:

1. Does this fit your perception of crime?

2. Does William Walters fit the description of a criminal?

3. Do you think he will be treated differently than other criminal offenders?

criminologist of the 20th century (for this and other work, such as the formation of differential association theory, see Chapter 10). In this presentation, which was the ASA presidential address, Sutherland did not provide a clear definition of white-collar crime but simply presented a variety of cases that seemed to apply.[9] For example, Sutherland discussed the racketeering cases against Chicago's Al Capone as well as the Federal Trade Commission investigations of automobile companies that falsely advertised low-interest-rate loans and the false claims of some of Hearst's publications, such as *Good Housekeeping*. His discussion also included cases in which judges and various officials accepted bribes or engaged in other unethical practices in which they abused the power of their positions. Perhaps the reason

United States Department of Justice

Al Capone's mug shot, taken by the Chicago police after his 1931 arrest.

why Sutherland did not provide a clear definition of crime in his address was because he first needed to convince other academics that white-collar crime is an actual, serious form of criminal activity, which at the time took some convincing. Perhaps the most profound statement he made in his address was "White-collar crime is real crime."[10]

Before we discuss the contents and importance of Sutherland's presidential address, it is important to note that there was a notable history of research in the study of corporate and occupational crimes—even back to the ancient Greeks, who had issued decrees against those who forced up prices of imported grain, the penalty for which was death for that person and his entire family.[11] Although most textbooks claim that Sutherland introduced the concept of corporate, occupational, or industrial crimes, that is not true. Specifically, prior to Sutherland's address, there were numerous scientific studies on "white-collar bandits," "robber-barons," "corporate crime," "muckrakers," and "industrial crime," all of which refer to forms of corporate, industrial, occupational, or political corruption.[12] In fact, some of these studies are considered seminal, classic studies on the topic, such as Matthew Josephson's classic *The Robber Barons: The Great American Capitalists*[13] and George Anderson's *Consolidation of Gas Companies in Boston*,[14] published in 1934 and 1905, respectively—well before Sutherland's address. So although Sutherland is often considered the scholar who created the concept of white-collar crime, this is far from true. There were many notable studies on corporate, occupational, and industrial offending prior to his 1939 address. Although similar terms, such as *white-collar bandits*, had been used many times before, Sutherland does deserve credit for coining the term *white-collar crime* and, more important, for bringing far more attention to the topic by making it the primary focus of his ASA presidential address, which was prominently reported by the mainstream press and significantly increased public attention for this type of offending.

At the end of Sutherland's presidential address at the ASA conference in 1939, he provided a summary list of his four primary propositions, the first (implying its importance) being that "white-collar criminality is real criminality, being in all cases in violation of the criminal law," which is a vague and weak definition.[15] In addition to this presidential address, Sutherland also published a study in 1945 on the prevalence of white-collar crime (discussed below); again, a clear definition of the concept was not provided.[16] However, in 1949, Sutherland published two works that supplied definitions, albeit still somewhat vague, for white-collar crime. One of these was *White-Collar*

white-collar crime:
criteria include (1) upper-class offender, (2) work-related violations, (3) work-related violations of blue-collar workers excluded, and (4) regular crimes committed by upper-class persons excluded.

Edwin Sutherland:
the man who coined the term *white-collar crime*; generally considered the most prominent criminologist of the 20th century.

Crime,[17] in which he provided the definition in a footnote. In this footnote, Sutherland stated that white-collar crime

> may be defined approximately as a crime committed by a person of respectability and high social status in the course of his occupation . . . [which] excludes many crimes of the upper class, such as . . . murder . . . since these are not customarily a part of their occupational procedures . . . and refer[s] principally to business managers and executives.[18]

There are a number of things to note about this definition, which was perhaps the first somewhat specific explanation ever provided, although still relatively vague compared with those of more modern researchers. First, as you can see from the wording, particularly use of the word *approximately*, even Sutherland (the man who coined the term) appears to lack confidence in what "white-collar crime" means.[19] However, the definition contains some key distinctions that separate it from descriptions of typical street crimes.

The first necessary condition is that the offenders are at the top of the socioeconomic structure, which is somewhat inherent due to the requirement of having a "white-collar" job as opposed to a "blue-collar" job or no job at all. According to this portion of Sutherland's definition, if a clerk at a fast-food restaurant steals money from the register, it is not considered white-collar crime because, although the person committed the crime while engaging in work-related duties, he or she clearly does not hold a white-collar position. Later, we will discuss modern criticisms of this requirement in defining white-collar crime.[20] Another key element of this definition is that offenses by upper-class individuals are considered white-collar crime only if they are employment related. A business executive may be a serial killer or a drug dealer, but if these violations do not pertain to his actual job, then they do not count as white-collar crime. Finally, the definition notes that this term refers "principally" to business executives, but such a word is vague (once again suggesting Sutherland's lack of confidence in specifying the exact meaning of the term) and therefore allows some deviation from including only violations committed by executives. Still, it is clear that the person must have a white-collar position to qualify, even if not that of a manager or high-ranking officer in the corporation.

The second relevant publication by Sutherland in 1949 was a brief, five-page entry titled "The White Collar Criminal" in Branham and Kutash's *Encyclopedia of Criminology*.[21] Despite its relative obscurity, this entry seemed to provide the most straightforward definition of this form of offending. Specifically, Sutherland wrote that the

> white-collar criminal is defined as a person with high socioeconomic status who violates the laws designed to regulate his occupational activities. . . . The white collar criminal should be differentiated . . . from the person of lower socio-economic status who violates the regular penal code or the special trade regulations which apply to him, and . . . from the person of high socio-economic status who violates the regular penal code in ways not connected with his occupation.[22]

For the most part, this definition is highly consistent with Sutherland's first definition, taken from *White-Collar Crime*. Specifically, in both definitions, Sutherland stipulates four criteria constituting white-collar crime: (1) The offender is upper-class, (2) the committed violations are work related, (3) the work-related violations of blue-collar workers are excluded, and (4) regular crimes (i.e., those occurring outside employment) committed by upper-class persons are excluded. Also in the encyclopedia entry, Sutherland stated that the laws violated by white-collar offenders are sometimes in the regular penal code but often found only in regulatory or trade codes (many of which are now created and enforced by agencies such as the Securities and Exchange Commission, or SEC).

WHY DO THEY DO IT?

CHARLES PONZI[32]

In 2009, Bernard Lawrence "Bernie" Madoff pled guilty to multiple federal felonies involving his defrauding investors of almost $50 billion. He was convicted of engaging in what has been termed a "Ponzi scheme."[33] A Ponzi scheme is an investment fraud which involves the initial investors receiving payment of their returns from monies of subsequent investors. They often collapse since there are little or no legitimate earnings and maintaining these schemes requires a constant influx of money from new investors.

The Ponzi scheme was named after Carlo Pietro Giovanni Guglielmo Tebaldo Ponzi, often referred to as Charles Ponzi. In 1903, Charles Ponzi emigrated from Italy and eventually resided in Boston. He worked as a grocery clerk and dishwasher. Later, he worked in an Italian bank, Banco Zarossi, in Montreal.[34] He was arrested for forging a signature on a check and was incarcerated in a Quebec prison for 20 months. Afterward, he returned to the United States and was convicted and incarcerated in an Atlanta prison for smuggling Italian immigrants into the country. Back in Boston, from 1919 to 1920, Ponzi swindled thousands of people by claiming that they could receive a 50% return on their investments in 90 days.[35] Ponzi's scheme consisted of an elaborate transaction involving international postage stamp rates. In 1920, Ponzi collected $5,000 from investors, but just five months later, he was taking in a million dollars a week.[36]

THINK ABOUT IT:

1. If we wanted to apply social control theory to understand Charles Ponzi's criminal behavior, we might ask, "Why would he want to obey the rules of society?" This is a key aspect of control theory—individuals conform because social controls prevent them from engaging in deviant and/or criminal behavior.

2. Does society view these types of offenses differently than violent offenses such as homicide?

3. What types of harm do victims of these offenses experience?

Perhaps the most important consequence of Sutherland's creation of the term *white-collar crime*, and his definition and promotion of the concept, was the almost immediate attention, particularly empirical studies, focused on the topic.[23] Although many of these studies failed to apply his definitional criteria to the offenses they examined and some clearly deviated from the parameters set by his criteria, there is no doubt that Sutherland's writings and presentations between 1939 and 1949—not to mention his subsequent work in the area— got the ball rolling in terms of research and theoretical development regarding white-collar crime. Still, despite the criteria established by Sutherland, the term *white-collar crime* was both criticized and loosely applied to a variety of behaviors,

Corporate workers have plenty of opportunities to commit white-collar crimes and are often under pressure from the corporation to engage in such activities, especially when the company is not performing well.

particularly by the researchers of the 1940s through the 1960s, while others questioned the limits that had been set or the use of the term *criminal* in such situations.

For instance, some argued that many, if not most, of the persons Sutherland referred to had not been convicted in criminal court and therefore could not be considered "criminals" who had committed "crimes."[24] Sutherland responded to this argument by noting the need to emphasize the actual harm done by such acts and to acknowledge that what these individuals did was in violation of the mandate of legal codes and stating that these factors should be emphasized more than what the criminal justice system and/or society was doing in response to such offenders.[25] Unfortunately, even today, white-collar criminals are far less likely than traditional street criminals to be investigated, caught, charged, and convicted, let alone sentenced to significant prison time. Perhaps the epitome of this type of minor "wrist-slapping" is seen in the case of Michael Milken, who admitted to stealing about a billion dollars via illegal business practices and was ordered to pay back only about 60% of that, also spending only a few years in prison. (He later received a standing ovation in Congress after donating some money—likely stolen via insider trading—to prostate cancer research—likely because he had just been diagnosed with this disease.)

Some of these criminologists acknowledged considering the criteria established by Sutherland when determining whether the offenses they were examining deserved the label "white-collar crime." For example, one researcher explicitly questioned whether embezzlers were white-collar offenders, considering that many of them were not persons of high status, although most had committed their crimes during the course of their occupational duties.[26] A similar consideration was expressed by a researcher who examined individuals who had violated wartime regulations regarding meat rationing, involving unauthorized distribution and/or consumption (i.e., the black market).[27] Other experts outright claimed that Sutherland's definitional criteria were far too restrictive and should allow for inclusion of any offenders working for a business.[28] These are just a couple of the many examples of offending that fall in the "gray area" between white-collar crimes and regular types of crime as well as bring up questions of what should be considered a true crime or criminal.

Another major cause of confusion when it comes to defining white-collar crime is that a variety of other terms have evolved that are typically used synonymously, although some would argue that these terms do have distinctions. These terms include, but are not limited to, *corporate crime, organizational crime, occupational crime, upperworld crime, business crime,* and *suite crime* (as opposed to traditional *street crime*).[29] Some have even claimed that there is virtually no distinction between white-collar crime and organized crime (this issue will be discussed further in a later section in this chapter).[30] The many different terms used to identify white-collar crime add to the difficulty in developing a clear, explicit definition of this behavior. For example, a strong argument has been made regarding the difference between occupational crime and corporate crime: The former includes offenders at all levels of the business/social structure, whereas the latter is generally crime committed by managers or executives (often under the direction of the CEO or board of directors).[31]

One summary of the early scientific works on white-collar crime, particularly regarding definitional issues, concluded that the primary criterion is that the acts occur in relation to the offender's occupational role, which the author claimed was more important than the types of offending or the person's socioeconomic standing.[37] Unfortunately, there is also debate over what behaviors are considered a part of one's occupational role and, thus, what activities constitute white-collar crime. Even in more recent times, experts have offered refined definitions, such as suggesting that the primary criterion is abuse of a position of authority or trust.[38] Still other theorists go as far as to claim that there is no reason at all to distinguish white-collar crimes from traditional crimes.[39] Interestingly, some recent recommendations have been to go back to using Sutherland's original criteria,[40] an idea that appears to be gaining support.[41]

Despite such pointed criticisms and ongoing disagreements among criminologists about a clear definition of white-collar crime, a short list of the general categories of various white-collar offenses includes (1) fraud, (2) labor violations, (3) manufacturing violations, (4) unfair business practices, (5) abuse of authority, and (6) regulatory or administrative violations.[42] Each of these categories contains many specific forms of crime; in this chapter, examples will be provided for each general type and variations will be discussed.

Examples of fraud include tax evasion and false advertising. Labor violations, discussed in detail later, include different forms of harassment and dangerous working conditions that can cause injuries and death. Manufacturing violations include the production and distribution of unsafe consumer products as well as environmental violations (e.g., toxic-waste dumping). The category of unethical business practices has likely gotten the most attention in the media recently due to the prosecution and/or conviction of many high-ranking business executives in the United States. Examples of unfair business practices include insider trading, bid rigging, antitrust violations, and illegal mergers. Perhaps one of the better-known categories for criminal justice practitioners is abuse of authority, which can take many forms, including bribery, extortion, brutality, kickbacks, and so forth. Finally, a host of rules and codes established by federal, state, and local agencies govern the functioning of businesses and other organizations; offenses against these codes are considered regulatory/administrative violations and include copyright, trademark, and patent infringements. There are literally thousands of other examples for these categories, but we have tried to provide some of the more common forms for each general grouping of white-collar offenses.

INCIDENCE AND IMPACT OF WHITE-COLLAR CRIME ON SOCIETY

After his presidential address to the ASA, Sutherland published a key study regarding corporate crime and violations by most of the largest companies in the United States at that time (the 1940s).[43] In this seminal study, Sutherland examined the decisions of courts and regulatory commissions against the 70 largest mercantile and industrial corporations in the nation. Considering that the study was done in the 1940s, the findings are quite startling. Sutherland found that a total of 547 adverse decisions had been made against these 70 companies, with an average of almost eight decisions per corporation. Even more surprising was the prevalence of the substantiated rule violations; specifically, every single one of the corporations that Sutherland included in

LEARNING CHECK 14.1

1. According to the text, which theorist is largely credited for coining the term *white-collar crime* in the late 1930s in his presidential address to the American Sociological Society?

   a. Hirschi

   b. Sutherland

   c. Lombroso

   d. Matza

   e. Agnew

2. According to the text, there were numerous studies of corporate crime prior to the above theorist's presidential address in the 1930s. True or false?

3. According to the text, "white-collar/corporate crime" has a clear definition. True or false?

Answers located at www.edge.sagepub.com/schram2e

his sample had a decision against it, which implies that all highly successful businesses in the United States had engaged in unethical practices (and been caught).

Perhaps most shocking, virtually every corporation had committed more than one offense, with 97.1% recidivating. It appears that being caught and charged once did not do much to deter the businesses from engaging in unethical behaviors again. Readers should keep in mind that corporate crime is usually not discovered when it occurs, so the fact that almost every business in this study was caught more than once implies that the most successful companies actively and repeatedly engage in unethical activity for a profit. Interestingly, although Sutherland made a strong argument that all these activities were criminal, only 9% (49 out of the 547) of the decisions were made by criminal courts. The others were made mostly by federal or state oversight agencies, which often lack the power that criminal courts can wield in terms of punishment and/or stigma.

It is amazing that every highly successful company in the United States was found by an authoritative body to have committed a rule violation, and most had committed more than a handful of such violations. When comparing these rates of violations, some may argue that there were a higher percentage of companies committing such violations in the 1940s due to less regulation of the rules. However, that doesn't seem to be a strong argument, because there was enough regulation to catch every single company (of the top 70) engaging in unethical practices and, furthermore, enough to catch most of them numerous times.

Has the increase in laws, regulatory codes, and investigation lowered this rate of violations among modern corporations? The scientific answer is that we do not know for sure if the rate is higher or lower, because there was no stable, consistent measure of such violations from the 1940s to now. But given the recent revelations regarding the extensive amount of grossly unethical practices at some of the nations most respected and "successful" corporations—especially those with strong political ties, such as Enron (see "Why Do They Do It?" on the next page) and others (e.g., WorldCom and Adelphia)—there has not likely been a significant reduction in the incidence of corporate criminality in the past 60 years.

After all, other investigations of the largest businesses in the nation have all found that corporate misbehavior is not the exception but the norm; in fact, it appears that the more successful the company, the more it has been charged with violations. For example, one analysis of the 582 largest manufacturing and retail/service corporations in the United States from 1975 to 1976 found that 60% of the corporations had at least one violation, and this was in just the two-year period of the study! Close to half the companies had more than one violation, and some had more than 30 violations in this short period of time, which of course represents a chronic state of corporate offending.[44] Furthermore, a review of corporate crime among the Fortune 500 companies found that well over half (62%) were involved in at least one violation between 1975 and 1984, while a more recent analysis found that every one (100%) of the 25 largest Fortune 500 corporations had been convicted of a violation between 1977 and 1990.[45] A recent review of the evidence of the rate (and causes) of modern white-collar crime concluded:

> The reality of corporate crime in U.S. society changes little from year to year. Corporate crime is rampant; corporations are criminal recidivists . . . and corporate crime is treated with kid gloves by government agencies and the criminal justice system.[46]

Enron Corporation was founded in 1985 by Kenneth Lay. It was an energy company based in Houston, Texas. When Enron was established, natural gas and energy were produced, transmitted, and sold by state-regulated monopolies. These procedures were largely ineffectual. Enron creatively transformed energy supplies into financial instruments, which subsequently could be traded online like stocks and bonds.[48] In 15 years, Enron grew to become the United States' seventh-largest company, with about 21,000 staff in more than 40 countries.[49] Apparently, the problems developed when Enron moved from trading energy to other trading ventures. So, "for a time, Enron swept its failures into creative hiding places, but ultimately the truth came out [and] confidence in the company collapsed."[50]

Enron attempted to hide its losses in an effort to protect company profits. The following is just one example of such an attempt:

Enron invested a bunch of money in a joint venture with Blockbuster to rent out movies online. The deal flopped eight months later. But in the meantime Enron had secretly set up a partnership with a Canadian bank. The bank essentially lent Enron $115 million in exchange for Enron's profits from the movie venture over its first 10 years. The Blockbuster deal never made a penny, but Enron counted the Canadian loan as a nice, fat profit.[51]

The fallout of one of the largest bankruptcies in U.S. history included several high-level executives being sentenced to prison and thousands of people losing their jobs and retirement savings.[52]

THINK ABOUT IT:

1. What are the similarities and differences between this crime and a robbery or a burglary? When answering this question, think in terms of type of harm experienced by the victims.

2. How would these similarities and differences be reflected in punishment of such offenses?

Economic Costs

There is now little doubt that white-collar crime causes far more financial damage to society than all other crimes combined. As one recent review concluded:

> The general public loses more money *by far* . . . from price fixing and monopolistic practices and from consumer deception and embezzlement than from all the property crimes in the Federal Bureau of Investigation's Index combined. Yet these far more costly acts are either not criminal, or, if technically criminal, not prosecuted, or if prosecuted, not punished, or if punished, only mildly. In any event, although the individuals responsible for these acts take more money out of the ordinary citizen's pocket than our Typical Criminal, they rarely show up in arrest statistics and almost never in prison populations.[47]

Some modern estimates by the FBI's Uniform Crime Reports have put the cost of all street crimes at close to $17 billion for the year 2002.[53] In a shocking comparison, just one act of corporate crime (Enron) in the early years of the millennium resulted in estimated losses of $60 billion, and it is estimated that the savings and loan industry bailout from 1989 will cost taxpayers $473 billion by the year 2020 (showing the long-term consequences of such events).[54]

So the "suite" crimes committed by Enron caused more than three times the financial damage of all "street" crimes combined, not to mention the impact of the savings and loan bailout. And these are just *two* cases discovered and brought to public attention. Furthermore, a "very conservative" estimate of the total economic costs from white-collar crimes each year is about $500 billion, about 30 times (i.e., 3,000%) greater than the total for combined street crimes.[55] Some readers will be surprised to know that this works out to an average loss of about $1,800 per person annually from corporate crimes, compared with the estimated loss of about $60 per person from combined street crimes. And yes, we are all paying for such corporate crimes, because such losses, bailouts, recovery funds, and so forth typically come out of federal or state funds, which means taxpayers are picking up the bill.

Physical Costs

The financial cost of white-collar crime is not the most disturbing type of damage that results from corporate misbehavior. Most experts now agree that the scientific evidence clearly shows that "corporate crime kills, maims, and injures enormously larger numbers of innocent people than all street crimes combined."[56] Empirical studies are consistent regarding the high numbers of deaths and physical injuries that directly result from the wrongdoings of business executives.

For example, one study showed that a conservative estimate of how many individuals die annually due to corporate crime is at least 105,000 persons, which includes about 55,000 employees who are harmed while working (including occupational illnesses), another 30,000 consumer deaths from unsafe products, and at least 20,000 citizen deaths from a variety of types of environmental pollution.[57] Of course, these estimates do not include how many persons are dying from falsely prescribed or marketed pharmaceutical drugs, which likely totals many thousands each year and, due to the aging population in the United States, is probably increasing every year—as is the number of people who die from criminally negligent nursing home or medical care.

Finally, these estimates do not include the estimated 4.7 million Americans harmed (but not killed) at work, which includes 4.4 million persons who suffer physical injuries and 300,000 who contract occupational illnesses (i.e., get sick due to work conditions),[58] with a high percentage of these being directly due to corporate crime. These workplace injuries are far more common than injuries due to traditional street crimes and, on average, are more serious than the common wounds suffered from assaults on the street. This was measured by comparing the number of workdays missed due to work-related injuries/illnesses versus workdays missed due to violent assaults; the average number of days missed from work was higher for those injured on the job.

It is important to keep in mind that there are only about 15,000 homicides due to street crimes in the United States each year (it was far higher in the early 1980s).[59] So, considering the previous estimates of annual deaths, it appears that corporate crime causes at least 7 times (and likely 10 times) more deaths than do traditional street crimes (i.e., 1,000% more deaths from corporate crimes than street crimes). Furthermore, it also appears that while the rate of homicides and assaults due to street crimes has been cut in half over the past 25 years (with most of this decrease coming in the past 15 years), there is no indication that deaths or injuries due to corporate crimes have decreased; on the contrary, there is evidence that such injuries are on the rise.[60] A recent review of the empirical evidence comparing the damages between traditional and white-collar crime concluded, "The total of all violent crime and all property crime combined is less of a threat to society than the crime committed by corporations."[61]

Breakdown in Social Fabric

Beyond the relatively high levels of economic and violent damage caused by white-collar crimes, a number of theorists have made the argument that these "suite" crimes are also far worse than "street" crimes in terms of the damage done to the moral and social fabric of society.[62] To clarify, they argue that corporate crime creates a higher level of immorality in American society because of the nature of hypocrisy typically inherent in the offenders and/or offending. After all, these offenders are often individuals who are looked up to by other members of society, and they are often persons, such as community leaders, politicians, or judges, who have condemned and even prosecuted others for street crimes that didn't inflict near the damage of their own "suite" crimes. As Clinard and Yeager (1980) claim in their classic work:

> It is hypocritical to regard theft and fraud among the lower classes with distaste and to punish such acts while countenancing upper-class deception and calling it "shrewd business practice." A review of corporate violations and how they are prosecuted and punished shows who controls what in law enforcement in American society and the extent to which this control is effective; . . . corporate crime is generally surrounded by an aura of politeness and respectability rarely if ever present in cases of ordinary crime.[63]

Furthermore, most high-profile businesses guilty of corporate wrongdoing had strong political ties to certain groups—namely, the Republican Party. Specifically, an analysis showed that virtually every corporate violator made more contributions to the Republican Party (which has a generally more pro-business or laissez-faire [hands-off] attitude) than to the Democratic Party.[64] However, the history of corporate and white-collar violations clearly is on both sides of the aisle in terms of political ideology.

When we poll our students about how serious they perceive white-collar crime to be compared with street crimes, they often claim that they don't care much about white-collar crime because it doesn't directly affect them. But indeed it does! After all, who will be paying for the Enron fallout, the savings and loan scandal of the late 1980s, fraudulent insurance claims, and the other thousands of corporate violations each year? American taxpayers and consumers. Furthermore, we are far less likely to be injured or killed by traditional street offenders than by corporate offenders, whether from unsafe pharmaceuticals, hazardous consumer products, or dangerous working conditions.

What are some of the negative effects experienced by victims of white-collar crime?

Ultimately, we hope readers will consider the argument that the damage caused by white-collar crimes outweighs the damage inflicted by all traditional street crimes combined in terms of property, violence, and destruction of the fabric of society. We will now examine several notable forms of white-collar crime. Although there are hundreds of varieties of corporate offending, due to space limitations, we concentrate here on what we consider to be the most influential and/or fastest-growing types of white-collar crime: violations against the environment, labor violations, and organized crime (i.e., racketeering).

TYPES OF WHITE-COLLAR CRIME

Crimes Against the Environment

Although forms of pollution have existed throughout human civilization, the real turn for the worst for the environment was the Industrial Revolution (mid-1700s to mid-1800s), which is generally considered by historians to be one of the most important periods in the world's history (and our nation's in particular) in terms of progress. After all, that period resulted in a dramatic shift from rural-based economies to industrial-based economies.

In the preindustrial period, the farmers were dependent on the land, so for the most part, they treated it well. Once the Industrial Revolution hit, there were countless numbers of factories and plants that had no concern for the environment, and this resulted in unprecedented dumping of deadly chemicals and waste products into bodies of water, toxins being released from endless streams of smoke coming out of factory chimneys, and massive destruction of majestic forests and natural resources. However, there was virtually no understanding of the damage being done, and pollution was not acknowledged as a concept, let alone a problem.

Environmental Protection Agency: started in 1970, charged with protecting human health and safeguarding the natural environment.

In the 20th century, it became obvious that much damage had been done, and efforts have since been made to repair and restrict harm to the environment. Many laws and regulations were passed, and entire federal, state, and local agencies were created, such as the most prominent federal agency, the Environmental Protection Agency (EPA; see http://www.epa.gov/). The EPA is not a Cabinet agency, but the administrator (appointed by the president) is normally given Cabinet rank, so he or she certainly has almost daily contact with the president of the United States.

The EPA, started in 1970, is charged with protecting human health and safeguarding the natural environment, which is quite a burden.[65] For instance, the United States contains 30,000 waste sites along with more than 10 billion pounds of toxic chemicals that pose a significant threat of pollution.[66] Furthermore, the EPA estimates that there are about 60,000 deaths—mostly among the elderly and young children—each year in

LEARNING CHECK 14.2

1. According to the text, studies show that what percentage of the largest 25 corporations in the Fortune 500 were convicted of a violation between 1977 and 1990?

   a. 20%

   b. 40%

   c. 60%

   d. 80%

   e. 100%

2. According to the text, white-collar/corporate crimes cost U.S. society far more each year in terms of injuries/deaths than all street crimes combined. True or false?

Answers located at www.edge.sagepub.com/schram2e

the United States as a direct result of toxic particles emitted from manufacturing plants. Also, in one recent year, the EPA identified 149 manufacturing plants throughout the nation where air in nearby communities was tested as being toxic and dangerous.[67]

The EPA often works with the U.S. Department of the Interior and U.S. Department of Agriculture in developing and enforcing regulations to protect the environment from corporate crimes. These include laws against air pollution, against water pollution, for preserving forests and other natural areas, for appropriate hazardous waste disposal, and for protecting endangered species. This has been one of the most common areas of corporate violation over the past few decades, and

Oil-covered pelicans sit in a pen waiting to be cleaned after the BP Oil Spill.

the EPA has been busy. Although the vast majority of the nearly 20,000 people working for the EPA are doing their best to protect us and the environment, imagine their shock, as well as the public's, when it was discovered that EPA executives in the early 1980s were committing corporate crime. Specifically, Rita Lavelle was appointed by President Reagan and put in charge of a large fund to clean up the most extreme cases of corporate pollution resulting from improper disposal of hazardous waste.[68] She participated in questionable decisions with some of the most chronic corporate polluters and used the dispersal of monies for political purposes; she was later convicted on four felony counts in 1983. So again, here is an example of the hypocrisy of white-collar crime and how it destroys the moral fabric of society. After all, why should any business respect the environmental codes when the very people who create and enforce the codes have been known to engage in high levels of corruption?

Labor Violations

One of the more common corporate violations involves crimes against the people who work for the business. Like environmental crimes, these types of offenses became far more common during and after the Industrial Revolution. Labor violations range from hiring illegal workers (e.g., children) to exploiting workers to keeping unsafe work conditions and many more variations.

The primary legislation developed to investigate labor violations is the Occupational Safety and Health Act (OSHA), passed in 1970. Among other things, this act made it a misdemeanor to cause the death of a worker by willfully violating safety laws; this remains a misdemeanor to this day.[69] Unfortunately, the maximum jail time for this offense was six months, which some theorists have noted is half the maximum term for a person caught riding a wild burro on federal lands.[70] OSHA inspectors are charged with establishing and enforcing standards for the safety of American workers; however, that means overseeing 115 million workers, which is near impossible, especially with only about 2,500 inspectors. So they remain busy and often find violators.

Occupational Safety and Health Act: among other things, this 1970 federal act established the Occupational Safety and Health Administration and made it a misdemeanor to cause the death of a worker by willfully violating safety laws.

This photograph illustrates the dangerous conditions associated with child labor. In 1836, Massachusetts was the first state to pass a minimum-age law for workers.

For example, OSHA conducted about 40,000 inspections in 2003 alone, finding about 83,600 violations.[71] Violators are sometimes fined, but even then these fines are usually relatively low in relation to the profits being made by the companies. Also, OSHA almost never pursues criminal charges; between 1970 and 2002, OSHA referred only 151 cases to the Department of Justice for criminal prosecution despite finding tens of thousands of violations each year. Of these 151 cases, only 11 resulted in prison sentences, with the maximum being six months. A comprehensive analysis of 170,000 workers killed during the 20-year period from 1982 to 2002 revealed that OSHA investigated only about 24% of these cases, and even in the cases where willful safety violations occurred, the fines were typically $70,000 or less and jail time was extremely rare.[72] Thus, it is obvious that little enforcement or deterrence is involved in labor violations, even by OSHA. So corporations simply have little or nothing to lose by even willfully violating the labor regulations and codes. Interestingly, labor issues, especially regarding worker unions, are often related to the next category of white-collar crime we will discuss later in the chapter—organized crime and racketeering.

TRANSNATIONAL COMPARISONS OF WHITE-COLLAR/CORPORATE CRIME

Although most of this chapter emphasizes white-collar and corporate crimes in the United States, it is now clear that similar crimes happen just as often, if not more, throughout various regions of the world. Unfortunately, the occurrence of such illegal activities is not measured well in virtually any of these regions, including the United States. Still, there are some indicators of such corporate offending across many countries, provided by the International Crime Victimization Survey (ICVS), the Corruption Perception Index, and Transparency International—with most of the focus on bribes among business experts (see "Comparative Criminology: Bribery").

In terms of more street-level corruption (such as bribing police officers or other local authorities), which is the best measure we have for the less-developed countries, one recent study by Van Dijk collected data from 92 countries and examined both the data from ICVS and Transparency International surveys from the early 2000s. These surveys focused on the percentage of the general public involved in paying bribes to local officials in a given year.[73] This study reported that such corruption was highest in two regions of the world: West/Central Africa and East Africa (South Asia ranked a distant third). These were by far the regions with the highest percentage of households reporting paying bribes to local authorities. Given the extreme deprivation in such areas, these results reveal that persons in even the lowest forms of power (e.g., police officers) likely take advantage of their relatively high status by victimizing those they can. Although this type of street-level corruption is often not seen as white-collar crime in the United States, we must understand that in many regions of the world, the local police authorities are the equivalent of our white-collar workers and CEOs.

Comparative Criminology: BRIBERY

Ranking Countries as Likeliest for Companies to Pay or Offer Bribes to Win or Retain Business

In this section, we examine findings and conclusions from the Transparency International Annual Report of 2011, which since 1999 has administered among business experts in 28 emerging market countries global surveys regarding the propensity of international companies to offer or pay bribes to win or retain business in their nations.[74]

This comparison is applicable to the chapter in the sense that it provides a relatively recent analysis of the extent to which countries are perceived to be corrupt in terms of soliciting bribes to encourage business opportunities in their countries. The portion of the Transparency International report that we are concerned with here is the ranking of countries based on responses of business experts to the question of how likely the companies from certain countries are to pay or offer bribes to win or retain business in that country. It should be noted that rankings are based on a scale of 10 (zero perceived propensity to pay bribes) to 1 (highest perceived propensity to pay bribes), with higher scores indicating lower likelihood for paying bribes. So the higher the score, the better the country's businesses are rated in terms of ethics, at least as related to offering bribes.

According to the findings in the Transparency International report (see Table 14.1), the countries that scored highest on this rating—meaning they had the lowest levels of perceived propensity to receive bribes—were the Netherlands and Switzerland, which were tied for least corrupt; Belgium and Germany closely followed as least perceived to take bribes.[75] This is not too surprising given the international respect for

business ethics in these countries, especially Switzerland, which consistently ranks in the top few countries for not being bribe-ridden in their business dealings. However, our focus is on the countries that scored lowest on this measure, Russia and China, the two countries that are consistently ranked by business executives as having the highest propensity to take and receive bribes.

Regarding Russia and China, this low ranking is very much in line with other rankings of corporate corruption, such as bribe taking and ICVS rankings of countries.[76] Furthermore, neither of these countries are members of the Organisation for Economic Co-operation and Development (OECD), which was adopted in 1997 after an urgent request by the U.S. government and other nations.[77] Ratified by the majority of industrialized countries, an obligation from the OECD requires countries to criminalize payment of bribes in their government legislation. Russia and China are not part of that coalition, and, as shown by the results, their reluctance to join is connected to their failure to crack down on bribery tactics.

THINK ABOUT IT:

1. Which countries consistently rank as least likely to take bribes in their major business practices?

2. Which countries consistently rank as most likely to take bribes in their business practices?

3. Do you see a pattern by region of the world in terms of which countries are ranked least or most likely to accept bribes in their business practices? Why do you think that is?

TABLE 14.1

Ranking of countries based on responses to the question "In the business sectors with which you are most familiar, how likely are companies from the following countries to pay or offer bribes to win or retain business in this country?"

RANKING BY COUNTRY	
COUNTRY	SCORE (10 = NEVER PAY BRIBES, 0 = ALWAYS PAY BRIBES)
Netherlands	8.8
Switzerland	8.8
Belgium	8.7
Germany	8.6
Japan	8.6
Australia	8.5

(Continued)

TABLE 14.1 (Continued)

COUNTRY	RANKING BY COUNTRY
	SCORE (10 = NEVER PAY BRIBES, 0 = ALWAYS PAY BRIBES)
Canada	8.5
Singapore	8.3
United Kingdom	8.3
United States	8.1
France	8.0
Spain	8.0
South Korea	7.9
Brazil	7.7
Hong Kong	7.6
Italy	7.6
Malaysia	7.6
South Africa	7.6
Taiwan	7.5
India	7.5
Turkey	7.5
Saudi Arabia	7.4
Argentina	7.3
United Arab Emirates	7.3
Indonesia	7.1
Mexico	7.0
China	6.5
Russia	6.1

Source: Transparency International. (2011). *Bribe payers index.*

At this time, it is virtually impossible to estimate the level of various white-collar crimes and corporate crimes committed in the numerous countries of the world. It is hoped that in the near future, far more information will be available regarding how often various countries are victimized by a larger range of white-collar and corporate crimes.

THEORETICAL EXPLANATIONS OF WHITE-COLLAR CRIME

Although historically the empirical research on theories explaining white-collar crime was limited, in the past few decades there has been a significant increase in attention to this area. A recent review of the extant scientific research testing the empirical validity of various theories discussed previously in this book found that some theories performed better than others in explaining white-collar crime.[78] Specifically, various studies were examined regarding the theories of differential association/social learning, techniques of neutralization, deterrence/rational choice, cultural/subcultural, routine activities/ opportunity, strain, and low self-control theory and the political/economic ideologies of capitalism versus communism/socialism.

Regarding the conclusions that can be reached from this recent review of the empirical research, the theory of differential association, techniques of neutralization, and other social learning principles are extremely valid in understanding the influence of the corporate world. In white-collar crime, however, it is not a person's significant others (e.g., friends, family, etc.) who form the important definitions of doing "good" but rather his or her supervisors and professional colleagues who are most likely to affect decisions to act unethically in business practices. Furthermore, this is consistent with the use of excuses or neutralization techniques to allow an individual to do what he or she knows is inherently wrong for the good of a higher authority (company, supervisors, loyalty to colleagues, etc.). In fact, one recent study showed that executive MBA candidates, who had much experience in the corporate world, were significantly more likely to use neutralization techniques in explaining why they agreed to marketing and selling an admittedly dangerous drug than were normal MBA students, who had far less experience in the corporate world.[79]

This may help explain why there is virtually no evidence for deterrence at the corporate level; after all, studies have shown that the more often a company is caught for violations, the more likely it is to engage in such acts in the future. This is easily understood by the simple fact that the companies that have been caught have gotten away with such violations for many years without being caught, and they know that the potential benefits far outweigh any sanctions they may face if they are caught for a few of their total violations. Relatedly, portions of rational choice theory are strongly supported by empirical research, in the sense that violating ethical business rules often gains much in terms of financial profit and/or employer recognition. This also relates to the cultural/subcultural findings regarding motivations to commit white-collar crime, which clearly show the significant cultural emphasis in most companies that focus solely on making a profit; thus, any other normative value system pales in comparison with helping contribute to the profit margin. And once a person starts working in a company, that individual tends to take on the mentality or normative culture of the company, with few exceptions. After all, that company is paying individuals and providing their livelihood, so it is only natural that a person would start internalizing the subcultural beliefs and goals promoted by the group directly responsible for his or her success or survival.

Such subcultural influences of peers and supervisors in a corporate environment likely take over as the dominating force, especially regarding the teaching of ethics for business majors at most universities. Such moral beliefs are key in social bonding theory as well as a key conditional variable in many rational choice theories of offending. However, as said before, studies show that the cultural norms of one's environment seem to overwhelm university-led ethical training.[85] Not surprisingly, an individual will typically follow the orders of superiors and/or subcultural pressures among colleagues to make a profit for the company, despite any ethical principles learned in school or personal beliefs.

Regarding opportunity theories, such as routine activities theory, the ready-made opportunity to commit various white-collar crimes is quite attractive, especially given the low likelihood of being caught and the ease of achieving economic gain via one's everyday job. After all, there doesn't seem to be much of a downside to engaging in illegal and unethical behavior in most white-collar positions, especially when one sees on the news that even when someone is caught and convicted, that person usually doesn't spend any

Applying Theory to Crime: *WHITE-COLLAR CRIME*

In this section, we discuss several theories that seem to explain some of the reasons why individuals engage in various forms of white-collar crime. First, it should be apparent that although most crimes don't pay well, white-collar crime often does come with a large pay-off. Second, the individuals in white-collar positions tend to have a low likelihood of getting caught; even if they are caught, they are typically not punished severely. So given the obvious failure of traditional, formal deterrence theory in trying to explain this phenomenon, we must turn to other theoretical frameworks.

Despite its similarity to traditional deterrence, one theoretical model that has shown much promise in understanding criminal decision-making in the corporate world is rational choice theory. In a recent review of the extant research, Paternoster and Tibbetts concluded that one of the key reasons for the empirical support of rational choice theory over formal deterrence theory is that the informal pressures and controls that exist within a corporation often override any possible deterrent effect from authorities outside the organization.[80] Rational choice theory places an emphasis on accounting for such informal factors and, thus, is an improvement over models focused on formal sanctions, or lack thereof.

Additional theoretical models found to be helpful in explaining white-collar crime include the social process/learning models of differential association/reinforcement theory, which place an emphasis on the influence of significant others in individuals' decisions of whether or not to engage in illegal behavior.[81] A study by Piquero, Tibbetts, and Blankenship showed that several components of the differential

association theoretical framework did, in fact, predict intentions to make unethical business decisions in a scenario presented to participants (MBA students). The scenario involved a drug that was known to cause detrimental (even fatal) side effects. However, it wasn't the perceived attitudes of peers or family or business professors that led to higher intentions to commit the unethical act of further marketing and selling the dangerous drug; it was the attitude of coworkers and the perceived beliefs of their employers/bosses that actually had a greater impact on participants' decision to commit this illegal act.[82]

Thus, it appears that social learning theory is supported for white-collar crime but not in the same way as for most street crimes, which typically are more influenced by family or good friends. Rather, the influence of such social learning factors in predicting white-collar/corporate crime is actually more due to the differential associations and reinforcements present in the workplace environment. These findings are consistent with additional research that has examined the validity of cultural/subcultural theory in understanding white-collar crime, with the vast majority of findings supporting the use of this framework in corporate offending.[83] What virtually all the studies reveal is that the climate in the corporation plays a much stronger role in individuals' decisions to commit white-collar crime than do other associations or learning from significant others, such as parents, peers, and/or professors from their college years.

Another theory tested in the Piquero et al. study was that of techniques of neutralization, which are strategies used by offenders to alleviate their guilt for committing an act they

know is wrong. In this study, there were numerous such neutralization techniques examined, and it was found that several of them (e.g., denial of responsibility, appeal to higher loyalties) were highly important in decisions to engage in illegal corporate activity. The participants noted the importance of making a profit for their company as trumping any type of hesitation in making their decision, despite what friends or family would think.[84]

Ultimately, the rational choice perspective has been supported as an important framework for understanding individuals' perceptions and intentions to engage in illegal business practices. Also, the social learning theories of differential association/reinforcement, as well as the concepts of techniques of neutralization, appear to be highly influential among individuals in their decisions to engage in unethical behavior when it comes to white-collar crime. These theories are consistent with the empirical validity found for cultural and subcultural models of unethical corporate decision-making.

Other theories can help explain why individuals engage in white-collar crime, but the three theories discussed in this section are the most supported models for understanding crime in the corporate realm.

THINK ABOUT IT:

1. Why do many scholars believe that rational choice theory and/or social learning theory may provide a better explanation for white-collar crime than formal deterrence?

2. How have techniques of neutralization been used to understand why individuals engage in corporate crime?

time in prison. And even when such persons do serve time, it is often at a minimum-security facility—quite a difference from serving "hard time." So there doesn't seem to be much certainty or severity of punishment, but there is likely to be a huge payoff or promotion if one does engage in unethical practices. Given the current lack of enforcement of laws against illegal behaviors among white-collar professionals, it only makes sense to engage in criminal activity. Until more certain enforcement and far more severe penalties are mandated, it is highly unlikely that the perceptions and motivations of white-collar workers will change, especially given the constant opportunities to engage in such activity.

Regarding strain theory, especially institutional anomie theory, there is believed to be an American cultural value of monetary success, which often takes priority over other important social factors (i.e., family, friends, education, etc.). This strain for success, or even greed, has its source in both individuals and corporations. Furthermore, the source of strain for monetary gain emanates from both internal and external sources to the company, ranging from the internal performance of specific employees to more macro-level economic trends in the market.

In terms of conflict theory, especially regarding the overall political or economic ideology of various corporations (such as across various countries), studies show that whether a company is based in more communistic countries or more capitalistic countries, the goal is profit. Specifically, studies have shown that white-collar crime existed at a high rate in more socialist and communist countries.[86] This is likely due to these countries not having much enforcement against such practices, since they are believed not to exist in such idealistic societies. But greed is a universal pattern, so you will find it everywhere, in any society and at any time.

After reviewing all the relevant empirical studies for each of the theories above, the authors concluded:

> The majority of empirical research in white-collar crime thus far has been built off traditional theories that were originally developed to explain conventional crimes. However, white-collar and conventional offenders . . . are distinctly different. . . . Our next step should be to move beyond conventional explanations.[87]

We agree with this assessment, and more topic-specific theories must be created to understand fully the reasons and motivations for committing white-collar crime. This is also true of another form of corporate-related offending, which we will discuss next—organized crime and racketeering.

WHAT IS ORGANIZED CRIME?

For decades, the American public has had a curious fascination with organized crime. For instance, when John Dillinger was gunned down by the Federal Bureau of Investigation in 1934, there were photographs of his body in the morgue. In fact, the Cook County (Chicago) morgue allowed the public to view his body. The public enjoys watching movies or television programs that depict the so-called mob lifestyle, such as *The Godfather*, *Goodfellas*, and *The Sopranos*. However, many of these movies and television programs contain some myths or "entertainment" license. In this section, we provide a general overview of issues pertaining to organized crime, beginning with a definition and followed by the historical context of organized crime in the United States. Next, we will review different types of criminal organizations as well as criminal justice responses to organized crime. We will conclude this section with a brief outline of various theoretical explanations for this type of criminal activity.

Actors from The Sopranos – a fictional series about a family involved in organized crime. What effect does the media have on our perceptions of organized crime?

Definition of Organized Crime

In the 1986 *Report to the President and the Attorney General*, the President's Commission on Organized Crime noted that when defining organized crime, the problem is not in the word *crime*; rather, the difficulty is with the term *organized*.[88] One approach to defining organized crime is to incorporate a typology. This typology includes such factors as the means of obtaining the goals (e.g., violence, theft, corruption) and the reasons for engaging in such activities—an economic objective (e.g., through common crime, illegal business, or legal business) or a political objective (e.g., through the existing order, against the existing order).[89]

While there is no agreed-on definition of organized crime, Howard Abadinsky listed various factors associated with this type of criminal activity as identified by law enforcement agencies and researchers.[90]

1. Organized crime is absent of political goals.

2. Organized crime is hierarchical.

3. Organized crime has limited or exclusive membership.

4. Organized crime constitutes a unique subculture.

5. Organized crime perpetuates itself.

6. Organized crime is willing to use illegal violence.

7. Organized crime is monopolistic.

8. Organized crime is governed by rules and regulations.

Historical Context of Organized Crime in the United States

> No sooner had crime become profitable in America than it became organized. And no sooner did it become organized than it became a regular part of the American way of life, thanks to the cooperation and collusion of government officials. Organized crime did not begin with twentieth century Prohibition. It began with the colonial pirates.[91]

organized crime: sometimes defined through a typology, such as the means of obtaining the goals and the reasons for engaging in such activity: an economic objective or a political objective.

Some argue that pirates during the American colonial era were a form of organized crime group. These pirates developed a well-structured, hierarchical organization; engaged in nonideological goals; and had a restricted membership.[92]

Crime at the end of the piracy era was essentially disorganized. By the turn of the 19th century, New York City was the "entrepreneurial center" of the country. Many immigrants entered the country to seek freedoms, opportunities, and fortunes. These factors also made New York the center for conspiracies, crooks, and criminals.[93] In the 1850s, gangs began to dominate the criminal arena. These gangs included the Forty Thieves, the Hudson Dusters, the Short Tails, and the Dead Rabbits; they evolved when groups of immigrants banded together for protection as well as for the exploitation of other immigrants. These gangs eventually formed partnerships with the political machines of the time in an effort to control their vice enterprises.[94] One notorious political machine was Tammany Hall. Tammany Hall got its name from the Indian chief Tamanend. It was founded in 1789 to oppose the ruling conservative Federalist party. A primary strength of Tammany Hall was its skill in electing candidates to the state legislature in Albany and to the board of aldermen in New York City.[95]

In 1919, the Eighteenth Amendment to the Constitution was passed, outlawing the manufacture, sale, distribution, and transportation of alcoholic beverages.[96] Prohibition created an opportunity for criminals. Even with the passage of the Eighteenth Amendment, they recognized the need for a major infrastructure to meet the public demand for alcohol, including production, transportation, and importation. Prohibition and the Chicago political machine created one of the most notorious criminal organizations in this country's history. One of the most infamous of these criminals, epitomizing Chicago during Prohibition, was Al Capone.[97] Prohibition provided an opportunity to transform Italian, Jewish, and Irish gangsters into more powerful groups. The profits earned from illegally supplying alcohol were great; however, even with a more powerful position, many of these gangs continued to operate as they did in their "wild early days."[98] This would often result in violence among various gangs to obtain control over this illegal market.

In response to the need for tax revenue during the Great Depression, the state of Nevada legalized gambling in 1931. Bugsy Siegel was the first prominent criminal to realize the potential of legalized gambling.[99] In 1947, the Flamingo Hotel in Las Vegas, Nevada, was opened. This opening designated the onset of organized crime control of the legal gambling industry.[100] Given their experience as "bootleggers," organized crime groups had the business acumen to control gambling. Many of the lavish hotels, such as the Flamingo, were controlled, albeit through hidden interests, by organized crime. Usually, monies were "skimmed" before being counted for tax purposes; this money was distributed to the organized crime bosses in proportion to their "hidden" ownership. In fact, from 1973 to 1983, at least $14 million was skimmed from just one hotel, the Stardust. Today, Las Vegas is not controlled by organized crime; rather, casinos are now major corporate entities.[101]

In 1986, the President's Commission on Organized Crime noted that of the various developments in organized crime during the preceding 20 years, three developments were significant. One was the increasing awareness that other organized crime groups exist. While many were ethnic based, others had originated in U.S. prisons and outlaw motorcycle gangs. Another development was the success of law enforcement against the leadership, membership, and associates of *La Cosa Nostra*, which is considered by some to be the best-known organized crime group in the past 30 years. The third significant development was organized crime's involvement in drug trafficking:[102] "It is essential that we broaden our view to include all significant facets of organized crime. There will be little lasting benefit in disabling *La Cosa Nostra* if other groups successfully claim its abandoned criminal franchise."[103]

Today there is growing concern over organized crime groups using advances in technology to engage in various criminal activities. While we specifically discuss cybercrime in the following section, Zambo claimed that cybergangs are organized in a similar fashion to the Mafia; the major difference is that cybergangs operate completely online.[104] Examples of such crimes include credit card cloning, phone card piracy, computer viruses, child pornography, electronic banking fraud, music piracy, counterfeit medicine, and software piracy.[105]

Tammany Hall: a notorious Democratic political machine in New York City from the 1790s through the 1960s with major influence in city and state politics.

Types of Criminal Organizations

As stated above, it is essential that law enforcement recognize that organized crime is not synonymous with the Mafia. In this section, we begin with a brief discussion of the Mafia followed by discussion of other types of criminal organizations, including outlaw motorcycle gangs, prison gangs, and urban street gangs.

The Mafia

The origins of the Mafia are unclear. One opinion is that the Mafia evolved as a ninth-century response to Arabic domination of Sicily. Another view is that the Mafia evolved in Palermo, Italy, in 1282 as a political organization to free Sicily from French domination. The group's rallying cry was *"Morte alla Francia Italia anela"* ("Death to the French is Italy's cry"). The acronym of this pledge is MAFIA.[106] The true origins of the term *Mafia* are convoluted by assorted use and personal preference.[107] Some of the most common references are listed in Table 14.2. Originally, the Mafia was similar to an extended social family. While not necessarily related by blood, members were related by home village and Sicilian nationality. The members took an oath, swearing under punishment of death to a code of silence. Initially, the Mafia was a self-protection group; by the 1860s, however, they had expanded to criminal activities such as smuggling, cattle rustling, and extortion.[108] While the term *Mafia* referred to beauty, perfection, grace, and excellence, the term Mafioso referred to characteristics of a man, such as pride, self-confidence, and an "arrogant" attitude.[109]

In 1878, the Italian government began concentrated efforts to eliminate the Sicilian Mafia. Thus, many Sicilian Mafiosi immigrated to the United States, settling in major urban cities such as Boston, Chicago, Kansas City, New Orleans, New York, and St. Louis.[110] The Mafiosi in the United States were similar to other immigrants. When these criminals entered the United States, they assimilated with others but continued their criminal activities. From 1890 to the 1920s, the Mafiosi preyed on other immigrants by forcing their participation in the protection scam. This was known as *La Mano Nero*, or "The Black Hand." Soon their activities expanded to other crimes, especially during Prohibition.[111] Michael Lyman and Gary Potter pose an interesting question: "Does the Mafia really exist?" They provide arguments from both positions. From the "yes" position, they note that there have been high-profile trials on such "mob bosses" as Al

Mafia: similar to an extended social family; members took an oath swearing, under punishment of death, to a code of silence. It started as a self-protection group, but by the 1860s expanded to criminal activities such as smuggling, cattle rustling, and extortion.

Mafioso: referred to characteristics of a man, such as pride, self-confidence, and a sense of "arrogant" behavior.

TABLE **14.2**   Common References to the Term *Mafia*

TERM	DEFINITION
Maffia	Tuscan word for misery
Mauvia	French word for bad
Ma-afir	Arabic tribe that settled in Sicily
MAFIA	*Mazzini autorizza furti incendi auvelenamenti*, or Massini authorizes thefts, arson, and poisons
Mu'afy	Arabic word meaning "protects from death in the night"
Mafia	The name of a stone quarry in Sicily
I Mafiusi di la Vicaria	The title of a play written in 1860 by Guiseppe Rizzotto, *The Heroes of the Penitentiary*.

Source: Albini, J. (1971). *Mafia: Genesis of a legend.* New York, NY: Appleton-Century-Crofts, p. 83.

Capone, Sam Giancana, "Lucky" Luciano, Vito Genovese, and John Gotti. While the convictions of these "bosses" did not result in total disbanding of the organization, they did provide law enforcement the opportunity to survey, monitor, arrest, interview, and collaborate with members of the Mafia and other organized crime groups. Some also maintain that in 1963, Joe Valachi revealed information about the structure of the Mafia, claiming that there were about 25 Italian gangs throughout the United States, referred to as "families."

From the "no" position, some argue that there is no single organization known as the Mafia; rather, there are loosely structured criminal gangs, some of which are of Italian descent. These Italian gangs, or families, do exist but are not as organized or structured as thought by law enforcement and the media. These individuals maintain, however, that by claiming the existence of a well-organized Mafia, law enforcement agencies can justify their existence.[112]

Police detain various motorcycle clubs outside the Twin Peaks restaurant in Waco, Texas on May 17, 2015.

Outlaw Motorcycle Gangs

During the late 1940s, outlaw motorcycle gangs (OMGs) evolved as disorganized and unruly groups made up of disgruntled World War II veterans. Through the decades, the tough-guy image was perpetuated and membership increased, along with the organization and sophistication of these groups.[113] Soon, some of these groups' behavior was more rebellious than openly criminal.[114] In fact, OMG members refer to themselves as "one-percenters":

> Some years ago . . . the American Motorcycle Association . . . [estimated] that outlaw motorcyclists comprised less than one per cent of the motorcycling population. Outlaw gangs immediately seized on the figure as a reflection of their belief that they are rebels, operating outside society's laws and norms.[115]

While the 1% figure is meaningless today, members refer to themselves as "one-percenters" to flaunt their status as lawless outsiders.

OMGs today are secretive and close-knit groups with selective membership. Membership in OMGs is symbolized by "colors," which are often displayed on denim or leather jackets with embroidered patches sewn on the back. These patches display a gang logo and may also include "rockers" that identify the name of the gang and home city of the chapter. The colors are the member's most prized possession and represent his primary commitment—to the gang and its criminal lifestyle. The outrageous treatment of women who associate with the members is also part of the OMG lifestyle. Women are considered less important than the gang itself or the member's motorcycle. In some gangs, women are used to generate money through prostitution as well as for the transportation of drugs and weapons.[116]

Some of the most notorious OMGs include the Hells Angels, the Outlaws, the Bandidos, and the Pagans (see Table 14.3). Among these, the Hells Angels are regarded as the wealthiest and most powerful of the OMGs. They have not only an extensive

outlaw motorcycle gangs: the tough-guy image of these groups was perpetuated and membership increased, along with organization and sophistication. Soon, behavior of some groups was less rebellious and more openly criminal; some members refer to themselves as "one-percenters."

TABLE 14.3 Hells Angels California Bylaws

BYLAW	FINE
1. All patches will be the same on the back, nothing will show on the back except the HELLS ANGELS patch. City patch is optional for each chapter. 1 patch and 1 membership card per member. Member may keep original patch if made into a banner. Prospects will wear California rocker on back and prospect patch left from where top of pocket is on a Levi jacket.	$100 for breaking above by-law.
2. No hypes. No use of Heroin in any form. Anyone using a needle for any reason other than having a doctor use it on you will be considered a hype.	Automatic kick-out from club.
3. No explosives of any kind will be thrown into the fire where there is one or more HELLS ANGELS in this area.	Ass-whipping and/or subject to California President's decision.
4. Guns on CA runs will not be displayed after 6 PM. They will be fired from dawn until 6 PM in a predetermined area only. Rule does not apply to anyone with a gun in a shoulder holster or belt that is seen by another member if it is not being shot or displayed.	$100 for breaking above by-law.
5. Brothers shall not fight with each other with weapons; when any HELLS ANGELS fights another HELLS ANGELS, it is one on one; prospects same as members. If members are from different chapters, fine goes to CA Treasurer.	$100 for breaking above by-law or possible loss of patch.
6. No narcotics burns. When making deals, persons get what they are promised or the deal is called off.	Automatic kick-out from club.
7. All HELLS ANGELS fines will be paid within 30 days. Fines will be paid to that chapter's treasurer to be held for the next CA run.	
8. One vote per chapter at CA officer's meetings. For CA 2 no votes instead of a majority to kill a new charter and a charter goes below 6 they must freeze or dissolve on the decision of CA Officers' Meeting.	
9. If kicked out, must stay out 1 year then back to original chapter. HELLS ANGEL tattoo will have an in-date and out-date when the member quits. If kicked out HELLS ANGELS tattoo will be completely covered with a ½ X through the tattoo.	
10. Runs are on the holidays; 3 mandatory runs are Memorial Day, July 4th, and Labor Day.	
11. No leave period except hospital, medical or jail.	

Source: Abadinsky, H. (2013). *Organized crime* (10th ed.). Belmont, CA: Cengage Learning, p. 230.

membership in the United States but also chapters in Brazil, Canada, Colombia, Australia, New Zealand, Japan, and seven Western European countries. The Hells Angels also have a sophisticated and wide-ranging counterintelligence structure as protection from arrest and prosecution.[117] There are sophisticated but smaller OMGs, including the Vagos (in the West and Southwest), the Warlocks (in the region of Pennsylvania, New Jersey, and Delaware), the Dirty Dozen (in Arizona), the Gypsy Jokers (in the Pacific Northwest), and the Sons of Silence (in Colorado).[118]

Prison Gangs

Some have attributed the growth of prison gangs to the 1964 U.S. Supreme Court decision Cooper v. Pate. As a result of this decision, prisoners were allowed to sue state officials in federal court, which resulted in a great deal of litigation and changed prison conditions in the 1970s. Gangs grew in the more liberal prison environment. Prior to *Cooper v. Pate*, only Washington and California reported the existence of prison gangs; by 1984, this number had risen to more than 60% of state and federal prisons reporting gang activity. By the 1990s, some of these prison gangs had evolved into well-organized crime groups. Some have attributed the growth of prison gangs to a void left with the dwindling influence of the convict code.[119] These gangs were different from previous gangs primarily in their demand for absolute obedience to the "parent" group. For instance, the "death oath," or "blood in and blood out," requires the member to remain a member forever.[120] Specifically, this oath requires that to become a member, an inmate must kill or assault another prisoner or staff member; if a member wants to leave the gang, then his blood "will be spilled."[121]

Organized in the late 1950s, one of the oldest prison gangs is the Mexican Mafia, whose members are primarily Mexican Americans from Southern California.[122] In some prisons, the Mexican Mafia controls homosexual prostitution, gambling, and narcotics. Both inside and outside prison, the Mexican Mafia is involved in burglary, assault, robbery, extortion, drug trafficking, and contract killing. Another major prison gang is La Nuestra Familia, considered an enemy of the Mexican Mafia. This prison gang was established in Soledad Prison (California) in 1967. La Nuestra Familia's outside prison operations include a protection racket, similar to more traditional organized crime groups. The Texas Syndicate originated in Folsom Prison (California) in 1974. The members are predominately Mexican Americans from the El Paso and San Antonio region. The gang has a reputation for being one of the most violent. The Black Guerilla Family was established at San Quentin Prison by black activist prisoner George Jackson in 1966. This gang is closely associated with the Crips street gang. The Black Guerilla Family is controlled by a central committee consisting of generals, captains, lieutenants, and soldiers. The Aryan Brotherhood is a motorcycle-oriented, white-supremacist gang founded in San Quentin Prison in the 1960s. The Aryan Brotherhood's criminal activities include extortion, protection rackets, drug trafficking, and contract killing.[123]

Urban Street Gangs

Using Maltz's[124] characteristics associated with organized crime groups, Dennis Kenney and James Finckenauer evaluated whether urban street gangs could be deemed organized crime groups. The first characteristic of organized crime groups is *corruption*. At this time, there is no evidence to support the notion that urban street gangs systematically engage in paying off public officials in an effort to avoid arrest and prosecution. The second characteristic, *violence* or the threat of violence, is a major feature of urban street gangs. The third characteristic, *continuity*, is a feature for certain street gangs. Some gangs, such as social or party gangs, are more spontaneous; they exist as a gang for a short period of time and quickly split up. The fourth characteristic is *multiple enterprises*. The drug "business" is essentially the only enterprise for urban street gangs. While some may be involved in other types of crime, such as property crime, they do not run illegal business enterprises such as gambling, prostitution, and loans.

Structure and involvement in legitimate businesses is the fifth characteristic. While some street gangs appear to have some type of organizational structure, there does not seem to be a great deal of expansion from illegal business into legitimate business. The last characteristic is *sophistication, discipline, and bonding*. While some gangs engage in sophisticated activities, such as speaking in code over the telephone, most gangs do not.

Cooper v. Pate: as a result of this decision, prisoners were allowed to sue state officials in federal court, which resulted in much litigation and changed the prison conditions in the 1970s.

In reference to discipline, many urban gangs, especially those involved in the drug business, do stress the need for discipline. Finally, many street gangs emphasize bonding, such as rituals and initiation rites.[125]

CRIMINAL JUSTICE RESPONSES TO ORGANIZED CRIME

Chicago Crime Commission

In 1919, a group of Chicago businessmen, concerned about Chicago's "gangland" reputation, formed the Chicago Crime Commission. While some would argue that the Commission was "a self-serving exercise in hypocrisy," it was able to demonstrate the city's crime problem through a successful public relations campaign. For instance, the public relations committee introduced the "Public Enemy" list prior to J. Edgar Hoover's version.

The Wickersham Commission

To assess the effect of Prohibition on criminal activity, the Wickersham Commission was formed in 1929. The findings from the commission revealed that organized criminal activity flourished around bootlegging activities. The commission recommended a more in-depth study of organized crime and its criminal activities. This study did not occur, however, until years later. This delay was attributed to various factors, including the well-publicized arrests and prosecutions of organized crime "bosses" such as Al Capone and "Lucky" Luciano, giving the public a sense that law enforcement and the criminal justice system were successfully deterring such activities. Further, the public's attention was focused on such social concerns as the Great Depression and World War II. Given these "diversions," organized crime prospered, and it was not until the formation of the Kefauver Committee that there was an extensive investigation into organized crime.[130]

The Kefauver Committee

In May 1950, Senator Estes Kefauver became chair of the Special Committee to Investigate Organized Crime in Interstate Commerce. The Kefauver Committee was charged with three responsibilities:

1. To conduct an extensive study and investigation to assess whether organized crime used the services, or avenues, of interstate commerce to promote any transactions that violated federal or state law

2. If such transactions did occur, to investigate the identification of the persons, firms, or corporations involved

3. To determine whether such interstate criminal operations were responsible for developing corrupting influences in violation of federal or state laws[131]

During Kefauver's term as chair, the committee heard from more than 600 witnesses in Miami, Tampa, New Orleans, Kansas City, Cleveland, St. Louis, Detroit, Los Angeles, San Francisco, Las Vegas, Philadelphia, Washington, Chicago, and New York.[132]

The Kefauver Committee provided invaluable information on organized crime; however, the committee did not provide support for the existence of an international Mafia conspiracy:[133]

> Neither the Senate Crime Committee in its testimony nor Kefauver in his book presented any real evidence that the Mafia exists as a functioning organization. . . . The only other "evidence" presented . . . is that certain crimes bear "the earmarks of the Mafia." [134]

Wickersham Commission: formed in 1929, this commission found that organized criminal activity flourished around bootlegging operations.

Kefauver Committee: in 1950, charged with three responsibilities that focused on whether organized crime used the services of interstate commerce to engage in illegal activities and identifying the persons, firms, or corporations involved in such activities.

Comparative Criminology: ORGANIZED CRIME

Ranking Regions/Countries as Most Likely for Organized Crime

In this section, we examine the findings and conclusions of various studies regarding organized crime, which typically includes certain elements, such as use of extreme violence, corruption of public officials (such as police and judicial officers), penetration of the legitimate economy (often through money laundering), and interference in the political process.[127] The findings of these recent studies on prevalence of organized crime across various regions/countries are surprising in many ways.

One of the key measures of organized crime in the world is the Organized Crime Perception (OCP) Index, which is a combined measure using data from various sources, such as the World Economic Forum (a survey of CEOs of large companies), the World Bank and European Bank of Reconstruction and Development, and The Merchant International Group Ltd (an internationally active security consultancy group). Although many factors go into the OCP Index, it is generally considered the most accurate measure to determine how much organized crime is perceived and how much is actually present in most regions/countries around the world.[128] According to the OCP Index, the traditional notion of Mafia-type activities being concentrated in Italy and other nearby locations can be largely dispelled. As seen in Figure 14.1, which plots the countries with the highest scores on the OCP Index against their rate of

FIGURE 14.1

Prevalence of Mafia-Type Activities as Perceived by Business Leaders and/or Security Experts and Rates of Unsolved Homicides (Ranked Variables)

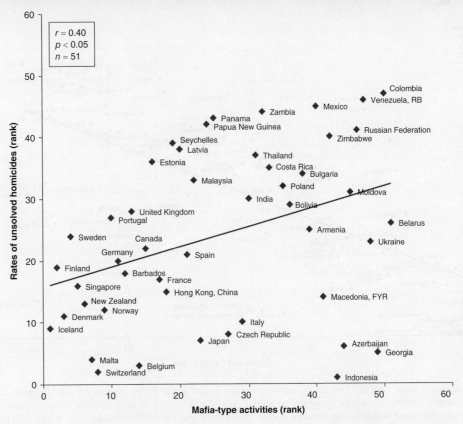

Sources: World Economic Forum. (2005). *The Global competitiveness report 2004–2005.* Hampshire, UK: Palgrave Macmillan; Merchant International Group Limited. (2004). *Gray-area dynamics, organized crime figures 2004.* Special analysis commissioned by UNICRI; BEEPS. (2014). *Business environment and enterprise performance survey.* World Bank and the EBRD. United Nations Office on Drugs and Crime. (2003). *The eighth United Nations survey on crime trends and the operations of criminal justice systems, 2001–2002.*

(Continued)

(Continued)

unsolved homicides, Italy ranked about in the middle in terms of Mafia-type activities and relatively low in terms of unsolved homicides. Rather, the countries of Colombia, Venezuela, Zimbabwe, and the Russian Federation have the highest scores on both Mafia-type activities and rates of unsolved homicides. (Note: The United States was absent from this comparison.)

In addition, Van Dijk correlated the OCP Index with another index that measured high-level corruption in many countries.[129] The findings of this analysis, as shown in Figure 14.2, reveal that the highest-scoring countries on both organized crime and political corruption included Iraq (the highest on both scores), Ukraine, Nigeria, Haiti, Pakistan, Venezuela, and the Russian Federation. It is interesting to note that the United States scored relatively low on both these measures. Given the noticeably high prevalence of organized crime and political corruption in the United States (as suggested by constant

media reports of political corruption and recent arrests for organized crime), it is shocking that we are doing better than most countries on these two types of criminal activity—at least according to these various measures. It is also notable that the countries that scored relatively higher on both organized crime and political corruption in this analysis were from scattered regions of the world, including the Middle East, Asia, Africa, North America/the Caribbean, and South America. Probably the only area that scored low on this analysis was the Australian continental region.

Thus, it can be concluded that organized crime is prevalent in virtually all parts of the world, as is political corruption. So the myth of Mafia-type organizations being largely present in Italy and the United States can be absolutely dismissed. Organized crime is alive and well throughout virtually all societies and, as shown in the results in Figure 14.2, is likely to be correlated with political corruption as well.

FIGURE 14.2

Prevalence of Perceived Organized Crime and Regional Scores on Composite Index Measuring High-Level Corruption/State Capture

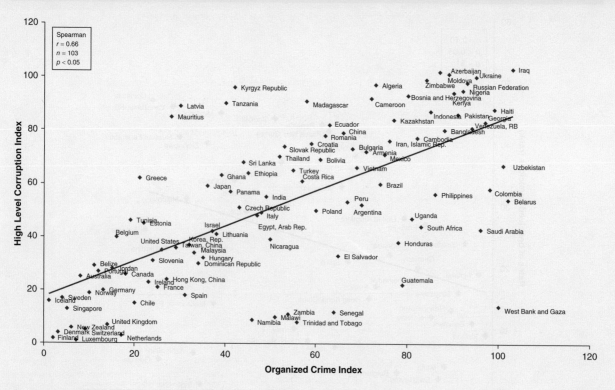

Sources: World Economic Forum. (2005). *The Global competitiveness report 2004–2005.* Hampshire, UK: Palgrave Macmillan; Merchant International Group Limited. (2004). *Gray-area dynamics, organized crime figures 2004.* Special analysis commissioned by UNICRI; BEEPS. (2014). *Business environment and enterprise performance survey.* World Bank and the EBRD. Buscaglia, E., & Van Dijk, J. (2003). Controlling organized crime and corruption in the public sector. *Forum on Crime and Society, 3,* 3–35.

The McClellan Committee

In the early 1960s, the Senate Permanent Subcommittee on Investigation, chaired by Senator John McClellan, was formed to investigate labor racketeering in the country's trade unions. In 1963, the committee held televised hearings, including the testimony of Joseph Valachi, the first "made member" of the Genovese crime family to testify on Italian American organized crime:[135]

> Valachi was a barely literate, low-echelon soldier whose firsthand knowledge of organized crime was limited to street-level experiences. Much of the information attributed to him is obviously well beyond his personal experience. . . . Nevertheless, this did not prevent his disclosures from becoming the core of a chapter on organized crime in the final report of the President's Commission on Law Enforcement and Administration of Justice.[136]

Valachi's testimony did not result in any convictions; further, the McClellan Committee failed to recommend a specific definition of organized crime. These hearings, however, did contribute to the government's understanding of this type of criminal activity.[137]

The President's Commission on Law Enforcement and the Administration of Justice

In 1965, President Lyndon Johnson established the President's Commission on Law Enforcement and the Administration of Justice; there were nine different task forces, one of which was the Task Force on Organized Crime. In its 1967 report to the commission, the task force noted:

> Today the core of organized crime in the United States consists of twenty-four groups operating as criminal cartels in large cities across the Nation. . . . To date, only the Federal Bureau of Investigation has been able to document fully the national scope of these groups, and the FBI intelligence indicates that the organization as a whole has changed its name from the Mafia to *Cosa Nostra*.[138]

The commission maintained that gambling was the largest source of revenue for organized crime, followed by loan sharking and narcotics trafficking.[139] The task force continued efforts initiated by the Kefauver Committee. Further, the task force made various recommendations, including a witness protection program, special federal grand juries, and legislation allowing electronic surveillance.[140]

Organized Crime Control Act of 1970

As a result of the President's Commission on Law Enforcement and the Administration of Justice, Congress passed the Organized Crime Control Act in 1970. A key component of this legislation was Title 9—specifically, the **Racketeer Influenced and Corrupt Organizations (RICO) Act**. It would take nearly a decade, however, for authorities to adequately apply RICO. There are three criminal penalties for RICO violations, which can be applied simultaneously: (1) a fine of no more than $25,000, (2) a prison term of no more than 20 years (for each racketeering count), and (3) the forfeiture of any interest obtained or maintained in the course of state violations.[141]

The President's Commission on Organized Crime

Under Executive Order Number 12435, President Reagan created the President's Commission on Organized Crime in 1983. During its three years of existence, the commission produced five reports. Some of the key issues highlighted by the commission

Racketeer Influenced and Corrupt Organizations (RICO) Act: provides for enhanced criminal and civil penalties for individuals engaging in activities with criminal organizations.

LEARNING CHECK 14.3

1. The President's Commission on Organized Crime noted that when defining organized crime, the problem is with the word _____.

2. Outlaw motorcycle gangs refer to themselves as "_____-percenters."

3. Some have attributed the growth of prison gangs to the 1964 U.S. Supreme Court decision _____.

4. A key component of the _____ was the Racketeer Influenced and Corrupt Organizations (RICO) Act.

Answers located at www.edge.sagepub.com/schram2e

included the problem of money laundering, labor union racketeering, and "mob lawyers." The commission avoided the primary focus on Italian American organized crime, focusing also on Colombian cocaine cartels and other criminal groups, such as outlaw motorcycle clubs.[142] The commission also provided a more meaningful definition of organized crime. Further, in an effort to enhance its understanding of organized crime groups, the commission developed a contingency model that highlighted levels of involvement of members and nonmembers; these levels included the criminal group (i.e., the core of the organized crime unit), the protectors (e.g., corrupt public officials, businesspersons, judges, attorneys, and financial advisers), specialized support (i.e., those who provide services that facilitate organized crime, such as pilots, chemists, arsonists, and hijackers), user support (i.e., consumers of organized crime's illegal goods and services, such as drug users and people knowingly buying stolen goods), and social support (i.e., those who provide the perception of legitimacy of these criminal groups, such as politicians who seek the support of organized crime members and community leaders who invite these crime members to social gatherings).[143]

Theoretical Explanations of Organized Crime

Dennis Kenney and James Finckenauer noted that while there had been some positive developments in understanding organized crime, there were criticisms that this type of criminal activity lacked a sound theoretical framework.[144] Kenney and Finckenauer reviewed various theoretical perspectives that attempt to provide an understanding of organized criminal behavior, such as cultural transmission, culture conflict, and strain theories as well as low self-control theory. Another theoretical perspective they discussed was ethnicity and ethnic succession:

> Organized crime has been described as being "caused" by the efforts of successive immigrant groups to make it in America. Cut off from legitimate opportunities for achieving socioeconomic and political success, immigrants have been forced by circumstances to climb . . . the "queer ladder" of upward social mobility, namely, crime, and especially organized crime.[145]

Another theoretical perspective presented was enterprise theory. This perspective maintains that the legitimate marketplaces do not provide an opportunity for customers to obtain goods and services; thus, illicit entrepreneurs fill this void by providing such goods and services themselves.[146]

The authors concluded this chapter with an outline of a theory proposed by Peter Reuter.[147] Reuter was attempting to understand under what circumstances some gangs are deemed organized crime groups. He contended that adult gangs are primarily in existence for economic purposes—specifically, to make money. Another key characteristic is the supply-and-demand conditions that help organized crime flourish. Thus, according to Reuter, three factors affect the extent of organized crime in a particular city:

1. Illegal market opportunities (e.g., gambling, drugs, and loan sharking) that are contingent on coordinated groups of people in frequent interaction

2. The extent of recent migration of significant ethnic groups into the community, allowing for recruitment as well as potential clients for goods and services

3. The strength and corruptness of local political authority[148]

Kenney and Finckenauer stress that Reuter's "mini-theory" provides an exploratory foundation for conceptual and empirical research in an effort to enhance our understanding of organized criminal behavior. Further, a sound theoretical framework is essential to providing effective intervention to prevent and control organized crime.

What Is Cybercrime?

In September 2011, Tony Perez, a 21-year-old Indiana man, was sentenced in U.S. District Court in Virginia after admitting to operating an online business that sold counterfeit credit cards encoded with stolen account information. He received a 14-year federal prison sentence and was ordered to pay $2.8 million in forfeiture and a $250,000 fine. Perez used various online personas in criminal "carding forums," Internet discussion groups established to assist in buying and selling stolen financial account information, as well as other avenues and services to promote credit card fraud. The U.S. Secret Service, upon executing a search warrant at Perez's apartment, found thousands of fraudulent transactions totaling more than $3 million.[149]

Cybercrime is a relatively new area of criminal activity. As there have been tremendous advances in technology in recent years, there have also been tremendous advances for criminal opportunities using this technology. In this chapter, we provide a brief definition of *cybercrime*, followed by a general overview of various types of cybercrime, such as hacking, identity theft, and cyberstalking. Next, we present some of the criminal justice responses to cybercrime. We conclude this section by reviewing some theoretical explanations of cybercrime.

Definition of Cybercrime

Scholars have recognized some of the issues surrounding terms and definitions for crimes committed by electronic means, terms such as *computer crime*, *computer-related crime*, and *cybercrime*. There is a question of whether this process of definitional clarification is "hyper-defining":

> The result of such hyper-definition is to negate some emerging legislation. This is not to suggest that legislators should cease efforts to specifically criminalize computer-specific criminal activity. Indeed, further legislation should be pursued to enhance prosecutorial toolboxes, not to replace or supplant traditional mechanisms.[150]

Another term was introduced for such crimes—*high-technology crime*. This refers to any criminal act involving the use of high-technology devices. Examples of high-technology devices include computers, telephones, check-reading machines, and credit card machines. High-technology crimes can comprise traditional crimes committed prior to technological developments and more recent crimes that use high-technology devices.[151] Thus, this term incorporates crimes that may involve *limited use* of computers and networks as well as those that *completely rely* on the use of computers and networks.[152]

Soumyo Moitra acknowledged that there were initially heated debates as to the various definitions for these crimes; however, he maintained that the term *cybercrime* has gained in both usage and popularity. Interestingly, *cybercrime* was derived from the term *cyberspace*, originated by the author William Gibson.[153] Cybercrime was defined as follows: "any unauthorized, or deviant, or illegal activity over the Internet that involves a computer (or computers) as the tool to commit the activity and a computer (or computers) as the target of that activity." **Cybercrime** consists of at least three features: The act was committed using (1) a computer, (2) a "victim" computer, and (3) an intermediary network.[154] Interestingly, the term "cybercrime" may have some limitations. Given the emergence of multiple technologies (e.g., mobile devices, social media), it has been suggested to use the term "digital technology crime" or "electronic crime."[155]

Types of Cybercrime

HACKING. The term *hacker* most likely emerged from the electrical engineering labs at the Massachusetts Institute of Technology (MIT). As at other universities, some MIT students engaged in attention-seeking pranks; these students were called "hacks." From this, the term soon took on the meaning of creative invention, especially as computing was developing as a discipline.[156] However, today individuals who claim to be **hackers** contend that true hackers are concerned with enhancing computer security. Later, the term *cracker* was suggested to replace *hacker* in the media. Although some use this term, it usually refers to an individual who violates copyright protection. In the computer science community, the distinction between these two terms is recognized; outside this community, the two terms often refer to the same activity.[157] One suggested definition of hackers is that used by those within the hacker community. A hacker is one who obtains unauthorized access to a computer system, file, or network.[158]

Robert Moore described six general types of hackers: black hat hackers, white hat hackers, gray hat hackers, script kiddies, hactivists, and cyber terrorists:[159]

• *Black hat hackers.* These individuals violate computer security essentially out of malice or for personal gain. They write programs to damage computer systems and networks. Because of these hackers, organizations have had to spend millions of dollars to develop protected computer networks and operating systems.

• *White hat hackers.* These hackers are involved in writing programs to protect systems and networks from being illegally and maliciously accessed. They attempt to hack into targeted computers. If successful, they subsequently notify the computer system's owner of its vulnerabilities.

• *Gray hat hackers.* A blend of black hat and white hat hackers, these individuals may be considered "opportunistic." They may successfully target and access a computer system and then notify the system's owner. Rather than informing the administrator of how the system was exposed, these hackers offer to correct the defect for a fee.

• *Script kiddies.* These hackers are deemed the lowest on the hacker ladder due to their limited technical ability. Essentially, they surf the Internet for hacker utility programs and then launch the programs at a target computer system. Due to their limited technical knowledge, they are considered risky because they are not aware of how programs will affect the attacked computer system. Some well-known hacking

cybercrime: cybercrime consists of at least three features: The act was committed using (1) a computer, (2) a "victim" computer, and (3) an intermediary network.

hackers: individuals who violate computer security.

attacks, such as the shutting down of the eBay and Amazon websites, were done by script kiddies.

• *Hactivists.* In reference to their methods, these individuals are similar to those hackers described above. They differ, however, in their motives. Hactivists attempt to hack computer systems or networks that will provide them an avenue to spread their political message. They may access the server that stores a webpage and then modify the page to reveal their message.

• *Cyber terrorists.* These individuals access computer systems linked to critical infrastructures, such as water purification, electricity, and nuclear power plants. Such "attacks" can cause damage or even death due to loss of service. These hackers are relatively new but are gaining attention and inspire a great deal of public fear.[160]

In 2015, a group of hackers stole data from the Ashley Madison website – a website that provides services to individuals wanting to engage in extramarital affairs.

Identity Theft

Identity theft is defined as "the procuring of . . . false identity regardless of its use . . . [often] to commit identity fraud, but in some cases, it is used by criminals and terrorists to establish false identities and escape detection."[161] There are generally three different types of identity theft. The first type is when the identity thief assumes the life of the victim. One possible motivation for this form of identity theft is that of someone engaging in organized criminal activities. The trail left behind would lead to someone else, with no affiliation to the criminal organization, rather than to the thief. This type of identity theft is rare, possibly because taking over an individual's life is extremely difficult.

The second form of identity theft is beginning to evolve but has received little attention, perhaps due to the lack of financial or physical harm to its victims. This type of identity theft is "virtual" identity theft. Today, most Internet users create a screen name. Recently, individuals have stolen others' screen names for the purpose of, for example, harassing people or spamming other users.

The third type of identity theft is the most common. It occurs when a victim's credit identity is stolen, such as his or her Social Security number or other identifying information. Subsequently, the offender will use this stolen information to apply for credit in the victim's name.[162] There are various approaches to obtaining an individual's identity, including the following:

1. *Carding.* This refers to stealing a victim's credit card information and subsequently using the information to purchase items, especially electronics. A key feature of carding is delivery of purchased items. One method has been to have the items delivered to a shipping facility (e.g., Mail Boxes Etc. or The UPS Store) where the offender can open a fake account to store these items.

2. *Dumpster diving.* This method involves offenders obtaining materials, such as credit card carbons or preapproval credit card forms, that include identity information. One new development in this area is dumpster diving in university unions, particularly

identity theft: occurs when an individual obtains a false identity to commit identity fraud; can be used by criminals and terrorists to establish false identities and escape detection.

those that provide postal service for students. Students often receive preapproval notices and usually throw them in the trash immediately.

3. *Credit card skimming.* A majority of companies no longer use slider machines that create credit card carbons. Rather, they use electronic card readers. When a credit card is slipped into this reader, the information is scanned from the magnetic strip on the back of the credit card. Subsequently, this information is sent to a credit card verification service through a call made by the machine. If the card is accepted, then the machine will save the authorization numbers in a separate digital file. Thus, offenders can implement various methods to steal this information during the scanning procedure.

4. *Shoulder surfing.* In this method, when a victim removes his or her credit card to pay for merchandise, the offender peers over the victim's shoulder and memorizes the card number. Interestingly, offenders need not memorize all 16 numbers. Experienced thieves may have a listing that includes information on the first eight numbers associated with the card. For instance, the gold Visa cards begin with a different eight-number sequence than do regular Visa cards. Thus, the offender needs to memorize only half the numbers and the expiration date.[163]

Child Pornography

Child pornography portrays children engaged in sexual acts or in a sexual way. These depictions are the same as those in adult pornography except that the media (e.g., photographs, video) include images of children, children and adults, or children and animals or objects.[164] As with adult pornography, child pornography exists to meet the demand for such material. From 2000 to 2009, arrests for child pornography steadily increased. In 2009, law enforcement agencies made approximately 4,901 arrests for child pornography. This is almost three times as many as in 2000 and a 33% increase for 2006 arrests.[165] Further, there are national and international organizations that support pedophiles and child sexual exploitation. One such organization is the North American Men/Boy Love Association (NAMBLA). A review of the literature identified four common categories of users of Internet child pornography:

1. Individuals who encourage prevailing or developing sexual interests in children

2. Individuals who communicate with other sexual offenders who use child pornography as a broader pattern of offending

3. Individuals who are impulsive and curious

4. Individuals who are involved in child pornography for nonsexual reasons, such as financial gain[166]

During the 1980s, federal law enforcement agencies aggressively focused on pursuing those involved in the manufacturing and distribution of child pornography. Such efforts resulted in the belief that the issue of child pornography was a "controllable problem." That all changed, however, with the advent of the Internet.[167] Deputy Assistant Attorney General Kevin V. Di Gregory testified before Congress that

the trafficking in child pornography by computer users has, in some ways, challenged the progress of nearly eighty years of aggressive child pornography investigation and prosecution. Whereas by the early 1990s, the government had largely eradicated the cottage trade within the United States for this material and distribution was typically limited to trading or sharing between individual pedophiles who actually knew each other, today computer technology has reinvigorated both the commercial and non-commercial distribution of obscene child pornography.[168]

With the ever-growing World Wide Web, there will be a continuous expansion of child pornography. Further, law enforcement efforts are difficult and characterized by legal definitional issues, overlapping jurisdictions, and entrapment problems.[169]

Internet Fraud

Businesses have the option of placing their operations, either entirely or as an added component, on the Internet. While this has allowed legitimate businesses to expand their customer base, it has also given illegitimate businesses or operations an opportunity to engage in Internet fraud. Some of the most common types of online frauds are listed below.

Fraudulent sales online. Online purchases create risks for both the merchant and the customer. The merchant does not want to release the goods until payment has been received and the customer does not want to pay before delivery. While offline purchases require payment upon delivery, more trust is required when making online purchases.[170] Yahoo Auctions and eBay are two of the most popular Internet auction sites. Some interesting items have been put up for auction, illustrating that practically anything can be sold:

- *A man's family.* The man promised that the highest bidder would receive a happy family ready for holidays and family events.

- *An island.* The island, apparently located off the coast of the United States, was advertised as ideal for a remote casino resort.

- *Escort services.* The winner was promised an "unforgettable afternoon."[171]

A major problem with online auction fraud is when an individual purchases merchandise but never receives it. Further, since these transactions can occur between a seller and purchaser living in different states or even different countries, there are issues pertaining to investigating and prosecuting these offenses. However, many states have statutes that criminalize fraudulent selling practices, and these statutes would apply to auction fraud cases just as they would to more traditional transactions between a buyer and seller.[172]

Advance fee frauds. With this type fraud, the victim is lured to pay monies with the expectation of receiving some service or benefit, but this never occurs. One of the most well-known is the Nigerian email scam (see Figure 14.3). Other types of advance fee frauds include dating scammers, someone impersonating an FBI or other government official requesting the payment of a fine, and computer support scams calling a victim to inform them that they have detected malware.[173]

Mail-order bride services/solicitation of prostitutes. Mail-order bride services and solicitation of prostitutes are not new offenses, but engaging in these crimes through the Internet is a relatively new phenomenon. For instance, there are more than 30,000 websites for mail-order brides. There are various types of mail-order bride fraud. One scam is when a woman contacts numerous men and states that she likes their letters. A man may then respond by asking her to visit, usually in the United States. He sends the woman money for the visit, but the woman stops communicating with him after receiving the money. In another type of scam, the woman is actually a man posing as a potential wife.[174]

Internet fraud: when individuals use the Internet to engage in fraud, often identity theft.

FIGURE **14.3**

Example of a Nigerian Email Scam

From Mrs Grace Kamara
Abidjan- Cote D'Ivoire
Phone 00(225) 0748 4681

My Dear ,

With due respect and humility I write you this proposal which I believe would be of great interest to you

I am Mrs Grace Kamara, a Sierra Leone National and the wife of Late Dr LAMINE Kamara of the blessed memory. Prior to my husband assassination by the rebel forces loyal to FODAY SANKOH , he was the Director General National Gold Diamond Mining Corporation of Sierra Leone. Two days before my husband was assassinated, he instructed me and my two sons TONY and FRANK to move out of Sierra Leone immediately. Before the powerful Economic Community of West African States (ECOMOG) forces intervened which eventually resulted into a brutal civil war. I and my children managed to escape to Abidjan, the Republic of Cote d'Ivoire through the help of my husband's friend who is a trawler. We came into Abidjan with some valuables including a cash sum of US 18 Million (EIGTHEEN MILLION UNITED STATES DOLLARS ONLY) in two trunk boxes which I deposited with a private security company here in Abidjan - Cote d'Ivoire in my son's name (TONY Kamara). For your information, we did not disclose the real content of the boxes to the security company and we do not wish them to know this under any circumstances. Rather, we deposited the boxes as containing family valuables.

Meanwhile, I want to leave Cote d'Ivoire entirely with this money for investment in your country because of the stable political situation and mostly for the future of my children. Right now I am seeking for a foreign partner who will assist me retrieve and serve as the guardian of this fund with whom I can plan the best way to move out this fund for investment purposes which is my motive for contacting you

 Moreover, you are requested to assist in the following areas:

1.That you will be required to negotiate on how best to transfer this fund without attracting much taxation

2.That you will assist in providing me and my family a permanent residence / Resident permit in your country after this money has been transferred to your country.

3.That you will be responsible in advising us to invest this fund a viable venture in your country.

4.That you will pay a short working visit (2 days) to meet with me and my family face to face here in Abidjan- Cote d'Ivoire to enable us establish a personal contact with you to ensure some amount of confidence between us. We have it in mind to reward you handsomely for your assistance.

We are prepared to give you 10 % of the total sum, and 25% share in the total investment to be made. Do not hesitate to call my son TONY on his line 00

Link: http://resources2.news.com.au/images/2012/06/21/1226404/301658-email-scam.jpg

Online prostitution refers to soliciting sexual acts through the Internet. The Internet can be used for prostitution in two ways. One involves using the Internet to facilitate communication between those seeking the services of prostitutes. The second uses the Internet for electronic communications and websites to facilitate meetings. It is this second form that involves fraudulent activities. One type of fraud occurs when a "date" is scheduled, with a required deposit prior to the arranged meeting. The website obtains the "customer's" credit card information, but the services are never provided.[175]

Cyberstalking

The term *stalking* has been in use since the early 1990s to describe a victim being harassed or physically threatened. Prior to this time, a victim of such harassment was informed that nothing could be done to the perpetrator until he or she made a physical attempt that threatened the victim's safety or well-being.[176] After five women were murdered by stalkers, California became the first state in the United States to criminalize this behavior.[177] These statutes, however, did not foresee how stalking behavior would emerge within cyberspace.

Florida statute explicitly defines cyberstalking as a

cyberstalking: when an individual engages in stalking behavior through such means as electronic mail or electronic communication

means to engage in a course of conduct to communicate, or to cause to be communicated, words, images, or language by or through the use of electronic mail or electronic communication, directed at a specific person, causing substantial emotional distress to that person and serving no legitimate purpose.[178]

Cyberstalking includes some of the following actions:

- Monitoring e-mail communication directly or by using some form of spyware or keystroke-logging hardware

- Sending e-mails that threaten, insult, or harass

- Disrupting e-mail communications by inundating a victim's inbox with unwanted mail

- Disrupting e-mail communications by sending a virus

- Using the victim's e-mail identity to send false messages to others or to purchase goods and services (i.e., committing virtual identity theft)

- Using the Internet to seek and collect a victim's personal information and whereabouts[179]

Various motivations have been offered as to why someone would stalk another individual. For instance, some may select their victims opportunistically and subsequently get a sense of satisfaction from intimidating them; this is a type of power-assertive motivation.[180] For instance, an abusive ex-husband was involved in a two-year crusade against his ex-wife through e-mail communications. Although the ex-wife obtained a restraining order against her ex-husband, he continued to send her more than 1,500 pages of threatening e-mails from numerous e-mail accounts. One such e-mail outlined his plans to shoot her children with a rifle and then beat, rape, and mutilate her with sulfuric acid before slashing her spinal cord so she could never walk again.[181] Other individuals may be obsessed with a need to retaliate against their victims for perceived wrongs; this is a type of anger-retaliatory motivation. Gary Dellapenta was a cyberstalker who went to extreme efforts to terrify Randi Barber. He stated that he had an "inner rage" toward her and that he was unable to control this rage. He would send messages that were degrading and intended to bring harm to Barber; he arranged to have other people harm her but was unwilling to do so himself.[182]

Criminal Justice Responses to Cybercrime

INVESTIGATION OF CYBERCRIME. Law enforcement has lagged behind the remarkable technological advances and the easy availability of this technology to millions of individuals. A number of large law enforcement agencies have devoted resources to electronic crime investigation; medium-sized agencies may be attempting to develop an electronic crime investigation unit or cross-train detectives from traditional fields. Small agencies, however, do experience computer crime in their area but are often not able to devote the resources to a specialized unit.[183] Further, law enforcement needs to determine whether they will be *reactive* or *proactive* when investigating the various types of cybercrimes:

> The question facing law enforcement has been whether to handle these crimes in a reactive or proactive manner. Cyberstalking and identity theft are almost always viewed in a reactive manner because a victim's complaint is necessary in order to begin an investigation. However, digital child pornography has become such a widespread problem that many agencies have begun employing proactive investigations in attempts to control the problems that develop from this activity.[184]

For instance, the Federal Bureau of Investigation, through Operation Innocent Images, has been proactively investigating pedophiles for years, and now local and state law enforcement agencies are also implementing these types of investigations. One method has

Subway restaurant spokesman Jared Fogle leaves his home. In 2015 he pled guilty to possessing child pornography and paying for sex with minors.

been for the officer to enter various chat rooms, pretending to be a child, usually between the ages of 6 and 14. The officer will spend a great deal of time chatting and interacting with others in an attempt to lure potential *groomers* (i.e., pedophiles). Another method is when the officer arranges a meeting between the groomer and the undercover officer, whom the groomer believes to be a child.[185]

Another important facet to investigating cybercrime involves search warrants. It is essential that operating systems, storage devices, and hard specifications be clearly articulated in the development of a comprehensive search warrant.[186] For instance, investigators may seize additional evidence under the "plain view" exception to search warrant requirements. In reference to computers, however, the concept of "plain view" may not be as clear. The case of *United States v. Carey* (1998) illustrated this point. Patrick Carey was under investigation for possible sale and possession of cocaine. During the arrest, officers observed in plain view a "bong." Subsequently, the officer asked Carey to consent to a search of his apartment. Carey consented to the search and signed a formal written consent. The officers recovered cocaine, marijuana, and hallucinogenic mushrooms. They also confiscated two computers, thinking they could be subject to forfeiture of evidence of drug dealing. The investigators then obtained a warrant to search the files on the computers for evidence related to drugs. Their investigation revealed that Carey had files containing child pornography; he was charged with one count of child pornography. On appeal, Carey challenged the admissibility of the child pornography because it was discovered as a result of a warrantless search. The court ruled that the investigators exceeded the scope of the warrant and reversed Carey's conviction. They noted that "the plain view doctrine may not be used to extend a general exploratory search from one object to another until something incriminating at last emerges."[187]

Thomas Holt and his colleagues noted that policies and practices targeting cybercrime should include such strategies as enhanced public awareness, more systematic data reporting, greater uniform training and certification courses, the establishment of onsite management assistance for electronic crime units and task forces, and improved cooperation with the high-tech industry.[188]

Relevant Legislation

Compared with state legislatures, the U.S. Congress has acted more swiftly to enact legislation establishing computer-specific statutes—specifically, legislation that addresses such crimes as electronic fraud and hacking.[189] Below, we present a brief overview of some legislation focusing on cybercrimes.

COMPUTER FRAUD AND ABUSE ACT. The Computer Fraud and Abuse Act (CFAA) was initially enacted in 1984; it was amended in 1986 and has been amended further since that time. It was originally designed to protect national security, financial, and commercial information; medical treatment; and interstate communication systems from malicious acts, including unauthorized access. In addition, the CFAA allows those who have been

Computer Fraud and Abuse Act: originally designed to protect national security, financial, and commercial information; medical treatment; and interstate communication systems from malicious acts, including unauthorized access; allows victims of such crimes to bring civil suits against violators.

victims of such crimes to bring a civil suit against violators. The CFAA does not exclude application of other laws, such as additional computer crime statutes that broaden the scope of CFAA.[190]

DIGITAL MILLENNIUM COPYRIGHT ACT. During the past several years, the music and video industries have modified their businesses in response to major technological advances. These industries have used the Internet as a vehicle for individuals to purchase (i.e., download) movies and music. A major problem with such availability, however, is Internet piracy.[191] Internet piracy is the "unauthorized copying of copyright material for commercial purposes and the unauthorized commercial dealing in copied materials."[192] The various entities claimed that they were losing millions of dollars due to copyright violations.[193] Under pressure from the motion picture industry, record labels, software publishers, and other entities whose profits are linked to copyrighted material, Congress passed the Digital Millennium Copyright Act in 1998. This act incorporates part of the Copyright Act; it criminalizes making, distributing, or using tools, such as software, to evade technological protection measures implemented by copyright owners to prevent access to copyrighted material.[194]

CHILD ONLINE PROTECTION ACT. In 1998, Congress passed the Child Online Protection Act, which prohibits individuals from knowingly engaging in communication for commercial purposes that includes material "harmful to minors" and available to minors.[195] Such prohibited material includes pictures, writings, recordings, and videos that are obscene—or what the average person would consider, in the context of minors, to appeal to prurient interests. A violation is a misdemeanor, punishable by up to six months' imprisonment and a $50,000 fine for each violation.[196] It is essential to note that this is just one example of legislation that has been enacted to address Internet child pornography. For instance, the Child Pornography Protection Act attempted to prohibit the use of electronically altered photographs depicting child pornography, such as artificial images of children (i.e., virtual images). This act has been challenged on the grounds of vague language and possible violation of the First Amendment right to free speech.[197]

ELECTRONIC COMMUNICATIONS PRIVACY ACT. In 1986, Congress passed the Electronic Communications Privacy Act, which regulates the interception of electronic communications by individuals as well as by the government. In reference to investigators, this act regulates the amount of information law enforcement can obtain based on the levels of service. Law enforcement is required to obtain a subpoena for basic subscriber information (e.g., name, address, local and long-distance telephone billing records, length of service, type of service). A court order is needed to acquire transactional information (e.g., records or logs pertaining to the subscriber, such as destinations of outgoing mail). Law enforcement needs to obtain a search warrant for obtaining the actual content of e-mail messages.[198]

EXECUTIVE ORDER 13694: BLOCKING THE PROPERTY OF CERTAIN PERSONS ENGAGING IN SIGNIFICANT MALICIOUS CYBER-ENABLED ACTIVITIES. In April 2015, President Obama issued Executive Order 13694, which provides the government the ability to impose sanctions against individuals and groups that threaten the United States' infrastructure through malicious activities in cyberspace.[199] As outlined by the executive order, these malicious activities would have the purpose or effect of:

- harming or significantly compromising the provision of services by entities in a critical infrastructure sector;

- significantly disrupting the availability of a computer or network of computers (for example, through a distributed denial-of-service attack); or

Digital Millennium Copyright Act: criminalizes making, distributing, or using tools, such as software, to evade technological protection measures implemented by copyright owners to prevent access to copyrighted material.

Child Online Protection Act: prohibits individuals from knowingly engaging in communication for commercial purposes that includes material "harmful to minors" and available to minors.

Electronic Communications Privacy Act: regulates the interception of electronic communications by individuals as well as the government.

- causing a significant misappropriation of funds or economic resources, trade secrets, personal identifiers, or financial information for commercial or competitive advantage or private financial gain (for example, by stealing large quantities of credit card information, trade secrets, or sensitive information).[200]

Theoretical Explanations of Cybercrime

Robert Taylor and his colleagues reviewed several theories to explain computer crime.[201] In this section, we highlight a few of these theoretical perspectives to illustrate how theories that have been applied to "traditional" types of criminal behavior can also explain more technologically advanced activities. Routine activities theory contends that when a motivated offender, a suitable target, and the absence of a capable guardian converge, a crime will occur. With the rapid increase in use of computers as well as the Internet, the number of suitable targets has also increased. The insufficient software protection for these types of crimes reveals the absence of a capable guardian. Thus, "when motivated offenders are present, they make rational choices by selecting suitable targets that lack capable guardianship."[202] This also lessens the chances of an offender being apprehended.

Social process theories, such as learning theory and differential reinforcement theory, can help explain crimes committed by individuals who develop and spread computer viruses. A person needs to have a certain level of technical competency to write a virus. This often involves a process that includes learning how to write the code necessary to develop a virus. In most instances, this learning does not take place face to face; rather, many learn these skills through chat rooms, bulletin boards, or distance learning. There are also positive reinforcements involved with this type of activity, including the excitement of propagating the virus and infecting systems, "admiration" from one's peer group, and possible financial gains. Negative reinforcements can include experiencing hostility from other virus writers and being wanted by law enforcement.[203] Social structure theories, specifically strain theory, can be applied when attempting to understand Internet fraud schemes and corporate espionage. From this theoretical perspective, criminal behavior may be linked to blocked legitimate opportunities. Thus, individuals who engage in this type of criminal behavior could be considered "innovators"; they use illegitimate means to attain the conventional goal of success, usually measured by financial gain. Interestingly, Merton initially applied this theoretical perspective to explain blocked legitimate opportunities of those predominantly from the lower class. Contemporary strain theorists, however, have attempted to apply this perspective to those from the middle and upper-middle classes. Specifically, individuals from higher socioeconomic classes may also enjoy a certain amount of success by *perceiving* that legitimate means to accumulating more wealth are blocked.[204]

LEARNING CHECK 14.4

1. _____ hackers are individuals who violate computer security essentially out of malice or for personal gain.

2. The _____ method of Internet fraud occurs when a victim removes his or her credit card to pay for merchandise and the offender peers over the victim's shoulder and memorizes the card numbers.

3. Activities associated with _____ include monitoring e-mail communication; sending e-mails that threaten, insult, or harass; and using the victim's e-mail identity to send false messages to others or to purchase goods and services.

4. The _____ Act was established to address various problems associated with the Internet, including piracy.

Answers located at www.edge.sagepub.com/schram2e

CONCLUSION

This chapter presented three general categories of crime that some may not consider as fitting in with traditional street crimes, such as murder, larceny, and assault. This does not mean that these types of crime are not associated with more traditional types of offenses. For instance, criminal organizations do engage in murder, and cybercrimes can involve theft. Rather, some would argue that there are unique aspects to these types of offenses that should be recognized. In the first section of this chapter, we attempted to illustrate how scholars have distinguished white-collar crime from traditional forms of offending. This section also explored the various ways corporate crimes have harmed society as well as responses to these types of offenses.

The next section focused on organized crime. Again, we presented the various complex factors involved in defining organized crime. We then briefly discussed the historical events that have influenced organized criminal behavior, including criminal justice responses to organized crime. We concluded this chapter with a discussion on cybercrime. This is a relatively new type of criminal activity; thus, there are growing challenges associated with investigating cybercrime as well as legislation that has been enacted to address it.

At the beginning of this chapter, we presented the case of William T. Walters. We asked you various questions about your perceptions and descriptions of crime and criminals as well as whether you thought Walters would be treated differently from other criminal offenders. As noted earlier, in this chapter we attempted to illustrate that criminal behavior is not restricted to what some deem traditional types of offenses; rather, criminal behavior can involve high-level executives and powerful corporations, groups organized around the purpose of engaging in criminal activity, and criminal behavior in which there is no physical contact between the victim and the offender.

KEY TERMS

Child Online Protection Act, 417

Computer Fraud and Abuse Act, 417

Cooper v. Pate, 403

cybercrime, 410

cyberstalking, 414

Digital Millennium Copyright Act, 417

Edwin Sutherland, 379

Electronic Communications Privacy Act, 417

Environmental Protection Agency, 390

hackers, 410

identity theft, 411

Internet fraud, 413

Kefauver Committee, 404

Mafia, 400

Mafioso, 400

Occupational Safety and Health Act, 391

organized crime, 398

outlaw motorcycle gangs, 401

Racketeer Influenced and Corrupt Organizations (RICO) Act, 407

Tammany Hall, 399

white-collar crime, 379

Wickersham Commission, 404

DISCUSSION QUESTIONS

1. How does white-collar crime differ from traditional street crimes?

2. How does white-collar crime compare with traditional street crimes in terms of property damage and damage to society? In terms of physical damage, such as injuries and death?

3. Can you provide recent examples of crimes against the environment in the United States?

4. What impact did OSHA seem to have on corporate labor violations?

5. What are some of the key features that distinguish organized crime from "just" crime?

6. How did Prohibition influence organized crime groups?

7. What are some of the different types of criminal organizations?

8. What are some of the major contributions from the Kefauver Committee?

9. What is RICO?

10. What is Reuter's "mini-theory" to explain and understand organized crime?

11. What are some of the similarities and differences between traditional forms of crime and cybercrime?

12. What are some of the different types of cybercrime?

13. What are some of the difficulties related to search warrants for cybercrimes?

14. What are some of the key statutes enacted by Congress to address problems associated with advanced technology?

15. How have some of the traditional theories of crime been applied to cybercrime?

WEB RESOURCES

From the CNN Money website, this story reports on President Bush's proposal to enforce tougher standards following the WorldCom scandal involving massive accounting irregularities.

http://money.cnn.com/2002/06/28/news/companies/worldcom/index.htm

On the CNN website, Professor John Coffee writes on the SEC being too passive in terms of overseeing Bernie Madoff's illegal investment operation.

http://www.cnn.com/2008/POLITICS/12/16/coffee.madoff/index.html?iref=allsearch

This is a documentary on the Pagans Outlaw Motorcycle Gang, published on December 19, 2014.

https://www.youtube.com/watch?v=lMZ2kkv3rJU

This *Cyberstalking Documentary* is from the Crime & Investigation Channel.

http://www.youtube.com/watch?v=BZ6LByl0pgw

STUDENT STUDY SITE

$SAGE edge™

WANT A BETTER GRADE ON YOUR NEXT TEST?

Get the tools you need to sharpen your study skills:

SAGE edge offers a robust online environment featuring an impressive array of tools and resources for review, study, and further exploration, keeping both instructors and students on the cutting edge of teaching and learning. Learn more at **edge.sagepub.com/schram2e**.

FOR FURTHER EXPLORATION AND APPLICATION, VISIT THE STUDENT STUDY SITE:

N.Y. Attorney General: Nation's Flood Insurance Program Defrauding Taxpayers

Uneasy Rider: The Origins of Motorcycle Gangs and How They Remain a Force

Cybersecurity: Who's Vulnerable to Attack?

Do women and men differ in their neutralizations of corporate crime?

Eating with the Mafia: Belonging and violence

Toward the adaptation of routine activity and lifestyle exposure theories to account for cyber abuse victimization

A Guide to White-Collar Crime

Giving Fraud a Bad Name

Enron Scandal

U. S. Labor Department says Austin restaurants violating labor laws

A Gangster's Hideaway

Cyberstalking

White Collar Crimes

Check Fraud

Human Trafficking

Jared Fogle

PREMIUM VIDEO:

Check out the Interactive eBook for premium videos, including videos from author Stephen Tibbetts, who discusses real-world examples and strange crimes; and videos from former offenders, who share their stories from a first-person view, and touch on key theories and concepts from the chapter.

CHAPTER 15

Hate Crimes, Mass Murder, Terrorism, and Homeland Security

INTRODUCTION

In recent years, increased attention has been given to certain types of criminal activities that were not often discussed in the newspaper, on television, or, for that matter, in criminology textbooks. Specifically, these activities include hate crimes and terrorism. These types of offenses illustrate the multicultural and multinational aspects of crime. It is essential for students to appreciate how crime, and the concept of crime, expands beyond national boundaries. There has been some debate, however, as to whether hate crime offending and terrorism should be considered as similar behavior. While scholars have recognized that there are legal distinctions, some have maintained that there are also similarities, such as motivations, objectives, and perpetrator characteristics.[3] These types of offenses focus on terrorizing a larger social group.[4] Others argue that hate crimes and terrorism are distinct types of behavior, conceptually and empirically. For instance, terrorism is often considered an upward crime; these offenses are committed by individuals from a lower social standing. Hate crimes are often deemed downward crimes; these offenses are often perpetrated by individuals from a majority or powerful group in society against minority-group victims.[5]

In this chapter, we present a discussion of both hate crimes and terrorism but do so in separate sections. The chapter begins with a discussion on hate crimes; this section presents issues pertaining to hate crimes, such as the definition and legislative responses to these offenses. Multicide, the killing of multiple individuals, is the next topic discussed in this chapter. The following section focuses on terrorism, including the definition and the types and extent of terrorism. The chapter concludes with a section on homeland security that covers such issues as agencies involved in homeland security and potential conflicts regarding civil liberties.

WHAT IS A HATE CRIME?

In February 2016, the *New York Times* reported that since the terrorist attacks in Paris on November 13, 2015, as well as the mass shooting in San Bernardino, California, on December 2, 2015, there have been an increasing number of attacks and threats against Muslims in the United States. Below are a few examples of such attacks and threats:

- Two mosques were vandalized in Hawthorne, California. At one mosque, "Jesus" graffiti was spray-painted on the wall. At another mosque, a hand grenade (later determined as a plastic replica) was left in the driveway.

- A Sikh temple in Buena Park, California, was vandalized with spray-painted obscenities referring to Islam and the Islamic State (known as ISIS and ISIL). The graffiti included gang codes, a racial slur, and profanity in reference to ISIS and Islam.

- In Coachella, California, Carl James Dial was charged with a hate crime, along with arson and burglary. He attempted to burn the Islamic Society of Coachella Valley prior to scheduled prayer services. There were no injuries as a result of the fire.

LEARNING OBJECTIVES

As you read this chapter, consider the following topics:

- Explain some of the bias motivations associated with hate crimes.

- Summarize some key anti-hate-crime legislation.

- Discuss theoretical explanations of hate crimes.

- Describe the various forms and rates of multicide in the United States.

- Distinguish terrorist activities from more conventional forms of criminal activities.

- Explain some of the factors that have contributed to the historical and current context of terrorism.

- Discuss theoretical explanations of terrorism.

- Describe homeland security, such as its origins and organizational structure.

- List some of the agencies that make up the Department of Homeland Security.

- Explain some of the controversial issues related to civil liberties and the efforts to counter terrorism.

CASE STUDY

CHARLESTON, SOUTH CAROLINA, SHOOTING

On the evening of June 17, 2015, Dylann Roof, a 21-year-old white male, entered the Emanuel African Methodist Episcopal Church in Charleston, South Carolina. The Emanuel African Methodist Episcopal Church is one of the oldest black churches in the United States; the church was founded in 1816. After participating in the prayer services with the other members for over an hour, Roof started venting against African-Americans and then opened fire on the members. He killed nine people, including the senior pastor; the victims ranged in age from 26 to 87 years of age.[1]

After a United States Department of Justice investigation, Roof was indicted on 33 federal hate crime charges. Further investigation revealed Roof's website, which contained numerous photographs of him posing with flags and emblems affiliated with white supremacy. Roof also included a manifesto that outlined his beliefs about race, of which a small portion is provided below:

"To take a saying from a film, 'I see all this stuff going on, and I don't see anyone doing anything about it. And it pisses me off.' To take a saying from my favorite film, 'Even if my life is worth less than a speck of dirt, I want to use it for the good of society.'

"I have no choice. I am not in the position to, alone, go into the ghetto and fight. I chose Charleston because it is most historic city in my state, and at one time had the highest ratio of blacks to Whites in the country. We have no skinheads, no real KKK, no one doing anything but talking on the internet. Well someone has to have the bravery to take it to the real world, and I guess that has to be me."

"Unfortunately at the time of writing I am in a great hurry and some of my best thoughts, actually many of them have been to be left out and lost forever. But I believe enough great White minds are out there already."

"Please forgive any typos, I didnt have time to check it."[2]

On December 15, 2016 a jury convicted Dylann Roof on all 33 federal charges. Subsequently, the jury will decide whether to sentence him to the death penalty.

> AFTER PARTICIPATING IN THE PRAYER SERVICES WITH THE OTHER MEMBERS FOR OVER AN HOUR, ROOF STARTED VENTING AGAINST AFRICAN-AMERICANS AND THEN OPENED FIRE ON THE MEMBERS.

THINK ABOUT IT:

1. Why was this considered a hate crime?

2. What makes this crime different than other types of crimes involving mass shootings?

3. Should Dylann Roof receive the death penalty?

We will address these questions at the end of this chapter.

- A convenience store worker in Grand Rapids, Michigan, was shot by a man attempting to rob the store. The attacker called the clerk a terrorist and then put the gun in the clerk's mouth, saying, "I killed guys like you in Iraq, so I never think about it when I shoot them anymore."

- In Brooklyn, New York, a postal worker was charged with menacing as a hate crime. He pushed and spat on a Muslim woman who was pushing a baby in a stroller. Using obscenities, the man said, "I'm gonna burn your Muslim temple down."[6]

Anti-Muslim hate crime of vandalism

How does a hate crime differ from a traditional crime? Are there various types of hate crimes? What is the extent of hate crimes in the United States? How has the criminal justice system responded to these crimes? Why do some people engage in these types of offenses? In this section, we attempt to answer these questions.

Definition of Hate Crimes

An incident designated as a hate crime is a traditional offense, such as murder or vandalism, with an additional factor of bias. Congress defined hate crime as follows: "A criminal offense against a person or property motivated in whole or in part by an offender's bias against a race, religion, disability, ethnic origin or sexual orientation."[7] The Federal Bureau of Investigation (FBI) has provided guidelines as to how one can identify a crime as being motivated by bias. The FBI stresses that when an individual commits an offense and has a bias against the victim's race, religion, disability, sexual orientation, and/or ethnicity/national origin there are not sufficient grounds to designate the offense a hate crime. Rather, this offense must be *motivated* by bias.[8]

The FBI recognizes the subjective nature of such an assessment; however, it provides various factors to consider when determining if such an offense is a crime motivated by bias:

- The offender and the victim were of a different race, religion, disability, sexual orientation, ethnicity, gender, and/or gender identity. For example, the victim was African-American and the offender was white.

- Bias-related oral comments, written statements, or gestures were made by the offender indicating his or her bias. For example, the offender shouted a racial epithet at the victim.

- Bias-related drawings, markings, symbols, or graffiti were left at the crime scene. For example, a swastika was painted on the door of a synagogue, mosque, or LGBT center.

- Certain objects, items, or things which indicate bias were used. For example, the offenders wore white sheets with hoods covering their faces or a burning cross was left in front of the victim's residence.

- The victim is a member of a specific group that is overwhelmingly outnumbered by other residents in the neighborhood where the victim lives and the incident took place.

- The victim was visiting a neighborhood where previous hate crimes had been committed because of race, religion, disability, sexual orientation, ethnicity, gender, or gender identity and where tensions remained high against the victim's group.

hate crimes: traditional offenses, such as murder and vandalism, with an additional factor of bias.

- Several incidents occurred in the same locality, at or about the same time, and the victims were all of the same race, religion, disability, sexual orientation, ethnicity, gender, or gender identity.

- A substantial portion of the community where the crime occurred perceived that the incident was motivated by bias.

- The victim was engaged in activities related to his or her race, religion, disability, sexual orientation, ethnicity, gender, or gender identity. For example, the victim was a member of the National Association for the Advancement of Colored People (NAACP) or participated in an LGBT pride celebration.

- The incident coincided with a holiday or a date of significance relating to a particular race, religion, disability, sexual orientation, ethnicity, gender, or gender identity, e.g., Martin Luther King Day, Rosh Hashanah, or the Transgender Day of Remembrance.

- The offender was previously involved in a similar hate crime or is a hate group member.

- There were indications that a hate group was involved. For example, a hate group claimed responsibility for the crime or was active in the neighborhood.

- A historically established animosity existed between the victim's and the offender's groups.

- The victim, although not a member of the targeted racial, religious, disability, sexual orientation, ethnicity, gender, or gender identity group, was a member of an advocacy group supporting the victim group.[9]

While a hate crime is not exclusively a federal offense, the federal government can, and does, investigate and prosecute hate crimes as civil rights violations.

The types of hate crimes are identified by bias motivations. Common biases include those against race and religion. There are, however, also biases against rich people, poor people, men with long hair, smokers, drinkers, and people with diseases such as AIDS. The biases reported to the FBI's Uniform Crime Reports (UCR) program are restricted to those mandated by the sanctioning act and subsequent amendments.[10] The bias categories and bias motivations are listed in Table 15.1.

Hate Groups

According to the Southern Poverty Law Center, Klan chapters grew from 72 in 2014 to 190 in 2015. They maintained that this increase may have been due to the 364 pro-Confederate battle flag rallies that were held after South Carolina removed the flag from its Capital grounds following the Charleston Church shooting. Overall, the number of hate groups increased by 14% in 2015 (see Figure 15.1).[11]

However, this 2015 number of hate groups most likely underestimates the extent of the American radical right. This is due, in part, to the increasing use and accessibility of the internet:

"White supremacists are increasingly opting to operate mainly online, where the danger of public exposure and embarrassment is far lower, where younger people tend to gather, and where it requires virtually no effort or cost to join in the conversation."[12]

One study revealed that an increase in access to the internet leads to an increase in racial hate crimes. Interestingly, there was no relation to an increase in internet access to an

hate crimes: traditional offenses, such as murder and vandalism, with an additional factor of bias.

TABLE **15.1** Bias Motivation by Category	

BIAS CATEGORY	BIAS MOTIVATION
Race/Ethnicity/Ancestry	Anti-American Indian or Alaska Native
	Anti-Arab
	Anti-Asian
	Anti–Black or African-American
	Anti-Hispanic or Latino
	Anti–Multiple Races, Group*
	Anti–Native Hawaiian or Other Pacific Islander
	Anti–Other Race/Ethnicity/Ancestry
	Anti-White
Religion	Anti-Buddhist
	Anti-Catholic
	Anti–Eastern Orthodox
	Anti-Hindu
	Anti-Islamic (Muslim)
	Anti–Jehovah's Witness
	Anti-Jewish
	Anti-Mormon
	Anti–Multiple Religions, Groups
	Anti–Other Christian
	Anti–Other Religion
	Anti-Protestant
	Anti-Sikh
	Anti–Atheism/Agnosticism
Sexual Orientation	Anti-Bisexual
	Anti-Gay (Male)
	Anti-Heterosexual
	Anti-Lesbian
	Anti–Lesbian, Gay, Bisexual, or Transgender (Mixed Group)**
Disability	Anti–Mental Disability
	Anti–Physical Disability
Gender	Anti-Female
	Anti-Male
Gender Identity	Anti–Gender Nonconforming
	Anti-Transgender

*Anti–Multiple Races, Group, is reported if more than one victim in the incident is of a different race. This also applies to the Anti–Multiple Religions, Group, category

**Lesbian, Gay, Bisexual, or Transgender is referred to as LGBT.

Source: Federal Bureau of Investigations. (2015). *Criminal Justice Information Services (CJIS) Division: Uniform Crime Reporting (UCR) Program. Hate crime data collection guidelines and training manual.* Washington, DC: U.S. Department of Justice, p. 11.

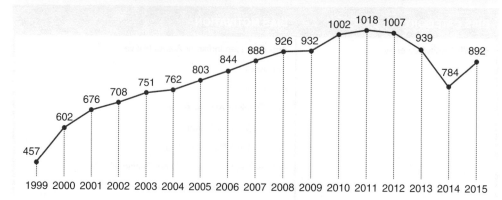

Number of Hate Groups in the U.S., 1999–2015

Source: Southern Poverty Law Center. The Year in hate and Extremism, Mark Potok, February 17, 2016.

increase in local hate group formation. Rather, there is a link with Internet access in terms of racial hate crimes committed by "lone-wolf" perpetrators (e.g., Dylann Roof).[13]

Table 15.2 provides a list of hate group ideologies as identified by the Southern Poverty Law Center. Next to each group is an icon. You can refer to this list and then access the Southern Poverty Law Center "Active Hate Groups" interactive map at https://www.splcenter.org/hate-map.

TABLE 15.2

List of Hate Groups and Their Ideologies

HATE GROUP	ICON
Anti-Immigrant Anti-immigrant hate groups are the most extreme of the hundreds of nativist and vigilante groups that have proliferated since the late 1990s, when anti-immigration xenophobia began to rise to levels not seen in the United States since the 1920s.	⬛
Anti-LGBT Opposition to equal rights for LGBT people has been a central theme of Christian right organizing and fundraising for the past three decades—a period that parallels the fundamentalist movement's rise to political power.	🔻
Anti-Muslim Anti-Muslim hate groups are a relatively new phenomenon in the United States, most of them appearing in the aftermath of the World Trade Center terrorist attacks on September 11, 2001. Earlier anti-Muslim groups tended to be religious in orientation and disputed Islam's status as a respectable religion.	☾
Antigovernment Movement The antigovernment movement has experienced a resurgence, growing quickly since 2008, when President Obama was elected to office. Factors fueling the antigovernment movement in recent years include changing demographics driven by immigration, the struggling economy, and the election of the first African-American president.	🐍
Black Separatist Black separatists typically oppose integration and racial intermarriage, and they want separate institutions—or even a separate nation—for blacks. Most forms of black separatism are strongly anti-white and anti-Semitic, and a number of religious versions assert that blacks are the Biblical "chosen people" of God.	★

HATE GROUP	ICON
Christian Identity Christian Identity is a unique anti-Semitic and racist theology that rose to a position of commanding influence on the racist right in the 1980s. "Christian" in name only, the movement's relationship with evangelicals and fundamentalists has generally been hostile due to the latter's belief that the return of Jews to Israel is essential to the fulfillment of end-time prophecy.	
General Hate These groups espouse a variety of rather unique hateful doctrines and beliefs that are not easily categorized. Many of the groups are vendors that sell a miscellany of hate materials from several different sectors of the white supremacist movement.	
Holocaust Denial Deniers of the Holocaust, the systematic murder of around 6 million Jews in World War II, either deny that such a genocide took place or minimize its extent. These groups (and individuals) often cloak themselves in the sober language of serious scholarship, call themselves "historical revisionists" instead of deniers, and accuse their critics of trying to squelch open-minded inquiries into historical truth.	
Ku Klux Klan The Ku Klux Klan, with its long history of violence, is the most infamous—and oldest—of American hate groups. Although black Americans have typically been the Klan's primary target, it also has attacked Jews, immigrants, gays and lesbians, and, until recently, Catholics.	
Neo-Confederate The term neo-Confederacy is used to describe twentieth- and twenty-first century revivals of pro-Confederate sentiment in the United States. Strongly nativist, neo-Confederacy claims to pursue Christianity and heritage and other supposedly fundamental values that modern Americans are seen to have abandoned.	
Neo-Nazi Neo-Nazi groups share a hatred for Jews and a love for Adolf Hitler and Nazi Germany. While they also hate other minorities, gays and lesbians, and even sometimes Christians, they perceive "the Jew" as their cardinal enemy.	
Phineas Priesthood The Phineas Priesthood is not an actual organization; it has no leaders, meetings, or any other institutional apparatus.	
Racist Music Racist music groups are typically white power music labels that record, publish, and distribute racist music in a variety of genres.	
Racist Skinhead Racist Skinheads form a particularly violent element of the white supremacist movement and have often been referred to as the "shock troops" of the hoped-for revolution. The classic Skinhead look is a shaved head, black Doc Martens boots, jeans with suspenders, and an array of typically racist tattoos.	
Radical Traditional Catholicism "Radical traditionalist" Catholics, who may make up the largest single group of serious anti-Semites in America, subscribe to an ideology that is rejected by the Vatican and some 70 million mainstream American Catholics.	
Sovereign Citizens Movement The strange subculture of the Sovereign Citizens movement, whose adherents hold truly bizarre, complex antigovernment beliefs, has been growing at a fast pace since the late 2000s. Sovereigns believe that they get to decide which laws to obey and which to ignore, and they don't think they should have to pay taxes.	
White Nationalist White nationalist groups espouse white supremacist or white separatist ideologies, often focusing on the alleged inferiority of nonwhites. Groups listed in a variety of other categories—Ku Klux Klan, neo-Confederate, neo-Nazi, racist Skinhead, and Christian Identity—could also be fairly described as white nationalist.	

Source: Southern Poverty Law Center. (n.d.). *Extremist file: Ideologies.*

Anti-Hate-Crime Legislation

Since 1990, Congress has passed various pieces of legislation that have greatly influenced hate crime initiatives and prevention measures. Below, we briefly review some of this legislation.

Hate Crime Statistics Act of 1990

On April 23, 1990, the president signed into law the Hate Crime Statistics Act of 1990. This was in response to increasing concern about these types of offenses.[14] As part of the UCR program, the attorney general was required to develop guidelines and collect data about crimes that manifest evidence of prejudice based on race, religion, sexual orientation, or ethnicity, including, where appropriate, the crimes of murder, nonnegligent manslaughter, forcible rape, aggravated assault, simple assault, intimidation, arson, and destruction, damage, or vandalism of property.[15]

To develop procedures for collecting national hate crime data, many emphasized avoiding any new data reporting responsibilities for those law enforcement agencies participating in the UCR program. Thus, the collection of hate crime data provides additional information on traditional UCR collection procedures.

Violent Crime Control and Law Enforcement Act of 1994

The Violent Crime Control and Law Enforcement Act of 1994 amended the Hate Crime Statistics Act to enhance penalties for offenses that involved a motivation bias.[16] Further, to complement the state hate crime penalty-enhancement statutes in the 1994 Crime Bill, Congress passed the Hate Crime Sentencing Enhancement Act. Specifically, this act directed the U.S. Sentencing Commission to enhance hate crime sentences to no fewer than three offense levels. The amendment took effect on November 1, 1995.[17]

Church Arson Prevention Act of 1996

From January 1, 1995, to January 7, 1997, the Department of Justice opened 328 investigations of suspicious fires, bombings, and attempted bombings. Of these, 138 attacks were on houses of worship, which were predominantly African-American institutions.[18]

In 1996, Congress unanimously enacted the Church Arson Prevention Act. This act prohibits

1. the intentional defacement, damage, or destruction of any religious real property, because of the religious, racial, or ethnic characteristics of that property, or

2. the intentional obstruction by force or threat of force, or attempts to obstruct any person in the enjoyment of that person's free exercise of religious beliefs.[19]

The punishment can vary from 1 year imprisonment and a fine to death. The punishment depends on such factors as whether any individuals were injured or killed as a result of the conduct prohibited by this act.

Campus Hate Crimes Right to Know Act of 1997

The Campus Hate Crimes Right to Know Act of 1997 amends a section of the Higher Education Act of 1965 that provides "for the disclosure of all criminal incidents that manifest evidence of prejudice based on race, gender, religion, sexual orientation, ethnicity, or disability."[20] Findings from the Congressional hearing include the following: The incidence of violence based on bias on college campuses poses a serious national problem; this violence disrupts the tranquility and safety of campuses and results in divisiveness;

Hate Crime Statistics Act of 1990: as part of the Uniform Crime Report program, the attorney general was required to develop guidelines and collect data about crimes that manifest evidence of prejudice based on race, religion, sexual orientation, or ethnicity.

Violent Crime Control and Law Enforcement Act of 1994: amended the Hate Crime Statistics Act to enhance penalties for offenses that involve a motivation bias.

Church Arson Prevention Act of 1996: prohibits intentional destruction of any religious real property or attempts to obstruct any person in the enjoyment of his or her free exercise of religious beliefs.

Campus Hate Crimes Right to Know Act of 1997: amends a section of the Higher Education Act of 1965 that provides for disclosure of all criminal incidents that indicate any evidence of prejudice based on race, gender, religion, sexual orientation, ethnicity, or disability.

Matthew Shepard was assaulted because he was perceived to be homosexual.

James Byrd Jr. was viciously attacked by white supremacists.

the existing reporting requirements are inadequate to deal with the problem of hate crimes, since the majority of hate crimes on college campuses do not result in murder, rape, or aggravated assault; and omitting certain hate crimes from official campus crime reports deprives students and their parents of important information needed to protect students and to make informed decisions in choosing a college or university.

Matthew Shepard and James Byrd Jr. Hate Crimes Prevention Act of 2009

The Matthew Shepard and James Byrd Jr. Hate Crimes Prevention Act of 2009 is named after two victims of hate crimes. Matthew Shepard attended the University of Wyoming. In 1998, he was assaulted because he was perceived to be a homosexual; he died from his injuries. Also in 1998, James Byrd Jr., an African-American man, was tied to a truck by white supremacists and then dragged and decapitated. The act states that it is unlawful to willfully cause bodily injury, or attempt to do so, with a dangerous weapon when the offense is committed because of the actual or perceived race, color, religion, national origin, gender, sexual orientation, gender identity, or disability of any person.[21] This act gives the FBI authority to investigate violent hate crimes, including those aimed at the gay, lesbian, bisexual, and transgender community.[22]

Model State Legislation: Hate Crimes/Violence Against People Experiencing Homelessness

The National Law Center on Homelessness and Poverty and the National Coalition for the Homeless advocated for state legislation that includes homelessness in hate crime statutes. They proposed a model state legislation for hate crimes/violence against people experiencing homelessness. The National Coalition for the Homeless reported that more communities across the country are actively addressing this problem. For instance,

Matthew Shepard and James Byrd Jr. Hate Crimes Prevention Act of 2009: makes it unlawful to willfully cause bodily injury, or attempt to do so, with a dangerous weapon when the offense is committed because of the actual or perceived race, color, religion, national origin, gender, sexual orientation, gender identity, or disability of any person.

WHY DO THEY DO IT?

MATTHEW SHEPARD

On October 9, 1998, a bicyclist was passing through a rural area in Laramie, Wyoming. When he glanced over, he thought he saw a scarecrow tied to a ranch fence. He stopped and realized that the form was not a scarecrow but the burned, battered, and nearly dead body of Matthew Shepard.

Shepard was a 22-year-old student at the University of Wyoming. Prior to his vicious assault that evening, he attended a meeting of the Lesbian, Gay, Bisexual, Transgendered Association. Later, he went to a bar. While he was drinking a beer, two men approached Shepard. The two men stated that they were gay; Shepard also indicated that he was gay. Just after midnight, the two men, Russell Henderson and Aaron McKinney, lured Shepard to Henderson's pickup truck. They beat Shepard inside the truck and then pulled into an isolated part of a rural subdivision. They tied Shepard to a fence and pistol-whipped him with a .357 magnum handgun "while he begged for

his life." They stole his wallet and shoes and left him there, where he was discovered by the bicyclist about 18 hours later.[25]

Five days after he was found tied to the fence, Shepard died from his injuries.[26] Henderson pled guilty and received two consecutive life sentences. McKinney was found guilty of felony murder and received two consecutive life terms without the possibility of parole. Shepard's death resulted in outrage across the country; many called for the need to develop federal hate crime legislation. As one writer noted in a New York Times opinion piece,

> In a nation sickened by the gratuitous thuggery of his murder, he may do much to dispel the stubborn belief in some quarters that homosexuals are not discriminated against. They are. Hatred can kill. . . . [H]is death makes clear the need for hate-crime laws to protect those who survive and punish those who attack others, whether fatally or not, just because of who they are.[27]

THINK ABOUT IT:

1. What could be done to prevent these types of hate crimes to occur?

2. Why did Henderson and McKinney brutally kill Shepard?

---

in 2008, Alaska added homeless status to a law that establishes more protection for vulnerable populations; in 2004, California passed a law requiring police officer training on hate crimes against persons who are homeless; and Florida passed a law in 2010 that added "homeless status" to hate crime legislation.[23]

The model state legislation designates the following acts as hate crimes motivated by a person's status as homeless:

model state legislation for hate crimes/violence against people experiencing homelessness: the National Law Center on Homelessness and Poverty and the National Coalition for the Homeless advocated state legislation that includes homelessness in hate crimes statutes.

- Assault, aggravated assault, battery, or aggravated battery on the person

- Acts that deface, damage, or destroy, or attempt to deface, damage, or destroy the personal property of the person

- Acts that result in the death of the person

- Any other crime against the person[24]

Theoretical Explanations of Hate Crimes

Byers and Crider examined hate crimes against the Amish using routine activities theory.[28] Specifically, they were studying offenders who engaged in acts called "claping." *Clape* is a derogatory term used by some non-Amish to insult and degrade Old Order Amish.

Claping is any act of persecution committed against the Amish. Examples of claping include verbal harassment, blowing up mailboxes, forcing Amish buggies off the road with motorized vehicles, killing Amish-owned animals, and spraying the Amish with fire extinguishers.

The qualitative data supported routine activities theory in that the participants (i.e., offenders) were motivated, the Amish were considered suitable targets, and there was a perception that guardians to discourage these types of crimes were absent. Based on interviews, the offenders revealed various motivations for engaging in these crimes, such as the perception that the Amish are "different," a desire for excitement, and the belief that the Amish deserve such treatment. The Amish were considered suitable targets for various reasons, such as the perceived absence of consequences, the belief that the Amish were inferior, and the belief that they were vulnerable or an "easy target." The participants cited various themes indicating the lack of capable guardians, such as the low probability of getting caught and a belief that society accepted claping and devalued the Amish.

Waldner and Berg applied a revision of routine activities theory to understanding anti-gay violence.[29] They employed Finkelhor and Asdigian's revised routine activities theory, which includes the concept of *target congruence*.[30] Target congruence is when various personal characteristics of individuals could possibly enhance their vulnerability to victimization since these characteristics have some congruence with the needs and motives of the offenders. Thus, certain offenders are attracted, or respond, to particular types of victims or particular characteristics in victims, making these victims more vulnerable.[31]

Some researchers have attempted to understand hate crime within the social disorganization theoretical framework. Further, those factors associated with non-hate crime are similar to factors related to hate crime (i.e., bias crime always consists of behavior that is criminalized).[32] Thus, low residential stability, poverty, and increased racial diversity may result in a breakdown of social relationships which leads to increase hate crimes as well as non-hate crimes.[33] Some research has supported the social disorganization theory.[34]

Another facet of studying hate crimes is examining individuals' *perceptions* of hate crimes, or how people view such offenses.[35] Plumm and her colleagues implemented a jury simulation model to explore different forms of victim blame involving an assault motivated by bias against sexual orientation.[36] They concluded that jurors may consider various factors in these types of cases. Jurors may not agree that a violent crime motivated by bias should necessarily be deemed a hate crime. Rather, other factors may be considered in the context of attributions of victim blaming. Thus, "prosecution of hate crimes may, therefore, be unsuccessful to the extent that extra-legal factors contribute to victim blaming."[37]

LEARNING CHECK 15.1

1. The _____ Act is named after two victims of hate crimes.

2. The _____ Act is part of the UCR program.

3. A hate crime is an offense that must be _____ by an individual with a bias against the victim's race, religion, disability, sexual orientation, and/or ethnicity/national origin.

4. _____ theory was applied to understanding hate crimes against the Amish.

Answers located at www.edge.sagepub.com/schram2e

MULTICIDE

There are several categories of *multicide*, or individuals who kill multiple victims. Some are *serial killers*, who kill single victims over time with a cooling period between the killings, whereas others are *mass murderers*, who kill multiple victims at one place at one

The deadliest mass shooting in U.S. history, by one gunman, occurred on June 12, 2016, at the Pulse nightclub in Orlando, Florida.

time. On the other hand, there are *spree killers* who kill victims in different places without a cooling-off time, typically driving/moving as fast as they can to the next place of violence.[38]

A good example of a serial killer is Ted Bundy, who committed his dozens of killings over many years (approximately five years in the 1970s). He would carefully plan his offenses, often planning the primary site, where he would rape and kill women, as well as the secondary site at a distant location, where he would dump the body. He would often go months between his murders as he traveled across the country, starting in Washington state and heading down through California and across the southern United States until his final murders in Tallahassee, Florida, at the Chi Omega sorority house at Florida State University. Therefore, this fits the definition of a cooling-off period between many killings over a very long period of time.

A good example of a mass murderer would be Omar Mateen, who, on June 12, 2016, killed 49 people (and wounded at least 50 others) at the Pulse nightclub in Orlando, Florida, a well-known hangout for LGBT (lesbian, gay, bisexual, and transgender) individuals. Notably, this was the deadliest mass attack in U.S. history. Prior to this incident, a married couple, Syed Farook and Tashfeen Malik, had killed 14 people in December 2015 at a workplace holiday event in San Bernardino. Both of these recent killings clearly fit the criteria of mass murder because they killed many people in a single incident.

A good example of a spree killer is Daniel Remeta, who drove across several states to kill his five victims in a six-day period. Specifically, in February 1985, Remeta went on a tristate crime spree, in which he first killed a 60-year-old convenience store clerk in Florida. His next victims were two individuals in Arkansas and two more in Kansas. The distinguishing feature of this killer is that he essentially had no cooling-down period; rather, he drove almost as fast as possible to different locations to kill his victims. Thus, he fits the definition of a spree killer.

There are many cases in which a killer fits more than one category. A good example is the notorious case of Charles Whitman, who in 1966 first killed his wife and mother in Austin, Texas, and the next day climbed the marquee tower at the University of Texas–Austin, killed the receptionist, and then waited for classes to break at noon, when he proceeded to shoot to death 15 victims from the top of the tower and wounded many others, including a pregnant woman who lost her baby. Whitman would fall into at least two categories, because he clearly was a mass murderer, but given his killing of his wife and mother the previous day, he is definitely either a spree killer or a serial killer, depending on whether you think a night is a "cooling-off" period. If you think one night was enough to cool off, then he would be a serial killer; more likely, he would be considered a spree killer, especially given his planning of the event and that it happened within 24 hours. (If you want to read more details about this case, see the section on Whitman in Chapter 6.)

It should be mentioned that some scholars consider or count incidents of the three categories discussed above as multicide if, and only if, at least three or more people died in the attacks.[39] In fact, some of the most cited researchers claim that at least four must be killed in a given incident.[40] Specifically, the notable scholar James Alan Fox has reported, based on this criterion of four or more killed by gunfire, that an average of 19 mass murders have occurred in the United States per year since 1976.

However, the authors of this book take issue with this criterion for both serial killers and mass murderers. After all, let's say in a given case that a serial killer murders one person, has a cooling-off period, and then kills another. Then, while the killer is carefully planning the next attack, the authorities catch the person. Shouldn't that person be counted as a serial killer? The same goes for the other categories. For example, if an individual shoots 20 people in a single attack but only two people die, why shouldn't this person be counted or labeled a mass murderer? Clearly, in such a case, the shooter intended for many more victims to die. It is understandable that researchers have drawn a certain line to produce criteria to use for a given study, but it seems to defy reason (especially with growing medical technology in keeping wounded people alive) that new definitions/criteria would not be developed that take into consideration how many victims were intended to be killed.

Categories of Mass Killers

Notable scholars have distinguished many types of categories of mass killers. We will define them, and then examine the final one—school shooters—in more detail.[41]

Disciple Mass Killer: The desire to kill is related to the relationship between the killer and the leader of a group/cult, such as in the Charles Manson case.

Family Annihilator Killer: Intends to kill victims he or she knows well, especially family members.

Disgruntled Employee Killer: As the label says, this is when angry (ex-)employees kill those whom they blame for either losing their job or having problems at work.

Ideological Mass Killer: Wants to kill people who are against the person's values, morals, or religious persuasion.

Disgruntled Citizen Killer: Angry with certain aspects of society (e.g., financial issues) and wants to take it out on people the person deems responsible.

Psychotic Mass Killer: Psychotic (often with schizophrenia) and perceive others as being out to get them.

School Killers: This category will be explored in depth below.

School Attacks

There has been much attention on school shootings and attacks in the last 20 years, so much that it led to a collaborative federal study by the U.S. Secret Service and Department of Education. This type of collaborative effort illustrates the importance of inter-agency cooperation when addressing various issues such as school shootings and attacks.[42] This study, examining all school attacks over a 25-year period, resulted in a comprehensive report. What is enlightening is that many of the findings are contrary to what many experts had claimed were the motivations/characteristics of school killers. It is likely that these experts did not examine the data and simply based their conclusions on a couple of high-profile anecdotes, such as that of Columbine High School in April 1999, in which Eric Harris and Dylan Klebold killed 12 students and one teacher (and injuring many more) with assault weapons.

The report from the Secret Service and Department of Education revealed that the Columbine attack did not fit the typical profile of school attacks. Specifically, the study of school attacks over 25 years (1975–2000) revealed that the vast majority were committed by only one student (not two or more) and that the most common weapon was a handgun (not an assault weapon). Perhaps even more surprising is that the study found that most attackers were socially "mainstream" (not social outcasts of peer culture or "grunge," as many media reports claimed). Additionally, most student attackers were receiving A's and B's in school, unlike the mistaken profile in the media of the attackers being poor students. Furthermore, the Secret Service study showed that the vast majority of student attackers were from two-headed households and not from split or single-headed households. It is also notable the 25-year examination found that most of the incidents didn't target any of the attacker's peers but rather a teacher or administrator. Finally, almost none of the attacks were stopped by law enforcement but rather by intervention by other teachers or staff at the school, likely due to the fact that most of the incidents took only a few minutes or less to complete. Most of these conclusions were the opposite of those provided by many experts in the media in the late 1990s and early 2000s.

One positive aspect of the Columbine High School incident and others during the late 1990s and early 2000s is that police agencies have changed the way they handle active shooters. Before, their tactics involved stopping to help victims, but in recent years, the strategy has changed to make the priority neutralizing the shooters and then to provide aid to the victims, which has likely saved lives in recent events.

Disparity in Rates of Committing Multicide Across Race and Religious Ideology

Recent studies have noted that it is a common myth that African-Americans are underrepresented as multicide offenders, especially serial killers. Specifically, a recent study by Allan Branson in 2012 revealed that African-American serial killers are actually overrepresented yet often not acknowledged by mainstream media.[43] Branson noted that over 90 black serial killers since 1945 are not typically highlighted by movies or journalistic reports, and thus, their notoriety and celebrity are absent from the popular cultural landscape in America. As Branson claims, "This is an interesting conundrum. The media show little reticence in portraying black males as low-level criminals, but rarely portray them as serial killers." Branson cites research by Eric Hickey, which found that approximately 20% of all serial killers are black, a number significantly higher than the 13% they make up of the population.[44] Branson concluded that the FBI was largely responsible for creating this profile of predominantly white serial killers, and that the media, as well as common myth in our society, followed in suit with this line of thought.

Regarding the notably horrible attacks in the United States by Muslims, it is also important to note the data on recent mass murders. Specifically, a recent review of the data on mass murders in the United States through most of 2015 showed that only 1 out of 207 incidents were committed by known Muslim offenders.[45] According to FBI data, 94% of terrorist attacks carried out in the United States from 1980 to 2005 were committed by non-Muslims.[46] Thus, an American terrorist suspect is over nine times more likely to be a non-Muslim than a Muslim. And the rate of terrorist attacks by radical Islamic offenders is even less in Europe (approximately 2%). Thus, to blame an entire religion for recent acts of terrorism would be the same as blaming all of Christianity for the killing of doctors who perform abortions or the violent actions of the Ku Klux Klan, who claim to be Christian.[47]

Still, there have been radical Islamic factions that do seek to forward their ideology via terrorism, especially in recent years; however, these radical Islamic groups do not represent the vast majority of the 1.6 billion Muslims around the world. There have always been terrorists, and there always will be, that represent all races and religions. But it is important to remember that while we should always be adamant in fighting and preventing such violent acts by any and all religious/ideological groups, by far the majority of the terrorist attacks and multicides on American soil, and Europe as well, are home-bred and non-Muslim.

WHAT IS TERRORISM?

In May 2011, Osama bin Laden was killed by Navy SEALs in the U.S. Naval Special Warfare Development Group. He was not found in a remote area near the Pakistani–Afghan border, where he was presumed to be hiding; rather, he was located in a large compound in the city of Abbottabad, about an hour's drive from the Pakistani capital of Islamabad. As noted in *the New York Times*, "Bin Laden's demise is a defining moment in the American-led fight against terrorism, a symbolic stroke affirming the relentlessness of the pursuit of those who attacked New York and Washington on Sept. 11, 2001."[48] President Barack Obama addressed the nation to announce Osama bin Laden's death. Part of his address included the following:

> After nearly 10 years of service, struggle, and sacrifice, we know well the costs of war. These efforts weigh on me every time I, as Commander-in-Chief, have to sign a letter to a family that has lost a loved one, or look into the eyes of a service member who's been gravely wounded. So Americans understand the costs of war. Yet as a country, we will never tolerate our security being threatened, nor stand idly by when our people have been killed. We will be relentless in defense of our citizens and our friends and allies. We will be true to the values that make us who we are. And on nights like this one, we can say to those families who have lost loved ones to al Qaeda's terror: Justice has been done.[49]

Terrorism has existed for hundreds of years. However, after the September 11 attacks, terrorism has become more intertwined with Americans and their lives than in previous years. For instance, we read about it more in the newspapers and have experienced changes in how we travel.

In this section, we attempt to provide students with an overview of terrorism, starting with the question, "What is terrorism?" Next, we provide a brief historical overview of terrorism, as well as a discussion on the context of modern terrorism, such as organizational networks and financial support. We conclude this section with a brief review of some theoretical explanations of terrorism.

In the past few years, through newspapers, television, the Internet, and personal conversations, we have heard a great deal about terrorism. Given that exposure, how would you define terrorism? What are some key features of terrorism? Who engages in terrorist activities? In this section, we will try to answer the question "What is terrorism?" First, we will discuss issues pertaining to the definition of terrorism. Then we will briefly review various types of terrorism, as well as the extent of terrorism.

Definition of Terrorism

In one respect, terrorism is a social construct, meaning it is defined through social and cultural practice. People have varying definitions for the term *terrorism*:

> It is a pejorative term in that it has extremely negative associations and always connotes death and destruction. Society is constantly exposed to the term by the news media, politicians, and popular entertainment venues, and it is applied to a wide variety of actors, conditions, activities, and situations. As a social construct, the term is used to demonize people, societies, and actions.[50]

Today, *terrorism* is a significant word in our vocabulary, evoking highly emotional responses and reactions. Billions of dollars are spent worldwide to control terrorism, and people die every day from acts of terrorism. However, "some people do not seem to bother to define terrorism nor do they consider it worthwhile defining the concept."[51] Thus, there is no clear and concise definition of the word.

During a presentation at the War Crime Research Symposium, Alex Schmid argued that the United Nations has found it difficult to agree on a common definition of terrorism. In fact, various agencies in the U.S. government with interests in counterterrorism missions have different definitions of terrorism (see Table 15.3). In an attempt to distinguish terrorism from other types of criminal activity and irregular warfare, Bruce Hoffman identified terrorism as follows:

- Inevitably political in aims and motives

- Violent or threatens violence

- Designed to have far-reaching psychological consequences beyond the immediate victim or target

- Conducted *either* by an organization with an identifiable chain of command or conspiratorial cell structure *or* by individuals or a small collection of individuals directly influenced, motivated, or inspired by the ideological aims or example of some existent terrorist movement and/or its leaders

- Perpetrated by a subnational group or nonstate entity[52]

Typologies of Terrorism

Identifying typologies of terrorism helps one focus on the varying forms of violence as well as the social meanings of terrorism while avoiding the controversial debates about the lack of a concise definition. It is essential to emphasize that while these typologies may enhance our understanding of terrorism, each incident should be appreciated within its particular social, historical, and political context.[53] There are a number of terrorist organizations and terrorist activities around the world.[54] The U.S. Department of State identified 60 foreign terrorist organizations including al-Shabaab, Revolutionary Struggle, Continuity Irish Republican Army (CIRA), and the National Liberation Army. The most resent foreign terrorist organization identified was the Islamic State of Iraq and the Levant's Branch in Libya (ISIL-Libya) on May 19, 2016.[55] Upon examining worldwide terrorism, Gus Martin developed a typology of terrorism founded on motivation: (1) state sponsored, (2) dissident, (3) religious, and (4) criminal.[56]

State-sponsored terrorism includes terrorist acts that transpire due to the guidance of the state or government against perceived enemies. Targets of this type of terrorism may include politicians and political parties or groups within the host country or in other countries.[61] The U.S. Department of State has identified three countries that are state sponsors of terrorism: Iran, Syria, and Sudan. In 1982, Cuba was designated as a state

state-sponsored terrorism: includes terrorist acts that transpire due to the guidance of the state or government against perceived enemies.

TABLE **15.3**   Definitions of Terrorism by Four U.S. Government Agencies

DEFINITIONS OF TERRORISM

1. Federal Emergency Management Agency (FEMA): "Terrorism is the use of force or violence against persons or property in violation of the criminal laws of the United States for purposes of intimidation, coercion, or ransom."[57]

2. U.S. State Department: Terrorism "means premeditated, politically motivated violence perpetrated against non-combatant targets by subnational groups or clandestine agents"[58]

3. Federal Bureau of Investigation (FBI): Terrorism is defined as "the unlawful use of force or violence against persons or property to intimidate or coerce a government, the civilian population, or any segment thereof in furtherance of political or social objectives."[59]

4. Department of Defense: Terrorism is "the unlawful use of violence or threat of violence, often motivated by religious, political, or other ideological beliefs, to instill fear and coerce governments or societies in pursuit of goals that are usually political."[60]

sponsor of terrorism; however, in 2015 the U.S. government removed Cuba from that list.[62] **Dissident terrorism** involves terrorist activities committed by rebellious groups against the government. In some instances, these terrorist acts are committed for power, wealth, and control; some are used to obtain independence. **Religious terrorism** involves terrorist acts legitimized by religious dogma. Terrorism motivated by religious philosophy has been the predominant form for the past several decades.[63] It is essential to stress that religious terrorism should not be associated with just the Muslim religion. For instance, American Christian white supremacists have engaged in various terrorist acts based on their faith and hatred for groups such as African-Americans and Jews. **Criminal terrorism** involves engaging in criminal activity for profits, as in the drug cartels in Mexico, for example. Traditional organized crime enterprises, such as the Italian Mafia, profit from criminal activity for personal gain; criminal-political enterprises, such as Sri Lanka's Tamil Tigers, profit from criminal activity to sustain the movement.[64]

Extent of Terrorism

A major resource to understanding the extent of terrorism is the Global Terrorism Index (GTI). This is a wide-ranging study that collects information on terrorism from 162 countries. In their 2015 report, GTI reported that terrorist activity increased by 80% in 2014. The number of deaths from terrorism in 2013 were 18,111; in 2014, this number increased to 32,681. Currently, the deadliest terrorist group in the world is Boko Haram. While deaths attributed to ISIL were 6,073, there were 6,644 deaths attributed to Boko Haram. Terrorist activity is highly concentrated; five countries accounted for 78% of deaths: Iraq, Nigeria, Afghanistan, Pakistan, and Syria (see Figure 15.2).

- The number of private citizens killed due to terrorist attacks increased by 172% from 2013 to 2014.

- Terrorist attacks on religious targets declined by 11% in 2014.

- Two groups are responsible for half the deaths from terrorism: Boko Haram and ISIL. Fifty-one percent of terrorist deaths attributed to a terrorist group were perpetrated by Boko Haram and ISIL.

- Nigeria experienced the largest increase in deaths from terrorism in 2014. Two of the five deadliest terrorist groups in 2014 are from Nigeria: Boko Haram and the Fulani militants.

dissident terrorism: involves terrorist activities against the government that are committed by rebellious groups.

religious terrorism: motivated by engaging in terrorist acts that are legitimized by religious dogma.

criminal terrorism: terrorism motivated by engaging in criminal activity for profit, such as in the drug cartels in Mexico.

FIGURE *15.2*

FIGURE *15.2*   Global Impact of Terrorism

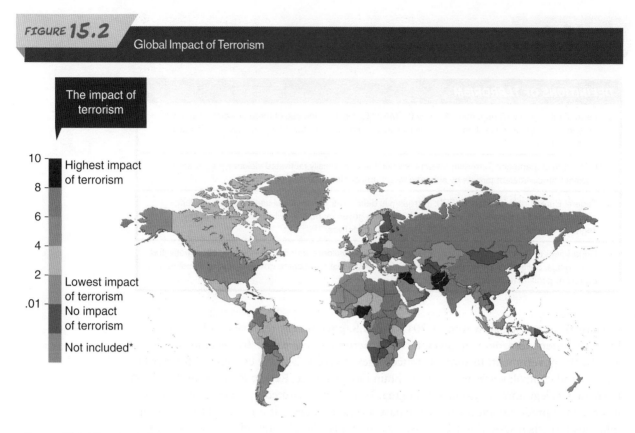

Source: Global Terrorism Index.

- ISIL inflicts more deaths on the battlefield than through terrorism.

- The movement of foreign fighters into Iraq and Syria continued in 2014 and 2015.

- Excluding Turkey, Europe accounted for 21% of all foreign fighters in 2014.

In reference to trends of terrorism in Western countries, the majority of deaths from terrorism do not occur in the West. Excluding the September 11, 2001, attacks, approximately 0.5% of deaths from terrorism have occurred in the West since 2000. (If one includes the September 11 attacks, the percentage increases to 2.6). Further, lone wolf attackers are the main perpetrators of terrorist activity in the West. In fact, during the last nine years, Islamic fundamentalism was not the main motivation of terrorism in the West. Approximately 80% of deaths by these lone-wolf terrorists were motivated by right wing extremism, nationalism, antigovernment sentiment and political extremism and other forms of supremacy.[65]

Historical Context of Modern Terrorism

Even though it is difficult to offer a clear and concise definition of terrorism, it is essential that we provide a brief historical overview. Presenting some historical context provides a better understanding of terrorism's origins and helps develop an appreciation of its implications.[66] Terrorism is a type of political warfare; thus, like war, while it retains its consistent nature, the causes, objectives, and motivations of terrorism evolve. The first known terrorist group was the Sicarii, an extremist group of the religious sect of Zealots who tried to banish the Romans and their Jewish collaborators from the Judean region from A.D. 66 to 73. The term *Sicarii* refers to the short sword or *sica*, their weapon of choice.[67] During the 11th century, a Shiite Muslim sect killed politicians and clerics who did not adhere to their form of Islam. These individuals became known as "assassins." Literally, the term *assassin* meant "hashish-eater." This may be a reference to the rumor, possibly false, that these individuals engaged in ritualistic drug use prior to their missions. Like other religiously inspired terrorists, when engaging in terrorist missions, the assassins perceived their deaths as sacrificial and believed that such a death would guarantee entrance into paradise.[68]

The French Revolution

The term *terrorism* originated from the *regime de la terreur* (reign of terror) that prevailed during the French Revolution. The regime was intended to consolidate the power of the new revolutionary government and protect it from what were considered "subversive" factors. Terrorism was initially considered a positive action.[69] In 1794, Maximilien Robespierre, the French revolutionary leader, stated that

> terror is nothing other than justice, prompt, severe, inflexible; it is therefore an emanation of virtue; it is not so much a special principle as it is a consequence of the general principle of democracy applied to our country's most urgent needs.[70]

Under this reign of terror, about 40,000 people were executed by guillotine. In fact, Robespierre and his top lieutenants were also put to death when he announced that he would be issuing a new list of subversives; some of the individuals in the revolutionary government feared their names were on this list. Soon, the French Revolution involved individuals turning on each other; the term *terrorism* eventually had a negative connotation, similar to today's value-laden meaning.[71]

Late-19th and Early-20th-Century Terrorism

From the 1800s into the early 1900s, anarchists and socialists were responsible for a great deal of terrorism.[72] Anarchism and radical socialism were leftist ideologies that advocated for the rights of the working class and abhorred central government control, as well as private property.[73] Thus, most of the acts involving the anarchists and socialists were directed toward those perceived as supporters of the oppressive government.[74] For example, many officials in the Serbian government and military were engaged in supporting, training, and arming Balkan terrorist groups, one of which was responsible for the assassination of Archduke Franz Ferdinand on June 28, 1914. This act has been attributed to initiating World War I. Terrorist acts during this time have been labeled *state-sponsored terrorism*.[75]

After World War II, there was shift in terrorist activity; this focus moved from Europe to its various colonies. There was an increase in national movements, as well as resistance to European attempts to continue colonization across the Middle East, Asia, and Africa. These nationalist and anticolonial groups were often involved in activity involving guerrilla warfare. Conflicts occurring in Kenya, Malaysia, Cyprus, and Palestine involved groups who learned how to exploit the increasing globalization of the international media:[76]

> They also began to target innocent civilians from other countries who often had little if anything to do with the terrorists' cause or grievance, simply in order to endow their acts with the power to attract attention and publicity that the attacks against their declared or avowed enemies often lacked. Their intent was to shock and, by shocking, to stimulate worldwide fear and alarm.[77]

These groups realized that terrorism, and the fear of terrorism, could be used to serve their needs.[78]

Applying Theory to Crime: *TERRORISM*

This section applies different theories of crime to one of the primary offenses discussed in this chapter—terrorism. Empirical studies show that the most likely theory to best explain this category of criminal behavior is strain theory, both traditional and more recent versions of this framework.[82] Further, social learning perspectives (differential association/reinforcement theory) are another theoretical framework that applies directly to such terrorist activities. Although other theories can also be applied to explaining terrorist behavior, versions of strain theory and social process/learning are currently among the leading theories for understanding why individuals engage in such activities.

Many notable recent acts of terrorism are based on the loss of some key positive element, whether it be land/territory (such as in the Israeli–Palestine conflict) or other types of principles/goals, such as what motivated Timothy McVeigh in his bombing of the Alfred P. Murrah Federal Building in Oklahoma City in 1995. These incidents of terrorism fit well in the framework of strain theory, including both Merton's traditional strain theory and the more modern versions of general strain theory, such as Agnew's. After all, most elements of terrorism are rooted in a feeling of strain or frustration, whether it be frustration with the current government structure or some other source (often anger with another government/state).

Specifically, in the case of the current dispute over land in Israel, the reason people revolt is because many feel that the Palestinian citizens' lands were taken from them (via the ruling by worldwide bodies that concluded that they belong to the state of Israel), which is clearly a case of losing a positive aspect of their livelihood. The Palestinian revolt over the past five decades or so has revealed this frustration and anger at having their land taken from them. This creates a great amount of strain and frustration, which has resulted in lashing out against the existing Israeli state that they believe took this important positive aspect. This type of anger and strain clearly fits into the general strain theory model of criminal offending, which emphasizes the loss of a positive stimulus (e.g., land/territory), without compensation for this loss.

A recent study by Agnew has shown that terrorism fits well in the framework of general strain theory, due to the feelings of anger and strain that create strong motivations for engaging in terrorist attacks against those who are primarily to blame for the loss of positive stimuli (in this case, land/territory, the Palestinian state, etc.).[83] And it certainly fits regarding the anger and frustration of the Palestinians in trying to reacquire their land in the face of an overwhelming force—the state of Israel (with the backing of the United States and other governments).

Another example is that of McVeigh, who was responsible for one of the worst cases of domestic terrorism. As a sympathizer of militia movements, McVeigh's goal in his bombings was to try to get revenge against the U.S. federal government regarding its handling of the 1993 siege (which killed 76 people) in Waco, Texas, as well as the killing of militia citizens at Ruby Ridge in 1992. Ultimately, his goals fit well in traditional strain theory,[84] especially regarding the adaptation of rebel or rebellion, in which a person desires certain means and goals for society but strongly disagrees with the current conventionally established means and goals and therefore seeks to change them. This is exactly what McVeigh sought to do by bombing the federal building. Unfortunately, many of the victims of his attack were children in the building's day care center. Thus, his act was seen not as an attack on authority or the current political state but, rather, as a massacre of innocent victims who had nothing to do with the ideological and political climate he was fighting against.

Other theories can also help explain the terrorism we have discussed in this section. For example, the social process/learning theories of differential association/reinforcement[85] offer a good explanation for why certain individuals engage in terrorist activity. To clarify, these theories emphasize the influence of significant others (e.g., peers, family) in promoting such behavior. Regarding the two notable incidents of terrorism described in this section, it is obvious that both cases involve a social learning element. Specifically, in both the Israeli/Palestinian conflict and the McVeigh bombing of the federal building, certain ideals are being internalized by the offenders via their peers and other significant others. In fact, a rather extensive doctoral dissertation study by Silverman supported the fact that social learning played an important role in various forms of terrorism.[86] It is quite certain that such social learning factors play a key role in the ongoing conflict within the state of Israel, which appears to be socialized from generation to generation via families and peers, as well as in McVeigh's motivation for bombing the federal building, which was documented by his association with coconspirator Terry Nichols, who taught him how to make explosives.

Ultimately, these two examples of terrorism fit well in the framework of strain theory (both traditional and modern versions), as well as various social learning components. There are other theories that also help explain modern terrorism (e.g., culture theory), but this section has showed that strain theory and social learning theory are two of the most likely explanatory models for understanding modern forms of terrorism.

THINK ABOUT IT:

1. What theoretical framework would help understanding the June 2016 shooting in the Orlando, Florida nightclub?

2. What theoretical framework would help understand the July 2016 attack with a cargo truck in Nice, France?

Comparative Criminology: *TERRORISM*

Quality of Rule of Law and Perceived Cost of Terrorism

Gupta[87] and Schmid[88] examined whether there was a link between the rule of law in a country and the prevalence of terrorist incidents. Their research revealed a negative association between these two factors. For instance, Gupta's research demonstrated that a lack of civil and political rights (i.e., the rule of law is weak) was related to terrorist incidents. Schmid's research also demonstrated a link between his index of terrorism and whether countries observed human rights or engaged in some form of state repression. Citing these works, Van Dijk replicated these studies by using the index of costs of terrorism for business as an indicator of terrorism; he used the World Bank index as an indicator of the rule of law.[89] Figure 15.3 illustrates the results of these analyses. A low score on the rule of law indicates high quality; a high score on the cost of terrorism indicates high prevalence of terrorist incidents. This figure reveals that terrorism incidents are more common, or thought to be more common, in those countries where the rule of law is weak. Interestingly, there were some countries that were considered "outliers"—specifically, the United

States and Israel. Van Dijk concluded that this was due to these countries being susceptible to international terrorism.

Further analyses noted a weak association between police performance and terrorism. Specifically, in those countries that ranked high on the Police Performance Index (i.e., practiced better policing), terrorist incidents are considered less of a threat. Van Dijk noted that terrorist "threats seem to be facilitated by institutional failures to maintain the rule of law, including through democratic and effective policing."[90]

THINK ABOUT IT:

1. Why do you think terrorist threats seem to be enhanced when there are institutional failures to maintain the rule of law?

2. Why do you think the United States is considered an "outlier?"

3. How would you explain that countries high on the Police Performance Index consider terrorist incidents less of a threat?

FIGURE 15.3   Quality of Perceived Cost of Terrorism per Country

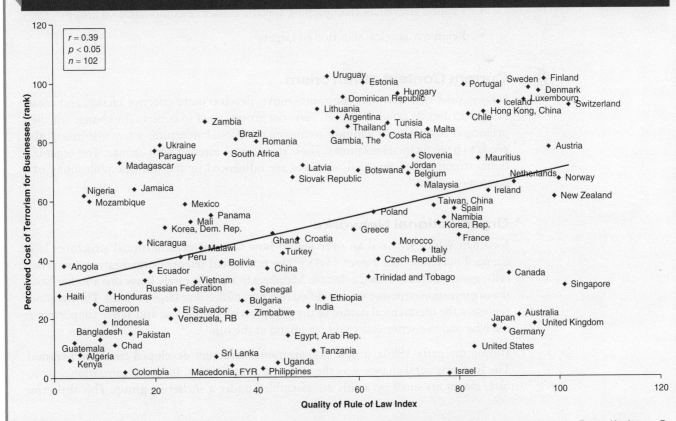

Sources: World Economic Forum. (2003). *The global competitiveness report 2002–2003.* New York, NY: Oxford University Press; Kaufmann, D., Kraay, A., & Mastruzzi, M. (2004). *Governance matters, III: Governance indicators for 1996–2002.* Policy Research Working Paper 3106. Washington, DC: World Bank; see www.worldbank.org/wbi/governance/govdata and the rule of law index (WBI).

During the 1960s and 1970s, groups engaging in terrorist activities increased; these groups expanded to include not only nationalists but those who were motivated by ethnic as well as ideological issues. Nationalist groups include the Palestinian Liberation Organization and the Provisional Irish Republican Army; groups motivated by ethnic and ideological issues include the Red Army Faction and the Italian Red Brigades.[79]

Contemporary Terrorism

Since the September 11 attacks, terrorism has had a tremendous influence not only in the United States but on the international stage as well. A great deal of emphasis has focused on the threat posed by al Qaeda. Interestingly, "the U.S. view of terrorism nonetheless remains, to a degree, largely ego-centric—despite the current administration's rhetoric concerning a so-called 'Global War Against Terrorism.'"[80] Gus Martin contends that the modern world is challenged by the "New Terrorism," which is characterized by the following:

- Loose, cell-based networks with minimal lines of command and control

- Desired acquisition of high-intensity weapons and weapons of mass destruction

- Politically vague, religious, or mystical motivations

Martin then compared the New Terrorism with traditional terrorism, characterized by the following:

- Clearly identifiable organizations or movements

- Use of conventional weapons, usually small arms and explosives

- Explicit grievances championing specific classes or ethno-national groups

- Relatively surgical selection of targets[81]

Current Context of Terrorism

It is essential that terrorists constantly move, develop more effective tactics, and create new structures to avoid detection. Terrorist groups need to continually change for their prolonged existence. In addition to an organizational structure, a terrorist group also needs to have financial resources. These two factors interact with change. The organizational structure and financial resources are influenced by the strategic philosophy of a given movement.[91]

Organizational Networks

Jonathan White provided an overview of how terrorist organizational structures have changed over time (see Figure 15.4).[92] The traditional terrorist organization comprised cells; groups of cells formed columns. Members in the cells rarely knew one another. Soon the organization structure was modified to a pyramid, either large or small. The pyramids represent the hierarchical nature of the groups, with the passive and active supporters at the base and the active cadre and command at the top.

During the early 1980s, a new organizational structure developed from the pyramid. The first structural change was the umbrella organization. In this organizational structure, numerous small pyramids are assembled under a sheltering group. This sheltering

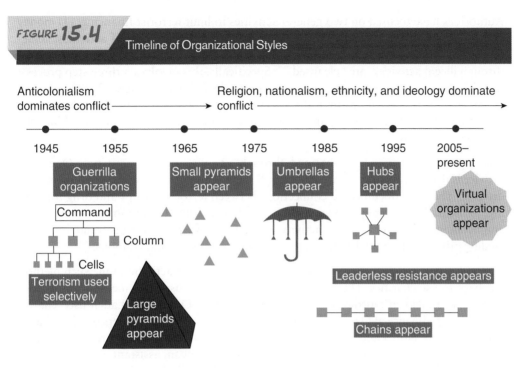

FIGURE 15.4 Timeline of Organizational Styles

Source: Adapted from White, J. R. (2012). *Terrorism and homeland security* (7th ed.). Belmont, CA: Wadsworth, p. 77.

group manages supplies, acquires resources, develops support structures, and obtains intelligence. The umbrella organization is disconnected from the terrorist activities. In the 1990s, the RAND Corporation identified other types of new organizational structures.[93] One is virtual organizations. This organizational structure evolves through communication, financial, and ideological links. A virtual organization has no central leadership. Another structure is chain organizations. Chain organizations are temporary associations with various groups. These groups gather for a specific operation; upon completion of that operation, they disperse. Hub organizations are established to manage or support cells; they function similarly to umbrella groups.

Financial Support

An essential method to combat terrorism is restricting the financing of such organizations.[94] Limiting their financial resources can result in the following: (1) It can directly or indirectly influence an organization's leadership, morale, and legitimacy (e.g., diminish support from members and other terrorist organizations), and (2) it can have strategic implications (e.g., a group may not have the necessary resources to accomplish a planned attack).[95] For example, in 2003, a terrorist group was planning to simultaneously bomb the Egyptian, American, and other Western embassies in Pakistan. Due to a lack of financial resources, the group focused solely on attacking the Egyptian embassy:

> A short time before the bombing of the [Egyptian] embassy the assigned group . . . told us that they could strike both the Egyptian and American embassies if we gave them enough money. We had already provided them with all that we had and we couldn't collect more money.[96]

Authorities have focused on two general activities to limit terrorist financing: (1) money laundering and (2) fundraising. While these are two different types of activities, sometimes they are interconnected. Money laundering is a process whereby funds, obtained through illegal activities, are "cleansed."[97] Specifically, this involves a three-step process: (1) The illegally obtained monies are placed into the financial system; (2) these monies are layered, or processed, through the system, usually internationally, and subsequently intermingled with legal monies; and (3) the monies are turned and reintegrated into the legitimate economy.[98]

These ill-gotten monies are obtained through various criminal activities. One such activity is drug trafficking: "If we cannot kill them with guns, . . . we will kill them with drugs."[99] There are documented connections between terrorist groups and drug trafficking, particularly in reference to smuggling pseudoephedrine (used to manufacture methamphetamine). Another criminal activity linked to terrorist financing is fraud, involving credit cards, welfare, Social Security, insurance, food stamps, and coupons.[100]

Terrorist organizations also use fundraising to finance their activities. One such method has been to use charities. The Irish Republican Army has used this method for decades to fund its attacks in Northern Ireland and England.[101] Osama bin Laden used charity fundraising to finance al Qaeda.[102] In November 2008, five former leaders of a U.S.-based Muslim charity, Holy Land Foundation, were convicted of channeling more than $12 million to the Palestinian terrorist group Hamas. Patrick Rowan, assistant attorney general for National Security, stated that "for many years, the Holy Land Foundation used the guise of charity to raise and funnel millions of dollars to the infrastructure of the Hamas terror organization."[103]

In 1989, the Financial Action Task Force (FATF) was established to set standards as well as promote the effective implementation of measures to combat money laundering, terrorist financing, and associated threats to the integrity of the international financial system. In their 2012 report, *International Standards on Combating Money Laundering and the Financing of Terrorism & Proliferation,* FATF outlined forty recommendations which included enhancing policies and coordination, targeting financial sanctions related to terrorism and terrorist financing, reporting of suspicious transactions, and transparency and beneficial ownership of legal arrangements.[104]

Influence of the Media

Much of what the general public knows about terrorism is from the media. Simon Cottle identified the various communication frames used to report on terrorism.[105] These frames include *reporting frames* that are short and blended with facts; *dominant frames* from one authority's viewpoint; *conflict frames* consisting of two perspectives; *contention frames* comprising various positions; *investigative frames* that expose corrupt or illegal behavior; *campaigning frames,* which are the broadcaster's opinion; *reportage frames* comprising comprehensive coverage; *community service frames,* which provide information to the public; *collective interest frames* that reinforce common values and viewpoints; *cultural recognition frames* that reflect a group's values and norms; and *mythic tales frames* consisting of hero stories.

As noted in the beginning of this section, terrorism is a social construct. One area that can shape the social construction of terrorism is the media; the meanings associated with terrorism can be shaped by the media. Terrorists are also attentive to the power of the media and will increase the use of various forms of media, such as the Internet, to convey their message and purpose.[106] White outlined some of the issues associated with the media and reporting terrorism.[107] One of these issues centers on whether the media present information on terrorism in an unbiased and objective manner. Governments and terrorists attempt to manipulate the news; thus, it is essential that the media take

money laundering: a process whereby funds, obtained through illegal activities, are "cleansed"

fundraising: used by terrorist organizations to finance their activities

an objective position and "just tell the truth." However, some maintain that this assumption is naive.[108] Another issue is the contention effect. This refers to whether media coverage of a terrorist incident inspires more terrorism. The issue of censorship is also raised when individuals assume that terrorist acts are influenced by irresponsible media coverage and that this coverage can provide terrorists with information. As White noted,

> These new media organizations not only cover the drama but add differing interpretations and flavors to their stories. An Algerian terrorist once said he would rather kill one victim in front of a news camera than one hundred in the desert where the world would not see them. His point should be noted: Modern terrorism is a media phenomenon.[109]

REUTERS/Christian Hartmann

TV5Monde, a French television network, experienced an "extremely powerful" cyber attack in 2015 by supporters of the Islamic State militant group.

Domestic Terrorism

While this section has focused on what some designate as *international terrorism*, another form of terrorism has been identified as domestic terrorism. Referring to the U.S. Code, the FBI identifies domestic terrorism as activities with the following characteristics:

- Involve acts dangerous to human life that violate federal or state law;

- Appear intended (i) to intimidate or coerce a civilian population; (ii) to influence the policy of a government by intimidation or coercion; or (iii) to affect the conduct of a government by mass destruction, assassination, or kidnapping; and

- Occur primarily within the territorial jurisdiction of the U.S.[110]

Essentially, this is when Americans attack other Americans, often based on extremist ideologies. The FBI contends that domestic terror threats include white supremacists, destructive eco-terrorists, violence-prone antigovernment extremists, and radical separatist groups, among others.[111]

Martin maintained that most of the political violence in the United States can be categorized as either *left* or *right*.[112] The *left* applies to those political trends and movements that stress group rights. Examples include labor activism, people's rights, single issues (e.g., environmentalists, peace movements), and questioning traditions.[113] Examples of single-issue groups from the left are the Animal Liberation Front (ALF) and the Earth Liberation Front (ELF). ALF's credo includes the following:

> The Animal Liberation Front (ALF) carries out direct action against animal abuse in the form of rescuing animals and causing financial loss to animal exploiters, usually through the damage and destruction of property. . . . Because ALF actions may be against the law, activists work anonymously, either in small groups or individually, and do not have any centralized organization or coordination.[114]

ELF was founded in England by a former activist of the group Earthfirst! These individuals separated from Earthfirst! because of that organization's decision to stop engaging in criminal activities. Some consider this group more radical than ALF.[115]

domestic terrorism: unlawful use, or threatened use, of force or violence by a group or individual based in the United States to intimidate or coerce others to further political or social objectives.

The *right* consists of political trends and movements that stress conventional and traditional principles such as family values, educational content, and social-order politics.[116] Right-wing terrorism is often motivated by racial supremacism and antigovernment viewpoints. Compared with left-wing groups, right-wing terrorist activities are rare, with an attack such as that in Oklahoma City being uncommon.[117] Moralist terrorism is one example of right-wing political violence. Most moral terrorist activities are motivated by a religious doctrine that is considered a "fringe interpretation" of Christianity. Abortion clinics and gay bars have often been the targets of moralist violence.[118] One such group is the Army of God, which opposes abortion and homosexuality. Apparently, the Army of God's ideology is an extreme interpretation of fundamentalist Protestantism. There are some racial supremacist predispositions as well.[119] For instance, on its website, when referring to individuals who have killed doctors who perform abortions, the Army of God used such phrases as these:

- This is why the shooting of babykilling abortionist George Tiller was Justifiable Homicide."

- "Thank you Scott Roeder for stopping Babykilling abortionist George Tiller from murdering any more innocent children."

- "Now George Tiller will never murder another child."[120]

In June of 2006, Director of the FBI Robert Mueller gave a speech to the City Club of Cleveland on the threat of homegrown terrorism:

> "I want to talk today about the changing shape of terrorism and, in particular, the threat of homegrown terrorism. I want to talk about the radicalization process—how an extremist becomes a terrorist."[121]

On December 2, 2015, Syed Rizwan Farook and his wife, Tashfeen Malik, entered a Christmas Party for employees of the San Bernardino County Public Health Department. Heavily armed, with military-style clothing, they started shooting at the unsuspecting partygoers. Farook and his wife killed 14 people. When learning about their backgrounds, investigators found that Farook and Malik were married. They were college graduates with no criminal records. He was a native-born American and she recently emigrated from Pakistan. What is surprising to many is that they were what some would consider a part of "mainstream American life" but this is exactly the strategy of homegrown terrorists.[122] Because homegrown terrorists are familiar with American culture, it makes it more difficult to detect prior to their terrorist activities. This is an ever growing concern for U.S. Homeland Security experts.[123]

Theoretical Explanations of Terrorism

Brian Forst noted that "the challenges presented by terrorism are in many ways more formidable than those presented by conventional crime."[124] He identified three general barriers to understanding terrorism. First, while terrorism cases are similar with respect to having a political motive, there are numerous differences as well. For instance, terrorism cases vary by type of extremism (e.g., Islamic, Christian fundamentalist, environmental), connection to a larger network, extent of planning, type of attack (e.g., assassination, hostage taking), ideological justification, nature of target, weapon of choice, and extent of fatalities.

Second, in most instances, terrorists, unlike other criminals, engage in unpredictable activities. These terrorists attempt to create fear and mayhem by purposely operating outside of conventional patterns. For instance, after the September 11 attacks, when terrorist screening procedures overlooked women as suicide bombers, terrorists enlisted women for this type of bombing. These unpredictable patterns are difficult to examine in the data.

Finally, compared with other types of crime, terrorism is difficult to analyze because there is a relatively small amount of reliable data on cases of each major form of terrorism to provide a foundation for statistical inference. As Forst notes, while a few terrorist cases in the United States have provided some empirical analysis, this lack of data "is a curse for empirically oriented analysts interested in understanding terrorism."[125]

Despite these barriers, however, there have been attempts to enhance our understanding of terrorism. As mentioned previously, the National
Counterterrorism Center is collecting data on terrorist incidents. This type of information is helpful in developing theoretical models to understand causal factors associated with terrorism. One such model is routine activities theory. In Chapter 4, we discussed key components of routine activities theory. For a crime to occur, there must be willing offenders, suitable targets, and an absence of adequate guardianship.[126] If any one of these factors is unmet or absent, there is no opportunity for a terrorist act to occur. One notable conclusion of this theory in explaining and preventing terrorism is to avoid situations where there is a lack of guardianship. Another factor to consider is diminishing willing offenders, such as by enhancing surveillance of extremists and targeting individuals and groups with terrorist affiliations.

Another theoretical model that could enhance our understating of terrorism is **game theory**. The military uses game theory for teaching, training, and operational studies. Another formal use of this theory is with business and economic games. However, game theory has also been used increasingly to study social and other problems such as political and social processes.[127] This analytic approach assesses various scenarios by applying simulation gaming models.[128] Generally, the analysis of games has two goals. The first goal is to understand why the parties (i.e., players) in competitive situations behave as they do. The second goal is to advise the players of the best way to play the game.[129] Thus, game theory "could prove equally useful for assessing alternative approaches to protecting any prospective target against threats posed by terrorism."[130]

WHAT IS HOMELAND SECURITY?

On September 11, 2001, the most horrible attacks of modern international terrorism occurred in the United States. Nineteen al Qaeda terrorists were responsible for these attacks. They were on a suicidal "martyrdom mission" to fight in the name of a holy cause against what they perceived to be an evil enemy from the West. Their purpose was to attack symbols of American, and Western, interests that they deemed responsible for the continuing domination and exploitation of Muslim countries.[131] These attacks were targeted at the World Trade Center in New York City and the Pentagon in northern Virginia. The attacks resulted in 3,047 deaths and 2,337 injuries. There were 343 firefighters and 71 police officers killed responding to these attacks.[132]

LEARNING CHECK 15.2

1. _____ includes terrorist acts that transpire due to the direct, or indirect, guidance of the state or government.

2. The term terrorism originated from the reign of terror that prevailed during the _____.

3. The traditional terrorist organization comprised _____.

4. Another theoretical model that could enhance our understating of terrorism, used in the military for teaching, training, and operational studies, is _____.

Answers located at www.edge.sagepub.com/schram2e

---

game theory: assesses various scenarios by applying simulation gaming models, usually to understand why parties in competitive situations behave as they do and to advise players of the best way to play the game.

After these attacks, the United States realized the need to develop a national security strategy. In this section, we will first attempt to answer the question "What is homeland security?" including a summary of the origins and definition. Next, we will provide an overview of the organizational structure of homeland security, including those agencies responsible for this task and some bureaucratic problems and solutions. Finally, we will cover some of the civil liberty issues that are challenged by national security concerns.

Origins of Homeland Security

When these attacks occurred, it was painfully clear not only that the United States was vulnerable to such attacks but that the country was ill equipped to prevent them. While there was a history of terrorist attacks throughout the world, and there had been a few in the United States, preparing for such attacks was a low priority.[133] The September 11 attacks, as well as the fear of subsequent attacks, "significantly changed the national philosophy and ushered in a new strategy and American defense system. Nonetheless, the country had little foundation from which to build a national prevention strategy."[134]

On October 8, 2001, President George W. Bush issued Executive Order 13228. The order established the Office of Homeland Security as well as the Homeland Security Council. Specifically, it laid the foundation for implementation of a new concept of homeland security as it relates to counterterrorist policies.[135] The initial responsibility of the Office of Homeland Security was to produce the first National Strategy for Homeland Security in 2002. This strategy was to address four questions:

- What is "homeland security," and what missions does it entail?

- What do we seek to accomplish, and what are the most important goals of homeland security?

- What is the federal executive branch doing now to accomplish these goals, and what should it do in the future?

- What should nonfederal governments, the private sector, and citizens do to help secure the homeland?[136]

In 2003, the Department of Homeland Security was created from the Office of Homeland Security.[137] This was considered the most noteworthy transformation of the U.S. government in more than 50 years, primarily because it transformed and realigned "the current confusing patchwork of government activities into a single department whose primary mission is to protect our homeland."[138]

Definition of Homeland Security

The 2002 National Strategy for Homeland Security defined homeland security as follows:

> Homeland security is a concerted national effort to prevent terrorist attacks within the United States, reduce America's vulnerability to terrorism, and minimize the damage and recover from attacks that do occur.[139]

homeland security:
a unified national effort to prevent terrorist attacks within the United States, lessen America's vulnerability to terrorism, and minimize the damage resulting from such attacks.

This strategy outlined a framework for achieving homeland security, which comprised four general goals: (1) Prevent and disrupt terrorist attacks; (2) protect the American people, critical infrastructure, and key resources; (3) respond to and recover from incidents that do occur; and (4) continue to strengthen the foundation to ensure long-term success.[140]

Upon examining the literature on homeland security, Christopher Bellavita recognized the various definitions of homeland security implemented since the September 11 attacks.[141] These definitions have been developed to address the events that have been the focus of homeland security programming; they include terrorism, all hazards, terrorism and

TABLE **15.4**   Definitions of Homeland Security

HOMELAND SECURITY DEFINITIONS

1. Terrorism. Homeland security is a concerted national effort by federal, state, and local governments, by the private sector, and by individuals to prevent terrorist attacks within the United States, reduce America's vulnerability to terrorism, and minimize the damage and recover from attacks that do occur.

2. All Hazards. Homeland security is a concerted national effort to prevent and disrupt terrorist attacks, protect against man-made and natural hazards, and respond to and recover from incidents that do occur.

3. Terrorism and Catastrophes. Homeland security is what the Department of Homeland Security—supported by other federal agencies—does to prevent, respond to, and recover from terrorist and catastrophic events that affect the security of the United States.

4. Jurisdictional Hazards. Homeland security means something different in each jurisdiction. It is a locally-directed effort to prevent and prepare for incidents most likely to threaten the safety and security of its citizens.

5. Meta Hazards. Homeland security is a national effort to prevent or mitigate any social trend or threat that can disrupt the long-term stability of the American way of life.

6. National Security. Homeland security is an element of national security that works with the other instruments of national power to protect the sovereignty, territory, domestic population, and critical infrastructure of the United States against threats and aggression.

7. Security *Uber Alles*. Homeland security is a symbol used to justify government efforts to curtail civil liberties.

Source: Bellavita, C. (2008). Changing homeland security: What is homeland security? *Homeland Security Affairs, 4,* 1–2.

catastrophes, jurisdictional hazards, meta hazards, national security, and security *uber alles* (see Table 15.4 for a detailed list of these definitions). For instance, under the definition of *jurisdictional hazards*, homeland security is founded more on a local jurisdiction and its experiences with various hazards (e.g., hurricanes, wildfires, floods, tornados) rather than on a federal decree.

Homeland Security Organizational Network

Since the creation of the Department of Homeland Security (DHS), there have been various modifications given the evolving nature of recognizing, and addressing, the range of threats faced by the United States. Eleven days after the September 11 attacks, Pennsylvania governor Tom Ridge was appointed the first director of the Office of Homeland Security. In November 2002, Congress passed the Homeland Security Act, making the DHS into a stand-alone, Cabinet-level department. In February 2005, Secretary Michael Chertoff took office and instigated a review of the DHS's operations, policies, and structures. Subsequently, additional modifications were adopted, including the Post-Katrina Emergency Management Reform Act of 2006 and the Security Accountability for Every Port (SAFE Port) Act of 2006.[142] In 2013, Jeh Johnson was named the fourth secretary of DHS. Figure 15.5 shows the department's organizational chart.

Agencies Responsible for Homeland Security

In this section, we provide a brief summary of some key agencies within the DHS, including the Transportation Security Administration, U.S. Customs and Border Protection, U.S. Citizenship and Immigration Services, the U.S. Secret Service, FEMA, and the U.S. Coast Guard (see Table 15.5).

Department of Homeland Security: a Cabinet department of the U.S. federal government, established in 2003 in response to the September 11 attacks; main responsibilities include protecting the United States from terrorist attacks and responding to terrorist attacks, man-made accidents, and natural disasters.

REUTERS/Brendan McDermid

A Transportation Security Administration agent works at JFK airport in the Queens borough of New York City.

TRANSPORTATION SECURITY ADMINISTRATION. With the passage of the Aviation and Transportation Security Act, the Transportation Security Administration (TSA) was established after the September 11 attacks to strengthen the security of the country's transportation system. The TSA issued three mandates: (1) take responsibility for security for all types of transportation; (2) recruit, assess, hire, train, and deploy security officers for 450 commercial airports; and (3) provide screening of all checked luggage for explosives. In March 2003, the TSA was moved from the Department of Transportation to the DHS.[143] Most people assume that the TSA is primarily concerned with airport security; as noted above, however, the TSA is responsible for all types of transportation, including aviation, waterways, rail, highways, public transportation, and pipelines.[144]

U.S. CITIZENSHIP AND IMMIGRATION SERVICES. In 2003, the services and functions of the U.S. Immigration and Naturalization Service (INS) were moved to the DHS, and the department was subsequently renamed the U.S. Citizenship and Immigration Services (USCIS).[148] As noted above, the enforcement and inspection functions of INS were moved to CBP.[148] USCIS is responsible for administration of immigration and naturalization adjudication functions. Some of these functions include granting U.S. citizenship, processing immigrant visa and naturalization petitions, adjudicating asylum and refugee applications, and issuing documents for employment authorization.[149]

Transportation Security Administration (TSA): provides security for all types of transportation; recruits, assesses, hires, trains, and deploys security officers for commercial airports; and provides screening of all checked luggage.

U.S. Citizenship and Immigration Services (USCIS): responsible for administration of immigration and naturalization adjudication functions.

U.S. Immigration and Customs Enforcement (ICE): focuses on identifying criminal activities and vulnerabilities that may be a threat to the country.

U.S. IMMIGRATION AND CUSTOMS ENFORCEMENT. U.S. Immigration and Customs Enforcement (ICE) was created as the primary investigative arm of the DHS.[150] ICE was created by merging the law enforcement branch of the INS, the intelligence and investigative sections of the former U.S. Customs Service, and the U.S. Federal Protective Services.[151] While CBP focuses on securing U.S. borders, ICE's responsibilities go beyond the borders. Thus, "ICE attempts to identify criminal activities and vulnerabilities that pose a threat to the nation, as well as enforcing economic, transportation, and infrastructure security."[152] The ICE Strategic Plan includes preventing terrorism and improving security; protecting the boarders against illicit trade, travel, and finance; and protecting the borders through enhanced interior immigration enforcement.[153]

U.S. SECRET SERVICE. The U.S. Secret Service was created in 1865 to suppress counterfeit currency. After the assassination of President William McKinley in 1901, the Secret Service became responsible for the protection of the president. In 1984, Congress passed legislation making the fraudulent use of credit and debit cards a federal violation; the Secret Service was authorized to investigate these violations. Under the PATRIOT Act of 2001 (discussed below), the Secret Service was authorized to investigate fraud and similar activities related to computers. The U.S. Secret Service was transferred from the Department of the Treasury to the DHS in 2003.[154] As noted in its mission statement,

the United States Secret Service is to safeguard the nation's financial infrastructure and payment systems to preserve the integrity of the economy, and to protect national leaders, visiting heads of state and government, designated sites and National Special Security Events.[155]

FIGURE **15.5** Organizational Chart for the Department of Homeland Security

U.S. DEPARTMENT OF HOMELAND SECURITY

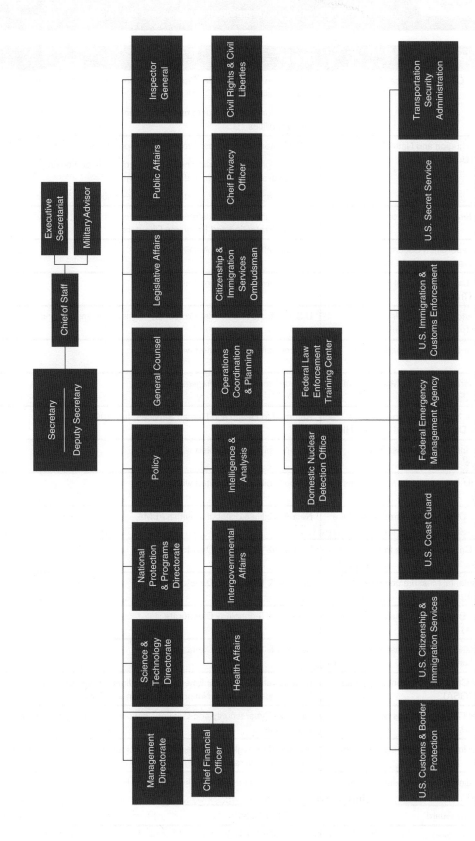

Source: Department of Homeland Security. (2016). *Organizational Chart*. Retrieved from http://www.dhs.gov/xabout/structure/editorial_0644.shtm .

TABLE 15.5

Agencies Transferred to the Department of Homeland Security

LEAD UP TO 9/11	TODAY
The U.S. Customs Service (Treasury)	U.S. Customs and Border Protection—inspection, border and ports of entry responsibilities U.S. Immigration and Customs Enforcement—customs law enforcement responsibilities
The Immigration and Naturalization Service (Justice)	U.S. Customs and Border Protection—inspection functions and the U.S. Border Patrol U.S. Immigration and Customs Enforcement—immigration law enforcement: detention and removal, intelligence, and investigations U.S. Citizenship and Immigration Services—adjudications and benefits programs
The Federal Protective Service	U.S. Immigration and Customs Enforcement until 2009; currently resides within the National Protection and Programs Directorate
The Transportation Security Administration (Transportation)	Transportation Security Administration
Federal Law Enforcement Training Center (Treasury)	Federal Law Enforcement Training Center
Animal and Plant Health Inspection Service (part) (Agriculture)	U.S. Customs and Border Protection—agricultural imports and entry inspections
Office for Domestic Preparedness (Justice)	Responsibilities distributed within FEMA
The Federal Emergency Management Agency (FEMA)	Federal Emergency Management Agency
Strategic National Stockpile and the National Disaster Medical System (HHS)	Returned to Health and Human Services, July 2004
Nuclear Incident Response Team (Energy)	Responsibilities distributed within FEMA
Domestic Emergency Support Teams (Justice)	Responsibilities distributed within FEMA
National Domestic Preparedness Office (FBI)	Responsibilities distributed within FEMA
CBRN Countermeasures Programs (Energy)	Science & Technology Directorate
Environmental Measurements Laboratory (Energy)	Science & Technology Directorate
National BW Defense Analysis Center (Defense)	Science & Technology Directorate
Plum Island Animal Disease Center (Agriculture)	Science & Technology Directorate
Federal Computer Incident Response Center (GSA)	United States Computer Emergency Readiness Team, Office of Cybersecurity and Communications in the National Protection and Programs Directorate
National Communications System (Defense)	Office of Cybersecurity and Communications in the National Protection and Programs Directorate
National Infrastructure Protection Center (FBI)	Dispersed throughout the Department, including Office of Operations Coordination and Office of Infrastructure Protection
Energy Security and Assurance Program (Energy)	Integrated into the Office of Infrastructure Protection
U.S. Coast Guard	U.S. Coast Guard
U.S. Secret Service	U.S. Secret Service

Source: Department of Homeland Security. (2015). *Who joined DHS*. Retrieved from http://www.dhs.gov/who-joined-dhs.

FEDERAL EMERGENCY MANAGEMENT AGENCY. The Federal Emergency Management Agency (FEMA) was created under the Robert T. Stafford Disaster Relief and Emergency Assistance Act of 1988. This act established the statutory authority for most federal response activities to prepare for, protect against, respond to, recover from, and alleviate all types of hazards. In 2003, FEMA became part of the DHS, along with many other agencies.[156] FEMA focuses on four initiatives: (1) Foster a whole community approach to emergency management nationwide, (2) build the country's ability to stabilize and recover from a catastrophic event, (3) build unity of effort and common strategic understanding among the emergency management team, and (4) enhance FEMA's ability to learn and innovate as an organization.[157] When the president declares an area a disaster, FEMA is then initiated to respond. FEMA activities include both short- and long-term responses; these activities also include coordinating with state and local personnel.[158]

U.S. COAST GUARD. Established in 1790, the U.S. Coast Guard's primary responsibility was to enforce the country's maritime laws, interests, and environment. The U.S. Coast Guard is one of the five armed forces of the United States; it is now the only military organization within the DHS.[159] The Coast Guard's homeland security role includes the following:

- Protecting ports, the flow of commerce, and the marine transportation system from terrorism

- Maintaining maritime borderer security against illegal drugs, illegal aliens, firearms, and weapons of mass destruction

- Ensuring that the United States can rapidly deploy and resupply military assets by maintaining the Coast Guard at a high state of readiness, as well as by keeping marine transportation open for other military services

- Protecting against illegal fishing and indiscriminate destruction of living marine resources

- Preventing and responding to oil and hazardous material spills

- Coordinating efforts and intelligence with federal, state, and local agencies[160]

Bureaucratic Problems and Solutions

Following the September 11 attacks, the United States took swift action to implement various measures to defend the country from further terrorist attacks. Numerous measures were established, including a major governmental reorganization for such a defense, the DHS. In view of the Boston Marathon bombing on April 15, 2013, there is a question as to whether the government's defense efforts have been effective. Further, "policy discussions of homeland security issues are driven not by rigorous analysis but by fear, perceptions of past mistakes, pork-barrel politics, and insistence on an invulnerability that cannot possibly be achieved."[161]

Since its establishment, there have been problems with the DHS, which is not unusual for a newly developed agency or organization. Larry Gaines and Victor Kappeler noted that one such problem is when conflicting political interests overshadow the organizational imperative. "Politicians were all too often more interested in managing appearances as opposed to solving real problems."[162] The White House and Congress have significant oversight responsibility, as well as authority over the DHS. For instance, about 80 committees and subcommittees in the House and Senate have some form of oversight responsibilities regarding homeland security. Many have realized that this is a problem and have suggested that the secretary of the DHS be given more autonomy to manage the department. However, some politicians are not willing to give up this oversight, especially

U.S. Secret Service: responsible for safeguarding the country's financial infrastructure and payment systems, as well as protecting national leaders and visiting heads of state and government.

Federal Emergency Management Agency (FEMA): focuses on emergency management and recovery from a catastrophic event on a local and national level.

U.S. Coast Guard: the only military organization within the Department of Homeland Security; its role includes protecting ports, maintaining border security, and coordinating intelligence with various government entities.

OMAR MATEEN

John Panella / Alamy Stock Photo

Below is a modified CNN timeline of the Orlando, Florida nightclub shooting:

- Sunday (June 12, 2016), 2:02 a.m. ET: Shooting erupts at Pulse, a gay nightclub in Orlando, Florida. There are approximately 320 that evening enjoying the club's "Latin flavor" event. An officer working extra duty in full uniform at the club responds. He and two officers nearby open fire on the shooter, and a gun battle ensues. The shooter goes inside the club, where a hostage situation develops. Over 100 officers from Orange County Sheriff's Office and the Orlando Police Department respond to the scene.

- 2:09 a.m. ET: A standoff follows. Police say they had to wait three hours to access the situation, get armored vehicles on the scene, and ensure they had enough personnel.

- 2:22 a.m. ET: Shooter calls 911 to pledge allegiance to ISIS. He also mentions the Boston Marathon bombers.

- Approximately 5:00 a.m. ET: Heavily armed SWAT team members use an armored vehicle to smash down a door at the club, clearing the way for some 30 people inside to flee to safety. SWAT officers confront the suspect in the doorway, then shoot and kill him.[164]

At least 49 people were killed that evening, and over 50 individuals were injured. It was the worst mass shooting in U.S. history. As the news unfolded, many were asking what could motivate someone to engage in such a horrific crime.

Omar Mir Seddique Mateen was 29 years old. His parents are from Afghanistan; he was born in New York but lived in an apartment in Fort Pierce, Florida. Interviews

People across the world, such as here in Seoul, South Korea, held vigils for the victims in the Orlando, Florida shooting.

with coworkers revealed that he was "scary." This was not just sometimes, but all the time. He had some anger management issues. Issues that would upset him revolved around women, race, or religion. In 2013, Mateen was interviewed two times by federal agents after co-workers reported he made "inflammatory" comments about radical Islamic propaganda. The next year, he raised concerns with the FBI because of his ties with an American who traveled to the Middle East to become a suicide bomber.

Sitora Yusufiy, Mateen's ex-wife, reported that he was a violent man and beat her. Not only did he physically abuse her, but he also isolated her from her family. They were married only a few months. They officially divorced in 2011. Mateen's father told reporters that Omar became enraged after a same-sex couple kissed in front of his family.[165]

On January 17, 2017 Mateen's wife at the time of the shooting, Noor Salman, was charged under anti-terrorism laws.

THINK ABOUT IT:

1. Was this a terrorist act?

2. Was this a hate crime?

3. Frida Ghitis of CNN asked this very question: terrorism or homophobia? Her answer was "both."[166] Do you agree?

when such "authority over some aspect of homeland security always plays well with their electorates."[163]

As noted previously, the establishment of the DHS—a major governmental reorganization—occurred in a rapid fashion. This resulted in a great deal of confusion among the newly formed departments and other agencies. Many would assume that the DHS has exclusive responsibility for homeland security; however, other agencies such as the Department of Defense, the FBI, and the Treasury Department also have major interests in homeland security. A related problem in this rapid reorganization is mission distortion. Those agencies involved in this reorganization not only acquired new responsibilities but also were expected to continue with their agency's missions prior to the merge. Thus, "homeland security duties, for the most part, were simply added to the agencies' original or traditional responsibilities."[167]

ISSUES RELATED TO CIVIL LIBERTIES

In recent years, efforts to counter terrorism have posed some serious challenges for civil liberties. For instance, some countries have engaged in torture to counter terrorism; other countries have disregarded monitoring of detention centers to prevent torture. Further, other countries have returned persons suspected of being involved with terrorist activities to countries where they may be tortured for these activities; this is a violation of international law, or *non-refoulement*. In this section, we briefly review some of the serious challenges to civil liberties as they relate to counterterrorism efforts.[168]

The Torture Debate

Gus Martin highlighted the issues concerning whether counterterrorist methods of torture should be used on terrorist suspects. This came to the forefront when there were reports of abuse at the U.S.-controlled Abu Ghraib prison, outside of Baghdad.[169] Once the Abu Ghraib prison was under U.S. control, there were several thousand civilian prisoners, including women and teenagers. They were picked up during random military sweeps and at highway checkpoints. These prisoners fell into three broadly designated categories: common criminals, security detainees suspected of "crimes against the coalition," and a few suspected "high-value" leaders of the insurgency against the coalition forces.

General Janis Karpinski, an Army reserve brigadier general, was named commander of the 800th Military Police Brigade and put in charge of the military prisons in Iraq. Later, General Karpinski was suspended and an investigation into the Army's prison system launched. Major General Antonio Taguba submitted his report, not meant for public release, on the conditions of the prison.[170] His report included the following:

> Breaking chemical lights and pouring the phosphoric liquid on detainees; pouring cold water on naked detainees; beating detainees with a broom handle and a chair; threatening male detainees with rape; allowing a military police guard to stitch the wound of a detainee who was injured after being slammed against the wall in his cell; sodomizing a detainee with a chemical light and perhaps a broom stick, and using military working dogs to frighten and intimidate detainees with threats of attack, and in one instance actually biting a detainee.[171]

Subsequently, incriminating photographs were released, several of which were broadcast on CBS's *60 Minutes II*. As a result, various criminal courts martial were convened and numerous guards convicted and imprisoned.

mission distortion: occurred when those agencies involved in the reorganization of the Department of Homeland Security acquired new responsibilities and also were to continue with their agency's missions prior to the merge.

According to Martin, the torture debate continues. On one side is the issue that the practice of torture has historically been disdained by the United States, both morally and as a questionable interrogation technique. On the other side, however, is that during a war on terrorism, one needs to consider the definition of torture. Further, one needs to determine whether certain forms of coercion, whether physical or psychological, are justifiable in this context. Martin then asks whether the following techniques should be considered torture:

- Waterboarding, during which prisoners feel as though they are drowning

- Sexual degradation, whereby prisoners are forced to pose in painful positions for performance of sex acts

- Stress positions, whereby prisoners are forced to pose in painful positions for extended periods

- Creating a chronic state of fear

- Environmental stress, accomplished by adjusting a detention cell's temperature

- Sleep deprivation

- Disorientation about one's whereabouts or the time of day

- Sensory deprivation, such as depriving suspects of sound or light[172]

He concludes this discussion by noting that policymakers are still involved in this debate and disagree as to whether certain situations necessitate the use of such techniques on terrorist suspects.

Human Rights

human rights:
universal values and legal guarantees that protect individuals against actions or omissions, primarily by government agents, that infringe on their fundamental freedoms, entitlements, and human dignity.

The United Nations has defined human rights as universal values and legal guarantees that protect individuals against actions or omissions, primarily by government agents, that infringe on their fundamental freedoms, entitlements, and human dignity. Further, these human rights include "respect for, and protection and fulfillment of, civil, cultural, economic, political and social rights as well as the right to development."[173] These rights are universal, meaning they are owed to all human beings.

Generally, there are two controversial areas involving the intersection of human rights with terrorism and homeland security.[174] The first is that terrorist attacks on innocent people violate the right of people to be free from such violence. Terrorists, however, justify their use of physical violence by maintaining that people are not innocent, because they live within the governmental system.[175] The second is that governments must recognize the human rights of their adversaries. Governments often justify inhumane actions against terrorists by arguing that such terrorists have forfeited their right to humane treatment due to their use of violence.[176]

DOD Photo / Alamy Stock Photo

U.S. Army military police escort a detainee to a cell in Guantanamo, Cuba.

The United Nations stressed that the issue of human rights within the context of terrorism and counterterrorism measures has often focused on the protection of civil and political rights. There has been little attention to how terrorism and counterterrorism measures affect economic, social, and cultural rights. Thus, "greater efforts must . . . be made to understand and address the linkages between terrorism and the enjoyment of economic, social, and cultural rights."[177]

The Constitution

The U.S. Constitution is the supreme law in the United States. It establishes the organizational framework of the government, including the relationship between federal and state governments, as well as U.S. citizens. The Bill of Rights, the first 10 amendments to the Constitution, also regulates the authority of government. Cole and Dempsey argue that some of the United States' fundamental rights are being challenged by new government policies focused on addressing terrorism. These fundamental rights include the presumption of innocence, the right to counsel, the right to confront witnesses, the right of access to the courts, and privacy rights.[178] One of the most controversial of these new government policies is the USA PATRIOT Act (discussed below).

An interesting facet involves the Equal Protection Clause for noncitizens:

> It might be argued that because noncitizens do not have a vested interest in American society the way that citizens do, they are more apt to commit acts of terrorism, even if they are no more practically capable of doing so. And, therefore, the distinction between citizens and aliens in counterterrorism law is appropriate. But this is plainly a false premise.[179]

Cohen concluded that the compromise to the Equal Protection Law after the September 11 attacks is not only problematic from a practical perspective when combating terrorism; it also undermines the most basic foundational principle of American government. Thus, the court needs to renew its commitment to the concept of equality under the law.

USA PATRIOT Act of 2001

Following the attacks on September 11, 2001, Congress responded quickly by passing the Uniting and Strengthening America by Providing Appropriate Tools Required to Intercept and Obstruct Terrorism Act (i.e., the USA PATRIOT Act) on October 26, 2001. Initially, the USA PATRIOT Act consists of 10 sections, or titles, that provide new powers for government operations.[180] The act focuses on four significant areas of concern for homeland security: (1) the collection of communications information and data, (2) conducting foreign intelligence investigations, (3) controlling money laundering, and (4) funding and enhancing national border security.[181] Examples of these provisions include the following:

- Revisions of the standards for government surveillance, including federal law enforcement access to private records

- Enhancement of electronic surveillance authority, such as tapping into e-mail, electronic address books, and computers

- The use of "roving wiretaps" by investigators, which permit surveillance of an individual's telephone conversations on any phone anywhere in the country

- Requiring banks to identify sources of money deposited in some private accounts and requiring foreign banks to report on suspicious transactions

USA PATRIOT Act: focuses on collecting communications information and data, conducting foreign intelligence investigations, controlling money laundering, and funding and enhancing national border security.

- The use of nationwide search warrants

- Deportation of immigrants who raise money for terrorist organizations

- The detention of immigrants without charge for up to 1 week on suspicion of supporting terrorism[182]

This act has sparked a great deal of controversy, especially those provisions that allow for intelligence gathering and sharing. Various groups, from constitutional conservatives to civil libertarian activists, were concerned that the law would encroach on civil freedoms, particularly those that protect citizens from government infringement on those freedoms guaranteed by the Constitution and the Bill of Rights.[183] However, there are others that are of the position that the act does not infringe on individuals' civil freedoms. Further, some emphasize the need to be less emotional and partisan when analyzing the provisions of the act:

> The Patriot Act headlines and sound bites that have permeated the print media and airwaves have created genuine public concern in the United States. . . . It is important for lawyers and scholars to stand back and look at the exact provisions of the Patriot Act, consider how they relate to established law, and identify where these provisions are consistent with the Constitution and case law and where they may have reached beyond the boundaries.[184]

In May 2011, President Obama approved a four-year extension of expiring provisions of the PATRIOT Act. These three provisions included extending the government's authority to conduct "roving wiretaps," allowing the government to access personal records of terrorism suspects (i.e., the "library provision"), and providing the government power to investigate foreigners who have no known affiliation with terrorist groups (i.e., the "lone-wolf" provision).[185] On June 1, 2015, the PATRIOT Act expired. A major issue was in reference to the bulk collection of telecommunication data on U.S. citizens by American intelligence agencies. On June 2, 2015, the USA Freedom Act was enacted. This restored several provisions of the PATRIOT Act.[186]

LEARNING CHECK 15.3

1. The establishment of the _____ was considered the most noteworthy transformation of the U.S. government in more than 50 years.

2. The problem of _____ arose when agencies involved in the reorganization not only acquired new responsibilities but also were to continue with their agencies' missions prior to the merge.

3. One of the most controversial of the new government policies after 9/11 is the _____.

Answers located at www.edge.sagepub.com/schram2e

POLICY IMPLICATIONS

When tragic events occur, such as the San Bernardino and Orlando shootings, the topic of gun control inevitably is raised as a policy that needs to be revisited in this country. After the December 2, 2015, shooting in San Bernardino, President Obama stated the following:

> The one thing we do know is that we have a pattern now of mass shootings in this country that has no parallel anywhere else in the world. And there are some steps we could take not to eliminate every one of these mass shootings, but to improve the odds that they don't happen as frequently: common-sense gun safety laws, stronger background checks.[187]

After the June 12, 2016, shooing in Orlando, President Obama stated the following:

> My concern is that we start getting into a debate, as has happened in the past, which is an either/or debate, and the suggestion is either we think about something as terrorism and we ignore the problems with easy access to firearms. Or it's all about firearms and we ignore the role, the very real role, that organizations like [the Islamic State] have in generating extremist views inside this country. It's not an either/or. It's a both/and.[188]

The term *gun control* is a very broad term. It can refer to restricting the types of firearms that can be sold and bought, who can possess or sell them, as well as where and how they can be stored or carried.[189] Interestingly, one journalist argued that some have maintained, particularly gun-control activists to get rid of the term. This is due to some associating *gun control* with confiscation. Some possible alternatives include "gun-violence prevention," "gun safety," and "firearms regulation." However, these alternatives have failed to become are part of our conversation regarding this topic.[190]

Over the past 25 years, Americans have revealed less support for stricter gun control. Thus, "[w]hile some high-profile shootings have resulted in calls for increased restrictions, that support has proved fleeting thus far. Gun control is one of the most sharply divisive issues in the U.S. today."[191] Table 15.6 provides a summary of the "pros" and "cons" for gun control.

TABLE 15.6   The Pro and Con Arguments on Gun Control

PRO	CON
The Second Amendment is not an unlimited right to own guns.	The Second Amendment of the U.S. Constitution protects individual gun ownership.
More gun control laws would reduce gun deaths.	Gun control laws do not deter crime; gun ownership deters crime.
High-capacity magazines should be banned because they too often turn murder into mass murder.	Gun control laws infringe upon the right to self-defense and deny people a sense of safety.
More gun control laws are needed to protect women from domestic abusers and stalkers.	Gun control laws, especially those that try to ban "assault weapons," infringe upon the right to own guns for hunting and sport.
Guns are rarely used in self-defense.	Gun control laws will not prevent criminals from obtaining guns or breaking laws.
Legally owned guns are frequently stolen and used by criminals.	Gun control laws give too much power to the government and may result in government tyranny and the government taking away all guns from citizens.
Gun control laws would reduce the societal costs associated with gun violence.	Gun control laws such as background checks and micro-stamping are an invasion of privacy.
A majority of adults, including gun owners, support commonsense gun control such as background checks, bans on assault weapons, and bans on high-capacity magazines.	More gun control is unnecessary because relatively few people are killed by guns.

(Continued)

TABLE 15.6   (Continued)

PRO	CON
More gun control leads to fewer suicides.	Gun control laws and lower gun ownership rates to not prevent suicides.
Enacting gun control laws such as mandatory safety features would reduce the number of accidental gun deaths.	More gun control is not needed; education about guns and gun safety is needed to prevent accidental gun deaths.
The presence of a gun makes a conflict more likely to become violent.	Gun control laws would prevent citizens from protecting themselves from foreign invaders.
Armed civilians are unlikely to stop crimes and are more likely to make dangerous situations, including mass shootings, more deadly.	Strict gun control laws do not work in Mexico and will not work in the United States.
Countries with restrictive gun control laws have lower gun homicide and suicide rates than the United States.	Gun control laws are racist.
The Second Amendment was intended to protect the right of militias to own guns, not the right of individuals.	The Second Amendment was intended to protect gun ownership of all able-bodied men so that they could participate in the militia to keep the peace and defend the country if needed.
Civilians, including hunters, should not own military-grade firearms or firearm accessories.	Gun control efforts have proved ineffective.

Source: ProCon.org. (n.d.). *Should more gun control laws be enacted?*

CONCLUSION

An essential purpose of this chapter is for readers to obtain a greater understanding of certain types of crime that have, in recent years, received significant attention in the media as well as in criminal justice courses. Criminal activities such as terrorism and hate crimes reveal the multicultural and multinational facets of crime.

The first section of this chapter discussed hate crimes. We started this section by attempting to answer the question "What is a hate crime?" It is essential for readers to realize that an incident designated as a hate crime is a conventional offense (e.g., murder, vandalism, robbery) with an additional factor of bias. Hate crimes must be motivated by some form of bias, such as the victim's race, religion, disability, sexual orientation, or ethnicity/national origin. Further, various types of hate crimes are identified by this particular motivation. The next portion provided a general overview of various anti-hate-crime legislation, such as the Hate Crime Statistics Act of 1990, the Violent Crime Control and Law Enforcement Act of 1994, and the Matthew Shepard and James Byrd Jr. Hate Crimes Prevention Act of 2009. One theoretical framework that has been applied to understanding hate crimes is routine activities theory. This section was followed by a summary of multicide, or the multiple killing of individuals. We discuss the various categories of mass killers while focusing on school attacks.

The next section of this chapter presented an overview of terrorism. These types of criminal activities have received a tremendous amount of media attention and government response, especially after the September 11 attacks. Again, we started this section with the question "What is terrorism?" It is interesting to note that there is no common definition of terrorism, even among the various agencies in the U.S. government. Next, we briefly reviewed various types of terrorism, such as state-sponsored and religious terrorism, as well as the extent of terrorist activities. The following portion of the chapter provided students with a brief historical context of modern terrorism. While many may consider terrorism a relatively "new" experience, this section illustrates that terrorism has deep historical roots. A noteworthy aspect to terrorism is the fluidity and constant flexibility of the organizational structure, as well as the financial support; this is especially evident given the major advances in technology. We concluded this section on terrorism with a few theoretical explanations, including routine activities and game theory.

The last section in this chapter began with an overview of homeland security, including its origins and definition. Next, we reviewed the organizational network by focusing on some of the agencies responsible for homeland security, such as TSA, CBP, ICE, and FEMA. With the establishment of the DHS, and the merging of these various agencies, there have been some bureaucratic problems, such as conflicting political interests and mission distortion. We concluded this section with a discussion of how counterterrorism efforts have raised some challenges for civil liberties; especially controversial is the USA PATRIOT Act of 2001.

At the beginning of this chapter, we presented the case study of the Charleston, South Carolina shootings. This was designated Dylann Roof was convicted of 33 hate crimes. What distinguishes this from a "conventional" mass shooting is the motivation. As illustrated in Roof's manifesto as well as photographs of him posted on the internet, his crimes were motivated by his bias against African-Americans.

KEY TERMS

Campus Hate Crimes Right to Know Act of 1997, 430

Church Arson Prevention Act of 1996, 430

criminal terrorism, 439

Department of Homeland Security, 451

dissident terrorism, 439

domestic terrorism, 447

Federal Emergency Management Agency (FEMA), 455

fundraising, 446

game theory, 449

Hate Crime Statistics Act of 1990, 430

hate crimes, 425

homeland security, 450

human rights, 458

Matthew Shepard and James Byrd Jr. Hate Crimes Prevention Act of 2009, 431

mission distortion, 457

model state legislation for hate crimes/violence against people experiencing homelessness, 432

money laundering, 446

National Counterterrorism Center, 000

religious terrorism, 439

state-sponsored terrorism, 438

Transportation Security Administration (TSA), 452

U.S. Citizenship and Immigration Services (USCIS), 452

U.S. Coast Guard, 455

U.S. Immigration and Customs Enforcement (ICE), 452

U.S. Secret Service, 452

USA PATRIOT Act, 459

Violent Crime Control and Law Enforcement Act of 1994, 430

DISCUSSION QUESTIONS

1. What are the various motivations associated with hate crimes?

2. What are some of the major legislative responses to hate crimes?

3. How would you apply routine activities theory to hate crimes?

4. What are some key features of terrorist activities?

5. What are some of the various motivations for engaging in terrorist activities?

6. What are the different organization networks associated with terrorist groups?

7. How do some terrorist groups finance their activities?

8. How would you apply routine activities theory to terrorist activities?

9. What is the purpose of homeland security?

10. What are some of the agencies that make up the Department of Homeland Security?

11. What are some of the bureaucratic problems associated with the Department of Homeland Security?

12. What are some of the controversial issues and challenges associated with counterterrorism efforts?

WEB RESOURCES

FBI's Terrorism

https://www.fbi.gov/about-us/investigate/terrorism

Hate Crime Statistics

https://www.fbi.gov/news/stories/2015/november/latest-hate-crime-statistics-available

Southern Poverty Law Center

https://www.splcenter.org/

Department of Homeland Security

https://www.dhs.gov/

WANT A BETTER GRADE ON YOUR NEXT TEST?

Get the tools you need to sharpen your study skills:

SAGE edge offers a robust online environment featuring an impressive array of tools and resources for review, study, and further exploration, keeping both instructors and students on the cutting edge of teaching and learning. Learn more at **edge.sagepub.com/schram2e**.

FOR FURTHER EXPLORATION AND APPLICATION, VISIT THE STUDENT STUDY SITE:

Authorities Probe Alleged Hate Crime Against Native American Kids

Louisiana Moves to Extend Hate Crime Protection for Police Officers

When to Call Attacks 'Terrorism'

Extreme hatred: Revisiting the hate crime and terrorism relationship to determine whether they are "close cousins" or "distant relatives"

Race and mass murder in the U. S.: A social and behavioral analysis

History of Terrorism History Channel

The Psychology of Hate

Oklahoma Teen 'Laughed' While Describing Killing Five Family Members as Part of Brothers' Gruesome Mass Murder Plan

Does Corruption Create or Help Fuel Global Terrorism?

Mass Murder

First Mass Murder in History

Jonestown

Homeland Security

Matthew Shepard

PREMIUM VIDEO:

Check out the Interactive eBook for premium videos, including videos from author Stephen Tibbetts, who discusses real-world examples and strange crimes; and videos from former offenders, who share their stories from a first-person view, and touch on key theories and concepts from the chapter.

CHAPTER 16

Drugs and Crime

AP Photo/Adrian Sainz

INTRODUCTION

Over the past few decades, there has been an increase in public attention on drug and alcohol abuse. For instance, some of the more popular antidrug and anti-alcohol slogans include "Just say no"; "This is your brain. This is your brain on drugs. Any questions?"; "Say not to pot"; "Hugs not drugs"; "Stay alive. Don't drink and drive"; "If you choose the booze, you lose"; and "Get high on life, not on drugs." During this time, there also has been tremendous emphasis on law enforcement strategies to combat illegal drug possession and sales in the United States. This has had some significant effects on the criminal justice system—from arrest to incarceration rates.[4] For instance, in 2014, there were 1,561,231 arrests for drug abuse violations and 1,117,852 arrests for driving under the influence. [5] In 2015, 46.3% of all federal prisoners were serving time for drug offenses;[6] in 2013, about 16% of prisoners under state jurisdiction were serving time for drug offenses.[7] This does not, however, include those individuals who committed a crime while under the influence of alcohol and/or drugs or those who committed a crime to support their drug habit.

Drugs (including alcohol) and crime go hand in hand, and this chapter illustrates that relationship for students. The chapter begins with a section on the various types of drugs. Next, we review trends over the past century regarding drug use, as well as society's response. Then, we examine the primary ways drugs contribute to the increasing crime rate, with an emphasis on violent crime. The next section of this chapter presents different strategies that have been implemented to address the drug problem in the United States, including eradication, interdiction, and drug courts. The chapter concludes with recommendations for future policies regarding drugs and alcohol.

COMMONLY ABUSED DRUGS

Depressants

With the exception of alcohol, most depressants are prescription drugs.[8] Depressants slow down, or "depress," the normal activity of the central nervous system (i.e., the brain and spinal cord). Thus, physicians often prescribe depressants for people who are anxious or cannot sleep.[9] Below, we briefly discuss various types of depressants that are routinely abused, including alcohol, barbiturates, and tranquillizers (including benzodiazepines).

ALCOHOL. In 2014, 52.7% of Americans age 12 and older reported using alcohol at least once in a 30-day period; 59.6% young adults between the ages of 18 to 25 were current alcohol users; and 11.5% of adolescents between the ages of 12 to 17 were current users of alcohol. Table 16.1 lists the general effects of alcohol, ranging by dose. In terms of binge alcohol use, less than one quarter (23.0%) of people aged 12 or older reported being binge alcohol users in the past 30 days. Figure 16.2 is a breakdown, by age groups, of binge drinking from 2002 to 2014. While it appears that reported binge drinking has decreased slightly for those 12 to 17 years old and 18 to 25 years old, individuals between the ages of 26 and older appear to remain steady.[10]

In this society, alcohol is often the drug of choice. Kuhn and her colleagues argue that this is clearly evident when one critically observes how alcohol is advertised in the United States:

LEARNING OBJECTIVES

As you read this chapter, consider the following questions:

- Distinguish between the different types of drugs.

- Identify trends pertaining to alcohol use in the United States.

- Describe key factors associated with the various trends of substance use in the United States.

- Summarize the key links between drugs and crime.

- Compare and contrast eradication and interdiction strategies.

- Discuss key aspects of drug courts, such as how they differ from traditional criminal courts.

- State the main features of harm reduction programs.

- Evaluate some of the pros and cons of maintenance and decriminalization policy.

- Determine what should be incorporated in future policies on substance use.

KENNETH SALTZMAN

On June 25, 2015, Samuel Ellis, a former star quarterback at Thomas S. Wooton High School in Maryland, drove his car off the road; it went over 100 feet airborne. The car struck a tree and flipped over. As a result, two of the passengers, his classmates, were killed and another passenger was injured. When police arrived on the scene, they found alcohol from a party, and it was still cold. Ellis pled guilty to two counts of vehicular manslaughter and was given a four-year prison sentence.[1]

A major issue surrounding this accident was where Ellis obtained the alcohol. Kenneth Saltzman, 49 years old at the time of the accident, was hosting a party for his daughter's friends. His teenage daughter invited her friends to the house. A 21-year-old bought vodka and a 17-year-old used a fake driver's license to buy beer. It was also reported that the teens were playing beer pong and were doing shots. The teenagers were in the basement while Kenneth Saltzman was upstairs.

Kenneth Saltzman pled guilty to furnishing alcohol to a minor. He was fined $2,500 for each criminal count, which amounted to a total of $5,000 in fines.[2] The parents of one of the victims, the Murks, viewed the fine "as the equivalent of nothing more than going to court, paying a parking fine and being done

with it." Following the accident, further investigation revealed that many teenagers reported that they thought of the Saltzman's house as a "safe place" to drink without the fear of getting into trouble.

Some maintain that the reason parents allow teenagers to have parties where alcohol is allowed is because "teens are going to drink anyway and it is safer at home."[3] States vary in terms of passing laws that impose liability against individuals deemed responsible for underage drinking events on property they own, lease, or control. These laws are referred to as "social host" laws. See Figure 16.1 for a summary of states that have "social host" laws.

THINK ABOUT IT:

1. Do you think some people consider drinking alcohol to be less of a problem that taking other types of drugs?

2. What do you think when you hear parents say, "I'd rather my kids drink in our home, with our knowledge, rather than somewhere else behind my back?"

3. Do you think all states should have "social host" laws?

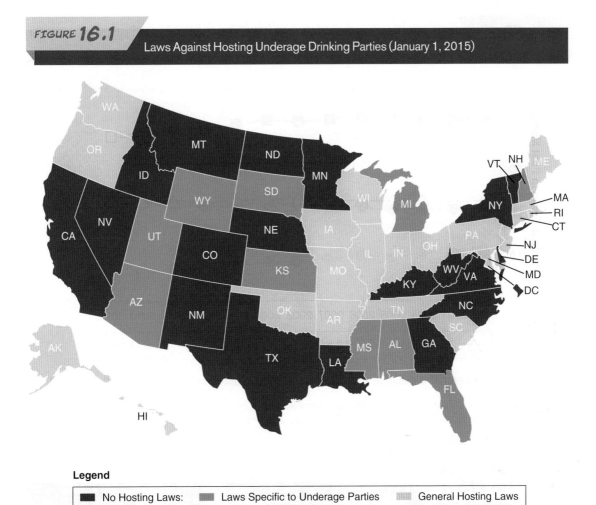

FIGURE **16.1**

Laws Against Hosting Underage Drinking Parties (January 1, 2015)

Legend

■ No Hosting Laws: ▦ Laws Specific to Underage Parties   ░ General Hosting Laws

Source: Alcohol Policy Information System. (n.d.). *Underage drinking: Prohibitions against hosting underage drinking parties.*

We use alcohol to celebrate successes, to mourn failures and losses, and to celebrate holidays of cultural and religious significance. Implicit in these uses are the hope and promise that alcohol will amplify the good times and help us through the bad ones.[11]

They also maintain that alcohol advertising is most often targeted toward adolescents and young adults, especially young men. Below are two examples of screening tests that are implemented to assess whether an individual may have an alcohol problem.

An issue related to alcohol use is **binge drinking**. According to the National Institute on Alcohol Abuse and Alcoholism, binge drinking, or heavy episodic drinking, refers to an individual who drinks so much alcohol within a two-hour period that it results in at least a.08 blood alcohol concentration.[13] According to the Substance Abuse and Mental Health Services Administration, binge drinking is defined for males as at least five drinks and for females as at least four drinks on the same occasion (i.e., at the same time or within a few hours of each other) on at least one day.[14]

One facet of binge drinking is *drinking games*. Drinking games have been known to be popular on college campuses. Binge drinking, however, does vary among student

depressants: slow down, or "depress," the normal activity of the central nervous system.

alcohol: ethanol is the only alcohol that should be consumed; rapidly absorbed through the stomach and small intestine into the bloodstream.

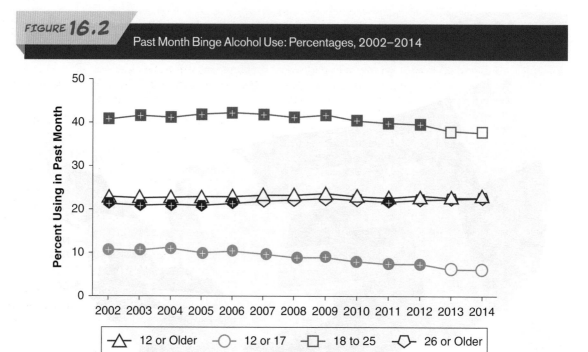

FIGURE **16.2**

Past Month Binge Alcohol Use: Percentages, 2002–2014

Legend: 12 or Older, 12 or 17, 18 to 25, 26 or Older

+ Difference between this estimate and the 2014 estimate is statistically significant at the .05 level.

Source: Substance Abuse and Mental Health Services Administration. (2015). *Results from the 2014 National Survey on Drug Use and Health: Volume I. Summary of national findings.* Washington, DC: U.S. Department of Health and Human Services, p. 20.

TABLE **16.1**

Effects of Alcohol on Behavior and Physical State

ETHANOL DOSE (OZ/HOUR)	BLOOD ETHANOL (MG/100 ML)	FUNCTION IMPAIRED	PHYSICAL STATE
1–4	up to 100	judgment fine motor coordination reaction time	happy talkative boastful
4–12	100–300	motor coordination reflexes	staggering slurred speech nausea, vomiting
12–16	300–400	voluntary responses to stimulation	hypothermia hyperthermia anesthesia
16–24	400–600	sensation movement self-protective reflexes	comatose
24–30	600–900	breathing heart function	dead

Source: Kuhn, C., Swartzwelder, S., & Wilson, W. (2003). *Buzzed: The straight facts about the most used and abused drugs from alcohol to ecstasy.* New York: W. W. Norton, p. 37. Copyright © 1998 by Cynthia Kuhn, Scott Swartzwelder, and Wilkie Wilson. Used by permission of W. W. Norton & Company, Inc.

DIAGNOSING ALCOHOL PROBLEMS

Kuhn, Swartzwelder, and Wilson provided two different screening tests that are used in doctors' offices and clinics as a first indicator that an individual may have an alcohol problem. They did stress that a diagnosis of alcohol abuse, alcohol dependency, or alcoholism can be made only by a health professional trained specifically in addiction; sometimes it does more harm than good to confront a friend or relative with the impression that he or she may have a drinking problem; and these screening techniques rely on one critical component—the individual's responses.

The first screening test is called CAGE:

- Have you ever felt the need to **C**ut down on your drinking?

- Have you ever felt **A**nnoyed by someone criticizing your drinking?

- Have you ever felt **G**uilty about your drinking?

- Have you ever felt the need for an **E**ye-opener (a drink at the beginning of the day)?

If an individual gives two or more positive responses to these questions, there is a chance that he or she has some type of alcohol problem.

The second screening test is called TWEAK; this has been especially useful with women:

- **T**olerance: How many drinks does it take to make you high?

- **W**orried: Have close friends or relatives worried or complained about your drinking?

- **E**ye-opener: Do you sometimes take a drink in the morning to wake up?

- **A**mnesia (memory loss): Has a friend or family member ever told you things you said or did while you were drinking that you could not remember?

- (**K**) Cut: Do you sometimes feel the need to cut down on your drinking?

This test is scored differently than CAGE; however, a positive score of three or more is considered to indicate that the person has a drinking problem.[12]

---

populations. For instance, African-American and Asian, female, and older students are less likely to engage in binge drinking compared with white, male, and younger students.[15] Zamboanga and his colleagues defined drinking games as consisting of a set of rules and guidelines that encourage heavy alcohol use.[16] Continued involvement in such games can result in an individual becoming more intoxicated and his or her skill at the game diminishing, leading to more drinking. Further, most drinking games include those individuals who are purposely "losing" to receive the penalty of drinking.

Individuals involved in such drinking games are at a higher risk of heavy alcohol consumption and negative alcohol-related consequences. For instance, this kind of drinking could result in increased aggression and driving under the influence.[17] Also, others on campus may experience the negative effects of this type of drinking in the form of physical assaults, property damage, and unwanted sexual advances.[18]

PYMCA/UIG via Getty Images

An intoxicated woman sitting on a bathroom floor is offered a glass of water. Nausea is a common effect of alcohol consumption.

BARBITURATES. The first barbiturate, barbital, was discovered in 1903 by two German scientists working at Bayer—Emil Fischer and Joseph von Mering. Barbital was marketed by Bayer under the trade name Veronal.[19] There are now about a dozen barbiturates in medical use.[20] The various types of barbiturates are often referred to "on the street" by their color; the most common types include Amytal (blue heavens), Nembutal (yellow jackets), Seconal (red birds), and Sombulex and Tuinal (rainbows, or reds and blues).[21] Barbiturates can induce a wide continuum of central nervous system depression, ranging from mild sedation to coma.[22] They can be physically and psychologically addictive. In general practice, barbiturates have essentially been replaced by benzodiazepines for treatment of anxiety and insomnia.[23]

TRANQUILIZERS (INCLUDING BENZODIAZEPINES). Kuhn and her colleagues noted that benzodiazepines are "remarkable because they are one of the closest drugs we have to a 'magic bullet' for anxiety."[24] If used properly, benzodiazepines can help individuals with anxiety without disrupting normal functions. In fact, these are among the most commonly prescribed drugs. Diazepam (Valium), alprazolam (Xanax), and estazolam (ProSom) are some types of benzodiazepines. However, this is not a "perfect" class of drug. Problems with benzodiazepines are that initial use causes sleepiness and incoordination, they can affect an individual's learning process, and they can cause amnesia.[25]

Recently, two specific types of tranquilizers have received a great deal of media attention and have been dubbed "date-rape drugs," or predatory drugs. The first is flunitrazepam, trade name Rohypnol. Some of the street names associated with Rohypnol are "forget-me-pill," "lunch money drug," "roofies," "ruffies," "wolfies," "pingus," and "R2." The Food and Drug Administration has never approved Rohypnol for medicinal use in the United States. It was brought to the public's attention when some individuals used it to physically and psychologically incapacitate women, for the purpose of then sexually assaulting them.[26] The second type of tranquilizer is gamma-hydroxybutyric acid (GHB). Some of the street names for GHB are "liquid ecstasy," "scoop," "easy lay," "liquid X," and "goop." GHB can come in the form of an odorless, colorless liquid or as a white powder. As with Rohypnol, offenders have used GHB as a predatory drug in the commission of sexual assaults because it renders the victim incapable of resisting, as well as causing memory problems.[27]

Narcotics

The term narcotics has been used historically, and often inaccurately, to refer to *all* illegal drugs. More accurately, *narcotics* refers to opiates (drugs derived from the opium poppy) or opioids (synthetically produced opiates).[28] In this section, we briefly discuss morphine, heroin, and other synthetic narcotics such as oxycodone.

MORPHINE. The term morphine is derived from the Greek god of dreams, Morpheus, who was often depicted with a handful of opium poppies. The effect of opiate use was even depicted in the film *The Wizard of Oz*, when Dorothy and her friends are running through the field of poppies. In 1805, morphine, the major active ingredient in the opium poppy, was purified. Coupled with the invention of the hypodermic syringe in 1853, the first major wave of morphine addiction occurred during the American Civil War.[29] Morphine has a high potential for abuse. It is also one of the most effective drugs for relieving severe physical pain. Street names include "dreamer," "God's drug," "Mister Blue," "morf," and "morpho."[30]

HEROIN. Perhaps the most infamous opiate drug is heroin, a chemically modified form of morphine. The color of heroin can range from white to black. Highly purified heroin is a white powder, but on the other end of the continuum, it is a black, sticky substance,

binge drinking: heavy episodic drinking; drinking so much alcohol within a two-hour period that it results in at least a .08 blood alcohol concentration.

barbiturate: a type of depressant; can induce a wide continuum of central nervous system depression, ranging from mild sedation to coma.

tranquilizers: a type of depressant; can help with anxiety without disrupting normal functions. Problems include sleepiness and incoordination, hampered learning process, and amnesia.

narcotics: opiates (drugs derived from the opium poppy) or opioids (synthetically produced opiates); includes morphine, heroin, and oxycodone.

morphine: one of the most effective drugs for relief of severe physical pain; has high potential for abuse.

sometimes referred to as "black tar heroin."[31] Heroin can be snorted/sniffed, smoked, or injected. Initially, it is often sniffed or snorted. When tolerance builds, one may use the method of "skin-popping" (injecting it into the skin but not into a vein). When tolerance builds further, one may "mainline" heroin (injecting it into the bloodstream).[32] Those users who inject heroin are at risk for infectious diseases, including HIV/AIDS and hepatitis. Further, street heroin usually contains toxic contaminants or additives that can lead to serious health issues.[33]

OTHER SYNTHETIC NARCOTICS. Synthetic narcotics are produced entirely within the laboratory, as opposed to other narcotics derived from opium.[34] Examples of synthetic opiates include hydrocodone (Vicodin, Lorcet, Lortab), hydromorphone (Dilaudid), meperidine (Demerol), oxycodone (OxyContin, Percodan, and Percocet), propoxyphene (Darvon), and codeine.[35] OxyContin has recently been the focus of much media attention. While the promotion and marketing of OxyContin could be deemed a commercial success, the result has also been a public health concern:

> The extraordinary amount of money spent in promoting a sustained-release opioid was unprecedented. During OxyContin's first 6 years on the market, Purdue spent approximately 6 to 12 times more on promoting it than the company had spent on promoting MS Contin. . . . Although OxyContin has not been shown to be superior to other available potent opioid preparations, by 2001 it had become the most frequently prescribed brand-name opioid in the United States for treating moderate to severe pain.[36]

Prescriptions for OxyContin have practically doubled every year since its release in 1996. In 2000, physicians issued more than 6.5 million prescriptions for OxyContin.[37]

Stimulants

As the name implies, stimulant drugs create a sense of energy, alertness, talkativeness, and well-being considered pleasurable to the user. Physiological effects include increased heart rate and blood pressure, as well as dilation of the bronchioles (breathing tubes) in the lungs.[38] Two of the most common forms of stimulants in our society, and perhaps the most popular drugs in the world, are caffeine (in coffee, tea, and a number of soft drinks) and nicotine (consumed through tobacco products such as cigarettes).[39] In this section, we briefly discuss stimulants such as cocaine, amphetamine, and methamphetamine.

COCAINE. Cocaine appears in the leaves of various species of plants grown in Bolivia, Peru, and Colombia. In fact, Colombia produces about 90% of the cocaine powder entering the United States. Street names for cocaine include "coca," "coke," "crack," "flake," "snow," and "soda cot." It is usually distributed as a white, crystalline powder and often diluted or "cut" with various substances such as sugars and local anesthetics. Cocaine base or crack comes in small, irregular-shaped pieces, or "rocks," of an opaque whitish color. Powdered cocaine can be snorted or, after dissolving it in water, injected into the veins. Crack cocaine is smoked, either by itself or with marijuana or

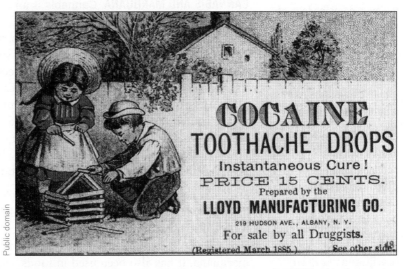

Public domain

An 1885 advertisement for toothache drops containing cocaine.

heroin: the most infamous opiate drug; a chemically modified form of morphine that ranges in color from white to black.

oxycodone: synthetic narcotic produced entirely in the laboratory; includes OxyContin, Percodan, and Percocet.

stimulant: creates a sense of energy, alertness, talkativeness, and well-being considered pleasurable to the user.

cocaine: a type of stimulant that appears in the leaves of various species of plants; usually distributed as a white, crystalline powder diluted with substances such as sugars and local anesthetics.

tobacco. Known as "speedballing," sometimes cocaine is used in combination with an opiate such as heroin.[40]

AMPHETAMINE. Like other stimulants, amphetamine boosts the body's functioning. A number of amphetamines are legally prescribed, in some instances to treat attention-deficit hyperactivity disorder and attention-deficit disorder. Adderall and Dexedrine are some commonly prescribed amphetamines. Street names include "bennies," "black beauties," "crank," "ice," "speed," and "uppers." The effects of amphetamines are similar to those of cocaine; however, the onset of these effects is slower and the duration longer.[41] As with cocaine, amphetamines decrease appetite. In fact, these drugs were used in the first diet pills, popular in the 1950s and 1960s.[42]

METHAMPHETAMINE. The most common form of amphetamine today is methamphetamine.[43] Methamphetamine can take the form of a white, odorless powder that dissolves in water; clear, "chunky" crystals (i.e., crystal meth); or small, brightly colored tablets. Street names include "meth," "poor man's cocaine," "crystal meth," "ice," "glass," and "speed." Methods of use include injecting, snorting, smoking, and oral ingestion. Some of the consequences associated with methamphetamine use are psychotic behavior and brain damage. Chronic use can result in violent behavior, anxiety, confusion, insomnia, auditory hallucinations, mood disturbances, delusions, and paranoia; brain damage due to methamphetamine use is similar to that occurring from Alzheimer's disease, stroke, and epilepsy.[44]

Methamphetamine was created in Japan in 1919 but did not become popular until the 1980s and 1990s.[45] Methamphetamine is most accessible in the Pacific region of the United States, followed by the West, Southwest, Southeast, Midwest, and Northeast regions; abuse of methamphetamine predominately occurs in the western, southwestern, and midwestern United States.[46] Another problem of the increased popularity of methamphetamine is that a major source of supply for use in the United States is clandestine laboratories in California and Mexico.[47] Methamphetamine can be made from a number of household products; thus, it is difficult to regulate the production of this drug and to prevent the dangers of such production to people and the environment.[48]

Other Drugs

CANNABIS AND MARIJUANA. Cannabis is an extremely useful plant. For instance, hemp, a strong fiber found in the stem of this plant, can be used to make rope, cloth, and paper. The leaves and flowers can be dried into marijuana and used for their psychoactive and medicinal effects. The most prevalent species of cannabis are *Cannabis sativa* and *Cannabis indica*. While the cannabis plant contains hundreds of psychoactive chemicals, the most psychoactive is delta-9-tetrahydrocannabinol (THC).[49] Large quantities of marijuana are grown in countries such as Colombia, Mexico, Jamaica, and the United States. In the United States, the largest marijuana-producing states are California, Kentucky, and Hawaii.[50] Hashish and hashish oil are drugs also derived from the cannabis plant; however, they are stronger than marijuana. The main sources of hashish are the Middle East, North Africa, Pakistan, and Afghanistan.[51]

Street names for marijuana include "Aunt Mary," "BC bud," "blunts," "hash," "indo," "joint," "Mary Jane," "pot," "reefer," "skunk," and "weed." It is usually smoked as a cigarette, called a joint, or in a pipe or bong. It can also be smoked in blunts, which are cigars that have been emptied of tobacco. Sometimes other drugs are used in combination with marijuana. It has also been used in foods, as well as brewed to make tea.[52] Some of the psychoactive effects of marijuana include problems with memory and learning, distorted perception, difficulty in thinking and problem solving, and loss of coordination. Some of

amphetamine: a type of stimulant; effects are similar to cocaine, but onset is slower and duration longer.

methamphetamine: the most common form of amphetamine today, it can take the form of a white, odorless powder that dissolves in water; clear, "chunky" crystals; or small, brightly colored tablets.

cannabis: an extremely useful plant that contains hundreds of psychoactive chemicals, particularly delta-9-tetrahydrocannabinol (THC).

marijuana: the dried leaves or flowers of the cannabis plant.

the physiological effects include sedation, bloodshot eyes, increased heart rate, coughing due to lung irritation, increased appetite, and decreased blood pressure.[53]

STEROIDS. Anabolic-androgenic steroids are synthetically produced variations of the male sex hormone testosterone.[54] Some steroids have been approved for medical and veterinary use. A legitimate use for humans is in replacement therapy for inadequate levels of hormones (e.g., delayed puberty, disease such as cancer and AIDS that results in loss of lean muscle mass). Steroids are also used in veterinary medicine for improving weight gain, increasing vigor, and enhancing coat.[55] Street names include "Arnolds," "gym candy," "pumpers," "roids," "stackers," "weight trainers," "gear," and "juice."[56] Research has revealed that abuse of steroids can lead to aggression and other negative effects.[57] While some users report "feeling good about themselves," others experience extreme mood swings and manic symptoms that could lead to violence.[58] Steroid abuse can lead to serious, and in some instances irreversible, health problems, including liver damage, jaundice, fluid retention, high blood pressure, renal failure, and severe acne.[59]

INHALANTS. Although other abused substances can be inhaled, the term Inhalants is used to refer to various substances whose primary trait is that they are rarely taken by any delivery method other than inhalation. Inhalants are volatile substances that produce chemical vapors. These vapors are inhaled to produce a psychoactive, or mind-altering, effect. The categorization of inhalants is difficult. One classification system identified four general categories: volatile solvents, aerosols, gases, and nitrites. These categories are based on the forms in which they are often found in household, industrial, and medical products. Inhalant use includes "sniffing" or "snorting" fumes from containers; spraying aerosols directly into the nose or mouth; "bagging," which is sniffing or inhaling fumes from substances in a plastic or paper bag; "huffing," which involves stuffing an inhalant-soaked rag over the mouth; and inhaling from balloons filled with nitrous oxide. The effects of intoxication last only a few minutes; thus, abusers often prolong the high by inhaling repeatedly over the course of several hours.[60]

HALLUCINOGENS. Hallucinogens are drugs that alter one's thought processes, mood, and perceptions. The word is derived from the Latin word *alucinare*, which means "to wander in mind, talk idly, or prate."[61] There are three general categories of hallucinogens. The first category, and the most familiar, is lysergic acid diethylamide (LSD). The second major category is belladonna alkaloids; these have been used for thousands of years for medical and ritual purposes. The third category is dissociative anesthetics, or "horse tranquilizers," including phencyclidine (PCP) and ketamine (an anesthetic used on children and in veterinary practices).[62] Since it is so individualized, it is difficult to describe a person's experience when using a hallucinogen. However, the onset of a "trip" includes nausea, feeling jittery, and a mild increase in blood pressure, heart rate, and breathing. Subsequently, the effects include a slight distortion of sensory perception, with

steroids: synthetically produced variations of the male sex hormone testosterone; some approved for medical and veterinary use.

inhalants: volatile substances that produce chemical vapors and whose primary trait is that they are rarely taken by any other delivery method than inhalation.

hallucinogens: drugs that alter one's thought processes, mood, and perceptions.

LEARNING CHECK 16.1

1. In this society, _____ is often the drug of choice.

2. Two types of _____ have received a great deal of media attention and have been dubbed "date-rape drugs," or predatory drugs.

3. The color of _____ ranges from white to black.

4. Prescriptions for _____ have practically doubled every year since its release in 1996.

5. _____ refers to when cocaine is used in combination with an opiate such as heroin.

6. The most common form of amphetamine today is _____.

7. Street names for _____ include "Mary Jane," "pot," "reefer," and "weed."

Answers located at www.edge.sagepub.com/schram2e

visual effects such as wavering images and distortion of size.[63] In some instances, these drugs can cause schizophrenia-like psychosis.[64]

TRENDS OF DRUG USE

The history of drug use can be traced back at least 10,000 years. Anthropologists have maintained that earlier cultures learned, through a process of trial and error, that chewing, sucking, or inhaling the leaves, fruits, or roots of certain types of plants would induce physical and psychological changes. Further, some anthropologists have speculated that the discovery of grain-derived alcohol, especially beer, may have been a reason why wandering hunter-gatherer tribes of the Old Stone Age established villages. By establishing villages, these tribes could pursue agriculture to ensure a stable supply of grain.[65] As Sally Freeman notes, "drug use is woven into the history of civilization. People have used drugs for pleasure, social interaction, medicine, rebellion, self-exploration, creativity, religious ceremonies, and as commodities in economic trade."[66]

Drugs have been an integral aspect of, and woven into, American history since the arrival of the first European colonists. Interactions between the Native American and European cultures exposed each group to drugs that were new to it but familiar to the other. For instance, in the early 17th century, the British found tobacco, which was smoked by Native Americans to achieve mystical states of mind and to strengthen social agreements. For the Europeans and the British, drinking was an integral aspect of life; the colonials introduced the Native Americans to alcohol.[67] In this section, we provide a brief overview of key trends of drug use in the United States, starting with the history of opioid and cocaine addiction.

Early History of Cocaine and Opioid Addiction

Around the time of the U.S. Civil War (1861–1865), opioid addiction was prevalent.[68] Soldiers were given morphine not only to ease the pain of their injuries but also to relieve the symptoms of dysentery. Upon returning home, many of the soldiers were dependent on morphine, and their addiction became known as the "soldier's disease." Some of England's most well-known literary talents were introduced to opiates through their physicians; American writer Louisa May Alcott, author of *Little Women*, used opium and morphine to address her physical ailments. Interestingly, under different pen names, she later authored thrillers that delved into topics such as drugs and violence.[69]

In 1898, the Bayer Company developed heroin, an opium derivative 10 times more powerful than morphine. It was extremely effective in relieving coughs, emphysema, asthma, and tuberculosis. As with previous opium derivatives, however, many soon realized that heroin was also highly addictive. In fact, by 1919, almost 1 million Americans were addicted to heroin or some form of opium. Physicians, pharmacists, and "opportunists" were able to prescribe opioids with no restrictions. Thus, patent medicines, claiming to treat a range of ailments, were often laced with opiates, cocaine, or alcohol.[70] To address this widespread addiction and questionable practices, the government enacted the 1906 Pure Food and Drug Act, which authorized federal regulations on any medication.[71] This was followed by additional regulations when Congress passed the **Harrison Act** in 1914. This required doctors to be licensed to prescribe narcotics.[72]

Harrison Act: passed by Congress in 1914, required doctors to have a license number to prescribe narcotics.

Like opiates, cocaine has some therapeutic properties but is also highly addictive. Cocaine was introduced in the United States initially for medicinal use, designated as a "wonder drug." In fact, cocaine was considered by many influential physicians as a cure for addiction to morphine, opium, and alcohol.[73] Before Sigmund Freud achieved fame as the founder of psychoanalysis, he was a neurologist. In several articles for medical journals, Freud maintained that cocaine could be used for a variety of ills, such as asthma, digestive upset, and morphine addiction.[74] In 1887, however, Freud conceded that cocaine should not be used for morphine addiction. It is also essential to note that in the early 1900s, medical viewpoints concerning cocaine (as for other forms of opium) were becoming more critical of its use in the field, with the exception of its use as a local anesthetic.[75]

Prohibition Era

On December 18, 1917, the U.S. Senate proposed the Eighteenth Amendment. Mississippi was the first state to ratify the amendment; on January 16, 1919, Nebraska was the 36th state to ratify the amendment. Thus, national Prohibition took effect on January 16, 1920.[76] The amendment has two operative sections:

> Section 1: After one year from the ratification of this article the manufacture, sale, or transportation of intoxicating liquors within, the importation thereof into, or the exportation thereof from the United States and all territory subject to the jurisdiction thereof for beverage purposes is hereby prohibited.
>
> Section 2: The Congress and the several States shall have concurrent power to enforce this article by appropriate legislation. (USCS Constitutional Amendment 18)

The passage of the amendment was influenced by such groups as the Prohibition Party, the Woman's Christian Temperance Union, and the Anti-Saloon League.[77]

During the Prohibition era, America's drinking patterns went through some changes. First, there was a significant drop in alcohol consumption among the working class; Prohibition made alcohol expensive, and many of these individuals could not afford to drink. Second, while beer and wine were difficult to manufacture and ship, distilled liquors (e.g., gin, rum, whiskey) were easy to produce and transport, which made these the more popular beverages. One of the most notable, and often cited, outcomes of Prohibition was the development of an underground system of producing and distributing alcohol.[78] While "Prohibition probably reduced per capita alcohol use and alcohol-related harm, . . . these benefits eroded over time as an organized black market developed and public support . . . declined."[79]

Prior to Prohibition, organized crime essentially comprised corrupt political machines, vice entrepreneurs, and, at the bottom, gangs. The onset of prohibition provided gangs an opportunity to engage in criminal activity that changed the power order, with gang leaders such as "Dutch Schultz" and Al Capone rising to the top of the organized crime "ladder."[80] On December 5, 1933, the Twenty-First Amendment was ratified, repealing the Eighteenth Amendment.

"Reefer Madness"

Although the cannabis plant has been used for various purposes since colonial times, it was not until the early 1900s that the act of smoking marijuana was considered a social problem in the United States. Further, those identified as smoking marijuana were from marginalized groups. Specifically, these individuals included Mexicans who came to America to work in the fields in the Southwest; sailors who brought back marijuana from South and Central American ports; and blacks in the South, where it was noted that as early as colonial times they smoked the hemp plant, having become familiar with the drug in Africa.[81]

Twenty-First Amendment: ratified on December 5, 1933, it repealed the Eighteenth Amendment.

Prior to the mid-1920s, there was not a great deal of public interest or concern about marijuana use. Soon thereafter, various articles appeared linking marijuana use with criminal activity.[82] For instance, in 1936, *Scientific American* reported, "Marijuana produces a wide variety of symptoms in the user, including hilarity, swooning, and sexual excitement. Combined with intoxicants, it often makes the smoker vicious, with a desire to fight and kill."[83]

Some have maintained that were it not for the zeal of Harry Anslinger, the commissioner of the new Federal Bureau of Narcotics in 1931, marijuana might be legal in the United States today. These articles, a number of which were written by Anslinger, stressed the negative effects of marijuana use. For instance, a 1927 article in the *New York Times* reported a story about a Mexican woman who went insane after eating cannabis leaves. At the Congressional hearings on the Marihuana Tax Act in 1937, Anslinger testified that a 21-year-old man from Florida axe-murdered his entire family because he was smoking marijuana. However, Anslinger failed to note that the authorities had attempted to institutionalize the man for insanity a year before he ever tried marijuana.[84]

On August 2, 1937, the 75th Congress passed the 1937 Marihuana Tax Act, and it became effective October 1, 1937. While this federal law did not criminalize marijuana or its preparations, it did tax the grower, distributor, seller, and buyer. This law essentially made it impossible for a person to have any involvement with marijuana. In 1969, the U.S. Supreme Court ruled that the Marihuana Tax Act was unconstitutional. The case involved Timothy Leary, who was found with marijuana in his car while going through Customs at Laredo, Texas. The Supreme Court stated that the act violated Leary's Fifth Amendment privilege against self-incrimination.[85] Some maintain that the Marihuana Tax Act of 1937 is one example of what one could characterize as a *racialized drug policy*. David Musto argued that the act was essentially a response to political pressure among those who feared the use of marijuana by individuals they labeled "Mexicans."[86] C. M. Goeth of Sacramento, a member of the American Coalition—a group whose goal was to "keep America American"—noted that

> marihuana, perhaps now the most insidious of our narcotics, is a direct by-product of unrestricted Mexican immigration. Easily grown, it has been asserted that it has recently been planted between rows in a California penitentiary garden. Mexican peddlers have been caught distributing sample marihuana cigarets [*sic*] to school children. Bills for our quota against Mexico have been blocked mysteriously in every Congress since the 1924 Quota Act. Our nation has more than enough laborers.[87]

As noted previously, there was a great deal of publicity regarding the "evils" of marijuana; this media attention exaggerated marijuana's effects.

In certain regions of the United States, the fear of marijuana was more intense. Specifically, a report published in 1932 noted that the abuse of marijuana is often associated with Latin American or Spanish-speaking populations; the sale of cannabis cigarettes usually occurs in states along the Mexican border, as well as in cities in the Southwest and West.[88] Musto concluded that initially the Federal Bureau of Narcotics resisted any involvement in terms of enforcing the anti-marijuana law. Pressure, most likely motivated by fear, from those in the Southwest and West regions of the country led to the implementation of federal legislation.

Marihuana Tax Act: effective October 1, 1937; did not criminalize marijuana or its preparations but did tax the grower, distributor, seller, and buyer.

The 1960s and the Baby Boomers

According to the U.S. Census, the population born between 1946 and 1964 is commonly referred to as the baby-boom generation. Due to a dramatic increase in birth rates following World War II, baby boomers now form what is considered to be one of the largest generations in U.S. history.[89] During the 1960s, these individuals were extremely influential to what has been identified as the "counterculture" of that time. Kenneth Westhues identified various characteristics of countercultures, including communistic relationships among members, sexual relationships that deviate from the nuclear family ideal, claims of superiority over the dominant society, members who look to spiritual leaders, and members who reject many of the status symbols of the larger society.[90]

The countercultural movement has also been associated with "mind-opening substances," or drugs such as LSD, mescaline, psilocybin, and other related chemicals, as well as marijuana.[91] Drugs were interwoven in various facets of this cultural movement. For instance, drug use was often referenced in music—appearing in songs by Bob Dylan, Jefferson Airplane, Jim Hendrix, The Beatles, and The Grateful Dead, just to name a few.

PYMCA/UIG via Getty Images

Example of psychedelic art. What role might drugs have played in the creation of such art?

Art, specifically psychedelic art, was also influential at this time. Some argue that psychedelic art was inspired by the effects of such drugs as LSD and mescaline.

The "War on Drugs" Era

The 1980s initiated what was designated as the **War on Drugs**:

> The drug "panic" or "crisis" of the mid-to-late 1980s illustrates the notion of the politics of social problems very nicely. Public concern about drugs, although building throughout the 1980s, *exploded* late in 1985 and early 1986—at a time, ironically, when the use of most drugs was actually *declining* [italics in original].[92]

There was extensive media coverage of drug use in the United States at this time. A well-known advertising campaign was "Just Say No." This phrase has been attributed to First Lady Nancy Reagan. During a presentation in Oakland, California, a schoolchild in the audience asked Mrs. Reagan what she and her friends should say when someone offered them drugs. The First Lady stated, "Just say no." Soon thereafter, thousands of "Just Say No" clubs had emerged in schools around the country.[93]

In the 1980s, Congress enacted mandatory minimum drug sentencing laws that resulted in lengthy prison terms for individuals convicted of nonviolent drug offenses.[94] In 1986, President Ronald Reagan stressed the need for a "nationwide crusade against drugs," such as $2 billion in federal monies to address the problem. This money included $56 million for drug testing federal employees. In September of 1986, the House of Representatives approved increased spending for education, treatment programs, and penalties against drug-producing countries. This was approved by the Senate in October. The Anti-Drug Abuse Act ultimately cost $1.7 billion.[95]

One particular drug often noted during this period was crack cocaine.[96] Witkin and his colleagues stated that it is amazing that crack cocaine did not become a social problem sooner. In fact, crack appeared throughout the 1970s. However, Witkin argues that crack became a craze due to mass marketing involving three groups of "sinister geniuses."

War on Drugs: public concern about drugs, building throughout the 1980s, exploded in late 1985 and early 1986.

The first group was the nameless kitchen chemists and drug traffickers who could set up small-scale operations. The second group comprised crime organizations, primarily in medium and large American cities; these organizations seized the local markets from smaller operators. Finally, the third group comprised gangs from both the East and West Coast; these gangs franchised crack operations.[97]

During the 1990s, there was intense focus and scrutiny on women who used illegal drugs during pregnancy; this was especially evident among women who gave birth to "crack babies." Again, the media played a prominent role in perpetuating the problem of crack babies. From the media perspective, "the inhumane actions of addicted mothers often produced children who were almost beyond the pale of humanity."[98] However, some researchers have noted that after years of research, medical experts have not identified a distinctive condition, syndrome, or disorder that merits the label "crack baby."[99]

Current Trends Regarding Drug Use

According to the 2014 National Survey on Drug Use and Health,

- about 27 million Americans aged 12 or older were current (i.e., in the past month) users of illicit drugs (i.e., marijuana/hashish, cocaine, heroin, hallucinogens, inhalants, or prescription-type psychotherapeutics used nonmedically), this is about 1 in 10 Americans;

- marijuana was the most commonly used illicit drug (with 22.2 million users);

- when comparing the percentage of young adults who were current cocaine users, the 2014 percentage was lower than the percentages in 2002 through 2007, and it was similar for most years between 2008 to 2014;

- approximately 435,000 people aged 12 or older were current heroin users in 2014;

- while nonmedical prescription-type psychotherapeutic drugs continues to be the second most common type of illicit drug used in 2014, the percentage has decreased (1.6%) in 2014 compared to most years from 2002 to 2012; and 569,000 individuals used methamphetamine.[100]

  U.S. Attorney Sally Quillian Yates stated,

  > Prescription drug abuse is our nation's fastest-growing segment of illegal drug use, causing significantly more overdose deaths than cocaine, methamphetamine, and heroin combined. Oxycodone remains one of the most widely abused prescription drugs, and it's also one of the most addictive and deadly drugs when not taken properly. The forging of prescriptions is an especially harmful situation because it completely removes the oversight of a physician from the equation.[101]

- The 2013 Partnership Attitude Tracking Study revealed that "there is encouraging evidence of behavioral and environmental trends that may help reduce teen misuse and abuse of prescription drugs in the future: The prevalence of teen prescription drug misuse and abuse has remained stable at 23 percent."

- There has been a decline over the past five years in the perceived accessibility of prescription opioids and peers' use of opioids without a prescription.

- The prevalence rate of prescription misuse or abuse has incrementally decreased over the past three years.[102]

The United States and New Zealand are the only countries that allow pharmaceutical companies to advertise their products directly to consumers, called direct-to-consumer

WHY DO THEY DO IT?

RYAN THOMAS HAIGHT

Ryan Thomas Haight attended Grossmont High School in La Mesa, California. He was outgoing and successful academically, and he enjoyed various athletic activities, such as skiboarding and swimming. Ryan also enjoyed using the computer.[103] On February 12, 2001, Francine Haight came home in the afternoon and noticed that her son's car had not moved. She knew then that something was wrong. She found Ryan dead in his bed. Later, one of the sheriff's deputies came out and said, "This is what we found in your son's room." It was a large bottle of Vicodin. Ryan had overdosed.

What made this situation even worse was that he had been able to purchase the Vicodin over the Internet with a debit card. This drug is strictly regulated by the DEA.[104] A physician on the Internet, whom he had never met, prescribed the drug to Ryan, and an Internet pharmacy mailed the Vicodin to his home. Ryan was only 17 years old when he purchased the drug; he was 18 when he died.[105] Due to the growing concern over distribution of controlled substances via the Internet, the Ryan Haight Online Pharmacy Consumer Protection Act of 2008 went into effect in April 2009.[106] Some of the requirements include the following:

- Face-to-face requirement for prescribing. With few exceptions, a doctor must conduct at least one in-person medical evaluation of the patient.

- Endorsement requirement. The DEA must provide an endorsement before a pharmacy can dispense controlled substances via the Internet.

- Enhanced penalties for Schedule III through V. Penalties will be enhanced for unlawfully dispensing controlled substances in Schedules III through V.

- Prohibition on advertising illegal sales.

- Requirement that Internet pharmacies post certain information on their websites.

DEA acting administrator Michele M. Leonhart stated, "Cyber-criminals illegally peddling controlled substances over the Internet have invaded households and threatened America's youth for far too long. . . . This landmark piece of legislation will bring rogue pharmacy operators out of the shadows."[107]

THINK ABOUT IT:

1. Do you think the Ryan Haight Online Pharmacy Consumer Protection Act will prevent these types of incidents?

2. Can you think of any other policies or laws that should be in place to address these cybercriminals who sell controlled substances over the Internet?

advertising. Since their beginning in the 1980s, the amount of advertising among these companies has significantly increased.[108] Further, researchers found that for every dollar pharmaceutical companies spend on "basic research," approximately $19 goes for promotion and marketing.[109] Access to prescription drugs becomes even more problematic when such drugs are available through the Internet. The Drug Enforcement Administration (DEA) has noted that the Internet has become one of the fastest-growing methods of distributing controlled pharmaceuticals (see "Why Do They Do It? Ryan Thomas Haight" above for an example).

There has been growing concern over a group of drugs called designer drugs. Designer drugs are substances considered to be for recreational use; they are derivatives of approved drugs, so they can circumvent existing legal restrictions. The term *designer drugs*, however, has been misused and popularized by the media.[110] Unfortunately, it appears as though the only use of the term is to differentiate between synthetic drugs and drugs that appear in nature. Interestingly, the term was coined by Gary Henderson, PhD, at the University of California at Davis in the 1970s. He

designer drugs: substances considered to be for recreational use; derivatives of approved drugs that can circumvent existing legal restrictions.

Two offenders were convicted of manufacturing and distributing synthetic cannabinoids sold in packages with brand names such as "Scooby Snax" and "Bizarro."

used the term to refer to analogues of fentanyl, a powerful synthetic opioid used in hospitals. One could use this substance only in controlled hospital settings. Henderson reported that an analogue of fentanyl, alpha-methylfentanyl, was being sold on the street as "China white"— synthetic heroin. The problem was that prosecuting the individuals selling this substance was not possible given the limitations of the Controlled Substances Act:[111]

> The Controlled Substances Act, as it was originally enacted, contained an unforeseen but, as it turned out, major flaw. It was very specific in describing the drugs within its several schedules. Unfortunately for the drug enforcement community, underground chemists, or cookers, had

become highly sophisticated. They were capable of altering the chemical structure of certain drugs, including fentanyl, so that their street products no longer fit the description of the controls.[112]

The number of designer drugs continues to grow. Two discussed often in the media are "spice" and "bath salts." In years past, K2 and spice were common. Numbers of other brands now exist such as Joker, Kush, and Kronic. "Spice," or synthetic cannabinoid, refers to various herbal mixtures intended to produce the same experiences as marijuana. These "spice" mixtures have been easily accessible in head shops (i.e., stores specializing in selling drug paraphernalia), at gas stations, and on the Internet. Interestingly, the DEA has designated five chemicals often found in spice as Schedule I controlled substances; thus, it is illegal to sell, buy, or possess these chemicals. However, manufacturers of spice products continue their attempts to evade the legal restrictions by substituting different chemicals in the mixture.[113]

"Bath salts" are another emerging designer drug. The active chemicals in bath salts are mephedrone, pyrovalerone, and methylenedioxypyrovalerone. These all have stimulant properties; thus, while they are different from such drugs as amphetamine and cocaine, they have similar effects on the brain.[114] Bath salts are sold under various brand names, such as Bloom, Cloud Nine, Lunar Wave, Vanilla Sky, White Lightning, and Scarface. The National Institute on Drug Abuse noted that there have been reports of severe intoxication and dangerous health effects related to the use of bath salts. The effects can include euphoria and increased sociability and sex drive; others can experience paranoia, agitation, and hallucinations. There have also been some instances of individuals displaying psychotic and violent behaviors while on bath salts.[115]

THE DRUG-CRIME LINK

From the general public's perspective, the relationship between drugs and crime is inseparable; the problem of crime and the problem of drugs are often discussed simultaneously.[116] James Inciardi maintains that "the pursuit of some simple cause-and-effect relationship may be futile."[117] The relationship between drugs and crime usually falls into one of three categories:

- *Drug-defined crimes* involve the sale and/or possession of an illegal substance.

- *Drug-related crimes* involve violent behaviors induced by the effects of a drug or illegal activity that is motivated by continued drug use.

- *Crimes associated with drug use* involve illegal activities that may have occurred while a person was under the influence of an illegal substance but those activities were not a direct result of the drug use.[118]

The time order of the drug–crime link (i.e., "Which came first?") has been the primary research focus of a number of investigators. Studies have revealed that individuals who engage in substance use, such as cocaine, heroin, or marijuana, have consistently engaged in criminal behavior prior to, or while, using illegal drugs.[119] Further, the research reveals that substance use does not necessarily precipitate an individual's involvement in criminal activity; however, substance use does influence the extent of crime, the types of crime, and the length of time an individual engages in criminal behavior.[120] In this vein, "existing data and research indicate that drug abuse and criminal activity are a part of a broader set of integrated deviant behaviors involving crime, drug use, and, often, high-risk sex."[121]

LEARNING CHECK 16.2

1. In 1898, the Bayer Company developed _____, an opium derivative that was 10 times more powerful than morphine.

2. The _____ Amendment prohibited the manufacture, sale, or transportation of intoxicating liquors in the United States.

3. Some have argued that were it not for the zeal of _____, the commissioner of the new Federal Bureau of Narcotics, marijuana might be legal in the United States today.

4. Some researchers have noted that after years of research, medical experts have not identified a distinctive condition, syndrome, or disorder among babies born of drug-abusing mothers that merits the label _____.

5. New Zealand and _____ are the only countries that allow pharmaceutical companies to advertise their products directly to consumers.

Answers located at www.edge.sagepub.com/schram2e

Duane McBride and Clyde McCoy suggest that to enhance our understanding of the relationship between drug use and criminal behavior, one should apply an analytical framework that incorporates the following issues: (1) the historical underpinnings of current perspectives; (2) the types of drugs and criminal behavior; (3) the statistical relationship, specifically the extent and type of criminal behavior among different types of drug users, as well as the extent and type of drug use among different types of criminals; (4) the etiological nature of the relationship, such as causality and interaction; (5) the theoretical interpretations of the relationships; and (6) the policy implications of research conclusions.[122] Benjamin Nordstrom and Charles Dackis conducted an extensive review of the literature that focuses on addiction and crime. They sought to assess whether there is support for any of the three leading hypotheses that attempt to explain the drug–crime association:

1. Drug use and criminal behavior have a common cause, which might be biological, psychological, or sociological.

2. Drug use influences criminal behavior by either disinhibiting behavior or creating the need to finance a drug habit.

3. Deviance increases the likelihood of drug use later, such as in seeking deviant, drug-using peers.[123]

For instance, they found research that examined various risk factors associated with *both* substance abuse and criminal behavior. These factors included the history of victimization, attachment to parents, a propensity for violence or aggression, and

AP Photo/Felipe Dana

A 2016 photograph of a drug gang leader in Rio de Janeiro, Brazil. He claims that drug dealers win the hearts and minds of locals by paying for food and medicine, providing a lifeline for many living in crushing poverty.

impulsivity. They also examined research that moves beyond psychological and social risk factors to explore whether meaningful life events can change the trajectory of an individual's criminal and drug-using behavior. These researchers noted that the review of the literature finds support for all the hypotheses listed above pertaining to the drug–crime association. They concluded by emphasizing that "drug users are not a monolithic group, as many drug users do not commit crimes. . . . Criminally active drug users are also not a monolithic group."[124]

The Tripartite Conceptual Framework

Paul Goldstein developed what has been designated the Tripartite Conceptual Framework of the relationship between drugs and violence.[125] This framework suggests that drugs and violence are related to each other in three ways: through psychopharmacological, economically compulsive, and systemic violence.

PSYCHOPHARMACOLOGICAL VIOLENCE. This model of drugs and violence contends that some individuals, due to either short-term or long-term use of certain drugs, may become excitable, irritable, and/or irrational. This may then result in some type of violent behavior. The most relevant drugs within this model include alcohol, stimulants, barbiturates, and PCP. There may also be instances when substance use has reverse psychopharmacological effects and subsequently offsets violent tendencies. Thus, individuals prone to violence may engage in self-medication to control their violent tendencies. Similarly, certain drugs may be used in a psychopharmacological manner because of their perceived effects. Such functional substance use includes use of tranquilizers and marijuana to control nervousness or use of barbiturates and alcohol to provide courage.

ECONOMICALLY COMPULSIVE VIOLENCE. This model maintains that some substance users engage in violent crime, such as robbery, to support their drug use. Heroin and cocaine are expensive drugs often associated with compulsive use; these substances are germane within this model. Individuals within this model are essentially motivated by economic incentives rather than impulses to act violently. Often, victims of economically compulsive drug-related violence are individuals living in the same neighborhood as the offenders. Sometimes the victims are involved in illegal activities themselves; they may be drug users, strangers coming into the neighborhood to buy drugs, or prostitutes.

Tripartite Conceptual Framework:

suggests that drugs and violence are related to each other through psychopharmacological, economically compulsive, and systemic violence.

SYSTEMIC VIOLENCE. This model denotes the aggressive behaviors associated with the system of drug distribution and use, such as

disputes over territory between rival drug dealers, assaults and homicides committed within dealing hierarchies as a means of enforcing normative codes, robberies of drug dealers and the usually violent retaliation by the dealers or their bosses, elimination of informers, disputes over drugs and/or drug paraphernalia, punishment for selling adulterated or phony drugs, punishment for failing to pay one's debts, and robbery violence related to the social ecology of copping areas.[126]

Some issues pertaining to systemic violence are unresolved. For instance, while there is no question that participating in the drug business increases likelihood of engaging in violence, there is no clear time order for this association. Specifically, does the drug business make people violent *or* are violence-prone individuals drawn to the violent roles associated with the drug business?

MODERN POLICIES RELATED TO REDUCING DRUG USE

Howard Abadinsky asks the question, "To what extent does knowledge actually affect drug policy?"[127] To address this question, he emphasizes the importance of distinguishing between *scientific* knowledge and *political* knowledge:

> Scientific knowledge in the field of drug use is the body of facts and theories related to the uses of drugs. Political knowledge concerns public attitudes and organization toward drug use, including scientific knowledge. . . . Scientific knowledge can be only one of a number of factors which bear upon the symbolic and instrumental character of official public opinion.[128]

Abadinsky concludes that reducing the consumption of drugs by enhancing law enforcement efforts and providing large-scale treatment programs will not solve other sociological problems associated with drug use. These problems include the lack of educational and employment opportunities, as well as residential instability.[129] Drug abuse is not an isolated problem; rather, it is linked to other problems such as family dysfunction, child abuse and neglect, delinquency, and alcohol abuse.[130]

In this section, we review some current policies and programs that have been implemented to reduce drug use. These include interdiction, eradication, drug courts, maintenance and decriminalization, and harm reduction. When examining these policies and programs, readers should consider how these efforts address the other sociological problems linked to substance abuse.

Interdiction Strategies

According to the *National Interdiction Command and Control Plan,* interdiction is a "general term used to describe the multi-step, usually sequential continuum of effort/events focused on interrupting illicit drug trafficking."[131] The various steps in the interdiction continuum start with *cueing* (providing intelligence), followed by *detection* (initial acquisition of a contact), *sorting/classifying* (distinguishing drug-smuggling traffic from legitimate traffic), *monitoring* (tracking and/or intercept of a contact), *hand-off* (shifting primary responsibility between forces or actors), *disruption* (halting an activity, usually the transportation of contraband), *apprehension* (detention, arrest, or seizure of suspects, evidentiary items, contraband, and/or vehicles), and *prosecution* (federal activities related to the conduct of criminal proceedings).[132]

With the Anti–Drug Abuse Act of 1988, Congress established the High Intensity Drug Trafficking Areas (HIDTA) program. The program's efforts focus on reducing drug trafficking and production in the United States by facilitating cooperation with federal, state, local, and tribal law enforcement agencies, such as information and intelligence sharing and coordinated law enforcement strategies to utilize resources. There are currently 28 HIDTAs in the United States, which includes about 17.2% of all U.S. counties. These HIDTA-designated counties are located in 48 states and Puerto Rico, the U.S. Virgin Islands, and the District of Columbia. The HIDTA program is involved in various activities, including multiagency investigative, interdiction, and prosecution activities, as well as prevention and treatment efforts. HIDTAs are directed and guided by executive boards.

interdiction:

describes the various steps implemented to interrupt illicit drug trafficking (e.g., cueing, detection, apprehension, prosecution).

A DEA agent involved in the eradication of marijuana plants.

These executive boards consist of both federal and nonfederal (i.e., state, local, and tribal) law enforcement leaders.[133] A key aspect of the HIDTA program is "the discretion granted to the Executive Boards to design and implement initiates that confront drug trafficking threats in each HIDTA."[134]

Ohio is designated as one of the HIDTAs; this area consists of 13 counties.[135] This area is also linked to major drug-source regions, including Chicago, Detroit, New York City, the Southwest Border, and Canada. The Ohio HIDTA emphasizes how the numerous interstate highways are often used by drug traffickers to move illegal drugs throughout the region. For instance, Ohio has the eighth-largest national highway system; it carries the seventh-highest volume of traffic in the nation. This traffic flow allows drug transporters to blend in with the natural flow of traffic. Key issues identified by the Ohio HIDTA include the following:

- The availability of heroin has increased in this region due to an increased supply of Mexican heroin.

- The availability and abuse of cocaine has declined in this region.

- The availability and abuse of controlled prescription drugs (CPD) has increased in this area, particularly with the abuse of prescription opioids.

- Availability and local production of methamphetamine have been low.[136]

Eradication Strategies

There are four recognized techniques of eradication: mechanical destruction (i.e., slashing or uprooting), bunting, chemical, and biological (including genetic).[140] Among these four techniques, mechanical and chemical destruction are the most commonly used eradication strategies.[141] Eradication efforts have focused on the opium poppy, the coca bush, and the cannabis plant.[142]

Colombia continues to be a major source country for cocaine, heroin, and marijuana. Peru is the world's second largest cocaine producing country. The government of Colombia maintains efforts to eliminate the production and trafficking of illegal drugs through eradication, interdiction and law enforcement strategies. However, the production of pure cocaine in 2014 increased 30% from 2013 production. According to the U.S. Drug Enforcement Administration, almost 90% of cocaine seized in the United States in 2014 came from Colombia. In terms of heroin, Colombia is the second largest supplier to the United States.[143] Interestingly, in 2015, Colombian officials stopped their eradication efforts, through aerial spraying, due to concerns that the spray may cause cancer. This decision ended a program that continued for over twenty years with the United States, to eradicate coca production.

Prior to this, however, the United States has been criticized for these eradication efforts. For instance, Colombian officials have condemned the United States for not adequately addressing the issue of consumption. During the Colombian presidential election of 1990, campaign speeches often included negative references to Marion Barry, the mayor of Washington, DC. Federal agents videotaped the mayor in the act of smoking crack

eradication: four recognized techniques: mechanical destruction (i.e., slashing or uprooting), bunting, chemical, and biological (including genetic).

Comparative Criminology: *DRUGS*

Contact With Drug-Related Problems in the Area of Residence

Since 1973, the European Commission has been involved in conducting public opinion surveys on various topics with participating member states. These surveys and studies focus on topics that affect European citizenship, such as enlargement, social situation, health, culture, technology, environment, and defense. These surveys are referred to as the "Eurobarometer."[137] One item on the 2002 *Public Safety, Exposure to Drug-Related Problems and Crime* public opinion survey asked respondents the following question:

> Over the last 12 months, how often were you personally in contact with drug related problems in the area where you live? For example, seeing people dealing in drugs, taking or using drugs in public spaces, or by finding syringes left by drug addicts? Was this often, from time to time, rarely or never?[138]

Van Dijk adapted the results from this survey (see Figure 16.3). The figure is based on results from 15 European Union

countries. About 19% of the respondents noted that they have been in contact with drug-related problems, either often or from time to time. This was the average percentage. One can note that countries such as the United Kingdom, the Netherlands, Portugal, Italy, and Greece were above this average. Van Dijk further noted that the United Kingdom and the Netherlands were also engaged in political debates about incivilities occurring in their countries. Thus, perceptions of feeling unsafe in the street were strongly associated with perceived exposure to drug problems.[139]

THINK ABOUT IT:

1. What other factors would you consider when asking United States citizens about their exposure to drug-related problems and crime?

2. Why do you think there is a strong association between the perceptions of feeling unsafe in the street with perceived exposure to drug problems?

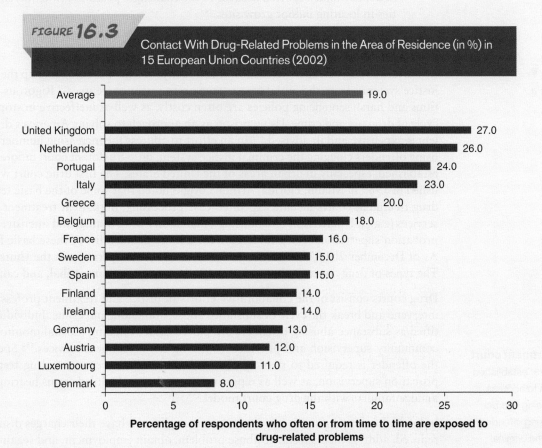

FIGURE 16.3

Contact With Drug-Related Problems in the Area of Residence (in %) in 15 European Union Countries (2002)

Country	Percentage
Average	19.0
United Kingdom	27.0
Netherlands	26.0
Portugal	24.0
Italy	23.0
Greece	20.0
Belgium	18.0
France	16.0
Sweden	15.0
Spain	15.0
Finland	14.0
Ireland	14.0
Germany	13.0
Austria	12.0
Luxembourg	11.0
Denmark	8.0

Percentage of respondents who often or from time to time are exposed to drug-related problems

Sources: Eurobarometer (2003), adapted, in Van Dijk, J. (2008). *The world of crime: Breaking the silence on problems of security, justice, and development across the world.* Thousand Oaks, CA: SAGE, p. 108.

cocaine, and his misdemeanor drug conviction inflamed Colombian public opinion.[144] There are similar criticisms among citizens of Peru and Bolivia. The cultivation of coca is intertwined with factors such as culture, tradition, and poverty. These social conditions render enforcement efforts ineffective.[145] Thus, when the most profitable crops are linked to an underground economy, and there is no viable, legal crop substitute, it is difficult to prevent coca cultivation.[146]

According to the DEA Domestic Cannabis Eradication/Suppression Program, in 2014, domestic cannabis eradication remained relatively consistent from 2013.[147] The primary marijuana cultivation states include California, Hawaii, Kentucky, Oregon, Tennessee, Washington, and West Virginia. While cannabis cultivation operations are more prevalent in western states, they are increasing in eastern states. Further, indoor cannabis cultivation continues to rise. Many cultivators have either relocated or established their operations indoors to avoid law enforcement detection. Indoor cultivators can generate higher profit margins since they can produce higher potency marijuana and cultivate year-round.[148] In their assessment of cannabis cultivation in the United States, the National Drug Intelligence Center noted the following intelligence gaps:

- No reliable estimates are available regarding the amount of domestically cultivated or processed marijuana.

- The amount of cannabis cultivated and marijuana produced in the United States by large-scale drug trafficking organizations, including Asian, Caucasian, and Mexican groups, is unknown.

- The extent of indoor cannabis cultivation in the United States is largely unknown and likely underreported because of the challenges posed to law enforcement entities in locating indoor grow sites.[149]

Drug Courts

By the late 1980s, offenders with substance abuse problems were clogging up the criminal justice system—from the initial arrest stage up to prisoner reentry.[150] Rigorous prosecutions and harsh sentencing policies are often costly, as well as ineffective in stopping the cycle of drug use and crime. Using prison as an approach to solving America's drug problem is expensive and ill-advised.[151] In an effort to address the increasing number of drug-using offenders clogging the criminal justice system, drug treatment court programs were established, especially in urban areas of the United States. The first drug court was established in 1989 in Miami, Florida. Arthur Lurigio noted that some of the basic features of drug treatment courts include expedited case processing, outpatient treatment, support services (e.g., job placement and housing), mandatory drug testing, and intensive court or probation supervision[152] (see Table 16.2 for a more detailed list of these basic features). As of December 2014, there are over 3,000 drug courts operating in the United States. The types of drug courts include adult, juvenile, family, veterans, tribal, and campus.[153]

Drug courts consist of the collaborative efforts of justice and treatment professionals to intervene and break the cycle of substance abuse, addiction, and crime. Individuals identified as substance-abusing offenders are placed under ongoing judicial monitoring and community supervision and provided with long-term treatment services.[154] Specifically, the offender is required to participate in substance abuse treatment, drug testing, and probation supervision, as well as reporting to regularly scheduled status hearings before a judge familiar with the drug court model.[155]

Individuals who participate in a drug court program can have their charges dismissed or reduced, address their substance abuse problem, obtain employment, and regain custody of their children. There are, however, additional rights not available to them, because

drug treatment court programs: established in an effort to address the increasing number of drug-using offenders clogging the criminal justice system.

TABLE 16.2

Basic Features of Drug Treatment Courts

- Prompt identification of clients and their immediate placement in treatment

- Nonadversarial court proceedings enacted by a team of judges, attorneys, and treatment providers and designed to protect community safety as well as defendants' and offenders' due-process rights

- Regular contact between clients and judges in judicial status hearings or other types of court sessions

- Intensive supervision practices that include close monitoring and frequent, random drug testing of clients

- Treatment interventions that are delivered on a continuum of care, evidence based, comprehensive, and integrated for individuals with co-occurring psychiatric disorders

- Contingencies of rewards and punishments that encourage compliance with treatment and other conditions of program participation

- Ongoing evaluations to monitor program implementation and measure the accomplishment of program objectives and goals

- Close working relationships with a wide range of community service providers and public agencies

- Interdisciplinary educational opportunities to help program staff stay current with the latest advances in offender drug treatment and case management strategies

Source: Lurigio, A. J. (2008). The first 20 years of drug treatment courts: A brief description of their history and impact. *Federal Probation, 72,* 15.

other aspects of public policy continue to consider addiction from a more punitive perspective. Individuals who have completed a drug court program but are charged or convicted of a drug offense may be denied welfare benefits, access to educational loans, public housing, and voting rights.[156] Jeanne Stinchcomb argues that the

> ongoing debate over the efficacy of drug courts . . . continues to raise questions concerning the strength of their conceptual foundation, the execution of their implementation strategies, and ultimately, the future potential of their ability to maintain a prominent position on the public-policy agenda.[157]

Loreen Wolfer conducted a qualitative exploration of individuals who participated and graduated from the drug treatment court program. When asked what changes should be implemented in the program, 13 of the 55 participants mentioned that there was a problem or weakness with how the court was conducting the urine screens. Nine of these individuals noted that more random screens should be conducted because the scheduled screens were "too predictable" and were "easy to beat." Another problem among these participants was the perceived unfairness of unequal treatment. The drug treatment court program is specifically designed to develop a treatment plan based on individual needs. Some individuals, however, considered this as differential treatment. Comments among these participants included the words "specialized treatment" and "lack of uniformity" in treatment.[158]

Sarah Messer and her colleagues applied the life course theory to drug courts. Specifically, they maintained that drug courts could be considered a *turning point* for an offender. They interviewed former drug court participants. During these interviews, the participants discussed how drug court helped them with various aspects of their lives such as self-esteem, general educational development, and relationships with family. Overall, recidivism rates for these participants were lower when compared to similarly situated offenders not participating in drug court.[159]

Maintenance and Decriminalization

A maintenance policy advocates for the accessibility of drugs through governmental regulation, such as distribution and legal age of use. A decriminalization policy supports the end of using criminal sanctions to address individual drug use. Often, this policy is advocated for marijuana possession.[160] Table 16.3 outlines three models of drug maintenance/decriminalization.

The pros for a maintenance/decriminalization policy are as follows:

- The resources that have been allocated for law enforcement efforts could be shifted to other areas of crime control, as well as treatment and education.

- Due to the low cost of psychoactive substances, there would be a reduction in secondary crime (i.e., crimes committed to support an expensive drug habit).

- Criminal organizations would no longer remain viable if they continued in drug trafficking.

- The aggressive marketing strategies of traffickers would no longer be operative.

- Individuals dependent on psychoactive substances could lead more productive lives; abusers would have an opportunity to become contributing members of society.

- Individuals using heroin intravenously would not be at risk for getting AIDS or hepatitis, because each user would have his or her own hypodermic kit.

- Decriminalization would enable use of social controls that inhibit antisocial, although legal, behavior. For example, various social controls attempt to influence the behavior of smokers and drunk drivers.[161]

maintenance: advocates for the accessibility of drugs through governmental regulation, such as distribution and legal age of use.

decriminalization: a policy related to labeling theory, which proposes less harsh punishments for some minor offenses, such as the possession of small amounts of marijuana.

TABLE 16.3 Three Models of Drug Maintenance/Decriminalization

1. Dangerous drugs can be dispensed only through government-controlled clinics or specially licensed medical personnel and only for short-term treatment purposes; unauthorized sale or possession entails criminal penalties. Long-term maintenance is limited to the use of methadone. This is basically the approach currently used in England.

2. Dangerous drugs can be prescribed by an authorized medical practitioner for treatment or maintenance; criminal penalties are imposed for sale or possession outside medical auspices. This is the old British system.

3. Dangerous drugs can be sold and used as tobacco and alcohol products are; that is, nonprescription use by adults is permitted. This was the case in the United States before the Harrison Act.

Source: Abadinsky, H. (2004). *Drug abuse: An introduction* (5th ed.). Belmont, CA: Wadsworth/Thomson Learning, p. 369 (table only).

The cons for a maintenance/decriminalization policy are as follows:

- Drugs such as cocaine, amphetamines, and heroin that are easily available to adults could also be abused by youths, similar to cigarettes and alcohol.

- More people would be tempted to try legalized controlled substances, which could result in an increase in abuse-related problems.

- Legalizing psychoactive substances would convey some form of acceptance of their use, similar to alcohol and tobacco use.

- Making psychoactive substances legal may reduce the incentive for individuals, addicted to these substances, to enter drug treatment or pursue a drug-free lifestyle.[162]

One current policy that continues to be controversial is legalized medical marijuana. Currently, 25 states—Alaska, Arizona, California, Colorado, Connecticut, Delaware, Hawaii, Illinois, Maine, Maryland, Massachusetts, Michigan, Minnesota, Montana, Nevada, New Hampshire, New Jersey, New Mexico, New York, Oregon, Pennsylvania, Rhode Island, Vermont, and Washington—and the District of Columbia have enacted laws to legalize medical marijuana (see Figure 16.4).[163] California was the first state to pass a legal medical marijuana law, designated as the Compassionate Use Act of 1996. This allows seriously ill Californians the right to obtain and use marijuana for medical

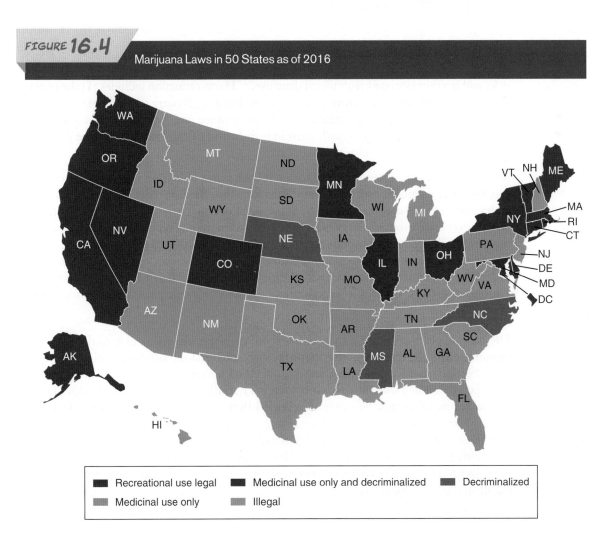

FIGURE **16.4**

Marijuana Laws in 50 States as of 2016

Recreational use legal   Medicinal use only and decriminalized   Decriminalized

Medicinal use only   Illegal

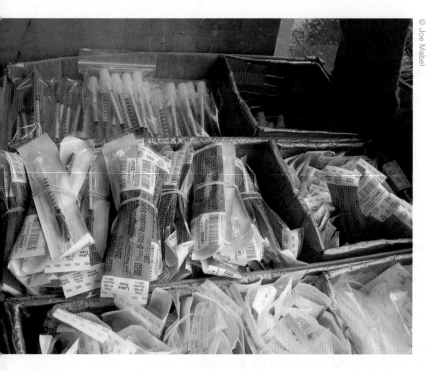

© Joe Mabel

One intervention associated with harm reduction policy is a needle exchange program.

purposes. According to the act, a physician needs to determine that an individual's health would benefit from the use of marijuana in treatment for such ailments as cancer, anorexia, AIDS, chronic pain, spasticity, glaucoma, arthritis, and migraines.[164]

After the November 2016 election, California, Massachusetts, and Nevada all passed laws that legalize recreational marijuana. There are, however, questions pertaining to voter support of this law. The major issue is the conflict between the federal government and the voters of of those states that have legalized recreational marijuana. The federal government still considers marijuana a Schedule I prohibited substance.[165] Interestingly, a month after Colorado and Washington legalized recreational marijuana, President Obama stated that federal law enforcement agencies have "bigger fish to fry" than prosecuting marijuana users in Colorado and Washington.[166]

Harm Reduction

A **harm reduction** policy attempts to incorporate a public health approach to lessen the risks and harms associated with illegal drug use.[167] Harm reduction includes (1) the provision of sterile injecting equipment (i.e., needle exchange), (2) outreach and peer education efforts, and (3) substitution therapies such as methadone and supervised injection facilities. Such interventions, it is argued, assist in transforming drug use contexts that promote safe drug use as well as healthier behaviors.[168]

As noted above, one intervention associated with harm reduction is a needle exchange program. The purpose of such programs is to exchange used syringes for unused syringes among intravenous drug users to prevent the reuse of contaminated injection equipment. Needle exchange programs may offer other related materials such as bleach bottles, cotton swabs, skin ointment, condoms, and educational materials pertaining to sexually transmitted diseases and other communicable illnesses. However, "most [needle exchange programs] combine a program goal of risk reduction through needle exchange with a program goal of offering counseling and referral of participants to drug treatment programs."[169]

The legal aspects pertaining to needle exchange programs focus essentially on drug paraphernalia. Specifically, the manufacture, possession, or distribution of drug paraphernalia is illegal in most states as well as a violation of federal law.[170] Kate Ksobiech examined outcome measures from 31 studies of U.S. and international needle exchange programs. Her results revealed that while injection frequency lessened slightly among those in needle exchange programs compared to those not in such programs, this could be considered positive given that one major criticism of these programs is that providing clean needles encourages increased drug use. However, participating in such a program was not strongly associated with a lessening of sharing drug paraphernalia.[171]

harm reduction:
attempts to incorporate a public health approach to lessen the risks and harms associated with illegal drug use.

Applying Theory to Crime: DRUG SELLING/TRAFFICKING AND DRUG USE

This section applies two theoretical frameworks of crime to two of the primary offenses discussed in this chapter—drug selling/trafficking and drug use. Although readers may think the theoretical explanations for these activities are similar because both deal with illegal drugs, the most likely theories supported by research are different. This is a good example of how theories can differ, even within the same general category of criminal behavior.

Specifically, regarding drug selling/trafficking, the most logical and empirically supported theory is traditional strain theory.[174] Traditional strain theory places a high emphasis on individuals' innovating ways they can obtain the goals of financial success, without having to go through common conventional means (e.g., education, employment). Drug selling/trafficking can be a fast, albeit risky, way of obtaining a lot of money, without having to work hard in school or at a conventional job. Scientific studies have shown that this theory is supported as a primary reason for why individuals engage in this activity. After all, the lure of a fast payoff, given the high demand for various drugs, provides an extremely high motivation for people who have low levels of education and/or mainstream work experience.

On the other hand, drug use is not as well explained by traditional strain theory. Although Merton[175] did identify a type of retreatist adaption to strain (i.e., escaping from reality), which would include chronic drug users, this is not a strong motivation for their behavior. Rather, other theories are likely better for explaining why some individuals become habitual drug users. Specifically, various types of social learning theory and subcultural theory have been shown by empirical research

to be highly supported as explanations of chronic drug use.[176]

Regarding the social learning theories of drug use, differential association/reinforcement theory emphasizes the importance of peer influences in decisions to commit certain behaviors. This is likely most important in terms of drug use. After all, virtually no individuals take drugs for the first time when they are alone; rather, their initial experience in taking any drug (from alcohol to marijuana to cocaine to heroin) is almost always with other persons providing it and showing them how to ingest it, which for higher drugs (e.g., freebasing and injecting heroin) can be a complicated process. To a large extent, the initial taking of any drug is typically a social process; the person does it because a friend or group motivates him or her to "try it."

Of course, later episodes of drug use often become more solo, but the first experience is almost always peer influenced, which highly supports the social learning theories of differential association/reinforcement models of offending. The initial experience of engaging in taking illegal substances goes back to one's significant others and what they are doing and, thus, what they are exposing one to regarding drug behavior. This is supported by recent empirical studies, such as that by Golub et al., which showed that the influence of friends, peers, and intimate partners was key in engaging in drug use.[177]

Furthermore, numerous empirical studies have shown a cultural or subcultural emphasis regarding the initial engagement in drug use. After all, it is likely that many individuals would not engage in drug use if it wasn't highly prevalent in their community or neighborhood

culture. Recent studies, such as that by Golub, Johnson, and Dunlap, have supported this drug subcultural effect among many individuals not only regarding their initial use but also their subsequent chronic use.[178]

General strain theory[179] is also a good explanation for such chronic drug use. This model places an emphasis on coping mechanisms (or lack thereof) to deal with various stressors and frustrations in our lives. When an individual has not developed healthy coping mechanisms for dealing with life stressors (e.g., exercise, watching television, religion), then he or she has a high likelihood for using drugs to self-medicate and "deal" with reality. Unfortunately, this usually leads such drug users into a downward spiral, in which the drugs create even more stressors, which in turn lead to further heavy drug use and addiction.

Ultimately, the key purpose of this section is to demonstrate that several different theories are likely explanations for various illegal behaviors regarding drugs. Furthermore, it is likely that the most fitting theories for drug selling/trafficking are somewhat different from those of chronic drug use, which reveals how important theory is for understanding certain criminal behaviors, even those within a given category of offending, such as drug activity.

THINK IT ABOUT:

Critical thinking question:

1. Can you think of any other theories that would be likely explanations for various illegal behaviors regarding drugs?

LEARNING CHECK 16.3

1. The _____ suggests that drugs and violence are related through psychopharmacological, economically compulsive, and systematic violence.

2. The _____ strategies refer to the multistep efforts or events that focus on interrupting illicit drug trafficking.

3. The four techniques associated with _____ include mechanical destruction, bunting, chemical, and biological.

4. Due to the growing number of substance problems clogging up the criminal justice system, the _____ courts were established.

5. The _____ policy attempts to incorporate a public health approach to lessen the risks and harms associated with illegal drug use.

Answers located at www.edge.sagepub.com/schram2e

There are also ethical issues surrounding needle exchange programs. Cheryl Delgado asserts,

> The principle risk reduction accepts that a dangerous behavior like intravenous drug use is inevitable. Health officials therefore have a responsibility to the general public to reduce risks associated with the acts (drug use) they cannot prevent. Risk reduction is a more reasonable goal than attempts to eradicate illegal intravenous drug use.[172]

From this perspective, one would maintain that the reduced risk is not just to the drug user but to the community as well, with respect to limiting the spread of communicable diseases. Some, however, would argue that providing such a service may encourage intravenous drug use. Further, the time, money, and effort to implement needle exchange programs could be more productively used for treatment programs.[173]

RECOMMENDATIONS FOR FUTURE POLICIES

Drug policies in the United States will never be simple; policy can often be contradictory, especially in those instances when state- and local-level policies conflict with national policy.[180] McBride and McCoy maintain that three policy implications result from the current research on the relation between drugs and crime:[181]

1. While there is no clear causal relation between drugs and crime, there is a link between substance use and levels of criminal involvement. Policy should be directed toward providing treatment services for drug users who are involved in criminal activity. Such an approach has the potential to reduce levels of crime.

2. It is essential to appreciate that the history of drug use is entangled with the differential social, political, and economic opportunities of certain marginalized groups. Policy needs to incorporate efforts to enhance educational and economic opportunities. Such efforts need to be a priority on both the local and national level.

3. Any drug policy that is implemented must never compromise an individual's civil rights. "Drug law enforcement must never be an excuse for a retreat on hard-won legal and civil rights, and drug law and policy must rest on a strong public support base.[182]

Elliott Currie argues that substance abuse is not an isolated problem limited to certain communities and groups; rather, it is intertwined with broader social problems such as family dissolution, child abuse and neglect, and alcohol abuse. If policy focuses only on treating individual substance abusers, "new" substance abusers will follow, given the broader social problems. Thus, "the best, most comprehensive programs to help addicts transform their lives will inevitably be compromised if we do not simultaneously address the powerful social forces that are destroying the communities to which they must return."[183]

WHY DO THEY DO IT?

PABLO ESCOBAR

Escobar also enjoyed a luxurious lifestyle. His favorite estate was a 7,000-acre ranch in Colombia, valued at an estimated $63 million. He imported various exotic animals such as giraffes, camels, bison, llamas, cockatoos, and a kangaroo. He is known to have actually burned $2 million just to stay warm when he was "on the lam" from U.S. authorities. Later, he wanted to give the impression that he was a legitimate businessman; so he owned his own radio station and many times was accompanied by Roman Catholic priests. At the peak of Escobar's criminal activities, he and others associated with the Medellin cartel produced 60% of the cocaine in Colombia; this was about 80% of the U.S. market. In fact, Forbes magazine listed him as one of the world's richest people.

In December 1993, Pablo Escobar was killed by security forces in his hometown of Medellin, Colombia. Escobar started his criminal career by selling tombstones he stole from a cemetery and sanded flat. His first arrest was in 1974 for stealing a car. He soon became known to fellow associates and enemies as intelligent, ambitious, a fast learner, having a knack for business, and possessing an unforgiving memory. He later engaged in the practice of kidnapping individuals from wealthy families and seeking ransom from their family members. However, these criminal endeavors apparently did not get him the riches he desired, so he switched to the drug business.[184] Ironically, Escobar did not enjoy taking cocaine or other hard drugs. His drug of choice was marijuana, which he was known to smoke on a consistent basis. Persons who knew him closely called him a "pothead."

In 1976, he had earned a reputation as an established drug smuggler. He also had a reputation for killing people and blowing up neighborhoods, shopping centers, and a jetliner. Escobar's innovations in the drug-smuggling business introduced new ways of transporting drugs that had not been common before, including soaking designer jeans in a liquid form of cocaine. Furthermore, he was likely the first to use submarines to carry large shipments of cocaine up the Pacific coastline, now a common practice.[185] However, he was considered by some as a type of Robin Hood. He built houses for the poor, paved roads, constructed sports stadiums, and gave employment opportunities to thousands. This is why 20,000 local citizens showed up for his funeral.

In 1991, after a massive manhunt, Escobar negotiated his surrender. The terms included his presiding over his drug business while incarcerated. He had cellular phones, computers, and meetings in board rooms. His living conditions were quite comfortable, with a waterbed, rugs, curtains, a stereo system, and a 60-inch television. He was soon concerned that his enemies would try to bomb the jail; officials built him a bomb shelter.

In 1992, the details of his luxurious incarceration were revealed and the government decided to transport him to a regular jail. During transport, however, he escaped. Escobar began targeting suspected traitors and rivals. When his cartel diminished, the government began to search for him, which resulted in his shooting death in December 1993.[186]

THINK ABOUT IT:

1. Why did Escobar engage in this criminal activity?

2. Why did the government and some of the Colombian citizens support Escobar and his activities?

3. How would you deter someone from wanting to engage in this type of criminal activity

CONCLUSION

A key purpose of this chapter is for readers to obtain a greater appreciation for the complex relationship between substance use and crime. This relation is dynamic and is influenced by factors on an individual, group, and societal level. First, a review of the various types of drugs reveals that the mere definition of "drugs" is not necessarily simple. For instance, some drugs are legal but highly addictive (e.g., nicotine); some drugs are legally prescribed for medical purposes but can be used illegally (e.g., OxyContin); and some drugs were initially deemed legal but are now considered illegal (e.g., heroin).

To further illustrate this complex link between drug use and crime, we briefly reviewed various trends of substance abuse, such as the early history of cocaine and opioid addiction, Prohibition, the "reefer madness" era, the 1960s and the baby boomers, the War on Drugs, and current patterns of substance abuse. For one to appreciate the current societal perspectives of substance use, it is essential to appreciate the historical context of such trends.[187] For instance, historically, certain drugs were legal and subsequently designated illegal (e.g., cocaine); other substances, such as alcohol, were legal, then illegal, and later deemed legal again.

The next section discussed the link between substance use and crime. While the general public's opinion may be that this relation is straightforward, it is essential for readers to appreciate that the link between drugs and crime is more complex than this simple causal explanation. We then briefly discussed the Tripartite Conceptual Framework of the relation between drugs and violence. This framework proposes that substance use and violent behavior are related in three ways: through psychopharmacological, economically compulsive, and systemic violence.

The following section reviewed modern policies that have been implemented to address the problem of substance use and criminal activity. These include interdiction and eradication strategies, drug courts, maintenance and decriminalization, and harm reduction. It is important for the reader to critically question whether such policies are effective, as well as what other policy approaches should be considered.

We started this chapter with the case study of Samuel Ellis, convicted of two counts of vehicular manslaughter, and Kenneth Saltzman, convicted of furnishing alcohol to a minor. This case study illustrates various influences and issues pertaining to alcohol use in this country. These influences and issues include peer pressure, and parental approval, of alcohol use; legal implications of such parental approval; and attitudes regarding drinking alcohol in private residences.

KEY TERMS

alcohol, 467

amphetamine, 474

barbiturate, 472

binge drinking, 469

cannabis, 474

cocaine, 473

decriminalization, 490

depressants, 467

designer drugs, 475

drug treatment court programs, 488

Eighteenth Amendment, 477

eradication, 486

hallucinogens, 475

harm reduction, 492

Harrison Act, 476

heroin, 472

inhalants, 475

interdiction, 485

maintenance, 490

Marihuana Tax Act, 478

marijuana, 474

methamphetamine, 474

morphine, 472

narcotics, 472

oxycodone, 473

Prohibition, 477

steroids, 475

stimulant, 473

tranquilizers, 472

Tripartite Conceptual Framework, 484

Twenty-First Amendment, 477

War on Drugs, 496

DISCUSSION QUESTIONS

1. What are the differences between stimulants and depressants?

2. What are the key features of the Prohibition era?

3. What are some key issues related to the 1937 Marihuana Tax Act?

4. What is meant by racialized drug policy?

5. How would you characterize the War on Drugs?

6. What is the main purpose of harm reduction programs?

7. Why were drug courts established?

8. What are the main arguments for and against maintenance and decriminalization policies?

9. What features should be eliminated from or incorporated in future policies on substance use?

WEB RESOURCES

National Institute on Drug Abuse

The National Institute on Drug Abuse web resource provides information on various aspects pertaining to drug abuse including a summary of related topics such as criminal justice and drug testing.

http://www.drugabuse.gov/

Drug Enforcement Administration

The Drug Enforcement Administration web resources provides readers with NEA news as well as discussing various operations and career opportunities.

http://www.justice.gov/dea/index.shtml

Substance Abuse and Mental Health Services

This web resource provides information on issues related to substance abuse and mental health including treatment, programs and campaigns, as well as publications.

http://www.samhsa.gov/

$SAGE edge™

WANT A BETTER GRADE ON YOUR NEXT TEST?

Get the tools you need to sharpen your study skills:

SAGE edge offers a robust online environment featuring an impressive array of tools and resources for review, study, and further exploration, keeping both instructors and students on the cutting edge of teaching and learning. Learn more at **edge.sagepub.com/schram2e**.

FOR FURTHER EXPLORATION AND APPLICATION, VISIT THE STUDENT STUDY SITE:

- As Adults Legally Smoke Pot in Colorado, More Minority Kids Arrested for It

- Deadly Opioid Overwhelms First Responders and Crime Labs in Ohio

- Drugs for kicks

- Committing economic crime for drug money

- Drug Free World - Real Life Drug Story - Drug Addiction Experiences

- Mexico's Feared Narcos: A Brief History of the Zetas Drug Cartel

- Branson: U.N. to Call for Drug Decriminalization

- Is Drinking with Your Kids at Home a Good Idea?

- Smuggling

- Crocodile - The Zombie Drug

- Heroin

- Bath Salts

- The Heroin Epidemic

PREMIUM VIDEO:

Check out the Interactive eBook for premium videos, including videos from author Stephen Tibbetts, who discusses real-world examples and strange crimes; and videos from former offenders, who share their stories from a first-person view, and touch on key theories and concepts from the chapter.

GLOSSARY

actus reus: in legal terms, whether the offender actually engaged in a given criminal act (2)

active victim precipitation: when an individual increases the likelihood they will be victimized, particularly by proactively doing something, such as yelling a racial slur or "throwing the first punch" (1)

adaptations to strain: as proposed by Merton, the five ways that individuals deal with feelings of strain; see conformity, innovation, rebellion, retreatism, and ritualism (7)

add women and stir: when one uses an existing theoretical perspective based on males and "adds" women (11)

adolescence-limited offenders: a type of offender who commits crimes only during adolescence and desists in his or her 20s or adulthood (12)

adoption studies: studies that examine the criminality of adoptees as compared to the criminality of their biological and adoptive parents (5)

Age of Enlightenment: a period of the late 17th century to 18th century in which philosophers and scholars began to emphasize the rights of individuals in society (2)

aggregate studies: collection of studies, generally on a particular topic (3)

alcohol: ethanol is the only alcohol that should be consumed; rapidly absorbed through the stomach and small intestine into the bloodstream (15)

American Law Institute's Model Penal Code (ALI/MPC): one standard for the insanity defense. A key difference between the M'Naghten and the ALI/MPC tests is the M'Naghten test stipulates that the offender demonstrate *total* mental impairment; the ALI/MPC test stipulates that the offender demonstrate a lack of *substantial capacity* (6)

amphetamine: a type of stimulant; effects are similar to cocaine, but onset is slower and duration longer (15)

anomie: a concept originally proposed by Durkheim, which meant *normlessness* or the chaos that takes place when a society (e.g., economic structure) changes very rapidly (7)

atavism: belief that certain characteristics or behaviors of a person are throwbacks to an earlier stage of evolutionary development (4)

attachment theory: there are seven essential features of this theoretical perspective focusing on attachment: specificity, duration, engagement of emotion, course of development, learning, organization, and biological function (6)

autonomic nervous system: the portion of the nervous system that consists of our anxiety levels, such as the fight or flight response, as well as our involuntary motor activities (e.g., heart rate) (5)

barbiturate: a type of depressant; can induce a wide continuum of central nervous depression, ranging from mild sedation to coma (15)

Benjamin Mendelsohn: an attorney who is generally considered the "Father of Victimology" and proposed the first typology or theory of victimization that categorized victims by the degree to which the victims contributed to the criminal act in which they were victimized (1)

binge drinking: heavy episodic drinking; drinking so much alcohol within a 2-hour period that it results in at least a .08 blood alcohol concentration (15)

bourgeoisie: a class or status Marx assigned to the dominant, oppressing owners of the means of production; believed to create and implement laws that helped retain their dominance over the working class (10)

brutalization effect: the predicted tendency of homicides to increase after an execution, particularly after high-profile executions (2)

Campus Hate Crimes Right to Know Act of 1997: amends a section of the Higher Education Act of 1965 that provides for disclosure of all criminal incidents that indicate any evidence of prejudice based on race, gender, religion, sexual orientation, ethnicity, or disability (14)

cannabis: An extremely resourceful plant that contains hundreds of psychoactive chemicals, particularly delta-9-tetrahydrocannibinol (THC) (15)

central nervous system: the portion of the nervous system that largely consists of the brain and spinal column and is responsible for our voluntary motor activities (5)

cerebrotonic: the type of temperament or personality associated with an ectomorphic (thin) body type; these people tend to be introverted and shy (4)

certainty of punishment: one of the key elements of deterrence; the assumption is that when people commit a crime, they will perceive a high likelihood of being caught and punished (2)

Cesare Lombroso: one of the earliest theorists focusing on the female offender; his book emphasized the physiological and psychological determinants of female criminality rather than socializing factors or social–structural constraints (11)

Chicago School of criminology: theoretical framework of criminal behavior that emphasizes the environmental impact of living in a high-crime neighborhood, applies ecological principles to explain how cities grow, and highlights levels of neighborhood organization to explain crime rates(8)

Child Online Protection Act: prohibits individuals from knowingly engaging in communication for commercial purposes that includes material "harmful to minors" and available to minors (13)

chivalry: pertains to behaviors and attitudes toward certain individuals that treat them as though they are on a pedestal(11)

Code of Hammurabi: created in 1754 B.C., this code had many laws, but the most relevant for this course is that it included a portion that called for a restoration of equity between the offender and the victim provided by the government, referred to now as compensation (1)

compensation: funds provided to victims of violent crime that are provided by local, state or federal governmental funds (1)

Church Arson Prevention Act of 1996: prohibits intentional destruction of any religious real property or attempts to obstruct any person in the enjoyment of his or her free exercise of religious beliefs

classical conditioning: a learning model that assumes that animals, as well as people, learn through associations between stimuli and responses (9)

Classical School: model of crime that assumes crime occurs after a rational individual mentally weighs the potential good and bad consequences of crime and then makes a decision about whether to engage in a given behavior (2)

cocaine: a type of stimulant that appears in the leaves of various species of plants; usually distributed as a white, crystalline powder diluted with substances such as sugars and local anesthetics (15)

collective conscience: according to Durkheim, the extent to which people in a society share similarities or likenesses; the stronger the collective conscience, the less crime in that community (7)

college boy: a type of lower class male youth who has experienced the same strains and status frustration as his peers but responds to his disadvantaged situation by dedicating himself to overcoming the odds and competing in the middle-class schools despite his unlikely chances for success (7)

comparative criminology: the study of crime across various cultures to identify similarities and differences in crime patterns (1)

Computer Fraud and Abuse Act: originally designed to protect national security, financial, and commercial information; medical treatment; and interstate communication systems from malicious acts, including unauthorized access; allows victims of such crimes to bring civil suits against violators (13)

concentric circles: model proposed by Chicago School theorists that assumes that all cities grow in a natural way with the same five zones (8)

concordance rates: rates at which twin pairs either share a trait (e.g., criminality) or the lack of the trait (5)

concurrent jurisdiction: original jurisdiction for certain cases is shared by both criminal and juvenile courts; the prosecutor has discretion to file such cases in either court (1)

conflict gangs: a type of gang identified by Cloward and Ohlin that tends to develop in neighborhoods with weak stability and little or no organization; gangs are typically relatively disorganized and lack the skills and knowledge to make a profit through criminal activity (7)

conflict perspective or conflict theory: criminal behavior theories that assume most people disagree on what the law should be and that law is used as a tool by those in power to keep down other groups (1)

conformity: in strain theory, an adaptation in which an individual buys into the conventional means of success and also buys into conventional goals (7)

consensus perspective: theories that assume that virtually everyone is in agreement on the laws and therefore assume no conflict in attitudes regarding the laws and rules of society (1)

control theories: theories of criminal behavior that emphasize the assumption that humans are born selfish and that their tendencies toward aggression and offending must be controlled (9)

conventional level of morality: level of morality considered the normal adult approach used to maintain the family and social order such as the principle of the golden rule and appreciating social order (6)

Cooper v. Pate: as a result of this decision, prisoners were allowed to sue state officials in federal court, which resulted in much litigation and changed the prison conditions in the 1970s (13)

corner boy: a type of lower-class male youth who has experienced the same strains and status frustration as others but responds to his disadvantaged situation by accepting his place in society as someone who will somewhat passively make the best of life at the bottom of the social order. As the label describes, they often hang out on corners (7)

correlation or covariation: a criterion of causality that requires a change in a predictor variable (X) to be consistently associated with some change in the explanatory variable (Y) (1)

craniometry: field of study that emphasized the belief that the size of the brain or skull reflected superiority or inferiority, with larger brains and skulls being considered superior (4)

crime: here are various definitions of crime. From a legalistic approach, crime is that which violates the law. (1)

criminal gangs: a type of gang identified by Cloward and Ohlin that forms in lower-class neighborhoods with an organized structure of adult criminal behavior. Such gangs tend to be highly organized and stable (7)

criminal justice: criminal justice often refers to the various criminal justice agencies and institutions (e.g., police, courts, and corrections) that were interrelated (1)

criminal terrorism: terrorism motivated by engaging in criminal activity for profit, such as in the drug cartels in Mexico (14)

criminology: the scientific study of crime and the reasons why people engage (or don't engage) in criminal behavior (1)

cross-sectional studies: a form of research design model in which a collection of data is taken at one point in time (often in survey format) (3)

cultural/subcultural theory: perspective of criminal offending that assumes that many offenders believe in a normative system distinctly different from and often at odds with the norms accepted by conventional society (8)

cybercrime: cybercrime consists of at least three features: The act was committed using (1) a computer, (2) a "victim" computer, and (3) an intermediary network (13)

cyberstalking: when an individual engages in stalking behavior through such means as electronic mail or electronic communication (13)

cytogenetic studies: studies of crime that focus on the genetic makeups of individuals, with a specific focus on abnormalities in chromosomal makeups (5)

decriminalization: A policy related to labeling theory, which proposes less harsh punishments for some minor offenses, such as the possession of small amounts of marijuana (15)

delinquent boy: a type of lower-class male youth, identified by Cohen, who responds to strains and status frustration by joining with similar others in a group to commit crime (7)

Department of Homeland Security: a Cabinet department of the U.S. federal government, established in 2003 in response to the September 11 attacks; main responsibilities include protecting the United States from terrorist attacks and responding to terrorist attacks, man-made accidents, and natural disasters (14)

depressants: slow down, or "depress," the normal activity of the central nervous system

designer drugs: substances considered to be for recreational use; derivatives of approved drugs that can circumvent existing legal restrictions (15)

determinism: the assumption that human behavior is caused by factors outside of free will and rational decision making (4)

deterrence theory: theory of crime associated with the Classical School; proposes that individuals will make rational decisions regarding their behavior (2)

developmental theories: perspectives of criminal behavior that emphasize the evolution of individuals' criminality over time, with the individual as the unit of analysis (12)

deviance: behaviors that are not normal; includes many illegal acts, as well as activities that are not necessarily criminal but are unusual and often violate social norms (1)

differential association theory: A theory of criminal behavior that emphasizes association with significant others (peers, parents, etc.) in learning criminal behavior (9)

differential identification: a theory of criminal behavior similar to differential association theory, the major difference being that this theory takes into account associations with persons and images presented in the media (9)

differential reinforcement theory: a theory of criminal behavior that emphasizes various types of social learning, specifically classical conditioning, operant conditioning, and imitation or modeling (9)

Digital Millennium Copyright Act: criminalizes making, distributing, or using tools, such as software, to evade technological protection measures implemented by copyright owners to prevent access to copyrighted material (13)

dissident terrorism: involves terrorist activities against the government that are committed by rebellious groups (14)

dizygotic twins: twin pairs that come from two separate eggs (zygotes) and thus share only 50% of the genetic makeup that can vary (5)

domestic terrorism: unlawful use, or threatened use, of force or violence by a group or individual based in the United States to intimidate or coerce others to further political or social objectives (14)

dopamine: a neurotransmitter that is largely responsible for good feelings in the brain; it is increased by many illicit drugs (e.g., cocaine)(5)

dramatization of evil: concept proposed by Tannenbaum in relation to labeling theory; states that when relatively minor laws are broken, the community tends to dramatize it (10)

drug treatment court programs: Established in an effort to address the increasing number of drug-using offenders clogging the criminal justice system (15)

Durham: offenders are not criminally responsible, even if they are aware of their conduct, if this behavior was the "product of mental disease or defect." (6)

ectoderm: medical term for the outer layer of tissue in our bodies (4)

ectomorphic: type of body shape associated with an emphasis on the outer layer of tissue (ectoderm) during development(4)

Edwin Sutherland: coined the term *white-collar crime*; generally considered the most prominent criminologist of the 20th century (13)

ego: the only conscious domain of the psyche; according to Freud, it functions to mediate the battle between id and superego (6)

Eighteenth Amendment: Put into effect national Prohibition on January 16, 1920 (15)

Electronic Communications Privacy Act: regulates the interception of electronic communications by individuals as well as the government (13)

empirical validity: refers to the extent to which a theoretical model is supported by scientific research (1)

endoderm: medical term for the inner layer of tissue in our bodies

endomorphic: type of body shape associated with an emphasis on the inner layer of tissue (endoderm) during development (4)

Environmental Protection Agency: started in 1970, charged with protecting human health and safeguarding the natural environment (13)

eradication: Four recognized techniques: mechanical destruction (i.e., slashing or uprooting), bunting, chemical, and biological (including genetic) (15)

eugenics: the study of and policies related to the improvement of the human race via discriminatory control over reproduction (4)

experiential effect: extent to which previous experience affects individuals' perceptions of how severe criminal punishment will be when deciding whether or not to offend again (3)

extroversion: in reference to the PEN-model, traits associated with extroversion include being sociable, lively, active, assertive, sensation-seeking, carefree, dominant, surgent, and venturesome cautious) (6)

falsely accused: based on Becker's typology, when an individual has been identified as disobeying the rules but did not violate the rules (10)

family studies: studies that examine the clustering of criminality in a given family (5)

Federal Emergency Management Agency (FEMA): focuses on emergency management and recovery from a catastrophic event on a local and national level (14)

feeble-mindedness: technical, scientific term in the early 1900s meaning those who had significantly below average levels of intelligence (4)

first wave of feminism: started in the mid-1800s when women demanded the right to vote

focal concerns: primary concept of Miller's theory, which asserts that all members of the lower class focus on concepts they deem important: fate, autonomy, trouble, toughness, excitement, and smartness (8)

formal/official deterrence: deterrent effects of law enforcement, courts, and corrections(3)

frontal lobes: a region of the brain located in the frontal portion of the brain; most of the executive functions of the brain, such as problem solving, take place here (5)

fundraising: used by terrorist organizations to finance their activities (14)

game theory: assesses various scenarios by applying simulation gaming models, usually to understand why parties in competitive situations behave as they do and to advise players of the best way to play the game (14)

gender: gender usually refers to social definitions of what it means to be a *woman* or a *man* (11)

gender-specific programming: programs targeted to juvenile girls; gives females an increased sense of community that has been associated with developing and integrating a healthy identity (11)

general deterrence: punishments given to an individual meant to prevent or deter other potential offenders from engaging in such criminal activity in the future (2)

group conflict theory: Vold argued that part of human nature is that people's lives are a part, and a product, of their group associations; groups come into conflict with one another due to conflicting and competitive interests (10)

hackers: individuals who violate computer security (13)

hallucinogens: Drugs that alter one's thought processes, mood, and perceptions (15)

harm reduction: Attempts to incorporate a public health approach to lessen the risks and harms associated with illegal drug use (15)

Harrison Act: Passed by Congress in 1914, required doctors to have a license number to prescribe narcotics (15)

Hate Crime Statistics Act of 1990: as part of the Uniform Crime Report program, the attorney general was required to develop guidelines and collect data about crimes that manifest evidence of prejudice based on race, religion, sexual orientation, or ethnicity (14)

hate crimes: traditional offenses, such as murder and vandalism, with an additional factor of bias (14)

heroin: The most infamous opiate drug; a chemically modified form of morphine that ranged in color from white to black (15)

highway patrol: one type of model characterizing statewide police departments. The primary focus is to enforce the laws that govern the operation of motor vehicles on public roads and highways (1)

homeland security: a unified national effort to prevent terrorist attacks within the United States, lessen America's vulnerability to terrorism, and minimize the damage resulting from such attacks (14)

human rights: universal values and legal guarantees that protect individuals against actions or omissions, primarily by government agents, that infringe on their fundamental freedoms, entitlements, and human dignity (14)

id: a subconscious domain of the psyche, according to Freud, with which we are all born; it is responsible for our innate desires and drives (such as libido [sex drive]) and it battles the moral conscience of the superego (6)

identity theft: occurs when an individual obtains a false identity to commit identity fraud; can be used by criminals and terrorists to establish false identities and escape detection (13)

informal deterrence: factors like family, church, or friends that do not involve official aspects of criminal justice, such as police, courts, and corrections (e.g., prisons) (3)

inhalants: volatile substances that produce chemical vapors and whose primary trait is that they are rarely taken by any other delivery method than inhalation (15)

innovation: in strain theory, an adaptation to strain in which an individual buys into the conventional goals of success but does not buy into the conventional means for getting to the goals (7)

insanity: the idea of excusing offenders for their criminal actions due to a mental disease has been in existence for centuries. The term *insanity* is not a medical term; rather it is a legal term(6)

intelligence quotient (IQ): a quantified measure of intelligence (6)

interdiction: describes the various steps implemented to interrupt illicit drug trafficking (e.g., cueing, detection, apprehension, prosecution) (15)

Internet fraud: when individuals use the Internet to engage in fraud, often identity theft (13)

irresistible impulse: one standard for the insanity defense. Offenders can claim that, due to a mental disease, they were unable to control their behavior (6)

jail: jails are often designated for individuals convicted of a minor crime, and to house individuals awaiting trial (1)

Kefauver Committee: in 1950, charged with three responsibilities that focused on whether organized crime used services of interstate commerce to engage in illegal activities and identifying the persons, firms, or corporations involved in such activities (13)

judicial waiver: the authority to waive juvenile court jurisdiction and transfer the case to criminal court (1)

labeling theory: theoretical perspective that assumes that criminal behavior increases because certain individuals are caught and labeled as offenders; their offending increases because they have been stigmatized (10)

learning theories: theoretical models that assume that criminal behavior of individuals is due to a process of learning from others the motivations and techniques for engaging in such behavior (9)

left realism: contends that previous criminological theories have been incomplete in that they emphasize only one part of the square of crime; attempts to provide an analysis of crime on all levels and develop a range of policy recommendations (10)

liberal feminism: one of the areas of feminist theories of crime that emphasize the assumption that differences between males and females in offending were due to the lack of female opportunities in education, employment, etc., compared with males (11)

liberation thesis: also referred to as the emancipation hypothesis; attempts to link the women's liberation movement with female crime rates (11)

life-course persistent offenders: a type of offender who starts offending early and persists through adulthood (12)

limited jurisdiction: the authority of a court to hear and decide cases within an area of the law or a geographic territory (1)

logical consistency: the extent to which concepts and propositions of a theoretical model makes sense in terms of both face value and consistency with what is readily known about crime rates and trends (1)

low self-control: a theory that proposes that individuals either develop self-control by age 10 or do not. Those who do not will manifest criminal or deviant behaviors throughout life (9)

Mafia: similar to an extended social family; members took an oath swearing, under punishment of death, to a code of silence. It started as a self-protection group, but by the 1860s expanded to criminal activities such as smuggling, cattle rustling, and extortion. (13)

Mafioso: referred to characteristics of a man such as pride, self-confidence, and a sense of "arrogant" behavior (13)

maintenance: advocates for the accessibility of drugs through governmental regulation, such as distribution and legal age of use (15)

mala in se: acts that are considered inherently evil (1)

mala prohibita: acts that are considered crimes primarily because they have been declared bad by the legal codes in that jurisdiction (1)

Marihuana Tax Act: effective October 1, 1937; did not criminalize marijuana or its preparations but did tax the grower, distributor, seller, and buyer (15)

marijuana: the dried leaves or flowers of the cannabis plant (15)

Marxist feminism: a perspective of crime that emphasizes men's ownership and control of the means of economic production; similar to critical or radical feminism but distinguished by its reliance on the concept of economic structure (11)

Matthew Shepard and James Byrd, Jr., Hate Crimes Prevention Act of 2009: makes it unlawful to willfully cause bodily injury, or attempt to do so, with a dangerous weapon when the offense is committed because of the actual or perceived race, color, religion, national origin, gender, sexual orientation, gender identity, or disability of any person (14)

mechanical societies: in Durkheim's theory, these societies were rather primitive with a simple distribution of labor (e.g., hunters & gatherers) and thus a high level of agreement regarding social norms and rules because nearly everyone is engaged in the same roles (7)

mens rea: concept regarding whether offenders actually knew what they were doing and meant to do it (2)

mental health courts: established to address the large proportion of individuals with mental illnesses involved in the criminal justice system (6)

mesoderm: medical term for the middle layer of tissue in our bodies (4)

mesomorphic: type of body shape associated with an emphasis on the middle layer of tissue (mesoderm) during development (4)

methamphetamine: The most common form of amphetamine today, it can take the form of a white, odorless powder that dissolves in water; clear, "chunky" crystals; or small, brightly colored tablets. (15)

minor physical anomalies: physical features, such as asymmetrical or low-seated ears, which are believed to indicate developmental problems (4)

mission distortion: occurred when those agencies involved in the reorganization of the Department of Homeland Security acquired new responsibilities and also were to continue with their agency's missions prior to the merge (14)

M'Naghten rule: the M'Naghten case introduced the modern concept of insanity into English Common Law. The legal standard is that "he didn't know what he was doing or didn't know it was wrong" (6)

model state legislation for hate crimes/violence against people experiencing homelessness: the National Law Center on Homelessness and Poverty and the National Coalition for the Homeless advocated for state legislation that includes homelessness in hate crimes statutes (14)

modeling/imitation: a major factor in differential reinforcement theory that proposes that much social learning takes place via imitation or modeling of behavior (9)

Moffitt's developmental theory or taxonomy: a theoretical perspective proposing that criminal behavior is caused by (1) adolescence-limited offenders and (2) life-course persistent offenders (12)

money laundering: a process whereby funds, obtained through illegal activities, are "cleansed" (14)

monozygotic twins: also referred to as identical twins, these are twin pairs that come from a single egg (zygote) and thus share 100% of their genetic makeup. (5)

morphine: one of the most effective drugs for relief of severe physical pain; has high potential for abuse (15)

multiracial feminism: an intersectional framework that includes such defining social characteristics as race, class, gender, sexuality, nationality, and age (11)

narcotics: opiates (drugs derived from the opium poppy) or opioids (synthetically produced opiates); includes morphine, heroin, and oxycodone (15)

National Counterterrorism Center: provides the Department of State with statistical information on terrorism (14)

National Crime Victimization Survey (NCVS): a primary measures of crime in the United States; collected by the DOJ and the Census Bureau, based on interviews with victims of crime (1)

natural areas: Chicago School's idea that all cities contain identifiable clusters, such as a Chinatown or Little Italy, and neighborhoods that have low or high crime rates (8)

negative reinforcement: a concept in social learning in which people are rewarded through removal of something they dislike (9)

negotiation: one of the key factors identified by Schur (i.e., labeling process); more noticeable in cases involving adults rather than juveniles (e.g., plea bargaining) (10)

Neoclassical School: assumes that aggravating and mitigating circumstances should be taken into account for purposes of sentencing and punishing an offender (2)

neuroticism: in reference to the PEN-model, neuroticism is often linked with such traits as being anxious, depressed, tense, irrational, shy, moody and emotional, and having guilty feelings and low self-esteem (6)

neurotransmitters: nervous system chemicals in the brain and body that help transmit electric signals from one neuron to another(5)

nonpartisan conflict perspective: according to Turk, the ideological position or political utilities of theories are irrelevant when assessing the validity of knowledge claims; *truth* should be independent of political ideology or personal values (10)

objectivity: refers to being "neutral," "value free," or "unbiased." Feminist scholars challenge research claims of objectivity (11)

Occupational Safety and Health Act: among other things, made it a misdemeanor to cause the death of a worker by willfully violating safety laws (13)

operant conditioning: a learning model based on the association between an action and feedback following the action (9)

organic societies: in the Durkheimian model, those societies that have a high division of labor and thus a low level of agreement about societal norms, largely because everyone has such different roles in society (7)

organized crime: sometimes defined through a typology, such as the means of obtaining the goals and the reasons for engaging in such activity: an economic objective or a political objective (13)

Otto Pollak: argued that women are more criminal in nature than has been generally perceived; suggested that criminologists should address the unknown criminality of women (11)

outlaw motorcycle gangs: the tough-guy image of these groups was perpetuated and membership increased, along with organization and sophistication. Soon, behavior of some groups was less rebellious and more openly criminal; some members refer to themselves as "one-percenters" (13)

oxycodone: synthetic narcotic produced entirely in the laboratory; includes OxyContin, Percodan, and Percocet (15)

parens patriae: a philosophical perspective that recognizes that the state has both the right and obligation to intervene on behalf of its citizens due to some impairment or impediment such as mental incompetence, or in the case of juveniles, age and immaturity (1)

parsimony: characteristic of a good theory, meaning that it explains a certain phenomenon, such as criminal behavior, with the fewest possible propositions or concepts. (1)

partisan conflict perspective: according to Quinney, provides a theory and practice with the purpose of changing the world; associated political objective (10)

paternalism: denotes that women need to be protected for their own good. In a broader social context, paternalism implies independence for men and dependence for women (11)

passive victim precipitation: when an individual increases the likelihood they will be victimized, particularly by *not* doing something, such not locking their home or car (1)

pathways research: typically collects data, usually through interviews, at one point in time that provide retrospective inquiry as to an individual's life and life experiences (11)

patriarchy: a social, legal, and political climate based on male dominance and hierarchy. A key aspect to this ideology is that women's nature is biologically, not culturally, determined (11)

peacemaking criminology: incorporates three intellectual traditions: religious, feminist, and critical; contends that society should attempt reconciliation through mediation and dispute settlement (10)

PEN model: discussions of this theory emphasize that human personality can be viewed in three dimensions: psychoticism, extraversion, and neuroticism (6)

"The personal is the political": refers to the notion that the "private sphere" is as structured by power relations involving gender, sexuality, race, class, and age as the "public sphere" (11)

phenotype: an observed manifestation of the interaction of genotypical traits with the environment, such as height (5)

phrenology: the science of determining human dispositions based on distinctions (e.g., bumps) in the skull, which is believed to conform to the shape of the brain (4)

physiognomy: the study of facial and other bodily aspects to identify developmental problems, such as criminality (4)

positive reinforcement: a concept in social learning in which people are rewarded by receiving something they want (9)

Positive School: a perspective that assumes individuals have no free will to control their behavior. (4)

postconventional level of morality: when a person attempts to balance between individual rights and societal rules (6)

postmodern feminism: a perspective that says women as a group cannot be understood, even by other women, because every person's experience is unique; therefore, there is no need to measure or research such experiences (11)

power–control theory: integrated theory of crime that assumes that, in households where the mother and father have relatively similar levels of power at work, mothers will be less likely to exert control over daughters, and in households where mothers and fathers have dissimilar levels of power in the workplace, mothers will be more likely to suppress criminal activity in daughters but not in sons (11)

praxis: refers not just to consciousness raising but also to the establishment of alternative arrangements that will provide models for change, which then change consciousness (11)

preconventional level of morality: level of morality characteristic of designating what is considered "right" and "wrong" (6)

primary deviance: in labeling theory, the type of minor, infrequent offending people commit before they are caught and labeled as offenders (10)

prison: generally for those convicted of more serious crimes with longer sentences, who may be housed in a supermax, maximum, medium, or minimum security prison (1)

probation: probation is essentially an *arrangement* between the sentencing authorities and the offender requiringthe offender to comply with certain terms for a specified amount of time (1)

Prohibition: After the passage of the Eighteenth Amendment, an era in which it was illegal to manufacture, sell, or transport intoxicating liquors within the United States (15)

proletariat: in Marx's conflict theory, the oppressed group of workers exploited by the bourgeoisie; they never profit from their own efforts because the upper class owns and controls the means of production (10)

psychoanalytic perspective: an individual's behavior is presumed to be due to the three aspects of his or her personality: the id, ego, and superego. Second, *anxiety, defense mechanisms,* and the *unconscious* are also key principles of the psychoanalytical perspective (6)

psychopath: refers to individuals whose antisocial behavior may be a result from a defect or abnormality within themselves rather than in their rearing or socialization (6)

psychoticism: individuals considered to have high psychoticism are associated with being aggressive, cold, egocentric, impersonal, impulsive, antisocial, unempathic, creative, and tough-minded; individuals with low psychoticism are characterized as being empathic, unselfish, altruistic, warm, peaceful, and generally more pleasant (6)

pure deviant: based on Becker's typology, an individual who disobeys the rules and is perceived as doing so (10)

qualitative: nonnumerical research methods; often compared with quantitative research methods (11)

quantitative: numerical research methods; often compared with qualitative research methods (11)

Racketeer Influenced and Corrupt Organizations (RICO) Act: provides for enhanced criminal and civil penalties for individuals engaging in activities with criminal organizations (13)

radical feminism: emphasizes the importance of personal feelings, experiences, and relationships; gender is a system of male dominance, and women's biology is the main cause of patriarchy (11)

rational choice theory: a modern, Classical School-based framework for explaining crime that includes the traditional formal deterrence aspects and other informal factors that studies show consistently and strongly influence behavior (3)

reaction formation: a Freudian defense mechanism applied to Cohen's theory of youth offending, which involves adopting attitudes or committing behaviors that are opposite of what is expected (7)

rebellion: in strain theory, an adaptation to strain in which an individual buys into the idea of conventional means and goals of success but does not buy into the current conventional means or goals (7)

relative deprivation: the perception that results when relatively poor people live in close proximity to relatively wealthy people (7)

religious terrorism: motivated by engaging in terrorist acts that are legitimized by religious dogma (14)

restitution: funds provided to victims of crime that are provided by the offender as a condition of his/her sentence (1)

restorative justice: refers to the repair of justice by reaffirming a shared consensus of values involving a joint or multisided approach; emphasizes victim, community, and offender (10)

retreatism: in strain theory, an adaptation to strain in which an individual does not buy into the conventional goals of success and also does not buy into the conventional means (7)

retreatist gangs: a type of gang identified by Cloward and Ohlin that tends to attract individuals who have failed to succeed in both the conventional world and the criminal or conflict gangs of their neighborhoods (7)

retributive justice: refers to the repair of justice through a one-sided approach of imposing punishment (10)

retrospective interpretation: in labeling theory, the process by which an individual is identified as a deviant and thereafter viewed in a "new light"(10)

ritualism: in strain theory, an adaptation to strain in which an individual buys into the conventional means of success (e.g., work, school, etc.) but does not buy into the conventional goals (7)

routine activities theory (lifestyle theory): explanation of crime that assumes crime and victimization are highest in places where three factors come together in time and place: motivated offenders, suitable or attractive targets, and absence of a guardian (3)

scenario research or vignettes: studies that involve providing participants with specific hypothetical scenarios and then asking them what they would do in each situation

scope: refers to the range of criminal behavior that a theory attempts to explain (1)

second wave of feminism: developed in the 1960s when other marginalized groups were also challenging the status quo (e.g., civil rights movement, prisoners' rights movement). Feminists of this wave argued that to be fully liberated, women needed to have equal access to economic opportunities and sexual freedoms as well as civil liberties (11)

secondary deviance: in labeling theory, the more serious, frequent offending people commit after they have been caught and labeled as offenders (10)

secret deviant: based on Becker's typology, an individual who violates the rules of society but elicits no reaction from society (10)

selective placement: an argument that adoptees tend to be placed in households that resemble that of their biological parents; thus, adoptees from rich biological parents are placed in rich adoptive households (5)

serotonin: a neurotransmitter that is key in information processing and most consistently linked to criminal behavior in its deficiency; low levels are linked to depression and other mental illnesses. (5)

severity of punishment: the assumption is that a given punishment must be serious enough to outweigh any potential benefits gained from a crime (2)

sex: sex differences typically refer to biological variations such as reproductive organs and hormones (11)

sex roles: research using the sex role approach has been criticized primarily because of the tendency to perceive these roles as being almost sex-linked, without incorporating a larger context for how these roles have been defined, leading to a form of biological determinism (11)

Sigmund Freud: originated psychoanalysis, founded on the perception of resistance used by individuals when therapists attempt to make them conscious of their unconscious; perceived women as anatomically inferior (11)

social bonding: a control theory that assumes that individuals are predisposed to commit crime and that conventional bonds prevent or reduce offending. This bond is made up of four constructs: attachments, commitment, involvement, and moral beliefs regarding committing crime (9)

social contract: an Enlightenment ideal or assumption that stipulates an unspecified arrangement among citizens in which they promise the state or government not to commit offenses against other citizens, and in turn, they gain protection from being violated by other citizens (2)

socialist feminism: feminist theories that moved away from economic structure (e.g., Marxism) and placed a focus on control of reproductive systems; believes that women should take control of their own bodies and reproductive functions via contraceptives (11)

sociopath: refers specifically to antisocial personalities that are due to social or familial dysfunction (6)

soft determinism: the assumption that both determinism and free will play a role in offenders' decisions to engage in criminal behavior (9)

somatotonic: type of temperament or personality associated with a mesomorphic (muscular) body type; tends to be risk taking and aggressive (4)

somatotyping: the area of study, primarily linked to William Sheldon, that links body type to risk for delinquent and criminal behavior. Also, as a methodology, it is a way of ranking body types based on three categories: *endomorphy, mesomorphy,* and *ectomorphy* (4)

specific deterrence: punishments given to an individual meant to prevent or deter that particular individual from committing crime in the future (2)

spuriousness: when other factors (often referred to as Z factors) are actually causing two variables (X and Y) to occur at the same time; it may appear as if X causes Y, when in fact they are both being caused by other Z factor(s) (1)

state police: agencies with general police powers to enforce state laws as well as to investigate major crimes, they may have intelligence units, drug trafficking units, juvenile units, and crime laboratories (1)

state-sponsored terrorism: includes terrorist acts that transpire due to the guidance of the state or government against perceived enemies (14)

status-degradation ceremony: the most dramatic way to initiate the process of giving an individual a new identity, such as a criminal trial (10)

statutory exclusion: excludes certain juvenile offenders from juvenile court jurisdiction; cases originate in criminal rather than juvenile court. (1)

stereotyping: in labeling theory, usually associated with racial prejudice and discrimination(10)

steroids: synthetically produced variations of the male sex hormone testosterone; some approved for medical and veterinary use (15)

stigmata: the physical manifestations of atavism (biological inferiority), according to Lombroso(4)

stimulant: creates a sense of energy, alertness, talkativeness, and well-being considered pleasurable to the user (15)

superego: a subconscious domain of the psyche; according to Freud, it is not part of our nature but must be developed through early social attachments (6)

swiftness of punishment: assumption is that the faster punishment occurs after a crime is committed, the more an individual will be deterred in the future (2)

symbolic interactionism: proposes that many social interactions involve symbolism, which occurs when individuals interpret each other's words or gestures and act based on the meaning of those gestures (10)

Tammany Hall: a notorious Democratic political machine in New York City from the 1790s through the 1960s, with major influence in city and state politics (13)

techniques of neutralization: a theory that suggests that individuals, especially in their teenage years and early adulthood, make excuses to alleviate guilt related to committing certain criminal acts (9)

temporal lobe: the region of the brain responsible for a variety of functions and that is located right above many primary limbic structures that govern our emotional and memory functions(5)

temporal ordering: the criterion for determining causality; requires that the predictor variable (X) precedes the explanatory variable (Y) in time(1)

testability: the extent that a theoretical model can be empirically or scientifically tested through observation and empirical research(1)

Thinking for a Change: an integrated cognitive behavioral change program that includes cognitive restructuring, social skill development, and the development of problem solving skills(6)

third wave of feminism: evolved around the late 1980s and into the 1990s; an extension of as well as a response to the shortcomings of the second wave (11)

Thornberry's interactional model: the first major perspective to emphasize reciprocal, or feedback, effects in the causal modeling of the theoretical framework (12)

traditional or conservative perspective: causes of gender inequality are due to biological sex differences, and social behavior is based on the biological sex differences; does not offer any strategies for social change since men's and women's behaviors reflect evolutionary adaptations of sex differences(11)

trajectories: paths people take in life, often due to life transitions (12)

tranquilizers: a type of depressant; can help with anxiety without disrupting normal functions. Problems include sleepiness and in coordination, hampered learning process, and amnesia. (15)

transitions: events important in altering trajectories toward or away from crime, such as marriage or employment (12)

Transportation Security Administration (TSA): provides security for all types of transportation; recruits, assesses, hires, trains, and deploys security officers for commercial airports; and provides screening of all checked luggage (14)

Tripartite Conceptual Framework: Suggests that drugs and violence are related to each other through psychopharmacological, economically compulsive, and systemic violence (15)

Twenty-First Amendment: Ratified on December 5, 1933, and repealed the Eighteenth Amendment (15)

twins separated at birth studies: studies that examine the similarities between identical twins who are separated in infancy(5)

twin studies: studies that examine the relative concordance rates for monozygotic versus dizygotic twins(5)

Uniform Crime Report (UCR): an annual report published by the FBI in the DOJ, which is meant to estimate most of the major street crimes in the United States(1)

USA PATRIOT Act: focuses on collecting communications information and data, conducting foreign intelligence investigations, controlling money laundering, and funding and enhancing national border security (14)

U.S. Citizenship and Immigration Services (USCIS): responsible for administration of immigration and naturalization adjudication functions (14)

U.S. Coast Guard: the only military organization within the Department of Homeland Security; its role includes protecting ports, maintaining border security, and coordinating intelligence with various government entities (14)

U.S. Customs and Border Protection (CBP): responsible for securing U.S. borders while also monitoring the flow of legitimate trade and travel (14)

U.S. Immigration and Customs Enforcement (ICE): focuses on identifying criminal activities and vulnerabilities that may be a threat to the country (14)

U.S. Secret Service: responsible for safeguarding the country's financial infrastructure and payment systems, as well as protecting national leaders and visiting heads of state and government (14)

utilitarianism: a philosophical concept that relates to the idea of the greatest good for the greatest number

victim impact statements or VIS: statements that are given by victims during the sentencing phase of a trial; these can be given in many ways, such as in person, a letter, or a video (1)

victim precipitation: when an individual increases the likelihood they will be victimized, by something they do or don't do (1)

victimology: the scientific study of victims of crime (1)

vignettes: short, descriptive sketches(2)

Violent Crime Control and Law Enforcement Act of 1994: amended the Hate Crime Statistics Act to enhance penalties for offenses that involve a motivation bias (14)

viscerotonic: the type of temperament or personality associated with an endomorphic (obese) body type; these people tend to be jolly, lazy, and happy-go-lucky (4)

War on Drugs: Public concern about drugs, building throughout the 1980s, exploded in late 1985 and early 1986 (15)

white-collar crime: criteria include (1) upper-class offender, (2) work-related violations, (3) work-related violations of blue-collar workers excluded, and (4) regular crimes committed by upper-class persons excluded(13)

W. I. Thomas: argued that there are basic biological differences between males and females (11)

Wickersham Commission: formed in 1929, the commission found that organized criminal activity flourished around bootlegging operations(13)

women's agency: the more traditional approach overlooks social locations of women's marginalization and places too much emphasis on female offenders as "active subjects" who pursue criminal opportunities. On the other end, women are denied agency and situated as mere instruments for the reproduction of determining social structures(11)

zone in transition: in the Chicago School, this zone (Zone II) was once residential but is becoming more industrial because of invading factories; tends to have the highest crime rates (8)

NOTES

CHAPTER 1

1. Rosner, L. (2011). *Anatomy murders: Being the true and spectacular history of Edinburgh's notorious Burke and Hare and of the man of science who abetted them in the commission of their most heinous crimes.* Philadelphia: University of Pennsylvania Press, pp. 240–244.

2. University of Edinburgh, Biomedical-Sciences/Anatomy. (2016, March 22). *William Burke.* Retrieved from http://www.ed.ac.uk/biomedical-sciences/anatomy/anatomy-museum/exhibits/burke

3. Wagner, M. (2016, January 30). Detroit couple accused of hacking donated corpses with chainsaw, selling diseased body parts to unwitting medical students. *New York Daily News.* Retrieved from http://www.nydailynews.com/news/crime/body-part-dealer-rented-infected-cadavers-students-article-1.2514657

4. Henry, S., & Lanier, M. (2001). *What is crime? Controversies over the nature of crime and what to do about it.* Lanham, MD: Rowman & Littlefield.

5. Black, H. C., Nolan, J. M., & Nolan-Haley, J. M. (1990). *Black's law dictionary* (6th ed.). St. Paul, MN: West, p. 959.

6. Ibid., p. 960.

7. Tibbetts, S. G. (2012). *Criminological theory: The essentials.* Thousand Oaks, CA: SAGE, pp. 3–4.

8. Adler, F., Mueller, G. O. W., & Laufer, W. S. (2007). *Criminology* (6th ed.). Boston, MA: McGraw-Hill, p. 10.

9. Sutherland, E. H. (1934). *Principles of criminology* (2nd ed.). Philadelphia, PA: Lippincott, p. 3.

10. Brown, S., Esbensen, F., & Geis, G. (2007). *Criminology* (6th ed.). Cincinnati, OH: LexisNexis.

11. Bernard, T. J., Paoline, E. A., & Pare, P. (2005). General systems theory and criminal justice. *Journal of Criminal Justice, 33,* 203–211, p. 205.

12. Belknap, J. (2007). *The invisible woman: Gender, crime, and justice* (3rd ed.). Belmont, CA: Thomson Wadsworth, p. 1.

13. Akers, R. L. (1997). *Criminological theories: Introduction and evaluation* (2nd ed.). Los Angeles, CA: Roxbury.

14. Ibid., p. 139.

15. Barkan, S. E. (2012). *Criminology: A sociological understanding* (5th ed.). Boston, MA: Prentice Hall.

16. Akers, R. L. (1997). *Criminological theories: Introduction and evaluation* (2nd ed.). Los Angeles, CA: Roxbury, p. 140.

17. Ibid.

18. Ibid., p. 141.

19. President's Commission on Law Enforcement and Administration of Justice. (1967). *The challenge of crime in a free society.* Washington, DC: Government Printing Office, p. 7.

20. Gaines, L. K., & Miller, R. L. (2011). *Criminal justice in action* (6th ed.). Belmont, CA: Wadsworth Cengage Learning, p. 11.

21. Inciardi, J. A. (1993). *Criminal justice* (4th ed.). Fort Worth, TX: Harcourt Brace College Publishers, p. 176.

22. Gaines, L. K., & Miller, R. L. (2011). *Criminal justice in action* (6th ed.). Belmont, CA: Wadsworth Cengage Learning, p. 13.

23. Inciardi, J. A. (1993). *Criminal justice* (4th ed.). Fort Worth, TX: Harcourt Brace College Publishers, p. 181.

24. Gaines, L. K., & Miller, R. L. (2011). *Criminal justice in action* (6th ed.). Belmont, CA: Wadsworth Cengage Learning, p. 13.

25. Ibid., p. 15.

26. Ibid., p. 275.

27. Inciardi, J. A. (1993). *Criminal justice* (4th ed.). Fort Worth, TX: Harcourt Brace College Publishers, p. 313.

28. Gaines, L. K., & Miller, R. L. (2010). *Criminal justice in action* (5th ed.). Belmont, CA: Wadsworth Cengage Learning, p. 433.

29. Allen, H. E., Latessa, E. J., & Ponder, B. S. (2010). *Corrections in America: An introduction* (12th ed.). Boston, MA: Pearson, p. 93.

30. Gaines, L. K., & Miller, R. L. (2011). *Criminal justice in action* (6th ed.). Belmont, CA: Wadsworth Cengage Learning, pp. 468–488.

31. Cromwell, P., Alarid, L. F., & del Carmen, R. V. (2005). *Community-based corrections* (6th ed.). Belmont, CA: Thomson Wadsworth.

32. Platt, A. M. (1977). *The child savers: The invention of delinquency.* Chicago, IL: University of Chicago Press.

33. This portion of our discussion on juvenile justice is primarily based on Trojanowicz, R. C., Morash, M., & Schram, P. J. (2001). *Juvenile delinquency: Concepts and control* (6th ed.). Upper Saddle River, NJ: Prentice Hall.

34. Gardner, M. R. (1995). Punitive juvenile justice: Some observations on a recent trend. In M. L. Frost (Ed.), *The new juvenile justice.* Chicago, IL: Nelson-Hall, pp. 103–108.

35. Rudman, C. J., Hartstone, E., Fagan, J. A., & Moore, M. (1986). Violent youth in adult court: Process and punishment. *Crime and Delinquency, 32,* 75–96.

36. Snyder, H. N., & Sickmund, M. (2006). *Juvenile offenders and victims: 2006 National report.* Washington, DC: Office of Juvenile Justice and Delinquency Prevention.

37. Ibid., p. 110.

38. Shahidullah, S. M. (2012). *Comparative criminal justice systems: Global and local perspectives*. Burlington, MA: Jones & Bartlett Learning.

39. Hardie-Bick, J., Sheptycki, J., & Wardak, A. (2005). Introduction: Transnational and comparative criminology in a global perspective. In J. Sheptycki & A. Wardak (Eds.), *Transnational and comparative criminology*. Portland, OR: Cavendish, p. 2.

40. Bennett, R. R. (2004). Comparative criminology and criminal justice research: The state of our knowledge. *Justice Quarterly, 21*, 1–21, pp. 2–3.

41. Winslow, R. W., & Zhang, S. X. (2008). *Criminology: A global perspective*. Upper Saddle River, NJ: Prentice Hall, p. 29.

42. Van Dijk, J. (2008). *The world of crime: Breaking the silence on problems of security, justice, and development across the world*. Thousand Oaks, CA: SAGE, p. 3.

43. Ibid., pp. 3–13.

44. Federal Bureau of Investigation. (2012). *Crime in the United States, 2011*. Washington, DC: U.S. Department of Justice. Retrieved from http://www.fbi.gov/about-us/cjis/ucr/crime-in-the-u.s/2011/crime-in-the-u.s.-2011/property-crime/motor-vehicle-theft

45. National Insurance Crime Bureau. (2015). *NICB's Hot Wheels: America's 10 most stolen vehicles*. Retrieved from https://www.nicb.org/newsroom/news-releases/hot-wheels-2015-report

46. National Insurance Crime Bureau. (n.d.). *Vehicle theft fraud: Taking an age-old crime to the next level*. Retrieved from https://www.nicb.org/theft_and_fraud_awareness/fact_sheets

47. Los Angeles Police Department. (2011). Northeast community newsletter. Retrieved from http://www.lapdonline.org/northeast_community_police_station/content_basic_view/6546

48. Schriffen, J. (2012). Car thief, 11, takes police "bait car" for joyride. *ABC News*. Retrieved from http://abcnews.go.com/blogs/headlines/2012/06/car-thief-11-takes-police-bait-car-for-joyride/

49. Akers, R., & Sellers, C. (2004). *Criminological theories* (4th ed.). Los Angeles, CA: Roxbury.

50. It should be noted that this discussion and the examples provided for the characteristics are taken from Akers, R., & Sellers, C. (2004). *Criminological theories* (4th ed.). Los Angeles, CA: Roxbury, pp. 5–12.

51. Van Dijk, J. (2008). *The world of crime: The silence on problems of security, justice and development across the world*. Thousand Oaks, CA: SAGE.

52. Gottfredson, M., & Hirschi, T. (1990). *A general theory of crime*. Palo Alto, CA: Stanford University Press.

53. Lombroso, C. (1876). *The criminal man*. Milan, Italy: Hoepli.

54. See Tibbetts, S. G., & Hemmens, C. (2010). *Criminological theory: A text reader*. Thousand Oaks, CA: SAGE, p. 9.

55. Akers, R. L. (1997). *Criminological theories: Introduction and evaluation* (2nd ed.). Los Angeles, CA: Roxbury, p. 9.

56. Ibid.

57. Salinger, T. (2016, January 21). Woman poisoned with antifreeze by her mother forgives her for killing father and brother, causing daughter's brain injuries. *New York Daily News*. Retrieved from http://www.nydailynews.com/news/crime/woman-poisoned-antifreeze-mother-forgives-article-1.2505120

58. Smith, J. (2016, April 15). Missouri woman recalls moment she suspected her mom tried to kill her. *ABC News*. Retrieved from http://abcnews.go.com/US/missouri-woman-recalls-moment-suspected-mom-kill/story?id=38036627#

59. Keegan, H. (2016, April 14). Watch chilling confessions of Springfield mother, daughter who poisoned family with antifreeze. *Springfield News-Leader*, pp. 14-18. Retrieved from http://www.news-leader.com/story/news/crime/2016/04/14/watch-chilling-confessions-springfield-mother-daughter-who-poisoned-family-antifreeze/83024972/

60. Ibid.

61. Faller, K. C. (1993). *Child sexual abuse: Intervention and treatment issues*. Washington, DC: U.S. Department of Health and Human Services, p. 11.

62. Walsh, A., & Ellis, L. (2007). *Criminology: An interdisciplinary approach*. Thousand Oaks, CA: SAGE, p. 135.

63. Ibid., p. 104.

64. Shichor, D., & Tibbetts, S. G. (2002). *Victims and victimization: Essential readings*. Prospect Heights, IL: Waveland Press, p. 1. See also Wallace, H., & Roberson, C. (2015). *Victimology: Legal, psychological, and social perspectives* (4th ed.). Boston, MA: Pearson, p. 1.

65. Wertham, F. (1949). *The show of violence*. New York, NY: Doubleday.

66. Mendelsohn, B. (1956, July–September). Victimology. *Etudes Internationales de Psycho-Sociologie Criminelle*, pp. 23–26.

67. Fattah, E. (1994). Some problematic concepts, unjustified criticism and popular misconceptions. In *International debates of victimology* (pp. 82–103). London, UK: USV.

68. Shichor, D., & Tibbetts, S. G. (2002). *Victims and victimization: Essential readings*. Prospect Heights, IL: Waveland Press, pp. 5-6. See also Wallace, H., & Roberson, C. (2015). *Victimology: Legal, psychological, and social perspectives* (4th ed.). Boston, MA: Pearson, pp. 5–6.

69. Wolfgang, M. (1958). *Patterns of criminal homicide*. Philadelphia, PA: University of Pennsylvania Press.

70. Truman, J. L., & Morgan, R. E. (2016). *Criminal victimization, 2015* (NCJ 250180). U.S. Department of Justice, Bureau of Justice Statistics, Table 7, p. 9.

71. Ibid.

72. Straus, M., & Gelles, R. (1989). *Physical violence in American families: Risk factors and adaptations to violence in 8,145 families*. New Brunswick, NJ: Transaction. For more recent estimates, see Office of Juvenile and Delinquency Prevention. (2015, September). Children's exposure to violence, crime, and abuse: An update. Washington, DC: Department of Justice, Office of Juvenile Justice and Delinquency Prevention.

73. OJJDP observes child abuse prevention month. (2016, March/April). *OJJDP News @ a Glance*. Retrieved from https://www.ojjdp.gov/newsletter/249801/topstory.html

74. Ibid.

75. Wallace, H., & Roberson, C. (2015). *Victimology: Legal, psychological, and social perspectives* (4th ed.). Boston, MA: Pearson.

76. *Payne v. Tennessee*, 111 S. Ct. 2597, 115 L. Ed. 2d 720 (1991).

77. Davis, R. C., & Smith, B. E. (1994). The effects of victim impact statements on sentencing decisions: A test in an urban setting. *Justice Quarterly, 11*(3), 453–470.

78. Akers, R.L. (1997). *Criminological theories: Introduction and evaluation* (2nd ed.). Los Angeles, CA: Roxbury, p. 11.

CHAPTER 2

1. Federal Bureau of Investigation. (2002). *Crime in the United States, 2001*. Washington, DC: U.S. Department of Justice, p. 306.

2. Ibid., p. 303.

3. Leighton, P. (2002, August 28). Decision on 9/11 victims is a crime. *Newsday*. Retrieved from http://www.newsday.com/decision-on-9-11-victims-is-a-crime-1.399909

4. Leighton, W. K., & Maximino, M. (2014, February 11). The effect of CCTV on public safety: Research roundup. *Journalist's Resource*. Retrieved from http://journalistsresource.org/ studies/government/criminal-justice/surveillance-cameras-and-crime

5. See McLean, S. J., Worden, R. E., & Kim, M. (2013). Here's looking at you: An evaluation of public CCTV cameras and their effects on crime and disorder. *Criminal Justice Review, 38*, 303–334; Piza, E., Caplan, J., & Kennedy, L. (2014). Analyzing the influence of micro-level factors on CCTV camera effect. *Journal of Quantitative Criminology, 30*, 237–264.

6. Maxim, P. S., & Whitehead, P. C. (1998). *Explaining crime* (4th ed.). Boston, MA: Butterworth-Heinemann, p. 55.

7. Duncan, B., & Eglin, P. (1979). Making sense of the reliability and validity of official crime statistics: Review and prospect. *Canadian Criminology Forum, 2*, 9.

8. Maltz, M. D. (1977). Crime statistics: A historical perspective. *Crime and Delinquency, 23*, 33.

9. Federal Bureau of Investigation. (2015). *Crime in the United States, 2014*. Washington, DC: U.S. Department of Justice.

10. Federal Bureau of Investigation. (2004). *Uniform Crime Reporting handbook*. Washington, DC: U.S. Department of Justice, p. 7.

11. Ibid., p. 19.

12. Federal Bureau of Investigation. (2015). *Crime in the United States, 2014*. Washington, DC: U.S. Department of Justice.

13. Ibid.

14. Vieraitis, L. M., Britto, S., & Morris, R. G. (2015). Assessing the impact of changes in gender equality on female homicide victimization: 1980–2000. *Crime and Delinquency, 61*, 428–453.

15. Studky, T. D., Ottensmann, J. R., & Payton, S. B. (2012). The effect of foreclosures on crime in Indianapolis, 2003–2008. *Social Science Quarterly, 93*, 602–624.

16. Monuteaux, M. C., Lee, L. K., Hemenway, D., Mannix, R., & Fleegler, E. W. (2015). Firearm ownership and violence crime in the U.S.: An ecologic study. *American Journal of Preventive Medicine, 49*, 207–214.

17. Sozer, M. A., & Merlo, A. V. (2013). The impact of community policing on crime rates: Does the effect of community policing differ in large and small law enforcement agencies? *Police Practice & Research, 14*, 506–521.

18. Lilley, D. (2015). The Weed and Seed Program: A nationwide analysis of crime outcomes. *Criminal Justice Policy Review, 26*, 423–447.

19. Federal Bureau of Investigation. (2004). *Uniform Crime Reporting handbook*. Washington, DC: U.S. Department of Justice, p. 6.

20. Federal Bureau of Investigation, Criminal Justice Information Services Division, Uniform Crime Reporting Program. (2013). *Summary Reporting System (SRS) user manual*. Washington, DC: U.S. Department of Justice, p. 20.

21. Ibid., p. 23.

22. Ibid., p. 20.

23. Sellin, T. (1931). The basis of a crime index. *Journal of Criminal Law and Corrections, 22*, 335–356.

24. Federal Bureau of Investigation. (2015). *Crime in the United States: About the Uniform Crime Report (UCR) Program*. Retrieved from https://ucr.fbi.gov/crime-in-the-u.s/2015/crime-in-the-u.s.-2015/resource-pages/aboutucrmain_final

25. Biderman, A. D., & Reiss, A. J. (1967). On exploring the "dark figure" of crime, *Annals*, pp. 1–15.

26. Skogan, W. G. (1977). The "dark figure" of unreported crime. *Crime and Delinquency, 23*, 41.

27. Simon, D. R. (2007). *Elite deviance* (9th ed.). London, UK: Pearson.

28. Brownstein, H. H. (1996). *The rise and fall of a violent crime wave: Crack cocaine and the social construction of a crime problem*. Guilderland, NY: Harrow & Heston. See also Leverentz, A. (2012). Narratives of crime and criminals: How places socially construct the crime problem. *Sociological Forum, 27*, 348–371; Herd, D. (2011). Voices from the field: The social construction of alcohol problems in inner-city communities. *Contemporary Drug Problems, 38*, 7–39; Brownstein, H. H. (1995). The social construction of crime problems: Insiders and the use of official statistics. *Journal of Crime and Justice, 18*, 17–30.

29. Brownstein, H. H. (1996). *The rise and fall of a violent crime wave: Crack cocaine and the social construction of a crime problem*. Guilderland, NY: Harrow & Heston, p. 27.

30. Maltz, M.D. (1999). *Bridging gaps in police crime data: A discussion paper for the BJS Fellows Program*. Washington, DC: U.S. Department of Justice, p. 16.

31. Brownstein, H. H. (1996). *The rise and fall of a violent crime wave: Crack cocaine and the social construction of*

a crime problem. Guilderland, NY: Harrow & Heston, p. 22.

32. Savitz, L. D. (1978). Official police statistics and their limitations. In L. D. Savitz & N. J. Johnston (Eds.), *Crime in society* (pp. 69–81). New York, NY: Wiley, p. 75.

33. National Law Center on Homelessness and Poverty. (2011). *Criminalizing crisis: The criminalization of homelessness in U.S. cities*. Washington, DC: Author.

34. Maxfield, M. G. (1999). The National Incident-Based Reporting System: Research and policy applications. *Journal of Quantitative Criminology, 15,* 121.

35. Maxfield, M. G., & Babbie, E. (2001). *Research methods for criminal justice and criminology*. Belmont, CA: Wadsworth, p. 134.

36. KHOU. (2016, March 28). Police department's hoax about contaminated meth leads to 1 arrest. Retrieved from http://www.kare11.com/news/local/police-departments-hoax-about-contaminated-meth-leads-to-1-arrest/106121366?utm_source=fark&utm_medium=website&utm_content=link

37. Uria, D. (2016, March 3). NY woman caught driving with an elaborate cardboard license plate. *UPI*. Retrieved from http://www.upi.com/Odd_News/2016/03/03/NY-Woman-caught-driving-with-elaborate-cardboard-license-plate/7981457032438/?spt=sec&or=on

38. Beer-battered fish defense unsuccessful in drunken driving case. (2016, February 8). *Milwaukee Wisconsin Journal Sentinel*. Retrieved from http://www.jsonline.com/news/beer-battered-fish-defense-unsuccessful-in-drunken-driving-defense-b99666865z1-368120921.html?utm_source=fark&utm_medium=website&utm_content=link

39. Usher accused of stealing offerings from Florida church during prayer. (2015, November 9). Retrieved from http://www.local10.com/news/usher-accused-of-stealing-offerings-from-florida-church-during-prayer?utm_medium=social&utm_source=facebook_WPLG_Local_10

40. Fox, J. A., & Zawitz, M. W. (n.d.). *Homicide trends in the United States*. Washington, DC: Bureau of Justice Statistics. Retrieved from http://www.bjs.gov/content/pub/pdf/htius.pdf

41. Regoeczi, W., Banks, D., Planty, M., Langton, L., Annest, J. L., Warner, M., & Barnett-Ryan, C. (2014). *The nation's two measures of homicide*. Washington, DC: U.S. Department of Justice, Bureau of Justice Statistics, Office of Justice Programs.

42. Federal Bureau of Investigation, Criminal Justice Information Services Division, Uniform Crime Reporting Program. (2013). *Summary Reporting System (SRS) user manual*. Washington, DC: U.S. Department of Justice, pp. 144–146.

43. Office of Juvenile Justice and Delinquency Prevention. (n.d.). *Easy access to the FBI's Supplementary Homicide Reports: 1980–2013*. Washington, DC: Bureau of Justice Statistics. Retrieved from http://www.ojjdp.gov/ojstatbb/ezashr/asp/methods.asp#modification

44. Ibid., para. 2.

45. Regoeczi, W., Banks, D., Planty, M., Langton, L., Annest, J. L., Warner, M., & Barnett-Ryan, C. (2014). *The nation's two measures of homicide*. Washington, DC: Department of Justice, Bureau of Justice Statistics, Office of Justice Programs, p. 3.

46. Maltz, M. D. (1999). *Bridging gaps in police crime data: A discussion paper for the BJS Fellows Program*. Washington, DC: U.S. Department of Justice, p. 31.

47. Gebo, E. (2002). A contextual exploration of siblicide. *Violence and Victims, 12,* 157–168.

48. Chan, H., & Beauregard, E. (2016). Choice of weapon or weapon of choice? Examining the interactions between victim characteristics in single-victim male sexual homicide offenders. *Journal of Investigative Psychology and Offender Profiling, 13,* 70–88.

49. Savolainen, J., Messner, S. F., & Kivivouri, J. (2000). Crime is part of the problem: Contexts of lethal violence in Finland and the USA. *Journal of Scandinavian Studies in Criminology and Crime Prevention, 1,* 41–55.

50. Bazley, T., & Mieczkowski, T. (2004). Researching workplace homicide: An assessment of the limitations of the Supplementary Homicide Reports. *Journal of Criminal Justice, 32,* 243–252.

51. Maltz, M. D. (1999). *Bridging gaps in police crime data: A discussion paper for the BJS Fellows Program*. Washington, DC: U.S. Department of Justice, p. 31.

52. Federal Bureau of Investigation. (2000). *Crime in the United States, 2000*. Washington, DC: U.S. Department of Justice.

53. Federal Bureau of Investigation, Criminal Justice Information Services Division, Uniform Crime Reporting Program. (2013). *Summary Reporting System (SRS) user manual*. Washington, DC: U.S. Department of Justice, p. 14.

54. Ibid.

55. Federal Bureau of Investigation. (2000). *National Incident-Based Reporting System: Vol. 1. Data collection guidelines*. Washington, DC: U.S. Department of Justice, p. 3.

56. Tillyer, M. S., & Tillyer, R. (2014). Violence in context: A multilevel analysis of victim injury in robbery incidents. *Justice Quarterly, 31,* 767–791.

57. Krienert, J., Walsh, J. A., & Turner, M. (2009). Elderly in America: A descriptive study of elder abuse examining National Incident-Based Reporting System (NIBRS) data, 2000–2005. *Journal of Elder Abuse and Neglect, 21,* 325–345.

58. Krienert, J. L., & Walsh, J. A. (2011). Sibling sexual abuse: An empirical analysis of offender, victim, and event characteristics in National Incident-Based Reporting System (NIBRS) data, 2000–2007. *Journal of Child Sexual Abuse, 20,* 353–372.

59. Warner, T. (2010). Violent acts and injurious consequences: An examination of competing hypotheses about intimate partner violence using agency-based data. *Journal of Family Violence, 25,* 183–193.

60. Krienert, J., & Walsh, J. (2011). My brother's keeper: A contemporary examination of reported sibling violence

using national level data, 2000–2005. *Journal of Family Violence, 26,* 331–342.

61. Federal Bureau of Investigation. (2000). *National Incident-Based Reporting System: Vol. 1. Data collection guidelines.* Washington, DC: U.S. Department of Justice, pp. 5–20.

62. Maxfield, M. G. (1999). The National Incident-Based Reporting System: Research and policy applications. *Journal of Quantitative Criminology, 15,* 121–122.

63. Ibid.

64. Federal Bureau of Investigation, Criminal Justice Information Services Division, Uniform Crime Reporting Program. (2013). *Summary Reporting System (SRS) user manual.* Washington, DC: U.S. Department of Justice, pp. 9–10.

65. Maxfield, M. G. (1999). The National Incident-Based Reporting System: Research and policy applications. *Journal of Quantitative Criminology, 15,* 145–146.

66. Federal Bureau of Investigation. (2015). *Uniform Crime Reports: 2014 hate crime statistics: About hate crime statistics.* Washington, DC: U.S. Department of Justice. Retrieved from https://ucr.fbi.gov/about-us/cjis/ucr/hate-crime/2014/resource-pages/about-hate-crime

67. Federal Bureau of Investigation, Criminal Justice Information Services Division, Uniform Crime Reporting Program. (2015). *Hate crime data collection guidelines and training manual.* Washington, DC: U.S. Department of Justice, p. 8.

68. Federal Bureau of Investigation, Criminal Justice Information Services Division, Uniform Crime Reporting Program. (2013). *Summary Reporting System (SRS) user manual.* Washington, DC: U.S. Department of Justice, p. 147.

69. Ibid.

70. Ibid., p. 148.

71. U.S. Census Bureau. (2012). *National Crime Victimization Survey: CAPI interviewing manual for field representatives.* Washington, DC: Author, p. A1-4.

72. Maxim, P. S., & Whitehead, P. C. (1998). *Explaining crime* (4th ed.) Boston, MA: Butterworth-Heinemann, pp. 91–92.

73. U.S. Census Bureau. (2012). *National Crime Victimization Survey: CAPI interviewing manual for field representatives.* Washington, DC: Author, pp. A1-11–A1-12.

74. Ibid., p. A1-11.

75. Carbone-Lopez, K., & Lauritsen, J. (2013). Season variation in violent victimization: Opportunity and the annual rhythm of the school calendar. *Journal of Quantitative Criminology, 29,* 399–422.

76. Bunch, J., Clay-Warner, J., & Lei, M. K. (2015). Demographic characteristics and victimization risk. *Crime and Delinquency, 61,* 1181–1205.

77. Hemenway, D., & Solnick, S. J. (2015). The epidemiology of self-defense gun use: Evidence from the National Crime Victimization Surveys 2007–2011. *Preventative Medicine, 79,* 22–27.

78. Lanier, D. N., & Dietz, T. L. (2012). Time dynamics of elder victimization: Evidence from the NCVS, 1992 to 2005. *Social Science Research, 41,* 444–463.

79. U.S. Census Bureau. (2012). *National Crime Victimization Survey: CAPI interviewing manual for field representatives.* Washington, DC: Author, p. A1-5.

80. Cantor, C., & Lynch, J. P. (2000). Self-report surveys as measures of crime and criminal victimization. In D. Duffee (Ed.), *Measurement and analysis of crime and justice* (Vol. 4), p. 108. Washington, DC: National Institute of Justice.

81. Penick, B. K. E, & Owens, M. (1976). *Surveying crime.* Washington, DC: National Academy Press.

82. U.S. Census Bureau. (2012). *National Crime Victimization Survey: CAPI interviewing manual for field representatives.* Washington, DC: Author, pp. A1-5–A1-6.

83. Barnett-Ryan, C., Langton, L., & Planty, M. (2014). *The nation's two crime measures.* Washington, DC: Bureau of Justice Statistics. Retrieved from http://www.bjs.gov/index.cfm?ty=dcdetail&iid=245

84. Walsh, A., & Ellis, L. (2007). *Criminology: An interdisciplinary approach.* Thousand Oaks, CA: SAGE, p. 35.

85. Maxim, P. S., & Whitehead, P. C. (1998). *Explaining crime* (4th ed.). Boston, MA: Butterworth-Heinemann, p. 93.

86. Walsh, A., & Ellis, L. (2007). *Criminology: An interdisciplinary approach.* Thousand Oaks, CA: SAGE, p. 35.

87. Maxim, P. S., & Whitehead, P. C. (1998). *Explaining crime* (4th ed.). Boston, MA: Butterworth-Heinemann, p. 94.

88. U.S. Department of Justice, Office of Justice Programs, Bureau of Justice Statistics. (2014). *The nation's two crime measures.* Washington, DC: Author. Retrieved from http://www.bjs.gov/content/pub/pdf/ntcm_2014.pdf

89. Weisberg, H. F., Krosnick, J. A., & Bowen, B. D. (1989). *An introduction to survey research and data analysis* (2nd ed.). Glenview, IL: Scott Foresman, pp. 14–15.

90. Porterfield, A. L. (1946). *Youth in trouble.* Fort Worth, TX: Leo Potisham.

91. Examples of this research include Jolliffe, D., Farrington, D. P., & Hawkins, D. J. (2003). Predictive, concurrent, prospective, and retrospective validity of self-reported delinquency. *Criminal Behaviour and Mental Health, 13,* 179–197; Farrington, D. P., Jolliffe, D., & Hawkins, D. J. (2003). Comparing delinquency careers in court records and self-reports. *Criminology, 41,* 933–958; Tompsett, C. J., Veits, G. M., & Amrhein, K. E. (2016). Peer delinquency and where adolescents spend time with peers: Mediation and moderation of home neighborhood effects on self-reported delinquency. *Journal of Community Psychology, 44,* 263–270; and Jencks, J. W., & Burton, D. L. (2013). The role of trait anxiety in reducing the relationship between childhood exposure to violence/victimization and subsequent violent behavior among male delinquent youth. *International Journal of Offender Therapy and Comparative Criminology, 57,* 985–995.

92. Komro, K., Perry, C. L., & Munson, K. A. (2004). Reliability and validity of self-report measures to evaluate drug and violence prevention program. *Journal of Child and Adolescent Substance Abuse, 13,* 17–51.

93. Torok, M., Darke, S., & Kaye, S. (2012). Predisposed violent drug users versus drug users who commit violence: Does the order of onset translate to differences in the severity of violent offending? *Drug and Alcohol Review, 31,* 558–565.

94. Goldstick, J. E., Lipton, R. I., Carter, P., Stoddard, S. A., Newton, M. F., Reischl, T., . . . Cunningham, R. M. (2015). The effect of neighborhood context on the relationship between substance misuse and weapons aggression in urban adolescents seeking ED care. *Substance Use and Misuse, 50,* 674–684.

95. Shorey, R. C., McNulty, J. K., Moore, T. M., & Stuart, G. L. (2016). Being the victim of violence during a date predicts next-day cannabis use among female college students. *Addiction, 111,* 492–498.

96. Cambron, C., Gringeri, C., & Vogel-Ferguson, M. B. (2014). Physical and mental health correlates of adverse childhood experiences among low-income women. *Health and Social Work, 39,* 221–229.

97. Thornton, A. J. V., Graham-Kevan, N., & Archer, J. (2012). Prevalence of women's violent and nonviolent offending behavior: A comparison of self-reports, victims' reports, and third-party reports. *Journal of Interpersonal Violence, 27,* 1399–1427.

98. Johnston, L. D., O'Malley, P. M., Miech, R. A., Bachman, J. G., & Schulenberg, J. E. (2016). *Monitoring the Future national survey results on drug use, 1975–2015: Overview, key findings on adolescent drug use.* Ann Arbor: University of Michigan, Institute for Social Research.

99. Johnston, L. D., Bachman J. G., O'Malley, P. M., Schulenberg, J. E., & Miech, R. A. (2014). *Monitoring the Future: A continuing study of American youth (8th- and 10th-grade surveys), 2014* (ICPSR36149-v1). Ann Arbor, MI: Inter-university Consortium for Political and Social Research. http://doi.org/10.3886/ICPSR36149.v1

100. Johnston, L. D., O'Malley, P. M., Miech, R. A., Bachman, J. G., & Schulenberg, J. E. (n.d.). *Purpose and design of the MTF.* Ann Arbor: University of Michigan, Institute for Social Research. Retrieved from http://www.monitoringthefuture.org/purpose.html

101. Substance Abuse and Mental Health Services Administration. (2014). *Results from the 2013 National Survey on Drug Use and Health: Summary of national findings* (NSDUH Series H-48, HHS Publication No. (SMA) 14-4863). Rockville, MD: Author.

102. Substance Abuse and Mental Health Services Administration. (n.d.). *National Survey on Drug Use and Health: About the survey.* Retrieved from https://nsduhweb.rti.org/respweb/project_description.html

103. DeLisi, M., Vaughn, M. G., & Salas-Wright, C. P. (2015). Rumble: Prevalence and correlates of group fighting among adolescents in the United States. *Behavioral Sciences, 5,* 214–229.

104. Liang, W., & Chikritzhs, T. (2015). Examining the relationship between heavy alcohol use and assaults: With adjustment for the effects of unmeasured confounders. *BioMed Research International, 2015,* 1–10.

105. Salas-Wright, C., Vaughn, M., Schwartz, S., & Cordova, D. (2016). An "immigrant paradox" for adolescent externalizing behavior? Evidence from a national sample. *Social Psychiatry and Psychiatric Epidemiology, 51,* 27–37.

106. Maynard, B., Salas-Wright, C., & Vaughn, M. (2015). High school dropouts in emerging adulthood: Substance use, mental health problems, and crime. *Community Mental Health Journal, 51,* 289–299.

107. See, for example, Lemert, E. M. (1972). *Human deviance, social problems, and social control* (2nd ed.). Upper Saddle River, NJ: Prentice Hall.

108. University of Colorado Boulder. (n.d.). *National Youth Survey: Family study.* Retrieved from http://www.colorado.edu/ibg/human-research-studies/national-youth-survey-family-study

109. Snyder, H. N., & Sickmund, M. (1999). *Juvenile offenders and victims: 1999 national report.* Washington, DC: Office of Juvenile Justice and Delinquency Prevention, p. 52.

110. Moore, J. P. (1997). *Highlights of the 1995 National Youth Gang Survey* (Fact Sheet No. 63). Washington, DC: Office of Juvenile Justice and Delinquency Prevention, p. 1.

111. National Youth Gang Center. (2000). *1998 National Youth Gang Survey.* Washington, DC: Office of Juvenile Justice and Delinquency Prevention.

112. National Gang Center. (n.d.). *National Youth Gang Survey analysis.* Retrieved from http://www.national-gangcenter.gov/Survey-Analysis

113. Eagley, A., Howell, J. C., & Harris, M. (2014). *Juvenile justice fact sheet.* Washington, DC: Office of Juvenile Justice and Delinquency Prevention.

114. Federal Bureau of Investigation. (2015). *Uniform Crime Reports: 2014 hate crime statistics.* Washington, DC: U.S. Department of Justice. Retrieved from https://www.fbi.gov/about-us/cjis/ucr/hate-crime/2014/topic-pages/incidentsandoffenses_final

115. Weiner, R. (2011, May 25). Hate Crimes Bill signed into law 11 years after Matthew Shepard's death. *Huffpost Politics.* Retrieved from http://www.huffingtonpost.com/2009/10/28/hate-crimes-bill-to-be-si_n_336883.html

116. Federal Bureau of Investigation. (2015). *Uniform Crime Reports: 2014 hate crime statistics.* Washington, DC: U.S. Department of Justice. Retrieved from https://www.fbi.gov/about-us/cjis/ucr/hate-crime/2014/topic-pages/incidentsandoffenses_final

117. Rocha, V. (2015, June 24). Man accused of skinny jeans hate crime against musicians turns himself in. *Los Angeles Times.* Retrieved from http://www.latimes.com/local/lanow/la-me-ln-musicians-attacked-hate-crime-20150623-story.html

118. Anselin, L., Cohen, J., Cook, D., Gorr, W., & Tita, G. (2000). Spatial analyses of crime. In D. Duffee (Ed.), *Measurement and analysis of crime and justice* (Vol. 4), p. 215. Washington, DC: National Institute of Justice.

119. Harries, K. (1999). *Mapping crime: Principle and Practice*. Washington, DC: Office of Justice Programs, pp. 18–19.

120. Ibid., p. 1.

121. See Cornish, D. B., & Clarke, R. V. (1986). *The reasoning criminal: Rational choice perspectives on offending*. New York, NY: Springer-Verlag; Cohen, L. E., & Felson, M. (1979). Social change and crime rate trends: A routine activity approach. *American Sociological Review, 44*, 588–605.

122. Murray, R. K. & Swatt, M. L. (2013). Disaggregating the relationship between schools and crime: A spatial analysis. *Crime and Delinquency, 59*, 163–190.

123. Sydes, M. L., Wickes, R. L., & Higginson, A. (2014). The spatial concentration of bias: An examination of the community factors that influence residents' receptions of bias crime. *Australian and New Zealand Journal of Criminology, 47*, 409–428.

124. Hodgkinson, T., Andresen, M. A., & Farrell, G. (2016). The decline and locational shift of automotive theft: A local level analysis. *Journal of Criminal Justice, 44*, 49–57.

125. Melsness, D., & Weichelt, R. (2014). Spatial crime displacement on Chicago's south side. *Geographical Bulletin, 55*, 63–80.

CHAPTER 3

1. Zagorin, A. (2008, May 1). D.C. Madam: Suicide before prison. *Time U.S.* Retrieved from http://www.time.com/time/nation/article/0,8599,1736687,00.html

2. Ibid.

3. Mumola, C. J. (2005, August). *Suicide and homicide in state prisons and local jails*. Washington, DC: U.S. Department of Justice, Office of Justice Programs. Retrieved from http://bjs.gov/content/pub/pdf/shsplj.pdf

4. Death Penalty Information Center. (2009). *Gap between the murder rate of death penalty states and non-death penalty states remains large*. Retrieved from http://www.deathpenaltyinfo.org/gap-between-murder-rate-death-penalty-states-and-non-death-penalty-states-remains-large

5. Brown, S. E., Esbensen, F., & Geis, G. (2004). *Criminology: Explaining crime and its context* (5th ed.). Cincinnati, OH: Anderson.

6. Tanacu exorcism. (n.d.). *Wikipedia.com*. Retrieved from https://en.wikipedia.org/wiki/Tanacu_exorcism

7. A good discussion of harsh punishment, such as quartering, can be found in Brown, S. E., Esbensen, F., & Geis, G. (2004). *Criminology: Explaining crime and its context* (5th ed.). Cincinnati, OH: Anderson.

8. Firdaus, I. (2005, June 25). Gamblers whipped in Muslim Indonesia. *Associated Press*.

9. Hobbes, T. (1958). *Leviathan*. New York, NY: Library of Liberal Arts. (Original work published 1651)

10. Ibid.; Montesquieu, C. (1949). *The spirit of the laws*. New York, NY: Library of Liberal Arts. (Original work published 1748)

11. Beccaria, C. (1963). *On crimes and punishments* (H. Paolucci, Trans.). New York, NY: MacMillan, p. 64. (Original work published 1764).

12. Ibid., pp. 30–31.

13. Ibid., p. 32.

14. Ibid.

15. Ibid., p. 21.

16. Ibid., p. 17.

17. Ibid., p. 99.

18. Ibid., p. 98.

19. Ibid., p. 45.

20. Ibid., p. 50.

21. For a review and analysis of the deterrent effect of capital punishment, see Stack, S. (1998). The effect of publicized executions on homicides in California. *Journal of Crime and Justice, 21*, 1–16. See also Ehrlich, I. (1975). The deterrent effect of capital punishment: A question of life and death. *American Economic Review, 65*, 397–417; Ehrlich, I. (1977). Capital punishment and deterrence. *Journal of Political Economy, 85*, 741–788; Layson, S. K. (1985). Homicide and deterrence: A reexamination of United States time-series evidence. *Southern Economic Journal, 52*, 68–89; Phillips, D. P. (1980). The deterrent effect of capital punishment: Evidence on an old controversy. *American Journal of Sociology, 86*, 139–148; Stack, S. (1987). Publicized executions and homicide, 1950–1980. *American Sociological Review, 52*, 532–540; Stack, S. (1990). Execution publicity and homicide in South Carolina. *Sociological Quarterly, 31*, 599–611; and Stack, S. (1995). The impact of publicized executions on homicide. *Criminal Justice and Behavior, 22*, 172–186.

22. Bailey, W. C. (1979). The deterrent effect of the death penalty for murder in California. *Southern California Law Review, 52*, 743–764; Bailey, W. C., & Peterson, R. D. (1989). Murder and capital punishment: A monthly time series analysis of execution publicity. *American Sociological Review, 54*, 722–743; Bowers, W. J. (1988). The effect of execution is brutalization, not deterrence. In K. Haas & J. Inciardi (Eds.), *Capital punishment: Legal and social science approaches* (pp. 49–89). Newbury Park, CA: SAGE; Cochran, J. K., Chamlin, M., & Seth, M. (1994). Deterrence or brutalization? An impact assessment of Oklahoma's return to capital punishment. *Criminology, 32*, 107–134; Fox, J. A., & Radelet, M. L. (1990). Persistent flaws in econometric studies of the deterrent effect of the death penalty. *Loyola of Los Angeles Law Review, 23*, 29–44; Lester, D. (1989). The deterrent effect of execution on homicide. *Psychological Reports, 64*, 306–314. For a review, see Bailey, W. C., & Peterson, R. D. (1999). Capital punishment, homicide, and deterrence: An assessment of the evidence. In M. D. Smith & M. A. Zahn (Eds.), *Studying and preventing homicide* (pp. 223–245). Thousand Oaks, CA: SAGE.

23. Cochran, J. K., & Chamlin, M. (2000). Deterrence and brutalization: The dual effects of executions. *Justice Quarterly, 17*, 685–706.

24. Beccaria, C. (1963). *On crimes and punishments* (H. Paolucci, Trans.). New York, NY: MacMillan, pp. 46–47. (Original work published 1764)

25. Ibid., p. 55.

26. Ibid.

27. Ibid., p. 56.

28. Ibid., p. 58.

29. Ibid.

30. Ibid., p. 43.

31. Tomislav, V., Kovandzic, J., Sloan, J., & Vieraitis, L. (2004). "Striking out" as crime reduction policy: The impact of "three strikes" laws on crime rates in U.S. cities. *Justice Quarterly, 21,* 207–240.

32. Beccaria, C. (1963). *On crimes and punishments* (H. Paolucci, Trans.). New York, NY: MacMillan, p. 42. (Original work published 1764)

33. Ibid., p. 93.

34. Ibid., p. 99.

35. Ibid., p. 68.

36. Vold, G., Bernard, T., & Snipes, J. (2002). *Theoretical criminology* (5th ed.). New York, NY: Oxford University Press.

37. Federal Bureau of Investigations. (2015). *Crime in the United States, 2014: Offense definitions.* Washington, DC: Department of Justice. Retrieved from https://www.fbi.gov/about-us/cjis/ucr/crime-in-the-u.s/2014/crime-in-the-u.s.-2014/cius-home

38. Ibid.

39. Bureau of Justice Statistics. (2015). *Criminal victimization, 2014.* Washington, DC: U.S. Department of Justice.

40. Buzawa, E. S., & Buzawa, C. G. (2003). *Domestic violence: The criminal justice response* (3rd ed.). Thousand Oaks, CA: SAGE, p. 104.

41. Sherman, L. W., & Berk, R. A. (1984). *The Minneapolis Domestic Violence Experiment.* Washington, DC: Police Foundation; Sherman, L. W., & Berk, R. A. (1984). The specific deterrent effects of arrest for domestic assault. *American Sociological Review, 49,* 261–272.

42. Mederer, H. J., & Gelles, R. J. (1989). Compassion or control: Intervention in cases of wife abuse. *Journal of Interpersonal Violence, 4,* 25–43. See also Binder, A., & Meeker, J. (1988). Experiments as reforms. *Journal of Criminal Justice, 16,* 347–358; Lembert, R. (1989). Humility is a virtue: On the publicization of policy relevant research. *Law and Society Review, 23,* 145–161.

43. Buzawa, E. S., & Buzawa, C. G. (2003). *Domestic violence: The criminal justice response* (3rd ed.). Thousand Oaks, CA: SAGE, p. 97.

44. See Berk, S. F., Campbell, A., Klap, R., & Western, B. (1992). Beyesian analysis of the Colorado Springs spouse abuse experiment. *Criminal Law and Criminology, 83,* 170–200; Dunford, F. W., Huizinga, D., & Elliott, D. (1989). *The Omaha domestic violence police experiment: Final report to the National Institute of Justice and the City of Omaha.* Boulder, CO: Institute of Behavioral Science; Hirschel, J. D., Hutchison, I. W., Dean, C. W., Kelley, J. J., & Pesackis, C. E. (1991). *Charlotte Spouse Assault Replication Project: Final report.* Washington, DC: U.S. Department of Justice; Pate, A., & Hamilton, E. (1992). Formal and informal deterrents to domestic violence: The Dade County Spouse Assault Experiment. *American Sociological Review, 57,* 691–697; Sherman, L. W., Schmidt, J. D., Rogan, D. P., Smith, D. A., Gartin, P. R., Cohn, E. G., . . . Bacich, A. R. (1992). The variable effects of arrest on criminal careers: The Milwaukee Domestic Violence Experiment. *Journal of Criminal Law and Criminology, 83,* 137–169.

45. Buzawa, E. S., & Buzawa, C. G. (2003). *Domestic violence: The criminal justice response* (3rd ed.). Thousand Oaks, CA: SAGE, p. 104.

46. United Nations Office on Drugs and Crime. (2001–2002). *United Nations survey on crime trends and the operations of criminal justice systems.* Retrieved from http://www.unodc.org/unodc/en/data-and-analysis/Eighth-United-Nations-Survey-on-Crime-Trends-and-the-Operations-of-Criminal-Justice-Systems.html

47. Ellis, L., Cooper, J., & Walsh, A. (2008). Criminologists' opinions about causes and theories of crime and delinquency: A follow-up. *The Criminologist, 33,* 23–26.

48. Henderson, P. (2012, October 13). California may lead prison-reform trend, ease "3 strikes." *NBCNews.com.* Retrieved from http://www.nbcnews.com/ID/49400913/ns/politics/t/california -may-lead-prison-reform-trend-ease -strikes/#.uvd3rRzCaSo

49. For a review and evaluations of these programs, see Lundman, R. (1993). *Prevention and control of juvenile delinquency* (2nd ed.). Oxford, UK: Oxford University Press.

50. See Pratt, T. (2008). Rational choice theory, crime control policy, and criminological relevance. *Criminology and Public Policy, 7,* 43–52.

51. Walker, S. (2005). *Sense and nonsense about crime and drugs* (6th ed.). Belmont, CA: West/Wadsworth.

CHAPTER 4

1. Dailey, J. (2012, August 24). Mom has son wear "Smoked pot, got caught" sign as punishment. *WTOC 11.* Retrieved from http://www.wtoc.com/story/19373395/mother-has-son-wear-smoked-pot-got-caught-sign-as-punishment

2. Martinson, R. (1974). What works? Questions and answers about prison reform. *Public Interest, 35,* 22–54. See also Bailey, W. C. (1966). Correctional outcome: An evaluation of 100 reports. *Journal of Criminal Law, Criminology, and Police Science, 57,* 153–160.

3. Becker, G. (1968). Crime and punishment: An economic approach. *Journal of Political Economy, 76,* 169–217; Chiricos, T. G., & Waldo, G. P. (1970). Punishment and crime: An examination of some empirical evidence. *Social Problems, 18,* 200–217; Gibbs, J. P. (1968). Crime, punishment and deterrence. *Southwestern Social Science Quarterly, 48,* 515–530; Tittle, C. R. (1969). Crime rates and legal sanctions. *Social Problems, 16,* 409–423.

4. Andenaes, J. (1974). *Punishment and deterrence.* Ann Arbor: University of Michigan Press; Gibbs, J. P. (1975). *Crime, punishment and deterrence.* New York, NY: Elsevier; Glaser, D., & Zeigler, M. S. (1974). Use of the death penalty v. outrage at murder. *Crime and Delinquency, 20,* 333–338; Tittle, C. R. (1969). Crime rates and legal sanctions. *Social Problems, 16,* 409–423; Zimring, F. E., & Hawkins, G. J. (1973). *Deterrence: The legal threat in crime control.* Chicago, IL: University of Chicago Press.

5. Blumstein, A., Cohen, J., & Nagin, D. (Eds.). (1978). *Deterrence and incapacitation: Estimating the effects of criminal sanctions on crime rates.* Washington, DC: National Academy of Sciences.

6. Paternoster, R. (1987). The deterrent effect of the perceived certainty and severity of punishment: A review of the evidence and issues. *Justice Quarterly, 4,* 173–217; Paternoster, R., Saltzman, L. E., Waldo, G. P., & Chiricos, T. G. (1983). Perceived risk and social control: Do sanctions really deter? *Law and Society Review, 17,* 457–480.

7. Ross, H. L. (1982). *Deterring the drunk driver: Legal policy and social control.* Lexington, MA: Lexington Books; Ross, H. L. (1992). *Confronting drunk driving: Social policy for saving lives.* New Haven, CT: Yale University Press; Ross, H. L. (1994). Sobriety checkpoints, American style. *Journal of Criminal Justice, 22,* 437–444; Ross, H. L., McCleary, R., & LaFree, G. (1990). Can mandatory jail laws deter drunk driving? The Arizona case. *Journal of Criminal Law and Criminology, 81,* 156–170.

8. Ross, H. L., McCleary, R., & LaFree, G. (1990). Can mandatory jail laws deter drunk driving? The Arizona case. *Journal of Criminal Law and Criminology, 81,* 164.

9. Simpson, S., & Koper, C. S. (1992). Deterring corporate crime. *Criminology, 30,* 347–376.

10. Pogarsky, G., Kim, K., & Paternoster, R. (2005). Perceptual change in the National Youth Survey: Lessons for deterrence theory and offender decision-making. *Justice Quarterly, 22,* 1–29.

11. For a review, see Brown, S., Esbensen, F., & Geis, G. (2004). *Criminology: Explaining crime and its context* (5th ed.). Cincinnati, OH: LexisNexis, pp. 201–204; Finley, N., & Grasmick, H. (1985). Gender roles and social control. *Sociological Spectrum, 5,* 317–330; Grasmick, H., Blackwell, B. S., & Bursik, R. (1993). Changes in the sex patterning of perceived threats of sanctions. *Law and Society Review, 27,* 679–705; Grasmick, H., Bursik, R., & Kinsey, K. (1991). Shame and embarrassment as deterrents to noncompliance with the law: The case of an antilittering campaign. *Environment and Behavior, 23,* 233–251; Loewenstein, G., Nagin, D., & Paternoster, R. (1997). The effect of sexual arousal on expectations of sexual forcefulness. *Journal of Research in Crime and Delinquency, 34,* 209–228; Makkai, T., & Braithwaite, J. (1994). The dialects of corporate deterrence. *Journal of Research in Crime and Delinquency, 31,* 347–373; Nagin, D., & Paternoster, R. (1993). Enduring individual differences and rational choice theories of crime. *Law and Society Review, 27,* 467–496; Nagin,

D., & Pogarsky, G. (2001). Integrating celerity, impulsivity, and extralegal sanction threats into a model of general deterrence: Theory and evidence. *Criminology, 39,* 404–430; Paternoster, R., & Simpson, S. (1996). Sanction threats and appeals to morality: Testing a rational choice model of corporate crime. *Law and Society Review, 30,* 549–583; Piquero, A., & Pogarsky, G. (2002). Beyond Stanford and Warr's reconceptualization of deterrence: Personal and vicarious experiences, impulsivity, and offending behavior. *Journal of Research in Crime and Delinquency, 39,* 153–186; Piquero, A., & Tibbetts, S. (1996). Specifying the direct and indirect effects of low self-control and situational factors in offenders' decision making: Toward a more complete model of rational offending. *Justice Quarterly, 13,* 481–510; Richards, P., & Tittle, C. (1981). Gender and perceived chances of arrest. *Social Forces, 59,* 1182–1199. For a recent review and altered explanation of these conclusions, see Pogarsky, G. (2002). Identifying "deterrable" offenders: Implications for research on deterrence. *Justice Quarterly, 19,* 431–452.

12. Ajzen, I., & Fishbein, M. (1977). Attitude-behavior relations: A theoretical analysis and review of empirical research. *Psychological Bulletin, 84,* 888–918; Ajzen, I., & Fishbein, M. (1980). *Understanding attitudes and predicting social behavior.* Englewood Cliffs, NJ: Prentice Hall; Fishbein, M., & Ajzen, I. (1975). *Belief, attitude, intention, and behavior.* Reading, MA: Addison-Wesley. *Psychological Bulletin, 84,* 888–918. For a recent review, see Pogarsky, G., Kim, K., & Paternoster, R. (2005). Perceptual change in the National Youth Survey: Lessons for deterrence theory and offender decision-making. *Justice Quarterly, 22,* 1–29.

13. Bachman, R., Paternoster, R., & Ward, S. (1992). The rationality of sexual offending: Testing a deterrence/rational choice conception of sexual assault. *Law and Society Review, 26,* 343–372; Grasmick, H., & Bursik, R. (1990). Conscience, significant others, and rational choice: Extending the deterrence model. *Law and Society Review, 24,* 837–861; Grasmick, H., & Green, D. (1980). Legal punishment, social disapproval and internalization as inhibitors of illegal behavior. *Journal of Criminal Law and Criminology, 71,* 325–335; Klepper, S., & Nagin, D. (1989). The deterrent effects of perceived certainty and severity of punishment revisited. *Criminology, 27,* 721–746; Loewenstein, G., Nagin, D., & Paternoster, R. (1997). The effect of sexual arousal on expectations of sexual forcefulness. *Journal of Research in Crime and Delinquency, 34,* 209–228; Nagin, D., & Paternoster, R. (1993). Enduring individual differences and rational choice theories of crime. *Law and Society Review, 27,* 467–496; Paternoster, R., & Simpson, S. (1996). Sanction threats and appeals to morality: Testing a rational choice model of corporate crime. *Law and Society Review, 30,* 549–583; Piquero, A., & Tibbetts, S. (1996). Specifying the direct and indirect effects of low self-control and situational factors in offenders' decision making: Toward a more complete model of rational offending. *Justice*

Quarterly, 13, 481–510; Tibbetts, S. (1997). Gender differences in students' rational decisions to cheat. *Deviant Behavior, 18,* 393–414; Tibbetts, S. (1997). Shame and rational choice in offending decisions. *Criminal Justice and Behavior, 24,* 234–255; Tibbetts, S., & Myers, D. (1999). Low self-control, rational choice, and student test cheating. *American Journal of Criminal Justice, 23,* 179–200.

14. Ajzen, I. (1987). From intentions to actions: A theory of planned behavior. In J. Kuhl & J. Beckmann (Eds.), *Action control: From cognition to behavior* (pp. 11–39). Berlin: Springer-Verlag; Ajzen, I., & Fishbein, M. (1969). The prediction of behavioral intentions in a choice situation. *Journal of Experimental Psychology, 5,* 400–416; Ajzen, I., & Fishbein, M. (1977). Attitude-behavior relations: A theoretical analysis and review of empirical research. *Psychological Bulletin, 84,* 888–918; Ajzen, I., & Fishbein, M. (1980). *Understanding attitudes and predicting social behavior.* Englewood Cliffs, NJ: Prentice Hall; Green, D. (1989). Measures of illegal behavior in individual behavior in individual-level deterrence research. *Journal of Research in Crime and Delinquency, 26,* 253–275.

15. Bouffard, J. A. (2002). Methodological and theoretical implications of using subject-generated consequences in tests of rational choice theory. *Justice Quarterly, 19,* 747–771.

16. Cornish, D., & Clarke, R. (1986). *The reasoning criminal: Rational choice perspectives on offending.* New York, NY: Springer-Verlag.

17. Katz, J. (1988). *Seductions of crime.* New York, NY: Basic Books.

18. Tibbetts, S. G., & Gibson, C. (2002). Individual propensities and rational decision-making: Recent findings and promising approaches. In A. Piquero & S. Tibbetts (Eds.), *Rational choice and criminal behavior* (pp. 3–24). New York, NY: Routledge.

19. Grasmick, H., Blackwell, B. S., & Bursik, R. B. (1993). Changes over time in gender differences in perceived risk of sanctions. *Law and Society Review, 27,* 679–705; Grasmick, H., & Bursik, R. (1990). Conscience, significant others, and rational choice: Extending the deterrence model. *Law and Society Review, 24,* 837–861; Grasmick, H., Bursik, R., & Arneklev, B. (1993). Reduction in drunk driving as a response to increased threats of shame, embarrassment, and legal sanctions. *Criminology, 31,* 41–67; Nagin, D., & Paternoster, R. (1993). Enduring individual differences and rational choice theories of crime. *Law and Society Review, 27,* 467–496; Pogarsky, G. (2002). Identifying "deterrable" offenders: Implications for research on deterrence. *Justice Quarterly, 19,* 431–452; Tibbetts, S. (1997). Gender differences in students' rational decisions to cheat. *Deviant Behavior, 18,* 393–414; Tibbetts, S. (1997). Shame and rational choice in offending decisions. *Criminal Justice and Behavior, 24,* 234–255; Tibbetts, S. G. (2004). Self-conscious emotions and criminal offending. *Psychological Reports, 93,* 101–131; Tibbetts, S. G., & Herz, D. (1996).

Gender differences in factors of social control and rational choice. *Deviant Behavior, 17,* 183–208; Tibbetts, S., & Myers, D. (1999). Low self-control, rational choice, and student test cheating. *American Journal of Criminal Justice, 23,* 179–200.

20. Finley, N., & Grasmick, H. (1985). Gender roles and social control. *Sociological Spectrum, 5,* 317–330; Grasmick, H., Blackwell, B. S., & Bursik, R. (1993). Changes in the sex patterning of perceived threats of sanctions. *Law and Society Review, 27,* 679–705; Pogarsky, G., Kim, K., & Paternoster, R. (2005). Perceptual change in the National Youth Survey: Lessons for deterrence theory and offender decision-making. *Justice Quarterly, 22,* 1–29; Tibbetts, S. G. (1997). Gender differences in students' rational decisions to cheat. *Deviant Behavior, 18,* 393–414; Tibbetts, S. G., & Herz, D. (1996). Gender differences in factors of social control and rational choice. *Deviant Behavior, 17,* 183–208.

21. Grasmick, H., Blackwell, B. S., & Bursik, R. (1993). Changes in the sex patterning of perceived threats of sanctions. *Law and Society Review, 27,* 679–705; Nagin, D., & Paternoster, R. (1993). Enduring individual differences and rational choice theories of crime. *Law and Society Review, 27,* 467–496; Tibbetts, S. G. (2004). Self-conscious emotions and criminal offending. *Psychological Reports, 93,* 101–131.

22. Pogarsky, G., Kim, K., & Paternoster, R. (2005). Perceptual change in the National Youth Survey: Lessons for deterrence theory and offender decision-making. *Justice Quarterly, 22,* 1–29.

23. Pogarsky, G. (2002). Identifying "deterrable" offenders: Implications for research on deterrence. *Justice Quarterly, 19,* 431–452.

24. Federal Bureau of Investigation. (2015). *Crime in the United States, 2014.* Washington, DC: U.S. Department of Justice.

25. Insurance Institute for Highway Safety. (2016, July). *Alcohol-impaired driving: DUI/DWI.* Retrieved from http://www.iihs.org/iihs/topics/laws/dui

26. Federal Bureau of Investigation. (2015). *Crime in the United States, 2014.* Washington, DC: U.S. Department of Justice. Retrieved from https://www.fbi.gov/about-us/cjis/ucr/crime-in-the-u.s/2014/crime-in-the-u.s.-2014/persons-arrested/main

27. Centers for Disease Control and Prevention. (2016). *Impaired driving: Get the facts.* Retrieved from http://www.cdc.gov/motorvehiclesafety/impaired_driving/impaired-drv_factsheet.html

28. Harrington, E. (2016, January 15). Feds want to lower legal driving limit to one drink. *Washington Free Beacon.* Retrieved from http://freebeacon.com/issues/feds-want-to-lower-legal-driving-limit-to-one-drink/.

29. Ignition Interlock Device.org. (n.d.). *How the ignition interlock device works.* Retrieved from http://www.ignitioninterlockdevice.org/ignitioninterlockdevice.html

30. National Conference on State Legislatures. (2016). *State ignition interlock laws.* Retrieved from http://www.ncsl.org/research/transportation/state-ignition-interlock-laws.aspx.

31. Florida Department of Highway Safety and Motor Vehicles. (n.d.). *Ignition interlock program*. Retrieved from http://www.flhsmv.gov/ddl/iid.html

32. Cohen, L., & Felson, M. (1979). Social change and crime rates: A routine activities approach. *American Sociological Review, 44*, 214–241.

33. Farrington, D. P., & Welsh, B. C. (2002). Improved street lighting and crime prevention. *Justice Quarterly, 19*, 313–343.

34. Sherman, L., Gartin, P. R., & Buerger, M. (1989). Hot spots of predatory crime: Routine activities and the criminology of place. *Criminology, 27*, 27–56.

35. Bernburg, J. G., & Thorlindsson, T. (2001). Routine activities in social context: A closer look at the role of opportunity in deviant behavior. *Justice Quarterly, 18*, 543–567; see also Bennett, R. (1991). Routine activity: A cross-national assessment of a criminological perspective. *Social Forces, 70*, 147–163; Hawdon, J. (1996). Deviant lifestyles: The social control of routine activities. *Youth and Society, 28*, 162–188; Massey, J. L., Krohn, M., & Bonati, L. (1989). Property crime and the routine activities of individuals. *Journal of Research in Crime and Delinquency, 26*, 378–400; Miethe, T., Stafford, M., & Long, J. (1987). Social differences in criminological victimization: A test of routine activities/lifestyles theories. *American Sociological Review, 52*, 184–194; Mustaine, E., & Tewksbury, R. (1998). Predicting risks of larceny theft victimization: A routine activity analysis using refined lifestyle measures. *Criminology, 36*, 829–857; Osgood, D., Wilson, J., O'Malley, P. M., Bachman, J., & Johnston, J. L. (1996). Routine activities and individual deviant behavior. *American Sociological Review, 61*, 635–655; Roncek, D., & Maier, P. (1991). Bars, blocks, and crimes revisited: Linking the theory of routine activities to the empiricism of hot spots. *Criminology, 29*, 725–753; Sampson, R., & Wooldredge, J. (1987). Linking the micro- and macro-level dimensions of lifestyle-routine activity and opportunity models of predatory victimization. *Journal of Quantitative Criminology, 3*, 371–393.

36. Brown, S., Esbensen, F., & Geis, G. (2004). *Criminology: Explaining crime and its context* (5th ed.). Cincinnati, OH: LexisNexis, p. 175.

37. Ibid.

38. Ibid.

39. Wilson, J. Q., & Kelling, G. (1982, March). Broken windows: The police and neighborhood safety. *Atlantic Monthly*, 29–38.

40. Shepherd, J. M. (2002). Fear of the first strike: The full deterrent effect of California's two- and three-strikes legislation. *Journal of Legal Studies, 31*, 159–201.

41. Males, M., & Macallair, D. (1999). Striking out: The failure of California's "three strikes and you're out" law. *Stanford Law and Policy Review, 11*, 65–72; Stolzenberg, L., & D'Alessio, S. J. (1997). Three strikes and you're out: The impact of California's new mandatory sentencing law on serious crime rates. *Crime and Delinquency, 43*, 457–469.

42. Marvell, T. B., & Moody, C. E. (2001). The lethal effects of three-strikes laws. *Journal of Legal Studies, 30*, 89–106; see also Kovandzic, T., Sloan, J. J., III, & Vieraitis, L. M. (2002). Unintended consequences of politically popular sentencing policy: The homicide-promoting effects of "three strikes" in U.S. cities (1980–1999). *Criminology and Public Policy, 1*, 399–424.

43. Tibbetts, S. G. (1997). Shame and rational choice in offending decisions. *Criminal Justice and Behavior, 24*, 234–255.

CHAPTER 5

1. Cohen, E., & Bonifield, J. (2012, March 15). California's dark legacy of forced sterilizations. *CNN Health*. Retrieved from http://www.cnn.com/2012/03/15/health/california-forced-sterilizations/index.html

2. For a good example of this perspective, see Morton, S. G. (1849). Observations on the size of the brain in various races and families of man. *Proceedings of the Academy of Natural Sciences (Philadelphia), 4*, 221–224; see also Broca, P. (1862). Sur la capacité des crânes parisiens des diverses époques. *Bulletin Societe d' Anthropologie Paris, 3*, 102–116; Morton, S. G. (1839). *Crania Americana: A comparative view of the skulls of various aboriginal nations of North and South America*. Philadelphia, PA: John Pennington. For a review of various studies, see Rafter, N. (2005). The murderous Dutch Fiddler. *Theoretical Criminology, 9*, 65–96.

3. For example, see Bean, R. (1906). Some racial peculiarities of the Negro brain. *American Journal of Anatomy, 5*, 353–432 (showed a distinct difference in the brains across race when brains were identified by race before comparison); Mall, F. P. (1909). On several anatomical characters of the human brain, said to vary according to race and sex, with especial reference to the weight of the frontal lobe. *American Journal of Anatomy, 9*, 1–32 (showed virtually no differences among the same brains when comparisons were made without knowing the races of the brains prior to comparison); for the comparison/contrast, see discussion in Gould, S. J. (1996). *The mismeasure of man* (2nd ed.). New York, NY: W. W. Norton.

4. See Mall, F. P. (1909). On several anatomical characters of the human brain, said to vary according to race and sex, with especial reference to the weight of the frontal lobe. *American Journal of Anatomy, 9*, 1–32; much of the discussion in this section is taken from Gould, S. J. (1996). *The mismeasure of man* (2nd ed.). New York: W. W. Norton.

5. Spitska, E. A. (1907). A study of the brains of six eminent scientists and scholars belonging to the anthropological society, together with a description of the skull of Professor E. D. Cope. *Transactions of the American Philosophical Society, 21*, 175–308.

6. Coren, S. (1993). *The left-hander syndrome*. New York, NY: Vintage; Kalat, J. (2004). *Biological psychology* (8th ed.). New York, NY: Wadsworth.

7. Fowler, O. S. (1842). *Fowler's practical phrenology: Giving a concise elementary view of phrenology*. New York, NY: Author.

8. For a review, see Raine, A. (1993). *The psychopathology of crime*. San Diego, CA: Academic Press.

9. Nott, J. C., & Gliddon, G. R. (1854). *Types of mankind*. Philadelphia, PA: Lippincott, Grambo; Nott, J. C., & Gliddon, G. R. (1868). *Indigenous races on Earth*. Philadelphia, PA: Lippincott.

10. Lombroso, C. (1876). *L'uomo delinquente* [The criminal man]. Milan, Italy: Hoepli; Lombroso, C. (1878). *The criminal man* (2nd ed.). Turin, Italy: Bocca.

11. Gould, S. J. (1996). *The mismeasure of man* (2nd ed.). New York, NY: W. W. Norton, p. 153.

12. Lombroso, C. (1876). *L'uomo delinquente* [The criminal man]. Milan, Italy: Hoepli, as cited and discussed in Taylor, I., Walton, P., & Young, J. (1973). *The new criminology: For a social theory of deviance*. London, UK: Routledge, p. 41.

13. See Gould, S. J. (1996). *The mismeasure of man* (2nd ed.). New York, NY: W. W. Norton; Taylor, I., Walton, P., & Young, J. (1973). *The new criminology: For a social theory of deviance*. London, UK: Routledge.

14. For a review of such identifications, see Gould, S. J. (1996). *The mismeasure of man* (2nd ed.). New York, NY: W. W. Norton.

15. Lombroso, C. (1911). *Crime: Its causes and remedies*. Boston, MA: Little, Brown, p. 436.

16. From Waldrop, M., & Halverson, C. (1971). Minor physical anomalies and hyperactive behavior in young children. In J. Hellmuth (Ed.), *Exceptional infant: Studies in abnormalities* (pp. 343–381). New York, NY: Brunner/Mazel, as cited in Fishbein, D. (2001). *Biobehavioral perspectives on criminology*. Belmont, CA: Wadsworth.

17. Agnew, R. (1984). Appearance and delinquency. *Criminology, 22,* 421–440.

18. Gould, S. J. (1996). *The mismeasure of man* (2nd ed.). New York, NY: W. W. Norton.

19. Again, most of this discussion is taken from Gould, S. J. (1996). *The mismeasure of man* (2nd ed.). New York, NY: W. W. Norton; his review is perhaps the best known in current literature.

20. Goddard, H. H. (1912). *The Kallikak family: A study of the heredity of feeble-mindedness*. New York, NY: Macmillan.

21. Goddard, H. H. (1913). The Binet tests in relation to immigration. *Journal of Psycho-Asthenics, 18,* 105–107; quote taken from p. 106, as cited in Gould, S. J. (1996). *The mismeasure of man* (2nd ed.). New York, NY: W. W. Norton.

22. Gould, S. J. (1996). *The mismeasure of man* (2nd ed.). New York, NY: W. W. Norton, p. 198.

23. Goddard, H. H. (1928). Feeblemindedness: A question of definition. *Journal of Psycho-Asthenics, 33,* 219–227, as discussed in Gould, S. J. (1996). *The mismeasure of man* (2nd ed.). New York, NY: W. W. Norton.

24. Goddard, H. H. (1928). Feeblemindedness: A question of definition. *Journal of Psycho-Asthenics, 33,* p. 224.

25. As quoted in Gould, S. J. (1996). *The mismeasure of man* (2nd ed.). New York, NY: W. W. Norton, p. 365.

26. Hirschi, T., & Hindelang, M. (1977). Intelligence and delinquency: A revisionist review. *American Sociological Review, 42,* 571–587.

27. For a review, see Paternoster, R., & Bachman, R. (2001). *Explaining criminals and crime*. Los Angeles, CA: Roxbury.

28. For a review, see Gibson, C. L., Piquero, A. R., & Tibbetts, S. G. (2001). The contribution of family adversity and verbal IQ to criminal behavior. *International Journal of Offender Therapy and Comparative Criminology, 45,* 574–592; see also Hirschi, T., & Hindelang, M. (1977). Intelligence and delinquency: A revisionist review. *American Sociological Review, 42,* 571–587; Moffitt, T. (1990). The neuropsychology of delinquency: A critical review of theory and research. In M. Tonry & N. Morris (Eds.), *Crime and justice: An annual review of research* (Vol. 12, pp. 99–169). Chicago, IL: University of Chicago Press; Moffitt, T., & Henry, B. (1991). Neuropsychological studies of juvenile delinquency and juvenile violence. In J. S. Miller (Ed.), *The neuropsychology of aggression* (pp. 67–91). Boston, MA: Kluwer; see also the conclusion in Paternoster, R., & Bachman, R. (2001). *Explaining criminals and crime*. Los Angeles, CA: Roxbury, p. 51.

29. Herrnstein, R. J., & Murray, C. (1994). *The bell curve: Intelligence and class structure in the United States*. New York, NY: Free Press.

30. See Brown, S., Esbensen, F., & Geis, G. (2009). *Criminology: Explaining crime and its context*. Cincinnati, OH: Anderson, p. 260.

31. Cullen, F., Gendreau, P., Jarjoura, G. R., & Wright, J. P. (1997). Crime and the bell curve: Lessons from intelligent criminology. *Crime and Delinquency, 43,* 387–411; Gould, S. J. (1996). *The mismeasure of man* (2nd ed.). New York, NY: W. W. Norton, pp. 367–390; Hauser, R. (1995). Review of the bell curve. *Contemporary Sociology, 24,* 149–153; Hudson, J. B. (1995). Scientific racism: The politics of tests, race and genes. *Black Scholar, 25,* 1–10; Perkins, D. (1995). *Outsmarting IQ: The emerging science of learnable intelligence*. New York, NY: Free Press; Taylor, H. (1995). Book review, *The Bell Curve. Contemporary Sociology, 24,* 153–158.

32. Greenfied, D. (2013, February 6). Chicago police will no longer respond to burglaries and robberies. *Frontpage Mag*. Retrieved from http://www.frontpagemag.com/point/176479/chicago-police-will-no-longer-respond-burglaries-daniel-greenfield

33. Van Dijk, J. (2008). *The world of crime: Breaking the silence on problems of security, justice, and development across the world*. Thousand Oaks, CA: SAGE, p. 54.

34. Ibid.

35. Sheldon, W., Hartl, E. M., & McDermott, E. (1949). *Varieties of delinquent youth*. New York, NY: Harper.

36. Greenberg, B. (1995, January 21). *Johnson City Press*, as cited in Brown, S., Esbensen, F., & Geis, G. (2009). *Criminology: Explaining crime and its context*. Cincinnati, OH: Anderson, p. 229.

37. Sheldon, W., Hartl, E. M., & McDermott, E. (1949). *Varieties of delinquent youth.* New York, NY: Harper.

38. Glueck, S., & Glueck, E. (1956). *Physique and delinquency.* New York, NY: Harper & Row; see also Cortes, J. (1972). *Delinquency and crime.* New York, NY: Seminar Press; Hartl, E. (1982). *Physique and delinquent behavior.* New York, NY: Academic Press. For the most recent applications, see Eysenck, H. J., & Gudjonsson, G. H. (1989). *The causes and cures of criminality.* New York, NY: Plenum.

39. Wilson, J. Q., & Herrnstein, R. J. (1985). *Crime and human nature.* New York, NY: McGraw-Hill.

40. Eysenck, H. J., & Gudjonsson, G. H. (1989). *The causes and cures of criminality.* New York, NY: Plenum.

41. Cortes, J. (1972). *Delinquency and crime.* New York, NY: Seminar Press; Glueck, S., & Glueck, E. (1956). *Physique and delinquency.* New York, NY: Harper & Row. For a review, see Eysenck, H. J., & Gudjonsson, G. H. (1989). *The causes and cures of criminality.* New York, NY: Plenum.

42. For a review, see Ellis, L. (2000). *Criminology: A global perspective.* Minot, ND: Pyramid Press.

43. Waldrop, M., & Halverson, C. (1971). Minor physical anomalies and hyperactive behavior in young children. In J. Hellmuth (Ed.), *Exceptional infant: Studies in abnormalities* (pp. 343–381). New York, NY: Brunner/Mazel. See discussion in Fishbein, D. (2001). *Biobehavioral perspectives on criminology.* Belmont, CA: Wadsworth.

44. Fishbein, D. (2001). *Biobehavioral perspectives on criminology.* Belmont, CA: Wadsworth.

45. Wright, J., Tibbetts, S., & Daigle, L. (2008). *Criminals in the making: Criminality across the life course.* Thousand Oaks, CA: SAGE.

46. Ibid.

CHAPTER 6

1. Ma, K. (2011, August 26). Top 10 weirdest twin-crime stories. *Time.* Retrieved from http://www.time.com/time/specials/packages/article/0,28804,2090549_2090540_2090537,00.html

2. Ibid.

3. Dugdale, R. L. (1910). *The Jukes: A study in crime, pauperism, disease, and heredity.* New York, NY: Putnam; Goddard, H. H. (1912). *The Kallikak family.* New York, NY: Macmillan.

4. For an excellent discussion of the alteration of Goddard's photographs, see Gould, S. J. (1996). *The mismeasure of man* (2nd ed.). New York, NY: W. W. Norton.

5. See the review in Raine, A. (1993). *The psychopathology of crime.* San Diego, CA: Academic Press; see also Christiansen, K. O. (1974). Seriousness of criminality and concordance among Danish twins. In R. Hood (Ed.), *Crime, criminology, and public policy* (pp. 63–77). New York, NY: Free Press; Cortes, J. B. (1972). *Delinquency and crime.* New York, NY: Seminar Press.

6. Raine, A. (1993). *The psychopathology of crime.* San Diego, CA: Academic Press.

7. Walters, G. (1992). A meta-analysis of the gene-crime relationship. *Criminology, 30,* 595–613.

8. Hutchings, B., & Mednick, S. A. (1977). Criminality in adoptees and their adoptive and biological parents: A pilot study. In S. Mednick & K. O. Christiansen (Eds.), *Biosocial bases of criminal behavior* (pp. 127–141). New York, NY: Gardner Press.

9. See Walters, G. (1992). A meta-analysis of the gene-crime relationship. *Criminology, 30,* 595–613; Wilson, J. Q., & Herrnstein, R. J. (1985). *Crime and human nature.* New York, NY: Simon & Schuster.

10. Bouchard, T. J., Lykken, D. T., McGue, M., Segal, N., & Tellegen, A. (1990). Sources of human psychological differences: The Minnesota study of twins reared apart. *Science, 250,* 223–228.

11. Jacobs, P., Brunton, M., Melville, M., Brittian, R., & McClemmot, W. (1965). Aggressive behavior, mental subnormality, and the XYY male. *Nature, 208,* 1351–1352.

12. See review in Paternoster, R., & Bachman, R. (2001). *Explaining criminals and crime.* Los Angeles, CA: Roxbury, p. 53.

13. Walsh, A. (1995). Genetic and cytogenetic intersex anomalies: Can they help us to understand gender differences in deviant behavior? *International Journal of Offender Therapy and Comparative Criminality, 39,* 151–166.

14. Booth, A., & Osgood, D. W. (1993). The influence of testosterone on deviance in adulthood: Assessing and explaining the relationship. *Criminology, 31,* 93–117; Soler, H., Vinayak, P., & Quadagno, D. (2000). Biosocial aspects of domestic violence. *Psychoneuroendocrinology, 25,* 721–773; for a review, see Ellis, L., & Walsh, A. (2000). *Criminology: A global perspective.* Boston, MA: Allyn & Bacon.

15. Sanchez-Martin, J. R., Fano, E., Ahedo, L., Cardas, J., Brain, P. F., & Azpiroz, A. (2000). Relating testosterone levels and free play social behavior in male and female preschool children. *Psychoneuroendocrinology, 25,* 773–783.

16. Halpern, D. (2000). *Sex differences in cognitive abilities.* Mahwah, NJ: Erlbaum.

17. Ibid.

18. Ellis, L. (2005). A theory explaining biological correlates of criminality. *European Journal of Criminality, 2,* 287–315.

19. Ibid.

20. Burr, C. (1993). Homosexuality and biology. *Atlantic Monthly, 271,* 47–65; Ellis, L. (2005). A theory explaining biological correlates of criminality. *European Journal of Criminality, 2,* 287–315; Ellis, L., & Ames, M. (1987). Neurohormonal functioning and sexual orientation: A theory of homosexuality-heterosexuality. *Psychological Bulletin, 101,* 233–258.

21. Badger, K., Simpson Craft, R., & Jensen, L. (1998). Age and gender differences in value orientation among American adolescents. *Adolescence, 33,* 591–596; Moll, J., Oliveira-Souza, R. de, Eslinger, P. J., Bramati, I. E., Mourão-Miranda, J., Andreiuolo, P. A., & Pessoa, L. (2002). The neural correlates of moral sensitivity:

A functional magnetic resonance imaging investigation of basic and moral emotions. *Journal of Neuroscience, 22,* 2730–2736; Reite, M., Cullum, C., Stocker, J., Teale, P., & Kozora, E. (1993). Neuropsychological test performance and MEG-based brain lateralization: Sex differences. *Brain Research Bulletin, 32,* 325–328.

22. For reviews, see Fishbein, D. (2001). *Biobehavioral perspectives in criminology.* Belmont, CA: Wadsworth/ Thomson Learning; Raine, A. (1993). *The psychopathology of crime.* San Diego, CA: Academic Press.

23. Beaver, K. (2008). *Biosocial criminology: A primer.* Dubuque, IA: Kendall/Hunt; Raine, A. (1993). *The psychopathology of crime.* San Diego, CA: Academic Press; Wright, J. P., Tibbetts, S. G., & Daigle, L. (2008). *Criminals in the making.* Thousand Oaks, CA: SAGE.

24. Burt, S. A., & Nikolajewski, A. J. (2008). Preliminary evidence that specific candidate genes are associated with adolescent-onset antisocial behavior. *Aggressive Behavior, 34,* 1–9; for a review, see Beaver, K. (2008). *Biosocial criminology: A primer.* Dubuque, IA: Kendall/Hunt.

25. Beaver, K., Wright, J. P., DeLisi, M., Daigle, L., Swatt, M. L., & Gibson, C. (2007). Evidence of a gene X environment interaction in the creation of victimization: Results from a longitudinal sample of adolescents. *International Journal of Offender Therapy and Comparative Criminology, 51,* 620–645. For a review, see Beaver, K. (2008). *Biosocial criminology: A primer.* Dubuque, IA: Kendall/Hunt.

26. For a review, see Beaver, K. (2008). *Biosocial criminology: A primer.* Dubuque, IA: Kendall/Hunt; see also Blumensohn, R., Ratzoni, G., Weizman, A., Apter, A., Tyano, S., Israeli, M., . . . Biegon, A. (1995). Reduction in serotonin 5HT$_2$ receptor binding on platelets of delinquent adolescents. *Psychopharmacology, 118,* 354–356; Coccaro, E. F., Kavoussi, R. J., Cooper, T. B., & Hauger, R. L. (1997). Central serotonin activity and aggression. *American Journal of Psychiatry, 154,* 1430–1435; Davidson, H., Putnam, K. M., & Larson, C. L. (2000). Dysfunction in the neural circuitry of emotion regulation: A possible prelude to violence. *Science, 289,* 591–594; Dolan, M., Deakin, W. J. F., Roberts, N., & Anderson, I. (2002). Serotonergic and cognitive impairment in impulsive aggressive personality disordered offenders: Are there implications for treatment? *Psychological Medicine, 32,* 105–117; Ellis, L. (2005). A theory explaining biological correlates of criminality. *European Journal of Criminality, 2,* 287–315.

27. For a review, see Raine, A. (1993). *The psychopathology of crime.* San Diego, CA: Academic Press, pp. 129–154; see also Tonkonogy, J. M. (1991). Violence and temporal lobe lesion: Head CT and MRI data. *Journal of Neuropsychiatry, 3,* 189–196; Wright, P., Nobrega, J., Langevin, R., & Wortzman, G. (1990). Brain density and symmetry in pedophilic and sexually aggressive offenders. *Annals of Sex Research, 3,* 319–328.

28. Ellis, L. (2005). A theory explaining biological correlates of criminality. *European Journal of Criminality, 2,* 294; see also Fishbein, D. (2003). Neuropsychological

and emotional regulatory processes in antisocial behavior. In A. Walsh & L. Ellis (Eds.), *Biosocial criminology: Challenging environmentalism's supremacy* (pp. 185–208). New York, NY: Nova Science.

29. Anderson, B. J., Holmes, M. D., & Ostresch, E. (1999). Male and female delinquents' attachments and effects of attachments on severity of self-reported delinquency. *Criminal Justice and Behavior, 26,* 435–452.

30. Ohlson, K. (2012, Fall). The good, the bad, and the brain. *Discover: The Brain* [Special issue].

31. Ibid.

32. For a review, see Piquero, A., & Tibbetts, S. G. (2002). *Rational choice and criminal behavior: Recent research and future challenges.* New York, NY: Routledge. See also Paternoster, R., & Simpson, S. (1996). Sanction threats and appeals to morality: Testing a rational choice model of corporate crime. *Law and Society Review, 30,* 378–399.

33. Bauer, L. O. (1997). Frontal P300 decrements, childhood conduct disorder, family history, and the prediction of relapse among abstinent cocaine abusers. *Drug and Alcohol Dependence, 44,* 1–10; Raine, A., & Venables, P. H. (1988). Enhanced P3 evoked potentials and longer P3 recovery times in psychopaths. *Psychophysiology, 25,* 30–38; for a review, see Ellis, L. (2005). A theory explaining biological correlates of criminality. *European Journal of Criminality, 2,* 287–315.

34. For a review, see Raine, A. (1993). *The psychopathology of crime.* San Diego, CA: Academic Press, pp. 174–178; see also Hare, R. D. (1970). *Psychopathy: Theory and practice.* New York, NY: Wiley; Venables, P. H. (1988). Psychophysiology and crime: Theory and data. In T. E. Moffitt & S. A. Mednick (Eds.), *Biological contributions to crime causation.* Dordrecht, Holland: Martinus Nijhoff; Venables, P. H., & Raine, A. (1987). Biological theory. In B. McGurk, D. Thornton, & M. Williams (Eds.), *Applying psychology to imprisonment: Theory and practice* (pp. 3–28). London, UK: Her Majesty's Stationery Office; Volavka, J. (1987). Electroencephalogram among criminals. In S. A. Mednick, T. E. Moffitt, & S. Stack (Eds.), *The causes of crime: New biological approaches* (pp. 137–145). Cambridge, UK: Cambridge University Press.

35. For further discussion and explanation, see Raine, A. (1993). *The psychopathology of crime.* San Diego, CA: Academic Press, pp. 174–177.

36. Boots, D. P. (2011). Neurobiological perspectives of brain vulnerability in pathways to violence over the life course. In K. Beaver & A. Walsh (Eds.), *The Ashgate research companion to biosocial theories of crime* (pp. 181–211). Burlington, VT: Ashgate.

37. Ibid., p. 197.

38. For a review, see Raine, A. (1993). *The psychopathology of crime.* San Diego, CA: Academic Press, pp. 159–173; see also reviews and studies by Bice, T. (1993). *Cognitive and psychophysiological differences in proactive and reactive aggressive boys.* Unpublished doctoral dissertation, University of Southern California, Department

of Psychology; Raine, A., & Venables, P. H. (1988). Skin conductance responsivity in psychopaths to orienting, defensive, and consonant-vowel stimuli. *Journal of Pyschophysiology, 2,* 221–225; Venables, P. H. (1989). Childhood markers for adult disorders. *Journal of Child Psychology and Psychiatric and Allied Disorders, 30,* 347–364.

39. See Kindlon, D. J., Tremblay, R. E., Mezzacappa, E., Earls, F., Laurent, D., & Schaal, B. (1995). Longitudinal patterns of heart rate and fighting behavior in 9- through 12-year-old boys. *Journal of the American Academy of Child and Adolescent Psychiatry, 34,* 371–377; Mezzacappa, E., Tremblay, R. E., Kindlon, D., Saul, J. P., Arseneault, L., Seguin, J., . . . Earls, F. (1997). Anxiety, antisocial behavior, and heart rate regulation in adolescent males. *Journal of Psychiatry, 38,* 457–469; Rogeness, G. A., Cepeda, C., Macedo, C. A., Fischer, C., & Harris, W. R. (1990). Differences in heart rate and blood pressure in children with conduct disorder, major depression, and separation anxiety. *Psychiatry Research, 33,* 199–206.

40. Armstrong, T. (2011). The relationship between low resting heart rate and antisocial behavior: Correlation or causation? In K. Beaver & A. Walsh (Eds.), *The Ashgate research companion to biosocial theories of crime* (pp. 45–68). Burlington, VT: Ashgate.

41. For a very recent review, see Rudo-Hutt, A., Gao, Y., Glenn, A., Peskin, M., Yang, Y., & Raine, A. (2011). Biosocial interactions and correlates of crime. In K. Beaver & A. Walsh (Eds.), *The Ashgate research companion to biosocial theories of crime* (pp. 17–44). Burlington, VT: Ashgate.

42. Tibbetts, S., & Piquero, A. (1999). The influence of gender, low birth weight, and disadvantaged environment in predicting early onset of offending: A test of Moffitt's interactional hypothesis. *Criminology, 37,* 843–878.

43. Piquero, A., & Tibbetts, S. (1999). The impact of pre/perinatal disturbances and disadvantaged familial environment in predicting criminal offending. *Studies on Crime and Crime Prevention, 8,* 52–71.

44. Gibson, C., & Tibbetts, S. (1998). Interaction between maternal cigarette smoking and Apgar scores in predicting offending. *Psychological Reports, 83,* 579–586.

45. Gibson, C., & Tibbetts, S. (2000). A biosocial interaction in predicting early onset of offending. *Psychological Reports, 86,* 509–518.

46. Raine, A., Brennan, P. A., & Mednick, S. A. (1994). Birth complications combined with early maternal rejection at age 1 year predispose to violent crime at age 18 years. *Archives of General Psychiatry, 51,* 984–988; for a thorough review of recent research, see Beaver, K. (2008). *Biosocial criminology: A primer.* Dubuque, IA: Kendall/Hunt.

47. Beaver, K. (2008). *Biosocial criminology: A primer.* Dubuque, IA: Kendall/Hunt.

48. Ibid.

49. Ibid.

50. Ibid. See also Lyons, M. J., True, W. R., Eisen, S. A., Goldberg, J., Meyer, J. M., Faraone, S. V., . . . Tsuang, M. T. (1995). Differential heritability of adult and juvenile antisocial traits. *Archives of General Psychiatry, 52,* 906–915.

51. Beaver, K., & Walsh, A. (2011). Biosocial criminology. In K. Beaver & A. Walsh (Eds.), *The Ashgate research companion to biosocial theories of crime* (pp. 3–16). Burlington, VT: Ashgate.

52. Shoenthaler, S. J. (1991). *Improve your child's IQ and behavior.* London: BBC Books.

53. For a review, see Beaver, K. (2008). *Biosocial criminology: A primer.* Dubuque, IA: Kendall/Hunt, pp. 174–176; see also the review in Wright, J., Tibbetts, S., & Daigle, L. (2008). *Criminals in the making.* Thousand Oaks, CA: SAGE.

54. For a recent review of such birth complications, see Tibbetts, S. (2011). Birth complications and the development of criminality: A biosocial perspective. In K. Beaver & A. Walsh (Eds.), *The Ashgate research companion to biosocial theories of crime* (pp. 273–290). Burlington, VT: Ashgate.

CHAPTER 7

1. Schechter, H., & Everitt, D. (1996). *The A to Z encyclopedia of serial killers.* New York, NY: Pocket Books, p. 92.

2. Rawlins, H. (2003). *The life of a cannibal: Albert Fish confession.* Retrieved from http://iml.jou.ufl.edu/projects/spring03/rawlins/fishconfess.htm

3. Schechter, H., & Everitt, D. (1996). *The A to Z encyclopedia of serial killers.* New York, NY: Pocket Books, p. 92.

4. Ibid.

5. Nietzel, M. T. (1979). *Crime and its modification: A social learning perspective.* New York, NY: Pergamon Press, p. 51.

6. Akers, R. L. (1997). *Criminological theories: Introduction and evaluation* (2nd ed.). Los Angeles, CA: Roxbury, p. 35.

7. Freud, S. (1964). *New introductory lectures on psychoanalysis.* New York, NY: W. W. Norton.

8. Freud, S. (1989). *An outline of psycho-analysis* (Standard ed.). New York, NY: W. W. Norton; see also Fodor, N., Gaynor, F., & Reik, T. (1975). *Freud: Dictionary of psychoanalysis.* Westport, CT: Greenwood Press, p. 90.

9. Coleman, J. C., Butcher, J. N., & Carson, R. C. (1984). *Abnormal psychology and modern life* (7th ed.). Glenview, IL: Scott, Foresman, p. 62.

10. Freud, S. (1960). *The ego and the id.* New York, NY: W. W. Norton.

11. Coleman, J. C., Butcher, J. N., & Carson, R. C. (1984). *Abnormal psychology and modern life* (7th ed.). Glenview, IL: Scott, Foresman, p. 63.

12. Ibid., p. 64.

13. Freud, S. (1964). *New introductory lectures on psychoanalysis.* New York: W. W. Norton.

14. Coleman, J. C., Butcher, J. N., & Carson, R. C. (1984). *Abnormal psychology and modern life* (7th ed.). Glenview, IL: Scott, Foresman, p. 64.

15. Fodor, N., Gaynor, F., & Reik, T. (1975). *Freud: Dictionary of psychoanalysis.* Westport, CT: Greenwood Press, pp. 29–30.

16. Aichhorn, A. (1935). *Wayward youth.* New York, NY: World Publishing Company.

17. Ibid., p. 31.

18. Erickson, E. (1968). *Identity, youth and crisis.* New York, NY: W. W. Norton.

19. Abrahamsen, D. (1944). *Crime and the human mind.* New York, NY: Columbia University Press.

20. Trojanowicz, R. C., Morash, M., & Schram, P. J. (2001). *Juvenile delinquency: Concepts and control* (6th ed.). Upper Saddle River, NJ: Prentice Hall, p. 49.

21. Eysenck, H. J. (1964). *Crime and personality.* London, UK: Routledge & Kegan Paul; see also Eysenck, H. J. (1977). *Crime and personality* (3rd ed.). London, UK: Routledge & Kegan Paul.

22. Eysenck, H. J., & Gudjonson, G. H. (1989). *The causes and cures of criminality.* New York, NY: Plenum Press, p. 44.

23. Ibid., pp. 44–45.

24. Rafter, N. H. (2006). H. J. Eysenck in Fagin's kitchen: The return to biological theory in 20th-century criminology. *History of the Human Sciences, 19,* 37–56.

25. Ibid., p. 43.

26. Eysenck, H. J. (1970). *Crime and personality* (2nd ed.). London, UK: Routledge & Kegan Paul, as cited in Rafter, N. H. (2006). H. J. Eysenck in Fagin's kitchen: The return to biological theory in 20th-century criminology. *History of the Human Sciences, 19,* p. 43.

27. Rafter, N. H. (2006). H. J. Eysenck in Fagin's kitchen: The return to biological theory in 20th-century criminology. *History of the Human Sciences, 19,* p. 43.

28. Eysenck, H. J., & Gudjonson, G. H. (1989). *The causes and cures of criminality.* New York, NY: Plenum Press, pp. 110–111.

29. Eysenck, H. J. (1970). *Crime and personality* (2nd ed.). London, UK: Routledge & Kegan Paul, p. 120, as cited in Rafter, N. H. (2006). H. J. Eysenck in Fagin's kitchen: The return to biological theory in 20th-century criminology. *History of the Human Sciences, 19,* p. 44.

30. Eysenck, H. J., & Gudjonson, G. H. (1989). *The causes and cures of criminality.* New York, NY: Plenum Press, p. 109.

31. Van Dam, C., De Bruyn, E. E. J., & Janssens, M. M. A. M. (2007). Personality, delinquency, and criminal recidivism. *Adolescence, 42,* 763–765.

32. See Blackburn, R. (1999). *The psychology of criminal conduct.* New York, NY: Wiley; Farrington, D. P., Biron, L., & LeBiron, M. (1982). Personality and delinquency in London and Montreal. In J. Gunn & D. P. Farrington (Eds.), *Abnormal offenders, delinquency, and the criminal justice system* (pp. 153–201). New York, NY: Wiley.

33. Levine, S. Z., & Jackson, C. J. (2004). Eysenck's theory of crime revisited: Factors or primary scales? *Legal and Criminological Psychology, 9,* 137.

34. Kohlberg, L. (1969). Stage and sequence: The cognitive-development approach to socialization. In D. A. Goslin (Ed.), *Handbook of socialization theory and research.* Chicago, IL: Rand McNally; Kohlberg, L. (1976). Moral stages and moralization: The cognitive-developmental approach. In T. Lickona (Ed.), *Moral development and behavior: Theory, research, and social issues* (pp. 31–53). New York, NY: Holt, Rinehart & Winston.

35. Kohlberg, L. (1986). A current statement on some theoretical issues. In S. Modgil & C. Modgil (Eds.), *Lawrence Kohlberg: Consensus and controversy* (pp. 485–586). Philadelphia, PA: Falmer Press, p. 491.

36. Ibid.

37. Ibid., p. 492.

38. Damon, W. (1980). Structural-developmental theory and the study of moral development. In M. Windmiller, N. Lambert, & E. Turiel (Eds.), *Moral development and socialization* (pp. 35–68). Boston, MA: Allyn & Bacon.

39. Ibid., p. 42.

40. Kohlberg, L. (1986). A current statement on some theoretical issues. In S. Modgil & C. Modgil (Eds.), *Lawrence Kohlberg: Consensus and controversy* (pp. 485–496). Philadelphia, PA: Falmer Press, p. 495.

41. Damon, W. (1980). Structural-developmental theory and the study of moral development. In M. Windmiller, N. Lambert, & E. Turiel (Eds.), *Moral development and socialization* (pp. 35–68). Boston, MA: Allyn & Bacon, p. 42.

42. Kohlberg, L. (1986). A current statement on some theoretical issues. In S. Modgil & C. Modgil (Eds.), *Lawrence Kohlberg: Consensus and controversy* (pp. 485–496). Philadelphia, PA: Falmer Press, p. 495.

43. Gilligan, C. (1982). *In a different voice: Psychological theory and women's development.* Cambridge, MA: Harvard University Press.

44. Damon, W. (1988). *The moral child: Nurturing children's natural moral growth.* New York, NY: Free Press, p. 96.

45. Gilligan, C. (1982). *In a different voice: Psychological theory and women's development.* Cambridge, MA: Harvard University Press.

46. Ibid., p. 18; see also Kohlberg, L. (1958). *The development of modes of thinking and choices in years 10 to 16.* Unpublished doctoral dissertation, University of Chicago; Kohlberg, L. (1981). *The philosophy of moral development.* San Francisco, CA: Harper & Row.

47. Van der Horst, F. C. P., & van der Veer, R. (2008). Loneliness in infancy: Harry Larlow, John Bowlby and issues of separation. *Integrative Psychological Behavior, 42,* 326.

48. Bretherton, I. (1992). The origins of attachment theory: John Bowlby and Mary Ainsworth. *Developmental Psychology, 28,* 759–775.

49. Bowlby, J. (1975). *Attachment and loss: Separation, anxiety and anger* (Vol. 2). New York, NY: Basic Books, p. 60.

50. Adler, F., Mueller, G. O. W., & Laufer, W. S. (2007). *Criminology* (6th ed.). Boston, MA: McGraw-Hill, p. 88. See also Bowlby, J. (1969, 1975). *Attachment and loss: Separation, anxiety and anger* (Vols. 1 & 2). New York, NY: Basic Books.

51. Bowlby, J. (1975). *Attachment and loss: Separation, anxiety and anger* (Vol. 2). New York, NY: Basic Books, p. 201.

52. Bretherton, I. (1992). The origins of attachment theory: John Bowlby and Mary Ainsworth. *Developmental Psychology, 28,* 759–775.

53. Bowlby, J. (1944). Forty-four juvenile thieves: Their character and home-life. *International Journal of Psychoanalysis, 25,* 19–52.

54. Source: Bowlby, J. (1944). Forty-four juvenile thieves: Their character and home-life. *International Journal of Psychoanalysis, 25,* 40–41.

55. Schneider, W. H. (1992). After Binet: French intelligence testing, 1900–1950. *Journal of the History of the Behavioral Sciences, 28,* 111–132.

56. Cravens, H. (1992). A scientific project locked in time: The Terman genetic studies of genius, 1920s–1950s. *American Psychologist, 47,* 183–189.

57. Ryan, P. J. (1997). Unnatural selection: Intelligence testing, eugenics, and American political cultures. *Journal of Social History, 30,* 669–685.

58. Tibbetts, S. (2012). *Criminological theory: The essentials.* Thousand Oaks, CA: SAGE, p. 73.

59. Holmes, R. M., & Holmes, S. T. (2002). *Profiling violent crimes: An investigative tool* (3rd ed.). Thousand Oaks, CA: SAGE, p. 671.

60. Sutherland, E. H. (1931). Mental deficiency and crime. In K. Young (Ed.), *Social attitudes* (pp. 357–375). New York, NY: Henry Holt.

61. Brownmiller, S. (1975). *Against our will: Men, women, and rape.* New York, NY: Simon & Schuster. See also Clark, A. (1987). *Women silence men's violence: Sexual assault in England 1770–1845.* London, UK: Pandora.

62. Ibid. See also Clark, A. (1987). *Women silence men's violence: Sexual assault in England 1770–1845.* London, UK: Pandora; Belknap, J. (2001). *The invisible woman: Gender, crime, and justice* (2nd ed.). Belmont, CA: Wadsworth, pp. 228–230; Burgess-Jackson, K. (1999). A history of rape law. In K. Burgess-Jackson (Eds.), *A most detestable crime: New philosophical essays on rape.* New York, NY: Oxford University Press, pp. 16–17.

63. Clark, A. (1987). *Women silence men's violence: Sexual assault in England 1770–1845.* London, UK: Pandora.

64. *State v. Sheline,* 955 S.W. 2d. 2, 44 (Tenn. 1997).

65. Burgess-Jackson, K. (1999). A history of rape law. In K. Burgess-Jackson (Eds.), *A most detestable crime: New philosophical essays on rape.* New York, NY: Oxford University Press, p. 22.

66. Ibid., p. 24.

67. Ibid.

68. Federal Bureau of Investigation. (2015). *Crime in the United States, 2014. Violent crimes: Rape.* Washington, DC: Department of Justice, para. 1. Retrieved from https://www.fbi.gov/about-us/cjis/ucr/crime-in-the-u.s/2014/crime-in-the-u.s.-2014/offenses-known-to-law-enforcement/rape

69. Holmes, R. M., & Holmes, S. T. (2002). *Profiling violent crimes: An investigative tool* (3rd ed.). Thousand Oaks, CA: SAGE, pp. 144–145.

70. Knight, R. A., & Prentky, R. A. (1987). The developmental antecedents and adult adaptations of rapist subtypes. *Criminal Justice and Behavior, 14,* 403–426.

71. Holmes, R. M., & Holmes, S. T. (2002). *Profiling violent crimes: An investigative tool* (3rd ed.). Thousand Oaks, CA: SAGE, p. 145.

72. Knight, R. A., & Prentky, R. A. (1987). The developmental antecedents and adult adaptations of rapist subtypes. *Criminal Justice and Behavior, 14,* 421.

73. Ibid., p. 411.

74. Holmes, R. M., & Holmes, S. T. (2002). *Profiling violent crimes: An investigative tool* (3rd ed.). Thousand Oaks, CA: SAGE, pp. 150–151.

75. Knight, R. A., & Prentky, R. A. (1987). The developmental antecedents and adult adaptations of rapist subtypes. *Criminal Justice and Behavior, 14,* 410.

76. Ibid., p. 411.

77. Van Dijk, J. (2008). The world of crime: Breaking the silence on problems of security, justice, and development across the world. Thousand Oaks, CA: SAGE, p. 83.

78. Ibid.

79. Kangaspunta, K. (2000). Secondary analysis of integrated sources of data. In A. Alvazzi del Frate & O. Hatalak (Eds.), *Surveying crime: A global perspective.* Rome: UNICRI/ISTAT.

80. Wilson, J. Q., & Herrnstein, R. J. (1985). *Crime and human nature.* New York, NY: Simon & Schuster.

81. Wrightsman, L. S. (1987). *Psychology and the legal system.* Monterey, CA: Brooks/Cole, p. 347.

82. Kaplin, J. (1985, September 22). Why people go to the bad. *New York Times Book Review,* p. 7, as cited in Wrightsman, L. S. (1987). *Psychology and the legal system.* Monterey, CA: Brooks/Cole, p. 348.

83. Lilly, J. R., Cullen, F. T., & Ball, R. A. (2011). *Criminological theory: Context and consequences* (5th ed.). Thousand Oaks, CA: SAGE, p. 307.

84. Gibbs, J. P. (1985). Review essay. *Criminology, 23,* 381.

85. Wilson, J. Q., & Herrnstein, R. J. (1985). *Crime and human nature.* New York, NY: Simon & Schuster, p. 103.

86. Wrightsman, L. S. (1987). *Psychology and the legal system.* Monterey, CA: Brooks/Cole, p. 348.

87. Ibid., p. 510.

88. Wilson, J. Q., & Herrnstein, R. J. (1985). *Crime and human nature.* New York, NY: Simon & Schuster, p. 61.

89. Lilly, J. R., Cullen, F. T., & Ball, R. A. (2011). *Criminological theory: Context and consequences* (5th ed.). Thousand Oaks, CA: SAGE, p. 308.

90. Wilson, J. Q., & Herrnstein, R. J. (1985). *Crime and human nature.* New York, NY: Simon & Schuster. See also Wrightsman, L. S. (1987). *Psychology and the legal system.* Monterey, CA: Brooks/Cole, p. 348.

91. Ibid., pp. 309–311.

92. Gibbs, J. P. (1985). Review essay. *Criminology, 23,* 382.

93. Lilly, J. R., Cullen, F. T., & Ball, R. A. (2011). *Criminological theory: Context and consequences* (5th ed.). Thousand Oaks, CA: SAGE, p. 309.

94. Cleckley, H. (1982). *The mast of sanity* (Rev. ed.). St. Louis, MO: C. V. Mosby.

95. Salekin, R. T., Neumann, C. S., Liestico, A. R., & Zalot, A. (2004). Psychopathy in youth and intelligence: An investigation of Cleckley's hypothesis. *Journal of Clinical Child and Adolescent Psychology, 33,* 731.

96. Hare, R. D. (1991). *Manual for the Revised Psychopathy Checklist.* Toronto, Ontario, Canada: Multi-Health Systems.

97. Vaughn, M. G., Edens, J. F., Howard, M. O., & Smith, S. T. (2009). An investigation of primary and secondary psychopathy in a statewide sample of incarcerated youth. *Youth Violence and Juvenile Justice, 7,* 172–188.

98. Ibid., p. 173.

99. Ibid.

100. Lykken, D. T. (1996). Psychopathy, sociopathy, and crime. *Society, 34,* 31.

101. Ibid., p. 32.

102. Ibid., pp. 33–34.

103. Hare, R. D. (1999). Psychopathy as a risk factor for violence. *Psychiatric Quarterly, 70,* 183–184.

104. Ibid., p. 186

105. See Hemphill, J. F., Hare, R. D., & Wong, S. (1998). Psychopathy and recidivism: A review. *Legal and Criminological Psychology, 3,* 141–172; Salekin, R. T., Rogers, R., & Sewell, K. W. (1996). A review and meta-analysis of the Psychopathy Checklist and Psychopathy Checklist–Revised: Predictive validity of dangerousness. *Clinical Psychology: Science and Practice, 3,* 203–215.

106. Hare, R. D. (1999). Psychopathy as a risk factor for violence. *Psychiatric Quarterly, 70,* 186.

107. Ibid., p. 191.

108. Teplin, L. A. (1994). Psychiatric and substance abuse disorders among male urban jail detainees. *American Journal of Public Health, 84,* 290–293. See also James, D. J., & Glaze, L. E. (2006). *Mental health problems of prison and jail inmates* [Bureau of Justice Statistics Special Report]. Washington, DC: U.S. Department of Justice.

109. Martin, M. S., Dorken, S. K., Wambolt, A. D., & Wooten, S. E. (2012). Stopping the revolving door: A meta-analysis on the effectiveness of interventions for criminally involved individuals with major mental disorders. *Law and Human Behavior, 36,* 1–12.

110. Torrey, E. F., Zdanowica, M. T., Kennard, A. D., Lamb, H. R., Eslinger, D. F., Biasotti, M. C., & Fuller, D. A. (2014). *The treatment of persons with mental illness in prisons and jails: A state survey.* Arlington, VA: The Treatment Advocacy Center. Retrieved from http://www.tacreports.org/storage/documents/treatment-behind-bars/treatment-behind-bars.pdf

111. Bush, J., Glick, B., & Taymans, J. (2006). *Thinking for a Change: Facilitator training.* Longmont, CO: National Institute of Corrections, U.S. Department of Justice.

112. Allen, H. E., Simonsen, C. E., & Latessa, E. J. (2004). *Corrections in America: An introduction* (10th ed.). Upper Saddle River, NJ: Prentice Hall, p. 277.

113. Bush, J., Glick, B., & Taymans, J. (1997). *Thinking for a Change: Facilitator training.* Longmont, CO: National Institute of Corrections, U.S. Department of Justice. See also Andrews, D. A., & Bonta, J. (1994). *The psychology of criminal conduct.* Cincinnati, OH: Anderson; Ross, R. R., & Fabiano, E. A. (1984). *Time to think: A cognitive model of delinquency prevention and offender rehabilitation.* Ottawa: Institute of Social Sciences and Arts.

114. Golden, L. S., Gatchel, R. J., & Cahill, M. A. (2006). Evaluating the effectiveness of the National Institute of Corrections' "Thinking for a Change" program among probationers. *Journal of Offender Rehabilitation, 43,* 55–73.

115. Wilson, R. J. (2005). Are cognitive problem-solving skills programmes really not working? A response to "evaluating evidence for the effectiveness of the reasoning and rehabilitation programme." *Howard Journal, 44,* 319–321.

116. O'Malley, N. (May 10, 2014). Betrayal: Michelle Knight tells of life inside Ariel Castro's house of hell. *Sidney Morning Herald.* Retrieved from http://www.smh.com.au/world/betrayal-michelle-knight-tells-of-life-inside-ariel-castros-house-of-hell-20140504-37r6h.html

117. Diaz, J., Pearle, L, & Valiente, A. (2015, April 27). What life in captivity was like for Cleveland kidnapping survivors Amanda Berry and Gina DeJesus. *ABC News.* Retrieved from http://abcnews.go.com/US/life-captivity-cleveland-kidnapping-survivors-amanda-berry-gina/story?id=30532737

118. Johnson, A. (2013, December 3). Ariel Castro blamed victims, addiction to porn for crimes. *Columbus Dispatch.* Retrieved from http://www.dispatch.com/content/stories/local/2013/12/03/Ariel-Castro-blamed-victims.html

119. Mueser, K. T., Torrey, W. C., Lynde, D., Singer, P., & Drake, R. E. (2003). Implementing evidence-based practices for people with severe mental illness. *Behavioral Modification, 27,* 387–411, as cited in Morgan, R. D., Flora, D. B., Kroner, D. G., Mills, J. F., Varghese, F., & Steffan, J. S. (2012). Treating offenders with mental illness: A research synthesis. *Law of Human Behavior, 36,* p. 40.

120. Steadman, H. J., Davidson, S., & Brown, C. (2001). Law & psychiatry: Mental health courts: Their promise and unanswered questions. *Psychiatric Services, 52,* 457.

121. Council of State Governments Justice Center. (2008). *Mental health courts: A primer for policymakers and practitioners.* Washington, DC: U.S. Department of Justice, p. 3.

122. Ibid., p. 8.

123. Ibid., p. 4.

124. Allnutt, S., Samuels, A., & O'Driscoll, C. (2007). The insanity defence: From wild beasts to M'Naghten. *Australian Psychiatry, 15,* 292.

125. Perlin, M. L. (1994). *The jurisprudence of the insanity defense.* Durham, NC: Carolina Academic Press.

126. Morris, N. (n.d.). Crime file: Insanity defense. Washington, DC: U.S. Department of Justice, National

Institute of Justice. Retrieved from https://www.ncjrs
.gov/pdffiles1/Digitization/100742NCJRS.pdf

127. Ibid. See also Slodov, M. D. (1990). Criminal responsibility and the noncompliant psychiatric offender: Risking madness. *Case Western Reserve Law Review, 40,* 271–330.

128. FindLaw. (n.d.). The insanity defense among the states. Retrieved from http://criminal.findlaw.com/criminal-procedure/the-insanity-defense-among-the-states.html

129. Wallace, H., & Roberson, C. (2008). *Principles of criminal law* (4th ed.). Boston, MA: Pearson, p. 95.

130. Allnutt, S., Samuels, A., & O'Driscoll, C. (2007). The insanity defence: From wild beasts to M'Naghten. *Australian Psychiatry, 15,* 292–293.

131. Ibid., pp. 293–294.

132. Morris, N. (n.d.). Crime file: Insanity defense. Washington, DC: U.S. Department of Justice, National Institute of Justice. Retrieved from https://www.ncjrs
.gov/pdffiles1/Digitization/100742NCJRS.pdf

133. Margolick, D. (1994). Lorena Bobbitt acquitted in mutilation of husband. *New York Times.* Retrieved from http://www.nytimes.com/1994/01/22/us/
lorena-bobbitt-acquitted-in-mutilation-of-husband
.html?pagewanted=all&src=pm

134. Cobun, L. S. (1984). The insanity defense: Effects of abolition unsupported by a moral consensus. *American Journal of Law and Medicine, 9,* 471–498.

135. Felthous, A. R. (2010). Psychopathic disorders and criminal responsibility in the USA. *European Archives of Psychiatry and Clinical Neuroscience, 260,* 138.

136. Wallace, H., & Roberson, C. (2008). *Principles of criminal law* (4th ed.). Boston, MA: Pearson, p. 96.

137. Martin, M. S., Dorken, S. K., Wamboldt, A. D., & Wootten, S. E. (2011). Stopping the revolving door: A meta-analysis on the effectiveness of interventions for criminally involved individuals with major mental disorders. *Law and Human Behavior, 36,* p. 1.

138. Lab, S. P. (2016). *Crime prevention: Approaches, practices, and evaluations* (9th ed.). New York, NY: Routledge, p. 53.

139. Siegel, L. J. (2013). *Criminology* (11th ed.). Belmont, CA: Wadsworth, p. 172.

140. Lab, S. P. (2016). *Crime prevention: Approaches, practices, and evaluations* (9th ed.). New York, NY: Routledge, p. 193.

141. Siegel, L. J. (2013). *Criminology* (11th ed.). Belmont, CA: Wadsworth, p. 172.

142. Lab, S. P. (2016). *Crime prevention: Approaches, practices, and evaluations* (9th ed.). New York, NY: Routledge, p. 309.

143. Siegel, L. J. (2013). *Criminology* (11th ed.). Belmont, CA: Wadsworth, p. 172.

144. Morgan, R. D., Flora, D. B., Kroner, D. G., Mills, J. F., Varghese, F., & Steffan, J. S. (2012). Treating offenders with mental illness: A research synthesis. *Law and Human Behavior, 36,* p. 39.

145. Mischel, W. (1968). *Personality and assessment.* New York, NY: Wiley.

146. Schmalleger, F. (2009). *Criminology today: An integrative introduction* (5th ed.). Upper Saddle River, NJ: Pearson/Prentice Hall, pp. 216–217.

CHAPTER 8

1. Ellis, L., & Walsh, A. (1999). Criminologists' opinions about causes and theories of crime and delinquency. *Criminologist, 24,* 1–4; Walsh, A., & Ellis, L. (1999). Political ideology and American criminologists' explanations for criminal behavior. *Criminologist, 24,* 1, 14.

2. Much of the discussion of the development of structural theories of the 19th century is drawn from Zanden, J. W. V. (2000). *Sociology: The core* (2nd ed.). New York, NY: McGraw-Hill, pp. 8–14.

3. Ibid., pp. 8–9.

4. For more thorough discussions of Guerry and Quetelet, see the sources from which we have drawn the information presented here: Beirne, P. (1993). *Inventing criminology.* Albany, NY: SUNY Press; Vold, G. B., Bernard, T. J., & Snipes, J. (2002). *Theoretical criminology* (5th ed.). New York, NY: Oxford University Press.

5. Morris, T. (1957). *The criminal area.* New York, NY: Routledge, pp. 42–53, as cited in Vold, G. B., Bernard, T. J., & Snipes, J. (2002). *Theoretical criminology* (5th ed.). New York, NY: Oxford University Press, p. 22.

6. U.S. Department of Justice, Bureau of Justice Statistics. (2001). *Sourcebook of criminal justice statistics, 2000* (NCJ-190251). Washington, DC: USGPO, Table 3.13, p. 194; U.S. Department of Justice, Bureau of Justice Statistics. (2001). *Sourcebook of criminal justice statistics, 2000* (NCJ-190251). Washington, DC: USGPO, Table 3.26, p. 202.

7. Beirne, P. (1993). *Inventing criminology.* Albany, NY: SUNY Press, pp. 78–81.

8. Vold, G. B., Bernard, T. J., & Snipes, J. (2002). *Theoretical criminology* (5th ed.). New York, NY: Oxford University Press, pp. 23–26.

9. Burton, V., & Cullen, F. (1992). The empirical status of strain theory. *Journal of Crime and Justice, 15,* 1–30; Passas, N. (1995). Continuities in the anomie tradition. In F. Adler & W. S. Laufer (Eds.), *Advances in criminological theory: Vol. 6. The legacy of anomie theory* (pp. 91–112). New Brunswick, NJ: Transaction; Passas, N. (1997). Anomie, reference groups, and relative deprivation. In N. Passas & R. Agnew (Eds.), *The future of anomie theory* (pp. 62–94). Boston, MA: Northeastern University Press.

10. U.S. Department of Justice, Bureau of Justice Statistics. (2001). *Sourcebook of criminal justice statistics, 2000* (NCJ-190251). Washington, DC: USGPO, Table 3.124, p. 290.

11. Lee, D. S. (1993). *An empirical investigation of the economic incentives for criminal behavior.* Bachelor of Arts thesis in economics, Harvard University, Boston, MA, as cited in Freeman, R. B. (1995). The labor market. In J. Q. Wilson & J. Petersilia (Eds.), *Crime* (pp. 103–105). San Francisco, CA: ICS Press.

12. Beirne, P. (1993). *Inventing criminology*. Albany, NY: SUNY Press, p. 88, as cited in Vold, G. B., Bernard, T. J., & Snipes, J. (2002). *Theoretical criminology* (5th ed.). New York, NY: Oxford University Press, p. 25.

13. Vold, G. B., Bernard, T. J., & Snipes, J. (2002). *Theoretical criminology* (5th ed.). New York, NY: Oxford University Press, pp. 25–26.

14. Much of this discussion of Durkheim is taken from Vold, G. B., Bernard, T. J., & Snipes, J. (2002). *Theoretical criminology* (5th ed.). New York, NY: Oxford University Press, Chapter 6, as well as Zanden, J. W. V. (2000). *Sociology: The core* (2nd ed.). New York, NY: McGraw-Hill, pp. 11–13.

15. Durkheim, E. (1965). *The rules of the sociological method* (G. E. G. Catlin, Ed.; S. A. Solovay & J. H. Mueller, Trans.). New York, NY: Free Press, as cited in Vold, G. B., Bernard, T. J., & Snipes, J. (2002). *Theoretical criminology* (5th ed.). New York, NY: Oxford University Press.

16. See discussion in Klein, M. (1995). Street gang cycles. In J. Q. Wilson & J. Petersilia (Eds.), *Crime* (pp. 217–236). San Francisco, CA: ICS Press.

17. For more details on these issues, see E. Durkheim's works *The division of labor in society*. (1965). New York, NY: Free Press. (Original work published 1893); *Suicide*. (1951). New York, NY: Free Press. (Original work published 1897).

18. U.S. Department of Justice, Bureau of Justice Statistics. (1996). *Violent crime in the United States*. Washington, DC: Author, as illustrated in Senna, J., & Siegel, L. G. (1999). *Introduction to criminal justice* (8th ed.). Belmont, CA: West/Wadsworth.

19. Chambliss, W. J. (1976). Functional and conflict theories of crime: The heritage of Emile Durkheim and Karl Marx. In W. J. Chambliss & M. Mankoff (Eds.), *Whose law what order? A conflict approach to criminology* (pp. 1–28). New York, NY: Wiley, pp. 11–16.

20. For reviews of Merton's theory, see both of his original and more recent works: Merton, R. K. (1938). Social structure and anomie. *American Sociological Review, 3*, 672–682; Merton, R. K. (1968). *Social theory and social structure*. New York, NY: Free Press; Merton, R. K. (1995). Opportunity structure: The emergence, diffusion, and differentiation as sociological concept, 1930s–1950s. In F. Adler & M. Laufer (Eds.), *Advances in criminological theory: The legacy of anomie theory* (Vol. 6, pp. 3–17). New Brunswick, NJ: Transaction Press. For reviews by others, see Akers, R. L., & Sellers, C. S. (2004). *Criminological theories: Introduction, evaluation, and application* (4th ed.). Los Angeles, CA: Roxbury, pp. 164–168; Bernard, T. J. (1987). Testing structural strain theories. *Journal of Research in Crime and Delinquency, 24*, 262–280; Brown, S. E., Esbensen, F., & Geis, G. (2004). *Criminology: Explaining crime and its context* (5th ed.). Cincinnati, OH: Anderson, pp. 297–307; Clinard, M. B. (1964). The theoretical implications of anomie and deviant behavior. In M. B. Clinard (Ed.), *Anomie and deviant behavior* (pp. 1–56). New York, NY: Free Press.

21. Clinard, M. B. (1964). The theoretical implications of anomie and deviant behavior. In M. B. Clinard (Ed.), *Anomie and deviant behavior* (pp. 1–56). New York, NY: Free Press; see also the discussion in Brown, S. E., Esbensen, F., & Geis, G. (2004). *Criminology: Explaining crime and its context* (5th ed.). Cincinnati, OH: Anderson, p. 297.

22. Senna, J., & Siegel, L. J. (1999). *Introduction to criminal justice* (8th ed.). Belmont, CA: Wadsworth, p. 44.

23. Merton, R. K. (1968). *Social theory and social structure*. New York, NY: Free Press.

24. Vold, G. B., Bernard, T. J., & Snipes, J. (2002). *Theoretical criminology* (5th ed.). New York, NY: Oxford University Press, p. 140.

25. For examples and reviews of this research, see Akers, R. L. (1964). Socio-economic status and delinquent behavior: A retest. *Journal of Research in Crime and Delinquency, 1*, 38–46; Dunaway, G. R., Cullen, F. T., Burton, V. S., & Evans, T. D. (2000). The myth of social class and crime revisited: An examination of class and adult criminality. *Criminology, 38*, 589–632; Hindelang, M. J. (1980). *Measuring delinquency*. Beverly Hills, CA: SAGE; Hindelang, M. J., Hirschi, T., & Weis, J. C. (1979). Correlates of delinquency: The illusion of discrepancy between self-report and official measures. *American Sociological Review, 44*, 995–1014; Nye, F. I. (1958). *Family relationships and delinquent behavior*. New York, NY: Wiley; Thornberry, T., & Farnworth, M. (1982). Social correlates of criminal involvement. *American Sociological Review, 47*, 505–517; Tittle, C. R., & Villemez, W. J. (1977). Social class and criminality. *Social Forces, 56*, 474–503; Tittle, C. R., Villemez, W. J., & Smith, D. A. (1978). The myth of social class and criminality: An empirical assessment of the empirical evidence. *American Sociological Review, 43*, 643–656; for one of the most thorough reviews, see Tittle, C. R., & Meier, R. F. (1990). Specifying the SES/delinquency relationship. *Criminology, 28*, 271–299.

26. Kleck, G., & Chiricos, T. (2000). Unemployment and property crime: A target-specific assessment of opportunity and motivation as mediating factors. *Criminology, 40*, 649–680.

27. Bernard, T. J. (1987). Testing structural strain theories. *Journal of Research in Crime and Delinquency, 24*, 262–280; Messner, S. F. (1988). Merton's "social structure and anomie": The road not taken. *Deviant Behavior, 9*, 33–53; see also discussion in Burton, V. S., & Cullen, F. T. (1992). The empirical status of strain theory. *Journal of Crime and Justice, 15*, 1–30.

28. For a review of these studies, see Land, K. C., McCall, P. L., & Cohen, L. E. (1990). Structural covariates of homicide rates: Are there any invariances across time and social space? *American Journal of Sociology, 95*, 922–963.

29. For examples and reviews of these types of studies, see Agnew, R. F., Cullen, F. T., Burton, V. S., Evans, T. D., & Dunaway, R. G. (1996). A new test of classic strain theory. *Justice Quarterly, 13*, 681–704; Burton, V., & Cullen, F.

(1992). The empirical status of strain theory. *Journal of Crime and Justice, 15,* 1–30; Burton, V. S., Cullen, F. T., Evans, T. D., & Dunaway, R. G. (1994). Reconsidering strain theory: Operationalization, rival theories, and adult criminality. *Journal of Quantitative Criminology, 10,* 213–239; Farnworth, M., & Leiber, M. J. (1989). Strain theory revisited: Economic goals, educational means, and delinquency. *American Sociological Review, 54,* 263–274; Hirschi, T. (1969). *Causes of delinquency.* Berkeley: University of California Press; Liska, A. E. (1971). Aspirations, expectations, and delinquency: Stress and additive models. *Sociological Quarterly, 12,* 99–107; see also discussion of this issue in Akers, R. L., & Sellers, C. S. (2004). *Criminological theories: Introduction, evaluation, and application* (4th ed.). Los Angeles: Roxbury, pp. 173–175.

30. Farnworth, M., & Leiber, M. J. (1989). Strain theory revisited: Economic goals, educational means, and delinquency. *American Sociological Review, 54,* 263–274.

31. Agnew, R. F., Cullen, F. T., Burton, V. S., Evans, T. D., & Dunaway, R. G. (1996). A new test of classic strain theory. *Justice Quarterly, 13,* 681–704.

32. Cohen, A. (1955). *Delinquent boys: The culture of the gang.* New York, NY: Free Press.

33. Hindelang, M. J., Hirschi, T., & Weis, J. C. (1979). Correlates of delinquency: The illusion of discrepancy between self-report and official measures. *American Sociological Review, 44,* 995–1014; Tittle, C. R., Villemez, W. J., & Smith, D. A. (1978). The myth of social class and criminality: An empirical assessment of the empirical evidence. *American Sociological Review, 43,* 643–656.

34. See Bernard, T. J. (1987). Testing structural strain theories. *Journal of Research in Crime and Delinquency, 24,* 262–280; Elliott, D., & Voss, H. (1974). *Delinquency and dropout.* Lexington, MA: D. C. Health; Jarjoura, G. R. (1993). Does dropping out of school enhance delinquent involvement? Results from a large-scale national probability sample. *Criminology, 31,* 149–172; Jarjoura, G. R. (1996). The conditional effect of social class on the dropout delinquency relationship. *Journal of Research in Crime and Delinquency, 33,* 232–255; Merton, R. K. (1995). Opportunity structure: The emergence, diffusion, and differentiation as sociological concept, 1930s–1950s. In F. Adler & M. Laufer (Eds.), *Advances in criminological theory: The legacy of anomie theory* (Vol. 6, pp. 3–17). New Brunswick, NJ: Transaction Press; Thornberry, T. P., Moore, M., & Christenson, R. L. (1985). The effect of dropping out of high school on subsequent criminal behavior. *Criminology, 23,* 3–18; see also discussion in Shoemaker, D. J. (2005). *Theories of delinquency* (5th ed.). New York, NY: Oxford University Press.

35. Hirschi, T. (1969). *Causes of delinquency.* Berkeley: University of California Press; Liazos, A. (1978). School, alienation, and delinquency. *Crime and Delinquency, 24,* 355–370; Rogers, J. W., & Mays, G. L. (1987). *Juvenile delinquency and juvenile justice.* New York: Wiley; Tygart, C. E. (1988). Strain theory and public school vandalism: Academic tracking, school social status, and students' academic achievement. *Youth and Society, 20,* 106–118.

36. Cloward, R. A., & Ohlin, L. E. (1960). *Delinquency and opportunity: A theory of delinquent gangs.* New York, NY: Free Press. For discussion and theoretical critique of the model, see Bernard, T. J. (1987). Testing structural strain theories. *Journal of Research in Crime and Delinquency, 24,* 262–280, and Merton, R. K. (1995). Opportunity structure: The emergence, diffusion, and differentiation as sociological concept, 1930s–1950s. In F. Adler & M. Laufer (Eds.), *Advances in criminological theory: The legacy of anomie theory* (Vol. 6, pp. 3–17). New Brunswick, NJ: Transaction Press.

37. Hirschi, T. (1969). *Causes of delinquency.* Berkeley: University of California Press; see discussion in Shoemaker, D. J. (2005). *Theories of delinquency* (5th ed.). New York, NY: Oxford University Press, pp. 121–130; Liska, A. E. (1971). Aspirations, expectations, and delinquency: Stress and additive models. *Sociological Quarterly, 12,* 99–107; Short, J. F. (1964). Gang delinquency and anomie. In M. B. Clinard (Ed.), *Anomie and deviant behavior.* New York, NY: Free Press, pp. 98–127; Short, J. F., Rivera, R., & Tennyson, R. A. (1965). Perceived opportunities, gang membership, and delinquency. *American Sociological Review, 30,* 56–67; Short, J. F., & Strodtbeck, F. L. (1965). *Group processes and gang delinquency.* Chicago, IL: University of Chicago Press.

38. Short, J. F., & Strodtbeck, F. L. (1965). *Group processes and gang delinquency.* Chicago, IL: University of Chicago Press; Spergel, I. (1964). *Racketville, Slumtown, and Haulburg.* Chicago, IL: University of Chicago Press; Tracy, P. E., Wolfgang, M. E., & Figlio, R. M. (1990). *Delinquency careers in two birth cohorts.* New York, NY: Plenum.

39. Empey, L. T. (1991). *American delinquency* (4th ed.). Homewood, IL: Dorsey.

40. Hindelang, M. J., Hirschi, T., & Weis, J. C. (1979). Correlates of delinquency: The illusion of discrepancy between self-report and official measures. *American Sociological Review, 44,* 995–1014; Tittle, C. R., Villemez, W. J., & Smith, D. A. (1978). The myth of social class and criminality: An empirical assessment of the empirical evidence. *American Sociological Review, 43,* 643–656.

41. For Agnew's works regarding this theory, see Agnew, R. (1985). A revised strain theory of delinquency. *Social Forces, 64,* 151–167; Agnew, R. (1992). Foundation for a general strain theory of crime and delinquency. *Criminology, 30,* 47–88; Agnew, R. (1995). Controlling delinquency: Recommendations from general strain theory. In H. Barlow (Ed.), *Crime and public policy: Putting theory to work* (pp. 43–70). Boulder, CO: Westview Press; Agnew, R. (2001). Building on the foundation of general strain theory: Specifying the types of strain most likely to lead to crime and delinquency. *Journal of Research in Crime and Delinquency, 38,*

319–361; Agnew, R., Cullen, F., Burton, V., Evans, T. D., & Dunaway, R. G. (1996). A new test of general strain theory. *Justice Quarterly, 13,* 681–704; Agnew, R., & White, H. R. (1992). An empirical test of general strain theory. *Criminology, 30,* 475–500.

42. Brezina, T., Piquero, A., & Mazerolle, P. (2001). Student anger and aggressive behavior in school: An initial test of Agnew's macro-level strain theory. *Journal of Research in Crime and Delinquency, 38,* 362–386.

43. Agnew, R., Cullen, F., Burton, V., Evans, T. D., & Dunaway, R. G. (1996). A new test of general strain theory. *Justice Quarterly, 13,* 681–704; Agnew, R., & White, H. R. (1992). An empirical test of general strain theory. *Criminology, 30,* 475–500; Baron, S. W. (2004). General strain, street youth and crime: A test of Agnew's revised theory. *Criminology, 42,* 457–484; Baron, S. W., & Hartnagel, T. F. (2002). Street youth and labor market strain. *Journal of Criminal Justice, 30,* 519–533; Brezina, T. (1996). Adapting to strain: An examination of delinquent coping responses. *Criminology, 34,* 39–60; Broidy, L. M. (2001). A test of general strain theory. *Criminology, 39,* 9–36; Hay, C. (2003). Family strain, gender, and delinquency. *Sociological Perspectives, 46,* 107–135; Hoffman, J. P., & Cerbone, F. G. (1999). Stressful life events and delinquency escalation in early adolescence. *Criminology, 37,* 343–374; Hoffman, J. P., & Miller, A. S. (1998). A latent variable analysis of general strain theory. *Journal of Quantitative Criminology, 14,* 83–110; Hoffman, J. P., & Su, S. S. (1998). Stressful life events and adolescent substance use and depression: Conditional and gender differentiated effects. *Substance Use and Misuse, 33,* 2219–2262; Jang, S. J., & Johnson, B. R. (2003). Strain, negative emotions, and deviant coping among African Americans: A test of general strain theory. *Journal of Quantitative Criminology, 19,* 79–105; Mazerolle, P. (1998). Gender, general strain, and delinquency: An empirical examination. *Justice Quarterly, 15,* 65–91; Mazerolle, P., Burton, V., Cullen, F., Evans, T. D., & Payne, G. (2000). Strain, anger, and delinquent adaptations: Specifying general strain theory. *Journal of Criminal Justice, 28,* 89–101; Mazerolle, P., & Maahs, J. (2000). General strain and delinquency: An alternative examination of conditioning influences. *Justice Quarterly, 17,* 753–778; Mazerolle, P., & Piquero, A. (1998). Linking exposure to strain with anger: An investigation of deviant adaptations. *Journal of Criminal Justice, 26,* 195–211; Mazerolle, P., Piquero, A., & Capowich, G. E. (2003). Examining the links between strain, situational and dispositional anger, and crime: Further specifying and testing general strain theory. *Youth and Society, 35,* 131–157; Paternoster, R., & Mazerolle, P. (1994). General strain theory and delinquency: A replication and extension. *Journal of Research in Crime and Delinquency, 31,* 235–263; Piquero, N. L., & Sealock, M. (2000). Generalizing general strain theory: An examination of an offending population. *Justice Quarterly, 17,* 449–484.

44. A recent review of this research can be found in Baron, S. W. (2004). General strain, street youth and crime: A test of Agnew's revised theory. *Criminology, 42,* 457–467.

45. For examples, see Hoffman, J. P., & Cerbone, F. G. (1999). Stressful life events and delinquency escalation in early adolescence. *Criminology, 37,* 343–374; Hoffman, J. P., & Su, S. S. (1998). Stressful life events and adolescent substance use and depression: Conditional and gender differentiated effects. *Substance Use and Misuse, 33,* 2219–2262; Paternoster, R., & Mazerolle, P. (1994). General strain theory and delinquency: A replication and extension. *Journal of Research in Crime and Delinquency, 31,* 235–263.

46. Baron, S. W. (2004). General strain, street youth and crime: A test of Agnew's revised theory. *Criminology, 42,* 457–467; Broidy, L. M. (2001). A test of general strain theory. *Criminology, 39,* 9–36.

47. See Brezina, T. (1996). Adapting to strain: An examination of delinquent coping responses. *Criminology, 34,* 39–60; Broidy, L. M. (2001). A test of general strain theory. *Criminology, 39,* 9–36; Mazerolle, P., & Piquero, A. (1998). Linking exposure to strain with anger: An investigation of deviant adaptations. *Journal of Criminal Justice, 26,* 195–211.

48. Mazerolle, P. (1998). Gender, general strain, and delinquency: An empirical examination. *Justice Quarterly, 15,* 65–91; Mazerolle, P., & Piquero, A. (1998). Linking exposure to strain with anger: An investigation of deviant adaptations. *Journal of Criminal Justice, 26,* 195–211; Piquero, N. L., & Sealock, M. (2000). Generalizing general strain theory: An examination of an offending population. *Justice Quarterly, 17,* 449–484.

49. Baron, S. W. (2004). General strain, street youth and crime: A test of Agnew's revised theory. *Criminology, 42,* 457–484; Mazerolle, P., Piquero, A., & Capowich, G. E. (2003). Examining the links between strain, situational and dispositional anger, and crime: Further specifying and testing general strain theory. *Youth and Society, 35,* 131–157.

50. For examples, see Baron, S. W. (2004). General strain, street youth and crime: A test of Agnew's revised theory. *Criminology, 42,* 457–484; Mazerolle, P., Burton, V., Cullen, F., Evans, T. D., & Payne, G. (2000). Strain, anger, and delinquent adaptations: Specifying general strain theory. *Journal of Criminal Justice, 28,* 89–101; see also discussion in Akers, R. L., & Sellers, C. S. (2004). *Criminological theories: Introduction, evaluation, and application* (4th ed.). Los Angeles: Roxbury, pp. 180–182; Mazerolle, P., Piquero, A., & Capowich, G. E. (2003). Examining the links between strain, situational and dispositional anger, and crime: Further specifying and testing general strain theory. *Youth and Society, 35,* 131–157.

51. Wright, J. P., Tibbetts, S. G., & Daigle, L. (2008). *Criminals in the making: Criminality across the life course.* Thousand Oaks, CA: SAGE, pp. 204–207.

52. Van Voorhis, P., Braswell, M. C., & Lester, D. (2009). *Correctional counseling and rehabilitation* (8th ed.). New Providence, NJ: Anderson.

CHAPTER 9

1. Romero, D. (2012, June 27). Gang map study shows crime happens along borders between sets in L.A. *LA Weekly*. Retrieved from http://blogs.laweekly.com/informer/2012/06/gang_maps_angeles_murder_attacks_borders_ucla_study.php?print=true. See also actual study: Brantingham, P. J., Tita, G. E., Short, M. B., & Reid, S. E. (2012). The ecology of gang territorial boundaries. *Criminology, 50*(3), 851–885. doi: 10.1111/j.1745-9125.2012.00281.x.

2. For an excellent discussion of the early history of Chicago, see Bernard, T. J. (1992). *The cycle of juvenile justice*. New York: Oxford University Press.

3. See discussion in Vold, G. B., Bernard, T. J., & Snipes, J. B. (2002). *Theoretical criminology* (5th ed.). Oxford, UK: Oxford University Press, pp. 117–122.

4. These dates were taken from Famighetti, R. (2000). *The world almanac and book of facts, 2000: Millennium collector's edition*. Mahwah, NJ: Primedia Reference.

5. Park, R. E. (1936). Human ecology. *American Journal of Sociology, 42*, 32–51; Park, R. E. (1952). *Human communities*. Glencoe, IL: Free Press.

6. Burgess, E. W. (1928). The growth of the city. In R. Park, E. W. Burgess, & R. D. McKenzie (Eds.), *The city*. Chicago, IL: University of Chicago Press.

7. See Vold, G. B., Bernard, T. J., & Snipes, J. B. (2002). *Theoretical criminology* (5th ed.). Oxford, UK: Oxford University Press, pp. 118–121.

8. Shaw, C., & McKay, H. D. (1969). *Juvenile delinquency and urban areas*. Chicago, IL: University of Chicago Press; Shaw, C., & McKay, H. D. (1972). *Juvenile delinquency and urban areas* (Rev. ed.). Chicago, IL: University of Chicago Press.

9. Shaw, C. (1930). *The Jackroller*. Chicago, IL: University of Chicago Press; Shaw, C. (1931). *The natural history of a delinquent career*. Chicago, IL: University of Chicago Press; Shaw, C. (1938). *Brothers in crime*. Chicago, IL: University of Chicago Press.

10. Shaw, C. (1938). *Brothers in crime*. Chicago, IL: University of Chicago Press, pp. 354–355.

11. Bursik, R. J. (1986). Ecological stability and the dynamics of delinquency. In A. J. Reiss & M. H. Tonry (Eds.), *Crime and community* (pp. 35–66). Chicago, IL: University of Chicago Press; Bursik, R. J. (1988). Social disorganization and theories of crime and delinquency: Problems and prospects. *Criminology, 26*, 519–551; Heitgard, J. L, & Bursik, R. J. (1987). Extracommunity dynamics and the ecology of delinquency. *American Journal of Sociology, 92*, 775–787; Laub, J. (1983). Urbanism, race, and crime. *Journal of Research in Crime and Delinquency, 20*, 283–298; Sampson, R. (1985). Structural sources of variation in race-age-specific rate of offending across major U.S. cities. *Criminology, 23*, 647–673; Sampson, R. (2002). Transcending tradition: New directions in community research, Chicago style—The American Society of Criminology 2001 Sutherland Address. *Criminology, 40*, 213–230; Sampson, R., Morenoff, J. D., & Gannon-Rowley, T. (2002). Assessing "neighborhood effects": Social processes and new directions in research. *Annual Review of Sociology, 28*, 443–478; Taylor, R., & Covington, J. (1988). Neighborhood changes in ecology and violence. *Criminology, 26*, 553–589; Wikstrom, P. O., & Loeber, R. (2000). Do disadvantaged neighborhoods cause well-adjusted children to become adolescent delinquents? *Criminology, 38*, 1109–1142.

12. Sampson, R., & Groves, W. B. (1989). Community structure and crime: Testing social disorganization theory. *American Journal of Sociology, 94*, 774–802.

13. Miller, W. B. (1962). The impact of a "total-community" delinquency control project. *Social Problems, 10*, 168–191.

14. For a review, see Lundman, R. (1993). *Prevention and control of juvenile delinquency* (2nd ed.). New York, NY: Oxford University Press. See also the review by Vold, G. B., Bernard, T. J., & Snipes, J. B. (2002). *Theoretical criminology* (5th ed.). Oxford, UK: Oxford University Press, pp. 125–126.

15. Schmalleger, F. (2006). *Criminology today* (4th ed.). Upper Saddle River, NJ: Prentice Hall; Vold, G. B., Bernard, T. J., & Snipes, J. B. (2002). *Theoretical criminology* (5th ed.). Oxford, UK: Oxford University Press, pp. 165–169.

16. Ferracuti, F., & Wolfgang, M. (1967). *The subculture of violence: Toward an integrated theory of criminology*. London, UK: Tavistock.

17. As quoted in Schmalleger, F. (2006). *Criminology today* (4th ed.). Upper Saddle River, NJ: Prentice Hall, pp. 230–231.

18. Miller, W. B. (1958). Lower class culture as a generating milieu of gang delinquency. *Journal of Social Issues, 14*, 5–19.

19. Anderson, E. (1999). *Code of the streets*. New York, NY: W. W. Norton.

20. Wright, J. P. (2009). Inconvenient truths: Science, race, and crime. In A. Walsh & K. M. Beaver (Eds.), *Biosocial criminology: New directions in theory and research* (pp. 137–153). New York, NY: Routledge.

21. Ibid., p. 144.

22. Ibid.

23. Laurence, J. (2015). Community disadvantage and race-specific rates of violent crime: An investigation into the "racial invariance" hypothesis in the United Kingdom. *Deviant Behavior, 36*, 974–995.

24. Sangmoon, K., Willis, C. L., Latterner, K, & LaGrange, R. (2016). When birds of a feather don't flock together: A macrostructural approach to interracial crime. *Sociological Inquiry, 86*, 166–188.

CHAPTER 10

1. Free, M. (1991). Clarifying the relationship between the broken home and juvenile delinquency: A critique of the current literature. *Deviant Behavior: An Interdisciplinary Journal, 12*, 109–167; Rankin, J. (1983). The family

context of delinquency. *Social Problems, 30,* 446–497; Thornberry, T. P., Smith, C. A., Rivera, C., Huizinga, D., & Stouthamer-Loeber, M. (1999). *Family disruption and delinquency* (Juvenile Justice Bulletin). Washington, DC: Office of Juvenile Justice and Delinquency Prevention.

2. Cernkovich, S., & Giordana, P. (1987). Family relationships and delinquency. *Criminology, 25,* 295–321; Wells, L. E., & Rankin, J. H. (1988). Direct parental controls and delinquency. *Criminology, 26,* 263–285.

3. Brezina, T. (1998). Adolescent maltreatment and delinquency. *Journal of Research in Crime and Delinquency, 35,* 71–98; Smith, C., & Thornberry, T. P. (1995). The relationship between childhood maltreatment and adolescent involvement in delinquency. *Criminology, 33,* 451–476; Widom, C. S. (1989). Child abuse, neglect, and violent criminal behavior. *Criminology, 27,* 251–271; Widom, C. S., & Ames, M. A. (1994). Criminal consequences of childhood sexual victimization. *Child Abuse and Neglect, 18,* 303–318.

4. Harlow, C. W. (1994). *Comparing federal and state prison inmates, 1991.* Washington, DC: Department of Justice; Kaufman, P., Klein, S., & Frase, M. (1999). *Dropout rates in the United States: 1997.* Washington, DC: U.S. Department of Education; Lotz, R., & Lee, L. (1999). Sociability, school experience, and delinquency. *Youth & Society, 31,* 199–223; Reed, M. D., & Rose, D. R. (1998). Doing what Simple Simon says? *Criminal Justice and Behavior, 25,* 383–393; Warr, M. (1996). Organization and instigation in delinquent groups. *Criminology, 34,* 863–864; Warr, M., & Stafford, M. (1991). The influence of delinquent peers. *Criminology, 29,* 851–866.

5. Crombie, N. (2014, February 19). Murder suspect Francis Weaver's family history spans four generations of violence. *The Oregonian.* Retrieved from http://www.oregonlive.com/oregon-city/index.ssf/2014/02/post_54.html. Original work published August 25, 2002.

6. Crombie, N. (2014, February 19). Ward Weaver III lived a life of cruelty and rage, reportedly raped son's fiancée. *The Oregonian.* Retrieved from http://www.oregonlive.com/oregon-city/index.ssf/2014/02/ward_weaver_iii_like_his_fathe.html. Original work published October 6, 2002.

7. Stepson of infamous child killer Ward Weaver receives life sentence for murder. (2016, March 11). *KGW.* Retrieved from http://www.kgw.com/news/crime/francis-weaver-stepson-of-infamous-child-killer-ward-weaver-pleads-guilty-to-murder/77722504.

8. Akers, R. L. (1997). *Criminological theories: Introduction and evaluation* (2nd ed.). Los Angeles, CA: Roxbury, pp. 59–

9. Shaw, C. R., & McKay, H. D. (1931). *Report on the causes of crime: Social factors in juvenile delinquency, 2* (National Commission on Law Observance and Enforcement, Report No. 13). Washington, DC: U.S. Government Printing Office; Shaw, C. R., & McKay, H. D. (1942). *Juvenile delinquency in urban areas.* Chicago, IL: University of Chicago Press.

10. Tarde, C. (1903). *The laws of imitation.* Gloucester, MA: Henry Holt; see also Tarde, G. (1972). Penal philosophy.

In S. F. Sylvester (Ed.), *The heritage of modern criminology.* Cambridge, MA: Schenkman. (Original work published 1912)

11. Vine, M. S. (1960). Gabriel Tarde. In H. Mannheim (Ed.), *Pioneers in criminology* (pp. 228–240). Chicago, IL: Quadrangle Books.

12. Sutherland, E. H. (1939). *Principles of criminology* (3rd ed.). Philadelphia, PA: Lippincott.

13. Sutherland, E. H., & Cressey, D. R. (2006). A theory of differential association. In F. T. Cullen & R. Agnew (Eds.), *Criminological theory: Past to present* (3rd ed.). Los Angeles, CA: Roxbury, pp. 123–124.

14. Pavlov, I. P. (1906). The scientific investigation of the psychical faculties or processes in the higher animals. *Science, 24,* 613–619; see also Pavlov, I. P. (1902). *The work of the digestive glands* (W. H. Gantt, Ed. & Trans.). London, UK: Charles Griffin.

15. See Abraham, A. J., Ducharme, L. J., & Roman, P. M. (2009). Counselor attitudes toward pharmacotherapies for alcohol dependence. *Journal of Studies on Alcohol and Drugs, 70,* 628–635; Krishnan-Sarin, S., O'Malley, S., & Krysta, J. H. (2008). Treatment implications. *Alcohol Research and Health, 31,* 400–407.

16. Sutherland, E. H., & Cressey, D. R. (1974). *Criminology* (9th ed.). Philadelphia, PA: Lippincott.

17. Matsueda, R. L., & Heimer, K. (1987). Race, family structure, and delinquency: A test of differential association and social control theories. *American Sociological Review, 47,* 489–504; Tittle, C. R., Burke, M. J., & Jackson, E. F. (1986). Modeling Sutherland's theory of differential association: Toward an empirical clarification. *Social Forces, 65,* 405–432.

18. Piquero, N. L., Tibbetts, S. G., & Blankenship, M. B. (2005). Examining the role of differential association and techniques of neutralization in explaining corporate crime. *Deviant Behavior, 26,* 159–188. This study also reviews other recent corporate crime studies that test differential association and other theoretical models.

19. Tittle, C. R., Burke, M. J., & Jackson, E. F. (1986). Modeling Sutherland's theory of differential association: Toward an empirical clarification. *Social Forces, 65,* 405–432.

20. Thornberry, T. (1987). Toward an interactional theory of delinquency. *Criminology, 25,* 863–887.

21. Tunnell, K. (1993). Inside the drug trade: Trafficking from the dealer's perspective. *Qualitative Sociology, 16,* 361–381.

22. Smith, D., Visher, C., & Jarjoura, G. R. (1991). Dimensions of delinquency: Exploring the correlates of participation, frequency, and persistence of delinquent behavior. *Journal of Research in Crime and Delinquency, 28,* 6–32.

23. Ploeger, M. (1997). Youth employment and delinquency: Reconsidering a problematic relationship. *Criminology, 35,* 659–675.

24. Adams, R. (1974). The adequacy of differential association theory. *Journal of Research in Crime and Delinquency, 1,* 1–8; Short, J. F. (1960). Differential

association as a hypothesis: Problems of empirical testing. *Social Problems, 8,* 14–25.

25. Glaser, D. (1956). Criminality theories and behavioral images. *American Journal of Sociology, 61,* 433–444.

26. Ibid., p. 440.

27. Dawes, K. J. (1973). *Family relationships, reference others, differential identification and their joint impact on juvenile delinquency.* Ann Arbor, MI: University Microfilms.

28. Jeffery, C. R. (1965). Criminal behavior and learning theory. *Journal of Criminal Law, Criminology, and Police Science, 56,* 294–300.

29. Burgess, R., & Akers, R. (1966). A differential association-reinforcement theory of criminal behavior. *Social Problems, 14,* 131.

30. Klotter, J. C. (2004). *Criminal law* (7th ed.). Cincinnati, OH: Anderson, p. 68.

31. Ibid., p. 69.

32. Federal Bureau of Investigation. (2015). *Crime in the United States, 2014.* Washington, DC: U.S. Department of Justice, n.p. Retrieved from https://www.fbi.gov/about-us/cjis/ucr/crime-in-the-u.s/2014/crime-in-the-u.s.-2014/offenses-known-to-law-enforcement/murder.

33. Ibid., n.p.

34. Klotter, J. C. (2004). *Criminal law* (7th ed.). Cincinnati, OH: Anderson, p. 580.

35. McGee, K. P. (1995). Comment: The absence of malice? In re Christian S., the second wind of the imperfect self-defense doctrine. *Golden Gate University Law Review, 25,* 297–330.

36. World Health Organization. (2002). *World report on violence and health.* Geneva, Switzerland: Author.

37. Van Dijk, J. (2008). *The world of crime: Breaking the silence on problems of security, justice, and development across the world.* Thousand Oaks, CA: SAGE.

38. Ibid.

39. Skinner, B. F. (1953). *Science and human behavior.* New York, NY: Macmillan.

40. Van Voorhis, P., Braswell, M., & Lester, D. (2000). *Correctional counseling* (4th ed.). Cincinnati, OH: Anderson.

41. Akers, R. L. (1977). *Deviant behavior: A social learning approach* (2nd ed.). Belmont, CA: Wadsworth, p. 57.

42. Tarde, G. (1972). Penal philosophy. In S. F. Sylvester (Ed.), *The heritage of modern criminology.* Cambridge, MA: Schenkman. (Original work published 1912)

43. See Bandura, A. (1969). Principles of behavior modification. New York, NY: Holt, Rinehart, & Winston; Bandura, A. (1973). Aggression: A social learning analysis. Englewood Cliffs, NJ: Prentice Hall; Bandura, A. (1977). Social learning theory. Englewood Cliffs, NJ: Prentice Hall.

44. Adams, R. (1973). Differential association and learning principles revisited. *Social Problems, 20,* 458–470.

45. Warr, M. (1991). Parents, peers, and delinquency. *Social Forces, 72,* 247–264; Warr, M., & Stafford, M. (1991). The influence of delinquent peers: What they think or what they do? *Criminology, 29,* 851–866.

46. See Akers, R., & Sellers, C. (2004). *Criminological theories* (4th ed.). Los Angeles, CA: Roxbury, pp. 98–101.

47. See studies such as Akers, R., & La Greca, A. J. (1991). Alcohol use among the elderly: Social learning, community context, and life events. In D. J. Pittman & H. Raskin White (Eds.), *Society, culture, and drinking patterns re-examined* (pp. 242–262). New Brunswick, NJ: Rutgers Center of Alcohol Studies; Akers, R., & Lee, G. (1996). A longitudinal test of social learning theory: Adolescent smoking. *Journal of Drug Issues, 26,* 317–343; Akers, R., & Lee, G. (1999). Age, social learning, and social bonding in adolescent substance abuse. *Deviant Behavior, 19,* 1–25; Hwang, S. (2000). *Substance use in a sample of South Korean adolescents: A test of alternative theories.* Ann Arbor, MI: University Microfilms; Hwang, S., & Akers, R. (2003). Adolescent substance use in South Korea: A cross-cultural test of three theories. In R. Akers & G. F. Jensen (Eds.), *Social learning theory and the explanation of crime: A guide for the new century.* New Brunswick, NJ: Transaction.

48. Akers, R., Krohn, M. D., Lanza-Kaduce, L., & Radosevich, M. (1979). Social learning and deviant behavior: A specific test of a general theory. *American Sociological Review, 44,* 638.

49. Ibid., p. 651.

50. Akers, R., & Lee, G. (1996). A longitudinal test of social learning theory: Adolescent smoking. *Journal of Drug Issues, 26,* 317–343; Krohn, M., Skinner, W., Massey, J., & Akers, R. (1985). Social learning theory and adolescent cigarette smoking: A longitudinal study. *Social Problems, 32,* 455–471; Lawrence, R. (1991). School performance, peers and delinquency: Implications for juvenile justice. *Juvenile and Family Court Journal, 42,* 59–69; Winfree, L. T., Sellers, C., & Clason, D. (1993). Social learning and adolescent deviance abstention: Toward understanding the reasons for initiating, quitting, and avoiding drugs. *Journal of Quantitative Criminology, 9,* 101–123.

51. Pratt, T. C., Cullen, F. T., Sellers, C. S., Winfree, L. T., Madensen, T. D., Daigle, L. E. . . . Gau, J. M. (2010). The empirical status of social learning theory: A meta-analysis. *Justice Quarterly, 27*(6), 765–802.

52. Sykes, G. M., & Matza, D. (1957). Techniques of neutralization: A theory of delinquency. *American Sociological Review, 22,* 664–670.

53. Matza, D. (1964). *Delinquency and drift.* New York, NY: Wiley.

54. Ibid., p. 28.

55. Sykes, G. M., & Matza, D. (1957). Techniques of neutralization: A theory of delinquency. *American Sociological Review, 22,* 664–670.

56. McCorkle, L., & Korn, R. (1954). Resocialization within walls. *Annals of the American Academy of Political and Social Science, 293,* 88–98.

57. Sykes, G. M., & Matza, D. (1957). Techniques of neutralization: A theory of delinquency. *American Sociological Review, 22,* 669.

58. Piquero, N. L., Tibbetts, S. G., & Blankenship, M. B. (2005). Examining the role of differential association

and techniques of neutralization in explaining corporate crime. *Deviant Behavior, 26,* 159–188.

59. Ibid., p. 164.

60. Agnew, R. (1994). The techniques of neutralization and violence. *Criminology, 32,* 563–564.

61. Minor, W. W. (1980). The neutralization of criminal offense. *Criminology, 18,* 116; Minor, W. W. (1984). Neutralization as a hardening process: Considerations in the modeling of change. *Social Forces, 62,* 995–1019. See also Austin, R. L. (1984). Commitment, neutralization, and delinquency. In T. N. Ferdinand (Ed.), *Juvenile delinquency: Little brother grows up.* Beverly Hills, CA: SAGE; Thurman, Q. C. (1984). Deviance and the neutralization of moral commitment: An empirical analysis. *Deviant Behavior, 5,* 291–304.

62. Hirschi, T. (1969). *Causes of delinquency.* Berkeley: University of California Press, p. 207. See also Hamlin, J. (1988). The misplaced concept of rational choice in neutralization theory. *Criminology, 26,* 425–438; Pogrebin, M., Poole, E., & Martinez, A. (1992). Accounts of professional misdeeds: The sexual exploitation of clients by psychotherapists. *Deviant Behavior, 13,* 229–252.

63. Lewis, M., Alessandri, S., and Sullivan, M. (1990). Expectancy, loss of control, and anger in young infants. *Developmental Psychology, 25,* 745–751; Restoin, A., Rodriguez, D., Ulmann, V., & Montagner, H. (1985). New data on the development of communication behavior in the young child with his peers. *Recherches de Psychologie Sociale, 5,* 31–56; Tremblay, R. E., Japel, C., Perusse, D., McDuff, P., Boivin, M., Zoccolillo, M., & Montplaisir, J. (1999). The search for the age of "onset" of physical aggression: Rousseau and Bandura revisited. *Criminal Behaviour and Mental Health, 9,* 8–23.

64. Tremblay, R., & LeMarquand, D. (2001). Individual risk and protective factors. In R. Loeber & D. Farrington (Eds.), *Child delinquents: Development, intervention, and service needs* (pp. 137–164). London, UK: SAGE.

65. For reviews of supporting studies, see Lewis, M. (1992). *Shame: The exposed self.* New York, NY: Macmillan; Tangney, J. P., & Fischer, K. W. (Eds.). (1995). *Self-conscious emotions: The psychology of shame, guilt, embarrassment, and pride.* New York, NY: Guilford Press.

66. Walsh, A., & Ellis, L. (1999). Political ideology and American criminologists' explanations for criminal behavior. *The Criminologist, 24,* 1, 14.

67. Hobbes, T. (1904). *Leviathan.* Cambridge, UK: Cambridge University Press. (Original work published 1651)

68. Durkheim, É. (1951). *Suicide.* New York, NY: Free Press. (Original work published 1897); Durkheim, É. (1965). *The division of labor in society.* New York, NY: Free Press. (Original work published 1893).

69. Durkheim, É. (1951). *Suicide.* New York: Free Press, pp. 246–247. (Original work published 1897). Also, much of this discussion is adapted from R. Paternoster & R. Bachman (Eds.). (2001). *Explaining criminals and crime.* Los Angeles, CA: Roxbury.

70. Durkheim, É. (1951). *Suicide.* New York, NY: Free Press, p. 254. (Original work published 1897).

71. A good discussion of Durkheim's concepts, particularly the collective conscience, can be found in Vold, G. B., Bernard, T. J., & Snipes, J. B. (1998). *Theoretical criminology* (4th ed.). New York, NY: Oxford University Press, pp. 124–139.

72. Freud, S. (1959). The ego and the id. In J. Strachey (Ed.), *The complete psychological works of Sigmund Freud* (Vol. 19). London, UK: Hogarth Press. (Original work published 1923).

73. Reiss, A. (1951). Delinquency as the failure of personal and social controls. *American Sociological Review, 16,* 196–207.

74. For a comprehensive review of studies of low self-control prior to year 2000, see Pratt, T., & Cullen, F. (2000). The empirical status of Gottfredson and Hirschi's general theory of crime: A meta-analysis. *Criminology, 38,* 931–964.

75. Vold, G. B., Bernard, T. J., & Snipes, J. B. (1998). *Theoretical criminology* (4th ed.). New York, NY: Oxford University Press, pp. 202–203.

76. Toby, J. (1957). Social disorganization and stake in conformity: Complementary factors in the predatory behavior of hoodlums. *Journal of Criminal Law, Criminology, and Police Science, 48,* 12–17.

77. Hirschi, T. (1969). *Causes of delinquency.* Berkeley: University of California Press; Sampson, R., & Laub, J. (1993). *Crime in the making: Pathways and turning points in life.* Cambridge, MA: Harvard University Press.

78. Nye, F. I. (1958). *Family relationships and delinquent behavior.* New York, NY: Wiley.

79. Seydlitz, R. (1993). Complexity in the relationships among direct and indirect parental controls and delinquency. *Youth and Society, 24,* 243–275.

80. Tittle, C. (1995). *Control balance: Toward a general theory of deviance.* Boulder, CO: Westview.

81. Reckless, W. (1967). *The crime problem* (4th ed.). New York, NY: Appleton-Century-Crofts.

82. Ibid., p. 479.

83. Dodder, R. A., & Long, J. R. (1980). Containment theory reevaluated: An empirical explication. *Criminal Justice Review, 5,* 74–84; Lawrence, R. (1985). School performance, containment theory, and delinquent behavior. *Youth and Society, 7,* 69–95.

84. Thompson, W. E., & Dodder, R. A. (1986). Containment theory and juvenile delinquency: A reevaluation through factor analysis. *Adolescence, 21,* 365–376.

85. Akers, R. L. (2000). *Criminological theories: Introduction, evaluation, and application* (3rd ed.). Los Angeles, CA: Roxbury, pp. 103–104.

86. Matza, D. (1964). *Delinquency and drift.* New York, NY: Wiley.

87. *OJJDP Statistical Briefing Book.* Arrest data for 1980–1997 from unpublished data from the Federal Bureau of Investigation, and for 1998, 1999, and 2000 from *Crime in the United States* reports. Washington, DC: U.S. Government Printing Office, 1999, 2000, and 2001, respectively.

88. "Age–arrest rate curve" is loosely based on data provided by Federal Bureau of Investigation. (1997). *Crime in the United States, 1996.* Washington, DC: U.S. Government Printing Office.

89. Vold, G. B., Bernard, T. J., & Snipes, J. B. (1998). *Theoretical criminology* (4th ed.). New York, NY: Oxford University Press, pp. 205–207.

90. Hirschi, T. (1969). *Causes of delinquency.* Berkeley: University of California Press.

91. Ibid, p. 31, in which Hirschi cites Durkheim.

92. Ibid., p. 18.

93. Ibid., p. 22.

94. For a review, see Akers, R. L. (2000). *Criminological theories: Introduction, evaluation, and application* (3rd ed.). Los Angeles, CA: Roxbury, pp. 105–110.

95. Ibid.

96. Elliott, D., Huizinga, D., & Ageton, S. (1985). *Explaining delinquency and drug use.* Beverly Hills, CA: SAGE.

97. Walsh, A., & Ellis, L. (1999). Political ideology and American criminologists' explanations for criminal behavior. *The Criminologist, 24,* 1, 14.

98. Eisner, M. (2002). Crime, problem drinking, and drug use: Patterns of problem behavior in cross-national perspective. *Annals of the American Academy of Political and Social Science, 580,* 201–225; Vazsonyi, A., & Killias, M. (2001). Immigration and crime among youth in Switzerland. *Criminal Justice and Behavior, 28,* 329–366; Wong, D. (2001). Pathways to delinquency in Hong Kong and Guangzhou, South China. *International Journal of Adolescence and Youth, 10,* 91–115.

99. Tittle, C. (1995). *Control balance: Toward a general theory of deviance.* Boulder, CO: Westview.

100. Hickman, M., & Piquero, A. (2001). Exploring the relationships between gender, control balance, and deviance. *Deviant Behavior, 22,* 323–351; Piquero, A., & Hickman, M. (1999). An empirical test of Tittle's control balance theory. *Criminology, 37,* 319–342.

101. Hickman, M., & Piquero, A. (2001). Exploring the relationships between gender, control balance, and deviance. *Deviant Behavior, 22,* 323–351.

102. Hagan, J. (1989). *Structural criminology.* Newark, NJ: Rutgers University Press; Hagan, J., Gillis, A., & Simpson, J. (1985). The class structure of gender and delinquency: Toward a power-control theory of common delinquent behavior. *American Journal of Sociology, 90,* 1151–1178; Hagan, J., Gillis, A., & Simpson, J. (1990). Clarifying and extending power-control theory. *American Journal of Sociology, 95,* 1024–1037; Hagan, J., Simpson, J., & Gillis, A. (1987). Class in the household: A power-control theory of gender and delinquency. *American Journal of Sociology, 92,* 788–816.

103. Hagan, J., Simpson, J., & Gillis, A. (1987). Class in the household: A power-control theory of gender and delinquency. *American Journal of Sociology, 92,* 788–816; McCarthy, B., & Hagan, J. (1987). Gender, delinquency, and the Great Depression: A test of power-control theory. *Canadian Review of Sociology and Anthropology, 24,* 153–177; Morash, M., & Chesney-Lind, M. (1991). A reformulation and partial test of the power-control theory of delinquency. *Justice Quarterly, 8,* 347–377; Singer, S., & Levine, M. (1988). Power-control theory, gender, and delinquency: A partial replication with additional evidence on the effects of peers. *Criminology, 26,* 627–647.

104. McCarthy, B., Hagan, J., & Woodward, T. (1999). In the company of women: Structure and agency in a revised power-control theory of gender and delinquency. *Criminology, 37,* 761–788.

105. Blackwell, B. S. (2000). Perceived sanction threats, gender, and crime: A test and elaboration of power-control theory. *Criminology, 38,* 439–488.

106. Ibid.; Bates, K., & Bader, C. (2003). Family structure, power-control theory, and deviance: Extending power-control theory to include alternate family forms. *Western Criminology Review, 4,* 170–190.

107. Gottfredson, M., & Hirschi, T. (1990). *A general theory of crime.* Palo Alto, CA: Stanford University Press.

108. For an excellent review of studies regarding low self-control theory, see Pratt, T., & Cullen, F. (2000). The empirical status of Gottfredson and Hirschi's general theory of crime: A meta-analysis. *Criminology, 38,* 931–964. For critiques of this theory, see Akers, R. (1991). Self-control as a general theory of crime. *Journal of Quantitative Criminology, 7,* 201–211. For a study that demonstrates the high popularity of the theory, see Walsh, A., & Ellis, L. (1999). Political ideology and American criminologists' explanations for criminal behavior. *The Criminologist, 24,* 1, 14.

109. Hay, C. (2001). Parenting, self-control, and delinquency: A test of self-control theory. *Criminology, 39,* 707–736; Hayslett-McCall, K., & Bernard, T. (2002). Attachment, masculinity, and self-control: A theory of male crime rates. *Theoretical Criminology, 6,* 15–33.

110. Piquero, A., & Tibbetts, S. (1996). Specifying the direct and indirect effects of low self-control and situational factors in offenders' decision making: Toward a more complete model of rational offending. *Justice Quarterly, 13,* 481–510.

111. Raine, A. (1993). *The psychopathology of crime.* San Diego, CA: Academic Press.

112. Walsh, A. (2002). *Biosocial criminology: Introduction and integration.* Cincinnati, OH: Anderson.

113. Fiorillo, C., Tobler, P., & Schultz, W. (2003). Discrete coding of reward probability and uncertainty by dopamine neurons. *Science, 299,* 1898–1902.

114. Grasmick, H., & Bursik, R. (1990). Conscience, significant others, and rational choice: Extending the deterrence model. *Law and Society Review, 24,* 837–861; Tibbetts, S. (1997). Shame and rational choice in offending decisions. *Criminal Justice and Behavior, 24,* 234–255.

115. Tibbetts, S., & Herz, D. (1996). Gender differences in factors of social control and rational choice. *Deviant Behavior, 17,* 183–208.

116. Montillo, R. (2015). *The wilderness of ruin: A tale of madness, fire, and the hunt for America's youngest serial killer.* New York, NY: William Morrow, p. 18.

117. Ibid.

118. The story of Jesse Pomeroy, 14-year-old serial killer. (2015, March 13). *CBS News.* Retrieved from http://www.cbsnews.com/news/the-story-of-jesse-pomeroy-14-year-old-serial-killer/

119. Jesse Pomeroy: The boy fiend. (n.d.). *Celebrate Boston.* Retrieved from http://www.celebrateboston.com/crime/jesse-pomeroy-serial-killer.htm.

120. McDade, T. M. (1961). *The annals of murder.* Norman: University of Oklahoma Press.

121. Walsh, A., & Ellis, L. (2007). *Criminology: An interdisciplinary approach.* Thousand Oaks, CA: SAGE, p. 135.

122. Nevada Board of Parole Commissioners. (2007). *Conditions of parole.* Retrieved from http://parole.nv.gov/FAQs/ConditionsOfParole/.

123. For example, Sandy, S. V., & Boardman, S. K. (2000). The peaceful kids conflict resolution program. *International Journal of Conflict Management, 11,* 337–357; Levine, E., & Tamburrino, M. (2014). Bullying among young children: Strategies for prevention. *Early Childhood Education Journal, 42,* 271–278.

124. Tremblay, R. E., & Craig, W. M. (1997). Developmental juvenile delinquency prevention. *European Journal on Criminal Policy and Research, 5,* p. 44.

125. Williams, F. P., & McShane, M. D. (1999). *Criminological theory* (3rd ed.). Upper Saddle River, NJ: Prentice Hall.

CHAPTER 11

1. Ganim, S., & Tran, L. (2016, January 13). How tap water became toxic in Flint, Michigan. *CNN.* Retrieved from http://www.cnn.com/2016/01/11/health/toxic-tap-water-flint-michigan/

2. Flint Judge Tracy Collier Nix and Attorney General Bill Schuette announced charges today against a Flint water official and two officials with the Michigan Department of Environmental Quality. (2016, April 20). *Detroit Free Press.* Retrieved from http://www.freep.com/story/news/local/michigan/flint-water-crisis/2016/04/20/flint-water-crisis-charges/83298608/

3. Ganim, S., & Tran, L. (2016, January 13). How tap water became toxic in Flint, Michigan. *CNN.* Retrieved from http://www.cnn.com/2016/01/11/health/toxic-tap-water-flint-michigan/

4. Barak, G. (2003). Revisionist history, visionary criminology, and needs-based justice. *Contemporary Justice Review, 63,* 217–225.

5. Ibid., pp. 218–219. See also Platt, T. (1974, Spring–Summer). Prospects for a radical criminology in the United States. *Crime and Social Justice, 1,* 2–6; Schwendinger, H., & Schwendinger, J. (1970). Defenders of order or guardians of human rights. *Issues in Criminology, 5,* 123–157.

6. Barak, G. (2003). Revisionist history, visionary criminology, and needs-based justice. *Contemporary Justice Review, 63,* 219.

7. Ibid.

8. Maxim, P. S., & Whitehead, P. C. (1998). *Explaining crime* (4th ed.). Boston: Butterworth-Heinemann, p. 347.

9. Akers, R. L. (1973). *Deviant behavior: A social learning approach.* Belmont, CA: Wadsworth, pp. 21–22; see also Becker, H. S. (Ed.). (1964). *The other side.* New York: Free Press.

10. Cooley, C. H. (1909). *Social organization.* New York: Scribner's; Cooley, C. H. (1922). *Human nature and social order* (Rev. ed.). New York: Scribner's.

11. Cooley, C. H. (1909). *Social organization.* New York: Scribner's, p. 23.

12. Reynolds, L. T. (1994). The early interactionists: Cooley and Thomas. In N. J. Herman & L. T. Reynolds (Eds.), *Symbolic interaction: An introduction to social psychology* (pp. 30–37). New York: General Hall.

13. Ibid., p. 36

14. Thomas, W. I., & Thomas, D. S. (1928). *The child in America.* New York: Knopf.

15. Thomas, W. I. (1923). *The unadjusted girl.* New York: Harper & Row.

16. Meltzer, B. N. (1994). Mead's social psychology. In N. J. Herman & L. T. Reynolds (Eds.), *Symbolic interaction: An introduction to social psychology* (pp. 38–54). New York: General Hall.

17. Blumer, H. (1968). *Symbolic interactionism: Perspective and method.* Berkeley: University of California Press, pp. 65–66.

18. Akers, R. L. (1997). *Criminological theories: Introduction and evaluation* (2nd ed.). Los Angeles: Roxbury, p. 101.

19. Goffman E. (1963). *Stigma: Notes on the management of spoiled identity.* Englewood Cliffs, NJ: Prentice Hall, p. 3.

20. Tannenbaum, F. (1938). *Crime and the community.* Boston: Ginn, pp. 17–18.

21. Ibid., pp. 19–20.

22. Lemert, E. M. (1951). *Social pathology: A systematic approach to the theory of sociopathic behavior.* New York: McGraw-Hill, p. 75.

23. Lemert, E. M. (1972). *Human deviance, social problems, and social control* (2nd ed.). Englewood Cliffs, NJ: Prentice Hall, p. 63.

24. Ibid., p. 48; see also Lemert, E. M. (1948). Some aspects of a general theory of sociopathic behavior. *Proceedings of Pacific Sociological Society, 16,* 23–29.

25. Lemert, E. M. (1951). *Social pathology: A systematic approach to the theory of sociopathic behavior.* New York: McGraw-Hill, p. 77.

26. Becker, H. S. (1963). *Outsiders: Studies in the sociology of deviance.* New York: Free Press, p. 15.

27. Ibid., p. 9.

28. Ibid., pp. 19–21. See also Arrigo, B. A. (2000). Social justice and critical criminology: On integrating knowledge. *Contemporary Justice Review, 3,* 7–37.

29. Schur, E. M. (1971). *Labeling deviant behavior: Its sociological implications.* New York: Harper & Row.

30. Ibid., p. 17.

31. Ibid., p. 24.

32. Schur, E. M. (1973). *Radical nonintervention: Rethinking the delinquency problem.* Englewood Cliffs, NJ: Prentice Hall, p. 120.

33. Piliavin, I., & Briar, S. (1964). Police encounters with juveniles. *American Journal of Sociology, 70,* 206–214.

34. Schur, E. M. (1973). Radical nonintervention: Rethinking the delinquency problem. Englewood Cliffs, NJ: Prentice Hall, pp. 120–121.

35. Ibid., p. 121.

36. Ibid., p. 122.

37. Cicourel, A. V. (1968). *The social organization of juvenile justice.* New York: Wiley, p. 132.

38. Schur, E. M. (1973). *Radical nonintervention: Rethinking the delinquency problem.* Englewood Cliffs, NJ: Prentice Hall, pp. 123–126.

39. Schrag, C. (1971). *Crime and justice: American style.* Washington, DC: Government Printing Office, pp. 89–91.

40. Wellford, W. (1975). Labelling theory and criminology: An assessment. *Social Problems, 22,* 333.

41. Horwitz, A., & Wasserman, M. (1979). The effect of social control on delinquent behavior: A longitudinal test. *Sociological Focus, 12,* 53–70; Shannon, L. W. (1988). *Criminal career continuity: Its social context.* New York: Human Sciences Press; Smith, D. A., & Paternoster, R. (1990). Formal processing and future delinquency: Deviance amplification as selection artifact. *Law & Society Review, 24,* 1109–1131; Wooldredge, J. (1988). Differentiating the effects of juvenile court sentences on eliminating recidivism. *Journal of Research in Crime and Delinquency, 25,* 264–300.

42. Matsueda, R. L. (1992). Reflected appraisals, parental labeling, and delinquency: Specifying a symbolic interactionist theory. *American Journal of Sociology, 97,* 1577–1611.

43. Adams, M. S., & Evans, D. T. (1996). Teacher disapproval, delinquent peers, and self-reported delinquency: A longitudinal test of labeling theory. *The Urban Review, 28,* 199–211.

44. Adams, M. S., Johnson, J. D., & Evans, D. T. (1998). Racial differences in informal labeling effects. *Deviant Behavior, 19,* 157–171; Albonetti, C. A., & Hepburn, J. R. (1996). Prosecutorial discretion to defer criminalization: The effects of defendant's ascribed and achieved status characteristics. *Journal of Quantitative Criminology, 12,* 63–81.

45. Rosenbaum, J. L., & Prinsky, L. (1991). The presumption of influence: Recent responses to popular music subcultures. *Crime and Delinquency, 37,* 528–535.

46. Kelley, T. M. (1983). Status offenders can be different: A comparative study of delinquent careers. *Crime and Delinquency, 29,* 365–380; Rausch, S. (1983). Court processing versus diversion of status offenders: A test of deterrence and labeling theories. *Journal of Research in Crime and Delinquency, 20,* 39–54.

47. Lopes, G., Krohn, M.D., Lizotte, A.J., Schmidt, N.M., Vasquez, B.E., & Bernburg, J.G. (2012). Labeling and cumulative disadvantage: The impact of formal police intervention on life changes and crime during emerging adulthood. *Crime & Delinquency, 58,* 456-488.

48. Powers, A. (May 25, 2012). A 10-year nightmare over rape conviction is over. *Los Angeles Times.* Retrieved from: http://articles.latimes.com/2012/may/25/local/la-me-rape-dismiss-20120525.

49. Schwartz, R. D., & Skolnick, J. H. (1962). Two studies of legal stigma. *Social Problems, 10,* 133–142.

50. Ibid., p. 136.

51. Rosenhan, D. L. (1973). On being sane in insane places. *Science, 179,* 250–258.

52. Tittle, C. R. (1976). Labelling and crime: An empirical evaluation. In W. R. Gove (Ed.), *The labelling of deviance: Evaluating a perspective* (p. 158). New York: John Wiley.

53. Ibid.

54. Smith, D. A., & Paternoster, R. (1990). Formal processing and future delinquency: Deviance amplification as selection artifact. *Law & Society Review, 24,* 1129.

55. Gibbs, J. P. (1970). Conceptions of deviant behavior: The old and the new. In H. L. Voss (Ed.), *Society, delinquency, and delinquent behavior* (p. 217). Boston: Little, Brown.

56. Rogers, J. W., & Buffalo, M. D. (1975). Fighting back: Nine modes of adaptation to a deviant label. *Social Problems, 22,* 101–118.

57. Hagan, J. (1973). Labelling and deviance: A case study in the 'sociology of the interesting.' *Social Problems, 20,* 456.

58. Martin, R., Mutchnick, R. J., & Austin, W. T. (1990). *Criminological thought: Pioneers past and present.* New York: Macmillan, p. 361.

59. Goode, E. (1975). On behalf of labeling theory. *Social Problems, 22,* 581.

60. Wellford, C. (1975). Labelling theory and criminology: An assessment. *Social Problems, 22,* 332–345. See also Goode, E. (1975). On behalf of labeling theory. *Social Problems, 22,* 570–583; Manning, P. K. (1975). Deviance and dogma: Some comments on the labeling perspective. *British Journal of Criminology, 15,* 1–20; Meade, A. C. (1974). The labeling approach to delinquency: State of the theory as a function of method. *Social Forces, 53,* 83–91.

61. Wellford, C. F., & Triplett, R. (1993). The future of labeling theory. In F. Adler & W. Laufer (Eds.), *New directions in criminological theory* (p. 22). New Brunswick, NJ: Transaction. See also Wellford, C. F. (1997). Controlling crime and achieving justice: The American Society of Criminology 1996 Presidential Address. *Criminology, 35,* 1–11.

62. Williams, F. P., & McShane, M. D. (1999). *Criminological theory* (3rd ed.). Upper Saddle River, NJ: Prentice Hall, p. 148.

63. See Braithwaite, J. (1989). *Crime, shame and reintegration.* Cambridge, UK: Cambridge University Press; Grasmick, H. G., Bursik, R. J., & Arneklev, B. J. (1993). Reduction in drunk driving as a response to increased threats of shame, embarrassment, and legal sanctions. *Criminology, 31,* 41–67; Grasmick, H. G., Bursik, R. J., & Kinsey, K. A. (1991). Shame and embarrassment as deterrents to noncompliance with the law: The case of an

antilittering campaign. *Environment and Behavior, 23,* 233–251.

64. Karp, D. R. (2000). The new debate about shame in criminal justice: An interactionist account. *Justice System Journal, 21,* 301–322.

65. Williams, F. P., & McShane, M. D. (1999). *Criminological theory* (3rd ed.). Upper Saddle River, NJ: Prentice Hall, p. 148.

66. Van de Mieroop, M. (2005). *King Hammurabi of Babylon: A biography.* Malden, MA: Blackwell.

67. Federal Bureau of Investigation. (2015). *Crime in the United States, 2014.* Washington, DC: U.S. Department of Justice. Retrieved from https://www.fbi.gov/about-us/cjis/ucr/crime-in-the-u.s/2014/crime-in-the-u.s.-2014/offenses-known-to-law-enforcement/larceny-theft.

68. Ibid.

69. Bureau of Justice Statistics. (n.d.). *Bureau of Justice Statistics (BJS): Property crime.* Retrieved from http:/bjs.ojp.usdoj.gov/index.cfm?ty=tp&tid=32.

70. Lynch, M. J., & Groves, W. B. (1989). *A primer in radical criminology* (2nd ed). New York: Harrow & Heston, pp. 19–20.

71. Ibid., p. 20.

72. Dahrendorf, R. (1959). *Class and class conflict in industrial society.* Stanford, CA: Stanford University Press.

73. Colvin, M., & Pauly, J. (1983). A critique of criminology: Toward an integrated structural-Marxist theory of delinquency production. *American Journal of Sociology, 89,* 513–551.

74. Ibid., p. 521.

75. Ibid.

76. Vold, G. B. (1958). *Theoretical criminology.* New York: Oxford University Press.

77. Vold, G. B., Bernard, T. J., & Snipes, J. B. (1998). *Theoretical criminology* (4th ed.). New York: Oxford University Press, pp. 4–7; see also Pelfrey, W. V. (1980). *The evolution of criminology.* Cincinnati, OH: Anderson.

78. Pelfrey, W. V. (1980). *The evolution of criminology.* Cincinnati, OH: Anderson, p. 62.

79. Vold, G. B. (1958). *Theoretical criminology.* New York: Oxford University Press, p. vii.

80. Vold, G. B., Bernard, T. J., & Snipes, J. B. (1998). *Theoretical criminology* (4th ed.). New York: Oxford University Press, p. 236.

81. Van Dijk, J. (2008). *The world of crime: The silence on problems of security, justice and development across the world.* Thousand Oaks, CA: Sage.

82. Vold, G. B., Bernard, T. J., & Snipes, J. B. (1998). *Theoretical criminology* (4th ed.). New York: Oxford University Press, p. 237.

83. Ibid.

84. Brown, S. E., Esbensen, F., & Geis, G. (1991). *Criminology: Explaining crime and its context.* Cincinnati, OH: Anderson, p. 401.

85. Pelfrey, W. V. (1980). *The evolution of criminology.* Cincinnati, OH: Anderson, p. 64.

86. Turk, A. (1969). *Criminality and legal order.* Chicago: Rand McNally, p. 10.

87. Pelfrey, W. V. (1980). *The evolution of criminology.* Cincinnati, OH: Anderson, pp. 64–65.

88. Turk, A. (1969). *Criminality and legal order.* Chicago: Rand McNally, p. 18.

89. Ibid., pp. 36–38.

90. Vold, G. B., Bernard, T. J., & Snipes, J. B. (1998). *Theoretical criminology* (4th ed.). New York: Oxford University Press, pp. 240–241.

91. Turk, A. T. (1979). Analyzing official deviance for nonpartisan conflict analyses in criminology. *Criminology, 16,* 459.

92. Quinney, R. (1977). *Class, state, and crime.* New York: David McKay, p. 165.

93. Turk, A. T. (1979). Analyzing official deviance for nonpartisan conflict analyses in criminology. *Criminology, 16,* 464.

94. Quinney, R. (1970). *The social reality of crime.* Boston: Little, Brown, pp. 15–16.

95. Ibid., pp. 16–18.

96. Ibid., pp. 18–20.

97. Ibid., pp. 20–22.

98. Ibid., pp. 22–23.

99. Ibid., p. 23.

100. Greenberg, D. F. (Ed.). (1981). *Crime and capitalism: Readings in Marxist criminology.* Palo Alto, CA: Mayfield; Williams, F. P., & McShane, M. D. (1999). *Criminological theory* (3rd ed.). Upper Saddle River, NJ: Prentice Hall, p. 168.

101. Marx, K. (2006). *The communist manifesto.* New York: Penguin Books.

102. Marx, K. (1962). *Selected works [of] Karl Marx and Frederick Engels.* Moscow: Foreign Languages Publishing House, p. 22.

103. Williams, F. P., & McShane, M. D. (1999). *Criminological theory* (3rd ed.). Upper Saddle River, NJ: Prentice Hall, pp. 169–170.

104. Chambliss, W., & Seidman, R. (1971). *Law, order, and power.* Reading, MA: Addison-Wesley, p. 502.

105. Ibid., p. 503.

106. Ibid., p. 7.

107. Ibid., p. 113.

108. Colvin, M., & Pauly, J. (1983). A critique of criminology: Toward an integrated structural-Marxist theory of delinquency production. *American Journal of Sociology, 89,* 542.

109. Ibid., pp. 536–537.

110. Ibid., p. 538.

111. Ibid., pp. 539–542.

112. Schwendinger, H., & Schwendinger, J. (1985). *Adolescent subcultures and delinquency.* New York: Praeger.

113. Ibid., p. xiii.

114. Steven Spitzer, S. (1975). Toward a Marxian theory of deviance. *Social Problems, 22,* 641.

115. Ibid., p. 649.

116. Williams, F. P. (1980). Conflict theory and differential processing: An analysis of the research literature. In J. A. Inciardi (Ed.), *Radical criminology: The coming crises.* Beverly Hills, CA: Sage, p. 215.

117. Chambliss, W. (1964). A sociological analysis of the laws of vagrancy. *Social Problems, 12,* 67–77.

118. Becker, H. S. (1963). *Outsiders: Studies in the sociology of deviance.* New York: Free Press.

119. Robinson, A. (1999). Conflicting consensus: Public reaction to a domestic violence pro-arrest policy. *Women and Criminal Justice, 10,* 95–120.

120. Lieber, M. J., & Stairs, J. M. (1999). Race, contexts, and the use of intake diversion. *Journal of Research in Crime and Delinquency, 36,* 56–86.

121. Cureton, S. R. (2001). An empirical test of the social threat phenomenon: Using 1990 census and uniform crime reports. *Journal of Criminal Justice, 29,* 157–166; Mosher, C. (2001). Predicting drug arrest rates: Conflict and social disorganization perspectives. *Crime and Delinquency, 47,* 84–104.

122. Frazier, C. E., Bishop, D. M., & Henretta, J. C. (1992). The social context of race differentials in juvenile justice dispositions. *Sociological Quarterly, 33,* 447–458.

123. Holmes, M. D., Hosch, H. M., Daudistel, H. C., Perez, D., & Graves, J. (1996). Ethnicity, legal resources, and felony dispositions in two Southwestern jurisdictions. *Justice Quarterly, 13,* 11–30.

124. Holmes, M. D. (2000). Minority threat and police brutality: Determinants of civil rights criminal complaints in U.S. municipalities. *Criminology, 38,* 343–367.

125. Chamlin, M. B. (1989). Conflict theory and police killings. *Deviant Behavior, 10,* 353–368.

126. Vold, G. B., Bernard, T. J., & Snipes, J. B. (1998). *Theoretical criminology* (4th ed.). New York: Oxford University Press, pp. 256–257.

127. Ibid., p. 256.

128. Lanza-Kanduce, L., & Greenleaf, R. (1994). Police-citizen encounters: Turk on norm resistance. *Justice Quarterly, 11,* 605–624.

129. Ibid., p. 257.

130. Federal Bureau of Investigation. (2008). *FBI 100: The Unabomber.* Retrieved from http://www.fbi.gov/news/stories/2008/april/unabomber_042408.

131. See The Unabomber manifesto. (1997). *Washington Post.* Retrieved from http://www.washingtonpost.com/wp-srv/national/longterm/unabomber/manifesto.text.htm.

132. Federal Bureau of Investigation. (2008). *FBI 100: The Unabomber.* Retrieved from http://www.fbi.gov/news/stories/2008/april/unabomber_042408.

133. Pepinsky, H. E. (1991). Peacemaking in criminology and criminal justice. In H. E. Pepinski & Quinney, R. (Eds.), *Criminology as peacemaking* (pp. 299–327). Bloomington: Indiana University Press.

134. Wheeldon, J. (2009). Finding common ground: Restorative justice and its theoretical construction(s). *Contemporary Justice Review, 12,* 93.

135. Pepinsky, H. E. (1988). Violence as unresponsiveness: Toward a new conception of crime. *Justice Quarterly, 5,* 539–563; Pepinsky, H. E. (1991). *The geometry of violence and democracy.* Bloomington: Indiana University Press; Pepinsky, H. E., & Quinney, R. (Eds.). (1991). *Criminology as peace-making.* Bloomington: University of Indiana Press; Quinney, R. (1988). Crime, suffering, service: Toward a criminology of peacemaking. *Quest, 1,* 66–75; Quinney, R. (1989). The theory and practice of peacemaking in the development of radical criminology. *Critical Criminologist, 1,* 5.

136. Wozniak, J. F. (2002). Toward a theoretical model of peacemaking criminology: An essay in honor of Richard Quinney. *Crime & Delinquency, 48,* 221.

137. Ibid., p. 214.

138. Wozniak, J. F. (2000). The voices of peacemaking criminology: Insights into a perspective with an eye toward teaching. *Contemporary Justice Review, 3,* 273–274.

139. Wozniak, J. F. (2002). Toward a theoretical model of peacemaking criminology: An essay in honor of Richard Quinney. *Crime & Delinquency, 48,* 219–220.

140. Caringella-MacDonald, S., & Humphries, D. (1991). Sexual assault, women, and the community: Organizing to prevent sexual violence. In H. E. Pepinsky & R. Quinney (Eds.), *Criminology as peacemaking* (pp. 98–113). Bloomington: Indiana University Press.

141. Rucker, L. (1991). Peacemaking in prisons: A process. In H. E. Pepinsky & R. Quinney (Eds.), *Criminology as peacemaking* (pp. 172–180). Bloomington: Indiana University Press.

142. Wenzel, M., Okimoto, T. G., Feather, N. T., & Platow, M. J. (2008). Retributive and restorative justice. *Law and Human Behavior, 32,* 375.

143. Bazemore, G., & Umbreit, M. (1999). *Balanced and restorative justice for juveniles: Framework for juvenile justice in the 21st century.* Washington, DC: Office of Juvenile Justice and Delinquency Prevention, p. 11.

144. Wheeldon, J. (2009). Finding common ground: Restorative justice and its theoretical construction(s). *Contemporary Justice Review, 12,* 93.

145. Young, J. (1992). Ten points of realism. In J. Young & R. Matthews (Eds.), *Rethinking criminology: The realist debate* (pp. 25–26). London: Sage.

146. See Dekeseredy, W. S., & Schwartz, M. D. (1991). British and U.S. left realism: A critical comparison. *International Journal of Offender Therapy and Comparative Criminology, 35,* 248–262; Lea, J. (1987). Left realism: A defense. *Contemporary Crises, 11,* 357–370.

147. Matthews, R., & Young, J. (1992). Reflections on realism. In J. Young & R. Matthews (Eds.), *Rethinking criminology: The realist debate* (pp. 19–20). London: Sage.

148. Ibid., pp. 17–19.

149. Schwartz, M., & DeKeseredy, W. (1993). *Contemporary criminology.* Belmont, CA: Wadsworth.

150. Coumarelos, C., & Weatherburn, D. (1995). Targeting intervention strategies to reduce juvenile recidivism. *Australian and New Zealand Journal of Criminology, 28,* 55–72; Levi, K. (1982). Relative redemption: Labeling in juvenile restitution. *Juvenile and Family Court Journal, 33,* 3–13.

151. Patrick, S., & March, R. (2005). Juvenile diversion: Results of a 3-year experimental study. *Criminal Justice Policy Review, 16,* 62.

152. Butts, J. A., & Buck, J. (2000). Teen courts: A focus on research. *Juvenile Justice Bulletin*. Washington, DC: Office of Juvenile Justice and Delinquency Prevention, n.p.

153. Inciardi, J. A., Pottieger, A. E., & Surrat, H. L. (1996). African Americans and the crack-crime connection. In D. D. Chitwood, J. E. Rivers, & J. A. Inciardi (Eds.), *The American pipe dream: Crack, cocaine and the inner city*. Fort Worth, TX: Harcourt Brace; Jensen, E. L., Gerber, J., & Mosher, C. (2004). Social consequences of the War on Drugs: The legacy of failed policy. *Criminal Justice Policy Review, 15*, 100–121.

CHAPTER 12

1. Stall, S. (October 21, 2015). Looking back on Indiana's most infamous crime, 50 years later. *Indianapolis Monthly*. Retrieved from http://www.indianapolis-monthly.com/features/looking-back-indianas-infamous-crime-50-years-later/

2. Bovsun, M. (April 6, 2913). Teen girl fatally bullied in Indiana house of horrors. *New York Daily News*. Retrieved from http://www.nydailynews.com/news/justice-story/teen-girl-fatally-bullied-indiana-house-horrors-article-1.1309751

3. Freedman, E. B. (2002). *No turning back: The history of feminism and the future of women*. New York, NY: Ballantine Books, p. 7.

4. Van Wormer, K. S., & Bartollas, C. (2000). *Women and the criminal justice system*. Boston: Allyn & Bacon, p. 5. See also Byers, M., & Crocker, D. (2012). Feminist cohorts and waves: Attitudes of junior female academics. *Women's Studies International Forum, 35*, 1–11.

5. Tong, R. (2009). *Feminist thought* (3rd ed.). Boulder, CO: Westview Press, pp. 21–22.

6. Lebedun, J. (1974). Harriet Beecher Stowe's interest in Sojourner Truth, black feminist. *American Literature, 46*, 359–363.

7. Boles, J. K., & Hoeveler, D. L. (2004). *Historical dictionary of feminism* (2nd ed.). Lanham, MD: Scarecrow Press, pp. 7–9.

8. Tong, R. (2009). *Feminist thought* (3rd ed.). Boulder, CO: Westview Press, p. 22; see also Hole, J., & Levine, E. (1971). *Rebirth of feminism*. New York, NY: Quadrangle Books, p. 3.

9. Schnittker, J., Freese, J., & Powell, B. (2003). Who are feminists and what do they believe? The role of generations. *American Sociological Review, 68*, 607–622; see also Van Wormer, K. S., & Bartollas, C. (2000). *Women and the criminal justice system*. Boston: Allyn & Bacon.

10. Tong, R. (2009). *Feminist thought* (3rd ed.). Boulder, CO: Westview Press, pp. 23–24; see also Freedman, E. B. (2002). *No turning back: The history of feminism and the future of women*. New York, NY: Ballantine Books, pp. 84–87.

11. Freedman, E. B. (2002). *No turning back: The history of feminism and the future of women*. New York, NY: Ballantine Books, pp. 84–87.

12. Tong, R. (2009). *Feminist thought* (3rd ed.). Boulder, CO: Westview Press, p. 24.

13. Krolokke, C., & Sorensen, A. S. (2006). *Gender communication theories and analyses: From silence to performance*. Thousand Oaks, CA: SAGE.

14. Byers, M., & Crocker, D. (2012). Feminist cohorts and waves: Attitudes of junior female academics. *Women's Studies International Forum, 35*, 1–11.

15. Tong, R. (2009). *Feminist thought* (3rd ed.). Boulder, CO: Westview Press, pp. 284–285.

16. Lorber, J., & Farrell, S. A. (1991). Principles of gender construction. In J. Lorber & S. A. Farrell (Eds.), *The social construction of gender* (pp. 7–8). Newbury Park, CA: SAGE.

17. West, C., & Zimmerman, D. H. (1991). Doing gender. In J. Lorber & S. A. Farrell (Eds.), *The social construction of gender* (pp. 13–37). Newbury Park, CA: SAGE, pp. 24–27.

18. Belknap, J. (2007). *The invisible woman: Gender, crime, and justice* (3rd ed.). Belmont, CA: Wadsworth, pp. 150–151; Moulds, E. F. (1980). Chivalry and paternalism: Disparities of treatment in the criminal justice system. In S. K. Datesman & F. R. Scarpitti (Eds.), *Women, crime, and justice* (pp. 277–299). New York, NY: Oxford University Press, p. 279.

19. Boles, J. K., & Hoeveler, D. L. (2004). *Historical dictionary of feminism*. Lanham, MD: Scarecrow Press, p. 253.

20. Belknap, J. (2007). *The invisible woman: Gender, crime, and justice* (3rd ed.). Belmont, CA: Wadsworth, p. 10; see also Edwards, A. (1987). Male violence in feminist theory: An analysis of the changing conception of sex/gender violence and male dominance. In J. Hanmer & M. Maynard (Eds.), *Women, violence, and social control* (pp. 13–29). Atlantic Highlands, NJ: Humanities Press International.

21. Daly, K., & Chesney-Lind, M. (1988). Feminism and criminology. *Justice Quarterly, 5*, 523.

22. Ibid., pp. 536–537.

23. Boles, J. K., & Hoeveler, D. L. (2004). *Historical dictionary of feminism*. Lanham, MD: Scarecrow Press, p. 192.

24. Daly, K., & Chesney-Lind, M. (1988). Feminism and criminology. *Justice Quarterly, 5*, p. 537.

25. Tong, R. (2009). *Feminist thought* (3rd ed.). Boulder, CO: Westview Press, p. 34.

26. Ibid., p. 35.

27. Ibid., p. 43.

28. Britton, D. B. (2000). Feminism in criminology: Engendering the law. Annals of the American Academy of Political and Social *Science, 571*, 57–76.

29. Belknap, J. (2007). *The invisible woman: Gender, crime, and justice* (3rd ed.). Belmont, CA: Wadsworth, p. 13.

30. Daly, K., & Chesney-Lind, M. (1988). Feminism and criminology. *Justice Quarterly, 5*, 525.

31. Ibid., p. 526.

32. Boles, J. K., & Hoeveler, D. L. (2004). *Historical dictionary of feminism*. Lanham, MD: Scarecrow Press, pp. 270–271.

33. Daly, K., & Chesney-Lind, M. (1988). Feminism and criminology. *Justice Quarterly, 5*, 538.

34. Tong, R. (2009). *Feminist thought* (3rd ed.). Boulder, CO: Westview Press, pp. 48–51.
35. Ibid., p. 51.
36. Daly, K., & Chesney-Lind, M. (1988). Feminism and criminology. *Justice Quarterly, 5*, 538.
37. Tong, R. (2009). *Feminist thought* (3rd ed.). Boulder, CO: Westview Press, pp. 92–93; see also Ferguson, A. (1984). Sex war: The debate between radical and libertarian feminist. *Signs: The Journal of Women in Culture and Society, 10*, 106–112.
38. Tong, R. (2009). *Feminist thought* (3rd ed.). Boulder, CO: Westview Press, p. 93.
39. Ibid., p. 96.
40. Boles, J. K., & Hoeveler, D. L. (2004). *Historical dictionary of feminism*. Lanham, MD: Scarecrow Press, pp. 204–205.
41. Daly, K., & Chesney-Lind, M. (1988). Feminism and criminology. *Justice Quarterly, 5*, 537.
42. Belknap, J. (2007). *The invisible woman: Gender, crime, and justice* (3rd ed.). Belmont, CA: Wadsworth, p. 13; see also Hardin, S. (2004). Can men be subjects of feminist thought? In S. N. Hesse-Biber & M. L. Yaiser (Eds.), Feminist perspectives on social *research* (pp. 39–64). New York, NY: Oxford University Press; Hartmann, H. I. (1987). The family as the locus of gender, class, and political struggle: The example of housework. In S. Harding (Ed.), *Feminism and methodology* (pp. 109–134). Bloomington, IN: Indiana University Press.
43. Belknap, J. (2007). *The invisible woman: Gender, crime, and justice* (3rd ed.). Belmont, CA: Wadsworth, p. 538.
44. Tong, R. (2009). *Feminist thought* (3rd ed.). Boulder, CO: Westview Press, p. 111.
45. Ibid., p. 115.
46. Boles, J. K., & Hoeveler, D. L. (2004). *Historical dictionary of feminism*. Lanham, MD: Scarecrow Press, pp. 262–263.
47. Tong, R. (2009). *Feminist thought* (3rd ed.). Boulder, CO: Westview Press; see also Moi, T. (1985). *Sexual/textual politics*. London: Methuen.
48. Tong, R. (2009). *Feminist thought* (3rd ed.). Boulder, CO: Westview Press, p. 270.
49. Sands, R. G., & Nuccio, K. (1992). Postmodern feminist theory and social work. *Social Work, 37*, 492.
50. Ibid., p. 492; see also Haraway, D. (1989). Situated knowledges: The science question in feminism and privilege of partial perspective. *Feminist Studies, 14*, 575–599.
51. Boles, J. K., & Hoeveler, D. L. (2004). *Historical dictionary of feminism*. Lanham, MD: Scarecrow Press, p. 109.
52. Tong, R. (2009). *Feminist thought* (3rd ed.). Boulder, CO: Westview Press, pp. 237–269.
53. Boles, J. K., & Hoeveler, D. L. (2004). *Historical dictionary of feminism*. Lanham, MD: Scarecrow Press, p. 109.
54. Tong, R. (2009). *Feminist thought* (3rd ed.). Boulder, CO: Westview Press, p. 215.
55. Pomeroy, S. B. (1975). *Goddesses, whores, wives, and slaves*. New York, NY: Schocken Books, p. 8.
56. Feinman, C. (1980). *Women in the criminal justice system*. New York, NY: Praeger.
57. Van Dijk, J. (2008). *The world of crime: The silence on problems of security, justice and development across the world*. Thousand Oaks, CA: SAGE.
58. Kangaspunta, K. (2003). Mapping the inhuman trade: Preliminary findings of the database on trafficking in human beings. *Forum on Crime and Society, 3*, 81–105.
59. Van Dijk, J. (2008). *The world of crime: The silence on problems of security, justice and development across the world*. Thousand Oaks, CA: SAGE, pp. 170–171.
60. Young, V. D. (1986). Gender expectations and their impact on black female offenders and victims. *Justice Quarterly, 3*, 305–327.
61. Ibid., p. 310.
62. Ibid., p. 322.
63. Dugger, K. (1991). Social location and gender-role attitudes: A comparison of black and white women. In J. Lorber, & S. A. Farrell (Eds.), *The social construction of gender* (pp. 38–59). Newbury Park, CA: SAGE.
64. Brownmiller, S. (1984). *Femininity*. New York, NY: Fawcett Columbine.
65. West, C., & Zimmerman, D. H. (1991). Doing gender. In J. Lorber, & S. A. Farrell (Eds.), *The social construction of gender* (pp. 13–37). Newbury Park, CA: SAGE, p. 15.
66. Carlen, P. (1982). Papa's discipline: An analysis of disciplinary modes in the Scottish women's prison. *Sociological Review, 30*, 97–124; Smith, B. A. (1990). The female prisoner in Ireland, 1855–1878. *Federal Probation, 54*, 69–81; Welter, B. (1973). The cult of true womanhood: 1820–1860. In J. E. Friedman & W. G. Shade (Eds.), *Our American sisters: Women in American life and thought* (pp. 96–123). Boston, MA: Allyn & Bacon.
67. Smart, C. (1977). Criminological theory: Its ideology and implications concerning women. *British Journal of Sociology, 28*, 91–92.
68. Hahn, N. R. (1980). Too dumb to know better: Cacogenic family studies and the criminology of women. *Criminology, 18*, 3.
69. Lombroso, C. (1898). *The female offender*. New York, NY: Appleton.
70. Belknap, J. (2007). *The invisible woman: Gender, crime, and justice* (3rd ed.). Belmont, CA: Wadsworth, p. 33.
71. Lombroso, C. (1898). *The female offender*. New York, NY: Appleton, p. 147.
72. Ibid., p. 216.
73. See Beaman, L. G. (1998). Women's defenses: Contextualizing dilemmas of difference and power. *Women and Criminal Justice, 9*, 87–115; Harry, B., & Balcer, C. M. (1987). Menstruation and crime: A critical review of the literature from the clinical criminology perspective. *Behavioral Sciences and the Law, 5*, 307–321; Welch, M. (1997). Regulating the reproduction and morality of women: The social control of body and soul. *Women and Criminal Justice, 9*, 17–38.
74. Thomas, W. I. (1907). Sex and society. Boston, MA: Little, Brown; see also Van Wormer, K. S., & Bartollas, C. (2000). *Women and the criminal justice system*. Boston, MA: Allyn & Bacon, p. 27.

75. Bowker, L. H. (1978). *Women, crime, and the criminal justice system.* Lexington, MA: D. C. Heath, p. 44.

76. Van Wormer, K. S., & Bartollas, C. (2000). *Women and the criminal justice system.* Boston, MA: Allyn & Bacon, p. 27.

77. Thomas, W. I. (1967). *The unadjusted girl.* New York, NY: Harper & Row, p. 4.

78. Bowker, L. H. (1978). *Women, crime, and the criminal justice system.* Lexington, MA: D. C. Heath, p. 45.

79. Thomas, W. I. (1967). *The unadjusted girl.* New York, NY: Harper & Row, p. 69.

80. Mann, C. R. (1984). *Female crime and delinquency.* University: University of Alabama Press, p. 79.

81. Klein, D. (1980). The etiology of female crime: A review of the literature. In S. Datesman & F. R. Scarpitti (Eds.), *Women, crime, and justice* (pp. 70–105). New York, NY: Oxford University Press, p. 87.

82. Freud, S. (1933). *New introductory lectures on psychoanalysis.* New York, NY: W. W. Norton; see also Van Wormer, K. S., & Bartollas, C. (2000). *Women and the criminal justice system.* Boston, MA: Allyn & Bacon, p. 28.

83. Klein, D. (1980). The etiology of female crime: A review of the literature. In S. Datesman & F. R. Scarpitti (Eds.), *Women, crime, and justice* (pp. 70–105). New York, NY: Oxford University Press, p. 88.

84. Pollak, O. (1950). *The criminality of women.* Philadelphia: University of Pennsylvania Press, p. 161.

85. Ibid., p. 1.

86. Ibid., p. 5.

87. Bowker, L. H. (1978). *Women, crime, and the criminal justice system.* Lexington, MA: D.C. Heath, p. 48.

88. Pollak, O. (1950). *The criminality of women.* Philadelphia: University of Pennsylvania Press, p. 10.

89. Smart, C. (1976). *Women, crime and criminology: A feminist critique.* London, UK: Routledge & Kegan Paul.

90. Klein, D. (1980). The etiology of female crime: A review of the literature. In S. Datesman & F. R. Scarpitti (Eds.), *Women, crime, and justice* (pp. 70–105). New York, NY: Oxford University Press.

91. Eichler, M. (1979). *The double standard: A feminist critique of feminist social science.* New York, NY: St. Martin's Press; Harding, S. (Ed.). (1987). *Feminism and methodology.* Bloomington: Indiana University Press; Keller, E. F. (1978). Gender and science. *Psychoanalysis and Contemporary Thought: A Quarterly of Integrative and Interdisciplinary Studies, 1,* 409–433; McHugh, M., Koeske, R., & Frieze, I. (1986). Issues to consider in conducting nonsexist psychological research. *American Psychologist, 41,* 879–890; Nielsen, J. M. (Ed.). *Feminist research methods: Exemplary readings in the social sciences.* Boulder, CO: Westview Press; Stanley, L., & Wise, S. (1979). Feminist research, feminist consciousness, and experiences of sexism. *Women's Studies International Quarterly, 2,* 359–374; Westkott, M. (1979). Feminist criticism of the social sciences. *Harvard Educational Review, 49,* 422–430.

92. West, C., & Zimmerman, D. H. (1991). Doing gender. In J. Lorber & S. A. Farrell (Eds.), *The social construction of gender* (pp. 13–37). Newbury Park, CA: SAGE, p. 24.

93. Belknap, J. (2007). *The invisible woman: Gender, crime, and justice* (3rd ed.). Belmont, CA: Wadsworth.

94. Smart, C. (1977). Criminological theory: Its ideology and implications concerning women. *British Journal of Sociology, 28,* 185.

95. Naffine, N. (1987). *Female crime: The construction of women in criminology.* Sydney, Australia: Allen & Unwin.

96. Daly, K. (1995). Looking back, looking forward: The promise of feminist transformation. In B. R. Price & N. J. Sokoloff (Eds.), *The criminal justice system and women: Offenders, victims, and workers* (pp. 443–457). New York, NY: McGraw-Hill.

97. West, C., & Zimmerman, D. H. (1991). Doing gender. In J. Lorber & S. A. Farrell (Eds.), *The social construction of gender* (pp. 13–37). Newbury Park, CA: SAGE, pp. 15–16.

98. Edwards, A. R. (1989). Sex/gender, sexism and criminal justice: Some theoretical considerations. *International Journal of the Sociology of Law, 17,* 165–184.

99. West, C., & Zimmerman, D. H. (1991). Doing gender. In J. Lorber & S. A. Farrell (Eds.), *The social construction of gender* (pp. 13–37). Newbury Park, CA: SAGE, p. 18.

100. Williams, F. P., & McShane, M. D. (1999). *Criminological theory* (3rd ed.). Upper Saddle River, NJ: Prentice Hall, p. 252.

101. Mann, C. R. (1984). *Female crime and delinquency.* University: University of Alabama Press, pp. 107–108.

102. Federal Bureau of Investigation. (2015). *Crime in the United States, 2014.* Washington, DC: U.S. Department of Justice. Retrieved from https://www.fbi.gov/about-us/cjis/ucr/crime-in-the-u.s/2014/crime-in-the-u.s.-2014/tables/table-33.

103. Valentine, L. (January 16, 2015). Teacher who had sex with 2 students gets probation. *New York Post.* Retrieved from http://nypost.com/2015/01/16/teacher-who-had-sex-with-2-students-gets-probation/

104. Teacher accused of sexual relationship with 13-year-old turns herself in. (2016, June 1). *ABC13 News.* Retrieved from http://abc13.com/news/teacher-accused-of-sex-with-13-year-old-turns-herself-in/1366303/

105. Ex-teacher Brianne Altice admits to sex with three teen boys. (2015, April 23). *Huffington Post.* Retrieved from http://www.huffingtonpost.com/2015/04/23/brianne-altice-guilty_n_7125596.html

106. Tanner, R. (2007). Abuse victims viewed differently. *Associated Press.* Retrieved from http://www.tdcaa.com/node/1277

107. Adler, F. (1975). *Sisters in crime.* Prospects Heights, IL: Waveland Press, p. 30.

108. Ibid., p. 251.

109. Simon, R. (1975). *Women and crime.* Lexington, MA: D.C. Heath.

110. Belknap, J. (2007). *The invisible woman: Gender, crime, and justice* (3rd ed.). Belmont, CA: Wadsworth, p. 56.

111. Naffine, N. (1987). *Female crime: The construction of women in criminology.* Sydney, Australia: Allen & Unwin, p. 95.

112. Belknap, J. (2007). *The invisible woman: Gender, crime, and justice* (3rd ed.). Belmont, CA: Wadsworth, p. 57.

113. See Leonard, E. B. (1982). *Women, crime, and society: A critique of criminology theory.* New York, NY: Longman; Radosh, P. (1990). Women and crime in the United States: A Marxian explanation. *Sociological Spectrum, 10,* 105–131; Steffensmeier, D., & Steffensmeier, R. H. (1980). Trends in female delinquency. *Criminology, 18,* 62–85.

114. Hagan, J., Gillis, A. R., & Simpson, J. (1985). The class structure of gender and delinquency: Toward a power-control theory of common delinquent behavior. *American Journal of Sociology, 90,* 1151–1178; Hagan, J., Simpson, J., & Gillis, A. R. (1987). Class in the household: A power-control theory of gender and delinquency. *American Journal of Sociology, 92,* 788–816.

115. Hagan, J., Gillis, A. R., & Simpson, J. (1985). The class structure of gender and delinquency: Toward a power-control theory of common delinquent behavior. *American Journal of Sociology, 90,* 1156–1157.

116. Hagan, J. (1991). A power-control theory of gender and delinquency. In R. J. Silverman, J. A. Teevan, & V. Sacco (Eds.), *Crime in Canadian society* (4th ed.). Toronto, Ontario, Canada: Butterworths, p. 130.

117. See Dornfeld, M., & Kruttschnitt, C. (1992). Do the stereotypes fit? Mapping gender-specific outcomes and risk factors. *Criminology, 30,* 397–420; Kruttschnitt, C. (1996). Contributions of quantitative methods to the study of gender and crime, or bootstrapping our way into the theoretical thicket. *Journal of Quantitative Criminology, 12,* 135–161; Morash, M., & Chesney-Lind, M. (1991). A re-formulation and patriarchal test of the power control theory of delinquency. *Justice Quarterly, 8,* 347–378.

118. Chesney-Lind, M. (1987). *Girls' crime and woman's place: Toward a feminist model of female delinquency.* Paper presented at the Annual Meeting of the American Society of Criminology, Montreal, Canada.

119. Harding, S. (Ed.). (1987). *Feminism and methodology.* Bloomington: Indiana University Press.

120. Ibid., pp. 8–9.

121. Campbell, R., & Schram, P. J. (1995). Feminist research methods: A content analysis of psychology and social science textbooks. *Psychology of Women Quarterly, 19,* 88.

122. Jayaratne, T. E., & Stewart, A. J. (1991). Quantitative and qualitative methods in social sciences: Current feminist issues and practical strategies. In M. M. Fonow & J. A. Cook (Eds.), *Beyond methodology: Feminist scholarship as lived research* (pp. 85–106). Bloomington: Indiana University Press; Stanley, L., & Wise, S. (1983). *Breaking out: Feminist consciousness and feminist research.* London, UK: Routledge & Kegan Paul.

123. Denmark, F., Russo, N. F., & Frieze, I. H. (1988). Guidelines for avoiding sexism in psychological research: A report of the Ad Hoc Committee on Nonsexist Research. *American Psychologist, 43,* 582–585; McHugh, M. C., Koeske, R. D., & Frieze, I. H. (1986). Issues to consider in conducting nonsexist psychological research. *American Psychologist, 41,* 879–890.

124. MacKinnon, C. A. (1987). Feminism, Marxism, methods and the state: Toward feminist jurisprudence. In S. Harding (Ed), *Feminism and methodology* (pp. 135–156). Bloomington: Indiana University Press, p. 136.

125. Sherif, C. W. (1987). Bias in psychology. In S. Harding (Ed.), *Feminism and methodology* (pp. 37–56). Bloomington: Indiana University Press.

126. Ibid., p. 47.

127. Campbell, R., & Schram, P. J. (1995). Feminist research methods: A content analysis of psychology and social science textbooks. *Psychology of Women Quarterly, 19,* 88.

128. Jayaratne, T. E., & Stewart, A. J. (1991). Quantitative and qualitative methods in social sciences: Current feminist issues and practical strategies. In M. M. Fonow & J. A. Cook (Eds.), *Beyond methodology: Feminist scholarship as lived research* (pp. 85–106). Bloomington: Indiana University Press.

129. White, J., & Farmer, R. (1992). Research methods: How they shape views of sexual violence. *Journal of Social Issues, 48,* 179.

130. Burgess-Proctor, A. (2006). Intersections of race, class, gender, and crime: Future directions for feminist criminology. *Feminist Criminology, 1,* 30.

131. Ibid.; see also Blumstein, A., Cohen, J., Roth, J. A., & Visher, C. (1986). Introduction: Studying criminal careers. In A. Blumstein, J. Cohen, J. A. Roth, & C. Visher (Eds.), *Criminal careers and "career criminals"* (pp. 12–30). Washington, DC: National Academy Press; Steffensmeier, D., & Allan, E. (1996). Gender and crime: Toward a gendered theory of female offending. *Annual Review of Sociology, 22,* 459–487.

132. Burgess-Proctor, A. (2006). Intersections of race, class, gender, and crime: Future directions for feminist criminology. *Feminist Criminology, 1,* 31.

133. Klein, D. (1995). The etiology of female crime: A review of the literature. In B. R. Price & N. J. Sokoloff (Eds.), *The criminal justice system and women: Offenders, victims, and workers* (2nd ed., pp. 48–52). New York: McGraw-Hill.

134. Belknap, J. (2007). The invisible woman: Gender, crime, and *justice* (3rd ed.). Belmont, CA: Wadsworth, pp. 36–56.

135. Daly, K., & Chesney-Lind, M. (1988). Feminism and criminology. *Justice Quarterly, 5,* 504.

136. Ibid., p. 504.

137. Burgess-Proctor, A. (2006). Intersections of race, class, gender, and crime: Future directions for feminist criminology. *Feminist Criminology, 1,* 27–47.

138. Ibid., p. 43.

139. Gaarder, E., & Belknap, J. (2002). Tenuous borders: Girls transferred to adult court. *Criminology, 40,* 484.

140. Belknap, J. (2007). *The invisible woman: Gender, crime, and justice* (3rd ed.). Belmont, CA: Wadsworth, p. 70.

141. Chesney-Lind, M. (1995). Girls, delinquency, and juvenile justice: Toward a feminist theory of young women's

crime. In B. F. Price & N. J. Sokoloff (Eds.), *The criminal justice system and women: Offenders, victims, and workers* (2nd ed., pp. 71–88). New York: McGraw-Hill.

142. Owen, B. (1998). *"In the mix": Struggle and survival in a women's prison.* Albany: State University of New York Press.

143. Ibid., p. 41.

144. Ibid., p. 192.

145. Sadeighi-Fassei, S., & Kendall, K. (2001). *Iranian women's pathways to imprisonment.* Women's Studies International Forum, 24, 701–710.

146. Gaarder, E., & Belknap, J. (2002). Tenuous borders: Girls transferred to adult court. *Criminology, 40,* 481–518.

147. Evans, R. D., Forsyth, C. J., & Gauthier, D. K. (2002). Gendered pathways into and experiences with crack cultures outside of the inner city. *Deviant Behaviors, 23,* 483–510.

148. Ullman, S. (2004). Sexual assault victimization and suicidal behavior in women: A review of the literature. *Aggression and Violent Behavior, 9,* 331–351.

149. Silverthorn, P., & Frick, P. J. (1999). Development pathways to antisocial behavior: The delayed-onset pathway in girls. *Development and Psychopathology, 11,* 101–126.

150. DeHart, D., Lynch, S., Belknap, J., Dass-Brailsford, P., & Green, B. (2014). Life history models of female offending: The roles of serious mental illness and trauma in women's pathways to jail. *Psychology of Women Quarterly, 38,* 138-151.

151. Shechory-Bitton, M., & Kamel, D. (2014). Pathways to crime and risk factors among Arab female adolescents in Israel. *Children & Youth Services Review, 44,* 363–369.

152. Zinn, M. B., & Thornton Dill, B. T. (1996). Theorizing difference from multiracial feminism. *Feminist Studies, 22,* 321–331.

153. Chafetz, J. S. (1997). Feminist theory and sociology: Underutilized contributions for mainstream theory. *Annual Review of Sociology, 23,* 97–120. See also Burgess-Proctor, A. (2006). Intersections of race, class, gender, and crime: Future directions for feminist criminology. *Feminist Criminology, 1,* 27–47.

154. Ginsberg, F., & Tsing, A. L. (1990). Introduction. In F. Ginsberg & A. L. Tsing (Eds.), *Uncertain terms, negotiating gender in American culture* (pp. 1–32). Boston, MA: Beacon Press.

155. Martin, S. (1994). "Outsider within" the station house: The impact of race and gender on black women police. *Social Problems, 41,* 383–400.

156. Zinn, M. B., & Thornton Dill, B. T. (1996). Theorizing difference from multiracial feminism. *Feminist Studies, 22,* 322.

157. Collins, P. H. (1999). *Black feminist thought: Knowledge, consciousness and the politics of empowerment* (2nd ed.). London, UK: HarperCollins.

158. Browne, I., & Misra, J. (2003). The intersection of gender and race in the labor market. *Annual Review of Sociology, 29,* 487–513.

159. Burgess-Proctor, A. (2006). Intersections of race, class, gender, and crime: Future directions for feminist criminology. *Feminist Criminology, 1,* 36–37.

160. Ibid., p. 37.

161. See Jagger, A. M., & Struhl, P. R. (1993). Feminist frameworks: Alternative theoretical accounts of the relations between women and men (3rd ed.). New York, NY: McGraw-Hill; Sandoval, C. (1991, Spring). U.S. Third World feminism: The theory and method of oppositional consciousness in the Postmodern World. *Genders, 10,* 1–24; Zinn, M. B., & Dill, B. T. (1996). Theorizing difference from multiracial feminism. *Feminist Studies, 22,* 321–331.

162. Gilfus, M. E. (1992). From victims to survivors to offenders: Women's routes of entry and immersion into street crime. *Women and Criminal Justice, 4,* 86.

163. Van de Mieroop, M. (2005). *King Hammurabi of Babylon: A biography.* Malden, MA: Blackwell.

164. Federal Bureau of Investigation. (2015). *Crime in the United States, 2014.* Washington, DC: U.S. Department of Justice. Retrieved from https://www.fbi.gov/about-us/cjis/ucr/crime-in-the-u.s/2014/crime-in-the-u.s.-2014/offenses-known-to-law-enforcement/robbery

165. Bureau of Justice Statistics. (n.d.). *NCVS Victimization Analysis Tool (NVAT).* Retrieved from http://www.bjs.gov/index.cfm?ty=nvat

166. Van Dijk, J. (2008). *The world of crime: The silence on problems of security, justice and development across the world.* Thousand Oaks, CA: SAGE.

167. Maher, L. (1997). *Sexed work: Gender, race and resistance in a Brooklyn drug market.* Oxford, UK: Clarendon Press.

168. Ibid., p. 1.

169. Williams, F. P., & McShane, M. D. (1999). *Criminological theory* (3rd ed.). Upper Saddle River, NJ: Prentice Hall, p. 260.

170. Griffin, C., & Phoenix, A. (1994). The relationship between qualitative and quantitative research: Lessons from feminist psychology. *Journal of Community & Applied Social Psychology, 4,* 290.

171. Ibid.

172. Ibid.

173. Donovan, J. (1985). *Feminist theory: The intellectual traditions of American feminism.* New York, NY: Frederick Ungar, p. 88.

174. Burgess-Proctor, A. (2006). Intersections of race, class, gender, and crime: Future directions for feminist criminology. *Feminist Criminology, 1,* 42. See also Andersen, M., & Collins, P. H. (2004). *Race, class, and gender* (5th ed.). Belmont, CA: Wadsworth; Weber, L. (2001). *Understanding race, class, gender, and sexuality: A conceptual framework.* Boston, MA: McGraw-Hill.

175. Van Wormer, K. S., & Bartollas, C. (2000). *Women and the criminal justice system.* Boston, MA: Allyn & Bacon.

176. Schwendinger, J. R., & Schwendinger, H. (1974). Rape myths: In legal, theoretical, and everyday practice. *Crime and Social Justice, 1,* 18–26.

177. Ibid., p. 21.

178. Searles, P., & Berger, R. J. (1987). The current status of rape reform legislation: An examination of state statutes. *Women's Rights Law Reporter, 10,* 25.

179. Ibid., pp. 25–27.

180. Bownes, D., & Albert, R. L. (1996, September). State challenge activities. *OJJDP Juvenile Justice Bulletin*; Kempf-Leonard, K., & Sample, L. (2000). Disparity based on sex: Is gender-specific treatment warranted? *Justice Quarterly, 17,* 89–128.

181. Smith, P., & Smith, W. A. (2005). Experiencing community through the eyes of young female offenders. *Journal of Contemporary Criminal Justice, 21,* 364–385.

182. Bond-Maupin, L., Maupin, J. R., & Leisenring, A. (2002). Girls' delinquency and the justice implications of intake workers' perspectives. *Women & Criminal Justice, 13,* 51–77.

183. Kakar, S., Friedemann, M., & Peck, L. (2002). Girls in detention: The results of focus group discussion interviews and official records review. *Journal of Contemporary Criminal Justice, 18,* 57–73; Walters, W., Dembo, R., Beaulaurier, R., Cocozza, J., La Rosa, M., Poythress, N., et al. (2005). The Miami-Dade Juvenile Assessment Center National Demonstration Project: An overview. *Journal of Offender Rehabilitation, 41,* 1–37.

184. Fendrich, M., Hubbell, A., & Lurigio, A. (2006). Providers' perceptions of gender-specific drug treatment. *Journal of Drug Issues, 36,* 667–686.

185. Van Wormer, K., & Kaplan, L. E. (2006). Results of a national survey of wardens in women's prisons: The case for gender specific treatment. *Women and Therapy, 29,* 133–151.

CHAPTER 13

1. 14-year-old suspected in nearly 100 Nashville burglaries. (2012, May 18). *WSMV.com.* Retrieved from http://www.wsmv.com/story/18151966/14-year-old-suspected-in-north-nashville-burglaries.

2. Glueck, S., & Glueck, E. (1950). *Unraveling juvenile delinquency.* New York, NY: Commonwealth Fund. See also Glueck, S., & Glueck, E. (1968). *Delinquents and nondelinquents in perspective.* Cambridge, MA: Harvard University Press.

3. Sampson, R. J., & Laub, J. H. (1993). *Crime in the making: Pathways and turning points through life.* Cambridge, MA: Harvard University Press. See also Laub, J. H., Nagin, D. S., & Sampson, R. J. (1998). Trajectories of change in criminal offending: Good marriages and the desistance process. *American Sociological Review, 63,* 225–238. For a brief discussion of how the Gluecks' work has influenced the current state of developmental theory, see Tibbetts, S. (2014). Prenatal and perinatal predictors of antisocial behavior: Review of research and interventions. In M. DeLisi & K. M. Beaver (Eds.), *Criminological theory: A life-course approach* (2nd ed., pp. 27–43). Boston, MA: Jones & Bartlett.

4. Brame, R., Turner, M., Paternoster, R., & Bushway, S. (2012). Cumulative prevalence of arrest from ages 8 to 23 in a national sample. *Pediatrics, 129,* 21–27.

5. For an excellent review, see Piquero, A. R., Farrington, D. P., & Blumstein, A. (2003). The criminal career paradigm: Background and recent developments. In M. Tonry (Ed.), *Crime and justice: A review of research* (Vol. 30, pp. 137–183). Chicago: University of Chicago Press.

6. For more discussion, see Gibson, C. L., & Tibbetts, S. (2000). A biosocial interaction in predicting early onset of offending. *Psychological Reports, 86,* 509–518; Tibbetts, S., & Piquero, A. (1999). The influence of gender, low birth weight, and disadvantaged environment in predicting early onset of offending: A test of Moffitt's interactional hypothesis. *Criminology, 37,* 843–878.

7. DeLisi, M. (2006). Zeroing in on early onset: Results from a population of extreme career criminals. *Journal of Criminal Justice, 34,* 17–26. For a recent review, see Tibbetts, S. (2009). Perinatal and developmental determinants of early onset of offending: A biosocial approach for explaining the two peaks of early antisocial behavior. In J. Savage (Ed.), *The development of persistent criminality* (pp. 179–201). New York, NY: Oxford University Press.

8. See numerous studies presented in Savage, J. (Ed.). (2009). *The development of persistent criminality.* New York, NY: Oxford University Press.

9. Lincoln Police arrest man for 226th time. (2006, August 14). *KETV.com.* Retrieved from http://www.ketv.com/Lincoln-Police-Arrest-Man-For-226th-Time/-/9675214/10057612/-/6v7e1kz/-/index.html.

10. Walker, S. (2001). *Sense and nonsense about crime and drugs: A policy guide* (5th ed.). Belmont, CA: Wadsworth.

11. For a review, see Piquero, A. R., Farrington, D. P., & Blumstein, A. (2003). The criminal career paradigm: Background and recent developments. In M. Tonry (Ed.), *Crime and justice: A review of research* (Vol. 30, pp. 137–183). Chicago, IL: University of Chicago Press.

12. Ellis, L., Cooper, J. A., & Walsh, A. (2008). Criminologists' opinions about causes and theories of crime and delinquency: A follow-up. *The Criminologist, 33,* 23–26.

13. For discussion of this ranking and past rankings, see Tibbetts, S. (2014). Prenatal and perinatal predictors of antisocial behavior: Review of research and interventions. In M. DeLisi & K. M. Beaver (Eds.), *Criminological theory: A life-course approach* (2nd ed., pp. 27–43). Boston, MA: Jones & Bartlett.

14. Gottfredson, M., & Hirschi, T. (1990). *A general theory of crime.* Palo Alto, CA: Stanford University Press.

15. For an excellent review of studies regarding low self-control theory, see Pratt, T., & Cullen, F. (2000). The empirical status of Gottfredson and Hirschi's general theory of crime: A meta-analysis. *Criminology, 38,* 931–64. For critiques of this theory, see Akers, R. (1991). Self-control as a general theory of crime. *Journal of Quantitative Criminology, 7,* 201–211. For a study that demonstrates the high popularity of the theory, see Walsh,

A., & Ellis, L. (1999). Political ideology and American criminologists' explanations for criminal behavior. *The Criminologist, 24,* 1, 14.

16. Hay, C. (2001). Parenting, self-control, and delinquency: A test of self-control theory. *Criminology, 39,* 707–736; Hayslett-McCall, K., & Bernard, T. (2002). Attachment, masculinity, and self-control: A theory of male crime rates. *Theoretical Criminology, 6,* 5–33.

17. Sampson, R., & Laub, J. (1990). Crime and deviance over the life course: The salience of adult social bonds. *American Sociological Review, 55,* 609–627; Sampson, R., & Laub, J. (1993). *Crime in the making: Pathways and turning points through life.* Cambridge, MA: Harvard University Press; Sampson, R., & Laub, J. (1993). Turning points in the life course: Why change matters to the study of crime. *Criminology, 31,* 301–326.

18. Piquero, A., Brame, R., Mazzerole, P., & Haapanen, R. (2002). Crime in emerging adulthood. *Criminology, 40,* 137–170; Uggen, C. (2000). Work as a turning point in the life course of criminals: A duration model of age, employment, and recidivism. *American Sociological Review, 65,* 529–546.

19. Moffitt, T. (1993). Adolescence limited and life course persistent antisocial behavioral: A developmental taxonomy. *Psychological Review, 100,* 674–701.

20. See Tibbetts, S., & Piquero, A. (1999). The influence of gender, low birth weight, and disadvantaged environment in predicting early onset of offending: A test of Moffitt's interactional hypothesis. *Criminology, 37,* 843–878.

21. Thornberry, T. (1987). Toward an interactional theory of delinquency. *Criminology, 25,* 863–887; see also Thornberry, T., Lizotte, A., Krohn, M., Farnworth, M., & Jang, S. (1991). Testing interactional theory: An examination of reciprocal causal relationships among family, school and delinquency. *Journal of Criminal Law and Criminology, 82,* 3–35; Thornberry, T., Lizotte, A., Krohn, M., Farnworth, M., & Jang, S. J. (1994). Delinquent peers, beliefs, and delinquent behavior: A longitudinal test of interactional theory. *Criminology, 32,* 47–83.

22. Much of this discussion is taken from Bernard, T. J., & Snipes, J. B. (1996). Theoretical integration in criminology. *Crime and Justice, 20,* 314–316; and also Akers, R. L., & Sellers, C. S. (2008). *Criminological theories: Introduction, evaluation, and application* (5th ed.). New York: Oxford University Press, p. 278.

23. Thornberry, T. (1987). Toward an interactional theory of delinquency. *Criminology, 25,* 876, as quoted in Bernard, T. J., & Snipes, J. B. (1996). Theoretical integration in criminology. *Crime and Justice, 20,* 315.

24. Bernard, T. J., & Snipes, J. B. (1996). Theoretical integration in criminology. *Crime and Justice, 20,* 316.

25. Thornberry, T., Lizotte, A., Krohn, M., Farnworth, M., & Jang, S. J. (1994). Delinquent peers, beliefs, and delinquent behavior: A longitudinal test of interactional theory. *Criminology, 32,* 47–83.

26. Ibid.

27. Jang, S. J. (1999). Age-varying effects of family, school, and peers on delinquency: A multilevel modeling test of interactional theory. *Criminology, 37,* 643–685.

28. Wright, J. P., Tibbetts, S. G., & Daigle, L. (2008). *Criminals in the making: Criminality across the life course.* Thousand Oaks, CA: SAGE, pp. 256–257.

29. Barnes, J. C. (2014). The impact of biosocial criminology on public policy: Where should we go from here? In M. DeLisi & K. M. Beaver (Eds.), *Criminological theory: A life-course approach* (2nd ed., pp. 83–98). Boston, MA: Jones & Bartlett, p. 93.

30. Wright, J. P., Tibbetts, S. G., & Daigle, L. (2008). *Criminals in the making: Criminality across the life course.* Thousand Oaks, CA: SAGE.

31. Wright, J. P. (2014). Prenatal insults and the development of persistent criminal behavior. In M. DeLisi & K. M. Beaver (Eds.), *Criminological theory: A life-course approach* (2nd ed., pp. 45–58). Boston, MA: Jones & Bartlett, p. 54.

32. Wright, J. P., Tibbetts, S. G., & Daigle, L. (2008). *Criminals in the making: Criminality across the life course.* Thousand Oaks, CA: SAGE.

33. Ibid.

CHAPTER 14

1. Goldstein, M., Protess, B., & Stevenson, A. (2016, May 19). Insider trading case links golfer, banker, and gambler. *New York Times.* Retrieved from http://www.nytimes.com/2016/05/20/business/dealbook/insider-trading-billy-walters-sports-gambler.html?_r=0

2. Fish, M. (February 6, 2015). A life on the line. *ESPN: The Magazine.* Retrieved from http://espn.go.com/espn/feature/story/_/id/12280555/how-billy-walters-became-sports-most-successful-controversial-bettor

3. Goldstein, M., Protess, B., & Stevenson, A. (2016, May 19). Insider trading case links golfer, banker, and gambler. *New York Times.* Retrieved from http://www.nytimes.com/2016/05/20/business/dealbook/insider-trading-billy-walters-sports-gambler.html?_r=0

4. Perez, A. J. (2016, May 19). Phil Mickelson to repay profits after being named in insider trading lawsuit. *USA Today.* Retrieved from http://www.usatoday.com/story/sports/golf/2016/05/19/phil-mickelson-insider-trading-sec-lawsuit/84584120/

5. Goldstein, M., Protess, B., & Stevenson, A. (2016, May 19). Insider trading case links golfer, banker, and gambler. *New York Times.* Retrieved from http://www.nytimes.com/2016/05/20/business/dealbook/insider-trading-billy-walters-sports-gambler.html?_r=0

6. Gerber, J. (2000). On the relationship between organized and white-collar crime: Government, business, and criminal enterprise in post-communist Russia. *European Journal of Crime, Criminal Law and Criminal Justice, 8,* 328.

7. For an excellent discussion of the origin, evolution, and recommendations regarding the definition of white-collar crime, see Geis, G. (2002). White-collar crime: What is

it? In D. Shichor, L. Gaines, & R. Ball (Eds.), *Readings in white-collar crime* (pp. 7–25). Prospect Heights, IL: Waveland Press.

8. Ibid., p. 8.

9. A full written version of E. Sutherland's 1939 presidential address at the American Sociological Association Conference in Philadelphia can be found in the 1940 *American Sociological Review, 5*, 1–12.

10. Ibid., p. 4.

11. For a comprehensive review of this research, see Geis, G. (2007). *White-collar and corporate crime.* Upper Saddle River, NJ: Pearson.

12. For a review of this research prior to Sutherland's address, see Schoepfer, A., & Tibbetts, S. (2012). From early white-collar bandits and robber barons to modern-day white-collar criminals: A review of the conceptual and theoretical research. In D. Shichor, L. Gaines, & A. Schoepfer (Eds.), *Reflecting on white-collar crime and corporate crime* (pp. 63–83). Long Grove, IL: Waveland Press.

13. Josephson, M. (1934). *The robber barons: The great American capitalists.* New York, NY: Harcourt Brace.

14. Anderson, G. W. (1905). *Consolidation of gas companies in Boston.* Boston, MA: Public Franchise League.

15. Sutherland, E. (1940). White-collar criminality. *American Sociological Review, 5*, 12.

16. Sutherland, E. (1945). Is "white-collar crime" crime? *American Sociological Review, 10*, 132–139.

17. Sutherland, E. (1949). *White-collar crime.* New York, NY: Dryden.

18. Ibid., p. 9.

19. For more discussion, see Geis, G. (2002). White-collar crime: What is it? In D. Shichor, L. Gaines, & R. Ball (Eds.), *Readings in white-collar crime* (pp. 7–25). Prospect Heights, IL: Waveland Press.

20. For example, see Gottfredson, M., & Hirschi, T. (1990). *A general theory of crime.* Stanford, CA: Stanford University Press, Chapter 9.

21. Sutherland, E. (1949). The white collar criminal. In V. C. Branham & S. B. Kutash (Eds.), *Encyclopedia of criminology* (pp. 511–515). New York, NY: Philosophical Library.

22. Ibid., p. 511; see further discussion about this entry and following discussion in Geis, G. (2002). White-collar crime: What is it? In D. Shichor, L. Gaines, & R. Ball (Eds.), *Readings in white-collar crime* (pp. 7–25). Prospect Heights, IL: Waveland Press.

23. For theoretical discussions and critiques, see Burgess, E. (1950). Comment & Concluding comment. *American Journal of Sociology, 56*, 32–34; Caldwell, R. G. (1958). A re-examination of the concept of white-collar crime. *Federal Probation, 22*, 30–36; Geis, G. (1962). Toward a delineation of white-collar offenses. *Sociological Inquiry, 32*, 160–171; Newman, D. (1958). White-collar crime: An overview and analysis. *Law and Contemporary Problems, 23*, 737–748; Quinney, R. (1964). The study of white collar crime: Toward a reorientation in theory and research. *Journal of Criminology, Criminal Law, and Police Science, 55*, 208–214; Tappan, P. W. (1947). Who is

the criminal? *American Sociological Review, 12*, 96–102; for empirical studies, see Clinard, M. (1952). *The black market: A study of white collar crime.* New York, NY: Rinehart; Cressey, D. (1953). *Other people's money: A study in the social psychology of embezzlement.* Glencoe, IL: Free Press; Hartung, F. (1950). White-collar offenses in the wholesale meat industry in Detroit. *American Journal of Sociology, 56*, 25–44.

24. Caldwell, R. G. (1958). A re-examination of the concept of white-collar crime. *Federal Probation, 22*, 30–36; Tappan, P. W. (1947). Who is the criminal? *American Sociological Review, 12*, 96–102.

25. Sutherland, E. (1945). Is "white-collar crime" crime? *American Sociological Review, 10*, 132–139; see discussion in Geis, G. (2002). White-collar crime: What is it? In D. Shichor, L. Gaines, & R. Ball (Eds.), *Readings in white-collar crime* (pp. 7–25). Prospect Heights, IL: Waveland Press.

26. Cressey, D. (1953). *Other people's money: A study in the social psychology of embezzlement.* Glencoe, IL: Free Press.

27. Hartung, F. (1950). White-collar offenses in the wholesale meat industry in Detroit. *American Journal of Sociology, 56*, 25–44.

28. Edelhertz, H. (1970). *The nature, impact and prosecution of white-collar crime.* Washington, DC: Law Enforcement Assistance Administration.

29. For the purposes of this chapter, these terms will all be considered relatively synonymous, considering that we are providing only a cursory review of the topic.

30. Smith, D. (1981). White-collar crime, organized crime, and the business establishment: Resolving a crisis in criminological theory. In P. Wickman & T. Dailey (Eds.), *White-collar and economic crime: Multidisciplinary and cross-national perspectives* (pp. 23–38). Lexington, MA: Lexington Books; Sparks, R. (1979). Crime as business and the female offender. In F. Adler & R. J. Simon (Eds.), *The criminology of deviant women* (pp. 171–179). Boston, MA: Houghton Mifflin.

31. Clinard, M. B., & Quinney, R. (1973). *Criminal behavior systems: A typology* (2nd ed.). New York, NY: Holt, Rinehart & Winston.

32. This section is from Schoepfer, A., & Schram, P. J. (forthcoming). "Controlling white-collar and corporate crime." In N. L. Piquero (Ed.), *Handbook in criminology and criminal justice.* Hoboken, NJ: Wiley-Blackwell.

33. Altman, A. (2009). A brief history of: Ponzi schemes." *Time, 173*, p. 18.

34. Zuckloff, M. (2005). *Ponzi's scheme: The true story of a financial legend.* New York, NY: Random House.

35. Robb, G. (2012). Before Madoff and Ponzi: 19th century business frauds. *Phi Kappa Phi Forum, 92*, 7–9.

36. Chernow, R. (2009). Madoff and his models. *New Yorker, 85*, 28–33.

37. Newman, D. (1958). White-collar crime: An overview and analysis. *Law and Contemporary Problems, 23*, 737; for further discussion, see Geis, G. (2002). White-collar crime: What is it? In D. Shichor, L. Gaines, &

R. Ball (Eds.), *Readings in white-collar crime* (pp. 7–25). Prospect Heights, IL: Waveland Press.

38. Shapiro, S. (1990). Collaring the crime, not the criminal: Liberating the concept of white-collar crime. *American Sociological Review, 55*, 346–367.

39. Gottfredson, M., & Hirschi, T. (1990). *A general theory of crime*. Stanford, CA: Stanford University Press. See also Hirschi, T., & Gottfredson, M. (1987). Causes of white-collar crime. *Criminology, 25*, 957–972.

40. Braithwaite, J. (1985). White collar crime. In R. H. Turner & J. F. Short (Eds.), *Annual review of sociology* (pp. 1–25). Palo Alto, CA: Annual Reviews.

41. See conclusion of Geis, G. (2002). White-collar crime: What is it? In D. Shichor, L. Gaines, & R. Ball (Eds.), *Readings in white-collar crime* (pp. 7–25). Prospect Heights, IL: Waveland Press.

42. Coleman, J. W. (1998). *The criminal elite: Understanding white-collar crime* (4th ed.). New York, NY: St. Martin's Press.

43. Sutherland, E. (1945). Is "white-collar crime" crime? *American Sociological Review, 10*, 132–139.

44. Clinard, M., & Yeager, P. (1980). *Corporate crime*. New York, NY: Macmillan.

45. Donahue, J. (1992). The missing rap sheet: Government records on corporate abuses. *Multinational Monitor, 14*, 37–51.

46. Much of our discussion on the impact of corporate crime is drawn from Chapter 7 in Kappeler, V. E., & Potter, G. (2005). *The mythology of crime and criminal justice* (4th ed.). Long Grove, IL: Waveland; quote from pp. 148–149.

47. Reiman, J. (2004). *The rich get richer and the poor get prison* (7th ed.). Boston: Allyn & Bacon; quote from p. 61.

48. Keller, B. (2002). Enron for dummies. *New York Times*. Retrieved from http://www.nytimes.com/2002/01/26/opinion/enron-for-dummies.html?pagewanted=all&src=pm

49. Enron scandal at-a-glance. (2002). *BBC News*. Retrieved from http://news.bbc.co.uk/2/hi/business/1780075.stm

50. Keller, B. (2002). Enron for dummies. *New York Times*. Retrieved from http://www.nytimes.com/2002/01/26/opinion/enron-for-dummies.html?pagewanted=all&src=pm

51. Ibid., para. 10.

52. Associated Press. (2011). Enron's victims: Still angry, but coping. *Omaha.com*. Retrieved from http://www.omaha.com/article/20111203/MONEY/712039931

53. Federal Bureau of Investigation. (2003). *Crime in the United States, 2002* (Uniform Crime Reports). Washington, DC: U.S. Department of Justice.

54. U.S. Congress, House of Representatives, Committee on Ways and Means. (1989). *Budget implications and current tax rules relating to troubled savings and loan institutions: Hearings before the Committee on Ways and Means, House of Representatives, 101st Congress, first session, February 22, March 9 and 15, 1989*. Washington, DC: Government Printing Office.

55. Eitzen, D. S., & Zinn, M. (2004). *Social problems* (9th ed.). Boston: Allyn & Bacon; Kappeler, V. E., & Potter, G.

(2005). *The mythology of crime and criminal justice* (4th ed.). Long Grove, IL: Waveland.

56. Kappeler, V. E., & Potter, G. (2005). *The mythology of crime and criminal justice* (4th ed.). Long Grove, IL: Waveland, p. 148.

57. Barkan, S. (2001). *Criminology: A sociological understanding* (2nd ed.). Upper Saddle River, NJ: Prentice Hall, as cited and discussed in Kappeler, V. E., & Potter, G. (2005). *The mythology of crime and criminal justice* (4th ed.). Long Grove, IL: Waveland.

58. Bureau of Labor Statistics. (2003). *Number and rates of fatal occupational injuries for select occupations, 2002*. Washington, DC: U.S. Government Printing Office.

59. Federal Bureau of Investigation. (2003). *Crime in the United States, 2002* (Uniform Crime Reports). Washington, DC: U.S. Department of Justice.

60. See discussion of corporate crime over recent years in Kappeler, V. E., & Potter, G. (2005). *The mythology of crime and criminal justice* (4th ed.). Long Grove, IL: Waveland, pp. 151–157.

61. Kappeler, V. E., & Potter, G. (2005). *The mythology of crime and criminal justice* (4th ed.). Long Grove, IL: Waveland, p. 148.

62. Clinard, M., & Yeager, P. (1980). *Corporate crime*. New York, NY: Macmillan; Mills, C. W. (1952). A diagnosis of moral uneasiness. In I. Horowitz (Ed.), *Power, politics and people* (pp. 330–339). New York, NY: Ballantine.

63. Clinard, M., & Yeager, P. (1980). *Corporate crime*. New York, NY: Macmillan, p. 21.

64. Kappeler, V. E., & Potter, G. (2005). *The mythology of crime and criminal justice* (4th ed.). Long Grove, IL: Waveland, pp. 164–169.

65. Some of this discussion is taken from "Environmental Protection Agency," *Wikipedia: The Free Encyclopedia*, retrieved from http://en.wikipedia.org/wiki/United_States_Environmental_Protection_Agency

66. Rosoff, S., Pontell, H., & Tillman, R. (2004). *Profit without honor: White-collar crime and the looting of America* (3rd ed.). Upper Saddle River, NJ: Prentice Hall.

67. Simon, D. (2002). *Elite deviance* (7th ed.). Boston: Allyn & Bacon.

68. See discussion in Kappeler, V. E., & Potter, G. (2005). *The mythology of crime and criminal justice* (4th ed.). Long Grove, IL: Waveland. See also Hagan, F. (2005). *Introduction to criminology* (5th ed.). Belmont, CA: Wadsworth.

69. Kappeler, V. E., & Potter, G. (2005). *The mythology of crime and criminal justice* (4th ed.). Long Grove, IL: Waveland.

70. Barstow, D. (2003, December 22). When workers die: U.S. rarely seeks charges for deaths in the workplace. *New York Times*. Retrieved from http://www.nytimes.com/2003/12/22/us/us-rarely-seeks-charges-for-deaths-in-workplace.html?pagewanted=all&src=pm

71. Kappeler, V. E., & Potter, G. (2005). *The mythology of crime and criminal justice* (4th ed.). Long Grove, IL: Waveland.

72. Barstow, D. (2003, December 22). When workers die: U.S. rarely seeks charges for deaths in the workplace.

New York Times. Retrieved from http://www.nytimes .com/2003/12/22/us/us-rarely-seeks-charges-for-deaths-in-workplace.html?pagewanted=all&src=pm

73. Van Dijk, J. (2008). *The world of crime.* Thousand Oaks, CA: SAGE, pp. 182–183.

74. For more information regarding this survey, see Van Dijk, J. (2008). *The world of crime.* Thousand Oaks, CA: SAGE, pp. 187–189.

75. Ibid.

76. Ibid., p. 188.

77. United Nations Office on Drugs and Crime. (2005). *Corruption: Compendium of international legal instruments on corruption* (2nd ed.). Vienna, Austria: Author.

78. Schoepfer, A., & Tibbetts, S. G. (2012). From early white-collar bandits and robber barons to modern-day white-collar criminals: A review of the conceptual and theoretical research. In D. Shichor, L. Gaines, & A. Schoepfer (Eds.), *Reflecting on white-collar and corporate crime: Discerning readings* (pp. 63–83). Long Grove, IL: Waveland.

79. See ibid., discussion of Piquero, N., Tibbetts, S., & Blankenship, M. (2005). Examining the role of differential association and techniques of neutralization in explaining corporate crime. *Deviant Behavior, 26,* 159–188.

80. Paternoster, R., & Tibbetts, S. G. (Forthcoming). White-collar crime and perceptual deterrence. In N. Shover (Ed.), *The Oxford handbook on white-collar crime.* Oxford, UK: Oxford University Press.

81. Akers, R. L. (1985). *Deviant behavior: A social learning approach* (3rd ed.). Belmont, CA: Wadsworth; Sutherland, E. H. (1939). *Principles of criminology* (3rd ed.). Philadelphia, PA: Lippincott.

82. Piquero, N. L., Tibbetts, S. G., & Blankenship, M. B. (2005). Examining the role of differential association and techniques of neutralization in explaining corporate crime. *Deviant Behavior, 26,* 159–188.

83. Shover, N., & Hochstetler, A. (2002). Cultural explanation and organizational crime. *Crime, Law and Social Change, 37,* 1–18; for a recent review of these studies, see Schoepfer, A., & Tibbetts, S. G. (2012). *From early white-collar bandits and robber barons to modern-day white-collar criminals: A review of the conceptual and theoretical research.* In D. Shichor, L. Gaines, & A. Schoepfer (Eds.), *Reflecting on white-collar and corporate crime: Discerning readings* (pp. 63–83). Long Grove, IL: Waveland.

84. Piquero, N. L., Tibbetts, S. G., & Blankenship, M. B. (2005). Examining the role of differential association and techniques of neutralization in explaining corporate crime. *Deviant Behavior, 26,* 159–188.

85. Schoepfer, A., & Tibbetts, S. G. (2012). From early white-collar bandits and robber barons to modern-day white-collar criminals: A review of the conceptual and theoretical research. In D. Shichor, L. Gaines, & A. Schoepfer (Eds.), *Reflecting on white-collar and corporate crime: Discerning readings* (pp. 63–83). Long Grove, IL: Waveland, pp. 72–73.

86. Ibid., p. 71.

87. Ibid., p. 79.

88. President's Commission on Organized Crime. (1986). *Report to the president and the attorney general. The impact: Organized crime today.* Washington, DC: U.S. Government Printing Office, p. 25.

89. Maltz, M. D. (1995). On defining "organized crime": The development of a definition and a typology. In N. Passas (Ed.), *Organized crime.* Brookfield, VT: Dartmouth, pp. 19–21.

90. Abadinsky, H. (2013). *Organized crime* (10th ed.). Belmont, CA: Cengage Learning, pp. 1–4.

91. Browning, F., & Gerassi, J. (1980). *The American way of crime.* New York, NY: G. P. Putnam, as cited in Kenney, D. J., & Finckenauer, J. O. (1995). *Organized crime in America.* Belmont, CA: Wadsworth, p. 52.

92. Kenney, D. J., & Finckenauer, J. O. (1995). *Organized crime in America.* Belmont, CA: Wadsworth, p. 69.

93. Ibid., p. 72.

94. Ryan, P. J. (1995). *Organized crime.* Santa Barbara, CA: ABC-CLIO, p. 95.

95. Lyman, M. D., & Potter, G. W. (2000). *Organized crime* (2nd ed.). Upper Saddle River, NJ: Prentice Hall, pp. 100–101; see also Kelly, R. J. (1999). United States. *Trends in Organized Crime, 5,* 85–114.

96. Hall, W. (2010). What are the policy lessons of National Alcohol Prohibition in the United States, 1920–1933? *Addiction, 105,* 1164.

97. Lyman, M. D., & Potter, G. W. (2000). *Organized crime* (2nd ed.). Upper Saddle River, NJ: Prentice Hall, pp. 108–111.

98. Reppetto, T. (2004). *American Mafia: A history of its rise to power.* New York, NY: Henry Holt.

99. Abadinsky, H. (2000). *Organized crime* (6th ed.). Belmont, CA: Wadsworth/Thompson, pp. 297–298.

100. Ryan, P. J. (1995). *Organized crime.* Santa Barbara, CA: ABC-CLIO, p. 98.

101. Abadinsky, H. (2000). *Organized crime* (6th ed.). Belmont, CA: Wadsworth/Thompson, pp. 298–299.

102. President's Commission on Organized Crime. (1986). *Report to the president and the attorney general. The impact: Organized crime today.* Washington, DC: U.S. Government Printing Office, p. 33.

103. Ibid., p. 34.

104. Zambo, S. (2007). Digital *La Cosa Nostra:* The Computer Fraud and Abuse Act's failure to punish and deter organized crime. *New England Journal on Criminal and Civil Confinement, 33*(2), 551.

105. Roth, M. P. (2010). *Organized crime.* Upper Saddle River, NJ: Prentice Hall, pp. 570–586.

106. Ryan, P. J. (1995). *Organized crime.* Santa Barbara, CA: ABC-CLIO, p. 33.

107. Albini, J. (1971). *Mafia: Genesis of a legend.* New York, NY: Appleton-Century-Crofts, p. 83.

108. Ryan, P. J. (1995). *Organized crime.* Santa Barbara, CA: ABC-CLIO, p. 35.

109. Hess, H. (1973). *Mafia and Mafioso: The structure of power.* Lexington, MA: D. C. Heath.

110. Ryan, P. J. (1995). *Organized crime.* Santa Barbara, CA: ABC-CLIO, p. 95.

111. Ibid., p. 37.

112. Lyman, M. D., & Potter, G. W. (2000). *Organized crime* (2nd ed.). Upper Saddle River, NJ: Prentice Hall, pp. 12–13.

113. Ibid., p. 264.

114. President's Commission on Organized Crime. (1986). *Report to the president and the attorney general. The impact: Organized crime today.* Washington, DC: U.S. Government Printing Office, p. 58.

115. Ibid., p. 61.

116. Ibid., p. 60.

117. Kenney, D. J., & Finckenauer, J. O. (1995). *Organized crime in America.* Belmont, CA: Wadsworth, p. 293.

118. Lyman, M. D., & Potter, G. W. (2000). *Organized crime* (2nd ed.). Upper Saddle River, NJ: Prentice Hall, p. 264.

119. Skarbek, D. (2014). *The social order of the underworld: How prison gangs govern the American penal system.* Oxford, UK: Oxford University Press.

120. Roth, M. P. (2010). *Organized crime.* Upper Saddle River, NJ: Prentice Hall, p. 287.

121. President's Commission on Organized Crime. (1986). *Report to the president and the attorney general. The impact: Organized crime today.* Washington, DC: U.S. Government Printing Office, p. 74.

122. Jackson, R. K., & McBride, W. D. (2000). *Understanding street gangs.* Incline Village, NV: Copperhouse.

123. Kenney, D. J., & Finckenauer, J. O. (1995). *Organized crime in America.* Belmont, CA: Wadsworth, pp. 303–304.

124. Maltz, M. (1985). Towards defining organized crime. In H. Alexander & G. Caiden (Eds.), *The politics and economics of organized crime.* Lexington, MA: D. C. Heath.

125. Kenney, D. J., & Finckenauer, J. O. (1995). *Organized crime in America.* Belmont, CA: Wadsworth, pp. 286–289.

126. Russo, G. (2006). *Supermob: How Sidney Korshak and his criminal associates became America's hidden power brokers.* New York, NY: Bloomsbury, as cited in Roth, M. P. (2010). *Organized crime.* Upper Saddle River, NJ: Prentice Hall, p. 27.

127. Van Dijk, J. (2008). *The world of crime.* Thousand Oaks, CA: SAGE, p. 146.

128. Ibid., pp. 154–157.

129. Ibid., pp. 159–161.

130. Lyman, M. D., & Potter, G. W. (2000). *Organized crime* (2nd ed.). Upper Saddle River, NJ: Prentice Hall, p. 14.

131. Kefauver, E. (1951). *Special committee to investigate organized crime in interstate commerce: Third interim report.* Washington, DC: U.S. Government Printing Office, p. 20.

132. Abadinsky, H. (2000). *Organized crime* (6th ed.). Belmont, CA: Wadsworth/Thompson, p. 441.

133. Lyman, M. D., & Potter, G. W. (2000). *Organized crime* (2nd ed.). Upper Saddle River, NJ: Prentice Hall, p. 27.

134. Bell, D. (1953). Crime as an American way of life. *Antioch Reviews, 13,* 139.

135. Kelly, R. J. (2000). *Encyclopedia of organized crime in the United States: From Capone's Chicago to the new urban underworld.* Westport, CN: Greenwood Press, p. 215.

136. Abadinsky, H. (2000). *Organized crime* (6th ed.). Belmont, CA: Wadsworth/Thompson, p. 444.

137. Lyman, M. D., & Potter, G. W. (2000). *Organized crime* (2nd ed.). Upper Saddle River, NJ: Prentice Hall, pp. 14–15.

138. Task Force on Organized Crime. (1967). *Task force report: Organized crime.* Washington, DC: U.S. Government Printing Office, p. 6.

139. Roth, M. P. (2010). *Organized crime.* Upper Saddle River, NJ: Prentice Hall, p. 31.

140. Abadinsky, H. (2000). *Organized crime* (6th ed.). Belmont, CA: Wadsworth/Thompson, pp. 444–445.

141. Roth, M. P. (2010). *Organized crime.* Upper Saddle River, NJ: Prentice Hall, p. 522.

142. Abadinsky, H. (2000). *Organized crime* (6th ed.). Belmont, CA: Wadsworth/Thompson, pp. 445–448.

143. Lyman, M. D., & Potter, G. W. (2000). *Organized crime* (2nd ed.). Upper Saddle River, NJ: Prentice Hall, pp. 39–43.

144. Kenney, D. J., & Finckenauer, J. O. (1995). *Organized crime in America.* Belmont, CA: Wadsworth, p. 29; see also Reuter, P. (1987). Methodological problems of organized crime research. In H. Edelhertz (Ed.), *Major issues in organized crime control: Symposium proceedings.* Washington, DC: National Institute of Justice; Walsh, M. (1983). *An overview of organized crime.* Washington, DC: National Institute of Justice.

145. Kenney, D. J., & Finckenauer, J. O. (1995). *Organized crime in America.* Belmont, CA: Wadsworth, p. 39; see also Bell, D. (1953). Crime as an American way of life. In M. E. Wolfgang, L. Savitz, & N. Johnston (Eds.), *The sociology of crime and delinquency* (pp. 213–225). New York, NY: Wiley; Ianni, F. (1972). *A family business.* New York, NY: Russell Sage; Ianni, F. (1974). *Black Mafia: Ethnic succession in organized crime.* New York, NY: Simon & Schuster.

146. Kenney, D. J., & Finckenauer, J. O. (1995). *Organized crime in America.* Belmont, CA: Wadsworth, p. 41; see also Fox, S. (1989). *Blood and power: Organized crime in 20th century America.* New York, NY: William Morrow; Smith, D. (1980). Paragons, pariahs, and pirates: A spectrum-based theory of enterprise. *Crime and Delinquency, 26,* 358–386.

147. Reuter, P. (1987). Methodological problems of organized crime research. In H. Edelhertz (Ed.), *Major issues in organized crime control: Symposium proceedings.* Washington, DC: National Institute of Justice, as cited in Kenney, D. J., & Finckenauer, J. O. (1995). *Organized crime in America.* Belmont, CA: Wadsworth.

148. Kenney, D. J., & Finckenauer, J. O. (1995). *Organized crime in America.* Belmont, CA: Wadsworth, p. 51.

149. U.S. Department of Justice. (2001). Online identity thief sentenced in Virginia to 14 years in prison for selling counterfeit credit cards leading to more than $3 million in losses [Press release]. Retrieved from http://www.justice.gov/opa/pr/2011/September/11 -crm-1163.html

150. Britz, M. T. (2004). *Computer forensics and cyber crime: An introduction.* Upper Saddle River, NJ: Pearson Prentice Hall, p. 4.

151. Moore, R. (2005). *Cybercrime: Investigating high-technology computer crime.* Cincinnati, OH: Anderson, p. 2.

152. Ibid., p. 5.

153. Moitra, S. D. (2005). Developing policies for cybercrime: Some empirical issues. *European Journal of Crime, Criminal Law and Criminal Justice, 13,* 438.

154. Ibid., pp. 445–446.

155. Mehan, J. E. (2014). *CyberWar, CyberTerror, CyberCrime and CyberActivism.* Ely, Cambridgeshire, UK: IT Governance Publishing, p. 26.

156. Wark, M. (2010). Hackers. In G. E. Higgins, *Cybercrime: An introduction to an emerging phenomenon.* Boston, MA: McGraw-Hill, p. 129.

157. Moore, R. (2005). *Cybercrime: Investigating high-technology computer crime.* Cincinnati, OH: Anderson, pp. 18–19.

158. Meyer, G. R. (1989). *The social organization of the computer underground.* Master's thesis, Northern Illinois University, as cited by Wade, C., Aldridge, J., Hopper, L., Drummond, H., Hopper, R., & Andrew, K. (2011). Hacking into the hacker: Separating fact from fiction. In T. J. Holt (Ed.), *Crime on-line: Correlates, causes, and context.* Durham, NC: Carolina Academic Press.

159. Ibid., 24–26.

160. See also Wall, D. S. (2008). Cybercrime, media and insecurity: The shaping of public perceptions of cybercrime. *International Review of Law Computers & Technology, 22,* 45–63.

161. Gaines, L. K., & Kappeler, V. E. (2012). *Homeland security.* Boston, MA: Prentice Hall, pp. 319–320.

162. Moore, R. (2005). *Cybercrime: Investigating high-technology computer crime.* Cincinnati, OH: Anderson, pp. 57–58.

163. Ibid., pp. 62–66.

164. Osanka, F., & Johann, S. L. (1989). *Sourcebook on pornography.* Lexington, MA: Lexington Books.

165. Wolak, J., Finkelhor, D., & Mitchell, K. J. (2012). *Trends in arrests for child pornography possession: The third National Juvenile Online Victimization Study.* Durham, NH: Crime Against Children Research Center.

166. Beech, R. B., Elliott, I. A., Birgden, A., & Findlater, D. (2008). The Internet and child sexual offending: A criminological review. *Aggression and Violent Behavior, 13,* 216–228.

167. Moore, R. (2005). *Cybercrime: Investigating high-technology computer crime.* Cincinnati, OH: Anderson, pp. 79–80.

168. Caeti, T. J. (2009). *Sex crimes, Part 1: Child pornography.* Law Enforcement Training Network, p. 8.

169. Ibid., p. 5.

170. Clough, J. (2015). *Principles of cybercrime* (2nd ed.). Cambridge, UK: Cambridge University Press.

171. Lieberman, J. (2001). Name your own price . . . for hookers?!? Ebay and Priceline.com muscle in on the world's oldest business model. *PCTyrant.com,* as cited in Moore, R. (2005). *Cybercrime: Investigating*

high-technology computer crime. Cincinnati, OH: Anderson, pp. 93–94.

172. Moore, R. (2005). *Cybercrime: Investigating high-technology computer crime.* Cincinnati, OH: Anderson, p. 92.

173. Clough, J. (2015). *Principles of cybercrime* (2nd ed.). Cambridge, UK: Cambridge University Press, pp. 214–216.

174. Ibid., p. 96.

175. Ibid., pp. 105–109.

176. Ibid., pp. 113–114.

177. Casey, E. (2004). *Digital evidence and computer crime: Forensic science, computers and the Internet* (2nd ed.). London, UK: Elsevier, p. 601.

178. Florida Statute § 784.048.

179. Baughman, L. L. (2007). Friend request or foe? Confirming the misuse of Internet and social networking sites by domestic violence perpetrators. *Widener Law Journal, 19,* 941.

180. Casey, E. (2004). *Digital evidence and computer crime: Forensic science, computers and the Internet* (2nd ed.). London, UK: Elsevier, p. 611.

181. Baughman, L. L. (2007). Friend request or foe? Confirming the misuse of Internet and social networking sites by domestic violence perpetrators. *Widener Law Journal, 19,* 942.

182. Casey, E. (2004). *Digital evidence and computer crime: Forensic science, computers and the Internet* (2nd ed.). London, UK: Elsevier, p. 611.

183. Taylor, R. W., Caeti, T. J., Loper, D. K., Fritsch, E. J., & Liederbach, J. (2006). *Digital crime and digital terrorism.* Upper Saddle River, NJ: Pearson Prentice Hall, p. 280.

184. Moore, R. (2005). *Cybercrime: Investigating high-technology computer crime.* Cincinnati, OH: Anderson, p. 134.

185. Ibid., p. 135.

186. Britz, M. T. (2004). *Computer forensics and cyber crime: An introduction.* Upper Saddle River, NJ: Pearson Prentice Hall, p. 177.

187. Casey, E. (2004). *Digital evidence and computer crime: Forensic science, computers and the Internet* (2nd ed.). London, UK: Elsevier, pp. 213–214.

188. Holt, T. J., Burruss, G. W., & Bossler, A. M. (2015). *Policing cybercrime and cyberterror.* Durham, NC: Carolina Academic Press, pp. 115–123.

189. Britz, M. T. (2004). *Computer forensics and cyber crime: An introduction.* Upper Saddle River, NJ: Pearson Prentice Hall, p. 83.

190. Casey, E. (2004). *Digital evidence and computer crime: Forensic science, computers and the Internet* (2nd ed.). London, UK: Elsevier, pp. 62–65.

191. Moore, R. (2005). *Cybercrime: Investigating high-technology computer crime.* Cincinnati, OH: Anderson, p. 118.

192. Piquero, N. L. (2010). Intellectual property theft. In G. E. Higgins (Ed.), *Cybercrime: An introduction to an emerging phenomenon.* Boston, MA: McGraw-Hill, p. 93.

193. Gillen, M., & Garrity, B. (2000). Industry's anti-piracy efforts: "Doomed to fail" says Forester. *Billboard, 112,* 9–11.

194. Casey, E. (2004). *Digital evidence and computer crime: Forensic science, computers and the Internet* (2nd ed.). London, UK: Elsevier, p. 60.

195. Ibid., p. 47.

196. Taylor, R. W., Caeti, T. J., Loper, D. K., Fritsch, E. J., & Liederbach, J. (2006). *Digital crime and digital terrorism*. Upper Saddle River, NJ: Pearson Prentice Hall, p. 188.

197. Britz, M. T. (2004). *Computer forensics and cyber crime: An introduction*. Upper Saddle River, NJ: Pearson Prentice Hall, p. 87.

198. Moore, R. (2005). *Cybercrime: Investigating high-technology computer crime*. Cincinnati, OH: Anderson, p. 145.

199. Boyd, A. (2015, April 1). Obama signs order authorizing sanctions against cyber criminals. *Federal Times*. Retrieved from http://www.federaltimes.com/story/government/cybersecurity/2015/04/01/obama-executive-order-sanctions-cyber-criminals/70770684/

200. Office of the Press Secretary. (2015, April 1). Executive Order Blocking the Property of Certain Persons Engaging in Significant Malicious Cyber-Enabled Activities (Fact Sheet), para. 4. Retrieved from https://www.whitehouse.gov/the-press-office/2015/04/01/fact-sheet-executive-order-blocking-property-certain-persons-engaging-si

201. Taylor, R. W., Caeti, T. J., Loper, D. K., Fritsch, E. J., & Liederbach, J. (2006). *Digital crime and digital terrorism*. Upper Saddle River, NJ: Pearson Prentice Hall.

202. Ibid., p. 38.

203. Ibid., pp. 58–59.

204. Ibid., pp. 45–46.

CHAPTER 15

1. Corasaniti, N., Pérez-Peña, R., & Alvarez, L. (2015, June 19). Church massacre suspect held as Charleston grieves. *New York Times*. Retrieved from http://mobile.nytimes.com/2015/06/19/us/charleston-church-shooting.html

2. McLaughlin, M. (2015, June 20). Racist manifesto purportedly written by Dylann Roof surfaces online. *HuffPost Crime*. Retrieved from http://www.huffingtonpost.com/2015/06/20/dylann-roof-manifesto-charleston-shooting_n_7627788.html.

3. Deloughery, K., King, R. D., & Asal, V. (2012). Close cousins or distant relatives? The relationship between terrorism and hate crime. *Crime & Delinquency, 58*, 664. See also Green, D. P., McFalls, L. H., & Smith, J. K. (2001). Hate crime: An emergent research agenda. *Annual Review of Sociology, 27*, 479–504; Herek, G. M., Cogan, J. C., & Gillis, J. R. (2002). Victim experiences in hate crimes based on sexual orientation. *Journal of Social Issues, 58*, 319–339.

4. Green, D. P., McFalls, L. H., & Smith, J. K. (2001). Hate crime: An emergent research agenda. *Annual Review of Sociology, 27*, 483.

5. Ibid., p. 665; see also Black, D. (2004). Terrorism as social control. *Sociology of Crime, Law and Deviance, 5*, 9–18; Messner, S. F., McHugh, S., & Felson, R. B. (2004). The distinctive characteristics of assaults motivated by bias. *Criminology, 42*, 585–618.

6. Stack, L. (February 15, 2016). American Muslims under attach. *The New York Times*. Retrieved from: http://www.nytimes.com/interactive/2015/12/22/us/Crimes-Against-Muslim-Americans.html?_r=0.

7. Federal Bureau of Investigation. (n.d.). *Hate crime: Overview*. Washington, DC: U.S. Department of Justice. Retrieved from http://www.fbi.gov/about-us/investigate/civilrights/hate_crimes/overview.

8. Federal Bureau of Investigations. (2015). *Criminal Justice Information Services (CJIS) Division: Uniform Crime Reporting (UCR) Program. Hate Crime Data Collection Guidelines and Training Manual*. Washington, D.C.: U.S. Department of Justice.

9. Ibid., pp. 12-13.

10. Ibid., p. 10.

11. Potok, M. (2016). The year in hate and extremism. *Intelligence Report*. Washington, D.C.: Southern Poverty Law Center.

12. Ibid., p. 36.

13. Chan, J., Ghose, An., & Seamans, R. (2016). The internet and racial hate crime: Offline spillovers from online access. *MIS Quarterly, 40*, 381-404.

14. Federal Bureau of Investigation. (1999). *Hate crime data collection guidelines*. Washington, DC: U.S. Department of Justice, p. 1.

15. Ibid., p. 37.

16. Ibid., p. 1; see also U.S. Department of Justice. (1994). *Violence Crime Control and Law Enforcement Act of 1994: Fact sheet*. Washington, DC: U.S. Department of Justice.

17. Hate Crime Sentencing Enhancement Act 28 U.S.C. 994.

18. National Church Arson Task Force. (n.d.). *Interim report to the president*. Retrieved from http://www.justice.gov/crt/church_arson/00000008.pdf.

19. Title 18, U.S.C., Section 247. Retrieved from http://www.fbi.gov/about-us/investigate/civilrights/federal-statutes.

20. 105th Congress, S. 1493IS. Retrieved from http://thomas.loc.gov/cgi-bin/query/z?c105:2.1493.

21. Title 18, U.S.C., Section 249.

22. U.S. Department of Justice. (n.d.). *Matthew Shepard/James Byrd, Jr., Hate Crimes Prevention Act of 2009*. Washington, DC: Author. Retrieved from http://www.justice.gov/crt/about/crm/matthewshepard.php.

23. National Coalition for the Homeless. (2012). *Hate crimes and violence against people experiencing homelessness*. Washington, DC: National Coalition for the Homeless. Retrieved from http://www.nationalhomeless.org/factsheets/hatecrimes.html.

24. National Law Center on Homelessness & Poverty (NLCHP) and National Coalition for the Homeless (NCH). (n.d.). *Model state legislation: Hate crimes/violence against homeless people*. Retrieved from http:/www.nlchp.org/content/pubs/Model%20State%20Legislation.pdf.

25. Brooke, J. (1998). Gay man beaten and left for dead; 2 are charged. *New York Times*. Retrieved from http://www.nytimes.com/1998/10/10/us/gay-man-beaten-and-left-for-dead-2-are-charged.html?ref=matthewshepard.

26. Brooke, J. (1998). Gay man dies from attack, fanning outrage and debate. *New York Times*. Retrieved from http://www.nytimes.com/1998/10/10/us/gay-man-beaten-and-left-for-dead-2-are-charged.html?ref=matthewshepard.

27. Murdered for who he was [Editorial]. (1998, October 13). *New York Times*. Retrieved from http://www.nytimes.com/1998/10/13/opinion/murdered-for -who-he-was.html?ref=matthewshepard.

28. Byers, B. D., & Crider, B. W. (2002). Hate crimes against the Amish: A qualitative analysis of bias motivation using routine activities theory. *Deviant Behavior, 23*, 115–148.

29. Waldner, L. K., & Berg, J. (2008). Explaining antigay violence using target congruence: An application of revised routine activities theory. *Violence and Victims, 23*, 267–287.

30. Finkelhor, D., & Asdigian, N. L. (1996). Risk factors for youth victimization: Beyond a lifestyles/routine activities theory approach. *Violence and Victims, 11*, 3–19.

31. Ibid., p. 6.

32. Grattet, R. (2009). The urban ecology of bias crime: A study of disorganized and defended neighborhoods'. *Social Problems, 56*, pp. 132–150.

33. Benier, K., Wickes, R., & Higginson, A. (2016). Ethnic hate crime in Australia: Diversity and change in the neighbourhood context. *British Journal of Criminology, 56*, pp. 480-481.

34. Hipp, J. R., Tita, G. E., &Boggess, L. N. (2009). Intergroup and intragroup violence: Is violent crime an expression of group conflict or social disorganisation? *Criminology, 47*, pp. 521–564; Lyons, C. J. (2007). Community (dis)organization and racially motivated crime. *American Journal of Sociology, 113*, pp. 815–863.

35. See Craig, K. M., & Waldo, C. R. (1996). "So what's a hate crime anyway?" Young adults' perceptions of hate crimes, victims, and perpetrators. *Law and Human Behavior, 20*, 113–129; Dunbar, E., & Molina, A. (2004). Opposition to the legitimacy of hate crime laws: The role of argument acceptance, knowledge, individual differences, and peer influence. *Analysis of Social Issues and Public Policy, 4*, 91–113.

36. Plumm, K. M., Terrance, C. A., Henderson, V. R., & Ellingson, H. (2010). Victim blame in a hate crime motivated by sexual orientation. *Journal of Homosexuality, 57*, 267–286.

37. Ibid., p. 282.

38. Holmes, R. M., & Holmes, S. T. (2001). *Mass murder in the United States*. Upper Saddle River, NJ: Prentice Hall.

39. Ibid.

40. J. A. Fox, as cited in Why did they die? (2016, June 27). *Time* magazine, pp. 31–41.

41. Holmes, R. M., & Holmes, S. T. (2001). *Mass murder in the United States*. Upper Saddle River, NJ: Prentice Hall.

42. U.S. Secret Service & U.S. Department of Education. (2004). *The final report and findings of the Safe School Initiative: Implications for the prevention of School attacks in the United States*. Washington, DC: U.S. Secret Service. Retrieved from https://www2.ed.gov/admins/lead/safety/preventingattacksreport.pdf.

43. Branson, A. (2012). African-American serial killers: Overrepresented yet underacknowledged. *Howard Journal of Criminal Justice, 52*, 1–18.

44. Hickey, E. (2002). *Serial murderers and their victims*. Belmont, CA: Wadsworth/Thomas Learning.

45. Clark, K. J. (2015, July 21). Muslims, mass shootings, and the media. *Huffington Post*.

46. Federal Bureau of Investigation. (2005). *Terrorism 2002–2005*. Retrieved from https://www.fbi.gov/stats-services/publications/terrorism-2002-2005, as reported by Alnatour, O. (2015, December 9). Muslims are not terrorists: A factual look at terrorism and Islam. *Huffington Post*.

47. Ibid.

48. Baker, P., Cooper, H., & Mazzetti, M. (2011). Bin Laden is dead, Obama says. *New York Times*. Retrieved from http://www.nytimes.com/2011/05/02/world/asia/osama-bin-laden-is-killed.html?pagewanted=all.

49. CNN Wire Staff. (2011). *Transcript: Obama's speech announcing the death of Osama bin Laden*. Retrieved from http://www.cnn.com/2011/WORLD/asiapcf/05/02/obama.bin.laden.transcript/index.html?iref=allsearch.

50. Gaines, L. K., & Kappeler, V. E. (2012). *Homeland security*. Boston: Prentice Hall, p. 109.

51. Schmid, A. (2004). Terrorism: The definitional problem. *Case Western Reserve Journal of International Law, 36*, 376.

52. Hoffman, B. (2009). Defining terrorism: Means, ends, and motives. In R. D. Howard, R. L. Sawyer, & N. E. Bajema (Eds.), *Terrorism and counterterrorism: Understanding the new security environment* (3rd ed.). Boston: McGraw-Hill, p. 33.

53. White, J. R. (2012). *Terrorism and homeland security* (7th ed.). Belmont, CA: Wadsworth, p. 13; see also Borum, R. (2004). *Psychology of terrorism*. Tampa: University of South Florida; Schmid, A. P., & Jongman, A. J. (2005). *Political terrorism: A new guide to actors, authors, concepts, data bases, theories, and literature*. Somerset, NJ: Transaction Books.

54. Gaines, L. K., & Kappeler, V. E. (2012). *Homeland security*. Boston: Prentice Hall, p. 123.

55. U.S. Department of State. (n.d.). *Foreign terrorist organizations*. Washington, D.C.: U.S. Department of State, Bureau of Counterterrorism. Retrieved from: http://www.state.gov/j/ct/rls/other/des/123085.htm

56. Martin, G. (2013). *Understanding terrorism: Challenges, perspectives, and issues* (4th ed.). Thousand Oaks, CA: Sage, p. 40.

57. Federal Emergency Management Agency. (n.d.) *General info about terrorism: Are you ready?* Washington, D.C.: FEMA. Retrieved from: http://www.fema.gov/pdf/areyouready/terrorism.pdf.

58. U.S. Department of State. (n.d.). Legislative requirements and key terms. Washington, D.C.: U.S. Department of

State. Retrieved from: http://www.state.gov/documents/organization/65464.pdf.

59. Federal Bureau of Investigation. (2010). *What we investigate*. Washington, D.C.: U.S. Department of Justice. Retrieved from: https://www.fbi.gov/albuquerque/about-us/what-we-investigate.

60. Department of Defense. (2015) *DOD Dictionary of Military Terms*. Washington, D.C.: Department of Defense. Retrieved from: http://www.dtic.mil/doctrine/dod_dictionary/.

61. Gaines, L. K., & Kappeler, V. E. (2012). *Homeland security*. Boston: Prentice Hall, pp. 123–125.

62. U.S. Department of State. (2015). *Country reports on terrorism, 2015*. Retrieved from: http://www.state.gov/j/ct/list/c14151.htm.

63. Hoffman, B. (2006). *Inside terrorism*. New York: Columbia University Press.

64. Martin, G. (2013). *Understanding terrorism: Challenges, perspectives, and issues* (4th ed.). Thousand Oaks, CA: Sage, p. 40.

65. Institute for Economics and Peace. (2015). *Global Terrorism Index, 2015*. New York: IEP. Retrieved from: http://economicsandpeace.org/wp-content/uploads/2015/11/Global-Terrorism-Index-2015.pdf.

66. Gaines, L. K., & Kappeler, V. E. (2012). *Homeland security*. Boston: Prentice Hall, p. 113.

67. Pratt, A. N. (2011). Terrorism's evolution: Yesterday, today, and forever. In C. C. Harmon, A. N. Pratt, & S. Gorka (Eds.), *Toward a grand strategy against terrorism*. New York: McGraw-Hill, p. 8.

68. Burgess, M. (2003). *A brief history of terrorism*. Washington, DC: Center for Defense Information.

69. Ibid.

70. Halsall, P. (1997). Maximilien Robespierre: Justification of the use of terror. *Modern History Sourcebook*. Retrieved from http://www.fordham.edu/halsall/mod/robespierre-terror.asp.

71. Burgess, M. (2003). *A brief history of terrorism*. Washington, DC: Center for Defense Information.

72. Gaines, L. K., & Kappeler, V. E. (2012). *Homeland security*. Boston: Prentice Hall, p. 113.

73. Martin, G. (2011). *Terrorism and homeland security*. Thousand Oaks, CA: Sage, p. 30.

74. Gaines, L. K., & Kappeler, V. E. (2012). *Homeland security*. Boston: Prentice Hall, p. 113.

75. Burgess, M. (2003). *A brief history of terrorism*. Washington, DC: Center for Defense Information.

76. Ibid.

77. Hoffman, B. (2006). *Inside terrorism*. New York: Columbia University Press, p. 64.

78. Gaines, L. K., & Kappeler, V. E. (2012). *Homeland security*. Boston: Prentice Hall, p. 114.

79. Burgess, M. (2003). *A brief history of terrorism*. Washington, DC: Center for Defense Information.

80. Ibid.

81. Martin, G. (2011). *Terrorism and homeland security*. Thousand Oaks, CA: Sage, p. 41.

82. Agnew, R. (2010). A general strain theory of terrorism. *Theoretical Criminology, 14,* 131–153; Merton, R. K. (1938). Social structure and anomie. *American Sociological Review, 3,* 672–682.

83. Agnew, R. (2010). A general strain theory of terrorism. *Theoretical Criminology, 14,* 131–153.

84. Merton, R. K. (1938). Social structure and anomie. *American Sociological Review, 3,* 672–682.

85. Akers, R. L. (1985). *Deviant behavior: A social learning approach* (3rd ed.). Belmont, CA: Wadsworth; Sutherland, E. H. (1939). *Principles of criminology* (3rd ed.). Philadelphia, PA: Lippincott.

86. Silverman, A. L. (2002). *Exploratory analysis of interdisciplinary theory of terrorism*. Ph.D. dissertation. University of Florida.

87. Gupta, D. K. (2001). *Rule of law and terrorism*. Unpublished paper, San Diego State University, San Diego, CA.

88. Schmid, A. (2005). Links between terrorist and organized crime networks: Emerging patterns and trends. In D. Vlassis (Ed.), *Trafficking: Networks and logistics of transnational crime and international terrorism*. Proceedings of the International Conference on "Trafficking: Networks and Logistics of Transnational Crime and International Terrorism," Courmayeur Mont Blanc, Italy.

89. Van Dijk, J. (2008). *The world of crime: The silence on problems of security, justice and development across the world*. Thousand Oaks, CA: Sage, p. 282.

90. Ibid., p. 284.

91. White, J. R. (2012). *Terrorism and homeland security* (7th ed.). Belmont, CA: Wadsworth, p. 64.

92. Ibid., pp. 64–78.

93. Arquilla, J., Ronfeldt, D., & Zanini, M. (1999). Networks, netwar, and information-age terrorism. In I. O. Lesser et al. (Eds.), *Countering the new terrorism*. Santa Monica, CA: RAND, as cited in White, J. R. (2012). *Terrorism and homeland security* (7th ed.). Belmont, CA: Wadsworth.

94. Levitt, M., & Jacobson, J. (2008). The U.S. campaign to squeeze terrorists' financing. *Journal of International Affairs, 62,* 67–85.

95. Gaines, L. K., & Kappeler, V. E. (2012). *Homeland security*. Boston: Prentice Hall, pp. 301–302.

96. Kochan, N. (2005). *The washing machine*. New York: Thompson, p. 32, as cited in Olson, D. T. (2007). *Financing terror*. Washington, DC: U.S. Department of Justice.

97. Gaines, L. K., & Kappeler, V. E. (2012). *Homeland security*. Boston: Prentice Hall, pp. 301–304.

98. Roberge, I. (2007). Misguided policies in the war on terror? The case for disentangling terrorist financing from money laundering. *Politics, 27,* 196–203, as cited in Gaines, L. K., & Kappeler, V. E. (2012). *Homeland security*. Boston: Prentice Hall, p. 304.

99. Ehrenfeld, R. (2003). *Funding evil: How terrorism is financed and how to stop it*. Seattle: National Press, p. 123, as cited in Olson, D. T. (2007). *Financing terror*. Washington, DC: U.S. Department of Justice.

100. Olson, D. T. (2007). *Financing terror*. Washington, DC: U.S. Department of Justice.

101. Gaines, L. K., & Kappeler, V. E. (2012). *Homeland security*. Boston: Prentice Hall, pp. 301–312.

102. Kohlmann, E. (2006). *The role of Islamic charities in international terrorist recruitment and financing*. Copenhagen: Danish Institute for International Studies.

103. Federal Bureau of Investigation. (2008). *No cash for terror: Convictions returned in Holy Land case*. Washington, DC: U.S. Department of Justice. Retrieved from http://www.fbi.gov/news/stories/2008/november/hlf112508.

104. FATF. (2012). *International Standards on Combating Money Laundering and the Financing of Terrorism & Proliferation*. (updated October 2015). FATF: Paris, France. Retrieved from: www.fatf-gafi.org/recommendations.html

105. Cottle, S. (2006). Mediatizing the global war on terror. In A. P. Kavoori & T. Fraley (Eds.), *Media, terrorism, and theory: A reader*. Lanham, MD: Rowman & Littlefield.

106. Ross, J. I. (2007). Deconstructing the terrorism news media relationship. *Crime, Media, Culture, 3*, 215–225.

107. White, J. R. (2012). *Terrorism and homeland security* (7th ed.). Belmont, CA: Wadsworth, pp. 116–125.

108. See Anderson, B. C. (2005). *South Park conservatives: The revolt against liberal media bias*. Washington, DC: Regnery; Goldberg, B. (2003). *Bias: A CBS insider exposes how the media distort the news*. New York: Perennial Editions (HarperCollins); Slisli, F. (2000). The Western media and the Algerian crisis. *Race and Class, 41*, 43–57.

109. White, J. R. (2012). *Terrorism and homeland security* (7th ed.). Belmont, CA: Wadsworth, p. 104.

110. Federal Bureau of Investigations. (2013). *Definitions of terrorism in the U.S. Code*. Washington, D.C.: U.S. Department of Justice. Retrieved from: https://www.fbi.gov/about-us/investigate/terrorism/terrorism-definition

111. Federal Bureau of Investigation. (2009). *Domestic terrorism: In the post-9/11 era*. Washington, DC: U.S. Department of Justice, para. 3. Retrieved from http://www.fbi.gov/news/stories/2009/september/domterror_090709.

112. Martin, G. (2013). *Understanding terrorism: Challenges, perspectives, and issues* (4th ed.). Thousand Oaks, CA: Sage, p. 382.

113. Ibid., pp. 383–384.

114. Animal Liberation Front (ALF). (n.d.). *The ALF credo and guidelines*. Retrieved from http://www.animalliberationfront.com/ALFront/alf_credo.htm.

115. Martin, G. (2013). *Understanding terrorism: Challenges, perspectives, and issues* (4th ed.). Thousand Oaks, CA: Sage, p. 401.

116. Ibid., pp. 383–384.

117. Ibid., p. 409.

118. Ibid., p. 417.

119. Ibid., p. 418.

120. Army of God. (n.d.). Retrieved from http://www.armyofgod.com/.

121. Mueller, R.S. (June 23, 2006). Speech to the City Club of Cleveland. Washington, D.C.: Federal Bureau of Investigation. Retrieved from: https://www.fbi.gov/news/speeches/the-threat-of-homegrown-terrorism.

122. Bergen, P. (January 22, 2016). Can we stop homegrown terrorists? *The Wall Street Journal*. Retrieved: http://www.wsj.com/articles/can-we-stop-homegrown-terrorists-1453491850

123. Olsson, P.A. (2015). The making of a homegrown terrorist. *Psychiatric Times, 34*, pp. 1-2.

124. Forst, B. (2010). Memorandum: Afterword to the State Department's country reports on terrorism for 2010—Challenges, accomplishments, and prospects. In National Counterterrorism Center. (2010). *2009 report on terrorism*. Washington, DC: Author, n.p.

125. Ibid., n.p.

126. Cohen, L., & Felson, M. (1979). Social change and crime rate trends: A routine activity approach. *American Sociological Review, 44*, 588–608.

127. Shubik, M. (1975). *The uses and methods of gaming*. New York: Elsevier, p. 6.

128. Forst, B. (2010). Memorandum: Afterword to the State Department's country reports on terrorism for 2010—Challenges, accomplishments, and prospects. In National Counterterrorism Center. (2010). *2009 report on terrorism*. Washington, DC: Author, n.p.

129. Morris, P. (1994). *Introduction to game theory*. New York: Springer-Verlag, p. vii.

130. Forst, B. (2010). Memorandum: Afterword to the State Department's country reports on terrorism for 2010—Challenges, accomplishments, and prospects. In National Counterterrorism Center. (2010). *2009 report on terrorism*. Washington, DC: Author, n.p.

131. Martin, G. (2011). *Terrorism and homeland security*. Thousand Oaks, CA: Sage, p. 270.

132. Federal Bureau of Investigation. (2002). *Crime in the United States, 2001*. Washington, D.C.: U.S. Department of Justice, p. 306.

133. Clarke, R. (2008). *Your government failed you: Breaking the cycle of national security disasters*. New York: HarperCollins.

134. Ibid., p. 6.

135. Martin, G. (2011). *Terrorism and homeland security*. Thousand Oaks, CA: Sage, p. 267.

136. Bush, G. W. (2002). Letter from the White House. *National Strategy for Homeland Security, 2002*. Washington, DC: Office of Homeland Security, n.p.

137. White, J. R. (2012). *Terrorism and homeland security* (7th ed). Belmont, CA: Wadsworth, p. 474.

138. White House. (2002). *The Department of Homeland Security*. Washington, DC: Department of Homeland Security. Retrieved from http://www.dhs.gov/xlibrary/assets/book.pdf.

139. Office of Homeland Security. (2002). *National strategy for homeland security, 2002*. Washington, DC: Author, p. 2.

140. Ibid., as cited in Gaines, L. K., & Kappeler, V. E. (2012). *Homeland security*. Boston: Prentice Hall, p. 6.

141. Bellavita, C. (2008). Changing homeland security: What is homeland security? *Homeland Security Affairs, 4,* 1–2.

142. Department of Homeland Security. (2015). *Creation of the Department of Homeland Security.* Washington, DC: Author. Retrieved from https://www.dhs.gov/creation-department-homeland-security

143. Transportation Security Administration. (n.d.). *About TSA.* Washington, DC: U.S. Department of Homeland Security. Retrieved from http://www.tsa.gov/about-tsa.

144. Gaines, L. K., & Kappeler, V. E. (2012). *Homeland security.* Boston: Prentice Hall, p. 37.

145. Ibid., p. 40.

146. U.S. Customs and Border Protection. (2011). *Snapshot: A summary of CBP facts and figures.* Washington, DC: Author, p. 1.

147. Gaines, L. K., & Kappeler, V. E. (2012). *Homeland security.* Boston: Prentice Hall, p. 40.

148. Ibid., p. 43.

149. U.S. Citizenship and Immigration Services. (2010). *USCIS overview: About the U.S. Citizenship and Immigration Services (USCIS).* Washington, DC: Author. Retrieved from http://www.uscitizenship.info/us-citizenship-and-immigration-services-uscis.html.

150. U.S. Immigration and Customs Enforcement. (n.d.). *Overview.* Washington, DC: U.S. Department of Homeland Security. Retrieved from http://www.ice.gov/about/overview/.

151. Gaines, L. K., & Kappeler, V. E. (2012). *Homeland security.* Boston: Prentice Hall, p. 43.

152. Ibid.

153. U.S. Immigration and Customs Enforcement. (n.d.). *Overview.* Washington, DC: U.S. Department of Homeland Security. Retrieved from http://www.ice.gov/about/overview/.

154. Gaines, L. K., & Kappeler, V. E. (2012). *Homeland security.* Boston: Prentice Hall, p. 45; see also U.S. Secret Service. (2010). *Secret Service history.* Washington, DC: Author. Retrieved from http://www.secretservice.gov/history.shtml.

155. U.S. Secret Service. (2010). *Mission statement.* Washington, DC: Author. Retrieved from http://www.secretservice.gov/mission.shtml.

156. Federal Emergency Management Agency. (2011). *About FEMA.* Washington, DC: Author. Retrieved from http://www.fema.gov/about-fema.

157. Federal Emergency Management Agency. (2011). *FEMA strategic plan: Fiscal years 2011–2014.* Washington, DC: U.S. Department of Homeland Security, p. 1.

158. Gaines, L. K., & Kappeler, V. E. (2012). *Homeland security.* Boston: Prentice Hall, p. 48.

159. U.S. Coast Guard. (2011). *About us.* Washington, DC: Author. Retrieved from http://www.uscg.mil/top/about/.

160. Haddal, C. C. (2010). *Border security: Key agencies and their missions.* Washington, DC: Congressional Research Service, p. 4.

161. Shapiro, J. (2007). *Managing homeland security: Develop a threat-based strategy.* Washington, DC: Brookings Institution, p. 1.

162. Gaines, L. K., & Kappeler, V. E. (2012). *Homeland security.* Boston: Prentice Hall, p. 35.

163. Ibid., p. 36.

164. Narayan, C. (June 13, 2016). Timeline of Orlando nightclub shooting. *CNN.* Retrieved from: http://www.cnn.com/2016/06/12/us/orlando-shooting-timeline/index.html.

165. Williams, P., Connor, T., Ortiz, E., & Gosk, S. (June 13, 2016). Gunman Omar Mateen described as belligerent, racist and toxic. *NBC News.* Retrieved from: http://www.nbcnews.com/storyline/orlando-nightclub-massacre/terror-hate-what-motivated-orlando-nightclub-shooter-n590496

166. Ghitis, F. (June 13, 2016). Was Orlando shooting terror or homophobia? Yes. *CNN.* Retrieved from: http://www.cnn.com/2016/06/12/opinions/orlando-terror-shooting-ghitis/index.html

167. Gaines, L. K., & Kappeler, V. E. (2012). *Homeland security.* Boston: Prentice Hall.

168. Office of the United Nations. (2008). *Human rights, terrorism and counter-terrorism.* Geneva, Switzerland: Author, p. 1.

169. Martin, G. (2013). *Understanding terrorism: Challenges, perspectives, and issues* (4th ed.). Thousand Oaks, CA: Sage, p. 401.

170. Hersh, S. M. (2004). Torture at Abu Ghraib. *New Yorker.* Retrieved from http://www.newyorker.com/archive/2004/05/10/040510fa_fact.

171. Ibid., para. 6.

172. Martin, G. (2013). *Understanding terrorism: Challenges, perspectives, and issues* (4th ed.). Thousand Oaks, CA: Sage, pp. 498–499.

173. Office of the United Nations. (2008). *Human rights, terrorism and counter-terrorism.* Geneva, Switzerland: Author, p. 3.

174. White, J. R. (2012). *Terrorism and homeland security* (7th ed). Belmont, CA: Wadsworth, p. 539.

175. Pew Foundation. (2005). *Pew global attitudes project.* Retrieved from http://pewglobal.org/reports/pdf/248.pdf, as cited in White, J. R. (2012). *Terrorism and homeland security* (7th ed). Belmont, CA: Wadsworth, p. 539.

176. Porteous, T. (2006). The al Qaeda myth. *TomPaine.com.* Retrieved from http://www.tompaine.com/articles/2006/04/12/the_al_qaeda_myth.php, as cited in White, J. R. (2012). *Terrorism and homeland security* (7th ed). Belmont, CA: Wadsworth, p. 539.

177. Office of the United Nations. (2008). *Human rights, terrorism and counter-terrorism.* Geneva, Switzerland: Author, p. 46.

178. Cole, D., & Dempsey, J. X. (2006). *Terrorism and the Constitution: Sacrificing civil liberties in the name of national security* (3rd ed.). New York: New Press.

179. Cohen, D. H. (2010). Post-9/11 anti-terrorism policy regarding noncitizens and the constitutional idea of equal protection under the laws. *Texas Law Review, 88,* 1339.

180. White, J. R. (2012). *Terrorism and homeland security* (7th ed.). Belmont, CA: Wadsworth, pp. 542–544.

181. Doyle, C. (2002). *CRS report for Congress: The USA PATRIOT Act: A sketch.* Washington, DC: Congressional Research Service; Executive Order 13025 of November 13, 1995, Amendment to Executive Order 13010, the President's Commission on Critical Infrastructure Protection, as cited in Gaines, L. K., & Kappeler, V. E. (2012). *Homeland security.* Boston: Prentice Hall, p. 96.

182. Martin, G. (2011). *Terrorism and homeland security.* Thousand Oaks, CA: Sage, p. 279.

183. White, J. R. (2012). *Terrorism and homeland security* (7th ed.). Belmont, CA: Wadsworth, pp. 542–544.

184. Sievert, R. J. (2007). PATRIOT 2005–2007: Truth, controversy, and consequences. *Texas Review of Law & Politics, 11,* 350.

185. Mascaro, L. (2011). PATRIOT Act provisions extended just in time. *Los Angeles Times.* Retrieved from http://articles.latimes.com/2011/may/27/nation/la-na-patriot-act-20110527.

186. Nelson, S. (June 2, 2015). Senate passes Freedom Act, ending PATRIOT Act provision lapse. *U.S. News World and Report.* Retrieved from http://www.usnews.com/news/articles/2015/06/02/senate-passes-freedom-act-ending-patriot-act-provision-lapse

187. The White House. (2015, December 5). Summary: President Obama speaks about the shooting in San Bernardino, California. Retrieved from https://www.whitehouse.gov/blog/2015/12/02/president-obama-shooting-san-bernardino

188. Nakamura, D. (2016, June 13). Orlando massacre turns triumphant week for Obama into referendum on terrorism. *Washington Post.* Retrieved from https://www.washingtonpost.com/politics/obama-ties-debate-over-terrorism-and-guns-together-after-orlando/2016/06/13/40ca1564-317b-11e6-8758-d58e76e11b12_story.html

189. Pérez-Peña, R. (2015, October 7). Gun control explained. *New York Times.* Retrieved from http://www.nytimes.com/interactive/2015/10/07/us/gun-control-explained.html?_r=0.

190. Ball, M. (2016, January 16). Don't call it "gun control." *The Atlantic.* Retrieved from http://www.theatlantic.com/politics/archive/2013/01/dont-call-it-gun-control/267259/

191. Pérez-Peña, R. (2015, October 7). Gun control explained. *New York Times.* Retrieved from http://www.nytimes.com/interactive/2015/10/07/us/gun-control-explained.html?_r=0 (para. 19)

CHAPTER 16

1. Kraut, A. (2016, June 9). Samuel Ellis sentenced to four years in prison. *Bethesda Magazine.* Retrieved from http://www.bethesdamagazine.com/Bethesda-Beat/Web-2016/Samuel-Ellis-Sentenced-to-Four-Years-in-Prison/.

2. Belt, D. (2015, December 11). Potomac party host pleads guilty in teen drinking case. *Patch.* Retrieved from http://patch.com/maryland/rockville/potomac-party-host-pleads-guilty-teen-drinking-case-0.

3. St. George, D., & Morse, D. (2015, December 23). Report: Teens said parent allowed parties "on a regular basis." *Washington Post.* Retrieved from https://www.washingtonpost.com/local/education/report-teens-said-parent-allowed-parties-on-a-regular-basis/2015/12/23/c228ce02-a5d5-11e5-ad3f-991ce3374e23_story.html

4. Lurigio, A. J. (2008). The first 20 years of drug treatment courts: A brief description of their history and impact. *Federal Probation, 72,* 13.

5. Federal Bureau of Investigation. (2015). *Crime in the United States, 2014.* Washington, DC: U.S. Department of Justice. Retrieved from https://www.fbi.gov/about-us/cjis/ucr/crime-in-the-u.s/2014/crime-in-the-u.s.-2014/tables/table-29.

6. Bureau of Prisons. (2016). *BOP statistics: Inmate offenses.* Retrieved from https://www.bop.gov/about/statistics/statistics_inmate_offenses.jsp

7. Carson, E.A. (2014). *Prisoners in 2013.* Washington, DC: U.S. Department of Justice.

8. Gaines, L. K. (2014). The psychopharmacology and prevalence of drugs. In L. K. Gaines & J. Kremling (Eds.), *Drugs, crime, and justice* (3rd ed., pp. 105-138). Prospect Heights, IL: Waveland Press, p. 113.

9. National Institute of Drug Abuse. (2011). *What are CNS depressants.* Washington, DC: U.S. Department of Health and Human Services. Retrieved from http://www.drugabuse.gov/publications/research-reports/prescription-drugs/cns-depressants/what-are-cns-depressants.

10. Substance Abuse and Mental Health Services Administration. (2015). *Results from the 2014 National Survey on Drug Use and Health: Volume I; Summary of national findings.* Washington, DC: U.S. Department of Health and Human Services.

11. Kuhn, C., Swartzwelder, S., & Wilson, W. (2003). *Buzzed: The straight facts about the most used and abused drugs from alcohol to ecstasy.* New York: W. W. Norton, p. 198.

12. Kuhn, C., Swartzwelder, S., & Wilson. W. (2003). Buzzed: The straight facts about the most used and abused drugs from alcohol to ecstasy. New York: W. W. Norton, pp. 49–50. Copyright © 1998 by Cynthia Kuhn, Scott Swartzwelder, and Wilkie Wilson. Used by permission of W. W. Norton & Company, Inc.

13. National Institute on Alcohol Abuse and Alcoholism. (n.d.). Moderate and binge drinking. Retrieved from http://www.niaaa.nih.gov/alcohol-health/overview-alcohol-consumption/moderate-binge-drinking.

14. Substance Abuse and Mental Health Services Administration. (2012). *Results from the 2011 National Survey on Drug Use and Health: Key definition for the 2011 detailed tables and national findings report.* Rockville, MD: Author, p. 4.

15. Wechsler, H., Dowdall, W., Davenport, A., & Castillo, S. (1995). Correlates of college student binge drinking. *American Journal of Public Health, 85,* 921–926.

16. Zamboanga, B. L., Schwartz, S. J., Van Tyne, K., Ham, L. S., Olthuis, J. V., Huang, S., et al. (2010). Drinking game

behaviors among college students: How often and how much? *American Journal of Drug and Alcohol Abuse, 36,* 176.

17. Borsari, B. (2004). Drinking games in the college environment: A review. *Journal of Alcohol and Drug Education, 48,* 29–51.

18. Perkins, H. W. (2002). Surveying the damage: A review of research on consequences of alcohol misuse in college populations. *Journal of Studies on Alcohol, 56,* 628–634.

19. Sneader, W. (2005). *Drug discovery.* New York: John Wiley.

20. U.S. Drug Enforcement Administration. (n.d.). *Barbiturates.* Washington, DC: U.S. Department of Justice. Retrieved from https://www.dea.gov/druginfo/drug_data_sheets/Barbiturates.pdf.

21. Gaines, L. K. (2014). The psychopharmacology and prevalence of drugs. In L. K. Gaines & J. Kremling (Eds.), *Drugs, crime, and justice* (3rd ed., pp. 105-138). Prospect Heights, IL: Waveland Press, p. 115.

22. U.S. Drug Enforcement Administration. (n.d.). *Barbiturates.* Washington, DC: U.S. Department of Justice. Retrieved from https://www.dea.gov/druginfo/drug_data_sheets/Barbiturates.pdf.

23. Ainsworth, S. (2011). Barbiturates: Soldiers, saints and spies. *Practice Nurse, 41,* 32–33.

24. Kuhn, C., Swartzwelder, S., & Wilson, W. (2003). *Buzzed: The straight facts about the most used and abused drugs from alcohol to ecstasy.* New York: W. W. Norton, p. 33.

25. Ibid., p. 199.

26. Zilney, L. A. (2011). *Drugs: Policy, social costs, crime, and justice.* Boston: Prentice Hall; see also U.S. Drug Enforcement Administration. (n.d.). *Drug fact sheet.* Washington, DC: U.S. Department of Justice. Retrieved from http://www.justice.gov/dea/druginfo/all_fact_sheets.pdf.

27. U.S. Drug Enforcement Administration. (n.d.). *Drug fact sheet.* Washington, DC: U.S. Department of Justice. Retrieved from http://www.justice.gov/dea/druginfo/all_fact_sheets.pdf.

28. Gaines, L. K. (2014). The psychopharmacology and prevalence of drugs. In L. K. Gaines & J. Kremling (Eds.), *Drugs, crime, and justice* (3rd ed., pp. 105-138). Prospect Heights, IL: Waveland Press, p. 118.

29. Kuhn, C., Swartzwelder, S., & Wilson, W. (2003). *Buzzed: The straight facts about the most used and abused drugs from alcohol to ecstasy.* New York: W. W. Norton, p. 176.

30. U.S. Drug Enforcement Administration. (n.d.). *Drug fact sheet.* Washington, DC: U.S. Department of Justice. Retrieved from http://www.justice.gov/dea/druginfo/all_fact_sheets.pdf.

31. Kuhn, C., Swartzwelder, S., & Wilson, W. (2003). *Buzzed: The straight facts about the most used and abused drugs from alcohol to ecstasy.* New York: W. W. Norton, p. 178.

32. Neaigus, A., Atillasoy, A., Friedman, S., Andrade, X., Miller, M., Ildefonso, G., et al. (1998). Trends in the noninjected use of heroin and factors associated with the transition to injecting. In J. Inciardi & L. Harrison (Eds.), *Heroin in the age of crack-cocaine* (pp. 131–159). Thousand Oaks, CA: Sage.

33. National Institute of Drug Abuse. (n.d.). *Drug facts: Heroin.* Washington, DC: National Institutes of Health. Retrieved from http://www.drugabuse.gov/infofacts/heroin.html.

34. U.S. Drug Enforcement Administration. (n.d.). *Drug fact sheet: Narcotics.* Washington, DC: U.S. Department of Justice. Retrieved from http://www.justice.gov/dea/druginfo/drug_data_sheets/Narcotics.pdf.

35. Gaines, L. K. (2014). The psychopharmacology and prevalence of drugs. In L. K. Gaines & J. Kremling (Eds.), *Drugs, crime, and justice* (3rd ed., pp. 105-138). Prospect Heights, IL: Waveland Press, p. 121.

36. Van Zee, A. (2009). The promotion and marketing of OxyContin: Commercial triumph, public health tragedy. *American Journal of Public Health, 99,* 225.

37. Tough, P. (2001). The alchemy of OxyContin: From pain relief to drug addiction. *New York Times.* Retrieved from http://www.nytimes.com/2001/07/29/magazine/290XYCONTIN.html?pagewanted=all.

38. Kuhn, C., Swartzwelder, S., & Wilson, W. (2003). *Buzzed: The straight facts about the most used and abused drugs from alcohol to ecstasy.* New York: W. W. Norton, p. 211.

39. Gaines, L. K. (2014). The psychopharmacology and prevalence of drugs. In L. K. Gaines & J. Kremling (Eds.), *Drugs, crime, and justice* (3rd ed., pp. 105-138). Prospect Heights, IL: Waveland Press, p. 121.

40. U.S. Drug Enforcement Administration. (n.d.). *Drug fact sheet.* Washington, DC: U.S. Department of Justice. Retrieved from http://www.justice.gov/dea/druginfo/all_fact_sheets.pdf.

41. Ibid.

42. Kuhn, C., Swartzwelder, S., & Wilson, W. (2003). *Buzzed: The straight facts about the most used and abused drugs from alcohol to ecstasy.* New York: W. W. Norton, p. 219.

43. Gaines, L. K. (2014). The psychopharmacology and prevalence of drugs. In L. K. Gaines & J. Kremling (Eds.), *Drugs, crime, and justice* (3rd ed., pp. 105-138). Prospect Heights, IL: Waveland Press, p. 122.

44. U.S. Drug Enforcement Administration. (n.d.). *Drug fact sheet.* Washington, DC: U.S. Department of Justice. Retrieved from http://www.justice.gov/dea/druginfo/all_fact_sheets.pdf.

45. Gahlinger, P. M. (2001). *Illegal drugs: A complete guide to their history, chemistry, use and abuse.* Salt Lake City, UT: Sagebrush Press.

46. National Drug Intelligence Center. (2005). *Methamphetamine drug threat assessment.* Johnstown, PA: Author, p. 10.

47. U.S. Drug Enforcement Administration. (n.d.). *Drug fact sheet.* Washington, DC: U.S. Department of Justice. Retrieved from http://www.justice.gov/dea/druginfo/all_fact_sheets.pdf.

48. Hunt, D., Kuck, S., & Truitt, L. (2005). *Methamphetamine use: Lessons learned.* Cambridge, MA: Abt Associates, pp. iv–v.

49. Kuhn, C., Swartzwelder, S., & Wilson, W. (2003). *Buzzed: The straight facts about the most used and abused drugs from alcohol to ecstasy.* New York: W. W. Norton, p. 137.

50. Gaines, L. K. (2014). The psychopharmacology and prevalence of drugs. In L. K. Gaines & J. Kremling (Eds.), *Drugs, crime, and justice* (3rd ed., pp. 105–138). Prospect Heights, IL: Waveland Press, p. 128.

51. U.S. Drug Enforcement Administration. (n.d.). *Drug fact sheet.* Washington, DC: U.S. Department of Justice. Retrieved from http://www.justice.gov/dea/druginfo/all_fact_sheets.pdf.

52. Ibid.

53. Ibid.

54. National Institute on Drug Abuse. (2012). *Drug facts: Anabolic steroids.* Washington, DC: National Institutes of Health. Retrieved from http://www.drugabuse.gov/infofacts/steroids.html; see also Mosher, C. J., & Akins, S. (2007). *Drugs and drug policy: The control of consciousness alternation.* Thousand Oaks, CA: Sage.

55. Gaines, L. K. (2014). The psychopharmacology and prevalence of drugs. In L. K. Gaines & J. Kremling (Eds.), *Drugs, crime, and justice* (3rd ed., pp. 105-138). Prospect Heights, IL: Waveland Press, p. 134; National Institute on Drug Abuse. (2012). *Drug facts: Anabolic steroids.* Washington, DC: National Institutes of Health. Retrieved from http://www.drugabuse.gov/infofacts/steroids.html.

56. U.S. Drug Enforcement Administration. (n.d.). *Drug fact sheet: Steroids.* Washington, DC: U.S. Department of Justice. Retrieved from http://www.justice.gov/dea/druginfo/drug_data_sheets/Steroids.pdf.

57. Pope, H. G., Kouri, E. M., & Hudson. J. I. (2000). Effects of supraphysiologic doses of testosterone on mood and aggression in normal men: A randomized controlled trial. *Archives of General Psychiatry, 57,* 133–140.

58. Pope, H. G., & Katz, D. L. (1988). Affective and psychotic symptoms associated with anabolic steroid use. *American Journal of Psychiatry, 145,* 487–490.

59. National Institute on Drug Abuse. (2012). *Drug facts: Anabolic steroids.* Washington, DC: National Institutes of Health. Retrieved from http://www.drugabuse.gov/infofacts/steroids.html.

60. National Institute on Drug Abuse. (2012). *Research report series: Inhalant abuse.* Washington, DC: National Institutes of Health. Retrieved from http://www.drugabuse.gov/publications/research-reports/inhalant-abuse.

61. Kuhn, C., Swartzwelder, S., & Wilson, W. (2003). *Buzzed: The straight facts about the most used and abused drugs from alcohol to ecstasy.* New York: W. W. Norton, p. 86.

62. Ibid., pp. 86–87.

63. Ibid., p. 89.

64. Mosher, C. J., & Akins, S. (2007). *Drugs and drug policy: The control of consciousness alteration.* Thousand Oaks, CA: Sage

65. Freeman, S. (1988). *Drugs and civilization.* New York: Chelsea House, pp. 19–20.

66. Ibid., p. 20.

67. Tracey, S. W., & Acker, C. J. (Eds.). (2004). *Altering American consciousness: The history of alcohol and drug use in the United States, 1800–2000.* Amherst: University of Massachusetts Press, pp. 2–3.

68. NIDA International Program. (n.d.). Question 2: What is the history of opioid addiction in the United States? Retrieved from https://www.drugabuse.gov/sites/default/files/pdf/parta.pdf.

69. Freeman, F. (1988). *Drugs and civilization.* New York: Chelsea House, pp. 64–67.

70. Ibid., p. 48.

71. NIDA International Program. (n.d.). Question 2: What is the history of opioid addiction in the United States? Retrieved from https://www.drugabuse.gov/sites/default/files/pdf/parta.pdf.

72. Freeman, F. (1988). *Drugs and civilization.* New York: Chelsea House, pp. 48–49.

73. Ibid., pp. 49–50.

74. Flynn, J. C. (1991). *Cocaine: An in-depth look at the facts, science, history and future of the world's most addictive drug.* New York: Carol Publishing Group, pp. 24–31.

75. Ibid.

76. Vick, D. (2011). *Drugs and alcohol in the 21st century: Theory, behavior, and policy.* Sudbury, MA: Jones & Bartlett, p. 128.

77. Clark, N. H. (1965). *The drug years: Prohibition and social change in Washington.* Seattle: University of Washington Press.

78. Levine, H. G. (1984). The alcohol problem in America: From temperance to alcoholism. *British Journal of Addiction, 79,* 114.

79. Hall, W. (2010). What are the policy lessons of National Alcohol Prohibition in the United States, 1920–1933? *Addiction, 105,* 1171.

80. Abadinsky, H. (2007). *Organized crime.* Belmont, CA: Wadsworth, pp. 43–53.

81. Sloman, L. R. (1998). *Reefer madness: A history of marijuana.* New York: St. Martin's Griffin, p. 29.

82. Ray, R. (1983). *Drugs, society, and human behavior* (3rd ed.). St. Louis, MO: C. V. Mosby, p. 424.

83. Marihuana menaces youth. (1936). *Scientific American, 154,* 151.

84. Morais, R. C. (1996). Reefer madness. *Forbes, 157,* 118.

85. 395 U.S. 6; 89 S. Ct. 1532; 23 L. Ed. 2d 57.

86. Musto, D. F. (1972). The history of the Marihuana Tax Act of 1937. *Archives of General Psychiatry, 26,* 101–108.

87. Ibid., 104.

88. Ibid., p. 105.

89. U.S. Census Bureau. (n.d.). *Selected characteristics of baby boomers 42 to 60 years old in 2006.* Retrieved from http://www.census.gov/population/age/publications/files/2006babyboomers.pdf.

90. Westhues, K. (1972). *Society's shadow: Studies in the sociology of countercultures.* Toronto: McGraw-Hill Ryerson, pp. 15–17.

91. Miller, T. (1999). *The 60s communes: Hippies and beyond,* Syracuse, NY: Syracuse University Press.

92. Goode, E. (1999). *Drugs in American society* (5th ed.). Boston: McGraw-Hill, p. 70.

93. *Remarks at the Nancy Reagan Drug Abuse Center Benefit Dinner in Los Angeles, California.* (1989, January 4). Retrieved from http://www.reagan.utexas.edu/archives/speeches/1989/010489a.htm.

94. Chitwood, D. D., Murphy, S., & Rosenbaum. M. (2009). Reflections on the meaning of drug epidemics. *Journal of Drug Issues, 39,* 29–39.

95. Goode, E. (1999). *Drugs in American society* (5th ed.). Boston: McGraw-Hill, pp. 70–71.

96. Chitwood, D. D., Murphy, S., & Rosenbaum. M. (2009). Reflections on the meaning of drug epidemics. *Journal of Drug Issues, 39,* 29–39.

97. Witkin, G., Mukenge, M., Guttman, M., Arrarte, A., Glastris, K., Burgower, B., et al. (1991). The men who created crack. *U.S. News & World Report, 111,* 44–53.

98. Logan, E. (2004). The wrong race, committing crime, doing drugs, and maladjusted for motherhood: The nation's fury over "crack babies." In P. J. Schram & B. Koons-Witt, *Gendered (in)justice: Theory and practice in feminist criminology.* Long Grove, IL: Waveland Press, p. 247.

99. Lewis, D. C. (2004). Stop perpetuating the "crack baby" myth. *Brown University Digest of Addiction Theory and Application, 23,* 8.

100. Substance Abuse and Mental Health Services Administration. (2015). *Results from the 2015 National Survey on Drug Use and Health: Volume I; Summary of national findings.* Rockville, MD: Author. http://www.samhsa.gov/data/sites/default/files/NSDUH-FRR1-2014/NSDUH-FRR1-2014.pdf

101. U.S. Drug Enforcement Administration. (2011, May 12). *Feds crack down on illegal trafficking of Oxycodone* [Press release]. Retrieved from http://www.justice.gov/usao/gan/press/2011/05–12–11b.html.

102. Partnership for Drug-Free Kids. (2013). *The Partnership Attitude Tracking Study.* New York: Author, p. 8.

103. RyansCause.org. (2006). About Ryan. Retrieved from http://www.ryanscause.org/section.php?id=1.

104. Mother crusades for online pharmacy regulation. (2005). *ABC10News.com.* Retrieved from http://www.10news.com/news/mother-crusades-for-online-pharmacy-regulation.

105. RyansCause.org. (2006). About Ryan. Retrieved from http://www.ryanscause.org/section.php?id=1.

106. Drug Enforcement Agency. (2009, April 31). *New rules governing Internet pharmacies go into effect next week* [News release]. Retrieved from http://www.justice.gov/dea/pubs/pressrel/pr041309.html.

107. Drug Enforcement Agency. (2008, October 1). *Congress passes Ryan Haight Online Pharmacy Consumer Protection Act* [News release]. Retrieved from http://www.justice.gov/dea/pubs/pressrel/pr100108.html.

108. Zilney, L.A. (2011). *Drugs: Policy, social costs, crime, and justice.* Boston: Prentice-Hall, p. 101.

109. Light, D.W., & Lexchin, J.R. (2012). Pharmaceutical research and development: what do we get for all that money? *British Journal of Medicine, 345,* pp. 22–25.

110. Buchanan, J. F., & Brown, C. R. (1988). 'Designer drugs': A problem in clinical toxicology. *Medical Toxicology and Adverse Drug Experience, 3,* 1.

111. Seymour, R. B. (1997). Some so-called designer drugs are not. *Brown University Psychopharmacology Update, 8,* 1–2.

112. Ibid., p. 2.

113. National Institute on Drug Abuse. (2015). *Drug facts: Spice (synthetic cannabinoids).* Retrieved from https://www.drugabuse.gov/publications/drugfacts/synthetic-cannabinoids.

114. Miller, M. C. (2011). Bath salts: A new way to get high? *Harvard Medical Health Letter, 28,* 8.

115. National Institute on Drug Abuse. (2016). *Drug facts: Synthetic cathinones ("bath salts").* Retrieved from ps://www.drugabuse.gov/publications/drugfacts/synthetic-cathinones-bath-salts.

116. Gaines, L.K. (2014). The relationship between drugs and crime. In L.K. Gaines & J. Kremling (Eds.), *Drugs, crime, and justice* (3nd ed., 511–108530). Prospect Heights, IL: Waveland Press, p. 511.

117. Indiardi, J. A. (1981). Heroin addiction and street crime. In *International narcotics trafficking: Hearings before the Permanent Subcommittee on Investigations.* Washington, DC: U.S. Government Printing Office, p. 59.

118. Walker, S. (2006). *Sense and non-sense about crime and drugs: A policy guide* (6th ed.). Belmont, CA: Thomson Wadsworth.

119. Gaines, L.K. (2014). The relationship between drugs and crime. In L.K. Gaines & J. Kremling (Eds.), *Drugs, crime, and justice* (3nd ed., 511–108530). Prospect Heights, IL: Waveland Press, p. 513.

120. Zilney, K. A. (2011). *Drugs: Policy, social costs, crime, and justice.* Boston: Prentice Hall, p. 173.

121. McBride, D. C., & McCoy, C. B. (2003). The drugs-crime relationship: An analytical framework. In L. K. Gaines & P. B. Kraska (Eds.), *Drugs, crime, and justice* (2nd ed., 87–108). Prospect Heights, IL: Waveland Press, p. 108.

122. Ibid.

123. Nordstrom, B., & Dackis, C. A. (2011). Drugs and crime. *Journal of Psychiatry & Law, 39,* 666. See also Brook, J. S., Whiteman, M., Finch, S. J., & Cohen, P. (1996). Young adult drug use and delinquency: Childhood antecedents and adolescent mediators. *Journal of the Academy of Child and Adolescent Psychiatry, 35,* 1584–1592; White, H. R., Pandina, R. J., & LaGrange, R. L. (1987). Longitudinal predictors of serious substance use and delinquency. *Criminology, 25,* 715–740.

124. Nordstrom, B., & Dackis, C. A. (2011). Drugs and crime. *Journal of Psychiatry & Law, 39,* 683.

125. Goldstein, P. J. (1989). Drugs and violent crime. In N. A. Weiner & M. E. Wolfgang (Eds.), *Pathways to criminal violence* (pp. 16–48). Newbury Park, CA: Sage.

126. Ibid., p. 30.

127. Abadinsky, H. (1997). *Drug abuse: An introduction* (3rd ed.). Chicago: Nelson-Hall, p. 308.

128. Gusfield. J. (1975). The (f)utility of knowledge? The relation of social science to public policy toward drugs. *Annals, 147, 13*.

129. Abadinsky, H. (1997). *Drug abuse: An introduction* (3rd ed.). Chicago: Nelson-Hall, p. 357.

130. Currie, E. (1993). *Reckoning: Drugs, the cities, and the American future*. New York: Hill & Wang.

131. Office of National Drug Control Policy. (2010, March 17). *National interdiction command and control plan*. Washington, DC: Author. Retrieved from http://www.whitehousedrugpolicy.gov/pdf/usic_2011_niccp.pdf.

132. Ibid., pp. 9–10.

133. Office of National Drug Control Policy. (n.d.). *High Intensity Drug Trafficking Areas (HIDTA) program*. Washington, DC: Author. Retrieved from https://www.whitehouse.gov/ondcp/high-intensity-drug-trafficking-areas-program.

134. Ibid., n.p.

135. Ohio HIDTA (High Intensity Drug Traffficking Areas). (n.d.). Retrieved from http://ohiohidta.net/.

136. U.S. Department of Justice. (2011). *Ohio High Intensity Drug Trafficking Area*. Washington, D.C.: National Drug Intelligence Center. Retrieved from: https://www.justice.gov/archive/ndic/dmas/Ohio_DMA-2011(U).pdf.

137. European Commission. (2013). *Public opinion*. Retrieved from http://ec.europa.eu/public_opinion/index_en.htm.

138. Europe Opinion Research Group. (2003). *Public safety, exposure to drug-related problems and crime: Public opinion survey* (p. 62). Retrieved from http://ec.europa.eu/public_opinion/archives/ebs/ebs_181_en.pdf.

139. Van Dijk, J. (2008). *The world of crime: Breaking the silence on problems of security, justice, and development across the world*. Thousand Oaks, CA: Sage, pp. 107–109.

140. Farrell, G. (1998). A global empirical review of drug crop eradication and United Nations' crop substitution and alternative development strategies. *Journal of Drug Issues, 28, 395–436*.

141. United National Economic and Social Council. (1996). *Crops from which drugs are extracted and appropriate strategies for their reduction* (Commission on Narcotic Drugs, 39th Session document E/CN.7/1996/11), pp. 16–25.

142. Farrell, G. (1998). A global empirical review of drug crop eradication and United Nations' crop substitution and alternative development strategies. *Journal of Drug Issues, 28, 395–436*.

143. Bureau of International Narcotics and Law Enforcement Affairs (INCSR). (2016). *Country Report: Colombia*. Retrieved from: http://www.state.gov/j/inl/rls/nrcrpt/2016/vol1/253252.htm.

144. Brooke, J. (1990). Near-acquittal of Barry is outraging Colombians. *New York Times*, p. 4, as cited in Abadinsky, H. (1997). *Drug abuse: An introduction* (3rd ed.). Chicago: Nelson-Hall, p. 344.

145. Wisotsky, S. (1987). *Breaking the impasse in the war on drugs*. Westport, CT: Greenwood, p. 57, as cited in Abadinsky, H. (1997). *Drug abuse: An introduction* (3rd ed.). Chicago: Nelson-Hall, p. 344.

146. Morales, E. (1986). Coca and cocaine economy and social change in the Andes of Peru. *Economic Development and Social Change, 35, 157*, as cited in Abadinsky, H. (1997). *Drug abuse: An introduction* (3rd ed.). Chicago: Nelson-Hall, pp. 344–345.

147. Drug Enforcement Administration. (2015). *Domestic Cannibis Eradication/Suppression Program*. Washington, DC: U.S. Department of Justice. Retrieved from: https://www.dea.gov/ops/cannabis.shtml.

148. National Drug Intelligence Center. (2009, July). *Domestic cannabis cultivation assessment, 2009*. Washington, DC: U.S. Department of Justice. Retrieved from http://www.justice.gov/archive/ndic/pubs37/37035/37035p.pdf.

149. Ibid., p. 29.

150. Lurigio, A. J. (2008). The first 20 years of drug treatment courts: A brief description of their history and impact. *Federal Probation, 72, 13*.

151. Hennessey, J. J. (2001). Introduction: Drug courts in operation. *Journal of Offender Rehabilitation, 33, 1–10*.

152. Lurigio, A. J. (2008). The first 20 years of drug treatment courts: A brief description of their history and impact. *Federal Probation, 72, 13–17*.

153. National Institute of Justice. (May 2016). *Drug Courts*. Retrieved from: http://www.nij.gov/topics/courts/drug-courts/pages/welcome.aspx.

154. Huddleston, C. W., Marlow, D. B., & Casebolt, R. (2008). *A national report card on drug courts and other problem-solving court programs in the United States*. Washington, DC: National Drug Court Institute, p. 2.

155. Fox, C. L., & Huddleston, C. W. (2003, May). Drug courts in the U.S. *Issues of Democracy, 8, 13–19*.

156. Cooper, C. S. (2007). Drug courts: Just the beginning; Getting other areas of public policy in sync. *Substance Use & Misuse, 42, 243–256*.

157. Stinchcomb, J. B. (2010). Drug courts: Conceptual foundation, empirical findings, and policy implications. *Drugs: Education, Prevention and Policy, 17, 161–162*.

158. Wolfer, L. (2006). Graduates speak: A qualitative exploration of drug court graduates' views of the strengths and weaknesses of the program. *Contemporary Drug Problems, 33, 303–320*.

159. Messer, S., Patten, R., & Candela, K. (2016). Drug courts and the facilitation of turning points: An expansion of life course theory. *Contemporary Drug Programs, 43, 6–24*.

160. McBride, D. C., Terry-McElrath, Y., Harwood, H., Inciardi, J. A., & Leukefeld, C. (2009). Reflections on drug policy. *Journal of Drug Issues, 39, 76*.

161. Abadinsky, H. (2004). *Drug abuse: An introduction* (5th ed.). Belmont, CA: Wadsworth/Thomson Learning, pp. 364-365.

162. Ibid., pp. 365-366.

163. ProCon.org. (2016). *Medical marijuana*. Retrieved from http://medicalmarijuana.procon.org/view.resource.php?resourceID=000881.

164. California Health and Safety Code Section 11362.5.

165. Healy, J. (2012). Voters ease marijuana laws in 2 states, but legal questions remain. *New York Times*. Retrieved from http://www.nytimes.com/ 2012/11/08/us/politics/ marijuana-laws-eased-in -colorado-and-washington .html.

166. Liptak, K. (2012). Obama: Enforcing pot laws in states that have legalized it not a top priority. *CNN Politics*. Retrieved from http://whitehouse.blogs.cnn .com/2012/12/14/obama-enforcing-pot-laws-in -states-that-have-legalized-it-not-a-top-priority/.

167. McBride, D. C., Terry-McElrath, Y., Harwood, H., Inciardi, J. A., & Leukefeld, C. (2009). Reflections on drug policy. *Journal of Drug Issues, 39*, 71.

168. Duff, C. (2010). Enabling places and enabling resources: New Directions for harm reduction research and practice. *Drug and Alcohol Review, 29*, 337.

169. Delgado, C. (2004). Evaluation of needle exchange programs. *Public Health Nursing, 21*, 171.

170. National Drug Intelligence Center. (2003). *Drug paraphernalia: Fast facts*. Retrieved from: https://www .justice.gov/archive/ndic/pubs6/6445/6445p.pdf.

171. Ksobiech, K. (2006). Beyond needle sharing: Meta-analyses of social context risk behaviors of injection drug users attending needle exchange programs. *Substance Use & Misuse, 41*, 1379-1394.

172. Delgado, C. (2004). Evaluation of needle exchange programs. *Public Health Nursing, 21*, 172.

173. Ibid.

174. Desroches, F. J. (2005). *The crime that pays: Drug trafficking and organized crime in Canada*. Toronto, Ontario: Canadian Scholars' Press; Merton, R. K. (1938). Social structure and anomie. *American Sociological Review, 3*, 672–682.

175. Merton, R. K. (1938). Social structure and anomie. *American Sociological Review, 3*, 672–682.

176. Akers, R. L. (1985). Social learning theory and adolescent cigarette smoking. *Social Problems, 32*, 455–473; Golub, A., Dunlap, E., & Benoit, E. (2010). Drug use and conflict in inner-city African-American relationships in the 2000s. *Journal of Psychoactive Drugs, 42*, 327–337.

177. Golub, A., Dunlap, E., & Benoit, E. (2010). Drug use and conflict in inner-city African-American relationships in the 2000s. *Journal of Psychoactive Drugs, 42*, 327–337.

178. Golub, A., Johnson, B. D., & Dunlap, E. (2005). Subcultural evolution and illicit drug use. *Addiction Research and Theory, 13*, 217–229;

179. Agnew, R., & Raskin White, H. (1992). An empirical test of general strain theory. *Criminology, 30*, 475–500.

180. McBride, D. C., Terry-McElrath, Y., Harwood, H., Inciardi, J. A., & Leukefeld, C. (2009). Reflections on drug policy. *Journal of Drug Issues, 39*, 81.

181. McBride, D. C., & McCoy, C. B. (2003). In L. K. Gaines & P. B. Kraska (Eds.), *Drugs, crime, and justice* (2nd ed.). Prospect Heights, IL: Waveland Press, pp. 114–115.

182. Ibid., p. 115.

183. Currie, E. (1993). *Reckoning: Drugs, the cities, and the American future*. New York: Hill & Wang, p. 279.

184. Penhaul, K. (2003, October 5). Drug kingpin's killer seeks Colombia office. *Boston Globe*. Retrieved from http://archive.boston.com/news/nation/arti cles/2003/10/05/drug_kingpins_killer_seeks_colombia_ office/.

185. Ceaser, M. (2008, June 2). At home on Pablo Escobar's ranch. *BBC News*. Retrieved from http://news.bbc .co.uk/2/hi/americas/7390584.stm.

186. McFadden, R.D. (1993). Head of Medellin cocaine cartel is killed by troops in Colombia. *New York Times*. Retrieved from: http://www.nytimes.com/1993/12/03/ world/head-of-medellin-cocaine-cartel-is-killed-by-troops-in-colombia.html?pagewanted=all.

187. McBride, D. C., & McCoy, C. B. (2003). In L. K. Gaines & P. B. Kraska (Eds.), *Drugs, crime, and justice* (2nd ed.). Prospect Heights, IL: Waveland Press, pp. 100–119.

INDEX

NOTE: Page references to boxes, figures, and tables are marked b, f, and t, respectively.